T0140449

Lecture Notes in Computer Science 13690

More information about this series at https://link.springer.com/bookseries/558

Shai Avidan · Gabriel Brostow ·
Moustapha Cissé · Giovanni Maria Farinella ·
Tal Hassner (Eds.)

Computer Vision – ECCV 2022

17th European Conference
Tel Aviv, Israel, October 23–27, 2022
Proceedings, Part XXX

 Springer

Editors
Shai Avidan
Tel Aviv University
Tel Aviv, Israel

Gabriel Brostow 🆔
University College London
London, UK

Moustapha Cissé
Google AI
Accra, Ghana

Giovanni Maria Farinella 🆔
University of Catania
Catania, Italy

Tal Hassner 🆔
Facebook (United States)
Menlo Park, CA, USA

ISSN 0302-9743   ISSN 1611-3349 (electronic)
Lecture Notes in Computer Science
ISBN 978-3-031-20055-7   ISBN 978-3-031-20056-4 (eBook)
https://doi.org/10.1007/978-3-031-20056-4

This Springer imprint is published by the registered company Springer Nature Switzerland AG
The registered company address is: Gewerbestrasse 11, 6330 Cham, Switzerland

Foreword

Organizing the European Conference on Computer Vision (ECCV 2022) in Tel-Aviv during a global pandemic was no easy feat. The uncertainty level was extremely high, and decisions had to be postponed to the last minute. Still, we managed to plan things just in time for ECCV 2022 to be held in person. Participation in physical events is crucial to stimulating collaborations and nurturing the culture of the Computer Vision community.

There were many people who worked hard to ensure attendees enjoyed the best science at the 16th edition of ECCV. We are grateful to the Program Chairs Gabriel Brostow and Tal Hassner, who went above and beyond to ensure the ECCV reviewing process ran smoothly. The scientific program includes dozens of workshops and tutorials in addition to the main conference and we would like to thank Leonid Karlinsky and Tomer Michaeli for their hard work. Finally, special thanks to the web chairs Lorenzo Baraldi and Kosta Derpanis, who put in extra hours to transfer information fast and efficiently to the ECCV community.

We would like to express gratitude to our generous sponsors and the Industry Chairs, Dimosthenis Karatzas and Chen Sagiv, who oversaw industry relations and proposed new ways for academia-industry collaboration and technology transfer. It's great to see so much industrial interest in what we're doing!

Authors' draft versions of the papers appeared online with open access on both the Computer Vision Foundation (CVF) and the European Computer Vision Association (ECVA) websites as with previous ECCVs. Springer, the publisher of the proceedings, has arranged for archival publication. The final version of the papers is hosted by SpringerLink, with active references and supplementary materials. It benefits all potential readers that we offer both a free and citeable version for all researchers, as well as an authoritative, citeable version for SpringerLink readers. Our thanks go to Ronan Nugent from Springer, who helped us negotiate this agreement. Last but not least, we wish to thank Eric Mortensen, our publication chair, whose expertise made the process smooth.

October 2022

Rita Cucchiara
Jiří Matas
Amnon Shashua
Lihi Zelnik-Manor

Preface

Welcome to the proceedings of the European Conference on Computer Vision (ECCV 2022). This was a hybrid edition of ECCV as we made our way out of the COVID-19 pandemic. The conference received 5804 valid paper submissions, compared to 5150 submissions to ECCV 2020 (a 12.7% increase) and 2439 in ECCV 2018. 1645 submissions were accepted for publication (28%) and, of those, 157 (2.7% overall) as orals.

846 of the submissions were desk-rejected for various reasons. Many of them because they revealed author identity, thus violating the double-blind policy. This violation came in many forms: some had author names with the title, others added acknowledgments to specific grants, yet others had links to their github account where their name was visible. Tampering with the LaTeX template was another reason for automatic desk rejection.

ECCV 2022 used the traditional CMT system to manage the entire double-blind reviewing process. Authors did not know the names of the reviewers and vice versa. Each paper received at least 3 reviews (except 6 papers that received only 2 reviews), totalling more than 15,000 reviews.

Handling the review process at this scale was a significant challenge. To ensure that each submission received as fair and high-quality reviews as possible, we recruited more than 4719 reviewers (in the end, 4719 reviewers did at least one review). Similarly we recruited more than 276 area chairs (eventually, only 276 area chairs handled a batch of papers). The area chairs were selected based on their technical expertise and reputation, largely among people who served as area chairs in previous top computer vision and machine learning conferences (ECCV, ICCV, CVPR, NeurIPS, etc.).

Reviewers were similarly invited from previous conferences, and also from the pool of authors. We also encouraged experienced area chairs to suggest additional chairs and reviewers in the initial phase of recruiting. The median reviewer load was five papers per reviewer, while the average load was about four papers, because of the emergency reviewers. The area chair load was 35 papers, on average.

Conflicts of interest between authors, area chairs, and reviewers were handled largely automatically by the CMT platform, with some manual help from the Program Chairs. Reviewers were allowed to describe themselves as senior reviewer (load of 8 papers to review) or junior reviewers (load of 4 papers). Papers were matched to area chairs based on a subject-area affinity score computed in CMT and an affinity score computed by the Toronto Paper Matching System (TPMS). TPMS is based on the paper's full text. An area chair handling each submission would bid for preferred expert reviewers, and we balanced load and prevented conflicts.

The assignment of submissions to area chairs was relatively smooth, as was the assignment of submissions to reviewers. A small percentage of reviewers were not happy with their assignments in terms of subjects and self-reported expertise. This is an area for improvement, although it's interesting that many of these cases were reviewers hand-picked by AC's. We made a later round of reviewer recruiting, targeted at the list of authors of papers submitted to the conference, and had an excellent response which helped provide enough emergency reviewers. In the end, all but six papers received at least 3 reviews.

The challenges of the reviewing process are in line with past experiences at ECCV 2020. As the community grows, and the number of submissions increases, it becomes ever more challenging to recruit enough reviewers and ensure a high enough quality of reviews. Enlisting authors by default as reviewers might be one step to address this challenge.

Authors were given a week to rebut the initial reviews, and address reviewers' concerns. Each rebuttal was limited to a single pdf page with a fixed template.

The Area Chairs then led discussions with the reviewers on the merits of each submission. The goal was to reach consensus, but, ultimately, it was up to the Area Chair to make a decision. The decision was then discussed with a buddy Area Chair to make sure decisions were fair and informative. The entire process was conducted virtually with no in-person meetings taking place.

The Program Chairs were informed in cases where the Area Chairs overturned a decisive consensus reached by the reviewers, and pushed for the meta-reviews to contain details that explained the reasoning for such decisions. Obviously these were the most contentious cases, where reviewer inexperience was the most common reported factor.

Once the list of accepted papers was finalized and released, we went through the laborious process of plagiarism (including self-plagiarism) detection. A total of 4 accepted papers were rejected because of that.

Finally, we would like to thank our Technical Program Chair, Pavel Lifshits, who did tremendous work behind the scenes, and we thank the tireless CMT team.

October 2022

Gabriel Brostow
Giovanni Maria Farinella
Moustapha Cissé
Shai Avidan
Tal Hassner

Organization

General Chairs

Rita Cucchiara	University of Modena and Reggio Emilia, Italy
Jiří Matas	Czech Technical University in Prague, Czech Republic
Amnon Shashua	Hebrew University of Jerusalem, Israel
Lihi Zelnik-Manor	Technion – Israel Institute of Technology, Israel

Program Chairs

Shai Avidan	Tel-Aviv University, Israel
Gabriel Brostow	University College London, UK
Moustapha Cissé	Google AI, Ghana
Giovanni Maria Farinella	University of Catania, Italy
Tal Hassner	Facebook AI, USA

Program Technical Chair

Pavel Lifshits	Technion – Israel Institute of Technology, Israel

Workshops Chairs

Leonid Karlinsky	IBM Research, Israel
Tomer Michaeli	Technion – Israel Institute of Technology, Israel
Ko Nishino	Kyoto University, Japan

Tutorial Chairs

Thomas Pock	Graz University of Technology, Austria
Natalia Neverova	Facebook AI Research, UK

Demo Chair

Bohyung Han	Seoul National University, Korea

Social and Student Activities Chairs

Tatiana Tommasi   Italian Institute of Technology, Italy
Sagie Benaim   University of Copenhagen, Denmark

Diversity and Inclusion Chairs

Xi Yin   Facebook AI Research, USA
Bryan Russell   Adobe, USA

Communications Chairs

Lorenzo Baraldi   University of Modena and Reggio Emilia, Italy
Kosta Derpanis   York University & Samsung AI Centre Toronto,
                                      Canada

Industrial Liaison Chairs

Dimosthenis Karatzas   Universitat Autònoma de Barcelona, Spain
Chen Sagiv   SagivTech, Israel

Finance Chair

Gerard Medioni   University of Southern California & Amazon,
                                      USA

Publication Chair

Eric Mortensen   MiCROTEC, USA

Area Chairs

Lourdes Agapito   University College London, UK
Zeynep Akata   University of Tübingen, Germany
Naveed Akhtar   University of Western Australia, Australia
Karteek Alahari   Inria Grenoble Rhône-Alpes, France
Alexandre Alahi   École polytechnique fédérale de Lausanne,
                                      Switzerland
Pablo Arbelaez   Universidad de Los Andes, Columbia
Antonis A. Argyros   University of Crete & Foundation for Research
                                      and Technology-Hellas, Crete
Yuki M. Asano   University of Amsterdam, The Netherlands
Kalle Åström   Lund University, Sweden
Hadar Averbuch-Elor   Cornell University, USA

Hossein Azizpour — KTH Royal Institute of Technology, Sweden
Vineeth N. Balasubramanian — Indian Institute of Technology, Hyderabad, India
Lamberto Ballan — University of Padova, Italy
Adrien Bartoli — Université Clermont Auvergne, France
Horst Bischof — Graz University of Technology, Austria
Matthew B. Blaschko — KU Leuven, Belgium
Federica Bogo — Meta Reality Labs Research, Switzerland
Katherine Bouman — California Institute of Technology, USA
Edmond Boyer — Inria Grenoble Rhône-Alpes, France
Michael S. Brown — York University, Canada
Vittorio Caggiano — Meta AI Research, USA
Neill Campbell — University of Bath, UK
Octavia Camps — Northeastern University, USA
Duygu Ceylan — Adobe Research, USA
Ayan Chakrabarti — Google Research, USA
Tat-Jen Cham — Nanyang Technological University, Singapore
Antoni Chan — City University of Hong Kong, Hong Kong, China
Manmohan Chandraker — NEC Labs America, USA
Xinlei Chen — Facebook AI Research, USA
Xilin Chen — Institute of Computing Technology, Chinese Academy of Sciences, China
Dongdong Chen — Microsoft Cloud AI, USA
Chen Chen — University of Central Florida, USA
Ondrej Chum — Vision Recognition Group, Czech Technical University in Prague, Czech Republic
John Collomosse — Adobe Research & University of Surrey, UK
Camille Couprie — Facebook, France
David Crandall — Indiana University, USA
Daniel Cremers — Technical University of Munich, Germany
Marco Cristani — University of Verona, Italy
Canton Cristian — Facebook AI Research, USA
Dengxin Dai — ETH Zurich, Switzerland
Dima Damen — University of Bristol, UK
Kostas Daniilidis — University of Pennsylvania, USA
Trevor Darrell — University of California, Berkeley, USA
Andrew Davison — Imperial College London, UK
Tali Dekel — Weizmann Institute of Science, Israel
Alessio Del Bue — Istituto Italiano di Tecnologia, Italy
Weihong Deng — Beijing University of Posts and Telecommunications, China
Konstantinos Derpanis — Ryerson University, Canada
Carl Doersch — DeepMind, UK

Matthijs Douze	Facebook AI Research, USA
Mohamed Elhoseiny	King Abdullah University of Science and Technology, Saudi Arabia
Sergio Escalera	University of Barcelona, Spain
Yi Fang	New York University, USA
Ryan Farrell	Brigham Young University, USA
Alireza Fathi	Google, USA
Christoph Feichtenhofer	Facebook AI Research, USA
Basura Fernando	Agency for Science, Technology and Research (A*STAR), Singapore
Vittorio Ferrari	Google Research, Switzerland
Andrew W. Fitzgibbon	Graphcore, UK
David J. Fleet	University of Toronto, Canada
David Forsyth	University of Illinois at Urbana-Champaign, USA
David Fouhey	University of Michigan, USA
Katerina Fragkiadaki	Carnegie Mellon University, USA
Friedrich Fraundorfer	Graz University of Technology, Austria
Oren Freifeld	Ben-Gurion University, Israel
Thomas Funkhouser	Google Research & Princeton University, USA
Yasutaka Furukawa	Simon Fraser University, Canada
Fabio Galasso	Sapienza University of Rome, Italy
Jürgen Gall	University of Bonn, Germany
Chuang Gan	Massachusetts Institute of Technology, USA
Zhe Gan	Microsoft, USA
Animesh Garg	University of Toronto, Vector Institute, Nvidia, Canada
Efstratios Gavves	University of Amsterdam, The Netherlands
Peter Gehler	Amazon, Germany
Theo Gevers	University of Amsterdam, The Netherlands
Bernard Ghanem	King Abdullah University of Science and Technology, Saudi Arabia
Ross B. Girshick	Facebook AI Research, USA
Georgia Gkioxari	Facebook AI Research, USA
Albert Gordo	Facebook, USA
Stephen Gould	Australian National University, Australia
Venu Madhav Govindu	Indian Institute of Science, India
Kristen Grauman	Facebook AI Research & UT Austin, USA
Abhinav Gupta	Carnegie Mellon University & Facebook AI Research, USA
Mohit Gupta	University of Wisconsin-Madison, USA
Hu Han	Institute of Computing Technology, Chinese Academy of Sciences, China

Bohyung Han	Seoul National University, Korea
Tian Han	Stevens Institute of Technology, USA
Emily Hand	University of Nevada, Reno, USA
Bharath Hariharan	Cornell University, USA
Ran He	Institute of Automation, Chinese Academy of Sciences, China
Otmar Hilliges	ETH Zurich, Switzerland
Adrian Hilton	University of Surrey, UK
Minh Hoai	Stony Brook University, USA
Yedid Hoshen	Hebrew University of Jerusalem, Israel
Timothy Hospedales	University of Edinburgh, UK
Gang Hua	Wormpex AI Research, USA
Di Huang	Beihang University, China
Jing Huang	Facebook, USA
Jia-Bin Huang	Facebook, USA
Nathan Jacobs	Washington University in St. Louis, USA
C.V. Jawahar	International Institute of Information Technology, Hyderabad, India
Herve Jegou	Facebook AI Research, France
Neel Joshi	Microsoft Research, USA
Armand Joulin	Facebook AI Research, France
Frederic Jurie	University of Caen Normandie, France
Fredrik Kahl	Chalmers University of Technology, Sweden
Yannis Kalantidis	NAVER LABS Europe, France
Evangelos Kalogerakis	University of Massachusetts, Amherst, USA
Sing Bing Kang	Zillow Group, USA
Yosi Keller	Bar Ilan University, Israel
Margret Keuper	University of Mannheim, Germany
Tae-Kyun Kim	Imperial College London, UK
Benjamin Kimia	Brown University, USA
Alexander Kirillov	Facebook AI Research, USA
Kris Kitani	Carnegie Mellon University, USA
Iasonas Kokkinos	Snap Inc. & University College London, UK
Vladlen Koltun	Apple, USA
Nikos Komodakis	University of Crete, Crete
Piotr Koniusz	Australian National University, Australia
Philipp Kraehenbuehl	University of Texas at Austin, USA
Dilip Krishnan	Google, USA
Ajay Kumar	Hong Kong Polytechnic University, Hong Kong, China
Junseok Kwon	Chung-Ang University, Korea
Jean-Francois Lalonde	Université Laval, Canada

Vittorio Murino	Istituto Italiano di Tecnologia, Italy
P. J. Narayanan	International Institute of Information Technology, Hyderabad, India
Ram Nevatia	University of Southern California, USA
Natalia Neverova	Facebook AI Research, UK
Richard Newcombe	Facebook, USA
Cuong V. Nguyen	Florida International University, USA
Bingbing Ni	Shanghai Jiao Tong University, China
Juan Carlos Niebles	Salesforce & Stanford University, USA
Ko Nishino	Kyoto University, Japan
Jean-Marc Odobez	Idiap Research Institute, École polytechnique fédérale de Lausanne, Switzerland
Francesca Odone	University of Genova, Italy
Takayuki Okatani	Tohoku University & RIKEN Center for Advanced Intelligence Project, Japan
Manohar Paluri	Facebook, USA
Guan Pang	Facebook, USA
Maja Pantic	Imperial College London, UK
Sylvain Paris	Adobe Research, USA
Jaesik Park	Pohang University of Science and Technology, Korea
Hyun Soo Park	The University of Minnesota, USA
Omkar M. Parkhi	Facebook, USA
Deepak Pathak	Carnegie Mellon University, USA
Georgios Pavlakos	University of California, Berkeley, USA
Marcello Pelillo	University of Venice, Italy
Marc Pollefeys	ETH Zurich & Microsoft, Switzerland
Jean Ponce	Inria, France
Gerard Pons-Moll	University of Tübingen, Germany
Fatih Porikli	Qualcomm, USA
Victor Adrian Prisacariu	University of Oxford, UK
Petia Radeva	University of Barcelona, Spain
Ravi Ramamoorthi	University of California, San Diego, USA
Deva Ramanan	Carnegie Mellon University, USA
Vignesh Ramanathan	Facebook, USA
Nalini Ratha	State University of New York at Buffalo, USA
Tammy Riklin Raviv	Ben-Gurion University, Israel
Tobias Ritschel	University College London, UK
Emanuele Rodola	Sapienza University of Rome, Italy
Amit K. Roy-Chowdhury	University of California, Riverside, USA
Michael Rubinstein	Google, USA
Olga Russakovsky	Princeton University, USA

Mathieu Salzmann	École polytechnique fédérale de Lausanne, Switzerland
Dimitris Samaras	Stony Brook University, USA
Aswin Sankaranarayanan	Carnegie Mellon University, USA
Imari Sato	National Institute of Informatics, Japan
Yoichi Sato	University of Tokyo, Japan
Shin'ichi Satoh	National Institute of Informatics, Japan
Walter Scheirer	University of Notre Dame, USA
Bernt Schiele	Max Planck Institute for Informatics, Germany
Konrad Schindler	ETH Zurich, Switzerland
Cordelia Schmid	Inria & Google, France
Alexander Schwing	University of Illinois at Urbana-Champaign, USA
Nicu Sebe	University of Trento, Italy
Greg Shakhnarovich	Toyota Technological Institute at Chicago, USA
Eli Shechtman	Adobe Research, USA
Humphrey Shi	University of Oregon & University of Illinois at Urbana-Champaign & Picsart AI Research, USA
Jianbo Shi	University of Pennsylvania, USA
Roy Shilkrot	Massachusetts Institute of Technology, USA
Mike Zheng Shou	National University of Singapore, Singapore
Kaleem Siddiqi	McGill University, Canada
Richa Singh	Indian Institute of Technology Jodhpur, India
Greg Slabaugh	Queen Mary University of London, UK
Cees Snoek	University of Amsterdam, The Netherlands
Yale Song	Facebook AI Research, USA
Yi-Zhe Song	University of Surrey, UK
Bjorn Stenger	Rakuten Institute of Technology
Abby Stylianou	Saint Louis University, USA
Akihiro Sugimoto	National Institute of Informatics, Japan
Chen Sun	Brown University, USA
Deqing Sun	Google, USA
Kalyan Sunkavalli	Adobe Research, USA
Ying Tai	Tencent YouTu Lab, China
Ayellet Tal	Technion – Israel Institute of Technology, Israel
Ping Tan	Simon Fraser University, Canada
Siyu Tang	ETH Zurich, Switzerland
Chi-Keung Tang	Hong Kong University of Science and Technology, Hong Kong, China
Radu Timofte	University of Würzburg, Germany & ETH Zurich, Switzerland
Federico Tombari	Google, Switzerland & Technical University of Munich, Germany

James Tompkin	Brown University, USA
Lorenzo Torresani	Dartmouth College, USA
Alexander Toshev	Apple, USA
Du Tran	Facebook AI Research, USA
Anh T. Tran	VinAI, Vietnam
Zhuowen Tu	University of California, San Diego, USA
Georgios Tzimiropoulos	Queen Mary University of London, UK
Jasper Uijlings	Google Research, Switzerland
Jan C. van Gemert	Delft University of Technology, The Netherlands
Gul Varol	Ecole des Ponts ParisTech, France
Nuno Vasconcelos	University of California, San Diego, USA
Mayank Vatsa	Indian Institute of Technology Jodhpur, India
Ashok Veeraraghavan	Rice University, USA
Jakob Verbeek	Facebook AI Research, France
Carl Vondrick	Columbia University, USA
Ruiping Wang	Institute of Computing Technology, Chinese Academy of Sciences, China
Xinchao Wang	National University of Singapore, Singapore
Liwei Wang	The Chinese University of Hong Kong, Hong Kong, China
Chaohui Wang	Université Paris-Est, France
Xiaolong Wang	University of California, San Diego, USA
Christian Wolf	NAVER LABS Europe, France
Tao Xiang	University of Surrey, UK
Saining Xie	Facebook AI Research, USA
Cihang Xie	University of California, Santa Cruz, USA
Zeki Yalniz	Facebook, USA
Ming-Hsuan Yang	University of California, Merced, USA
Angela Yao	National University of Singapore, Singapore
Shaodi You	University of Amsterdam, The Netherlands
Stella X. Yu	University of California, Berkeley, USA
Junsong Yuan	State University of New York at Buffalo, USA
Stefanos Zafeiriou	Imperial College London, UK
Amir Zamir	École polytechnique fédérale de Lausanne, Switzerland
Lei Zhang	Alibaba & Hong Kong Polytechnic University, Hong Kong, China
Lei Zhang	International Digital Economy Academy (IDEA), China
Pengchuan Zhang	Meta AI, USA
Bolei Zhou	University of California, Los Angeles, USA
Yuke Zhu	University of Texas at Austin, USA

Todd Zickler   Harvard University, USA
Wangmeng Zuo   Harbin Institute of Technology, China

Technical Program Committee

Davide Abati
Soroush Abbasi
   Koohpayegani
Amos L. Abbott
Rameen Abdal
Rabab Abdelfattah
Sahar Abdelnabi
Hassan Abu Alhaija
Abulikemu Abuduweili
Ron Abutbul
Hanno Ackermann
Aikaterini Adam
Kamil Adamczewski
Ehsan Adeli
Vida Adeli
Donald Adjeroh
Arman Afrasiyabi
Akshay Agarwal
Sameer Agarwal
Abhinav Agarwalla
Vaibhav Aggarwal
Sara Aghajanzadeh
Susmit Agrawal
Antonio Agudo
Touqeer Ahmad
Sk Miraj Ahmed
Chaitanya Ahuja
Nilesh A. Ahuja
Abhishek Aich
Shubhra Aich
Noam Aigerman
Arash Akbarinia
Peri Akiva
Derya Akkaynak
Emre Aksan
Arjun R. Akula
Yuval Alaluf
Stephan Alaniz
Paul Albert
Cenek Albl

Filippo Aleotti
Konstantinos P.
   Alexandridis
Motasem Alfarra
Mohsen Ali
Thiemo Alldieck
Hadi Alzayer
Liang An
Shan An
Yi An
Zhulin An
Dongsheng An
Jie An
Xiang An
Saket Anand
Cosmin Ancuti
Juan Andrade-Cetto
Alexander Andreopoulos
Bjoern Andres
Jerone T. A. Andrews
Shivangi Aneja
Anelia Angelova
Dragomir Anguelov
Rushil Anirudh
Oron Anschel
Rao Muhammad Anwer
Djamila Aouada
Evlampios Apostolidis
Srikar Appalaraju
Nikita Araslanov
Andre Araujo
Eric Arazo
Dawit Mureja Argaw
Anurag Arnab
Aditya Arora
Chetan Arora
Sunpreet S. Arora
Alexey Artemov
Muhammad Asad
Kumar Ashutosh

Sinem Aslan
Vishal Asnani
Mahmoud Assran
Amir Atapour-Abarghouei
Nikos Athanasiou
Ali Athar
ShahRukh Athar
Sara Atito
Souhaib Attaiki
Matan Atzmon
Mathieu Aubry
Nicolas Audebert
Tristan T.
   Aumentado-Armstrong
Melinos Averkiou
Yannis Avrithis
Stephane Ayache
Mehmet Aygün
Seyed Mehdi
   Ayyoubzadeh
Hossein Azizpour
George Azzopardi
Mallikarjun B. R.
Yunhao Ba
Abhishek Badki
Seung-Hwan Bae
Seung-Hwan Baek
Seungryul Baek
Piyush Nitin Bagad
Shai Bagon
Gaetan Bahl
Shikhar Bahl
Sherwin Bahmani
Haoran Bai
Lei Bai
Jiawang Bai
Haoyue Bai
Jinbin Bai
Xiang Bai
Xuyang Bai

Yang Bai
Yuanchao Bai
Ziqian Bai
Sungyong Baik
Kevin Bailly
Max Bain
Federico Baldassarre
Wele Gedara Chaminda
    Bandara
Biplab Banerjee
Pratyay Banerjee
Sandipan Banerjee
Jihwan Bang
Antyanta Bangunharcana
Aayush Bansal
Ankan Bansal
Siddhant Bansal
Wentao Bao
Zhipeng Bao
Amir Bar
Manel Baradad Jurjo
Lorenzo Baraldi
Danny Barash
Daniel Barath
Connelly Barnes
Ioan Andrei Bârsan
Steven Basart
Dina Bashkirova
Chaim Baskin
Peyman Bateni
Anil Batra
Sebastiano Battiato
Ardhendu Behera
Harkirat Behl
Jens Behley
Vasileios Belagiannis
Boulbaba Ben Amor
Emanuel Ben Baruch
Abdessamad Ben Hamza
Gil Ben-Artzi
Assia Benbihi
Fabian Benitez-Quiroz
Guy Ben-Yosef
Philipp Benz
Alexander W. Bergman

Urs Bergmann
Jesus Bermudez-Cameo
Stefano Berretti
Gedas Bertasius
Zachary Bessinger
Petra Bevandić
Matthew Beveridge
Lucas Beyer
Yash Bhalgat
Suvaansh Bhambri
Samarth Bharadwaj
Gaurav Bharaj
Aparna Bharati
Bharat Lal Bhatnagar
Uttaran Bhattacharya
Apratim Bhattacharyya
Brojeshwar Bhowmick
Ankan Kumar Bhunia
Ayan Kumar Bhunia
Qi Bi
Sai Bi
Michael Bi Mi
Gui-Bin Bian
Jia-Wang Bian
Shaojun Bian
Pia Bideau
Mario Bijelic
Hakan Bilen
Guillaume-Alexandre
    Bilodeau
Alexander Binder
Tolga Birdal
Vighnesh N. Birodkar
Sandika Biswas
Andreas Blattmann
Janusz Bobulski
Giuseppe Boccignone
Vishnu Boddeti
Navaneeth Bodla
Moritz Böhle
Aleksei Bokhovkin
Sam Bond-Taylor
Vivek Boominathan
Shubhankar Borse
Mark Boss

Andrea Bottino
Adnane Boukhayma
Fadi Boutros
Nicolas C. Boutry
Richard S. Bowen
Ivaylo Boyadzhiev
Aidan Boyd
Yuri Boykov
Aljaz Bozic
Behzad Bozorgtabar
Eric Brachmann
Samarth Brahmbhatt
Gustav Bredell
Francois Bremond
Joel Brogan
Andrew Brown
Thomas Brox
Marcus A. Brubaker
Robert-Jan Bruintjes
Yuqi Bu
Anders G. Buch
Himanshu Buckchash
Mateusz Buda
Ignas Budvytis
José M. Buenaposada
Marcel C. Bühler
Tu Bui
Adrian Bulat
Hannah Bull
Evgeny Burnaev
Andrei Bursuc
Benjamin Busam
Sergey N. Buzykanov
Wonmin Byeon
Fabian Caba
Martin Cadik
Guanyu Cai
Minjie Cai
Qing Cai
Zhongang Cai
Qi Cai
Yancheng Cai
Shen Cai
Han Cai
Jiarui Cai

Bowen Cai
Mu Cai
Qin Cai
Ruojin Cai
Weidong Cai
Weiwei Cai
Yi Cai
Yujun Cai
Zhiping Cai
Akin Caliskan
Lilian Calvet
Baris Can Cam
Necati Cihan Camgoz
Tommaso Campari
Dylan Campbell
Ziang Cao
Ang Cao
Xu Cao
Zhiwen Cao
Shengcao Cao
Song Cao
Weipeng Cao
Xiangyong Cao
Xiaochun Cao
Yue Cao
Yunhao Cao
Zhangjie Cao
Jiale Cao
Yang Cao
Jiajiong Cao
Jie Cao
Jinkun Cao
Lele Cao
Yulong Cao
Zhiguo Cao
Chen Cao
Razvan Caramalau
Marlène Careil
Gustavo Carneiro
Joao Carreira
Dan Casas
Paola Cascante-Bonilla
Angela Castillo
Francisco M. Castro
Pedro Castro

Luca Cavalli
George J. Cazenavette
Oya Celiktutan
Hakan Cevikalp
Sri Harsha C. H.
Sungmin Cha
Geonho Cha
Menglei Chai
Lucy Chai
Yuning Chai
Zenghao Chai
Anirban Chakraborty
Deep Chakraborty
Rudrasis Chakraborty
Souradeep Chakraborty
Kelvin C. K. Chan
Chee Seng Chan
Paramanand Chandramouli
Arjun Chandrasekaran
Kenneth Chaney
Dongliang Chang
Huiwen Chang
Peng Chang
Xiaojun Chang
Jia-Ren Chang
Hyung Jin Chang
Hyun Sung Chang
Ju Yong Chang
Li-Jen Chang
Qi Chang
Wei-Yi Chang
Yi Chang
Nadine Chang
Hanqing Chao
Pradyumna Chari
Dibyadip Chatterjee
Chiranjoy Chattopadhyay
Siddhartha Chaudhuri
Zhengping Che
Gal Chechik
Lianggangxu Chen
Qi Alfred Chen
Brian Chen
Bor-Chun Chen
Bo-Hao Chen

Bohong Chen
Bin Chen
Ziliang Chen
Cheng Chen
Chen Chen
Chaofeng Chen
Xi Chen
Haoyu Chen
Xuanhong Chen
Wei Chen
Qiang Chen
Shi Chen
Xianyu Chen
Chang Chen
Changhuai Chen
Hao Chen
Jie Chen
Jianbo Chen
Jingjing Chen
Jun Chen
Kejiang Chen
Mingcai Chen
Nenglun Chen
Qifeng Chen
Ruoyu Chen
Shu-Yu Chen
Weidong Chen
Weijie Chen
Weikai Chen
Xiang Chen
Xiuyi Chen
Xingyu Chen
Yaofo Chen
Yueting Chen
Yu Chen
Yunjin Chen
Yuntao Chen
Yun Chen
Zhenfang Chen
Zhuangzhuang Chen
Chu-Song Chen
Xiangyu Chen
Zhuo Chen
Chaoqi Chen
Shizhe Chen

Xiaotong Chen
Xiaozhi Chen
Dian Chen
Defang Chen
Dingfan Chen
Ding-Jie Chen
Ee Heng Chen
Tao Chen
Yixin Chen
Wei-Ting Chen
Lin Chen
Guang Chen
Guangyi Chen
Guanying Chen
Guangyao Chen
Hwann-Tzong Chen
Junwen Chen
Jiacheng Chen
Jianxu Chen
Hui Chen
Kai Chen
Kan Chen
Kevin Chen
Kuan-Wen Chen
Weihua Chen
Zhang Chen
Liang-Chieh Chen
Lele Chen
Liang Chen
Fanglin Chen
Zehui Chen
Minghui Chen
Minghao Chen
Xiaokang Chen
Qian Chen
Jun-Cheng Chen
Qi Chen
Qingcai Chen
Richard J. Chen
Runnan Chen
Rui Chen
Shuo Chen
Sentao Chen
Shaoyu Chen
Shixing Chen

Shuai Chen
Shuya Chen
Sizhe Chen
Simin Chen
Shaoxiang Chen
Zitian Chen
Tianlong Chen
Tianshui Chen
Min-Hung Chen
Xiangning Chen
Xin Chen
Xinghao Chen
Xuejin Chen
Xu Chen
Xuxi Chen
Yunlu Chen
Yanbei Chen
Yuxiao Chen
Yun-Chun Chen
Yi-Ting Chen
Yi-Wen Chen
Yinbo Chen
Yiran Chen
Yuanhong Chen
Yubei Chen
Yuefeng Chen
Yuhua Chen
Yukang Chen
Zerui Chen
Zhaoyu Chen
Zhen Chen
Zhenyu Chen
Zhi Chen
Zhiwei Chen
Zhixiang Chen
Long Chen
Bowen Cheng
Jun Cheng
Yi Cheng
Jingchun Cheng
Lechao Cheng
Xi Cheng
Yuan Cheng
Ho Kei Cheng
Kevin Ho Man Cheng

Jiacheng Cheng
Kelvin B. Cheng
Li Cheng
Mengjun Cheng
Zhen Cheng
Qingrong Cheng
Tianheng Cheng
Harry Cheng
Yihua Cheng
Yu Cheng
Ziheng Cheng
Soon Yau Cheong
Anoop Cherian
Manuela Chessa
Zhixiang Chi
Naoki Chiba
Julian Chibane
Kashyap Chitta
Tai-Yin Chiu
Hsu-kuang Chiu
Wei-Chen Chiu
Sungmin Cho
Donghyeon Cho
Hyeon Cho
Yooshin Cho
Gyusang Cho
Jang Hyun Cho
Seungju Cho
Nam Ik Cho
Sunghyun Cho
Hanbyel Cho
Jaesung Choe
Jooyoung Choi
Chiho Choi
Changwoon Choi
Jongwon Choi
Myungsub Choi
Dooseop Choi
Jonghyun Choi
Jinwoo Choi
Jun Won Choi
Min-Kook Choi
Hongsuk Choi
Janghoon Choi
Yoon-Ho Choi

Yukyung Choi
Jaegul Choo
Ayush Chopra
Siddharth Choudhary
Subhabrata Choudhury
Vasileios Choutas
Ka-Ho Chow
Pinaki Nath Chowdhury
Sammy Christen
Anders Christensen
Grigorios Chrysos
Hang Chu
Wen-Hsuan Chu
Peng Chu
Qi Chu
Ruihang Chu
Wei-Ta Chu
Yung-Yu Chuang
Sanghyuk Chun
Se Young Chun
Antonio Cinà
Ramazan Gokberk Cinbis
Javier Civera
Albert Clapés
Ronald Clark
Brian S. Clipp
Felipe Codevilla
Daniel Coelho de Castro
Niv Cohen
Forrester Cole
Maxwell D. Collins
Robert T. Collins
Marc Comino Trinidad
Runmin Cong
Wenyan Cong
Maxime Cordy
Marcella Cornia
Enric Corona
Huseyin Coskun
Luca Cosmo
Dragos Costea
Davide Cozzolino
Arun C. S. Kumar
Aiyu Cui
Qiongjie Cui

Quan Cui
Shuhao Cui
Yiming Cui
Ying Cui
Zijun Cui
Jiali Cui
Jiequan Cui
Yawen Cui
Zhen Cui
Zhaopeng Cui
Jack Culpepper
Xiaodong Cun
Ross Cutler
Adam Czajka
Ali Dabouei
Konstantinos M. Dafnis
Manuel Dahnert
Tao Dai
Yuchao Dai
Bo Dai
Mengyu Dai
Hang Dai
Haixing Dai
Peng Dai
Pingyang Dai
Qi Dai
Qiyu Dai
Yutong Dai
Naser Damer
Zhiyuan Dang
Mohamed Daoudi
Ayan Das
Abir Das
Debasmit Das
Deepayan Das
Partha Das
Sagnik Das
Soumi Das
Srijan Das
Swagatam Das
Avijit Dasgupta
Jim Davis
Adrian K. Davison
Homa Davoudi
Laura Daza

Matthias De Lange
Shalini De Mello
Marco De Nadai
Christophe De
    Vleeschouwer
Alp Dener
Boyang Deng
Congyue Deng
Bailin Deng
Yong Deng
Ye Deng
Zhuo Deng
Zhijie Deng
Xiaoming Deng
Jiankang Deng
Jinhong Deng
Jingjing Deng
Liang-Jian Deng
Siqi Deng
Xiang Deng
Xueqing Deng
Zhongying Deng
Karan Desai
Jean-Emmanuel Deschaud
Aniket Anand Deshmukh
Neel Dey
Helisa Dhamo
Prithviraj Dhar
Amaya Dharmasiri
Yan Di
Xing Di
Ousmane A. Dia
Haiwen Diao
Xiaolei Diao
Gonçalo José Dias Pais
Abdallah Dib
Anastasios Dimou
Changxing Ding
Henghui Ding
Guodong Ding
Yaqing Ding
Shuangrui Ding
Yuhang Ding
Yikang Ding
Shouhong Ding

Haisong Ding
Hui Ding
Jiahao Ding
Jian Ding
Jian-Jiun Ding
Shuxiao Ding
Tianyu Ding
Wenhao Ding
Yuqi Ding
Yi Ding
Yuzhen Ding
Zhengming Ding
Tan Minh Dinh
Vu Dinh
Christos Diou
Mandar Dixit
Bao Gia Doan
Khoa D. Doan
Dzung Anh Doan
Debi Prosad Dogra
Nehal Doiphode
Chengdong Dong
Bowen Dong
Zhenxing Dong
Hang Dong
Xiaoyi Dong
Haoye Dong
Jiangxin Dong
Shichao Dong
Xuan Dong
Zhen Dong
Shuting Dong
Jing Dong
Li Dong
Ming Dong
Nanqing Dong
Qiulei Dong
Runpei Dong
Siyan Dong
Tian Dong
Wei Dong
Xiaomeng Dong
Xin Dong
Xingbo Dong
Yuan Dong

Samuel Dooley
Gianfranco Doretto
Michael Dorkenwald
Keval Doshi
Zhaopeng Dou
Xiaotian Dou
Hazel Doughty
Ahmad Droby
Iddo Drori
Jie Du
Yong Du
Dawei Du
Dong Du
Ruoyi Du
Yuntao Du
Xuefeng Du
Yilun Du
Yuming Du
Radhika Dua
Haodong Duan
Jiafei Duan
Kaiwen Duan
Peiqi Duan
Ye Duan
Haoran Duan
Jiali Duan
Amanda Duarte
Abhimanyu Dubey
Shiv Ram Dubey
Florian Dubost
Lukasz Dudziak
Shivam Duggal
Justin M. Dulay
Matteo Dunnhofer
Chi Nhan Duong
Thibaut Durand
Mihai Dusmanu
Ujjal Kr Dutta
Debidatta Dwibedi
Isht Dwivedi
Sai Kumar Dwivedi
Takeharu Eda
Mark Edmonds
Alexei A. Efros
Thibaud Ehret

Max Ehrlich
Mahsa Ehsanpour
Iván Eichhardt
Farshad Einabadi
Marvin Eisenberger
Hazim Kemal Ekenel
Mohamed El Banani
Ismail Elezi
Moshe Eliasof
Alaa El-Nouby
Ian Endres
Francis Engelmann
Deniz Engin
Chanho Eom
Dave Epstein
Maria C. Escobar
Victor A. Escorcia
Carlos Esteves
Sungmin Eum
Bernard J. E. Evans
Ivan Evtimov
Fevziye Irem Eyiokur
Yaman
Matteo Fabbri
Sébastien Fabbro
Gabriele Facciolo
Masud Fahim
Bin Fan
Hehe Fan
Deng-Ping Fan
Aoxiang Fan
Chen-Chen Fan
Qi Fan
Zhaoxin Fan
Haoqi Fan
Heng Fan
Hongyi Fan
Linxi Fan
Baojie Fan
Jiayuan Fan
Lei Fan
Quanfu Fan
Yonghui Fan
Yingruo Fan
Zhiwen Fan

Zicong Fan
Sean Fanello
Jiansheng Fang
Chaowei Fang
Yuming Fang
Jianwu Fang
Jin Fang
Qi Fang
Shancheng Fang
Tian Fang
Xianyong Fang
Gongfan Fang
Zhen Fang
Hui Fang
Jiemin Fang
Le Fang
Pengfei Fang
Xiaolin Fang
Yuxin Fang
Zhaoyuan Fang
Ammarah Farooq
Azade Farshad
Zhengcong Fei
Michael Felsberg
Wei Feng
Chen Feng
Fan Feng
Andrew Feng
Xin Feng
Zheyun Feng
Ruicheng Feng
Mingtao Feng
Qianyu Feng
Shangbin Feng
Chun-Mei Feng
Zunlei Feng
Zhiyong Feng
Martin Fergie
Mustansar Fiaz
Marco Fiorucci
Michael Firman
Hamed Firooz
Volker Fischer
Corneliu O. Florea
Georgios Floros

Wolfgang Foerstner
Gianni Franchi
Jean-Sebastien Franco
Simone Frintrop
Anna Fruehstueck
Changhong Fu
Chaoyou Fu
Cheng-Yang Fu
Chi-Wing Fu
Deqing Fu
Huan Fu
Jun Fu
Kexue Fu
Ying Fu
Jianlong Fu
Jingjing Fu
Qichen Fu
Tsu-Jui Fu
Xueyang Fu
Yang Fu
Yanwei Fu
Yonggan Fu
Wolfgang Fuhl
Yasuhisa Fujii
Kent Fujiwara
Marco Fumero
Takuya Funatomi
Isabel Funke
Dario Fuoli
Antonino Furnari
Matheus A. Gadelha
Akshay Gadi Patil
Adrian Galdran
Guillermo Gallego
Silvano Galliani
Orazio Gallo
Leonardo Galteri
Matteo Gamba
Yiming Gan
Sujoy Ganguly
Harald Ganster
Boyan Gao
Changxin Gao
Daiheng Gao
Difei Gao

Chen Gao
Fei Gao
Lin Gao
Wei Gao
Yiming Gao
Junyu Gao
Guangyu Ryan Gao
Haichang Gao
Hongchang Gao
Jialin Gao
Jin Gao
Jun Gao
Katelyn Gao
Mingchen Gao
Mingfei Gao
Pan Gao
Shangqian Gao
Shanghua Gao
Xitong Gao
Yunhe Gao
Zhanning Gao
Elena Garces
Nuno Cruz Garcia
Noa Garcia
Guillermo
    Garcia-Hernando
Isha Garg
Rahul Garg
Sourav Garg
Quentin Garrido
Stefano Gasperini
Kent Gauen
Chandan Gautam
Shivam Gautam
Paul Gay
Chunjiang Ge
Shiming Ge
Wenhang Ge
Yanhao Ge
Zheng Ge
Songwei Ge
Weifeng Ge
Yixiao Ge
Yuying Ge
Shijie Geng

Zhengyang Geng
Kyle A. Genova
Georgios Georgakis
Markos Georgopoulos
Marcel Geppert
Shabnam Ghadar
Mina Ghadimi Atigh
Deepti Ghadiyaram
Maani Ghaffari Jadidi
Sedigh Ghamari
Zahra Gharaee
Michaël Gharbi
Golnaz Ghiasi
Reza Ghoddoosian
Soumya Suvra Ghosal
Adhiraj Ghosh
Arthita Ghosh
Pallabi Ghosh
Soumyadeep Ghosh
Andrew Gilbert
Igor Gilitschenski
Jhony H. Giraldo
Andreu Girbau Xalabarder
Rohit Girdhar
Sharath Girish
Xavier Giro-i-Nieto
Raja Giryes
Thomas Gittings
Nikolaos Gkanatsios
Ioannis Gkioulekas
Abhiram
    Gnanasambandam
Aurele T. Gnanha
Clement L. J. C. Godard
Arushi Goel
Vidit Goel
Shubham Goel
Zan Gojcic
Aaron K. Gokaslan
Tejas Gokhale
S. Alireza Golestaneh
Thiago L. Gomes
Nuno Goncalves
Boqing Gong
Chen Gong

Yuanhao Gong
Guoqiang Gong
Jingyu Gong
Rui Gong
Yu Gong
Mingming Gong
Neil Zhenqiang Gong
Xun Gong
Yunye Gong
Yihong Gong
Cristina I. González
Nithin Gopalakrishnan
    Nair
Gaurav Goswami
Jianping Gou
Shreyank N. Gowda
Ankit Goyal
Helmut Grabner
Patrick L. Grady
Ben Graham
Eric Granger
Douglas R. Gray
Matej Grcić
David Griffiths
Jinjin Gu
Yun Gu
Shuyang Gu
Jianyang Gu
Fuqiang Gu
Jiatao Gu
Jindong Gu
Jiaqi Gu
Jinwei Gu
Jiaxin Gu
Geonmo Gu
Xiao Gu
Xinqian Gu
Xiuye Gu
Yuming Gu
Zhangxuan Gu
Dayan Guan
Junfeng Guan
Qingji Guan
Tianrui Guan
Shanyan Guan

Denis A. Gudovskiy
Ricardo Guerrero
Pierre-Louis Guhur
Jie Gui
Liangyan Gui
Liangke Gui
Benoit Guillard
Erhan Gundogdu
Manuel Günther
Jingcai Guo
Yuanfang Guo
Junfeng Guo
Chenqi Guo
Dan Guo
Hongji Guo
Jia Guo
Jie Guo
Minghao Guo
Shi Guo
Yanhui Guo
Yangyang Guo
Yuan-Chen Guo
Yilu Guo
Yiluan Guo
Yong Guo
Guangyu Guo
Haiyun Guo
Jinyang Guo
Jianyuan Guo
Pengsheng Guo
Pengfei Guo
Shuxuan Guo
Song Guo
Tianyu Guo
Qing Guo
Qiushan Guo
Wen Guo
Xiefan Guo
Xiaohu Guo
Xiaoqing Guo
Yufei Guo
Yuhui Guo
Yuliang Guo
Yunhui Guo
Yanwen Guo

Akshita Gupta
Ankush Gupta
Kamal Gupta
Kartik Gupta
Ritwik Gupta
Rohit Gupta
Siddharth Gururani
Fredrik K. Gustafsson
Abner Guzman Rivera
Vladimir Guzov
Matthew A. Gwilliam
Jung-Woo Ha
Marc Habermann
Isma Hadji
Christian Haene
Martin Hahner
Levente Hajder
Alexandros Haliassos
Emanuela Haller
Bumsub Ham
Abdullah J. Hamdi
Shreyas Hampali
Dongyoon Han
Chunrui Han
Dong-Jun Han
Dong-Sig Han
Guangxing Han
Zhizhong Han
Ruize Han
Jiaming Han
Jin Han
Ligong Han
Xian-Hua Han
Xiaoguang Han
Yizeng Han
Zhi Han
Zhenjun Han
Zhongyi Han
Jungong Han
Junlin Han
Kai Han
Kun Han
Sungwon Han
Songfang Han
Wei Han

Xiao Han
Xintong Han
Xinzhe Han
Yahong Han
Yan Han
Zongbo Han
Nicolai Hani
Rana Hanocka
Niklas Hanselmann
Nicklas A. Hansen
Hong Hanyu
Fusheng Hao
Yanbin Hao
Shijie Hao
Udith Haputhanthri
Mehrtash Harandi
Josh Harguess
Adam Harley
David M. Hart
Atsushi Hashimoto
Ali Hassani
Mohammed Hassanin
Yana Hasson
Joakim Bruslund Haurum
Bo He
Kun He
Chen He
Xin He
Fazhi He
Gaoqi He
Hao He
Haoyu He
Jiangpeng He
Hongliang He
Qian He
Xiangteng He
Xuming He
Yannan He
Yuhang He
Yang He
Xiangyu He
Nanjun He
Pan He
Sen He
Shengfeng He

Songtao He
Tao He
Tong He
Wei He
Xuehai He
Xiaoxiao He
Ying He
Yisheng He
Ziwen He
Peter Hedman
Felix Heide
Yacov Hel-Or
Paul Henderson
Philipp Henzler
Byeongho Heo
Jae-Pil Heo
Miran Heo
Sachini A. Herath
Stephane Herbin
Pedro Hermosilla Casajus
Monica Hernandez
Charles Herrmann
Roei Herzig
Mauricio Hess-Flores
Carlos Hinojosa
Tobias Hinz
Tsubasa Hirakawa
Chih-Hui Ho
Lam Si Tung Ho
Jennifer Hobbs
Derek Hoiem
Yannick Hold-Geoffroy
Aleksander Holynski
Cheeun Hong
Fa-Ting Hong
Hanbin Hong
Guan Zhe Hong
Danfeng Hong
Lanqing Hong
Xiaopeng Hong
Xin Hong
Jie Hong
Seungbum Hong
Cheng-Yao Hong
Seunghoon Hong

Yi Hong
Yuan Hong
Yuchen Hong
Anthony Hoogs
Maxwell C. Horton
Kazuhiro Hotta
Qibin Hou
Tingbo Hou
Junhui Hou
Ji Hou
Qiqi Hou
Rui Hou
Ruibing Hou
Zhi Hou
Henry Howard-Jenkins
Lukas Hoyer
Wei-Lin Hsiao
Chiou-Ting Hsu
Anthony Hu
Brian Hu
Yusong Hu
Hexiang Hu
Haoji Hu
Di Hu
Hengtong Hu
Haigen Hu
Lianyu Hu
Hanzhe Hu
Jie Hu
Junlin Hu
Shizhe Hu
Jian Hu
Zhiming Hu
Juhua Hu
Peng Hu
Ping Hu
Ronghang Hu
MengShun Hu
Tao Hu
Vincent Tao Hu
Xiaoling Hu
Xinting Hu
Xiaolin Hu
Xuefeng Hu
Xiaowei Hu

Yang Hu
Yueyu Hu
Zeyu Hu
Zhongyun Hu
Binh-Son Hua
Guoliang Hua
Yi Hua
Linzhi Huang
Qiusheng Huang
Bo Huang
Chen Huang
Hsin-Ping Huang
Ye Huang
Shuangping Huang
Zeng Huang
Buzhen Huang
Cong Huang
Heng Huang
Hao Huang
Qidong Huang
Huaibo Huang
Chaoqin Huang
Feihu Huang
Jiahui Huang
Jingjia Huang
Kun Huang
Lei Huang
Sheng Huang
Shuaiyi Huang
Siyu Huang
Xiaoshui Huang
Xiaoyang Huang
Yan Huang
Yihao Huang
Ying Huang
Ziling Huang
Xiaoke Huang
Yifei Huang
Haiyang Huang
Zhewei Huang
Jin Huang
Haibin Huang
Jiaxing Huang
Junjie Huang
Keli Huang

Lang Huang
Lin Huang
Luojie Huang
Mingzhen Huang
Shijia Huang
Shengyu Huang
Siyuan Huang
He Huang
Xiuyu Huang
Lianghua Huang
Yue Huang
Yaping Huang
Yuge Huang
Zehao Huang
Zeyi Huang
Zhiqi Huang
Zhongzhan Huang
Zilong Huang
Ziyuan Huang
Tianrui Hui
Zhuo Hui
Le Hui
Jing Huo
Junhwa Hur
Shehzeen S. Hussain
Chuong Minh Huynh
Seunghyun Hwang
Jaehui Hwang
Jyh-Jing Hwang
Sukjun Hwang
Soonmin Hwang
Wonjun Hwang
Rakib Hyder
Sangeek Hyun
Sarah Ibrahimi
Tomoki Ichikawa
Yerlan Idelbayev
A. S. M. Iftekhar
Masaaki Iiyama
Satoshi Ikehata
Sunghoon Im
Atul N. Ingle
Eldar Insafutdinov
Yani A. Ioannou
Radu Tudor Ionescu

Umar Iqbal
Go Irie
Muhammad Zubair Irshad
Ahmet Iscen
Berivan Isik
Ashraful Islam
Md Amirul Islam
Syed Islam
Mariko Isogawa
Vamsi Krishna K. Ithapu
Boris Ivanovic
Darshan Iyer
Sarah Jabbour
Ayush Jain
Nishant Jain
Samyak Jain
Vidit Jain
Vineet Jain
Priyank Jaini
Tomas Jakab
Mohammad A. A. K. Jalwana
Muhammad Abdullah Jamal
Hadi Jamali-Rad
Stuart James
Varun Jampani
Young Kyun Jang
YeongJun Jang
Yunseok Jang
Ronnachai Jaroensri
Bhavan Jasani
Krishna Murthy Jatavallabhula
Mojan Javaheripi
Syed A. Javed
Guillaume Jeanneret
Pranav Jeevan
Herve Jegou
Rohit Jena
Tomas Jenicek
Porter Jenkins
Simon Jenni
Hae-Gon Jeon
Sangryul Jeon

Boseung Jeong
Yoonwoo Jeong
Seong-Gyun Jeong
Jisoo Jeong
Allan D. Jepson
Ankit Jha
Sumit K. Jha
I-Hong Jhuo
Ge-Peng Ji
Chaonan Ji
Deyi Ji
Jingwei Ji
Wei Ji
Zhong Ji
Jiayi Ji
Pengliang Ji
Hui Ji
Mingi Ji
Xiaopeng Ji
Yuzhu Ji
Baoxiong Jia
Songhao Jia
Dan Jia
Shan Jia
Xiaojun Jia
Xiuyi Jia
Xu Jia
Menglin Jia
Wenqi Jia
Boyuan Jiang
Wenhao Jiang
Huaizu Jiang
Hanwen Jiang
Haiyong Jiang
Hao Jiang
Huajie Jiang
Huiqin Jiang
Haojun Jiang
Haobo Jiang
Junjun Jiang
Xingyu Jiang
Yangbangyan Jiang
Yu Jiang
Jianmin Jiang
Jiaxi Jiang

Jing Jiang
Kui Jiang
Li Jiang
Liming Jiang
Chiyu Jiang
Meirui Jiang
Chen Jiang
Peng Jiang
Tai-Xiang Jiang
Wen Jiang
Xinyang Jiang
Yifan Jiang
Yuming Jiang
Yingying Jiang
Zeren Jiang
ZhengKai Jiang
Zhenyu Jiang
Shuming Jiao
Jianbo Jiao
Licheng Jiao
Dongkwon Jin
Yeying Jin
Cheng Jin
Linyi Jin
Qing Jin
Taisong Jin
Xiao Jin
Xin Jin
Sheng Jin
Kyong Hwan Jin
Ruibing Jin
SouYoung Jin
Yueming Jin
Chenchen Jing
Longlong Jing
Taotao Jing
Yongcheng Jing
Younghyun Jo
Joakim Johnander
Jeff Johnson
Michael J. Jones
R. Kenny Jones
Rico Jonschkowski
Ameya Joshi
Sunghun Joung

Felix Juefei-Xu
Claudio R. Jung
Steffen Jung
Hari Chandana K.
Rahul Vigneswaran K.
Prajwal K. R.
Abhishek Kadian
Jhony Kaesemodel Pontes
Kumara Kahatapitiya
Anmol Kalia
Sinan Kalkan
Tarun Kalluri
Jaewon Kam
Sandesh Kamath
Meina Kan
Menelaos Kanakis
Takuhiro Kaneko
Di Kang
Guoliang Kang
Hao Kang
Jaeyeon Kang
Kyoungkook Kang
Li-Wei Kang
MinGuk Kang
Suk-Ju Kang
Zhao Kang
Yash Mukund Kant
Yueying Kao
Aupendu Kar
Konstantinos Karantzalos
Sezer Karaoglu
Navid Kardan
Sanjay Kariyappa
Leonid Karlinsky
Animesh Karnewar
Shyamgopal Karthik
Hirak J. Kashyap
Marc A. Kastner
Hirokatsu Kataoka
Angelos Katharopoulos
Hiroharu Kato
Kai Katsumata
Manuel Kaufmann
Chaitanya Kaul
Prakhar Kaushik

Yuki Kawana
Lei Ke
Lipeng Ke
Tsung-Wei Ke
Wei Ke
Petr Kellnhofer
Aniruddha Kembhavi
John Kender
Corentin Kervadec
Leonid Keselman
Daniel Keysers
Nima Khademi Kalantari
Taras Khakhulin
Samir Khaki
Muhammad Haris Khan
Qadeer Khan
Salman Khan
Subash Khanal
Vaishnavi M. Khindkar
Rawal Khirodkar
Saeed Khorram
Pirazh Khorramshahi
Kourosh Khoshelham
Ansh Khurana
Benjamin Kiefer
Jae Myung Kim
Junho Kim
Boah Kim
Hyeonseong Kim
Dong-Jin Kim
Dongwan Kim
Donghyun Kim
Doyeon Kim
Yonghyun Kim
Hyung-Il Kim
Hyunwoo Kim
Hyeongwoo Kim
Hyo Jin Kim
Hyunwoo J. Kim
Taehoon Kim
Jaeha Kim
Jiwon Kim
Jung Uk Kim
Kangyeol Kim
Eunji Kim

Daeha Kim
Dongwon Kim
Kunhee Kim
Kyungmin Kim
Junsik Kim
Min H. Kim
Namil Kim
Kookhoi Kim
Sanghyun Kim
Seongyeop Kim
Seungryong Kim
Saehoon Kim
Euyoung Kim
Guisik Kim
Sungyeon Kim
Sunnie S. Y. Kim
Taehun Kim
Tae Oh Kim
Won Hwa Kim
Seungwook Kim
YoungBin Kim
Youngeun Kim
Akisato Kimura
Furkan Osman Kınlı
Zsolt Kira
Hedvig Kjellström
Florian Kleber
Jan P. Klopp
Florian Kluger
Laurent Kneip
Byungsoo Ko
Muhammed Kocabas
A. Sophia Koepke
Kevin Koeser
Nick Kolkin
Nikos Kolotouros
Wai-Kin Adams Kong
Deying Kong
Caihua Kong
Youyong Kong
Shuyu Kong
Shu Kong
Tao Kong
Yajing Kong
Yu Kong

Zishang Kong
Theodora Kontogianni
Anton S. Konushin
Julian F. P. Kooij
Bruno Korbar
Giorgos Kordopatis-Zilos
Jari Korhonen
Adam Kortylewski
Denis Korzhenkov
Divya Kothandaraman
Suraj Kothawade
Iuliia Kotseruba
Satwik Kottur
Shashank Kotyan
Alexandros Kouris
Petros Koutras
Anna Kreshuk
Ranjay Krishna
Dilip Krishnan
Andrey Kuehlkamp
Hilde Kuehne
Jason Kuen
David Kügler
Arjan Kuijper
Anna Kukleva
Sumith Kulal
Viveka Kulharia
Akshay R. Kulkarni
Nilesh Kulkarni
Dominik Kulon
Abhinav Kumar
Akash Kumar
Suryansh Kumar
B. V. K. Vijaya Kumar
Pulkit Kumar
Ratnesh Kumar
Sateesh Kumar
Satish Kumar
Vijay Kumar B. G.
Nupur Kumari
Sudhakar Kumawat
Jogendra Nath Kundu
Hsien-Kai Kuo
Meng-Yu Jennifer Kuo
Vinod Kumar Kurmi

Yusuke Kurose
Keerthy Kusumam
Alina Kuznetsova
Henry Kvinge
Ho Man Kwan
Hyeokjun Kweon
Heeseung Kwon
Gihyun Kwon
Myung-Joon Kwon
Taesung Kwon
YoungJoong Kwon
Christos Kyrkou
Jorma Laaksonen
Yann Labbe
Zorah Laehner
Florent Lafarge
Hamid Laga
Manuel Lagunas
Shenqi Lai
Jian-Huang Lai
Zihang Lai
Mohamed I. Lakhal
Mohit Lamba
Meng Lan
Loic Landrieu
Zhiqiang Lang
Natalie Lang
Dong Lao
Yizhen Lao
Yingjie Lao
Issam Hadj Laradji
Gustav Larsson
Viktor Larsson
Zakaria Laskar
Stéphane Lathuilière
Chun Pong Lau
Rynson W. H. Lau
Hei Law
Justin Lazarow
Verica Lazova
Eric-Tuan Le
Hieu Le
Trung-Nghia Le
Mathias Lechner
Byeong-Uk Lee

Chen-Yu Lee
Che-Rung Lee
Chul Lee
Hong Joo Lee
Dongsoo Lee
Jiyoung Lee
Eugene Eu Tzuan Lee
Daeun Lee
Saehyung Lee
Jewook Lee
Hyungtae Lee
Hyunmin Lee
Jungbeom Lee
Joon-Young Lee
Jong-Seok Lee
Joonseok Lee
Junha Lee
Kibok Lee
Byung-Kwan Lee
Jangwon Lee
Jinho Lee
Jongmin Lee
Seunghyun Lee
Sohyun Lee
Minsik Lee
Dogyoon Lee
Seungmin Lee
Min Jun Lee
Sangho Lee
Sangmin Lee
Seungeun Lee
Seon-Ho Lee
Sungmin Lee
Sungho Lee
Sangyoun Lee
Vincent C. S. S. Lee
Jaeseong Lee
Yong Jae Lee
Chenyang Lei
Chenyi Lei
Jiahui Lei
Xinyu Lei
Yinjie Lei
Jiaxu Leng
Luziwei Leng

Jan E. Lenssen
Vincent Lepetit
Thomas Leung
María Leyva-Vallina
Xin Li
Yikang Li
Baoxin Li
Bin Li
Bing Li
Bowen Li
Changlin Li
Chao Li
Chongyi Li
Guanyue Li
Shuai Li
Jin Li
Dingquan Li
Dongxu Li
Yiting Li
Gang Li
Dian Li
Guohao Li
Haoang Li
Haoliang Li
Haoran Li
Hengduo Li
Huafeng Li
Xiaoming Li
Hanao Li
Hongwei Li
Ziqiang Li
Jisheng Li
Jiacheng Li
Jia Li
Jiachen Li
Jiahao Li
Jianwei Li
Jiazhi Li
Jie Li
Jing Li
Jingjing Li
Jingtao Li
Jun Li
Junxuan Li
Kai Li

Kailin Li
Kenneth Li
Kun Li
Kunpeng Li
Aoxue Li
Chenglong Li
Chenglin Li
Changsheng Li
Zhichao Li
Qiang Li
Yanyu Li
Zuoyue Li
Xiang Li
Xuelong Li
Fangda Li
Ailin Li
Liang Li
Chun-Guang Li
Daiqing Li
Dong Li
Guanbin Li
Guorong Li
Haifeng Li
Jianan Li
Jianing Li
Jiaxin Li
Ke Li
Lei Li
Lincheng Li
Liulei Li
Lujun Li
Linjie Li
Lin Li
Pengyu Li
Ping Li
Qiufu Li
Qingyong Li
Rui Li
Siyuan Li
Wei Li
Wenbin Li
Xiangyang Li
Xinyu Li
Xiujun Li
Xiu Li

Xu Li
Ya-Li Li
Yao Li
Yongjie Li
Yijun Li
Yiming Li
Yuezun Li
Yu Li
Yunheng Li
Yuqi Li
Zhe Li
Zeming Li
Zhen Li
Zhengqin Li
Zhimin Li
Jiefeng Li
Jinpeng Li
Chengze Li
Jianwu Li
Lerenhan Li
Shan Li
Suichan Li
Xiangtai Li
Yanjie Li
Yandong Li
Zhuoling Li
Zhenqiang Li
Manyi Li
Maosen Li
Ji Li
Minjun Li
Mingrui Li
Mengtian Li
Junyi Li
Nianyi Li
Bo Li
Xiao Li
Peihua Li
Peike Li
Peizhao Li
Peiliang Li
Qi Li
Ren Li
Runze Li
Shile Li

Sheng Li
Shigang Li
Shiyu Li
Shuang Li
Shasha Li
Shichao Li
Tianye Li
Yuexiang Li
Wei-Hong Li
Wanhua Li
Weihao Li
Weiming Li
Weixin Li
Wenbo Li
Wenshuo Li
Weijian Li
Yunan Li
Xirong Li
Xianhang Li
Xiaoyu Li
Xueqian Li
Xuanlin Li
Xianzhi Li
Yunqiang Li
Yanjing Li
Yansheng Li
Yawei Li
Yi Li
Yong Li
Yong-Lu Li
Yuhang Li
Yu-Jhe Li
Yuxi Li
Yunsheng Li
Yanwei Li
Zechao Li
Zejian Li
Zeju Li
Zekun Li
Zhaowen Li
Zheng Li
Zhenyu Li
Zhiheng Li
Zhi Li
Zhong Li

Zhuowei Li
Zhuowan Li
Zhuohang Li
Zizhang Li
Chen Li
Yuan-Fang Li
Dongze Lian
Xiaochen Lian
Zhouhui Lian
Long Lian
Qing Lian
Jin Lianbao
Jinxiu S. Liang
Dingkang Liang
Jiahao Liang
Jianming Liang
Jingyun Liang
Kevin J. Liang
Kaizhao Liang
Chen Liang
Jie Liang
Senwei Liang
Ding Liang
Jiajun Liang
Jian Liang
Kongming Liang
Siyuan Liang
Yuanzhi Liang
Zhengfa Liang
Mingfu Liang
Xiaodan Liang
Xuefeng Liang
Yuxuan Liang
Kang Liao
Liang Liao
Hong-Yuan Mark Liao
Wentong Liao
Haofu Liao
Yue Liao
Minghui Liao
Shengcai Liao
Ting-Hsuan Liao
Xin Liao
Yinghong Liao
Teck Yian Lim

Che-Tsung Lin
Chung-Ching Lin
Chen-Hsuan Lin
Cheng Lin
Chuming Lin
Chunyu Lin
Dahua Lin
Wei Lin
Zheng Lin
Huaijia Lin
Jason Lin
Jierui Lin
Jiaying Lin
Jie Lin
Kai-En Lin
Kevin Lin
Guangfeng Lin
Jiehong Lin
Feng Lin
Hang Lin
Kwan-Yee Lin
Ke Lin
Luojun Lin
Qinghong Lin
Xiangbo Lin
Yi Lin
Zudi Lin
Shijie Lin
Yiqun Lin
Tzu-Heng Lin
Ming Lin
Shaohui Lin
SongNan Lin
Ji Lin
Tsung-Yu Lin
Xudong Lin
Yancong Lin
Yen-Chen Lin
Yiming Lin
Yuewei Lin
Zhiqiu Lin
Zinan Lin
Zhe Lin
David B. Lindell
Zhixin Ling

Zhan Ling
Alexander Liniger
Venice Erin B. Liong
Joey Litalien
Or Litany
Roee Litman
Ron Litman
Jim Little
Dor Litvak
Shaoteng Liu
Shuaicheng Liu
Andrew Liu
Xian Liu
Shaohui Liu
Bei Liu
Bo Liu
Yong Liu
Ming Liu
Yanbin Liu
Chenxi Liu
Daqi Liu
Di Liu
Difan Liu
Dong Liu
Dongfang Liu
Daizong Liu
Xiao Liu
Fangyi Liu
Fengbei Liu
Fenglin Liu
Bin Liu
Yuang Liu
Ao Liu
Hong Liu
Hongfu Liu
Huidong Liu
Ziyi Liu
Feng Liu
Hao Liu
Jie Liu
Jialun Liu
Jiang Liu
Jing Liu
Jingya Liu
Jiaming Liu

Jun Liu
Juncheng Liu
Jiawei Liu
Hongyu Liu
Chuanbin Liu
Haotian Liu
Lingqiao Liu
Chang Liu
Han Liu
Liu Liu
Min Liu
Yingqi Liu
Aishan Liu
Bingyu Liu
Benlin Liu
Boxiao Liu
Chenchen Liu
Chuanjian Liu
Daqing Liu
Huan Liu
Haozhe Liu
Jiaheng Liu
Wei Liu
Jingzhou Liu
Jiyuan Liu
Lingbo Liu
Nian Liu
Peiye Liu
Qiankun Liu
Shenglan Liu
Shilong Liu
Wen Liu
Wenyu Liu
Weifeng Liu
Wu Liu
Xiaolong Liu
Yang Liu
Yanwei Liu
Yingcheng Liu
Yongfei Liu
Yihao Liu
Yu Liu
Yunze Liu
Ze Liu
Zhenhua Liu

Zhenguang Liu
Lin Liu
Lihao Liu
Pengju Liu
Xinhai Liu
Yunfei Liu
Meng Liu
Minghua Liu
Mingyuan Liu
Miao Liu
Peirong Liu
Ping Liu
Qingjie Liu
Ruoshi Liu
Risheng Liu
Songtao Liu
Xing Liu
Shikun Liu
Shuming Liu
Sheng Liu
Songhua Liu
Tongliang Liu
Weibo Liu
Weide Liu
Weizhe Liu
Wenxi Liu
Weiyang Liu
Xin Liu
Xiaobin Liu
Xudong Liu
Xiaoyi Liu
Xihui Liu
Xinchen Liu
Xingtong Liu
Xinpeng Liu
Xinyu Liu
Xianpeng Liu
Xu Liu
Xingyu Liu
Yongtuo Liu
Yahui Liu
Yangxin Liu
Yaoyao Liu
Yaojie Liu
Yuliang Liu

Yongcheng Liu

Yuan Liu

Yufan Liu

Yu-Lun Liu

Yun Liu

Yunfan Liu

Yuanzhong Liu

Zhuoran Liu

Zhen Liu

Zheng Liu

Zhijian Liu

Zhisong Liu

Ziquan Liu

Ziyu Liu

Zhihua Liu

Zechun Liu

Zhaoyang Liu

Zhengzhe Liu

Stephan Liwicki

Shao-Yuan Lo

Sylvain Lobry

Suhas Lohit

Vishnu Suresh Lokhande

Vincenzo Lomonaco

Chengjiang Long

Guodong Long

Fuchen Long

Shangbang Long

Yang Long

Zijun Long

Vasco Lopes

Antonio M. Lopez

Roberto Javier
   Lopez-Sastre

Tobias Lorenz

Javier Lorenzo-Navarro

Yujing Lou

Qian Lou

Xiankai Lu

Changsheng Lu

Huimin Lu

Yongxi Lu

Hao Lu

Hong Lu

Jiasen Lu

Juwei Lu

Fan Lu

Guangming Lu

Jiwen Lu

Shun Lu

Tao Lu

Xiaonan Lu

Yang Lu

Yao Lu

Yongchun Lu

Zhiwu Lu

Cheng Lu

Liying Lu

Guo Lu

Xuequan Lu

Yanye Lu

Yantao Lu

Yuhang Lu

Fujun Luan

Jonathon Luiten

Jovita Lukasik

Alan Lukezic

Jonathan Samuel Lumentut

Mayank Lunayach

Ao Luo

Canjie Luo

Chong Luo

Xu Luo

Grace Luo

Jun Luo

Katie Z. Luo

Tao Luo

Cheng Luo

Fangzhou Luo

Gen Luo

Lei Luo

Sihui Luo

Weixin Luo

Yan Luo

Xiaoyan Luo

Yong Luo

Yadan Luo

Hao Luo

Ruotian Luo

Mi Luo

Tiange Luo

Wenjie Luo

Wenhan Luo

Xiao Luo

Zhiming Luo

Zhipeng Luo

Zhengyi Luo

Diogo C. Luvizon

Zhaoyang Lv

Gengyu Lyu

Lingjuan Lyu

Jun Lyu

Yuanyuan Lyu

Youwei Lyu

Yueming Lyu

Bingpeng Ma

Chao Ma

Chongyang Ma

Congbo Ma

Chih-Yao Ma

Fan Ma

Lin Ma

Haoyu Ma

Hengbo Ma

Jianqi Ma

Jiawei Ma

Jiayi Ma

Kede Ma

Kai Ma

Lingni Ma

Lei Ma

Xu Ma

Ning Ma

Benteng Ma

Cheng Ma

Andy J. Ma

Long Ma

Zhanyu Ma

Zhiheng Ma

Qianli Ma

Shiqiang Ma

Sizhuo Ma

Shiqing Ma

Xiaolong Ma

Xinzhu Ma

Gautam B. Machiraju
Spandan Madan
Mathew Magimai-Doss
Luca Magri
Behrooz Mahasseni
Upal Mahbub
Siddharth Mahendran
Paridhi Maheshwari
Rishabh Maheshwary
Mohammed Mahmoud
Shishira R. R. Maiya
Sylwia Majchrowska
Arjun Majumdar
Puspita Majumdar
Orchid Majumder
Sagnik Majumder
Ilya Makarov
Farkhod F.
 Makhmudkhujaev
Yasushi Makihara
Ankur Mali
Mateusz Malinowski
Utkarsh Mall
Srikanth Malla
Clement Mallet
Dimitrios Mallis
Yunze Man
Dipu Manandhar
Massimiliano Mancini
Murari Mandal
Raunak Manekar
Karttikeya Mangalam
Puneet Mangla
Fabian Manhardt
Sivabalan Manivasagam
Fahim Mannan
Chengzhi Mao
Hanzi Mao
Jiayuan Mao
Junhua Mao
Zhiyuan Mao
Jiageng Mao
Yunyao Mao
Zhendong Mao
Alberto Marchisio

Diego Marcos
Riccardo Marin
Aram Markosyan
Renaud Marlet
Ricardo Marques
Miquel Martí i Rabadán
Diego Martin Arroyo
Niki Martinel
Brais Martinez
Julieta Martinez
Marc Masana
Tomohiro Mashita
Timothée Masquelier
Minesh Mathew
Tetsu Matsukawa
Marwan Mattar
Bruce A. Maxwell
Christoph Mayer
Mantas Mazeika
Pratik Mazumder
Scott McCloskey
Steven McDonagh
Ishit Mehta
Jie Mei
Kangfu Mei
Jieru Mei
Xiaoguang Mei
Givi Meishvili
Luke Melas-Kyriazi
Iaroslav Melekhov
Andres Mendez-Vazquez
Heydi Mendez-Vazquez
Matias Mendieta
Ricardo A. Mendoza-León
Chenlin Meng
Depu Meng
Rang Meng
Zibo Meng
Qingjie Meng
Qier Meng
Yanda Meng
Zihang Meng
Thomas Mensink
Fabian Mentzer
Christopher Metzler

Gregory P. Meyer
Vasileios Mezaris
Liang Mi
Lu Mi
Bo Miao
Changtao Miao
Zichen Miao
Qiguang Miao
Xin Miao
Zhongqi Miao
Frank Michel
Simone Milani
Ben Mildenhall
Roy V. Miles
Juhong Min
Kyle Min
Hyun-Seok Min
Weiqing Min
Yuecong Min
Zhixiang Min
Qi Ming
David Minnen
Aymen Mir
Deepak Mishra
Anand Mishra
Shlok K. Mishra
Niluthpol Mithun
Gaurav Mittal
Trisha Mittal
Daisuke Miyazaki
Kaichun Mo
Hong Mo
Zhipeng Mo
Davide Modolo
Abduallah A. Mohamed
Mohamed Afham
 Mohamed Aflal
Ron Mokady
Pavlo Molchanov
Davide Moltisanti
Liliane Momeni
Gianluca Monaci
Pascal Monasse
Ajoy Mondal
Tom Monnier

Aron Monszpart
Gyeongsik Moon
Suhong Moon
Taesup Moon
Sean Moran
Daniel Moreira
Pietro Morerio
Alexandre Morgand
Lia Morra
Ali Mosleh
Inbar Mosseri
Sayed Mohammad
  Mostafavi Isfahani
Saman Motamed
Ramy A. Mounir
Fangzhou Mu
Jiteng Mu
Norman Mu
Yasuhiro Mukaigawa
Ryan Mukherjee
Tanmoy Mukherjee
Yusuke Mukuta
Ravi Teja Mullapudi
Lea Müller
Matthias Müller
Martin Mundt
Nils Murrugarra-Llerena
Damien Muselet
Armin Mustafa
Muhammad Ferjad Naeem
Sauradip Nag
Hajime Nagahara
Pravin Nagar
Rajendra Nagar
Naveen Shankar Nagaraja
Varun Nagaraja
Tushar Nagarajan
Seungjun Nah
Gaku Nakano
Yuta Nakashima
Giljoo Nam
Seonghyeon Nam
Liangliang Nan
Yuesong Nan
Yeshwanth Napolean

Dinesh Reddy
  Narapureddy
Medhini Narasimhan
Supreeth
  Narasimhaswamy
Sriram Narayanan
Erickson R. Nascimento
Varun Nasery
K. L. Navaneet
Pablo Navarrete Michelini
Shant Navasardyan
Shah Nawaz
Nihal Nayak
Farhood Negin
Lukáš Neumann
Alejandro Newell
Evonne Ng
Kam Woh Ng
Tony Ng
Anh Nguyen
Tuan Anh Nguyen
Cuong Cao Nguyen
Ngoc Cuong Nguyen
Thanh Nguyen
Khoi Nguyen
Phi Le Nguyen
Phong Ha Nguyen
Tam Nguyen
Truong Nguyen
Anh Tuan Nguyen
Rang Nguyen
Thao Thi Phuong Nguyen
Van Nguyen Nguyen
Zhen-Liang Ni
Yao Ni
Shijie Nie
Xuecheng Nie
Yongwei Nie
Weizhi Nie
Ying Nie
Yinyu Nie
Kshitij N. Nikhal
Simon Niklaus
Xuefei Ning
Jifeng Ning

Yotam Nitzan
Di Niu
Shuaicheng Niu
Li Niu
Wei Niu
Yulei Niu
Zhenxing Niu
Albert No
Shohei Nobuhara
Nicoletta Noceti
Junhyug Noh
Sotiris Nousias
Slawomir Nowaczyk
Ewa M. Nowara
Valsamis Ntouskos
Gilberto Ochoa-Ruiz
Ferda Ofli
Jihyong Oh
Sangyun Oh
Youngtaek Oh
Hiroki Ohashi
Takahiro Okabe
Kemal Oksuz
Fumio Okura
Daniel Olmeda Reino
Matthew Olson
Carl Olsson
Roy Or-El
Alessandro Ortis
Guillermo Ortiz-Jimenez
Magnus Oskarsson
Ahmed A. A. Osman
Martin R. Oswald
Mayu Otani
Naima Otberdout
Cheng Ouyang
Jiahong Ouyang
Wanli Ouyang
Andrew Owens
Poojan B. Oza
Mete Ozay
A. Cengiz Oztireli
Gautam Pai
Tomas Pajdla
Umapada Pal

Simone Palazzo
Luca Palmieri
Bowen Pan
Hao Pan
Lili Pan
Tai-Yu Pan
Liang Pan
Chengwei Pan
Yingwei Pan
Xuran Pan
Jinshan Pan
Xinyu Pan
Liyuan Pan
Xingang Pan
Xingjia Pan
Zhihong Pan
Zizheng Pan
Priyadarshini Panda
Rameswar Panda
Rohit Pandey
Kaiyue Pang
Bo Pang
Guansong Pang
Jiangmiao Pang
Meng Pang
Tianyu Pang
Ziqi Pang
Omiros Pantazis
Andreas Panteli
Maja Pantic
Marina Paolanti
Joao P. Papa
Samuele Papa
Mike Papadakis
Dim P. Papadopoulos
George Papandreou
Constantin Pape
Toufiq Parag
Chethan Parameshwara
Shaifali Parashar
Alejandro Pardo
Rishubh Parihar
Sarah Parisot
JaeYoo Park
Gyeong-Moon Park

Hyojin Park
Hyoungseob Park
Jongchan Park
Jae Sung Park
Kiru Park
Chunghyun Park
Kwanyong Park
Sunghyun Park
Sungrae Park
Seongsik Park
Sanghyun Park
Sungjune Park
Taesung Park
Gaurav Parmar
Paritosh Parmar
Alvaro Parra
Despoina Paschalidou
Or Patashnik
Shivansh Patel
Pushpak Pati
Prashant W. Patil
Vaishakh Patil
Suvam Patra
Jay Patravali
Badri Narayana Patro
Angshuman Paul
Sudipta Paul
Rémi Pautrat
Nick E. Pears
Adithya Pediredla
Wenjie Pei
Shmuel Peleg
Latha Pemula
Bo Peng
Houwen Peng
Yue Peng
Liangzu Peng
Baoyun Peng
Jun Peng
Pai Peng
Sida Peng
Xi Peng
Yuxin Peng
Songyou Peng
Wei Peng

Weiqi Peng
Wen-Hsiao Peng
Pramuditha Perera
Juan C. Perez
Eduardo Pérez Pellitero
Juan-Manuel Perez-Rua
Federico Pernici
Marco Pesavento
Stavros Petridis
Ilya A. Petrov
Vladan Petrovic
Mathis Petrovich
Suzanne Petryk
Hieu Pham
Quang Pham
Khoi Pham
Tung Pham
Huy Phan
Stephen Phillips
Cheng Perng Phoo
David Picard
Marco Piccirilli
Georg Pichler
A. J. Piergiovanni
Vipin Pillai
Silvia L. Pintea
Giovanni Pintore
Robinson Piramuthu
Fiora Pirri
Theodoros Pissas
Fabio Pizzati
Benjamin Planche
Bryan Plummer
Matteo Poggi
Ashwini Pokle
Georgy E. Ponimatkin
Adrian Popescu
Stefan Popov
Nikola Popović
Ronald Poppe
Angelo Porrello
Michael Potter
Charalambos Poullis
Hadi Pouransari
Omid Poursaeed

Shraman Pramanick
Mantini Pranav
Dilip K. Prasad
Meghshyam Prasad
B. H. Pawan Prasad
Shitala Prasad
Prateek Prasanna
Ekta Prashnani
Derek S. Prijatelj
Luke Y. Prince
Véronique Prinet
Victor Adrian Prisacariu
James Pritts
Thomas Probst
Sergey Prokudin
Rita Pucci
Chi-Man Pun
Matthew Purri
Haozhi Qi
Lu Qi
Lei Qi
Xianbiao Qi
Yonggang Qi
Yuankai Qi
Siyuan Qi
Guocheng Qian
Hangwei Qian
Qi Qian
Deheng Qian
Shengsheng Qian
Wen Qian
Rui Qian
Yiming Qian
Shengju Qian
Shengyi Qian
Xuelin Qian
Zhenxing Qian
Nan Qiao
Xiaotian Qiao
Jing Qin
Can Qin
Siyang Qin
Hongwei Qin
Jie Qin
Minghai Qin

Yipeng Qin
Yongqiang Qin
Wenda Qin
Xuebin Qin
Yuzhe Qin
Yao Qin
Zhenyue Qin
Zhiwu Qing
Heqian Qiu
Jiayan Qiu
Jielin Qiu
Yue Qiu
Jiaxiong Qiu
Zhongxi Qiu
Shi Qiu
Zhaofan Qiu
Zhongnan Qu
Yanyun Qu
Kha Gia Quach
Yuhui Quan
Ruijie Quan
Mike Rabbat
Rahul Shekhar Rade
Filip Radenovic
Gorjan Radevski
Bogdan Raducanu
Francesco Ragusa
Shafin Rahman
Md Mahfuzur Rahman
   Siddiquee
Hossein Rahmani
Kiran Raja
Sivaramakrishnan
   Rajaraman
Jathushan Rajasegaran
Adnan Siraj Rakin
Michaël Ramamonjisoa
Chirag A. Raman
Shanmuganathan Raman
Vignesh Ramanathan
Vasili Ramanishka
Vikram V. Ramaswamy
Merey Ramazanova
Jason Rambach
Sai Saketh Rambhatla

Clément Rambour
Ashwin Ramesh Babu
Adín Ramírez Rivera
Arianna Rampini
Haoxi Ran
Aakanksha Rana
Aayush Jung Bahadur
   Rana
Kanchana N. Ranasinghe
Aneesh Rangnekar
Samrudhdhi B. Rangrej
Harsh Rangwani
Viresh Ranjan
Anyi Rao
Yongming Rao
Carolina Raposo
Michalis Raptis
Amir Rasouli
Vivek Rathod
Adepu Ravi Sankar
Avinash Ravichandran
Bharadwaj Ravichandran
Dripta S. Raychaudhuri
Adria Recasens
Simon Reiß
Davis Rempe
Daxuan Ren
Jiawei Ren
Jimmy Ren
Sucheng Ren
Dayong Ren
Zhile Ren
Dongwei Ren
Qibing Ren
Pengfei Ren
Zhenwen Ren
Xuqian Ren
Yixuan Ren
Zhongzheng Ren
Ambareesh Revanur
Hamed Rezazadegan
   Tavakoli
Rafael S. Rezende
Wonjong Rhee
Alexander Richard

Christian Richardt
Stephan R. Richter
Benjamin Riggan
Dominik Rivoir
Mamshad Nayeem Rizve
Joshua D. Robinson
Joseph Robinson
Chris Rockwell
Ranga Rodrigo
Andres C. Rodriguez
Carlos Rodriguez-Pardo
Marcus Rohrbach
Gemma Roig
Yu Rong
David A. Ross
Mohammad Rostami
Edward Rosten
Karsten Roth
Anirban Roy
Debaditya Roy
Shuvendu Roy
Ahana Roy Choudhury
Aruni Roy Chowdhury
Denys Rozumnyi
Shulan Ruan
Wenjie Ruan
Patrick Ruhkamp
Danila Rukhovich
Anian Ruoss
Chris Russell
Dan Ruta
Dawid Damian Rymarczyk
DongHun Ryu
Hyeonggon Ryu
Kwonyoung Ryu
Balasubramanian S.
Alexandre Sablayrolles
Mohammad Sabokrou
Arka Sadhu
Aniruddha Saha
Oindrila Saha
Pritish Sahu
Aneeshan Sain
Nirat Saini
Saurabh Saini

Takeshi Saitoh
Christos Sakaridis
Fumihiko Sakaue
Dimitrios Sakkos
Ken Sakurada
Parikshit V. Sakurikar
Rohit Saluja
Nermin Samet
Leo Sampaio Ferraz
   Ribeiro
Jorge Sanchez
Enrique Sanchez
Shengtian Sang
Anush Sankaran
Soubhik Sanyal
Nikolaos Sarafianos
Vishwanath Saragadam
István Sárándi
Saquib Sarfraz
Mert Bulent Sariyildiz
Anindya Sarkar
Pritam Sarkar
Paul-Edouard Sarlin
Hiroshi Sasaki
Takami Sato
Torsten Sattler
Ravi Kumar Satzoda
Axel Sauer
Stefano Savian
Artem Savkin
Manolis Savva
Gerald Schaefer
Simone Schaub-Meyer
Yoni Schirris
Samuel Schulter
Katja Schwarz
Jesse Scott
Sinisa Segvic
Constantin Marc Seibold
Lorenzo Seidenari
Matan Sela
Fadime Sener
Paul Hongsuck Seo
Kwanggyoon Seo
Hongje Seong

Dario Serez
Francesco Setti
Bryan Seybold
Mohamad Shahbazi
Shima Shahfar
Xinxin Shan
Caifeng Shan
Dandan Shan
Shawn Shan
Wei Shang
Jinghuan Shang
Jiaxiang Shang
Lei Shang
Sukrit Shankar
Ken Shao
Rui Shao
Jie Shao
Mingwen Shao
Aashish Sharma
Gaurav Sharma
Vivek Sharma
Abhishek Sharma
Yoli Shavit
Shashank Shekhar
Sumit Shekhar
Zhijie Shen
Fengyi Shen
Furao Shen
Jialie Shen
Jingjing Shen
Ziyi Shen
Linlin Shen
Guangyu Shen
Biluo Shen
Falong Shen
Jiajun Shen
Qiu Shen
Qiuhong Shen
Shuai Shen
Wang Shen
Yiqing Shen
Yunhang Shen
Siqi Shen
Bin Shen
Tianwei Shen

Xi Shen
Yilin Shen
Yuming Shen
Yucong Shen
Zhiqiang Shen
Lu Sheng
Yichen Sheng
Shivanand Venkanna
    Sheshappanavar
Shelly Sheynin
Baifeng Shi
Ruoxi Shi
Botian Shi
Hailin Shi
Jia Shi
Jing Shi
Shaoshuai Shi
Baoguang Shi
Boxin Shi
Hengcan Shi
Tianyang Shi
Xiaodan Shi
Yongjie Shi
Zhensheng Shi
Yinghuan Shi
Weiqi Shi
Wu Shi
Xuepeng Shi
Xiaoshuang Shi
Yujiao Shi
Zenglin Shi
Zhenmei Shi
Takashi Shibata
Meng-Li Shih
Yichang Shih
Hyunjung Shim
Dongseok Shim
Soshi Shimada
Inkyu Shin
Jinwoo Shin
Seungjoo Shin
Seungjae Shin
Koichi Shinoda
Suprosanna Shit

Palaiahnakote
    Shivakumara
Eli Shlizerman
Gaurav Shrivastava
Xiao Shu
Xiangbo Shu
Xiujun Shu
Yang Shu
Tianmin Shu
Jun Shu
Zhixin Shu
Bing Shuai
Maria Shugrina
Ivan Shugurov
Satya Narayan Shukla
Pranjay Shyam
Jianlou Si
Yawar Siddiqui
Alberto Signoroni
Pedro Silva
Jae-Young Sim
Oriane Siméoni
Martin Simon
Andrea Simonelli
Abhishek Singh
Ashish Singh
Dinesh Singh
Gurkirt Singh
Krishna Kumar Singh
Mannat Singh
Pravendra Singh
Rajat Vikram Singh
Utkarsh Singhal
Dipika Singhania
Vasu Singla
Harsh Sinha
Sudipta Sinha
Josef Sivic
Elena Sizikova
Geri Skenderi
Ivan Skorokhodov
Dmitriy Smirnov
Cameron Y. Smith
James S. Smith
Patrick Snape

Mattia Soldan
Hyeongseok Son
Sanghyun Son
Chuanbiao Song
Chen Song
Chunfeng Song
Dan Song
Dongjin Song
Hwanjun Song
Guoxian Song
Jiaming Song
Jie Song
Liangchen Song
Ran Song
Luchuan Song
Xibin Song
Li Song
Fenglong Song
Guoli Song
Guanglu Song
Zhenbo Song
Lin Song
Xinhang Song
Yang Song
Yibing Song
Rajiv Soundararajan
Hossein Souri
Cristovao Sousa
Riccardo Spezialetti
Leonidas Spinoulas
Michael W. Spratling
Deepak Sridhar
Srinath Sridhar
Gaurang Sriramanan
Vinkle Kumar Srivastav
Themos Stafylakis
Serban Stan
Anastasis Stathopoulos
Markus Steinberger
Jan Steinbrener
Sinisa Stekovic
Alexandros Stergiou
Gleb Sterkin
Rainer Stiefelhagen
Pierre Stock

Ombretta Strafforello
Julian Straub
Yannick Strümpler
Joerg Stueckler
Hang Su
Weijie Su
Jong-Chyi Su
Bing Su
Haisheng Su
Jinming Su
Yiyang Su
Yukun Su
Yuxin Su
Zhuo Su
Zhaoqi Su
Xiu Su
Yu-Chuan Su
Zhixun Su
Arulkumar Subramaniam
Akshayvarun Subramanya
A. Subramanyam
Swathikiran Sudhakaran
Yusuke Sugano
Masanori Suganuma
Yumin Suh
Yang Sui
Baochen Sun
Cheng Sun
Long Sun
Guolei Sun
Haoliang Sun
Haomiao Sun
He Sun
Hanqing Sun
Hao Sun
Lichao Sun
Jiachen Sun
Jiaming Sun
Jian Sun
Jin Sun
Jennifer J. Sun
Tiancheng Sun
Libo Sun
Peize Sun
Qianru Sun

Shanlin Sun
Yu Sun
Zhun Sun
Che Sun
Lin Sun
Tao Sun
Yiyou Sun
Chunyi Sun
Chong Sun
Weiwei Sun
Weixuan Sun
Xiuyu Sun
Yanan Sun
Zeren Sun
Zhaodong Sun
Zhiqing Sun
Minhyuk Sung
Jinli Suo
Simon Suo
Abhijit Suprem
Anshuman Suri
Saksham Suri
Joshua M. Susskind
Roman Suvorov
Gurumurthy Swaminathan
Robin Swanson
Paul Swoboda
Tabish A. Syed
Richard Szeliski
Fariborz Taherkhani
Yu-Wing Tai
Keita Takahashi
Walter Talbott
Gary Tam
Masato Tamura
Feitong Tan
Fuwen Tan
Shuhan Tan
Andong Tan
Bin Tan
Cheng Tan
Jianchao Tan
Lei Tan
Mingxing Tan
Xin Tan

Zichang Tan
Zhentao Tan
Kenichiro Tanaka
Masayuki Tanaka
Yushun Tang
Hao Tang
Jingqun Tang
Jinhui Tang
Kaihua Tang
Luming Tang
Lv Tang
Sheyang Tang
Shitao Tang
Siliang Tang
Shixiang Tang
Yansong Tang
Keke Tang
Chang Tang
Chenwei Tang
Jie Tang
Junshu Tang
Ming Tang
Peng Tang
Xu Tang
Yao Tang
Chen Tang
Fan Tang
Haoran Tang
Shengeng Tang
Yehui Tang
Zhipeng Tang
Ugo Tanielian
Chaofan Tao
Jiale Tao
Junli Tao
Renshuai Tao
An Tao
Guanhong Tao
Zhiqiang Tao
Makarand Tapaswi
Jean-Philippe G. Tarel
Juan J. Tarrio
Enzo Tartaglione
Keisuke Tateno
Zachary Teed

Ajinkya B. Tejankar
Bugra Tekin
Purva Tendulkar
Damien Teney
Minggui Teng
Chris Tensmeyer
Andrew Beng Jin Teoh
Philipp Terhörst
Kartik Thakral
Nupur Thakur
Kevin Thandiackal
Spyridon Thermos
Diego Thomas
William Thong
Yuesong Tian
Guanzhong Tian
Lin Tian
Shiqi Tian
Kai Tian
Meng Tian
Tai-Peng Tian
Zhuotao Tian
Shangxuan Tian
Tian Tian
Yapeng Tian
Yu Tian
Yuxin Tian
Leslie Ching Ow Tiong
Praveen Tirupattur
Garvita Tiwari
George Toderici
Antoine Toisoul
Aysim Toker
Tatiana Tommasi
Zhan Tong
Alessio Tonioni
Alessandro Torcinovich
Fabio Tosi
Matteo Toso
Hugo Touvron
Quan Hung Tran
Son Tran
Hung Tran
Ngoc-Trung Tran
Vinh Tran

Phong Tran
Giovanni Trappolini
Edith Tretschk
Subarna Tripathi
Shubhendu Trivedi
Eduard Trulls
Prune Truong
Thanh-Dat Truong
Tomasz Trzcinski
Sam Tsai
Yi-Hsuan Tsai
Ethan Tseng
Yu-Chee Tseng
Shahar Tsiper
Stavros Tsogkas
Shikui Tu
Zhigang Tu
Zhengzhong Tu
Richard Tucker
Sergey Tulyakov
Cigdem Turan
Daniyar Turmukhambetov
Victor G. Turrisi da Costa
Bartlomiej Twardowski
Christopher D. Twigg
Radim Tylecek
Mostofa Rafid Uddin
Md. Zasim Uddin
Kohei Uehara
Nicolas Ugrinovic
Youngjung Uh
Norimichi Ukita
Anwaar Ulhaq
Devesh Upadhyay
Paul Upchurch
Yoshitaka Ushiku
Yuzuko Utsumi
Mikaela Angelina Uy
Mohit Vaishnav
Pratik Vaishnavi
Jeya Maria Jose Valanarasu
Matias A. Valdenegro Toro
Diego Valsesia
Wouter Van Gansbeke
Nanne van Noord

Simon Vandenhende
Farshid Varno
Cristina Vasconcelos
Francisco Vasconcelos
Alex Vasilescu
Subeesh Vasu
Arun Balajee Vasudevan
Kanav Vats
Vaibhav S. Vavilala
Sagar Vaze
Javier Vazquez-Corral
Andrea Vedaldi
Olga Veksler
Andreas Velten
Sai H. Vemprala
Raviteja Vemulapalli
Shashanka
  Venkataramanan
Dor Verbin
Luisa Verdoliva
Manisha Verma
Yashaswi Verma
Constantin Vertan
Eli Verwimp
Deepak Vijaykeerthy
Pablo Villanueva
Ruben Villegas
Markus Vincze
Vibhav Vineet
Minh P. Vo
Huy V. Vo
Duc Minh Vo
Tomas Vojir
Igor Vozniak
Nicholas Vretos
Vibashan VS
Tuan-Anh Vu
Thang Vu
Mårten Wadenbäck
Neal Wadhwa
Aaron T. Walsman
Steven Walton
Jin Wan
Alvin Wan
Jia Wan

Jun Wan
Xiaoyue Wan
Fang Wan
Guowei Wan
Renjie Wan
Zhiqiang Wan
Ziyu Wan
Bastian Wandt
Dongdong Wang
Limin Wang
Haiyang Wang
Xiaobing Wang
Angtian Wang
Angelina Wang
Bing Wang
Bo Wang
Boyu Wang
Binghui Wang
Chen Wang
Chien-Yi Wang
Congli Wang
Qi Wang
Chengrui Wang
Rui Wang
Yiqun Wang
Cong Wang
Wenjing Wang
Dongkai Wang
Di Wang
Xiaogang Wang
Kai Wang
Zhizhong Wang
Fangjinhua Wang
Feng Wang
Hang Wang
Gaoang Wang
Guoqing Wang
Guangcong Wang
Guangzhi Wang
Hanqing Wang
Hao Wang
Haohan Wang
Haoran Wang
Hong Wang
Haotao Wang

Hu Wang
Huan Wang
Hua Wang
Hui-Po Wang
Hengli Wang
Hanyu Wang
Hongxing Wang
Jingwen Wang
Jialiang Wang
Jian Wang
Jianyi Wang
Jiashun Wang
Jiahao Wang
Tsun-Hsuan Wang
Xiaoqian Wang
Jinqiao Wang
Jun Wang
Jianzong Wang
Kaihong Wang
Ke Wang
Lei Wang
Lingjing Wang
Linnan Wang
Lin Wang
Liansheng Wang
Mengjiao Wang
Manning Wang
Nannan Wang
Peihao Wang
Jiayun Wang
Pu Wang
Qiang Wang
Qiufeng Wang
Qilong Wang
Qiangchang Wang
Qin Wang
Qing Wang
Ruocheng Wang
Ruibin Wang
Ruisheng Wang
Ruizhe Wang
Runqi Wang
Runzhong Wang
Wenxuan Wang
Sen Wang

Shangfei Wang
Shaofei Wang
Shijie Wang
Shiqi Wang
Zhibo Wang
Song Wang
Xinjiang Wang
Tai Wang
Tao Wang
Teng Wang
Xiang Wang
Tianren Wang
Tiantian Wang
Tianyi Wang
Fengjiao Wang
Wei Wang
Miaohui Wang
Suchen Wang
Siyue Wang
Yaoming Wang
Xiao Wang
Ze Wang
Biao Wang
Chaofei Wang
Dong Wang
Gu Wang
Guangrun Wang
Guangming Wang
Guo-Hua Wang
Haoqing Wang
Hesheng Wang
Huafeng Wang
Jinghua Wang
Jingdong Wang
Jingjing Wang
Jingya Wang
Jingkang Wang
Jiakai Wang
Junke Wang
Kuo Wang
Lichen Wang
Lizhi Wang
Longguang Wang
Mang Wang
Mei Wang

Congcong Wen
Chuan Wen
Jie Wen
Sijia Wen
Song Wen
Chao Wen
Xiang Wen
Zeyi Wen
Xin Wen
Yilin Wen
Yijia Weng
Shuchen Weng
Junwu Weng
Wenming Weng
Renliang Weng
Zhenyu Weng
Xinshuo Weng
Nicholas J. Westlake
Gordon Wetzstein
Lena M. Widin Klasén
Rick Wildes
Bryan M. Williams
Williem Williem
Ole Winther
Scott Wisdom
Alex Wong
Chau-Wai Wong
Kwan-Yee K. Wong
Yongkang Wong
Scott Workman
Marcel Worring
Michael Wray
Safwan Wshah
Xiang Wu
Aming Wu
Chongruo Wu
Cho-Ying Wu
Chunpeng Wu
Chenyan Wu
Ziyi Wu
Fuxiang Wu
Gang Wu
Haiping Wu
Huisi Wu
Jane Wu

Jialian Wu
Jing Wu
Jinjian Wu
Jianlong Wu
Xian Wu
Lifang Wu
Lifan Wu
Minye Wu
Qianyi Wu
Rongliang Wu
Rui Wu
Shiqian Wu
Shuzhe Wu
Shangzhe Wu
Tsung-Han Wu
Tz-Ying Wu
Ting-Wei Wu
Jiannan Wu
Zhiliang Wu
Yu Wu
Chenyun Wu
Dayan Wu
Dongxian Wu
Fei Wu
Hefeng Wu
Jianxin Wu
Weibin Wu
Wenxuan Wu
Wenhao Wu
Xiao Wu
Yicheng Wu
Yuanwei Wu
Yu-Huan Wu
Zhenxin Wu
Zhenyu Wu
Wei Wu
Peng Wu
Xiaohe Wu
Xindi Wu
Xinxing Wu
Xinyi Wu
Xingjiao Wu
Xiongwei Wu
Yangzheng Wu
Yanzhao Wu

Yawen Wu
Yong Wu
Yi Wu
Ying Nian Wu
Zhenyao Wu
Zhonghua Wu
Zongze Wu
Zuxuan Wu
Stefanie Wuhrer
Teng Xi
Jianing Xi
Fei Xia
Haifeng Xia
Menghan Xia
Yuanqing Xia
Zhihua Xia
Xiaobo Xia
Weihao Xia
Shihong Xia
Yan Xia
Yong Xia
Zhaoyang Xia
Zhihao Xia
Chuhua Xian
Yongqin Xian
Wangmeng Xiang
Fanbo Xiang
Tiange Xiang
Tao Xiang
Liuyu Xiang
Xiaoyu Xiang
Zhiyu Xiang
Aoran Xiao
Chunxia Xiao
Fanyi Xiao
Jimin Xiao
Jun Xiao
Taihong Xiao
Anqi Xiao
Junfei Xiao
Jing Xiao
Liang Xiao
Yang Xiao
Yuting Xiao
Yijun Xiao

Yao Xiao

Zeyu Xiao

Zhisheng Xiao

Zihao Xiao

Binhui Xie

Christopher Xie

Haozhe Xie

Jin Xie

Guo-Sen Xie

Hongtao Xie

Ming-Kun Xie

Tingting Xie

Chaohao Xie

Weicheng Xie

Xudong Xie

Jiyang Xie

Xiaohua Xie

Yuan Xie

Zhenyu Xie

Ning Xie

Xianghui Xie

Xiufeng Xie

You Xie

Yutong Xie

Fuyong Xing

Yifan Xing

Zhen Xing

Yuanjun Xiong

Jinhui Xiong

Weihua Xiong

Hongkai Xiong

Zhitong Xiong

Yuanhao Xiong

Yunyang Xiong

Yuwen Xiong

Zhiwei Xiong

Yuliang Xiu

An Xu

Chang Xu

Chenliang Xu

Chengming Xu

Chenshu Xu

Xiang Xu

Huijuan Xu

Zhe Xu

Jie Xu

Jingyi Xu

Jiarui Xu

Yinghao Xu

Kele Xu

Ke Xu

Li Xu

Linchuan Xu

Linning Xu

Mengde Xu

Mengmeng Frost Xu

Min Xu

Mingye Xu

Jun Xu

Ning Xu

Peng Xu

Runsheng Xu

Sheng Xu

Wenqiang Xu

Xiaogang Xu

Renzhe Xu

Kaidi Xu

Yi Xu

Chi Xu

Qiuling Xu

Baobei Xu

Feng Xu

Haohang Xu

Haofei Xu

Lan Xu

Mingze Xu

Songcen Xu

Weipeng Xu

Wenjia Xu

Wenju Xu

Xiangyu Xu

Xin Xu

Yinshuang Xu

Yixing Xu

Yuting Xu

Yanyu Xu

Zhenbo Xu

Zhiliang Xu

Zhiyuan Xu

Xiaohao Xu

Yanwu Xu

Yan Xu

Yiran Xu

Yifan Xu

Yufei Xu

Yong Xu

Zichuan Xu

Zenglin Xu

Zexiang Xu

Zhan Xu

Zheng Xu

Zhiwei Xu

Ziyue Xu

Shiyu Xuan

Hanyu Xuan

Fei Xue

Jianru Xue

Mingfu Xue

Qinghan Xue

Tianfan Xue

Chao Xue

Chuhui Xue

Nan Xue

Zhou Xue

Xiangyang Xue

Yuan Xue

Abhay Yadav

Ravindra Yadav

Kota Yamaguchi

Toshihiko Yamasaki

Kohei Yamashita

Chaochao Yan

Feng Yan

Kun Yan

Qingsen Yan

Qixin Yan

Rui Yan

Siming Yan

Xinchen Yan

Yaping Yan

Bin Yan

Qingan Yan

Shen Yan

Shipeng Yan

Xu Yan

Yan Yan
Yichao Yan
Zhaoyi Yan
Zike Yan
Zhiqiang Yan
Hongliang Yan
Zizheng Yan
Jiewen Yang
Anqi Joyce Yang
Shan Yang
Anqi Yang
Antoine Yang
Bo Yang
Baoyao Yang
Chenhongyi Yang
Dingkang Yang
De-Nian Yang
Dong Yang
David Yang
Fan Yang
Fengyu Yang
Fengting Yang
Fei Yang
Gengshan Yang
Heng Yang
Han Yang
Huan Yang
Yibo Yang
Jiancheng Yang
Jihan Yang
Jiawei Yang
Jiayu Yang
Jie Yang
Jinfa Yang
Jingkang Yang
Jinyu Yang
Cheng-Fu Yang
Ji Yang
Jianyu Yang
Kailun Yang
Tian Yang
Luyu Yang
Liang Yang
Li Yang
Michael Ying Yang

Yang Yang
Muli Yang
Le Yang
Qiushi Yang
Ren Yang
Ruihan Yang
Shuang Yang
Siyuan Yang
Su Yang
Shiqi Yang
Taojiannan Yang
Tianyu Yang
Lei Yang
Wanzhao Yang
Shuai Yang
William Yang
Wei Yang
Xiaofeng Yang
Xiaoshan Yang
Xin Yang
Xuan Yang
Xu Yang
Xingyi Yang
Xitong Yang
Jing Yang
Yanchao Yang
Wenming Yang
Yujiu Yang
Herb Yang
Jianfei Yang
Jinhui Yang
Chuanguang Yang
Guanglei Yang
Haitao Yang
Kewei Yang
Linlin Yang
Lijin Yang
Longrong Yang
Meng Yang
MingKun Yang
Sibei Yang
Shicai Yang
Tong Yang
Wen Yang
Xi Yang

Xiaolong Yang
Xue Yang
Yubin Yang
Ze Yang
Ziyi Yang
Yi Yang
Linjie Yang
Yuzhe Yang
Yiding Yang
Zhenpei Yang
Zhaohui Yang
Zhengyuan Yang
Zhibo Yang
Zongxin Yang
Hantao Yao
Mingde Yao
Rui Yao
Taiping Yao
Ting Yao
Cong Yao
Qingsong Yao
Quanming Yao
Xu Yao
Yuan Yao
Yao Yao
Yazhou Yao
Jiawen Yao
Shunyu Yao
Pew-Thian Yap
Sudhir Yarram
Rajeev Yasarla
Peng Ye
Botao Ye
Mao Ye
Fei Ye
Hanrong Ye
Jingwen Ye
Jinwei Ye
Jiarong Ye
Mang Ye
Meng Ye
Qi Ye
Qian Ye
Qixiang Ye
Junjie Ye

Sheng Ye
Nanyang Ye
Yufei Ye
Xiaoqing Ye
Ruolin Ye
Yousef Yeganeh
Chun-Hsiao Yeh
Raymond A. Yeh
Yu-Ying Yeh
Kai Yi
Chang Yi
Renjiao Yi
Xinping Yi
Peng Yi
Alper Yilmaz
Junho Yim
Hui Yin
Bangjie Yin
Jia-Li Yin
Miao Yin
Wenzhe Yin
Xuwang Yin
Ming Yin
Yu Yin
Aoxiong Yin
Kangxue Yin
Tianwei Yin
Wei Yin
Xianghua Ying
Rio Yokota
Tatsuya Yokota
Naoto Yokoya
Ryo Yonetani
Ki Yoon Yoo
Jinsu Yoo
Sunjae Yoon
Jae Shin Yoon
Jihun Yoon
Sung-Hoon Yoon
Ryota Yoshihashi
Yusuke Yoshiyasu
Chenyu You
Haoran You
Haoxuan You
Yang You

Quanzeng You
Tackgeun You
Kaichao You
Shan You
Xinge You
Yurong You
Baosheng Yu
Bei Yu
Haichao Yu
Hao Yu
Chaohui Yu
Fisher Yu
Jin-Gang Yu
Jiyang Yu
Jason J. Yu
Jiashuo Yu
Hong-Xing Yu
Lei Yu
Mulin Yu
Ning Yu
Peilin Yu
Qi Yu
Qian Yu
Rui Yu
Shuzhi Yu
Gang Yu
Tan Yu
Weijiang Yu
Xin Yu
Bingyao Yu
Ye Yu
Hanchao Yu
Yingchen Yu
Tao Yu
Xiaotian Yu
Qing Yu
Houjian Yu
Changqian Yu
Jing Yu
Jun Yu
Shujian Yu
Xiang Yu
Zhaofei Yu
Zhenbo Yu
Yinfeng Yu

Zhuoran Yu
Zitong Yu
Bo Yuan
Jiangbo Yuan
Liangzhe Yuan
Weihao Yuan
Jianbo Yuan
Xiaoyun Yuan
Ye Yuan
Li Yuan
Geng Yuan
Jialin Yuan
Maoxun Yuan
Peng Yuan
Xin Yuan
Yuan Yuan
Yuhui Yuan
Yixuan Yuan
Zheng Yuan
Mehmet Kerim Yücel
Kaiyu Yue
Haixiao Yue
Heeseung Yun
Sangdoo Yun
Tian Yun
Mahmut Yurt
Ekim Yurtsever
Ahmet Yüzügüler
Edouard Yvinec
Eloi Zablocki
Christopher Zach
Muhammad Zaigham
    Zaheer
Pierluigi Zama Ramirez
Yuhang Zang
Pietro Zanuttigh
Alexey Zaytsev
Bernhard Zeisl
Haitian Zeng
Pengpeng Zeng
Jiabei Zeng
Runhao Zeng
Wei Zeng
Yawen Zeng
Yi Zeng

Yiming Zeng
Tieyong Zeng
Huanqiang Zeng
Dan Zeng
Yu Zeng
Wei Zhai
Yuanhao Zhai
Fangneng Zhan
Kun Zhan
Xiong Zhang
Jingdong Zhang
Jiangning Zhang
Zhilu Zhang
Gengwei Zhang
Dongsu Zhang
Hui Zhang
Binjie Zhang
Bo Zhang
Tianhao Zhang
Cecilia Zhang
Jing Zhang
Chaoning Zhang
Chenxu Zhang
Chi Zhang
Chris Zhang
Yabin Zhang
Zhao Zhang
Rufeng Zhang
Chaoyi Zhang
Zheng Zhang
Da Zhang
Yi Zhang
Edward Zhang
Xin Zhang
Feifei Zhang
Feilong Zhang
Yuqi Zhang
GuiXuan Zhang
Hanlin Zhang
Hanwang Zhang
Hanzhen Zhang
Haotian Zhang
He Zhang
Haokui Zhang
Hongyuan Zhang

Hengrui Zhang
Hongming Zhang
Mingfang Zhang
Jianpeng Zhang
Jiaming Zhang
Jichao Zhang
Jie Zhang
Jingfeng Zhang
Jingyi Zhang
Jinnian Zhang
David Junhao Zhang
Junjie Zhang
Junzhe Zhang
Jiawan Zhang
Jingyang Zhang
Kai Zhang
Lei Zhang
Lihua Zhang
Lu Zhang
Miao Zhang
Minjia Zhang
Mingjin Zhang
Qi Zhang
Qian Zhang
Qilong Zhang
Qiming Zhang
Qiang Zhang
Richard Zhang
Ruimao Zhang
Ruisi Zhang
Ruixin Zhang
Runze Zhang
Qilin Zhang
Shan Zhang
Shanshan Zhang
Xi Sheryl Zhang
Song-Hai Zhang
Chongyang Zhang
Kaihao Zhang
Songyang Zhang
Shu Zhang
Siwei Zhang
Shujian Zhang
Tianyun Zhang
Tong Zhang

Tao Zhang
Wenwei Zhang
Wenqiang Zhang
Wen Zhang
Xiaolin Zhang
Xingchen Zhang
Xingxuan Zhang
Xiuming Zhang
Xiaoshuai Zhang
Xuanmeng Zhang
Xuanyang Zhang
Xucong Zhang
Xingxing Zhang
Xikun Zhang
Xiaohan Zhang
Yahui Zhang
Yunhua Zhang
Yan Zhang
Yanghao Zhang
Yifei Zhang
Yifan Zhang
Yi-Fan Zhang
Yihao Zhang
Yingliang Zhang
Youshan Zhang
Yulun Zhang
Yushu Zhang
Yixiao Zhang
Yide Zhang
Zhongwen Zhang
Bowen Zhang
Chen-Lin Zhang
Zehua Zhang
Zekun Zhang
Zeyu Zhang
Xiaowei Zhang
Yifeng Zhang
Cheng Zhang
Hongguang Zhang
Yuexi Zhang
Fa Zhang
Guofeng Zhang
Hao Zhang
Haofeng Zhang
Hongwen Zhang

Hua Zhang
Jiaxin Zhang
Zhenyu Zhang
Jian Zhang
Jianfeng Zhang
Jiao Zhang
Jiakai Zhang
Lefei Zhang
Le Zhang
Mi Zhang
Min Zhang
Ning Zhang
Pan Zhang
Pu Zhang
Qing Zhang
Renrui Zhang
Shifeng Zhang
Shuo Zhang
Shaoxiong Zhang
Weizhong Zhang
Xi Zhang
Xiaomei Zhang
Xinyu Zhang
Yin Zhang
Zicheng Zhang
Zihao Zhang
Ziqi Zhang
Zhaoxiang Zhang
Zhen Zhang
Zhipeng Zhang
Zhixing Zhang
Zhizheng Zhang
Jiawei Zhang
Zhong Zhang
Pingping Zhang
Yixin Zhang
Kui Zhang
Lingzhi Zhang
Huaiwen Zhang
Quanshi Zhang
Zhoutong Zhang
Yuhang Zhang
Yuting Zhang
Zhang Zhang
Ziming Zhang

Zhizhong Zhang
Qilong Zhangli
Bingyin Zhao
Bin Zhao
Chenglong Zhao
Lei Zhao
Feng Zhao
Gangming Zhao
Haiyan Zhao
Hao Zhao
Handong Zhao
Hengshuang Zhao
Yinan Zhao
Jiaojiao Zhao
Jiaqi Zhao
Jing Zhao
Kaili Zhao
Haojie Zhao
Yucheng Zhao
Longjiao Zhao
Long Zhao
Qingsong Zhao
Qingyu Zhao
Rui Zhao
Rui-Wei Zhao
Sicheng Zhao
Shuang Zhao
Siyan Zhao
Zelin Zhao
Shiyu Zhao
Wang Zhao
Tiesong Zhao
Qian Zhao
Wangbo Zhao
Xi-Le Zhao
Xu Zhao
Yajie Zhao
Yang Zhao
Ying Zhao
Yin Zhao
Yizhou Zhao
Yunhan Zhao
Yuyang Zhao
Yue Zhao
Yuzhi Zhao

Bowen Zhao
Pu Zhao
Bingchen Zhao
Borui Zhao
Fuqiang Zhao
Hanbin Zhao
Jian Zhao
Mingyang Zhao
Na Zhao
Rongchang Zhao
Ruiqi Zhao
Shuai Zhao
Wenda Zhao
Wenliang Zhao
Xiangyun Zhao
Yifan Zhao
Yaping Zhao
Zhou Zhao
He Zhao
Jie Zhao
Xibin Zhao
Xiaoqi Zhao
Zhengyu Zhao
Jin Zhe
Chuanxia Zheng
Huan Zheng
Hao Zheng
Jia Zheng
Jian-Qing Zheng
Shuai Zheng
Meng Zheng
Mingkai Zheng
Qian Zheng
Qi Zheng
Wu Zheng
Yinqiang Zheng
Yufeng Zheng
Yutong Zheng
Yalin Zheng
Yu Zheng
Feng Zheng
Zhaoheng Zheng
Haitian Zheng
Kang Zheng
Bolun Zheng

Haiyong Zheng
Mingwu Zheng
Sipeng Zheng
Tu Zheng
Wenzhao Zheng
Xiawu Zheng
Yinglin Zheng
Zhuo Zheng
Zilong Zheng
Kecheng Zheng
Zerong Zheng
Shuaifeng Zhi
Tiancheng Zhi
Jia-Xing Zhong
Yiwu Zhong
Fangwei Zhong
Zhihang Zhong
Yaoyao Zhong
Yiran Zhong
Zhun Zhong
Zichun Zhong
Bo Zhou
Boyao Zhou
Brady Zhou
Mo Zhou
Chunluan Zhou
Dingfu Zhou
Fan Zhou
Jingkai Zhou
Honglu Zhou
Jiaming Zhou
Jiahuan Zhou
Jun Zhou
Kaiyang Zhou
Keyang Zhou
Kuangqi Zhou
Lei Zhou
Lihua Zhou
Man Zhou
Mingyi Zhou
Mingyuan Zhou
Ning Zhou
Peng Zhou
Penghao Zhou
Qianyi Zhou

Shuigeng Zhou
Shangchen Zhou
Huayi Zhou
Zhize Zhou
Sanping Zhou
Qin Zhou
Tao Zhou
Wenbo Zhou
Xiangdong Zhou
Xiao-Yun Zhou
Xiao Zhou
Yang Zhou
Yipin Zhou
Zhenyu Zhou
Hao Zhou
Chu Zhou
Daquan Zhou
Da-Wei Zhou
Hang Zhou
Kang Zhou
Qianyu Zhou
Sheng Zhou
Wenhui Zhou
Xingyi Zhou
Yan-Jie Zhou
Yiyi Zhou
Yu Zhou
Yuan Zhou
Yuqian Zhou
Yuxuan Zhou
Zixiang Zhou
Wengang Zhou
Shuchang Zhou
Tianfei Zhou
Yichao Zhou
Alex Zhu
Chenchen Zhu
Deyao Zhu
Xiatian Zhu
Guibo Zhu
Haidong Zhu
Hao Zhu
Hongzi Zhu
Rui Zhu
Jing Zhu

Jianke Zhu
Junchen Zhu
Lei Zhu
Lingyu Zhu
Luyang Zhu
Menglong Zhu
Peihao Zhu
Hui Zhu
Xiaofeng Zhu
Tyler (Lixuan) Zhu
Wentao Zhu
Xiangyu Zhu
Xinqi Zhu
Xinxin Zhu
Xinliang Zhu
Yangguang Zhu
Yichen Zhu
Yixin Zhu
Yanjun Zhu
Yousong Zhu
Yuhao Zhu
Ye Zhu
Feng Zhu
Zhen Zhu
Fangrui Zhu
Jinjing Zhu
Linchao Zhu
Pengfei Zhu
Sijie Zhu
Xiaobin Zhu
Xiaoguang Zhu
Zezhou Zhu
Zhenyao Zhu
Kai Zhu
Pengkai Zhu
Bingbing Zhuang
Chengyuan Zhuang
Liansheng Zhuang
Peiye Zhuang
Yixin Zhuang
Yihong Zhuang
Junbao Zhuo
Andrea Ziani
Bartosz Zieliński
Primo Zingaretti

Nikolaos Zioulis
Andrew Zisserman
Yael Ziv
Liu Ziyin
Xingxing Zou
Danping Zou
Qi Zou

Shihao Zou
Xueyan Zou
Yang Zou
Yuliang Zou
Zihang Zou
Chuhang Zou
Dongqing Zou

Xu Zou
Zhiming Zou
Maria A. Zuluaga
Xinxin Zuo
Zhiwen Zuo
Reyer Zwiggelaar

Contents – Part XXX

Fast Two-View Motion Segmentation Using Christoffel Polynomials

Bengisu Ozbay⬤, Octavia Camps$^{(\boxtimes)}$⬤, and Mario Sznaier⬤

ECE Department, Northeastern University, Boston, MA 02115, USA
ozbay.b@northeastern.edu, {camps,msznaier}@coe.neu.edu

Abstract. We address the problem of segmenting moving rigid objects based on two-view image correspondences under a perspective camera model. While this is a well understood problem, existing methods scale poorly with the number of correspondences. In this paper we propose a fast segmentation algorithm that scales linearly with the number of correspondences and show that on benchmark datasets it offers the best trade-off between error and computational time: it is at least one order of magnitude faster than the best method (with comparable or better accuracy), with the ratio growing up to three orders of magnitude for larger number of correspondences. We approach the problem from an algebraic perspective by exploiting the fact that all points belonging to a given object lie in the same quadratic surface. The proposed method is based on a characterization of each surface in terms of the Christoffel polynomial associated with the probability that a given point belongs to the surface. This allows for efficiently segmenting points "one surface at a time" in $\mathscr{O}$(number of points).

Keywords: Motion segmentation · Epipolar geometry · Algebraic clustering

1 Introduction

Motion segmentation –segmenting distinct moving objects in a sequence of frames– has a wide range of applications in computer vision and robotics [1–5].

While it is possible to perform trajectory association and object segmentation jointly [6,7], this requires solving expensive optimization problems. Hence, most algorithms require feature correspondences between two or more frames to be given as input.

Most multi-frame approaches segment moving objects by clustering feature trajectories, under the assumption of an affine camera projection model. In this scenario, the trajectories lie in linear or affine subspaces and can be found by using subspace clustering [8–18], or factorization algorithms [19–23]. While these approaches perform

This work was supported in part by NSF grants IIS–1814631 and CNS–2038493, ONR grant N00014-21-1-2431 and U.S. DHS grant 22STESE00001-01-00.

Supplementary Information The online version contains supplementary material available at https://doi.org/10.1007/978-3-031-20056-4_1.

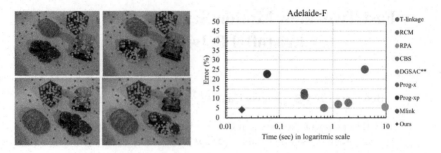

Fig. 1. Left: Sample motion segmentation results for the Adelaide-F data-set. Segmentation for two views of ground truth (1st col.) and our algorithm (2nd col.) each view in one row. Colors of feature points indicate their label where red shows outliers. Right: Comparison of time versus average segmentation error for the entire Adelaide-F data-set. The proposed method is both the most accurate (4.15% error) and fastest (0.02 s per image pair). (Color figure online)

well on benchmarks such as the Hopkins 155 dataset [24] they have several drawbacks. Since they rely on an affine projection model they do not perform well when images have perspective distortion. In addition, point trajectories require tracking features across multiple frames, which is more expensive and difficult than finding singleton correspondences between a pair of frames. Finally, occlusions and missing features in intermediate frames often result in a relatively low number of reliable trajectories to work with. [25–28] handle perspective effects by combining results from two-view correspondences. However, they still require tracked trajectories. More recent approaches [29–32] avoid this requirement, for instance by using triplets of images [31]. However, despite achieving higher accuracy, trifocal tensors fail to classify a high percent of available pairs.

Two-view methods avoid the need for trajectory acquisition, by using the epipolar geometry between correspondences to cluster feature pairs. Thus, they can work with full perspective views. These approaches [33–38] relate pairs of corresponding features through geometric constraints, such as the Longuet-Higgins equation and enforce that features which belong to the same rigid object must be related by the same fundamental matrix. However, while it is easier to find a large number of correspondences between two frames than to obtain many long trajectories across multiple frames, these correspondences are often corrupted with outliers, making the segmentation task more difficult.

A popular approach to eliminate outliers while estimating a single fundamental matrix between two views of a static scene [39–44] is to use random sample consensus (RANSAC) [45]. RANSAC and related sampling methods have also been used when seeking multiple structures [46–48], including motion segmentation. However, the presence of multiple structures necessitates relatively expensive sampling in order to guarantee a given probability of achieving the correct segmentation. Other techniques [49–54] follow a preference-based approach, where the distribution of residuals of individual data points with respect to the models is inspected. However, the model step in these approaches suffers from low accuracy and depends on the bin size. Perhaps the closest approach in spirit to the one proposed in this paper is [12], where two-view motion segmentation is recast into a sparse subspace clustering form. While effective, this approach requires solving first a computationally expensive optimization, followed by a spectral clustering step. Hence, its computational complexity scales at least as (number of points)^3.

In this paper we introduce a robust, computationally efficient algebraic approach for motion segmentation from feature correspondences between two perspective images (Fig. 1). The approach is based on a Christoffel polynomial characterization of the support set of the (unknown) probability distribution associated with data in each of the quadratic surfaces corresponding to points in the same object. This polynomial, which has low (high) values at inliers (outliers) to a given surface allows for efficiently segmenting the objects "one at a time", by identifying all points with high probability of belonging to the same object (Fig. 2). These points are removed from the population and the process is repeated until all points have been labeled. If desired, an outlier removal step can be implemented prior to starting the process, by considering the Christoffel polynomial corresponding to the joint distribution over all objects and identifying correspondences with high probability of being outliers. Notably, computing the Christoffel polynomial from the correspondence data involves the singular value decomposition (SVD) of a matrix whose size depends only on the number of objects, leading to an algorithm whose computational complexity scales linearly with the number of data points. These results are illustrated with standard datasets, show-

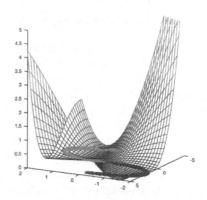

Fig. 2. One at a time segmentation of two second order curves. Since the green points are outliers to the red curve, the Christoffel polynomial of the latter has values higher than 0.5 at these points.

ing that the proposed approach offers the best trade-off between error and computational time (Fig. 1): it is at least one order of magnitude faster than the best method (with comparable or better accuracy), with the ratio growing up to three orders of magnitude for image pairs with larger number of correspondences. In terms of computational time, it is always the fastest, with an error rate at least 50% smaller than the runner up, with this number growing up to 3 times as the number of correspondences increases.

2 Related Work

Two view motion segmentation methods can be roughly grouped into sampling based and model fitting based.

2.1 Sampling Based Approaches

Most of the sampling based methods build on RANSAC [45], which searches for consensus between randomly sampled minimal sets to estimate a single model. Some extensions of RANSAC, including [40,42,55], use a similar methodology on problems with multiple structures and depend on some form of prior knowledge such as matching scores, spatial distance or super-pixel information. Other variations [39,56,57], use the knowledge collected from previous steps to guide sampling in subsequent steps and speed up model estimation. For a more comprehensive overview of variations of RANSAC please see [58,59]. Note that although there are many advances in model estimation for both homography and fundamental matrix estimation [60–62] since these methods are tailored towards obtaining accurate models rather than accurate segmentation, they are not considered in the scope of this work.

2.2 Model Fitting Based Approaches

The T-linkage approach [52] starts with random sampling to generate m hypothesis from minimum sample sets. Then, each data point is described by a *preference function* taking values between 0 and 1. Finally, a greedy bottom-up agglomerative clustering yields a partition of the data by merging points with similar preferences. Later in RPA [54] the authors exploited a robust M-estimator, combined with robust component analysis and non-negative matrix factorization. Some of the more recent preference based methods are MCT [63], HF [64], HOMF [65] and MultiLink [66]. MCT extends T-linkage to handle nested models such as planar sides of a cube whereas MultiLink extends preference representations to multiple, not necessarily nested, mixed classes of models. Although these model fitting based approaches generally achieve good performance on the fitting accuracy, they have a high computational complexity.

[53] learns a Random Cluster Models (RCM) to generate hypotheses using non-minimal subsets of samples. Point preferences are organized in a graph and then graph cuts are used to optimize the fitting. The MSHF method [67] clusters model hypotheses using hypergraphs constructed from data where each hypothesis indicates an instance in data. However, this method seeks modes from the generated model hypotheses which may lead to suboptimal fitting results, for cases where the generated model hypotheses do not contain all model instances. A similar method, Prog-x (P-x) [68], interleaves sampling and geometric multi-model fitting using a modified RANSAC to progressively explore the data through model proposal and optimization steps. Prog-xp (P-xp) [69] extends P-x by introducing a new problem formulation which allows points to be assigned to more than one model. These consensus analysis based methods can achieve a high fitting accuracy if provided by a high quality model hypothesis.

All the above approaches use random sampling to grow clusters and reject outliers. In contrast, our approach is deterministic and proceeds by selecting the most reliable data available at each step.

3   Notation

$\mathbf{A} \succeq 0$	matrix $\mathbf{A}$ is positive semidefinite.
$\mathscr{P}_n^d$	subspace of nth degree homogeneous multivariate polynomials in d variables.
$s_{n,d} \doteq \binom{n+d-1}{d-1}$	number of monomials of degree n in d variables.
$\mathbf{v}_n(\mathbf{x}) \doteq$	$\begin{bmatrix} x_1^n & x_1^{n-1}x_2 & \dots & x_d^n \end{bmatrix}^T$ degree n Veronese map of $\mathbf{x} = \left(x_1 \dots x_d \right)^T$
$\mathscr{E}_\mu(x)$	Expected value of x with respect to the probability density function μ.
$|\mathscr{S}|$	number of elements in the set $\mathscr{S}$.

4   Problem Setup

The goal of this paper is to assign correspondences to objects. As discussed below, this problem is equivalent to algebraic variety clustering, where points need to be assigned to a known number of unknown second order varieties. Consider a set of N (inlier) correspondences $\mathscr{C} = \{(\mathbf{x}_1, \mathbf{x}_2)_i, i = 1, \dots, N\}$ between two perspective views of a scene with a known number M of rigid objects. If $\mathbf{x}_1$ and $\mathbf{x}_2$ are corresponding features that belong to object j, they must satisfy the epipolar constraint:

$$\mathbf{x}_1^T \mathbf{F}^{(j)} \mathbf{x}_2 = 0 \tag{1}$$

where $\mathbf{F}^{(j)} \in \mathbb{R}^{3\times3}$ is the Fundamental matrix for object j and $\mathbf{x}_k = (x_k, y_k, 1)^T$ are the homogeneous coordinates of the feature in view $k = 1, 2$. Therefore, $[x_1, y_1, x_2, y_2]^T$ is a root of a second order polynomial with four variables and hence belongs to the second order algebraic variety associated with this polynomial (or, equivalently, it lies on the quadratic surface defined by all the roots of the polynomial).

4.1   Two View Motion Segmentation as Algebraic Variety Clustering

Since all two-view correspondences associated with a given object satisfy (1), the problem addressed in this paper is a special case of algebraic variety clustering where the goal is to segment points lying on a surface defined by the union of n_v algebraic varieties of the form $V_i \doteq \{\mathbf{x} : p_{2,i}(\mathbf{x}) = 0\}$, where $p_{2,i}(.)$ are quadratic multivariate polynomials.

The algebraic segmentation problem (and hence two view segmentation) can be solved by first estimating the polynomials that define each variety and then assigning points $\mathbf{x}_i$ to the polynomial that yields the smallest fitting error $|p_{2,i}(\mathbf{x}_j)|$. In the case of linear subspaces, this is precisely the approach used by GPCA [15,70]. In principle, a straightforward approach to extend GPCA to second order algebraic varieties, is to simply use a polynomial lifting to lift the problem from its original space to the space defined by the Veronese map $\mathbf{v}_2(\mathbf{x})$. Under this lifting, the problem reduces to subspace clustering, where each subspace is of the form $\mathbf{v}_2(\mathbf{x})^T \mathbf{p}_k = 0$, where the vector $\mathbf{p}_k$ contains the coefficients of the polynomial $p_{2,k}(.)$. However, even for the linear case it is well known that GPCA is fragile to noise and outliers. This situation is exacerbated when extending the approach to algebraic varieties, since the noise is polynomially lifted. In addition, this lifting ignores the specific structure of each of the polynomials that define the varieties (1), potentially introducing spurious solutions. As we show in the paper, these difficulties can be circumvented by considering a "one-at-a-time" approach that combines algebraic and Christoffel function arguments.

4.2   Approximating Support Sets via Christoffel Polynomials

Given a probability measure μ supported on $\mathbb{R}^d$, its associated moments sequence is given by

$$m_\alpha = \mathcal{E}_\mu(\mathbf{x}^\alpha) = \int_{\mathbb{R}^d} \mathbf{x}^\alpha d\mu \tag{2}$$

where $\mathbf{x} \doteq [x_1 \ x_2 \ \dots \ x_d]^T$, $\alpha \doteq [\alpha_1 \ \alpha_2 \ \dots \ \alpha_d]$ and $\mathbf{x}^\alpha$ stands for $x_1^{\alpha_1} x_2^{\alpha_2} \cdots x_d^{\alpha_d}$. Each sequence m can be associated with a moment matrix $\mathbf{M}_n$, with entries $\mathbf{M}_{i,j} = m_{\alpha_i + \alpha_j}$, containing moments of order up to $2n$. In the sequel, we will use the submatrix $\mathbf{L}_n$ of $\mathbf{M}_n$, containing only moments of order $2n$. For instance, for moments of order 4 in two variables, we have

$$\mathbf{L}_2 = \begin{bmatrix} m_{(4,0)} & m_{(3,1)} & m_{(2,2)} \\ m_{(3,1)} & m_{(2,2)} & m_{(1,3)} \\ m_{(2,2)} & m_{(1,3)} & m_{(0,4)} \end{bmatrix}$$

By construction $\mathbf{L}_n \succeq 0$ thus it induces a reproducing Kernel $K_n(\mathbf{x}, \mathbf{y}) \doteq \mathbf{v}_n^T(\mathbf{x}) \mathbf{L}_n^{-1} \mathbf{v}_n(\mathbf{y})$[1]. The non-negative function $Q_n^{-1}(\mathbf{x}) \doteq \mathbf{v}_n^T(\mathbf{x}) \mathbf{L}_n^{-1} \mathbf{v}_n(\mathbf{x})$ is known as the Christoffel function associated with the Kernel $\mathbf{K}$ [71]. It is related to the measure μ that induces $\mathbf{L}_n$ through the following optimization problem over homogeneous polynomials of degree n [71,72]:

$$p_{\mathbf{y}}^*(.) = \underset{p \in \mathscr{P}_n^d}{argmin} \int_{\mathbb{R}^p} p^2(\xi) d\mu \ \text{ s.t. } p(\mathbf{y}) = 1$$

$$Q_n^{-1}(\mathbf{y}) = \mathcal{E}_\mu[(p_{\mathbf{y}}^*(.))^2] \tag{3}$$

where $\mathbf{y}$ is an arbitrary given data point. That is, given the data point $\mathbf{y}$, $p_{\mathbf{y}}^*(.)$ is the minimum mean square value homogeneous polynomial of degree n, subject to the constraint $p_{\mathbf{y}}^*(\mathbf{y}) = 1$, and the Christoffel function evaluated at $\mathbf{y}$, $Q_n^{-1}(\mathbf{y})$, is precisely its mean square value. In this paper, with a slight abuse of notation, we will refer to $p_{\mathbf{y}}^*(.)$ as the Christoffel *polynomials*. An explicit expression for $p_{\mathbf{y}}^*(.)$ in terms of the singular vectors $\mathbf{u}_i$ and singular values σ_i of $\mathbf{L}_n$ is given by [73]:

$$p_{\mathbf{y}}^*(.) = \mathbf{v}_n(.)^T \mathbf{c}_{\mathbf{y}}^*$$

$$\text{where } \mathbf{c}_{\mathbf{y}}^* = \frac{1}{\sum_{i=1}^{S_{n,d}} (\frac{1}{\sqrt{\sigma_i}} \mathbf{u}_i^T \mathbf{v}_n(\mathbf{y}))^2} \sum_{i=1}^{S_{n,d}} \frac{1}{\sigma_i} \mathbf{u}_i^T \mathbf{v}_n(\mathbf{y}) \mathbf{u}_i \tag{4}$$

As noted in [72], both $Q_n(.)$ and $p_{\mathbf{y}}^*(.)$ can be used to approximate the support of the

---

[1] For a singular $\mathbf{L} \doteq \mathbf{U} \begin{bmatrix} \Sigma & \mathbf{0} \\ \mathbf{0} & \mathbf{0} \end{bmatrix} \mathbf{U}^T, \mathbf{L}^{-1} \doteq \mathbf{U} \begin{bmatrix} \Sigma^{-1} & \mathbf{0} \\ \mathbf{0} & \mathbf{0} \end{bmatrix} \mathbf{U}^T.$

distribution μ and to detect outliers. Specifically, it can be easily shown that $\mathscr{E}_\mu(Q_n) = s_{n,d} \doteq \binom{n+d-1}{d-1}$. Direct application of Markov's inequality yields:

$$\text{prob}\{Q_n(\mathbf{y}) \geq t.s_{n,d}\} \leq \frac{1}{t} \quad (5)$$

Thus, high values of Q_n correspond to points with a high probability of being outliers. Similarly, for the polynomial $p_{\mathbf{y}}^{*2}(.)$ we have:

$$\text{prob}\left\{(p_{\mathbf{y}}^*(\mathbf{x}))^2 \geq \frac{1}{tQ_n(\mathbf{y})}\right\} \leq t \quad (6)$$

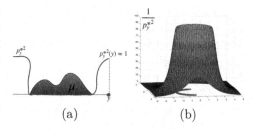

Fig. 3. (a) The square Christoffel polynomial $p_{\mathbf{y}}^{*2}$ for an outlier $\mathbf{y}$ is small at inlier points. (b) The inverse of the square Christoffel polynomial, $p_{\mathbf{y}}^{*-2}$, estimated from partial data of a circle (shown in red). It has *high values at the inliers* and approximates the support of the data.

Remark 1. From the equations above it follows that if $\mathbf{y}$ is chosen to be an outlier to the distribution μ, then the polynomial $p_{\mathbf{y}}^{*2}(.)$ will approximate the complement of the support of μ, in the sense that its value will be large in places where μ is small and viceversa (Fig. 3). This follows from the observation that if $\mathbf{y}$ is an outlier to the distribution μ, then $Q_n(\mathbf{y})$ is large and, from (6), $(p_{\mathbf{y}}^*(\mathbf{x}))^2$ is small if $\mathbf{x}$ is an inlier. Intuitively, if $\mathbf{y}$ is an outlier, a solution to (3) will be a polynomial that is close to one in a neighborhood of $\mathbf{y}$, to satisfy the constraint $p(\mathbf{y}) = 1$, and small in regions where μ is large, to minimize the overall integral (Fig. 3(a)). Since the region around $\mathbf{y}$ has low density, it contributes little to the integral of p^2, while setting p^2 small in regions where μ is large minimizes their cost. This observation will be key in developing the clustering algorithm.

Note in passing that since the distribution μ is typically unknown, $\mathbf{L}_n$ cannot be computed. Rather, it is approximated by the empirical moments matrix:

$$\mathbf{L}_n \approx \frac{1}{N} \sum_{i=1}^{N} \mathbf{v}_n(\mathbf{x})\mathbf{v}_n^T(\mathbf{x}).$$

5 Methodology and Algorithm

In this section we present a computationally efficient algorithm to segment the given data. For simplicity, we will cover the basic ideas of the algorithm for the generic algebraic variety clustering case and then indicate refinements to improve performance in the specific case of two view motion segmentation.

5.1 One at a Time Algebraic Clustering

The proposed iterative algorithm is based on the observation made in Remark 1 that the polynomial $p_{\mathbf{y}}^*$ constructed based on a point $\mathbf{y}$ that is an outlier to the distribution μ, provides a good approximation to the support of its complement. Consider again the arrangement of n_v varieties $\mathscr{A} \doteq \cup_{j=1}^{n_v} V_j$, and suppose that we select a point $\mathbf{y}_i \in V_i$. Since this point is an outlier to the distribution over the partial arrangement $\mathscr{A}_{partial} = \cup_{j \neq i} V_j$, then it is expected that $p_{\mathbf{y}_i}^*$ will approximate, at least around $\mathbf{y}_i$ the support of its complement $\overline{\mathscr{A}}_{partial} = V_i$. Thus, a "reliable" subset $V_{i,rel}$ of V_i can be found by simply collecting points where $p_{\mathbf{y}_i}^*$ is above a threshold, related to the probability of misclassification. These "reliable" inliers can be used to refine the estimates of the coefficients of the polynomial $p_{\mathbf{y}_i}^*$ and grow the set $V_{i,rel}$ by adding new points where $p_{\mathbf{y}_i}^*$ is above the threshold. Points on this set are removed from the population and the process is repeated for the remaining varieties. A heuristic for choosing $\mathbf{y}_i$ is to select, at each stage, the point corresponding to the minimum Q. The rationale behind this choice is to select a point located in a "high mass" region of the distribution, and hence likely to have a large number of points from the same variety in its neighborhood, maximizing the number of reliable inliers used to estimate the set $V_{i,rel}$. An illustration of how to apply these ideas to a simple case is shown in Fig. 4. The corresponding conceptual Algorithm is outlined in Algorithm 1.

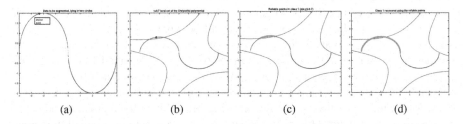

(a)   (b)   (c)   (d)

Fig. 4. Applying Algorithm 1 to segment two circles. (a): Original data (red and blue points) and selected anchor (green) point (Alg. 1, step 2). (b): $t = 0.7$ level set of the Christoffel polynomial. The anchor point and its neighborhood are outside the set (Alg. 1, step 3). (c): Points outside the level set are "reliable points", used to estimate the parameters of the circle (Alg. 1, step 4). (d): Final segmentation using the circle estimated from the reliable points (Alg. 1, step 5). (Color figure online)

5.2   Refinements for Two View Motion Segmentation

For the specific case of interest to this paper, the basic conceptual algorithm can be refined to improve robustness as follows. Firstly, note that the polynomial $\mathbf{x}_1^T \mathbf{F} \mathbf{x}_2$ does not contain pure quadratic terms. Thus, when computing the moment matrix $\mathbf{L}$, rather that using the standard veronese map, one can use the restricted one:

$$\mathbf{v}_r(x_1, y_1, x_2, y_2, 1) \doteq [1\; x_1\; y_1\; x_2\; y_2\; x_1 x_2 x_1 y_2\; y_1 x_2\; y_1 y_2]^T$$

Algorithm 1. Conceptual one-at-a-time segmentation.

1: **for** $k := 1$ to $n_v - 1$ **do**
2:     **Selecting** $\mathbf{y}_k$: Compute $Q_{n_v+1-k}(\mathbf{x})$ and choose $\mathbf{y}_k = \arg\min_{\mathbf{x}} Q_{n_v+1-k}(\mathbf{x})$
3:     Compute $p^*_{\mathbf{y}_k}(\mathbf{x})$, the Christoffel support polynomial, for the union of $n_v - k$ clusters treating the point $\mathbf{y}_k$ as an outlier.
4:     Assign points where $(p^*_{\mathbf{y}_k}(\mathbf{x}))^2 \geq t$ to the set $\mathscr{X}_k$. This set approximates a subset of V_k, the variety that contains $\mathbf{y}_k$.
5:     Using the points in $\mathscr{X}_k$ and available structural information, estimate the polynomial p_k that characterizes V_k. Estimate $\hat{V}_k = \mathscr{X}_k \cup \{\mathbf{y}: |p_k(\mathbf{y})| \leq \text{noise level}\}$.
6:     Remove the points in $\hat{V}_k$ from the population $\mathbf{x}$.

This avoids spurious solutions that do not correspond to fundamental matrices when computing $p_{\mathbf{x}_{o,k}}$. Secondly, once the initial set of reliable points has been computed, it can be used to estimate the Fundamental matrix, using for instance the 8 points algorithm, possibly combined with RANSAC. In turn, this estimated Fundamental matrix can be used to find additional correspondences belonging to this object. The complete two view segmentation algorithm is given in Algorithm 2.

6 Experimental Evaluation

In this section we evaluate the performance of the proposed two-view motion segmentation method using the following benchmark datasets: Adelaide-F [74], two-view versions of Hopkins [24], with and without outliers, two-view version of KT3D dataset [28], two image pairs, named as BC and BCD, introduced in [75] and pairwise indoor scenes dataset introduced in [30]. For all datasets, we use the same thresholds as shown in lines 3 and 7 in Algorithm 2. We report the performance in terms of segmentation error [53] and computation time, and compare against the state-of-art algorithms: T-linkage [52], RCM [53], RPA [54], CBS [57], DGSAC [76], P-x [68], P-xp [69] and MLink [66]. In all cases we used code provided by their authors (except for DGSAC for which we report values from [76].

    A summary of our experiments is given in Table 1, followed by a detailed analysis of each data set. As noted before, the proposed method is at least one order of magnitude faster than the best method (with comparable or better accuracy), with the ratio growing up to three orders of magnitude for larger number of correspondences. Further, it is always the fastest, with an error rate at least 50% smaller than the runner up, with this number growing up to 3 times as the number of correspondences increases.

6.1 Adelaide-F

Adelaide-F is part of a larger dataset, Adelaide-RMF, widely used for homography and Fundamental matrix fitting problems. Since this paper deals with two-view motion segmentation, the only relevant portion of this dataset is the subset Adelaide-F, consisting of group of images intended for Fundamental matrix estimation problems. The Adelaide-F dataset has 19 image pairs of different sizes, with correspondences between

---

Algorithm 2. Two-view motion segmentation algorithm. Lines 2-8 perform outlier rejection; 9-26 implement one at a time clustering on the estimated inliers; 27-34 assign all inlier correspondences to clusters; 35-39 use the model of each cluster to classify the unreliable points found in Step 1. Code is available at https://github.com/BengisuOzbay/TwoViewMotSeg

---

1: **Input:** Data matrix $\mathbf{X} \in \mathbb{R}^{5 \times N}$ where each column is $[x_1, y_1, x_2, y_2, 1]^T$, number of objects M
2: **Find a reliable set for arrangement $\mathscr{A}_M = \bigcup_{i=1}^{m} V_i$:**
3:     $t = 0.6 \times mean(Q_M)$ ▷ Initialize threshold
4:     $\mathbf{X}_{rel} \leftarrow \mathbf{X}(:, Q_M < t)$ ▷ Pick the most reliable data
5: **Outlier rejection:**
6:     $\mathbf{y}_o = \arg\min_{\mathbf{x}} Q_M(\mathbf{x})$ ▷ Grossest outlier
7:     $t = 0.001 \times M$ ▷ Initialize threshold
8:     $\mathbf{X}_{in} \leftarrow \mathbf{X}(:, p_{\mathbf{y}_o, M}(\mathbf{x} \mid \mathbf{X}_{rel}) < t)$ ▷ Remove outliers
9: **Clustering:**
10:    $\mathbf{X}_{av} \leftarrow \mathbf{X}_{in}$ ▷ Initialize available
11: **for** $k := 1$ to M **do**
12:     $m \leftarrow M - k$ ▷ Available clusters
13:     **if** $k \neq M$ or $|\mathbf{X}_{av}| \geq 18^{\dagger}$ **then**
14:        $\mathbf{y}_a \leftarrow \arg\min_{\mathbf{x}}(Q_{m+1}(\mathbf{x}))$ ▷ "anchor" point
15:        $t \leftarrow$ otsu threshold for $p_{\mathbf{y}_a, m}^2(\mathbf{x})$
16:        $V_{o,k} \leftarrow \mathbf{X}_{av}(:, p_{\mathbf{y}_a, m}^2(\mathbf{x}) \geq t)$ ▷ $\mathbf{y}_a \in V_{o,k} \subset V_k$
17:     **else**   ▷ last cluster or $|\mathbf{X}_{av}|$ is too small
18:        $V_{o,k} \leftarrow \mathbf{X}_{av}$
19:     **Grow the variety $V_{o,k}$ using Fundamental Matrix**
20:     $V_{o,k,cl} \leftarrow V_{o,k}(Q_1(x \mid V_{o,k}) < mean(Q_1) \times 1.2)$ ▷ Clean the variety $V_{o,k}$
21:     $\mathbf{F}_k \leftarrow norm8Point(V_{o,k,cl})$ ▷ Normalized 8 pt. alg.
22:     **fit** $\leftarrow abs(p_1^T \mathbf{F}_k p_2)$ ▷ $[p_1^T \ p_2^T \ 1]^T \in \mathbf{X}_{av}$
23:     $t_F \leftarrow 0.05$, $V_{id,k} \leftarrow \mathbf{X}_{av}(:, \textbf{fit} < t_F)$
24:     **Find a reliable set $V_{rel,k} \subset V_{id,k} \subset V_k$**
25:     $V_{rel,k} \leftarrow V_{id,k}(Q_1(x \mid V_{id,k}) < mean(Q_1) \times 1.4)$
26:     Update available data: $\mathbf{X}_{av} \leftarrow \mathbf{X}_{av} \setminus V_{id,k}$
27: **Assign all correspondences to found clusters:**
28: **for** $j := 1$ to M **do**   ▷ Find the score for each variety
29:     $\textbf{score}_Q(j) \leftarrow Q_1(\mathbf{x} \mid V_{rel,j}) / norm(Q_1(\mathbf{x} \mid V_{rel,j}))$
30:     $\mathbf{F}_j \leftarrow norm8Point(V_{rel,j})$
31:     $\textbf{fits}_j \leftarrow abs(p_1^T \mathbf{F}_k p_2)$ ▷ $[p_1^T \ p_2^T \ 1]^T \in \mathbf{X}$
32: $V_{rel,all} = V_{rel,1} \bigcup V_{rel,2} \bigcup \dots V_{rel,M}$
33: $\textbf{score}_Q(0) \leftarrow (Q_M(\mathbf{x} \mid V_{rel,all}) / norm(Q_M(\mathbf{x} \mid V_{rel,all}))$
34: **labels** $\leftarrow \arg\min_j \textbf{score}_Q(j)$ ▷ Assign each pair to the cluster with lowest score, cluster $j = 0$ represents outliers
35: **Refine outliers by cross checking using F_k**
36: $[\textbf{fits}_{min} \ \textbf{fits}_{idx}] = min(\textbf{fits})$ ▷ Find the cluster associated with min fit for each point
37: $\textbf{idx}_{in} \leftarrow \textbf{fits}_{idx}(\textbf{fits}_{min} < 0.02)$ ▷ Inlier index according to their fit with subspaces
38: **if labels**$(\textbf{idx}_{in}) == 0$ **then**
39:     $\textbf{labels}(\textbf{idx}_{in}) = \textbf{idx}_{in}$

---

† The dimension of the modified Veronese mapping for a single cluster is 9

Table 1. Summary of our experiments: Average segmentation errors in %; 5 random runs on each scene, and the average processing times per scene (in secs) for each problem: two-view motion fitting on the two view subsets of Adelaide (2nd–3rd cols), Hopkins dataset without outliers (4th–5th) and with uniformly added outliers (6th–7th), KT3D dataset (8th–9th), a single image pair with 2 motions and 1116 feature correspondences (10th–11th), a single image pair with 3 motions and 1227 feature correspondences (12th–13th), Pairwise dataset (14th–15th) a subset of the original data set containing all pairs with more than 700 correspondences. Best results are shown in italic red and second best results are blue. *Entries for DGSAC from [76]. In all cases the proposed method is the fastest one and has the best or second best average segmentation error.

	Adelaide-F		H-C		H-O		KT3D		BC		BCD		Pairwise	
	SE%	Time	SE%	Time	SE%	Time	SE%	Time	SE%	Time	SE%	Time	SE%	Time
T-L	25.1	4.00	33.6	6.27	26.2	37.2	28.5	3.90	15.8	137	30.8	172	40.1	95.4
RCM	7.65	1.96	18.2	4.72	9.83	4.36	24.7	2.00	44.3	7.88	30.6	10.3	12.1	6.93
RPA	5.49	9.65	6.41	11.3	8.5	50.9	46.4	12.4	7.56	153	5.3	210	2.63	142
CBS	5.03	0.69	10.2	1.6	15.7	1.5	44.9	0.58	39.6	3.83	28.8	2.84	22.8	3.08
DGSAC*	6.95	1.27	-	-	-	-	-	-	-	-	-	-	-	-
P-x	11.5	0.30	17.6	0.39	9.77	0.71	15.0	0.257	10.3	1.73	27.3	1.07	18.0	0.996
P-xp	22.7	0.06	32.2	0.03	29.2	0.29	25.6	0.017	30.1	0.08	16.7	0.27	30.7	0.091
MLink	13.1	0.29	16.9	0.28	16.1	1.92	19.6	0.178	22.1	3.40	22.5	3.77	10.7	2.45
Ours	4.15	0.02	7.42	0.02	7.79	0.03	17.2	0.016	9.23	0.05	7.25	0.09	4.93	0.036

two frames manually annotated. In each image pair there are from one to four rigid motions as well as outliers.

Figure 1(b) compares the segmentation error, averaged over five random runs versus the average computational time per image pair. As shown there, our method has the best performance both in terms of mean error (4.15%) and runtime (0.02 s). Our method is 30 times faster than the runner-up in error (CBS) and has 1/5 of the error and is 3 times faster than the second fastest method, P-xp.

6.2 Hopkins-Clean (H-C) and Hopkins-Outliers (H-O)

The original Hopkins dataset has 156 sequences with two and three moving objects, and a single sequence with 5 moving objects. This dataset is one of the most widely used benchmarks for subspace clustering and motion segmentation problems. In the original dataset each sequence consists of 30 frames long videos of moving objects where each feature point is tracked through the entire video. [38] uses this dataset for two-view motion segmentation problem by using the first and last frames of each video as image pairs.

For this experiment, following [38] we initially used the first and last frames of the each video and referred to this as Hopkins-clean (H-C). To evaluate the effects of the displacement, we also run experiments where we selected the 1st and 10th frames of each sequence as the image pairs. Finally, since the Hopkins dataset does not have outliers, we generated a Hopkins-outlier (H-O) dataset, contaminated by synthetic outliers generated by declaring as matches uniformly distributed random pixels from each view. The overall results are given in Table 1 and Fig. 5, for the case where

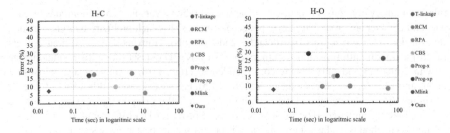

Fig. 5. Average error versus time for Hopkins (left) and Hopkins with outliers (right)

$r = (number\ of\ outliers) \div (number\ of\ inliers) = 0.9$. As shown there, our method is the second best for H-C and best for H-O, and provides the best error versus time trade-off, running more than 2 orders of magnitude faster than the method with the best/second-best error.

Robustness to Outliers: In order to evaluate the performance of the proposed method under changing number of outliers, we tested it with different outlier ratios.

As before, these outliers where generated by matching randomly chosen pixels from both views. The results, shown in Table 2, illustrate that the proposed method is indeed robust to outliers, since performance degrades gracefully even when the outlier ratio is substantially increased. This behavior matches the observation in [73] that algebraic methods are robust to

Table 2. Hopkins dataset with varying outlier ratio where $r = (number\ of\ outliers) \div (number\ of\ inliers)$.

	$r = 0.9$	$r = 1.5$	$r = 2.1$
SE%	7.79	9.37	10.72
Time	0.03	0.03	0.04

outliers as long as enough reliable inliers are available to estimate the polynomials associated with the algebraic varieties.

Displacement: To investigate the effect of displacement of the objects on the performance, we tested the proposed method and state-of-the-art methods on different image pairs of the Hopkins-clean. Table 3 compares results using pairs of 1st-10th frames and 1st-last. As shown there, although the performance of our method slightly decreases, it is still the second best performance in terms of accuracy with the shortest run time.

Table 3. Comparison of segmentation results on H-C using frames 1 and 10 versus 1 and last.

Frames	1st–10th		1st–last	
	SE%	Time	SE%	Time
T-L	33.4	8.25	33.6	6.27
RCM	24.8	3.87	18.2	4.72
RPA	5.5	14.7	6.4	11.4
CBS	17.9	1.5	10.2	1.6
P-x	10.7	0.28	17.6	0.39
P-xp	33.1	0.19	32.2	0.03
MLink	12.1	0.249	16.9	0.28
Ours	9.9	0.014	7.4	0.02

Categorical Analysis: Figure 6 provides a detailed analysis of the Hopkins results separated by number of motions. For two motion cases our method has the second best accuracy in both clean and the outlier version of Hopkins, whereas the performance degrades in the 3-motion cases. The reasons for performance drop in our method when moving to 3 motions are: (a) In this case there are less points per object so estimation of the moment matrix is less accurate. Our method is designed to work well for scenarios with large number of correspondences, where computational complexity may render other methods impractical. (b) The results for 3-motion seem to be poisoned by the checkerboard scenes where the camera is very close to the objects and has a significant movement, while the objects have small displacements. As a consequence, the dominant motion of all objects is the same as the background category leading to clusters of two objects becoming corrupted with points belonging to the background. This is illustrated in Fig. 6 (right panel) showing that dropping this sequence leads to substantially smaller average segmentation error. In all cases our method has a lower error than P-xp, the fastest amongst existing methods. The method that yields the best error (RPA) is 500 times slower than ours.

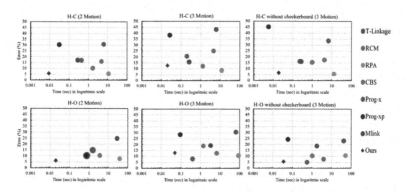

Fig. 6. Hopkins categorical analysis: H-C (top) and H-O (bottom) with 2 motion (left), 3 motion (middle) and 3 motion without checkerboard scenes (right). Segmentation error (%) and times (secs) are averaged over 5 random runs.

6.3 KT3D

KT3D was introduced by [28] as a dataset with more realistic and challenging real world effects such as strong perspective effects in the background, foreground moving objects with limited depth reliefs, background objects with non-compact shapes, small or intermittent foreground object movement compared to that of the camera, objects moving along the epipolar line etc. We use this dataset in order to test robustness of our method against these real world challenges. The KT3D dataset has 22 videos, each 10–20 frames long with two to four moving objects. To perform 2-view motion segmentation we picked frame pairs where all the moving objects are present and frames have large perspective effects. Note that since most of the time either one or more objects appear later in the video or disappear before the last frame we could not pick the first and last

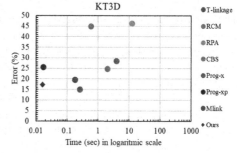

Fig. 7. Results for the KT3D data set. Our method gives the best error-time tradeoff

frame for KT3D as we did for Hopkins. Table 1 and Fig. 7 show that our method is the fastest, with the second best error, and the best error-time trade-off. It runs one order of magnitude faster than P-x, at the price of 10% increase in error.

6.4   BC and BCD

We selected two image pairs Box-Car (BC) and Box-Car-Dinosaurs (BCD) [75] to illustrate the scaling benefits of our method. BC and BCD have two and three moving rigid objects with 1116 and 1227 feature correspondences, respectively. Both pairs are also mildly contaminated by outliers. For comparison, the Adelaide-F and Hopkins datasets have only 260 and 295 feature correspondences on average.

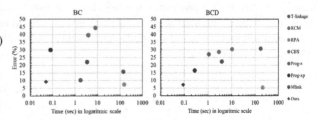

Fig. 8. Results for the KT3DMoSeg data set. Our method gives the best error-time tradeoff

Thus, the number of correspondences in these image pairs is significantly larger, allowing for observing its effect on the time complexity. As shown in Table 1, the proposed algorithm has the second lowest error and is the fastest method in both cases (Fig. 8). Further, the best performing algorithm (RPA) is 3 orders of magnitude slower. Note also that RPA scales quadratically with the number of correspondences, while the proposed method scales linearly.

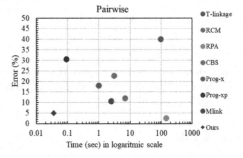

Fig. 9. Results for the Pairwise dataset. Our method gives the best error-time tradeoff

6.5   Pairwise

The Pairwise dataset was introduced in [30] as a small benchmark for pairwise matching purposes. It consists of five sequences each having six to ten different indoor scenes containing two or three motions where one object is fixed. The main challenge in these image pairs is having noisy SIFT correspondences. Since our goal is different from the original purpose for which this dataset was created [30], we used a subset consisting of 29 image pairs each having at least 700 feature correspondences to illustrate the performance and time scaling of our method. In this case the proposed method is the fastest, with second best error (Table 1 and Fig. 9). Further, the only method that has lower segmentation error is 10^3 times slower.

7 Conclusions

In this paper, we address the problem of segmenting moving rigid objects based on two-view image correspondences under a perspective camera model. We approach the problem from an algebraic perspective by exploiting the fact that, due to the geometric constraints, all correspondences from the same object lie on a quadratic surface defined by the Fundamental matrix. The proposed method is based on a characterization of each surface in terms of the Christoffel polynomial associated with the probability that a given point belongs to the surface. This allows for efficiently segmenting points "one surface at a time" by first estimating a set of points $V_{i,rel}$, the "reliable" inlier set, that, with high probability, belong to the same variety (and hence to the same object). We use these reliable inliers to estimate the parameters of the polynomial defining the variety. Finally, using this polynomial we identify additional points on the variety by simply collecting points where its absolute value is below a given threshold. It is worth emphasizing that estimating the Christoffel polynomial requires only a singular value decomposition of a matrix whose size is independent of n_p, the number of data points. Further, since this matrix is formed by adding n_p outer products, the computational complexity of the method scales linearly with the number of correspondences, which makes it well suited for applications where n_p is large.

The effectiveness of the proposed approach was demonstrated on several benchmark datasets. The experiments show that the proposed method yields the best trade-off error versus computation time. Our approach has error comparable (or better) than the most accurate method, while being at least one order of magnitude faster. In terms of execution time, the proposed algorithm is the fastest, while the runner up in execution time (P-xp) has an error rate that is at least 50% higher. Further, these gaps increase with the number of correspondences: for the largest datasets the proposed algorithm is 3 orders of magnitude faster than RPA and achieves an error less than half of the one achieved by P-xp. An additional advantage is that, since the Christoffel polynomial approximates the distribution of the inliers, it automatically provides robustness against outliers, as shown with the experiments with the Hopkins data set, where performance degraded gracefully, even in a scenario where the number of outliers was twice as high as the number of inliers.

References

1. Kim, J.B., Kim, H.J.: Efficient region-based motion segmentation for a video monitoring system. Pattern Recogn. Lett. **24**(1–3), 113–128 (2003)
2. Ess, A., Mueller, T., Grabner, H., Van Gool, L.: Segmentation-based urban traffic scene understanding. In: BMVC, vol. 1, p. 2. Citeseer (2009)
3. Weinland, D., Ronfard, R., Boyer, E.: A survey of vision-based methods for action representation, segmentation and recognition. Comput. Vis. Image Underst. **115**(2), 224–241 (2011)
4. Geiger, A., Lenz, P., Urtasun, R.: Are we ready for autonomous driving? The KITTI vision benchmark suite. In: 2012 IEEE Conference on Computer Vision and Pattern Recognition, pp. 3354–3361. IEEE (2012)
5. Saputra, M.R.U., Markham, A., Trigoni, N.: Visual SLAM and structure from motion in dynamic environments: a survey. ACM Comput. Surv. (CSUR) **51**(2), 1–36 (2018)

6. Ji, P., Li, H., Salzmann, M., Dai, Y.: Robust motion segmentation with unknown correspondences. In: Fleet, D., Pajdla, T., Schiele, B., Tuytelaars, T. (eds.) ECCV 2014. LNCS, vol. 8694, pp. 204–219. Springer, Cham (2014). https://doi.org/10.1007/978-3-319-10599-4_14

7. Wang, Y., Liu, Y., Blasch, E., Ling, H.: Simultaneous trajectory association and clustering for motion segmentation. IEEE Signal Process. Lett. **25**(1), 145–149 (2017)

8. Gear, C.W.: Multibody grouping from motion images. Int. J. Comput. Vis. **29**(2), 133–150 (1998)

9. Elhamifar, E., Vidal, R.: Sparse subspace clustering. In: 2009 IEEE Conference on Computer Vision and Pattern Recognition, pp. 2790–2797. IEEE (2009)

10. Kanatani, K.: Motion segmentation by subspace separation and model selection. In: Proceedings Eighth IEEE International Conference on computer Vision, ICCV 2001, vol. 2, pp. 586–591. IEEE (2001)

11. Yan, J., Pollefeys, M.: A general framework for motion segmentation: independent, articulated, rigid, non-rigid, degenerate and non-degenerate. In: Leonardis, A., Bischof, H., Pinz, A. (eds.) ECCV 2006. LNCS, vol. 3954, pp. 94–106. Springer, Heidelberg (2006). https://doi.org/10.1007/11744085_8

12. Liu, G., Lin, Z., Shuicheng Yan, J., Sun, Y.Y., Ma, Y.: Robust recovery of subspace structures by low-rank representation. IEEE Trans. Pattern Anal. Mach. Intell. **35**(1), 171–184 (2012)

13. Elhamifar, E., Vidal, R.: Sparse subspace clustering: algorithm, theory, and applications. IEEE Trans. Pattern Anal. Mach. Intell. **35**(11), 2765–2781 (2013)

14. Liu, G., Yan, S.: Latent low-rank representation for subspace segmentation and feature extraction. In: 2011 International Conference on Computer Vision, pp. 1615–1622. IEEE (2011)

15. Vidal, R., Ma, Y., Sastry, S.: Generalized principal component analysis (GPCA). IEEE Trans. PAMI **27**(12), 1945–1959 (2005)

16. Rao, S., Tron, R., Vidal, R., Ma, Y.: Motion segmentation in the presence of outlying, incomplete, or corrupted trajectories. IEEE Trans. Pattern Anal. Mach. Intell. **32**(10), 1832–1845 (2009)

17. Zappella, L., Provenzi, E., Lladó, X., Salvi, J.: Adaptive motion segmentation algorithm based on the principal angles configuration. In: Kimmel, R., Klette, R., Sugimoto, A. (eds.) ACCV 2010. LNCS, vol. 6494, pp. 15–26. Springer, Heidelberg (2011). https://doi.org/10.1007/978-3-642-19318-7_2

18. Keuper, M., Andres, B., Brox, T.: Motion trajectory segmentation via minimum cost multicuts. In: Proceedings of the IEEE International Conference on Computer Vision, pp. 3271–3279 (2015)

19. Costeira, J.P., Kanade, T.: A multibody factorization method for independently moving objects. Int. J. Comput. Vision **29**(3), 159–179 (1998)

20. Gruber, A., Weiss, Y.: Multibody factorization with uncertainty and missing data using the EM algorithm. In: Proceedings of the 2004 IEEE Computer Society Conference on Computer Vision and Pattern Recognition, CVPR 2004, vol. 1, p. I. IEEE (2004)

21. Vidal, R., Tron, R., Hartley, R.: Multiframe motion segmentation with missing data using powerfactorization and GPCA. Int. J. Comput. Vision **79**(1), 85–105 (2008)

22. Sugaya, Y., Kanatani, K.: Geometric structure of degeneracy for multi-body motion segmentation. In: Comaniciu, D., Mester, R., Kanatani, K., Suter, D. (eds.) SMVP 2004. LNCS, vol. 3247, pp. 13–25. Springer, Heidelberg (2004). https://doi.org/10.1007/978-3-540-30212-4_2

23. Flores-Mangas, F., Jepson, A.D.: Fast rigid motion segmentation via incrementally-complex local models. In: Proceedings of the IEEE Conference on Computer Vision and Pattern Recognition, pp. 2259–2266 (2013)

24. Tron, R., Vidal, R.: A benchmark for the comparison of 3-d motion segmentation algorithms. In: 2007 IEEE Conference on Computer Vision and Pattern Recognition, pp. 1–8. IEEE (2007)

25. Schindler, K., U, J., Wang, H.: Perspective *n*-view multibody structure-and-motion through model selection. In: Leonardis, A., Bischof, H., Pinz, A. (eds.) ECCV 2006. LNCS, vol. 3951, pp. 606–619. Springer, Heidelberg (2006). https://doi.org/10.1007/11744023_47

26. Dragon, R., Rosenhahn, B., Ostermann, J.: Multi-scale clustering of frame-to-frame correspondences for motion segmentation. In: Fitzgibbon, A., Lazebnik, S., Perona, P., Sato, Y., Schmid, C. (eds.) ECCV 2012. LNCS, vol. 7573, pp. 445–458. Springer, Heidelberg (2012). https://doi.org/10.1007/978-3-642-33709-3_32

27. Li, Z., Guo, J., Cheong, L.-F., Zhou, S.Z.: Perspective motion segmentation via collaborative clustering. In: Proceedings of the IEEE International Conference on Computer Vision, pp. 1369–1376 (2013)

28. Xu, X., Cheong, L.F., Li, Z.: Motion segmentation by exploiting complementary geometric models. In: Proceedings of the IEEE Conference on Computer Vision and Pattern Recognition, pp. 2859–2867 (2018)

29. Arrigoni, F., Pajdla, T.: Motion segmentation via synchronization. In: Proceedings of the IEEE/CVF International Conference on Computer Vision Workshops (2019)

30. Arrigoni, F., Pajdla, T.: Robust motion segmentation from pairwise matches. In: Proceedings of the IEEE/CVF International Conference on Computer Vision, pp. 671–681 (2019)

31. Arrigoni, F., Magri, L., Pajdla, T.: On the usage of the trifocal tensor in motion segmentation. In: Vedaldi, A., Bischof, H., Brox, T., Frahm, J.-M. (eds.) ECCV 2020. LNCS, vol. 12365, pp. 514–530. Springer, Cham (2020). https://doi.org/10.1007/978-3-030-58565-5_31

32. Arrigoni, F., Ricci, E., Pajdla, T.: Multi-frame motion segmentation by combining two-frame results. Int. J. Comput. Vision **130**(3), 696–728 (2022)

33. Torr, P.H.S.: Geometric motion segmentation and model selection. Philos. Trans. R. Soc. Lond. Ser. A Math. Phys. Eng. Sci. **356**(1740), 1321–1340 (1998)

34. Vidal, R., Soatto, S., Ma, Y., Sastry, S.: Segmentation of dynamic scenes from the multibody fundamental matrix. In: ECCV Workshop on Vision and Modeling of Dynamic Scenes (2002)

35. Li, H.: Two-view motion segmentation from linear programming relaxation. In: 2007 IEEE Conference on Computer Vision and Pattern Recognition, pp. 1–8. IEEE (2007)

36. Jian, Y.-D., Chen, C.-S.: Two-view motion segmentation with model selection and outlier removal by RANSAC-enhanced Dirichlet process mixture models. Int. J. Comput. Vision **88**(3), 489–501 (2010)

37. Jung, H., Ju, J., Kim, J.: Rigid motion segmentation using randomized voting. In: Proceedings of the IEEE Conference on Computer Vision and Pattern Recognition, pp. 1210–1217 (2014)

38. Poling, B., Lerman, G.: A new approach to two-view motion segmentation using global dimension minimization. Int. J. Comput. Vision **108**(3), 165–185 (2014)

39. Chum, O., Matas, J., Kittler, J.: Locally optimized RANSAC. In: Michaelis, B., Krell, G. (eds.) DAGM 2003. LNCS, vol. 2781, pp. 236–243. Springer, Heidelberg (2003). https://doi.org/10.1007/978-3-540-45243-0_31

40. Kanazawa, Y., Kawakami, H.: Detection of planar regions with uncalibrated stereo using distributions of feature points. In: BMVC, pp. 1–10. Citeseer (2004)

41. Tordoff, B.J., Murray, D.W.: Guided-MLESAC: faster image transform estimation by using matching priors. IEEE Trans. Pattern Anal. Mach. Intell. **27**(10), 1523–1535 (2005)

42. Chum, O., Matas, J.: Matching with PROSAC-progressive sample consensus. In: 2005 IEEE Computer Society Conference on Computer Vision and Pattern Recognition (CVPR 2005), vol. 1, pp. 220–226. IEEE (2005)

43. Brahmachari, A.S., Sarkar, S.: Blogs: balanced local and global search for non-degenerate two view epipolar geometry. In: 2009 IEEE 12th International Conference on Computer Vision, pp. 1685–1692. IEEE (2009)

44. McIlroy, P., Rosten, E., Taylor, S., Drummond, T.: Deterministic sample consensus with multiple match hypotheses. In: BMVC, pp. 1–11. Citeseer (2010)
45. Fischler, M.A., Bolles, R.C.: Random sample consensus: a paradigm for model fitting with applications to image analysis and automated cartography. Commun. ACM **24**(6), 381–395 (1981)
46. Vincent, E., Laganiére, R.: Detecting planar homographies in an image pair. In: Proceedings of the 2nd International Symposium on Image and Signal Processing and Analysis, ISPA 2001. Conjunction with 23rd International Conference on Information Technology Interfaces (IEEE Cat.), pp. 182–187. IEEE (2001)
47. Zuliani, M., Kenney, C.S., Manjunath, B.S.: The multiRANSAC algorithm and its application to detect planar homographies. In: IEEE International Conference on Image Processing, vol. 3, pp. III-153. IEEE (2005)
48. Magri, L., Fusiello, A.: Multiple model fitting as a set coverage problem. In: Proceedings of the IEEE Conference on Computer Vision and Pattern Recognition, pp. 3318–3326 (2016)
49. Zhang, W., Kŏsecká, J.: Nonparametric estimation of multiple structures with outliers. In: Vidal, R., Heyden, A., Ma, Y. (eds.) WDV 2005–2006. LNCS, vol. 4358, pp. 60–74. Springer, Heidelberg (2007). https://doi.org/10.1007/978-3-540-70932-9_5
50. Toldo, R., Fusiello, A.: Robust multiple structures estimation with J-linkage. In: Forsyth, D., Torr, P., Zisserman, A. (eds.) ECCV 2008. LNCS, vol. 5302, pp. 537–547. Springer, Heidelberg (2008). https://doi.org/10.1007/978-3-540-88682-2_41
51. Chin, T.-J., Suter, D., Wang, H.: Multi-structure model selection via kernel optimisation. In: 2010 IEEE Computer Society Conference on Computer Vision and Pattern Recognition, pp. 3586–3593. IEEE (2010)
52. Magri, L., Fusiello, A.: T-linkage: a continuous relaxation of j-linkage for multi-model fitting. In: Proceedings of the IEEE Conference on Computer Vision and Pattern Recognition, pp. 3954–3961 (2014)
53. Pham, T.T., Chin, T.-J., Yu, J., Suter, D.: The random cluster model for robust geometric fitting. IEEE Trans. Pattern Anal. Mach. Intell. **36**(8), 1658–1671 (2014)
54. Magri, L., Fusiello, A.: Robust multiple model fitting with preference analysis and low-rank approximation. In: BMVC, vol. 20, p. 12 (2015)
55. Torr, P.H., Nasuto, S.J., Bishop, J.M.: NAPSAC: high noise, high dimensional robust estimation-it's in the bag. In: British Machine Vision Conference (BMVC) (2002)
56. Chin, T.-J., Yu, J., Suter, D.: Accelerated hypothesis generation for multistructure data via preference analysis. IEEE Trans. Pattern Anal. Mach. Intell. **34**(4), 625–638 (2011)
57. Tennakoon, R., Sadri, A., Hoseinnezhad, R., Bab-Hadiashar, A.: Effective sampling: fast segmentation using robust geometric model fitting. IEEE Trans. Image Process. **27**(9), 4182–4194 (2018)
58. Raguram, R., Frahm, J.-M., Pollefeys, M.: A comparative analysis of RANSAC techniques leading to adaptive real-time random sample consensus. In: Forsyth, D., Torr, P., Zisserman, A. (eds.) ECCV 2008. LNCS, vol. 5303, pp. 500–513. Springer, Heidelberg (2008). https://doi.org/10.1007/978-3-540-88688-4_37
59. Kim, T., Yu, W.: Performance evaluation of RANSAC family. In: Proceedings of the British Machine Vision Conference (BMVC), pp. 1–12 (2009)
60. Kluger, F., Brachmann, E., Ackermann, H., Rother, C., Yang, M.Y., Rosenhahn, B.: CONSAC: robust multi-model fitting by conditional sample consensus. In: Proceedings of the IEEE/CVF Conference on Computer Vision and Pattern Recognition, pp. 4634–4643 (2020)
61. Ivashechkin, M., Barath, D., Matas, J.: VSAC: efficient and accurate estimator for H and F. In: Proceedings of the IEEE/CVF International Conference on Computer Vision, pp. 15243–15252 (2021)

62. Tennakoon, R., Suter, D., Zhang, E., Chin, T.-J., Bab-Hadiashar, A.: Consensus maximisation using influences of monotone boolean functions. In: Proceedings of the IEEE/CVF Conference on Computer Vision and Pattern Recognition, pp. 2866–2875 (2021)
63. Magri, L., Fusiello, A.: Fitting multiple heterogeneous models by multi-class cascaded t-linkage. In: Proceedings of the IEEE/CVF Conference on Computer Vision and Pattern Recognition, pp. 7460–7468 (2019)
64. Xiao, G., Wang, H., Lai, T., Suter, D.: Hypergraph modelling for geometric model fitting. Pattern Recogn. **60**, 748–760 (2016)
65. Lin, S., Xiao, G., Yan, Y., Suter, D., Wang, H.: Hypergraph optimization for multi-structural geometric model fitting. In: Proceedings of the AAAI Conference on Artificial Intelligence, vol. 33, pp. 8730–8737 (2019)
66. Magri, L., Leveni, F., Boracchi, G.: Multilink: multi-class structure recovery via agglomerative clustering and model selection. In: Proceedings of the IEEE/CVF Conference on Computer Vision and Pattern Recognition, pp. 1853–1862 (2021)
67. Wang, H., Xiao, G., Yan, Y., Suter, D.: Searching for representative modes on hypergraphs for robust geometric model fitting. IEEE Trans. Pattern Anal. Mach. Intell. **41**(3), 697–711 (2018)
68. Barath, D., Matas, J.: Progressive-X: efficient, anytime, multi-model fitting algorithm. In: Proceedings of the IEEE International Conference on Computer Vision, pp. 3780–3788 (2019)
69. Barath, D., Rozumny, D., Eichhardt, I., Hajder, L., Matas, J.: Progressive-X+: clustering in the consensus space. arXiv preprint arXiv:2103.13875 (2021)
70. Vidal, R., Soatto, S., Ma, Y., Sastry, S.: An algebraic geometric approach to the identification of a class of linear hybrid systems. In: 42nd IEEE International Conference on Decision and Control, vol. 1, pp. 167–172 (2003)
71. Xu, Y.: On orthogonal polynomials in several variables. Spec. Funct. Q-Ser. Related Topics Fields Inst. Res. Math. Sci. Commun. Ser. **14**, 247–270 (1997)
72. Pauwels, E., Lasserre, J.B.: Sorting out typicality with the inverse moment matrix SOS polynomial. In: Advances in Neural Information Processing Systems, pp. 190–198 (2016)
73. Sznaier, M., Camps, O.: SOS-RSC: a sum-of-squares polynomial approach to robustifying subspace clustering algorithms. In: IEEE CVPR, pp. 8033–8041 (2018)
74. Wong, H.S., Chin, T.-J., Yu, J., Suter, D.: Dynamic and hierarchical multi-structure geometric model fitting. In: 2011 International Conference on Computer Vision, pp. 1044–1051. IEEE (2011)
75. Wang, H., Chin, T.-J., Suter, D.: Simultaneously fitting and segmenting multiple-structure data with outliers. IEEE Trans. Pattern Anal. Mach. Intell. **34**(6), 1177–1192 (2011)
76. Tiwari, L., Anand, S.: DGSAC: density guided sampling and consensus. In: 2018 IEEE Winter Conference on Applications of Computer Vision (WACV), pp. 974–982. IEEE (2018)

UCTNet: Uncertainty-Aware Cross-Modal Transformer Network for Indoor RGB-D Semantic Segmentation

Xiaowen Ying[ID] and Mooi Choo Chuah[(✉)][ID]

Lehigh University, Bethlehem, USA
`xiy517@lehigh.edu, chuah@cse.lehigh.edu`

Abstract. In this paper, we tackle the problem of RGB-D Semantic Segmentation. The key challenges in solving this problem lie in 1) how to extract features from depth sensor data and 2) how to effectively fuse the features extracted from the two modalities. For the first challenge, we found that the depth information obtained from the sensor is not always reliable (*e.g.* objects with reflective or dark surfaces typically have inaccurate or void sensor readings), and existing methods that extract depth features using ConvNets did not explicitly consider the reliability of depth value at different pixel locations. To tackle this challenge, we propose a novel mechanism, namely Uncertainty-Aware Self-Attention that explicitly controls the information flow from unreliable depth pixels to confident depth pixels during feature extraction. For the second challenge, we propose an effective and scalable fusion module based on Cross-Attention that can perform adaptive and asymmetric information exchange between the RGB and depth encoder. Our proposed framework, namely UCTNet, is an encoder-decoder network that naturally incorporates these two key designs for robust and accurate RGB-D Segmentation. Experimental results show that UCTNet outperforms existing works and achieves state-of-the-art performances on two RGB-D Semantic Segmentation benchmarks.

1   Introduction

Semantic Segmentation is a task that aims to gain pixel-level understandings of the scene. Given an input RGB image, the goal of Semantic Segmentation is to classify each pixel into a set of predefined semantic categories. A single monocular RGB image can be seen as a 2D projection of a 3D scene. During the imaging procedure, the information in the depth dimension is inevitably lost. With the development of sensor technology, depth sensors are becoming widely

---

Supplementary Information The online version contains supplementary material available at https://doi.org/10.1007/978-3-031-20056-4_2.

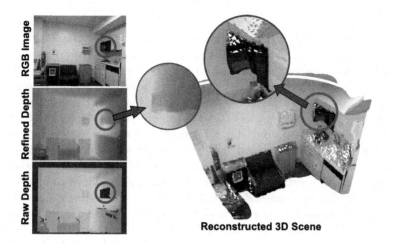

Fig. 1. An example RGB-D image and its reconstructed 3D scene. The raw depth map has no valid measurements on the surface of the microwave (highlighted in Red Circle) and such missing values are filled by certain algorithms (Refined Depth). These uncertain area looks reasonable in the refined depth map but leads to a largely distorted reconstruction and therefore should not be completely trusted. (Color figure online)

accessible and can help recover the missing information in the depth dimension which is valuable for scene understanding.

In this paper, we focus on the task of depth-assisted (RGB-D) Semantic Segmentation. There are two major challenges in this task: 1) how to effectively extract features from the additional depth input (since feature extraction from RGB images has been extensively studied for decades), and 2) how to aggregate and fuse the features extracted from two input modalities.

For the first challenge, existing approaches typically consider depth maps as single-channel images and employ CNNs (Convolutional Neural Networks) to extract features from the depth map similar to the RGB input. However, such approaches omit an important characteristic of the depth sensor, *i.e.* not every depth value in the depth maps is reliable. Most of the depth sensors available nowadays, either based on *structured light*, *ToF*, or *Lidar*, rely on measuring the reflection of the light signals they sent out. Due to the physical constraint, it is difficult to correctly measure the depth values on some surfaces such as glasses or dark materials. Figure 1 illustrates an example where we can see the raw depth map does not have valid measurements on the microwave since it has a reflective surface. To avoid feeding the *raw depth map* with missing values to the Neural Networks, a common practice is to use the *refined depth* map as input instead, which is generated by filling the missing values using certain algorithms such as colorization [29]. However, as the filled values are estimated by algorithms, we should not completely trust them. We can see from Fig. 1 that even though the refined depth map itself looks reasonable, the resulting reconstructed object in the 3D space is largely distorted.

To tackle this problem, our goal is to design a framework that explicitly considers the reliability of the input values during feature extraction. This goal may not be easily achieved using traditional CNNs since Convolutions are input-agnostic (always applies the same set of kernels during inference regardless of different inputs), and we found that the recently developed Vision Transformers (ViTs) are more suitable for achieving our goal. Instead of using Convolution operations to extract features, ViTs are built upon the Self-Attention (SA) operations which are input-specific [36]. A SA operation can be seen as propagating information on a fully connected *undirected graph* where nodes are the pixels and edges are their attentions. Based on this point-of-view, we proposed a novel mechanism called Uncertainty-Aware Self-Attention (UASA), by re-modeling the attention operation as a *directed graph* and explicitly controlling the information flow coming out from the uncertain nodes. Concretely, UASA limits the information flows coming out from uncertain nodes (since such information is unreliable) but allows uncertain nodes to accept information from other confident nodes (so the features of uncertain nodes can be gradually refined). We replace all the SA operations in our depth encoder with the proposed UASA, and our experimental results demonstrate its effectiveness compared to the traditional SA operation for extracting features from the depth map.

The second challenge is how to fuse the information extracted from two input modalities. We review and analyze the pros and cons of existing fusion strategies in the literature and summarize four design principles. Following these principles, we design a new fusion module that can perform adaptive and asymmetric information exchange between two branches. Our fusion module is based on the Cross-Attention (CA) technique that aligns well with our ViT backbone and we propose two modifications to make it scalable to high-resolution feature maps and easier to train. We demonstrate the effectiveness of our fusion module compared to baselines and other fusion strategies with our ablation studies.

Our final framework, namely UCTNet, is an encoder-decoder network that incorporates our proposed two designs for RGB-D Semantic Segmentation. Since the transformer-based backbones are shown to be more powerful feature extractors compared to traditional CNN-based backbones [31], we also perform careful ablation studies to demonstrate the effectiveness of our contributions over the strong baselines. Finally, we evaluate our framework on two public benchmarks for RGB-D Semantic Segmentation and show that UCTNet significantly outperforms previous approaches on both benchmarks.

Our contributions can be summarized as follow:

- We introduce a novel Uncertainty-Aware Self-Attention mechanism to explicitly handle the feature extraction from inputs with uncertain values.
- We design an effective and scalable fusion module that can perform adaptive and asymmetric information exchange between two branches.
- Our proposed framework, namely UCTNet, achieves new state-of-the-art performance on two public benchmarks and outperforms all existing methods with significant improvements.

2   Related Work

Semantic Segmentation. Traditional Semantic Segmentation takes as input an RGB image and aims to predict every pixel in the image into a set of predefined categories. FCN [32] proposed one of the first deep learning-based semantic segmentation frameworks by replacing the fully-connected layer in a deep image classification model with a convolution layer to support pixel-wise classification. Following works [1,3,17,35,48] explored to add different types of decoder networks and skip-connections to produce finer segmentation results. This architecture, which is also referred to as the *Encoder-decoder Network*, is the most popular architecture for semantic segmentation and is still being used in many state-of-the-art approaches. Following the encoder-decoder architecture, a line of works [13,19,23,24,30,55] explore to incorporate multi-scale analysis to the semantic segmentation network. Another line of works [5–8] explores the use of Dilated Convolutions to increase the receptive field while maintaining similar computational costs.

RGB-D Semantic Segmentation. A depth map provides complementary information to the corresponding RGB image that helps recover the information in the missing dimension. Earlier works [22,28] have shown that adding depth information can improve the segmentation results. As we discussed in the previous section, extracting features from depth maps and incorporating the features from two modalities are not trivial problems since the depth maps have different input distribution and characteristics compared to RGB images. To solve these problems, a line of works [9,11,46,51,53] try to design special "depth-aware" convolution operations to handle the depth information. These new operations can be seen as the augmented version of convolution and they technically have similar complexities compared to the original convolution; however, they usually run much slower in practice due to the lack of efficient and optimized implementation. Another line of works [10,16,22,25,28,37,40,45,52] simply employ a dual-encoder design, in which two separate encoders are used to extract features from the RGB image and depth map, respectively. Most of the state-of-the-art approaches follow this dual-encoder architecture as it allows different encoders to focus on extracting modality-specific features and typically yields better performance. However, none of the aforementioned approaches explicitly consider the uncertainty of the depth map—those modified convolutions only added "depth-aware" functionality to the convolution, and the dual-encoder network typically employs the same encoder structure for both branches and lets the network learn the modality-specific features implicitly. Our proposed framework follows the dual-encoder design but has a specifically designed uncertainty-aware encoder for the depth modality.

RGB-D Fusion. For all dual-encoder approaches that extract features from two modalities using separate encoders, a key problem is how to fuse and combine modality-specific features from two encoders. Within the scope of RGB-D Semantic Segmentation, early works [22,28] adopt a naive fusion strategy by fusing the depth features to the RGB encoder using element-wise addition. Seichter et al. [40] perform fusion using channel-wise weighted addition where the weight is produced by a Squeeze-and-Excitation (SE) module. However, their fusion weights are generated from each input feature, respectively, and are not adaptive to both inputs. The fusion module in [10] uses attentive addition and produces the fusion weight by considering both input features. They additionally pass the combined feature back to both encoders to enhance not only the RGB encoder but also the depth encoder. However, their fusion module only outputs one combined feature, meaning that both encoders receive the same fused feature regardless of the input modality they process. This problem inspires us to come up with the *Asymmetric* principle in Sect. 3.4.

Fusion techniques in other RGB-D-related tasks are typically not directly compatible with our framework. [27] fuses the features from RGB and depth encoders into a third encoder-decoder network which introduces high computational overheads. Fusion techniques in [4,18,34,39,43] all involve customization of the entire decoding stage and hence are not compatible with other existing semantic decoders. Our fusion module follows the modular design principle and is compatible with most of the well-designed encoders and decoders in the existing Semantic Segmentation literature.

Vision Transformers. Convolutional Neural Networks (CNNs) have been the most popular architecture in building the encoder-decoder architecture for semantic segmentation in the past decade. Recently, a novel architecture called Vision Transformers (ViTs) has attracted much interest in the Computer Vision community. The Transformer has proven to be a very powerful feature extractor in the Natural Language Processing (NLP) problems and was recently introduced to the Computer Vision tasks [12,14,21,44,47,54]. At this point, the major problem of ViTs is the high computational cost as the Self-Attention operation has quadratic complexity. Liu et al. [31] solved this problem by substituting the Self-Attention operation with their proposed Shifted Window Self-Attention (SWSA) which reduces the complexity to linear. While our proposed method is compatible with any ViTs, we choose to use the Swin Transformer [31] as the base architecture of our encoder network for it is one of the first ViTs that are both powerful and efficient.

3 Proposed Method

3.1 Overall Architecture

The framework of UCTNet, as illustrated in Fig. 2, consists of two parallel encoders (RGB Encoder and Depth Encoder) to extract modality-specific features from the image and depth modalities, respectively, followed by a Semantic Decoder to generate the final segmentation results.

RGB Encoder. The RGB Encoder takes a single RGB image as input and adopts the Swin-S [31] architecture which is a powerful and efficient ViT backbone. Given an input RGB image, the RGB Encoder first generates patch features via a Patch Embedding layer. The patch features will go through four

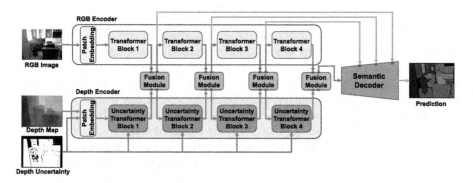

Fig. 2. The architecture of our proposed framework.

sequential Transformer Blocks that produces image features in $\frac{1}{4}$, $\frac{1}{8}$, $\frac{1}{16}$ and $\frac{1}{32}$ resolutions, respectively.

Depth Encoder. Different from existing methods, our Depth Encoder not only takes as input a Depth Map but also a Depth Uncertainty Map (described in Sect. 3.2). The Depth Encoder shares the same architecture as the RGB Encoder except that 1) we substitute all Self-Attention (SA) layers with our proposed Uncertainty-Aware Self-Attention (UASA) layer, and 2) we additionally feed the Depth Uncertainty to the Patch Embedding layer by concatenating it with the Depth Map. More details of the UASA are described in Sect. 3.3.

Fusion Module. At the output of each encoder block, we use our proposed Fusion Module to fuse and exchange information between the RGB Encoder and the Depth Encoder. The Fusion Module takes inputs from both RGB and depth branches and returns the updated features back to their corresponding encoders for the next block (as illustrated in Fig. 2). More details of our fusion module are described in Sect. 3.4.

Semantic Decoder. The Semantic Decoder takes as inputs the fused features from each Fusion Module and generates the final segmentation results. Similar to [31], we use the UperNet decoder [50] as our semantic decoder in this paper for its efficiency. More details of the architecture can be found in our supplementary materials.

3.2 Depth Uncertainty

In this section, we describe how to generate the Depth Uncertainty input for the Depth Encoder (as shown in Fig. 2). Depth measurements from the sensors could be affected by the physical environment. In general, existing depth sensors typically have difficulties in measuring depth for surfaces that are highly reflective or have high light absorption. Traditional depth sensors such as Kinect simply return a void value if the depth cannot be accurately measured. In these cases, we represent its uncertainty map as a binary map $\mathcal{U} \in \{0, 1\}^{H \times W}$ where zeros denote no sensor reading at this location and one denotes a valid sensor reading. Some newer sensors can provide multi-level confidence maps (e.g. three-level confidence map in Apple's Lidar Scanner). In such cases, we can normalize the confident map to $\mathcal{U} \in [0,1]$. In the following subsection, we formulate our Uncertainty-Aware Self-Attention for any generic type of uncertainty map $\mathcal{U} \in [0,1]$ consists of either binary, multi-level discrete, or continuous values. It is worth mentioning that most of the major benchmarks for RGB-D Semantic Segmentation (e.g. NYUv2 and SUN RGB-D) are collected using traditional sensors such as Kinect which only provides binary uncertainty maps. Yet our experimental results show that the performance is improved significantly by incorporating such simple uncertainty into the framework.

3.3   From Self-attention to Uncertainty-Aware Self-attention

Self-Attention (SA). Self-attention is the core layer in a Vision Transformer Encoder. Unlike a Convolution layer that extracts features from a local kernel, self-attention allows information propagation between every single pair of input features. Given an input feature map $\mathcal{X} \in \mathbb{R}^{H \times W \times C}$, the traditional Self-Attention operation is computed as:

$$SA(Q, K, V) = softmax(\frac{QK^T}{\sqrt{d}})V, \tag{1}$$

where $Q, K, V \in \mathbb{R}^{H \times W \times d}$ are the *query*, *key* and *value* produced by mapping each C-dimensional feature in $\mathcal{X}$ to d-dimensional embeddings via three different linear layers, respectively.

One can see that SA can be interpreted as a fully-connected graph $\mathcal{G}(\mathcal{X}, \mathcal{E})$ where each feature in $\mathcal{X}$ is a node and the edge between two nodes are the attention weights between two features computed by QK^T in Eq. 1. After each SA operation, each node in the graph gets updated by gathering information flow from other nodes it connects to, and the edge values (attention weights) control how much information it should keep from different nodes. This graph is also an undirected graph since $\mathcal{E}_{i \rightarrow j} = \mathcal{E}_{j \rightarrow i}$, meaning that the attention weight from node i to node j is the same as the other way around.

Uncertainty-Aware Self-Attention. The proposed Uncertainty-Aware Self-Attention (UASA) operation extends the SA operation by considering a bidirected graph $\mathcal{G}(\mathcal{X}, \mathcal{E})$ where $\mathcal{E}_{i \rightarrow j} \neq \mathcal{E}_{j \rightarrow i}$. In this way, we can explicitly control the information flow between a confident node and an uncertain node. Here, we introduce two variants of UASA: **Cut-off** and **Suppression**.

UASA (Cut-Off). Given an uncertainty map $\mathcal{U} \in [0,1]^{H \times W}$, the cut-off variant of the UASA can be computed as:

$$UASA_{cut}(Q, K, V) = softmax(\frac{QK^T}{\sqrt{d}} - M)V, \tag{2}$$

where $M \in \mathbb{R}^{HW \times HW}$ and:

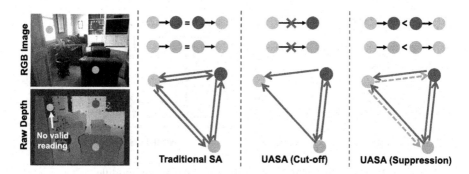

Fig. 3. High-level illustration of the Uncertainty-Aware Self-Attention among three selected pixels (● ● ●) in an example scene. In this example ● is an uncertain node since the depth sensor has no valid reading in this location. An arrow in the figure represents the attention weight $A_{i,j}$ from node i to node j. Comparing to Tradition SA that has symmetric attention matrices (i.e. $A_{i,j} = A_{j,i}$), our UASA (Cut-off) discards the information flows from uncertain nodes to confident nodes, while UASA (Suppression) keeps these edges but reduce their attention weights. (Color figure online)

$$M_{i,j} = \begin{cases} 0, & \text{if } \mathcal{U}_j \geq \theta \\ \infty, & \text{if } \mathcal{U}_j < \theta \end{cases} \qquad (3)$$

The $UASA_{cut}$ operation simply cuts off the outward information flow from all uncertain nodes in which their confidences are less than a threshold θ, such that their features will not be propagated to other nodes ($-\infty$ becomes 0 after the *softmax* operation). However, they can still receive information from other confident nodes and use them to update their node features.

UASA (Suppression). The $UASA_{cut}$ operation may be too aggressive since the information from those uncertain nodes may still be useful. On one hand, as we mentioned in Sect. 1, their initial values can be filled by using an estimation algorithm. On the other hand, as the input goes through multiple transformer layers, those uncertain nodes already got updated multiple times by features from confident nodes, and hence their uncertainties are reduced. To this end we consider a softer variant of UASA:

$$UASA_{sup}(Q, K, V) = softmax(\frac{QK^\top \cdot \mathcal{S}}{\sqrt{d}})V, \qquad (4)$$

where $\mathcal{S} \in \mathbb{R}^{HW \times HW}$ and:

$$\mathcal{S}_{i,j} = \frac{1}{\mathcal{T} + \mathcal{U}_j \cdot (1 - \mathcal{T})}, \qquad (5)$$

where $\mathcal{T}$ is a hyper-parameter indicating the maximum temperature (corresponding to those nodes with zero confidences).

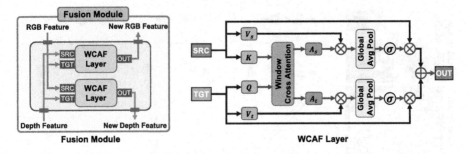

Fig. 4. The architecture of the proposed fusion module.

Instead of simply cutting off all the information from uncertain nodes, Eq. 4 and 5 suppress these uncertain features by dividing their attention weights with a temperature (calculated based on the node uncertainty) before applying the Softmax operation. Figure 3 provides a high-level illustration of the UASA using three selected pixels.

UASA for Shift-Window Attention. The above formulations define our UASA based on the traditional Self-Attention operation, while the Swin-S backbone we employed for our encoder uses a modified version of SA named Shift-Window Self-Attention (SWSA). However, the above formulations also work for SWSA as we simply need to do the same window-partition operation on uncertainty map $\mathcal{U}$ along with the input image before we perform UASA on each window. We omit the detail of the window-partition operation in our formulation for simplicity and refer readers to its original paper [31].

3.4 Fusion Module

The design goal of our fusion module is to achieve feature fusion and information exchange between two encoding streams. We choose not to modify the decoder to allow our approach compatible with any existing decoder.

Based on the analysis of existing fusion modules in Sect. 2, we summarize the following design principles for our fusion module:

- **Attentive:** The features from different modalities should be combined in an attentive way instead of simple element-wise addition.
- **Adaptive:** The attention/weight to perform attentive fusion should be generated by adaptively considering both input modalities.
- **Bidirectional:** Instead of one-way passing the feature from one modality to another, we prefer to exchange the information between two modalities.
- **Asymmetric:** The combined features passing back to different encoders should be different, *i.e.* $F_{depth \rightarrow rgb} \neq F_{rgb \rightarrow depth}$, where F denotes the fusion function.

Apart from these design principles, we also prefer to design the fusion module using the Attention mechanism to align with our ViT backbone. The architecture of our Fusion Module is illustrated in Fig. 4. The core layer in our fusion module, namely the Window Cross Attentive Fusion (WCAF) layer, takes a *source* feature and a *target* feature as inputs, and the goal is to fuse the information from *source* feature into the *target* feature. The *source* and *target* features may come from either RGB or depth modalities depending on the fusion direction. The WCAF layer is based on the Cross-Attention mechanism with two key modifications: (1) the vanilla cross-attention has quadratic complexity which scales badly to high-resolution features, and we proposed Window Cross-Attention (inspired by [31]) that has linear complexity and can be used to fuse high-resolution features from the early stages of the encoder. (2) it is very difficult to learn a Cross-Attention layer that performs well to directly fuse dense features. We address this by combining cross-attention with channel-attention so that the cross-attention only needs to produce channel weighting which greatly reduces the training difficulties.

The design of WCAF layer met our first two design principles, *i.e. Attentive* and *Adaptive*. To further achieve the last two principles, we employ two independent WCAF layers in our fusion module (as shown in Fig. 4) to approximate $F_{depth \rightarrow rgb}$ and $F_{rgb \rightarrow depth}$, respectively. These two WCAF layers have identical architectures except the input order is reversed. This allows us to enhance the features in both RGB and depth encoders while keeping them independent to extract their own modality-specific features.

4   Experiments

4.1   Implementation Details

Architecture. We implement and train our networks using the PyTorch [38] framework. We use the default configuration of Swin-S [31] for our encoders except we change the input channel in the first layer of the depth encoder to match its input modality. The input resolutions for both RGB and depth encoders are set to 640×480.

Losses. The main training loss is a pixel-wise Cross-Entropy loss with *frequency class balancing* strategy [15] applied to the final decoder output. During training, we follow the common practices to attach an auxiliary FCN head to the stage 3 features that produce an auxiliary prediction at 1/16 resolution and apply the same Cross-Entropy loss to this output as an auxiliary loss. The final loss for optimization is a weighted sum of the main loss and the auxiliary loss, where the weights are set to 1.0 and 0.4, respectively.

Training. As in [31], we employ the AdamW [33] as our optimizer during training with a learning rate of 6e-6. During training, we initialize the network with weights pretrained on ADE20K datasets provided by [31] except for the first layer of the depth encoder which is randomly initialized (since the input channel is different). All the experiments in this paper are trained for 500 epochs with batches of size 2.

4.2 Datasets

We train and evaluate the performance of our networks on two public datasets for indoor RGBD Semantic Segmentation—NYUv2 [41] and SUN RGB-D [42].

NYUv2. NYUv2 dataset is comprised of RGB-D images taken from a variety of indoor scenes. The raw depth image is captured using a Microsoft Kinect sensor and the refined depth is generated using the colorization scheme proposed in [29]. It provides 1,449 densely labeled data which is split into a training set of 795 samples and a testing set of 654 samples. The annotations are provided in 13, 40, and 894 class settings but we adopt the most-common 40-class setting as in most of the existing works.

SUN RGB-D. SUN RGB-D is a large-scale benchmark for RGB-D scene understanding tasks. It not only consists of a significant amount of newly captured data but also combines samples from multiple existing datasets including NYUv2 [41], Berkeley B3DO [26] and SUN3D [49]. SUN RGB-D consists of 10,335 indoor RGB-D images which are split into a training set with 5,285 samples and a testing set of 5,050 samples. All images are densely annotated with 37-classes semantic labels.

4.3 Ablation Study

Baselines. Our framework employs a Vision Transformer backbone for this task while most of the existing works use CNN-based backbones. To reveal the real contribution of our proposed approach, we first design two baselines for our ablation study. The first baseline model (*Baseline-1* in Table 1) is a typical encoder-decoder network for semantic segmentation using *RGB* images as input (w/o depth image). The second baseline model (*Baseline-2*) uses the same architecture as Baseline-1 except that it takes *RGB-D* images as input by simply concatenating the RGB image with the depth map along the channel axis, resulting in a 4-channel input image. Note that these two baseline models do not involve depth encoders and hence no fusion module is needed. The result of *Baseline-1* demonstrates the power of ViT backbones for the Semantic Segmentation task since the performance it achieves using merely RGB image is already a very strong baseline. *Baseline-2* is a naive solution for RGB-D segmentation by simply concatenating RGB image and depth image as a 4-channel input and processing it with the same encoder-decoder architecture. The result shows that the segmentation performance benefits from this additional information but the improvement is minor.

Different Fusion Module. Once we start adding depth encoder to extract better depth-specific features, we will need a fusion module to exchange information between the two encoders. The *Ablation 1-4* in Table 1 compare our fusion module with three existing fusion modules used in recent state-of-the-arts. We can see that the result using our fusion module (*Ablation-4*) is better than the other three existing fusion modules, which demonstrates the effectiveness of our proposed fusion module. It is worth mentioning that the design of

Table 1. Ablation study on NYUv2 dataset. **TR-Enc.**: Encoder consists of standard transformer blocks. **UATR-Enc.**: Encoder consists of uncertainty-aware transformer blocks.

Method	RGB Enc.	Depth Enc.	Fusion	mIoU (%)
Baseline-1 (RGB only)	TR-Enc.	N/A	N/A	52.2
Baseline-2 (RGB cat. D)	TR-Enc.	N/A	N/A	52.4
Ablation-1	TR-Enc.	TR-Enc.	Element-Add [22, 28]	54.3
Ablation-2	TR-Enc.	TR-Enc.	SE-Add [40]	54.6
Ablation-3	TR-Enc.	TR-Enc.	SA-Gate [10]	53.8
Ablation-4	TR-Enc.	TR-Enc.	Our fusion	55.3
Ablation-5	TR-Enc.	UATR-Enc. (cut-off)	Our fusion	56.8
Ablation-6 (final model)	TR-Enc.	UATR-Enc. (suppression)	Our fusion	**57.6**

Table 2. Sensitivity analysis of the temperature T in UASA.

Value of T	5	10	**15**	20
mIoU(%)	57.2	57.2	**57.6**	56.8

SA-Gate [10] meets the first three design principles yet its performance is not as good as expected. This may be caused by that the design of SA-Gate being optimized for the HHA [20] depth encoding instead of a normal single-channel depth image.

Uncertainty-Aware Transformer Encoder. One of our core contributions in this paper is the Uncertainty-Aware Encoder that explicitly considers the input uncertainties during feature extraction. As shown in Table 1 *Ablation 4-6*, replacing the standard encoder with our Uncertainty-Aware encoder for the depth branch leads to significant performance improvements. We can also see that the *Suppression* variant of our UASA performs better than the *Cut-off* variant, which supports our hypothesis that the features from those uncertain nodes are not completely unreliable and should not be completely dropped out. Therefore, we choose the *Suppression* variant of our UASA in our final model.

Choice of Temperature T in UASA. A key hyperparameter in our UASA (Suppression) is the temperature that controls the suppression strength for the outward information from uncertain nodes. Intuitively, if the temperature is too small, the information from uncertain nodes may interfere with and mess up the features in the confident nodes; if the temperature is too large, the information from uncertain nodes will be almost dropped out, which could lead to negative impacts as we discussed in previous ablation studies. Table 2 shows the sensitivity analysis of the temperature T in the UASA module. We can see that the performance improves by increasing T from 5 to 15 but starts to drop when T increases to 20. We also notice that the performance of $T = 20$ is the same as the *Cut-off* version of UASA in Table 1, which implies that $T = 20$ is a fairly strong suppression factor that almost cuts off most of the uncertain information.

Table 3. Quantitative results (MIoU) on the NYUv2 dataset and SUN RGB-D benchmark compared to state-of-the-art RGB-D semantic segmentation methods. Mod. Conv: Methods based on modified convolutions. Dual Enc.: Methods based on dual encoder architectures. *: Multi-scale testing.

Method	Category	Architecture	NYUv2	SUN RGB-D
2.5D Conv [53]	Mod. Conv	1 × R101	48.5	48.2
SGNet [9]	Mod. Conv	1 × R101	49.0	47.1
ShapeConv [2]	Mod. Conv	1 × R50	47.3	46.3
ShapeConv [2]	Mod. Conv	1 × R101	50.2	47.6
FuseNet [22]	Dual Enc.	2 × VGG16	-	37.3
RedNet [28]	Dual Enc.	2 × R34	-	47.8
SSMA [45]	Dual Enc.	2 × R50	-	44.4
ACNet [25]	Trio Enc.	3 × R50	48.3	48.1
MMAF-Net [16]	Dual Enc.	2 × R152	44.8	47.0
Idempotent [52]	Dual Enc.	2 × R101	49.9	47.6
RDFNet [37]	Dual Enc.	2 × R152	50.1*	47.7*
ESANet [40]	Dual Enc.	2 × R50	50.5	48.3
SA-Gate [10]	Dual Enc.	2 × R101	52.4*	49.4*
UCTNet (ours)	Dual Enc.	2 × Swin-S	**57.6**	**51.2**

4.4 Comparison with State-of-the-Arts

We compare our proposed framework with existing state-of-the-art methods on two public benchmarks—Table 3 lists all the results on the NYUv2 dataset the SUN RGB-D benchmark. On the NYUv2 dataset, our approach outperforms all existing methods with significant improvement where we achieve 7.1% absolute improvement in terms of mIoU compared to the previous best method without using multi-scale testing.

The SUN RGB-D benchmark is a large-scale benchmark with much more training and testing samples compared to the NYUv2 dataset. One can observe that recent works all have very similar performances on this dataset. For example, RDFNet [37] performs 5.3% better than MMAF-Net [16] on NYUv2 dataset, but the gap between them is 0.7% on the SUN RGB-D benchmark. We suspect that this is not only because the SUN RGB-D benchmark is more challenging, but also because it provides more training data that may narrow down the performance gaps between different models. With that being said, our approach still achieves ∼3% absolute performance improvement compared to the previous best number (those without multi-scale testing), which demonstrates that our approach can generalize to a larger dataset.

We also list the main architecture used in different methods in Table 3 for references. According to [31], the complexity (# of parameters and FLOPs) of the Swin-S backbone we use in our framework is similar to a ResNet-101 backbone.

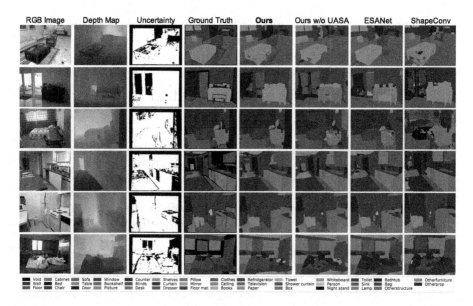

Fig. 5. Qualitative results of our approach compared to our baseline and selected existing works.

4.5 Qualitative Results

Figure 5 shows the qualitative results of our methods compared to the variant of our method *w/o* UASA and other selected state-of-the-art approaches. We can see that our approach produces decent segmentation results and the quality is consistently better than existing work. We can also observe that adding UASA improves the segmentation results on reflective surfaces such as the glass door in row 1 and row 2, the sink in row 4, and the upper part of the refrigerator in row 6. These qualitative results further demonstrate the effectiveness of our proposed method.

5 Conclusion

In this paper, we present a novel framework for indoor RGB-D semantic segmentation. We tackle the two major challenges in this task: 1) how to better extract features from the depth image, and 2) how to effectively fuse and combine information from two modalities. For the first challenge, we propose an Uncertainty-Aware Self-Attention to replace the traditional Self-Attention in a transformer encoder to explicitly control the information flow between uncertain and confident nodes. For the second challenge, we review and analyze the problems of existing fusion modules and design a new fusion module following four design principles. We perform various ablation studies to demonstrate the effectiveness of our proposed methods, and our experimental results show that our approach achieves new state-of-the-art on two public benchmarks with significant improvements compared to existing works.

Acknowledgement. This work was partially supported by a gift from Qualcomm Inc.

References

1. Badrinarayanan, V., Kendall, A., Cipolla, R.: SegNet: a deep convolutional encoder-decoder architecture for image segmentation. IEEE Trans. Pattern Anal. Mach. Intell. **39**(12), 2481–2495 (2017)
2. Cao, J., Leng, H., Lischinski, D., Cohen-Or, D., Tu, C., Li, Y.: ShapeConv: shape-aware convolutional layer for indoor RGB-D semantic segmentation. In: Proceedings of the IEEE/CVF International Conference on Computer Vision, pp. 7088–7097 (2021)
3. Chaurasia, A., Culurciello, E.: LinkNet: exploiting encoder representations for efficient semantic segmentation. In: 2017 IEEE Visual Communications and Image Processing (VCIP), pp. 1–4. IEEE (2017)
4. Chen, C., Wei, J., Peng, C., Zhang, W., Qin, H.: Improved saliency detection in RGB-D images using two-phase depth estimation and selective deep fusion. IEEE Trans. Image Process. **29**, 4296–4307 (2020)
5. Chen, L.C., Papandreou, G., Kokkinos, I., Murphy, K., Yuille, A.L.: Semantic image segmentation with deep convolutional nets and fully connected CRFs. arXiv preprint arXiv:1412.7062 (2014)
6. Chen, L.C., Papandreou, G., Kokkinos, I., Murphy, K., Yuille, A.L.: DeepLab: semantic image segmentation with deep convolutional nets, atrous convolution, and fully connected CRFs. IEEE Trans. Pattern Anal. Mach. Intell. **40**(4), 834–848 (2017)
7. Chen, L.C., Papandreou, G., Schroff, F., Adam, H.: Rethinking atrous convolution for semantic image segmentation. arXiv preprint arXiv:1706.05587 (2017)
8. Chen, L.-C., Zhu, Y., Papandreou, G., Schroff, F., Adam, H.: Encoder-decoder with atrous separable convolution for semantic image segmentation. In: Ferrari, V., Hebert, M., Sminchisescu, C., Weiss, Y. (eds.) ECCV 2018. LNCS, vol. 11211, pp. 833–851. Springer, Cham (2018). https://doi.org/10.1007/978-3-030-01234-2_49
9. Chen, L.Z., Lin, Z., Wang, Z., Yang, Y.L., Cheng, M.M.: Spatial information guided convolution for real-time RGBD semantic segmentation. IEEE Trans. Image Process. **30**, 2313–2324 (2021)
10. Chen, X., et al.: Bi-directional cross-modality feature propagation with separation-and-aggregation gate for RGB-D semantic segmentation. In: Vedaldi, A., Bischof, H., Brox, T., Frahm, J.-M. (eds.) ECCV 2020. LNCS, vol. 12356, pp. 561–577. Springer, Cham (2020). https://doi.org/10.1007/978-3-030-58621-8_33
11. Chen, Y., Mensink, T., Gavves, E.: 3D neighborhood convolution: Learning depth-aware features for RGB-D and RGB semantic segmentation. In: 2019 International Conference on 3D Vision (3DV), pp. 173–182. IEEE (2019)
12. Chu, X., Zhang, B., Tian, Z., Wei, X., Xia, H.: Do we really need explicit position encodings for vision transformers? arXiv e-prints pp. arXiv-2102 (2021)
13. Ding, H., Jiang, X., Shuai, B., Liu, A.Q., Wang, G.: Context contrasted feature and gated multi-scale aggregation for scene segmentation. In: Proceedings of the IEEE Conference on Computer Vision and Pattern Recognition, pp. 2393–2402 (2018)

14. Dosovitskiy, A., et al.: An image is worth 16×16 words: transformers for image recognition at scale. arXiv preprint arXiv:2010.11929 (2020)
15. Eigen, D., Fergus, R.: Predicting depth, surface normals and semantic labels with a common multi-scale convolutional architecture. In: Proceedings of the IEEE International Conference on Computer Vision, pp. 2650–2658 (2015)
16. Fooladgar, F., Kasaei, S.: Multi-modal attention-based fusion model for semantic segmentation of RGB-depth images. arXiv preprint arXiv:1912.11691 (2019)
17. Fu, J., Liu, J., Wang, Y., Zhou, J., Wang, C., Lu, H.: Stacked deconvolutional network for semantic segmentation. IEEE Trans. Image Process. (2019)
18. Fu, K., Fan, D.P., Ji, G.P., Zhao, Q.: JL-DCF: joint learning and densely-cooperative fusion framework for RGB-D salient object detection. In: Proceedings of the IEEE/CVF Conference on Computer Vision and Pattern Recognition, pp. 3052–3062 (2020)
19. Ghiasi, G., Fowlkes, C.C.: Laplacian pyramid reconstruction and refinement for semantic segmentation. In: Leibe, B., Matas, J., Sebe, N., Welling, M. (eds.) ECCV 2016. LNCS, vol. 9907, pp. 519–534. Springer, Cham (2016). https://doi.org/10.1007/978-3-319-46487-9_32
20. Gupta, S., Girshick, R., Arbeláez, P., Malik, J.: Learning rich features from RGB-D images for object detection and segmentation. In: Fleet, D., Pajdla, T., Schiele, B., Tuytelaars, T. (eds.) ECCV 2014. LNCS, vol. 8695, pp. 345–360. Springer, Cham (2014). https://doi.org/10.1007/978-3-319-10584-0_23
21. Han, K., Xiao, A., Wu, E., Guo, J., Xu, C., Wang, Y.: Transformer in transformer. arXiv preprint arXiv:2103.00112 (2021)
22. Hazirbas, C., Ma, L., Domokos, C., Cremers, D.: FuseNet: incorporating depth into semantic segmentation via fusion-based CNN Architecture. In: Lai, S.-H., Lepetit, V., Nishino, K., Sato, Y. (eds.) ACCV 2016. LNCS, vol. 10111, pp. 213–228. Springer, Cham (2017). https://doi.org/10.1007/978-3-319-54181-5_14
23. He, J., Deng, Z., Qiao, Y.: Dynamic multi-scale filters for semantic segmentation. In: Proceedings of the IEEE/CVF International Conference on Computer Vision, pp. 3562–3572 (2019)
24. He, J., Deng, Z., Zhou, L., Wang, Y., Qiao, Y.: Adaptive pyramid context network for semantic segmentation. In: Proceedings of the IEEE/CVF Conference on Computer Vision and Pattern Recognition, pp. 7519–7528 (2019)
25. Hu, X., Yang, K., Fei, L., Wang, K.: ACNet: attention based network to exploit complementary features for RGBD semantic segmentation. In: 2019 IEEE International Conference on Image Processing (ICIP), pp. 1440–1444. IEEE (2019)
26. Janoch, A., et al.: A category-level 3D object dataset: putting the kinect to work. In: Fossati, A., Gall, J., Grabner, H., Ren, X., Konolige, K. (eds.) Consumer Depth Cameras for Computer Vision. Advances in Computer Vision and Pattern Recognition, pp. 141–165. Springer, London (2013). https://doi.org/10.1007/978-1-4471-4640-7_8
27. Ji, W., et al.: Calibrated RGB-D salient object detection. In: Proceedings of the IEEE/CVF Conference on Computer Vision and Pattern Recognition, pp. 9471–9481 (2021)
28. Jiang, J., Zheng, L., Luo, F., Zhang, Z.: RedNet: residual encoder-decoder network for indoor RGB-D semantic segmentation. arXiv preprint arXiv:1806.01054 (2018)
29. Levin, A., Lischinski, D., Weiss, Y.: Colorization using optimization. In: ACM SIGGRAPH 2004 Papers, pp. 689–694 (2004)
30. Lin, T.Y., Dollár, P., Girshick, R., He, K., Hariharan, B., Belongie, S.: Feature pyramid networks for object detection. In: Proceedings of the IEEE Conference on Computer Vision and Pattern Recognition, pp. 2117–2125 (2017)

31. Liu, Z., et al.: Swin transformer: hierarchical vision transformer using shifted windows. In: Proceedings of the IEEE/CVF International Conference on Computer Vision (ICCV) (2021)
32. Long, J., Shelhamer, E., Darrell, T.: Fully convolutional networks for semantic segmentation. In: Proceedings of the IEEE Conference on Computer Vision and Pattern Recognition, pp. 3431–3440 (2015)
33. Loshchilov, I., Hutter, F.: Decoupled weight decay regularization. arXiv preprint arXiv:1711.05101 (2017)
34. Luo, A., Li, X., Yang, F., Jiao, Z., Cheng, H., Lyu, S.: Cascade graph neural networks for RGB-D salient object detection. In: Vedaldi, A., Bischof, H., Brox, T., Frahm, J.-M. (eds.) ECCV 2020. LNCS, vol. 12357, pp. 346–364. Springer, Cham (2020). https://doi.org/10.1007/978-3-030-58610-2_21
35. Noh, H., Hong, S., Han, B.: Learning deconvolution network for semantic segmentation. In: Proceedings of the IEEE International Conference on Computer Vision, pp. 1520–1528 (2015)
36. Park, N., Kim, S.: How do vision transformers work? In: International Conference on Learning Representations (2022)
37. Park, S.J., Hong, K.S., Lee, S.: RDFNet: RGB-D multi-level residual feature fusion for indoor semantic segmentation. In: Proceedings of the IEEE International Conference on Computer Vision, pp. 4980–4989 (2017)
38. Paszke, A., et al.: PyTorch: An imperative style, high-performance deep learning library. In: Advances in Neural Information Processing Systems 32, pp. 8026–8037 (2019)
39. Piao, Y., Ji, W., Li, J., Zhang, M., Lu, H.: Depth-induced multi-scale recurrent attention network for saliency detection. In: Proceedings of the IEEE/CVF International Conference on Computer Vision, pp. 7254–7263 (2019)
40. Seichter, D., Köhler, M., Lewandowski, B., Wengefeld, T., Gross, H.M.: Efficient RGB-D semantic segmentation for indoor scene analysis. In: 2021 IEEE International Conference on Robotics and Automation (ICRA), pp. 13525–13531. IEEE (2021)
41. Silberman, N., Hoiem, D., Kohli, P., Fergus, R.: Indoor segmentation and support inference from RGBD images. In: Fitzgibbon, A., Lazebnik, S., Perona, P., Sato, Y., Schmid, C. (eds.) ECCV 2012. LNCS, vol. 7576, pp. 746–760. Springer, Heidelberg (2012). https://doi.org/10.1007/978-3-642-33715-4_54
42. Song, S., Lichtenberg, S.P., Xiao, J.: Sun RGB-D: a RGB-D scene understanding benchmark suite. In: Proceedings of the IEEE Conference on Computer Vision and Pattern Recognition, pp. 567–576 (2015)
43. Sun, P., Zhang, W., Wang, H., Li, S., Li, X.: Deep RGB-D saliency detection with depth-sensitive attention and automatic multi-modal fusion. In: Proceedings of the IEEE/CVF Conference on Computer Vision and Pattern Recognition, pp. 1407–1417 (2021)
44. Touvron, H., Cord, M., Douze, M., Massa, F., Sablayrolles, A., Jégou, H.: Training data-efficient image transformers & distillation through attention. In: International Conference on Machine Learning, pp. 10347–10357. PMLR (2021)
45. Valada, A., Mohan, R., Burgard, W.: Self-supervised model adaptation for multi-modal semantic segmentation. Int. J. Comput. Vision 128(5), 1239–1285 (2020)
46. Wang, W., Neumann, U.: Depth-aware CNN for RGB-D segmentation. In: Ferrari, V., Hebert, M., Sminchisescu, C., Weiss, Y. (eds.) ECCV 2018. LNCS, vol. 11215, pp. 144–161. Springer, Cham (2018). https://doi.org/10.1007/978-3-030-01252-6_9
47. Wang, W., et al.: Pyramid vision transformer: a versatile backbone for dense prediction without convolutions. arXiv preprint arXiv:2102.12122 (2021)

48. Xia, X., Kulis, B.: W-Net: a deep model for fully unsupervised image segmentation. arXiv preprint arXiv:1711.08506 (2017)
49. Xiao, J., Owens, A., Torralba, A.: Sun3D: a database of big spaces reconstructed using SFM and object labels. In: Proceedings of the IEEE International Conference on Computer Vision, pp. 1625–1632 (2013)
50. Xiao, T., Liu, Y., Zhou, B., Jiang, Y., Sun, J.: Unified perceptual parsing for scene understanding. In: Ferrari, V., Hebert, M., Sminchisescu, C., Weiss, Y. (eds.) ECCV 2018. LNCS, vol. 11209, pp. 432–448. Springer, Cham (2018). https://doi.org/10.1007/978-3-030-01228-1_26
51. Xing, Y., Wang, J., Chen, X., Zeng, G.: 2.5D convolution for RGB-D semantic segmentation. In: 2019 IEEE International Conference on Image Processing (ICIP), pp. 1410–1414. IEEE (2019)
52. Xing, Y., Wang, J., Chen, X., Zeng, G.: Coupling two-stream RGB-D semantic segmentation network by idempotent mappings. In: 2019 IEEE International Conference on Image Processing (ICIP), pp. 1850–1854. IEEE (2019)
53. Xing, Y., Wang, J., Zeng, G.: Malleable 2.5D convolution: learning receptive fields along the depth-axis for RGB-D scene parsing. In: Vedaldi, A., Bischof, H., Brox, T., Frahm, J.-M. (eds.) ECCV 2020. LNCS, vol. 12364, pp. 555–571. Springer, Cham (2020). https://doi.org/10.1007/978-3-030-58529-7_33
54. Yuan, L., et al.: Tokens-to-token ViT: training vision transformers from scratch on ImageNet. arXiv preprint arXiv:2101.11986 (2021)
55. Zhao, H., Shi, J., Qi, X., Wang, X., Jia, J.: Pyramid scene parsing network. In: Proceedings of the IEEE Conference on Computer Vision and Pattern Recognition, pp. 2881–2890 (2017)

Bi-directional Contrastive Learning for Domain Adaptive Semantic Segmentation

Geon Lee, Chanho Eom, Wonkyung Lee, Hyekang Park, and Bumsub Ham[✉]

Yonsei University, Seoul, South Korea
bumsub.ham@yonsei.ac.kr
https://cvlab.yonsei.ac.kr/projects/DASS

Abstract. We present a novel unsupervised domain adaptation method for semantic segmentation that generalizes a model trained with source images and corresponding ground-truth labels to a target domain. A key to domain adaptive semantic segmentation is to learn domain-invariant and discriminative features without target ground-truth labels. To this end, we propose a bi-directional pixel-prototype contrastive learning framework that minimizes intra-class variations of features for the same object class, while maximizing inter-class variations for different ones, regardless of domains. Specifically, our framework aligns pixel-level features and a prototype of the same object class in target and source images (i.e., positive pairs), respectively, sets them apart for different classes (i.e., negative pairs), and performs the alignment and separation processes toward the other direction with pixel-level features in the source image and a prototype in the target image. The cross-domain matching encourages domain-invariant feature representations, while the bidirectional pixel-prototype correspondences aggregate features for the same object class, providing discriminative features. To establish training pairs for contrastive learning, we propose to generate dynamic pseudo labels of target images using a non-parametric label transfer, that is, pixel-prototype correspondences across different domains. We also present a calibration method compensating class-wise domain biases of prototypes gradually during training. Experimental results on standard benchmarks including GTA5 → Cityscapes and SYNTHIA → Cityscapes demonstrate the effectiveness of our framework.

Keywords: Bi-directional contrastive learning · Domain adaptive semantic segmentation · Dynamic pseudo label

1 Introduction

Semantic segmentation is to assign a semantic label to each pixel in an image. In the past decade, supervised methods based on convolutional neural networks

Supplementary Information The online version contains supplementary material available at https://doi.org/10.1007/978-3-031-20056-4_3.

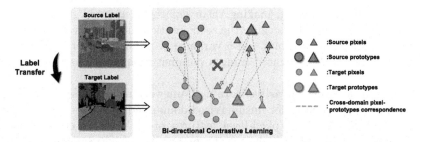

Fig. 1. An illustration of our framework for UDASS. We generate pseudo labels of target images using a nonparametric label transfer. We then perform bi-directional pixel-prototype contrastive learning. This encourages pixel-level features in a target image and a prototype of the same object class in a source domain to pull each other, while setting them apart for different ones. We also perform the alignment and separation in a reverse direction, with pixel-level features of source images and prototypes of a target domain.

(CNNs) [1,17,26,33,41,56] have achieved remarkable improvements in semantic segmentation. Training networks for the dense prediction task generally requires lots of pixel-level labels. Annotating pixel-level labels of high-resolution images is, however, significantly labor-intensive and time-consuming. For example, annotating the labels for an image of size 2048×1024 in Cityscapes [6] takes about 90 min. One alternative is to leverage synthetic datasets, *e.g.*, GTA5 [32] and SYNTHIA [34], that contain realistic images and corresponding pixel-level labels. The annotation cost is much cheaper than the manual labeling, but CNNs trained with synthetic datasets do not work well on real images, due to the domain discrepancy between synthetic and real images.

To reduce the domain discrepancy, several methods [4,15,16,23,43,44] have exploited an unsupervised domain adaptation approach. It transfers knowledge learned from a source domain (*e.g.*, a synthetic dataset) to a target one (*e.g.*, a real dataset), with labels for the source domain alone. Many unsupervised domain adaptation methods leverage an adversarial training scheme [12] that aligns distributions of source and target domains by fooling a domain classifier [3–5,10,15,16,23,27,28,30,36,42,44,48,49,55]. However, they typically focus on reducing the domain discrepancy globally, and fail to keep pixel-level semantics [50]. For example, regions corresponding to a car class in a source image might align with those for a bus class in a target image. Self-training methods [22,50,51,58,59] enable a class-aware alignment. They generate pseudo labels for target images iteratively in a parametric approach, typically using CNNs trained with a source dataset, and then retrain a segmentation model on both source and target samples with the pseudo labels. This aligns cross-domain features in a class-level, improving performance of the model on target images progressively. The pseudo labels obtained using a parametric approach have the following drawbacks: First, they are very sparse, since low confident predictions are discarded to obtain reliable labels. Second, estimating pseudo labels is also computationally demanding, making them not to be updated frequently during training. These problems cause the segmentation model to overfit to pseudo labels, resulting in a large bias and a variance of predictions. In the following, we will call the labels estimated using a parametric approach as *static pseudo labels*.

We present a novel contrastive learning framework using cross-domain pixel-prototype correspondences for unsupervised domain adaptive semantic segmentation (UDASS). It aligns pixel-level features of each object class in target images, obtained by pseudo labels, with prototypes of corresponding class in a source domain, computed by ground truth, while setting them apart for different classes (Fig. 1). The alignment and separation process is also performed in a reverse direction, with pixel-level features of source images and prototypes of a target domain. The cross-domain matching encourages domain-invariant feature representations, and the bidirectional pixel-prototype correspondences provide compact and discriminative representations. We also present a nonparametric approach to generating *dynamic pseudo labels* using pixel-prototype correspondences. Specifically, we calibrate prototypes of individual object classes in a source domain, while considering the domain discrepancy in target images, and establish correspondences for each prototype with individual pixel-level features in target images. We then transfer ground-truth labels of prototypes to corresponding pixels in target images. In contrast to the parametric approach in current self-training methods, our nonparametric approach provides denser pseudo labels, and generates the labels dynamically, whenever source images are changed during training. This helps to obtain more accurate pseudo labels, and prevents the overfitting problem. Experimental results on standard benchmarks including GTA5-to-Cityscapes [6,32] and SYNTHIA-to-Cityscapes [6,34] demonstrate that our contrastive learning framework provides domain-invariant and discriminative features for UDASS. The main contributions can be summarized as follows:

- We introduce a novel contrastive learning framework using bi-directional pixel-prototype correspondences to learn domain-invariant and discriminative feature representations for UDASS.
- We propose a nonparametric approach to generating dynamic pseudo labels. We also present a calibration method to reduce domain biases for pixel-prototype correspondences between target and source domains.
- We set a new state of the art on standard benchmarks for UDASS, and demonstrate the effectiveness of our contrast learning framework.

2   Related Work

UDASS. UDASS leverages knowledge learned from a label-rich source domain to predict semantic labels of a scene in a target domain, where ground-truth annotations are not available. Synthetic images (*e.g.*, GTA5 [32] and SYN-THIA [34]) are widely used as source samples, as pixel-level labels can be generated automatically using computer graphics engines. The key factor for UDASS is hence to learn domain-invariant features to reduce the discrepancy between source and target domains. To this end, many UDASS methods adopt an adversarial learning framework [12] to fool a domain discriminator. They can generally be categorized into image-level and feature-level alignment methods. Motivated by image translation techniques [18,57], image-level alignment methods [5,15,23, 30,49] transfer the styles (*e.g.*, texture and illumination) of target images to the source, so that segmentation models can accommodate both domains. Feature-level alignment methods [3,4,10,16,27,28,36,42,44,48,55] align the feature distributions of source and target images explicitly. These adversarial approaches, however, align source and target distributions globally. Namely, they perform a class-agnostic alignment, and ignore positional information of a scene. This suggests that the adversarial approaches fail to transfer pixel-level semantics, related to the structural information of a scene, from source to target domains.

UDASS methods based on self-training [22,58,59] have recently been introduced. The self-training approach first segments target images using a model trained on a source dataset, and obtains pseudo labels if the confidence of semantic labels predicted by the model exceeds a pre-defined threshold. It then retrains the model iteratively with both ground-truth and pseudo labels of source and target datasets, respectively. The representative work of [58] proposes to use different thresholds for individual object categories to consider a class imbalance problem. In [59], soft pseudo labels have been introduced, together with a confidence regularization technique that helps transfer discriminative feature representations from source to target domains. The self-training approaches [22,52,58,59] are, however, likely to overfit to pseudo labels. The reasons are as follows: (1) Pseudo labels are fixed for a few epochs during training, due to computational overheads, which accumulates error from incorrect pseudo labels; (2) Pseudo labels are very sparse, as high confident predictions are chosen only as the labels. Our method alleviates these limitations by generating denser pseudo labels dynamically in a nonparametric way using pixel-prototype correspondences. Most similar to ours is PLCA [20] using pixel-wise matches. It adopts a contrastive learning scheme to reduce the distances between source and target features directly at a pixel-level. The pixel-level domain alignment, however, does not consider contextual information, and fails to obtain compact representations between corresponding object categories in source and target domains. Our method instead uses bidirectional pixel-prototype correspondences for contrastive learning, which encourages intra-class compactness and inter-class separability across domains.

Prototypical Learning. The seminal work of [40] introduces prototypical networks that extract prototype representations for individual object categories. The prototypical features have proven useful in the limited-data regime for the task of, *e.g.*, few-/zero-shot classification. PL [9] extends the idea of prototypical learning for few-shot semantic segmentation in such a way that class prototypes obtained from a support set are matched to pixel-level features in a query image. PANet [46] presents a bidirectional framework exploiting correspondences between prototypical features for a support set and pixel-level ones for query images, and vice versa, for few-shot semantic segmentation. Similar to these methods, we exploit prototypical features for semantic segmentation. Differently, we leverage them within a framework of contrastive learning for UDASS. We use pixel-prototype correspondences to obtain domain-invariant and discriminative feature representations. We also leverage the correspondences to obtain dynamic pseudo labels, which alleviates the limitations of current self-training methods using static pseudo labels.

Contrastive Learning. Contrastive learning [2,13] is a de facto approach to learning generic feature representations in a self-supervised way. The basic idea is to encourage positive pairs with the same label to be close, while negative ones with different labels to be distant. In order to set positive and negative pairs without ground-truth labels, contrastive learning augments a single input image, *e.g.*, using random cropping and color jittering. It then considers the original image and the augmented one as a positive pair, while setting the pairs composed of the original and other images as negative ones. Similar to ours, CANet [19] adopts contrastive learning for unsupervised domain adaptive classification. It computes the domain discrepancies using image-level features, and then performs a class-wise alignment using target labels obtained by a clustering method. Differently, our method leverages contrastive learning using correspondences between pixels and prototypes across domains. Optimizing bidirectional correspondences jointly in our method also enables aggregating features for the same object category, regardless of domains.

Nonparametric Label Transfer. Label transfer has been widely used in object localization [29], scene segmentation [25,31,35,39], automatic image annotation [45], and image translation [38]. Label transfer methods first search visually similar images or patches in large datasets for given queries, and then transfer labels of retrieved samples to the queries. Similar to our approach, the work of [8] adopts a nonparametric label transfer method for scene parsing under different domains (*e.g.*, weather or illumination). Specifically, it extracts features from query images with pre-trained networks, finds the best matching images using SIFT flow [24], and transfers labels of the images to the queries via a probabilistic MRF model, suggesting that this approach requires source images and ground-truth labels at both training and test time. Our method, on the other hand, uses source images and corresponding ground-truth labels only at training time. Namely, we leverage non-parametric label transfer to train a parametric segmentation model.

3 Approach

3.1 Overview

We introduce a cross-domain contrastive learning framework for UDASS using pixel-prototype correspondences (Fig. 2). It first extracts feature maps from

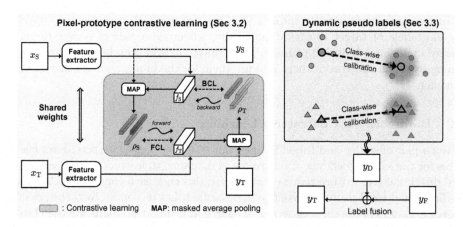

Fig. 2. An overview of our framework. (Left) Bi-directional contrastive learning: We first extract feature maps, f_S and f_T, from source and target images, x_S and x_T, respectively. We then obtain prototypes in a source domain, ρ_S using ground-truth labels of source images y_S. Prototypes in a target domain ρ_T are similarly computed but with dynamic pseudo labels of target images y_T. Bidirectional contrastive terms, FCL and BCL, exploit pixel-prototype correspondences across domains to learn domain-invariant and discriminative features for UDASS. (Right) Hybrid pseudo labels: We generate dynamic pseudo labels y_D using pixel-prototype correspondences across domains, while calibrating the prototypes to reduce domain discrepancies. We then combine them with static ones y_F using a parametric approach to obtain hybrid pseudo labels y_T.

source and target images, respectively, using a siamese network. We obtain prototypes of source and target domains using ground-truth labels of source images and pseudo labels of target ones, respectively. Our method then establishes correspondences between the prototypes and pixel-level features across domains, and leverages them to learn domain-invariant and discriminative representations via contrastive learning. To this end, we introduce a bi-directional contrastive loss that consists of a forward contrastive term (FCL) and a backward contrastive term (BCL). FCL matches individual pixel-level features of a target image with prototypes of a source domain, and enforces pixel-prototype pairs with the same class labels to be aligned closely than other ones. BCL performs the alignment process in a reverse direction, with pixel-level features of a source image and prototypes of a target domain, encouraging our model to provide discriminative and compact features. In order to establish training pairs for computing the bi-directional contrastive loss, we require pseudo labels of target images. To this end, we use dynamic pseudo labels obtained by a nonparametric label transfer, addressing the drawbacks of static pseudo labels. Specifically, given a pair of source-target images, we establish correspondences between prototypes of a source domain and pixel-level features of a target image, while calibrating the prototypes progressively during training to compensate domain discrepancies. We then set the pseudo labels of pixel-level features to the class labels of the corresponding prototypes in a source domain. Unlike static pseudo labels estimated by a parametric approach [22,58], our approach can generate novel pseudo labels of target images dynamically, whenever a pair of source-target images are changed, during training. We estimate hybrid pseudo labels by combining dynamic and static labels, and use them for the bi-directional contrastive learning.

3.2   Bi-directional Contrastive Learning

Given a pair of source and target images, our goal is to aggregate pixel-level features for the same object class, regardless of domains, to learn domain-invariant and discriminative feature representations. To this end, we formulate UDASS as bi-directional pixel-prototype contrastive learning. Let us denote by $\mathcal{C}$ the set of object classes. We obtain prototypes of source and target domains for the class $c \in \mathcal{C}$, $\rho_S(c)$ and $\rho_T(c)$, using masked average pooling (MAP) as follows:

$$\rho_S(c) = \frac{\sum_p f_S(p) y_S(p, c)}{\sum_p y_S(p, c)}, \rho_T(c) = \frac{\sum_p f_T(p) y_T(p, c)}{\sum_p y_T(p, c)}, \tag{1}$$

where we denote by $f_S(p)$ and $f_T(p)$ pixel-level features of source and target images, respectively, at position p. $y_S(p, c)$ and $y_T(p, c)$ are one-hot labels, *i.e.*, 1 if the class label at position p correspond to c and 0 otherwise. Note that we use ground-truth labels of source images y_S and hybrid pseudo labels of target ones y_T to set the labels, y_S and y_T, respectively. Using the prototypes of source and target domains, we perform cross-domain contrastive learning in a bi-directional way. We leverage a bi-directional constative loss that consists of FCL and BCL. FCL exploits prototypes of a source domain and pixel-level features of a target image. To be specific, given pixel-level features of a target image, we select the prototypes of a source domain having the same class labels as the features, and set them as positive pairs, while other prototypes are used to set negative ones. FCL maximizes the similarities between positive pairs as follows:

$$\mathcal{L}_{FC} = -\sum_c \sum_p y_T(p, c) \log \frac{\exp\big(s(f_T(p), \rho_S(c))/\tau\big)}{\sum_c \exp\big(s(f_T(p), \rho_S(c))/\tau\big)}, \tag{2}$$

where τ is a temperature parameter, and $s(\cdot, \cdot)$ computes cosine similarity. Similarly, BCL exploits prototypes of a target domain and pixel-level features of a source image. It encourages positive pairs sharing the same labels to pull each other, while making others set apart as follows:

$$\mathcal{L}_{BC} = -\sum_c \sum_p y_S(p, c) \log \frac{\exp\big(s(f_S(p), \rho_T(c))/\tau\big)}{\sum_c \exp\big(s(f_S(p), \rho_T(c))/\tau\big)}. \tag{3}$$

In summary, using the bidirectional contrastive loss, pixel-level features for the same object class are embedded closely, regardless of domains, while those for different classes are distinguished from each other. That is, by jointly optimizing FCL and BCL, we can minimize intra-class variations and maximize inter-class variations of pixel-level features progressively during training. In contrast to current UDASS methods [22,50,51,54,58,59] that do not consider such variations for domain adaptation, our approach provides more discriminative and compact features. This in turn allows to perform more accurate class-wise alignments across domains, and enables our model to generalize better on a target domain.

3.3   Dynamic Pseudo Labels

Current self-training methods [22,50,51,54,58,59] employ a parametric model trained with ground-truth labels of source images to obtain static pseudo labels of target images. Specifically, using the parametric segmentation model, confidence scores for individual object classes are computed for each pixel-level feature from entire target images. The pixel-level features with high confidence scores are chosen, and corresponding object classes are used as pseudo labels. Although exploiting static pseudo labels of target images enables performing class-aware UDASS, they have the following drawbacks: First, computing the pixel-level confidence scores for all target images to obtain the pseudo labels is computationally demanding. Current self-training methods perform this process for a few iterations (e.g., 10000) during training, and update the pseudo labels of target images very occasionally. The error from incorrect pseudo labels might hence be accumulated. Second, current self-training methods choose highly confident pixel-level features only for static pseudo labels, and thus they are very sparse. These problems cause a model to overfit to the static pseudo labels, and induce suboptimal class-wise alignments between domains. To overcome the limitations, we introduce a novel approach to generating dynamic pseudo labels. It leverages a nonparametric label transfer technique using pixel-prototype correspondences between source and target images. That is, we estimate pseudo labels using pairs of source and target images. This suggests that our approach generates pseudo labels of target images dynamically, whenever source images are changed during training. In other words, the pseudo labels for the same target image could be different, depending on which source images are used to establish pixel-prototype correspondences w.r.t the target one (Fig. 3).

Concretely, given a pair of source and target images, we establish correspondences between prototypes of a source image and pixel-level features of a target one. To obtain reliable correspondences, we alleviate domain biases between source and target domains. We could estimate the degree of domain biases by calculating average class-wise features for each domain using all source and target images, followed by computing differences between the average features, which however requires lots of computational overheads. We instead leverage prototypes of source and target images. We first update prototypes of source and target domains progressively during training using an exponential moving average with a momentum parameter of λ as follows:

$$\mu_S(c) \leftarrow \lambda\mu_S(c) + (1 - \lambda)\rho_S(c), \tag{4}$$

$$\mu_T(c) \leftarrow \lambda\mu_T(c) + (1 - \lambda)\rho_T(c), \tag{5}$$

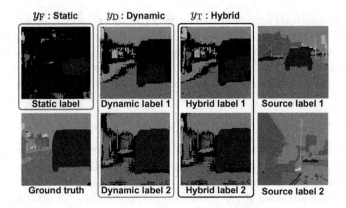

Fig. 3. Visual comparison of static, dynamic, and hybrid pseudo labels for a target image. In contrast to the static label (the first column), estimated using a parametric segmentation model, dynamic labels are obtained by a nonparametric label transfer between source and target images. This suggests that they are denser and cheap to update. We can also obtain different dynamic labels (the second column), according to source images (the fourth column). We combine both labels to get hybrid pseudo labels (the third column), and use them to augment the number of positive and negative pairs for contrastive learning.

where we denote by $\mu_S(c)$ and $\mu_T(c)$ updated prototypes of source and target domains, respectively, for the class c. We then estimate class-wise domain biases:

$$\xi(c) = \mu_T(c) - \mu_S(c), \tag{6}$$

and obtain calibrated prototypes for each object class in a source domain as follows:

$$\rho_{S \to T}(c) = \rho_S(c) + \xi(c). \tag{7}$$

Using the calibrated prototypes, we can establish more correct correspondences across domains. We consider the correspondences are correct, if similarity scores between the pixel-prototype matches are larger than a pre-defined threshold, and set dynamic pseudo labels of target images to corresponding object categories of the prototypes, as follows:

$$y_D(p, c) = \begin{cases} 1, & \text{if } s(f_T(p)), \rho_{S \to T}(c)) > \mathcal{T} \text{ and } c = c' \\ 0, & \text{otherwise} \end{cases}, \tag{8}$$

where $y_D(p, c)$ is a dynamic pseudo label for the class c at position p, $\mathcal{T}$ is a pre-defined threshold, and

$$c' = \underset{c}{\operatorname{argmax}}(s(f_T(p)), \rho_{S \to T}(c))). \tag{9}$$

Hybrid Pseudo Labels. We can obtain diverse pseudo labels even for the same target image every iteration, and the dynamic labels are much denser than static ones. Static pseudo labels, on the other hand, are sparse but reliable. In order to take advantage of both, we combine them and obtain hybrid pseudo labels y_T as follows:

$$y_T(p,c) = \begin{cases} y_D(p,c), & \text{if } y_D(p,c) = 1 \\ y_F(p,c), & \text{if } y_D(p,c') = 0 \text{ for } c' \in C, \text{ and } y_F(p,c) = 1 , \\ 0, & \text{otherwise} \end{cases} \quad (10)$$

where $y_F(p,c)$ is a static pseudo label for the class c at position p.

3.4 Training Loss

Following the previous works [22,50,51,58,59], we exploit segmentation and entropy terms using ground-truth and pseudo labels of source and target images, respectively. The former encourages our model to provide accurate pixel-wise predictions, and the latter minimizes the entropy of the predictions. We define a loss for training a baseline model as follows:

$$\mathcal{L}_{\text{base}} = \lambda_{seg}^S \mathcal{L}_{seg}^S + \lambda_{seg}^T \mathcal{L}_{seg}^T + \lambda_{ent}^S \mathcal{L}_{ent}^S + \lambda_{ent}^T \mathcal{L}_{ent}^T, \quad (11)$$

where $\mathcal{L}_{seg}^S$ and $\mathcal{L}_{seg}^T$ are segmentation losses for source and target domains, respectively. $\mathcal{L}_{ent}^S$ and $\mathcal{L}_{ent}^T$ are entropy terms for source and target domains, respectively. λ_{seg}^S, λ_{seg}^T, λ_{ent}^S, and λ_{ent}^T are balance parameters for each term. For the baseline, we obtain static pseudo labels using the method of [58]. As our final model, we additionally use a bi-directional contrastive loss to learn domain-invariant and discriminative representations as follows:

$$\mathcal{L} = \mathcal{L}_{\text{base}} + \lambda_{FC} \mathcal{L}_{FC} + \lambda_{BC} \mathcal{L}_{BC}, \quad (12)$$

where λ_{FC} and λ_{BC} are weighting factors for forward and backward contrastive terms, respectively.

4 Experiments

4.1 Implementation Details

Dataset and Evaluation Metric. We evaluate our framework on two standard benchmarks (GTA5 [32] $\rightarrow$ Cityscapes [6], and SYNTHIA [34] $\rightarrow$ Cityscapes [6]). GTA5 and SYNTHIA provide 24,996 and 9400 images, respectively. Cityscapes consists of 2975, 500, and 1525 images for training, validation, and testing, respectively. Following the standard protocol in [15,43,58,59], we report the mean intersection over Union (mIoU) on 19 classes for GTA5 $\rightarrow$ Cityscapes and 13 (or 16) classes for Synthia $\rightarrow$ Cityscapes.

Table 1. Quantitative comparison with state-of-the-art methods on GTA5 → Cityscapes in terms of mIoU. AT: methods based on adversarial training; ST: methods based on self-training. †: a method using a different network architecture.

GTA5 → Cityscapes

Split	Methods	Type	Road	Side	Build	Wall	Fence	Pole	Light	Sign	Veg.	Terrian	Sky	Person	Rider	Car	Truck	Bus	Train	Motor	Bike	mIoU
Validation	Source-only	-	45.4	16.5	66.4	14.4	21.6	25.1	36.3	17.2	80.1	16.3	69.1	61.4	24.9	68.6	28.4	4.7	4.4	40.8	27.5	35.2
	AdaptSeg [43]	AT	86.5	36.0	79.9	23.4	23.3	23.9	35.2	14.8	83.4	33.3	75.6	58.5	27.6	73.7	32.5	35.4	3.9	30.1	28.1	42.4
	CBST [58]	ST	91.8	53.5	80.5	32.7	21.0	34.0	28.9	20.4	83.9	34.2	80.9	53.1	24.0	82.7	30.3	35.9	16.0	25.9	42.8	45.9
	CRST [59]	ST	91.0	55.4	80.0	33.7	21.4	37.3	32.9	24.5	85.0	34.1	80.8	57.7	24.6	84.1	27.8	30.1	26.9	26.0	42.3	47.1
	PLCA [20]	-	84.0	30.4	82.4	35.3	24.8	32.2	36.8	24.5	85.5	37.2	78.6	66.9	32.8	85.5	40.4	48.0	8.8	29.8	41.8	47.7
	CAG_UDA [53]	ST	90.4	51.6	83.8	34.2	27.8	38.4	25.3	48.4	85.4	38.2	78.1	58.6	34.6	84.7	21.9	42.7	41.1	29.3	37.2	50.2
	FDA [51]	ST	92.5	53.5	82.4	26.5	27.6	36.4	40.6	38.9	82.3	39.8	78.0	62.6	34.4	84.9	34.1	53.1	16.9	27.7	46.4	50.5
	TPLD [37]	ST	94.2	60.5	82.8	36.6	16.6	39.3	29.0	25.5	85.6	44.9	84.4	60.6	27.4	84.1	37.0	47.0	31.2	36.1	46.4	51.2
	CorDA [47]	ST	**94.7**	**63.1**	87.6	30.7	40.6	40.2	47.8	51.6	87.6	**47.0**	89.7	66.7	35.9	90.2	**48.9**	57.5	0.0	39.8	56.0	56.6
	ProDA [52]	ST	87.1	55.1	78.1	**45.6**	**43.8**	**44.6**	52.5	**53.4**	89.1	44.7	82.1	70.1	**39.1**	88.4	43.8	**59.1**	1.0	**48.7**	54.4	56.5
	Ours	ST	93.5	60.2	**88.1**	31.1	37.0	41.9	**54.7**	37.8	**89.9**	45.5	**89.9**	**72.7**	38.2	**90.7**	34.3	53.2	4.4	47.2	**58.5**	**57.1**
Test	AdaptSeg [43]	AT	88.5	40.4	81.0	26.3	20.6	25.6	36.0	12.9	84.8	45.5	87.2	63.7	35.8	76.4	27.7	28.0	2.9	33.0	26.1	44.3
	CBST [58]	ST	91.0	55.4	80.0	33.7	21.4	37.3	32.9	24.5	85.0	34.1	80.8	57.7	24.6	84.1	27.8	30.1	26.9	26.0	42.3	47.1
	CRST [59]	ST	93.5	57.6	84.6	**39.3**	24.1	25.2	35.0	17.3	85.0	40.6	86.5	58.7	28.7	85.8	**49.0**	56.4	5.4	31.9	43.2	49.9
	FDA-MBT [51]	ST	93.4	55.8	83.6	25.4	23.1	33.2	39.0	36.9	84.0	47.2	88.8	66.3	40.6	87.4	26.9	49.6	12.8	35.2	42.8	51.2
	CorDA [47]	ST	**94.2**	**62.9**	88.1	30.2	41.2	40.1	49.1	49.9	89.1	49.1	90.1	69.1	28.9	86.2	46.2	59.5	1.2	35.2	52.3	57.5
	ProDA [52]	ST	88.1	57.1	81.2	46.1	**45.2**	41.5	**55.1**	**56.2**	86.1	45.1	78.1	73.2	40.1	88.8	48.7	**60.1**	1.1	50.3	53.1	57.6
	Ours	ST	93.8	59.7	**90.1**	38.0	33.4	39.9	45.3	30.5	**92.2**	58.2	**94.8**	**81.9**	**47.9**	**93.2**	40.1	53.1	13.1	**51.2**	**58.2**	**58.5**

Table 2. Quantitative comparison with state-of-the-art methods on SYNTHIA → Cityscapes results in terms of mIoU. We report the results for 13 classes (mIoU*) and 16 classes (mIoU). AT: methods based on adversarial training; ST: methods based on self-training.

SYNTHIA → Cityscapes

Methods	Type	Road	Side.	Build.	Wall*	Fence*	Pole*	Light	Sign	Veg.	Sky	Person	Rider	Car	Bus	Motor	Bike	mIoU	mIoU*
Source-only	AT	53.4	23.4	73.0	5.5	0.0	25.7	6.6	7.0	77.9	55.3	52.9	21.0	60.9	6.6	21.8	33.7	32.5	37.6
AdaptSeg [43]	AT	84.3	42.7	77.5	-	-	-	4.7	7.0	77.9	82.5	54.3	21.0	72.3	32.2	18.9	32.3	-	46.7
CBST [58]	ST	68.0	29.9	76.3	10.8	1.4	33.9	22.8	29.5	77.6	78.3	60.6	28.3	81.6	23.5	18.8	39.8	38.9	42.6
CRST [59]	ST	67.7	32.2	73.9	10.7	1.6	37.4	22.2	31.2	80.8	80.5	60.8	29.1	82.8	25.0	19.4	45.3	43.8	50.1
CAG_UDA [53]	ST	84.7	40.8	81.7	7.8	0.0	35.1	13.3	22.7	84.5	77.6	64.2	27.8	80.9	19.7	22.7	48.3	44.5	51.5
FDA [51]	ST	79.3	35.0	73.2	-	-	-	19.9	24.0	61.7	82.6	61.4	31.1	83.9	40.8	38.4	51.1	-	52.5
PLCA [20]	-	82.6	29.0	81.0	11.2	0.2	33.6	24.9	18.3	82.8	82.3	62.1	26.5	85.6	48.9	26.8	52.2	46.8	54.0
TPLD [37]	ST	80.9	44.3	82.2	19.9	0.3	40.6	20.5	30.1	77.2	80.9	60.6	25.5	84.8	41.1	24.7	43.7	47.3	53.5
CorDA [47]	ST	**93.3**	**61.6**	85.3	19.6	5.1	37.8	36.6	**42.8**	84.9	90.4	69.7	41.8	85.6	38.4	32.6	53.9	55.0	62.8
ProDA [52]	ST	87.3	45.1	84.2	**36.5**	0.0	**43.3**	**54.7**	36.0	88.3	83.1	71.5	24.4	88.4	**50.1**	40.1	45.6	55.1	61.3
Ours	ST	83.8	42.2	**85.3**	16.4	**5.7**	43.1	48.3	30.2	**89.3**	**92.1**	68.2	43.1	**89.7**	47.2	**42.2**	**54.2**	**55.6**	**62.9**

Training. We adopt the DeepLab-V2 [1] architecture with ResNet-101 [14] as a backbone network pretrained for ImageNet classification [7]. We first train DeepLab-V2 with a source dataset, and use it as an initial segmentation model for UDASS. We train the model for $100k$ iterations with a batch size of 4, using stochastic gradient descent (SGD) [21] of a momentum of 0.9 and weight decay of 5×10^{-4}. We use a poly learning rate scheduling with an initial learning rate of 7.5×10^{-5}. We update static pseudo labels y_F every $10k$ iterations. We resize a shorter side of images to 850, and crop them into a patch of size 730×730. For data augmentation, we use horizontal flipping and random scaling with the factor of $[0.8, 1.2]$. We use a weighted sampling strategy to select source images containing objects that rarely appear in a source domain, mitigating low co-occurrence rates for the rare object categories. Following [11,52], we additionally apply a self-distillation technique to our final model. Detailed descriptions for the weighted sampling and hyperparameter settings are available in the supplement.

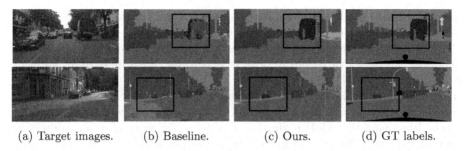

(a) Target images.   (b) Baseline.   (c) Ours.   (d) GT labels.

Fig. 4. Qualitative comparisons on GTA5 → Cityscapes. Our model gives better results than the baseline. (Best viewed in color).

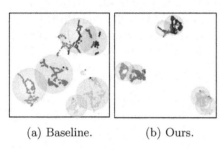

(a) Baseline.   (b) Ours.

Fig. 5. t-SNE visualization of a baseline (a) and our model (b). (Best viewed in color).

Table 3. Quantitative results for variants of our model. We report mIoU scores for 19 and 16 classes on GTA5 → Cityscapes and SYNTHIA → Cityscapes, respectively.

$\mathcal{L}_{base}$	$\mathcal{L}_{FC}$	$\mathcal{L}_{BC}$	$+y_D$ (w/o cal.)	$+y_D$ (w/ cal.)	Source dataset	
					GTA5	SYNTHIA
✓					49.5	45.1
✓	✓				51.2	48.8
✓	✓	✓			53.5	51.3
✓	✓	✓	✓		55.3	53.5
✓	✓	✓		✓	57.1	55.6

4.2 Results

Quantitative Results. We compare our method with the state-of-the-art methods on GTA5 → Cityscapes and SYNTHIA → Cityscapes in Tables 1 and 2, respectively. Note that all methods in the tables are based on the DeepLab-V2 [1] architecture with ResNet-101, except for CAG-UDA [53]. For a fair comparison, we report the results of ProDA [52] using the same network architecture as other methods, reproduced using an official source code. CBST [58] uses a self-training-based method to perform a class-aware alignment. This method is similar to our baseline, but it uses a limited number of pseudo labels, being outperformed by our approach on both benchmarks. PLCA [20] uses a pixel-wise association method to align source and target domains in a pixel-level. This method, however, fails to obtain compact feature representations, and it is hence outperformed by our approach on both benchmarks. CorDA [47] uses depth maps of source and target domains to transfer the knowledge of a source domain to a target one. Our method outperforms CorDA [47] on both benchmarks even without using the depth information, indicating that our contrastive learning framework effectively transfers the knowledge across domains using pseudo labels. ProDA [52] focuses on removing false-positives of pseudo labels [58] and uses sparse labels. Different from ProDA [52], we are interested in generating additional labels based upon the ones obtained by the approach of [58]. That is, our method focuses on obtaining more true-positives and generating denser labels using pixel-prototype correspondences. Other than ProDA [52], we additionally use the bi-directional contrastive loss to minimize intra-class variations and maximize inter-class variations of pixel-level features. We achieve mIoU gains of 0.6% and 1.6% for GTA5 → Cityscapes and SYNTHIA → Cityscapes, respectively, compared to ProDA [52]. The results imply that our method effectively learns domain-invariant and discriminative representations with denser pseudo labels, improving the mIoU performance of semantic segmentation. Additional comparisons with ProDA [52] are available in the supplement. We also report mIoU scores for the test split of Cityscapes, obtained from an official evaluation server, which has been ignored by most previous works. We use official source codes provided by the authors to obtain the results of state-of-the-art methods. We achieve non-trivial mIoU gains over CorDA [47] and ProDA [52] for the test split of Cityscapes, demonstrating that ours can generalize better than them. Considering the performance gains of recent UDASS methods, the results are significant. For example, FDA [51] achieves a mIoU gain of 0.3% over CAG_UDA [53], and TPLD [37] gets the gain of 0.7% over FDA [51]. CorDA [47] and ProDA [52] provide large mIoU gains compared to other methods, but the improvements mainly come from exploiting additional depth maps and applying post-processing method, respectively.

Qualitative Results. We show in Fig. 4 segmentation results on the GTA5 → Cityscapes task. Compared to the baseline model, our model provides more accurate segmentation results (*e.g.*, the bus in the first row, and the road and the rider in the second row). We show in Fig. 5 the t-SNE plot of feature representations of our model and the baseline. We visualize features of source and target images for each method by red and blue circles, respectively. The results show that our method successfully aligns the features for the same object category and separates them for different ones. That is, it minimizes intra-class variations, and maximizes inter-class variations, regardless of domains.

Ablation Study. We present in Table 3 an ablation analysis for each component of our framework on GTA5 → Cityscapes and SYNTHIA → Cityscapes. We show mIoU scores for variants of our model on the validation split of Cityscapes. As a baseline in the first row, we use static pseudo labels, obtained by the method of [58], to perform a class-aware alignment between source and target domains. We can see from the second row that FCL gives better mIoU scores, demonstrating the effectiveness of our approach to aligning prototypes and pixel-level features across domains. From the first and third rows, we can clearly see that jointly optimizing two contrastive terms is effective to UDASS. The fourth row demonstrates that leveraging additional dynamic pseudo labels provides better results than exploiting the static ones alone in terms of the mIoU score, even without the calibration (w/o cal.). We can observe from the fifth row that the calibration (w/ cal.) reduces domain discrepancies, and further improves the performance significantly.

(a) w/o cal.   (b) w/ cal.   (c) GT labels.

Fig. 6. Visualization of dynamic pseudo labels. (a–b) Pseudo labels obtained without and with calibrating prototypes of a source domain; (c) Target labels.

Table 4. Quantitative results for various pseudo labels of a target domain. We report the densities of static, dynamic, and hybrid pseudo labels and corresponding label accuracies.

Pseudo labels	Density (%)	Accuracy (%)
Static [58]	20.1	98.5
Dyn. (w/o cal.)	22.2	98.6
Dyn. (w/ cal.)	34.3	98.6
Hybrid	42.3	98.8

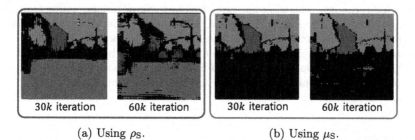

(a) Using ρ_S.   (b) Using μ_S.

Fig. 7. Pseudo labels at $30k$ and $60k$ iterations using ρ_S (a) and μ_S (b), respectively.

Comparison of Pseudo Labels. We measure the densities of various pseudo labels and corresponding label accuracies, and report the results in Table 4. We can see that the densities of dynamic pseudo labels are slightly higher than that of a static one, even without calibrating domain biases, while maintaining the label accuracies. Using pixel-prototype correspondences between target and source domains leads to obtaining denser labels than [58]. The calibration process largely densifies dynamic pseudo labels. We can establish more correct correspondences between source and target domains by using the calibration process. The approach of [58] neglects the biases between source and target domains. Different from [58], ours compensate for the class-wise domain biases and generate more accurate and denser labels than [58]. Hybrid pseudo labels that combine static and dynamic ones provide the best result in terms of the label density and accuracy. When obtaining hybrid pseudo labels, we can reduce the number of incorrect static labels [58] by comparing them with dynamic ones. We show in Fig. 6 examples of dynamic pseudo labels obtained with and without the class-wise calibration. The results show that calibrating class-wise domain biases for source prototypes leads to establishing more correct pixel-prototype correspondences, providing denser and more accurate pseudo labels.

In Fig. 7, we compare generated pseudo labels using instance-wise prototypes ρ_S and momentum-based ones μ_S. We can see that using instance-wise prototypes ρ_S provides more diverse pseudo labels. They are more various than the other ones μ_S slowly moving with momentum, and lead our model to establish diverse pixel-prototype correspondences.

5   Conclusion

We have introduced a novel contrastive learning framework for UDASS. Our key idea is to use cross-domain pixel-prototype correspondences to learn domain-invariant and discriminative representations. We have introduced a bi-directional contrastive loss to align the features for the same object category and seperate them for different ones. We have also introduced an approach to generating pseudo labels dynamically in a nonparametric way using pixel-prototype correspondences, while compensating class-wise domain biases between source and target domains. Experimental results show the effectiveness of our framework, setting a new state of the art on standard benchmarks.

Acknowledgements. This work was supported by Institute of Information & communications Technology Planning & Evaluation (IITP) grant funded by the Korea government (MSIT) (No. RS-2022-00143524, Development of Fundamental Technology and Integrated Solution for Next-Generation Automatic Artificial Intelligence System, and No. 2022-0-00124, Development of Artificial Intelligence Technology for Self-Improving Competency-Aware Learning Capabilities), and the Yonsei Signature Research Cluster Program of 2022 (2022-22-0002).

References

1. Chen, L.C., Papandreou, G., Kokkinos, I., Murphy, K., Yuille, A.L.: Semantic image segmentation with deep convolutional nets and fully connected CRFs. ICLR (2015)
2. Chen, T., Kornblith, S., Norouzi, M., Hinton, G.: A simple framework for contrastive learning of visual representations. In: ICML (2020)
3. Chen, Y.H., Chen, W.Y., Chen, Y.T., Tsai, B.C., Frank Wang, Y.C., Sun, M.: No more discrimination: cross city adaptation of road scene segmenters. In: ICCV (2017)
4. Chen, Y., Li, W., Van Gool, L.: ROAD: reality oriented adaptation for semantic segmentation of urban scenes. In: CVPR (2018)
5. Chen, Y.C., Lin, Y.Y., Yang, M.H., Huang, J.B.: CrDoCo: pixel-level domain transfer with cross-domain consistency. In: CVPR (2019)
6. Cordts, M., et al.: The cityscapes dataset. In: CVPR Workshop (2015)
7. Deng, J., Dong, W., Socher, R., Li, L.J., Li, K., Fei-Fei, L.: ImageNet: a large-scale hierarchical image database. In: CVPR (2009)
8. Di, S., Zhang, H., Li, C.G., Mei, X., Prokhorov, D., Ling, H.: Cross-domain traffic scene understanding: a dense correspondence-based transfer learning approach. IEEE Trans. ITS **19**(3), 745–757 (2017)
9. Dong, N., Xing, E.P.: Few-shot semantic segmentation with prototype learning. In: BMVC (2018)
10. Du, L., et al.: SSF-DAN: separated semantic feature based domain adaptation network for semantic segmentation. In: ICCV (2019)
11. Fang, Z., Wang, J., Wang, L., Zhang, L., Yang, Y., Liu, Z.: SEED: self-supervised distillation for visual representation. ICLR (2021)
12. Ganin, Y., et al.: Domain-adversarial training of neural networks. JMLR **17**(1), 1–35 (2016)

13. He, K., Fan, H., Wu, Y., Xie, S., Girshick, R.: Momentum contrast for unsupervised visual representation learning. In: CVPR (2020)
14. He, K., Zhang, X., Ren, S., Sun, J.: Deep residual learning for image recognition. In: CVPR (2016)
15. Hoffman, J., et al.: CyCADA: cycle-consistent adversarial domain adaptation. In: ICML (2018)
16. Hoffman, J., Wang, D., Yu, F., Darrell, T.: FCNs in the wild: pixel-level adversarial and constraint-based adaptation. arXiv preprint arXiv:1612.02649
17. Huang, Z., Wang, X., Huang, L., Huang, C., Wei, Y., Liu, W.: CCNet: criss-cross attention for semantic segmentation. In: ICCV (2019)
18. Isola, P., Zhu, J.Y., Zhou, T., Efros, A.A.: Image-to-image translation with conditional adversarial networks. In: CVPR (2017)
19. Kang, G., Jiang, L., Yang, Y., Hauptmann, A.G.: Contrastive adaptation network for unsupervised domain adaptation. In: CVPR (2019)
20. Kang, G., Wei, Y., Yang, Y., Zhuang, Y., Hauptmann, A.: Pixel-level cycle association: a new perspective for domain adaptive semantic segmentation. In: NeurIPS (2020)
21. Kiefer, J., Wolfowitz, J.: Stochastic estimation of the maximum of a regression function. Ann. Math. Stat. **23**, 462–466 (1952)
22. Li, G., Kang, G., Liu, W., Wei, Y., Yang, Y.: Content-consistent matching for domain adaptive semantic segmentation. In: Vedaldi, A., Bischof, H., Brox, T., Frahm, J.-M. (eds.) ECCV 2020. LNCS, vol. 12359, pp. 440–456. Springer, Cham (2020). https://doi.org/10.1007/978-3-030-58568-6_26
23. Li, Y., Yuan, L., Vasconcelos, N.: Bidirectional learning for domain adaptation of semantic segmentation. In: CVPR (2019)
24. Liu, C., Yuen, J., Torralba, A.: SIFT flow: dense correspondence across scenes and its applications. IEEE Trans. PAMI **33**(5), 978–994 (2010)
25. Liu, C., Yuen, J., Torralba, A.: Nonparametric scene parsing via label transfer. IEEE Trans. PAMI **33**(12), 2368–2382 (2011)
26. Long, J., Shelhamer, E., Darrell, T.: Fully convolutional networks for semantic segmentation. In: CVPR (2015)
27. Luo, Y., Liu, P., Guan, T., Yu, J., Yang, Y.: Significance-aware information bottleneck for domain adaptive semantic segmentation. In: ICCV (2019)
28. Luo, Y., Zheng, L., Guan, T., Yu, J., Yang, Y.: Taking a closer look at domain shift: category-level adversaries for semantics consistent domain adaptation. In: CVPR (2019)
29. Malisiewicz, T., Gupta, A., Efros, A.A.: Ensemble of Exemplar-SVMs for object detection and beyond. In: ICCV (2011)
30. Murez, Z., Kolouri, S., Kriegman, D., Ramamoorthi, R., Kim, K.: Image to image translation for domain adaptation. In: CVPR (2018)
31. Najafi, M., Namin, S.T., Salzmann, M., Petersson, L.: Sample and filter: nonparametric scene parsing via efficient filtering. In: CVPR (2016)
32. Richter, S.R., Vineet, V., Roth, S., Koltun, V.: Playing for data: ground truth from computer games. In: Leibe, B., Matas, J., Sebe, N., Welling, M. (eds.) ECCV 2016. LNCS, vol. 9906, pp. 102–118. Springer, Cham (2016). https://doi.org/10.1007/978-3-319-46475-6_7
33. Ronneberger, O., Fischer, P., Brox, T.: U-Net: convolutional networks for biomedical image segmentation. In: Navab, N., Hornegger, J., Wells, W.M., Frangi, A.F. (eds.) MICCAI 2015. LNCS, vol. 9351, pp. 234–241. Springer, Cham (2015). https://doi.org/10.1007/978-3-319-24574-4_28

34. Ros, G., Sellart, L., Materzynska, J., Vazquez, D., Lopez, A.M.: The SYNTHIA dataset: a large collection of synthetic images for semantic segmentation of urban scenes. In: CVPR (2016)
35. Russell, B.C., Efros, A., Sivic, J., Freeman, W.T., Zisserman, A.: Segmenting scenes by matching image composites (2009)
36. Sankaranarayanan, S., Balaji, Y., Jain, A., Lim, S.N., Chellappa, R.: Unsupervised domain adaptation for semantic segmentation with GANs. arXiv preprint arXiv:1711.06969
37. Shin, I., Woo, S., Pan, F., Kweon, I.S.: Two-phase pseudo label densification for self-training based domain adaptation. In: Vedaldi, A., Bischof, H., Brox, T., Frahm, J.-M. (eds.) ECCV 2020. LNCS, vol. 12358, pp. 532–548. Springer, Cham (2020). https://doi.org/10.1007/978-3-030-58601-0_32
38. Shrivastava, A., Malisiewicz, T., Gupta, A., Efros, A.A.: Data-driven visual similarity for cross-domain image matching. In: SIGGRAPH Asia (2011)
39. Singh, G., Kosecka, J.: Nonparametric scene parsing with adaptive feature relevance and semantic context. In: CVPR (2013)
40. Snell, J., Swersky, K., Zemel, R.S.: Prototypical networks for few-shot learning. In: NeurIPS (2017)
41. Song, L., et al.: Learnable tree filter for structure-preserving feature transform. In: NeurIPS (2019)
42. Sun, R., Zhu, X., Wu, C., Huang, C., Shi, J., Ma, L.: Not all areas are equal: transfer learning for semantic segmentation via hierarchical region selection. In: CVPR (2019)
43. Tsai, Y.H., Hung, W.C., Schulter, S., Sohn, K., Yang, M.H., Chandraker, M.: Learning to adapt structured output space for semantic segmentation. In: CVPR (2018)
44. Tsai, Y.H., Sohn, K., Schulter, S., Chandraker, M.: Domain adaptation for structured output via discriminative patch representations. In: ICCV (2019)
45. Uricchio, T., Ballan, L., Seidenari, L., Del Bimbo, A.: Automatic image annotation via label transfer in the semantic space. PR **71**, 144–157 (2017)
46. Wang, K., Liew, J.H., Zou, Y., Zhou, D., Feng, J.: PANet: few-shot image semantic segmentation with prototype alignment. In: ICCV (2019)
47. Wang, Q., Dai, D., Hoyer, L., Van Gool, L., Fink, O.: Domain adaptive semantic segmentation with self-supervised depth estimation. In: ICCV (2021)
48. Wang, Z., et al.: Differential treatment for stuff and things: a simple unsupervised domain adaptation method for semantic segmentation. In: CVPR (2020)
49. Yang, J., An, W., Wang, S., Zhu, X., Yan, C., Huang, J.: Label-driven reconstruction for domain adaptation in semantic segmentation. In: Vedaldi, A., Bischof, H., Brox, T., Frahm, J.-M. (eds.) ECCV 2020. LNCS, vol. 12372, pp. 480–498. Springer, Cham (2020). https://doi.org/10.1007/978-3-030-58583-9_29
50. Yang, Y., Lao, D., Sundaramoorthi, G., Soatto, S.: Phase consistent ecological domain adaptation. In: CVPR (2020)
51. Yang, Y., Soatto, S.: FDA: Fourier domain adaptation for semantic segmentation. In: CVPR (2020)
52. Zhang, P., Zhang, B., Zhang, T., Chen, D., Wang, Y., Wen, F.: Prototypical pseudo label denoising and target structure learning for domain adaptive semantic segmentation. In: CVPR (2021)
53. Zhang, Q., Zhang, J., Liu, W., Tao, D.: Category anchor-guided unsupervised domain adaptation for semantic segmentation. In: NeurIPS (2019)
54. Zhang, Y., David, P., Gong, B.: Curriculum domain adaptation for semantic segmentation of urban scenes. In: ICCV (2017)

55. Zhang, Y., Qiu, Z., Yao, T., Liu, D., Mei, T.: Fully convolutional adaptation networks for semantic segmentation. In: CVPR (2018)
56. Zheng, S., et al.: Conditional random fields as recurrent neural networks. In: ICCV (2015)
57. Zhu, J.Y., Park, T., Isola, P., Efros, A.A.: Unpaired image-to-image translation using cycle-consistent adversarial networks. In: ICCV (2017)
58. Zou, Y., Yu, Z., Vijaya Kumar, B.V.K., Wang, J.: Unsupervised domain adaptation for semantic segmentation via class-balanced self-training. In: Ferrari, V., Hebert, M., Sminchisescu, C., Weiss, Y. (eds.) ECCV 2018. LNCS, vol. 11207, pp. 297–313. Springer, Cham (2018). https://doi.org/10.1007/978-3-030-01219-9_18
59. Zou, Y., Yu, Z., Liu, X., Kumar, B., Wang, J.: Confidence regularized self-training. In: ICCV (2019)

Learning Regional Purity for Instance Segmentation on 3D Point Clouds

Shichao Dong[1,2], Guosheng Lin[1,2(✉)], and Tzu-Yi Hung[3]

[1] S-Lab, Nanyang Technological University, Singapore, Singapore
{scdong,gslin}@ntu.edu.sg
[2] School of Computer Science and Engineering, Nanyang Technological University,
Singapore, Singapore
[3] Delta Research Center, Singapore, Singapore
tzuyi.hung@deltaww.com

Abstract. 3D instance segmentation is a fundamental task for scene understanding, with a variety of applications in robotics and AR/VR. Many proposal-free methods have been proposed recently for this task, with remarkable results and high efficiency. However, these methods heavily rely on instance centroid regression and do not explicitly detect object boundaries, thus may mistakenly group nearby objects into the same clusters in some scenarios. In this paper, we define a novel concept of "regional purity" as the percentage of neighboring points belonging to the same instance within a fixed-radius 3D space. Intuitively, it indicates the likelihood of a point belonging to the boundary area. To evaluate the feasibility of predicting regional purity, we design a strategy to build a random scene toy dataset based on existing training data. Besides, using toy data is a "free" way of data augmentation on learning regional purity, which eliminates the burdens of additional real data. We propose Regional Purity Guided Network (RPGN), which has separate branches for predicting semantic class, regional purity, offset, and size. Predicted regional purity information is utilized to guide our clustering algorithm. Experimental results demonstrate that using regional purity can simultaneously prevent under-segmentation and over-segmentation problems during clustering.

Keywords: 3D instance segmentation · Point cloud representation learning · Clustering algorithm

1 Introduction

Semantic scene understanding is a crucial component for many real-world computer vision applications, such as indoor robots, autonomous driving, drones, AR/VR devices, etc. Although processing visual information for scene understanding is an instinctive ability for humans, it remains a fairly challenging task for robots. Many robotic applications cannot fully handle various situations due to the lack of semantic understanding of the target objects in the working environment. In recent times, with the rapid development of deep learning techniques, computer vision has achieved remarkable success

Supplementary Information The online version contains supplementary material available at https://doi.org/10.1007/978-3-031-20056-4_4.

Fig. 1. Example of regional purity. Green point indicates high regional purity, since all its surrounding points belong to the same instance. Red point indicates low regional purity, since some of its neighboring points are from a different instance. (Color figure online)

in 2D image tasks. Different from 2D data captured from a conventional camera, 3D data are usually collected by Lidar sensor or RGB-D based 3D scanner. Point cloud data involves a bunch of discrete points with their XYZ coordinates. Compared with images, 3D data retains the original geometric information and does not suffer from depth information loss during projection.

Existing approaches on 3D instance segmentation task can be classified into two categories, proposal-based methods [9,17,27,39,40] and proposal-free methods [8,13,18,19,21,24,26,28,36,37]. Proposal-based methods perform object detection task first and predict a point-level mask for each proposed box. Whereas, proposal-free methods start solving the problem based on semantic segmentation result and discriminate points into clusters via post-processing steps [5]. Generally, proposal-free methods have relatively lower objectness since they do not perform computationally expensive object detection task.

Majority of the methods with good performance, including [13,19,19,21,29,30] follows a same way of predicting instance centers and group nearby points into proposals or clusters. Although this has been proven to be very effective, there are some situations that are fairly challenging to predict accurate centroid from a single point. Specifically, points near object boundary or belonging to objects with distorted shapes are difficult to be predicted precisely. These points with inaccurate center prediction may potentially cause two nearby objects with the same semantic class to be wrongly grouped into the same cluster. Can we find an efficient way to tackle such problems without even performing object detection task? The answer is yes.

In this paper, we look at this problem from a different point of view and aim to find a more robust way to deal with these hard cases. Our work focus on approximating boundary area via predicting regional purity. On ground-truth, we explore the surrounding space for each point and calculate the percentage of the points with the same instance label. As shown in Fig. 1, if most neighbor points belong to the same instance, this point is said to have high regional purity and vice versa. We build a random scene toy dataset and let our network learn to predict regional purity on it. Based on the predicted results, we can know which points are more likely to be in the boundary area between objects and need to be cautious when grouping them. Comparing with bounding box detection, our approximated boundary areas own more adaptive shapes and are not constrained by rigid rectangular boxes. Meanwhile, our regional prediction is a direct output from one branch after the backbone network, thus does not bring much computational burden during processing.

To sum up, the key contributions of our work are following:

- We define a novel concept of regional purity, which encodes instance-aware contextual information of the surrounding region. Regional purity information can be employed to guide the clustering algorithm and provide good objectness for 3D instance segmentation.
- We propose a pretraining pipeline for learning regional purity and design rules to generate random toy scenes by extracting samples from existing training data.
- Our proposed method achieves state-of-the-art performance and the fastest processing speed among all the methods.

2   Related Work

To handle unstructured point cloud data [2], existing proposed feature learning methods can be classified into point-based methods [23,31,32,35,38,43] and projection-based methods [10,12,16,22]. Inspired by the success of convolution on images, projection-based methods transform original data into regular format and then implement with convolution operation. On the other hand, point-based methods directly work on irregular point cloud with different ways of feature extraction.

Similarity Group Proposal Network (SGPN) [36] is a pioneering work that directly tackles instance segmentation task with deep learning technique on 3D point cloud data. It learns point feature using PointNet++ [32] backbone and merges group proposals from similarity matrix for instance segmentation. Submanifold sparse convolution [12] has been proven to be a very effective backbone network for 3D semantic segmentation, which transforms sparse point cloud into voxels and performs convolution only on non-empty voxels. Liu et al. [26] proposed MASC, a U-net architecture with submanifold sparse convolution [12]. It predicts semantic scores for every voxel and the affinity between neighbouring voxels at different scales. Wang et al. [37] introduced Associatively Segmenting Instance and Semantics(ASIS), which has two separate branches for semantic segmentation and instance segmentation that can mutually support each other. JSIS3D [28] uses multi-value Conditional Random Field (CRF) for joint optimization. MTML [21] introduced directional loss and discriminative loss for feature embedding into 3D instance segmentation. Since then, center based methods dominate this area. PointGroup [19] finds the void space between objects and leverage dual set of proposals to boost performance. Occuseg [13] introduces occupancy signal to guide graph-based clustering algorithm. Overall, these proposal-free methods do not require region proposal network which makes them less computational expensive. Proposal-based methods including GSPN [36], 3D-SIS [17] and 3D-BoNet [39] explicitly detect object boundaries and perform binary mask prediction on top of the detection result. The recent 3D-MPA [9] makes dense center predictions on all points and aggregate the features between proposals via graph convolutional network for mask prediction.

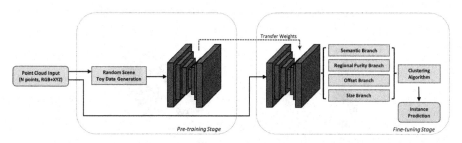

Fig. 2. Pipeline of the proposed pretraining scheme for learning regional purity. First, we extract samples from training set of point cloud data and use our montage assembly method to generate random scenes. Then, we pretrain our backbone network on toy dataset and fine tune on real dataset. Our network has four branches for point feature prediction and a clustering algorithm to output final result.

3 Method

In this work, the predominant objective is to evaluate if our defined regional purity signal can be well learned and predicted. Therefore we start by building a toy dataset with clean data. Following that, the next question is to show how those useful information can be utilized.

As shown in Fig. 2, we proposed a pipeline of the training scheme, consisting of pre-training stage and fine-tuning stage. Our random scene toy dataset serves two main purposes: 1) to evaluate the feasibility of predicting regional purity; and 2) to introduce "free" additional data for data augmentation.

3.1 Random Scene Toy Dataset

For the network to learn regional purity in a generalized way, we need a large amount of data that contains different combined cases of nearby objects. However, scenes in public dataset usually only have limited high-quality data for learning regional purity. Moreover, many objects are not close enough to each other, which makes the unbalance problem between high purity class and low purity class even worse. Excessive background points are not helpful for learning regional purity but inevitably lead to additional computational costs. To tackle these issues, we design a novel strategy of building a toy dataset by sample extraction and montage assembly. The created toy dataset contains foreground points only and keeps objects highly compacted.

Sample Extraction. As the preparation step, we select and crop those points belonging to a particular instance from the training set. Since cropped point clouds can be at different positions in the original coordinate system, its coordinates need to be normalized by shifting the origin of the coordinate system to its mean center. To make the object on the floor, we then shift all points upwards until no negative Z values exist. The semantic labels are kept but instance labels will be reassigned in the next steps (Fig. 3).

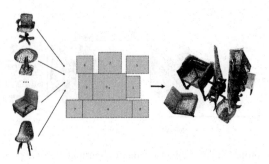

Fig. 3. Illustration of random toy scene generation. Extracted toy samples are flexibly joined into new scenes via a template-based montage assembly method.

Montage Assembly. To create more cases of the boundary area, we use a template-based assembling method. Specifically, nine samples from extraction stages will be randomly selected and stitched into a toy scene. The template is designed on the bird-view of objects. Instance samples are added to the template sequentially. Oversized objects can cause the next object to be shifted aside. Afterward, we shift all surrounding objects towards the center object by a Gaussian random distance. These hard cases can benefit network training. All objects are augmented with random rotation. The whole scene is also randomly adjusted and one object is randomly dropped out, to prevent any potential possibility of over-fitting. In summary, our assembly method creates random scene toy dataset with high coverage and few overlaps, meanwhile keeping the data size consistent.

Regional Purity Label. For automatically generating ground-truth regional purity labels, we use k-d tree which organizes points in a space partitioning data structure. This allows fast retrieval of neighboring points in 3D space. Given a seed point q, we search and find all points within a fixed radius r. Its receptive space can be expressed as:

$$\mathcal{N}(q,r) = \{p \in \mathcal{P} \mid \|p - q\| < r\}, \tag{1}$$

where r is the radius of the receptive space and p is taken from the set of points $\mathcal{P}$ of the entire point cloud scene.

Here, we define the following rules for regional purity label generation. We consider $id1$ as high purity, $id2$ as low purity and $id0$ as medium purity.

$$\text{regional purity label} = \begin{cases} 1 & \frac{\mathcal{M}}{\mathcal{N}} \geq \theta_1 \\ 2 & \frac{\mathcal{M}}{\mathcal{N}} \leq \theta_2 \\ 0 & otherwise \end{cases}, \tag{2}$$

where $\mathcal{M}$ is the number of points with the same instance label as the seed point, $\mathcal{N}$ is the number of total found points. We empirically set θ_1 to be 95% and θ_2 to be 80%.

3.2   Network Architecture

Our network uses a shared U-net backbone and several branches for joint task learning. Proposed clustering algorithm considers predicted information and directly outputs instance segmentation result.

3.3   Multi-task Learning

As a necessary preliminary step, the major role of backbone network is to extract the contextual and geometric information from input data. Subsequently, we apply linear transformation for different branches to predict semantic labels, regional purity labels, offsets and size labels. The training of our network is supervised by following the joint loss function,

$$L_{joint} = L_{sem} + L_{purity} + L_{offset} + L_{size}. \tag{3}$$

Semantic Segmentation Branch. Based on point feature vectors, semantic score can be predicted for N classes. The training process is supervised by a conventional cross entropy loss [11] L_{sem}.

Regional Purity Branch. As mentioned in the previous section, we assigned regional purity labels to be either 0, 1, or 2 on ground-truth. Normal data distribution may include much more label id 1 than id 2. To deal with the class imbalance issue, we propose a joint loss with three terms for regional purity,

$$L_{purity} = L_{CE} + L_{dice} + 0.1 * L_{dist}. \tag{4}$$

For learning regional purity, Cross-Entropy loss with softmax activation is applied for three equally weighted categories,

$$L_{CE} = -\frac{1}{N} \sum_{i=1}^{N} H_{CE}(y_i, c_i). \tag{5}$$

where N is the number of points, i is the index of point, c_i is the one-hot-encoding of the ground-truth regional purity label of point i and H_{CE} is the cross-entropy function.

Accuracy in class imbalance tasks can be misleading sometimes. $F1$ score, as known as Dice coefficient [3, 34], is a more reliable measure. It represents the harmonic mean of precision and recall.

$$Dice = \frac{2 \mid A \cap B \mid}{\mid A \mid + \mid B \mid} = \frac{2TP}{2TP + FP + FN}. \tag{6}$$

This metric is directly adapted in dice loss function [4,20,33]. Here, we add different weight coefficients for FP (false positives) and FN (false negatives). For predicting low purity label, a false positive prediction will surfer more punishment than a false negative prediction. In other words, we think precision is more important than recall in this task. Comparing with predicting nothing, wrong prediction hurts performance more. This loss term is formulated as:

$$L_{dice} = 1 - \frac{1 + p\hat{p}}{1 + p\hat{p} + \alpha p(1 - \hat{p}) + \beta(1 - p)\hat{p}}. \tag{7}$$

where α is the coefficient for FP (false positives) and β is the coefficient for FN (false negatives). The sum of these two factors must be 1. If both are set to 0.5, it is just same as regular Dice loss. A value of 1 is added at both numerator and denominator of the fraction to smooth the loss.

A distance map [15] is derived on ground-truth by searching the distance to the nearest low purity point for each point. The purpose of using distance penalty term is to treat false positive point differently. For example, a point wrongly predicted as low purity point but just nearby other positive points is much tolerable, but predicting a low purity point at the center of an object is beyond reasonable limits. Using distance penalty term, it guides the network to focus towards the target area at boundary regions. This term is defined as:

$$L_{dist} = \frac{1}{M} \sum_{i=1}^{M} (1 + \Phi) \odot L_{CE}, \tag{8}$$

Here, M is the number of predicted low purity points, Φ is the distance map created, i is the index of Φ. This is an additional term to the Cross-Entropy loss.

Offset Branch. Following previous work [19], we use L1 loss to regress object centroid for all points on instances. Offset labels are three dimensional vectors which generated on ground-truth.

$$L_{o\_reg} = \frac{1}{\sum_i m_i} \sum_i ||o_i - (\hat{c}_i - p_i)|| \cdot m_i, \tag{9}$$

where m is a binary mask to filter out background points.

Directly regressing instance center is a challenging task. Here, an additional direction loss term is introduced to guide the network based on cosine similarity.

$$L_{o\_dir} = 1 - \frac{1}{\sum_i m_i} \sum_i \frac{o_i}{||o_i||_2} \cdot \frac{\hat{c}_i - p_i}{||\hat{c}_i - p_i||_2} \cdot m_i, \tag{10}$$

Note that we add a constant of 1 to avoid negative loss value, since the range of cosine similarity is between -1 and 1. The combined offset loss can be written as

$$L_{offset} = L_{o\_reg} + L_{o\_dir}. \tag{11}$$

Size Branch. For the network to learn instance-level contextual feature, we also introduce a size branch for auxiliary purposes. Based on the length of diagonal of bird view 2D bounding box, instance size is classified into six categories and the fixed interval between classes is 0.4 m.

3.4   Regional Purity Guided Clustering Algorithm

In this section, we employ predicted regional purity to guide a standard breath-first search algorithm. Figure 4 shows a typical grouping process towards some ungrouped points (in grey). In (a), a new cluster starts from a random initial seed point (in blue). The seed point will search and find target points in space. If target points satisfy its criteria, they are grouped into the cluster and becoming the seed points in next grouping iteration.

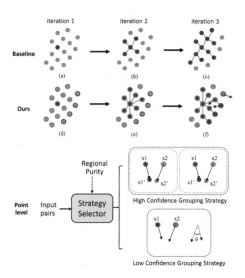

Fig. 4. Illustration of clustering algorithm grouping strategy (Color figure online)

In our method, points are not treated equally. On point-level, before grouping of each pair, we check the regional purity prediction of the seed point and target point (represented by the outline color of points in $(d)(e)(f)$). Based on that, strategy selector makes decision to go for high confidence grouping strategy or low confidence grouping strategy, other cases will block and skip. The core idea is to better group the inner part of objects with high purity while isolating instances by utilizing low purity points.

High purity pairs are more likely at inner part of objects and their offset prediction is relatively reliable. Thus we use high confidence strategy by shifting their coordinates to their predicted object centers. Real point cloud data are often holey and inconsistent, which can potentially cause an over-segmentation problem. To reduce the impact, we also make the grouping criteria more tolerable by introducing additional radius Δr_1.

Low confidence grouping strategy is defined towards low purity points. At boundary area, offset prediction is often not reliable, if we use shift coordinates may cause two clusters to be mistakenly merged. To make the grouping more robust, we use the cosine similarity of the direction between their offset vectors as an additional criteria. Here only medium purity points can be used as seed points, because they are geometrically closer to low purity points and comparing the offset vector directions between nearby points has more reference value.

Algorithm 1. Clustering algorithm. N is the number of points. M is the number of clusters found by the algorithm.

Input: clustering radius r;

         clustering additional radius Δr_1 and Δr_2;

         cluster point number threshold N_θ;

         cosine similarity threshold ϕ;

         coordinates $\mathbf{X} = \{x_1, x_2, ..., x_N\} \in \mathbb{R}^{N \times 3}$

         offset $\mathbf{D} = \{d_1, d_2, ..., d_N\} \in \mathbb{R}^{N \times 3}$; and

         semantic labels $\mathbf{S} = \{s_1, ..., s_N\} \in \mathbb{R}^{N}$.

         regional purity labels $\mathbf{P} = \{p_1, ..., p_N\} \in \mathbb{R}^{N}$.

Output: clusters $\mathbf{C} = \{C_1, ..., C_M\}$.

1:   initialize an array v (visited) of length N with all zeros

2:   initialize an empty cluster set $\mathbf{C}$

3:   **for** $i = 1$ to N **do**

4:      **if** s_i is a background class **then**

5:         $v_i = 1$

6:   **for** $i = 1$ to N **do**

7:      **if** $v_i == 0$ **then**

8:         **if** $p_i == 1$ **then**

9:            initialize an empty queue Q

10:        initialize an empty cluster C

11:        $v_i = 1$; Q.enqueue(i); add i to C

12:      **while** Q is not empty **do**

13:        $k = Q$.dequeue()

14:        **for** $j \in [1, N]$ **do**

15:          **if** $s_j == s_k$ and $v_j == 0$ **then**

16:            ▶high confidence grouping strategy

17:            **if** $p_i == 1$ and $p_j\ != 2$ **then**

18:              $r\prime \leftarrow r + \Delta r_1$

19:              $x_j\prime \leftarrow x_j + d_j$

20:              $x_k\prime \leftarrow x_k + d_k$

21:              **if** $||x_j\prime - x_k\prime||_2 < r\prime$ **then**

22:                 $v_j = 1$

23:                 Q.enqueue(j);add j to C

24:            ▶low confidence grouping strategy

25:            **if** $p_i == 0$ and $p_j == 2$ **then**

26:              $r\prime = r + \Delta r_2$

27:              **if** $||x_j\prime - x_k\prime||_2 < r\prime$ **then**

28:                 $cos\theta(d_j, d_k) = \frac{d_j}{||d_j||} * \frac{d_k}{||d_k||}$

29:                 **if** $cos\theta < \phi$ **then**

30:                    $v_j = 1$

31:                    Q.enqueue(j);add j to C

32:       **if** number of points in $C > N_\theta$ **then**

33:         add C to $\mathbf{C}$

34: **return C**

Our algorithm only takes one set of points as input. Since each point can only be visited once, there will be no overlapping clusters. Thus non-maximum-suppression (NMS) [14] is not needed as a post-processing step.

4 Experiment

In this section, we evaluate our method on created toy dataset and public dataset of ScanNet v2 [7] and S3DIS [1] to show the effectiveness of our approach.

Table 1. Evaluation of regional purity prediction at different scales on toy dataset validation set.

Radius	0.2m		0.3m	
Purity label	High	Low	High	Low
Precision	97.4	88.5	95.1	89.2
Recall	99.0	86.4	98.7	88.2
$F1$ score	98.2	87.4	96.9	88.7
IoU	96.5	77.7	93.9	79.6

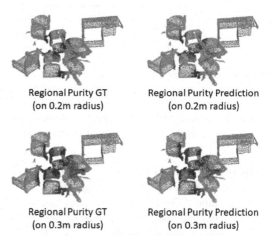

Regional Purity GT
(on 0.2m radius)

Regional Purity Prediction
(on 0.2m radius)

Regional Purity GT
(on 0.3m radius)

Regional Purity Prediction
(on 0.3m radius)

Fig. 5. Visualization of regional purity prediction at different scales on toy dataset validation set. (Color figure online)

4.1 Evaluation on Random Scene Toy Dataset

Toy scenes are randomly generated by our introduced assembly method and split into training set and validation set at a ratio of 4:1. The network takes coordinates with RGB color information of points as input and predicts regional purity at point-level.

We evaluate on two different scales of regional purity on 0.2 m and 0.3 m searching radius, with same 95% and 80% criteria for label generation. The results in Table 1 and Fig. 5 show that our network is able to learn the contextual information of defined regional purity. For regional purity, green color represents high purity with $id1$, red color represents low purity with $id2$, yellow color represents medium purity with $id0$.

4.2 Evaluation on ScanNet Dataset

To demonstrate the effectiveness of our approach, we conduct experiments on ScanNet dataset [7]. It is a popular point cloud dataset containing 1513 real-world indoor scenes. The 3D meshed data are annotated with point-level semantic label and instance label.

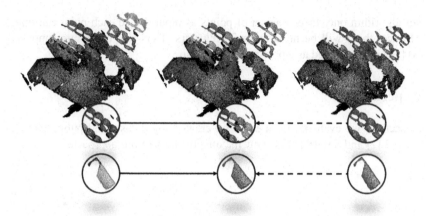

Fig. 6. Result analysis on ScanNet validation set. From left to right: (1) instance prediction by baseline algorithm without regional purity (2) instance prediction by regional purity guided clustering algorithm (3) regional purity prediction (red color area represents low regional purity, green color area represents high regional purity). This shows that using regional purity information can simultaneously resolve under-segmentation and over-segmentation problem. (Color figure online)

Implementation Details. We use Adam solver for optimization with an initial learning rate of 0.001. At pretraining stage, the network takes 10k randomly generated toy scenes as input. The backbone network are initially frozen when transferring to real dataset. After the last two linear layers are well trained, we unfreeze whole network and continue to train it until convergence. The training takes 4–5 days on a single GPU.

Table 2. 3D instance segmentation results on ScanNet v2 [7] on 18 classes.

mAP@0.25	bath	bed	bkshf	cab	chair	cntr	curt	desk	door	ofurn	pic	fridg	showr	sink	sofa	tabl	toil	wind	avg
SGPN [36]	90.3	8.1	0.8	23.3	17.5	28.0	10.6	15.0	20.3	17.5	48.0	21.8	14.3	54.2	40.4	15.3	39.3	4.9	26.1
3D-BEVIS [8]	66.7	68.7	41.9	13.7	58.7	18.8	23.5	35.9	21.1	9.3	8.0	31.1	57.1	38.2	75.4	30.0	87.4	35.7	40.1
R-PointNet	50.0	65.5	66.1	66.3	76.5	43.2	21.4	61.2	58.4	49.9	20.4	28.6	42.9	65.5	65.0	53.9	95	49.9	54.4
3D-SIS [17]	100	77.3	61.4	50.3	69.1	20.0	41.2	49.8	54.6	31.1	10.3	60.0	85.7	38.2	79.9	44.5	93.8	37.1	55.8
MASC [26]	71.1	80.2	54.0	75.7	77.7	2.9	57.7	58.8	52.1	60.0	43.6	53.4	69.7	61.6	83.8	52.6	98	53.4	61.5
3D-BoNet [39]	100	88.7	83.6	58.7	64.3	55.0	62.0	72.4	52.2	50.1	24.3	51.2	100	75.1	80.7	66.1	90.9	61.2	68.7
PanopticFusion [27]	100	85.2	65.5	61.6	78.8	33.4	76.3	77.1	45.7	55.5	65.2	51.8	85.7	76.5	73.2	63.1	94.4	57.7	69.3
SSEN [42]	100	92.6	78.1	66.1	84.5	59.6	52.9	76.4	65.3	48.9	46.1	50.0	85.9	76.5	87.2	76.1	100	57.7	72.4
MTML [21]	100	99.2	77.9	60.9	74.6	30.8	**86.7**	60.1	60.7	53.9	51.9	55.0	100	82.4	86.9	72.9	100	61.6	73.1
3D-MPA [9]	100	93.3	78.5	**79.4**	83.1	27.9	58.8	69.5	61.6	55.9	55.6	65.0	100	80.9	87.5	69.6	100	60.8	73.7
OccuSeg [13]	100	92.3	78.5	74.5	86.7	55.7	57.8	72.9	67.0	64.4	48.8	57.7	100	79.4	83.0	62.0	**100**	55.0	74.2
PE [41]	100	90.0	86.0	72.8	86.9	40.0	85.7	77.4	56.8	70.1	60.2	64.6	93.3	84.3	**89.0**	69.1	99.7	70.9	77.6
PointGroup [19]	100	90.0	79.8	71.5	86.3	49.3	70.6	**89.5**	56.9	**70.1**	57.6	63.9	100	88	85.1	71.9	99.7	70.9	77.8
SSTNet [25]	100	84	**88.8**	71.7	83.5	**71.7**	68.4	62.7	**72.4**	65.2	**72.7**	60	100	**91.2**	82.2	75.7	100	69.1	78.9
HAIS [6]	100	**99.4**	82	75.9	85.5	55.4	88.2	82.7	61.5	67.6	63.8	64.6	100	**91.2**	79.7	**76.7**	99.4	**72.6**	80.3
RPGN (ours)	**100**	99.2	78.9	72.3	**89.1**	65.0	81	83.2	66.5	69.9	65.8	**70.0**	**100**	88.1	83.2	77.4	99.7	61.3	**80.6**

The results of 3D instance segmentation on ScanNet [7] are presented in Table 2, Table 3 and Fig. 8, which show our predicted regional purity information can be leveraged to improve the performance of instance segmentation.

Table 3. 3D instance segmentation results on ScanNet v2 [7] validation set with on 18 classes.[†] represents using refined semantic prediction via label smoothing.

mAP@0.5	cab	bed	chair	sofa	tabl	door	wind	bkshf	pic	cntr	desk	curt	fridg	showr	toil	sink	bath	ofurn	avg
SegCluster	10.4	11.9	15.5	12.8	12.4	10.1	10.1	10.3	0.0	11.7	10.4	11.4	0.0	13.9	17.2	11.5	14.2	10.5	10.8
MRCNN	11.2	10.6	10.6	11.4	10.8	10.3	0.0	0.0	11.1	10.1	0.0	10.0	12.8	0.0	18.9	13.1	11.8	11.6	9.1
SGPN [36]	10.1	16.4	20.2	20.7	14.7	11.1	11.1	0.0	0.0	10.0	10.3	12.8	0.0	0.0	48.7	16.5	0.0	0.0	11.3
3D-SIS [17]	19.7	37.7	40.5	31.9	15.9	18.1	0.0	11.0	0.0	0.0	10.5	11.1	18.5	24.0	45.8	15.8	23.5	12.9	18.7
MTML [21]	14.5	54.0	79.2	48.8	42.7	32.4	32.7	21.9	10.9	0.8	14.2	39.9	42.1	64.3	96.5	36.4	70.8	21.5	40.2
PointGroup [19]	48.1	69.6	87.7	**71.5**	62.9	42.0	46.2	54.9	37.7	22.4	41.6	44.9	37.2	64.4	98.3	**61.1**	80.5	53.0	56.9
3D-MPA [9]	51.9	72.2	83.8	66.8	63.0	43.0	44.5	58.4	38.8	**31.1**	43.2	47.7	61.4	80.6	99.2	50.6	**87.1**	40.3	59.1
RPGN (ours)	50.9	76.6	92.1	62.6	70.6	47.2	52.1	59.8	41.7	17.6	45.7	**51.9**	63.3	**91.5**	100	42.7	**87.1**	61.4	61.9
RPGN† (ours)	**57.3**	75	**92.6**	63.6	**71.9**	**49.8**	**56.4**	**62.6**	**46.6**	22.1	**54.8**	51.2	**65.3**	90.0	100	48.0	83.9	**64.3**	**64.2**

Discussion. In Fig. 6, we compare the instance segmentation results before and after adding the regional purity prediction into the algorithm. In case 1, four chairs are wrongly grouped into one cluster. By using our well predicted regional purity information, the clustering algorithm can successfully separate them into different clusters. In case 2, the table is predicted as two instances due to the inaccuracy in offset prediction. Since all points on the table have high purity label, we give more tolerance for grouping them into one piece.

4.3 Evaluation on S3DIS Dataset

To study the generalizability of our pretrained model, we also evaluate our proposed RPGN model on S3DIS dataset [1]. The dataset has 272 scenes under six large-scale indoor areas. Different from ScanNet [7], all 13 classes including background are annotated as instances and require prediction. Following previous methods, we use the mean precision (mPre) and mean recall (mRec) with an IoU threshold of 0.5 as evaluation metric. We report results on both Area 5 and 6-fold cross validation over six areas in Table 4. Using pretrained model reduces overfitting on small dataset and dramatically boost the performance (Fig. 7).

Table 4. 3D instance segmentation results on S3DIS dataset [1]

	Area 5		6-fold	
	mPrec	mRec	mPrec	mRec
ASIS [37]	55.3	42.4	63.6	47.5
PointGroup [19]	61.9	62.1	69.6	69.2
OccuSeg [13]	-	-	72.8	60.3
SSTNet [25]	65	64.2	73.5	**73.4**
HAIS [6]	**71.1**	**65.0**	73.2	69.4
RPGN (ours)	64.0	63.0	**84.5**	70.5

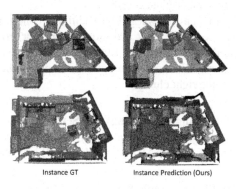

Instance GT   Instance Prediction (Ours)

Fig. 7. Instance segmentation result on S3DIS dataset [1].

5   Ablation Study

To evaluate the effectiveness of each component in proposed method, we conduct ablation studies on the validation set of ScanNet dataset in Table 5.

Table 5. Ablation results of instance segmentation task for clustering algorithm on ScanNet v2 [7] validation set

	High purity	Low purity	Offset	Direction	mAP	mAP@0.5
Baseline	×	×	×	×	0.284	0.508
(a)	✓	×	×	×	0.294	0.518
(b)	✓	✓	×	×	0.322	0.545
(c)	✓	✓	✓	×	0.352	0.572
(d)	✓	✓	✓	✓	0.359	0.582

Ablation on Clustering Algorithm. To analysis our proposed clustering algorithm, we use mentioned baseline algorithm and step-by-step add our components onto it.

In step (a), we utilize high purity points by allowing an additional Δr_1 radius when grouping other high purity points. We argue that regions with high purity prediction should be safer to group other nearby points. By bringing additional tolerance, high purity points can help to step over the gaps inside objects.

In step (b), we define low purity points can only be grouped by medium purity points within $(r + \Delta r_2)$ radius on original coordinates and cannot group any other points. This constrains the grouping direction to be regional purity guided, only from high to low. Allowing inverse direction grouping can potentially cause different instances to be connected. Our soft barrier formed by low purity points can help to prevent such cases.

In step (c), predicted offset feature is used for high purity points to be better grouped. Note that we only shift high purity points to their predicted instance center. We argue that points with low purity labels can hardly predict accurate offset to their center, since they are more likely on the boundary. Therefore, grouping low purity points only considers the original coordinates.

In step (d), we add an additional condition to compare the angle of offset vector between seed point and target point. The grouping is only proceeded if their cosine similarity is above 0.8. Even though we have low confidence in their predicted instance centers to be precise, rough directions still have value for assigning low purity points into the right clusters.

Pretraining vs Training from Scratch. We compare two training strategies for the network to predict regional purity. The proposed pre-training strategy brings an improvement of 3.8% mAP on ScanNet v2 [7] validation set.

Dual Set vs Single Set. The previous work [19] uses two sets of points for proposal generation and filter out duplicated cases by a scoring network and Non-Maximum Suppression (NMS). In this work, we make rational use of predicted information. Our clustering algorithm can directly generate high-quality proposals and get rid of NMS.

Ground-truth   Prediction

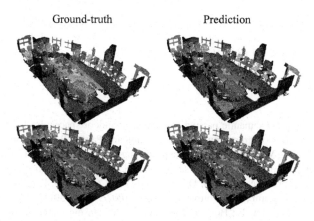

Fig. 8. Qualitative results of instance segmentation and regional purity prediction on ScanNet v2 [7] validation set.

Runtime Analysis. In Table 6, we compare the processing time on full validation set of ScanNet (312 scenes) with other methods according to [13, 39]. In general, the inference time of our network for a single scene with 20k points is around 0.3 s.

Table 6. Total processing time (in seconds) on the validation set of ScanNet v2 [7]

	Total processing time
SGPN [36]	49433
ASIS [37]	56757
3D-SIS [17]	38841
GSPN [40]	3963
3D-BoNet [39]	2871
OccuSeg [13]	594
PointGroup [19]	141
HAIS [6]	128
RPGN (ours)	**89**

6   Conclusion

In this paper, we have presented our defined regional purity concept and its learning strategy with the random scene toy dataset generation and pretraining scheme. Predicted regional purity can be used to guide the clustering process for 3D instance segmentation. Without performing object detection tasks, we use regional purity area to approximate object boundaries in a more flexible and robust form.

Acknowledgements. This research is supported under the RIE2020 Industry Alignment Fund - Industry Collaboration Projects (IAF-ICP) Funding Initiative, as well as cash and in-kind contribution from the industry partner(s). This research is also supported by the National Research

Foundation, Singapore under its AI Singapore Programme (AISG Award No: AISG-RP-2018-003), the Ministry of Education, Singapore, under its Academic Research Fund Tier 2 (MOE-T2EP20220-0007) and Tier 1 (RG95/20).

References

1. Armeni, I., et al.: 3D semantic parsing of large-scale indoor spaces. In: Proceedings of the IEEE International Conference on Computer Vision and Pattern Recognition (2016)
2. Bello, S.A., Yu, S., Wang, C.: Review: deep learning on 3D point clouds (2020)
3. Bertels, J., et al.: Optimizing the dice score and Jaccard index for medical image segmentation: theory and practice. In: Shen, D., et al. (eds.) MICCAI 2019. LNCS, vol. 11765, pp. 92–100. Springer, Cham (2019). https://doi.org/10.1007/978-3-030-32245-8_11
4. Bokhovkin, A., Burnaev, E.: Boundary loss for remote sensing imagery semantic segmentation. In: Lu, H., Tang, H., Wang, Z. (eds.) ISNN 2019. LNCS, vol. 11555, pp. 388–401. Springer, Cham (2019). https://doi.org/10.1007/978-3-030-22808-8_38
5. Brabandere, B.D., Neven, D., Gool, L.V.: Semantic instance segmentation with a discriminative loss function (2017)
6. Chen, S., Fang, J., Zhang, Q., Liu, W., Wang, X.: Hierarchical aggregation for 3D instance segmentation. In: Proceedings of the IEEE/CVF International Conference on Computer Vision (ICCV), pp. 15467–15476, October 2021
7. Dai, A., Chang, A.X., Savva, M., Halber, M., Funkhouser, T., Nießner, M.: ScanNet: richly-annotated 3D reconstructions of indoor scenes. In: Proceedings of Computer Vision and Pattern Recognition (CVPR). IEEE (2017)
8. Elich, C., Engelmann, F., Kontogianni, T., Leibe, B.: 3D bird's-eye-view instance segmentation. Pattern Recogn. 48–61 (2019). https://doi.org/10.1007/978-3-030-33676-9_4. http://dx.doi.org/10.1007/978-3-030-33676-9_4
9. Engelmann, F., Bokeloh, M., Fathi, A., Leibe, B., Nießner, M.: 3D-MPA: multi proposal aggregation for 3D semantic instance segmentation (2020)
10. Gojcic, Z., Zhou, C., Wegner, J.D., Guibas, L.J., Birdal, T.: Learning multiview 3D point cloud registration. In: IEEE/CVF Conference on Computer Vision and Pattern Recognition (CVPR), June 2020
11. Goodfellow, I., Bengio, Y., Courville, A.: Deep Learning. MIT Press (2016). http://www.deeplearningbook.org
12. Graham, B., van der Maaten, L.: Submanifold sparse convolutional networks. CoRR abs/1706.01307 (2017)
13. Han, L., Zheng, T., Xu, L., Fang, L.: OccuSeg: occupancy-aware 3D instance segmentation (2020)
14. Hosang, J., Benenson, R., Schiele, B.: Learning non-maximum suppression (2017)
15. Jadon, S.: A survey of loss functions for semantic segmentation (2020)
16. Jaritz, M., Gu, J.Y., Su, H.: Multi-view PointNet for 3D scene understanding. arXiv abs/1909.13603 (2019)
17. Ji, H., Dai, A., Nießner, M.: 3D-SIS: 3D semantic instance segmentation of RGB-D scans. In: Proceedings of Computer Vision and Pattern Recognition (CVPR). IEEE (2019)
18. Jiang, H., Yan, F., Cai, J., Zheng, J., Xiao, J.: End-to-end 3D point cloud instance segmentation without detection. In: Proceedings of the IEEE/CVF Conference on Computer Vision and Pattern Recognition (CVPR), June 2020
19. Jiang, L., Zhao, H., Shi, S., Liu, S., Fu, C.W., Jia, J.: Pointgroup: dual-set point grouping for 3D instance segmentation (2020)

20. Kervadec, H., Bouchtiba, J., Desrosiers, C., Granger, E., Dolz, J., Ben Ayed, I.: Boundary loss for highly unbalanced segmentation. In: Proceedings of Machine Learning Research, London, UK, 08–10 July 2019, vol. 102, pp. 285–296. PMLR (2019). http://proceedings.mlr.press/v102/kervadec19a.html

21. Lahoud, J., Ghanem, B., Pollefeys, M., Oswald, M.R.: 3D instance segmentation via multi-task metric learning (2019)

22. Li, L., Zhu, S., Fu, H., Tan, P., Tai, C.L.: End-to-end learning local multi-view descriptors for 3D point clouds. In: IEEE/CVF Conference on Computer Vision and Pattern Recognition (CVPR), June 2020

23. Li, Y., Bu, R., Sun, M., Wu, W., Di, X., Chen, B.: PointCNN: convolution on x-transformed points. In: NeurIPS, pp. 820–830. Curran Associates, Inc. (2018)

24. Liang, Z., Yang, M., Wang, C.: 3D graph embedding learning with a structure-aware loss function for point cloud semantic instance segmentation. IEEE Robot. Autom. Lett. **5**(3), 4915–4922 (2019)

25. Liang, Z., Li, Z., Xu, S., Tan, M., Jia, K.: Instance segmentation in 3D scenes using semantic superpoint tree networks. In: Proceedings of the IEEE/CVF International Conference on Computer Vision (ICCV), pp. 2783–2792, October 2021

26. Liu, C., Furukawa, Y.: MASC: multi-scale affinity with sparse convolution for 3D instance segmentation. CoRR (2019)

27. Narita, G., Seno, T., Ishikawa, T., Kaji, Y.: PanopticFusion: online volumetric semantic mapping at the level of stuff and things (2019)

28. Pham, Q.H., Nguyen, T., Hua, B.S., Roig, G., Yeung, S.K.: JSIS3D: joint semantic-instance segmentation of 3D point clouds with multi-task pointwise networks and multi-value conditional random fields. In: The IEEE Conference on Computer Vision and Pattern Recognition (CVPR) (2019)

29. Qi, C.R., Chen, X., Litany, O., Guibas, L.J.: ImVoteNet: boosting 3D object detection in point clouds with image votes. In: IEEE/CVF Conference on Computer Vision and Pattern Recognition (CVPR), June 2020

30. Qi, C.R., Litany, O., He, K., Guibas, L.J.: Deep hough voting for 3D object detection in point clouds. In: Proceedings of the IEEE International Conference on Computer Vision (2019)

31. Qi, C.R., Su, H., Mo, K., Guibas, L.J.: PointNet: deep learning on point sets for 3D classification and segmentation. In: 2017 IEEE Conference on Computer Vision and Pattern Recognition (CVPR), pp. 77–85 (2016)

32. Qi, C.R., Yi, L., Su, H., Guibas, L.J.: Pointnet++: deep hierarchical feature learning on point sets in a metric space. In: NIPS (2017)

33. Salehi, S.S.M., Erdogmus, D., Gholipour, A.: Tversky loss function for image segmentation using 3D fully convolutional deep networks. In: Wang, Q., Shi, Y., Suk, H.-I., Suzuki, K. (eds.) MLMI 2017. LNCS, vol. 10541, pp. 379–387. Springer, Cham (2017). https://doi.org/10.1007/978-3-319-67389-9_44

34. Shamir, R.R., Duchin, Y., Kim, J., Sapiro, G., Harel, N.: Continuous dice coefficient: a method for evaluating probabilistic segmentations (2019)

35. Thomas, H., Qi, C.R., Deschaud, J.E., Marcotegui, B., Goulette, F., Guibas, L.J.: KPConv: flexible and deformable convolution for point clouds. arXiv abs/1904.08889 (2019)

36. Wang, W., Yu, R., Huang, Q., Neumann, U.: SGPN: similarity group proposal network for 3D point cloud instance segmentation. In: CVPR (2018)

37. Wang, X., Liu, S., Shen, X., Shen, C., Jia, J.: Associatively segmenting instances and semantics in point clouds. In: CVPR (2019)

38. Wu, W., Qi, Z., Fuxin, L.: PointConv: deep convolutional networks on 3D point clouds. arXiv preprint arXiv:1811.07246 (2018)

39. Yang, B., et al.: Learning object bounding boxes for 3D instance segmentation on point clouds (2019)

40. Yi, L., Zhao, W., Wang, H., Sung, M., Guibas, L.: GSPN: generative shape proposal network for 3D instance segmentation in point cloud. arXiv preprint arXiv:1812.03320 (2018)
41. Zhang, B., Wonka, P.: Point cloud instance segmentation using probabilistic embeddings (2019)
42. Zhang, D., Chun, J., Cha, S.K., Kim, Y.M.: Spatial semantic embedding network: fast 3D instance segmentation with deep metric learning (2020)
43. Zhao, H., Jiang, L., Fu, C.W., Jia, J.: PointWeb: enhancing local neighborhood features for point cloud processing. In: CVPR (2019)

Cross-Domain Few-Shot Semantic Segmentation

Shuo Lei[1], Xuchao Zhang[2], Jianfeng He[1], Fanglan Chen[1], Bowen Du[3(✉)], and Chang-Tien Lu[1]

[1] Department of Computer Science, Virginia Tech, Falls Church, VA, USA
[2] NEC Laboratories America, Princeton, NJ, USA
[3] State Key Laboratory of Software Development Environment, Beihang University, Beijing, China
dubowen@buaa.edu.cn

Abstract. Few-shot semantic segmentation aims at learning to segment a novel object class with only a few annotated examples. Most existing methods consider a setting where base classes are sampled from the same domain as the novel classes. However, in many applications, collecting sufficient training data for meta-learning is infeasible or impossible. In this paper, we extend few-shot semantic segmentation to a new task, called Cross-Domain Few-Shot Semantic Segmentation (CD-FSS), which aims to generalize the meta-knowledge from domains with sufficient training labels to low-resource domains. Moreover, a new benchmark for the CD-FSS task is established and characterized by a task difficulty measurement. We evaluate both representative few-shot segmentation methods and transfer learning based methods on the proposed benchmark and find that current few-shot segmentation methods fail to address CD-FSS. To tackle the challenging CD-FSS problem, we propose a novel Pyramid-Anchor-Transformation based few-shot segmentation network (PATNet), in which domain-specific features are transformed into domain-agnostic ones for downstream segmentation modules to fast adapt to unseen domains. Our model outperforms the state-of-the-art few-shot segmentation method in CD-FSS by 8.49% and 10.61% average accuracies in 1-shot and 5-shot, respectively. Code and datasets are available at https://github.com/slei109/PATNet.

Keywords: Few-shot learning · Cross-domain transfer learning · Semantic segmentation

1 Introduction

Deep neural networks for semantic segmentation, such as FCN [26], DeepLab [5] and PSPNet [52], typically require large-scale annotations for training, which is

Supplementary Information The online version contains supplementary material available at https://doi.org/10.1007/978-3-031-20056-4_5.

S. Avidan et al. (Eds.): ECCV 2022, LNCS 13690, pp. 73–90, 2022.
https://doi.org/10.1007/978-3-031-20056-4_5

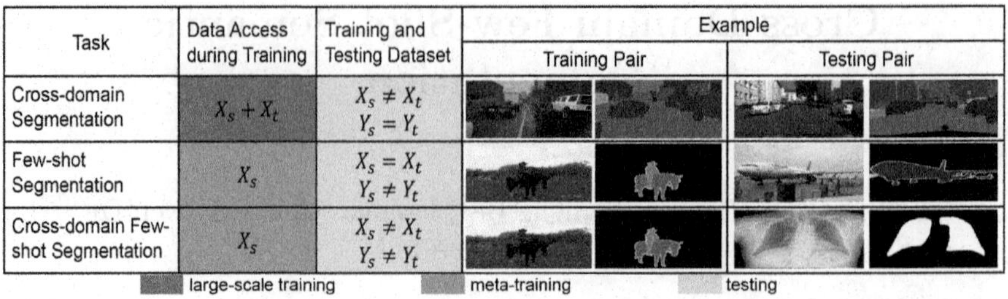

Task	Data Access during Training	Training and Testing Dataset	Example	
			Training Pair	Testing Pair
Cross-domain Segmentation	$X_s + X_t$	$X_s \neq X_t$ $Y_s = Y_t$		
Few-shot Segmentation	X_s	$X_s = X_t$ $Y_s \neq Y_t$		
Cross-domain Few-shot Segmentation	X_s	$X_s \neq X_t$ $Y_s \neq Y_t$		

large-scale training   meta-training   testing

Fig. 1. Differences between the cross-domain few-shot segmentation and existing tasks. X_s and X_t denote the data distribution in the source and target domain, respectively. Y_s represents the source label space and Y_t represents the target label space.

costly to obtain. To reduce such burden on data annotation, *Few-Shot Semantic Segmentation (FSS)* task has been proposed [33], which aims to learn a model that can perform segmentation on novel classes with only a few pixel-level annotated images. Although significant progress has been made in the FSS task [34,45,46,49,50], it is hard to apply existing methods to cross-domain scenarios. Since the methods still require a large number of base class samples for training, it is infeasible for low-resource domains where few training annotations can be obtained. For instance, it is too expensive to collect sufficient satellite images for meta-training purposes, remaining a large obstacle to applying the few-shot segmentation methods directly into the satellite image domain. To tackle the issue, we extend FSS to a new Cross-Domain Few-Shot Segmentation (CD-FSS) task that aims at generalizing the meta-knowledge from domains with sufficient training labels (*e.g.* PASCAL VOC [13]) to low-resource domains.

The conceptual comparisons between the existing tasks and our CD-FSS task are shown in Fig. 1. First, most works on cross-domain semantic segmentation (or domain adaptation for semantic segmentation) focus on the problem setting where the target domain data can be *accessed* during training and share the *same* label space as the source domain. For example, in the first row of Fig. 1, street photo-realistic synthetic images are usually used as training data for real-world urban scene understanding tasks. In contrast, we study the CD-FSS problem, where the source and target domains have completely *disjoint* label space and *cannot* access target domain data during the training stage. Second, the classic few-shot semantic segmentation only focuses on segmenting novel classes sampled from the *same* domain in the training stage. In other words, the input data distributions from source and target domains are the *same* while the label spaces are *disjoint* in the training and testing stages. In contrast, both data distributions and label spaces in the testing stage are *different* from the training stage in the CD-FSS task.

In this paper, we establish a new benchmark for the CD-FSS task to evaluate the cross-domain generalization ability of segmentation models under different domain gaps. It consists of four different domains characterized by domain shifts of different size: FSS-1000 [23], Deepglobe [11], ISIC2018 [10,42], and Chest X-ray datasets [4, 21]. These datasets cover daily objects images, satellite images, dermoscopic images of skin lesions, and X-ray images, respectively. The selected datasets have class diversity and reflect the real-world scenario for few-shot semantic segmentation.

Furthermore, both representative few-shot segmentation methods and transfer learning based methods are evaluated on the proposed benchmark. Experiment results show that: 1) the performances of existing few-shot semantic segmentation methods degrade significantly under large domain shifts. Those methods even underperform the simple transfer learning baselines when the target domain is drastically different from the source domain; 2) meta-learning approaches are more effective than all transfer learning baselines in the setting of limited domain differences.

A major challenge in CD-FSS is that the feature space learned from the source domain cannot be applied to the target domain. Concretely, existing methods learn a support-query matching/comparing model in a single domain and their basic assumption is that the pretrained encoder is powerful enough to embed the image into distinguishable features. However, the backbone only pretrained in the source domain fails in the target domain due to the different data distribution. To address this problem, we propose a novel Pyramid Anchor-based Transformation Module (PATM) to transform the domain-specific features into domain-agnostic ones. Thus, the downstream model can be well adapted to the novel domains by matching domain-agnostic features of support and query sets to make the segmentation. To further refine the predicted mask of the query image, we also propose a Task-adaptive Fine-tuning Inference (TFI) strategy for fast adaptation to unseen domain. In the testing phase, only PATM is updated with the prototype similarity between support images and query predictions to avoid over-fitting in few-shot scenarios. In this way, the predicted mask is refined with the calibrated features produced by the fine-tuned PATM.

Our main contributions are summarized as follows:

- We extend few-shot semantic segmentation to a new task, called Cross-Domain Few-Shot Semantic Segmentation (CD-FSS), which aims to segment a novel object class in *unseen domains* with only *a few* annotated examples.
- A practical evaluation benchmark for CD-FSS is established, consisting of four different domains. We also measure the task difficulty for each domain according to 1) domain shift and 2) discrimination between foreground and background classes.
- We propose a Pyramid Anchor-based Transformation Module (PATM) to transform the domain-specific features into domain-agnostic ones. Downstream segmentation modules can be adapted to unseen domains by learning with domain-agnostic features. A novel Task-adaptive Fine-tuning Inference (TFI) strategy is proposed to refine the prediction in unseen domains.
- We investigate a practical evaluation of few-shot segmentation methods and transfer learning based methods in the proposed benchmark. Results show that current few-shot segmentation methods fail to address CD-FSS and are even inferior to the transfer learning baseline methods when a large domain

gap exists. In contrast, Our model outperforms the state-of-the-art few-shot segmentation method in CD-FSS by 8.49% and 10.61% average accuracies in 1-shot and 5-shot, respectively.

2   Related Work

The prior works related to this paper are summarized below in domain adaptation for semantic segmentation, cross-domain few-shot learning and few-shot semantic segmentation.

Domain Adaptation for Semantic Segmentation. Recent works in domain adaptation for semantic segmentation are mainly divided into two directions. One group of studies aims to learn domain-invariant representations of instances by domain adversarial training [8,9,12,41]. Hoffman et al. [20] combine global and local alignment methods with adversarial training. Similar ideas are also explored using different techniques, such as distillation loss [9], output space alignment [40], class-balanced self-training [54], conservative loss [53], etc. The other group is learning from a pre-defined curriculum [31,51].

However, these methods operate in the setting where the target domain data can be *accessed* during training to drive the model adaptation and compensate for the domain shift. In addition, most existing works exploit photo-realistic synthetic data. Thus, the source and target domain share the *same* label space and still retain a high degree of visual similarity. In contrast, we study the cross-domain few-shot semantic segmentation problem, where the source and target domains have completely *disjoint* label space and *cannot* require target domain data during the training stage. The goal of this work is to learn a task-adaptive few-shot semantic segmentation model under large domain shifts.

Few-Shot Learning. Few-shot learning aims to learn a new concept representation from only a few annotated examples. Most existing works can be categorized into metric learning methods [35,37,44], gradient-based meta learners [14,29], and graph neural network [15,24] based methods. Yoon et al. [47] introduce a reference vector set to construct a linear transformer that performed task-specific null-space projection for classification, which is the theoretical basis of our method. In cross-domain few-shot learning [7,39,43], both data distribution and the label space in the meta-testing stage are different from the meta-training stage. Tseng et al. [43] propose feature-wise transformation layers to improve the generalization of metric-based few-shot classification approaches to unseen domains. Guo et al. [16] propose a harder cross-domain few-shot benchmark (BSCD-FSL), where there is a large shift between base and novel class domains. It covers several target domains with varying similarities to natural images. Our proposed benchmark can be seen as an extension of BSCD-FSL in the few-shot segmentation task to evaluate the cross-domain generalization ability of few-shot segmentation models under different domain shifts.

Few-Shot Semantic Segmentation. In contrast to the domain adaptation for semantic segmentation, few-shot semantic segmentation has no access to the target domain during training stage. It aims at segmenting novel semantic objects in an image with only a few densely annotated examples. Based on the optimized module in the meta-training process, existing works can be divided into two groups, metric-based and relation-based methods. Specifically, metric-based methods (e.g. PANet [45] and AMP [34]) adopt non-parametric decoder and aim to train the encoder to construct a consistent metric space. In contrast, relation-based methods (e.g. CaNet [49], RPMM [46], PGNet [48], PFENet [38] and HSNet [27]) freeze the pre-trained encoder during training process and train a decoder to compare the support and query samples. In other words, metric-based methods focus on separating foreground and background classes in each task, while relation-based methods focus on recognizing the foreground classes based on the pre-trained features. RePRI [3] foregoes meta-learning and adopts a transductive inference with a feature extraction trained on the base classes. However, these methods only focus on segmenting novel classes sampled from the same domain. They fail to generalize to unseen domains due to large discrepancy of the feature distribution across domains.

3   Benchmark

The proposed benchmark for CD-FSS consists of four datasets characterized by domain shifts of different sizes. The proposed benchmark includes images and pixel-level annotations from FSS-1000 [23], Deepglobe [11], ISIC2018 [10, 42], and Chest X-ray datasets [4,21]. As shown in Fig. 2, These datasets cover daily objects images, satellite images, dermoscopic images of skin lesions, and X-ray images, respectively. The selected datasets have class diversity and reflect the real-world scenario for few-shot semantic segmentation tasks. To provide a better overview, in Table 1, the task difficulty for each domain is measured from two aspects: 1) domain shift (cross the datasets) and 2) class distinction in a single image (within the dataset). Fréchet Inception Distance (FID) [19] is adopted to measure the domain shift [1] of these four datasets with respect to the PASCAL [13]. Since the discrimination between classes in a single image has an important impact on the segmentation task, we measure the similarity between foreground and background classes using KL-divergence. For more details, please refer to the supplementary material.

FSS-1000 [23] is a natural image dataset for few-shot segmentation, consisting of 1,000 object classes and each class has 10 samples. The official split for semantic segmentation is used in our experiment. We report the results on the official testing set, which contains 240 classes and 2,400 testing images.

Deepglobe [11] is a satellite image dataset. Each image is densely annotated at pixel-level with 7 categories: areas of urban, agriculture, rangeland, forest, water, barren, and unknown. As the ground-truth label is only available in the training set, thus we adopt the official training set to report the results, which contains 803 images. The images have a fixed spatial resolution of 2448 × 2448 pixels. To increase the number of testing images and reduce the size of images, we cut each image into 6 pieces. As the categories labeled in this dataset have no

Table 1. Conceptual difference between PAS-CAL and the four cross-domain datasets. The domain shift and class distinction in a single image is measured by FID and DisFB, respectively.

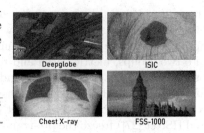

Dataset	Perspective distortion	Natural content	Color depth	FID	DisFB
Deepglobe	×	×	3	213.58	0.143
ISIC	×	×	3	275.28	0.187
Chest X-ray	×	×	1	316.56	0.126
FSS-1000	✓	✓	3	238.41	0.112

Fig. 2. Example of segmentation in the benchmark.

regular shape, the cutting operation has little effect on the segmentation. After filtering the single class images and the 'unknown' class, we get 5,666 images to report the results and each image has 408 × 408 pixels.

ISIC2018 [10,42] is a dataset on lesion images, consisting of skin cancer screening samples. Every lesion image contains exactly one primary lesion. As the ground-truth label is only available in the training set, thus we report the results on the official training set, containing 2,596 images. The images have a spatial resolution around 1022 × 767. As a common practice we down-size the images to 512 × 512 pixels.

Chest X-ray [4,21] is an X-ray image dataset for Tuberculosis. It includes 566 images with a resolution of 4020 × 4892, which are collected from 58 cases with a manifestation of Tuberculosis and 80 normal cases. Due to the large size of image, we down-size the images to 1024 × 1024 pixels as a common practice.

4   Problem Setting

The cross-domain few-shot semantic segmentation (CD-FSS) problem can be formalized as follows. We have a source domain $(\mathcal{X}_s, \mathcal{Y}_s)$ and a target domain $(\mathcal{X}_t, \mathcal{Y}_t)$, where $\mathcal{X}$ is the input data distribution and $\mathcal{Y}$ is the label space. In CD-FSS, the input data distribution in source domains $\mathcal{X}_s$ is different from target domains and the label space in source domains has no overlap with target domains $\mathcal{X}_t$, i.e., $\mathcal{X}_s \neq \mathcal{X}_t$, $\mathcal{Y}_s \cap \mathcal{Y}_t = \emptyset$.

Suppose that the model is trained on the source domain, CD-FSS aims to use the trained model to perform segmentation on the novel classes in the target domain with only a few annotated images per class. The training set $\mathcal{D}_{train}$ is constructed from $(\mathcal{X}_s, \mathcal{Y}_s)$ and the testing set $\mathcal{D}_{test}$ is constructed from $(\mathcal{X}_t, \mathcal{Y}_t)$. We align training and testing with the episodic paradigm [44] to handle the few-shot scenario. Specifically, given a N-way K-shot learning task, both the training set $\mathcal{D}_{train}$ and testing set $\mathcal{D}_{test}$ consist of several episodes. Each episode is constructed by 1) a support set $\mathcal{S} = \{(\mathbf{I}_i^s, \mathbf{M}_i^s)\}_{i=1}^{N \times K}$ and 2) a query set $\mathcal{Q} = \{(\mathbf{I}_i^q, \mathbf{M}_i^q)\}_{i=1}^{Q}$, where $\mathbf{I}$ is an image, $\mathbf{M}$ is a corresponding mask and Q is the number of query samples. Note that the model is trained on $\mathcal{D}_{train}$ from the

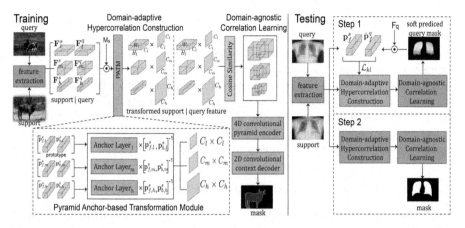

Fig. 3. Overview of our method in a 1-way 1-shot example. After obtaining the pyramid features of support and query images, PATM is introduced to transform the domain-specific hypercorrelations into domain-agnostic ones by producing linear transformation matrices. Then, the transformed features are fed into Domain-agnostic Correlation Learning part for the final query segmentation mask prediction. In the testing phase, the anchor layers are fine-tuned with the foreground prototype similarity between support and query predictions. Yellow parts are trainable and blue parts are frozen. (Color figure online)

source domain and has *no access* to the target domain data. During the testing (or meta-testing) process, the model is presented with a support set and a query set from the target domain is used to evaluate the model performance.

5   Model

The main challenge in CD-FSS is to reduce the performance degradation brought by domain shifts. Previous works focus on learning a support-query matching model and their basic assumption is that the pretrained encoder is powerful enough to embed the image into distinguishable features for the downstream matching model. However, the backbone only pretrained in the source domain fails in the target domain, especially under the large domain gap, like daily life object images to X-ray images. To address the problem, our model learns to transform the domain-specific features into domain-agnostic ones. In this way, the downstream model can be well adapted to the novel domain by matching domain-agnostic features of support and query sets to make the segmentation.

As shown in Fig. 3, our method consists of three major parts, feature extraction backbone, domain-adaptive hypercorrelation construction and domain-agnostic correlation learning. Given support and query images, we first extract all the intermediate features with feature extractor. Then, we introduce a particularly novel module in the Domain-adaptive Hypercorrelation Construction part, dubbed Pyramid Anchor-based Transformation Module (PATM), to transform the domain-specific features into domain-agnostic ones. Next, we compute multi-level correlation maps with all transformed feature maps to feed into Domain-agnostic Correlation Learning part. Two off-the-shelf modules, 4D convolutional pyramid encoder and 2D convolutional context decoder [27], are adopted to produce the prediction mask in a coarse-to-fine manner with efficient 4D convolutions. In the testing phase, we also propose a Task-adaptive Fine-tuning Inference (TFI) strategy to encourage the model to fast adapt to the target domain by fine-tuning PATM with $\mathcal{L}_{kl}$ loss, which measures the foreground prototype similarity between support and query predictions.

5.1   Pyramid Anchor-Based Transformation Module

The core idea of Pyramid Anchor-based Transformation Module (PATM) aims at learning pyramid anchor layers to transform the domain-specific features into domain-agnostic ones. Intuitively, if we can find a transformer to transform the domain-specific features into a domain-agnostic metric space, it will reduce the detrimental effects brought by the domain drift. Since the domain-agnostic metric space is constant, it will be much easier for the downstream segmentation modules to make predictions in such a stable space.

Ideally, features belonging to the same class will produce similar results when they are transformed in the same way. Thus, if we transform the support features to the corresponding anchor points in the domain-agnostic space, then by using the same transformation, we can also make query features belonging to the same class transform close to the anchor points in the domain-agnostic space. Inspired by TAFT module [32], we adopt a linear transformation matrix as the transformation mapper since it introduces fewer learnable parameters. As shown in Fig. 3, we use the anchor layer and the prototype set of the support image to compute the transformation matrix. Let $\mathbf{A}$ represent the weight matrix of the anchor layer and $\mathbf{P}$ denote the prototype matrix of the support image. We construct the transformation matrix $\mathbf{W}$ by finding a matrix such that $\mathbf{WP} = \mathbf{A}$.

Specifically, for an 1-way 1-shot task, once the intermediate feature maps in L layers of the support image, $\{\mathbf{F}_l^s\}_{l=1}^L$, are obtained, we can calculate the foreground prototype of each feature map $\mathbf{F}_l^s \in \mathbb{R}^{C_l \times H_l \times W_l}$ with the support mask $\mathbf{M}^s \in \{0,1\}^{H \times W}$ via masked average pooling, i.e. $\mathbf{p}_{f,l}^s = \frac{\sum_i \mathbf{F}_{l,i}^s \zeta_l(\mathbf{M}^s)_i}{\sum_i \zeta_l(\mathbf{M}^s)_i}$, where $\mathbf{p}_{f,l}^s \in \mathbb{R}^{C_l}$ and i is 2D spatial positions of the feature map. $\zeta_l(\cdot)$ denotes a function that bilinearly interpolates input tensor to the spatial size of the feature map $\mathbf{F}_l^s$ at intermediate layer l by expanding along channel dimension, $\zeta_l : \mathbb{R}^{H \times W} \rightarrow \mathbb{R}^{C_l \times H_l \times W_l}$. Similarly, the background prototype $\mathbf{p}_{b,l}^s$ for $\mathbf{F}_l^s$ can be obtained in the same way and the prototype matrix $\mathbf{P}_l^s$ is defined as $[\frac{\mathbf{p}_{f,l}^s}{\|\mathbf{p}_{f,l}^s\|}, \frac{\mathbf{p}_{b,l}^s}{\|\mathbf{p}_{b,l}^s\|}]$. Accordingly, the anchor weight matrix $\mathbf{A}_l$ is defined as $[\frac{\mathbf{a}_{f,l}}{\|\mathbf{a}_{f,l}\|}, \frac{\mathbf{a}_{b,l}}{\|\mathbf{a}_{b,l}\|}]$, where $\mathbf{a}_{\cdot,l} \in \mathbb{R}^{C_l}$. In general, $\mathbf{P}_l^s$ is a non-square matrix and we can calculate its generalized inverse [2] with $\mathbf{P}_l^{s+} = \{\mathbf{P}_l^{sT} \mathbf{P}_l^s\}^{-1} \mathbf{P}_l^{sT}$. Thus, the transformation matrix at intermediate layer l is computed as $\mathbf{W}_l = \mathbf{A}_l \mathbf{P}_l^{s+}$, where $\mathbf{W}_l \in \mathbb{R}^{C_l \times C_l}$.

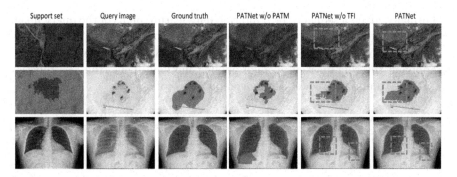

Fig. 4. Visual comparison results of several 1-shot tasks. For each task, the first three columns show the ground truth of support and query sets. The next two columns represent the prediction mask without anchor layers and the prediction mask without fine-tuning, respectively. The last column shows the final predicted segmentation after fine-tuning with $\mathcal{L}_{kl}$. Best viewed in colors.

For the subsequent hypercorrelation construction, a pair of transformed query and masked support features $\hat{\mathbf{F}}_l^s$ at each layer forms a 4D correlation tensor $\mathbf{C}_l \in \mathbb{R}^{H_l \times W_l \times H_l \times W_l}$ using cosine similarity:

$$\mathbf{C}_l(i,j) = \mathrm{ReLU}\left(\frac{\mathbf{W}_l\mathbf{F}_l^q(i) \cdot \mathbf{W}_l\hat{\mathbf{F}}_l^s(j)}{\parallel \mathbf{W}_l\mathbf{F}_l^q(i) \parallel \parallel \mathbf{W}_l\hat{\mathbf{F}}_l^s(j) \parallel}\right) \tag{1}$$

where i and j denote 2D spatial positions of $\mathbf{F}_l^q$ and $\hat{\mathbf{F}}_l^s$, respectively.

To avoid adding too many learnable parameters, we set three anchor layers for low-, medium- and high-level feature maps respectively. Note that only three anchor layers are introduced for different feature dimensions. Even though feature maps with the same dimension share one anchor layer, each of them still can obtain its unique transformation matrix with its own prototype set.

5.2   Task-Adaptive Fine-Tuning Inference

To further refine the prediction mask of query images, we propose a Task-adaptive Fine-tuning Inference (TFI) strategy for fast adaptation to unseen domains in the testing phase. The motivation is that if the model can predict a good segmentation mask for the query image, the foreground class prototype of the segmented query image should be similar to that of the support set. Different from optimizing all parameters in the model, we only fine-tune the anchor layers to avoid overfitting in few-shot scenarios. Figure 3 shows the pipeline of the strategy. In the testing phase, during step 1, only anchor layers are updated accordingly using the proposed $\mathcal{L}_{kl}$, which measures the similarity between the foreground class prototype of support and query sets. In step 2, all layers in the model are frozen and make the final prediction for query images. In this way, the model is encouraged to fast adapt to the target domain and the predicted mask is refined with calibrated features produced by fine-tuned anchor layers.

Formally, given a sequence of L intermediate feature maps of the query image $\{\mathbf{F}_l^q\}_{l=1}^L$ and its predicted probability map $\hat{\mathbf{M}}$, we compute the foreground class prototype of the query image at layer l with the probability map $\hat{\mathbf{M}}_l = \zeta_l(\hat{\mathbf{M}})$ by applying the soft masked average pooling method. Thus, the loss function $\mathcal{L}_{kl}$ for fine-tuning the model can be computed as follows:

$$\mathcal{L}_{kl} = \sum_{l=1}^L D_{KL}(\mathbf{p}_{f,l}^s \| \hat{\mathbf{p}}_{f,l}^q), \text{ where } \hat{\mathbf{p}}_{f,l}^q = \frac{\sum_i \mathbf{F}_{l,i}^q \hat{\mathbf{M}}_{l,i} \mathbb{1}[\hat{\mathbf{M}}_{l,i} \geq \tau]}{\sum_i \hat{\mathbf{M}}_{l,i}} \tag{2}$$

Here, $D_{KL}(\cdot)$ denotes the Kullback-Leibler divergence loss function and i denotes 2D spatial positions of the feature map. $\mathbb{1}(\cdot)$ is an indicator function to extract the binary predicted mask from $\hat{\mathbf{M}}_l$, outputting value 1 if the argument is true or 0 otherwise. Pixels will be predicted as the foreground class if their values are larger than threshold τ. We set $\tau = 0.5$ in our experiments.

6 Experiment

6.1 Evaluation Setup

Datasets. We use PASCAL VOC 2012 [13] with SBD [17] augmentation as training domain and then evaluate the trained models on the proposed benchmark introduced in Sect. 3.

Baseline. To evaluate the performance of existing few-shot semantic segmentation models on CD-FSS, we adopt eight representative few-shot segmentation models: AMP [34], CaNet [49], PANet [45], RPMMs [46], PGNet [48], PFENet [38], RePRI [3] and HSNet [27]. We use the publicly available codes and follow the default training configuration of these models. For CaNet [49] method, we iteratively optimize the predicted results for 4 times after the initial prediction at inference time, which is same as their recommended settings. For a fair comparison, we also adopt ResNet-50 [18] as a feature extractor in PANet [45] to be our baseline model, denoted as PANet*. An alternative way to tackle CD-FSS is based on transfer learning, where an initial model is trained on the source dataset in a standard supervised learning way and reused on the novel datasets. We adapt the FCN [26] and DeeplabV3 [6] to serve as baselines by fine-tuning their last k layers on the support set, denoted as "Ft-last-k.". For example, "Ft-last-1$_{FCN}$" represents the performance of fine-tuning the last-1 (fc-8) fully connected layers of FCN-32s pretrained on PASCAL VOC. In addition, the trained segmentation networks followed by the base classifier are also evaluated on the benchmark. The base classifier is trained to map dense features from the support set to their corresponding labels and uses it to generate the predicted mask in the query set. We experimented with various classifiers including 1-NN and logistic regression. For more details, please refer to the supplementary materials.

Training and Testing Strategy. We meta-train all methods on all the classes of PASCAL VOC with SBD augmentation and meta-test the trained models on each dataset of the proposed benchmark. For each evaluation, we average the mean-IoU of 5 runs [44] with different random seeds. Each run contains 1200 tasks for all datasets except FSS-1000. FSS-1000 has 2400 tasks in each run, which is the same as the setting in [23,27].

6.2 Evaluation Metric

Mean intersection over-union (mIoU), which is defined as the mean IoUs of all image categories, was employed as the metric for performance evaluation. For each category, the IoU is calculated by $IoU = \frac{TP}{TP+FP+FN}$, where TP, FP and FN respectively denote the number of true positive, false positive and false negative pixels of the predicted segmentation masks.

6.3 Implementation Details

We adopt VGG-16 [36] and ResNet-50 [18] as feature extractors, which are initialized with weights pre-trained on ILSVRC [30] and kept frozen during training, following previous works [25,27,45,49]. For the VGG backbone, we use feature maps from conv4_x to conv5_x, and after the last max-pooling layer. The channel dimensions of the three anchor layers are set to 512. For the ResNet backbone, we use feature maps from conv3_x, conv4_x and conv5_x. The channel dimensions of the three anchor layers are set to 512, 1024 and 2048, respectively. To reduce the memory consumption and speed up training process, we set spatial sizes of both support and query images to 400 × 400. We implement the model in PyTorch [28] and utilize the Adam [22] optimizer with a learning rate of 1e-3. At inference, all images are resized to a fixed 400 × 400 resolution. An Adam optimizer is used to fine-tune PATM, with a learning rate of 1e−3 for Deepglobe and ISIC, 5e−5 for Chest X-ray and FSS-1000. For each task, a total of 50 iterations are performed. More details can be found in the supplementary material.

6.4 Baseline Performance Analysis

Meta-learning Based Results. Table 2 shows the results using mIoU, in terms of different datasets, methods, and shot levels in the benchmark. The results reveal that the performance of existing few-shot semantic segmentation methods degrades significantly under domain shifts, especially under large domain gaps. The main reason is that the frozen pretrained encoder cannot generate distinguishable features for the downstream decoder when a large domain gap exists. Furthermore, when the target domain is similar to the source domain, like on FSS-1000, the relation-based methods generally perform better than the metric-based methods. But when the domain gap becomes larger (*e.g.* Deepglobe and Chest X-ray), the metric-based methods are more effective than the relation-based methods. For instance, PANet surpasses HSNet by 5.87% (1-shot) and 14.95% (5-shot) on Chest X-ray, but underperforms HSNet by 8.38% (1-shot)

Table 2. Mean-IoU of 1-way 1-shot and 5-shot results of meta-learning and transfer learning methods on the CD-FSS benchmark. **Note that all methods are trained on PASCAL VOC and tested on CD-FSS.** Bold denotes the best performance among *all* methods and underlined shows the best performance in *each* method group. * denotes the model implemented by ourselves.

Methods	Backbone	Deepglobe		ISIC		Chest X-ray		FSS-1000		Average	
		1-shot	5-shot	1-shot	5-shot	1-shot	5-shot	1-shot	5-shot	1-shot	5-shot
Transfer learning methods											
Ft-last-1$_{FCN}$	Vgg-16	29.80	32.25	15.17	19.75	33.63	48.08	32.51	53.62	27.78	38.43
Ft-last-2$_{FCN}$	Vgg-16	32.90	35.34	17.52	21.65	36.35	53.85	32.15	57.44	29.82	42.07
Ft-last-3$_{FCN}$	Vgg-16	32.91	35.54	17.91	25.58	45.61	56.05	33.32	<u>60.86</u>	32.34	44.51
1NN$_{FCN}$	Vgg-16	32.42	38.63	15.68	23.66	46.26	52.70	41.51	46.64	33.97	40.41
Linear$_{FCN}$	Vgg-16	<u>33.56</u>	38.75	15.51	<u>30.65</u>	37.69	50.07	41.09	49.16	31.96	42.16
Ft-last-1$_{Deeplab}$	Res-50	28.11	28.65	11.08	16.57	30.43	35.54	25.14	35.86	23.69	29.41
Ft-last-2$_{Deeplab}$	Res-50	24.09	36.74	10.22	17.56	31.16	51.57	20.68	42.50	21.29	37.10
1NN$_{Deeplab}$	Res-50	32.28	35.96	<u>21.44</u>	26.04	<u>47.76</u>	57.93	<u>45.81</u>	55.95	<u>36.82</u>	43.97
Linear$_{Deeplab}$	Res-50	32.95	<u>39.69</u>	19.42	30.04	43.52	<u>60.29</u>	40.50	58.36	34.10	<u>47.10</u>
Few-shot segmentation methods											
AMP [34]	Vgg-16	<u>37.61</u>	40.61	28.42	30.41	51.23	53.04	57.18	59.24	43.61	45.83
PGNet [48]	Res-50	10.73	12.36	21.86	21.25	33.95	27.96	62.42	62.74	32.24	31.08
PANet* [45]	Res-50	36.55	**45.43**	25.29	33.99	57.75	<u>69.31</u>	69.15	71.68	47.19	<u>55.10</u>
CaNet [49]	Res-50	22.32	23.07	25.16	28.22	28.35	28.62	70.67	72.03	36.63	37.99
RPMMs [46]	Res-50	12.99	13.47	18.02	20.04	30.11	30.82	65.12	67.06	31.56	32.85
PFENet [38]	Res-50	16.88	18.01	23.50	23.83	27.22	27.57	70.87	70.52	34.62	34.98
RePRI [3]	Res-50	25.03	27.41	23.27	26.23	<u>65.08</u>	65.48	70.96	74.23	46.09	48.34
HSNet [27]	Res-50	29.65	35.08	<u>31.20</u>	<u>35.10</u>	51.88	54.36	<u>77.53</u>	<u>80.99</u>	<u>47.57</u>	51.38
PATNet	Vgg-16	28.74	34.83	33.07	45.83	57.83	60.55	71.60	76.17	47.81	54.35
PATNet	Res-50	**37.89**	<u>42.97</u>	**41.16**	**53.58**	**66.61**	**70.20**	**78.59**	**81.23**	**56.06**	**61.99**

and 9.31% (5-shot) on FSS-1000. This indicates that if the target domain is drastically different from the source domain, it may be more effective to make the encoder obtain the meta-transfer ability than the decoder. Finally, we observed that all the methods achieved the best performance on the FSS-1000 dataset among the four selected datasets because the data distribution of the FSS-1000 is most similar to the source dataset (PASCAL VOC) compared to the other datasets.

Transfer Learning Based Results. We observe that the base classifier methods significantly outperform simple fine-tuning methods on CD-FSS. The main reason is that limited samples in support set are insufficient for the deep segmentation networks to be adapted to a novel distribution. Furthermore, when the target domain is similar to the source domain (*e.g.* FSS-1000), those meta-learning based methods outperform transfer learning based methods with a large margin. In contrast, the base classifier methods surprisingly achieve comparable performance when a large domain shift gap exists. For example, the pre-trained Deeplab with a simple linear classifier achieves 39.69% on Deepglobe for 5-shot, outperforming most few-shot segmentation methods. It is worth noting

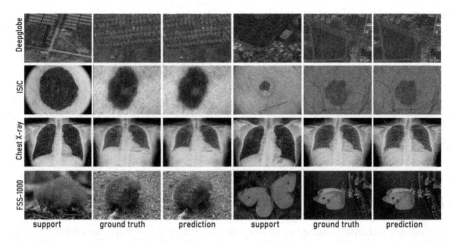

Fig. 5. Qualitative results of our model in 1-way 1-shot segmentation on CD-FSS. Note that the model is trained with PASCAL. Support labels are overlaid in blue. Prediction and ground truth of query images are in plum. Best view in color and zoom in.

that RePRI [3] is also a kind of transfer learning method designed for few-shot segmentation tasks. It performs well on Chest X-ray and FSS-1000, but fails on Deepglobe and ISIC. This indicates that it is inefficient only to fine-tune the classifier during inference. Generating distinguishable features for the downstream segmentation modules is a key to reducing the performance degradation brought by domain shifts.

6.5   Experimental Results of PATNet

As shown in Table 2, across all the datasets, our model outperforms both meta-learning methods and transfer learning based methods with a sizable margin. Specifically, our 1-shot and 5-shot results respectively achieve **8.49%** and **10.61%** of mean-IoU improvements over HSNet (achieves the best performance among meta-learning methods on CD-FSS), 21.96% and 14.89% of mean-IoU improvements over DeeplabV3 combined with a linear classifier (achieves the best performance among transfer learning based methods on CD-FSS), verifying its superiority on the CD-FSS task. In particular, our model outperforms recent methods with a sizable margin under large domain gaps, surpassing HSNet by 14.73% (1-shot) and 15.84% (5-shot) on Chest X-ray, and 9.96% (1-shot) and 18.48% (5-shot) on ISIC. In addition, we present some of the qualitative results of the proposed model for 1-way 1-shot segmentation in Fig. 5. These results validate that the proposed method can significantly improve the generalization ability under large domain gaps while achieving a comparable accuracy in a similar domain shift.

Table 3. Ablation study on PATM on CD-FSS. Results are averaged over 4 datasets for 1-shot and 5-shot.

Method	CD-FSS		#params
	1-shot	5-shot	to train
w/o PAT	47.57	51.38	2.574M
Explicit PAT	54.16	59.38	2.602M
PATNet	**56.06**	**61.99**	2.581M

Table 4. Ablation study on the choice of fine-tuning anchor layers on Deepglobe.

Ft_{high}	Ft_{med}	Ft_{low}	1-shot	5-shot
×	×	×	35.10	40.72
✓	×	×	37.52	42.03
×	✓	×	34.56	39.74
×	×	✓	**37.89**	**42.97**

6.6 Ablation Study

We conduct extensive ablation studies to investigate the impacts of PATM and TFI strategy. All ablation study experiments are performed with ResNet-50.

Effect of Pyramid Anchor Layers. To study the effect of the number of pyramid anchor layers in PATM, we compare our method with and without the anchor layers. We also form an explicit transformation module using a unique anchor layer for each intermediate feature map. From Table 3 we can observe that introducing the anchor layers for feature transformation improves the segmentation performance with 8.25% and 7.64% gain in 1-shot and 5-shot, respectively. This suggests that our proposed PATM is able to enhance the generalization ability by transforming the domain-specific features into domain-agnostic ones. One may ask why not make each feature map have its own anchor layer. We compare the results with the explicit transformation module, introducing the anchor layer for each intermediate feature map (denoted as 'explicit PAT' in Table 3). Performance degradation from PATNet to explicit PAT indicates that the light-weight anchor layers are more reliable to construct the domain transformation matrices in few-shot scenarios. Thus, we only introduce one anchor layer for each feature dimension and feature maps with the same dimension share one anchor layer to compute their corresponding transformation matrices.

Choice of Fine-Tuning Anchor Layers. Table 4 provides a quantitative evaluation of the TFI strategy. We present the results of fine-tuning each anchor layer: low-, medium- and high-level feature dimensions, respectively. We observe that fine-tuning the anchor layer of the low feature map achieves the best performance, indicating that the correlation patterns from low intermediate CNN layers are crucial in effective domain transfer. Qualitative results on how TFI affects the final prediction are provided in Fig. 4. We adopt fine-tuning the anchor layer for low dimensions to report all the experiment results.

7 Conclusion

In this paper, we extend few-shot semantic segmentation to a new task, called Cross-Domain Few-Shot Semantic Segmentation (CD-FSS), which aims to learn a model that can segment the novel classes in *unseen* domains with only *a few* pixel-level annotated images. Moreover, a new benchmark for CD-FSS is established to evaluate the cross-domain generalization ability of few-shot segmentation models under different domain shifts. Experiments show that SOTA few-shot segmentation models do not generalize well to categories from different domains, due to the large discrepancy of the feature distribution across domains. In addition, we propose a novel model, PATNet, to tackle the CD-FSS problem by transforming domain-specific features into domain-agnostic ones for downstream segmentation modules to fast adapt to unseen domains. Extensive experimental results show that our method outperforms the prior art with a sizable margin under domain shifts. We believe this work will help the community understand existing methods in a practical way and dive into further advances for real-world applications.

References

1. Adler, T., et al.: Cross-domain few-shot learning by representation fusion. arXiv preprint arXiv:2010.06498 (2020)
2. Ben-Israel, A., Greville, T.N.: Generalized Inverses: Theory and Applications, vol. 15. Springer, Heidelberg (2003)
3. Boudiaf, M., Kervadec, H., Masud, Z., et al.: Few-shot segmentation without meta-learning: a good transductive inference is all you need? In: Proceedings of the IEEE/CVF Conference on Computer Vision and Pattern Recognition, pp. 13979–13988 (2021)
4. Candemir, S., et al.: Lung segmentation in chest radiographs using anatomical atlases with nonrigid registration. IEEE Trans. Med. Imaging **33**(2), 577–590 (2013)
5. Chen, L., Papandreou, G., Kokkinos, I., Murphy, K., Yuille, A.: DeepLab: semantic image segmentation with deep convolutional nets, atrous convolution, and fully connected CRFs. IEEE Trans. Pattern Anal. Mach. Intell. **40**(4), 834–848 (2018)
6. Chen, L.C., Papandreou, G., Schroff, F., Adam, H.: Rethinking atrous convolution for semantic image segmentation. arXiv preprint arXiv:1706.05587 (2017)
7. Chen, W.Y., Liu, Y.C., Kira, Z., Wang, Y.C.F., Huang, J.B.: A closer look at few-shot classification. arXiv preprint arXiv:1904.04232 (2019)
8. Chen, Y.H., Chen, W.Y., Chen, Y.T., Tsai, B.C., Frank Wang, Y.C., Sun, M.: No more discrimination: cross city adaptation of road scene segmenters. In: Proceedings of the IEEE International Conference on Computer Vision, pp. 1992–2001 (2017)
9. Chen, Y., Li, W., Van Gool, L.: Road: Reality oriented adaptation for semantic segmentation of urban scenes. In: Proceedings of the IEEE Conference on Computer Vision and Pattern Recognition, pp. 7892–7901 (2018)
10. Codella, N., et al.: Skin lesion analysis toward melanoma detection 2018: a challenge hosted by the international skin imaging collaboration (ISIC). arXiv preprint arXiv:1902.03368 (2019)
11. Demir, I., et al.: DeepGlobe 2018: a challenge to parse the earth through satellite images. In: The IEEE Conference on Computer Vision and Pattern Recognition (CVPR) Workshops, June 2018

12. Du, L., et al.: SSF-DAN: separated semantic feature based domain adaptation network for semantic segmentation. In: Proceedings of the IEEE International Conference on Computer Vision, pp. 982–991 (2019)
13. Everingham, M., Van Gool, L., Williams, C.K., Winn, J., Zisserman, A.: The pascal visual object classes (VOC) challenge. Int. J. Comput. Vision 88(2), 303–338 (2010)
14. Finn, C., Abbeel, P., Levine, S.: Model-agnostic meta-learning for fast adaptation of deep networks. arXiv preprint arXiv:1703.03400 (2017)
15. Garcia, V., Bruna, J.: Few-shot learning with graph neural networks. arXiv preprint arXiv:1711.04043 (2017)
16. Guo, Y., Codella, N.C., Karlinsky, L., Smith, J.R., Rosing, T., Feris, R.: A new benchmark for evaluation of cross-domain few-shot learning. arXiv preprint arXiv:1912.07200 (2019)
17. Hariharan, B., Arbeláez, P., Bourdev, L., Maji, S., Malik, J.: Semantic contours from inverse detectors. In: 2011 International Conference on Computer Vision, pp. 991–998. IEEE (2011)
18. He, K., Zhang, X., Ren, S., Sun, J.: Deep residual learning for image recognition. In: Proceedings of the IEEE Conference on Computer Vision and Pattern Recognition, pp. 770–778 (2016)
19. Heusel, M., Ramsauer, H., Unterthiner, T., Nessler, B., Hochreiter, S.: GANs trained by a two time-scale update rule converge to a local nash equilibrium. In: Proceedings of the 31st International Conference on Neural Information Processing Systems, pp. 6629–6640 (2017)
20. Hoffman, J., Wang, D., Yu, F., Darrell, T.: FCNs in the wild: pixel-level adversarial and constraint-based adaptation. arXiv preprint arXiv:1612.02649 (2016)
21. Jaeger, S., et al.: Automatic tuberculosis screening using chest radiographs. IEEE Trans. Med. Imaging 33(2), 233–245 (2013)
22. Kingma, D.P., Ba, J.: Adam: a method for stochastic optimization. arXiv preprint arXiv:1412.6980 (2014)
23. Li, X., Wei, T., Chen, Y.P., Tai, Y.W., Tang, C.K.: FSS-1000: a 1000-class dataset for few-shot segmentation. In: Proceedings of the IEEE/CVF Conference on Computer Vision and Pattern Recognition, pp. 2869–2878 (2020)
24. Liu, Y., et al.: Learning to propagate labels: transductive propagation network for few-shot learning. arXiv preprint arXiv:1805.10002 (2018)
25. Liu, Y., Zhang, X., Zhang, S., He, X.: Part-aware prototype network for few-shot semantic segmentation. arXiv preprint arXiv:2007.06309 (2020)
26. Long, J., Shelhamer, E., Darrell, T.: Fully convolutional networks for semantic segmentation. In: Proceedings of the IEEE Conference on Computer Vision and Pattern Recognition., pp. 3431–3440 (2015)
27. Min, J., Kang, D., Cho, M.: Hypercorrelation squeeze for few-shot segmentation. In: Proceedings of the IEEE/CVF International Conference on Computer Vision, pp. 6941–6952 (2021)
28. Paszke, A., et al.: Automatic differentiation in PyTorch (2017)
29. Ravi, S., Larochelle, H.: Optimization as a model for few-shot learning (2016)
30. Russakovsky, O., et al.: ImageNet large scale visual recognition challenge. Int. J. Comput. Vision 115(3), 211–252 (2015)
31. Sakaridis, C., Dai, D., Gool, L.V.: Guided curriculum model adaptation and uncertainty-aware evaluation for semantic nighttime image segmentation. In: Proceedings of the IEEE International Conference on Computer Vision, pp. 7374–7383 (2019)
32. Seo, J., Park, Y.H., Yoon, S.W., Moon, J.: Task-adaptive feature transformer for few-shot segmentation. arXiv preprint arXiv:2010.11437 (2020)

33. Shaban, A., Bansal, S., Liu, Z., Essa, I., Boots, B.: One-shot learning for semantic segmentation. arXiv preprint arXiv:1709.03410 (2017)

34. Siam, M., Oreshkin, B.N., Jagersand, M.: AMP: adaptive masked proxies for few-shot segmentation. In: Proceedings of the IEEE International Conference on Computer Vision, pp. 5249–5258 (2019)

35. Simon, C., Koniusz, P., Nock, R., Harandi, M.: Adaptive subspaces for few-shot learning. In: Proceedings of the IEEE/CVF Conference on Computer Vision and Pattern Recognition, pp. 4136–4145 (2020)

36. Simonyan, K., Zisserman, A.: Very deep convolutional networks for large-scale image recognition. arXiv preprint arXiv:1409.1556 (2014)

37. Snell, J., Swersky, K., Zemel, R.: Prototypical networks for few-shot learning. In: Advances in Neural Information Processing Systems, pp. 4077–4087 (2017)

38. Tian, Z., Zhao, H., Shu, M., Yang, Z., Li, R., Jia, J.: Prior guided feature enrichment network for few-shot segmentation. IEEE Trans. Pattern Anal. Mach. Intell. (TPAMI) **44**, 1050–1065 (2020)

39. Triantafillou, E., et al.: Meta-dataset: a dataset of datasets for learning to learn from few examples. arXiv preprint arXiv:1903.03096 (2019)

40. Tsai, Y.H., Hung, W.C., Schulter, S., Sohn, K., Yang, M.H., Chandraker, M.: Learning to adapt structured output space for semantic segmentation. In: Proceedings of the IEEE Conference on Computer Vision and Pattern Recognition, pp. 7472–7481 (2018)

41. Tsai, Y.H., Sohn, K., Schulter, S., Chandraker, M.: Domain adaptation for structured output via discriminative patch representations. In: Proceedings of the IEEE International Conference on Computer Vision, pp. 1456–1465 (2019)

42. Tschandl, P., Rosendahl, C., Kittler, H.: The HAM10000 dataset, a large collection of multi-source dermatoscopic images of common pigmented skin lesions. Sci. Data **5**, 180161 (2018)

43. Tseng, H.Y., Lee, H.Y., Huang, J.B., Yang, M.H.: Cross-domain few-shot classification via learned feature-wise transformation. arXiv preprint arXiv:2001.08735 (2020)

44. Vinyals, O., Blundell, C., Lillicrap, T., Wierstra, D., et al.: Matching networks for one shot learning. In: Advances in Neural Information Processing Systems, pp. 3630–3638 (2016)

45. Wang, K., Liew, J.H., Zou, Y., Zhou, D., Feng, J.: PANet: few-shot image semantic segmentation with prototype alignment. In: Proceedings of the IEEE International Conference on Computer Vision, pp. 9197–9206 (2019)

46. Yang, B., Liu, C., Li, B., Jiao, J., Ye, Q.: Prototype mixture models for few-shot semantic segmentation. arXiv preprint arXiv:2008.03898 (2020)

47. Yoon, S.W., Seo, J., Moon, J.: TapNet: neural network augmented with task-adaptive projection for few-shot learning. In: International Conference on Machine Learning, pp. 7115–7123. PMLR (2019)

48. Zhang, C., Lin, G., Liu, F., Guo, J., Wu, Q., Yao, R.: Pyramid graph networks with connection attentions for region-based one-shot semantic segmentation. In: Proceedings of the IEEE/CVF International Conference on Computer Vision, pp. 9587–9595 (2019)

49. Zhang, C., Lin, G., Liu, F., Yao, R., Shen, C.: CANet: class-agnostic segmentation networks with iterative refinement and attentive few-shot learning. In: Proceedings of the IEEE Conference on Computer Vision and Pattern Recognition, pp. 5217–5226 (2019)

50. Zhang, X., Wei, Y., Yang, Y., Huang, T.S.: SG-One: similarity guidance network for one-shot semantic segmentation. IEEE Trans. Cybern. **50**(9), 3855–3865 (2020)

51. Zhang, Y., David, P., Foroosh, H., Gong, B.: A curriculum domain adaptation approach to the semantic segmentation of urban scenes. IEEE Trans. Pattern Anal. Mach. Intell. **42**(8), 1823–1841 (2019)
52. Zhao, H., Shi, J., Qi, X., Wang, X., Jia, J.: Pyramid scene parsing network. In: Proceedings of the IEEE Conference on Computer Vision and Pattern Recognition, pp. 2881–2890 (2017)
53. Zhu, X., Zhou, H., Yang, C., Shi, J., Lin, D.: Penalizing top performers: conservative loss for semantic segmentation adaptation. In: Ferrari, V., Hebert, M., Sminchisescu, C., Weiss, Y. (eds.) ECCV 2018. LNCS, vol. 11211, pp. 587–603. Springer, Cham (2018). https://doi.org/10.1007/978-3-030-01234-2_35
54. Zou, Y., Yu, Z., Vijaya Kumar, B.V.K., Wang, J.: Unsupervised domain adaptation for semantic segmentation via class-balanced self-training. In: Ferrari, V., Hebert, M., Sminchisescu, C., Weiss, Y. (eds.) ECCV 2018. LNCS, vol. 11207, pp. 297–313. Springer, Cham (2018). https://doi.org/10.1007/978-3-030-01219-9_18

Generative Subgraph Contrast for Self-Supervised Graph Representation Learning

Yuehui Han, Le Hui, Haobo Jiang, Jianjun Qian[✉], and Jin Xie[✉]

Key Lab of Intelligent Perception and Systems for High-Dimensional Information
of Ministry of Education, Jiangsu Key Lab of Image and Video Understanding
for Social Security PCA Lab, School of Computer Science and Engineering,
Nanjing University of Science and Technology, Nanjing, China
{hanyh,le.hui,jiang.hao.bo,csjqian,csjxie}@njust.edu.cn

Abstract. Contrastive learning has shown great promise in the field
of graph representation learning. By manually constructing posi-
tive/negative samples, most graph contrastive learning methods rely
on the vector inner product based similarity metric to distinguish the
samples for graph representation. However, the handcrafted sample construction (e.g., the perturbation on the nodes or edges of the graph) may
not effectively capture the intrinsic local structures of the graph. Also,
the vector inner product based similarity metric cannot fully exploit
the local structures of the graph to characterize the graph difference
well. To this end, in this paper, we propose a novel adaptive subgraph
generation based contrastive learning framework for efficient and robust
self-supervised graph representation learning, and the optimal transport
distance is utilized as the similarity metric between the subgraphs. It
aims to generate contrastive samples by capturing the intrinsic structures of the graph and distinguish the samples based on the features
and structures of subgraphs simultaneously. Specifically, for each center node, by adaptively learning relation weights to the nodes of the
corresponding neighborhood, we first develop a network to generate the
interpolated subgraph. We then construct the positive and negative pairs
of subgraphs from the same and different nodes, respectively. Finally,
we employ two types of optimal transport distances (i.e., Wasserstein
distance and Gromov-Wasserstein distance) to construct the structured
contrastive loss. Extensive node classification experiments on benchmark
datasets verify the effectiveness of our graph contrastive learning method.
Source code is available at https://github.com/yh-han/GSC.git.

Keywords: Graph representation learning · Contrastive learning ·
Subgraph generation · Optimal transport distance

Supplementary Information The online version contains supplementary material
available at https://doi.org/10.1007/978-3-031-20056-4_6.

1 Introduction

Graph representation learning [11] has received intensive attention in recent years due to its superior performance in various downstream tasks, such as node/graph classification [17,19], link prediction [41] and graph alignment [7]. Most graph representation learning methods [10,17,31] are supervised, where manually annotated nodes are used as the supervision signal. Since the acquisition of supervision signals is time-consuming and labor-intensive, these methods are difficult to be applied to real scenarios.

Recent efforts have been devoted to unsupervised graph representation learning [15,18,22,34,35,43]. Among these methods, graph contrastive learning is a powerful manner for learning node or graph representation. By manually constructing positive/negative samples based on the perturbation (e.g., attribute masking, nodes shuffling or edge perturbation), it aims to enforce similar samples to be closer and dissimilar samples far from each other. However, dropping edges or masking node attributes randomly may change the original properties of the graph. For example, by adding or discarding graph nodes to construct positive samples, edge perturbation based methods [9,30,44,45] may change the local geometric structures of the original graph, resulting in generating dissimilar positive samples. Thus, with GNNs for feature extraction, the features of positive samples cannot be guaranteed to be as close as possible in the graph contrastive learning framework. Moreover, since the perturbation-based positive/negative sample augmentation methods are dataset-specific, it is difficult to adaptively select the suitable augmentation method for the specific dataset. Besides, the readout function is usually used to construct the vector-wise similarity metric between nodes/graphs, which ignores the structures of the graph [12,14,32]. Thus, the vector inner product based similarity metrics cannot characterize the graph difference well.

In this paper, instead of manually constructing contrastive samples, we propose a novel subgraph generation based contrastive learning framework for efficient self-supervised graph representation learning, where the optimal transport distance is employed to capture the difference between the subgraphs for robust similarity evaluation. Specifically, we first sample the neighbor subgraph of the center node based on the breadth first search (BFS). We then develop a subgraph generation network to adaptively generate subgraphs whose nodes are interpolated in the feature space with the learned weights. For each node, we can assign different attentional weights to the neighboring nodes to obtain the weighted node so that the formed subgraph can capture the intrinsic geometric structure of the graph. Consequently, we construct the positive pair with the sampled subgraph and the generated subgraph of the same center node and the negative pair with the sampled and generated subgraphs of different center nodes. Finally, based on the constructed positive/negative subgraphs, we formulate the structured contrastive loss to learn the node representation with the Wasserstein distance and Gromov-Wasserstein distance [2]. The structured contrastive loss can minimize the geometry difference between the positive subgraphs and maximize the difference between the negative subgraphs. Experimental results on five benchmark node classification datasets demonstrate that our proposed graph contrastive learning method can yield good classification performance.

To summarize, the main contributions include:

- We propose a novel adaptive sample generation based contrastive learning framework for self-supervised graph representation learning.
- We develop a subgraph generation module to adaptively generate contrastive subgraphs with neighborhood interpolation.
- We employ the optimal transport distance as the similarity metric for subgraphs, which can distinguish the contrastive samples by fully exploiting the local attributes (i.e., features and structures) of the graph.

2   Related Work

2.1   Graph Neural Networks

The purpose of graph neural networks (GNNs) is to use graph structures and node features to learn the node representations. Formally, classical GNNs follow a two-step processing: neighborhood node aggregation and feature transformation. It first updates the node representations by aggregating the representations of its neighboring nodes as well as its representations. Then, the representations of each node are mapped into a new feature space by the shared linear transformation. Graph Convolutional Network (GCN) [17] employs a weighted sum of the 1-hop neighboring node features to update the node features, where the weights of each node come from the node degree. Graph Attention Network (GAT) [31] calculates the weights by using the interaction between the neighboring nodes to replace the node degree. However, they usually need the complete graph as the input. Therefore, limited by the hardware resources, these methods are not suitable to be applied to large-scale graph data. To solve this issue, Hamilton et al. [10] propose the sampling-based method, GraphSAGE. They first sample the neighborhood nodes for the mini-batch of the center nodes and update the node features by aggregating the sampled neighborhood nodes. Then, the batch nodes are iteratively updated until the entire graph is updated. These methods mainly focus on supervised learning and require a lot of manual labels. However, the acquisition of manually annotated labels is costly in labor and time.

2.2   Graph Contrastive Learning

Graph contrastive learning has recently been considered a promising approach for self-supervised graph representation learning. Its main objective is to train the encoder with an annotation-free pretext task. The trained encoder can transform the data into low-dimensional representations, which can be used for downstream tasks. The basic idea of graph contrastive learning aims at embedding positive samples close to each other while pushing away each embedding of the negative samples. In general, we can divide graph contrastive learning into two categories: pretext task based and data augmentation based methods.

Pretext Task. In graph contrastive learning, many early works design pretext tasks from the scale of the contrastive samples, i.e., node, subgraph or graph. Inspired by Deep InfoMax (DIM) [13], Deep Graph Infomax (DGI) [32] and Mutual Information Graph (INFOGRAPH) [29] learn the representations of nodes or graph by maximizing mutual information between the node and global graph. Also based on the contrast of nodes and graph, Multi-View Graph Representation Learning (MVGRL) [12] expands DGI to multiple views. By adding the cross-view contrast between the representation of nodes and graph, MVGRL further enhances the guidance performance of the pretext task. In order to avoid the problem of sharing positive samples (global graph) among multiple nodes in these methods, some works try to construct exclusive positive sample for each sample. Graphical Mutual Information (GMI) [23] proposes to maximize the mutual information between the neighborhood in input and the center node in output. Sub-graph Contrast (Subg-Con) [14] learns node features by taking the induced subgraphs of the center node as the input of the encoder and treating the center node and context subgraph as the contrastive sample pairs. This method can also alleviate the problem of memory overload caused by large-scale graphs. By treating top-k similar nodes from T-hop neighbors as positive samples, Augmentation-Free Graph Contrastive Learning (AF-GCL) [33] proposes the augmentation-free methods. Graph Contrastive Coding (GCC) [27] proposes to contrast between subgraphs. It takes the subgraphs from the same r-ego network as positive samples and subgraphs from the different r-ego networks as negative samples. However, GCC only considers the structure information neglecting the node features.

In addition to the scale of the contrastive samples, some works design pretext tasks to better exploit contrastive information. To solve the problem of false-negative samples, [42] proposes to jointly perform representation learning and clustering, where feature representation and clustering can be promoted from each other. With the same motivation, Curriculum Contrastive Learning (CuCo) [5] proposes a scoring function to sort the negative samples from easy to hard, and a pacing function to automatically select the negative samples in the training process. For better selection of positive samples, Augmentation-Free Graph Representation Learning (AFGRL) [20] proposes to discover the positive node that share the local structural information and the global semantics. Besides, Local-instance and Global-semantic Learning (GraphLoG) [36] proposes to capture the local similarities and the global semantic clusters to learn the whole-graph representation.

Data Augmentation. Data augmentation based graph contrastive learning methods usually design different perturbation manners (e.g., attribute masking, nodes shuffling or edge perturbation) to construct contrastive samples. Deep Graph Contrastive Representation Learning (GRACE) [44] augments the graph by setting the probability of edge removal and node features mask. Then, it takes the corresponding nodes of the augmented graph as positive samples and all the other nodes as negative samples. Graph Contrastive Learning (GraphCL) [9] proposes the sample augmentation manner from the subgraph level. For the induced subgraphs of the center nodes, it employs two stochastic perturbations and a shared encoder to produce two representations of the same node. You et al. propose [39] for molecular property prediction in chemistry and protein function prediction in biology. They systematically study the effects of various combinations of graph augmentations on multiple datasets, and found that the choice of data augmentation is closely related to the specific datasets. However, these perturbation-based methods heavily rely on handcraft settings. To solve this problem, various efforts have been made. On the one hand, some works try to optimize the setting of perturbation probability. Based on the node centrality, Graph Contrastive Learning with Adaptive Augmentation (GCA) [45] can adaptively learn the probability of edge removal. Besides, by adding more noise to the unimportant node features, it can enforce the model to recognize underlying semantic information. Based on the min-max principle, Adversarial Graph Contrastive Learning (AD-GCL) [30] proposes a trainable edge-dropping graph augmentation manner. On the other hand, some works try to optimize the choice of perturbation methods. Joint Augmentation Optimization (JOAO) [38] proposes to adaptively select data augmentation manners of graph by adversarial training. With the same motivation, Automated Graph Contrastive Learning (AutoGCL) [37] proposes to adaptively select data augmentation manners of nodes by the learnable graph view generator.

3   Proposed Method

In this section, we present our subgraph generation based graph contrastive learning method. As shown in Fig. 1, based on the sampled subgraphs with the breadth first search, we first adaptively generate the contrastive subgraphs to construct positive/negative samples. Then, we employ the optimal transport distance (i.e., Wasserstein distance and Gromov-Wasserstein distance) to formulate the contrastive loss between the constructed samples.

3.1   Adaptive Subgraph Generation

Before introducing our method, we first provide the preliminary concepts about our graph representation learning. Let $G = (V, E)$ represent an undirected graph, where V and E denote the vertex set and the edge set, respectively. The feature matrix of the graph is denoted as $X = \{x_1, x_2, ..., x_N\}$, where $x_i \in R^C$ is the feature of the node i, C represents the dimension of input features and N is the number of the nodes. The adjacency matrix $A \in \mathbb{R}^{N \times N}$ indicates the topological structure of the graph where if node i and j are linked, $A_{ij} = 1$, otherwise, $A_{ij} = 0$. Let $\mathcal{G}_i = (V_i, E_i)$ denote the induced subgraph of center node i, where V_i and E_i represent the vertex set and the edge set of the induced subgraph i, respectively. We denote the adjacency matrix of subgraph i induced from graph as $A_i \in R^{k \times k}$, where k is the number of nodes of subgraph i. The goal of self-supervised graph representation learning is to learn the nodes embeddings $H = \varepsilon(A, X)$ via an encoder $\varepsilon : R^{N \times C} \times R^{N \times N} \rightarrow R^{N \times F}$ without supervised information, where F is the dimension of embeddings.

The construction of contrastive samples is critical in graph contrastive learning. Most graph contrastive learning methods generate positive and negative samples with the perturbation of nodes, edges, or graphs. The perturbation

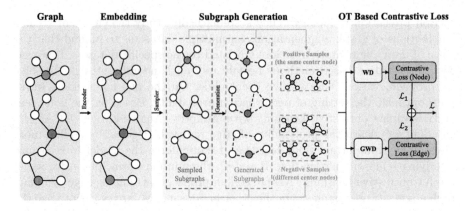

Fig. 1. The architecture of our method. We first employ an encoder to obtain the node embeddings. Based on the BFS sampling, we obtain the subgraphs of each node. Next, we use the proposed generation module to generate the contrastive samples of the sampled subgraphs. Then we take the sampled and generated subgraphs with the same center node as the positive samples while the subgraphs with the different center nodes as the negative samples. In order to fully exploit local structure information of the graph, we further introduce two types of optimal transport distances (i.e., Wasserstein distance and Gromov-Wasserstein distance) to calculate the similarity between the subgraphs. Finally, we use the combination of the WD-based contrastive loss $\mathcal{L}_1$ and GWD-based contrastive loss $\mathcal{L}_2$ to train the network.

operation may lose important information or even destroy the intrinsic structures of the graph. Thus, the constructed samples may be not discriminative enough to train the contrastive learning model. In order to construct more effective contrastive samples, we propose a learnable subgraph generation module to generate positive/negative subgraph samples. It is expected that the generated subgraphs can characterize the intrinsic local structures of the graph well.

The proposed generation module can adaptively generate the contrastive subgraph of the sampled subgraph. (For the specific sampling process, please refer to the supplementary materials). As shown in Fig. 2(a), (b), based on the local structure information interpolation, we first generate the subgraph nodes. Then, we generate the edges of the subgraph based on the interpolated nodes.

For a specific sampled subgraph node i, we can formulate the interpolation-based generation as:

$$\hat{h}_i = \sum_{j=1}^{\mathcal{N}_i} a_j h_j \tag{1}$$

where $h_j \in R^F$ is the representations of neighborhood node of center node i. $j \in \mathcal{N}_i$, $\mathcal{N}_i$ is the neighborhood of node i in the graph. $\hat{h}_i \in R^F$ is the representations of generated subgraph node. a_j is the learned relationship weight between the neighborhood node j and the center node i. For each sampled subgraph node, we perform the interpolation based on learned neighborhood relation weights to generate new nodes. As for the learned relation weight a_j, we can define it as:

$$a_j = \frac{exp(\theta(\boldsymbol{h}_i, \boldsymbol{h}_j))}{\sum_{k=1}^{\mathcal{N}_i} exp(\theta(\boldsymbol{h}_i, \boldsymbol{h}_k))} \tag{2}$$

where $\theta(\boldsymbol{h}_i, \boldsymbol{h}_j)$ represents the relationship between center node i and neighborhood node j. We can define the $\theta(\boldsymbol{h}_i, \boldsymbol{h}_j)$ as:

$$\theta(\boldsymbol{h}_i, \boldsymbol{h}_j) = \text{LeakyReLU}(\boldsymbol{W}_\theta[\boldsymbol{W}_\phi \boldsymbol{h}_i \| \boldsymbol{W}_\phi \boldsymbol{h}_j]) \tag{3}$$

where LeakyReLU is the activation function (with negative input slope 0.2), $\boldsymbol{W}_\theta \in R^{1 \times 2F}$ and $\boldsymbol{W}_\phi \in R^{F \times F}$ are the weight matrixes to be learned, and $\|$ represents the feature concatenation.

As shown in Fig. 2(c), based on the generated nodes, we directly generate the edges of the contrastive subgraph. For the node s_i and s_j in the subgraph, $s_i, s_j = 1, 2, ..., k$, k is the number of subgraph nodes, the generated edge between nodes s_i and s_j of the subgraph can be denoted as:

$$\hat{\boldsymbol{A}}(s_i, s_j) = \varphi(\hat{\boldsymbol{h}}_{s_i}, \hat{\boldsymbol{h}}_{s_j}) \tag{4}$$

where $\hat{\boldsymbol{A}}$ is the adjacency matrix of generated subgraph, $\hat{\boldsymbol{h}}_{s_i}$ is the generated features of subgraph node s_i. $\varphi(., .)$ is the similarity calculation function, here, we use the cosine similarity, i.e., $\varphi(\hat{\boldsymbol{h}}_{s_i}, \hat{\boldsymbol{h}}_{s_j}) = \frac{\hat{\boldsymbol{h}}_{s_i}^T \hat{\boldsymbol{h}}_{s_j}}{\|\hat{\boldsymbol{h}}_{s_i}\|_2 \|\hat{\boldsymbol{h}}_{s_j}\|_2}$.

So far, we obtain the generated contrastive subgraph that contains the nodes features and edges. Essentially, we use the adaptively generated samples to replace the perturbation-based samples. Different from perturbation-based method that randomly discards the information of the graph, the proposed generation module could maintain the integrity of the graph. Our generation module, by assigning the learned attentional weights to the neighborhood nodes, can adaptively exploit the intrinsic geometric structure of the graph and generate more effective contrastive samples. Besides, since the similarity between adjacent nodes in the graph is an inherent attribute, there is a strong correlation between the central node and its neighborhood. Therefore, the generated subgraphs by neighborhood interpolation are inherently similar to the original subgraphs. And it is reasonable and effective to treat the generated subgraph as positive sample.

3.2 OT Distance Based Contrastive Learning

Most graph contrastive learning methods use node pairs or node-subgraph pairs or subgraph pairs as contrastive samples. Particularly, the features of subgraphs can be extracted with the readout function. Thus, these methods mainly employ the vector-wise similarity metrics to calculate the similarity between these samples. However, the vector inner product based similarity metrics cannot fully exploit the local structures of the graph to characterize the graph difference well. Instead of using the vector-wise similarity metrics, in our method, we introduce the optimal transport distance (i.e., Wasserstein distance and Gromov-Wasserstein distance) as the similarity metric for contrastive subgraphs. Therefore, we can accurately characterize the geometric difference between the subgraphs.

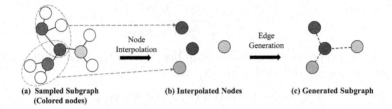

(a) Sampled Subgraph   (b) Interpolated Nodes   (c) Generated Subgraph
   (Colored nodes)

Fig. 2. The proposed interpolation-based adaptive subgraph generation module. For the sampled subgraph in (a), we use the neighborhood of each subgraph node to interpolate the new node in the subgraph (b). Based on the interpolated nodes features, we then generate the edges between the interpolated nodes. Finally, we obtain the generated subgraph (c).

Wasserstein Distance (WD). WD is commonly used for matching two discrete distributions (e.g., two sets of node embeddings) [2]. It can represent the cost of converting one subgraph to another by counting the difference between all node pairs in the two subgraphs. In our settings, WD is employed to measure the similarity between the nodes of the subgraphs. The WD for similarity calculation between subgraphs can be described as follows.

Let u and v represent discrete distributions of two subgraphs, where $u = \{u_1, u_2, ..., u_n\}$ and $v = \{v_1, v_2, ..., v_m\}$, $\sum_{i=1}^{n} u_i = \sum_{j=1}^{m} v_j = 1$, n and m are the number of the subgraph nodes, respectively. The WD between the two discrete distributions u and v can be defined as:

$$D_w(\boldsymbol{u}, \boldsymbol{v}) = \min_{\boldsymbol{T} \in \pi(\boldsymbol{u}, \boldsymbol{v})} \sum_{i=1}^{n} \sum_{j=1}^{m} \boldsymbol{T}_{ij} c(\boldsymbol{h}_{1i}, \boldsymbol{h}_{2j}) \tag{5}$$

where $\pi(\boldsymbol{u}, \boldsymbol{v})$ represents all the joint distributions between two subgraphs nodes. $c(\boldsymbol{h}_{1i}, \boldsymbol{h}_{2j}) = exp(-\varphi(\boldsymbol{h}_{1i}, \boldsymbol{h}_{2j})/\tau)$ denotes the transport cost between node i in subgraph 1 and node j in subgraph 2, $\boldsymbol{h}_{1i}$ and $\boldsymbol{h}_{2j}$ represent the node features, τ is a temperature parameter, and $\varphi(., .)$ denotes the cosine similarity between the node features. The matrix $\boldsymbol{T}$ represents the transport plan, where $\boldsymbol{T}_{ij}$ denotes the amount of mass shifted from u_i to v_j. And $\boldsymbol{T}$ can be achieved by applying the Sinkhorn algorithm [6,26] with an entropic regularizer [1].

$$\min_{\boldsymbol{T} \in \pi(\boldsymbol{u}, \boldsymbol{v})} \sum_{i=1}^{n} \sum_{j=1}^{m} \boldsymbol{T}_{ij} c(\boldsymbol{h}_{1i}, \boldsymbol{h}_{2j}) + \beta H(\boldsymbol{T}) \tag{6}$$

where $H(\boldsymbol{T}) = \sum_{i,j} \boldsymbol{T}_{ij} log \boldsymbol{T}_{ij}$, and β is the hyperparameter controlling the importance of the entropy term.

WD-Based Contrastive Loss. Based on the Wasserstein distance, we define the loss as:

$$\mathcal{L}_1 = \frac{-1}{N(M+1)} \sum_{i=1}^{N} [log(exp(-D_w(\boldsymbol{s}_i, \boldsymbol{s}_p)/\tau)) + \sum_{j=1}^{M} log(1 - exp(-D_w(\boldsymbol{s}_i, \boldsymbol{s}_{nj})/\tau))]$$

$$\tag{7}$$

where N is the number of sampled subgraphs, M is the number of negative samples of each subgraph, and τ is a temperature parameter. (s_i, s_p) denotes the positive sample pair, (s_i, s_{nj}) denotes the negative sample pair. To speed up the calculation efficiency, we only randomly select two negative samples, i.e., $M = 2$, one from the sampled subgraphs and the other from the generated subgraphs.

Compared with readout function-based manner, WD can exploit similar information among all nodes and distinguish the contrastive samples more effectively. Therefore, with the WD-based contrastive loss, we can maximize the similarity between the nodes across the positive subgraphs and minimize the similarity between the nodes across the negative subgraphs.

Gromov-Wasserstein Distance (GWD). Unlike WD, which can directly calculate the distance of node pairs between two subgraphs, GWD [4,25] can be used when we can only get the distances between pairs of nodes within each subgraph. GWD can be used to calculate the distance between node pairs within the subgraph, as well as to measure the differences in these distances across the subgraphs. That is to say, GWD can measure the distances between node pairs within each subgraph compare to those in the counterpart subgraph. Therefore, GWD can be used to capture the similarity between the edges of the subgraphs. The GWD for similarity calculation between subgraphs can be described as:

Let $\boldsymbol{u}$ and $\boldsymbol{v}$ represent discrete distributions of two subgraphs, where $\boldsymbol{u} = \{u_1, u_2, ..., u_n\}$ and $\boldsymbol{v} = \{v_1, v_2, ..., v_m\}$, $\sum_{i=1}^{n} u_i = \sum_{j=1}^{m} v_j = 1$, n and m is the number of subgraph nodes. The GWD between the two discrete distributions $\boldsymbol{u}$, $\boldsymbol{v}$ can be defined as:

$$D_{gw}(\boldsymbol{u}, \boldsymbol{v}) = \min_{\boldsymbol{T} \in \pi(\boldsymbol{u}, \boldsymbol{v})} \sum_{i,i',j,j'} \boldsymbol{T}_{ij} \boldsymbol{T}_{i'j'} \hat{c}(\boldsymbol{h}_{1i}, \boldsymbol{h}_{2j}, \boldsymbol{h}_{1i'}, \boldsymbol{h}_{2j'}) \tag{8}$$

where $\pi(\boldsymbol{u}, \boldsymbol{v})$ denotes all the joint distributions, the matrix $\boldsymbol{T}$ represents the transport plan between two subgraphs, $\boldsymbol{T}_{ij}$ denotes the amount of mass shifted from u_i to v_j. $\hat{c}(\boldsymbol{h}_{1i}, \boldsymbol{h}_{2j}, \boldsymbol{h}_{1i'}, \boldsymbol{h}_{2j'}) = \|c(\boldsymbol{h}_{1i}, \boldsymbol{h}_{1i'}) - c(\boldsymbol{h}_{2j}, \boldsymbol{h}_{2j'})\|_2$ is the cost function to measure the edge difference between two subgraphs. $c(.,.)$ represents the distance between nodes within the subgraph.

Given the adjacent matrix of the sampled subgraph, for the nodes s_1 and s_2 of sampled subgraph s, the distance $c(\boldsymbol{h}_{s_1}, \boldsymbol{h}_{s_2})$ can be defined as:

$$c(\boldsymbol{h}_{s_1}, \boldsymbol{h}_{s_2}) = exp(-\boldsymbol{A}_s(s_1, s_2)/\tau) \tag{9}$$

where $\boldsymbol{A}_s(s_1, s_2)$ represents the connection relationship between node s_1 and node s_2 of the sampled subgraph, τ is a temperature parameter.

The distance between the generated subgraph nodes can be defined as:

$$c(\hat{\boldsymbol{h}}_{s_1}, \hat{\boldsymbol{h}}_{s_2}) = exp(-\hat{\boldsymbol{A}}_s(s_1, s_2)/\tau) \tag{10}$$

where $\hat{\boldsymbol{A}}_s(s_1, s_2) = \varphi(\hat{\boldsymbol{h}}_{s_1}, \hat{\boldsymbol{h}}_{s_2})$ represents the connection relationship between the node s_1 and node s_2 of generated subgraph, $\varphi(.,.)$ represents the consine similarity, τ is a temperature parameter.

GWD-Based Contrastive Loss. Based on the Gromov-Wasserstein distance, we define the loss as:

$$\mathcal{L}_2 = \frac{-1}{N(M+1)} \sum_{i=1}^{N} [log(exp(-D_{gw}(\boldsymbol{s}_i, \boldsymbol{s}_p)/\tau)) + \sum_{j=1}^{M} log(1-exp(-D_{gw}(\boldsymbol{s}_i, \boldsymbol{s}_{nj})/\tau))]$$

(11)

where N is the number of sampled subgraphs, M is the number of negative samples of each subgraph and we also set $M = 2$, τ is a temperature parameter. $(\boldsymbol{s}_i, \boldsymbol{s}_p)$ and $(\boldsymbol{s}_i, \boldsymbol{s}_{nj})$ denote positive and negative sample pairs. The GWD-based contrastive loss can maximize the similarity between the edges of the positive subgraphs and minimize the similarity between the edges of the negative subgraphs so that the geometry difference between the subgraphs can be captured.

Finally, we obtain the final loss function $\mathcal{L}$, which is defined as follows:

$$\mathcal{L} = \lambda \mathcal{L}_1 + (1 - \lambda)\mathcal{L}_2 \tag{12}$$

where λ is the hyper-parameter for controlling the importance of different loss functions. Here, we set $\lambda = 0.5$. To the best of our knowledge, we are the first to introduce OT into subgraph-based graph contrastive learning. We use WD to exploit contrastive information based on the subgraph node features, and GWD to exploit contrastive information based on the edges of the subgraph. Therefore, the OT-based contrastive loss can better guide the training of the encoder.

4 Experiment

In this section, extensive experiments are conducted to evaluate the performance of our method in a self-supervised manner on the transductive and inductive node classification tasks. And we compare our method with other baselines, including unsupervised and supervised methods. Besides, we conduct ablation studies to verify the effectiveness of our proposed method.

4.1 Datasets

In order to evaluate the effectiveness of our method, we conduct experiments on five benchmark datasets of three real-world networks. Following [10,17], three tasks are performed: (1) classifying the topics of the documents on the citation network datasets of Cora, Citeseer and Pubmed [28]; (2) classifying protein roles of protein-protein interaction (PPI) networks [46], and generalizing to unseen networks; (3) predicting the community structure of the social network on Reddit posts [40]. More detailed descriptions can be found in the supplementary materials.

4.2   Implementation Details

Due to different attributes of datasets, we employ distinct encoders for three experimental settings, i.e., transductive learning for the small graph, inductive learning for the large graph and multiple graphs. For more specific information of encoders may be found in [32], or please refer to the supplementary materials.

All experiments are implemented using PyTorch [3] and the geometric deep learning extension library [8]. The experiments are conducted on a single TITAN RTX GPU. Our method is used to learn node representations in a self-supervised manner, followed by evaluating the learned representations with the node classification task. This is performed by training and testing a simple linear (logistic regression) classifier in the downstream tasks using the learned representations. We train the model by minimizing the loss function provided in Eq. (12). And we use Adam optimizer [16] with an initial learning rate of 0.0001 (especially, 0.0005 on Pubmed). The dimension of node representations is 1024 (256 with 4 heads for PPI). In order to avoid the excessive calculation, in every epoch, we randomly sample some subgraphs to calculate the OT distance for the loss calculation. Besides, parameter T is shared by WD and GWD. The detailed parameter settings can be found in the supplementary materials.

4.3   Results

Classification Results. We choose four state-of-the-art graph contrastive learning methods to evaluate graph embeddings, DGI [32], GMI [23], GraphCL [9] and Subg-Con [14]. And two traditional unsupervised methods, DeepWalk [24] and the unsupervised variant of GraphSAGE [10] are also compared with our method. Specially, we also provide results for training the classifier on the raw input features. Besides, we report the results of three supervised graph neural networks, GCN [17], GAT [31] and GraphSAGE [10]. For the node classification task, we employ mean classification accuracy to evaluate the performance on Cora, Citeseer, and Pubmed datasets, while the micro-averaged F1 score for the Reddit and PPI datasets.

The evaluation results on the five datasets are listed in Table 1. The results demonstrate that our method has achieved good performance across all five datasets. As can be seen in Table 1, our method successfully outperforms all the competing graph contrastive learning approaches, which implies the potential of our proposed method for the node classification task. Compared with the traditional subgraph perturbation based GraphCL, our method has the gain of at least 1% improvement on all data sets, even 3.2% on PPI. This indicates that our subgraph generation module can effectively capture the intrinsic local structures of the graph. We further observe that the performance of our method is better than other vector inner product based methods, which verifies that our OT-based similarity metric can effectively characterize the graph difference by exploiting local structures of the graph. From this table, one can also see that although the labels of the nodes are used in the supervised graph representation learning

Table 1. Performance comparison of node classification with different methods on the transductive and inductive tasks. The third column illustrates the data used by each algorithm in the training phase, where X, A, and Y denote features, adjacency matrix, and labels, respectively. For simple expression, we abbreviate our method as GSC.

	Algorithm	Data	Transductive			Inductive	
			Cora	Citeseer	Pubmed	PPI	Reddit
Supervised	GCN [17]	X, A, Y	81.4 ± 0.6	70.3 ± 0.7	76.8 ± 0.6	51.5 ± 0.6	93.3 ± 0.1
	GAT [31]	X, A, Y	83.0 ± 0.7	72.5 ± 0.7	79.0 ± 0.3	$\mathbf{97.3 \pm 0.2}$	-
	GraphSAGE [10]	X, A, Y	79.2 ± 1.5	71.2 ± 0.5	73.1 ± 1.4	51.3 ± 3.2	92.1 ± 1.1
Unsupervised	Raw features	X	56.6 ± 0.4	57.8 ± 0.2	69.1 ± 0.2	42.5 ± 0.3	58.5 ± 0.1
	DeepWalk [24]	A	67.2	43.2	65.3	52.9	32.4
	GraphSAGE [10]	X, A	75.2 ± 1.5	59.4 ± 0.9	70.1 ± 1.4	46.5 ± 0.7	90.8 ± 1.1
	DGI [32]	X, A	82.3 ± 0.6	71.8 ± 0.7	76.8 ± 0.6	63.8 ± 0.2	94.0 ± 0.1
	GMI [23]	X, A	83.0 ± 0.3	73.0 ± 0.3	79.9 ± 0.2	65.0 ± 0.0	95.0 ± 0.0
	GraphCL [9]	X, A	83.6 ± 0.5	72.5 ± 0.7	79.8 ± 0.5	65.9 ± 0.6	95.1 ± 0.1
	Subg-Con [14]	X, A	83.5 ± 0.5	73.2 ± 0.2	81.0 ± 0.1	66.9 ± 0.2	95.2 ± 0.0
	GSC (ours)	X, A	$\mathbf{84.6 \pm 0.1}$	$\mathbf{73.7 \pm 0.1}$	$\mathbf{82.1 \pm 0.2}$	69.1 ± 0.3	$\mathbf{95.3 \pm 0.1}$

methods, the proposed graph contrastive learning method can still outperform most of the supervised methods.

We also conduct node classification experiments with few contrastive training samples to evaluate our method. When using 70%, 50%, 30% and 10% contrastive samples on the Cora dataset, the performance of Subg-Con is 83.0%, 82.3%, 81.2% and 79.6%, while the performance of GraphCL is 83.2%, 82.5%, 81.6% and 80.1%, respectively. Nonetheless, by generating multiple positive samples for each original subgraph, the performance of our method is 84.6%, 84.1%, 83.6% and 82.9%, respectively. Particularly, in the case of 10% contrastive samples, our method can obtain the gain of 3.3%. Since Subg-Con can only construct one positive sample by pooling the top-k important neighbors for each subgraph, the performance is limited in the cases of few contrastive training samples. Different from Subg-Con, based on neighborhood interpolation, our subgraph generation module can generate multiple positive samples for each samples, which can effectively handle the situation of insufficient contrastive samples. Although GraphCL can also construct multiple positive samples, the perturbation-based data augmentation manner may change the original attributes of the graph. Compared with GraphCL, our neighborhood interpolation based generation module can effectively preserve the local structures of the graph. For more results, please refer to supplementary materials.

Visual Results. As shown in Fig. 3, we also visualize the raw features and learned embeddings of the graphs with the t-SNE [21] plot for different graph contrastive learning methods, including DGI, Subg-Con and GSC (ours). From the visualization results in Fig. 3, one can see that the embeddings generated by GSC can exhibit closer clusters than the other three methods. This means that our graph contrastive learning can obtain more discriminative features.

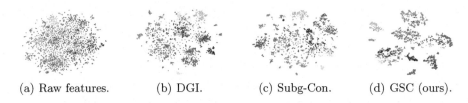

(a) Raw features.   (b) DGI.   (c) Subg-Con.   (d) GSC (ours).

Fig. 3. Visualization of t-SNE embeddings of raw features, DGI, Sub-Con, and GSC (ours) on Cora dataset.

4.4   Ablation Studies

Effectiveness of Generation Module and OT Distance. To further verify the effectiveness of different modules, we conduct three sets of comparative experiments on Cora, Citeseer and, Pubmed datasets. To verify the effectiveness of the OT distance based contrastive loss, we use the readout function to obtain the feature vectors of the subgraphs and calculate the vector-wise similarity. As can be seen from Table 2, in comparison with Readout, the use of the OT distance can improve the classification performance. This demonstrates that the OT distance can effectively capture local structure information of the graph and distinguish different subgraphs.

To demonstrate the effectiveness of the generation module, we use the traditional perturbation on the subgraph to replace the generation module and calculate the similarity between subgraphs with the OT distance. From Table 2, we can see that the classification performance of Generation + OT outperforms that of Perturbation + OT. This can verify that our generation module can effectively capture the intrinsic local structures of the graph. The generated samples can improve the performance of graph contrastive learning.

Table 2. Ablation studies on different modules

	Cora	Citeseer	Pubmed
Gene + Readout	83.6	72	78.5
Perturbation + OT	84.1	72.3	80.4
Gene + OT (ours)	**84.6**	**73.7**	**82.1**

Table 3. Ablation studies on different sampling methods

	Cora	Citeseer	Pubmed
Importance Score	83.5	71.68	80.6
Random Walk	84.2	72.4	81.2
BFS (ours)	**84.6**	**73.7**	**82.1**

Effectiveness of Different Sampling Methods. We compare different subgraph sampling methods (i.e., importance score [14] and random walk [39]) and list the experiment results in Table 3. To make the comparisons fair, we sample subgraphs of the same size. As can be seen from Table 3, BFS-based method can achieve the best performance compared with other sampling methods. This can verify that BFS-based sampled subgraphs can better cover local information and can be more beneficial to distinguish between subgraphs.

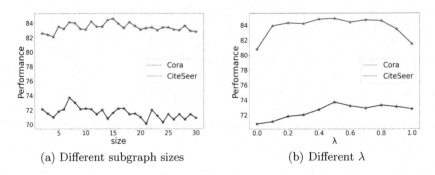

(a) Different subgraph sizes   (b) Different λ

Fig. 4. Ablation studies of different subgraph sizes and parameter λ.

Influence of the Subgraph Size and Parameter λ. To study the influence of
the subgraph size in our method, conduct experiments on the Cora and Citeseer
datasets by varying the numbers of subgraph nodes from 2 to 30. As can be seen
from Fig. 4(a), the classification performance is slightly fluctuated with different
subgraph sizes. Besides, we vary the parameter λ from 0 to 1 to study the effects
on the final classification accuracy. Different λ can control different weights of
the loss terms. As shown in Fig. 4(b), both node and edge features have effects on
the final performance and the classification performance can be kept relatively
stable in $[0.4, 0.8]$. The best performance can be achieved when λ is set to 0.5,
where the contributions of node and edge features reach a balance.

5   Conclusion

In this paper, we proposed a novel subgraph generation method for graph contrastive learning. Based on the neighborhood interpolation, we developed the
subgraph generation module, which can adaptively generate the contrastive subgraphs. Furthermore, we employed two types of optimal transport distances (i.e.,
Wasserstein distance and Gromov-Wasserstein distance) to calculate the similarity between subgraphs. In particular, generated subgraphs and the OT distance
based similarity metric can effectively capture the intrinsic local structures of the
graph to characterize the graph difference well. By conducting extensive experiments on multiple benchmark datasets, we demonstrate that our proposed graph
contrastive learning method can yield better performance in comparison with the
supervised and unsupervised graph representation learning methods.

Acknowledgments. The authors would like to thank reviewers for their detailed comments and instructive suggestions. This work was supported by the National Science
Fund of China (Grant Nos. 61876084, 61876083, 62176124).

References

1. Benamou, J.D., Carlier, G., Cuturi, M., Nenna, L., Peyré, G.: Iterative Bregman projections for regularized transportation problems. SIAM J. Sci. Comput. **37**(2), A1111–A1138 (2015)
2. Chen, L., Gan, Z., Cheng, Y., Li, L., Carin, L., Liu, J.: Graph optimal transport for cross-domain alignment. In: International Conference on Machine Learning, pp. 1542–1553. PMLR (2020)
3. Chollet, F.: Deep learning with Python. Simon and Schuster (2017)
4. Chowdhury, S., Mémoli, F.: The Gromov-Wasserstein distance between networks and stable network invariants. Inf. Inference J. IMA **8**(4), 757–787 (2019)
5. Chu, G., Wang, X., Shi, C., Jiang, X.: CuCo: graph representation with curriculum contrastive learning. In: IJCAI (2021)
6. Cuturi, M.: Sinkhorn distances: lightspeed computation of optimal transport. In: Advances in Neural Information Processing Systems, vol. 26, pp. 2292–2300 (2013)
7. Faerman, E., Voggenreiter, O., Borutta, F., Emrich, T., Berrendorf, M., Schubert, M.: Graph alignment networks with node matching scores. In: Proceedings of Advances in Neural Information Processing Systems (NIPS) (2019)
8. Fey, M., Lenssen, J.E.: Fast graph representation learning with PyTorch geometric. arXiv preprint arXiv:1903.02428 (2019)
9. Hafidi, H., Ghogho, M., Ciblat, P., Swami, A.: GraphCL: contrastive self-supervised learning of graph representations. arXiv preprint arXiv:2007.08025 (2020)
10. Hamilton, W.L., Ying, R., Leskovec, J.: Inductive representation learning on large graphs. In: Proceedings of the 31st International Conference on Neural Information Processing Systems, pp. 1025–1035 (2017)
11. Hamilton, W.L., Ying, R., Leskovec, J.: Representation learning on graphs: methods and applications. arXiv preprint arXiv:1709.05584 (2017)
12. Hassani, K., Khasahmadi, A.H.: Contrastive multi-view representation learning on graphs. In: International Conference on Machine Learning, pp. 4116–4126. PMLR (2020)
13. Hjelm, R.D., et al.: Learning deep representations by mutual information estimation and maximization. arXiv preprint arXiv:1808.06670 (2018)
14. Jiao, Y., Xiong, Y., Zhang, J., Zhang, Y., Zhang, T., Zhu, Y.: Sub-graph contrast for scalable self-supervised graph representation learning. arXiv preprint arXiv:2009.10273 (2020)
15. Jin, W., et al.: Self-supervised learning on graphs: deep insights and new direction. arXiv preprint arXiv:2006.10141 (2020)
16. Kingma, D.P., Ba, J.: Adam: a method for stochastic optimization. arXiv preprint arXiv:1412.6980 (2014)
17. Kipf, T.N., Welling, M.: Semi-supervised classification with graph convolutional networks. arXiv preprint arXiv:1609.02907 (2016)
18. Kipf, T.N., Welling, M.: Variational graph auto-encoders. arXiv preprint arXiv:1611.07308 (2016)
19. Lee, J., Lee, I., Kang, J.: Self-attention graph pooling. In: International Conference on Machine Learning, pp. 3734–3743. PMLR (2019)
20. Lee, N., Lee, J., Park, C.: Augmentation-free self-supervised learning on graphs. In: Proceedings of the AAAI Conference on Artificial Intelligence, vol. 36, pp. 7372–7380 (2022)
21. Van der Maaten, L., Hinton, G.: Visualizing data using t-SNE. J. Mach. Learn. Res. **9**(11) (2008)

22. Manessi, F., Rozza, A.: Graph-based neural network models with multiple self-supervised auxiliary tasks. Pattern Recogn. Lett. **148**, 15–21 (2021)
23. Peng, Z., et al.: Graph representation learning via graphical mutual information maximization. In: Proceedings of the Web Conference 2020, pp. 259–270 (2020)
24. Perozzi, B., Al-Rfou, R., Skiena, S.: DeepWalk: online learning of social representations. In: Proceedings of the 20th ACM SIGKDD International Conference on Knowledge Discovery and Data Mining, pp. 701–710 (2014)
25. Peyré, G., Cuturi, M., Solomon, J.: Gromov-Wasserstein averaging of kernel and distance matrices. In: International Conference on Machine Learning, pp. 2664–2672. PMLR (2016)
26. Peyré, G., Cuturi, M., et al.: Computational optimal transport: with applications to data science. Found. Trends® Mach. Learn. **11**(5–6), 355–607 (2019)
27. Qiu, J., et al.: GCC: graph contrastive coding for graph neural network pre-training. In: Proceedings of the 26th ACM SIGKDD International Conference on Knowledge Discovery & Data Mining, pp. 1150–1160 (2020)
28. Sen, P., Namata, G., Bilgic, M., Getoor, L., Galligher, B., Eliassi-Rad, T.: Collective classification in network data. AI Mag. **29**(3), 93 (2008)
29. Sun, F.Y., Hoffmann, J., Verma, V., Tang, J.: InfoGraph: unsupervised and semi-supervised graph-level representation learning via mutual information maximization. arXiv preprint arXiv:1908.01000 (2019)
30. Suresh, S., Li, P., Hao, C., Neville, J.: Adversarial graph augmentation to improve graph contrastive learning. arXiv preprint arXiv:2106.05819 (2021)
31. Veličković, P., Cucurull, G., Casanova, A., Romero, A., Lio, P., Bengio, Y.: Graph attention networks. arXiv preprint arXiv:1710.10903 (2017)
32. Veličković, P., Fedus, W., Hamilton, W.L., Liò, P., Bengio, Y., Hjelm, R.D.: Deep graph infomax. arXiv preprint arXiv:1809.10341 (2018)
33. Wang, H., Zhang, J., Zhu, Q., Huang, W.: Augmentation-free graph contrastive learning. arXiv preprint arXiv:2204.04874 (2022)
34. Wu, L., Lin, H., Gao, Z., Tan, C., Li, S., et al.: Self-supervised on graphs: contrastive, generative, or predictive. arXiv preprint arXiv:2105.07342 (2021)
35. Wu, Z., Pan, S., Chen, F., Long, G., Zhang, C., Philip, S.Y.: A comprehensive survey on graph neural networks. IEEE Trans. Neural Netw. Learn. Syst. **32**(1), 4–24 (2020)
36. Xu, M., Wang, H., Ni, B., Guo, H., Tang, J.: Self-supervised graph-level representation learning with local and global structure. arXiv preprint arXiv:2106.04113 (2021)
37. Yin, Y., Wang, Q., Huang, S., Xiong, H., Zhang, X.: AutoGCL: automated graph contrastive learning via learnable view generators. In: Proceedings of the AAAI Conference on Artificial Intelligence, vol. 36, pp. 8892–8900 (2022)
38. You, Y., Chen, T., Shen, Y., Wang, Z.: Graph contrastive learning automated. arXiv preprint arXiv:2106.07594 (2021)
39. You, Y., Chen, T., Sui, Y., Chen, T., Wang, Z., Shen, Y.: Graph contrastive learning with augmentations. In: Advances in Neural Information Processing Systems, vol. 33 (2020)
40. Zeng, H., Zhou, H., Srivastava, A., Kannan, R., Prasanna, V.: GraphSAINT: graph sampling based inductive learning method. arXiv preprint arXiv:1907.04931 (2019)
41. Zhang, M., Chen, Y.: Link prediction based on graph neural networks. In: Advances in Neural Information Processing Systems, vol. 31, pp. 5165–5175 (2018)
42. Zhao, H., Yang, X., Wang, Z., Yang, E., Deng, C.: Graph debiased contrastive learning with joint representation clustering. In: IJCAI (2021)

43. Zhu, Q., Du, B., Yan, P.: Self-supervised training of graph convolutional networks. arXiv preprint arXiv:2006.02380 (2020)

44. Zhu, Y., Xu, Y., Yu, F., Liu, Q., Wu, S., Wang, L.: Deep graph contrastive representation learning. arXiv preprint arXiv:2006.04131 (2020)

45. Zhu, Y., Xu, Y., Yu, F., Liu, Q., Wu, S., Wang, L.: Graph contrastive learning with adaptive augmentation. In: Proceedings of the Web Conference 2021, pp. 2069–2080 (2021)

46. Zitnik, M., Leskovec, J.: Predicting multicellular function through multi-layer tissue networks. Bioinformatics **33**(14), i190–i198 (2017)

SdAE: Self-distillated Masked Autoencoder

Yabo Chen[1], Yuchen Liu[2], Dongsheng Jiang[3], Xiaopeng Zhang[3], Wenrui Dai[1], Hongkai Xiong[2], and Qi Tian[3(✉)]

[1] Department of Computer Science and Engineering, Shanghai Jiao Tong University, Shanghai, China
{chenyabo,daiwenrui}@sjtu.edu.cn
[2] Department of Electronic Engineering, Shanghai Jiao Tong University, Shanghai, China
{liuyuchen6666,xionghongkai}@sjtu.edu.cn
[3] Huawei Cloud EI, Shenzhen, China
dongsheng_jiang@outlook.com, zxphistory@gmail.com, tian.qi1@huawei.com

Abstract. With the development of generative-based self-supervised learning (SSL) approaches like BeiT and MAE, how to learn good representations by masking random patches of the input image and reconstructing the missing information has grown in concern. However, BeiT and PeCo need a "pre-pretraining" stage to produce discrete codebooks for masked patches representing. MAE does not require a pre-training codebook process, but setting pixels as reconstruction targets may introduce an optimization gap between pre-training and downstream tasks that good reconstruction quality may not always lead to the high descriptive capability for the model. Considering the above issues, in this paper, we propose a simple Self-distillated masked AutoEncoder network, namely SdAE. SdAE consists of a student branch using an encoder-decoder structure to reconstruct the missing information, and a teacher branch producing latent representation of masked tokens. We also analyze how to build good views for the teacher branch to produce latent representation from the perspective of information bottleneck. After that, we propose a multi-fold masking strategy to provide multiple masked views with balanced information for boosting the performance, which can also reduce the computational complexity. Our approach generalizes well: with only 300 epochs pre-training, a vanilla ViT-Base model achieves an 84.1% fine-tuning accuracy on ImageNet-1 k classification, 48.6 mIOU on ADE20K segmentation, and 48.9 mAP on COCO detection with only 300 epochs pre-training, which surpasses other methods by a considerable margin. Code is available at https://github.com/AbrahamYabo/SdAE.

Keywords: Self-supervised learning · Masked image modeling · Vision transformer

Y. Chen, Y. Liu, D. Jiang—Equal contribution.

Supplementary Information The online version contains supplementary material available at https://doi.org/10.1007/978-3-031-20056-4_7.

S. Avidan et al. (Eds.): ECCV 2022, LNCS 13690, pp. 108–124, 2022.
https://doi.org/10.1007/978-3-031-20056-4_7

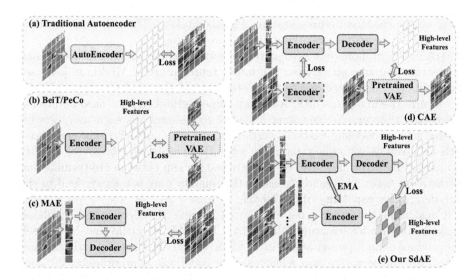

Fig. 1. Comparison of typical generative-based self-supervised learning methods. (a) The inpainting-based methods aim to regress the whole image. (b) BeiT [4] and PeCo [18] model the discrete visual correlation using a pre-trained VAE. They need a pre-trained stage to get the discrete codebooks. (c) MAE [22] mainly models the masked image modeling task as a simply pixel restoration task. (d) Although CAE [13] builds a two-branch structure, it still needs an offline tokenizer. CAE only designs the two-branch to build alignment between masked and unmasked features. (e) Without the need of a pre-trained codebook, our SdAE can build discrete correlations by self-distillating and constructing the reconstruction targets with high-level features, which can eliminate the representation gaps between the actual reconstruction targets. SdAE also proposes a masking strategy to organize the mask tokens for the teacher branch.

1   Introduction

The masked language modeling task (MLM) [16] has shown great success in self-supervised learning (SSL) for natural language processing. In computer vision, contrastive learning/instance discrimination [11,21,23,28] is a promising direction recently, which regards each instance in the training dataset as a single category. Based on instance discrimination [6,12,14], some methods show the effectiveness in many computer vision tasks. With the development of vision transformer [19], inspired by natural language processing (NLP), the generative based self-supervised learning (SSL) methods [3,4,13,18,22] using masked image modeling (MIM) task have grown in concern. MIM first randomly masks some proportion of image patches, and then recovers the masked patches based on the corrupted image.

BeiT [4] transfers the MIM task into discrete token classification using a pre-trained discrete autoencoder dVAE (DALL-E [30]). PeCO [18] modifies the generating procedure of codebook by enforcing the perceptual similarity during the VAE training. Similarly, these methods rely on a pre-trained feature descriptor to obtain the latent representation of masked tokens. These designs requiring an additional codebook are a kind of "pre-pretraining".

MAE [22] proposes an asymmetric encoder-decoder architecture that can reconstruct the raw pixels from the latent representation. MaskFeat [34] uses the hand-crafted feature descriptor Histograms of Oriented Gradients (HOG) to tokenize the image features. Although these methods do not need additional codebooks, they employ restoring low-level representations such as pixels for masked image modeling tasks. Nevertheless, restoring low-level representations such as pixels is redundant for high semantic level tasks. Moreover, directly reconstructing pixels may lead to an optimization gap between pre-training and downstream tasks, *i.e.*, good reconstruction quality may not always lead to the high descriptive capability of the model.

Considering the above issue, we propose a simple yet effective self-distillated masked autoencoder structure called SdAE. In SdAE, we claim that MAE itself can produce good representations in an effective and efficient way, and can eliminate the representation gap when used as codebook appropriately. Without needing a codebook in advance nor modeling a low-level representation, SdAE uses a self-distillated teacher-student network to produce the latent representation as reconstruction targets. The student branch consists of the asymmetric encoder-decoder architecture that feeds unmasked images, and the teacher branch contains an encoder to produce latent representation and updates weights from the student using Exponential Moving Average (EMA).

When introducing the teacher branch into the masked autoencoder structure, the easiest way is to feed the full image into the teacher network directly. However, there is no computational loss on the unmasked tokens. Obviously, due to the spatial redundancy that exists in the image, it is not optimal to put the whole image into the teacher branch. In addition, simply putting all masked tokens is still resource-consuming and faced with performance degradation compared with using the whole image as input. So there grows another concern about how to produce better latent representation using the raw images.

We further discuss this problem from the perspective of information bottleneck and propose a multi-fold masking strategy to produce good views for the self-distillated masked autoencoders as well as reduce the computational complexity. The contributions of this paper are summarized as below:

- We propose a novel self-distillated masked autoencoder structure that can construct a learnable high-level reconstruction target rather than extra pre-trained codebooks or low-level pixels, and find that MAE itself can produce a better codebook.
- We discuss how to produce good views for the teacher branch and propose a multi-fold masking strategy to keep mutual information from the teacher branch relevant to the student one. This strategy can also save computation resources.

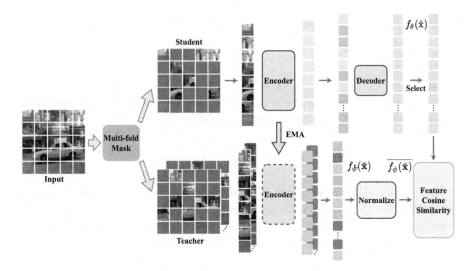

Fig. 2. An overall framework of SdAE. SdAE adopts ViT [19] as the backbone and consists of two branches. The student branch with an asymmetric encoder-decoder reconstructs the missing patches, referring to the teacher branch's latent representation. The teacher branch is simply an exponential moving average (EMA) of the student one. Specifically, all masked tokens are divided into several "small parts" to fit the information bottleneck between two branches for the multi-fold masking strategy.

2   Methods

Firstly, we elaborate the basic framework of masked image modeling and derive the objective function of our masked feature reconstruction methods in Sect. 2.1. Figure 2 depicts our proposed self-distilled masked autoencoder that consists of a two-branch network, *i.e.*, teacher and student branches. After that, we present theoretical discussions on how to produce good views for the teacher branch to build latent representation. In addition, we propose a multi-fold masking strategy, which is tailored for balancing the information between the teacher and student branches as in Sect. 2.2. Finally, in Sect. 2.3, the distillation strategy for the teacher-student framework is demonstrated.

2.1   Framework

Inspired by Masked Language Modeling (MLM) as the pre-training tasks in BERT [16], Masked Image Modeling (MIM) has been proposed in several recent works [4,22,36]. Specifically, an image $\mathbf{x} \in \mathbb{R}^{H \times W \times C}$ is reshaped and tokenized into a sequence of flattened 2D patches as $\mathbf{x} = \{\mathbf{x}_i\}_{i=1}^{N}$, where $\mathbf{x}_i \in \mathbb{R}^{N \times (P^2 \cdot C)}$ and (P, P) is the resolution of each image patch. MIM firstly samples a random binary mask $\mathbf{M} \in \{0,1\}^N$ to be $\{m^1, m^2, \cdots, m^N\}$, where $m^i \in \{0,1\}$ and N is the number of tokens. The patch token $\mathbf{x}_i$ with $m^i = 1$ is masked and we denote the mask ratio as $r = \frac{\sum_{i=1}^{N} m^i}{N} \in (0,1)$. All the masked tokens $\tilde{\mathbf{x}} \triangleq \{\mathbf{x}_i \mid m^i = 1\}_{i=1}^{N}$ are discarded for efficiency, resulting in a corrupted image $\hat{\mathbf{x}} \triangleq \{\hat{\mathbf{x}}_i \mid (1 - m^i)\, \mathbf{x}_i\}_{i=1}^{N}$. In summarize, we have $\tilde{\mathbf{x}} \in \mathbb{R}^{N \cdot r \times (P^2 \cdot C)}$ and $\hat{\mathbf{x}} \in \mathbb{R}^{N \cdot (1-r) \times (P^2 \cdot C)}$. The objective of MIM is to recover the masked tokens $\tilde{\mathbf{x}}$ by using the corrupted image $\hat{\mathbf{x}}$ as $\log q_\psi(\tilde{\mathbf{x}}|\hat{\mathbf{x}})$. Assuming the reconstruction of each masked token is independent to each other [4,39], the objective can be reformulated as:

$$\log q_\psi(\tilde{\mathbf{x}}|\hat{\mathbf{x}}) \approx \sum_{i=1}^{N} m^i \cdot \log q_\psi(\mathbf{x}_i|\hat{\mathbf{x}}) \tag{1}$$

Considering MIM is essentially a reconstruction task. It is related more to regression tasks than to classification tasks. Thus, we assume the noise in the deviation of reconstructed and ground truth values follow the standard Gaussian distribution as $\eta \sim N(0,1)$, and the objective is to minimize

$$\sum_{i=1}^{N} m^i \cdot \log q_\psi(\mathbf{x}_i|\hat{\mathbf{x}}) = \sum_{i=1}^{N} m^i \cdot \log e^{\frac{-(f_\phi(\mathbf{x}_i) - f_\theta(\hat{\mathbf{x}}))^2}{2}} = \sum_{i=1}^{N} -\frac{1}{2} m^i (f_\phi(\mathbf{x}_i) - f_\theta(\hat{\mathbf{x}}))^2. \tag{2}$$

Specifically, for MAE [22], f_ϕ is the identity function, and f_θ is the masked autoencoder that reconstructs masked patches in the pixel spatial space. However, we argue that (1) The f_ϕ is a fixed identity function without adaptation during pre-training that undermines the effectiveness of the self-supervised training; (2) Memorying each pixel of the images by reconstruction in the low semantic level space is sub-optimal and less efficient for capturing representations for high-level tasks. There exists an optimization direction gap in that the quality of the reconstruction may not always increase the descriptive capability of the model.

Correspondingly, we introduce a self-distillation architecture, $i.e.$, f_θ is the student network trained by gradient descent using $\hat{\mathbf{x}}$ as inputs and f_ϕ is the teacher network updated by exponential moving average (EMA) from the parameters of the student network. The teacher network use $\tilde{\mathbf{x}}$ as inputs and conduct the missing information reconstruction in the high-level latent representation space rather than in the pixel space.

Inspired by MAE [22], we propose a value normalization function upon teacher outputs. Specifically, we compute the mean and standard deviation of feature values within a patch and use them to normalize the teacher outputs as

$$\overline{f_\phi(\mathbf{x}_i)} = \frac{f_\phi(\mathbf{x}_i) - mean(f_\phi(\mathbf{x}_i))}{\sqrt{var(f_\phi(\mathbf{x}_i)) + \epsilon}} \tag{3}$$

where ϵ is a small value to prevent the denominator from being 0. We find that using normalized features as the reconstruction target improves the representation quality.

Then we minimize the normalized teacher features with the output features of the student decoder based on the feature cosine similarity, and Eq. (2) is reformulated as:

$$\log q_\psi(\tilde{\mathbf{x}}|\hat{\mathbf{x}}) \approx \frac{\sum_{i=1}^{n} m^i \overline{f_\phi(\mathbf{x}_i)} f_\theta(\hat{\mathbf{x}})}{\sqrt{\sum_{i=1}^{n} m^i \left(\overline{f_\phi(\mathbf{x}_i)}\right)^2} \sqrt{\sum_{i=1}^{n} m^i \left(f_\theta(\hat{\mathbf{x}})\right)^2}} \tag{4}$$

2.2 Discussions on the Teacher Branch Feeding

As mentioned in MAE [22], languages are human-generated signals that are highly semantic and information-dense. Predicting a few missing words per sentence can induce sophisticated language understanding, but images are natural signals with heavy spatial redundancy. Directly feeding the whole image into the teacher network to produce features may be sub-optimal.

Before discussing the better feeding of the teacher branch, we provide a brief introduction here to show alternatives to the teacher branch feeding. As shown in Fig. 3 (a), MAE [22] and MaskFeat [34] take the whole image as input to produce normalized tokens (normalized raw image pixels) or HOG from the whole images as the reconstruction target. Correspondingly, another simply modeling way is to feed the whole image into the teacher network directly as Fig. 3 (b). However, since we have mentioned that the reconstruction loss only computes for masked tokens, there is no need to feed all the patches, and visible patches may be spatial redundant. Only feeding the masked patches $\hat{x}$ into the network can relieve the spatial redundancy to some extent. Furthermore, to reduce more spatial redundancy and save the computational resource, we can mask some of the target tokens and feed the remaining tokens into the teacher. We called this operation as teacher crop. In the experiment, we can achieve comparable performance between teacher crop and reconstruct all masked patches. As shown in Fig. 3 (c). We formulate this teacher crop masking as another random binary mask $\mathbf{M^t} \in \{0,1\}^{N \cdot \mathrm{r}}$ to be $\{m_t^1, m_t^2, \cdots, m_t^{N \cdot \mathrm{r}}\}$, where $m_t^i \in \{0,1\}$ and $N \cdot \mathrm{r}$ is the number of total target tokens. Similarly, we formulate the teacher crop mask ratio as $\mathrm{r}_c \in (0,1)$. Based on this binary mask, we can randomly select a group of target tokens as: $\tilde{\mathbf{x}}^* \triangleq \{\tilde{\mathbf{x}}_i \mid m_t^i = 1\}_{i=1}^{N \cdot \mathrm{r}}$, and the latent representation is denoted as $f_\theta(\tilde{\mathbf{x}}^*)$.

Multi-fold Masking Strategy. Furthermore, we propose a multi-fold masking strategy that groups several teacher crops to sufficiently use masked tokens. As shown in Fig. 3 (d), given a number of fold t, all the masked tokens are divided into t groups of teacher crops without overlap as $\tilde{\mathbf{x}} = \{\tilde{\mathbf{x}}^{*1}, \tilde{\mathbf{x}}^{*2}, ..., \tilde{\mathbf{x}}^{*t}\}$. Each fold containing masked tokens will be fed into a shared teacher network independently. The outputs of the teacher network will be rearranged together to calculate the cosine similarity loss in a parallel way. Specifically, the output of the teacher branch can be reformulated as: $f_\theta(\tilde{\mathbf{x}}) = \{f_\theta(\tilde{\mathbf{x}}^{*1}), f_\theta(\tilde{\mathbf{x}}^{*2}), ..., f_\theta(\tilde{\mathbf{x}}^{*t})\}$. As shown in Table 1, from the view of computational cost, the main difference between multi-fold masking strategy and all masked patches feeding is that in the teacher branch, the self-attention is only calculated in each teacher crop of tokens instead of all masked tokens. So the multi-mask strategy can save complexities by a factor of t. Detailed theoretical complexity can be seen in Table 1.

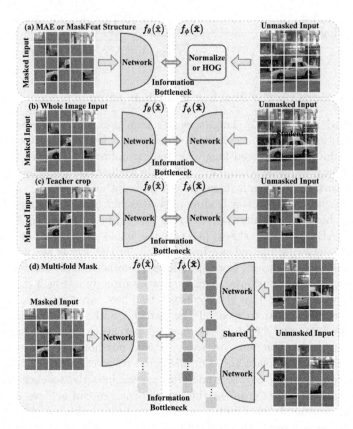

Fig. 3. (a) MAE [22] and MaskFeat [34] reconstruct the low-level representations. (b) Feeding the whole image into the teacher network is the simplest way. (c) We experiment with teacher-crop reconstructing only parts of tokens. (d) Multi-fold masking divides unmasked tokens into independent groups and feeds them into shared networks.

In practice, directly feeding the whole image into the teacher network will increase almost half of the computation costs compared with MAE, as shown in Table 1. Using all masked patches as input like CAE [13] will also increase 38.1% pre-training time. Using multi-fold masking strategy, we can save the extra pre-training time costs by only 28.1%.

The main difference between our multi-fold masking and previous work multi-crop [6] is discussed as follows. The multi-crop strategy needs to train multiple random views with different sizes without concern of complexity. By contrast, multi-fold masking just rearranges the mask tokens and does not create new views. Multi-fold masking can also save training complexity by calculating self-attention on only a small group of tokens.

Table 1. Alternatives for the input of the teacher branch network. The multi-mask strategy captures content only within each fold at a reduced memory cost compared with all masked patches fed. Comparatively, using a multi-mask strategy reduces complexities by a factor of t. n: input length, d: dimension of channels, r: mask ratio, r_c the teacher crop mask ratio, t: number of fold. The training time is the computational costs for per epoch with NVIDIA V100 GPUs and the memory cost is the maximum usage on per GPU.

Operation	Theoretical complexity	Training time	GPU memory
MAE(baseline)	–	551 s	14.93 G
Full image input	$\Theta(n^2 d)$	826s(+49.9%)	16.24 G
Only masked patches input	$\Theta(n^2 r^2 d)$	761s(+38.1%)	16.01 G
Teacher crop input	$\Theta(n^2 r_c{}^2 r^2 d)$	616s(+11.8%)	15.54 G
Multi-fold masking strategy	$\Theta((n/t)^2 t r^2 d)$	706s(+28.1%)	16.02 G

Information Bottleneck and Multi-fold Masking. In this section, we will follow the assumption from the views of information bottleneck theory in [1,33] to discuss the benefits of multi-fold masking except for saving costs.

Denote $\tilde{\mathbf{x}}$ and $\hat{\mathbf{x}}$ as the input of the teacher and student network, respectively. From the perspective of information theory, maximizing Eq. (2) is equivalent to maximizing the mutual information $I(\tilde{\mathbf{x}}, \hat{\mathbf{x}})$ as

$$I(\tilde{\mathbf{x}}, \hat{\mathbf{x}}) = H(f_\phi(\tilde{\mathbf{x}})) - H(f_\phi(\tilde{\mathbf{x}})|f_\theta(\hat{\mathbf{x}})) = H(f_\phi(\tilde{\mathbf{x}})) + \mathbb{E}_{\tilde{\mathbf{x}}, \hat{\mathbf{x}}}[\log p(f_\phi(\tilde{\mathbf{x}})|f_\theta(\hat{\mathbf{x}}))] \quad (5)$$

Since the true distribution of $p(\tilde{\mathbf{x}}|\hat{\mathbf{x}})$ is unknown, a variational distribution $q(\tilde{\mathbf{x}}|\hat{\mathbf{x}})$ is employed for approximation, and Eq. (5) can be written as:

$$I(\tilde{\mathbf{x}}, \hat{\mathbf{x}}) = H(f_\phi(\tilde{\mathbf{x}})) + \mathbb{E}_{\tilde{\mathbf{x}}, \hat{\mathbf{x}}}[\log q(f_\phi(\tilde{\mathbf{x}})|f_\theta(\hat{\mathbf{x}}))] + \mathbb{E}_{\hat{\mathbf{x}}}[KL(p(f_\phi(\tilde{\mathbf{x}})|f_\theta(\hat{\mathbf{x}}))||q(f_\phi(\tilde{\mathbf{x}})|f_\theta(\hat{\mathbf{x}})))]$$
$$(6)$$

where $f_\phi(\tilde{\mathbf{x}})$ and $f_\theta(\hat{\mathbf{x}})$ are the representations from the teacher and student networks, and $H(\cdot)$ is the entropy function. Since $KL(\cdot)$ function is non-negative and $H(\tilde{\mathbf{x}})$ is constant w.r.t the parameters to be optimized, maximizing $I(\tilde{\mathbf{x}}, \hat{\mathbf{x}})$ is equivalent to maximizing $\mathbb{E}_{\tilde{\mathbf{x}}, \hat{\mathbf{x}}}[\log q(f_\phi(\tilde{\mathbf{x}})|f_\theta(\hat{\mathbf{x}}))]$ with q modeled by a Gaussian distribution, which is in consistent with Eq. (2). Thus, the objective of MIM can be reinterpreted as $I(\tilde{\mathbf{x}}, \hat{\mathbf{x}})$ in the information theory view.

Definition 1. *(Sufficient Encoder) The encoder f_θ of $\hat{\mathbf{x}}$ is sufficient in the self-supervised learning framework if and only if $|I(\tilde{\mathbf{x}}, \hat{\mathbf{x}}) - I(\tilde{\mathbf{x}}, f_\theta(\hat{\mathbf{x}}))| < \epsilon$.*

Ideally, the encoder f_θ is sufficient if the amount of information in $\hat{\mathbf{x}}$ about $\tilde{\mathbf{x}}$ is lossless during the encoding procedure. In other words, $f_\theta(\hat{\mathbf{x}})$ has kept all the information that the reconstruction objective requires. Symmetrically, f_ϕ is sufficient if $|I(\tilde{\mathbf{x}}, \hat{\mathbf{x}}) - I(\tilde{\mathbf{x}}, f_\theta(\hat{\mathbf{x}}))| < \epsilon$.

Definition 2. *(Minimal Sufficient Encoder) A sufficient encoder f_θ of $\hat{\mathbf{x}}$ is minimal if and only if $I(f_\theta(\hat{\mathbf{x}}), \hat{\mathbf{x}}) \leq I(f(\hat{\mathbf{x}}), \hat{\mathbf{x}}), \forall f$ that is sufficient.*

Among these sufficient encoders, the minimal ones only keep relevant information of the reconstruction task and throw away other irrelevant information.

Proposition 1. *Suppose f_θ and f_ϕ are minimal sufficient encoders. Given a downstream task T with label $\mathbf{y}$, the optimal views created from the data $\mathbf{x}$ are $(\tilde{\mathbf{x}}^*, \hat{\mathbf{x}}^*) = \arg\min_{\tilde{\mathbf{x}}, \hat{\mathbf{x}}} I(\tilde{\mathbf{x}}, \hat{\mathbf{x}})$, subject to $|I(\tilde{\mathbf{x}}, \mathbf{y}) - I(\hat{\mathbf{x}}, \mathbf{y})| < \epsilon$.*

Specifically, based on Proposition 1, we can model the multi-fold masking tokens as multi-views from reconstructed images, which can be formulated as $\{\tilde{\mathbf{x}}^{*1}, \tilde{\mathbf{x}}^{*2}, ..., \tilde{\mathbf{x}}^{*t}\}$ and the unmasked tokens is another view of input images $\hat{\mathbf{x}}$. Then, we draw insights for views that feed into the teacher and student networks: (1) Ours method satisfies with $\arg\min_{\tilde{\mathbf{x}}, \hat{\mathbf{x}}} I(\tilde{\mathbf{x}}, \hat{\mathbf{x}})$, since the feeding of the teacher and student networks do not contains overlap tokens, reducing the shared mutual information. (2) Due to the need to satisfy $|I(\tilde{\mathbf{x}}, \mathbf{y}) - I(\hat{\mathbf{x}}, \mathbf{y})| < \epsilon$, the amount of mutual information between $\tilde{\mathbf{x}}$ and $\hat{\mathbf{x}}$ should be comparable. We propose a multi-fold masking strategy to divide the masked patches into groups to make the number of masked patches feeding into the teacher network equal with that feeding into the student. Thus, their shared mutual information with the downstream task is comparable. As shown in Fig. 4 (b), we experimentally verify this proposition that when the number of masked patches from each fold is equal with the unmasked patches (25% of total image patches in practice), our SdAE achieves the best performance. (3) Considering the objective function of MIM tasks is $\max I(\tilde{\mathbf{x}}, \mathbf{y})$, we also need to $\max I(\hat{\mathbf{x}}, \mathbf{y})$, so we try to utilize almost all masked tokens to keep as more task related information as possible.

2.3 Distillation Strategy

Considering a teacher network, we hypothesize that it is desirable to build the reconstruction target representations in the (i) online and (ii) consistent way. Now that the student network f_θ is trained by back-propagation to minimize the feature reconstruction loss. The teacher network is updated in a momentum update way using exponential moving average (EMA). Specifically, denoting the parameters of f_ϕ as ϕ and those of f_θ as θ, we update ϕ by:

$$\phi \leftarrow \eta \cdot \phi + (1 - \eta) \cdot \theta \tag{7}$$

Here $\eta \in [0, 1)$ is a momentum coefficient to control the frequency of updates from the student model. The codebook should not update too often. Otherwise, the model may fail to converge.

3   Experiments

This section evaluates our pre-trained feature representation on several unsupervised benchmarks. We first evaluate the classification performance on ImageNet-1 k under fine-tuning and linear probing. Then we transfer the pre-trained features to several downstream tasks, *i.e.*, semantic segmentation and object detection. Finally, we conducted an ablation study on the key components of SdAE.

Table 2. Image classification results on the ILSVRC-2012 ImageNet dataset with top 1 accuracy. "Epochs" refers to the number of pre-training epochs. MoCo v3 and DINO adopt multi-crop augmentation for pre-training. MoCo v3: 2 global crops of 224 × 224. DINO: 2 global crops of 224 × 224 and 10 local crops of 96 × 96.

Method	Epochs	Crops	Finetune	Linear
Methods using ViT-B:				
Train from Scratch	300	–	81.8	–
MoCo v3	300	2	83.2	76.2
DINO	400	12	83.3	**77.3**
BEiT	300	1	83.0	49.4
MAE	100	1	82.1	54.8
MAE	300	1	82.9	61.5
MAE	1600	1	83.6	67.8
CAE	300	1	83.3	64.2
SdAE	100	1	83.5	60.3
SdAE	300	1	**84.1**	64.9

3.1   Fine-Tuning on ImageNet-1 k

We study the fine-tuning on the ILSVRC-2012 ImageNet dataset [31] with 1 k classes and 1.3 M images. For a fair comparison, we directly follow most of the hyperparameters of MAE [22] in our fine-tuning experiments. All experiments reported are only fine-tuning for 100 epochs (vs. 300 training from scratch). We compare our SdAE with Vision Transformers trained by random initialization and previous self-supervised learning methods. As shown in Table 2, compared with the models trained by random initialization which only achieves 81.8% top-1 accuracy with ViT-B, our SdAE achieves 84.1%, demonstrating the effectiveness of pre-training with unlabeled data.

Compared with previous self-supervised methods, our proposed SdAE surpasses them on ImageNet fine-tuning by a large margin. For ViT-B, our SdAE outperforms MAE by 1.2% top-1 accuracy with the same number of training epochs, demonstrating that MIM on high-level latent feature space is more effective than low-level pixel space. Besides, our SdAE outperforms BEiT by 1.1% top-1 accuracy. Moreover, compared to the recently proposed CAE, our SdAE achieves 0.8% top-1 accuracy gain, demonstrating the effectiveness of our self-distillated design and multi-fold masking strategy. In addition, with only 100 epochs pre-training, SdAE can achieve comparable performance with MAE using 1600 epochs pre-training and surpass 300 epochs pre-trained CAE. Our proposed SdAE also surpasses above methods on ImageNet linear probing with the same training epochs. As a MIM based method, SdAE can also surpasses MIM based methods with the same pre-training epochs. The phenomenon that contrastive based methods surpass the MIM based ones on linear probing is also discussed in MAE [22] and CAE [13]. In terms of linear probing, contrastive

Table 3. Semantic segmentation on ADE20K. All methods use ViT-B backbone based on the same implementation. "Epochs" refers to the number of pre-training epochs.

Method	Epochs	Crops	Supervised	Self-supervised	mIoU
DeiT	300	–	✓	✗	47.0
MoCo v3	300	2	✗	✓	47.2
DINO	400	12	✗	✓	47.2
BEiT	300	1	✗	✓	45.5
BEiT	800	1	✗	✓	46.5
MAE	300	1	✗	✓	45.8
MAE	1600	1	✗	✓	48.1
CAE	300	1	✗	✓	47.7
SdAE	300	1	✗	✓	**48.6**

Table 4. Object detection and instance segmentation on COCO. All the results are based on the same implementations. Mask R-CNN is adopted and trained with the 1× schedule. "Epochs" refers to the number of pre-training epochs on ImageNet-1 K. "Sup" and "Self-sup" refer to the methods that are supervised or self-supervised.

Methods	Epochs	Sup	Self-sup	Object Detection			Instance segmentation		
				AP^b	AP^b_{50}	AP^b_{75}	AP^m	AP^m_{50}	AP^m_{75}
Methods using ViT-B:									
DeiT	300	✓	✗	46.9	68.9	51.0	41.5	65.5	44.4
MoCo v3	300	✗	✓	45.5	67.1	49.4	40.5	63.7	43.4
DINO	400	✗	✓	46.8	68.6	50.9	41.5	65.3	44.5
BEiT	300	✗	✓	39.5	60.6	43.0	35.9	57.7	38.5
BEiT	800	✗	✓	42.1	63.3	46.0	37.8	60.1	40.6
MAE	300	✗	✓	45.4	66.4	49.6	40.6	63.4	43.7
MAE	1600	✗	✓	48.4	69.4	53.1	42.6	66.1	45.9
CAE	300	✗	✓	48.0	68.7	52.7	42.3	65.6	45.4
SdAE	300	✗	✓	**48.9**	69.6	53.3	**43.0**	66.2	46.2

learning mainly cares about the 1000 classes and MIM methods may care about the classes beyond the 1000 classes. So fine-tuning measurement may better validate the effectiveness of MIM based methods.

3.2   Semantic Segmentation

We evaluate the learned representation of our SdAE on the ADE20K benchmark [38] with 25 K images and 150 semantic categories. The mean Intersection of Union (mIoU) averaged over all semantic categories is reported as the evaluation metric. Table 3 shows that our SdAE achieves the state-of-the-art performance with 48.6 mIoU for 300 pre-training epochs. Our SdAE outperforms BEiT,

MAE, and CAE by 3.1, 2.8, and 1.9 mIoU, respectively. Besides, our SdAE with 300 pre-training epochs even outperforms MAE with 1600 pre-training epochs.

3.3 Object Detection

Following CAE [13], we fine-tune Mask R-CNN [25] in an end-to-end manner on COCO [27]. The ViT backbone is adapted for use with FPN [26]. The box AP for object detection and the mask AP for instance segmentation is reported in Table 4. Our method (300 epochs, ViT-B) is consistently superior to all the other models. Our SdAE performs better than the recent published CAE (48.9 *vs.* 48.0 AP^b). Besides, it is worth mentioning that our SdAE (300 epochs) even outperforms MAE (1600 epochs) by 0.5 AP^b. As an effective framework for self-supervised learning, we achieve better performance with fewer training epochs.

4 Ablation Studies

In this section, we present ablation studies to better evaluate the contributions of each component and hyperparameter settings in our proposed SdAE. Unless specified, all results are compared with models pre-trained for 100 epochs for efficiency, and we report the top-1 accuracy after fine-tuning for 100 epochs.

4.1 Ablation Studies on Each Component

In this subsection, we present ablation studies on each component. Table 5 shows that our proposed teacher normalization achieves 0.3% top-1 accuracy gain. Only inputting the masked tokens into the teacher network suffers from 0.5% performance degradation due to insufficient information exploration. While using our proposed multi-fold masking strategy, we can achieve 0.6% improvement compared with only masked token inputs. Besides, multi-fold masking even outperforms taking full image as inputs more efficiently.

Table 5. Ablation studies on each component. "Full image" refers to the teacher network taking the whole image as input. "Only masked" refers to only the masked patches that are fed into the teacher network. "Multi fold" indicates our multi-fold masking strategy. Teacher normalization refers to whether adding feature values normalization within patches or not.

Full image	Only masked	Multi fold	Teacher normalize	Accuracy
✓	✗	✗	✗	83.7
✓	✗	✗	✓	84.0
✗	✓	✗	✓	83.5
✗	✗	✓	✓	**84.1**

4.2   The EMA Strategy

This experiment is conducted without the multi-fold masking strategy to evaluate the raw performance of the EMA strategy. Specifically, we have two settings for the EMA strategy: (1) update the parameters of the teacher branch with EMA for each training iteration. (2) update the parameters of the teacher branch with EMA for each training epoch. As shown in Fig. 4 (a), conducting the EMA strategy to update the teacher branch each training iteration is extremely sensitive to the value of the momentum coefficient. Specifically, only changing the value by 0.001 results in the sharply degraded performance. In contrast, the EMA strategy to update the teacher branch per batch is more robust to the momentum coefficient. Besides, conducting the EMA strategy per epoch can better benefit from long training epochs.

4.3   The Multi-fold Masking Strategy

We further conduct an ablation study on the multi-fold masking strategy. Firstly, we study experiments on the teacher crop that mask some of the target tokens and feed the remaining tokens into the teacher. The whole image is divided into 196 image patches with the size of 16×16, and we randomly sample a different number of total patches, *e.g.*, 36, 49, 79, 122, 147 and 196 as whole image input into the teacher network. As shown in Fig. 4 (b), for the case that 36 image patches (roughly 18% of the whole image) are input to the teacher network, our method can achieve 82.81% top-1 accuracy. 83.04% top-1 accuracy is achieved when we take the whole image as input. Comparably, only 0.23% performance gain is achieved when five times as many image patches are input. The problem of spatial redundancy is also common in the input views of the teacher network.

Correspondingly, we take the multi-fold masking strategy. Apart from the 49 patches that are input to the student network, the left 147 image patches are divided into 2 fold as 2×79 patches, 3 fold as 3×49 patches or 4 fold as 4×36 patches. As shown in Fig. 4 (b), a multi-fold masking strategy can consistently improve the performance. For 3 fold with 49 patches, our method achieves the best performance. This experiment also proves our information bottleneck discussion, that with comparable mutual information between each fold and the student input, we can get the best performance.

4.4   Evaluation of Teacher and Student Models

As shown in Fig. 4 (c), for every 20 epochs of our training, we finetune our pre-trained teacher and student models for 5 epochs on ImageNet-1 K. The student model performs better than the teacher model in the initial epochs when the learning rate is relatively low due to warm up and then is very close to the teacher when the learning rate increases. We demonstrate that the teacher model and student model trained by our SdAE achieve similar performance. That proves the teacher branch can really learn high semantic level related representations. The teacher model can be seen as an ensemble over many student models. We follow most previous works to use the student model as the final model.

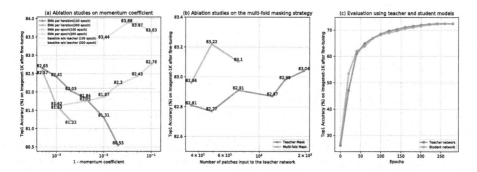

Fig. 4. (a) Ablation studies on the EMA update strategy for the coefficient of the momentum teacher. (b) Ablation studies on the multi-fold masking strategy. (c) Ablation studies on the evaluation of teacher and student models.

5   Related Work

Previous self-supervised methods utilize different priors of images to design clever pretext tasks, such as predicting the patch positions [17], inpainting [29], colorization [37], and rotation prediction [20]. Recent progress in self-supervised learning focuses on contrastive learning and masked image modeling.

Masked Image Modeling. Motivated by BERT [16] for masked language modeling(MLM), masked image modeling(MIM) is proposed to learn representations from images corrupted by masking. Recent works leverage the powerful Vision Transformer, which matches the masked image modeling task. iGPT [9] operates on sequences of pixels and predicts unknown pixels. Vision transformer [19] studies masked average value prediction for self-supervised learning. BEiT [4] proposes to predict discrete tokens based on a pre-trained image tokenizer while iBOT [39] proposes an online tokenizer. MAE [22] proposes a masked autoencoder for reconstructing the image pixels. CAE [13] provides a two-branch network for MIM, and the masked features are modeled as a regularization to align the mask and unmasked features.

Contrastive Learning. Contrastive learning is proposed based on the InfoMax principle, which aims at maximizing the mutual information [35] across different augmentations of the same image [10,32]. This augmentation invariance is achieved by enforcing the similarity over different views of the same image while avoiding model collapse. Model collapse can be avoided by introducing negative samples for noise-contrastive estimation [10,12,24,35]. The models typically regard various data augmentations as different views of an image and then make the representations of positive pairs similar while pushing negative pairs away. Large memory banks or large batch size is leveraged to obtain more informative negative samples. BYOL [21] and SimSiam [15] employ an asymmetric network and eliminate the requirement of negative samples. Other methods use clustering [2,5,7,8] to organize image examples.

6   Conclusion

In this paper, we propose a novel Self-distillated Masked Autoencoder for masked feature reconstruction, namely SdAE. We first formulate the framework of the masked image modeling task, based on which we analyze that existing methods are sub-optimal due to the need of pre-trained codebooks or just reconstructing the low-level pixels. We propose a self-distillated framework for reconstruction in the high-level feature space. Besides, we analyze how to build good views for the teacher branch to produce latent representation from the perspective of information bottleneck theory and propose a multi-fold masking strategy that can also relieve the spatial redundancy. Experimentally, based on a vanilla ViT-Base model, our SdAE achieves a new state-of-the-art of 84.1% top-1 accuracy with only 300 epochs pre-training.

Acknowledgments. This work was supported in part by the National Natural Science Foundation of China under Grant 61932022, Grant 61931023, Grant 61971285, Grant 62120106007, and in part by the Program of Shanghai Science and Technology Innovation Project under Grant 20511100100.

References

1. Alemi, A.A., Fischer, I., Dillon, J.V., Murphy, K.: Deep variational information bottleneck. arXiv: Learning (2016)
2. Asano, Y.M., Rupprecht, C., Vedaldi, A.: Self-labelling via simultaneous clustering and representation learning. arXiv preprint. arXiv:1911.05371 (2019)
3. Baevski, A., Hsu, W.N., Xu, Q., Babu, A., Gu, J., Auli, M.: Data2vec: a general framework for self-supervised learning in speech, vision and language. arXiv preprint. arXiv:2202.03555 (2022)
4. Bao, H., Dong, L., Wei, F.: Beit: bert pre-training of image transformers. arXiv: Computer Vision and Pattern Recognition (2021)
5. Caron, M., Bojanowski, P., Joulin, A., Douze, M.: Deep clustering for unsupervised learning of visual features. In: Ferrari, V., Hebert, M., Sminchisescu, C., Weiss, Y. (eds.) Computer Vision – ECCV 2018. LNCS, vol. 11218, pp. 139–156. Springer, Cham (2018). https://doi.org/10.1007/978-3-030-01264-9_9
6. Caron, M., Misra, I., Mairal, J., Goyal, P., Bojanowski, P., Joulin, A.: Unsupervised learning of visual features by contrasting cluster assignments. In: Neural Information Processing Systems (2020)
7. Caron, M., Misra, I., Mairal, J., Goyal, P., Bojanowski, P., Joulin, A.: Unsupervised learning of visual features by contrasting cluster assignments. In: Advances in Neural Information Processing Systems, vol. 33, pp. 9912–9924 (2020)
8. Caron, M., Touvron, H., Misra, I., Jégou, H., Mairal, J., Bojanowski, P., Joulin, A.: Emerging properties in self-supervised vision transformers. In: Proceedings of the IEEE/CVF International Conference on Computer Vision, pp. 9650–9660 (2021)
9. Chen, M., et al.: Generative pretraining from pixels. In: International Conference on Machine Learning, pp. 1691–1703. PMLR (2020)
10. Chen, T., Kornblith, S., Norouzi, M., Hinton, G.: A simple framework for contrastive learning of visual representations. In: International Conference on Machine Learning, pp. 1597–1607. PMLR (2020)

11. Chen, T., Kornblith, S., Norouzi, M., Hinton, G.E.: A simple framework for contrastive learning of visual representations. arXiv: Learning (2020)

12. Chen, T., Kornblith, S., Swersky, K., Norouzi, M., Hinton, G.E.: Big self-supervised models are strong semi-supervised learners. arXiv: Learning (2020)

13. Chen, X., et al.: Context autoencoder for self-supervised representation learning (2022)

14. Chen, X., Fan, H., Girshick, R., He, K.: Improved baselines with momentum contrastive learning. arXiv: Computer Vision and Pattern Recognition (2020)

15. Chen, X., He, K.: Exploring simple siamese representation learning. In: Proceedings of the IEEE/CVF Conference on Computer Vision and Pattern Recognition, pp. 15750–15758 (2021)

16. Devlin, J., Chang, M.W., Lee, K., Toutanova, K.: Bert: pre-training of deep bidirectional transformers for language understanding. In: North American Chapter of the Association for Computational Linguistics (2018)

17. Doersch, C., Gupta, A., Efros, A.A.: Unsupervised visual representation learning by context prediction. In: Proceedings of the IEEE International Conference on Computer Vision, pp. 1422–1430 (2015)

18. Dong, X., et al.: Peco: perceptual codebook for Bert Pre-training of Vision Transformers (2022)

19. Dosovitskiy, A., et al.: An image is worth 16x16 words: transformers for image recognition at scale. In: International Conference on Learning Representations (2021)

20. Gidaris, S., Singh, P., Komodakis, N.: Unsupervised representation learning by predicting image rotations. arXiv preprint. arXiv:1803.07728 (2018)

21. Grill, J.B., et al.: Bootstrap your own latent: a new approach to self-supervised learning. arXiv: Learning (2020)

22. He, K., Chen, X., Xie, S., Li, Y., Dollár, P., Girshick, R.: Masked autoencoders are scalable vision learners. arXiv preprint. arXiv:2111.06377 (2021)

23. He, K., Fan, H., Wu, Y., Xie, S., Girshick, R.: Momentum contrast for unsupervised visual representation learning. In: Computer Vision and Pattern Recognition (2020)

24. He, K., Fan, H., Wu, Y., Xie, S., Girshick, R.: Momentum contrast for unsupervised visual representation learning. In: Proceedings of the IEEE/CVF Conference on Computer Vision and Pattern Recognition, pp. 9729–9738 (2020)

25. He, K., Gkioxari, G., Dollár, P., Girshick, R.: Mask r-cnn. In: Proceedings of the IEEE international conference on computer vision, pp. 2961–2969 (2017)

26. Lin, T.Y., Dollár, P., Girshick, R., He, K., Hariharan, B., Belongie, S.: Feature pyramid networks for object detection. In: Proceedings of the IEEE Conference on Computer Vision and Pattern Recognition, pp. 2117–2125 (2017)

27. Lin, T.Y., et al.: Microsoft COCO: common objects in context. In: Fleet, D., Pajdla, T., Schiele, B., Tuytelaars, T. (eds.) ECCV 2014. LNCS, vol. 8693, pp. 740–755. Springer, Cham (2014). https://doi.org/10.1007/978-3-319-10602-1_48

28. van den Oord, A., Li, Y., Vinyals, O.: Representation learning with contrastive predictive coding. arXiv: Learning (2018)

29. Pathak, D., Krahenbuhl, P., Donahue, J., Darrell, T., Efros, A.A.: Context encoders: feature learning by inpainting. In: Proceedings of the IEEE Conference on Computer Vision and Pattern Recognition, pp. 2536–2544 (2016)

30. Ramesh, A., et al.: Zero-shot text-to-image generation. arXiv: Computer Vision and Pattern Recognition (2021)

31. Russakovsky, O., et al.: ImageNet large scale visual recognition challenge. International Journal of Computer Vision **115**(3), 211–252 (2015). https://doi.org/10.1007/s11263-015-0816-y

32. Tian, Y., Krishnan, D., Isola, P.: Contrastive multiview coding. In: Vedaldi, A., Bischof, H., Brox, T., Frahm, J.-M. (eds.) ECCV 2020. LNCS, vol. 12356, pp. 776–794. Springer, Cham (2020). https://doi.org/10.1007/978-3-030-58621-8_45

33. Tian, Y., Sun, C., Poole, B., Krishnan, D., Schmid, C., Isola, P.: What makes for good views for contrastive learning? Advances in Neural Information Processing Systems, vol. 33, pp. 6827–6839 (2020)

34. Wei, C., Fan, H., Xie, S., Wu, C.Y., Yuille, A., Feichtenhofer, C.: Masked feature prediction for self-supervised visual pre-training. arXiv preprint. arXiv:2112.09133 (2021)

35. Wu, Z., Xiong, Y., Yu, S.X., Lin, D.: Unsupervised feature learning via non-parametric instance discrimination. In: Proceedings of the IEEE Conference on Computer Vision and Pattern Recognition, pp. 3733–3742 (2018)

36. Xie, Z., et al.: Simmim: a simple framework for masked image modeling. In: International Conference on Computer Vision and Pattern Recognition (CVPR) (2022)

37. Zhang, R., Isola, P., Efros, A.A.: Colorful image colorization. In: Leibe, B., Matas, J., Sebe, N., Welling, M. (eds.) ECCV 2016. LNCS, vol. 9907, pp. 649–666. Springer, Cham (2016). https://doi.org/10.1007/978-3-319-46487-9_40

38. Zhou, B., et al.: Semantic understanding of scenes through the ADE20K dataset. Int. J. Comput. Vis. **127**(3), 302–321 (2018). https://doi.org/10.1007/s11263-018-1140-0

39. Zhou, J., et al.: ibot: Image bert pre-training with online tokenizer (2022)

Demystifying Unsupervised Semantic Correspondence Estimation

Mehmet Aygün[⊠] and Oisin Mac Aodha

University of Edinburgh, Edinburgh, UK
m.aygun@sms.ed.ac.uk
https://mehmetaygun.github.io/demistfy

Abstract. We explore semantic correspondence estimation through the lens of unsupervised learning. We thoroughly evaluate several recently proposed unsupervised methods across multiple challenging datasets using a standardized evaluation protocol where we vary factors such as the backbone architecture, the pre-training strategy, and the pre-training and finetuning datasets. To better understand the failure modes of these methods, and in order to provide a clearer path for improvement, we provide a new diagnostic framework along with a new performance metric that is better suited to the semantic matching task. Finally, we introduce a new unsupervised correspondence approach which utilizes the strength of pre-trained features while encouraging better matches during training. This results in significantly better matching performance compared to current state-of-the-art methods.

Keywords: Semantic correspondence · Self-supervised learning

1 Introduction

In metaphysics, the correspondence theory of truth posits that without the notion of correspondence, there cannot be truth [15]. Analogously, correspondence estimation also holds a very important place as one of the core problems in computer vision. The ability to reliably obtain accurate pixel-level correspondence underpins a diverse range of tasks from stereo estimation, optical flow, structure-from-motion, through to visual tracking. Distinct from these lower-level objectives, semantic correspondence estimation, the task of matching different regions, parts, and landmarks across distinct object instances, is crucial to developing systems that can perform higher-level visual reasoning in diverse environments with objects that can vary significantly in both appearance and the configuration of their constituent parts.

Manually obtaining semantic correspondence supervision, for example in the form of annotated object landmarks, is an arduous and time consuming task. As a result, several works have instead attempted to understand to what extent

---

Supplementary Information The online version contains supplementary material available at https://doi.org/10.1007/978-3-031-20056-4_8.

semantic regions and parts emerge from conventionally trained supervised image classification networks [17,43,72,78]. These works have shown such semantic information is indeed present in the representations encoded by these networks, at least to some degree. Recently, a body of work has emerged that aims to learn semantic correspondence through self-supervision alone, i.e. without the need for ground truth supervision at training time [11,29,61,63].

While we have observed progress on unsupervised semantic correspondence estimation, a number of questions are still underexplored and unanswered. For instance, it is not clear how well current approaches generalize beyond more simplified object categories such as human faces to more complex non-rigidly deforming categories that vary in terms of both pose and appearance. Recent works have also been able to avail of advances in self-supervised learning of general visual representations [11,29], thus making it difficult to properly understand how they compare to older methods that do not utilize such self-supervised pre-training. In this work, we attempt to shine light on the above questions in addition to exploring the role other factors such as the impact of pre-training and finetuning data, backbone models, and the underlying evaluation criteria used to asses performance. Inspired by detailed benchmarking investigation in human pose estimation [55], we provide a thorough evaluation of the success and failure modes of current methods to provide guidance for future progress.

We make the following three contributions: (i) A standardized evaluation of multiple existing approaches for unsupervised semantic correspondence estimation across five challenging datasets. (ii) A new, conceptually simple, unsupervised training objective that results in superior semantic matching performance. (iii) A detailed breakdown of the current failure cases for current best performing approaches and our proposed new unsupervised method.

2   Related Work

Supervised Semantic Correspondence. Pre-deep learning work tackled semantic correspondence estimation as a local region matching problem using hand crafted features [6,31,40], or as offset matching using object proposals [19]. In the deep learning era, several works investigated if objects parts and regions emerge from image classification models [17,72,78], i.e. models trained only with image-level class supervision. [43] showed that deep CNN features could actually be used for semantic matching. Subsequent work built on this by proposing new architectures specifically designed for semantic matching [14,20,24,32,33,38,51]. Some of these approaches focused on combining multilevel features (i.e. hypercolumn features) from deep networks [45,47,64,76], aggregating information from features using 4D convolutions [37,39,52,53], leveraging geometric relations via Hough transforms [44], or using optimal transport [41,59]. Some matching methods formulate the problem as one of flow estimation between images [40,45]. However, unlike optical flow, semantic correspondence methods need to be able to handle intra and inter class variations when matching points. Recently, the use of transformer-based models has also been explored [12,27]. In contrast to most of the above works, we focus on the unsupervised setting, whereby no supervised keypoint annotations are used to train our models.

Unsupervised Semantic Correspondence. Recent progress in self-supervised learning has resulted in a suite of methods that are capable of extracting discriminative whole image representations without requiring explicit supervision [8,18,21,50,70]. While the majority of these methods optimize objectives to discriminate global image representations by using augmented image pairs, [11,29] showed that these approaches can also be utilized in correspondence estimation. Recently, several approaches proposed optimizing alternative objectives on a denser level [3,49,54,67–69,77]. However, these methods have been applied to tasks such as object detection and segmentation, but not directly for semantic correspondence. Another line of work proposed methods to discover semantic keypoint locations in an unsupervised way [25,26,36,58,74].

For the problem of correspondence estimation, images augmented with artificial spatial deformations were used by [28,51] to learn transformations between image pairs without any external supervision. Instead of learning a function to match image pairs, [62,63] framed the problem as one of learning a function that can extract local features which can be used for semantic matching across all instances of a category of interest. To introduce greater invariance for intra-category differences, DVE [61] extended EQ [62] with the use of additional non-augmented auxiliary images during training.

More recent work has been able to make use of advances in self-supervised learning in order to learn more effective representations. CL [11] proposed a two-stage approach, combining image-level instance-based discrimination [21] together with dense equivariant learning. They trained a linear projection head on top of frozen learned features computed via an image-level self-supervised pre-training task, where the goal of the projection step was to enforce the dense features to be spatially distinct within an image. LEAD [29] also followed a similar two-stage approach, starting with instance-level discrimination using [18]. In the second stage, instead of encouraging the features to be spatially distinct, their projection operation minimized the dissimilarity between feature correlation maps from the instance-level features and correlation maps from the projected features. This can be viewed as a form of dimensionality reduction as the projected features are smaller in size compared to the original features.

The above methods, while effective on some datasets, have limitations. EQ [62] is only able to learn invariances that can be expressed via image augmentations. DVE [61] assumes that the images have the same visible keypoints, and can thus be negatively impacted by incorrect matches on background pixels. The projection step used by CL [11] runs the risk of discarding invariances learned during the pre-training stage. While LEAD [29] maintains learned invariances from the first stage, if the pre-trained features generate incorrect matches, their loss can end up optimizing possibly incorrect feature correlations. In this work, we thoroughly benchmark the performance of these approaches by evaluating them on several challenging datasets. We also propose a new semantic correspondence loss, which learns more effective dense features by both preserving the learned invariances while also making the features more distinct.

Performance Evaluation and Error Diagnosis. Benchmarking model performance with a single summary metric is one of the best tools that we have for objectively measuring progress on a given task. However, accurately under-standing the limitations and improvements provided by new methods is even more crucial for future progress. Several works have introduced different diag-nostic tools and frameworks to analyze methods across a variety of problems [1,16,23,56,60,73]. For the semantic correspondence problem, the vast majority of existing works only report performance via single summary metrics, e.g. the Percentage of Correct Keypoints (PCK) with a fixed distance threshold. This allows us to get an overall sense of performance but does not reveal *why* a given method performs better than others. Recent works [13,48] have emphasized the importance of detailed evaluation in order to better understand what compo-nents specific performance improvements can be attributed to. In this work, in the spirit of [55], we introduce a more thorough evaluation for analyzing semantic correspondence methods. We also propose a new version of PCK which better captures correspondence errors and present standardized baseline results across multiple datasets to fairly compare semantic correspondence performance.

3   Semantic Correspondence Estimation

3.1   Problem Setup

Given a source-target image pair, $\mathbf{x}_s$ and $\mathbf{x}_t$, the goal of correspondence estima-tion is to find the locations of a set of points of interest from the source image in the target image. Unlike in optical flow or stereo estimation, where the task is to compute correspondence across time or viewpoint, in the case of semantic cor-respondence, the goal is to find matching locations across different depictions of the same object category. This is a challenging setting as the objects of interest can vary in terms of appearance, pose, and shape, in addition to difficulty arising from other nuisance factors such as the background, occlusion, and lighting.

We pose the correspondence problem as a nearest-neighbor matching task in a learned local feature embedding space. Formally, for a pixel location, $u \in \Omega = \{1, ..., H\} \times \{1, ..., W\}$, in a source image of size $H \times W$, we find the cor-responding point $\hat{u}$ in the target image $\mathbf{x}_t$ as, $\hat{u} = \arg\max_{k \in \Omega} f(\Phi_u(\mathbf{x}_s), \Phi_k(\mathbf{x}_t))$, where $\Phi_u(\mathbf{x}_s)$ represents an embedding vector of the point u from image $\mathbf{x}_s$, and f is a similarity function. We use a deep neural network as our embedding func-tion Φ, and the similarity is computed via the dot product of the ℓ_2 normalized embedding vectors. In practice, we decompose the embedding function into a feature encoder, followed by a projection step, i.e. $\Phi(\mathbf{x}) = \rho(\Psi(\mathbf{x}))$, where the encoder is deep network. The purpose of the projection is to reduce the dimen-sionality of the feature, and could be a linear operation [11] or a network [29].

In the next section, we review several existing unsupervised methods designed for learning dense representations with an emphasis on matching (see Fig. 1 for an overview). While more sophisticated methods have been proposed for esti-mating semantic correspondence, e.g. using optimal transport [41,59], distance re-weighting with spatial regularizers [45], or restricting the search area with class activation maps [78] as in [41], we focus on learning embedding functions as recent work has shown that combining self-supervised representation learning with correspondence specific finetuning produces state of the art results [11,29].

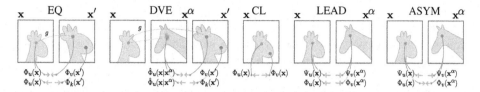

Fig. 1. Unsupervised approaches for semantic correspondence estimation. $\mathbf{x}'$ is a synthetically augmented version of image $\mathbf{x}$, and $\mathbf{x}^\alpha$ is a different image of the same semantic category. EQ [62] minimizes the distance between embeddings of point pairs with known geometric transformations g. DVE [61] builds on EQ by using an additional auxiliary image. CL [11] maximizes distance between embeddings of points within an image. LEAD [29] enforces the same distance between pre-trained and projected embeddings. Our ASYM method extends LEAD by enforcing projected embeddings to be closer in the feature space.

3.2 Unsupervised Semantic Correspondence Learning

EQ [62] proposed an unsupervised method that utilizes the equivariance principle to learn dense matchable features. During training, their model takes an image $\mathbf{x}$ along with an augmented version of it $\mathbf{x}'$ and tries to minimize feature similarity of known corresponding pixel locations u and v. Here, $\mathbf{x}'$ is derived from $\mathbf{x}$ using artificial spatial and appearance-based augmentations and the pixel coordinates u and v are locations from the two images which are related by a known transformation g, such that $v = gu$. They minimize the following loss,

$$\mathcal{L}_{eq} = \frac{1}{|\Omega|^2} \sum_{u \in \Omega} \sum_{v \in \Omega} \|gu - v\| \, p(v|u; \Phi, \mathbf{x}, \mathbf{x}', \tau), \tag{1}$$

$$p(v|u; \Phi, \mathbf{x}, \mathbf{x}', \tau) = \frac{\exp(\langle \Phi_u(\mathbf{x}), \Phi_v(\mathbf{x}') \rangle / \tau)}{\sum_{k \in \Omega} \exp(\langle \Phi_u(\mathbf{x}), \Phi_k(\mathbf{x}') \rangle / \tau)}, \tag{2}$$

where τ is temperature parameter for the softmax function and Ω is the set of possible pixel locations on the image grid. In essence, the model aims to embed corresponding points nearby in the learned embedding space, while also pushing other points further away.

EQ uses artificially augmented image pairs and can thus only learn invariances up to those expressible by these augmentations. Subsequently, DVE [61] extended EQ using an auxiliary image, $\mathbf{x}^\alpha$, to calculate correspondence from $\mathbf{x} \rightarrow \mathbf{x}^\alpha$ and then $\mathbf{x}^\alpha \rightarrow \mathbf{x}'$. This is achieved by replacing the $\Phi_u(\mathbf{x})$ term in Eq. 2 with $\hat{\Phi}_u(\mathbf{x}|\mathbf{x}^\alpha) = \sum_w \Phi_u(\mathbf{x}^\alpha) p(w|u; \Phi, \mathbf{x}, \mathbf{x}^\alpha, \tau)$. Importantly, the ground truth correspondence to the auxiliary image does not need to be known as the mapping from $\mathbf{x} \rightarrow \mathbf{x}'$ is available.

Recently, two stage methods for learning dense embeddings have been proposed [11,29]. In these approaches, the first stage makes use of an image-level self-supervised training objective (e.g. [18,21]) in order to train the feature encoder. Then the projection head is tuned to refine the representation so that it is better for matching. Like EQ, CL [11] also aims to make features distinct within the image. However, in contrast to EQ, the dense D dimensional feature vectors from $\Psi(\mathbf{x})$ are linearly projected to a lower dimension D' using a linear projection with weights $\mathbf{w} \in \mathbb{R}^{D \times D'}$. They use the same loss as Eq. 1, but simply use $\mathbf{x}$ instead of $\mathbf{x}'$, i.e. they do *not* use a pair of augmented images.

LEAD [29] also employs a two stage approach, but aims to maximize the similarity between feature correlation maps calculated using the original self-supervised features $\Psi(\mathbf{x})$ and the projected features $\Phi(\mathbf{x})$. The first term in their loss represents the probability that point u from image $\mathbf{x}$ is matched with point v in image $\mathbf{x}^\alpha$ using embeddings from the feature encoder Ψ. In the second term, embeddings are projected to a lower dimensional space using the combined encoder and projection head,

$$\mathcal{L}_{lead} = \frac{1}{|\Omega|^2} \sum_{u \in \Omega} \sum_{v \in \Omega} - p(v|u; \Psi, \mathbf{x}, \mathbf{x}^\alpha, \tau) \log p(v|u; \Phi, \mathbf{x}, \mathbf{x}^\alpha, \tau). \qquad (3)$$

LEAD uses 'real' image pairs, as opposed to augmented images, i.e. $\mathbf{x}^\alpha$ is not a synthetically augmented version of $\mathbf{x}$, but instead it is an auxiliary real image depicting the same object class. This is possible as their formulation does not require any ground truth correspondence during training. In essence, LEAD implements a form of learned dimensionality reduction, which can be effective if the pre-trained features already contain useful information for matching.

EQ and DVE were originally designed such that their embedding network Φ was trained in an end-to-end manner, while CL and LEAD separately trained the encoder network Ψ, followed by the learned projection function ρ. Existing methods often use different network architectures for the encoder and decoder which makes it challenging to compare the objective functions directly. To fairly evaluate these approaches, in our experiments we use frozen pre-trained networks as the encoder Ψ, and train a separate linear projection head ρ, i.e. $\Phi(\mathbf{x}) = \rho(\Psi(\mathbf{x}))$, for each of the losses.

3.3 Unsupervised Asymmetric Correspondence Loss

The LEAD objective aims to preserve distances between features before and after they have been projected into a lower dimensional feature space. Given two points, u and v, from different images, the loss term effectively tries to enforce $f(\Psi_u(\mathbf{x}), \Psi_v(\mathbf{x}^\alpha))$ and $f(\Phi_u(\mathbf{x}), \Phi_v(\mathbf{x}^\alpha))$ to be as close as possible. The projection tries to maintain both what is similar and not similar between point pairs by preserving their distance. However, the structure of the embedding space does *not* change after this projection step which means that performance is bounded by the quality of the features in the original feature space.

We make a conceptually simple change to the LEAD objective in order to provide the flexibility to allow the model to change distances in the projected feature space. Unlike LEAD, instead of using the same temperature value in the softmax function for both feature spaces, we utilize a different temperature when we calculate the similarity between point embeddings. Specially, we use a smaller temperature for the original feature space and a larger one for the projected feature space, i.e. $\tau_1 < \tau_2$, resulting in the following loss,

$$\mathcal{L}_{asym} = \frac{1}{|\Omega|^2} \sum_{u \in \Omega} \sum_{v \in \Omega} || \, p(v|u; \Psi, \mathbf{x}, \mathbf{x}^\alpha, \tau_1) - p(v|u; \Phi, \mathbf{x}, \mathbf{x}^\alpha, \tau_2)||. \qquad (4)$$

A smaller temperature makes the distance between closer points smaller and far away points larger. To match these same distance scores, the projection needs to make embeddings of closer points closer and vice versa. Moreover, the objective also preserves the order of distances of point pairs, i.e. close points remain closer compared to further away ones. As a result, the projection needs to capture what is common between already matching point pairs in order to optimize the loss which leads to better embeddings for matching. While this is a relatively small change in the loss formulation, it results in a significant improvement in the performance. As we use different temperature parameters, we refer to our asymmetric projection loss as ASYM. The other difference between ASYM and LEAD is that we make use of Euclidean distance instead of cross entropy as we found this to be more effective. We compare the impact of these design choices via detailed ablation experiments in our supplementary material.

4   Evaluation Protocol

4.1   Evaluation Metrics

There are two dominant approaches for benchmarking the performance of unsupervised correspondence estimation methods: (i) landmark regression and (ii) feature matching. For landmark regression, an additional supervised regression head is trained for each of the landmarks of interest (e.g. the keypoints of a human face) on top of the representation learned by the correspondence network. For matching, one simply computes the distance in feature space to all the points in the second image for a given point of interest in a source image and then selects the closest match as the corresponding point.

We argue that matching is a better task for evaluating the power of learned feature embeddings as regression requires ground truth supervision to train the additional parameters. As matching uses raw feature embeddings it cannot incorporate biases from datasets, e.g. exploiting the average locations of keypoints. While current literature tends to focus on regression evaluation, there are some exceptions to this. However, by and large, matching results are only presented for comparably easier datasets. For example, [11,29,61] only present matching results on the MAFL dataset [75]. MAFL contains cropped and aligned images of human faces, and current methods perform very well on it, with matching errors close to two pixels on average.

Percentage of Correct Keypoints (PCK). Traditionally, matching performance is measured using the PCK metric. Given a set of ground truth keypoints $\mathcal{P} = \{\mathbf{p}_m\}_{m=1}^M$ and predictions $\hat{\mathcal{P}} = \{\hat{\mathbf{p}}_m\}_{m=1}^M$, PCK is calculated as

(a) Source   (b) Match   (c) Miss   (d) Jitter   (e) Swap

Fig. 2. For the keypoint denoted in red in the source image (a), we see the correct match in (b). If the point matches with the background it is a miss (c), if it is close to the correct location it is a jitter (d). If the match is in the correct vicinity but closer to another semantic part, it is a swap error (e). (Color figure online)

$PCK(\mathcal{P}, \hat{\mathcal{P}}) = \frac{1}{M} \sum_{m=1}^{M} \mathbb{1}[\|\hat{\mathbf{p}}_m - \mathbf{p}_m\| \leq d]$. Here, $d = \alpha \max(W^b, H^b)$ is a distance threshold, chosen as a proportion (e.g. $\alpha = 0.1$ of the maximum side length) of the object bounding box (with width W^b and height H^b) size. A prediction is counted as correct if it is inside of the target keypoint area.

Detailed Error Evaluation. Inspired by [55], we define additional error metrics to analyze performance of different methods in more detail. A visual overview is illustrated in Fig. 2. If a point is matched with a point that not is close to any of the keypoints in the target image, we denote this error as a 'miss'. This error generally occurs when a point is matched with the image background: $E_{miss} = \mathbb{1}[d < \min\{\|\hat{\mathbf{p}}_m - \mathbf{p}\| \mid \mathbf{p} \in \mathcal{P}\}]$. If a prediction is in the correct vicinity, but outside of the defined distance threshold, we denote this a 'jitter', $E_{jitter} = \mathbb{1}[d < \|\hat{\mathbf{p}}_m - \mathbf{p}_m\| < 2d]$. The last error type is a 'swap' which occurs when a point matches in an area that is closer to a different keypoint, $E_{swap} = \mathbb{1}[\delta \neq \|\hat{\mathbf{p}}_m - \mathbf{p}_m\| \wedge d > \delta]$, where $\delta = \min\{\|\hat{\mathbf{p}}_m - \mathbf{p}\| \mid \mathbf{p} \in P\}$.

The miss and jitter errors are also counted as incorrect by the PCK metric, but swaps may still be counted as correct. For instance, a prediction which is in the middle of a pair of eyes might still be counted as correct according to PCK even if it closer to the wrong eye since it could be still within the distance threshold. As our goal is to estimate semantic correspondence, we should aim to match with the *correct* semantic part. As a result, we propose a new version of PCK which penalizes these swaps. Under this metric, to make a correct prediction, a point needs to both match close to the corresponding keypoint *and* the closest keypoint should be the same semantic keypoint,

$$PCK^{\dagger}(\mathcal{P}, \hat{\mathcal{P}}) = \frac{1}{M} \sum_{m=1}^{M} \mathbb{1}[\|\hat{\mathbf{p}}_m - \mathbf{p}_m\| \leq d \wedge \delta = \|\hat{\mathbf{p}}_m - \mathbf{p}_m\|]. \quad (5)$$

4.2   Evaluation Datasets

In order to evaluate semantic correspondence performance we perform experiments on five different datasets: AFLW [34], Spair-71k [46], CUB-200-2011 (CUB) [66], Stanford Dogs Extra (SDog) [5,30], and Awa-Pose [4,71]. These

Table 1. Summary of the different datasets that we use for evaluating semantic correspondence performance. We also report the metadata that is provided with each dataset: KP (keypoints/landmarks) and Bbox (bounding boxes). With the exception of Spair-71k, there is no pre-defined evaluation pairs for the datasets.

Dataset name	# Images	# Pairs	# Classes	Annotations	Matching diversity
SPair-71k [46]	2k	70k	18	KP (3–30), Bbox	Med
Stanford Dogs (SDog) [5]	10k	10k	120	KP (24), Bbox	Med
CUB-200-2011 (CUB) [66]	11k	10k	200	KP (15), Bbox	Med
AFLW [34]	13k	10k	–	KP (5)	Low
Awa-Pose [4]	10k	10k	36	KP (30–40), Bbox	High

datasets were chosen as they span a range of object category types (e.g. from man made to natural world classes) and exhibit different levels of difficultly (e.g. from topologically simply human faces to deformable animals). AFLW [34] contains images of human faces with various backgrounds from different view points. However, due to structured nature of faces, the visual difference between images are limited and thus the task is relatively easy compared to the other datasets. SDog [5,30] and CUB [66] contain images of fine-grained visual categories (dogs and birds respectively) and include highly varying appearance, diverse backgrounds, and non-rigid poses which results in a challenging matching task. Awa-Pose [4,71] contains images from 35 different animal species and allows us to asses inter-class correspondence as the keypoints are shared across the species. SPair-71k [46] contains scenes with multiple man made objects present with complex backgrounds, but the pairs come from same class and the size of the datasets is relatively small. An overview can be found in Table 1.

Only the annotations in SPair-71K were explicitly collected with a focus on semantic correspondence evaluation. For the other datasets there are no predefined image pairs or standardized correspondence evaluation splits. In the existing literature random image pairs are selected that makes direct comparison between alternative methods challenging [14,39,76]. As the keypoint annotations are semantically consistent across instances in these datasets, we create splits for each dataset, where random image pairs are selected from test splits of the datasets. We will publish these splits in order to aid future evaluation.

4.3 Implementation Details

We perform experiments with two different types of backbones models for our feature encoder Ψ. For the CNN, unless otherwise specified, we extract features from images resized to 384×384, and use the 1024 dimensional features from the conv3 layer of a ResNet-50 [22]. For the Transformer, 8×8 patches from 224×224 images with stride 8 are used as input (similar to [2]) and we extract 736 dimensional features from 9th layer. We also investigate supervised and self-supervised trained backbones. The supervised and self-supervised CNNs are from [22] and [10] and the Transformer models are from [35] and [7] respectively.

Unless stated otherwise, we report results using the standard PCK metric with $\alpha = 0.1$ for direct comparison to other methods. We set the temperature τ_1 to 0.2 and τ_2 to 0.4 for ASYM. We provide an evaluation of different temperature values and additional implementation details in the supplementary material.

5   Experiments

In our experiments, we attempt to answer the following questions: i) how well do current unsupervised correspondence methods perform on challenging datasets, ii) how does the choice of backbone architecture and pre-training objective impact performance, iii) how does the pre-training data source impact performance, iv) how does the data source used for finetuning the correspondence model impact performance, and finally, v) what are the current source of errors, and thus what needs to be done to close the gap between current state-of-the art supervised and unsupervised methods.

5.1   Impact of Unsupervised Correspondence Objective

To evaluate the unsupervised correspondence methods outlined in Sect. 3, in Table 2 we train a linear projection head ρ on top of the embeddings from a frozen pre-trained backbone Ψ. Additional baselines are also presented, including: pre-trained features directly from the backbone models with no projection (None), Non-Negative Matrix Factorization (NMF), Principal Component Analysis (PCA), projection using a Random weight matrix, and Supervised projection where we optimize the objective in Eq. 1 using ground truth keypoint pairs. We explore CNNs and Transformers as backbones that are pre-trained either in a supervised or self-supervised fashion.

Overall, our proposed ASYM approach obtains better scores than other unsupervised methods on all datasets, independent of the choice of backbone or pre-training method, with the exception of the AFLW face dataset. Compared to LEAD, our proposed adaptation improves performance on datasets where the visual diversity is high (i.e. non-face datasets). EQ and DVE perform poorly on the datasets where the visual appearance is high across instances, but it is worth noting that these methods were originally designed for the end-to-end trained setting. CL obtains good performance in some cases and is the best on AFLW. However, our ASYM method is still consistently strong. Perhaps somewhat surprisingly, PCA based projection performs better than most of the baselines, while NMF did not perform well. PCA's performance can be partially explained by the strength of the original features (i.e. None). Although the performance of unsupervised methods differs across different backbones, the relative ordering stays the same – Sup, ASYM, CL, PCA, NONE, LEAD, NMF, EQ, and DVE.

5.2   Impact of Backbone Model and Pre-training Objective

While [12] claims that the choice of CNNs or Transformers as the backbone model does not affect the performance, recently [2] presented impressive correspondence results using a Transformer-based model. In order to explore further,

Table 2. Comparison of different unsupervised semantic correspondence methods. Here we vary the backbone models and pre-training strategies. The unsupervised correspondence methods are trained on the respective evaluation datasets.

(a) Ψ = Sup. pre-trained - CNN

Projection(ρ)	Spair-71K	SDogs	CUB	AFLW	Awa
None	31.8	34.9	51.3	57.4	28.8
NMF	27.4	33.9	49.6	53.6	28.0
PCA	32.2	35.5	53.1	57.8	29.7
Random	26.9	30.5	43.1	54.9	23.4
Supervised	38.7	53.2	72.7	80.8	46.1
EQ [62]	16.4	21.2	28.1	48.5	15.6
DVE [61]	16.3	20.5	27.7	58.7	15.4
CL [11]	30.8	37.0	54.5	**67.3**	31.7
LEAD [29]	31.7	35.1	51.5	58.0	29.1
ASYM (ours)	**34.0**	**40.4**	**60.8**	63.6	**34.1**

(b) Ψ = Unsup. pre-trained - CNN

Projection(ρ)	Spair-71K	SDogs	CUB	AFLW	Awa
None	30.7	34.3	47.5	64.3	27.6
NMF	20.6	19.9	44.0	40.8	15.6
PCA	27.4	29.8	50.7	51.0	24.1
Random	26.6	31.5	40.0	60.2	23.3
Supervised	39.5	54.0	73.4	83.8	48.2
EQ [62]	14.3	20.5	26.4	62.8	15.5
DVE [61]	15.0	19.4	28.7	60.6	14.7
CL [11]	29.7	37.9	54.1	**77.1**	**33.4**
LEAD [29]	30.5	34.4	48.3	64.9	28.1
ASYM (ours)	**33.2**	**38.2**	**54.4**	69.7	32.1

(c) Ψ = Sup. pre-trained - Transformer

Projection(ρ)	Spair-71K	SDogs	CUB	AFLW	Awa
None	**33.5**	38.0	66.3	54.1	34.1
NMF	23.3	29.2	55.5	51.5	24.7
PCA	33.0	38.1	66.4	53.9	34.1
Random	31.9	36.9	63.3	52.9	31.8
Supervised	38.5	48.2	78.2	70.5	47.9
EQ [62]	15.5	15.9	24.0	60.2	11.7
DVE [61]	15.4	17.5	23.8	55.6	11.8
CL [11]	30.5	35.8	67.1	**68.4**	31.0
LEAD [29]	32.7	37.6	65.8	53.8	33.9
ASYM (ours)	33.2	**41.7**	**72.2**	54.2	**38.5**

(d) Ψ = Unsup. pre-trained - Transformer

Projection(ρ)	Spair-71K	SDogs	CUB	AFLW	Awa
None	**34.1**	42.7	61.0	64.2	36.1
NMF	26.3	39.0	51.9	61.0	32.9
PCA	34.0	42.7	61.0	64.2	36.1
Random	32.3	42.1	59.6	61.9	34.6
Supervised	38.1	52.7	72.9	92.0	47.4
EQ [62]	9.0	12.5	15.0	62.5	8.8
DVE [61]	8.5	13.1	14.1	60.6	9.0
CL [11]	25.8	32.3	54.1	**81.8**	25.0
LEAD [29]	33.6	42.5	60.8	64.2	35.8
ASYM (ours)	32.9	**45.2**	**65.2**	65.9	**39.9**

we compared features from models pre-trained on Imagenet with either supervised (Sup.) or unsupervised (Unsup.) objectives.

When a projection layer is trained with keypoint supervision, the performance difference between architectures diminishes, as can be observed by comparing the supervised baseline to original embeddings (None) in Table 2. However, when the projection layer is trained using no supervision, the best results are obtained in the cases where the initial embeddings were the best on a given dataset. For instance, the unsupervised pre-trained Transformer obtains the best results with no projection on the SDog and Awa datasets compared to other backbone models. Training the unsupervised methods from these embeddings also results in the best performance compared to other pre-trained backbones. In summary, if keypoint supervision is available, the choice of backbone does not significantly impact the end result. However, in the unsupervised case, starting with good performing embeddings is important. Furthermore, the pre-training strategy does not affect the performance of CNNs, while unsupervised Transformers generally performs better than supervised one (see Table 2).

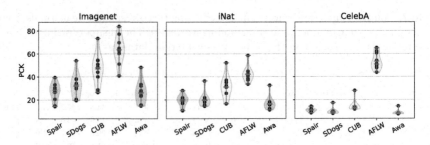

Fig. 3. Impact of different pre-training datasets used to train a CNN feature encoder using self-supervised training. For each of the three datasets we report the performance of different methods shown as individual dots.

5.3 Impact of Pre-training Dataset

Here we explore the impact of the pre-training data source used to train the feature encoder. We train correspondence losses using embeddings from a CNN trained via contrastive self-supervision on either Imagenet [57] (various categories), iNat2021 [65] (natural world categories), or Celeb-A [42] (human faces). Specifically, we use MoCov3 from [10] for Imagenet, MoCov2 [9] for iNat from [65], and MoCov2 from [11] for CelebA. These results are presented in Fig. 3.

It is clear that the choice of pre-training data has an impact on all unsupervised methods, with Imagenet outperforming other sources. The CelebA model performs poorly on all tasks with the exception of AFLW, as the features likely only contain information about faces. iNat2021 does not contain any man-made objects or dog categories, and as a result, models trained on it perform worse on SDog and Spair. While iNat2021 contains many bird images, it contains an order of magnitude less mammals making it less effective on Awa-Pose.

5.4 Impact of Finetuning Correspondence Dataset

Next we explore how transferable are the embeddings trained on one dataset and evaluated on another. For instance, what happens if the linear projection is trained on dog images and then tested on birds, or in an extreme case, trained on human faces and tested on animal categories. The correspondence losses are trained on top of the sup. CNN from Table 2. The results are outlined in Fig. 4.

The generalization performance across other datasets is poor for supervised losses compared to the unsupervised ones. The performance drop is largest for models trained on faces, but when training on other data and tested on faces, the performance does not drop significantly. Models trained on Spair-71k generally perform reasonably well on other datasets.

5.5 Detailed Error Analysis

Here we break down the different error types in order to better understand where the different methods fail and thus require improvement. We compare

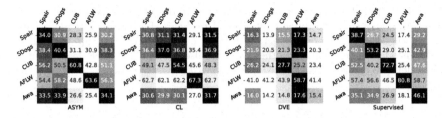

Fig. 4. Cross dataset evaluation results. Each row represents the test source data, and each column is the dataset that a given correspondence loss is trained on. Note that the colormaps are row normalized. These results use the same initial encoder as the 'Sup. pre-trained - CNN' results in Table 2.

unsupervised correspondence losses and supervised projection to the current best performing methods CATs [12], CHM [44], and MMNet [76] on Spair-71K. Results are presented in Table 3.

For the supervised methods, MMNet has significantly lower miss errors compared to all other methods, although it results in a lot of swaps. As this method combines correlation maps from different layers, it is able to capture more global context, which helps reduce misses. However, while CATs and CHM produce more misses compared to MMNet, swaps are reduced, as they use more sophisticated aggregation methods (6D convolution and attention) to resolve ambiguities during matching. Moreover, as these two lines of work complement each other in the error types, they could potentially be combined to obtain better results.

For the unsupervised methods, we see that the most common error type is miss across all methods. While ASYM reduces misses compared to other unsupervised methods, it is not as good as the supervised approaches. As swaps are instances where a match has occurred, but to the wrong keypoint, methods with high number of misses will not have many swaps by definition. ASYM results in fewer misses, which is desirable, but this increases the chance that swaps can occur. The 'Supervised' baseline reduces misses, but compared to the more sophisticated supervised approaches it generates more swaps. We argue that while more supervision might help to reduce misses, in order to reduce swaps, better matching mechanisms are needed, as in [12,44].

Finally, we can see that our $PCK^{\dagger}$ metric is reduced by $\sim$20% compared to the original PCK metric in all cases. This indicates that in one in five cases, the source point matches an area closer to another keypoint instead of the correct corresponding point. For some applications these errors might not affect the end performance drastically, while for others, this disparity could be significant. We provide additional analysis and $PCK^{\dagger}$ scores for other datasets in the supplementary material.

5.6 Discussion and Limitations

Our exhaustive experiments show that evaluating with varied challenging datasets is crucial in order to see the benefits of current methods as human

Table 3. Detailed error types for both unsupervised and supervised correspondence losses on Spair using two different distance thresholds. FT indicates if the backbone was finetuned with keypoint supervision. Our baselines use the 'Sup. pre-trained - CNN' encoder from Table 2, in other cases we use the public models by the authors. All models use a ResNet backbone, except MMNet-FCN [76].

(a) $\alpha = 0.1$

	FT	Method	Miss↓	Jitter↓	Swap↓	PCK↑	PCK†↑
Unsup.		CL	51.5	13.7	24.3	30.8	24.2
		EQ	68.3	15.0	18.9	16.4	12.8
		DVE	67.9	14.9	19.7	16.3	12.4
		LEAD	47.1	13.6	27.4	31.7	25.4
		ASYM	44.1	13.2	28.6	34.0	27.2
Sup.		Supervised	40.2	14.9	29.4	38.7	30.4
		CATs [12]	46.3	21.0	21.9	42.4	31.7
	✓	CATs [12]	40.1	19.1	20.3	49.9	39.6
	✓	CHM [44]	40.3	18.2	23.8	44.2	35.8
	✓	MMNet-FCN [76]	28.5	14.7	28.8	52.2	42.6

(b) $\alpha = 0.05$

	FT	Method	Miss↓	Jitter↓	Swap↓	PCK↑	PCK†↑
Unsup.		CL	71.5	13.2	12.9	17.7	15.6
		EQ	85.1	8.8	8.0	7.6	6.9
		DVE	85.3	9.0	8.3	7.3	6.5
		LEAD	66.9	12.4	15.9	19.3	17.3
		ASYM	63.3	12.6	17.5	21.5	19.2
Sup.		Supervised	61.1	14.6	17.6	24.1	21.3
		CATs [12]	71.0	20.7	10.8	21.6	18.1
	✓	CATs [12]	64.8	22.2	10.7	27.7	24.4
	✓	CHM [44]	64.5	18.7	12.4	25.6	23.1
	✓	MMNet-FCN [76]	51.7	19.0	18.1	33.3	30.2

face data results (e.g. AFLW) alone can be misleading (Table 2). While unsupervised performance may not yet be at the level of fully supervised baselines, they are not far off but have the benefit of generalizing better across datasets (Fig. 4). Current performance metrics (i.e. PCK) do not penalize all error types and thus result in overly optimistic performance (Table 3). The choice of pretraining can have a big impact, but in most instances Imagenet pre-training is superior (Fig. 3).

It is not feasible to control all hyper-parameter values as the space too large. As a result, to ensure fair and controlled comparisons, we adopted a two stage pipeline, with frozen backbone models, as advocated in recent start-of-the-art work [11]. We justified the important design choices and provide additional experiments in the supplementary material. Finally, the keypoints used for evaluating correspondence are derived from object landmarks which are detectable and salient by design. In future work, it would be interesting to use additional annotations from other object parts which are not necessarily easily annotated but still have semantically meaningful correspondences across instances.

6 Conclusion

We presented a thorough evaluation of existing unsupervised methods for semantic correspondence estimation and presented a new approach that consistently outperforms existing methods. We showed that while matching performance on human face data is strong, there is still a way to go on more challenging datasets. Our analysis sheds light on some of the reasons for failure as well as providing some further insight into the role of data, models, and losses which we hope will enable others to make further progress on this important task.

Acknowledgements. Thanks to Hakan Bilen and Omiros Pantazis for their valuable feedback. This work was in part supported by the Turing 2.0 'Enabling Advanced Autonomy' project funded by the EPSRC and the Alan Turing Institute.

References

1. Alwassel, H., Caba Heilbron, F., Escorcia, V., Ghanem, B.: Diagnosing error in temporal action detectors. In: Ferrari, V., Hebert, M., Sminchisescu, C., Weiss, Y. (eds.) ECCV 2018. LNCS, vol. 11207, pp. 264–280. Springer, Cham (2018). https://doi.org/10.1007/978-3-030-01219-9_16

2. Amir, S., Gandelsman, Y., Bagon, S., Dekel, T.: Deep ViT features as dense visual descriptors. arXiv:2112.05814 (2021)

3. Araslanov, N., Schaub-Meyer, S., Roth, S.: Dense unsupervised learning for video segmentation. In: NeurIPS (2021)

4. Banik, P., Li, L., Dong, X.: A novel dataset for keypoint detection of quadruped animals from images. arXiv:2108.13958 (2021)

5. Biggs, B., Boyne, O., Charles, J., Fitzgibbon, A., Cipolla, R.: Who left the dogs out? 3D animal reconstruction with expectation maximization in the loop. In: Vedaldi, A., Bischof, H., Brox, T., Frahm, J.-M. (eds.) ECCV 2020. LNCS, vol. 12356, pp. 195–211. Springer, Cham (2020). https://doi.org/10.1007/978-3-030-58621-8_12

6. Bristow, H., Valmadre, J., Lucey, S.: Dense semantic correspondence where every pixel is a classifier. In: ICCV, pp. 4024–4031 (2015)

7. Caron, M., et al.: Emerging properties in self-supervised vision transformers. In: ICCV (2021)

8. Chen, T., Kornblith, S., Norouzi, M., Hinton, G.: A simple framework for contrastive learning of visual representations. In: ICML (2020)

9. Chen, X., Fan, H., Girshick, R., He, K.: Improved baselines with momentum contrastive learning. arXiv:2003.04297 (2020)

10. Chen, X., Xie, S., He, K.: An empirical study of training self-supervised vision transformers. arXiv:2104.02057 (2021)

11. Cheng, Z., Su, J.C., Maji, S.: On equivariant and invariant learning of object landmark representations. In: ICCV (2021)

12. Cho, S., Hong, S., Jeon, S., Lee, Y., Sohn, K., Kim, S.: CATs: cost aggregation transformers for visual correspondence. In: NeurIPS (2021)

13. Choe, J., Oh, S.J., Lee, S., Chun, S., Akata, Z., Shim, H.: Evaluating weakly supervised object localization methods right. In: CVPR, pp. 3133–3142 (2020)

14. Choy, C.B., Gwak, J., Savarese, S., Chandraker, M.: Universal correspondence network. In: NeurIPS (2016)

15. David, M.: The correspondence theory of truth. In: The Oxford Handbook of Truth (2016)

16. Everingham, M., Eslami, S.A., Van Gool, L., Williams, C.K., Winn, J., Zisserman, A.: The pascal visual object classes challenge: a retrospective. IJCV 111, 98–136 (2015). https://doi.org/10.1007/s11263-014-0733-5

17. Gonzalez-Garcia, A., Modolo, D., Ferrari, V.: Do semantic parts emerge in convolutional neural networks? IJCV 126(5), 476–494 (2017). https://doi.org/10.1007/s11263-017-1048-0

18. Grill, J.B., et al.: Bootstrap your own latent-a new approach to self-supervised learning. In: NeurIPS (2020)

19. Ham, B., Cho, M., Schmid, C., Ponce, J.: Proposal flow. In: CVPR (2016)

20. Han, K., et al.: SCNet: learning semantic correspondence. In: ICCV, pp. 1831–1840 (2017)

21. He, K., Fan, H., Wu, Y., Xie, S., Girshick, R.: Momentum contrast for unsupervised visual representation learning. In: CVPR (2020)

22. He, K., Zhang, X., Ren, S., Sun, J.: Deep residual learning for image recognition. In: CVPR (2016)
23. Hoiem, D., Chodpathumwan, Y., Dai, Q.: Diagnosing error in object detectors. In: Fitzgibbon, A., Lazebnik, S., Perona, P., Sato, Y., Schmid, C. (eds.) ECCV 2012. LNCS, vol. 7574, pp. 340–353. Springer, Heidelberg (2012). https://doi.org/10.1007/978-3-642-33712-3_25
24. Huang, S., Wang, Q., Zhang, S., Yan, S., He, X.: Dynamic context correspondence network for semantic alignment. In: ICCV, pp. 2010–2019 (2019)
25. Jakab, T., Gupta, A., Bilen, H., Vedaldi, A.: Unsupervised learning of object landmarks through conditional image generation. In: NeurIPS (2018)
26. Jakab, T., Gupta, A., Bilen, H., Vedaldi, A.: Self-supervised learning of interpretable keypoints from unlabelled videos. In: CVPR (2020)
27. Jiang, W., Trulls, E., Hosang, J., Tagliasacchi, A., Yi, K.M.: COTR: correspondence transformer for matching across images. In: ICCV, pp. 6207–6217 (2021)
28. Kanazawa, A., Jacobs, D.W., Chandraker, M.: WarpNet: weakly supervised matching for single-view reconstruction. In: CVPR (2016)
29. Karmali, T., Atrishi, A., Harsha, S.S., Agrawal, S., Jampani, V., Babu, R.V.: LEAD: self-supervised landmark estimation by aligning distributions of feature similarity. In: WACV (2022)
30. Khosla, A., Jayadevaprakash, N., Yao, B., Li, F.F.: Novel dataset for fine-grained image categorization: stanford dogs. In: CVPR Workshop on Fine-Grained Visual Categorization (2011)
31. Kim, J., Liu, C., Sha, F., Grauman, K.: Deformable spatial pyramid matching for fast dense correspondences. In: CVPR, pp. 2307–2314 (2013)
32. Kim, S., Lin, S., Jeon, S.R., Min, D., Sohn, K.: Recurrent transformer networks for semantic correspondence. In: NeurIPS (2018)
33. Kim, S., Min, D., Ham, B., Jeon, S., Lin, S., Sohn, K.: FCSS: fully convolutional self-similarity for dense semantic correspondence. In: CVPR, pp. 6560–6569 (2017)
34. Koestinger, M., Wohlhart, P., Roth, P.M., Bischof, H.: Annotated facial landmarks in the wild: a large-scale, real-world database for facial landmark localization. In: ICCV Workshops (2011)
35. Kolesnikov, A., et al.: An image is worth 16×16 words: transformers for image recognition at scale. In: ICLR (2021)
36. Kulkarni, T.D., et al.: Unsupervised learning of object keypoints for perception and control. In: NeurIPS (2019)
37. Lee, J.Y., DeGol, J., Fragoso, V., Sinha, S.N.: Patchmatch-based neighborhood consensus for semantic correspondence. In: CVPR, pp. 13153–13163 (2021)
38. Lee, J., Kim, D., Ponce, J., Ham, B.: SFNet: learning object-aware semantic correspondence. In: CVPR, pp. 2278–2287 (2019)
39. Li, S., Han, K., Costain, T.W., Howard-Jenkins, H., Prisacariu, V.: Correspondence networks with adaptive neighbourhood consensus. In: CVPR, pp. 10196–10205 (2020)
40. Liu, C., Yuen, J., Torralba, A.: Sift flow: dense correspondence across scenes and its applications. PAMI **33**(5), 978–994 (2010)
41. Liu, Y., Zhu, L., Yamada, M., Yang, Y.: Semantic correspondence as an optimal transport problem. In: CVPR, pp. 4463–4472 (2020)
42. Liu, Z., Luo, P., Wang, X., Tang, X.: Deep learning face attributes in the wild. In: ICCV (2015)
43. Long, J.L., Zhang, N., Darrell, T.: Do convnets learn correspondence? In: NeurIPS (2014)

44. Min, J., Cho, M.: Convolutional hough matching networks. In: CVPR (2021)
45. Min, J., Lee, J., Ponce, J., Cho, M.: Hyperpixel flow: semantic correspondence with multi-layer neural features. In: ICCV (2019)
46. Min, J., Lee, J., Ponce, J., Cho, M.: SPair-71k: a large-scale benchmark for semantic correspondence. arXiv:1908.10543 (2019)
47. Min, J., Lee, J., Ponce, J., Cho, M.: Learning to compose hypercolumns for visual correspondence. In: Vedaldi, A., Bischof, H., Brox, T., Frahm, J.-M. (eds.) ECCV 2020. LNCS, vol. 12360, pp. 346–363. Springer, Cham (2020). https://doi.org/10. 1007/978-3-030-58555-6_21
48. Musgrave, K., Belongie, S., Lim, S.-N.: A metric learning reality check. In: Vedaldi, A., Bischof, H., Brox, T., Frahm, J.-M. (eds.) ECCV 2020. LNCS, vol. 12370, pp. 681–699. Springer, Cham (2020). https://doi.org/10.1007/978-3-030-58595-2_41
49. Pinheiro, P.O.O., Almahairi, A., Benmalek, R., Golemo, F., Courville, A.C.: Unsupervised learning of dense visual representations. In: NeurIPS (2020)
50. Van den Oord, A., Li, Y., Vinyals, O.: Representation learning with contrastive predictive coding. arXiv:1807.03748 (2018)
51. Rocco, I., Arandjelovic, R., Sivic, J.: Convolutional neural network architecture for geometric matching. In: CVPR, pp. 6148–6157 (2017)
52. Rocco, I., Arandjelović, R., Sivic, J.: Efficient neighbourhood consensus networks via submanifold sparse convolutions. In: Vedaldi, A., Bischof, H., Brox, T., Frahm, J.-M. (eds.) ECCV 2020. LNCS, vol. 12354, pp. 605–621. Springer, Cham (2020). https://doi.org/10.1007/978-3-030-58545-7_35
53. Rocco, I., Cimpoi, M., Arandjelović, R., Torii, A., Pajdla, T., Sivic, J.: Neighbourhood consensus networks. In: NeurIPS (2018)
54. Roh, B., Shin, W., Kim, I., Kim, S.: Spatially consistent representation learning. In: CVPR, pp. 1144–1153 (2021)
55. Ruggero Ronchi, M., Perona, P.: Benchmarking and error diagnosis in multi-instance pose estimation. In: ICCV (2017)
56. Russakovsky, O., Deng, J., Huang, Z., Berg, A.C., Fei-Fei, L.: Detecting avocados to Zucchinis: what have we done, and where are we going? In: ICCV (2013)
57. Russakovsky, O., et al.: ImageNet large scale visual recognition challenge. IJCV 115, 211–252 (2015). https://doi.org/10.1007/s11263-015-0816-y
58. Ryou, S., Perona, P.: Weakly supervised keypoint discovery. arXiv:2109.13423 (2021)
59. Sarlin, P.E., DeTone, D., Malisiewicz, T., Rabinovich, A.: SuperGlue: learning feature matching with graph neural networks. In: CVPR, pp. 4938–4947 (2020)
60. Sigurdsson, G.A., Russakovsky, O., Gupta, A.: What actions are needed for understanding human actions in videos? In: ICCV, pp. 2137–2146 (2017)
61. Thewlis, J., Albanie, S., Bilen, H., Vedaldi, A.: Unsupervised learning of landmarks by descriptor vector exchange. In: ICCV (2019)
62. Thewlis, J., Bilen, H., Vedaldi, A.: Unsupervised learning of object frames by dense equivariant image labelling. In: NeurIPS (2017)
63. Thewlis, J., Bilen, H., Vedaldi, A.: Unsupervised learning of object landmarks by factorized spatial embeddings. In: ICCV (2017)
64. Ufer, N., Ommer, B.: Deep semantic feature matching. In: CVPR, pp. 6914–6923 (2017)
65. Van Horn, G., Cole, E., Beery, S., Wilber, K., Belongie, S., Mac Aodha, O.: Benchmarking representation learning for natural world image collections. In: CVPR (2021)
66. Wah, C., Branson, S., Welinder, P., Perona, P., Belongie, S.: The Caltech-UCSD Birds-200-2011 dataset (2011)

67. Wang, X., Zhang, R., Shen, C., Kong, T., Li, L.: Dense contrastive learning for self-supervised visual pre-training. In: CVPR, pp. 3024–3033 (2021)
68. Wang, Z., et al.: Exploring set similarity for dense self-supervised representation learning. arXiv:2107.08712 (2021)
69. Wei, F., Gao, Y., Wu, Z., Hu, H., Lin, S.: Aligning pretraining for detection via object-level contrastive learning. In: NeurIPS (2021)
70. Wu, Z., Xiong, Y., Yu, S.X., Lin, D.: Unsupervised feature learning via non-parametric instance discrimination. In: CVPR (2018)
71. Xian, Y., Lampert, C.H., Schiele, B., Akata, Z.: Zero-shot learning-a comprehensive evaluation of the good, the bad and the ugly. PAMI 41(9), 2251–2265 (2018)
72. Zeiler, M.D., Fergus, R.: Visualizing and understanding convolutional networks. In: Fleet, D., Pajdla, T., Schiele, B., Tuytelaars, T. (eds.) ECCV 2014. LNCS, vol. 8689, pp. 818–833. Springer, Cham (2014). https://doi.org/10.1007/978-3-319-10590-1_53
73. Zhang, S., Benenson, R., Omran, M., Hosang, J., Schiele, B.: How far are we from solving pedestrian detection? In: CVPR, pp. 1259–1267 (2016)
74. Zhang, Y., Guo, Y., Jin, Y., Luo, Y., He, Z., Lee, H.: Unsupervised discovery of object landmarks as structural representations. In: CVPR (2018)
75. Zhang, Z., Luo, P., Loy, C.C., Tang, X.: Learning deep representation for face alignment with auxiliary attributes. PAMI 38(5), 918–930 (2015)
76. Zhao, D., Song, Z., Ji, Z., Zhao, G., Ge, W., Yu, Y.: Multi-scale matching networks for semantic correspondence. In: ICCV, pp. 3354–3364 (2021)
77. Zhong, Y., Yuan, B., Wu, H., Yuan, Z., Peng, J., Wang, Y.X.: Pixel contrastive-consistent semi-supervised semantic segmentation. In: ICCV, pp. 7273–7282 (2021)
78. Zhou, B., Khosla, A., Lapedriza, A., Oliva, A., Torralba, A.: Learning deep features for discriminative localization. In: CVPR (2016)

Open-Set Semi-Supervised Object Detection

Yen-Cheng Liu[1]([✉]), Chih-Yao Ma[2], Xiaoliang Dai[2], Junjiao Tian[1],
Peter Vajda[2], Zijian He[2], and Zsolt Kira[1]

[1] Georgia Tech, Atlanta, USA
ycliu@gatech.edu
[2] Meta, Menlo Park, USA

Abstract. Recent developments for Semi-Supervised Object Detection
(SSOD) have shown the promise of leveraging unlabeled data to improve
an object detector. However, thus far these methods have assumed that
the unlabeled data does not contain out-of-distribution (OOD) classes,
which is unrealistic with larger-scale unlabeled datasets. In this paper,
we consider a more practical yet challenging problem, Open-Set Semi-
Supervised Object Detection (OSSOD). We first find the existing SSOD
method obtains a lower performance gain in open-set conditions, and this
is caused by the semantic expansion, where the distracting OOD objects
are mispredicted as in-distribution pseudo-labels for the semi-supervised
training. To address this problem, we consider online and offline OOD
detection modules, which are integrated with SSOD methods. With the
extensive studies, we found that leveraging an offline OOD detector
based on a self-supervised vision transformer performs favorably against
online OOD detectors due to its robustness to the interference of pseudo-
labeling. In the experiment, our proposed framework effectively addresses
the semantic expansion issue and shows consistent improvements on
many OSSOD benchmarks, including large-scale COCO-OpenImages. We
also verify the effectiveness of our framework under different OSSOD
conditions, including varying numbers of in-distribution classes, different
degrees of supervision, and different combinations of unlabeled sets.

1 Introduction

The success of deep neural networks relies on large collections of labeled data,
although creating such large-scale datasets is expensive and time-consuming.
The recent development of successful Semi-Supervised Learning (SSL) methods
alleviates this requirement by making better use of unlabeled data, narrowing
the performance gap between the SSL models and the fully-supervised model.

Inspired by SSL methods for image classification [1,10,13,20,35,36,39,46,48],
recent works on semi-supervised object detection (SSOD) [25,37,38,49] have
applied the self-training method, which trains the model with the pseudo-labels

---

Y.-C. Liu—Work done partially while interning at Meta.

Supplementary Information The online version contains supplementary material
available at https://doi.org/10.1007/978-3-031-20056-4_9.

S. Avidan et al. (Eds.): ECCV 2022, LNCS 13690, pp. 143–159, 2022.
https://doi.org/10.1007/978-3-031-20056-4_9

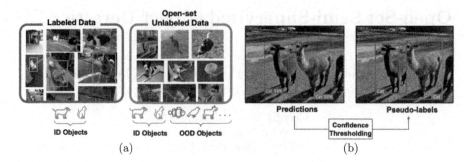

Fig. 1. (a) Open-Set Semi-Supervised Object Detection aims to learn an in-distribution object detector with a number of labeled images and another set of unconstrained/open-set unlabeled images. The objects appearing in the labeled data are defined as in-distribution (ID) objects, while some objects in the open-set unlabeled data are out-of-distribution (OOD) objects, which are unseen, unknown, and undefined in the labeled set. (b) While most of the self-training methods [25,36] rely on thresholding for filtering unreliable pseudo-labels, some OOD objects in unlabeled images are mispredicted as inlier objects with high confidence. These OOD objects are then mis-labeled, trained on, and lead to worse performance.

of the unlabeled data. These works often consider a scenario where the labeled set is randomly sampled from a dataset (*e.g.,* MS-COCO [23]) and use the remaining images as the unlabeled set. This implicitly assumes the label spaces of labeled and unlabeled data are identical. However, this closed-set assumption is unlikely to happen in real-world situations, where unlabeled images collected in the wild might contain out-of-distribution (OOD) objects, which are unseen, undefined, and unknown in the available labeled set.

We are thus interested in a more practical yet challenging problem, Open-Set Semi-Supervised Object Detection (OSSOD), which aims to leverage the **unconstrained** unlabeled images (*i.e.,* images containing unseen OOD objects), to improve an object detector trained with the available labeled data as shown in Fig. 1a. When adding unlabeled data containing open-set categories, we observe that the existing successful SSOD method leads to a lower performance gain or even *degraded* results. This is different from the common belief that SSL methods can benefit from using more unlabeled data. We attribute the above phenomena to the *semantic expansion* issue, where OOD objects are mispredicted as in-distribution objects with high confidence and misused as pseudo-labels with confidence thresholding (Fig. 1b).

To eliminate the detrimental effect of OOD samples, we propose to add an additional OOD filtering process into the existing SSOD training pipeline. More concretely, we first consider **online** OOD detectors to perform OOD filtering. An online OOD detector is a prediction head/branch we straightforwardly add on the object detector using existing OOD methods [12,14,21,41]. However, we find that such methods cannot produce satisfactory results due to interference with other tasks, *e.g.,* bounding box localization and box classification (See Sect. 4.2 for further discussion). In order to address this, we propose a simple but effective strategy that uses an **offline** OOD detection module, which is disentangled from the architecture of the object detector. This OOD detector is based on a self-supervised DINO [2] model, and it provides several advantages. First, the pre-training of DINO does not require label annotations, so it is suitable for the low-label setting and alleviates the concern of limited amounts of labels for OOD detection tasks. Secondly, it is more effective in detecting OOD objects in the pseudo-labels compared with other (online) OOD methods as shown in Sect. 5.2, and this eliminates the detrimental effect of OOD samples for OSSOD tasks. Lastly, since the architecture of OOD detector and object detector are independent, the training of the two models can be done separately and prevent interference as we observed in online OOD detectors.

In our experiments, we first provide a systematic analysis between several OOD detection methods, and our results suggest that offline methods show consistent improvements over the online detection methods. We also show that using the offline OOD detector can filter the OOD objects in pseudo-labels and consistently improve against the existing SSOD methods under different open-set scenarios, including under different combination of unlabeled sets, varying number of in-distribution (ID) classes, and different number of images. We also find that using the pseudo-labels generated from our framework is even more effective than using the ground-truth labels provided in OpenImages (see Sect. 5.3).

We highlight the contributions of this paper as follows:

- To the best of our knowledge, we are the *first* to address the open-set semi-supervised object detection tasks, and we analyze the limitation of existing SSOD methods on OSSOD tasks.
- We identify the challenges in designing OOD detection in OSSOD tasks, present online and offline OOD detectors, and provide a systematic comparison between these two modules.
- Through our extensive experiments, we demonstrate that an offline OOD detector can effectively remove OOD objects in pseudo-labels, and this leads to a significant improvements under different OSSOD scenarios, including a varying number of ID/OOD classes, different degrees of supervision, and different scales of datasets.

2   Related Work

Open-set semi-supervised object detection focuses on improving an in-distribution object detector with in-the-wild unlabeled data and preventing the detrimental effects caused by distracting OOD objects in a more practical semi-supervised setup. This task is different from the existing works on open-vocabulary/open-world object detection [9,16–18,33,47,50], where the goal is to improve the recall and accuracy of novel/OOD objects.

Semi-Supervised Object Detection. Recent successful methods on semi-supervised learning for image classification have applied various data augmentation and consistency regularization on unlabeled data [1,10,13,20,35,36,39,46, 48]. These techniques have also promoted the development of semi-supervised learning in object detection tasks. For example, several works [25,37,38,49] apply the self-training method, which is based on the Teacher-Student framework. For example, STAC [37] uses the labeled data to train the Teacher, which generates pseudo-labels to supervise the Student model. To refine the quality of pseudo-labels, existing works propose several techniques, including exponential moving average (EMA) [25,43,44,49], co-rectify mechanism [49], replacing hard pseudo-labels with soft pseudo-labels [38], and addressing class imbalance in pseudo-labels [25]. While promising results have been made, existing SSOD works usually experiment on datasets where the labeled and unlabeled sets have the same object categories. We are interested in a more challenging scenario, where some objects in the unlabeled set are novel and never appear in the labeled set.

Out-of-Distribution Detection. Out-of-distribution (OOD) classes are object categories that do not appear in the training label space and are not known *a-priori*, and OOD detection, which plays a vital role in OSSOD tasks, is a binary classification problem that decides whether a sample is an ID or OOD. Early works use different scoring functions to estimate the likelihood of a sample being OOD, including maximum softmax probability (MSP) [11,22] and Mahalanobis distance [21]. Another line of works [12,24,28] exploit large sets of OOD samples during training and they generally achieve better performance on detecting the outlier objects. There are also several generative-based methods [29,30,32,52] for OOD detection tasks, though it is difficult and prohibitively challenging to apply them on large-scale semi-supervised object detection tasks. Among the existing OOD works, Fort *et al.* [7] shows state-of-the-art performance on OOD detection by simply fine-tuning the pretrained vision transformer with the available inlier data. While promising results have been made on OOD detection tasks, most of the existing works only experiment on small-scale image classification tasks, and their extension to the large-scale object detection tasks is not verified. The only work on OOD detection for object detection is VOS [6], but the interference with pseudo-labeling in SSOD tasks and computation cost of virtual negative sampling make it incompatible with the existing SSOD methods.

Open-Set Semi-Supervised Learning. Existing works on open-set semi-supervised learning focus on image classification tasks [15,26,34,45] or image generation [8]. For example, MTC [45] estimates the OOD score for each unlabeled image, and both the network parameters and OOD scores are updated alternately. Based on the estimated OOD scores, MTC eliminates the OOD samples with low OOD scores and improves the image classifier in a semi-supervised scenario. OpenMatch [34] applies a consistency regularization on a one-vs-all classifier, which is used as an OOD detector to filter the OOD samples during semi-supervised learning. Despite the promising results, no prior work has addressed open-set semi-supervised learning for object detection tasks, which have more challenges than image classification tasks. For instance, in image classification, each image only contains one single object/class, whereas, in object detection, each image may contain an arbitrary number of ID/OOD objects, making pseudo-labeling integrated with OOD detection much more challenging. Additionally, we also observed that balancing object detection losses against OOD detector is difficult as we showed in Sect. 4.2.

3   Revisiting Semi-Supervised Object Detection

Semi-supervised object detection (SSOD) aims to learn an object detector by using a set of labeled images $D_s = \{x_i^s, y_i^s\}_{i=1}^{N_s}$ and unlabeled images $D_u = \{x_i^u\}_{i=1}^{N_u}$, where $N_s << N_u$. Existing SSOD works [25,37,43,49] apply the self-training method and have shown significant improvements in this semi-supervised scenario. The typical strategy of such methods is to generate pseudo-labels (*i.e.*, pseudo-boxes and the corresponding class labels) of unlabeled images and then train the object detector using both labeled data and unlabeled data with pseudo-labels.

These works adopt the Teacher-Student framework, where the **Teacher** model generates pseudo-labels to train the **Student** model. Specifically, the **Teacher** model takes the weakly-augmented unlabeled data as input and generates the box predictions, and the bounding boxes with confidence higher than a pre-defined threshold τ are selected as the pseudo-boxes. The **Student** then takes as input the same images with stronger augmentation, and we enforce the consistency loss $\mathcal{L}_{unsup}$ (*i.e.*, unsupervised loss) between its predictions and the generated pseudo-labels. To train the **Student**, we combine both the supervised loss $\mathcal{L}_{sup}$ and the unsupervised loss $\mathcal{L}_{unsup}$.

$$\mathcal{L}_{ssod} = \mathcal{L}_{sup} + \lambda \mathcal{L}_{unsup} = \sum_i \mathcal{L}(x_i^s, y_i^s) + \lambda \sum_i \mathcal{L}(x_i^u, \hat{y}_i^u), \tag{1}$$

where λ is the unsupervised loss weight and $\hat{y}_i^u = \delta(\tilde{y}_i^u; \tau)$ represents the pseudo-labels, which are derived from the bounding box prediction $\tilde{y}_i^u$ after the confidence thresholding function $\delta(\cdot)$ with the pre-defined threshold τ.

To further refine the quality of pseudo-labels, some existing works [25,38,43] update the **Teacher** model (θ_t) by exploiting the model weights of **Student** (θ_s) via the exponential moving average (*i.e.*, $\theta_t \leftarrow \alpha \theta_t + (1 - \alpha)\theta_s$).

To verify the effectiveness of the models, existing works often experiment on a setting where the labeled and unlabeled sets are randomly sampled from the same dataset. This implicitly assumes the set of object categories are the same across the labeled and unlabeled sets, and we formalize this setup as the **closed-set** SSOD.

4   Open-Set Semi-Supervised Object Detection

While the above self-training methods show promising results in closed-set SSOD, it restricts the set of object categories in the unlabeled set to be the same as the labeled set. This setting, however, is less practical since unlabeled datasets collected in the wild might contain images with novel objects beyond what were presented in the labeled dataset. We are thus interested in OSSOD, a more practical yet challenging problem setup, where novel and undefined objects appear in the unconstrained unlabeled set and are not available in the labeled set with a limited amount of data.

4.1 Semantic Expansion in Open-Set Scenarios

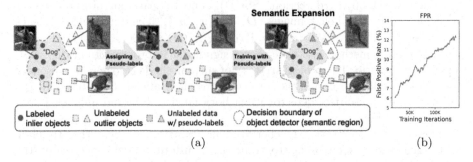

(a)   (b)

Fig. 2. Illustration of **semantic expansion**. (a) With the object detector trained with the labeled data, some OOD objects in unlabeled data are predicted as ID objects, and solely using the confidence thresholding based on the box score cannot effectively suppress these OOD objects in pseudo-labels. Using the noisy pseudo-labels in self-training methods makes the open-set issue become more severe after several training iterations, and (b) thus the false-positive rate (*i.e.,* percentage of OOD objects predicted as ID) increases over time.

We first analyze the existing successful SSOD work[1] on OSSOD tasks. Interestingly, we found it shows limited performance gain in the open-set scenario compared with closed-set scenario as shown in Fig. 3. We attribute this lower performance gain to *semantic expansion* as presented in Fig. 2a. To be more specific, when OOD/novel objects exist in the unlabeled set, the closed-set classifier (*e.g.,* ROIhead classifier in Faster-RCNN [31]) might mispredict these OOD instances as ID objects with high confidence (a similar observation

Fig. 3. Performance comparison between closed-set and open-set SSOD. The performance gain of the existing SSOD method [25] is much smaller in the open-set conditions. Note that we randomly select 0.5%/1% data as the labeled set for both conditions.

is also made recently in prior works [4,27]). These over-confident and incorrect OOD instances are prone to be selected as the pseudo-labels of ID objects even after confidence thresholding, and using these incorrect OOD pseudo-labels in the training makes the EMA-updated Teacher mispredict more OOD objects as ID objects. After the iterative EMA updates between the Teacher and Student, the semantic discrimination of ID objects is *enlarged* and incorrectly covers more OOD objects. This causes the false-positive rate of the OOD pseudo-labels to increase as the model is trained longer, as presented in Fig. 2b.

---

[1] As all SoTA SSOD methods [25,38,43,49] use the Teacher-student mechanism and pseudo-labeling method, we choose UT [25] as an example while our framework is not restricted to it.

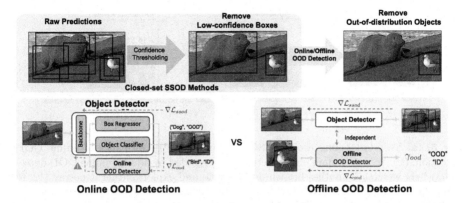

Fig. 4. Illustration of online and offline OOD detection frameworks for OSSOD tasks. Combined with the existing closed-set SSOD methods, OOD detection aims to remove the OOD objects in pseudo-labels and prevent *semantic expansion* in OSSOD. For the online OOD detector, we add an additional branch on the object detector, but it suffers from the instability of pseudo-labels used for SSOD and leads to degraded performance of the object detector. In contrast, the offline OOD detector does not have these limitations and produce better results on OOD detection due to its nature of independent model architecture.

To address the above issue and improve the performance on OSSOD tasks, we propose an integrated framework to detect the OOD instances in the pseudo-boxes and eliminate their detrimental effect during semi-supervised learning. With the goal of deciding whether a sample is an ID or OOD data (*i.e.*, binary classification), prior works have proposed several OOD detection methods [11, 12, 21, 24, 34], although most of these works only verify the effectiveness of the methods on the image-level vision tasks. To further advance to OOD detection for instance-level tasks (*e.g.*, object detection), we consider **online** and **offline** OOD detectors in the following sections.

4.2 Online OOD Detection

As illustrated in Fig. 4, online OOD detection expands the architecture of the existing object detector so that it can perform OOD detection in addition to bounding box classification and localization. One simple way to detect the OOD objects is to use the maximum softmax probability (MSP) [11] of ROIhead classifier as an indicator for identifying OOD samples. In a similar spirit, another way is to apply a range of existing OOD detection methods [11,12,21,24,34,41] and add an additional OOD branch on the ROIhead. We combine the semi-supervised object detection loss $\mathcal{L}_{ssod}$ as mentioned in Eq. 3 and OOD detection loss $\mathcal{L}_{ood}$ defined in the original works, and we train the model in an end-to-end manner.

However, these online OOD detectors have several limitations in OSSOD tasks. On the one hand, as presented in Fig. 5a, pseudo-labeling used for SSOD significantly degrades the performance of online OOD detection (we use MSP [11] as an example), and such a trend is hypothetically caused by the instability of pseudo-labels (*i.e.*, classification noise in pseudo-labels). On the other hand,

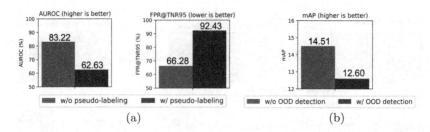

Fig. 5. (a) Pseudo-labeling used in SSOD degrades the performance of online OOD detection. (b) Accuracy of an object detector is degraded by adding online OOD detection, where we create another branch on ROIhead and exploit outlier exposure [12] to detect OOD samples. Both AUROC and FPR@TNR95 are standard evaluation metrics for OOD detection (defined in Sect. 5.2).

bundling two different tasks (*e.g.*, OOD detection and object detection) in a shared architecture leads to sub-optimal performance of object detection task as shown in Fig. 5b, making the online OOD detection less favorable to be applied for OSSOD tasks.

4.3   Offline OOD Detection

To ameliorate the above issues, as shown in Fig. 4, we alternatively propose to use **offline** OOD detection, where we construct an OOD detector that is disentangled from the architecture of the object detector and *not* jointly trained with the object detector. This framework design provides two advantages: 1) the offline OOD detector is compatible with *any* existing SSOD methods [25,37,49,51], since the offline OOD detector is modularized and independent from the object detector. 2) Such a framework design alleviates the concern about competing task objectives between OOD detection and object detection.

To design the offline OOD detector, we exploit the current state-of-the-art OOD method, which is simple yet effective on image-level OOD tasks. Specifically, as pointed out by Fort *et al.* [7], one highly successful method for OOD detection is to simply fine-tune a pretrained ViT-B [5] with available ID data. Despite its promising results, pre-training a ViT-B requires ImageNet-21k images and the corresponding large amount of annotated labels, which is not suitable for our semi-supervised setting and would result in an unfair comparison to prior works.

DINO as an Offline OOD Detector. We therefore utilize the self-supervised DINO [2], which is only trained with ImageNet-1k images without using any label annotations[2]. To perform the OOD detection, we fine-tune DINO with multi-class training and then compute different OOD scores (described below) to decide whether an object is an ID or an OOD sample. To be more concrete, the OOD detector is trained as a simple classifier with $K + 1$ output classes (K

---

[2] The backbone of object detectors is usually pretrained on the ImageNet1k classification [3,42], and both images and ground-truth labels are required for pretraining of the model weights. A systematic comparison between using DINO and ViT will be discussed in supplementary material.

is the number of ID object classes), where the additional node is for the OOD and novel samples. Unlike prior works [12,24,28] that used a large amount of additional OOD data during training, we do not assume the availability of such data. We therefore only use the available ID labeled data and propose to regard the background proposal patches as the OOD samples. Specifically, we crop the image patches according to the ground-truth boxes, and the background patches are randomly sampled from the proposal boxes labeled with the low IoU to the ground-truth boxes. We compute the OOD detection loss $\mathcal{L}_{ood}$ with the cross-entropy which enforces the ID patches as the corresponding ID foreground labels and enforces the background patches as the OOD class. While it is sub-optimal to use background instances as OOD class, they still provide sufficient negative gradients for distinguishing the ID objects when the novel OOD objects are not available in the labeled set.

After the fine-tuning of the DINO model, we freeze the DINO model and experiment the following common scores for OOD detection:

1. **Mahalanobis Distance** [21]:

$$\gamma_{ood} = \max_k -(f(x) - \tilde{\mu}_k)^\mathsf{T} \tilde{\Sigma}^{-1}(f(x) - \tilde{\mu}_k). \tag{2}$$

where $f(x)$ represents the DINO intermediate feature vector of patch x, $\tilde{\mu}_k$ is the estimated mean vector of class k, and $\tilde{\Sigma}$ is the estimated covariance matrix. Both $\tilde{\mu}_k$ and $\tilde{\Sigma}$ are estimated by using the available labeled data.

2. **Inverse Abstaining Confidence** [28,40]:

$$\gamma_{ood} = 1 - \tilde{p}_{K+1}, \tag{3}$$

where $\tilde{p}_{K+1}$ is the prediction confidence of $K+1$-th class (*i.e.*, abstention class) from the DINO classifier.

3. **Energy Score** [24]:

$$\gamma_{ood} = -T \log \sum_i^K e^{f_i(x)/T}, \tag{4}$$

where T is the temperature value, K is the number of classes, $f_i(x)$ represents the i-th index of the logit corresponding to the class i. We also consider **Shannon Entropy** and **Euclidean Distance** for the OOD scores. To decide whether an object is an ID or OOD class, we set a threshold δ_{ood} on the OOD score, and the objects with OOD scores lower than the threshold are regarded as OOD samples.

Integration with Semi-Supervised Object Detection. With the goal of filtering the OOD objects in pseudo-labels, we integrate the trained OOD detector with the SSOD method by inserting the OOD filtering after the confidence thresholding as shown in Fig. 4. In other words, the pseudo-boxes are derived by sequentially applying both confidence thresholding and OOD filtering on predicted boxes from Teacher model, and they are then used to compute the unsupervised loss defined in Eq. 3 to train the Student. Note that our OOD detector is complementary to the existing semi-supervised object detection works [25,37,49,51] and can also be combined with these SSOD methods to address the open-set issue.

5   Experiments

5.1   Experimental Setting and Datasets

COCO-Open. `COCO2017-train` contains 117k images with box-level labels from 80 object categories. We randomly sample 20/40/60 classes as the ID classes and the remaining classes as the OOD classes. Specifically, since each image contains multiple objects, `COCO2017-train` is divided into the pure-ID, mixed, and pure-OOD image sets. Each image in the pure-ID set has at least one ID object and no OOD object, and each image in the pure-OOD set has at least one OOD object and no ID object. As for the mixed set, each image has at least one ID object and at least one OOD object. To make sure that OOD objects are not in the labeled set, we randomly sample the pure-ID images as a labeled set and the remaining data as the unlabeled set. Thus, the unlabeled set contains images from the pure-ID, pure-OOD, and mixed sets.

COCO-OpenImages. To examine all methods in a large-scale OSSOD experiment, we use `COCO2017-train` as the labeled set and `OpenImagesv5` [19] as the unlableed set. `OpenImagesv5` contains 1.7M images with 601 object categories, and most object categories do not exist in COCO (and are hence OOD).

We also include more experiments in the supplementary material.

5.2   Comparison Between Online and Offline OOD Detection

We first present a comparison between online and offline detectors on **OOD detection** tasks (object detection results shown in Sect. 5.3), and we evaluate them with the standard OOD detection metrics, including area under the ROC curve (AUROC) and false-positive rate under the true-false rate with $x\%$ (FPR@TNRx). We consider several OOD detection methods [11,12,14,21,24, 34,34,41][3]. For a fair and thorough comparison, we adapt these methods from image classification to object detection tasks and implement them in a unified framework with the same implementation details such as batch size and optimization. To better understand the efficacy of each OOD method and prevent the interference of pseudo-labeling from affecting the performance, we do not use the pseudo-labels of unlabeled data and only use the available labeled data to train all OOD detectors (adding pseudo-labels worsen online OOD detection methods as we discussed in Sect. 4.2).

As presented in Table 1, we list our observations as follows,

1) *offline OOD detectors are significantly better than online OOD detectors on all evaluation metrics*, and this trend also supports that the disentanglement between OOD detector and object detector can alleviate the interference between OOD detection and object detection. It is worth repeating that the feature backbone of Faster-RCNN is pretrained on ImageNet1k with label annotations, so the superiority of the DINO on OOD detection does not come from using extra

---

[3] As the problem setting of GODIN [14] and GSD [41] is OOD detection without OOD samples, we adapt them to our setup and enhance the performance by using an linear classifier to predict background samples.

Table 1. Evaluation of OOD detection for object detection. We sample 20 classes from COCO as ID objects, and $4k$ pure-ID images are selected as labeled images.

OOD models	Methods	OoD scores γ_{ood}	AUROC↑	FPR75↓	FPR95↓
Online (ROIhead)	Vanilla	MSP [11]	67.0	58.4	92.3
		Energy [24]	75.5	36.8	83.6
		Entropy	75.9	38.5	83.1
		Mahalanobis [21]	50.2	83.0	98.1
		Euclidean	56.3	74.3	96.1
	OE [12]	MSP	67.0	55.0	89.1
	OVA [34]	MSP	73.0	45.7	90.0
	GODIN [14]	Cosine $h(x)$	77.8	33.8	77.4
	GSD [41]	Feat. angle	78.7	32.1	73.9
Offline (DINO)	Ours	IAC [40]	83.6	22.4	61.7
		Energy	89.6	12.2	47.5
		Entropy	88.9	12.6	51.1
		Mahalanobis [21]	81.8	25.6	57.6
		Euclidean	**90.8**	**10.7**	**38.6**

images and labels. In addition, as mentioned in Sect. 4.3, another merit of the offline OOD detector is its robustness to the instability to pseudo-labeling used in SSOD due to the isolated training of OOD detectors and object detectors.

2) Among the OOD scores used in offline detectors, simply applying the Euclidean distance performs the bests on all metrics. The popular Mahalanobis distance cannot lead to satisfactory results due to the inaccurate covariance matrix estimated limited amounts of labeled data.

Additionally, in the supplementary material, we also list other in-depth analyses and discussions on OOD detection, including using supervised ViT-B as an offline OOD detector, and other offline OOD detection methods with different ID/OOD class splits and different degrees of supervision. Owing to the superior performance on OOD detection, we apply the offline OOD detectors in the following OSSOD experiments.

5.3   Experiments on Open-set Semi-Supervised Object Detection

In addition to the OOD detection performance shown in the previous section, we further advance to OSSOD tasks and assess the object detection performance under different OSSOD conditions, including different combinations of unlabeled sets, varying numbers of ID classes, different degrees of supervision, and larger-scale OSSOD tasks (COCO-additional and COCO-GOI).

Effect of Different Combinations of Unlabeled Sets. We experiment with the existing SSOD method (UT [25]) and our proposed OOD detectors by using different combinations of unlabeled data, including the pure-ID, the mixed, and the pure-OOD sets. The purpose of this experiment is to verify the existence of open-set issue/semantic expansion and investigate whether the OOD samples affect the SSOD methods.

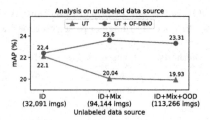

Fig. 6. Using more unlabeled images containing OOD objects (*i.e.,* Mix and OOD) cannot lead to a better result for UT, while applying our OOD filtering can alleviate the performance drop and improve the accuracy. We experiment on COCO-open with $4k$ images from 40 ID classes.

Table 2. Mean average precision of COCO-Open when **varying the number of ID objects**. We experiment on COCO-Open with $4k$ labeled images from 20/40/60 ID classes. We run each method 3 times and report the standard deviation.

Num. of ID/OOD objects	20/60	40/40	60/20
Label-only	16.89±2.6	15.98±0.49	16.64±0.59
UT	18.37±1.67 (+1.48)	20.28±0.85 (+4.29)	23.09±0.25 (+6.45)
UT + OF-DINO	**23.43±2.19** (+6.54)	**22.91±0.28** (+6.93)	**24.89±0.34** (+8.25)

As shown in Fig. 6, UT achieves 22.10 mAP when the pure-ID images are used in the unlabeled set, while the performance drops when the mixed and pure-OOD sets, containing OOD objects, are added. This shows that OOD objects in the unlabeled set do affect the effectiveness of the existing SS-OD method, and the trend is also contrary to the common belief that semi-supervised methods can derive more performance gains by using more unlabeled data. Therefore, with our proposed OOD filtering (OF-DINO), the performance of the object detector does not degrade but instead improves by using the mixed set, and this reflects the importance of eliminating the detrimental effect of OOD objects.

Varying Numbers of ID Classes. We also experiment by varying the number of ID classes in COCO-Open, and we first find that UT shows less performance gain against label-only baseline when there are fewer ID classes (see Table 2). This is because the semantic expansion/open-set issue becomes more severe when more OOD objects appear in the unlabeled set, and such an issue can be alleviated by the OOD filtering. With the OOD filtering, we can obtain a larger improvement gain against UT, and it improves 6.54 mAP against the labeled-only baseline and 5.06 mAP against UT in the case of 20 ID classes. This verifies the efficacy of the OOD filtering using the different number of ID/OOD classes.

Different Degrees of Supervision. In addition, we consider varying the number of labeled images in COCO-Open as shown in Table 3, and we find that using the OOD detector can also consistently improve against the label-only baseline and UT under different numbers of labeled images. When fewer labeled images are used, we could obtain more improvement gain by filtering OOD samples.

Table 3. Mean average precision of COCO-open under **different degree of super-vision**. We experiment on COCO-Open with $1/2/4k$ labeled images from 20 selected ID classes. We run each method 3 times and report the standard deviation.

Num. of Labeled Images	1,000	2,000	4,000
Label-only	10.20± 0.34	11.84± 0.33	16.35± 0.28
UT	11.77±0.38 (+1.57)	13.87±0.68 (+2.03)	18.23±0.47 (+1.88)
UT + OF-DINO	**16.80±0.53** (+6.60)	**18.10±0.71** (+6.26)	**22.56±0.51** (+6.21)

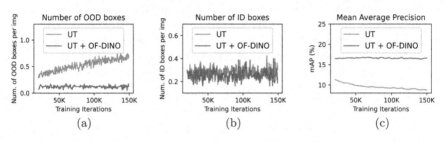

(a)   (b)   (c)

Fig. 7. Using OOD detector can (a) suppress the OOD objects while (b) maintain the ID objects in pseudo-labels, and this leads to (c) the improvement on OSSOD. We experiment on COCO-Open with 500 labeled images from 20 ID classes.

Analysis on Pseudo-Labels. To better understand how our OOD detector helps the learning of the SSOD method in the open-set condition, we use the ground-truth labels to measure the number of ID/OOD boxes in pseudo-labels (note that we only use ground-truth labels for the analysis and do not use them in the training). As illustrated in Fig. 7, our OOD detector can effectively suppress OOD objects in pseudo-labels without sacrificing the ID objects, and thus this alleviates the semantic expansion issue mentioned in Sect. 4.1 and leads to improvement for the OSSOD task.

COCO-GOI. We also consider a more challenging experiment, where we use unlabeled `OpenImagesv5` to improve the object detector trained on `COCO2017-train`. Although `OpenImagesv5` is substantially larger than COCO datasets, the object categories in `OpenImagesv5` (601 classes) are more diverse than the object categories in MSCOCO (80 classes). This implies there are more distracting OOD objects that can affect the performance of existing SSOD methods. In addition to UT, we also consider a fully-supervised baseline, which uses ground-truth labels from *both* `COCO2017-train` and `OpenImagesv5` to train an object detector. To be more specific, we first manually label the correspondence between 601 classes in `OpenImagesv5` and 80 classes in `COCO2017-train`, and we only use labels of 80 COCO-classes in `OpenImagesv5`. We present the details of the correspondence in our supplementary material.

As presented in Table 4, with our OOD filtering mechanism (DINO) we can improve UT from 41.81 mAP to 43.14 mAP. Another interesting result is that our framework can perform *even better than the model with the ground-truth labels from OpenImages*, and this indicates that using pseudo-labels generated from

Table 4. Experimental results of COCO-OpenImages.

Methods	Labeled	Unlabeled	mAP
Fully-supervised	COCO	–	40.90
Fully-supervised	COCO+OpenImage	–	42.91
Unbiased teacher [25]	COCO	OpenImage	41.81
Unbiased teacher+OF-DINO	COCO	OpenImage	**43.14**

our framework might be more effective than the ground-truth labels provided in `OpenImages`. This is potentially caused by noisy labels from human annotations. In addition, we also find that some COCO object categories are rare in `OpenImages`, and this potentially limits further improvements by exploiting `OpenImages` as an unlabeled set (more discussion in the supplementary material).

Limitations and Future Works. While addressing OSSOD, we do not address other issues such as covariate shift and mismatch in object category distributions between datasets. The offline OOD detector is an individual module from the object detector, so it requires more computational resources in the training stage. However, this concern does not exist as we remove the offline OOD detector and only use the object detector in the inference stage. Our key message is that combining an offline OOD detection module and an SSOD method is a simple yet effective solution to address OSSOD tasks. Based on this integrated framework, there will be more advanced techniques for both SSOD and OOD detection methods, which can potentially improve the performance on OSSOD tasks.

6   Conclusion

Unlike traditional closed-set Semi-Supervised Object Detection, where the majority of the unlabeled images are from in-distribution datasets, we aim to train object detector with *unconstrained* unlabeled images – Open-Set Semi-Supervised Object Detection (OSSOD). In our proposed setting, unlabeled training images can contain object classes that are out-of-distribution, *i.e.,* classes not included in the labeled set. To the best of our knowledge, this is the first work investigating OSSOD. We present comprehensive studies to understand the challenges for OSSOD and analyze why the performance of existing SoTA methods degrade even when trained with more unlabeled images. To overcome the challenges, we consider both online and offline OOD detectors and show that a simple yet effective offline OOD detector can further improve the SSOD models when training with large-scale unlabeled datasets, *e.g.,* COCO-OpenImage. We achieved state-of-the-art results across existing and new benchmark settings, and some interesting directions such as more accurate and efficient OOD detectors are worth exploring for future research.

Acknowledgments. We thank Ross Girshick for many helpful suggestions and valuable discussions. Yen-Cheng Liu and Zsolt Kira were partly supported by DARPA's Learning with Less Labels (LwLL) program under agreement HR0011-18-S-0044, as part of their affiliation with Georgia Tech.

References

1. Berthelot, D., Carlini, N., Goodfellow, I., Papernot, N., Oliver, A., Raffel, C.A.: Mixmatch: a holistic approach to semi-supervised learning. In: Advances in Neural Information Processing Systems (NeurIPS), pp. 5049–5059 (2019)
2. Caron, M., et al.: Emerging properties in self-supervised vision transformers. arXiv preprint arXiv:2104.14294 (2021)
3. Chen, K., et al.: MMDetection: open MMLab detection toolbox and benchmark. arXiv preprint arXiv:1906.07155 (2019)
4. Dhamija, A., Gunther, M., Ventura, J., Boult, T.: The overlooked elephant of object detection: open set. In: Proceedings of the IEEE Winter Conference on Applications of Computer Vision (WACV) (2020)
5. Dosovitskiy, A., et al.: An image is worth 16x16 words: transformers for image recognition at scale. In: Proceedings of the International Conference on Learning Representations (ICLR) (2021)
6. Du, X., Wang, Z., Cai, M., Li, Y.: Vos: learning what you don't know by virtual outlier synthesis. arXiv preprint arXiv:2202.01197 (2022)
7. Fort, S., Ren, J., Lakshminarayanan, B.: Exploring the limits of out-of-distribution detection. In: Advances in Neural Information Processing Systems (NeurIPS) (2021)
8. Girish, S., Suri, S., Rambhatla, S.S., Shrivastava, A.: Towards discovery and attribution of open-world GAN generated images. In: Proceedings of the IEEE/CVF International Conference on Computer Vision, pp. 14094–14103 (2021)
9. Gu, X., Lin, T.Y., Kuo, W., Cui, Y.: Open-vocabulary object detection via vision and language knowledge distillation. In: Proceedings of the International Conference on Learning Representations (ICLR) (2022)
10. Guo, H., Mao, Y., Zhang, R.: MixUP as locally linear out-of-manifold regularization. In: Proceedings of the AAAI Conference on Artificial Intelligence (AAAI), vol. 33, pp. 3714–3722 (2019)
11. Hendrycks, D., Gimpel, K.: A baseline for detecting misclassified and out-of-distribution examples in neural networks. In: Proceedings of the International Conference on Learning Representations (ICLR) (2017)
12. Hendrycks, D., Mazeika, M., Dietterich, T.: Deep anomaly detection with outlier exposure. In: Proceedings of the International Conference on Learning Representations (ICLR) (2019)
13. Hendrycks, D., Mu, N., Cubuk, E.D., Zoph, B., Gilmer, J., Lakshminarayanan, B.: AugMix: a simple data processing method to improve robustness and uncertainty. In: Proceedings of the International Conference on Learning Representations (ICLR) (2020)
14. Hsu, Y.C., Shen, Y., Jin, H., Kira, Z.: Generalized ODIN: detecting out-of-distribution image without learning from out-of-distribution data. In: Proceedings of the IEEE Conference on Computer Vision and Pattern Recognition (CVPR) (2020)
15. Huang, J., et al.: Trash to treasure: harvesting OOD data with cross-modal matching for open-set semi-supervised learning. In: Proceedings of the IEEE/CVF International Conference on Computer Vision, pp. 8310–8319 (2021)
16. Huynh, D., Kuen, J., Lin, Z., Gu, J., Elhamifar, E.: Open-vocabulary instance segmentation via robust cross-modal pseudo-labeling. arXiv preprint arXiv:2111.12698 (2021)

17. Joseph, K., Khan, S., Khan, F.S., Balasubramanian, V.N.: Towards open world object detection. In: Proceedings of the IEEE Conference on Computer Vision and Pattern Recognition (CVPR) (2021)
18. Kim, D., Lin, T.Y., Angelova, A., Kweon, I.S., Kuo, W.: Learning open-world object proposals without learning to classify. IEEE Robot. Autom. Lett. **7**(2), 5453–5460 (2022)
19. Krasin, I., et al.: Openimages: a public dataset for large-scale multi-label and multi-class image classification (2017). https://storage.googleapis.com/openimages/web/index.html
20. Laine, S., Aila, T.: Temporal ensembling for semi-supervised learning. In: Proceedings of the International Conference on Learning Representations (ICLR) (2017)
21. Lee, K., Lee, K., Lee, H., Shin, J.: A simple unified framework for detecting out-of-distribution samples and adversarial attacks. In: Advances in Neural Information Processing Systems (NeurIPS) (2018)
22. Liang, S., Li, Y., Srikant, R.: Enhancing the reliability of out-of-distribution image detection in neural networks. In: Proceedings of the International Conference on Learning Representations (ICLR) (2018)
23. Lin, T.Y., et al.: Microsoft coco: common objects in context. In: Proceedings of the European Conference on Computer Vision (ECCV) (2014)
24. Liu, W., Wang, X., Owens, J.D., Li, Y.: Energy-based out-of-distribution detection. In: Advances in Neural Information Processing Systems (NeurIPS) (2020)
25. Liu, Y.C., et al.: Unbiased teacher for semi-supervised object detection. In: Proceedings of the International Conference on Learning Representations (ICLR) (2021)
26. Luo, H., et al.: On the consistency training for open-set semi-supervised learning. arXiv preprint arXiv:2101.08237 (2021)
27. Miller, D., Sünderhauf, N., Milford, M., Dayoub, F.: Uncertainty for identifying open-set errors in visual object detection. arXiv preprint arXiv:2104.01328 (2021)
28. Mohseni, S., Pitale, M., Yadawa, J., Wang, Z.: Self-supervised learning for generalizable out-of-distribution detection. In: Proceedings of the AAAI Conference on Artificial Intelligence (AAAI) (2020)
29. Nalisnick, E., Matsukawa, A., Teh, Y.W., Gorur, D., Lakshminarayanan, B.: Do deep generative models know what they don't know? In: Proceedings of the International Conference on Learning Representations (ICLR) (2019)
30. Pidhorskyi, S., Almohsen, R., Adjeroh, D.A., Doretto, G.: Generative probabilistic novelty detection with adversarial autoencoders. In: Advances in Neural Information Processing Systems (NeurIPS) (2018)
31. Ren, S., He, K., Girshick, R., Sun, J.: Faster R-CNN: towards real-time object detection with region proposal networks. In: Advances in neural information processing systems (NeurIPS), pp. 91–99 (2015)
32. Sabokrou, M., Khalooei, M., Fathy, M., Adeli, E.: Adversarially learned one-class classifier for novelty detection. In: Proceedings of the IEEE Conference on Computer Vision and Pattern Recognition (CVPR) (2018)
33. Saito, K., Hu, P., Darrell, T., Saenko, K.: Learning to detect every thing in an open world. arXiv preprint arXiv:2112.01698 (2021)
34. Saito, K., Kim, D., Saenko, K.: OpenMatch: open-set consistency regularization for semi-supervised learning with outliers. In: Advances in Neural Information Processing Systems (NeurIPS) (2021)
35. Sajjadi, M., Javanmardi, M., Tasdizen, T.: Regularization with stochastic transformations and perturbations for deep semi-supervised learning. In: Advances in Neural Information Processing Systems (NeurIPS), pp. 1163–1171 (2016)

36. Sohn, K., et al.: FixMatch: simplifying semi-supervised learning with consistency and confidence. In: Advances in Neural Information Processing Systems (NeurIPS) (2020)
37. Sohn, K., Zhang, Z., Li, C.L., Zhang, H., Lee, C.Y., Pfister, T.: A simple semi-supervised learning framework for object detection. arXiv preprint arXiv:2005.04757 (2020)
38. Tang, Y., Chen, W., Luo, Y., Zhang, Y.: Humble teachers teach better students for semi-supervised object detection. In: Proceedings of the IEEE/CVF Conference on Computer Vision and Pattern Recognition, pp. 3132–3141 (2021)
39. Tarvainen, A., Valpola, H.: Mean teachers are better role models: weight-averaged consistency targets improve semi-supervised deep learning results. In: Advances in Neural Information Processing Systems (NeurIPS), pp. 1195–1204 (2017)
40. Thulasidasan, S., Thapa, S., Dhaubhadel, S., Chennupati, G., Bhattacharya, T., Bilmes, J.: An effective baseline for robustness to distributional shift. arXiv preprint arXiv:2105.07107 (2021)
41. Tian, J., Yung, D., Hsu, Y.C., Kira, Z.: A geometric perspective towards neural calibration via sensitivity decomposition. In: Advances in Neural Information Processing Systems (NeurIPS) (2021)
42. Wu, Y., Kirillov, A., Massa, F., Lo, W.Y., Girshick, R.: Detectron2 (2019). https://github.com/facebookresearch/detectron2
43. Xu, M., et al.: End-to-end semi-supervised object detection with soft teacher. arXiv preprint arXiv:2106.09018 (2021)
44. Yang, Q., Wei, X., Wang, B., Hua, X.S., Zhang, L.: Interactive self-training with mean teachers for semi-supervised object detection. In: Proceedings of the IEEE Conference on Computer Vision and Pattern Recognition (CVPR) (2021)
45. Yu, Q., Ikami, D., Irie, G., Aizawa, K.: Multi-task curriculum framework for open-set semi-supervised learning. In: Proceedings of the European Conference on Computer Vision (ECCV) (2020)
46. Yun, S., Han, D., Oh, S.J., Chun, S., Choe, J., Yoo, Y.: CutMix: regularization strategy to train strong classifiers with localizable features. In: Proceedings of the IEEE International Conference on Computer Vision (ICCV), pp. 6023–6032 (2019)
47. Zareian, A., Rosa, K.D., Hu, D.H., Chang, S.F.: Open-vocabulary object detection using captions. In: Proceedings of the IEEE Conference on Computer Vision and Pattern Recognition (CVPR) (2021)
48. Zhang, H., Cisse, M., Dauphin, Y.N., Lopez-Paz, D.: mixup: beyond empirical risk minimization. In: Proceedings of the International Conference on Learning Representations (ICLR) (2018)
49. Zhou, Q., Yu, C., Wang, Z., Qian, Q., Li, H.: Instant-teaching: an end-to-end semi-supervised object detection framework. In: Proceedings of the IEEE Conference on Computer Vision and Pattern Recognition (CVPR) (2021)
50. Zhou, X., Girdhar, R., Joulin, A., Krähenbühl, P., Misra, I.: Detecting twenty-thousand classes using image-level supervision. arXiv preprint arXiv:2201.02605 (2022)
51. Zhu, C., Chen, F., Shen, Z., Savvides, M.: Soft anchor-point object detection. In: Proceedings of the European Conference on Computer Vision (ECCV) (2020)
52. Zong, B., et al.: Deep autoencoding gaussian mixture model for unsupervised anomaly detection. In: Proceedings of the International Conference on Learning Representations (ICLR) (2018)

Vibration-Based Uncertainty Estimation for Learning from Limited Supervision

Hengtong Hu[1], Lingxi Xie[3], Xinyue Huo[3], Richang Hong[1,2(✉)], and Qi Tian[3(✉)]

[1] School of Computer Science and Information Engineering,
Hefei University of Technology, Hefei, China
[2] Institute of Data Space, Hefei Comprehensive National Science Center,
Hefei, China
hongrc@hfut.edu.cn
[3] Huawei Inc., Shenzhen, China
tian.qi1@huawei.com

Abstract. We investigate the problem of estimating uncertainty for training data, so that deep neural networks can make use of the results for learning from limited supervision. However, both prediction probability and entropy estimate uncertainty from the instantaneous information. In this paper, we present a novel approach that measures uncertainty from the vibration of sequential data, *e.g.*, the output probability during the training procedure. The key observation is that, a training sample that suffers heavier vibration often offers richer information when it is manually labeled. Motivated by Bayesian theory, we sample the sequences from the latter part of training. We make use of the Fourier Transformation to measure the extent of vibration, deriving a powerful tool that can be used for semi-supervised, active learning, and one-bit supervision. Experiments on the CIFAR10, CIFAR100, mini-ImageNet and ImageNet datasets validate the effectiveness of our approach.

Keywords: Uncertainty estimation · Semi-supervised learning · Active learning · One-bit supervision

1 Introduction

Recently deep learning [28] has become the main methodology for the computer vision tasks. However, training deep neural network usually needs tremendous labeled data which costs amounts of labors. Researchers have proposed some approaches for learning from limited supervision, including semi-supervised learning [15,27,40] and active learning [10,17,32,38]. All of them aim to utilize the large amounts of unlabeled data to improve the model training. Hence, obtaining an accurate estimation to the predictive uncertainty for unlabeled data is quite important. The existing uncertainty estimated methods, *e.g.*, the predictive probabilities [30] and the entropy [52], usually estimate uncertainty using

S. Avidan et al. (Eds.): ECCV 2022, LNCS 13690, pp. 160–176, 2022.
https://doi.org/10.1007/978-3-031-20056-4_10

the instantaneous information, and achieves unsatisfied performance. We aim to utilize the sequential information from training procedure to obtain a more accurate estimation.

In general, a series of predictive probabilities for unlabeled samples can be obtained by a forward pass after each training epoch, and we use the probabilities of the class predicted by the last epoch model. We consider to estimate uncertainty by measuring the vibration of this sequence. The description to vibration consists of two keys: (i) where the baseline it fluctuates around, and (ii) how large are its fluctuations. This inspires us to utilize the Fourier Transformation (FT) to measure it. The direct component of its results represents the fluctuation baseline, while the high frequency parts reflect the fluctuation degree. By combining the two parts, an accurate estimation of the uncertainty will be obtained. To further improve this measure, we equip it with the label flipping information, in which each element indicates whether the label changed.

To obtain the appropriate sequence from training process, we utilize Bayesian methods [36,37] which offer a natural probabilistic representation of uncertainty in deep learning. By sampling from the latter training epochs we connect the model optimization with the Bayesian procedure, which offers theory foundation for our approach. As shown in Fig. 1, the instantaneous probabilities might provide inaccurate estimation to uncertainty, e.g., the images with high probability and high vibration own wrong predictions. Our approach that considers both the fluctuation baseline and intensity will alleviate this issue.

We develop methods to apply this uncertainty measure to the tasks of learning from limited supervision, e.g., semi-supervised learning, active learning and the recently proposed one-bit supervision [19]. To improve SSL, we use the proposed measure to select reliable pseudo labels, to further improve the semi-supervised baselines. Also a strategy of class weights is utilized to alleviate the class imbalance issue. Different from SSL that directly utilizes unlabeled data to enhance generalization ability, active learning aims to select informative samples from the unlabeled set to annotate. This is also an appropriate application scenario for our approach. We select and annotate the highly uncertain samples to conduct active learning to verify its effectiveness in uncertainty estimation. Finally, we propose a mix annotation approach to improve one-bit supervision. It utilized a weakly annotation method to efficiently utilize the supervision information, while only negative labels can be obtained for the most uncertain samples. Hence, we propose to incorporate full-bit annotation with one-bit annotation, i.e., using the proposed approach to select appropriate samples to conduct this two kinds of annotation respectively.

We evaluate our approach on CIFAR10, CIFAR100, Mini-ImageNet and ImageNet for this three tasks. Extensive experiments demonstrate that, the proposed approach enjoys superiority in selecting no matter reliable pseudo labels and informative samples, and most of all, making accurate uncertainty estimation for unlabeled data.

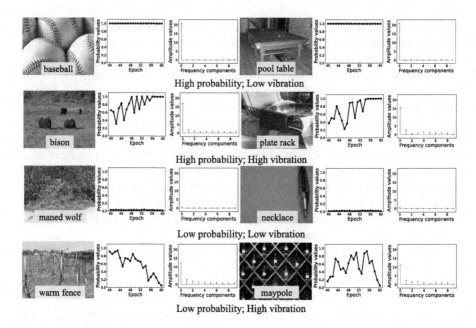

Fig. 1. The four types of selected samples. The first and fourth columns are the images, the second and fifth columns are their corresponding scatter diagram of probabilities sequence, and the third and sixth columns are their magnitude spectra. The textboxes on the images represent their predictive labels, where the red text denotes a correct prediction while the black texts denote incorrect ones. The experiments are conducted on ImageNet trained using ~3% labels (Color figure online)

2   Related Work

2.1   Semi-supervised Learning

Semi-supervised learning [27,34,40] often can be categorised into two types according to their usages of unlabeled data. The first type assigns pseudo labels [6,29] to unlabeled data and optimizes them with labeled data together. Iscen *et al.* [22] used the transductive label propagation method to obtain more accurate pseudo labels. Hu *et al.* [20] proposed a pair loss to minimize the distance between high confidence pseudo labels. The second type utilizes the consistency regularization [17,26] to facilitate model training. The methods of encouraging the consistency are various, *e.g.*, Mean Teacher [48] inputted a sample with different perturbations into two models to make their outputs be similar. WCP [56] imposed additive noise on network weights and making structural changes. In addition, some methods aim to combine two types of approaches, *e.g.*, MixMatch [4] introduced a single loss to seamlessly reduce the entropy while maintaining consistency. ReMixMatch [3] improved it by extra introducing distribution alignment and augmentation anchoring.

2.2   Active Learning

Active learning aims to reduce labeling cost by selecting informative samples to annotate. According to the selection criterion it can be classified into two groups. Firstly, the diversity-based methods [44] select samples that can represent the whole distribution of the unlabeled pool, *e.g.*, Shi *et al.* [45] proposed to identify a small number of samples that best represent the overall data space. Sinha *et al.* [46] utilized the variational autoencoder and adversarial network to choose samples that are not well represented in the labeled set. The second type utilizes uncertainty [2] to select samples that can decrease the model uncertainty, *e.g.*, using the prediction probability [30], the entropy [52], and the target losses [54]. Gao *et al.* [12] used the consistency-based metric for selecting uncertain samples. Huang *et al.* [21] did this by evaluating the discrepancy of outputs of different optimization steps.

2.3   Uncertainty Estimation Approaches

Bayesian neural networks usually are used to estimate uncertainty, while they are inefficient and computationally intractable. Then some approximated Bayesian inference methods [5,31] were proposed to alleviate this. Gal *et al.* [11] proposed to estimate uncertainty by interpreting dropout neural networks as variational Bayes. The similar approaches include SpatialDropout [49] and DropBlock [14]. SDE-Net [24] proposed to quantify uncertainty from a dynamical system perspective. AUM [39] utilized the average difference between the logit values for a sample's assigned class and its highest non-assigned class to identify the mislabeled data.

3   Approach

3.1   Learning from Limited Supervision

For the setting of learning from limited supervision, we often have a dataset $\mathcal{D} = \{\mathbf{x}_n\}_{n=1}^N$, where $\mathbf{x}_n$ is the n-th sample of image data and N is the total number of training samples. Let $y_n^\star$ denote the ground-truth class label of $\mathbf{x}_n$ and C is the number of classes, and they are mostly unseen in the setting. An initial set of samples S^0 is chose randomly to partition the dataset into two subsets $\mathcal{D}^S$ and $\mathcal{D}^U$, where the superscripts respectively represent 'supervised' and 'unsupervised'. Learning from limited supervision aims to utilize unlabeled data to reduce model uncertainty. Therefore, we write the objective as,

$$\mathcal{L}(\boldsymbol{\theta}) = \mathbb{E}_{\mathbf{x} \in \mathcal{D}^S} \ell(\mathbf{y}_n^\star, \ \mathbf{f}(\mathbf{x}; \boldsymbol{\theta})) + \lambda \cdot \mathbb{E}_{\mathbf{x} \in \mathcal{D}^S \cup \mathcal{D}^U} \mathbf{h}(q, \ \mathbf{f}(\mathbf{x}; \boldsymbol{\theta})), \tag{1}$$

where $\mathbf{f}(\mathbf{x}; \boldsymbol{\theta})$ represents the model function and $\boldsymbol{\theta}$ is the learnable parameters. The $\ell(\cdot, \cdot)$ is cross-entropy loss for labeled samples. The $\mathbf{h}(\cdot, \cdot)$ denotes the loss that utilizes unlabeled data by q, which is obtained via the semi-supervised or active learning methods. Since the main idea for this task is the use strategy of unlabeled data, measuring uncertainty to distinguish each of them is very significant. Hence, it is necessary to develop an accurate uncertainty estimation approach for learning from limited supervision.

3.2 Vibration-Based Approach

The conventional measures, *e.g.*, the maximum predictive probabilities, the entropy and the gradients, often used instantaneous information to estimate uncertainty. We do this from another view, *i.e.*, evaluating it using information from training procedure. Supposing an initial model is trained for T epochs in a semi-supervised type, *e.g.*, the Mean Teacher algorithm. If we sample the model weights from the training process, *e.g.*, from M-th epoch to L-th epoch, and conducting forward pass at each epoch, a sequence of outputs $\{\mathbf{y}_n^M, \mathbf{y}_n^{M+1}, \ldots, \mathbf{y}_n^L\}$ can be obtained, where $\mathbf{y}_n^i$ is the C-dimension vector for n-th sample of i-th epoch. To better describe vibration, we form the sequence as $\mathbf{s}_n = \{s_n^i\}_{i=M}^{i=L}$ where s_n^i is the c-th element of $\mathbf{y}_n^i$ and c is the class with maximum probability predicted in L-th epoch. We aim to utilize this sequential information to estimate uncertainty for unlabeled data. To achieve this, we consider to calculate vibration for this sequence. In general, if the sequence has higher vibration intensity around a lower baseline, the prediction will be more uncertain. This inspires us to utilize Fourier Transformation to capture its vibration. It is denoted as

$$\mathbf{S}_k = \mathscr{L}\{\mathbf{s}^n\} = \sum_{i=M}^{L} s_n^i \cdot e^{-j\frac{2\pi}{L-M}ki}. \tag{2}$$

By calculating the real part of $\mathbf{S}_k$, the amplitude sequence $\{A_0, A_1, \ldots, A_{L-M+1}\}$ can be obtained for the corresponding frequency components. Because of the conjugate symmetry of Discrete Fourier Transformation, we use half part of the obtained amplitudes $\{A_0, \cdots, A_{(L-M+1)/2}\}$. A_0 represents the direct component of the frequency, which reveals the baseline where the sequence fluctuates, and $\{A_1, \ldots, A_{(L-M+1)/2}\}$ represents the high frequency part which tells the vibration intensity. Therefore, we define the predictive uncertainty by

$$v_c = \sum_{i=1}^{(L-M+1)/2} A_i - \mu \cdot A_0, \tag{3}$$

where μ is the weight coefficient for balancing high frequency parts and direct component. The summation to the high frequency parts lets the sequence lose its order and makes it have no conflict with the sampling theory. While there may other methods to extract uncertainty, we believe that Eq. (3) is a straightforward and effective method that combines the direct and high frequency parts of the amplitudes. In addition, another kind of information within the outputs, namely label flipping, is also useful for estimating uncertainty. Generally, a prediction is more uncertain when the predicted label flips more frequent in the training process. Hence, we define a sequence with binary values $\{b_M, b_{M+1}, \ldots, b_L\}$ for each unlabeled sample, where $b_i = 1$ denotes $\arg\max \mathbf{y}_n^i$ equals to $\arg\max \mathbf{y}_n^L$ and $b_i = 0$ represents they are different.

For the label flipping sequence, we also conduct Discrete Fourier Transformation to it and calculate its vibration according to Eq. (3), which denoted as v_l. To conveniently combine the two measures, we conduct min-max normalization for them and obtain the results $\hat{v}_c$ and $\hat{v}_l$ respectively. We verify the effectiveness of this fused measure by the experiments on active learning in Sect. 4.2. Finally, the predictive uncertainty is defined by a weight α as:

$$v_f = (1 - \alpha) \cdot \hat{v}_c + \alpha \cdot \hat{v}_l \tag{4}$$

3.3 Theoretical Foundation

Since we estimate uncertainty by using sequential information from training process, the important question to be solved is how to sample the sequence. One can use the whole sequence (from 0-th epoch to the last) or part of it. To solve this, we make use of Bayesian probability theory which provides a mathematical tool to analysis model uncertainty. The predictive distribution for a Bayesian procedure is defined as:

$$p(\mathbf{y}_*|\mathbf{x}_*, \mathcal{D}) = \int p(\mathbf{y}_*|\boldsymbol{\theta}, \mathbf{x}_*)p(\boldsymbol{\theta}|\mathcal{D})d\boldsymbol{\theta}, \tag{5}$$

where $\mathbf{x}_*$ and $\mathbf{y}_*$ are test inputs and outputs. The posterior distribution $p(\boldsymbol{\theta}|\mathcal{D})$ in Eq. (5) is intractable. Next we will show how to develop a Gaussian approximation to the posterior by stochastic gradient descent (SGD) iterations. According to the deduction in [33], when the gradients or the learning rates are small enough and the optimization is confined to a sufficiently small region, the SGD iterations is equivalent to a stochastic process known as the Ornstein-Uhlenbeck (OU) process [51]. The OU process has an analytic stationary distribution $q(\boldsymbol{\theta})$ which follows a Gaussian distribution of:

$$q(\boldsymbol{\theta}) \propto \exp\left\{-\frac{1}{2}\boldsymbol{\theta}^\top \boldsymbol{\Sigma}^{-1}\boldsymbol{\theta}\right\}, \tag{6}$$

where $\boldsymbol{\Sigma}$ is the corresponding covariance matrix. We can approximate $q(\boldsymbol{\theta})$ by Monte Carlo sampling procedure, *e.g.*, drawing $\boldsymbol{\theta}$ from the latter part of the training procedure. To approximate the $p(\boldsymbol{\theta}|\mathcal{D})$, the variational inference [23] is utilized by minimizing the KL divergence between it and the stationary distribution $q(\boldsymbol{\theta})$, which is written as $\arg\min_{\epsilon,S} \mathrm{KL}\left(q(\boldsymbol{\theta})\|p(\boldsymbol{\theta}|\mathcal{D})\right)$. It involves with the learning rate ϵ and mini-batch size S. The learning rate to satisfy this is $\epsilon = 2\frac{S}{N}\frac{D}{\mathrm{Tr}(\mathbf{BB}^T)}$, where D is the dimension of $\boldsymbol{\theta}$ and $\mathbf{BB}^T = \mathbf{C}$ is the gradient noise covariance. For an explicit deduction, please kindly refer to [33]. To achieve the requirement of minimization, the learning rate needs to be a small value, and the norm of gradients needs to be small but larger than zero. These conditions are satisfied when we sample $\boldsymbol{\theta}$ from the late training epochs (close to converging). Hence, the approximated predictive distribution is given by:

$$q(\mathbf{y}_*|\mathbf{x}_*,\mathcal{D}) = \int p(\mathbf{y}_*|\boldsymbol{\theta},\mathbf{x}_*)q(\boldsymbol{\theta})d\boldsymbol{\theta}. \tag{7}$$

Since the optimization in the late training epochs can agree with Bayesian procedure, we estimate uncertainty by using the sampled sequence information. This can be viewed as sampling from the distribution $q(\mathbf{y}_*|\mathbf{x}_*,\mathcal{D})$.

Relationship to Previous Works. Similarly, Temporal Ensembling [27] utilized sequential outputs to obtain weights or predictions. AUM [39] proposed to exploits differences in the training dynamics of clean and mislabeled samples. Though they both aim to make use of the outputs in training epochs, our approach is different from them in many aspects. TE only conducted self-ensembling to obtain more accurate predictions, while our approach estimates uncertainty for unlabeled samples. AUM used the front part outputs in training to calculate area under the margin values, which is inapplicable to unlabeled samples for the margins are very close at those epochs. Also, AUM neglects the semantic changes in training epochs while our approach considers this by calculating v_l. In addition, the idea of forgetting events [50] is similar to the used label flipping sequence. Lastly, SG-MCMC [7,9] is also a Bayesian method that used for uncertainty estimation. However, Our approach is different from them in theory, *i.e.*, our approach utilizes a stationary distribution to approximate the posterior, while SG-MCMC samples from an asymptotically exact posterior.

3.4 Application to Different Scenarios of Learning from Limited Supervision

In this section, we apply the proposed approach to the tasks of learning from limited supervision, including semi-supervised learning, active learning, and one-bit supervision. The difference among them is their usage to unlabeled data. SSL utilizes unlabeled data to enhance generalization ability. In particular, the consistency-based type defines the $h(\cdot,\cdot)$ in Eq. (1) as a mean square error loss and sets q as the outputs for the perturbative samples. The pseudo-labeling based type sets q as the pseudo labels and uses a cross-entropy loss to optimize them. Compared to SSL, AL selects informative samples from unlabeled data to annotate. Its objective equals to set $h(\cdot,\cdot)$ as the cross entropy and let q be the ground-truth of the selected samples. Different from AL that annotates true labels for samples, one-bit supervision annotates by asking the labeler if it belongs to a guessed class. All of the three tasks start by training the initial model using $\mathcal{D}^S$ and $\mathcal{D}^U$.

Semi-Supervised Learning. For SSL, we utilize the proposed uncertainty measurement to mine reliable pseudo labels to improve semi-supervised baselines. In particular, after training the initial model $\mathbb{M}_0$, we calculate uncertainty for unlabeled samples by Eq. (4) via the outputted probabilities and label flipping information. Then we select K samples with the smallest vibration values from $\mathcal{D}^U$, and use $\mathbb{M}_0$ to generate pseudo labels for them. Then adding them to $\mathcal{D}^S$ and fine-tuning the model to obtain the first stage model $\mathbb{M}_1$. We adopt appropriate strategies to utilize the mined pseudo labels for the used baseline. For Mean Teacher [48], we inject the pseudo labels according to each unlabeled batch. For FixMatch [47], we replace the pseudo labels generated by the weak-augmented images with ours.

In the next iteration, we moderately increase the number of selected samples to obtain more reliable pseudo labels. The cycle of selecting pseudo labels and fine-tuning continues until the training converges. One issue for pseudo-label selection is about class imbalance, *i.e.*, the correct predictions may focus on partial classes. Especially when the model is not strong enough, this issue will be more obvious. To alleviate this, we assign weight for each class by $w_i = \frac{A}{n_i}$, where A is the average number of samples in each class in labeled set (including pseudo labels), and $\mathbf{n}_i$ denotes the actual number of samples in i-th class. Here we normalize the weights by $\hat{w} = w / \max(w)$.

Active Learning. We apply the proposed approach to AL by selecting the informative samples. The training process of AL often consists of several iterations, and in each of them a batch of samples is selected for annotating. To obtain more accurate estimation, we train the model in each stage in semi-supervised type. In our algorithm, for the t-th cycle, we estimate uncertainty for unlabeled data by Eq. (3) and Eq. (4) according to the model $\mathbb{M}_{t-1}$. Then selecting J samples with the largest uncertainty and checking their ground-truth to imitate the process of annotating. Then adding them to $\mathcal{D}^S_{t-1}$, and removing from $\mathcal{D}^U_{t-1}$. Finally we update to obtain new model $\mathbb{M}_t$ using both $\mathcal{D}^S_t$ and $\mathcal{D}^U_t$. This iteration continues until the satisfied performance is achieved.

One-Bit Supervision. We apply our approach to one-bit supervision via conducting mix annotation, which efficiently acquires supervision by combining full-bit and one-bit annotation. Since the multi-stage training framework in one-bit supervision is similar to the process of AL, we omit the introduction to the iterations. For t-th stage, after calculating uncertainty for unlabeled samples by Eq. (4), we select I samples with the largest vibrations to conduct full-bit annotation, then adding them to $\mathcal{D}^F$, the subset of full-bit annotated samples. Next, we select a subset $\mathcal{D}^O_t$ from $\mathcal{D}^U_t$ and use the model $\mathbb{M}_{t-1}$ to make predictions for them to conduct one-bit annotation. Generally, selecting samples with predictive probabilities around 0.5 will obtain the highest gains for one-bit annotation. Hence, the middle-uncertain samples are selected according to the model precision. By checking their ground-truth, we add correctly guesses to the positively labeled set $\mathcal{D}^{O+}$, and add incorrectly guesses to the negatively labeled set $\mathcal{D}^{O-}$. Finally, we retrain the model by combining the labeled set $\mathcal{D}^S \cup \mathcal{D}^F \cup \mathcal{D}^{O+}$, the negatively labeled set $\mathcal{D}^{O-}$ and the unlabeled set $\mathcal{D}^U_t$.

4   Experiments

4.1   Datasets and Implementation Details

Dataset. For both SSL and AL, we do experiments on three classification benchmarks CIFAR10, CIFAR100 [25] and Mini-ImageNet. CIFAR10 and CIFAR100 are standard datasets with 10 and 100 classes respectively. They contain 60K images in which 50K for training and 10K for testing. All of them are 32×32 RGB images and uniformly distributed over all classes. For Mini-ImageNet, we use the training/testing split created in [41], which contains 100 classes, 50K training images and 10K testing images. For one-bit supervision, the experiments are conducted on CIFAR100 and Mini-ImageNet. In addition, the experiments on ImageNet [43] are also conducted for SSL. This dataset contains 1.2M images from 1000 classes.

Implementation Details. For SSL, we use Wide ResNet-28-2 [55], a commonly used backbone for CIFAR10 and CIFAR100, and ResNet-18 [18] for Mini-ImageNet. For AL, WRN-28-2 is used for all three datasets. For one-bit supervision, we follow the experimental setting in [19] to use ResNet-50 for Mini-ImageNet, and ResNet-26 [18] with Shake-Shake regularization [13] for CIFAR100. The SSL experiments are based on two famous baselines, Mean Teacher [48] and FixMatch [47]. The experiments for AL are conducted using Mean Teacher. We refer to their original paper to set our parameters. We use the SGD optimizer with momentum. For the hyper-parameters in our approach, we set the balance coefficient μ to 0.1 for all experiments. The fused weight α is set to 0.6 for CIFAR10 and Mini-ImageNet, and 0.2 for CIFAR100. For the value of K in SSL, we choose it according the model precision. We follow the general rules to set the parameter I in AL. Specifically, on CIFAR10, we randomly select 100 samples as the initial labeled set, and add 500 samples in each of the following stage, except for the last two which 1000 samples are added; on CIFAR100, we randomly select 5000 samples as the initial labeled set and add 1000 samples in the next stage; on Mini-ImageNet, we randomly select 20% samples as the initial set and add 5% in the following stage. For one-bit supervision, we split the quota of supervision used in each stage into two parts, 1000 full-bit annotations (about 6644 bits of supervision) and the remaining one-bit annotations.

4.2 Main Results

Semi-Supervised Learning. The results for combining with two semi-supervised baselines are shown in Table 1. We run 5 iterations for three datasets for their performance approaches to converge. We can observe that our approach both achieves higher performance when applied to Mean Teacher [48] and Fix-Match [47]. Also, more accuracy gains are obtained when combined with the MT algorithm, *e.g.*, it achieves 7.00% gains for CIFAR100 with 4000 labels. Except for the used weak baseline, we also own this to that our approach is more applicable to consistency-based approaches. Meanwhile, our approach still achieves 0.82% gains when combined with FixMatch. Specifically, to our knowledge, we report the best results on Mini-ImageNet both with 4000 and 10000 labels when using ResNet-18. We also list some popular semi-supervised methods in Table 1, and among them UPS [42] is most similar with our approach. It also used an uncertainty estimation method (MC Dropout [11]) to mine pseudo labels. The results show that our approach outperforms UPS both with the two baselines, which verifies the superiority of the proposed uncertainty measure.

Table 1. Test error (%) of semi-supervised methods on CIFAR10, CIFAR100 and Mini-ImageNet. The methods with * represent that using the CNN-13 architecture. "RA" represents the Randaugment [8] approach. For our method and two baselines Mean Teacher and FixMatch, we report the mean and standard deviation over 3 runs

Total labels	CIFAR10			CIFAR100			Mini-ImageNet	
	250	1000	4000	2500	4000	10000	4000	10000
PL [29]	49.78 ± 0.43	30.91 ± 1.73	16.09 ± 0.28	–	–	36.21 ± 0.19	–	–
DeepLP [22]	–	22.02 ± 0.88*	12.69 ± 0.29*	–	46.20 ± 0.76*	38.43 ± 1.88*	70.29 ± 0.81	57.58 ± 1.47
Π model [27]	–	–	14.01 ± 0.38	–	–	37.88 ± 0.11	–	–
VAT [34]	–	18.64 ± 0.40	11.05 ± 0.31	–	–	–	–	–
PLCB [1]	24.81 ± 5.35	–	6.28 ± 0.30	–	37.55 ± 1.09*	32.15 ± 0.50*	56.49 ± 0.51	46.08 ± 0.11
MixMatch [4]	11.29 ± 0.75	–	6.24 ± 0.07	39.70 ± 0.27	–	28.59 ± 0.31	49.79 ± 0.11	44.27 ± 0.23
UPS [42] (RA)	–	8.18 ± 0.15*	6.39 ± 0.02*	–	40.77 ± 0.10*	32.00 ± 0.49*	–	–
SemCo [35]	5.87 ± 0.31	–	4.43 ± 0.01	33.80 ± 0.57	29.40 ± 0.18	25.07 ± 0.04	46.01 ± 0.93	41.25 ± 0.76
MT [48]	52.30 ± 0.95	21.54 ± 0.12	11.48 ± 0.21	–	52.36 ± 0.39	38.00 ± 0.17	70.58 ± 0.37	56.91 ± 0.16
Ours+MT	48.05 ± 1.17	16.94 ± 0.18	9.33 ± 0.08	–	46.56 ± 0.43	34.55 ± 0.21	69.46 ± 0.13	54.91 ± 0.08
MT (RA)	16.50 ± 0.18	11.72 ± 0.10	9.48 ± 0.29	49.83 ± 0.10	43.86 ± 0.56	35.60 ± 0.36	61.97 ± 0.32	52.98 ± 0.27
Ours+MT (RA)	10.37 ± 0.53	7.63 ± 0.64	5.87 ± 0.05	42.12 ± 0.22	36.86 ± 0.46	29.84 ± 0.23	57.02 ± 0.26	49.73 ± 0.29
FixMatch [47] (RA)	6.16 ± 0.79	5.21 ± 0.08	4.73 ± 0.03	34.28 ± 0.23	31.22 ± 0.16	26.87 ± 0.05	40.02 ± 0.35	38.47 ± 0.39
Ours+FM (RA)	**6.06 ± 0.76**	**4.84 ± 0.04**	**4.63 ± 0.12**	**33.53 ± 0.21**	**30.40 ± 0.20**	**26.18 ± 0.12**	**39.21 ± 0.58**	**37.72 ± 0.20**

To reveal the quality of uncertainty estimated by our approach, we analyze the relationship between it and the Expected Calibration Error (ECE) score [16]. Experiments are conducted on CIFAR10 with 1000 and 4000 labels and CIFAR100 with 4000 and 10000 labels, and trained using MT. The results are presented in Fig. 2, which show that the ECE scores are positively associated with the uncertainty values. It means reliable pseudo labels can be obtained by selecting samples with low uncertainty defined in our approach. Experiments on CIFAR100 with 5000 labels are also conducted to verify this.

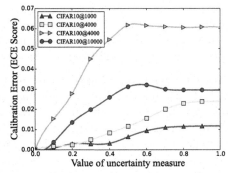

Fig. 2. The relationship between the expected calibration error (ECE) and the value of our uncertainty measure (v_f) on unlabeled samples.

Our approach achieves (95.7%/88.73%) accuracy with top-5,000/10,000 selected samples, while the numbers for Consistency, Confidence, and Entropy are (88.94%/82.26%), (92.6%/84.7%), and (92.56%/84.86%), respectively.

Also, with the training iteration increases, uncertainty for unlabeled samples becomes lower. For example, in SSL on CIFAR100 with 10000 labels, the average uncertainty decreases throughout training: the values after 1st, 5th, 10th iterations are 0.3516, 0.2570, and 0.2434, respectively. In addition, we also do ablations for pseudo labels selection and class weights. The experiments are conducted on Mini-ImageNet with 4000 and 10000 labels by using MT. Only mining pseudo labels achieves 42.12% and 49.32% accuracy respectively, and further using the generated class weights brings 0.86% and 0.85% gains. Finally, we test the computation cost on a RTX 2080Ti GPU, in SSL in CIFAR10/100, each

Table 2. Test error (%) of our approach on CIFAR10, CIFAR100, and Mini-ImageNet for active learning. They are all based on the Mean Teacher algorithm. The comparison methods include K-center [44], MC dropout [11], AUM [39] and Consistency [12]. The Initial labels for these three datasets respectively are 100, 5000 and 10000

Methods		Random	Confidence	K-center	MC Dropout	AUM	Consistency	Vibration	Vibration_fused
CIFAR10	iter 1	37.98	42.39	35.53	33.27	40.75	40.95	35.37	27.33
	iter 2	24.26	23.24	23.20	25.74	25.00	28.38	26.75	20.43
	iter 3	20.85	18.25	16.87	21.46	18.93	18.58	18.79	15.14
	iter 4	15.69	12.80	12.40	13.42	12.28	12.49	11.58	10.53
	iter 5	12.39	10.55	10.70	11.46	10.06	10.05	10.04	9.47
CIFAR100	iter 1	45.49	45.37	45.35	45.31	45.77	46.18	45.64	43.99
	iter 2	43.40	43.15	42.53	42.10	42.37	43.24	41.97	41.22
	iter 3	42.25	41.08	40.03	39.46	39.22	40.30	38.78	38.42
	iter 4	39.67	38.72	38.67	38.01	38.56	38.36	37.61	37.11
	iter 5	38.19	37.37	37.20	37.06	37.33	37.9	37.01	36.51
Mini-ImageNet	iter 1	45.23	46.07	45.13	44.33	45.58	45.00	44.68	43.14
	iter 2	42.24	42.89	42.29	42.43	41.47	42.22	42.41	40.30
	iter 3	40.34	40.95	40.77	40.30	40.07	40.45	38.98	38.62
	iter 4	38.90	39.50	38.82	37.57	38.63	37.43	37.87	36.77
	iter 5	37.51	37.11	37.98	36.55	36.85	36.63	36.96	35.95

training epoch takes 76.72 s, in which, after forward/backward prop, using the newest model to update sequential information takes 10.73 s, then uncertainty estimation plus pseudo label selection takes 5.44 s.

Active Learning. The experiments for AL are conducted on CIFAR10, CIFAR100 and Mini-ImageNet. From the results on Table 2 we can obtain some observations. Firstly, the fused vibration measure achieves higher performance than the single measure on all four iterations for three datasets. This verifies the effectiveness of the approach which utilizes both the outputted probabilities and label flipping sequences. Secondly, compared to the basic AL methods, e.g., Random, Confidence and K-center [44], our approach obviously outperform them in all iterations. For example, on CIFAR10, it achieves 8.20% accuracy gains compared to K-center in the first iteration. Though these three methods are simple, we argue that they still provide strong baselines when combined with semi-supervised algorithms.

Thirdly, compared to other uncertainty estimation methods, such as MC Dropout [11] and AUM [39], our approach still achieves higher performance in four iterations on three datasets. In particular, the gains are 5.94% and 13.42% respectively in the first iteration on CIFAR10. This demonstrates the superiority of our approach for uncertainty estimation. Here AUM was originally designed to identify the mislabeled data, we adapt it to active learning by calculating the average difference between the prediction probabilities for a sample's pseudo-labeled class and its highest non-pseudo-labeled class. Lastly, on all datasets, the proposed approach outperforms Consistency [12] for all iterations. Notably, it is also designed for SSL algorithm, which is appropriate to verify our approach as a comparison. In addition, another observation on these three datasets is, our approach obtains the highest gains on the first stage, which shows that it enjoys more advantages when the supervision is scarce.

One-Bit Supervision. The experiments for one-bit supervision are conducted on CIFAR100 and Mini-ImageNet. The proposed mix annotation approach achieves **23.93%** and **50.29%** test error respectively on these two datasets. Compared to the baseline Mean Teacher, our approach brings 6.31% and 8.65% accuracy gains respectively. The gains still have 2.31% and 4.17% when compared to the original one-bit supervision. In addition, MixMatch [4] and UDA [53] achieves 25.88% and 24.50% test error on CIFAR100 using Wide ResNet-28-8 backbone, which is inferior to our approach. These results demonstrate the effectiveness of the proposed mix annotation approach, for which efficiently utilize the annotation information to maximize the labeling gains. And we own this to that our approach accurately estimates uncertainty for all unlabeled samples.

We also apply the proposed approach to noise learning and conduct experiments on CIFAR10 by assigning random labels to a random subset of training data. Our approach is based on MT and trains using predicted noisy data as unlabeled data. It achieves 10.06%, 12.77% test error for 0.2, 0.4 noise level respectively, which are obviously better than the standard training (using all data) achieves, *i.e.*, 13.82%, 18.19% test error.

4.3   Diagnostic Experiments

Transferring to Large-Scale Dataset. To verify the effectiveness of our approach on large scale datasets, we do experiments on ImageNet [43] for semi-supervised learning. The results are still based on the two baselines, Mean Teacher [48] and FixMatch [47]. For MT, we use ResNet-50 as the backbone. Our approach achieves 47.30% and 59.88% test error respectively for using 5% and 10% labels, and brings 4.89% and 2.87% gains when compared to the baseline. For FixMatch, we use VGG-16 as the backbone and train using 10% labeled samples. The error rate of our approach is 30.84%, which outperforms the baseline by 3.38% gains. These results reveal the potential of the proposed approach in applying to large scale datasets.

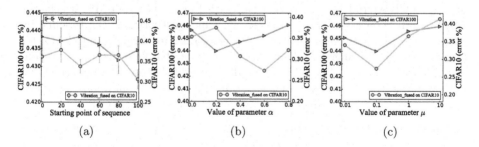

(a)   (b)   (c)

Fig. 3. Analysis to the starting epoch of the sampled sequence, balance coefficient μ and fused weight α. Experiments are conducted on CIFAR10 and CIFAR100 for the first iteration of active learning, using WRN-28-2 backbone. Results about starting epoch are ran for 10 times.

Position of Starting Epoch. We conduct experiments for the first active learning iteration on CIFAR10 and CIFAR100, to investigate the effect of different starting epoch of the sequence. The results are shown on the subfigure (a) of Fig. 3. We can obtain some observations from them. Firstly, most of the results are higher than the "Random" approach on two datasets, which shows the superiority of estimating uncertainty from sequential data. Secondly, the best results are obtained when setting the starting point to the latter epoch, *e.g.*, 80 and 100 for CIFAR10 and CIFAR100 respectively. This is in accord with the sampling theory for approximating the posterior, which is introduced in Sect. 3.3.

Lastly, we observe that sampling from early epochs does not show dramatic accuracy drop, *i.e.*, violating the constraints necessary for the theoretical guarantee still yield good results. We argue that this is quite often in practice, *e.g.*, for SVMs. Also, sampling from the latter epochs is advantage in computation cost. We also analyze the curve changing of learning rate and norm of gradients in training process. The results are shown in Fig. 4. According to the deduction in Sect. 3.3, to better approximate the posterior, the learning rate needs to be small while the norm of gradients needs to be larger than zero. Hence, the sequence needs to be sampled from about epoch 80 to 140 for this training stage.

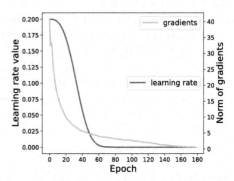

Fig. 4. Value of learning rate and the Frobenius norm of gradients in the training procedure on CIFAR100 with 5000 labels. The gradients are obtained from the last fully-connected layer

Transferring to Other Network Architecture. We also verify the proposed approach by using WRN-28-8 as the backbone for semi-supervised learning. The experiments are based on Mean Teacher [48] and FixMatch [47] and are conducted on CIFAR100 and Mini-ImageNet with 10000 labels. For MT, it achieves 24.99% and 34.06% test error respectively, which outperforms the baseline by 2.93% and 3.83% gains. For FixMatch, the error rates are 22.58% and 21.11% for two datasets, and brings 0.75% and 0.94% than the baseline. As a comparison, MixMatch [4] and UDA [53] achieves 28.31% and 24.50% test error on CIFAR100 in the same setting respectively. These results are inferior to our approach, which demonstrates the effectiveness of our approach by a stronger backbone.

Robustness to Hyperparameters. Our approach introduces two new hyperparameters, namely the balance coefficient μ and the fused coefficient α. Here we investigate the effect of different choice for them. The parameter μ plays the role of balancing the high frequency part and the direct component. As shown in the subfigure (c) in Fig. 3, we can observe that $\mu = 0.1$ achieves the best results on both two datasets. When μ becomes too large, the performance degrades obviously. It shows the significance of making a balance between the vibration baseline and its intensity. We set $\mu = 0.1$ in all our experiments for the robustness of our approach to it. The parameter α is used to balance the two components in the fused measure. As shown in the subfigure (b) in Fig. 3, setting α to 0.6 and 0.2 achieves the best accuracy respectively on CIFAR10 and CIFAR100. Also, the performance for different α varies relatively smoothly on two datasets. In general, the proposed uncertainty estimation approach enjoys flexibility in hyperparameter adjustment for its robustness and limited numbers.

5   Conclusions

In this paper, we propose a novel approach for uncertainty estimation, and use it to improve learning from limited supervision. The conventional methods including the probabilities and the entropy often estimate uncertainty from instantaneous information. Different from them, we do this by using the sequential data from training process, e.g., the probabilities. In particular, we measure the vibration of the obtained sequence via Fourier Transformation. By equipping with label flipping, a more accurate estimation will be obtained. Inspired by the Bayesian theory which provides a probabilistic representation of uncertainty, the sequence is sampled from latter optimization iterations. The effectiveness of the proposed approach for semi-supervised learning, active learning and one-bit supervision is verified by the extensive experiments on CIFAR10, CIFAR100, Mini-ImageNet and ImageNet.

Acknowledgements. This work was supported by the National Key Research and Development Program of China under grant 2019YFA0706200, 2018AAA0102002, and in part by the National Natural Science Foundation of China under grant 61732007, 61932009.

References

1. Arazo, E., Ortego, D., Albert, P., O'Connor, N.E., McGuinness, K.: Pseudo-labeling and confirmation bias in deep semi-supervised learning. In: 2020 International Joint Conference on Neural Networks (IJCNN), pp. 1–8. IEEE (2020)
2. Ash, J.T., Zhang, C., Krishnamurthy, A., Langford, J., Agarwal, A.: Deep batch active learning by diverse, uncertain gradient lower bounds. arXiv preprint arXiv:1906.03671 (2019)
3. Berthelot, D., et al.: ReMixMatch: semi-supervised learning with distribution alignment and augmentation anchoring. arXiv preprint arXiv:1911.09785 (2019)
4. Berthelot, D., Carlini, N., Goodfellow, I., Papernot, N., Oliver, A., Raffel, C.: MixMatch: a holistic approach to semi-supervised learning. arXiv preprint arXiv:1905.02249 (2019)
5. Blundell, C., Cornebise, J., Kavukcuoglu, K., Wierstra, D.: Weight uncertainty in neural network. In: International Conference on Machine Learning, pp. 1613–1622. PMLR (2015)
6. Cascante-Bonilla, P., Tan, F., Qi, Y., Ordonez, V.: Curriculum labeling: revisiting pseudo-labeling for semi-supervised learning. arXiv preprint arXiv:2001.06001 (2020)

7. Chen, T., Fox, E., Guestrin, C.: Stochastic gradient Hamiltonian Monte Carlo. In: International Conference on Machine Learning, pp. 1683–1691. PMLR (2014)
8. Cubuk, E.D., Zoph, B., Shlens, J., Le, Q.V.: Randaugment: practical automated data augmentation with a reduced search space. In: Proceedings of the IEEE/CVF Conference on Computer Vision and Pattern Recognition Workshops, pp. 702–703 (2020)
9. Ding, N., Fang, Y., Babbush, R., Chen, C., Skeel, R.D., Neven, H.: Bayesian sampling using stochastic gradient thermostats. Adv. Neural Inf. Process. Syst. **27** (2014)
10. Freytag, A., Rodner, E., Denzler, J.: Selecting influential examples: active learning with expected model output changes. In: Fleet, D., Pajdla, T., Schiele, B., Tuytelaars, T. (eds.) ECCV 2014. LNCS, vol. 8692, pp. 562–577. Springer, Cham (2014). https://doi.org/10.1007/978-3-319-10593-2_37
11. Gal, Y., Ghahramani, Z.: Dropout as a Bayesian approximation: representing model uncertainty in deep learning. In: International Conference on Machine Learning, pp. 1050–1059. PMLR (2016)
12. Gao, M., Zhang, Z., Yu, G., Arık, S.Ö., Davis, L.S., Pfister, T.: Consistency-based semi-supervised active learning: towards minimizing labeling cost. In: Vedaldi, A., Bischof, H., Brox, T., Frahm, J.-M. (eds.) ECCV 2020. LNCS, vol. 12355, pp. 510–526. Springer, Cham (2020). https://doi.org/10.1007/978-3-030-58607-2_30
13. Gastaldi, X.: Shake-shake regularization. arXiv preprint arXiv:1705.07485 (2017)
14. Ghiasi, G., Lin, T.Y., Le, Q.V.: DropBlock: a regularization method for convolutional networks. arXiv preprint arXiv:1810.12890 (2018)
15. Grandvalet, Y., Bengio, Y., et al.: Semi-supervised learning by entropy minimization. CAP **367**, 281–296 (2005)
16. Guo, C., Pleiss, G., Sun, Y., Weinberger, K.Q.: On calibration of modern neural networks. In: International Conference on Machine Learning, pp. 1321–1330. PMLR (2017)
17. Han, T., Tu, W.W., Li, Y.F.: Explanation consistency training: facilitating consistency-based semi-supervised learning with interpretability. In: Proceedings of the AAAI Conference on Artificial Intelligence, vol. 35, pp. 7639–7646 (2021)
18. He, K., Zhang, X., Ren, S., Sun, J.: Deep residual learning for image recognition. In: Proceedings of the IEEE Conference on Computer Vision and Pattern Recognition, pp. 770–778 (2016)
19. Hu, H., Xie, L., Du, Z., Hong, R., Tian, Q.: One-bit supervision for image classification. Adv. Neural Inf. Process. Syst. **33** (2020)
20. Hu, Z., Yang, Z., Hu, X., Nevatia, R.: SimPLE: similar pseudo label exploitation for semi-supervised classification. In: Proceedings of the IEEE/CVF Conference on Computer Vision and Pattern Recognition, pp. 15099–15108 (2021)
21. Huang, S., Wang, T., Xiong, H., Huan, J., Dou, D.: Semi-supervised active learning with temporal output discrepancy. arXiv preprint arXiv:2107.14153 (2021)
22. Iscen, A., Tolias, G., Avrithis, Y., Chum, O.: Label propagation for deep semi-supervised learning. In: Proceedings of the IEEE/CVF Conference on Computer Vision and Pattern Recognition, pp. 5070–5079 (2019)
23. Kingma, D.P., Welling, M.: Auto-encoding variational bayes. arXiv preprint arXiv:1312.6114 (2013)
24. Kong, L., Sun, J., Zhang, C.: SDE-Net: equipping deep neural networks with uncertainty estimates. arXiv preprint arXiv:2008.10546 (2020)
25. Krizhevsky, A., Hinton, G., et al.: Learning multiple layers of features from tiny images (2009)

26. Kuo, C.-W., Ma, C.-Y., Huang, J.-B., Kira, Z.: FeatMatch: feature-based augmentation for semi-supervised learning. In: Vedaldi, A., Bischof, H., Brox, T., Frahm, J.-M. (eds.) ECCV 2020. LNCS, vol. 12363, pp. 479–495. Springer, Cham (2020). https://doi.org/10.1007/978-3-030-58523-5_28
27. Laine, S., Aila, T.: Temporal ensembling for semi-supervised learning. arXiv preprint arXiv:1610.02242 (2016)
28. LeCun, Y., Bengio, Y., Hinton, G.: Deep learning. Nature 521(7553), 436–444 (2015)
29. Lee, D.H., et al.: Pseudo-Label: the simple and efficient semi-supervised learning method for deep neural networks. In: Workshop on challenges in representation learning, ICML, vol. 3, p. 896 (2013)
30. Lewis, D.D., Gale, W.A.: A sequential algorithm for training text classifiers. In: Croft, B.W., van Rijsbergen, C.J. (eds) SIGIR 1994. Springer, London (1994). https://doi.org/10.1007/978-1-4471-2099-5_1
31. Louizos, C., Welling, M.: Multiplicative normalizing flows for variational Bayesian neural networks. In: International Conference on Machine Learning, pp. 2218–2227. PMLR (2017)
32. Luo, W., Schwing, A., Urtasun, R.: Latent structured active learning. Adv. Neural. Inf. Process. Syst. 26, 728–736 (2013)
33. Mandt, S., Hoffman, M.D., Blei, D.M.: Stochastic gradient descent as approximate Bayesian inference. arXiv preprint arXiv:1704.04289 (2017)
34. Miyato, T., Maeda, S.I., Koyama, M., Ishii, S.: Virtual adversarial training: a regularization method for supervised and semi-supervised learning. IEEE Trans. Pattern Anal. Mach. Intell. 41(8), 1979–1993 (2018)
35. Nassar, I., Herath, S., Abbasnejad, E., Buntine, W., Haffari, G.: All labels are not created equal: enhancing semi-supervision via label grouping and co-training. In: Proceedings of the IEEE/CVF Conference on Computer Vision and Pattern Recognition, pp. 7241–7250 (2021)
36. Neal, R.M.: Bayesian learning for neural networks, vol. 118, p. 204. Springer, NY (2012). https://doi.org/10.1007/978-1-4612-0745-0
37. Paisley, J., Blei, D., Jordan, M.: Variational Bayesian inference with stochastic search. arXiv preprint arXiv:1206.6430 (2012)
38. Pinsler, R., Gordon, J., Nalisnick, E., Hernández-Lobato, J.M.: Bayesian batch active learning as sparse subset approximation. Adv. Neural. Inf. Process. Syst. 32, 6359–6370 (2019)
39. Pleiss, G., Zhang, T., Elenberg, E.R., Weinberger, K.Q.: Identifying mislabeled data using the area under the margin ranking. arXiv preprint arXiv:2001.10528 (2020)
40. Rasmus, A., Valpola, H., Honkala, M., Berglund, M., Raiko, T.: Semi-supervised learning with ladder networks. arXiv preprint arXiv:1507.02672 (2015)
41. Ravi, S., Larochelle, H.: Optimization as a model for few-shot learning (2016)
42. Rizve, M.N., Duarte, K., Rawat, Y.S., Shah, M.: In defense of pseudo-labeling: an uncertainty-aware pseudo-label selection framework for semi-supervised learning. In: International Conference on Learning Representations (2020)
43. Russakovsky, O., et al.: ImageNet large scale visual recognition challenge. Int. J. Comput. Vis. 115(3), 211–252 (2015). https://doi.org/10.1007/s11263-015-0816-y
44. Sener, O., Savarese, S.: Active learning for convolutional neural networks: a core-set approach. arXiv preprint arXiv:1708.00489 (2017)
45. Shi, W., Yu, Q.: Integrating Bayesian and discriminative sparse kernel machines for multi-class active learning. Adv. Neural Inf. Process. Syst. (2019)

46. Sinha, S., Ebrahimi, S., Darrell, T.: Variational adversarial active learning. In: Proceedings of the IEEE/CVF International Conference on Computer Vision, pp. 5972–5981 (2019)

47. Sohn, K., et al.: FixMatch: simplifying semi-supervised learning with consistency and confidence. arXiv preprint arXiv:2001.07685 (2020)

48. Tarvainen, A., Valpola, H.: Mean teachers are better role models: weight-averaged consistency targets improve semi-supervised deep learning results. arXiv preprint arXiv:1703.01780 (2017)

49. Tompson, J., Goroshin, R., Jain, A., LeCun, Y., Bregler, C.: Efficient object localization using convolutional networks. In: Proceedings of the IEEE Conference on Computer Vision and Pattern Recognition, pp. 648–656 (2015)

50. Toneva, M., Sordoni, A., Combes, R.T.D., Trischler, A., Bengio, Y., Gordon, G.J.: An empirical study of example forgetting during deep neural network learning. arXiv preprint arXiv:1812.05159 (2018)

51. Uhlenbeck, G.E., Ornstein, L.S.: On the theory of the Brownian motion. Phys. Rev. **36**(5), 823 (1930)

52. Wang, K., Zhang, D., Li, Y., Zhang, R., Lin, L.: Cost-effective active learning for deep image classification. IEEE Trans. Circuits Syst. Video Technol. **27**(12), 2591–2600 (2016)

53. Xie, Q., Dai, Z., Hovy, E., Luong, M.T., Le, Q.V.: Unsupervised data augmentation for consistency training. arXiv preprint arXiv:1904.12848 (2019)

54. Yoo, D., Kweon, I.S.: Learning loss for active learning. In: Proceedings of the IEEE/CVF Conference on Computer Vision and Pattern Recognition, pp. 93–102 (2019)

55. Zagoruyko, S., Komodakis, N.: Wide residual networks. arXiv preprint arXiv:1605.07146 (2016)

56. Zhang, L., Qi, G.J.: WCP: worst-case perturbations for semi-supervised deep learning. In: Proceedings of the IEEE/CVF Conference on Computer Vision and Pattern Recognition, pp. 3912–3921 (2020)

Concurrent Subsidiary Supervision for Unsupervised Source-Free Domain Adaptation

Jogendra Nath Kundu[1]([✉])[iD], Suvaansh Bhambri[1][iD], Akshay Kulkarni[1][iD],
Hiran Sarkar[1][iD], Varun Jampani[2][iD], and R. Venkatesh Babu[1][iD]

[1] Indian Institute of Science, Bengaluru, India
jogendrak@iisc.ac.in
[2] Google Research, Cambridge, USA

Abstract. The prime challenge in unsupervised domain adaptation (DA) is to mitigate the domain shift between the source and target domains. Prior DA works show that pretext tasks could be used to mitigate this domain shift by learning domain invariant representations. However, in practice, we find that most existing pretext tasks are ineffective against other established techniques. Thus, we theoretically analyze how and when a subsidiary pretext task could be leveraged to assist the goal task of a given DA problem and develop objective subsidiary task suitability criteria. Based on this criteria, we devise a novel process of sticker intervention and cast sticker classification as a supervised subsidiary DA problem concurrent to the goal task unsupervised DA. Our approach not only improves goal task adaptation performance, but also facilitates privacy-oriented source-free DA i.e. without concurrent source-target access. Experiments on the standard Office-31, Office-Home, DomainNet, and VisDA benchmarks demonstrate our superiority for both single-source and multi-source source-free DA. Our approach also complements existing non-source-free works, achieving leading performance.

1 Introduction

The prevalent trend in supervised deep learning systems is to assume that training and testing data follow the same distribution. However, such models often fail [6] when deployed in a new environment (target domain) due to the discrepancy in the training (source domain) and target distributions. A standard approach to deal with this problem of *domain shift* is Unsupervised Domain Adaptation (DA) [10,30], which aims to minimize the domain discrepancy [3] between source

---

J. N. Kundu, S. Bhambri and A. Kulkarni—Equal contribution | Webpage: https://sites.google.com/view/sticker-sfda.

Supplementary Information The online version contains supplementary material available at https://doi.org/10.1007/978-3-031-20056-4_11.

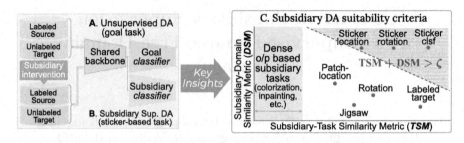

Fig. 1. We tackle **A.** unsupervised goal task DA by introducing **B.** a concurrent subsidiary supervised DA. **C.** Our theoretical insights reveal that subsidiary tasks having both higher TSM (X-axis) and DSM (Y-axis) are most suitable for concurrent goal-subsidiary adaptation (*i.e.* the shaded blue area). The proposed sticker-based tasks better suit concurrent goal-subsidiary DA among other self-supervised pretext tasks. (Color figure online)

and target. The prime challenge in DA is to facilitate the effective utilization of the unlabeled samples while adapting to the target domain.

Drawing motivation from self-supervised pretext task literature [13,35], recent DA works [5,31] have adopted subsidiary tasks as side-objectives to improve the adaptation performance. The intuition is that subsidiary task objectives enforce learning of domain-generic representations, leading to improved domain alignment [51] and consequently, better feature clustering for unlabeled target [31]. We aim to design a similar framework but, contrary to prior works, we adopt a novel perspective of subsidiary supervised DA for the subsidiary task concurrent to unsupervised goal task DA. Specifically, the framework involves a shared backbone with a goal classifier and a subsidiary classifier (Fig. 1A, B).

To better understand how subsidiary supervised DA objectives support goal task DA, we intend to theoretically analyze the proposed framework. While several subsidiary tasks are available in the literature, there has been little attention on identifying the desirable properties of a subsidiary task that would better aid the unsupervised DA. A recent self-supervised work [55] studied the effectiveness of pretraining with existing subsidiary tasks [13,35] on different downstream supervised settings such as fine-grained or medical image classification [37,56]. We argue that our intended theoretical analysis is necessary to understand the same for DA settings as DA presents a different set of challenges compared to downstream supervised learning paradigms.

Thus, we attempt to answer two interconnected questions,

1. *How does subsidiary supervised DA help goal task unsupervised DA?*
2. *What kind of subsidiary tasks better suit concurrent goal-subsidiary DA?*

For the first question, we uncover theoretical insights based on generalization bounds in DA [3,64]. These bounds define distribution shift or domain discrepancy between source and target as the worst discrepancy for a given hypothesis space. We analyze the effect of adding the subsidiary supervised DA problem on the hypothesis space of the shared backbone. Based on this, we find that a higher domain similarity between goal and subsidiary task samples leads to a lower domain discrepancy. This leads to better adaptation for concurrent goal-subsidiary DA w.r.t. naive goal DA. Further, we observe that a higher goal-subsidiary task similarity aids effective learning of both tasks with the shared backbone, which is crucial for subsidiary DA to positively impact the goal DA.

For the second question, we first devise a subsidiary-domain similarity metric (DSM) and a subsidiary-task similarity metric (TSM) to measure the domain similarity and task similarity between any subsidiary task with a given goal task. Based on our theoretical insights, we propose a subsidiary task suitability criteria using both DSM and TSM to identify *DA-assistive* subsidiary tasks. With this criteria, we evaluate the commonly used subsidiary tasks from the pretext task literature like rotation prediction [31], patch location [51], and jigsaw permutation prediction [5] in Fig. 1C. We observe that these existing tasks have significantly low DSM. On the other hand, dense output based tasks like colorization [22] or inpainting [38] severely lack in TSM as goal task is classification-based. Understanding these limitations, we devise a sticker-intervention that facilitates domain preservation (high DSM) and propose a range of sticker-based subsidiary tasks (Fig. 2). For general shape-based goal tasks, it turns out that sticker classification task has the best TSM among other sticker-based tasks. This yields higher adaptation performance thereby validating the proposed criteria.

To evaluate our theoretical insights and the proposed concurrent subsidiary DA, we particularly focus on source-free DA regime [17,21,23]. In this, the source and target data are not concurrently accessible while model sharing is permitted.

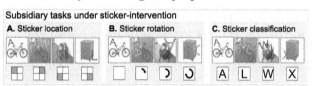

Fig. 2. Sticker intervention involves mixup of input with a masked sticker. We devise the following sticker-based tasks; **A.** locating the quadrant of the sticker, **B.** predicting sticker rotation, **C.** classifying sticker category.

While this challenging setting holds immense practical value by working within the data privacy regulations, we choose source-free DA as it can prominently highlight our advantages. The well-developed discrepancy minimization techniques, tailored to general DA scenarios, guide the adaptation more significantly than our proposed approach but cannot be used for source-free DA. Further, existing source-free works [26] rely heavily on pseudo-label based self-training on target data. Our proposed subsidiary supervised adaptation implicitly regularizes target-side self-training, leading to improved adaptation.

To summarize, our main contributions are:

- We introduce concurrent subsidiary supervised DA, for a subsidiary task, that not only improves unsupervised goal task DA but also facilitates source-free adaptation. We provide theoretical insights to analyze the impact of subsidiary DA on the domain discrepancy, and hence, the goal task DA.

– Based on our insights, we devise a subsidiary DA suitability criteria to identify *DA-assistive* subsidiary tasks that better aid the unsupervised goal task DA. We also propose novel sticker intervention based subsidiary tasks that demonstrate the efficacy of the criteria.
– Our proposed approach achieves state-of-the-art performance on source-free single-source DA (SSDA) as well as source-free multi-source DA (MSDA) for image classification. The proposed approach also complements existing non-source-free works, achieving leading performance.

2 Related Work

Pretext Tasks in Self-supervised Learning. Pretext tasks are used to learn deep feature representations from unlabeled data, in a self-supervised manner, for downstream tasks. There are several pretext tasks such as image inpainting [38], colorization [22,62,63], spatial context prediction [7], contrastive predictive coding [36], image rotation [13], and jigsaw puzzle solving [35]. Pretext tasks are commonly used for pre-training on unlabeled data followed by finetuning on labeled data. Conversely, we perform supervised DA for the pretext-like task along with the unsupervised goal task DA, resulting in a representation that aligns the domains while maintaining the goal task performance.

Source-Free DA. Recently, several methods have investigated source-free DA. USFDA [19] and FS [20] investigate universal DA [61] and open-set DA [46], in a source-free setting by synthesizing training samples to make the decision boundaries compact. SHOT [26,27], NRC [59] maximize mutual information and propose pseudo-labeling, using global structure to match target features to that of a fixed source classifier. To provide adaptation supervision, 3C-GAN [23] generates labeled target-style images from a GAN. Finally, SFDA [28], UR [49], and GtA [18] are semantic segmentation specific source-free DA techniques.

Pretext Task Based DA. Several DA works have demonstrated the efficacy of learning meaningful representations using pretext tasks. Early works [11,12] used reconstruction as a pretext task to extract domain-invariant features. [4] captured both domain-specific and shared features by separating the feature space into domain-private and domain-shared spaces. [5] used jigsaw puzzles as a side-objective to tackle domain generalization. [51] proposed that adaptation can be accomplished by learning many self-supervision tasks at the same time. [16] suggested a cross-domain SSL strategy for adaptation with minimal source labels based on instance discrimination [57]. [15] recommended employing SSL pretext tasks like rotation prediction and patch placement prediction. [45] solved the challenge of universal domain adaptation by unsupervised clustering. [43] employed easy labels for synthetic images, such as the surface normal, depth, and instance contour, to train a network. [9] employed SSL pretext tasks like rotation prediction as part of their domain generalization technique.

3 Approach

In this section, we introduce required preliminaries (Sect. 3.1), followed by theoretical insights (Sect. 3.2) that motivate our training algorithm design (Sect. 3.4).

3.1 Preliminaries

3.1.1 Goal Task Unsupervised DA

For closed set DA problem, consider a labeled source dataset $\mathcal{D}_s = \{(x_s, y_s) : x_s \in \mathcal{X}, y_s \in \mathcal{C}_g\}$ where $\mathcal{X}$ is the input space and $\mathcal{C}_g$ denotes the label set for the goal task. x_s is drawn from the marginal distribution p_s. Let $\mathcal{D}_t = \{x_t : x_t \in \mathcal{X}\}$ be an unlabeled target dataset with $x_t \sim p_t$. The goal is to assign labels for each target image x_t. The usual approach [10,29,50] is to use a backbone feature extractor $h : \mathcal{X} \to \mathcal{Z}$ followed by a goal classifier $f_g : \mathcal{Z} \to \mathcal{C}_g$ (see Fig. 3A). The expected source risk with h and an optimal labeling function $f_S : \mathcal{X} \to \mathcal{C}_g$, is $\epsilon_s(h) = \mathbb{E}_{x \sim p_s}[\mathbb{1}(f_g \circ h(x) \neq f_S(x))]$, where $(.)$ is an indicator function. Similarly, $\epsilon_t(h)$ is the target risk with optimal labeling function $f_T : \mathcal{X} \to \mathcal{C}_g$. We restate the theoretical upper bound on target risk from [64]. For backbone hypothesis $h \in \mathcal{H}$ with $\mathcal{H}$ being the hypothesis space and a domain classifier $f_d : \mathcal{Z} \to \{0, 1\}$ (0 for source, 1 for target),

$$\epsilon_t(h) \leq \epsilon_s(h) + d_{\mathcal{H}}(p_s, p_t) + \lambda_g;$$

$$\text{where, } \lambda_g = \min\left\{ \mathbb{E}_{p_s}[\mathbb{1}(f_S(x) \neq f_T(x))], \mathbb{E}_{p_t}[\mathbb{1}(f_S(x) \neq f_T(x))] \right\}$$

$$\text{and, } d_{\mathcal{H}}(p_s, p_t) = \sup_{h \in \mathcal{H}} \left| \mathbb{E}_{x \sim p_s}[\mathbb{1}(f_d \circ h(x) = 1)] - \mathbb{E}_{x \sim p_t}[\mathbb{1}(f_d \circ h(x) = 1)] \right| \quad (1)$$

Here, $d_{\mathcal{H}}$ is the $\mathcal{H}$-divergence [3] that indicates the distribution shift or worst-case domain discrepancy between the two domains. λ_g is a constant that represents the optimal cross-domain error of the labeling functions. Thus, the target risk $\epsilon_t(h)$ is upper bounded by these two terms along with the source risk $\epsilon_s(h)$.

3.1.2 Subsidiary Supervised DA

Next, we introduce a subsidiary supervised DA problem concurrent to the goal task unsupervised DA. To this end, we aim to devise a subsidiary classification task with a new label set $\mathcal{C}_n$. The label-set specific attributes are inflicted on $x \in \mathcal{X}$ via an intervention, to form supervised pairs. These pairs form labeled source, $(x_{s,n}, y_n) \in \mathcal{D}_{s,n}$ and labeled target, $(x_{t,n}, y_n) \in \mathcal{D}_{t,n}$ datasets. Here, the inputs $x_{s,n}$ and $x_{t,n}$ are drawn from marginal distributions $p_{s,n}$ and $p_{t,n}$ respectively. We also define the optimal labeling functions for source and target subsidiary task as $f_{S,n} : \mathcal{X} \to \mathcal{C}_n$ and $f_{T,n} : \mathcal{X} \to \mathcal{C}_n$. Next, the prediction mapping involves the shared goal-task backbone h followed by a subsidiary classifier $f_n : \mathcal{Z} \to \mathcal{C}_n$ (see Fig. 3A). Here, the source-subsidiary task error is $\epsilon_{s,n}(h) = \mathbb{E}_{x \sim p_{s,n}}[\mathbb{1}(f_n \circ h(x) \neq f_{S,n}(x))]$. Similarly, $\epsilon_{t,n}(h)$ for target and λ_n

A. Architecture overview

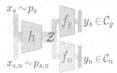

B. Hypothesis space analysis

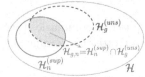

C. Sticker intervention

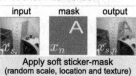

Fig. 3. A. Our method uses a shared backbone h with goal classifier f_g and subsidiary classifier f_n. **B.** Hypothesis space analysis for only goal DA, only subsidiary DA and concurrent goal-subsidiary DA (Sect. 3.2.1). **C.** Sticker intervention.

defined as in Eq. 1. Thus, generalization bounds for subsidiary DA with the same $\mathcal{H}$ is stated as,

$$\epsilon_{t,n}(h) \leq \epsilon_{s,n}(h) + d_{\mathcal{H}}(p_{s,n}, p_{t,n}) + \lambda_n \tag{2}$$

3.1.3   Metrics

We introduce two metrics that form the basis of our insights.

a) Subsidiary-Domain Similarity Metric (DSM), $\gamma_{DSM}(.,.)$. DSM measures the similarity between two domains as the inverse of the standard $\mathcal{A}$-distance [3]. $\mathcal{A}$-distance can be thought of as a proxy [10] for $\mathcal{H}$-divergence.
b) Subsidiary-Task Similarity Metric (TSM), $\gamma_{TSM}(.,.)$. TSM measures the task similarity of a subsidiary task w.r.t. the goal task. TSM is computed using the standard linear evaluation protocol [47] borrowed from transfer learning and self-supervised literature. It is the performance of a subsidiary-task linear classifier attached to a goal-task pretrained backbone feature extractor $h_{s,g}$. Intuitively, it indicates the extent of compatibility between the two tasks.

For a dataset pair of source-goal and source-subsidiary, *i.e.* $(\mathcal{D}_s, \mathcal{D}_{s,n})$;

$$\gamma_{DSM}(\mathcal{D}_s, \mathcal{D}_{s,n}) = 1 - \frac{1}{2}d_{\mathcal{A}}(\mathcal{D}_s, \mathcal{D}_{s,n}); \quad \gamma_{TSM}(\mathcal{D}_s, \mathcal{D}_{s,n}) = 1 - \min_{f_n} \hat{\epsilon}_{s,n}(h_{s,g}) \tag{3}$$

Here, $d_{\mathcal{A}}(.,.)$ denotes $\mathcal{A}$-distance and $\hat{\epsilon}_{s,n}(.)$ denotes empirical error for subsidiary task on source data. Note that $0 \leq \hat{\epsilon}_{s,n}(h_{s,g}) \leq 1$ while $0 \leq d_{\mathcal{A}}(\mathcal{D}_1, \mathcal{D}_2) \leq 2$.

3.2   Theoretical Insights

We analyze the impact of solving subsidiary supervised DA on the goal task unsupervised DA. We first consider the combined bounds (combining Eq. 1, 2),

$$\epsilon_t(h) + \epsilon_{t,n}(h) \leq \epsilon_s(h) + \epsilon_{s,n}(h) + d_{\mathcal{H}}(p_s, p_t) + d_{\mathcal{H}}(p_{s,n}, p_{t,n}) + \lambda_g + \lambda_n \tag{4}$$

Among the six terms on the right side, the two λ terms are constants as they do not involve the hypothesis h or hypothesis space $\mathcal{H}$. We analyze the source error duet, $\epsilon_s(h) + \epsilon_{s,n}(h)$, and the domain discrepancy duet $d_{\mathcal{H}}(p_s, p_t) + d_{\mathcal{H}}(p_{s,n}, p_{t,n})$.

3.2.1 Analyzing the Domain Discrepancy Duet

(Figure 3B). We analyze w.r.t. the domain discrepancy duet considering three configurations:

a) While performing only unsupervised goal task DA, the backbone optimization would operate on a limited hypothesis space $\mathcal{H}_g^{(uns)} \subset \mathcal{H}$ where $\mathcal{H}_g^{(uns)} = \{h \in \mathcal{H} : |\epsilon_t(h) - \epsilon_s(h)| \leq \zeta_g^{(uns)}\}$. Here, $\zeta_g^{(uns)}$ is a threshold on the source-target error gap.

b) While performing supervised adaptation only for subsidiary domain adaptation, the optimization would operate on a limited hypothesis space $\mathcal{H}_n^{(sup)} \subset \mathcal{H}$ i.e., $\mathcal{H}_n^{(sup)} = \{h \in \mathcal{H} : |\epsilon_{t,n}(h) - \epsilon_{s,n}(h)| \leq \zeta_n^{(sup)}\}$. Here, $\zeta_n^{(sup)}$ is a threshold on the subsidiary-task source-target error gap.

c) While concurrently performing a) unsupervised goal task DA and b) subsidiary supervised DA (i.e. the proposed approach), the optimization would operate on a limited hypothesis space $\mathcal{H}_{g,n} \subset \mathcal{H}$. Specifically, $\mathcal{H}_{g,n} = \mathcal{H}_n^{(sup)} \cap \mathcal{H}_g^{(uns)}$. This is because the backbone is shared between the two DA tasks and hence, would be limited to the intersection space.

Different configurations lead to different $\mathcal{H}$-spaces and consequently, different $\mathcal{H}$-divergences. Comparing the $\mathcal{H}$-divergences leads us to the following insight.

Insight 1 ($\mathcal{H}$-divergence in concurrent goal DA and subsidiary DA). *The backbone hypothesis space for concurrent unsupervised goal DA and subsidiary supervised DA, i.e. $\mathcal{H}_{g,n} = \mathcal{H}_n^{(sup)} \cap \mathcal{H}_g^{(uns)}$ will yield a lower $\mathcal{H}$-divergence than $\mathcal{H}_g^{(uns)}$ (hypothesis space for only unsupervised goal task DA), i.e.*

$$d_{\mathcal{H}_{g,n}}(p_s, p_t) \leq d_{\mathcal{H}_g^{(uns)}}(p_s, p_t) \;\; and \;\; d_{\mathcal{H}_{g,n}}(p_{s,n}, p_{t,n}) \leq d_{\mathcal{H}_g^{(uns)}}(p_{s,n}, p_{t,n}) \quad (5)$$

Remarks. In Eq. 1, $d_{\mathcal{H}}(p_s, p_t)$ is the supremum over the hypothesis space $\mathcal{H}$ i.e. a worst-case measure. Since $\mathcal{H}_{g,n} \subset \mathcal{H}_g^{(uns)}$, $\mathcal{H}_{g,n}$ would have a lower $\mathcal{H}$-divergence as the worst-case hypothesis of $\mathcal{H}_g^{(uns)}$ may be absent in the subset $\mathcal{H}_{g,n}$. This applies to both pairs, (p_s, p_t) and $(p_{s,n}, p_{t,n})$. While a lower $\mathcal{H}$-divergence duet leads to improved goal DA, the equality may hold when the worst hypothesis of $\mathcal{H}_g^{(uns)}$ remains in $\mathcal{H}_{g,n}$. In such a case, concurrent DA would perform the same as naive goal DA. To this end, we put forward the following insight.

Insight 2 (When is concurrent DA strictly better than naive DA?). *A subsidiary task supports the strict inequality $d_{\mathcal{H}_{g,n}}(p_s, p_t) < d_{\mathcal{H}_g^{(uns)}}(p_s, p_t)$ if with at least $(1-\delta)$ probability, the subsidiary-domain similarity $\gamma_{DSM}(\mathcal{D}_s, \mathcal{D}_{s,n})$ exceeds a threshold ζ_d by no less than ξ; $\mathbb{P}[\gamma_{DSM}(\mathcal{D}_s, \mathcal{D}_{s,n}) \geq \zeta_d - \xi] \geq 1 - \delta$.*

Remarks. In other words, the strict inequalities in Eq. 5 would hold if the DSM $\gamma_{DSM}(.,.)$ exceeds a threshold ζ_d. The supports for this insight are twofold. First, a subsidiary task may heavily alter domain information [32], *e.g.* jigsaw shuffling [5]. Then, the backbone will be updated using out-of-domain samples which is undesirable as such samples are unlikely for inference. This will be avoided if Insight 2 is satisfied. Second, if DSM is high, we can approximate $p_s \approx p_{s,n}$ and $p_t \approx p_{t,n}$. Thus, more samples from subsidiary task data will be available for training the backbone to be domain-invariant (as subsidiary task uses samples from both the domains) *i.e.* reducing $d_{\mathcal{H}}$ against the same in naive goal DA.

3.2.2 Analyzing the Source Error Duet

Now we analyze w.r.t. the source error duet of Eq. 4. While the $\mathcal{H}$-divergence is lower for concurrent goal task DA and subsidiary supervised DA, a logical concern is that simultaneous minimization of errors, *i.e.* $\epsilon_s(h) + \epsilon_{s,n}(h)$, for both tasks may be difficult with the shared backbone h. Further, it may happen that simultaneous training for both tasks in target domain may hamper the goal task performance as it is unsupervised. In such cases, the subsidiary task would be ill-equipped to assist the goal task adaptation. To avoid these, we propose another empirical criterion as follows.

Insight 3 (Goal and subsidiary task similarity for concurrent DA). *Higher goal-subsidiary task similarity (TSM) aids effective minimization of both task errors with the shared backbone, which is crucial for subsidiary supervised DA to positively affect the goal task DA. The criterion is* $\gamma_{TSM}(\mathcal{D}_s, \mathcal{D}_{s,n}) > \zeta_n$.

Remarks. Here, ζ_n is a threshold. The TSM γ_{TSM} indicates the compatibility of goal task features to support the subsidiary task. Intuitively, a higher TSM implies more overlap in the discriminative features of the two tasks, which would allow better simultaneous minimization of both task errors.

Based on Insight 1, concurrent subsidiary supervised DA and goal task DA yields a lower domain discrepancy. Further, based on Insight 2, a subsidiary task can be selected such that effective minimization of both source errors is possible simultaneously. Thus, using Eq. 1, we can infer that $\sup_{h \in \mathcal{H}_{g,n}} \epsilon_t(h) \leq \sup_{h \in \mathcal{H}_g^{(uns)}} \epsilon_t(h)$ *i.e.* a lower target error upper bound for our approach w.r.t. naive goal task DA. Now, we summarize the criteria (Insight 2, 3).

Definition 1 (Subsidiary DA suitability criteria). *A subsidiary task is termed DA-assistive i.e. suitable for subsidiary supervised DA if the sum of DSM γ_{DSM} and TSM γ_{TSM} exceeds a threshold ζ,*

$$\gamma_{DSM}(\mathcal{D}_s, \mathcal{D}_{s,n}) + \gamma_{TSM}(\mathcal{D}_s, \mathcal{D}_{s,n}) > \zeta \tag{6}$$

Remarks. In other words, a subsidiary task which is domain-preserving and has high task similarity w.r.t. the goal task is *DA-assistive i.e.* suitable for subsidiary supervised DA to aid the goal task DA. We employ this criteria empirically for a diverse set of subsidiary tasks (shown in Fig. 1C). Next, we describe the motivation for our proposed sticker intervention and corresponding subsidiary tasks as well as training algorithms tailored for source-free DA.

3.3 Sticker Intervention Based Subsidiary Task Design

While one may consider pretext tasks from the self-supervised learning literature as candidates for subsidiary DA, almost all such tasks fail to satisfy subsidiary DA suitability criteria in Eq. 6. For instance, dense output based tasks such as colorization [22,62], inpainting [38], *etc.*exhibit markedly low task similarity (TSM) against the non-dense goal tasks. Further, the input intervention for certain pretext tasks such as jigsaw [5], patch-location [51], rotation [15,31], significantly alter the domain information leading to low domain similarity (DSM).

Insight 4 (Sticker-intervention based tasks well suit subsidiary DA). *Sticker intervention is the process of pasting a sticker x_n (i.e., a symbol with random texture and scale) on a given image sample $x_s \in \mathcal{D}_s$ to obtain a stickered sample, i.e. $x_{s,n} = \mathcal{T}(x_s, x_n) \in \mathcal{D}_{s,n}$. Following this, the subsidiary task could be defined as the classification of some sticker attribute (e.g. shape, location, or orientation). Such a formalization provides effective control to maximize $\gamma_{DSM}(\mathcal{D}_s, \mathcal{D}_{s,n})$ and $\gamma_{TSM}(\mathcal{D}_s, \mathcal{D}_{s,n})$, in line with our suitability criteria.*

Remarks. The sticker intervention (Fig. 3C) facilitates domain preservation while simultaneously supporting a range of subsidiary tasks. Since the proposed sticker intervention alters only a local area of the sample, the original content is not suppressed which in turn preserves the domain information, implying high DSM. Following this, one can ablate over a range of sticker-based tasks in order to select a suitable subsidiary task based on the given goal task. Below, we discuss some possible subsidiary tasks under the sticker intervention.

a) **Sticker location** (Fig. 2A). We draw motivation from patch-location [51], where the task is to classify the quadrant to which a patch-input belongs. With sticker intervened images, the task is to classify the quadrant with the sticker. Our use of whole images as input is more domain-preserving than patch-input.

b) **Sticker rotation** (Fig. 2B). Motivated by the image rotation task [31], we propose sticker rotation task where the rotation of the sticker has to be classified ($0°$, $90°$, $180°$ and $270°$ rotations possible). Note that our sticker rotation does not affect the domain information while rotating the entire image does.

c) **Sticker classification** (Fig. 2C). While the discriminative features in the previous two tasks were location and rotation, we propose sticker classification task with primary discriminative features as shape. In other words, the task is to classify the sticker shape (*i.e.* the symbol) given a stickered sample.

3.4 Training Algorithm Design Under Source-Free Constraints

For the standard DA setting with concurrent access to source and target data [10,50], the subsidiary supervised DA can be implemented simply by optimizing the subsidiary classification loss simultaneously for source and target. This would yield a lower domain discrepancy as discussed in Sect. 3.2. However, in the more practical source-free setting [19,23] where concurrent source-target access is prohibited, this simple approach would not be possible. We believe the improvements will be prominent in source-free DA based on the following insight:

Insight 5 (Subsidiary DA better suits challenging source-free DA). *Existing source-free DA works heavily rely on pseudo-label or clustering based self-training on unlabeled target with no obvious alternative. The proposed subsidiary supervised adaptation helps to implicitly regularize the target-side self-training, leading to improved adaptation performance. The subsidiary DA not only aids goal DA as a result of high DSM but also preserves the goal task inductive bias as a result of high TSM, while adhering to the source-free constraints.*

Remarks. The source-free setting presents new challenges which highlight the advantages of our proposed method more prominently. This is because, the performance in non-source-free DA is strongly influenced by well-developed discrepancy minimization techniques. However, these techniques cannot be leveraged in a source-free setting due to their requirement of concurrent source-target data access. Thus, we primarily operate in the source-free regime to evaluate our theoretical insights and the proposed concurrent subsidiary supervised DA problem.

We perform the training in three steps. First two steps involve pre-training of goal task and subsidiary task respectively with source data. The final step involves adapting both tasks to target domain. For clarity, we first summarize available and intervened datasets required for training and their notations.

Datasets. The goal task source data is denoted by $(x_s, y_s) \in \mathcal{D}_s$ while the corresponding unlabeled target is denoted by $x_t \in \mathcal{D}_t$. The intervened stickered-source data, coupled with both goal and sticker task labels, is denoted by $(x_{s,n}, y_s, y_n) \in \mathcal{D}_{s,n}$. The corresponding stickered-target data, with only subsidiary sticker task labels, is denoted by $(x_{t,n}, y_n) \in \mathcal{D}_{t,n}$. We introduce a pseudo-OOS (out-of-source) dataset, $\mathcal{D}_s^{(od)}$ further in this section.

3.4.1   Goal Task Source Pre-training

(Figure 4A). We train the backbone h and goal classifier f_g with source data $\mathcal{D}_s$ and stickered-source data $\mathcal{D}_{s,n}$:

$$\min_{\theta_h, \theta_{f_g}} \mathbb{E}_{(x,y) \in \mathcal{D}_s \cup \mathcal{D}_{s,n}} [\mathcal{L}_{s,g}]; \quad \mathcal{L}_{s,g} = \mathcal{L}_{ce}(f_g \circ h(x), y) \tag{7}$$

Here, θ_h and θ_{f_g} are the parameters of h and f_g, $\mathcal{L}_{ce}$ is the cross-entropy loss, y is the goal task label, and expectation is implemented by sampling mini-batches.

3.4.2   Sticker Task Source Pre-training

(Figure 4A). We pretrain the sticker classifier f_n while inculcating the ability to reject samples out of the source distribution. Specifically, f_n predicts a $(|\mathcal{C}_n| +$

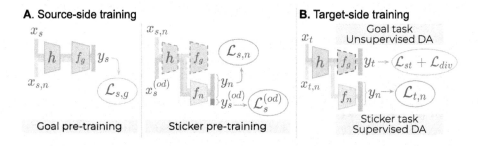

Fig. 4. A. Source-side training involves goal pre-training (Sect. 3.4.1) and sticker pre-training (Sect. 3.4.2). **B.** Target-side training involves concurrent goal-task unsupervised DA and sticker-task supervised DA (Sect. 3.4.3).

1)-sized vector and is trained to classify *out-of-source* (OOS) samples to the $(|\mathcal{C}_n| + 1)^{\text{th}}$ class.

Insight 6. *The OOS node in the sticker classifier implicitly behaves as a domain discriminator from adversarial alignment methods. Minimizing the OOS probability only for the target data aligns the target with the source.*

Remarks. In source training, the OOS objective forces the sticker classifier to discriminate between source and OOS samples. This is done with the intuition that OOS samples simulate the role of target samples in adversarial alignment methods. This domain discriminatory knowledge will support future source-free target alignment. Concretely, the shared backbone can be adapted to the target, by minimizing OOS probability for target samples, as source knowledge is preserved by freezing f_g. Thus, we require OOS data to prepare f_n for adaptation.

Obtaining the OOS Dataset. A naive approach is to use a dataset unrelated to the goal task label set. Conversely, we devise a pseudo-OOS dataset using only already available source samples. Mitsuzumi *et al.* [32] show that, beyond a certain grid size, shuffling grid patches makes the domain unrecognizable. Hence, we generate a pseudo-OOS dataset by shuffling grid patches of source images.

We also add stickers to shuffled images, at random, to further instill differences between source and pseudo-OOS (see Suppl). Formally, $(x_s^{(od)}, y_s^{(od)}) \in \mathcal{D}_s^{(od)}$ where $y_s^{(od)}$ denotes OOS category *i.e.* $(|\mathcal{C}_n| + 1)^{\text{th}}$ category of f_n.

We train only the sticker classifier f_n, keeping backbone h and goal classifier f_g frozen, using cross-entropy loss $\mathcal{L}_{ce}$. With $\mathcal{L}_{s,n} = \mathcal{L}_{ce}(f_n \circ h(x_{s,n}), y_n)$, the overall objective for stickered source data $\mathcal{D}_{s,n}$ and pseudo-OOS data $\mathcal{D}_s^{(od)}$ is,

$$\min_{\theta_{f_n}} \mathop{\mathbb{E}}_{\mathcal{D}_{s,n}} [\mathcal{L}_{s,n}] + \mathop{\mathbb{E}}_{\mathcal{D}_s^{(od)}} [\mathcal{L}_s^{(od)}]; \quad \text{where } \mathcal{L}_s^{(od)} = \mathcal{L}_{ce}(f_n \circ h(x_s^{(od)}), y_s^{(od)}) \quad (8)$$

Table 1. Single-Source Domain Adaptation (SSDA) on Office-Home benchmarks. SF indicates *source-free* adaptation.

Method	SF	Office-Home											
		Ar→Cl	Ar→Pr	Ar→Rw	Cl→Ar	Cl→Pr	Cl→Rw	Pr→Ar	Pr→Cl	Pr→Rw	Rw→Ar	Rw→Cl	Rw→Pr	Avg
FixBi [33]	✗	58.1	77.3	80.4	67.7	79.5	78.1	65.8	57.9	81.7	76.4	62.9	86.7	72.7
SENTRY[41]	✗	61.8	77.4	80.1	66.3	71.6	74.7	66.8	63.0	80.9	74.0	66.3	84.1	72.2
SCDA [24]	✗	60.7	76.4	82.8	69.8	77.5	78.4	68.9	59.0	82.7	74.9	61.8	84.5	73.1
SHOT [26]	✓	57.1	78.1	81.5	68.0	78.2	78.1	67.4	54.9	82.2	73.3	58.8	84.3	71.8
A²Net [58]	✓	58.4	79.0	82.4	67.5	79.3	78.9	68.0	56.2	82.9	74.1	60.5	85.0	72.8
GSFDA [60]	✓	57.9	78.6	81.0	66.7	77.2	77.2	65.6	56.0	82.2	72.0	57.8	83.4	71.3
CPGA [42]	✓	59.3	78.1	79.8	65.4	75.5	76.4	65.7	**58.0**	81.0	72.0	64.4	83.3	71.6
NRC [59]	✓	57.7	80.3	82.0	68.1	79.8	78.6	65.3	56.4	83.0	71.0	58.6	85.6	72.2
SHOT++ [27]	✓	57.9	79.7	82.5	68.5	79.6	79.3	68.5	57.0	**83.0**	73.7	60.7	84.9	73.0
Ours	✓	**61.0**	**80.4**	**82.5**	**69.1**	**79.9**	**79.5**	**69.1**	57.8	82.7	**74.5**	**65.1**	**86.4**	**74.0**

3.4.3   Source-Free Target Adaptation

(Figure 4B). For unsupervised goal task adaptation, we use the general self training loss $\mathcal{L}_{st}$ and diversity loss $\mathcal{L}_{div}$ [26]. See Suppl. for more details. The goal task objective is given in Eq. 9 (left),

$$\min_{\theta_h} \underset{\mathcal{D}_t \cup \mathcal{D}_{t,n}}{\mathbb{E}} [\mathcal{L}_{st} + \mathcal{L}_{div}]; \text{ and } \min_{(\theta_h, \theta_{f_n})} \underset{\mathcal{D}_{t,n}}{\mathbb{E}} [\mathcal{L}_{t,n}]; \; \mathcal{L}_{t,n} = \mathcal{L}_{ce}(f_n \circ h(x_{t,n}), y_n) \tag{9}$$

The goal classifier f_g is frozen to preserve its inductive bias and only the backbone h is updated for both original and stickered samples in Eq. 9 (left).

For subsidiary supervised sticker adaptation, we use a simple cross-entropy loss with sticker labels. We implicitly minimize OOS probability by maximizing label class probability. We observe that this works well and explicit minimization of OOS probability is not required. As per Insight 6, *out-of-target* (OOT) samples are not required. Further, using OOT samples to update the backbone could be undesirable as discussed under Insight 2. The objective is given in Eq. 9 (right). Both backbone h and sticker classifier f_n are updated as the task is supervised.

4   Experiments

We provide the implementation details of our experiments and thoroughly evaluate our approach w.r.t. state-of-the-art prior works across multiple settings. Unless mentioned, *Ours* implies sticker classification as the subsidiary task.

4.1   Experimental Setup

Datasets. We evaluate on four standard DA benchmarks; Office-31 [44], Office-Home [54], VisDA [40], and DomainNet [39]. See Suppl. for more details.

Implementation Details. We use a ResNet-101 [14] backbone for VisDA, and ResNet-50 for other benchmarks. We employ the same network design as SHOT [26]. For the subsidiary classifier, we use the same architecture after ResLayer-3. The number of sticker classes is 10. See Suppl. for more details.

Table 2. Multi-Source Domain Adaptation (MSDA) on DomainNet and Office-Home. We outperform *source-free* (denoted by SF) prior arts despite not using domain labels.

Method	SF	w/o domain labels	DomainNet							Office-Home				
			→C	→I	→P	→Q	→R	→S	Avg	→Ar	→Cl	→Pr	→Rw	Avg
WAMDA [1]	✗	✗	59.3	21.8	52.1	9.5	65.0	47.7	42.6	71.9	61.4	84.1	82.3	74.9
SImpAl$_{50}$ [53]	✗	✗	66.4	26.5	56.6	18.9	68.0	55.5	48.6	70.8	56.3	80.2	81.5	72.2
CMSDA [48]	✗	✗	70.9	26.5	57.5	21.3	68.1	59.4	50.4	71.5	67.7	84.1	82.9	76.6
DRT [25]	✗	✗	71.0	31.6	61.0	12.3	71.4	60.7	51.3	–	–	–	–	–
STEM [34]	✗	✗	72.0	28.2	61.5	25.7	72.6	60.2	53.4	–	–	–	–	–
Source-combine	✗	✓	57.0	23.4	54.1	14.6	67.2	50.3	44.4	58.0	57.3	74.2	77.9	66.9
SHOT [26]-Ens	✓	✗	58.6	25.2	55.3	15.3	**70.5**	52.4	46.2	72.2	59.3	82.8	82.9	74.3
DECISION [2]	✓	✗	61.5	21.6	54.6	**18.9**	67.5	51.0	45.9	74.5	59.4	84.4	83.6	75.5
SHOT++ [27]	✓	✗	–	–	–	–	–	–	–	73.1	61.3	84.3	84.0	75.7
CAiDA [8]	✓	✗	–	–	–	–	–	–	–	**75.2**	60.5	84.7	84.2	76.2
NRC [59]	✓	✓	65.8	24.1	56.0	16.0	69.2	53.4	47.4	70.6	60.0	84.6	83.5	74.7
Ours	✓	✓	**70.3**	**25.7**	**57.3**	17.1	69.9	**57.1**	**49.6**	75.1	**64.1**	**86.6**	84.4	**77.6**

4.2   Discussion

a) Single Source Domain Adaptation (SSDA). We compare with prior source-free SSDA works in Table 1 on Office-Home. We achieve *state-of-the-art* results exceeding the source-free SHOT++ and non-source-free SCDA [24] by 1% and 0.9% respectively. See Suppl. for Office-31 and VisDA results.

b) Multi Source Domain Adaptation (MSDA). In Table 2, we compare with the source-only baseline (*source-combine*) and source-free works. Even without domain labels, our approach achieves *state-of-the-art* results, even w.r.t. non-source-free works on Office-Home (+1%). On DomainNet, we outperform source-free works (+2.2%) with comparable results to non-source-free works.

c) Evaluating the subsidiary DA suitability criteria. We empirically evaluate DSM and TSM for our sticker-based tasks as well as existing tasks from self-supervised literature in Fig. 5A, 5B. Compared to patch location [51] and image rotation [31], sticker location and sticker rotation tasks exhibit higher DSM and thus, are more suitable with better adaptation performance (Table 3). However, sticker classification task is the most suitable due to its higher TSM as shape is the primary discriminative features, same as in goal task. We observe a positive correlation between DA performance and both DSM and TSM, which empirically verifies our suitability criteria. In Table 3, we also compare dense output based tasks like colorization and inpainting, which give marginal gains.

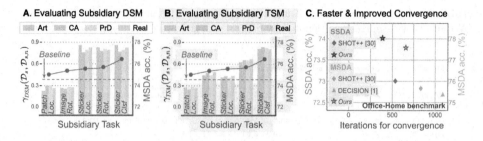

Fig. 5. We observe higher **A.** domain similarity (DSM) and **B.** task similarity (TSM) for our sticker-based tasks compared to existing subsidiary tasks like patch-location and image-rotation. This correlates with the better MSDA performance of sticker-based tasks on Office-Home and validates our criteria (Definition 1). **C.** Faster and improved convergence w.r.t.prior source-free works on both SSDA and MSDA for Office-Home.

d) Faster and improved convergence. Figure 5C illustrates our better and faster convergence w.r.t. source-free prior arts for both SSDA and MSDA. The hypothesis space for concurrent subsidiary supervised DA and unsupervised goal task DA, $\mathcal{H}_{g,n}$, is a subset of the hypothesis space for only unsupervised goal task DA, $\mathcal{H}_g^{(uns)}$. Thus, we achieve faster convergence. Further, as per Insight 1, lower domain discrepancy leads to lower target error $i.e.$ improved convergence.

Table 3. Subsidiary task comparisons on **Office-Home** for source-free DA. Here, baseline is same as #3 in Table 5.

Method	SSDA	MSDA
Baseline (B)	66.2	74.3
B + inpainting	66.3	74.5
B + colorization	66.8	74.7
B + jigsaw	67.0	74.8
B + patch-loc	67.6	75.0
B + rotation	67.9	75.4
B + sticker-loc	68.8	75.5
B + sticker-rot	69.0	75.7
B + sticker-clsf	**69.7**	**76.2**

e) Compatibility with non-source-free DA. In Table 4, we evaluate the compatibility of concurrent subsidiary supervised DA with existing non-source-free SSDA techniques [10,30,52]. MSDA results are obtained by combining the multiple sources for each target. Compared to the original reported results, all four perform better with our proposed subsidiary DA. Note that our non-source-free variant outperforms these results (#7 in Table 5).

4.2.1 Ablation Study.

Below, we discuss a thorough ablation study.

a) Effect of subsidiary supervised DA and OOS node. In Table 5, we compare the baseline $i.e.$ only unsupervised goal task DA (#3) with the addition of only OOS classifier (#4). Here, a binary classifier is used for OOS detection. We observe gains of 0.8% and 0.6% for SSDA and MSDA respectively. This indicates that only OOS helps, but subsidiary classifier

Table 4. Evaluating compatibility of subsidiary DA with non-source-free DA works on Office-Home. SSDA and MSDA indicate single-source and multi-source DA.

Method	Office-Home	
	SSDA	MSDA
CDAN [30]	65.8	69.4
+ *Subsidiary-DA*	**67.1**	**71.2**
SRDC [52]	71.3	73.1
+ *Subsidiary-DA*	**71.9**	**75.2**
FixBi [33]	72.7	–
+ *Subsidiary-DA*	**73.7**	–
CMSDA [48]	–	76.6
+ *Subsidiary-DA*	–	**78.1**

Table 5. Ablation analysis. Here, *sticker-w-OOS-clsf* denotes learning with all the proposed components unlike in *only-OOS-clsf* (all losses except $\mathcal{L}_{s,n}, \mathcal{L}_{t,n}$) and *only-sticker-clsf* (all losses except $\mathcal{L}_s^{(od)}$). SF denotes source-free constraint.

#	Variation	SF	Office-Home	
			SSDA	MSDA
1	Source-only baseline	–	60.2	66.9
2	+ *sticker-w-OOS-clsf*	–	61.9	71.4
3	Adaptation baseline (B)	✓	66.2	74.3
4	B + *only-OOS-clsf*	✓	67.0	74.9
5	B + *only-sticker-clsf*	✓	69.7	76.2
6	B + *sticker-w-OOS-clsf*	✓	73.1	77.6
7	B + *sticker-w-OOS-clsf*	✗	**74.5**	**78.3**

is essential for further improvements. Next, we compare the baseline (#3) with concurrent goal-subsidiary DA without using OOS (#5). We observe an improvement of 3.5% and 1.9% for SSDA and MSDA. Adding the OOS objective to the subsidiary supervised DA (#6 vs. #4) improves the source-target alignment as explained in Insight 6, resulting in improvements of 3.1% and 1.4% for SSDA and MSDA.

b) Subsidiary-goal task similarity. As per Insight 3, higher goal-subsidiary task similarity is important for effective learning of both tasks. Thus, in Table 5, we compare the source-only baseline (#1) with only subsidiary supervised DA without goal task target adaptation (#2). We observe gains of 1.7% and 1.3% for SSDA and MSDA respectively. This illustrates the positive correlation between sticker classification and goal task even when target goal losses are not used.

5   Conclusion

In this work, we introduced concurrent subsidiary supervised DA for a pretext-like task to aid the unsupervised goal task DA. We provide theoretical insights to analyze the effect of subsidiary supervised DA on the domain discrepancy and consequently on the goal task adaptation. Based on the insights, we introduce a subsidiary DA suitability criteria to determine DA-assistive subsidiary tasks that improve the goal task DA performance. We also propose a novel sticker intervention based pretext task that follows our criteria. The proposed approach outperforms prior state-of-the-art source-free SSDA and MSDA works on four standard benchmarks, establishing the usefulness of our approach.

Acknowledgments. This work was supported by MeitY (Ministry of Electronics and Information Technology) project (No. 4(16)2019-ITEA), Govt. of India and a research grant by Google.

References

1. Aggarwal, S., Kundu, J.N., Babu, R.V., Chakraborty, A.: WAMDA: weighted alignment of sources for multi-source domain adaptation. In: BMVC (2020)
2. Ahmed, S.M., Raychaudhuri, D.S., Paul, S., Oymak, S., Roy-Chowdhury, A.K.: Unsupervised multi-source domain adaptation without access to source data. In: CVPR (2021)
3. Ben-David, S., Blitzer, J., Crammer, K., Pereira, F.: Analysis of representations for domain adaptation. In: NeurIPS (2006)
4. Bousmalis, K., Silberman, N., Dohan, D., Erhan, D., Krishnan, D.: Unsupervised pixel-level domain adaptation with generative adversarial networks. In: CVPR (2017)
5. Carlucci, F.M., D'Innocente, A., Bucci, S., Caputo, B., Tommasi, T.: Domain generalization by solving jigsaw puzzles. In: CVPR (2019)
6. Chen, Y.H., Chen, W.Y., Chen, Y.T., Tsai, B.C., Frank Wang, Y.C., Sun, M.: No more discrimination: cross city adaptation of road scene segmenters. In: ICCV (2017)
7. Doersch, C., Gupta, A., Efros, A.A.: Unsupervised visual representation learning by context prediction. In: ICCV (2015)
8. Dong, J., Fang, Z., Liu, A., Sun, G., Liu, T.: Confident anchor-induced multi-source free domain adaptation. In: NeurIPS (2021)
9. Feng, Z., Xu, C., Tao, D.: Self-supervised representation learning from multi-domain data. In: ICCV (2019)
10. Ganin, Y., et al.: Domain-adversarial training of neural networks. J. Mach. Learn. Res. **17**(1), 2096–2130 (2016)
11. Ghifary, M., Kleijn, W.B., Zhang, M., Balduzzi, D.: Domain generalization for object recognition with multi-task autoencoders. In: ICCV (2015)
12. Ghifary, M., Kleijn, W.B., Zhang, M., Balduzzi, D., Li, W.: Deep reconstruction-classification networks for unsupervised domain adaptation. In: Leibe, B., Matas, J., Sebe, N., Welling, M. (eds.) ECCV 2016. LNCS, vol. 9908, pp. 597–613. Springer, Cham (2016). https://doi.org/10.1007/978-3-319-46493-0_36
13. Gidaris, S., Singh, P., Komodakis, N.: Unsupervised representation learning by predicting image rotations. In: ICLR (2018)
14. He, K., Zhang, X., Ren, S., Sun, J.: Deep residual learning for image recognition. In: CVPR (2016)
15. Jiaolong, X., Liang, X., López, A.M.: Self-supervised domain adaptation for computer vision tasks. IEEE Access **7**, 156694–156706 (2019)
16. Kim, D., Saito, K., Oh, T.H., Plummer, B.A., Sclaroff, S., Saenko, K.: CDS: cross-domain self-supervised pre-training. In: ICCV (2021)
17. Kundu, J.N., et al.: Balancing discriminability and transferability for source-free domain adaptation. In: ICML (2022)
18. Kundu, J.N., Kulkarni, A., Singh, A., Jampani, V., Babu, R.V.: Generalize then adapt: source-free domain adaptive semantic segmentation. In: ICCV (2021)
19. Kundu, J.N., Venkat, N., M V, R., Babu, R.V.: Universal source-free domain adaptation. In: CVPR (2020)
20. Kundu, J.N., Venkat, N., Revanur, A., Rahul, M.V., Babu, R.V.: Towards inheritable models for open-set domain adaptation. In: CVPR (2020)
21. Kundu, J.N., Venkatesh, R.M., Venkat, N., Revanur, A., Babu, R.V.: Class-incremental domain adaptation. In: Vedaldi, A., Bischof, H., Brox, T., Frahm, J.-M. (eds.) ECCV 2020. LNCS, vol. 12358, pp. 53–69. Springer, Cham (2020). https://doi.org/10.1007/978-3-030-58601-0_4

22. Larsson, G., Maire, M., Shakhnarovich, G.: Colorization as a proxy task for visual understanding. In: CVPR (2017)
23. Li, R., Jiao, Q., Cao, W., Wong, H.S., Wu, S.: Model adaptation: unsupervised domain adaptation without source data. In: CVPR (2020)
24. Li, S., Xie, M., Lv, F., Liu, C.H., Liang, J., Qin, C., Li, W.: Semantic concentration for domain adaptation. In: ICCV (2021)
25. Li, Y., Yuan, L., Chen, Y., Wang, P., Vasconcelos, N.: Dynamic transfer for multi-source domain adaptation. In: CVPR (2021)
26. Liang, J., Hu, D., Feng, J.: Do we really need to access the source data? source hypothesis transfer for unsupervised domain adaptation. In: ICML (2020)
27. Liang, J., Hu, D., Wang, Y., He, R., Feng, J.: Source data-absent unsupervised domain adaptation through hypothesis transfer and labeling transfer. IEEE Trans. Pattern Anal. Mach. Intell. (2021)
28. Liu, Y., Zhang, W., Wang, J.: Source-free domain adaptation for semantic segmentation. In: CVPR (2021)
29. Long, M., Cao, Y., Wang, J., Jordan, M.: Learning transferable features with deep adaptation networks. In: ICML (2015)
30. Long, M., Cao, Z., Wang, J., Jordan, M.I.: Conditional adversarial domain adaptation. In: NeurIPS (2017)
31. Mishra, S., Saenko, K., Saligrama, V.: Surprisingly simple semi-supervised domain adaptation with pretraining and consistency. In: BMVC (2021)
32. Mitsuzumi, Y., Irie, G., Ikami, D., Shibata, T.: Generalized domain adaptation. In: CVPR (2021)
33. Na, J., Jung, H., Chang, H.J., Hwang, W.: FixBi: bridging domain spaces for unsupervised domain adaptation. In: CVPR (2021)
34. Nguyen, V.A., Nguyen, T., Le, T., Tran, Q.H., Phung, D.: STEM: an approach to multi-source domain adaptation with guarantees. In: ICCV (2021)
35. Noroozi, M., Favaro, P.: Unsupervised learning of visual representations by solving jigsaw puzzles. In: Leibe, B., Matas, J., Sebe, N., Welling, M. (eds.) ECCV 2016. LNCS, vol. 9910, pp. 69–84. Springer, Cham (2016). https://doi.org/10.1007/978-3-319-46466-4_5
36. Oord, A.v.d., Li, Y., Vinyals, O.: Representation learning with contrastive predictive coding. arXiv preprint arXiv:1807.03748 (2018)
37. Parkhi, O.M., Vedaldi, A., Zisserman, A., Jawahar, C.V.: Cats and dogs. In: CVPR (2012)
38. Pathak, D., Krahenbuhl, P., Donahue, J., Darrell, T., Efros, A.A.: Context encoders: feature learning by inpainting. In: CVPR (2016)
39. Peng, X., Bai, Q., Xia, X., Huang, Z., Saenko, K., Wang, B.: Moment matching for multi-source domain adaptation. In: ICCV (2019)
40. Peng, X., Usman, B., Kaushik, N., Hoffman, J., Wang, D., Saenko, K.: VisDA: the visual domain adaptation challenge. arXiv preprint arXiv:1710.06924 (2017)
41. Prabhu, V., Khare, S., Kartik, D., Hoffman, J.: SENTRY: selective entropy optimization via committee consistency for unsupervised domain adaptation. In: ICCV (2021)
42. Qiu, Z., Zhang, Y., Lin, H., Niu, S., Liu, Y., Du, Q., Tan, M.: Source-free domain adaptation via avatar prototype generation and adaptation. In: IJCAI (2021)
43. Ren, Z., Lee, Y.J.: Cross-domain self-supervised multi-task feature learning using synthetic imagery. In: CVPR (2018)
44. Saenko, K., Kulis, B., Fritz, M., Darrell, T.: Adapting visual category models to new domains. In: Daniilidis, K., Maragos, P., Paragios, N. (eds.) ECCV 2010.

LNCS, vol. 6314, pp. 213–226. Springer, Heidelberg (2010). https://doi.org/10. 1007/978-3-642-15561-1_16

45. Saito, K., Kim, D., Sclaroff, S., Saenko, K.: Universal domain adaptation through self supervision. In: NeurIPS (2020)

46. Saito, K., Yamamoto, S., Ushiku, Y., Harada, T.: Open set domain adaptation by backpropagation. In: Ferrari, V., Hebert, M., Sminchisescu, C., Weiss, Y. (eds.) ECCV 2018. LNCS, vol. 11209, pp. 156–171. Springer, Cham (2018). https://doi. org/10.1007/978-3-030-01228-1_10

47. Salman, H., Ilyas, A., Engstrom, L., Kapoor, A., Madry, A.: Do adversarially robust ImageNet models transfer better? In: NeurIPS (2020)

48. Scalbert, M., Vakalopoulou, M., Couzini'e-Devy, F.: Multi-source domain adaptation via supervised contrastive learning and confident consistency regularization. In: BMVC (2021)

49. Sivaprasad, P.T., Fleuret, F.: Uncertainty reduction for model adaptation in semantic segmentation. In: CVPR (2021)

50. Sun, B., Saenko, K.: Deep CORAL: correlation alignment for deep domain adaptation. In: Hua, G., Jégou, H. (eds.) ECCV 2016. LNCS, vol. 9915, pp. 443–450. Springer, Cham (2016). https://doi.org/10.1007/978-3-319-49409-8_35

51. Sun, Y., Tzeng, E., Darrell, T., Efros, A.A.: Unsupervised domain adaptation through self-supervision. arXiv preprint arXiv:1909.11825 (2019)

52. Tang, H., Chen, K., Jia, K.: Unsupervised domain adaptation via structurally regularized deep clustering. In: CVPR (2020)

53. Venkat, N., Kundu, J.N., Singh, D.K., Revanur, A., Babu, R.V.: Your classifier can secretly suffice multi-source domain adaptation. In: NeurIPS (2020)

54. Venkateswara, H., Eusebio, J., Chakraborty, S., Panchanathan, S.: Deep hashing network for unsupervised domain adaptation. In: CVPR (2017)

55. Wallace, B., Hariharan, B.: Extending and analyzing self-supervised learning across domains. In: Vedaldi, A., Bischof, H., Brox, T., Frahm, J.-M. (eds.) ECCV 2020. LNCS, vol. 12371, pp. 717–734. Springer, Cham (2020). https://doi.org/10.1007/ 978-3-030-58574-7_43

56. Wang, X., Peng, Y., Lu, L., Lu, Z., Bagheri, M., Summers, R.: ChestX-ray8: hospital-scale chest X-ray database and benchmarks on weakly-supervised classification and localization of common thorax diseases. In: CVPR (2017)

57. Wu, Z., Xiong, Y., Yu, S.X., Lin, D.: Unsupervised feature learning via nonparametric instance discrimination. In: CVPR (2018)

58. Xia, H., Zhao, H., Ding, Z.: Adaptive adversarial network for source-free domain adaptation. In: ICCV (2021)

59. Yang, S., Wang, Y., van de Weijer, J., Herranz, L., Jui, S.: Exploiting the intrinsic neighborhood structure for source-free domain adaptation. In: NeurIPS (2021)

60. Yang, S., Wang, Y., van de Weijer, J., Herranz, L., Jui, S.: Generalized source-free domain adaptation. In: ICCV (2021)

61. You, K., Long, M., Cao, Z., Wang, J., Jordan, M.I.: Universal domain adaptation. In: CVPR (2019)

62. Zhang, R., Isola, P., Efros, A.A.: Colorful image colorization. In: Leibe, B., Matas, J., Sebe, N., Welling, M. (eds.) ECCV 2016. LNCS, vol. 9907, pp. 649–666. Springer, Cham (2016). https://doi.org/10.1007/978-3-319-46487-9_40

63. Zhang, R., Isola, P., Efros, A.A.: Split-brain autoencoders: unsupervised learning by cross-channel prediction. In: CVPR (2017)

64. Zhao, H., Combes, R.T.D., Zhang, K., Gordon, G.: On learning invariant representations for domain adaptation. In: ICML (2019)

Weakly Supervised Object Localization Through Inter-class Feature Similarity and Intra-class Appearance Consistency

Jun Wei[1,2,3], Sheng Wang[6], S. Kevin Zhou[1,4,5], Shuguang Cui[1,2,3], and Zhen Li[1,2,3(✉)]

[1] The Future Network of Intelligence Institute, School of Science and Engineering, Shenzhen Research Institute of Big Data, The Chinese University of Hong Kong (Shenzhen), Shenzhen, China
junwei@link.cuhk.edu.cn, lizhen@cuhk.edu.cn
[2] Shenzhen Research Institute of Big Data, Shenzhen, China
[3] The Future Network of Intelligence Institute, Shenzhen, China
[4] School of Biomedical Engineering and Suzhou Institute for Advanced Research, University of Science and Technology of China, Suzhou, China
[5] Institute of Computing Technology, Chinese Academy of Sciences, Beijing, China
[6] Shanghai Key Laboratory of Metabolic Remodeling and Health, Institute of Metabolism and Integrative Biology, Fudan University, Shanghai, China

Abstract. Weakly supervised object localization (WSOL) aims at detecting objects through only image-level labels. Class activation maps (CAMs) are the commonly used features for WSOL. However, existing CAM-based methods tend to excessively pursue discriminative features for object recognition and hence ignore the feature similarities among different categories, thereby leading to CAMs incomplete for object localization. In addition, CAMs are sensitive to background noise due to over-dependence on the holistic classification. In this paper, we propose a simple but effective WSOL model (named **ISIC**) through Inter-class feature **S**imilarity and **I**ntra-class appearance **C**onsistency. In practice, our ISIC model first proposes the inter-class feature similarity (ICFS) loss against the original cross entropy loss. Such an ICFS loss sufficiently leverages the shared features together with the discriminative features between different categories, which significantly reduces the model over-fitting risk to background noise and brings more complete object masks. Besides, instead of CAMs, a non-negative matrix factorization mask module is applied to extract object masks from multiple intra-class images. Thanks to intra-class appearance consistency, the achieved pseudo masks are more complete and robust. As a result, extensive experiments confirm that our ISIC model achieves state-of-the-art on both CUB-200 and ImageNet-1K benchmarks *i.e.*, **97.3%** and **70.0%** GT-Known localization accuracy, respectively.

Keywords: Weak supervision · Object localization · Inter-class similarity

© The Author(s), under exclusive license to Springer Nature Switzerland AG 2022
S. Avidan et al. (Eds.): ECCV 2022, LNCS 13690, pp. 195–210, 2022.
https://doi.org/10.1007/978-3-031-20056-4_12

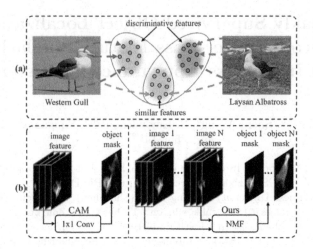

Fig. 1. (a) Visualization of discriminative (eye, beak and foot) and similar (body and feather) features between two categories. (b) The comparison between the CAM-based method and non-negative matrix factorization (NMF)-based one. NMF utilizes features of multiple images of the same category to assist the object mask prediction, while CAM performs on the single image features and highly relies on the classification layer.

1   Introduction

Thanks to the breakthrough of deep learning, recent years have witnessed great progress in object detection [7]. However, training a high-performance object detector requires massive bounding box annotations. These annotations are expensive and sometimes unavailable. To alleviate the model's thirst for annotations, weakly-supervised object localization (WSOL) has gained lots of attentions [1–4,9,12,15,16,24,27,28,31,32,34,35] as it aims at predicting objects' bounding boxes through cheap image-level annotations. Therefore, it largely reduces the annotation cost and is of great practical significance. Previous WSOL methods mainly rely on the class activation maps (CAMs) [35]. However, CAMs tend to cover only small discriminative regions of an object, causing incomplete predictions. Hence, lots of approaches have been proposed to improve CAMs, such as erasing based methods [3,14,19,26,32], feature refining based methods [4,16,24,27,29] and regression based methods [6,12,31]. All these methods have achieved remarkable localization performance. However, these methods mostly are based on classification models, whose goals are inconsistent with object localization due to the following two defects.

First, the similarity between classes has been ignored. Previous classification models [8,18,20] usually adopt cross entropy loss for model training, thus finding the discriminative features of each category. However, for WSOL, focusing too much on differences between images will lead to incomplete predictions. Because images from different categories might share highly similar features. Forcing the model to distinguish between them causes the model to focus only on the most

ignored channel

noise channel

redundant channel

input image

CAM prediction

our prediction

(a) feature maps   (b) input & output

Fig. 2. Visualization of feature maps and predictions. (a) shows some feature maps before the classification layer, where red rectangle in the first row shows the unused features by CAM. (b) compares the predictions between CAM and our model. (Color figure online)

discriminative object regions. To better elaborate this statement, we present an illustrative example in Fig. 1(a). Two images come from different categories and each of them could be regarded as a bag of features, such as beak, eye, body, feather and foot. Among these two images, beak, eye and foot show different colors or shapes, as shown in blue and red areas. These features are usually regarded as the discriminative features and will be extracted to assist the classification model in making decisions. However, there also exist some similar features in the two images, namely body and feather, as shown in the green area. Overemphasizing the differences between images results in these similar features being ignored, which leads to incomplete predictions for WSOL. Besides, due to the classification supervision, even though there are no discriminative features in the image, the model still is forced to learn the differences between images, thus overfitting to the background noise.

Second, as shown in Fig. 1(b), the generation of CAMs is highly dependent on the final classifier (*i.e.*, the last fully connected layer), suffering from false positives (*i.e.*, noise) and false negatives (*i.e.*, content missing) in the final predictions. Because CAM-based methods [32,35] generally adopt parameters of the classification layer as the coefficients to combine feature maps for final prediction. However, these parameters are optimized for classification, where only the most discriminative feature maps are selected out for combination and the rest maps are ignored. But we argue that those overlooked feature maps actually contain helpful information for WSOL. To explain it, we visualize some feature maps extracted from the CAM-based model, as shown in Fig. 2. The body region (red rectangle) of the bird has been activated in feature maps. But in the final prediction, the body region is ignored and only the head region stands out. Namely, CAM-based methods could not make full use of the extracted feature maps. Besides, CAMs are generated based on a single image, which is not robust to background noise. As shown in the blue rectangle in Fig. 2, many background areas are also activated, which interferes with the model's predictions.

To address the above concerns, we propose the Inter-class feature similarity and Intra-class appearance Consistency (named ISIC) model, which improves WSOL from two aspects: supervision and object mask generation. For supervision, we introduce the inter-class feature similarity (ICFS) loss to supplement the widely used cross entropy (CE) loss. In practice, CE loss focuses on the discriminative features of each category (*i.e.*, red and blue areas in Fig. 1(a)), and ICFS loss focuses on the similarities between different categories (green area in Fig. 1(a)). These two losses work against each other and eventually reach an equilibrium. Therefore, ISIC can better balance the localization task and the classification task and is not easy to overfit to the background noise, resulting in more complete predictions.

For object mask generation, instead of relying on the classification layer, we apply the non-negative matrix factorization module (NMFM) to obtain the object mask. NMFM is based on features of multiple images from the same category, which achieves the object mask by extracting the commonness of these images, as shown in Fig. 1(b). Compared with previous methods, NMFM does not rely on the high-level classification layer, so it will not ignore the body region in Fig. 2 and fully exploit all the feature maps. Besides, NMFM is based on multiple images, which is more robust to background noise than that based on a single image. After getting the predicted mask, we follow [24] to train a class-agnostic segmentation model to get the final mask and apply a bounding box extractor to obtain the final object localization. In summary, our contributions fall into three parts:

– Opposite to classification, we propose the ICFS loss to constrain and maintain the similarity between classes. Such ICFS loss can largely reduce the model risk of over-optimizing the discriminative features, thus more complete regions of the object can be activated.
– We propose to replace the original CAMs with non-negative matrix factorization for object mask generation, which avoids the over-discriminative effect of the classification layer and the background noise.
– With negligible computational cost overheads, our proposed methods achieve consistent and substantial gains, *i.e.*, state-of-the-art on both CUB-200–2011 and ImageNet-1K benchmarks for WSOL.

2   Related Works

2.1   Class Activation Maps (CAMs) Based WSOL

Weakly supervised object localization (WSOL) is a challenging task, aiming to localize objects with inexpensive image-level annotations. Zhou *et al.* [35] firstly propose the class activation maps (CAMs) to extract the object location. But restricted by the classification mechanism, CAMs only cover the discriminative object parts. To make CAMs complete, HaS [19] proposes the random erasure of image patches to force the model to mine more object regions. ACoL [32], ADL [3], EIL [14] and AE [26] follow the erasure paradigm and drop the most discriminative features to reduce the model's dependency on them. CutMix [30] assembles patches from different images to guide model to learn more object parts. These methods greatly improve the quality of CAMs, but have the risk of spreading to the background regions when discriminative features are insufficient.

2.2 Pseudo Label Based WSOL

[6,12,31] take object localization as a regression task. Specifically, GCNet [12] utilizes a detector to regress the object bounding box, and produces the object mask by a generator to maximize the score of the classifier. But the indirect supervision brings unstable predictions. Inspired by GCNet, SLTNet [6] supervises the regressor to learn through the pseudo bounding box generated by a newly designed locator. On the contrary, PSOL [31] divides WSOL into two separate tasks, classification and localization. It applies DDT [25] to produce pseudo bounding boxes from the pre-trained model, which are exploited afterward to train a detector. However, these pseudo labels come from the pre-trained model, which are inexact and lower the upper limit of the detector. Different from pseudo bounding box label, SPOL [24] proposes to generate the pseudo mask to train a lass-agnostic segmentation model and achieves higher performance.

2.3 Attention Based WSOL

SPG [33] adopts a stage-wise manner to refine object mask, which regards high confident object regions as the foreground seeds and uses the self-produced guidance maps to progressively expand these seeds. SPOL [24] focuses on shallow features and proposes a multiplication feature fusion to combine the complementary features of different layers. To capture the long-range feature dependency, TS-CAM [4] proposes to generate the token semantic coupled attention map by visual transformer [22], which extracts both semantics and positioning information. Similarly, SPA [16] proposes the self-correlation to capture long-range structural information of objects. All these methods have achieved great progress in WSOL. However, the similarity between categories has been ignored. In this paper, we explicitly use inter-class similarity to boost WSOL performance.

3 Methodology

3.1 Pipeline

Figure 3 depicts the pipeline of our proposed ISIC model, which consists of two stages (*i.e.*, object mask generation and class-agnostic segmentation). During training, both stages are involved, where the object mask generation stage is used to generate pseudo masks for the input images, and the class-agnostic segmentation stage adopts these pseudo masks as labels to train a binary (*i.e.*, object or no-object) segmentation model. But during inference, only the class-agnostic segmentation stage is involved, where we directly derive the segmentation mask

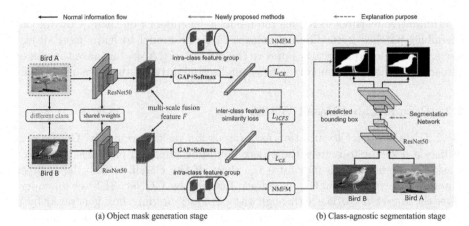

(a) Object mask generation stage   (b) Class-agnostic segmentation stage

Fig. 3. Pipeline for the proposed ISIC model. In the object mask generation stage, to improve the similarity between different categories, inter-class feature similarity loss $\mathcal{L}_{ICFS}$ is applied. Besides, based on non-negative matrix factorization, we design NMFM module to generate the object masks instead of CAM, which flows into the subsequent segmentation stage as the pseudo labels. After training, a class-agnostic segmentation model is achieved, which is adopted as the final model to predict the object bounding boxes during inference.

for each input image and extract the object bounding box from the mask. This decoupled design brings three benefits. First, the complex design (*i.e.*, ICFS and NMFM) in object mask generation will not be brought into the inference phase. Hence, the time complexity of the model depends entirely on the segmentation network and is not affected by ICFS or NMFM. Second, unlike the CAM-based methods, which deal with the classification task and the location task at once, our class-agnostic segmentation model focuses only on localization and is not disturbed by the classification task, thus it can derive more complete object regions. Third, the bounding box extraction from a segmentation mask is much easier and less sensitive to the threshold selection than from a class activation map, because values in the segmentation mask are more consistent (tending to 0 or 1), compared with the class activation map. After getting the bounding box, we follow SPOL [24] to use a separate classification network(SPOL adopts the EfficientNet-B7 [21]) to predict the category of the input image. Combining the bounding box and the category, we derive the final results. In fact, this step of obtaining the object category can be omitted, if we focus only on object localization without category information.

3.2   Baseline

As shown in the left part of Fig. 3, our proposed methods (*i.e.*, ICFS and NMFM) are concentrated in the object mask generation stage, which aims to improve the accuracy of the pseudo masks. Before introducing the specific methods, let's

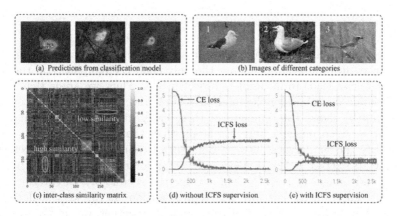

Fig. 4. (a) visualizes incomplete predictions of CAM-based models. (b) shows images from three categories. Obviously, the appearance similarity between image 1 and 2 is larger than that between image 1 and 3. (c) shows the inter-class similarity matrix, where the horizontal and vertical axes both represent the category index. The bright areas (*i.e.*, blue circle) and dark areas (*i.e.*, green circle) indicate the high similarity and low similarity between categories, respectively. (d) shows the loss curve of cross-entropy (CE), where ICFS loss is not adopted as the supervision. (e) shows that ICFS loss is adopted as the supervision.

first introduce the baseline model that we used. Our model is based SPOL [24], which combines the complementarity of deep and shallow features and designs the multiplication fusion strategy to improve the completeness of the object regions. Specifically, SPOL adopts the ResNet50 [8] as the backbone network. For each input image with the size $H \times W$, SPOL extracts its features at five scales (denoted as $\{f_i | i = 1, ..., 5\}$) with the resolutions $[\frac{H}{2^i}, \frac{W}{2^i}]$. Considering the calculation cost, SPOL only uses the last three scale features (*i.e.*, f_3, f_4 and f_5). These features are firstly upsampled to the same scale $[\frac{H}{8}, \frac{W}{8}]$ and then aggregated by element-wise multiplication. In this way, the details of the shallow features and the semantics of the deep features are combined, both of which are helpful for WSOL. We call these aggregated features as the multi-scale fusion features, as shown in Fig. 3. More than that, SPOL also introduces the Gaussian prior pseudo label, self-distillation and auxiliary loss to further enhance the WSOL model. Readers can refer to the specific paper [24] for more details. But to keep the model simple, only the most effective multiplication strategy is involved in our baseline model and the other parts are directly ignored.

3.3 Inter-class and Intra-class Features Analysis

For WSOL, most of previous methods [1,24,32,35] rely on classification models to predict the object masks and then obtain the bounding boxes. Unfortunately, limited by classification models, these masks only cover the most discriminative object regions while other less discriminative ones are ignored. As shown in Fig. 4(a), only the head regions of the birds are highlighted but the body parts are ignored. Because classification models focus only on the differences (*i.e.*, head parts) between classes. To maximize the classification accuracy, features that have the similar appearance (*i.e.*, body parts) will be discarded. But for WSOL, classification accuracy is not the only goal. Overemphasis on the inter-class differences leads to incomplete object masks. Thus, we argue that WSOL models should also consider the inter-class similarity.

Figure 4(b) shows three images of three categories. From appearance, the similarity between image 1 and 2 is larger than that between image 1 and 3. To quantify the similarities between different categories, we use the pretrained ResNet50 to extract a 128 dimensional vector for each image in both CUB-200 [23] and ImageNet-1k [17], then average the vectors of i-th category as its class representation c_i. For any two representations c_i, c_j, we calculate their cosine similarity $s_{ij} = \frac{c_i c_j}{||c_i||_2 ||c_j||_2}$. Bringing all s_{ij} together, we get the similarity matrix S. As shown in Fig. 4(c), S is not evenly distributed. The highlighted areas (*e.g.*, blue circle) show the high similarity between categories and the dark areas (*e.g.*, green circle) show the low similarity between categories. However, previous methods ignore the inter-class similarity, thus leading to incomplete predictions.

3.4 Inter-class Similarity Feature Loss

To address the above concerns, we propose the inter-class feature similarity (ICFS) loss, which aims at reducing the feature distance between similar categories. Specifically, we first derive the representation c_i for i-th category according to Sect. 3.3 and then find the similar categories of c_i by $M_i = \{j \mid S_{ij} > \gamma\}$, where i and j are the category indexes, γ is a threshold, M_i is the index collection of categories that similar to c_i and S is the inter-class similarity matrix, as shown in Fig. 4(c). Finally, we could define the distance $\mathcal{D}_i$ between c_i and $c_j (j \in M_i)$ and derive ICFS loss $\mathcal{L}_{\text{ICFS}}$ by Eq. 1

$$\mathcal{D}_i = \frac{1}{N_i} \sum_{j \in M_i} ||c_i - c_j||_2^2, \quad \mathcal{L}_{\text{ICFS}} = \frac{1}{N_k} \sum_{i=1}^{N_k} \mathcal{D}_i \tag{1}$$

where N_i is element number of M_i and N_k is the total number of categories. The challenge is how to get the representation c for each category during training. The naive way is feeding the entire training set into the model at each iteration and calculate the class representation for each category, which is totally unacceptable due to the high cost of computation and storage. Alternatively, we regard c_i, c_j as the expectations of the image vectors of i-th and j-th categories, respectively.

$$c_i = E[X_i], \quad c_j = E[X_j] \tag{2}$$

where $E[\cdot]$ is the expectation and X_i, X_j are the image vectors corresponding to i-th and j-th categories, respectively. Hence, we derive the upper bound of $\mathcal{D}_i$.

$$\mathcal{D}_i = \frac{1}{N_i} \sum_{j \in M_i} ||E[X_i] - E[X_j]||_2^2 \leq \frac{1}{N_i} \sum_{j \in M_i} E||X_i - X_j||_2^2 \tag{3}$$

In Eq. 4, we use Monte Carlo sampling to approximate the upper bound, where i and j are the category indexes. p and q are the sample indexes. x_i^p and x_j^q are specific vectors. N_{ip} and N_{iq} are the numbers of x_i^p and x_j^q, respectively.

$$\mathcal{D}_i \le \mathcal{U}_i = \frac{1}{N_i N_{ip} N_{iq}} \sum_{j \in M_i} \sum_{p=1}^{N_{ip}} \sum_{q=1}^{N_{iq}} ||x_i^p - x_j^q||_2^2 \tag{4}$$

Finally, we replace $\mathcal{D}_i$ with its upper bound $\mathcal{U}_i$ in $\mathcal{L}_{\text{ICFS}}$ and get Eq. 5.

$$\mathcal{L}_{\text{ICFS}} = \frac{1}{N_k} \sum_{i=1}^{N_k} \frac{1}{N_i N_{ip} N_{iq}} \sum_{j \in M_i} \sum_{p=1}^{N_{ip}} \sum_{q=1}^{N_{iq}} ||x_i^p - x_j^q||_2^2 \tag{5}$$

The total training loss consists of cross-entropy loss (*i.e.*, $\mathcal{L}_{\text{CE}}$) and $\mathcal{L}_{\text{ICFS}}$, as shown in Eq. 6, where λ is a hyper-parameter. $\mathcal{L}_{\text{CE}}$ supervises the model to learn the discriminative features between categories. In contrast, $\mathcal{L}_{\text{ICFS}}$ forces the model to learn the similarities between categories. These two losses work against each other so that the model will not go to extremes and eventually reach an equilibrium. Figure 4(d) shows the loss curves for $\mathcal{L}_{\text{CE}}$ and $\mathcal{L}_{\text{ICFS}}$ when $\lambda = 0$ in CUB-200. The model minimizes the $\mathcal{L}_{\text{CE}}$ as much as possible, and the inter-class difference gradually becomes large. However, when $\lambda = 1$, as shown in Fig. 4(e), inter-class difference is constrained and the model does not go to extremes for classification, thus could get more complete predictions. Note that, ICFS loss aims at improving the integrity of pseudo masks and does not care about the classification performance. Following SPOL [24], a separate classification model is adopted to predict the object category.

$$\mathcal{L}_{\text{total}} = \mathcal{L}_{\text{CE}} + \lambda \mathcal{L}_{\text{ICFS}} \tag{6}$$

3.5 Intra-class Appearance Consistency

Most of the previous WSOL methods obtain the object mask based on class activation maps, where the parameters of the classifier play an important role. Specifically, given a group of feature maps $\{F_1, F_2, ..., F_N\}$ (extracted before the classifier) with spatial size $W \times H$ and the parameters L of the final classifier with shape $N \times C$, where N and C is the number of maps and categories, respectively. Then the class activation map M_c for the c-th class is derived as Eq. 7. With a threshold, M_c can be binarized to extract the object bounding box.

$$M_c = \sum_{i=1}^{N} L_{i,c} F_i \tag{7}$$

However, CAM-based methods are flawed in two ways. First, the goals of classification and localization are inconsistent. Directly using the parameters of the final classifier to generate the class activation maps is harmful. As shown in Fig. 2, although the bird's body have been included in the feature maps, the final prediction suffers from the under-utilization of feature maps and get incomplete predictions. Second, for CAM-based methods, each image is processed separately, which is exposed to the risk of accidental noise. Namely, some cluttered background may lead to the prediction failure. In contrast, predictions based on multiple images (Fig. 1(b)) are statistically more robust to noise. By extracting the commonality of multiple images of the same category, accidental risk is reduced and the complementarity between images is fully explored.

Given the above concerns, we propose the non-negative matrix factorization mask (NMFM) module to generate object masks. Different from CAMs [35], NMFM does not rely on the final classifier. Instead, it achieves the object mask based on the appearance consistency of multiple images from the same category. Specifically, NMFM utilizes the non-negative matrix factorization (NMF) to extract the commonalities between images. NMF was first proposed in [10] and has been widely used in face recognition [5], recommender system [13] and data compression [11]. Given a non-negative matrix $V \in R^{m \times n}$, NMF finds two non-negative matrices $P \in R^{m \times c}$ and $Q \in R^{c \times n}$, so that $V \approx PQ$. The specific optimization function is shown in the Eq. 8.

$$\min_{P,Q} \quad f(P,Q) = \frac{1}{2} \sum_{i=1}^{n} \sum_{j=1}^{m} (V_{ij} - (PQ)_{ij})^2 \tag{8}$$

$$\text{subject to} \quad P_{ia} \geq 0, Q_{bj} \geq 0, \quad \forall i, a, b, j$$

Instead of relying on the classifier, we apply NMF to compress the feature maps $F \in R^{W \times H \times N}$ into the object mask $M \in R^{W \times H}$. Namely, we find a project direction vector $S \in R^{N \times 1}$ so that $M = F \cdot S$ (dot production), where S is derived from the statistics of multiple F of the same category rather than the parameters of the classifier. Specifically, we split F into $W \times H$ vectors, each of which has N dimensions. Supposing there are T images in each category, then we could get $T \times W \times H$ vectors. Lining up these vectors together, we get a big matrix $\Theta \in R^{TWH \times N}$. To find the optimal projection direction S, we use NMF to decompose Θ into two small matrices $\theta_1 \in R^{TWH \times 1}$ and $\theta_2 \in R^{1 \times N}$ so that $\Theta \approx \theta_1 \cdot \theta_2$ (dot production), where θ_1 represents the set of vectors reduced in dimension, which is discarded. θ_2 is what we need, which represents the projection direction and combines the commonality of multiple images. Namely, $S = \theta_2^T$. According to $M = F \cdot S$, the object mask could be derived by $M = F \cdot \theta_2^T$.

Compared with CAMs, NMFM does not rely on the classifier, hence making better use of feature maps, as shown in Fig. 2. Besides, NMFM extracts the commonality of a category of images, which is more robust to background noise. Note that, NMFM is not involved in the training or inference phase. It is just applied to generate the pseudo masks after the classification model has been trained. Thus, it is called only once and will not bring any time complexity for the training or inference phase. With these pseudo masks, we train a class-agnostic segmentation model. The final object bounding boxes are extracted from the predictions of the class-agnostic segmentation model rather than the pseudo masks generated by NMFM.

3.6 Class-Agnostic Segmentation Stage

Although NMFM generates accurate object masks, too many modules are involved in the object mask generation stage, which brings a lot of computation and complexity. To make the inference faster and easier, we use the object masks (generated by NMFM) as the pseudo labels to train a separate class-agnostic segmentation model for prediction. Specifically, we use ResNet50 as the backbone network to extract the features of five scales (denoted as $\{f_i | i = 1, ..., 5\}$) for each image. Similar to the baseline model in Sect. 3.2, only features of the last three scales are utilized, namely f_3, f_4, f_5. We upsample these features to the same scale and aggregate them by element-wise multiplication. Finally, we send the aggregated features to a 1×1 convolutional layer to generate the binary object mask, which is supervised by the pseudo labels derived from NMFM. During inference, for each image, we use the segmentation model to get the object mask and the complex object mask generation stage is discarded. Hence, the whole inference process is simple and quick. Besides, compared with the class activation maps, the predictions of the segmentation are already binary. So precise threshold adjustment for bounding box extraction is no longer required.

4 Experiments

4.1 Experimental Setup

Datasets. CUB-200 [23] and ImageNet-1K [17] are adopted for model evaluation, where CUB-200 consists of 200 categories, with 5,994 training images and 5,794 testing images. ImageNet-1K consists of 1000 categories, with 1,281,197 training images and 50,000 testing images. All the training images have only image-level labels, but the testing images have bounding box annotations.

Metrics. Following [3,24,35], three metrics are adopted to quantify the model performance. 1) Top-1 localization (*Top-1 Loc*): top-1 prediction is exactly the right image class and the IoU (Intersection over Union) between the predicted bounding box and the ground truth one is larger than 0.5. 2) Top-5 localization (*Top-5 Loc*): top-5 predictions contain the right image class and the IoU between the predicted bounding box and the ground truth one is larger than 0.5. 3) GT-known localization (*GT-known Loc*): the IoU between the predicted bounding box and the ground truth one is larger than 0.5.

Data Augmentation and Training Settings. During training, we follow previous methods [3,24,31,32,35] to first resize each input image to 256×256 then randomly crop it to 224×224. Also, a random flip is adopted to increase the diversity of input images. During inference, the random cropping is replaced by the center cropping and the random flip is removed [3,31]. We use the SGD optimizer to train our model, where the learning rates for both CUB-200 [23] and ImageNet-1K [17] are 0.02 and remain constant throughout the training process. Besides, due to the difference in dataset size, the training epochs for CUB-200 and ImageNet-1K are set to 32 and 5, respectively.

Table 1. Performance comparison between the state-of-the-art methods. '–' means no given. The highest scores are highlighted in bold.

Model	Backbone	CUB-200			ImageNet-1K		
		Top-1 Loc	Top-5 Loc	GT-known	Top-1 Loc	Top-5 Loc	GT-known
CAM [35]	VGG16	36.13	–	–	42.80	54.86	59.00
ACoL [32]	VGG16	45.92	56.51	62.96	45.83	59.43	62.96
SPG [33]	InceptionV3	46.64	57.72	–	48.60	60.00	64.69
ADL [3]	VGG16	52.36	–	73.96	44.92	–	–
I^2C [34]	InceptionV3	65.99	68.34	72.60	53.11	64.13	68.50
GC-Net [12]	InceptionV3	58.58	71.10	75.30	49.06	58.09	–
PSOL [31]	InceptionV3	65.51	83.44	–	54.82	63.25	65.21
SPA [16]	VGG16	60.27	72.5	77.29	49.56	61.32	65.05
ORNet [27]	VGG16	67.74	80.77	86.2	52.05	63.94	68.27
TS-CAM [4]	Deit-S	71.3	83.8	87.7	53.4	64.3	67.6
RCAM [1]	ResNet50-SE	58.39	–	74.51	51.96	–	64.40
ADL [3]	ResNet50-SE	62.29	–	71.99	48.53	–	–
SPOL [24]	ResNet50	80.12	93.44	96.46	59.14	67.15	69.02
SLT-Net [6]	ResNet50	72.3	–	90.7	56.2	–	68.5
PSOL [31]	ResNet50	70.68	86.64	90.00	53.98	63.08	65.44
FAM [15]	ResNet50	73.74	–	85.73	54.46	–	64.56
ISIC (Ours)	ResNet50	**80.68**	**94.08**	**97.32**	**59.61**	**67.84**	**70.01**

4.2   Comparison with State-of-the-Arts

Quantitative Comparison. To evaluate the performance of the proposed ISIC, we train it both on CUB-200 [23] and ImageNet-1k [17], as shown in Table 1. Many state-of-the-art methods [1,3,4,12,15,16,24,27,31–35] are also included in Table 1 for comparison. The highest scores are highlighted in bold. Among all these methods, ISIC achieves the highest accuracy on both CUB-200 and ImageNet-1K in terms of **Top-1 Loc**, **Top-5 Loc** and **GT-Known Loc** metrics. Especially for **GT-Known Loc** metric, ISIC achieves a pronounced performance boost, demonstrating its superiority in object localization.

Visual Comparison. Figure 5 shows some localization maps for CUB-200 and ImageNet-1k, where the bottom row and the middle row visualize the predictions derived from CAM [35] and our proposed ISIC, respectively. Obviously, compared with CAM, ISIC could cover more complete object regions rather than only focus on the most discriminative ones. Besides, ISIC predictions preserve sharper object boundaries and more detailed shapes.

4.3   Ablation Studies

Ablation Study for Each Component. We use CUB-200 to evaluate each component of the proposed ISIC. As shown in Table 2, ICFS loss largely improve the localization accuracy of the baseline model by 4.9% in the GT-Known Loc metric, surpassing a lot of SOTA methods, which proves the significance of inter-class similarity for WSOL. Compared with the excessive pursuit of inter-class

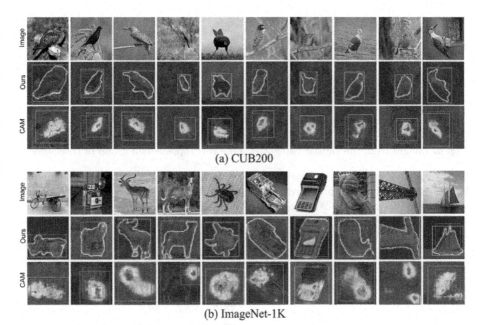

(a) CUB200

(b) ImageNet-1K

Fig. 5. Visualization of the localization maps with CAM [35] (bottom row) and the proposed ISIC (middle row). Ground truth bounding boxes and the predicted bounding boxes are shown in red and green color, respectively. (Color figure online)

difference in classification models, ICFS loss guides the model to a better balance between inter-class similarity and inter-class difference, thus achieving more complete predictions. Besides, NMFM also boosts the model performance by suppressing noise and improving feature utilization. With all components, the object localization capability of ISIC is largely enhanced.

Ablation Study for λ. In Eq. 6, λ is set to balance $\mathcal{L}_{CE}$ and $\mathcal{L}_{ICFS}$. To study its disturbance with the performance, different values are chosen for CUB-200, as shown in Table 3. $\lambda = 0$ means no ICFS supervision. When $\lambda = 1.0$, the model reaches an equilibrium between inter-class similarity and inter-class difference, achieving the best performance. However, when λ keeps increasing, the balance is broken and the model degrades.

Ablation Study for γ. In Sect. 3.4, we set a threshold γ to find the similarity categories. Table 4 shows its effect at different values. When $\gamma = 0.3$, our model achieves the best performance.

Visualization of the similar categories. Figure 6 shows some images of the similar categories (Sect. 3.4). As shown, category similarity is widespread both in the fine-grained dataset (CUB-200) and the general dataset (ImageNet-1k).

Fig. 6. Images from the similar categories. One row represents a group of categories.

Table 2. Ablation studies for each component of ISIC. BASE is the baseline model. ICFS and NMFM are the proposed components of ISIC. SEG means the class-agnostic segmentation model. CUB-200 is adopted for evaluation.

BASE	ICFS	NMFM	SEG	CUB-200		
				Top-1	Top-5	GT-Known
✓				73.0	85.2	88.3
✓	✓			77.3	90.1	93.2
✓		✓		75.7	88.6	91.5
✓	✓	✓		77.4	90.8	94.1
✓	✓	✓	✓	**80.7**	**94.1**	**97.3**

Table 3. Ablation studies for λ.

λ	0	0.5	1.0	1.5
Top-1	73.0	76.5	77.3	75.4
Top-5	85.2	89.2	90.1	89.8
Gt-Known	88.3	92.3	93.2	92.7

Table 4. Ablation studies for γ.

γ	0.2	0.3	0.4	0.5
Top-1	76.9	77.3	76.7	75.6
Top-5	89.7	90.1	89.5	88.7
Gt-Known	92.8	93.2	92.6	91.9

5   Conclusion

In this paper, we investigate the effect of inter-class similarity on WSOL and propose the ICFS loss against the widely used cross entropy loss. Besides, considering predictions from the classifier are biased to classification task, we propose to abandon CAMs and apply the non-negative matrix factorization to generate object masks. All the proposed modules greatly improve the WSOL performance.

Acknowledgement. This work was supported in part by NSFC-Youth 61902335, by the Basic Research Project No. HZQB-KCZYZ-2021067 of Hetao Shenzhen HK S&T Cooperation Zone, by the National Key R&D Program of China with grant No. 2018YFB1800800, by Shenzhen Outstanding Talents Training Fund, by Guangdong Research Project No. 2017ZT07X152 and No. 2019CX01X104, by the Guangdong Provincial Key Laboratory of Future Networks of Intelligence (Grant No. 2022B1212010001), by zelixir biotechnology company Fund, by Tencent Open Fund, and by ITSO at CUHKSZ.

References

1. Bae, W., Noh, J., Kim, G.: Rethinking class activation mapping for weakly supervised object localization. In: Vedaldi, A., Bischof, H., Brox, T., Frahm, J.-M. (eds.) ECCV 2020. LNCS, vol. 12360, pp. 618–634. Springer, Cham (2020). https://doi.org/10.1007/978-3-030-58555-6_37

2. Bai, H., Zhang, R., Wang, J., Wan, X.: Weakly supervised object localization via transformer with implicit spatial calibration. In: ECCV (2022)

3. Choe, J., Shim, H.: Attention-based dropout layer for weakly supervised object localization. In: CVPR, pp. 2219–2228 (2019)

4. Gao, W., et al.: Ts-cam: token semantic coupled attention map for weakly supervised object localization. In: ICCV, pp. 2886–2895 (2021)

5. Guillamet, D., Vitria, J.: Non-negative matrix factorization for face recognition. In: CCAI, pp. 336–344 (2002)

6. Guo, G., Han, J., Wan, F., Zhang, D.: Strengthen learning tolerance for weakly supervised object localization. In: CVPR, pp. 7403–7412 (2021)

7. He, K., Gkioxari, G., Dollar, P., Girshick, R.: Mask r-cnn. In: ICCV, pp. 2961–2969 (2017)

8. He, K., Zhang, X., Ren, S., Sun, J.: Deep residual learning for image recognition. In: CVPR, pp. 770–778 (2016)

9. Kim, J., Choe, J., Yun, S., Kwak, N.: Normalization matters in weakly supervised object localization. In: ICCV, pp. 3427–3436 (2021)

10. Lee, D.D., Seung, H.S.: Learning the parts of objects by non-negative matrix factorization. Nature 401(6755), 788–791 (1999)

11. Liu, W., Zheng, N., Lu, X.: Non-negative matrix factorization for visual coding. In: ICASSP, pp. 111–293 (2003)

12. Lu, W., Jia, X., Xie, W., Shen, L., Zhou, Y., Duan, J.: Geometry constrained weakly supervised object localization. In: Vedaldi, A., Bischof, H., Brox, T., Frahm, J.-M. (eds.) ECCV 2020. LNCS, vol. 12371, pp. 481–496. Springer, Cham (2020). https://doi.org/10.1007/978-3-030-58574-7_29

13. Luo, X., Zhou, M., Xia, Y., Zhu, Q.: An efficient non-negative matrix-factorization-based approach to collaborative filtering for recommender systems, pp. 1273–1284 (2014)

14. Mai, J., Yang, M., Luo, W.: Erasing integrated learning: a simple yet effective approach for weakly supervised object localization. In: CVPR, pp. 8766–8775 (2020)

15. Meng, M., Zhang, T., Tian, Q., Zhang, Y., Wu, F.: Foreground activation maps for weakly supervised object localization. In: ICCV, pp. 3385–3395 (2021)

16. Pan, X., et al.: Unveiling the potential of structure preserving for weakly supervised object localization. In: CVPR, pp. 11642–11651 (2021)

17. Russakovsky, O.: ImageNet large scale visual recognition challenge. IJCV 115(3), 211–252 (2015)

18. Simonyan, K., Zisserman, A.: Very deep convolutional networks for large-scale image recognition. In: ICLR, pp. 1–14 (2015)

19. Singh, K.K., Lee, Y.J.: Hide-and-seek: forcing a network to be meticulous for weakly-supervised object and action localization. In: ICCV, pp. 3544–3553 (2017)

20. Szegedy, C., Vanhoucke, V., Ioffe, S., Shlens, J., Wojna, Z.: Rethinking the Inception architecture for computer vision. In: CVPR, pp. 2818–2826 (2016)

21. Tan, M., Le, Q.: Efficientnet: rethinking model scaling for convolutional neural networks. In: ICML, pp. 6105–6114 (2019)

22. Vaswani, A., et al.: Attention is all you need. In: NIPS, pp. 5998–6008 (2017)

23. Wah, C., Branson, S., Welinder, P., Perona, P., Belongie, S.: The Caltech-UCSD birds-200-2011 dataset. Technical Rep. CNS-TR-2011-001, California Institute of Technology (2011)
24. Wei, J., Wang, Q., Li, Z., Wang, S., Zhou, S.K., Cui, S.: Shallow feature matters for weakly supervised object localization. In: CVPR, pp. 5993–6001 (2021)
25. Wei, X.S., Zhang, C.L., Wu, J., Shen, C., Zhou, Z.H.: Unsupervised object discovery and co-localization by deep descriptor transformation, vol. 88, pp. 113–126 (2019)
26. Wei, Y., Feng, J., Liang, X., Cheng, M.M., Zhao, Y., Yan, S.: Object region mining with adversarial erasing: a simple classification to semantic segmentation approach. In: CVPR, pp. 1568–1576 (2017)
27. Xie, J., Luo, C., Zhu, X., Jin, Z., Lu, W., Shen, L.: Online refinement of low-level feature based activation map for weakly supervised object localization. In: ICCV, pp. 132–141 (2021)
28. Xue, H., Liu, C., Wan, F., Jiao, J., Ji, X., Ye, Q.: Danet: divergent activation for weakly supervised object localization. In: ICCV, pp. 6589–6598 (2019)
29. Yang, S., Kim, Y., Kim, Y., Kim, C.: Combinational class activation maps for weakly supervised object localization. In: WACV, pp. 2941–2949 (2020)
30. Yun, S., Han, D., Oh, S.J., Chun, S., Choe, J., Yoo, Y.: Cutmix: regularization strategy to train strong classifiers with localizable features. In: CVPR, pp. 6023–6032 (2019)
31. Zhang, C.L., Cao, Y.H., Wu, J.: Rethinking the route towards weakly supervised object localization. In: CVPR, pp. 13460–13469 (2020)
32. Zhang, X., Wei, Y., Feng, J., Yang, Y., Huang, T.S.: Adversarial complementary learning for weakly supervised object localization. In: CVPR, pp. 1325–1334 (2018)
33. Zhang, X., Wei, Y., Kang, G., Yang, Y., Huang, T.: Self-produced guidance for weakly-supervised object localization. In: Ferrari, V., Hebert, M., Sminchisescu, C., Weiss, Y. (eds.) ECCV 2018. LNCS, vol. 11216, pp. 610–625. Springer, Cham (2018). https://doi.org/10.1007/978-3-030-01258-8_37
34. Zhang, X., Wei, Y., Yang, Y.: Inter-image communication for weakly supervised localization. In: Vedaldi, A., Bischof, H., Brox, T., Frahm, J.-M. (eds.) ECCV 2020. LNCS, vol. 12364, pp. 271–287. Springer, Cham (2020). https://doi.org/10.1007/978-3-030-58529-7_17
35. Zhou, B., Khosla, A., Lapedriza, A., Oliva, A., Torralba, A.: Learning deep features for discriminative localization. In: CVPR, pp. 2921–2929 (2016)

Active Learning Strategies
for Weakly-Supervised Object Detection

Huy V. Vo[1,2(✉)], Oriane Siméoni[2], Spyros Gidaris[2], Andrei Bursuc[2],
Patrick Pérez[2], and Jean Ponce[1,3]

[1] Inria and DI/ENS (ENS-PSL, CNRS, Inria), Paris, France
{van-huy.vo,jean.ponce}@inria.fr
[2] Valeo.ai, Paris, France
{oriane.simeoni,spyros.gidaris,andrei.bursuc,patrick.perez}@valeo.com
[3] Center for Data Science, New York University, New York, USA

Abstract. Object detectors trained with weak annotations are affordable alternatives to fully-supervised counterparts. However, there is still
a significant performance gap between them. We propose to narrow this
gap by fine-tuning a base pre-trained weakly-supervised detector with
a few fully-annotated samples automatically selected from the training
set using "box-in-box" (BiB), a novel active learning strategy designed
specifically to address the well-documented failure modes of weakly-
supervised detectors. Experiments on the VOC07 and COCO benchmarks show that BiB outperforms other active learning techniques and
significantly improves the base weakly-supervised detector's performance
with only a few fully-annotated images per class. BiB reaches 97% of
the performance of fully-supervised Fast RCNN with only 10% of fully-
annotated images on VOC07. On COCO, using on average 10 fully-
annotated images per class, or equivalently 1% of the training set, BiB
also reduces the performance gap (in AP) between the weakly-supervised
detector and the fully-supervised Fast RCNN by over 70%, showing a
good trade-off between performance and data efficiency. Our code is publicly available at https://github.com/huyvvo/BiB.

Keywords: Object detection · Weakly-supervised · Active learning

1   Introduction

Object detectors are critical components of visual perception systems deployed
in real-world settings such as robotics or surveillance. Many methods have
been developed to build object detectors with high predictive performance [31–
33,36,54] and fast inference [52,53]. They typically train a neural network in
a fully-supervised manner on large datasets annotated manually with bounding boxes [23,24,47]. In practice, the construction of these datasets is a major

Supplementary Information The online version contains supplementary material
available at https://doi.org/10.1007/978-3-031-20056-4_13.

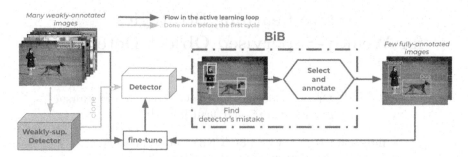

Fig. 1. Overview of our approach. A base object detector is first trained only with image-level tags, then fine-tuned in successive stages using few *well-selected* images that are fully annotated. For their selection, we propose *"box-in-box"* (BiB), an acquisition function designed to discover recurring failure cases of the weakly-supervised detector, e.g., failure to localize whole objects or to separate distinct instances of the same class.

bottleneck since it involves large, expensive and time-consuming data acquisition, selection and annotation campaigns. To address this challenge, much effort has been put in devising object detection approaches trained with less (or even no) human annotation. This includes semi-supervised [39,51,63,76], weakly-supervised [7,15,29,38,55,69,80], few-shot [25,41,43,66], active [1,8,14, 35,58,59] and unsupervised [13,60,62,67,72,74] learning frameworks for object detection.

Weakly-supervised object detection (WSOD) typically only uses image-level category labels during training [7,55,69]. This type of annotation is much cheaper than bounding boxes and, in some cases, it can be even obtained automatically, e.g., leveraging tags on online photos, photo captions in media or time-stamped movie scripts. WSOD is thus an affordable alternative to fully-supervised object detection in terms of annotation cost. However, weakly-supervised detectors often struggle to correctly localize the full extent of objects [55,69]. Several recent works [6,49] show that a good trade-off between performance and annotation cost can be achieved by annotating bounding boxes in a small set of randomly selected training images and by training the detector with a mix of weak and full supervision. However, there are better alternatives to random selection. Active learning (AL) methods [14,79] offer means to *select* images that should be the most helpful for the training of an object detector model, given some criterion.

In this work, we propose to combine both worlds, by augmenting the weakly-supervised framework with an active learning scheme. Our active learning strategy specifically targets the known failure modes of weakly-supervised detectors. We show that it can be used to significantly narrow the gap between weakly-supervised detectors and expensive fully-supervised ones with a few fully-annotated images per class. We start with a weakly-annotated dataset, e.g., a set of images and their class labels, with which we train a weakly-supervised detector. We apply our new active learning strategy that we call *box-in-box* (BiB) to iteratively select from the dataset a few images to be fully annotated. New full annotations are added to the training set and used to fine-tune the detector. Given the fine-tuned detector, we select another batch of images to be fully annotated. This process is repeated several times to improve the detector (Fig. 1). Previous works have attempted to combine weak supervision with active learning, but they all start with an initial set of hundreds to thousands of fully-annotated images. As shown in Sect. 4, our approach only requires a small number of fully-annotated images (50–250 on VOC07 [24] and 160–800 on COCO [47]) to significantly improve the performance of weakly-supervised detectors. Our main contributions are: (1) We propose a new approach to improve weakly-supervised object detectors, by using a few fully-annotated images, carefully selected with the help of active learning. Contrary to typical active learning approaches, we initiate the learning process without any fully-annotated data; (2) We introduce BiB, an active selection strategy that is tailored to address the limitations of weakly-supervised detectors; (3) We validate our proposed approach with extensive experiments on VOC07 and COCO datasets. We show that BiB outperforms other active strategies on both datasets, and reduce significantly the performance gap between weakly- and fully-supervised object detectors.

2   Related Work

Weakly-supervised object detection is a data-efficient alternative to fully-supervised object detection which only requires image-level labels (object categories) for training a detector. It is typically formulated as a multiple instance learning problem [19] where images are bags and region proposals [71,83] are instances. The model is trained to classify images using scores aggregated from their regions, through which it also learns to distinguish *object* from *non-object* regions. Since training involves solving a non-convex optimization problem, adapted initialization and regularization techniques [15,17,44,64,65] are necessary for good performance. Bilen *et al.* [7] proposes WSDDN, a CNN-based model for WSOD which is improved in subsequent works [18,40,55,68,69]. Tang *et al.* [69] proposes OICR which refines WSDDN's output with parallel detector heads in a self-training fashion. Trained with only image-level labels, weakly-supervised object detectors are often confused between object parts and objects, or between objects and groups of objects [55]. Although mitigating efforts with better pseudo labels [55,68], better representation [38,55] or better optimization [3,75] achieve certain successes, such confusion issues of weakly-supervised detectors remain due to the lack of a formal definition of objects and their performance is still far behind that of fully-supervised counterparts. In this work, we show that fine-tuning weakly-supervised detectors with strong annotation on *a few carefully selected* images can alleviate these limitations and significantly narrow the gap between weakly- and fully-supervised object detectors.

Semi-supervised object detection methods exploits a mix of some fully-annotated and many unlabelled-data. Two dominant strategies arise among these methods: consistency-based [39,70] and pseudo-labeling [45,51,63,76,77, 84]. The latter can be further extended with strategies inspired by active learning [45,76] for selecting boxes to be annotated by humans.

Combining weakly- and semi-supervised object detection. These approaches seek a better trade-off between performance and annotation cost than individual strategies. All images from the training set have weak labels and a subset is also annotated with bounding boxes. This setup enables the exploration of the utility of additional types of weak labels, e.g., points [10,56] or scribbles [56]. Others leverage fully-annotated images to train detectors that can correct wrong predictions of weakly-supervised detectors [49] or compute more reliable pseudo-boxes [6]. Similarly to [6,49], we train a detector with only a few annotated images, but different from them, we focus on how to best select the images to annotate towards maximizing the performance of the detector.

Active learning for object detection aims at carefully *selecting* images to be fully annotated by humans, in order to minimize human annotation efforts. Most methods exploit *data diversity* [30,58] or *model uncertainty* [8,14] to identify such images. These strategies, originally designed for generic classification tasks [59], have been recently derived and adapted to object detection [14,79], a complex task involving both classification (object class) and regression (bounding box location). Data diversity can be ensured by selecting data samples using image features and applying k-means [82], k-means++ initialization [35] or identifying a core-set – a *representative* subset of a dataset [1,30,58]. Model uncertainty for AL can be computed from image-level scores aggregated from class predictions over boxes [8,35,50], comparing predictions of the same image from different corrupted versions of it [22,28,42] or from different steps of model training [37,57], voting over predictions from an ensemble of networks [5,12,35], Bayesian Neural Networks [27,35] or single forward networks mimicking an ensemble [14,79]. Multiple other strategies have been proposed for selecting informative, difficult or confusing samples to annotate by: learning to discriminate between labeled and unlabeled data [20,21,34,81], learning to predict the detection loss [78], the gradients [4] or the influence of data on gradient [48]. In contrast to classical active learning methods in which the initial model is trained in a fully-supervised fashion using a randomly sampled initial set of images, our initial model is only trained with weakly-annotated data. This is a challenging problem, but often encountered in practice when new collections of data arrive only with weak annotations and significant effort is required to select which images to annotate manually prior to active learning.

Combining weak supervision and active learning. Closer to us, [16,26,50] investigate how weakly-supervised learning and active learning can be conducted together in the context of object detection. Desai et al. [16] propose to use clicks in the center of the object as weak labels which include localization information and are stronger than image-level tags. Pardo et al. [50] also mix strong supervision, tags and pseudo-labels in an active learning scenario. Both [16,50] rely on Faster R-CNN [26,54] on a FPN [46] – detectors that are hard to train only

---

Algorithm 1: WSOD with Active Learning.

Input: Set $\mathcal{I}$ of weakly-labelled images, set $\mathcal{Q}$ of weak annotations, number of cycles T, budget per cycle B.

Result: Detector M^T, bounding box annotations $\mathcal{G}^T$.

1 $M^0 \leftarrow \texttt{train}(\mathcal{I}, \mathcal{Q})$ ▷ weakly-supervised pre-training

2 **for** $t = 1$ *to* T **do**

3      $A^t \leftarrow \texttt{select}(W^{t-1}, M^{t-1}, \mathcal{I}, \mathcal{Q}, B)$ ▷ select a batch A^t of B images

4      $\mathcal{G}^t \leftarrow \mathcal{G}^{t-1} \cup \texttt{label}(\mathcal{I}, A^t)$ ▷ annotate new selection

5      $S^t \leftarrow S^{t-1} \cup A^t$, $W^t \leftarrow W^{t-1} \setminus A^t$ ▷ update the sets

6      $M^t \leftarrow \texttt{fine-tune}(\mathcal{I}, \mathcal{Q}, \mathcal{G}^t, M^0)$ ▷ fine-tune the model

7 **end**

---

with weak labels. All start with 10% of the dataset fully labeled, which is more than the total amount of fully annotated data we consider in this work.

3 Proposed Approach

3.1 Problem Statement

We assume that we are given n images $\mathcal{I} = \{\mathbf{I}_i\}_{i \in \{1...n\}}$ annotated with labels $\mathcal{Q} = \{\mathbf{q}_i\}_{i \in \{1...n\}}$. Here $\mathbf{q}_i \in \{0,1\}^C$ is the class label of image $\mathbf{I}_i$, with C being the number of classes in the dataset. Let M^0 be a weakly-supervised object detector trained using only $\mathcal{Q}$. The goal of our work is to iteratively select a *very small set of images* to fully annotate with bounding boxes and fine-tune M^0 on the same images with both weak and full annotation so as to maximize its performance. To that end, we propose a novel *active learning* method properly adapted to the aforementioned problem setting.

3.2 Active Learning for Weakly-Supervised Object Detection

As typical in active learning, our approach consists of several cycles in which an acquisition function first uses the available detector to select images that are subsequently annotated by a human with bounding boxes. The model is then updated with this additional data. With the updated detector, a new cycle of acquisition is performed (see Algorithm 1).

Let $W^t \subset \{1, \ldots, n\}$ be the set of indices of images with class labels only, and $S^t \subset \{1, \ldots, n\}$ the set with bounding-box annotations at the t-th active learning cycle. The active learning process starts with $W^0 = \{1, \ldots, n\}$ and $S^0 = \varnothing$. Then, at each cycle $t > 0$, the acquisition function selects from W^{t-1} a set A^t of B images to be annotated with bounding boxes, with B the fixed annotation budget per cycle. By definition, we have that $A^t \subset W^{t-1}$ and $|A^t| = B$. For the selection, the acquisition function exploits the detector M^{t-1} obtained at the end of the previous cycle. After selecting A^t, the sets of fully and weakly-annotated images are updated with $S^t = S^{t-1} \cup A^t$ and $W^t = W^{t-1} \setminus A^t$ respectively. We

Fig. 2. Example of box-in-box (BiB) pairs among the predictions of the weakly-supervised object detector. The existence of such pairs is an indicator of the detector's failure on those images. Best viewed in color.

define as $\mathcal{G}^t = \{\mathbf{G}_i\}_{i \in S^t}$ the bounding-box annotations for images with indices in S^t. Finally, at the end of cycle t, we fine-tune M^0 on the entire dataset, using the bounding box annotations for images with indices in S^t and the original image-level annotations for others.

3.3   BiB: An Active Learning Strategy

With a very small annotation budget, we aim at selecting the "best" training examples to "fix" the mistakes of the base weakly-supervised detector. We propose *BiB*, an acquisition strategy tailored for this purpose. It first *discovers (likely) detection mistakes* of the weakly-supervised detector, and then selects *diverse detection mistakes*. Our selection strategy is summarized in Algorithm 2.

Discovering BiB Patterns. Weakly-supervised detectors often fail to accurately localize the full extent of the objects in an image, and tend to focus instead on the most *discriminative parts* of an object or to group together multiple object instances [55]. Several examples of these errors are shown in Fig. 2. In the first column, a predicted box focuses on the most discriminative part of an object while a bigger one encompasses a much larger portion of the same object. Another recurring mistake is when two or more distinct objects are grouped together in a box, but some correct individual predictions are also provided for the same class (second column). The two kinds of mistakes can also be found in the same image (third column). We name "box-in-box" (BiB) such detection patterns where two boxes are predicted for a same object class, a small one being "contained" (within some tolerance, see below) in a larger one. We take BiB pairs as an indicator of model's confusion on images.

   More formally, let $\mathbf{D}_i$ be the set of boxes detected in image $\mathbf{I}_i$ and let d_A and d_B be two of them. We consider that (d_A, d_B) is a BiB pair, which we denote with

---

Algorithm 2: BiB acquisition strategy.

Result: Set A^t of selected images.
Input: Budget B, model M^{t-1}, image set $\mathcal{I}$, index set W^{t-1} of
         weakly-annotated images, set $\hat{\mathcal{P}}$ of already selected BiB pairs (if empty,
         see text for initialization)

1   **for** $i \in W^{t-1}$ **do**
2      $\mathbf{D}_i \leftarrow \texttt{Detect}(\mathbf{I}_i|M^{t-1})$ ▷ Predict boxes
3      $P_i \leftarrow \{p_{i,j}\}_{j=1}^{|P_i|} = \text{find-bib}(\mathbf{D}_i)$ ▷ Discover BiB patterns
4   **end**
5   # Select diverse detection mistakes
6   $A^t \leftarrow \varnothing$
7   **while** $|A^t| < B$ **do**
8   **for** $p \in \cup_{i \in W^{t-1} \setminus A^t} P_i$ **do**
9         $w_p \leftarrow \min_{\tilde{p} \in \hat{\mathcal{P}}} \|F(p) - F(\tilde{p})\|$ ▷ Comp. dist. to selected pairs
10   **end**
11     $p^* \sim \text{Prob}(\{w_p\}_p)$ ▷ Randomly select a pair
12     $i^* \leftarrow \texttt{get-imid}(p)$ ▷ Get index of the image containing p
13     $\hat{\mathcal{P}} \leftarrow \hat{\mathcal{P}} \cup P_{i^*}, A^t \leftarrow A^t \cup \{i^*\}$ ▷ Updates
14   **end**

---

is-bib$(d_A, d_B) = \texttt{True}$, when: (i) d_A and d_B are predicted for the same class, (ii) d_B is at least μ times larger than d_A (i.e., $\frac{\text{Area}(d_B)}{\text{Area}(d_A)} \geq \mu$), and (iii) the intersection of d_B and d_A over the area of d_A is at least δ (i.e., $\frac{\text{Intersection}(d_A, d_B)}{\text{Area}(d_A)} \geq \delta$). Hence, the set $P_i = \{p_{i,j}\}_{j=1}^{|P_i|}$ of BiB pairs is found in image $\mathbf{I}_i$ by the procedure

$$\text{find-bib}(\mathbf{D}_i) = \{(d_A, d_B) \in \mathbf{D}_i \times \mathbf{D}_i | \text{is-bib}(d_A, d_B)\}. \tag{1}$$

We observe that in such a BiB pair, it is likely that at least one of the boxes is a detection mistake. We thus propose to select images to be fully annotated among those containing BiB pairs.

Selecting Diverse Detection Mistakes. Given the set of all BiB pairs over $\mathcal{I}$, the acquisition function considers the *diversity* of the pairs in order to select images. In particular, we follow *k-means++ initialization* [2] – initially developed to provide a good initialization to k-means clustering by iteratively selecting as centroids data points that lie further away from the current set of selected ones. This initialization has previously been applied onto image features in the context of active learning for object detection [35] or on model's gradients for active learning applied to image classification [4]. Here we focus and apply the algorithm to pairs of detected boxes.

We denote with $\hat{\mathcal{P}}$ the set of BiB pairs from the already selected images. For each pair p not in $\hat{\mathcal{P}}$, we compute the minimum distance w_p to the pairs in $\hat{\mathcal{P}}$: $w_p \leftarrow \min_{\tilde{p} \in \hat{\mathcal{P}}} \|F(p) - F(\tilde{p})\|$, where $F(p)$ is the feature vector of p, i.e., the concatenation of the region features corresponding to the two boxes of p each extracted using the model M^{t-1}. We then randomly pick a new pair p^*, using a weighted probability distribution where a pair p is chosen with probability proportional to w_p. We finally select the image $\mathbf{I}_{i^*}$ that contains p^*, add its index i^* to A^t and its BiB pairs to $\hat{\mathcal{P}}$. Note that at the beginning of the selection process in each cycle, $\hat{\mathcal{P}}$ contains the pairs of images selected in the previous cycles and is empty when the first cycle begins. In the latter case, we start by selecting the image $\mathbf{I}_{i^*}$ that has the greatest number of pairs $|P_{i^*}|$[1] and add the pairs in P_{i^*} to $\hat{\mathcal{P}}$ before starting the selection process above.

With this design, BiB selects a diverse set of images that are representative of the dataset while addressing the known mistakes of the weakly-supervised detector. We show some examples selected by BiB and demonstrate its effectiveness in boosting the performance of the weakly-supervised detector in Sect. 4.

3.4   Training Detectors with both Weak and Strong Supervision

We provide below details about the step of model fine-tuning performed at each cycle. For clarity, we drop the image index i and the cycle index t in this section.

Training with Weak Annotations. We adopt the state-of-the-art weakly-supervised method MIST [55] as our base detector. MIST follows [69] which adapts the detection paradigm of Fast R-CNN [32] to weak annotations. It leverages pre-computed region proposals extracted from unsupervised proposal algorithms, such as Selective Search [71] and EdgeBoxes [83]. In particular, given image $\mathbf{I}$ which has only weak labels q (class labels) and its set of region proposals $\mathcal{R}$, simply called regions, the detection network extracts the image features with a CNN backbone and compute for each region a feature vector using a region-wise pooling [32]. Then, the network head(s) on top of the CNN backbone process the extracted region features in order to predict for each of them the object class and modified box coordinates. To build a detector that can be effectively trained using only image-wise labels, MIST has two learning stages, *coarse detection with multiple instance learning* and *detection refinement with pseudo-boxes*, each implemented with different heads but trained simultaneously in an online fashion [69].

The *Multiple Instance Learner* (MIL) head is trained to minimize the multi-label classification loss $\mathcal{L}^{\mathrm{MIL}}$ using weak labels through which it produces classification scores for all regions in $\mathcal{R}$. MIST selects from them the regions with the highest scores (with non-maximum suppression) as coarse predictions, which we denote with $\mathbf{D}^{(0)}$. Then, such predictions are iteratively refined using K consecutive *refinement heads*. Each refinement head $k \in \{1 \ldots K\}$ predicts for all regions in $\mathcal{R}$ their classification scores for the $C+1$ classes (C object classes plus 1 background class) and box coordinates per object class. The refinement head k is trained by minimizing:

$$\mathcal{L}_w^{(k)}(\mathbf{I}, \mathcal{R}, \mathbf{D}^{(k-1)}) = \mathcal{L}_{\mathrm{cls}}^{(k)}(\mathbf{I}, \mathcal{R}, \mathbf{D}^{(k-1)}) + \mathcal{L}_{\mathrm{reg}}^{(k)}(\mathbf{I}, \mathcal{R}, \mathbf{D}^{(k-1)}), \qquad (2)$$

---

[1] In case of a draw, an image is randomly selected.

which combines an adapted instance classification loss, $\mathcal{L}_{cls}^{(k)}$, and the box regression loss $\mathcal{L}_{reg}^{(k)}$ of Fast R-CNN [32], using as targets the pseudo-boxes $\mathbf{D}^{(k-1)}$ generated by MIST from the region scores of the previous head. The final loss for image $\mathbf{I}$ is:

$$\mathcal{L}_w = \mathcal{L}^{\mathrm{MIL}}(\mathbf{I}, \mathcal{R}, \mathbf{q}) + \sum_{k=1}^{K} \mathcal{L}_w^{(k)}(\mathbf{I}, \mathcal{R}, \mathbf{D}^{(k-1)}). \tag{3}$$

For more details about MIST, please refer to the appendix and [55].

Adding Strong Annotations. In our proposed approach, we obtain ground-truth bounding boxes for *very few* images in the set $\mathcal{I}$. In order to integrate such strong annotations to the weakly-supervised framework, we simply replace the pseudo-annotations in Eq. 2 with box annotations $\mathbf{G}$, now supposed available for image $\mathbf{I}$. The resulting loss for the refinement head k reads $\mathcal{L}_s^{(k)}(\mathbf{I}, \mathcal{R}, \mathbf{G}) = \mathcal{L}_{cls}^{(k)}(\mathbf{I}, \mathcal{R}, \mathbf{G}) + \mathcal{L}_{reg}^{(k)}(\mathbf{I}, \mathcal{R}, \mathbf{G})$, and the final loss on image $\mathbf{I}$ in this case is $\mathcal{L}_s = \mathcal{L}^{\mathrm{MIL}}(\mathbf{I}, \mathcal{R}, \mathbf{q}) + \sum_{k=1}^{K} \mathcal{L}_s^{(k)}(\mathbf{I}, \mathcal{R}, \mathbf{G})$. As such, during the fine-tuning of the detector M^0, we use $\mathcal{L}_w$ to train on images for which only class labels are available and $\mathcal{L}_s$ when images are provided with bounding-boxes.

Difficulty-Aware Proposal Sampling. In this framework, we use thousands of pre-computed proposals in $\mathcal{R}$ for each image. This is necessary when no box annotations are provided. However, when ground-truth boxes are available, better training can be achieved by sampling a smaller number of proposals [32,56]. In particular, we select a subset of 512 proposals with 25% of *positive* boxes, i.e., those whose IoU with one of the ground-truth boxes exceeds 0.5, and 75% of *negative* boxes, i.e., those whose IoU ≤ 0.3 with all ground-truth boxes. However, we have noticed that negatives are over-sampled from the background or often appear uninformative. We propose to improve negative proposal sampling by using the network predictions to select those classified as objects. We perform a first forward pass and average classification scores obtained over the K refinement heads; we then apply row-wise softmax and select proposals with the highest class scores, excluding background. We show in our experiments that this sampling method allows better training and yields better performance.

4   Experimental Results

In this section, we first introduce the general setup of our experiments. We then present an ablation study of different components of BiB before comparing BiB to different existing active learning strategies. Finally, we demonstrate the effectiveness of our proposed pipeline compared to the state of the art.

4.1   Experimental Setup

Datasets and Evaluation. We evaluate our method on two well-known object detection datasets, Pascal VOC2007 [24] (noted VOC07) and COCO2014 [47] (COCO). Following previous works [6,55], we use the *trainval* split of VOC07 for training and the *test* split for evaluation, respectively containing 5011 and 4952 images. On COCO, we train detectors with the *train* split (82783 images) and evaluate on the *validation* split (40504 images) following [6]. We use the average precision metrics AP50 and AP, computed respectively with an IoU threshold of 0.5 and with thresholds in [0.5 : 0.95]. We report results corresponding to N-shot experiments – where $N \times C$ images are selected – and $N\%$ experiments, where about N percents of the training set are selected to be fully-annotated.

Architecture. Though BiB can be applied on any weakly-supervised detector, we use MIST [55] as our base weakly-supervised detector for it has public code and has been shown to be a strong baseline. We modify MIST to account for images containing bounding box annotations during training as detailed in Sect. 3.4. The Concrete Drop Block (CDB) [55] technique is used in MIST in experiments on VOC07 but dropped in COCO experiments to save computational cost. We use our difficulty-aware proposal sampling in all experiments unless stated otherwise. We train with a batch size of 8 during training and a learning rate of 4e−4 for MIST and 4e−6 for CDB when the latter is used. During training, images are drawn from the sets of images with weak and strong annotation uniformly at random such that the numbers of weakly- and fully-annotated images considered are asymptotically equal.

Active Learning Setup. We emulate an active learning setup by ignoring available bounding box annotations of images considered weakly annotated in our experiments. On both dataset, we run MIST [55] three times to account for the training's instability and obtain three base weakly-supervised detectors. We fine-tune each base weakly-supervised detector twice on VOC07 and once on COCO, giving respectively 6 and 3 repetitions. We always report averaged results, and in some cases also their standard deviation. Detailed results for all experiments are provided in supplemental material. The number of fine-tuning iterations is scaled linearly with the number of strong images in the experiment. Concretely, the base weakly-supervised detector is fine-tuned over 300 iterations for every 50 strong images in VOC07 and 1200 iterations for every 160 images on COCO.

Active Learning Baselines. We compare BiB to existing active learning strategies. We first compare our method to random selections, either uniform sampling (*u-random*) or balanced per class sampling (*b-random*). We compare to uncertainty-based selection and aggregate box entropy scores per image using sum or max pooling, noted *entropy-sum* and *entropy-max* respectively. Finally, we leverage weak detection losses to select high impact images (*loss*). We report here results obtained with the detection loss of the last refinement branch in MIST, which we find outperforms others losses; a detailed comparison can be found in supplemental material along with a complete description of other methods. We also use the greedy version of the *core-set* selection method [58]; and a weighted version that weights distances in core-set with uncertainty scores (entropy-max) [35], named *coreset-ent*. For our BiB, we set $\mu = 3$ and $\delta = 0.8$, and provide a study on their influence in the supplemental material.

4.2   Ablation Studies

We perform in Table 1 an ablation study to understand the relative importance of the difficulty-aware proposal sampling (*DifS*), the selection based on k-means++ initialization and the use of box-in-box pairs in our method. The second row corresponds to *u-random*. We apply the diversity selection (e.g., following k-means++ initialization) on image-level features, predictions, and BiB pairs. The experiments are conducted on VOC07 and for each variant of our method, we perform five active learning cycles with a budget of 50 images per cycle. It appears that *DifS* significantly improves results over both random and BiB, confirming that targeting the model's most confusing regions is helpful. K-means++ initialization does not help when applied on image-level features but yields significant performance boosts over random when combined with region-level features. Finally, the use of BiB pairs shows consistent improvements over *region*, confirming our choices in BiB's design.

Table 1. Ablation study. Results in AP50 on VOC07 with 5 cycles and a budget $B = 50$. We provide averages and standard deviation results over 6 repetitions. *DifS* stands for the difficulty-aware region sampling module. Images are selected by applying k-means++ init. (*K selection*) on image-level features (*im.*), confident predictions' features (*reg.*) or BiB pairs.

DifS	K selection			Number of images annotated				
	im	reg	BiB	50	100	150	200	250
				56.3 ± 0.4	58.0 ± 0.5	58.9 ± 0.4	60.0 ± 0.3	60.5 ± 0.4
✓				56.5 ± 0.4	58.4 ± 0.4	59.3 ± 0.7	60.2 ± 0.4	61.1 ± 0.5
✓	✓			57.1 ± 0.4	58.3 ± 0.5	59.3 ± 0.6	59.8 ± 0.4	60.3 ± 0.4
✓		✓		**58.4** ± 0.4	60.2 ± 0.4	61.5 ± 0.6	62.6 ± 0.4	**63.4** ± 0.3
			✓	57.9 ± 0.7	60.1 ± 0.4	61.2 ± 0.5	62.1 ± 0.5	62.6 ± 0.4
✓			✓	**58.5** ± 0.8	**60.8** ± 0.5	**61.9** ± 0.4	**62.9** ± 0.5	**63.5** ± 0.4

4.3   Comparison of Active Strategies

In order to compare BiB to baselines, we conduct 5 active learning cycles with a budget of $B = 50$ images (1% of the training set) per cycle on VOC07 and

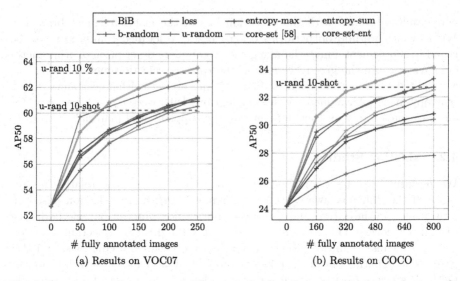

Fig. 3. Detection performances of different active learning strategies in our framework on VOC07 [24] (a) and COCO datasets [47] (b). We perform 5 annotation cycles for each strategy with the budget of $B = 50$ on VOC07 and $B = 160$ on COCO. This corresponds to annotating 1% and 0.2% of the training set per cycle respectively for VOC07 and COCO. Dashed lines in purple and red highlight results obtained with *10-shot* and *10%* images selected with *u-random*. Best viewed in color. (Color figure online)

of $B = 160$ images (0.2% of the training set, 2 fully annotated images per class on average) on COCO. We present results in Fig. 3. The detailed numbers are provided in the supplemental material. It can be seen that the ranking of the examined baseline methods w.r.t. their detection performance is different on the two datasets. This is explained by the fact that the two datasets have different data statistics. COCO dataset contains many cluttered images, with an average of 7.4 objects in an image, and VOC07 depicts simpler scenes, with an average of only 2.4 objects. However, BiB consistently improves over other baselines.

Results on VOC07 (Fig. 3a) show that BiB and *loss* significantly outperform every method in all cycles. BiB also surpasses *loss* except in the first cycle. Entropy and variants of *random* perform comparably and slightly better than variants of core-set. Balancing the classes consistently improves the performance of random strategy, albeit with a small margin. Interestingly, BiB reaches the performance of *random* at 10% setting (≈ 500 images) with only ≈ 200 fully-annotated images. Similarly, it needs fewer than 100 fully annotated images to attain *random*'s performance in the 10-shot (≈ 200 images) setting.

On COCO, BiB again shows consistent improvement over competitors. However, surprisingly, *loss* fares much worse than BiB and even *random*. To understand these results, we present a representative subset of selected images in Fig. 4. It appears that images selected by the *loss* strategy tend to depict com-

BiB   entropy-sum   loss

Fig. 4. Images selected by BiB, *entropy-max* and *loss* strategies on COCO dataset.

Table 2. Performance of BiB compared to the state of the art on VOC07 ($B = 50$) and COCO ($B = 160$) datasets. The *10-shot* setting corresponds to 4 and 5 AL cycles resp. on VOC07 and COCO. All of the compared methods use VGG16 [61] as the backbone.

Setting	Method	VOC07	COCO	
		AP50	AP50	AP
		100%		
Fully supervised	Fast RCNN [32]	66.9	38.6	18.9
	Faster RCNN [54]	69.9	41.5	21.2
		0%		
WSOD	WSDDN [7]	34.8	–	–
	OICR [69]	41.2	–	–
	C-MIDN [29]	52.6	21.4	9.6
	WSOD2 [80]	53.6	22.7	10.8
	MIST-CDB [55]	54.9	24.3	11.4
	CASD [38]	56.8	26.4	12.8
		10-shot		
Weak & few strong	BCNet [49]	57.1	–	–
	OAM [6]	59.7	31.2	14.9
	Ours (u-rand)	60.2	32.7	16.4
	Ours (BiB)	62.9	34.1	17.2

plex scenes. Many of them are indoors scenes with lots of objects (people, foods, furniture, ...). The supervision brought by these images is both redundant (two many images for certain classes) and insufficient (no or too few images for others). This result agrees with those obtained in [14,48] on COCO with the predicted loss method [78]. On the other hand, variants of entropy strategy tend to select very difficult images that are outliers and not representative of the training dataset. They do not perform well on COCO, especially *entropy-sum* which obtains significantly worse results than other strategies. This observation is similar to that of [79]. Diversity-based methods fare better than uncertainty-based methods, with *core-set* and *core-set-ent* performing much better than *entropy* variants. Among the latter two methods, *core-set* performs unsurprisingly better than *core-set-ent*, given *entropy*'s bad performance. BiB outperforms all other methods. It obtains significantly better results than *random*, which other methods fail to do. In addition, BiB attains the same performance as *u-random* (see dashed line) with only half as many annotated images, reducing the performance gap (in AP50) between the base weak detector and the fully-supervised Fast RCNN by nearly 70% with only ten fully annotated images per class on average. It can be seen in Fig. 4 that BiB selects a diverse set of images that reflect the model's confusion on object extent.

4.4 Comparison to the State of the Art

We compare the 10-shot performance of our proposed method to the state of the art in Table 2. For BiB, we report the performance of previous experiments (Fig. 3) at cycle 4 on VOC07 and cycle 5 on COCO. All compared methods use a Fast R-CNN or Faster R-CNN architecture with a VGG16 [61] backbone. Most related to us, OAM [6] and BCNet [49] also seek to improve the performance of weakly-supervised detectors with a few fully-annotated images. We can see that BiB significantly outperforms them in this setting. In particular, on COCO, we observe from Table 2 and Fig. 3 that BiB obtains comparable results to 10-shot OAM with only 2 shots (160 images) and significantly better results with 4 shots. Similarly, on VOC07, BiB surpasses the performance of OAM with only a half of the number of fully-annotated images used by the latter. We additionally consider the 10% setting and compare BiB to other baselines on the VOC07 dataset (see Table 3). In this setting, a random selection following our method ('Ours (u-rand)') gives an AP50 of 63.1, outperformed by BiB ('Ours (BiB)') which achieves an AP50 of 65.1. In comparison, our main competitors perform worse: OAM (63.3), BCNet (61.8), EHSOD [26] (55.3) and BAOD [50] (50.9).

Compared to WSOD methods, we obtain significantly better results with a small amount of full annotations. BiB enables a greater boost over weakly-supervised detectors than *random* and narrows significantly the performance gap between weakly-supervised detectors and fully-supervised detectors. It reduces the gap between the state of the art weakly-supervised detector CASD [38] and Fast RCNN [32] by 5.5 times with 10% of the training images fully annotated on VOC07 and by 3.5 times with only 10 fully annotated images on average per class on COCO. This is arguably a better trade-off between detection performance and data efficiency than both weakly- and fully-supervised detectors.

Per-class Study. Additionally, we present in Table 3 the per-class results for different methods on VOC07. It can be seen that variants of our approach (u-random and BiB) consistently boost the performance on all classes over MIST [55] (except on *aeroplane* and *motorbike* where they perform slightly worse than MIST). Notably, BiB yields larger boosts on *hard* classes such as *table* (+23 points w.r.t.our baseline MIST), *chair* (+17.3), *bottle* (+23) and *potted plant* (+19.2). On those classes, a random selection with our approach is

Table 3. Per-class AP50 results on VOC07. BiB yields significant boosts in hard classes such as *bottle, chair, table* and *potted plant*. Results of MIST are the average of three runs using the authors' public code and differ from the numbers in the original paper.

Method	Sup	Aero	Bike	Bird	Boat	Bottl	Bus	Car	Cat	Chair	Cow	Table	Dog	Horse	Moto	Pers	Plant	Sheep	Sofa	Train	Tv	Mean
MIST*	✗	69.0	75.6	57.4	22.5	24.8	71.5	76.1	55.9	27.6	70.3	43.9	37.5	50.8	**75.9**	18.5	23.9	60.8	54.7	69.3	68.1	52.7
BAOD [50]	10%	51.6	50.7	52.6	41.7	36.0	52.9	63.7	69.7	34.4	65.4	22.1	66.1	63.9	53.5	59.8	24.5	60.2	43.3	59.7	46.0	50.9
BCNet [49]	10%	64.7	73.1	55.2	37.0	39.1	**73.3**	74.0	75.4	35.9	69.8	56.3	**74.7**	77.6	71.6	66.9	25.4	61.0	61.4	**73.8**	69.3	61.8
OAM [6]	10%	65.6	73.1	59.0	**49.4**	42.5	72.5	78.3	**76.4**	35.4	72.3	57.6	73.6	**80.0**	72.5	**71.1**	28.3	64.6	55.3	71.4	66.2	63.3
Ours (u-r.)	10%	**70.5**	77.2	62.3	38.5	38.5	72.3	**79.4**	73.6	38.6	73.8	55.7	66.5	71.4	75.3	65.5	33.8	65.4	62.7	72.3	69.7	63.1
Ours (BiB)	10%	68.9	**78.1**	**62.7**	41.4	**47.8**	72.4	79.2	70.3	**44.9**	**74.7**	**66.2**	62.2	72.1	75.6	69.8	**43.1**	**66.2**	**65.0**	71.4	**70.7**	**65.1**

worse than BiB by more than 7 points. Overall, BiB obtains the best results on most classes.

5   Conclusion and Future Work

We propose a new approach to boost the performance of weakly-supervised detectors using a few fully annotated images selected following an active learning process. We introduce BiB, a new selection method specifically designed to tackle failure modes of weakly-supervised detectors and show a significant improvements over random sampling. Moreover, BiB is effective on both VOC07 and COCO datasets, narrowing significantly the performance between weakly- and fully-supervised object detectors, and outperforming all methods mixing many weak and a few strong annotations in the low annotation regime.

In this work, we combine weakly-supervised and active learning for reducing human annotation effort for object detectors. There are other types of methods that require no annotation at all, such as unsupervised object discovery [60, 73] and self-supervised pre-training [9,11], that could help improving different component of our pipeline, e.g., region proposals or the detection architecture. Future work will be dedicated to improving our approach by following those directions.

Acknowledgements. This work was supported in part by the Inria/NYU collaboration, the Louis Vuitton/ENS chair on artificial intelligence and the French government under management of Agence Nationale de la Recherche as part of the "Investissements d'avenir" program, reference ANR19-P3IA-0001 (PRAIRIE 3IA Institute). It was performed using HPC resources from GENCI-IDRIS (Grant 2021-AD011013055). Huy V. Vo was supported in part by a Valeo/Prairie CIFRE PhD Fellowship.

References

1. Agarwal, S., Arora, H., Anand, S., Arora, C.: Contextual diversity for active learning. In: Vedaldi, A., Bischof, H., Brox, T., Frahm, J.-M. (eds.) ECCV 2020. LNCS, vol. 12361, pp. 137–153. Springer, Cham (2020). https://doi.org/10.1007/978-3-030-58517-4_9

2. Arthur, D., Vassilvitskii, S.: K-means++: the advantages of careful seeding. In: Proceedings of the Eighteenth Annual ACM-SIAM Symposium on Discrete Algorithms (SODA), pp. 1027–1035 (2007)

3. Arun, A., Jawahar, C., Kumar, M.P.: Dissimilarity coefficient based weakly supervised object detection. In: Proceedings of the IEEE/CVF Conference on Computer Vision and Pattern Recognition (CVPR) (2019)

4. Ash, J.T., Zhang, C., Krishnamurthy, A., Langford, J., Agarwal, A.: Deep batch active learning by diverse, uncertain gradient lower bounds. In: Proceedings of the International Conference on Learning Representations (ICLR) (2020)

5. Beluch, W.H., Genewein, T., Nürnberger, A., Köhler, J.M.: The power of ensembles for active learning in image classification. In: Proceedings of the IEEE/CVF Conference on Computer Vision and Pattern Recognition (CVPR) (2018)

6. Biffi, C., McDonagh, S., Torr, P., Leonardis, A., Parisot, S.: Many-shot from low-shot: learning to annotate using mixed supervision for object detection. In: Vedaldi, A., Bischof, H., Brox, T., Frahm, J.-M. (eds.) ECCV 2020. LNCS, vol. 12353, pp. 35–50. Springer, Cham (2020). https://doi.org/10.1007/978-3-030-58598-3_3
7. Bilen, H., Vedaldi, A.: Weakly supervised deep detection networks. In: Proceedings of the IEEE Conference on Computer Vision and Pattern Recognition (CVPR) (2016)
8. Brust, C.A., Kading, C., Denzler, J.: Active learning for deep object detection. In: Proceedings of the International Joint Conference on Computer Vision, Imaging and Computer Graphics Theory and Applications (VISIGRAPP) (2019)
9. Caron, M., Touvron, H., Misra, I., Jégou, H., Mairal, J., Bojanowski, P., Joulin, A.: Emerging properties in self-supervised vision transformers. In: Proceedings of the International Conference on Computer Vision (ICCV) (2021)
10. Chen, L., Yang, T., Zhang, X., Zhang, W., Sun, J.: Points as queries: weakly semi-supervised object detection by points. In: Proceedings of the IEEE/CVF Conference on Computer Vision and Pattern Recognition (CVPR), pp. 8819–8828 (2021)
11. Chen, X., Fan, H., Girshick, R., He, K.: Improved baselines with momentum contrastive learning. arXiv preprint arXiv:2003.04297 (2020)
12. Chitta, K., Alvarez, J.M., Lesnikowski, A.: Large-scale visual active learning with deep probabilistic ensembles. arXiv preprint arXiv:1811.03575 (2019)
13. Cho, M., Kwak, S., Schmid, C., Ponce, J.: Unsupervised object discovery and localization in the wild: Part-based matching with bottom-up region proposals. In: Proceedings of the IEEE Conference on Computer Vision and Pattern Recognition (CVPR) (2015)
14. Choi, J., Elezi, I., Lee, H.J., Farabet, C., Alvarez, J.M.: Active learning for deep object detection via probabilistic modeling. In: Proceedings of the IEEE/CVF International Conference on Computer Vision (ICCV) (2021)
15. Cinbis, R., Verbeek, J., Schmid, C.: Weakly supervised object localization with multi-fold multiple instance learning. IEEE Trans. Pattern Anal. Mach. Intell. (TPAMI) **39**, 189–203 (2017)
16. Desai, S.V., Lagandula, A.C., Guo, W., Ninomiya, S., Balasubramanian, V.N.: An adaptive supervision framework for active learning in object detection. In: Proceedings of the British Machine Vision Conference (BMVC) (2019)
17. Deselaers, T., Alexe, B., Ferrari, V.: Localizing objects while learning their appearance. In: Daniilidis, K., Maragos, P., Paragios, N. (eds.) ECCV 2010. LNCS, vol. 6314, pp. 452–466. Springer, Heidelberg (2010). https://doi.org/10.1007/978-3-642-15561-1_33
18. Diba, A., Sharma, V., Pazandeh, A., Pirsiavash, H., Van Gool, L.: Weakly supervised cascaded convolutional networks. In: Proceedings of the IEEE Conference on Computer Vision and Pattern Recognition (CVPR) (2017)
19. Dietterich, T.G., Lathrop, R.H., Lozano-Pérez, T.: Solving the multiple instance problem with axis-parallel rectangles. Artif. Intell. **89**(1–2), 31–71 (1997)
20. Ebrahimi, S., Gan, W., Salahi, K., Darrell, T.: Minimax active learning. ArXiv abs/2012.10467 (2020)
21. Ebrahimi, S., Sinha, S., Darrell, T.: Variational adversarial active learning. In: Proceedings of the IEEE/CVF International Conference on Computer Vision (ICCV) (2019)
22. Elezi, I., Yu, Z., Anandkumar, A., Leal-Taixe, L., Alvarez, J.M.: Not all labels are equal: Rationalizing the labeling costs for training object detection. In: Proceedings of the IEEE/CVF Conference on Computer Vision and Pattern Recognition (CVPR) (2021)

23. Everingham, M., Van Gool, L., Williams, C.K.I., Winn, J., Zisserman, A.: The PASCAL Visual Object Classes Challenge 2012 (VOC 2012) Results (2012)
24. Everingham, M., Van Gool, L., Williams, C.K., Winn, J., Zisserman, A.: The PASCAL visual object classes challenge 2007 (VOC 2007) results (2007)
25. Fan, Q., Zhuo, W., Tang, C.K., Tai, Y.W.: Few-shot object detection with attention-rpn and multi-relation detector. In: Proceedings of the IEEE/CVF Conference on Computer Vision and Pattern Recognition, pp. 4013–4022 (2020)
26. Fang, L., Xu, H., Liu, Z., Parisot, S., Li, Z.: Ehsod: cam-guided end-to-end hybrid-supervised object detection with cascade refinement. In: Proceedings of the AAAI Conference on Artificial Intelligence (AAAI), pp. 10778–10785 (2020)
27. Gal, Y., Islam, R., Ghahramani, Z.: Deep bayesian active learning with image data. arXiv preprint arXiv:1703.02910 (2017)
28. Gao, M., Zhang, Z., Yu, G., Arık, S.Ö., Davis, L.S., Pfister, T.: Consistency-based semi-supervised active learning: towards minimizing labeling cost. In: Vedaldi, A., Bischof, H., Brox, T., Frahm, J.-M. (eds.) ECCV 2020. LNCS, vol. 12355, pp. 510–526. Springer, Cham (2020). https://doi.org/10.1007/978-3-030-58607-2_30
29. Gao, Y., et al.: C-midn: Coupled multiple instance detection network with segmentation guidance for weakly supervised object detection. In: Proceedings of the International Conference on Computer Vision (ICCV) (2019)
30. Geifman, Y., El-Yaniv, R.: Deep active learning over the long tail. ArXiv abs/1711.00941 (2017)
31. Gidaris, S., Komodakis, N.: Object detection via a multi-region and semantic segmentation-aware cnn model. In: Proceedings of the International Conference on Computer Vision (ICCV) (2015)
32. Girshick, R.: Fast R-CNN. In: Proceedings of the International Conference on Computer Vision (ICCV) (2015)
33. Girshick, R., Donahue, J., Darrell, T., Malik, J.: Rich feature hierarchies for accurate object detection and semantic segmentation. In: Proceedings of the Conference on Computer Vision and Pattern Recognition (CVPR) (2014)
34. Gissin, D., Shalev-Shwartz, S.: Discriminative active learning. ArXiv abs/1907.06347 (2019)
35. Haussmann, E., et al.: Scalable active learning for object detection. In: Proceedings of the IEEE Intelligent Vehicles Symposium (IV) (2020)
36. He, K., Gkioxari, G., Dollar, P., Girshick, R.: Mask R-CNN. In: Proceedings of the International Conference on Computer Vision (ICCV) (2017)
37. Huang, S., Wang, T., Xiong, H., Huan, J., Dou, D.: Semi-supervised active learning with temporal output discrepancy. In: Proceedings of the IEEE/CVF International Conference on Computer Vision (ICCV) (2021)
38. Huang, Z., Zou, Y., Kumar, B., Huang, D.: Comprehensive attention self-distillation for weakly-supervised object detection. In: Advances in Neural Information Processing Systems (NeurIPS) (2020)
39. Jeong, J., Lee, S., Kim, J., Kwak, N.: Consistency-based semi-supervised learning for object detection. In: Advances in Neural Information Processing Systems (NeurIPS) (2019)
40. Jie, Z., Wei, Y., Jin, X., Feng, J., Liu, W.: Deep self-taught learning for weakly supervised object localization. In: Proceedings of the Conference on Computer Vision and Pattern Recognition (CVPR) (2017)
41. Kang, B., Liu, Z., Wang, X., Yu, F., Feng, J., Darrell, T.: Few-shot object detection via feature reweighting. In: Proceedings of the IEEE/CVF International Conference on Computer Vision (ICCV), pp. 8420–8429 (2019)

42. Kao, C.C., Lee, T.Y., Sen, P., Liu, M.Y.: Localization-aware active learning for object detection. In: Proceedings of the Asian Conference on Computer Vision (ACCV) (2018)

43. Karlinsky, L., et al.: Repmet: representative-based metric learning for classification and few-shot object detection. In: Proposal Learning for Semi, pp. 5197–5206 (2019)

44. Kumar, M., Packer, B., Koller, D.: Self-paced learning for latent variable models. In: Advances in Neural Information Processing Systems (NIPS) (2010)

45. Li, Y., Huang, D., Qin, D., Wang, L., Gong, B.: Improving object detection with *selective* self-supervised self-training. In: Vedaldi, A., Bischof, H., Brox, T., Frahm, J.-M. (eds.) ECCV 2020. LNCS, vol. 12374, pp. 589–607. Springer, Cham (2020). https://doi.org/10.1007/978-3-030-58526-6_35

46. Lin, T.Y., Dollár, P., Girshick, R.B., He, K., Hariharan, B., Belongie, S.J.: Feature pyramid networks for object detection. Proceedings of the IEEE Conference on Computer Vision and Pattern Recognition (CVPR), pp. 936–944 (2017)

47. Lin, T.-Y., et al.: Microsoft COCO: common objects in context. In: Fleet, D., Pajdla, T., Schiele, B., Tuytelaars, T. (eds.) ECCV 2014. LNCS, vol. 8693, pp. 740–755. Springer, Cham (2014). https://doi.org/10.1007/978-3-319-10602-1_48

48. Liu, Z., Ding, H., Zhong, H., Li, W., Dai, J., He, C.: Influence selection for active learning. In: Proceedings of the IEEE/CVF International Conference on Computer Vision (ICCV), pp. 9274–9283 (2021)

49. Pan, T., Wang, B., Ding, G., Han, J., Yong, J.: Low shot box correction for weakly supervised object detection. In: Proceedings of the International Joint Conference on Artificial Intelligence (IJCAI), pp. 890–896 (2019)

50. Pardo, A., Xu, M., Thabet, A.K., Arbeláez, P., Ghanem, B.: Baod: budget-aware object detection. Proceedings of the IEEE/CVF Conference on Computer Vision and Pattern Recognition Workshops (CVPRW), pp. 1247–1256 (2021)

51. Radosavovic, I., Dollár, P., Girshick, R.B., Gkioxari, G., He, K.: Data distillation: towards omni-supervised learning. In: Proceedings of the IEEE/CVF Conference on Computer Vision and Pattern Recognition (CVPR), pp. 4119–4128 (2018)

52. Redmon, J., Divvala, S., Girshick, R., Farhadi, A.: You only look once: unified, real-time object detection. In: Proceedings of the IEEE Conference on Computer Vision and Pattern Recognition (CVPR) (2016)

53. Redmon, J., Farhadi, A.: Yolo9000: better, faster, stronger. In: Proceedings of the IEEE Conference on Computer Vision and Pattern Recognition (CVPR) (2017)

54. Ren, S., He, K., Girshick, R., Sun, J.: Faster R-CNN: towards real-time object detection with region proposal networks. In: Advances in Neural Information Processing Systems (NIPS) (2015)

55. Ren, Z., et al.: Instance-aware, context-focused, and memory-efficient weakly supervised object detection. In: Proceedings of the IEEE/CVF Conference on Computer Vision and Pattern Recognition (CVPR) (2020)

56. Ren, Z., Yu, Z., Yang, X., Liu, M.-Y., Schwing, A.G., Kautz, J.: UFO^2: a unified framework towards omni-supervised object detection. In: Vedaldi, A., Bischof, H., Brox, T., Frahm, J.-M. (eds.) ECCV 2020. LNCS, vol. 12364, pp. 288–313. Springer, Cham (2020). https://doi.org/10.1007/978-3-030-58529-7_18

57. Roy, S., Unmesh, A., Namboodiri, V.P.: Deep active learning for object detection. In: Proceedings of the British Machine Vision Conference (BMVC) (2018)

58. Sener, O., Savarese, S.: Active learning for convolutional neural networks: a core-set approach. In: Proceedings of the International Conference on Learning Representations (ICLR) (2018)

59. Settles, B.: Active Learning Literature Survey. Technical Report, University of Wisconsin-Madison Department of Computer Sciences (2009). https://minds.wisconsin.edu/handle/1793/60660

60. Siméoni, O., et al.: Localizing objects with self-supervised transformers and no labels. In: Proceedings of the British Machine Vision Conference (BMVC) (2021)

61. Simonyan, K., Zisserman, A.: Very deep convolutional networks for large-scale image recognition. In: Proceedings of the International Conference on Learning Representations (ICLR) (2015)

62. Sivic, J., Russell, B., Efros, A., Zisserman, A., Freeman, W.: Discovering objects and their location in images. In: Proceedings of the International Conference on Computer Vision (ICCV) (2005)

63. Sohn, K., Zhang, Z., Li, C.L., Zhang, H., Lee, C.Y., Pfister, T.: A simple semi-supervised learning framework for object detection. In: arXiv:2005.04757 (2020)

64. Song, H.O., Girshick, R., Jegelka, S., Mairal, J., Harchaoui, Z., Darrell, T.: On learning to localize objects with minimal supervision (2014)

65. Song, H.O., Lee, Y.J., Jegelka, S., Darrell, T.: Weakly-supervised discovery of visual pattern configurations. In: Advances in Neural Information Processing Systems (NIPS) (2014)

66. Sun, B., Li, B., Cai, S., Yuan, Y., Zhang, C.: FSCE: few-shot object detection via contrastive proposal encoding. In: Proceedings of the IEEE/CVF Conference on Computer Vision and Pattern Recognition (CVPR), pp. 7352–7362 (2021)

67. Tang, J., Lewis, P.H.: Non-negative matrix factorisation for object class discovery and image auto-annotation. In: Proceedings of the International Conference on Content-Based Image and Video Retrieval (CIVR) (2008)

68. Tang, P., et al.: PCL: proposal cluster learning for weakly supervised object detection. IEEE Trans. Pattern Anal. Mach. Intell. (TPAMI) **42**(1), 176–191 (2020)

69. Tang, P., Wang, X., Bai, X., Liu, W.: Multiple instance detection network with online instance classifier refinement. In: Proceedings of the IEEE Conference on Computer Vision and Pattern Recognition (CVPR) (2017)

70. Tang, P., Ramaiah, C., Xu, R., Xiong, C.: Proposal learning for semi-supervised object detection. In: Proceedings of the IEEE Winter Conference on Applications of Computer Vision (WACV), pp. 2290–2300 (2021)

71. Uijlings, J., van de Sande, K., Gevers, T., Smeulders, A.: Selective search for object recognition. Int. J. Comput. Vision **104**, 154–171 (2013)

72. Vo, H.V., et al.: Unsupervised image matching and object discovery as optimization. In: Proceedings of the IEEE/CVF Conference on Computer Vision and Pattern Recognition (CVPR) (2019)

73. Vo, H.V., Pérez, P., Ponce, J.: Toward unsupervised, multi-object discovery in large-scale image collections. In: Vedaldi, A., Bischof, H., Brox, T., Frahm, J.-M. (eds.) ECCV 2020. LNCS, vol. 12368, pp. 779–795. Springer, Cham (2020). https://doi.org/10.1007/978-3-030-58592-1_46

74. Vo, H.V., Sizikova, E., Schmid, C., Pérez, P., Ponce, J.: Large-scale unsupervised object discovery. In: Advances in Neural Information Processing Systems (NeurIPS), vol. 34 (2021)

75. Wan, F., Liu, C., Ke, W., Ji, X., Jiao, J., Ye, Q.: C-mil: Continuation multiple instance learning for weakly supervised object detection. In: Proceedings of the Conference on Computer Vision and Pattern Recognition (CVPR) (2019)

76. Wang, K., Yan, X., Zhang, D., Zhang, L., Lin, L.: Towards human-machine cooperation: self-supervised sample mining for object detection. In: Proceedings of the IEEE Conference on Computer Vision and Pattern Recognition (CVPR) (2018)

77. Xu, M., et al.: End-to-end semi-supervised object detection with soft teacher. In: Proceedings of the IEEE/CVF International Conference on Computer Vision (ICCV) (2021)
78. Yoo, D., Kweon, I.S.: Learning loss for active learning. In: Proceedings of the IEEE/CVF Conference on Computer Vision and Pattern Recognition (CVPR) (2019)
79. Yuan, T., et al.: Multiple instance active learning for object detection. In: Proceedings of the IEEE/CVF Conference on Computer Vision and Pattern Recognition (CVPR) (2021)
80. Zeng, Z., Liu, B., Fu, J., Chao, H., Zhang, L.: Wsod2: learning bottom-up and top-down objectness distillation for weakly-supervised object detection. In: Proceedings of the IEEE International Conference on Computer Vision (ICCV) (2019)
81. Zhang, B., Li, L., Yang, S., Wang, S., Zha, Z., Huang, Q.: State-relabeling adversarial active learning. In: Proceedings of the IEEE/CVF Conference on Computer Vision and Pattern Recognition (CVPR), pp. 8753–8762 (2020)
82. Zhdanov, F.: Diverse mini-batch active learning. ArXiv abs/1901.05954 (2019)
83. Zitnick, C.L., Dollár, P.: Edge boxes: locating object proposals from edges. In: Fleet, D., Pajdla, T., Schiele, B., Tuytelaars, T. (eds.) ECCV 2014. LNCS, vol. 8693, pp. 391–405. Springer, Cham (2014). https://doi.org/10.1007/978-3-319-10602-1_26
84. Zoph, B., et al.: Rethinking pre-training and self-training. In: Advances in Neural Information Processing Systems (NeurIPS) (2020)

mc-BEiT: Multi-choice Discretization for Image BERT Pre-training

Xiaotong Li[1], Yixiao Ge[2], Kun Yi[2], Zixuan Hu[1], Ying Shan[2],
and Ling-Yu Duan[1,3(✉)]

[1] Peking University, Beijing, China
lixiaotong@stu.pku.edu.cn, {hzxuan,lingyu}@pku.edu.cn
[2] ARC Lab, Tencent PCG, Beijing, China
{yixiaoge,kunyi,yingsshan}@tencent.com
[3] Peng Cheng Laboratory, Shenzhen, China

Abstract. Image BERT pre-training with masked image modeling (MIM) becomes a popular practice to cope with self-supervised representation learning. A seminal work, BEiT, casts MIM as a classification task with a visual vocabulary, tokenizing the continuous visual signals into discrete vision tokens using a pre-learned dVAE. Despite a feasible solution, the improper discretization hinders further improvements of image pre-training. Since image discretization has no ground-truth answers, we believe that the masked patch should not be assigned with a unique token id even if a better "tokenizer" can be obtained. In this work, we introduce an improved BERT-style image pre-training method, namely mc-BEiT, which performs MIM proxy tasks towards eased and refined multi-choice training objectives. Specifically, the multi-choice supervision for the masked image patches is formed by the soft probability vectors of the discrete token ids, which are predicted by the off-the-shelf image "tokenizer" and further refined by high-level inter-patch perceptions resorting to the observation that similar patches should share their choices. Extensive experiments on classification, segmentation, and detection tasks demonstrate the superiority of our method, $e.g.$, the pre-trained ViT-B achieves 84.1% top-1 fine-tuning accuracy on ImageNet-1K classification, 49.2% AP^b and 44.0% AP^m of object detection and instance segmentation on COCO, 50.8% mIOU on ADE20K semantic segmentation, outperforming the competitive counterparts. The code is available at https://github.com/lixiaotong97/mc-BEiT.

Keywords: Self-supervised learning · Vision transformers · Image BERT pre-training

1 Introduction

Self-supervised pre-training [1,2,6,11,36,43,45] is attracting emerging attention due to its effectiveness and flexibility in exploiting large-scale uncurated data,

Supplementary Information The online version contains supplementary material available at https://doi.org/10.1007/978-3-031-20056-4_14.

S. Avidan et al. (Eds.): ECCV 2022, LNCS 13690, pp. 231–246, 2022.
https://doi.org/10.1007/978-3-031-20056-4_14

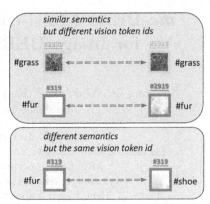

Fig. 1. The improper token ids for image discretization, where a better tokenizer [17] is used here. We observe that semantically-similar patches might be allocated with different token ids while patches with different semantics might be allocated with the same token id, indicting that the hard-label classification with unique token ids in BEiT [1] may hinder the pre-training performance.

which demonstrates its superiority to supervised pre-training in a wide range of downstream applications, such as classification, detection, and segmentation, *etc.* Recently, the introduction of vision Transformers [16,33,38] brings about a new revolution to self-supervised learning [1,5,11].

Inspired by the great success of BERT [13] in natural language processing (NLP) tasks, masked image modeling (MIM) has been introduced for visual pre-training as a new pretext task. It is not trivial, because one key barrier lies in that the visual signal is continuous and cannot be properly classified as is done in masked language modeling (MLM) of BERT. A pioneer work, BEiT [1], tackles the challenge by "tokenizing" continuous visual signals into discrete vision tokens resorting to a pre-learned codebook [37], which plays the role of a pre-defined vocabulary in MLM. The pre-training objective is to predict the vision token id of the masked image patch based on its context and semantics.

Despite the impressive performances of BEiT on image pre-training, there remain some questions under-developed. (1) *Does the masked patch prediction have ground-truth answers?* Unlike the linguistic vocabulary which is naturally composed of discrete words, the image tokenizer is relatively subjective, *i.e.,* there is no perfect answer to visual discretization and the tokenizer carries inevitable label noise even a better tokenizer is obtained in [17]. For example, as shown in Fig. 1, patches of the dog and the shoe are discretized into the same vision token (#319) due to their similar pixel-level representations. (2) *Should the masked patch be assigned a unique token id given a pre-learned tokenizer?* Not really. As illustrated in Fig. 1, semantically-similar patches of the grass are discretized into different vision tokens, *i.e.,* they are classified into distinct and unique ids in BEiT pre-training, neglecting their semantic relations.

Given the observation of the above two issues, we argue that performing MIM with a strict mapping between patch predictions and unique token ids by a hard-label classification loss in BEiT limits the visual context capturing and the pre-training performance. To tackle the challenge, we introduce to effectively boost BERT-style image pre-training with eased and refined masked prediction targets, that is, *multi-choice vision token ids*. Rather than retraining the tokenizer with perceptual regularizations [15, 45], we efficiently inject the semantic relations into off-the-shelf vision tokens without any extra computational overhead.

Specifically, to enable multi-choice answers for masked patches, we adopt the soft id probability vectors, rather than the hard predicted id over a pre-learned codebook, as the supervision signals for masked image modeling. Although the off-the-shelf image tokenizer [17] can capture some local semantics with the training objectives of both pixel-level and perceptually-aware regularizations, it is proven to be still vulnerable to various low-level changes (see Fig. 1). Therefore, we introduce to refine the predicted soft id probabilities by inter-patch semantic similarities, which are estimated by the vision Transformers being trained. Under the observation that patches with similar high-level visual perceptions ought to share their predictions, we propagate the soft id probabilities of different patches in an image based on their semantic similarities and form ensembled learning targets for masked image patches (see Fig. 2). The final training objective is formulated as a soft-label cross-entropy loss.

To fully evaluate our novel, flexible and effective method, we pre-train the vision Transformers with various scales on the widely-acknowledged ImageNet-1K [12] dataset and fine-tune the pre-trained models on multiple downstream tasks, including image classification, instance/semantic segmentation, and object detection. The empirical results show that our method impressively outperforms supervised pre-training as well as recent self-supervised learning methods [1,5,11,45]. Concretely, we achieve 84.1% top-1 accuracy on ImageNet-1K classification with a ViT-B model, outperforming the state-of-the-art iBOT [45] by +0.3% with 800 fewer epochs. Regarding the transfer learning ability on different downstream tasks, our pre-trained ViT-B model achieves 49.2% AP^b and 44.0% AP^m of object detection and instance segmentation on COCO [30], 50.8% mIOU on downstream ADE20K [44] semantic segmentation, outperforming all existing methods.

2 Related Works

Self-supervised learning (SSL) has gained great popularity benefiting from its capability of exploiting the tremendous amounts of unlabeled data, which leverages input data itself as supervision. Substantial works [1,3,6,13,19,23,25,31,35] have shown that the pre-training can be beneficial for downstream tasks and enable faster training convergence, which shows its impressive potentials on various machine learning tasks, especially in the fields of natural language processing and computer vision.

2.1 BERT Pre-training with Masked Language Modeling

Self-supervised learning has been studied in NLP for decades. Masked language modeling (MLM) is firstly widely acknowledged because of BERT [13]. BERT encourages bidirectional textual context understanding and adopts the masked language modeling approach for pre-training, which randomly masks 15% tokens and predicts the missing words as the target. After that, various MLM variants are proposed, *e.g.,* GPT [3], XLM [27], and RoBERTa [32], *etc.* These MLM works achieve huge success and show impressive performances on various downstream tasks, which greatly advance the development of language pre-training.

2.2   Self-supervised Visual Pre-training

In the past few years, various pretext tasks are designed for self-supervised visual pre-training. For example, earlier pretext-based works adopt the pseudo labels based on the attributes of images to learn the representation, such as image colorization [28], jigsaw puzzle [34], context prediction [14], and rotation prediction [20], etc. Besides these approaches, there are two mainstream paradigms, *i.e.,* contrastive learning and masked image modeling approaches, which will be further analyzed in the following subsection.

Contrastive Learning: Contrastive learning is an instance-level discriminative approach and has occupied a dominant position in visual pre-training. Contrastive learning methods, such as SimCLR [6,7], MoCo [9,11,23], and Swav [4], *etc.,* typically rely on data augmentation to create the counterparts of the images and aim at learning such an embedding space, where similar sample pairs are close to each other while dissimilar ones are far apart. Swav [4] proposes a cluster-based contrastive learning method to enforce consistency between cluster assignments under different augmentations. BYOL [21] and SiamSim [10] abandons the negative samples and avoids the collapse with either an additional momentum network or the stop-gradient operation. MoCov3 [11] extends the contrastive learning framework for transformers and further promotes the development of self-supervised vision Transformers.

Masked Image Modeling: Motivated by the great success of BERT, masked image modeling (MIM) [1,8,22,39,41,42,45] becomes a new trend in self-supervised visual pre-training, which randomly masks parts of images and reconstructs them based on the corrupted image. ViT [16] attempts to adopt masked patch prediction for self-supervised learning. BEiT [1] predicts the discrete tokens of masked token resorting to an off-the-shelf discrete VAE. Instead of discretizing the visual information, MAE [22] and SimMIM [41] propose to directly predict the pixel-level value as the reconstruction target. MaskFeat [39] further exploits different supervision signals such as HOG feature to be the objective. iBOT [45] performs masked prediction and adopts the teacher network as an online tokenizer to provide the supervision. PeCo [15] further provides the evidence that the perceptually-aware tokenizer will provide better pre-training performance for the masked image modeling.

3   Preliminaries

3.1   Image BERT Pre-training with Masked Image Modeling

The paradigm of mask-and-then-predict is first introduced in BERT pre-training [13] of NLP tasks to encourage bidirectional context understanding of the textual signals. Recent works [1,45] reproduce the success of BERT by employing the proxy task of masked image modeling (MIM) on image pre-training of vision Transformers [16,33,38]. MIM requires randomly masking a proportion of the image patches and then training the vision Transformer to recover the corrupted image via reasoning among the visual context. The pretext task of MIM enables a more fine-grained understanding of the local visual semantics compared to the contrastive counterparts [6,23]. Vision Transformers pre-trained with MIM objectives can be well transferred to a wide range of downstream tasks, *i.e.*, classification, segmentation, and detection, after fine-tuning.

3.2   Masked Image Modeling as Single-Choice Classification

Introducing the mask-and-then-predict paradigm into image pre-training is actually non-trivial, because the visual signals are continuous and cannot be predicted resorting to a well-defined vocabulary. A pioneering work, BEiT [1], tackles the challenge by casting masked patch prediction as a single-choice classification problem via discretizing the image into vision tokens with an off-the-shelf "tokenizer". The "tokenizer" can be a discrete auto-encoder [17,37] pre-learned towards the reconstruction objective.

Formally, given a raw image $x \in \mathbb{R}^{C \times H \times W}$, it is initially divided into N patches $\{x_i\}_{i=1}^N$ and then mapped into compact patch embeddings. We denote the corrupted image as $\hat{x}$, which is formed by masking part of the patches in x, and we denote the set of masked patch indices as $\mathcal{M}$. We encode the image patch features $f(\hat{x}) \in \mathbb{R}^{N \times D}$ with high-level perceptions by feeding $\hat{x}$ into the vision Transformer. The patch features are further projected to the probabilities of the vision token ids using an MLP head which will be dropped for downstream tasks. We denote the probability vectors as $q(f(\hat{x})) \in \mathbb{R}^{N \times V}$ where V is the length of the visual vocabulary defined by the pre-learned image "tokenizer".

To receive the answers for the masked image modeling, we discrete the raw image x into vision tokens $\{z_i\}_{i=1}^N$ using the image "tokenizer", where $z_i \in \mathbb{R}^V$. The assigned token id with the maximal probability in z_i is termed as y_i. The pre-training objective is formulated as a hard-label cross-entropy loss to encourage masked patch prediction with unique token ids as follow,

$$\mathcal{L}_{\mathrm{mim}}(x) = \mathbb{E}_{i \in \mathcal{M}} \left[-\log q\left(y_i | f(\hat{x}_i) \right) \right]. \tag{1}$$

4   *mc*-BEiT

BEiT provides inspiring insights of casting masked image modeling (MIM) as a classification problem to bridge the gap between discrete words in NLP tasks

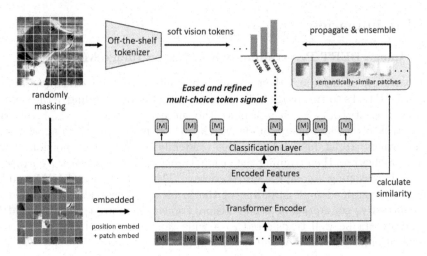

Fig. 2. The overview of the proposed method, *mc*-BEiT. We improve image BERT pre-training with multi-choice training objectives, which is composed of the soft probability vectors predicted by the off-the-shelf image "tokenizer" and further refined by high-level inter-patch perceptions. A proportion of image patches are randomly masked and then fed into the vision Transformer. The masked patch prediction is optimized towards eased and refined multi-choice token ids in the form of a soft-label cross-entropy loss.

and continuous visual signals in computer vision tasks. However, as there are no perfect answers for visual discretization, performing a strict mapping between patch predictions and unique token ids as a single-choice classification problem is actually a sub-optimal solution for MIM pre-training. As illustrated in Fig. 1, there may exist multiple appropriate token ids for a certain patch, motivating us to boost the BEiT pre-training with multi-choice classification.

4.1   Masked Image Modeling as Multi-choice Classification

We introduce an improved BERT-style image pre-training with eased and refined masked prediction targets, *i.e.*, multi-choice vision token ids, rather than a unique answer. All possible token ids in the visual vocabulary will be assigned possibilities to be chosen. To this end, we soften the training objective from the original hard-label cross-entropy loss to a soft-label cross-entropy loss with the multi-choice targets $\hat{z} \in \mathbb{R}^{N \times V}$ as follow,

$$\mathcal{L}_{\text{mc-mim}}(x) = \mathbb{E}_{i \in \mathcal{M}} \left[-\sum_{k=1}^{V} \hat{z}_{i,k} \log q \left(f(\hat{x}_i) \right)_k \right], \tag{2}$$

where $\sum_{k=1}^{V} \hat{z}_{i,k} = 1, \forall i$ and $q\left(f(\hat{x}_i)\right) \in \mathbb{R}^V$. We will go over how to produce such refined multi-choice answers for MIM pre-training in the following section.

4.2   Multi-choice Visual Discretization

To produce multi-choice discretization without extra training stages or computational overhead, we attempt to exploit the predictions from the off-the-shelf image tokenizer. Given the discretization predictions $z \in \mathbb{R}^{N \times V}$ from the image tokenizer, we estimate the soft probabilities $p(z) \in \mathbb{R}^{N \times V}$ rather than using the unique predicted token id as done in the single-choice version. Specifically, the soft probability vector is obtained using a softmax operation, where a temperature coefficient τ is used to move between the sharpness (single-choice) and smoothness (multi-choice),

$$p(z_i)_k = \frac{\exp(z_{i,k}/\tau)}{\sum_{j=1}^{V} \exp(z_{i,j}/\tau)}. \tag{3}$$

As discussed in the introduction section and illustrated in Fig. 1, semantically-similar patches may be allocated with discrepant token ids and semantically-dissimilar patches may be allocated with the same token id due to their low-level similarities, indicating that the raw predictions from the off-the-shelf tokenizer are sub-optimal to fully represent the semantic relations among patches. The phenomenon motivates us to refine the predictions of the tokenizer with inter-patch relations. The inter-patch relations can be estimated with their high-level perceptions, which are encoded by the in-training vision Transformer. Specifically, we calculate the cosine similarity between patch features to measure their affinities,

$$W(\hat{x}_i)_k = \frac{\exp\langle f(\hat{x}_i), f(\hat{x}_k)\rangle}{\sum_{j=1}^{N} \exp\langle f(\hat{x}_i), f(\hat{x}_j)\rangle}, \tag{4}$$

where $W(\hat{x}) \in \mathbb{R}^{N \times N}$ and $\langle \cdot, \cdot \rangle$ indicates the inner product between two feature vectors after ℓ_2 normalization. Based on the observation that perceptually-similar patches ought to share their choices, we propagate the soft probabilities p of different patches in an image x to form a refined target $W(\hat{x})p(z) \in \mathbb{R}^{N \times V}$. In this way, patches with similar high-level perceptions can provide complementary supervision signals for the masked patches.

The overall objective of multi-choice image discretization is composed of the weighted sum of the aforementioned parts, where the semantic equilibrium coefficient ω is introduced to move between low-level semantics (directly predicted by the tokenizer) and high-level semantics (ensembled from the perceptually-similar patches). The former one adopts the eased supervision directly predicted from the tokenizer, while the latter one injects high-level perceptions by propagating among other semantically-similar patches, together forming the refined multi-choice targets $\hat{z} \in \mathbb{R}^{N \times V}$ as follow:

$$\hat{z} = \omega p(z) + (1 - \omega)W(\hat{x})p(z), \tag{5}$$

which is further used as the objectives for masked patch predictions in Eq. (2).

Table 1. The top-1 fine-tuning accuracy of ImageNet-1K using ViT-Base and ViT-Large with different pre-training methods.

Method	Reference	Pre-train epoch	Acc. (%)
Supervised pre-training (training from scratch):			
ViT-B/16 [16]	ICLR 2021	–	77.9
ViT-L/16 [16]	ICLR 2021	–	76.5
DeiT-B/16 [38]	ICML 2021	–	81.8
Self-supervised pre-training using ViT-B/16:			
MoCo v3 [11]	CVPR 2021	300	83.2
DINO [5]	ICCV 2021	300	82.8
BEiT [1]	ICLR 2022	800	83.2
iBOT [45]	ICLR 2022	1600	83.8
MAE [22]	CVPR 2022	1600	83.6
SimMIM [41]	CVPR 2022	800	83.8
Ours	This paper	800	**84.1**
Self-supervised pre-training using ViT-L/16:			
MoCo v3 [11]	CVPR 2021	300	84.1
BEiT [1]	ICLR 2022	800	85.2
MAE [22]	CVPR 2022	1600	**85.9**
Ours	This paper	800	85.6

5 Experiments

5.1 Pre-training Setup

In our experiments, the images of 224×224 resolution are divided into 14×14 image sequences with 16×16 patch size. We use different architectures such as ViT-Base/16 and ViT-Large/16 for pre-training and the backbone implementation follows [16] for fair comparisons. For the BERT-style visual pre-training, we randomly mask 75% patches for masked image modeling. Inspired by PeCo [15], we employ the off-the-shelf VQGAN of [17] as a better tokenizer, which is pre-trained on OpenImages [26] with the vocabulary size of 8192. In our experiments, the semantic equilibrium coefficient ω is 0.8 and the temperature coefficient τ is 4.0 by default. The vision Transformers are pre-trained for 800 epochs on the widely-acknowledged ImageNet-1K [12] dataset, which includes 1.28 million images. Note that the ground-truth labels are disabled for pre-training. We use 16 Nvidia A100 GPUs for pre-training and a batch size of 128 per GPU. We adopt simple image augmentation for pre-training, including random resized cropping and horizontal flipping. The detailed recipe of pre-training and finetuning is summarized in the Appendix.

5.2 Image Classification

For the ImageNet classification task, the fully-connected layer is employed as the classifier after the average pooling of the feature embeddings. We adopt top-1 accuracy after fine-tuning as the evaluation metric and we thoroughly compare our method with the supervised methods, *i.e.*, ViT [16], DeiT [38], and recently published state-of-the-art self-supervised learning methods, *i.e.*, MoCo v3 [11], DINO [5], BEiT [1], and iBOT [45]. Besides, we also compare with the very recent pixel-level MIM methods, *i.e.*, MAE [22] and SimMIM [41]. The experiment results are listed in Table 1. As observed from the results, the proposed method obtains 84.1% top-1 accuracy on ViT-B, outperforming the competing methods and achieving state-of-the-art performance. We can see that our *mc*-BEiT shows significant gains compared to the baseline BEiT, which verifies the effectiveness of our introduced multi-choice objectives. Concretely, our method outperforms the recent state-of-the-art method iBOT [45] by +0.3% with the fewer 800 epochs pre-training. It is noted that iBOT adopts an extra teacher network and enables multi-crops for pre-training, showing lower efficiency than our method.

Table 2. The top-1 fine-tuning accuracy of ImageNet-1K using our *mc*-BEiT with different training epochs and backbone architectures.

Method	Arch	Model size	Pre-train epoch	Acc. (%)
Self-supervised pre-training using ViT-B/16:				
Ours	ViT-B	86M	100	83.3
Ours	ViT-B	86M	300	83.9
Ours	ViT-B	86M	800	**84.1**
Self-supervised pre-training using ViT-L/16:				
Ours	ViT-L	307M	300	85.2
Ours	ViT-L	307M	800	**85.6**

Different Training Epochs and Architectures: We also provide more comprehensive results of different training epochs and architectures in Table 2. From the table, we can see that our method can adapt well to different scales of vision tranformers, *e.g.*, the mostly used ViT-B and ViT-L. It is worth noting that our method obtains a relatively high accuracy (already achieves the state-of-the-art performance) when pre-training for only 300 epochs. Moreover, the performance can be further improved with longer pre-training epochs, *e.g.*, the accuracy reaches 84.1% pre-training for 800 epochs.

Convergence Curve: In Fig. 3, we further demonstrate the convergence curve of the supervised learning method and self-supervised learning methods, *i.e.*, the baseline BEiT and our method, when fine-tuning ViT-B models. As shown in the figure, the proposed method achieves faster convergence as well as better performance than training DeiT from scratch [38]. Meanwhile, our method obtains obvious and consistent performance gains compared to the baseline method BEiT, showing the superiority of the proposed multi-choice training objectives.

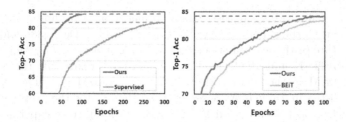

Fig. 3. The convergence curves when fine-tuning ViT-B models on ImageNet-1K classification. The models are pre-trained by different methods.

5.3 Object Detection and Instance Segmentation

For object detection and instance segmentation tasks, COCO [30] benchmark is employed to validate the pre-training performances. We follow the implementation of [18,29] and the model is trained for 25 epochs (we also provide another evaluation setting following iBOT [45] in the Appendix). ViT-B is adopted as the backbone and Mask-RCNN [24] is used as the task head. The evaluation metrics for objection detection and instance segmentation are bounding box AP and mask AP, respectively.

Table 3. Experiment results of object detection and instance segmentation on COCO. We follow the implementation of [18,29] and the model is trained for 25 epochs. Intermediate fine-tuning denotes the model is further fine-tuned on ImageNet-1K.

Method	Reference	Object det. AP^b	Instance seg. AP^m
Supervised [38]	ICML 2021	46.5	41.7
MoCo v3 [11]	CVPR 2021	46.6	41.9
DINO [5]	ICCV 2021	47.6	42.3
MAE [22]	CVPR 2022	48.0	43.0
iBOT [45]	ICLR 2022	48.4	42.9
BEiT [1]	ICLR 2022	47.6	42.2
Ours	This paper	48.5	43.1
+Intermediate Fine-tuning			
BEiT [1]	ICLR 2022	48.4	43.5
Ours	This paper	**49.2**	**44.0**

As observed in Table 3, the BERT style pre-training shows superiority to supervised pre-training in terms of performances. Our method achieves 48.5% and 43.1% in AP^b and AP^m. Meanwhile, the proposed method outperforms the competitor BEiT with +0.9%/+0.9% gain in AP^b and AP^m. We also evaluate the performance after intermediate fine-tuning, the relative improvement is still

Table 4. Results of semantic segmentation on ADE20K. Intermediate fine-tuning denotes the pre-trained model has been fine-tuned on ImageNet-1K classification.

Method	Reference	mIOU
Supervised [38]	ICML 2021	45.3
MoCo v3 [11]	CVPR 2021	47.2
DINO [5]	ICCV 2021	46.8
MAE [22]	CVPR 2022	48.1
iBOT [45]	ICLR 2022	50.0
BEiT [1]	ICLR 2022	45.6
Ours	This paper	47.0
+Intermediate Fine-tuning		
BEiT [1]	ICLR 2022	47.7
Ours	This paper	**50.8**

obvious, *i.e.*, +0.8%/+0.5% to BEiT. Our method even outperforms the recent pixel-level MIM method MAE and obtains better performances compared to state-of-the-art methods.

5.4 Semantic Segmentation

Semantic segmentation belongs to the pixel-level classification task and is often adopted to evaluate the pre-training performance on downstream tasks. Here we evaluate the performance on ADE20k [44] benchmark and mean intersection over union (mIOU) averaged over all semantic categories is adopted as the evaluation metric. Following the common setting in [1, 45], ViT-B is adopted as the default backbone and UPerNet [40] is used for semantic segmentation task head.

Because the pre-training process does not introduce the instance discrimination, the performance can be further improved after intermediate fine-tuning on ImageNet-1K according to BEiT [1]. Therefore we also compare the performance after intermediate fine-tuning. Table 4 shows that our method significantly improves the transferability of pre-trained models compared to the supervised learning, with +5.5% performance gain. It is also noticed that our method outperforms recent state-of-the-art self-supervised methods. It achieves better results as 47.0%/50.8% mIOU and improves +1.4%/3.1% gain to its pre-training only version.

6 Ablation Study

In this section, we conduct an extensive ablation study of our method on ImageNet-1K. Considering the time expenditure, all ablation experiments are performed under 100-epoch pre-trained ViT-B/16 on ImageNet-1K.

6.1   The Temperature Coefficient τ

The hyper-parameter of temperature coefficient τ is to scale the logits from the tokenizer, which moves between the sharpness (single-choice) and smoothness (multi-choice). We adopt the common values for temperature to ablate its effect. In general, the small temperature will sharp the probability distribution and the large one will smooth it conversely. When τ is extremely small, it is an approximate single-choice classification task. The ablation is shown in the Fig. 4(a), where *single-choice label* indicates training with the strict mapping to the unique answer. From the result, we can observe that multi-choice vision token improves the BERT style pre-training performance and it behaves better when setting temperature factor at 4.0 empirically.

6.2   The Semantic Equilibrium Coefficient ω

The semantic equilibrium coefficient ω is introduced to move between low-level semantics (directly predicted by the tokenizer) and high-level semantics (ensembled from the perceptually-similar patches). The ablation study is shown in Fig. 4(b). When setting ω to 0, the objective relies on totally the inter-relationship guided objective and it achieves only 81.8% accuracy, which is because the inevitable noise of calculating patch similarity, especially in the early epochs, will cause collapse and degrade the pre-learning performance. As the coefficient goes larger, it shows consistent gains over baseline. When setting ω to 1.0, the objective comes only from the low-level signals of the tokenizer and the performance is still higher than baseline, which shows the superiority of multi-choice to single-choice. As observed from the results, the semantic equilibrium coefficient is thus set to be 0.8 for better performances.

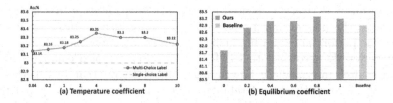

Fig. 4. Ablation study on the hyper-parameters.

6.3   Masking Strategy

In the masked image modeling approach, the masking strategy determines the difficulty of inferring the missing patches. Table 3 shows the influence of different mask strategies, where *Block* and *Random* masking types and different mask ratios are conducted for ablation. It is observed from the results that the random masking strategy with 75% masking ratio makes the best performances, which is thus adopted as the default setting for pre-training.

Table 5. Ablation study on different masking strategies.

Masking strategy	Masking ratio	Acc. (%)
Block	45%	83.2
Block	60%	83.2
Block	75%	82.8
Random	45%	83.0
Random	60%	83.1
Random	75%	**83.3**
Random	90%	83.0

6.4 Tokenizer

In the BERT-style visual pre-training, the tokenizer plays the role of a vocabulary in texts and is used to produce the discrete vision token as supervision. As discussed in PeCo [15], perceptually-aware tokenizer may benefit the image BERT pre-training, so we introduce to use off-the-shelf VQGAN [17] as a better tokenizer throughout our experiments. Besides, we would like to also verify the effectiveness of our multi-choice objectives on top of the vanilla BEiT.

Table 6. Ablation study on the different tokenizer.

	Training data		Top 1 acc. (100/800 epochs)	
	Source	Scale	BEiT	Ours
DALL-E [37]	Private	250M	82.3/83.2	82.6/83.7
VQGAN [17]	OpenImage	9M	82.9/83.8	83.3/84.1

The influence of tokenizers is shown in Table 6. It is shown that adopting the VQGAN as the tokenizer brings better performance than DALL-E, which verify our observation that tokenizer with high semantics can indeed improve the pre-training performance. It also indicates that enhancing the semantic relation is beneficial to visual pre-training. Meanwhile, it is noticed that the relative improvement of our method is consistent regardless of different kinds of tokenizers, which demonstrates the effectiveness of the proposed method.

6.5 Visualization

Besides the quantitative experiment results, we further provide some visualizations in Fig. 5 for better understanding the effects of our multi-choice answers. 75% patches of the images are randomly masked for prediction.

It can be observed from the blue box in Fig. 5(a), the adjacent patches with similar semantics are still allocated with different vision token ids, indicating

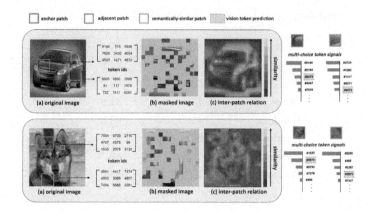

Fig. 5. The visualization is obtained using the off-the-shelf tokenizer and our pre-trained vision Transformer. The inter-patch perception relation is equipped with contour lines for better visual effect. (Color figure online)

that the hard vision token id directly from the tokenizer neglects the semantic relations and is a sub-optimal objective. In contrast, the proposed eased and refined objective can provide diverse possible vision tokens for the prediction. As shown in our multi-choice token signals, the semantically-similar patches have the possibility to be allocated with the same vision token, which refines the objective with inter-patch perceptions. Furthermore, we randomly select a masked patch and shows the inter-patch perception relations (obtained from the patch feature similarity) learned by the pre-trained model in Fig. 5(c). The similar patches can still be well estimated even under heavy random masking and the inter-patch relation shows higher responses, *e.g*, the skeleton of the car. It demonstrates that the informative semantic relations estimated by the in-training vision Transformer can properly enhance the multi-choice discretization for pre-training.

7   Conclusion

In this paper, we propose the *mc*-BEiT, *i.e.,* multi-choice discretization for improving image BERT pre-training. Instead of adopting the unique label signals from the tokenizer, we introduce an eased and refined objective for providing multi-choice answers. Extensive experiments are conducted to evaluate the performances of our method. The empirical results show that *mc*-BEiT achieves the state-of-the-art performances on various tasks, such as image classification, semantic/instance segmentation, and objection detection.

Acknowlegement. This work was supported by the National Natural Science Foundation of China under Grant 62088102, and in part by the PKU-NTU Joint Research Institute (JRI) sponsored by a donation from the Ng Teng Fong Charitable Foundation.

References

1. Bao, H., Dong, L., Piao, S., Wei, F.: BEit: BERT pre-training of image transformers. In: ICLR (2022)
2. Bardes, A., Ponce, J., LeCun, Y.: VICReg: variance-invariance-covariance regularization for self-supervised learning. In: ICLR (2022)
3. Brown, T., et al.: Language models are few-shot learners. In: NIPS, vol. 33, pp. 1877–1901 (2020)
4. Caron, M., Misra, I., Mairal, J., Goyal, P., Bojanowski, P., Joulin, A.: Unsupervised learning of visual features by contrasting cluster assignments. In: NIPS, pp. 9912–9924 (2020)
5. Caron, M., Touvron, H., Misra, I., Jégou, H., Mairal, J., Bojanowski, P., Joulin, A.: Emerging properties in self-supervised vision transformers. In: ICCV (2021)
6. Chen, T., Kornblith, S., Norouzi, M., Hinton, G.: A simple framework for contrastive learning of visual representations. In: ICML, pp. 1597–1607 (2020)
7. Chen, T., Kornblith, S., Swersky, K., Norouzi, M., Hinton, G.E.: Big self-supervised models are strong semi-supervised learners. In: NIPS, pp. 22243–22255 (2020)
8. Chen, X., et al.: Context autoencoder for self-supervised representation learning. arXiv preprint arXiv:2202.03026 (2022)
9. Chen, X., Fan, H., Girshick, R., He, K.: Improved baselines with momentum contrastive learning. arXiv preprint arXiv:2003.04297 (2020)
10. Chen, X., He, K.: Exploring simple siamese representation learning. In: CVPR, pp. 15750–15758 (2021)
11. Chen, X., Xie, S., He, K.: An empirical study of training self-supervised vision transformers. In: ICCV, pp. 9640–9649 (2021)
12. Deng, J., Dong, W., Socher, R., Li, L.J., Li, K., Fei-Fei, L.: Imagenet: a large-scale hierarchical image database. In: CVPR, pp. 248–255
13. Devlin, J., Chang, M.W., Lee, K., Toutanova, K.: BERT: pre-training of deep bidirectional transformers for language understanding. In: ACL, pp. 4171–4186 (2019)
14. Doersch, C., Gupta, A., Efros, A.A.: Unsupervised visual representation learning by context prediction. In: ICCV, pp. 1422–1430 (2015)
15. Dong, X., et al.: Peco: perceptual codebook for bert pre-training of vision transformers. arXiv preprint arXiv:2111.12710 (2021)
16. Dosovitskiy, A., et al.: An image is worth 16×16 words: transformers for image recognition at scale. In: ICLR (2021)
17. Esser, P., Rombach, R., Ommer, B.: Taming transformers for high-resolution image synthesis. In: CVPR, pp. 12873–12883 (2021)
18. Fang, Y., Yang, S., Wang, S., Ge, Y., Shan, Y., Wang, X.: Unleashing vanilla vision transformer with masked image modeling for object detection. arXiv preprint arXiv:2204.02964 (2022)
19. Ge, Y., et al.: Miles: visual bert pre-training with injected language semantics for video-text retrieval. arXiv preprint arXiv:2204.12408 (2022)
20. Gidaris, S., Singh, P., Komodakis, N.: Unsupervised representation learning by predicting image rotations. arXiv preprint arXiv:1803.07728 (2018)
21. Grill, J.B., et al.: Bootstrap your own latent-a new approach to self-supervised learning. In: NIPS, pp. 21271–21284 (2020)
22. He, K., Chen, X., Xie, S., Li, Y., Dollár, P., Girshick, R.: Masked autoencoders are scalable vision learners. arXiv preprint arXiv:2111.06377 (2021)

23. He, K., Fan, H., Wu, Y., Xie, S., Girshick, R.: Momentum contrast for unsupervised visual representation learning. In: CVPR, pp. 9729–9738 (2020)
24. He, K., Gkioxari, G., Dollár, P., Girshick, R.: Mask r-cnn. In: ICCV, pp. 2980–2988 (2017)
25. Henaff, O.: Data-efficient image recognition with contrastive predictive coding. In: ICML, pp. 4182–4192 (2020)
26. Krasin, I., et al.: Openimages: a public dataset for large-scale multi-label and multi-class image classification (2017)
27. Lample, G., Conneau, A.: Cross-lingual language model pretraining. In: NIPS (2019)
28. Larsson, G., Maire, M., Shakhnarovich, G.: Colorization as a proxy task for visual understanding. In: CVPR, pp. 6874–6883 (2017)
29. Li, Y., Xie, S., Chen, X., Dollar, P., He, K., Girshick, R.: Benchmarking detection transfer learning with vision transformers. arXiv preprint arXiv:2111.11429 (2021)
30. Lin, T.-Y., et al.: Microsoft COCO: common objects in context. In: Fleet, D., Pajdla, T., Schiele, B., Tuytelaars, T. (eds.) ECCV 2014. LNCS, vol. 8693, pp. 740–755. Springer, Cham (2014). https://doi.org/10.1007/978-3-319-10602-1_48
31. Liu, X., et al.: Self-supervised learning: generative or contrastive. TKDE (2021)
32. Liu, Y., et al.: Roberta: a robustly optimized bert pretraining approach. arXiv preprint arXiv:1907.11692 (2019)
33. Liu, Z., et al.: Swin transformer: hierarchical vision transformer using shifted windows. In: ICCV (2021)
34. Noroozi, M., Favaro, P.: Unsupervised learning of visual representations by solving jigsaw puzzles. In: Leibe, B., Matas, J., Sebe, N., Welling, M. (eds.) ECCV 2016. LNCS, vol. 9910, pp. 69–84. Springer, Cham (2016). https://doi.org/10.1007/978-3-319-46466-4_5
35. Oord, A.V.d., Li, Y., Vinyals, O.: Representation learning with contrastive predictive coding. arXiv preprint arXiv:1807.03748 (2018)
36. Radford, A., et al.: Learning transferable visual models from natural language supervision. In: ICML, pp. 8748–8763 (2021)
37. Ramesh, A., et al.: Zero-shot text-to-image generation. In: ICML, pp. 8821–8831 (2021)
38. Touvron, H., Cord, M., Douze, M., Massa, F., Sablayrolles, A., Jegou, H.: Training data-efficient image transformers and distillation through attention. In: ICML, pp. 10347–10357 (2021)
39. Wei, C., Fan, H., Xie, S., Wu, C.Y., Yuille, A., Feichtenhofer, C.: Masked feature prediction for self-supervised visual pre-training. arXiv preprint arXiv:2112.09133 (2021)
40. Xiao, T., Liu, Y., Zhou, B., Jiang, Y., Sun, J.: Unified perceptual parsing for scene understanding. In: Ferrari, V., Hebert, M., Sminchisescu, C., Weiss, Y. (eds.) ECCV 2018. LNCS, vol. 11209, pp. 432–448. Springer, Cham (2018). https://doi.org/10.1007/978-3-030-01228-1_26
41. Xie, Z., et al.: Simmim: a simple framework for masked image modeling. arXiv preprint arXiv:2111.09886 (2021)
42. Yi, K., et al.: Masked image modeling with denoising contrast. arXiv preprint arXiv:2205.09616 (2022)
43. Zbontar, J., Jing, L., Misra, I., LeCun, Y., Deny, S.: Barlow twins: self-supervised learning via redundancy reduction. In: ICML, pp. 12310–12320 (2021)
44. Zhou, B., Zhao, H., Puig, X., Fidler, S., Barriuso, A., Torralba, A.: Scene parsing through ade20k dataset. In: CVPR, pp. 5122–5130 (2017)
45. Zhou, J., et al.: Image BERT pre-training with online tokenizer. In: ICLR (2022)

Bootstrapped Masked Autoencoders for Vision BERT Pretraining

Xiaoyi Dong[1]👁, Jianmin Bao[2], Ting Zhang[2], Dongdong Chen[3(✉)],
Weiming Zhang[1], Lu Yuan[3], Dong Chen[2], Fang Wen[2], and Nenghai Yu[1]

[1] University of Science and Technology of China, Hefei, China
dlight@mail.ustc.edu.cn, {zhangwm,ynh}@ustc.edu.cn
[2] Microsoft Research Asia, Beijing, China
{jianbao,Ting.Zhang,doch,fangwen}@microsoft.com
[3] Microsoft Cloud + AI, Redmond, USA
cddlyf@gmail.com, luyuan@microsoft.com

Abstract. We propose bootstrapped masked autoencoders (Boot-MAE), a new approach for vision BERT pretraining. BootMAE improves the original masked autoencoders (MAE) with two core designs: 1) momentum encoder that provides online feature as extra BERT prediction targets; 2) target-aware decoder that tries to reduce the pressure on the encoder to memorize target-specific information in BERT pretraining. The first design is motivated by the observation that using a pretrained MAE to extract the features as the BERT prediction target for masked tokens can achieve better pretraining performance. Therefore, we add a momentum encoder in parallel with the original MAE encoder, which bootstraps the pretraining performance by using its own representation as the BERT prediction target. In the second design, we introduce target-specific information (e.g., pixel values of unmasked patches) from the encoder directly to the decoder to reduce the pressure on the encoder of memorizing the target-specific information. Thus, the encoder focuses on semantic modeling, which is the goal of BERT pretraining, and does not need to waste its capacity in memorizing the information of unmasked tokens related to the prediction target. Through extensive experiments, our BootMAE achieves 84.2% Top-1 accuracy on ImageNet-1K with ViT-B backbone, outperforming MAE by +0.8% under the same pre-training epochs. BootMAE also gets +1.0 mIoU improvements on semantic segmentation on ADE20K and +1.3 box AP, +1.4 mask AP improvement on object detection and segmentation on COCO dataset. Code is released at https://github.com/LightDXY/BootMAE.

Keywords: Vision transformer · Bert pre-training · Bootstrap · Masked autoencoder

---

X. Dong—Work done during an internship at Microsoft Research Asia.

Supplementary Information The online version contains supplementary material available at https://doi.org/10.1007/978-3-031-20056-4_15.

S. Avidan et al. (Eds.): ECCV 2022, LNCS 13690, pp. 247–264, 2022.
https://doi.org/10.1007/978-3-031-20056-4_15

1 Introduction

Self-supervised representation learning [11,25,31,43,53,55,60], aiming to learn transferable representation from unlabeled data, has been a longstanding problem in the area of computer vision. Recent progress has demonstrated that large-scale self-supervised representation learning leads to significant improvements over the supervised learning counterpart on challenging datasets. Particularly, masked image modeling (MIM) in self-supervised pre-training for vision transformers has shown remarkably impressive downstream performance in a wide variety of computer vision tasks [4,22], attracting increasing attention.

MIM aims to recover the masked region based on remaining visible patches. Essentially, it learns the transferable representation through modeling the image structure itself by content prediction. A very recent work, masked autoencoder (MAE) [28], introduces an asymmetric encoder-decoder structure where the encoder only operates on visible patches, and the output representation of the encoder along with masked tokens are fed into a lightweight decoder. Shifting the mask tokens into the small decoder results in a large reduction in computation. Besides efficiency, it also achieves competitive accuracy (87.8%), equipped with the ViT-Huge backbone, among methods that only use ImageNet-1K data.

In this paper, we introduce bootstrapped masked autoencoders (BootMAE), a new framework for self-supervised representation learning with two core designs. Firstly, we observe that with the same structure design as MAE, just changing the MIM prediction target from the pixels to the representation of a pretrained MAE encoder boosts the ImageNet classification accuracy from 83.4% to 83.8% using a ViT-Base backbone. Motivated by this observation, we propose to use a momentum encoder to provide an extra prediction target. The momentum encoder is a temporal ensemble of the MAE encoder, *i.e.*, the weights are parameterized by an exponential moving average (EMA) of the MAE encoder parameters [27,29]. For each iteration, we pass the full image to the momentum encoder to provide ground-truth representation for masked patches, and pass the masked image to the encoder followed by a predictor to generate predictions for masked patches. We hypothesize that as the training proceeds, the momentum encoder provides dynamically deeper semantics than fixed targets via bootstrapping. We keep the pixel regression branch in MAE as a good regularization in differentiating images. Moreover, it also provides guidance for the model to learn reasoning about low-level textures. Such multiple supervision helps learn the representation that benefits broader tasks including high-level recognition and accurate pixel-wise prediction that requires low-level information.

Secondly, we propose the target-aware decoder that tries to reduce the pressure on the encoder to memorize target-specific information and encourage the encoder focus on semantic modeling that benefits for pre-training. Recall that MIM aims to recover the missing region given the visible patches. It is based on the fact that natural images, regardless of their diversity, are highly structured (for example, the regular pattern of buildings, the structured shape of cars). The goal of MIM is to enable the model to understand this structure, or so-called semantics, or equivalently the relationship of different patches in the prediction target space (either pixel space or feature space). Afterwards, the predictions are made by two indispensable ingredients: the knowledge of this structure and the target-specific information (*e.g.*, pixel values) of the visible patches. Yet previous MIM methods couple the two ingredients in a single module, wasting the model capability in "memorizing" the target-specific information of visible patches. In comparison, we try to decouple them so that the encoder exploits its whole model capability for structure learning. More specifically, the target-specific information is explicitly and continuously given to the decoder, just like we humans always see the visible patches when making visual predictions.

In summary, our framework, as illustrated in Fig. 1, contains four components: (1) an encoder that aims to capture the structure knowledge; (2) a regressor that takes the structure knowledge from the encoder along with the low-level context information for pixel-level regression; (3) a predictor that takes the structure knowledge from the encoder and the high-level context information for latent representation prediction; (4) feature injection modules in both regressor decoder and predictor decoder, responsible for incorporating each own necessary target-specific information.

In addition, we find that masking strategy is crucial for these two different prediction targets. They favor different masking strategies. Particularly, pixel regression relies on random masking while block-wise masking is better for feature prediction. The reason might be that block-wise masking tends to remove large blocks, which is a difficult task for pixel regression as pixel regression heavily relies on hints from local neighbors for prediction. While for feature prediction not compelled by precise pixel-wise alignment, a large masked patch is more helpful for the model to reason about the semantic structure.

In the experiments we demonstrate the effectiveness of our framework in various downstream tasks including image classification, object detection and semantic segmentation. Our approach achieves superior performance than previous supervised methods as well as self-supervised methods. We also provide extensive ablation studies validating that the two core designs in our model works. We further provide comprehensive comparison with MAE in various epochs and various models and show our framework achieves consistently better performance.

2   Related Works

Computer vision has made tremendous progress on image content understanding in the past decade. The features learned by neural networks trained on ImageNet using over 1 million images associated with labels usually generalize very well across tasks [9,19,34,46]. Another line of image content understanding explores whether such semantically informative features can be learned through raw images alone [11,18,23,25,29,31,43,53,55,60]. Representative methods along this line include autoencoding, clustering based, contrastive learning and masked image modeling.

Autoencoding. Autoencoding (AE) [5,32] is a type of neural networks used to learn a representation (embedding) for unlabeled data. It consists of an encoder that maps data to a low-dimensional latent embedding and a decoder that recovers the data from the latent embedding, with the goal of learning a compact feature representation for the data. AE is commonly used for feature selection and feature extraction. The denoising autoencoder (DAE) [48] learns the representation robust to noise as the observed data in encoder is an addition of the original data and the noise. The decoder aims to undo the noise and recover the original data. Numerous efforts generalize DAE using different noise modelings, such as masking pixels [10,45,49], removing color channels [35,56], and shuffling image patches [42] and so on.

Clustering Based Methods. Clustering is a class of unsupervised learning methods that has been widely studied in the computer vision community. Traditional works are mostly designed under the assumption that feature representation is fixed. With the emerging of deep learning area, lots of efforts [53,55] explore adapting clustering to the end-to-end training to jointly learn the feature representation as well as clustering. The representative work DeepCluster [6] utilizes k-means to generate pseudo-labels to alternatively update the weights of the convnets and the clustering assignments of the image descriptors. Recently, several attempts [1,7] aim to maximize the mutual information between the pseudo labels and the input data, scaling up to large datasets.

Contrastive Learning. Contrastive learning aims to learn an embedding space where similar data pairs stay close to each other while dissimilar data pairs are far apart. In the self-supervised scenario, it can be interpreted as a special case of clustering where each instance itself forms a class. Thus, the positive pairs are formed by two augmented views of the same image and the negative paris are views from different images. The typical methods include MOCO [14,15,29], SimCLR [11,12], BYOL [27] and more [2,36,44]. However, contrastive-based methods rely heavily on the data augmentation strategies that need to introduce non-essential variations while without modifying semantic meanings. Crucial augmentations include random cropping and random color distortion. Meanwhile, large quantities of negative samples are usually required in order to avoid trivial solution in which the model outputs a constant representation for all data.

Masked Image Modeling. Masked image modeling for self-supervised pre-training has recently grown in popularity motivated by the success of BERT pre-training in NLP [17]. ViT [22] and BEiT [4] are two initiatives along this direction. MIM that predicts masked patches from visible ones in a sense can be viewed as context prediction. Feature representation learned through such within-image context prediction shows surprisingly strong performance in downstream tasks. Recently, lots of works [26,28] exploring MIM have been concurrently developed from different perspectives. The efforts include (i) framework design, such as MAE [28], SplitMask [24], SimMIM [54], CAE [13]; (ii) prediction targets, such as PeCo [21], MaskFeat [51], data2vec [3], iBOT [59]; (iii) video extension BEVT [50]; (iv) integration with vision-language contrastive learning FaRL [57]. Our work belongs to the first group and introduces a novel framework called Bootstrapped MAE. We progressively bootstrap the latent representation

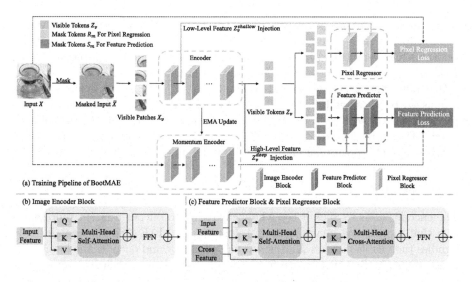

Fig. 1. Illustrating the details of our BootMAE in (a) the overall framework and training pipeline, (b) the image encoder block, (c) the feature predictor block & pixel regressor block.

in MAE to learn dynamically deeper semantics. Moreover, in comparison with previous methods coupling the context information with semantic modeling in a single model, we separate them by explicitly passing the context information to the decoder so that the encoder leverage the whole model for structure learning.

3 Approach

In this section, we introduce our Bootstrapped MAE framework in details. As illustrated in Fig. 1, our framework contains four components: 1) the encoder network focusing on learning the structure knowledge; 2) the pixel regressor decoder network aiming to predict the missing pixels of the masked region given the structure knowledge from the encoder and the context information from the visible patches,i.e., pixel values or low-level features in this case; 3) the feature predictor decoder network attempting to make feature predictions for the masked region given the same structure knowledge from the encoder and the context information of the visible patches, i.e., high-level feature information in this case; and 4) feature injection modules that feed each own context information into the regressor and the predictor explicitly and continuously in each decoder layer. After self-supervised pre-training with our BootMAE, we adopt the encoder network for various downstream tasks.

Formally, suppose an input image is $X \in \mathbb{R}^{H \times W \times C}$, where H and W denote the image height and image width and C denotes the channel number, we first split it into non-overlapping patches. This results in $N = H \times W/P^2$ patches with P denotes the resolution of each patch. In this way, an image is represented by a number of patches $\boldsymbol{X} = \{x^1, x^2, \cdots, x^N\}$ with $x^n \in \mathbb{R}^{P^2C}$ denotes a vector reshaped from the image patch. Thereafter, a large fraction of, say N_m patches are randomly sampled to be masked and leave the remaining N_v patches to be visible, $N = N_m + N_v$. Let $\mathcal{M}$ be the index set of masked patches, $\boldsymbol{X}_v = \{x^k | k \notin \mathcal{M}\}$ denotes the set of visible patches and $\boldsymbol{X}_m = \{x^k | k \in \mathcal{M}\}$ denotes the set of masked patches, we have $\boldsymbol{X} = \boldsymbol{X}_v \cup \boldsymbol{X}_m$ and $\boldsymbol{X}_v \cap \boldsymbol{X}_m = \emptyset$. Generally, each patch is associated with a positional embedding indicating the location of each patch. Therefore similarly, we have $\boldsymbol{P}_v$, positional embeddings for the visible patches and $\boldsymbol{P}_m$, positional embeddings for the masked patches.

3.1   Encoder

The encoder aims to exploit the whole capability to output a latent representation that models the image structure. Inspired by MAE [28], the encoder only handles the visible patches $\boldsymbol{X}_v$ for training efficiency and outputs the latent representation $\boldsymbol{Z}_v$. Specifically, we first project each visible patch into an embedding and add a positional embedding on each embedding to ensure the awareness of position for each patch. After this, the combined embedding is fed to a ViT [22] composed of a stack of standard vision Transformer blocks based on self-attention. That is,

$$\boldsymbol{Z}_v = \text{Enc}(\boldsymbol{X}_v, \boldsymbol{P}_v). \tag{1}$$

The computation and memory are really efficient even for large scale models as only a small subset (e.g., 25%) of the image patches needs to be handled by the encoder. Moreover, the elimination of the special mask tokens bridges the gap between pre-training and fine-tuning as the fine-tuning stage sees real visible patches without any mask token [26,28]. The mask region (e.g., 75%) is randomly sampled from the image.

We find that the masking strategy is crucial as different prediction targets favor different masking strategies. We study this masking strategy and provide more analysis in the experiments. We provide explanations about which masking strategy is suitable for which prediction target, and reach a conclusion offering guidance about the choice of masking strategy. In our implementation, we adopt the block-wise masking strategy. The output is further normalized to $\hat{\boldsymbol{Z}}_v = \text{norm}(\boldsymbol{Z}_v)$ which captures the image structure and is fed to the subsequent decoders.

3.2   Feature Injection Module

As mentioned in the introduction, there are two indispensable ingredients for the decoder to make predictions: the structure knowledge and the corresponding context information from the visible patches. Our feature injection module is designed to directly feed the context information into each layer of the decoder. We argue that in this way, the encoder exploits the whole model capability to learn structure knowledge without considering "memorizing" the context information of visible patches that is related to prediction target.

In particular, different prediction targets require different context information. Specifically, pixel-level prediction focusing on low-level details probably favors low-level context information of the visible patches while feature-level prediction attempting to predict semantic feature representation probably needs high-level context information of the visible patches. Therefore, we feed the features from the shallow layer of the encoder to the regressor decoder and the features from the deep layer of the encoder to the predictor decoder. We use $Z_v^{shallow}$ to represent the shallow features and Z_v^{deep} to represent the deep features of the encoder.

Instead of using addition or concatenation, we adopt a very elegant operator cross-attention. To be specific, we leverage the feature from the encoder as keys and values and the features from the regressor/predictor as queries to perform cross-attention. This operator helps leverage the low-level information for better pixel reconstruction and the high-level semantics for feature prediction. We apply this cross attention right after the self-attention in each transformer block of the regressor and predictor.

3.3 Regressor

The regressor aims to recover the missing pixels as in [28]. The pixel-level regression not only helps prevent the model from collapsing but also guide the model to learn reasoning about low-level textures. The input of the regressor includes (1) the normalized latent representation output from the encoder and (2) the shallow features providing context information. We add mask tokens R_m containing N_m learnable vectors representing masked patches to be predicted. To ensure that each mask token is aware of its location in the image, we add the positional embedding to each mask token. We adopt a lightweight architecture for the regressor, consisting of two vision transformer blocks and a fully-connected layer to predict missing pixels. Let the output of the regressor be $\bar{X}$, the formulation can be written as,

$$\bar{X} = \text{Reg}(\hat{Z}_v, Z_v^{shallow}, R_m, P_m). \tag{2}$$

The regressor makes prediction based on the structure knowledge in $\hat{Z}_v$ and the context information in $Z_v^{shallow}$.

3.4 Predictor

The predictor aims to predict the feature representation of the masked patches. This high-level feature prediction target guides the model to learn reasoning about high-level semantics. Moreover, the prediction groundtruth is the representation itself which evolves along with the training, providing richer and deeper semantics than fixed targets. The input of the predictor includes (1) the normalized latent representation same with the regressor and (2) the deep features providing context information different from the regressor. We also add another set of mask tokens S_m representing the masked patches to be predicted and associate them with positional embeddings. The predictor decoder network consists of two transformer blocks with a MLP layer for prediction. Say the output of the predictor is $\bar{F}$, the formulation can be written as,

$$\bar{F} = \text{Pre}(\hat{Z}_v, Z_v^{deep}, S_m, P_m). \tag{3}$$

Similarly, the predictor makes prediction based on the structure knowledge in $\hat{Z}_v$ and the context information in Z_v^{deep}.

3.5   Objective Function

The regressor and the predictor output all predictions for both visible patches as well as masked patches, but only the predictions for masked patches are involved in the loss calculation. For the regressor, each element in the output is a vector of pixel values representing a patch. We use normalized pixels as the reconstruction target for groundtruth as MAE [28]. The objective function for the regressor is,

$$\mathcal{L}_R = \sum_{k \in \mathcal{M}} \frac{1}{P^2 C} ||g_m^k - \bar{x}_m^k||_2^2, \tag{4}$$

where g_m^k is the normalized patch of x_m^k using the mean and standard deviation computed from all pixels in that patch. $\bar{x}_m^k$ is the reconstructed masked patch in $\bar{X}$.

For the predictor, the prediction feature groundtruth is the latent representation itself by passing a full image into the momentum encoder where the weights are parameterized by an exponential moving average of the MAE encoder. Let $F = \mathrm{Enc}_{ema}(X, P)$ be the groundtruth, the objective function over the masked patches for predictor is,

$$\mathcal{L}_P = \sum_{k \in \mathcal{M}} \frac{1}{\#\mathrm{dim}} ||f_m^k - \bar{f}_m^k||_2^2, \tag{5}$$

where #dim denotes the feature dimension of the token, and $f, \bar{f}$ is one of token in $F, \bar{F}$. The overall loss is a weighted sum,

$$\mathcal{L} = \mathcal{L}_R + \lambda \mathcal{L}_P, \tag{6}$$

where λ is the hyperparameter tuning the loss weight.

4   Experiments

4.1   Implementations

We experiment with the standard ViT[1] base and large architectures, ViT-B (12 transformer blocks with dimension 768) and ViT-L (24 transformer blocks with dimension 1024) for the encoder. The regressor and the predictor consist of 2 transformer blocks as mentioned above. The dimension of the regressor is set to 512 while the dimension of the predictor is set to the same as the encoder for feature prediction. The input is partitioned 14×14 patches from the image of 224×224, and each patch is of size 16×16. Following the setting in MAE, we only

---

[1] we didn't use some recent techniques like relative position or layer scaling.

Table 1. The effect of bootstrapped feature prediction. The performance with pre-trained 300 epochs gets improvement from 83.2% to 83.6%, achieving the same performance with the vanilla MAE with pre-trained 1600 epochs.

Model	Pre-train epoch	Fine-tuning
MAE	1600	83.6
MAE	800	83.4
MAE	300	83.2
MAE w bootstrapped feature prediction	300	83.6

Table 2. Ablation studies showing the effect of feature injection module in our framework. Providing context for both regressor and predictor achieves the best performance, suggesting that in this target-aware decoder design, the encoder indeed learns stronger semantic modeling.

Model	Context for regressor	Context for predictor	Fine-tuning
BootMAE	✗	✗	83.6
BootMAE	✓	✗	83.9
BootMAE	✓	✓	84.0

use standard random cropping and horizontal flipping for data augmentation. We find that the different prediction tasks favor different masking strategies. We choose the block-wise masking strategy to benefit for feature prediction. The total masking ratio is 75%, same with that in MAE [28]. Both ViT-B and ViT-L model are trained for 800 epochs with batch size set to 4096. We use Adam [33] and a cosine schedule [41] with a single cycle where we warm up the learning rate for 40 epochs to $2.4e^{-3}$. The learning rate is further annealed following the cosine schedule. Our proposed method is pre-trained on ImageNet. The regressor and the predictor are only used during pre-training. After pre-training, only the encoder is used to generate the image representation.

For ImageNet experiments, we average pool the output of the last transformer of the encoder and feed it to a softmax-normalized classifier. We evaluate the pre-trained feature representation using end-to-end fine-tuning along with the backbone model. We fine-tune 100 epochs for ViT-B and 50 epochs for ViT-L. The learning rate are warmed up to 0.005 for 20 epochs for ViT-B and 0.0015 for 5 epochs for ViT-L, after which followed by cosine schedule. The evaluation metric is top-1 validation accuracy of a single 224×224 crop.

4.2 Analysis of BootMAE

Bootstrapped Feature Prediction. One core design of our framework is the bootstrapped feature prediction that predicts the iteratively evolved latent representation of the image to enable the model to learn from dynamically richer semantic information. Here we investigate the effect of adding this proposed bootstrapped feature prediction branch. The compared models are the vanilla

Table 3. Results comparison of two different masking strategies, random masking and block-wise masking, with two different prediction targets, pixel-level target and feature-level target. This validates our hypothesis that pixel-level target favors random masking while feature-level target favors block-wise masking.

Prediction target	Mask strategy		Fine-tuning accuracy
	Random	Block	
Pixel-level	✓		83.2
Pixel-level		✓	82.8
Feature-level	✓		83.1
Feature-level		✓	83.6

Table 4. We study the regressor and predictor design and ablate the performance in terms of (a) the regressor and predictor depth and (b) the feature dimension of the regressor.

(a) The regressor and predictor depth		(b) The feature dimension of regressor	
Depth	Fine-tuning	#Dim	Fine-tuning
1	83.4	256	83.8
2	84.0	384	84.0
4	83.9	512	84.0
8	84.0	768	84.0

MAE and the MAE with an additional bootstrapped feature prediction without the feature injection module. The comparison results are presented in Table 1. We observe that the performance with pre-trained 300 epochs gets improvement from 83.2% to 83.6%, achieving the same performance with the vanilla MAE with pre-trained 1600 epochs. This demonstrates the effectiveness of the proposed bootstrapped feature prediction. Based on this result, we further analysis BootMAE under the 300 epoch pre-training setting in the following.

Feature Injection. Another important design in our framework is the feature injection module, which provides different features representing different level of context information for the regressor and the predictor. Specifically, we explicitly feed the feature outputted from the first layer of the encoder to each layer of the regressor to ease the burden of the encoder in "memorizing" the low-level details so that the encoder focuses on structure modeling. Similarly, we directly feed the features from the last layer of the encoder to each layer of the predictor. Here we study the effect of the proposed feature injection and the ablated results are shown in Table 2. We can see that providing both regressor and predictor with each own necessary context achieves the best performance, the encoder indeed learns stronger semantic modeling due to the target-aware decoder design.

Masking Strategy. Then we study two widely used masking strategies in masked image modeling: random block-wise masking in [4] and random masking

Table 5. We study the pre-training efficiency with the momentum encoder and report the performance as well as iteration time cost when feeding different fractions of the image to the momentum encoder.

Model	Fraction of image for momentum encoder	Fine-tuning	Training iter time (s)	Speed up
MAE	—	83.2	0.473	1×
BootMAE	25%	83.8	0.407	1.16×
BootMAE	50%	83.8	0.479	0.98×
BootMAE	75%	83.9	0.588	0.80×
BootMAE	100% (Default)	84.0	0.660	0.72×

in [28]. The masking ratio is the same and is set to 75%. It has been observed in MAE [28] that block-wise masking degrades at such a large ratio for their model. While in other scenarios, we find that block-wise masking is better than random masking. Here we provide explanations about why this is the case.

We suspect that the reason may come from the prediction target. Pixel-level prediction target pursuing precise pixel-wise alignment requires visible neighboring patches to provide texture information, thus favoring that the masked region should be close to the visible region. While in block-wise masking, there always exists a larger continuous block of the image being masked and more masked patches are near the image center, making it difficult to the pixel-level prediction. As for feature-level prediction which cares less about the textures/details, block-wise masking largely reduces the redundancy and most center patches are masked, forcing the model to learn reasoning about the semantics.

We experiment the two masking strategies when using two different prediction targets and the results are given in Table 3. Here we train MAE for 300 epochs with different prediction target: pixel (MAE default setting) or output feature of a 800 epoch pretrained MAE model. The comparison validates our hypothesis analyzed above that pixel-level (feature-level) target favors random masking (block-wise masking). We adopt block-wise masking as bootstrapped feature prediction is key in our framework.

Regressor and Predictor Design. Our regressor and predictor are pretty lightweight consisting of two transformer layers. In this section, we vary the network depth (number of Transformer blocks) and experiment the performance when setting the depth to 1, 2, 4 and 8. The results are reported in Table 4 (a). We can see that using depth 2 or 8 achieves the best fine-tuning performance while depth 2 enjoys more efficiency. In addition we also study the feature dimension in regressor. Note that the feature dimension in predictor is set as the same with the encoder width. As shown in Table 4 (b). The fine-tuning accuracy with different dimensions is similar, except dim = 256 which is too small.

Pre-training Efficiency with the Momentum Encoder. In our framework, we feed the full image to the momentum encoder to provide the feature prediction

Table 6. Image classification accuracy (%) comparison on ImageNet-1K of different methods using various backbones. -B, -L stands for using ViT-B, ViT-L model, respectively. We report the fine-tuning and linear probing accuracy and our method BootMAE outperforms previous self-supervised methods.

Methods	Pre-train dataset	Pre-train epochs	ViT-B		ViT-L	
			Fine-tuning	Linear	Fine-tuning	Linear
Training from scratch (i.e., random initialization)						
ViT$_{384}$ [22]	–	–	77.9	–	76.5	–
DeiT [47]	–	–	81.8	–	–	–
ViT [28]	–	–	82.3	–	82.6	–
Self-supervised pre-training on ImageNet-1K						
DINO [8]	IN-1K	300	82.8	78.2	–	–
MoCo v3 [15]	IN-1K	300	83.2	76.7	84.1	77.6
BEiT [4]	IN-1K + DALLE	800	83.2	56.7	85.2	73.5
MAE [28]	IN-1K	800	83.4	64.4	85.4	73.9
MAE* [28]	IN-1K	1600	83.6	68.0	85.9	76.6
BootMAE	IN-1K	300	84.0	64.1	85.4	74.8
BootMAE	IN-1K	800	<u>84.2</u>	66.1	**85.9**	77.1

ground-truth. We observe that this extra inference incurs additional computation cost compared with MAE. Here we present specific training iteration time in Table 5. The validation is conducted with A100 GPU and batch size 256 per GPU for all models. We further study several variants that only a subset of the masked patches are fed into the momentum encoder and the prediction loss is only evaluated on this subset of masked patches. As the masking ratio is 75%, we study three fractions: 75% (all the masked patches), 50% (sampled from masked patches), 25% (also sampled from masked patches). We report the iteration time as well as the performance in Table 5. We can see that as with a smaller fraction of patches to the momentum encoder, the iteration time cost gets fewer while the performance gets lower due to the model only learns from a fraction of the masked tokens. It is worth noting that our method when feeding 25% image patches to the momentum encoder achieves better performance than MAE while is more efficient. This is because MAE adopt 8 layers for the decoder while our regressor and predictor only consist of 2 layers.

4.3   ImageNet Classification Comparison

We compare our methods with previous state-of-the-art works on ImageNet-1K classification task. We report the top-1 validation accuracy for both fine-tuning and linear probing results in Table 6. Compared to the supervised models trained from scratch, self-supervised pre-training methods achieve significant improvement, suggesting the effectiveness of pre-training.

We further compare our framework with prior self-supervised pre-training models. We can see that the proposed BootMAE achieves the best fine-tuning

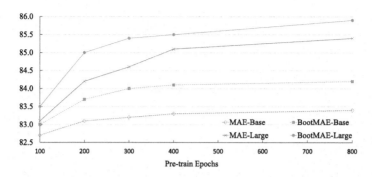

Fig. 2. Performance comparison with MAE in different pre-training epochs using ViT-B and ViT-L, showing that our BootMAE consistently outperforms MAE.

performance either based on ViT Base network or based on ViT Large network. For example, compared with the recent work MAE [28], our bootMAE with ViT-B achieves 84.2% top-1 accuracy with 0.8% gain, and with ViT-L achieves 85.9% with 0.5% improvement. We also report the linear probing accuracy. Our approach performs better than MIM based self-supervised methods, but not as good as the contrastive-based methods. We suspect that contrastive learning methods pursue linear features by comparing across images while MIM based methods exploit within image structure.

In addition, we present comprehensive comparison with MAE under different pre-training epochs for both ViT-B and ViT-L. We plot the results in Fig. 2. We can see that our approach consistently performs better than MAE. It is worth mentioning that the proposed bootMAE at 200 epochs achieves 83.7% accuracy, which is alredy better than MAE pre-trained at 800 epochs. This demonstrate that our approach is more efficient to achieve similar performance, though with the extra inference of the momentum encoder. To be specific, under the same setting that using 16 V100 GPUs, MAE takes 51 h for 800 epochs to get an 83.4% accuracy, while our BootMAE only takes 18 h for 200 epochs to get a better result 83.7%.

4.4   Downstream Tasks

To further validate the learned visual representation of our BootMAE, we present transfer learning experiments on two popular downstream tasks.

Semantic Segmentation. We compare our model on the widely used semantic segmentation dataset ADE20K [58]. We adopt UperNet framework [52] in the experiments. We train Upernet 160K iterations with batch size set as 16. We report the results in Table 7 (a). The evaluation metric is mean Intersection of Union (mIoU) averaged over all semantic categories and we report single-scale test results here. We compare our method with supervised pre-training on ImageNet-1K as well as state-of-the-art self-supervised models. We can see that

Table 7. (a) Semantic segmentation mIoU (%) comparison on ADE20K. (b) Object detection and instance segmentation comparison in terms of box AP (AP^{bb}) and mask AP (AP^{mk}) on COCO. The same ViT-B backbone is used.

(a) Semantic segmentation			(b)Object detection and instance segmentation			
Models	Pre-train epochs	ADE-20K mIoU	Models	Pre-train epochs	COCO	
					AP^{bb}	AP^{mk}
Supervised	300	47.4	Supervised	300	44.1	39.8
MoCo [16]	300	47.3	MoCo [16]	300	44.9	40.4
BEiT [4]	800	47.1	BEiT [4]	800	46.3	41.1
MAE [28]	800	47.6	MAE [28]	800	46.8	41.9
MAE* [28]	1600	48.1	MAE* [28]	1600	47.2	42.0
BootMAE	800	**49.1**	BootMAE	800	**48.5**	**43.4**

the proposed BootMAE gets superior performance than all the other baselines, further validating the effectiveness of our framework.

Object Detection and Segmentation. We perform fine-tuning on the COCO object detection and segmentation [39]. We choose the Mask R-CNN [30] framework. Concretely, we adopt FPNs [38] to scale the feature map into different size as introduced in [37]. The fine-tuning is conducted with "1×" (12 training epochs) schedule and single-scale input on the COCO training set. The performance is tested on COCO validation set, following the strategy used in previous works [20,40]. The results are reported in Table 7 (b) in terms of box AP for detection and mask AP for segmentation. We observe that our model achieves 48.5% for object detection and 43.4% for segmentation, surpassing MAE by 1.3% and 1.4% respectively.

5   Discussion and Conclusion

In this paper, we introduce a new framework BootMAE with two core designs. (1) We propose to bootstrap the latent feature representation in MAE for better performance since the prediction target evolves with training, providing progressively richer information. (2) We propose to decouple the target-specific context from the encoder so that the encoder focuses on modeling the image structure. We present extensive experiments on various downstream tasks and comprehensive ablation studies to validate the effectiveness of the proposed framework. In addition, we find that different prediction targets likely favor different masking strategies.

Previous MIM methods couple the target-specific information with structure learning in a single model. We argue that as the goal of MIM through inpainting is essentially modeling the within image structure, it is advantageous to enable the whole encoder to focus on semantic modeling which we empirically demonstrate its advantage in the experiments. In the future, we would like to seek theoretical connection between semantic modeling and representation learning.

Acknowledgement. This work was supported in part by the Natural Science Foundation of China under Grant U20B2047, 62072421, 62002334, and 62121002, Exploration Fund Project of University of Science and Technology of China under Grant YD3480002001, and by Fundamental Research Funds for the Central Universities under Grant WK2100000011.

References

1. Asano, Y.M., Rupprecht, C., Vedaldi, A.: Self-labelling via simultaneous clustering and representation learning. arXiv preprint arXiv:1911.05371 (2019)
2. Bachman, P., Hjelm, R.D., Buchwalter, W.: Learning representations by maximizing mutual information across views. arXiv preprint arXiv:1906.00910 (2019)
3. Baevski, A., Hsu, W.N., Xu, Q., Babu, A., Gu, J., Auli, M.: Data2vec: a general framework for self-supervised learning in speech, vision and language. arXiv preprint arXiv:2202.03555 (2022)
4. Bao, H., Dong, L., Wei, F.: Beit: bert pre-training of image transformers. arXiv preprint arXiv:2106.08254 (2021)
5. Bengio, Y.: Learning Deep Architectures for AI. Now Publishers Inc. (2009)
6. Caron, M., Bojanowski, P., Joulin, A., Douze, M.: Deep clustering for unsupervised learning of visual features. In: Proceedings of the European Conference on Computer Vision (ECCV), pp. 132–149 (2018)
7. Caron, M., Misra, I., Mairal, J., Goyal, P., Bojanowski, P., Joulin, A.: Unsupervised learning of visual features by contrasting cluster assignments. Adv. Neural Inf. Process. Syst. **33**, 9912–9924 (2020)
8. Caron, M., et al.: Emerging properties in self-supervised vision transformers. arXiv preprint arXiv:2104.14294 (2021)
9. Carreira, J., Zisserman, A.: Quo vadis, action recognition? a new model and the kinetics dataset. In: proceedings of the IEEE Conference on Computer Vision and Pattern Recognition, pp. 6299–6308 (2017)
10. Chen, M., et al.: Generative pretraining from pixels. In: International Conference on Machine Learning, pp. 1691–1703. PMLR (2020)
11. Chen, T., Kornblith, S., Norouzi, M., Hinton, G.: A simple framework for contrastive learning of visual representations. In: International Conference on Machine Learning, pp. 1597–1607. PMLR (2020)
12. Chen, T., Kornblith, S., Swersky, K., Norouzi, M., Hinton, G.: Big self-supervised models are strong semi-supervised learners. arXiv preprint arXiv:2006.10029 (2020)
13. Chen, X., et al.: Context autoencoder for self-supervised representation learning. arXiv preprint arXiv:2202.03026 (2022)
14. Chen, X., Fan, H., Girshick, R., He, K.: Improved baselines with momentum contrastive learning. arXiv preprint arXiv:2003.04297 (2020)
15. Chen, X., Xie, S., He, K.: An empirical study of training self-supervised vision transformers. arXiv preprint arXiv:2104.02057 (2021)
16. Chen, X., Xie, S., He, K.: An empirical study of training self-supervised vision transformers. In: Proceedings of the IEEE/CVF International Conference on Computer Vision, pp. 9640–9649 (2021)
17. Devlin, J., Chang, M.W., Lee, K., Toutanova, K.: Bert: pre-training of deep bidirectional transformers for language understanding. arXiv preprint arXiv:1810.04805 (2018)

18. Doersch, C., Gupta, A., Efros, A.A.: Unsupervised visual representation learning by context prediction. In: Proceedings of the IEEE International Conference on Computer Vision, pp. 1422–1430 (2015)

19. Donahue, J., et al.: Decaf: a deep convolutional activation feature for generic visual recognition. In: International Conference on Machine Learning, pp. 647–655. PMLR (2014)

20. Dong, X., et al.: Cswin transformer: a general vision transformer backbone with cross-shaped windows. arXiv preprint arXiv:2107.00652 (2021)

21. Dong, X., et al.: Peco: perceptual codebook for bert pre-training of vision transformers. arXiv preprint arXiv:2111.12710 (2021)

22. Dosovitskiy, A., et al.: An image is worth 16×16 words: transformers for image recognition at scale. arXiv preprint arXiv:2010.11929 (2020)

23. Dosovitskiy, A., Springenberg, J.T., Riedmiller, M., Brox, T.: Discriminative unsupervised feature learning with convolutional neural networks. Adv. Neural Inf. Process. Syst. **27**, 766–774 (2014)

24. El-Nouby, A., Izacard, G., Touvron, H., Laptev, I., Jegou, H., Grave, E.: Are large-scale datasets necessary for self-supervised pre-training? arXiv preprint arXiv:2112.10740 (2021)

25. Ermolov, A., Siarohin, A., Sangineto, E., Sebe, N.: Whitening for self-supervised representation learning. In: International Conference on Machine Learning, pp. 3015–3024. PMLR (2021)

26. Fang, Y., Dong, L., Bao, H., Wang, X., Wei, F.: Corrupted image modeling for self-supervised visual pre-training. arXiv preprint arXiv:2202.03382 (2022)

27. Grill, J.B., et al.: Bootstrap your own latent: a new approach to self-supervised learning. arXiv preprint arXiv:2006.07733 (2020)

28. He, K., Chen, X., Xie, S., Li, Y., Dollár, P., Girshick, R.: Masked autoencoders are scalable vision learners. arXiv preprint arXiv:2111.06377 (2021)

29. He, K., Fan, H., Wu, Y., Xie, S., Girshick, R.: Momentum contrast for unsupervised visual representation learning. In: Proceedings of the IEEE/CVF Conference on Computer Vision and Pattern Recognition,pp. 9729–9738 (2020)

30. He, K., Gkioxari, G., Dollár, P., Girshick, R.: Mask r-cnn. In: Proceedings of the IEEE International Conference on Computer Vision, pp. 2961–2969 (2017)

31. Henaff, O.: Data-efficient image recognition with contrastive predictive coding. In: International Conference on Machine Learning, pp. 4182–4192. PMLR (2020)

32. Hinton, G.E., Salakhutdinov, R.R.: Reducing the dimensionality of data with neural networks. Science **313**(5786), 504–507 (2006)

33. Kingma, D.P., Ba, J.: Adam: a method for stochastic optimization. arXiv preprint arXiv:1412.6980 (2014)

34. Kolesnikov, A., Beyer, L., Zhai, X., Puigcerver, J., Yung, J., Gelly, S., Houlsby, N.: Big Transfer (BiT): general visual representation learning. In: Vedaldi, A., Bischof, H., Brox, T., Frahm, J.-M. (eds.) ECCV 2020. LNCS, vol. 12350, pp. 491–507. Springer, Cham (2020). https://doi.org/10.1007/978-3-030-58558-7_29

35. Larsson, G., Maire, M., Shakhnarovich, G.: Learning representations for automatic colorization. In: Leibe, B., Matas, J., Sebe, N., Welling, M. (eds.) ECCV 2016. LNCS, vol. 9908, pp. 577–593. Springer, Cham (2016). https://doi.org/10.1007/978-3-319-46493-0_35

36. Li, S., et al.: Improve unsupervised pretraining for few-label transfer. In: ICCV (2021)

37. Li, Y., Xie, S., Chen, X., Dollar, P., He, K., Girshick, R.: Benchmarking detection transfer learning with vision transformers. arXiv preprint arXiv:2111.11429 (2021)

38. Lin, T.Y., Dollár, P., Girshick, R., He, K., Hariharan, B., Belongie, S.: Feature pyramid networks for object detection. In: Proceedings of the IEEE Conference on Computer Vision and Pattern Recognition, pp. 2117–2125 (2017)

39. Lin, T.-Y., et al.: Microsoft COCO: common objects in context. In: Fleet, D., Pajdla, T., Schiele, B., Tuytelaars, T. (eds.) ECCV 2014. LNCS, vol. 8693, pp. 740–755. Springer, Cham (2014). https://doi.org/10.1007/978-3-319-10602-1_48

40. Liu, Z., et al.: Swin transformer: hierarchical vision transformer using shifted windows. arXiv preprint arXiv:2103.14030 (2021)

41. Loshchilov, I., Hutter, F.: SGDR: stochastic gradient descent with warm restarts. arXiv preprint arXiv:1608.03983 (2016)

42. Noroozi, M., Favaro, P.: Unsupervised learning of visual representations by solving jigsaw puzzles. In: Leibe, B., Matas, J., Sebe, N., Welling, M. (eds.) ECCV 2016. LNCS, vol. 9910, pp. 69–84. Springer, Cham (2016). https://doi.org/10.1007/978-3-319-46466-4_5

43. Van den Oord, A., Li, Y., Vinyals, O.: Representation learning with contrastive predictive coding. arXiv e-prints pp. arXiv-1807 (2018)

44. Oord, A.V.d., Li, Y., Vinyals, O.: Representation learning with contrastive predictive coding. arXiv preprint arXiv:1807.03748 (2018)

45. Pathak, D., Krahenbuhl, P., Donahue, J., Darrell, T., Efros, A.A.: Context encoders: feature learning by inpainting. In: Proceedings of the IEEE Conference on Computer Vision and Pattern Recognition, pp. 2536–2544 (2016)

46. Sun, C., Shrivastava, A., Singh, S., Gupta, A.: Revisiting unreasonable effectiveness of data in deep learning era. In: Proceedings of the IEEE International Conference on Computer Vision, pp. 843–852 (2017)

47. Touvron, H., Cord, M., Douze, M., Massa, F., Sablayrolles, A., Jégou, H.: Training data-efficient image transformers & distillation through attention. In: International Conference on Machine Learning, pp. 10347–10357. PMLR (2021)

48. Vincent, P., Larochelle, H., Bengio, Y., Manzagol, P.A.: Extracting and composing robust features with denoising autoencoders. In: Proceedings of the 25th International Conference on Machine Learning, pp. 1096–1103 (2008)

49. Vincent, P., Larochelle, H., Lajoie, I., Bengio, Y., Manzagol, P.A., Bottou, L.: Stacked denoising autoencoders: learning useful representations in a deep network with a local denoising criterion. J. Mach. Learn. Res. **11**(12) (2010)

50. Wang, R., et al.: Bevt: bert pretraining of video transformers. In: IEEE Conference on Computer Vision and Pattern Recognition (CVPR 2022) (2022)

51. Wei, C., Fan, H., Xie, S., Wu, C.Y., Yuille, A., Feichtenhofer, C.: Masked feature prediction for self-supervised visual pre-training. arXiv preprint arXiv:2112.09133 (2021)

52. Xiao, T., Liu, Y., Zhou, B., Jiang, Y., Sun, J.: Unified perceptual parsing for scene understanding. In: Proceedings of the European Conference on Computer Vision (ECCV), pp. 418–434 (2018)

53. Xie, J., Girshick, R., Farhadi, A.: Unsupervised deep embedding for clustering analysis. In: International Conference on Machine Learning, pp. 478–487. PMLR (2016)

54. Xie, Z., et al.: Simmim: a simple framework for masked image modeling. arXiv preprint arXiv:2111.09886 (2021)

55. Yang, J., Parikh, D., Batra, D.: Joint unsupervised learning of deep representations and image clusters. In: Proceedings of the IEEE Conference on Computer Vision and Pattern Recognition, pp. 5147–5156 (2016)

56. Zhang, R., Isola, P., Efros, A.A.: Colorful image colorization. In: Leibe, B., Matas, J., Sebe, N., Welling, M. (eds.) ECCV 2016. LNCS, vol. 9907, pp. 649–666. Springer, Cham (2016). https://doi.org/10.1007/978-3-319-46487-9_40

57. Zheng, Y., et al.: General facial representation learning in a visual-linguistic manner. In: IEEE Conference on Computer Vision and Pattern Recognition (CVPR 2022) (2022)

58. Zhou, B., Zhao, H., Puig, X., Fidler, S., Barriuso, A., Torralba, A.: Scene parsing through ade20k dataset. In: Proceedings of the IEEE Conference on Computer Vision and Pattern Recognition, pp. 633–641 (2017)

59. Zhou, J., et al.: ibot: image bert pre-training with online tokenizer. arXiv preprint arXiv:2111.07832 (2021)

60. Zhuang, C., Zhai, A.L., Yamins, D.: Local aggregation for unsupervised learning of visual embeddings. In: Proceedings of the IEEE/CVF International Conference on Computer Vision, pp. 6002–6012 (2019)

Unsupervised Visual Representation Learning by Synchronous Momentum Grouping

Bo Pang[1], Yifan Zhang[1], Yaoyi Li[2], Jia Cai[2], and Cewu Lu[1]($\boxtimes$)

[1] Shanghai Jiao Tong University, Shanghai, China
{pangbo,zhangyf_sjtu,lucewu}@sjtu.edu.cn
[2] HuaWei Technologies Co., Ltd., Shenzhen, China
{liyaoyi,caijiai1}@huawei.com

Abstract. In this paper, we propose a genuine group-level contrastive visual representation learning method whose linear evaluation performance on ImageNet surpasses the vanilla supervised learning. Two mainstream unsupervised learning schemes are the instance-level contrastive framework and clustering-based schemes. The former adopts the extremely fine-grained instance-level discrimination whose supervisory signal is not efficient due to the false negatives. Though the latter solves this, they commonly come with some restrictions affecting the performance. To integrate their advantages, we design the SMoG method. SMoG follows the framework of contrastive learning but replaces the contrastive unit from instance to group, mimicking clustering-based methods. To achieve this, we propose the momentum grouping scheme which synchronously conducts feature grouping with representation learning. In this way, SMoG solves the problem of supervisory signal hysteresis which the clustering-based method usually faces, and reduces the false negatives of instance contrastive methods. We conduct exhaustive experiments to show that SMoG works well on both CNN and Transformer backbones. Results prove that SMoG has surpassed the current SOTA unsupervised representation learning methods. Moreover, its linear evaluation results surpass the performances obtained by vanilla supervised learning and the representation can be well transferred to downstream tasks.

1 Introduction

In the era of adopting deep learning and data-driving as the mainstream framework [33], the quality of the learned representation largely determines the performance of models on a majority of tasks [75]. For a long time, people utilize supervised tasks and adopt a large amount of annotations to train models and get good representations. Nevertheless, this simple and efficient scheme faces the problems of expensive and time-consuming annotating costs [2,17,18,57], and non-ideal generalization performance caused by bias from the annotation information [4,51]. To solve these problems, people extensively study the unsupervised representation learning method [58], including the generative models providing expressive latent features [30,55] and self-supervised methods with different pretext tasks [48,53,62]. However, there are still performance gaps between these methods and the supervised scheme. In recent years, unsupervised representation learning achieves great improvements, SOTA contrastive learning [6,8,21,23] based unsupervised methods reduce the performance gap to less than 3%. We continue the study of the unsupervised representation learning, stand on the shoulder of previous contrastive and clustering-based methods, and finally, push the performance of unsupervised methods above the level of the vanilla supervised scheme.

Traditional contrastive learning methods adopt instance discrimination as the pretext task. This kind of refinement of classification treats every sample as a category to conduct discrimination. Thus, it will introduce many false-negative pairs, leading to inefficient supervisory signals. And another problem is that the accurate instance discrimination requires pair-wise comparison on the entire dataset. However, with limited resources, most implementations compromise to adopt a subset of the comparison with a large batch size or memory bank [23,67], which further decreases the efficiency of learning.

Previous clustering-based methods relax instance discrimination into group discrimination to solve these problems. The core task of clustering is how to split instances into groups. They try to adopt K-means clustering method [5,71] or optimal transport [3,6] method to achieve this, but due to the limitations they introduce (asynchronous two-stage training or local equipartition respectively), they don't show an advantage in terms of performance.

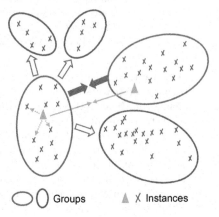

Fig. 1. Group contrastive *vs.* instance contrastive learning. Compared with instance contrasting (red parts), group contrasting (blue part) learns representations through higher-level semantics, which can reduce the chance that the already learned similar instances are still treated as negative pairs (false negatives). The significant reduction of contrast elements after the grouping process also makes global contrasting easier to calculate. The colorized instances or groups denote the positive pairs and the grey ones are negatives. (Color figure online)

Here, we integrate the advantages of instance contrastive and clustering-based methods to the newly proposed SMoG method which follows the instance contrastive framework, and extend it to group-level (see Fig. 1). One major design is the momentum grouping scheme that allows gradient propagating through groups to synchronously conduct the instance grouping process together with the representation learning. It is the first method to apply contrasting directly on groups instead of instances, since no gradient can propagate through group features in previous methods, With it, SMOG avoids the false negatives in instance contrasting and wipes off limiting factors in previous clustering-based methods.

The proposed SMoG method is effective and pretty simple. We evaluate it on several standard self-supervised benchmarks and multiple downstream tasks. In particular, under the linear protocol, it achieves 76.4% top-1 accuracy on ImageNet with a standard ResNet-50 [25], which surpasses the vanilla supervised-level performance for the first time! Extensive experiments show that SMoG works robustly and we observe consistent SOTA performance under linear (+0.8%), semi-supervised classification (+2%), detection, and segmentation tasks. Besides, SMoG works well on both CNN and Transformer backbones.

2 Related Work

2.1 Handcraft Pretext Task

Adopting pretext tasks to provide training supervisory signals is an effective unsupervised representation learning scheme. By now, well studied pretext tasks include jigsaw solving [48,49], colorization [32,62,73], denoising [62], inpainting [53], super-resolution [34], and patch position prediction [13,14]. In addition, for video visual inputs with temporal dimension, sequential-related pretext tasks are proved useful, such as ordering frames [19,46,66], motion estimation [1,29,39,61], and further frame estimation [43,44,56,63,64]. Due to the specificity of these tasks, the learned representation often carry a certain bias, leading to relatively limited performances on downstream tasks.

2.2 Instance Discrimination Method

Present mainstream contrastive learning methods [6,8,20,21,23,37,47,52,59,74] learn representations by instance discrimination which treats each image (pixel) in a training set as its own category. This scheme achieves state-of-the-art performances on downstream tasks. Its common training direction provided by InfoNCE [8,22,50] or its variations is to maximize the mutual information [27,50], which requires a large number of negative pairs to get good performances [8]. Adopting a large batch size is a straightforward method, but it consumes lots of resources. To solve this, MoCo [23] and [67] propose to utilize memory structures. Some latest designs [7,9,21] conduct contrasting without negative samples by an asymmetry Siamese structure or normalization techniques. Recent work [37] proposes self-supervised learning with the Hilbert-Schmidt Independence Criterion, which yields a new understanding of InfoNCE. While RELIC [47] improves the generalization performance through an invariance regularizer under the causal framework. NNCLR [15] adopts the nearest neighbour from the dataset as the positives. UniGrad [59] provides a unified contrastive formula through gradient analysis. Instance discrimination, as an excessive fine-grained classification setting implies some problems like false-negative pairs [76].

2.3 Group Discrimination Method

Our work follows the group discrimination scheme. DeepClustering [5] adopts the K-means clustering method to get the groups and learn features from them in an iterative manner. However, the two-step training scheme (clustering, learning) leads to delayed supervisory signal, against effective representation learning. ODC [71] and CoKe [54] shortens the two-step circulation period but does not solve the delay problem. SeLa [3] and SwAV [6] treat the grouping problem as pseudo-labelling and solve it as a optimal transport task. But, to avoid degeneracy, they add an equipartition constraint, decreasing the validity of grouping. Our work stands on the shoulders of these works, solves the mentioned problems, and finally achieves the level of vanilla supervised learning for the first time.

3 Approach

Present SOTA methods commonly adopt the instance contrastive learning, apply a two-stream Siamese network structure, and take InfoNCE or its variants as the loss function to conduct the contrasting. This is an eminent and robust structure that has been proved by many models. However, there are two potential problems: 1) In terms of the problem setting, instance discrimination is too fine-grained and the learned representation goes against the downstream tasks that rely on the high-level semantics to some extent, because for high-level semantics, instance-level contrasting introduces many false-negative pairs which damage the quality of representation learning. 2) In terms of technical practice, contrastive learning based on InfoNCE needs a large number of negative pairs to improve the upper bound of the theoretical performance [8,23], which poses a challenge on computing resources or needs specific model designs.

To deal with the above two problems, previous works [5,6,65] propose the clustering-based method: adopting groups as negatives to reduce false-negatives and the total number of negative pairs. However, these methods introduce some limitations and lose the advantages of contrastive methods: the always-updating optimization signal and totally unrestricted feature distribution. To integrate the advantages of contrastive and clustering-based method, we propose to contrast in the group unit and design the first group-level contrastive learning algorithm Synchronous Momentum Grouping (SMoG) which inherits and develops current contrastive learning techniques, and pushes the performance of unsupervised methods to the level of vanilla supervised scheme.

3.1 Group-Level Contrastive Learning

In general, given a dataset $\mathbf{X} = \{\mathbf{x}_1, \mathbf{x}_2, ...\mathbf{x}_n\}$ with n instances and a visual model f_θ with parameter set θ which maps each instance to a vector representation $f_\theta(\mathbf{x})$, the pipeline of the instance contrastive learning framework can be expressed as:

$$L_i = -\log \frac{\exp(\mathrm{sim}(f_\theta(\mathbf{x}_i^a), \hat{f}_\eta(\mathbf{x}_i^b)/\tau)}{\sum_{\mathbf{x}_j \neq \mathbf{x}_i^a, \mathbf{x}_j \in \mathbf{Y} \subseteq \mathbf{X}} \exp(\mathrm{sim}(f_\theta(\mathbf{x}_i^a), \hat{f}_\eta(\mathbf{x}_j))/\tau)}, \tag{1}$$

where $\text{sim}(\mathbf{u}, \mathbf{v})$ is commonly instantiated as the normalized inner product, $\hat{f}_\eta$ is just f_θ or a variant of f_θ such as its momentum updated version or the version without the last few layers (predictor). $\mathbf{x}_i^a$ and $\mathbf{x}_i^b$ are two different augmented views of $\mathbf{x}_i$. In theory, $\mathbf{x}_j$ should come from the training set $\mathbf{X}$, but in practical, taking computing complexity into account, $\mathbf{x}_j$ is commonly selected from a much smaller subset $\mathbf{Y} \subseteq \mathbf{X}$.

In order to extend this framework to the group level, we need to first define and generate a certain number of groups with group feature $\mathbf{g}$, attach each instance to a certain group, allow gradients propagating through groups, and update them synchronously during training: $\mathbf{c}_i^a, \{\mathbf{g}\} \leftarrow \phi(f_\theta(\mathbf{x}_i^a)|\{\mathbf{g}\})$, where ϕ is the group assigning function that takes in instance and group features, generates instances' corresponding group $\mathbf{c}_i^a$, and updates the groups $\{\mathbf{g}\}$. Thus, $\mathbf{c}_i = \mathbf{g}_k$ means that instance $\mathbf{x}_i$ is attached to group k. With the group-level features, we can derive the group-level contrastive learning framework as:

$$L_i = -\log \frac{\exp(\text{sim}(\mathbf{c}_i^a, \mathbf{c}_i^b)/\tau)}{\sum_{\mathbf{g}_j \in \mathbf{G}} \exp(\text{sim}(\mathbf{c}_i^a, \mathbf{g}_j)/\tau)}, \tag{2}$$

where $\mathbf{G}$ is the set of group features. Since the number of groups is a certain small value, we can conduct group contrasting globally with all the group pairs.

The algorithm of gaining group features (ϕ) will be detailed introduced in the next section. Here, we emphasize that besides well expressing a group of similar instances without extra limitation, a qualified ϕ also needs to make sure every group feature $\mathbf{c}_i$ is updated synchronously with the instance feature $f_\theta(\mathbf{x}_i)$ since the gradients need to be back-propagated through $\mathbf{c}_i$ to $f_\theta(\mathbf{x}_i)$ for training the parameters which means $\mathbf{c}_i$ can replace the latest $f_\theta(\mathbf{x}_i)$ to participate in contrasting. This is the core difference from the previous clustering-based method, since their group features gained by clustering cannot back-propagate the gradi-

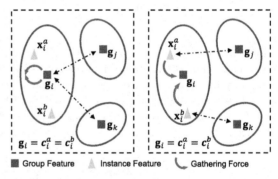

Group Feature   **Instance Feature**   **Gathering Force**

Fig. 2. The left part illustrates the group contrastive target described by Eq. 2. As the training progresses, preliminary formed meaningful representations have a large chance to make $\mathbf{x}_i^a$ and $\mathbf{x}_i^b$ belong to the same group. In this case, the gathering force (the green arrow) cannot make them get closer. Thus, we modify it to the version in Eq. 3 illustrated in the right part, where the push and pull force required by contrastive learning can always take effect. (Color figure online)

ent, and directly contrasting group features cannot train the network.

Intuitively, the newly designed group contrastive learning method aims at directly adjusting the distribution of group features, and since gradients can propagate through group features to instance features, this algorithm can grad-

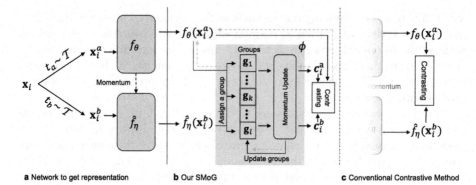

a Network to get representation   **b** Our SMoG   **c** Conventional Contrastive Method

Fig. 3. Pipeline of our SMoG *vs.* conventional contrastive method. Like typical contrastive learning methods, SMoG gets instance features from two augmentation views of the same image by a Siamese structure. Rather than directly contrasting the instance features, SMoG works at the group level. Specifically, it dynamically splits the already seen instances into groups, assigns the new instance to the closest group (the red one in the figure), and adopts the group feature which replaces the instance one to conduct the contrasting. Synchronous with the representation learning, group features are updated by the new instances in a momentum manner. The yellow dashed lines show the back-propagation paths, and we can see that the group feature can also back-propagate gradients. (Color figure online)

ually learn the instance representation. However, unfortunately, it has flaws in the second half of the training process. With the meaningful representations gradually formed, c_i^a and c_i^b tend to be the same group feature. This will make the supervisory signal fail to gather similar instances and get them closer (see Fig. 2). To solve this problem, considering that c_i^a is the combination of a group of $f_\theta(\mathbf{x})$, we change the group contrastive learning loss to:

$$L_i = -\log \frac{\exp(\text{sim}(f_\theta(\mathbf{x}_i^a), c_i^b)/\tau)}{\sum_{\mathbf{g}_j \in \mathbf{G}} \exp(\text{sim}(f_\theta(\mathbf{x}_i^a), \mathbf{g}_j)/\tau)}. \tag{3}$$

When $c_i^a \neq c_i^b$ Eq. 3 can be seen as the "stochastic-batch" version of Eq. 2, which splits an intact loss into several batches, similar to SGD and GD. When $c_i^a = c_i^b$, Eq. 3 can still gather instances, which solves the problem. This formulation looks similar to previous clustering-based methods, but remember that we still conduct group contrasting instead of instance classification that previous methods do, since group features c_i and $\mathbf{g}_j$ can propagate the gradient, thus has the same status with $f_\theta(\mathbf{x}_i^a)$ in contrasting and directly guide the learning direction.

3.2 Synchronous Momentum Grouping

SMoG's network structure and training settings are identical to conventional contrastive learning frameworks as Fig. 3 shows. That is generating $\mathbf{x}_i^a$ and $\mathbf{x}_i^b$

through two different groups of augmentation $t_a, t_b \sim \mathcal{T}$, and gaining their features through a Siamese network. Following MoCo [23], we adopt a momentum network: $\hat{f}_\eta \leftarrow \alpha * \hat{f}_\eta + (1 - \alpha) * f_\theta$, where α is the momentum ratio and here, f_θ denotes layers that also exist in $\hat{f}_\eta$. So far, SMoG is consistent with the typical contrastive learning methods. By adding the group assigning function ϕ, we can get the complete SMoG method.

Generating Group Features. As mentioned in last section, group-level contrasting optimizes instance features through group features. Thus, group features must represent the latest instance ones to propagate gradients, namely, c_i needs to be synchronously updated with $f_\theta(x_i)$ and calculated by a differentiable function. Directly adopting conventional global clustering as ϕ is not feasible to synchronously update c_i with $f_\theta(x_i)$ at each iteration due to the computing cost. Thus, we simply modify it to the momentum grouping scheme, generating c_i through an iterative algorithm synchronized with representation learning.

Before the training start, we initialize the l group features $\{g_1, ..., g_k, ..., g_l\}$ randomly or using a clustering method such as k-means. Then along with the training process, we update g_k and get c_i in each iteration by:

$$c_i = \mathrm{argmax}_{g_k}(\mathrm{sim}(f_\theta(x_i), g_k))$$
$$g_k \leftarrow \beta * g_k + (1 - \beta) * \mathrm{mean}_{c_t = g_k} f_\theta(x_t), \tag{4}$$

where β is the momentum ratio, x_t comes from a mini-batch, and we omit the normalization. Importantly, this mechanism does not introduce extra limitation.

The momentum grouping scheme assigns each instance to the closest group and iteratively updates the group features in a momentum manner. In this way, the group features are always the latest representative of the instance visual features and more importantly, for each iteration, the updated g_k is adopted to conduct contrasting and the gradient can be back-propagated through g_k to $f_\theta(x_i)$. This is the main difference from previous clustering-based methods.

Avoiding Collapse. The momentum grouping scheme ensures that the group features g_k always represent the latest learned instance representations. However, because the algorithm is based on the iterative updating with a local subset of instances (a batch), at the early training stage, it might be unstable. The scale of the groups may be unbalanced or all the instances collapse into few groups. To deal with this, we periodically apply an extra grouping process on a cached relatively large feature set to relocate the groups. There will be long intervals among groupings which are light and quick, thus, the overhead can be ignored.

3.3 Compared with Previous Clustering Methods

Group discrimination is not a first proposed concept. Previous clustering based methods DeepClustering [5] and SwAV [6] also conduct it and in terms of the loss function, the three algorithms have a similar form. The main difference lies on the method to generate the groups and the way to utilize them. Our SMoG aims at conducting the contrasting among the groups like Eq. 2 shows. This is impossible for previous clustering-based methods since their group features have to be detached out and cannot back-propagate the gradients to the parameters. Thus, they do not contrast the groups but classify the instances into groups. To achieve the group contrasting, we propose the momentum grouping scheme which allows us directly contrasting the groups and propagate gradients. Although we modify the final loss to Eq. 3 for better performance, our SMoG is still a group-level contrastive algorithm, since the group features directly guide the optimization direction. This is the reason we call our method "grouping contrasting" instead of "clustering" to distinguish them. SMoG conducts contrasting among groups instead of classifying instances based on clusters.

3.4   Implementation Details

Augmentation. We adopt the asymmetrical augmentation method used in BYOL [21], where there are two augmentation schemes for the two streams of the Siamese network. The two schemes adopt the same color jittering but one has a stronger Gaussian blur and the other one has stronger solarization. Since the contrasting loss we adopt is also asymmetrical (contrasting among instance and group features), the two streams of the Siamese network are not assigned to a fixed augmentation scheme, instead, they adopt one of them in an alternate manner. In this way, the two streams can generate instance features under the same distribution so that they can be mapped to the same group feature set.

SMoG Setting. Like many previous works [10,21,68], both f_θ and $\hat{f}_\eta$ have a backbone and a projection head. And f_θ has an extra prediction head stacked on the projection head. The backbone's output is adopted as the learning representation. The two kinds of head are both a two-layer MLP and their hidden layer is followed by a BatchNorm [28] and an activation function (ReLU for ResNet and GELU [26] for SwinTransformer [40]). The output layer of projection head also has BN. The dimension of the hidden layer is 2048, while for the output layer, it is 128 for CNN and 256 for Transformer. The Siamese's momentum ratio α is 0.999. In experiments, we group all the instances into 3k groups and the group features **g** are initialized with the K-means algorithm. The momentum ratio β of grouping follows a linear schedule from 1.0 to 0.99. To avoid collapse, we reset the group features every 300 iterations with K-means on cached features of the past 300 iterations and $\hat{f}_\eta$ is synchronously reset with the parameters of f_θ.

Pre-training Details. We pre-train the models on ImageNet dataset [12]. For CNN backbones, we train with the LARS [69] optimizer with 4096 mini-batchsize on 64 GPUS (when adopting ResNet50). The base learning rate is set to $lr = 0.3 \times$ batchsize/256, following first a 10-epoch warm-up and then the cosine scheduler. The weight decay and temperature τ are set to 10^{-6} and 0.1. For Transformer based backbones, we adopt the Adamw optimizer [42]. The base learning rate and weight decay are $5e^{-4} \times$ batchsize/2048 and 0.05. Other settings are the same with CNN backbones. For efficient training, we also adopt the multi-crop training scheme [6,7] with two large views (224×224) and 4 small views (96×96). When adopting multi-crop, the scale of the random crops are [0.2, 1.0] and [0.05, 0.2] respectively for large and small views.

4 Experiments

We evaluate SMoG firstly on the standard benchmark on ImageNet with both CNN and Transformer backbones. We then compare the performance on several downstream tasks and give a detailed ablation study.

4.1 Linear Evaluation

Following the standard benchmarks [6–8,10,21,23,68], we first evaluate the representation of ResNet-50 [25] and Swin Transformer Tiny [40] trained with the proposed SMoG by the linear protocol: linear classification on frozen features.

Results on ResNet-50 is shown in Table 1 and we can see that previous group-based methods have no advantages over instance contrastive ones (about -2% top-1 accuracy) due to the introduced restrictions. While the proposed SMoG improves the best performance of group-based methods by 2.3% top-1 accuracy and achieves the SOTA performances among all the unsupervised representation methods. More importantly, after adopting the multi-crop training strategy [6,7], for the first time, the unsupervised representation of ResNet-50 surpasses the performance of the vanilla supervised one ($+0.3\%$) on ImageNet.

We adopt Swin-Transformer to evaluate the performance of SMoG on Transformer backbones. Results are shown in Table 2. For the two-view setting, most Transformer-based backbones perform worse than the CNNs with similar parameters. But Transformers benefit more from the multi-view training. We hold the

Table 1. Linear protocol results on ImageNet. ResNet50 is adopted. † denotes the model adopts the multi-crop training strategy. "acc" means accuracy.

Model	Epoch	Batchsize	Top1 acc	Top5 acc
Supervised	100ep	256	76.1	92.7
Instance contrastive method				
ReSSL [74]	200	256	69.6	–
MoCoV2 [23]	800	256	71.1	90.1
SimSiam [9]	800	256	71.3	–
InfoMin Aug. [60]	800	256	73.0	91.1
MoCoV3 [10]	400	4096	73.1	–
MoCoV3	800	4096	73.8	–
BYOL [21]	400	4096	73.2	–
BYOL	800	4096	74.3	91.6
Barlow Twins [70]	1000	2048	73.2	91.0
RELIC [47]	1000	4096	74.8	92.2
SSL-HSIC [37]	1000	4096	74.8	92.2
Group-based method				
DeepCluster	400	256	52.2	–
ODC [71]	400	256	57.6	–
PCL [36]	200	256	67.6	–
DeepClusterV2	400	4096	70.2	–
SwAV	400	4096	70.1	–
CoKe [54]	800	1024	72.2	–
SMoG	400	2048	73.6	91.3
SMoG	800	4096	74.5	91.9
With multi-crop				
SwAV†	400	4096	74.6	–
SwAV†	800	4096	75.3	–
DC-v2†	800	4096	75.2	–
DINO † [7]	800	4096	75.3	–
UniGrad † [59]	800	4096	75.5	–
NNCLR † [15]	1000	4096	75.6	92.4
SMoG†	400	4096	**76.4**	**93.1**

opinion that the self-attention, a global operator, needs more data to train. Thus, stronger augmentation leads to better performances. SMoG, in the two-view setting, achieves SOTA performances compared to DINO (+2%), MoCo (+2%), EsViT (+4%), and MOBY (−0.5%). Note that, for fair comparison, we report the performance of EsViT with only $\mathcal{L}_V$. In the multi-crops setting, SMoG achieves the supervised performance without Mixup [72] augmentation. Since mixup needs labels, it is not straightforwardly suitable for the unsupervised setting. This comparison reveals a landmark progress in contrastive learning.

Table 2. Linear protocol results on ImageNet. † denotes adopting the multi-crop training strategy. The throughput (im/s) is calculated on a NVIDIA V100 GPU with 128 samples per forward. We report performances without Mixup and standard ones for supervised methods.

Model	Backbone	Throughput	Param	Top1 acc
Supervised	SwinT	808	28	77.8/81.3
Supervised	DeiT-S/16	1007	21	77.5/79.8
MoBY	DeiT-S/16	1007	21	72.8
MoBY	SwinT	808	28	75.0
MoCoV3	DeiT-S/16	1007	21	72.5
MoCoV3	ViT-B/16	312	85	76.7
DINO	DeiT-S/16	1007	21	72.5
DINO †	DeiT-S/16	1007	21	77.0
EsViT [35]	SwinT	808	28	70.5
EsViT †	SwinT	808	28	77.0
SMoG	SwinT	808	28	74.5
SMoG †	SwinT	808	28	**77.7**

Large Architectures. Table 3 shows the results on several varients of ResNet-50 with larger widths [31]. The performance increases with a similar trend of supervised method and previous unsupervised framework. And it is worth noting that in previous works [8,21], with larger architectures, their gap with the supervised learning decreases, but it is a pity that we do not observe an increasing superiority of SMoG over the supervised one. In Fig. 4, we

Table 3. Linear protocol results on ImageNet with larger backbones. We experiment on wider ResNet. The pre-training details are the same with the ResNet-50 × 1.

Model	Backbone	Param	Top1 acc	Top5 acc
Supervised	Res50 (x2)	188	77.8	93.8
	Res50 (x4)	375	78.9	94.5
BYOL	Res50 (x2)	188	77.4	93.6
	Res50 (x4)	375	78.6	94.2
SwAV	Res50 (x2)	188	77.3	–
	Res50 (x4)	375	77.9	–
SMoG	Res50 (x2)	188	78.0	93.9
	Res50 (x4)	375	79.0	94.4

demonstrate that on both CNN and Transformer, SMoG is comparable with the vanilla supervised method.

4.2 Semi-supervised Fine-Tune Evaluation

Next, we evaluate the proposed SMoG through semi-supervised fine-tuning the unsupervised representation on a subset of training data of ImageNet. We follow the protocol adopted in [8] and the 1% and 10% labeled splits of ImageNet we adopt are the fixed ones provided in [8].

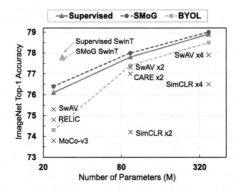

Fig. 4. ResNet linear evaluation on ImageNet compared with supervised training. We can see that for different model sizes, our SMoG achieves comparable performance with supervised method.

As shown in Table 4, SMoG consistently outperforms all the previous methods in both 1% and 10% settings on ResNet-50 × 1 and ×2. Besides, we also fine-tune the unsupervised representation on the full ImageNet. With SMoG pre-training, ResNet-50 achieves 78.3% top-1 accuracy under the standard training recipe, surpassing the directly supervised learning by 2.2%. Similarly, the ResNet-50 × 2 also outperforms the directly supervised training by 2.4%.

Table 4. Semi-supervised results on ImageNet.

Method	Top-1 acc (%)			Top-5 acc (%)		
	1%	10%	100%	1%	10%	100%
resnet-50 ×1						
Supervised	25.4	56.4	76.1	48.4	80.4	92.9
SimCLR	48.3	65.6	76.0	75.5	87.8	93.1
BYOL	53.2	68.8	77.7	78.4	89.0	93.9
SwAV	53.9	70.2	–	78.5	89.9	–
Barlow Twins	55.0	69.7	–	79.2	89.3	–
SSL-HSIC	52.1	67.9	77.2	77.7	88.6	93.6
NNCLR	56.4	69.8	–	80.7	89.3	–
SMoG	**58.0**	**71.2**	**78.3**	**81.6**	**90.5**	**94.2**
resnet-50 ×2						
Supervised	–	–	77.8	–	–	93.8
SimCLR	58.5	71.7	–	83.0	91.2	–
BYOL	62.2	73.5	–	84.1	91.7	–
SMoG	**63.6**	**74.4**	**80.2**	**85.6**	**92.4**	**95.2**

4.3 Transfer to Other Vision Tasks

We further transfer the unsupervised representations of ResNet-50 learned with the proposed SMoG to several downstream tasks, namely semantic segmentation, object detection, and instance segmentation.

We first evaluate SMoG on Cityscapes [11] and VOC-2012 [16] semantic segmentation tasks. For fair comparison, we align all the methods with the same training recipe of FCN [41]. Results of mean accuracy and mean IoU are provided in Table 5, we can

Table 5. Transfer learning results on semantic segmentation task. We fine-tune the representations on VOC2012 and Cityscapes dataset. The segmentation model is FCN with ResNet-50.

Model	Cityscapes		VOC-2012	
	mIoU	mAcc	mIoU	mAcc
Supervised	73.83	82.56	73.59	83.74
MoCoV2	74.30	83.37	70.86	80.37
SwAV	74.80	83.01	74.97	84.27
BYOL	74.90	83.73	74.76	84.37
SMoG	**76.03**	**83.97**	**76.22**	**85.01**

see that nearly all the unsupervised representations outperform the conventional supervised one which reveals that in this downstream task, unsupervised representation is already a better choice. And again, SMoG performs better than the original SOTAs on Cityscapes (+1.1 mIoU) and VOC-2012 (+1.4 mIoU) datasets.

Then, we evaluate on object detection and instance segmentation tasks on COCO [38] dataset. Similarly, all the unsupervised representations are transferred with the same fine-tuning recipe of Mask-RCNN [24]. We provide AP results in Table 6. The same with semantic segmentation, on these two downstream tasks, our unsupervised pre-training representations are better than the supervised one. And still, SMoG improves the current SOTA results, +0.7 AP on object detection and +1.1 AP on instance segmentation.

4.4 Ablation Study

We provide ablation studies on key components of SMoG. ResNet-50 is adopted. Network is trained for 100 epochs without multi-crop. The representation is evaluated under the linear protocol.

Grouping Quality. To evaluate the grouping quality, in Fig. 5, we provide the density distribution of group entropy. All the three group-discrimination methods (our SMoG, SwAV, and Deep-Clusteringv2) have 3k groups. For each group, its entropy is $\sum_i -p_i *$

Table 6. Transfer learning results on object detection and instance segmentation tasks. We adopt COCO as the fine-tuning dataset. Mask RCNN with ResNet-50-FPN is the detection and segmentation model. We report the AP metrics.

Method	COCO det			COCO instance seg.		
	AP^{bb}	AP^{bb}_{50}	AP^{bb}_{75}	AP^{mk}	AP^{mk}_{50}	AP^{mk}_{75}
Rand Init	31.0	49.5	33.2	28.5	46.8	30.4
Supervised	38.9	59.6	42.7	35.4	56.5	38.1
InsDis [67]	37.4	57.6	40.6	34.1	54.6	36.4
PIRL [45]	38.5	57.6	41.2	34.0	54.6	36.2
MoCoV2	39.4	59.9	43.0	35.8	56.9	38.4
SwAV	38.5	60.4	41.4	35.4	57.0	37.7
DC-v2 [6]	38.3	60.3	41.3	35.4	56.7	38.0
BYOL	39.4	59.9	43.0	35.8	56.8	38.5
Barlow Twins	39.2	58.7	42.6	34.3	55.4	36.5
SMoG	**40.1**	**61.6**	**43.7**	**36.9**	**58.7**	**39.3**

$\log(p_i)$ where p_i is the ratio of instances that belong to class i (data annotation) in this group. A lower entropy means a group has more unitary semantics and is more meaningful. Thus, more groups with low entropy indicate higher grouping quality. From Fig. 5, we can see SMoG has twice more low-entropy groups than the two baselines, proving its superiority.

Momentum Ratio β of Group Features. From Table 7a, we can see that the linearly decreasing schedule for β is much better than the fixed schedule. This is because our momentum grouping scheme updates the group features with only a small part of features (a batch) in each iteration and at the beginning of training, the feature distribution changes drastically, a small β will lead to unstable groups. Thus, we need a large β at the beginning to solve the problem and the linear schedule is a straightforward solution. After adopting the linearly decreasing schedule, our SMoG is not sensitive to the final value of β and we adopt 0.99 as the default value for all the experiments on both CNN and Transformer.

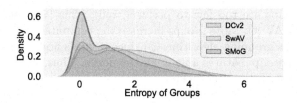

Fig. 5. Entropy of each groups. SMoG produces groups with much lower entropy which represents a better grouping quality in terms of high-level semantics.

Avoiding Collapse. Still, because the group feature updating process cannot access the global feature distribution, there is a possibility of collapse during training. Thus, we adopt the periodical clustering (pd) trick to avoid this. The first two rows of Table 7b prove its necessity. We can see that it successfully makes the backbone learn useful representations but the performance is not good enough. We believe this is because the group features are always generated and updated based on the instance features generated by only f_θ, leading to misalignment with features from $\hat{f}_\eta$. Thus, we also reset $\hat{f}_\eta$ with the parameters of f_θ after each clustering. The integrated pd with $\hat{f}_\eta$ reset leads to ideal performance. And surprisingly, we find that only resetting $\hat{f}_\eta$ without the clustering can avoid the collapse too. We think the sudden change of $\hat{f}_\eta$ feature distribution also helps to avoid the network gradually falling into degeneration.

Number of Groups. In Table 7c, we evaluate the influence of the number of groups used in SMoG under the linear protocol. The results show that SMoG is not sensitive to the group number. Even if we tune it in a wide range (1k–30k), the performance is maintained at a stable level (±0.2), as long as there are enough

Table 7. Ablation study on SMoG. We adopt ResNet50 as the backbone and train the unsupervised algorithm on ImageNet for 100 epochs without multi-crop training strategy. We report the linear evaluation results (Top-1 accuracy).

(a) Momentum ratio β. Linearly decreasing schedule performs better.

Schedule	Top1 acc
fixed 0.99 β	65.9
1.0 $\beta \rightarrow$ 0.9 β	67.0
1.0 $\beta \rightarrow$ 0.99 β	67.2
1.0 $\beta \rightarrow$ 0.999 β	67.1

(b) Tricks dealing with collapse. The periodical clustering is necessary.

Tricks	Top1 acc
None	0.1
+ periodical clustering (pd)	53.7
+ reset $\hat{f}_\eta$ periodically	53.4
+ pd & reset $\hat{f}_\eta$ periodically	67.2

(c) Number of groups. 3k is enough for SMoG.

# Groups	Top1 acc
300	65.2
1000	67.0
3000	67.2
10000	67.2

(d) Grouping algo. Momentum update better balances grouping and learning.

method	Top1 acc
Randomly select	30.2
Adopt latest	42.1
Averaging update	65.8
Momentum update	67.2

groups (300 groups are too few to perform well). This is consistent with the conclusion of SwAV [6]. More groups increase the computation time consuming of the momentum grouping algorithm (ϕ) since it needs node communication to synchronize the group features among all the nodes. Thus, we adopt 3K as the default setting for all the experiments.

Method for Updating Group Features. In Table 7d, we evaluate different operators for updating the group features. We consider 4 operators here: 1) Randomly select (RS): randomly select a group of latest instance features and adopt them as the group features. 2) Adopt latest (AL): $\mathbf{g}_k \leftarrow \text{mean}_{\mathbf{c}_t = \mathbf{g}_k} f_\theta(\mathbf{x}_t)$. 3) Averaging update (AU): $\mathbf{g}_k \leftarrow \mathbf{g}_k + (1/n) * (\text{mean}_{\mathbf{c}_t = \mathbf{g}_k} f_\theta(\mathbf{x}_t) - \mathbf{g}_k)$, where n is the total number of instances belonging to group k, including ones in current iteration. 4) Momentum update (MU): the proposed method described in Eq. 4.

As the random baseline, RS's poor performance shows us that the grouping algorithm plays an important role in our SMoG method. AL also does not perform well, which implies that the local grouping method will not provide an efficient training signal for representation learning. AU follows the sequential k-means algorithm and achieves a relatively great performance. But compared to our MU, it is not the best choice for conducting grouping together with the representation learning. The specifically designed MU which gives new features more weights is more suitable for the group-level contrastive learning.

5 Conclusion

We extend the recently popular contrastive learning to group level with the proposed SMoG and push the performance of unsupervised representation under linear protocol to the vanilla supervised level. SMoG synchronously conducts the representation learning and grouping process to effectively achieve the group-level contrasting. We hope the newly designed group-level contrastive learning will be useful for the community to further develop visual unsupervised method.

Acknowledgement. This work was supported by the National Key R&D Program of China (2021ZD0110700), Shanghai Municipal Science and Technology Major Project (2021SHZDZX0102), Shanghai Qi Zhi Institute, and SHEITC (018-RGZN-02046).

References

1. Agrawal, P., Carreira, J., Malik, J.: Learning to see by moving. In: ICCV, pp. 37–45 (2015)
2. Asano, Y.M., Patrick, M., Rupprecht, C., Vedaldi, A.: Labelling unlabelled videos from scratch with multi-modal self-supervision. arXiv preprint arXiv:2006.13662 (2020)
3. Asano, Y.M., Rupprecht, C., Vedaldi, A.: Self-labelling via simultaneous clustering and representation learning. arXiv preprint arXiv:1911.05371 (2019)
4. Ben-David, S., Blitzer, J., Crammer, K., Pereira, F., et al.: Analysis of representations for domain adaptation. In: NeurIPS, vol. 19, p. 137 (2007)

5. Caron, M., Bojanowski, P., Joulin, A., Douze, M.: Deep clustering for unsupervised learning of visual features. In: Ferrari, V., Hebert, M., Sminchisescu, C., Weiss, Y. (eds.) Computer Vision – ECCV 2018. LNCS, vol. 11218, pp. 139–156. Springer, Cham (2018). https://doi.org/10.1007/978-3-030-01264-9_9

6. Caron, M., Misra, I., Mairal, J., Goyal, P., Bojanowski, P., Joulin, A.: Unsupervised learning of visual features by contrasting cluster assignments. arXiv preprint arXiv:2006.09882 (2020)

7. Caron, M., et al.: Emerging properties in self-supervised vision transformers. arXiv preprint arXiv:2104.14294 (2021)

8. Chen, T., Kornblith, S., Norouzi, M., Hinton, G.: A simple framework for contrastive learning of visual representations. In: ICML, pp. 1597–1607. PMLR (2020)

9. Chen, X., He, K.: Exploring simple siamese representation learning. In: CVPR, pp. 15750–15758 (2021)

10. Chen, X., Xie, S., He, K.: An empirical study of training self-supervised visual transformers. arXiv e-prints, p. arXiv–2104 (2021)

11. Cordts, M., et al.: The cityscapes dataset for semantic urban scene understanding. In: CVPR, pp. 3213–3223 (2016)

12. Deng, J., Dong, W., Socher, R., Li, L.J., Li, K., Fei-Fei, L.: ImageNet: a large-scale hierarchical image database. In: CVPR, pp. 248–255. IEEE (2009)

13. Doersch, C., Gupta, A., Efros, A.A.: Unsupervised visual representation learning by context prediction. In: ICCV, pp. 1422–1430 (2015)

14. Doersch, C., Zisserman, A.: Multi-task self-supervised visual learning. In: ICCV, pp. 2051–2060 (2017)

15. Dwibedi, D., Aytar, Y., Tompson, J., Sermanet, P., Zisserman, A.: With a little help from my friends: nearest-neighbor contrastive learning of visual representations. arXiv preprint arXiv:2104.14548 (2021)

16. Everingham, M., Van Gool, L., Williams, C.K., Winn, J., Zisserman, A.: The pascal visual object classes (VOC) challenge. IJCV **88**(2), 303–338 (2010)

17. Fabbri, M., Lanzi, F., Calderara, S., Palazzi, A., Vezzani, R., Cucchiara, R.: Learning to detect and track visible and occluded body joints in a virtual world. In: Ferrari, V., Hebert, M., Sminchisescu, C., Weiss, Y. (eds.) ECCV 2018. LNCS, vol. 11208, pp. 450–466. Springer, Cham (2018). https://doi.org/10.1007/978-3-030-01225-0_27

18. Fang, H.S., Sun, J., Wang, R., Gou, M., Li, Y.L., Lu, C.: InstaBoost: boosting instance segmentation via probability map guided copy-pasting. In: ICCV, pp. 682–691 (2019)

19. Fernando, B., Bilen, H., Gavves, E., Gould, S.: Self-supervised video representation learning with odd-one-out networks. In: CVPR, pp. 3636–3645 (2017)

20. Ge, C., Liang, Y., Song, Y., Jiao, J., Wang, J., Luo, P.: Revitalizing CNN attentions via transformers in self-supervised visual representation learning. arXiv preprint arXiv:2110.05340 (2021)

21. Grill, J.B., et al.: Bootstrap your own latent: a new approach to self-supervised learning. arXiv preprint arXiv:2006.07733 (2020)

22. Gutmann, M., Hyvärinen, A.: Noise-contrastive estimation: a new estimation principle for unnormalized statistical models. In: International Conference on Artificial Intelligence and Statistics, pp. 297–304. JMLR Workshop and Conference Proceedings (2010)

23. He, K., Fan, H., Wu, Y., Xie, S., Girshick, R.: Momentum contrast for unsupervised visual representation learning. In: CVPR, pp. 9729–9738 (2020)

24. He, K., Gkioxari, G., Dollár, P., Girshick, R.: Mask R-CNN. In: ICCV, pp. 2961–2969 (2017)

25. He, K., Zhang, X., Ren, S., Sun, J.: Deep residual learning for image recognition. In: CVPR, pp. 770–778 (2016)
26. Hendrycks, D., Gimpel, K.: Gaussian error linear units (GELUs). arXiv preprint arXiv:1606.08415 (2016)
27. Hjelm, R.D., et al.: Learning deep representations by mutual information estimation and maximization. arXiv preprint arXiv:1808.06670 (2018)
28. Ioffe, S., Szegedy, C.: Batch normalization: accelerating deep network training by reducing internal covariate shift. In: ICML, pp. 448–456. PMLR (2015)
29. Jayaraman, D., Grauman, K.: Learning image representations tied to ego-motion. In: ICCV, pp. 1413–1421 (2015)
30. Kingma, D.P., Welling, M.: Auto-encoding variational bayes. arXiv preprint arXiv:1312.6114 (2013)
31. Kolesnikov, A., Zhai, X., Beyer, L.: Revisiting self-supervised visual representation learning. In: CVPR, pp. 1920–1929 (2019)
32. Larsson, G., Maire, M., Shakhnarovich, G.: Colorization as a proxy task for visual understanding. In: CVPR, pp. 6874–6883 (2017)
33. LeCun, Y., Bengio, Y., Hinton, G.: Deep learning. Nature **521**(7553), 436–444 (2015)
34. Ledig, C., et al.: Photo-realistic single image super-resolution using a generative adversarial network. In: CVPR, pp. 4681–4690 (2017)
35. Li, C., et al.: Efficient self-supervised vision transformers for representation learning. arXiv preprint arXiv:2106.09785 (2021)
36. Li, J., Zhou, P., Xiong, C., Hoi, S.C.: Prototypical contrastive learning of unsupervised representations. arXiv preprint arXiv:2005.04966 (2020)
37. Li, Y., Pogodin, R., Sutherland, D.J., Gretton, A.: Self-supervised learning with kernel dependence maximization. arXiv preprint arXiv:2106.08320 (2021)
38. Lin, T.-Y., Maire, M., Belongie, S., Hays, J., Perona, P., Ramanan, D., Dollár, P., Zitnick, C.L.: Microsoft COCO: common objects in context. In: Fleet, D., Pajdla, T., Schiele, B., Tuytelaars, T. (eds.) ECCV 2014. LNCS, vol. 8693, pp. 740–755. Springer, Cham (2014). https://doi.org/10.1007/978-3-319-10602-1_48
39. Liu, S., et al.: Switchable temporal propagation network. In: Ferrari, V., Hebert, M., Sminchisescu, C., Weiss, Y. (eds.) ECCV 2018. LNCS, vol. 11211, pp. 89–104. Springer, Cham (2018). https://doi.org/10.1007/978-3-030-01234-2_6
40. Liu, Z., et al.: Swin transformer: hierarchical vision transformer using shifted windows. arXiv preprint arXiv:2103.14030 (2021)
41. Long, J., Shelhamer, E., Darrell, T.: Fully convolutional networks for semantic segmentation. In: CVPR, pp. 3431–3440 (2015)
42. Loshchilov, I., Hutter, F.: Fixing weight decay regularization in adam (2018)
43. Lotter, W., Kreiman, G., Cox, D.: Deep predictive coding networks for video prediction and unsupervised learning. arXiv preprint arXiv:1605.08104 (2016)
44. Mathieu, M., Couprie, C., LeCun, Y.: Deep multi-scale video prediction beyond mean square error. arXiv preprint arXiv:1511.05440 (2015)
45. Misra, I., Maaten, L.V.D.: Self-supervised learning of pretext-invariant representations. In: CVPR, pp. 6707–6717 (2020)
46. Misra, I., Zitnick, C.L., Hebert, M.: Shuffle and learn: unsupervised learning using temporal order verification. In: Leibe, B., Matas, J., Sebe, N., Welling, M. (eds.) ECCV 2016. LNCS, vol. 9905, pp. 527–544. Springer, Cham (2016). https://doi.org/10.1007/978-3-319-46448-0_32
47. Mitrovic, J., McWilliams, B., Walker, J., Buesing, L., Blundell, C.: Representation learning via invariant causal mechanisms. arXiv preprint arXiv:2010.07922 (2020)

48. Noroozi, M., Favaro, P.: Unsupervised learning of visual representations by solving jigsaw puzzles. In: Leibe, B., Matas, J., Sebe, N., Welling, M. (eds.) ECCV 2016. LNCS, vol. 9910, pp. 69–84. Springer, Cham (2016). https://doi.org/10.1007/978-3-319-46466-4_5

49. Noroozi, M., Vinjimoor, A., Favaro, P., Pirsiavash, H.: Boosting self-supervised learning via knowledge transfer. In: CVPR, pp. 9359–9367 (2018)

50. Oord, A.v.d., Li, Y., Vinyals, O.: Representation learning with contrastive predictive coding. arXiv preprint arXiv:1807.03748 (2018)

51. Pan, S.J., Tsang, I.W., Kwok, J.T., Yang, Q.: Domain adaptation via transfer component analysis. IEEE Trans. Neural Netw. **22**(2), 199–210 (2010)

52. Pang, B., et al.: Unsupervised representation for semantic segmentation by implicit cycle-attention contrastive learning. In: AAAI (2022)

53. Pathak, D., Krahenbuhl, P., Donahue, J., Darrell, T., Efros, A.A.: Context encoders: feature learning by inpainting. In: CVPR, pp. 2536–2544 (2016)

54. Qian, Q., Xu, Y., Hu, J., Li, H., Jin, R.: Unsupervised visual representation learning by online constrained k-means. arXiv preprint arXiv:2105.11527 (2021)

55. Rezende, D.J., Mohamed, S., Wierstra, D.: Stochastic backpropagation and variational inference in deep latent gaussian models. In: ICML, vol. 2, p. 2. Citeseer (2014)

56. Srivastava, N., Mansimov, E., Salakhudinov, R.: Unsupervised learning of video representations using LSTMs. In: ICML, pp. 843–852. PMLR (2015)

57. Sun, J., Fang, H.S., Zhu, X., Li, J., Lu, C.: Correlation field for boosting 3D object detection in structured scenes. In: Proceedings of the AAAI conference on artificial intelligence, vol. 36, no. 1 (2022)

58. Sun, J., Li, Y., Chai, L., Fang, H.S., Li, Y.L., Lu, C.: Human trajectory prediction with momentary observation. In: CVPR, pp. 6467–6476 (2022)

59. Tao, C., et al.: Exploring the equivalence of siamese self-supervised learning via a unified gradient framework. arXiv preprint arXiv:2112.05141 (2021)

60. Tian, Y., Sun, C., Poole, B., Krishnan, D., Schmid, C., Isola, P.: What makes for good views for contrastive learning? arXiv preprint arXiv:2005.10243 (2020)

61. Tung, H.F., Tung, H., Yumer, E., Fragkiadaki, K.: Self-supervised learning of motion capture. CoRR (2017)

62. Vincent, P., Larochelle, H., Bengio, Y., Manzagol, P.A.: Extracting and composing robust features with denoising autoencoders. In: ICML, pp. 1096–1103 (2008)

63. Vondrick, C., Pirsiavash, H., Torralba, A.: Anticipating visual representations from unlabeled video. In: CVPR, pp. 98–106 (2016)

64. Vondrick, C., Pirsiavash, H., Torralba, A.: Generating videos with scene dynamics. arXiv preprint arXiv:1609.02612 (2016)

65. Wang, X., Liu, Z., Yu, S.X.: Unsupervised feature learning by cross-level instance-group discrimination. In: CVPR, pp. 12586–12595 (2021)

66. Wei, D., Lim, J.J., Zisserman, A., Freeman, W.T.: Learning and using the arrow of time. In: CVPR, pp. 8052–8060 (2018)

67. Wu, Z., Xiong, Y., Yu, S.X., Lin, D.: Unsupervised feature learning via non-parametric instance discrimination. In: CVPR, pp. 3733–3742 (2018)

68. Xie, Zet al.: Self-supervised learning with swin transformers. arXiv preprint arXiv:2105.04553 (2021)

69. You, Y., Gitman, I., Ginsburg, B.: Scaling SGD batch size to 32k for ImageNet training. arXiv preprint arXiv:1708.03888, **6**, 12 (2017)

70. Zbontar, J., Jing, L., Misra, I., LeCun, Y., Deny, S.: Barlow twins: self-supervised learning via redundancy reduction. arXiv preprint arXiv:2103.03230 (2021)

71. Zhan, X., Xie, J., Liu, Z., Ong, Y.S., Loy, C.C.: Online deep clustering for unsupervised representation learning. In: CVPR, pp. 6688–6697 (2020)
72. Zhang, H., Cisse, M., Dauphin, Y.N., Lopez-Paz, D.: Mixup: beyond empirical risk minimization. ICLR (2018)
73. Zhang, R., Isola, P., Efros, A.A.: Colorful image colorization. In: Leibe, B., Matas, J., Sebe, N., Welling, M. (eds.) ECCV 2016. LNCS, vol. 9907, pp. 649–666. Springer, Cham (2016). https://doi.org/10.1007/978-3-319-46487-9_40
74. Zheng, M., et al.: ReSSL: relational self-supervised learning with weak augmentation. arXiv preprint arXiv:2107.09282 (2021)
75. Zhou, B., Khosla, A., Lapedriza, A., Oliva, A., Torralba, A.: Learning deep features for discriminative localization. In: CVPR, pp. 2921–2929 (2016)
76. Zhuang, C., Zhai, A.L., Yamins, D.: Local aggregation for unsupervised learning of visual embeddings. In: ICCV, pp. 6002–6012 (2019)

Improving Few-Shot Part Segmentation Using Coarse Supervision

Oindrila Saha[✉], Zezhou Cheng, and Subhransu Maji

University of Massachusetts, Amherst, USA
{osaha,zezhoucheng,smaji}@cs.umass.edu

Abstract. A significant bottleneck in training deep networks for part segmentation is the cost of obtaining detailed annotations. We propose a framework to exploit coarse labels such as figure-ground masks and keypoint locations that are readily available for some categories to improve part segmentation models. A key challenge is that these annotations were collected for different tasks and with different labeling styles and cannot be readily mapped to the part labels. To this end, we propose to jointly learn the dependencies between labeling styles and the part segmentation model, allowing us to utilize supervision from diverse labels. To evaluate our approach we develop a benchmark on the Caltech-UCSD birds and OID Aircraft dataset. Our approach outperforms baselines based on multi-task learning, semi-supervised learning, and competitive methods relying on loss functions manually designed to exploit coarse supervision.

Keywords: Part segmentation · Few-shot learning · Semi-supervised learning

1 Introduction

Accurate models for labeling parts of an object can aid fine-grained recognition tasks such as estimating the shape and size of animals, and support applications in graphics such as image editing and animation. But a significant bottleneck is the cost of collecting annotations for supervising part labeling models. In many situations however, one can find datasets with alternate labels such as object bounding boxes, figure-ground masks, or keypoints, which may serve as a source of supervision. However the variations in their level of detail and structure, e.g., bounding boxes and masks are coarser than part labels while keypoints are sparse, implies that they cannot be readily "translated" to part labels to directly supervise learning.

We propose a framework to learn part segmentation models using existing datasets with coarse labels such as figure-ground masks and keypoints. The approach illustrated in Fig. 1 treats part labels as latent variables and jointly learns the part segmentation model and the *unknown* dependencies between the

Supplementary Information The online version contains supplementary material available at https://doi.org/10.1007/978-3-031-20056-4_17.

S. Avidan et al. (Eds.): ECCV 2022, LNCS 13690, pp. 283–299, 2022.
https://doi.org/10.1007/978-3-031-20056-4_17

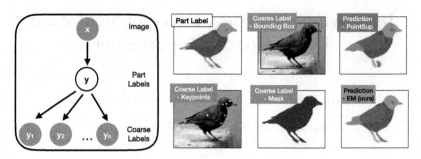

Fig. 1. Overview of our approach. The graphical model over an image x, parts labels y and coarse labels $y_1, \ldots, y_n$, is shown on the left. Coarse labels such as bounding boxes, figure-ground masks, or keypoint locations are easier to annotate than per-pixel part labels, and our learning framework can utilize datasets with coarse labels to train part segmentation models, outperforming previous work - PointSup (Fig. 7).

labeling styles in a Bayesian setting (Sect. 3). The dependencies are represented using deep networks to model complex relationships between labeling styles, allowing supervision from a variety of coarse labels. One technical challenge is that inference requires sampling over high-dimensional latent distributions which is typically intractable. We address this by making certain conditional independence assumptions and develop an amortized inference procedure for learning. Our method allows the use off-the-shelf image segmentation networks and standard back-propagation machinery for training.

To evaluate our approach we design a benchmark for labeling parts on the Caltech-UCSD birds (CUB) [31] and OID Aircraft [30] dataset (Sect. 4). We utilize the keypoint and masks from the CUB dataset and the part-segmentation labels of the birds of PASCAL VOC to segment birds into 10 parts. Our approach achieves a performance of 49.25% mIoU compared to baseline of fine-tuning an ImageNet pre-trained network on all the available part labels (45.37% mIoU), as well as multi-tasking (41.27% mIoU) and semi-supervised learning baseline (46.01% mIoU). It also outperforms PointSup [4] (46.76% mIoU), an approach for training using point-supervision – for this approach we manually assign keypoints to parts and combine it with the figure-ground mask to provide a set of part segmentation labels. On the OID Aircraft dataset we observed a similar trend, where our approach (58.68% mIoU) outperforms the fine-tuning (55.3% mIoU) and multi-tasking (55.61% mIoU) baselines. These experiments are consistent across different initializations of the network (e.g., ImageNet pre-trained vs. random), as well as the types and combinations of coarse labels (Sect. 5 & Sect. 6).

Our approach is also relatively efficient—fine-tuning on all the labeled parts of the CUB dataset requires 1 h, PointSup [2] requires 2.5 h, while our approach requires 7.5 h on a single NVIDIA RTX-8000 GPU. Importantly, our approach requires little additional labeling ($\approx$300 or <3% instances for CUB dataset), and benefits from *existing* part labels on PASCAL and coarse labels on CUB. These experiments suggest that diverse coarse labels across datasets can be used to effectively guide part labeling tasks within our framework.

To summarize our contributions include: 1) a framework to learning part segmentation models using diverse coarse supervision from existing datasets; 2) an amortized inference procedure that is efficient, roughly 3× slower than the leading alternate methods for coarse supervision (e.g., PointSup [4]), and is more accurate; 3) two benchmarks for evaluating part-segmentation from a few-labeled examples on the CUB and OID Aircraft dataset; and 4) a systematic evaluation of various design choices including the role of initialization for transfer learning and the relative benefits of various forms of coarse labels. The source code and data associated with the paper are publicly available at https://people.cs.umass. edu/~osaha/coarsesup.

2   Related Work

Weakly Supervised Image Segmentation. Previous work use supervision from classification labels, bounding boxes or at sparse locations in the image such as points or lines. Zhou *et al.* [36] use class response at every image location for a given class and train by mapping the response peaks to more informative parts of an object instance. Other approaches generate pseudo ground truth labels using previous image classification models [1,37]. Khoreva *et al.* [14] use bounding boxes as weak supervision. They generate pseudo ground truth using classical approaches such as GrabCut [22] inside given bounding box and use that to train the segmentation model. Hsu *et al.* [12] use a bounding box tightness prior and train a Mask-RCNN [10] using horizontal and vertical patches from the tight bounding box as positive signals and those outside as negative signals. BoxInst [26] uses a projection loss that forces horizontal and vertical lines inside bounding boxes to predict at least one foreground pixel and an affinity loss that forces pixels with similar colors to have the same label. Laradji *et al.* [16] introduce a proposal-based instance segmentation method that uses a single point per instance as supervision. Cheng *et al.* [4] uses multiple points randomly sampled per instance as well as bounding boxes as supervision to train a Mask-RCNN model. ScribbleSup [17] uses a graphical model that jointly propagates information from scribbles to unmarked pixels to learn network parameters. Another stream of work [3,38] train two models simultaneously with cross supervision from one model to train the other. Naha *et al.* [19] use keypoint guidance to predict part segmentation labels for unseen classes but require keypoint inputs during evaluation time. All these methods design algorithms specific to one kind of supervision and the annotation style has a clear mapping to the desired part labels. *In contrast, our method handles a variety of label styles allowing opportunistic use of existing datasets to learn part segmentation labels.*

Unsupervised Learning. A number of previous work use self-supervision for learning segmentations. SCOPS [13] uses geometric concentration (areas of the same object part are spatially concentrated), equivariance (enforcing part segmentation to be aligned with geometric transformations) and semantic consistency (over different instances). Wang *et al.* [32] also use equivariance constraints to refine class activation maps which in turn form the final segmentation maps.

Another method [20] uses pixel-level contrastive learning to learn feature representations for downstream tasks such as segmentation. Yang *et al.* [34] use a layered GAN to produce background and foreground layers for an image where the discriminator predicts on the overlayed image. PiCIE [5] enforces invariance to photometric transformations and equivariance to geometric transformations for different views of the same image. A number of recent techniques based on generative [28,35] and contrastive learning [18] approaches have also been proposed (See [24] for a systematic evaluation). These methods can be used to initialize networks to boost performance in few-shot learning and are complementary to our approach. *For example, we compare the benefits of self-supervised learning over randomly initialized networks and ImageNet pre-trained networks.*

Multi-task learning benefits from diverse source of supervision by sharing parts of the model across tasks. For image segmentation, a prior work [6] proposes multi-task cascaded networks where three networks predict instances, masks and categorize objects respectively. Heuer *et al.* [11] combine the tasks of object detection, semantic segmentation and human pose estimation but fails to perform better than the single task network for segmentation—a trend we also observe in our experiments. Standley *et al.* [25] show that combining some tasks in multi-task setting can degrade performance while for other cases performance can get boosted. To design a multi-task network able to handle different tasks, some methods [8,9] group tasks that would perform well together. Other works such as [15,27] use keypoints and bounding box information to predict instance segmentation but use a multistage framework. Mask-RCNN [10] adds a mask segmentation head to Faster-RCNN [21] to predict bounding box and instance segmentation. *Unlike generic multi-tasking approaches, our approach exploits the hierarchical label structure to guide learning and consistently outperforms them.*

3   A Joint Model of Labeling Styles

For an image x denote $y \in S$ the part segmentation label, i.e., pixel-wise label for each part, and $y_1 \in S_1$, $y_2 \in S_2$, $\ldots$, $y_n \in S_n$ denote coarse labels corresponding to various labeling styles. For example, y_1 might denote the coordinates of a set of keypoints and y_2 might denote the figure-ground mask. We call a labeling S_a coarser than S_b if S_a can be derived from S_b *independent* of the image x. For example, the figure-ground mask can be derived from the part label of an object, or the bounding-box can be derived from the figure-ground mask. *Our goal is to learn a part segmentation model $p(y|x)$ given a small set of images with part labels $y \in S$, and a large set of images with coarse labels $y_k \in S_k$.*

This assumption that the coarse labels can be derived from the part labels leads to the following joint probability distribution over the image and the labels:

$$p(y, y_1, \ldots, y_n | x) = p(y|x) \prod_{i=1}^{n} p(y_1|y),$$

and is illustrated by the graphical model in Fig. 1. The assumption might appear to be strong, but we find that it holds for the styles of labels we consider. For example, a convolutional network can accurately predict the location of keypoints given the part segmentation labels with >92 PCK which is as good as the accuracy of keypoints given image. However, the form of $p(y_k|y)$ is complex in this case as it involves reasoning about the extent and location of various parts. The distribution might also be unknown, especially when combining existing datasets which may have been collected with a different set of labels and annotation guidelines. For example, there might not be a direct correspondence between the names of parts used for keypoint annotations and those for segmentation task. In contrast, the form is simple and deterministic for figure-ground masks or bounding boxes given part labels. We incorporate this factorization in a Bayesian setup to learn both the part segmentation model and the dependencies between the labeling styles described next.

3.1 Variational EM for Learning

Assume that an image x contains coarse labels $y_1, y_2, \ldots, y_n$. We will estimate parameters θ to maximize the log-likelihood of the data:

$$\max_{\theta} \mathcal{L}(\theta) = \log p(y_1, y_2, \ldots, y_n | x, \theta). \tag{1}$$

Given a distribution $q(y)$ over the latent variables[1] the $\mathcal{L}(\theta)$ can be bounded as:

$$\mathcal{L}(\theta) = \log \sum_y p(y, y_1, y_2, \ldots, y_n | x, \theta)$$

$$= \log \sum_y q(y) \frac{p(y, y_1, y_2, \ldots, y_n | x, \theta)}{q(y)}$$

$$\geq \sum_y q(y) \log \frac{p(y, y_1, y_2, \ldots, y_n | x, \theta)}{q(y)} \tag{2}$$

$$= \sum_y q(y) \log p(y, y_1, y_2, \ldots, y_n | x, \theta) + H(q)$$

$$= \sum_y q(y) \left[\log p(y|x) \prod_{i=1}^{n} p(y_i|y, \theta) \right] + H(q) := \mathcal{F}(q, \theta).$$

where $H(q) = -\sum_y q(y) \log q(y)$ is the entropy of the distribution q. The EM algorithm alternates between:

– **E step:** maximize $\mathcal{F}(q, \theta)$ wrt distribution over y given the parameters:

$$q^{(k)}(y) = \arg\max_{q(y)} \mathcal{F}(q(y), \theta^{(k-1)}).$$

– **M step:** maximize $\mathcal{F}(q, \theta)$ wrt parameters given the distribution $q(y)$:

$$\theta^{(k)} = \arg\max_{\theta} \mathcal{F}(q^{(k)}(y), \theta) = \arg\max_{\theta} \sum_y q^{(k)}(y) \log p(y, y_1, y_2, \ldots y_n | x, \theta)$$

---

[1] $q(y) \geq 0$ and $p(y, y_1, y_2, \ldots, y_n) > 0 \Rightarrow q(y) > 0$.

Note that in the above we have derived the EM algorithm for a single example x, but the overall approach requires estimating the distribution over latent variables $q(y)$ for each training example and parameters across all the training examples. However, optimizing $q(y)$ for each training sample x is typically intractable for high-dimensional distributions like ours. In "Hard EM" the distribution $q(y)$ is replaced by the mode of the posterior distribution but estimating this can also be challenging when the probabilities are expressed using deep networks. In the next section we present an amortized inference procedure where we estimate $q(y)$ using a separate network conditioned on all the observed variables.

3.2   Coarse Supervision from Keypoints and Figure-Ground Mask

As a concrete example consider that two types of coarse labeling styles are available – $y_{\mathrm{mask}} \in S_{\mathrm{mask}}$ denoting the figure-ground mask of the same size as the image, and $y_{\mathrm{kp}} \in S_{\mathrm{kp}}$ denoting the locations of a set of keypoints in an image. To make inference tractable we adopt a Laplace approximation and model the conditional distributions as a random variable centered around a mean as follows:

- $p(y|x) \propto \exp(-\alpha|y - \mu(x)|)$ where $\mu(x)$ is the mean distribution of the part labels for the image estimated using a deep network with parameters θ.
- $p(y_{\mathrm{kp}}|y) \propto \exp(-\lambda|y_{kp} - \mu_{\mathrm{kp}}(y)|)$ where $\mu_{\mathrm{kp}}(y)$ is the mean location of the keypoints estimated using a deep network with parameters θ_{kp} that takes part labels as input and predicts the locations of keypoints.
- $p(y_{\mathrm{mask}}|y) = B(y_{\mathrm{mask}}, \mu_{\mathrm{mask}}(y))$ a Binomial distribution where $\mu_{\mathrm{mask}}(y)$ is obtained by summing over the parts probabilities at each pixel. This function has no learnable parameters.

In the E Step we optimize $q(y)$ for each training example x as:

$$\arg\max_{q(y)} \sum_y q(y) \left[\log p(y|x) \prod_{i=1}^n p(y_i|y) \right] + H(q). \tag{3}$$

Given the form of the probability distributions this corresponds to maximizing $q(y)$ given $\mu(x), y_{kp}$ and y_{mask} (ignoring the entropy term):

$$\sum_y q(y) \exp\big(-\alpha|y - \mu(x)|\big) \exp\big(-\lambda|y_{kp} - \mu_{\mathrm{kp}}(y)|\big) B\big(y_{\mathrm{mask}}, \mu_{\mathrm{mask}}(y)\big). \tag{4}$$

For hard EM, it is possible to solve for the optimal y using gradient ascent as each of these functions $\mu, \mu_{\mathrm{kp}}(y)$ and $\mu_{\mathrm{mask}}(y)$ are differentiable wrt y. Similarly, one can construct a sample estimate for $q(y)$ using gradient-based techniques such as SGLD [33]. However, both these choices require many gradient iterations and can get stuck in local minima as y is very high-dimensional. Thus, instead of optimizing for each example x individually we approximate the mode with another distribution $q_x(y) \approx q(y|x, y, y_{kp}, y_{mask}, \theta_q)$ parameterized using a deep network with parameters θ_q shared across all training examples. The network takes as input the image and coarse labels and predicts the part labels. In the

E step we optimize θ_q using gradient descent over *all* examples allowing us to amortize the inference cost across examples.

In the M step, for each unlabeled image x we sample labels y using the variational distribution $q(y|x, y, y_{kp}, y_{mask}, \theta_q)$ and update the parameters θ and θ_{kp} of the model for predicting $p(y|x)$ and $p(y_{kp}|y)$ respectively. In practice we sample the mode of each input x predicted by the feed-forward network. This is simple and has worked well for our experiments, though techniques for sampling from deep networks might lead to better estimates. The entire algorithm is outlined in Algorithm 1. Here ℓ, ℓ_{kp} and ℓ_{mask} correspond to the loss functions for the part labels, keypoints, mask obtained as the negative log-likelihood of the corresponding probability functions in Eq. 2 and ℓ_q is the negative entropy.

Remark. (1) In the above derivation we assumed all the images have the same set of coarse labels. But the method can be generalized to handle images with different number of coarse labels as the log-likelihood (Eq. 2) decomposes over the labels. However, the model for estimating the variational distribution $q(y)$ should be adapted to condition on the provided labels for the image. One possibility is to train separate models, e.g., $q(y|x, y_{mask})$ and $q(y|x, y_{kp}, y_{mask})$, or treat the missing labels as latent variables and infer them during training. (2) The method can handle different styles of coarse supervision by simply adding $p(y_k|y)$ for the corresponding label style. For example, supervision from object bounding-boxes can be incorporated by treating the box as two keypoints corresponding to the top-left and bottom-right corners or as a mask. Similarly, box-level annotations for the parts can also be used as coarse supervision.

4   Benchmarks for Evaluation

In this section we describe the datasets used for our experiments. Figure 2 shows the PASCUB dataset for bird part segmentation. The top row is examples we annotated from the CUB dataset and bottom row are examples from the PASCAL parts dataset for the birds category after removing low-resolution and truncated instances (Appendix A). Figure 3 shows examples from the OID Aircraft dataset. Below we describe the details and evaluation metrics of both.

4.1   Bird Part Segmentation Benchmark

Our goal is to segment each bird into 10 parts: 'beak', 'head', 'left eye', 'left leg', 'left wing', 'right eye', 'right leg', 'right wing', 'tail' and 'torso'. The bird category in the PASCAL parts dataset contains several labeled examples, but most instances are small and truncated as the dataset is primarily designed for object detection. On the other hand, the CUB dataset has higher resolution instances and includes keypoint and figure-ground masks but does not contain part labels. So, we combine the two and provide part labels for a few instances on the CUB dataset to create a benchmark for few-shot part segmentation.

CUB. The Caltech-UCSD birds dataset [31] has 11,788 images centered on individual birds across 200 species. We annotate 299 randomly chosen images

---

Algorithm 1. Stochastic Variational EM for Part Segmentation

Input: $\mathcal{D}^p := \{(x^p, y^p, y^p_{\text{mask}}, y^p_{\text{kp}})\}$ ▷ Dataset with part labels
Input: $\mathcal{D} := \{(x, y_{\text{mask}}, y_{\text{kp}})\}$ ▷ Dataset with coarse labels
Input: params $= \{\#epochs, b^p, b, \alpha, \lambda_1, \lambda_2, \delta_1, \delta_2\}$

1: **function** TRAINPARTSEGSGDVAREM($\mathcal{D}^p, \mathcal{D}$, params)
2:      Initialize $f(y|x, \theta)$, $f(y_{\text{mask}}|y)$, $f(y_{\text{kp}}|y, \theta_{\text{kp}})$ and $f(y|x, y_{\text{mask}}, y_{\text{kp}}, \theta_q)$
3:      **for** $epoch \leftarrow 1$ to $\#epochs$ **do**
4:          $[x^p, y^p, y^p_{\text{mask}}, y^p_{\text{kp}}] = \text{next-batch}(\mathcal{D}^p, b^p)$
5:          $[x, y_{\text{mask}}, y_{\text{kp}}] = \text{next-batch}(\mathcal{D}, b)$
6:          **#E Step**
7:          $\mu_q = f(y|x, y_{\text{mask}}, y_{\text{kp}}, \theta_q)$ ▷ Variational distribution
8:          $\mu = f(y|x, \theta)$ ▷ Part segmentation model
9:          $\mu_{\text{kp}} = f(y_{\text{kp}}|\mu_q, \theta_{\text{kp}})$.   ▷ Keypoint model
10:         $\mu_{\text{mask}} = f(y_{\text{mask}}|\mu_q)$ ▷ Mask model
11:         $L = \alpha\ell(\mu_q, \mu) + \lambda_1\ell_{\text{kp}}(y_{\text{kp}}, \mu_{\text{kp}}) + \lambda_2\ell_{\text{mask}}(y_{\text{mask}}, \mu_{\text{mask}}) + \ell_q(\mu_q)$
12:         gradient-update(L, θ_q)
13:         **#M Step**
14:         $\mu_q = f(y|x, y_{\text{mask}}, y_{\text{kp}}, \theta_q)$ ▷ Sample labels
15:         $\mu^p = f(y|x^p, \theta)$ ▷ Part segmentation model
16:         $\mu_{\text{kp}} = f(y_{\text{kp}}|\mu_q, \theta_{\text{kp}})$ ▷ Keypoint model
17:         gradient-update($\delta_1\ell(y^p, \mu^p) + \delta_2\ell(\mu_q, \mu), \theta$)
18:         gradient-update($\ell_{\text{kp}}(y_{\text{kp}}, \mu_{\text{kp}}), \theta_{\text{kp}}$)
19:      **end for**
20: **end function**

Table 1. Data splits for PASCUB.

Part segmentation data

Split	PASCAL	CUB
#Train	271	150
#Val	132	74
#Test	133	75

Coarsely labelled data

#Train	5994
#Val	2897
#Test	2897

Fig. 2. Example images from the PASCUB dataset.

with pixel-wise part labels (referred to as CUB Part) for the 10 classes mentioned above. We divide the 299 images we annotated into train, val and test in a 2:1:1 split (Table 1). The CUB dataset also includes keypoints and figure-ground masks for all images. We use the full data divided into the official splits as our coarsely labelled data for PASCUB experiments (Table 1).

PASCAL. The PASCAL VOC [7] dataset has 625 images that contain at least one bird. Chen *et al.* [2] provide part segmentations where each bird has pixel-wise part labels for 13 classes – we group classes such as 'neck' and 'head' to a single category 'head' resulting in the 11 classes listed above. We also removed

Fig. 3. Part labels on the OID Aircraft dataset.

instances that are truncated and are of low resolution to make for a cleaner training and evaluation set—the pre-processing is detailed in Appendix A. Now we are left with 536 centered bird images. Using the official split of PASCAL VOC results in a training set of 271 images. One image can contain more than one bird in PASCAL. Crops originating from an image from train split go in the train split of our dataset. Since the official split does not have val/test demarcation we randomly divide the rest of the images into validation and test sets equally (Table 1). Figure 2 shows the data after pre-processing.

The overall dataset contains 570 instances with part labels, and roughly 12k instances with keypoint and mask labels, divided into training, validation, and test sets. Annotating part segmentations requires roughly 5–10× more effort than masks based on our own experience, and this benchmark contains such labels for less than 5% of the objects.

4.2 Aircraft Part Segmentation Benchmark

The OID Aircraft dataset [30] has 7543 images. Each image has an associated figure ground mask and part labels for four parts—'nose', 'wings', 'wheels' and 'vertical stabilizer'. The figure ground masks provided are quite accurate, but the part labels are noisy. Thus, we manually select 300 images for which the part labels are visually correct. In keeping with the splits of the datasets described above, we divide these 300 images into 150 for training, 75 each for validation and testing. We refer to this subset as OID Part. For the rest of the dataset, we use the official train/val/test split. Note that the part labels in this case do not collectively form the figure ground masks. Each pixel of the image also can have more than one part label marked. Thus, we handle the segmentation training in a different way for Aircrafts as described in the section below.

5 Part Segmentation Algorithms

For all the baselines and for our approach, we use an encoder-decoder based fully convolutional network. We present details of all architectures in Appendix B. We use colour jittering and flipping augmentations for training all models. We resize images and corresponding labels to 256 × 256. The hyperparameters for each approach were chosen on the validation set of each benchmark.

5.1   Baselines

In this section, we describe training and design details for all baselines that we compare our method with.

Fine-Tuning. We start with a network pre-trained on another task and fine-tune it for part segmentation. We replace the final fully connected layer to predict part labels and train the network using a cross entropy loss for PASCUB experiments. For Aircrafts, we treat segmentation as a pixel-wise multi-label classification task and use binary cross entropy (BCE) on each channel. We train this using Adam optimizer with a learning rate of 0.0001 for 200 epochs.

Semi-supervised Learning. We use the method described in PseudoSup [3] as a semi-supervised learning baseline. The method uses an ensemble of two networks obtained by fine-tuning starting from two different initializations. Note that for the 'Random' case (see Table 2), both networks start with different random init before fine-tuning, while for 'Keypoint'/'ImageNet' cases only the last layer/decoder has different random inits. After obtaining the two different fine-tuning checkpoints, PseudoSup training uses one ensemble to train the other and vice versa using pseudo-labels on all coarsely labelled images. Pseudo-labels refers to converting the predictions to one-hot labels by computing the argmax over all channels. We also add the fully-supervised loss from images with part labels. We use SGD optimizer with learning rate of 1E−4, momentum of 0.9 and weight decay of 1E−4 for both networks. We train for 90 epochs with cosine learning rate scheduling.

Multi-task Learning. Here we train a single model to accomplish both the tasks of keypoint prediction and part segmentation. We use a common encoder based on a ResNet-34 and attach decoders for each task described below.

– For PASCUB, the first decoder is for part segmentation labels where we use cross entropy loss over the prediction and ground truth labels. The second decoder predicts keypoints where we use pixel-wise ℓ_1-loss over the predicted and ground-truth keypoints which are represented as Gaussians around each keypoint. The output of the first decoder also receives supervision from the figure-ground masks by summing over channel dimension for the foreground classes of the prediction and taking a cross-entropy loss. The sum of all these losses is backpropagated through the encoder during training. The weights for the figure-ground loss and part segmentation loss are set to be 1 and that of the keypoint loss is set to be 10. We use SGD optimizer with learning rate of 0.1, momentum of 0.9 and weight decay of 0.0001 for both networks. We train for 90 epochs with cosine learning rate scheduling.
– For Aircrafts, the first decoder performs part segmentation and is trained with binary cross-entropy loss for on each channel as parts are not mutually exclusive. The second decoder predicts the figure ground mask and is trained with cross-entropy loss. The weightages for losses from both decoders are set to be 1. Using an initial learning rate of 0.2, the rest of the training procedure remains the same as above.

Handcrafted Loss Functions. We base this method on PointSup [4]—a method to train segmentation models using point supervision. We evaluate this on PASCUB since it has keypoint annotations. The procedure is illustrated in Fig. 7 in the Appendix. We first assign keypoints to each part manually based on their co-occurrence, e.g. the 'head', 'crown' and 'throat' keypoints are assigned the 'head' part. We then dilate these locations using a 5×5 pixel window—we choose 5×5 so as to not exceed the area of the smallest part, the eyes. We then train the network with a pixel-wise cross entropy loss computed on all these annotated points and the corresponding figure-ground mask. This is mask-loss is computed across all pixels by summing over the foreground channels and using a cross entropy loss. For the loss over part labels points we set the weightage as 0.5, for loss from figure-ground mask as 1 and for that from part label we set weightage to 2. We use SGD optimizer with learning rate of 0.001, momentum of 0.9 and weight decay of 0.0001. We train for 90 epochs with cosine lr scheduling.

5.2   Details for Our Approach

In this section we specify how we initialize each model of the EM algorithm before training and describe the training details of the EM method.

Part Segmentation Model: $f(y|x)$. We initialize this using a checkpoint obtained by fine-tuning, i.e., a model trained using the provided part labels.

Posterior Inference Model: $f(y|x, y_{\mathrm{mask}}, y_{\mathrm{kp}})$. We use a split encoders for this model (Fig. 5 in supp.). The first is a ResNet34 pretrained on ImageNet [23] to extract features from the image and second a shallow ResNet-based encoder to process the masks and keypoint heatmaps concatenated in channel dimension. We concatenate the features of the encoders and use a common decoder to create y. For PASCUB, we train using images from CUB for which we have both labelled part segmentations and keypoint annotations. For Aircrafts, similarly we use those images which have both figure ground masks and clean part labels. We provide details on architecture in Appendix B. We use flipping and color jitter augmentations while training. We use a learning rate of 0.1 for the whole network except the image encoder branch for which we set learning rate to 0.01. We use cosine learning rate scheduling and train for 90 epochs. We use SGD optimizer with momentum of 0.9 and weight decay of 1e−4.

Keypoint Model: $f(y_{\mathrm{kp}}|y)$. This refers to the model for predicting keypoints given part labels. On PASCUB using the checkpoint from the finetuned $p(y|x)$ model we generate part segmentations for all CUB images. We use y_{kp} from ground truth and generated y from $f(y|x)$ for an initial training. We then fine-tune the model on the images that have both ground truth y and y_{kp}. For this stage we use color jitter and flipping augmentations. For the initial training we use a learning rate of 0.1 with cosine lr scheduling and train for 90 epochs. For fine-tuning, we use a learning rate of 0.001 and train for 10 epochs. We use SGD optimizer with momentum of 0.9 and weight decay of 1e−4 for both. This model achieves a PCK@10% of **92.85** on the CUB test set which is higher than that obtained by training using image inputs (92.65) for the same architecture.

Mask Model: $f(y_{\text{mask}}|y)$. This is the model for predicting figure-ground masks from part labels. For PASCUB, we can predict the mask directly by marginalizing (summing) over the all the part labels. For Aircrafts, we need to use a model to predict $f(y_{\text{mask}}|y)$ since the part labels do not cover the whole mask and are not mutually exclusive. We use a model similar to the $f(y_{\text{kp}}|y)$ for PASCUB and follow the same initialization procedure.

EM Training. As described in Algorithm 1, the EM training proceeds by updating the posterior model $p(y|x, y_{\text{kp}}, y_{\text{mask}})$ (E Step), followed by updating the part $p(y|x)$ and keypoint $p(y_{\text{kp}}|y)$ models (M Step) over batches of training data. For PASCUB with keypoint and ImageNet initialization, we use learning rate for part model as 1e−5, that of posterior model as 1e−3 and coarse supervision model $p(y_k|y)$ as 1e−8. For random initialization, we set learning rates as 5e−4, 1e−5 and 1e−8 respectively. We use SGD optimizer with momentum of 0.9 and weight decay of 1e−4. We train the model for 40 epochs and choose the best checkpoint based on lowest cross entropy loss of $p(y|x)$ on validation set of PASCUB dataset. We use batch size of 32 for the coarse labelled dataset and a batch size of 4 for the part labelled dataset. We detail rest of the hyperparameters in Appendix C. We follow a very similar procedure for the Aircrafts. The loss for the E step comes from the predicted labels and the figure-ground mask, while for the M step we train the part model $p(y|x)$ using posterior mode. We use learning rate for part model as 0.005, that of posterior model as 1e−6 and coarse supervision model $p(y_m|y)$ as 1e−8. For Aircrafts we perform experiments for ImageNet init and share details of all hyperparameters in Appendix C. Figure 4 shows the progress segmentation models using EM over epochs on an image.

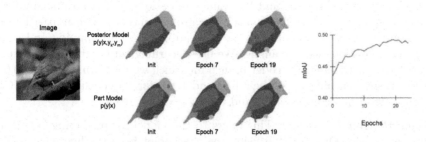

Fig. 4. EM training. The top row shows the output of the posterior model $p(y|x, y_{\text{mask}}, y_{\text{kp}})$ and the bottom shows the output of the part model $p(y|x)$ for the image at various epochs. Both models improve and influence each other – the posterior model learns to recognise the eyes while the part model learns to segment the feet. The right shows that the validation mIoU increases over epochs.

6   Results

Below we summarize the key conclusions of our experiments.

Our Approach Outperforms Alternatives. Table 2 compares our approach
to baselines on the PASCUB dataset for various network initializations. Performance is reported as the mean intersection-over-union (mIoU) across parts.
Note that the benchmark has train/val sets for CUB and PASCAL. Table 2
shows the results on CUB, while those for PASCAL are included in the supp.
Our approach handily outperforms the fine-tuning baseline—with the largest
gains when the network is randomly initialized. We also outerform PointSup, a
strong baseline based on handcrafted labels obtained from keypoints. Designing
handcrafted labels might be challenging if keypoints are densely labeled, or if
the annotation style varies. In comparison, our approach does not assume prior
knowledge on the style of labels and learns them as part of training. Table 4
shows the same results for the OID Part dataset, where our approach outperforms fine-tuning and multi-tasking baseline. For this dataset we use ImageNet
initialization. PointSup is not applicable as keypoints are not annotated on this
dataset.

Multi-tasking is Rarely Effective. The simple strategy of multi-tasking was
effective only when the models are trained from scratch. Despite careful hyper-
parameter search, we found that the overall performance degrades when better
initializations are used. A staged strategy, where the network is trained to predict
keypoints on the whole CUB dataset and then fine-tuned to predict part labels
was more effective (Table 2 Keypoint init. + Fine-tuning outperforms Multi-
task).

Semi-supervised Learning Provides Minor Benefits. The semi-supervised
learning approach based on PseusoSup provides relatively small (0.5–1% MIoU)
improvement over the fine-tuning baseline.

Our Approach Benefits from Various Coarse Labels. Table 3 shows the
results on the CUB test set using various forms of coarse supervision. A model
trained using mask supervision only obtain 46.30% mIoU, one with Keypoint
only obtains 47.96% mIoU, while using both Keypoints and masks obtains
49.25% mIoU. All these models are better than the fine-tuning baseline (45.37%
mIoU) and the semi-supervised learning baseline (46.01% mIoU).

Our Approach is Relatively Efficient. The key benefit of our approach is
that it is relatively efficient. First, we were able to utilize existing labels on
PASCAL and CUB dataset to train the part segmentation model. Our model
required labeling 300 part labels on CUB, half of which were used for evaluation.
Considering that it takes on the order of a minute or two to label parts for each
instance, the ability to train part-segmentation models using existing coarse
labels is a compelling alternative to labeling large datasets of parts. Second, the
overall training for our approach (7.5 h) is also a small factor increase over fine-
tuning (1 h), semi-supervised learning (6.2 h), multitasking (4 h) and PseudoSup
(2.5 h) on a single NVIDIA RTX8000 GPU.

Table 2. Performance on birds. Comparison of the EM method with baselines described in Sect. 5.1 on the testing and validation set of CUB parts. Our method (in green) outperforms baselines for all initializations. We present results on PASCAL val/test splits in Appendix D. The std-deviation over runs for Fine-tuning, MultiTask, PseudoSup and EM is $< \pm 1$ mIoU. For PointSup the std-deviation is $\sim \pm 2$ mIoU.

Method	CUB part test			CUB part val		
	Random	Keypoint	ImageNet	Random	Keypoint	ImageNet
Fine-tuning	29.88	41.12	45.37	35.28	44.64	48.62
MultiTask	36.96	38.00	41.27	40.24	41.74	43.93
PseudoSup [3]	30.77	41.62	46.01	36.32	45.03	48.67
PointSup [4]	35.18	46.45	46.76	38.05	48.01	48.84
Ours	37.98	49.25	48.05	40.85	52.19	51.11

Table 3. Effect of coarse supervision. The mIoU on the CUB test using various coarse labels.

EM supervision	mIOU
Keypoint + Mask	49.25
Mask only	46.30
Keypoint only	47.96

Table 4. Performance on OID. Our method (in green) outperforms baselines based on multi-tasking and fine-tuning.

Method	OID val	OID test
Fine-tune	54.17	55.30
MultiTask	55.94	55.61
Ours	57.46	58.68

7   Conclusions

We present a framework for learning part segmentation models using a few part labels by exploiting existing coarsely labelled datasets. Our approach jointly learns the dependencies between labeling styles allowing supervision from diverse labels. This allowed us to train a bird part segmentation model by combining the part labels on PASCAL VOC with figure-ground mask and keypoint labels on CUB dataset. The model outperforms baselines based on fine-tuning, semi-supervised learning, multi-tasking, as well as learning with handcrafted labels and loss functions. We also presented results on the Aircraft dataset where we improve over the baselines. Our framework can handle multiple types of annotations (e.g., boxes, keypoints, masks, etc.) providing a way to combine existing labels across datasets without requiring manual translation across styles. For example, we could combine annotations from the NABirds dataset [29] which contains keypoints and object bounding-box to improve results.

Acknowledgements. The research is supported in part by NSF grants # 1749833 and #1908669. Our experiments were performed on the University of Massachusetts GPU cluster funded by the Mass. Technology Collaborative.

References

1. Ahn, J., Cho, S., Kwak, S.: Weakly supervised learning of instance segmentation with inter-pixel relations. In: Proceedings of the IEEE/CVF Conference on Computer Vision and Pattern Recognition, pp. 2209–2218 (2019)
2. Chen, X., Mottaghi, R., Liu, X., Fidler, S., Urtasun, R., Yuille, A.: Detect what you can: detecting and representing objects using holistic models and body parts. In: Proceedings of the IEEE Conference on Computer Vision and Pattern Recognition, pp. 1971–1978 (2014)
3. Chen, X., Yuan, Y., Zeng, G., Wang, J.: Semi-supervised semantic segmentation with cross pseudo supervision. In: Proceedings of the IEEE/CVF Conference on Computer Vision and Pattern Recognition, pp. 2613–2622 (2021)
4. Cheng, B., Parkhi, O., Kirillov, A.: Pointly-supervised instance segmentation. arXiv preprint arXiv:2104.06404 (2021)
5. Cho, J.H., Mall, U., Bala, K., Hariharan, B.: PiCIE: unsupervised semantic segmentation using invariance and equivariance in clustering. In: Proceedings of the IEEE/CVF Conference on Computer Vision and Pattern Recognition, pp. 16794–16804 (2021)
6. Dai, J., He, K., Sun, J.: Instance-aware semantic segmentation via multi-task network cascades. In: Proceedings of the IEEE Conference on Computer Vision and Pattern Recognition (CVPR) (2016)
7. Everingham, M., Van Gool, L., Williams, C.K.I., Winn, J., Zisserman, A.: The pascal visual object classes (VOC) challenge. Int. J. Comput. Vis. **88**(2), 303–338 (2010)
8. Fifty, C., Amid, E., Zhao, Z., Yu, T., Anil, R., Finn, C.: Efficiently identifying task groupings for multi-task learning. Adv. Neural Inf. Process. Syst. **34**, 27503–27516 (2021)
9. Guo, P., Lee, C.Y., Ulbricht, D.: Learning to branch for multi-task learning. In: III, H.D., Singh, A. (eds.) Proceedings of the 37th International Conference on Machine Learning. Proceedings of Machine Learning Research, vol. 119, pp. 3854–3863. PMLR, 13–18 July 2020. https://proceedings.mlr.press/v119/guo20e.html
10. He, K., Gkioxari, G., Dollár, P., Girshick, R.: Mask R-CNN. In: Proceedings of the IEEE International Conference on Computer Vision, pp. 2961–2969 (2017)
11. Heuer, F., Mantowsky, S., Bukhari, S., Schneider, G.: Multitask-CenterNet (MCN): efficient and diverse multitask learning using an anchor free approach. In: Proceedings of the IEEE/CVF International Conference on Computer Vision (ICCV) Workshops, pp. 997–1005 (2021)
12. Hsu, C.C., Hsu, K.J., Tsai, C.C., Lin, Y.Y., Chuang, Y.Y.: Weakly supervised instance segmentation using the bounding box tightness prior. Adv. Neural Inf. Process. Syst. **32** (2019)
13. Hung, W.C., Jampani, V., Liu, S., Molchanov, P., Yang, M.H., Kautz, J.: SCOPS: self-supervised co-part segmentation. In: Proceedings of the IEEE/CVF Conference on Computer Vision and Pattern Recognition, pp. 869–878 (2019)
14. Khoreva, A., Benenson, R., Hosang, J., Hein, M., Schiele, B.: Simple does it: weakly supervised instance and semantic segmentation. In: Proceedings of the IEEE Conference on Computer Vision and Pattern Recognition, pp. 876–885 (2017)
15. Kocabas, M., Karagoz, S., Akbas, E.: MultiPoseNet: fast multi-person pose estimation using pose residual network. In: Proceedings of the European Conference on Computer Vision (ECCV) (2018)

16. Laradji, I.H., Rostamzadeh, N., Pinheiro, P.O., Vazquez, D., Schmidt, M.: Proposal-based instance segmentation with point supervision. In: 2020 IEEE International Conference on Image Processing (ICIP), pp. 2126–2130. IEEE (2020)

17. Lin, D., Dai, J., Jia, J., He, K., Sun, J.: ScribbleSup: scribble-supervised convolutional networks for semantic segmentation. In: Proceedings of the IEEE Conference on Computer Vision and Pattern Recognition, pp. 3159–3167 (2016)

18. Liu, W., Wu, Z., Ding, H., Liu, F., Lin, J., Lin, G.: Few-shot segmentation with global and local contrastive learning. arXiv preprint arXiv:2108.05293 (2021)

19. Naha, S., Xiao, Q., Banik, P., Reza, M., Crandall, D.J., et al.: Part segmentation of unseen objects using keypoint guidance. In: Proceedings of the IEEE/CVF Winter Conference on Applications of Computer Vision, pp. 1742–1750 (2021)

20. O Pinheiro, P.O., Almahairi, A., Benmalek, R., Golemo, F., Courville, A.C.: Unsupervised learning of dense visual representations. Adv. Neural. Inf. Process. Syst. **33**, 4489–4500 (2020)

21. Ren, S., He, K., Girshick, R., Sun, J.: Faster r-cnn: Towards real-time object detection with region proposal networks. Adv. Neural. Inf. Process. Syst. **28** (2015)

22. Rother, C., Kolmogorov, V., Blake, A.: "GrabCut" interactive foreground extraction using iterated graph cuts. ACM Trans. Graph. (TOG) **23**(3), 309–314 (2004)

23. Russakovsky, O., et al.: ImageNet large scale visual recognition challenge. Int. J. Comput. Vis. (IJCV) **115**(3), 211–252 (2015). https://doi.org/10.1007/s11263-015-0816-y

24. Saha, O., Cheng, Z., Maji, S.: GANORCON: are generative models useful for few-shot segmentation? In: Conference on Computer Vision and Pattern Recognition (CVPR), pp. 9991–10000 (2022)

25. Standley, T., Zamir, A., Chen, D., Guibas, L., Malik, J., Savarese, S.: Which tasks should be learned together in multi-task learning? In: III, H.D., Singh, A. (eds.) Proceedings of the 37th International Conference on Machine Learning. Proceedings of Machine Learning Research, vol. 119, pp. 9120–9132. PMLR, 13–18 July 2020. https://proceedings.mlr.press/v119/standley20a.html

26. Tian, Z., Shen, C., Wang, X., Chen, H.: BoxInst: high-performance instance segmentation with box annotations. In: Proceedings of the IEEE/CVF Conference on Computer Vision and Pattern Recognition, pp. 5443–5452 (2021)

27. Tripathi, S., Collins, M., Brown, M., Belongie, S.: Pose2Instance: harnessing keypoints for person instance segmentation. arXiv preprint arXiv:1704.01152 (2017)

28. Tritrong, N., Rewatbowornwong, P., Suwajanakorn, S.: Repurposing gans for one-shot semantic part segmentation. In: Proceedings of the IEEE/CVF Conference on Computer Vision and Pattern Recognition, pp. 4475–4485 (2021)

29. Van Horn, G., et al.: Building a bird recognition app and large scale dataset with citizen scientists: the fine print in fine-grained dataset collection. In: 2015 IEEE Conference on Computer Vision and Pattern Recognition (CVPR), pp. 595–604 (2015). https://doi.org/10.1109/CVPR.2015.7298658

30. Vedaldi, A., et al.: Understanding objects in detail with fine-grained attributes. In: Proceedings of the IEEE Conference on Computer Vision and Pattern Recognition (CVPR) (2014)

31. Wah, C., Branson, S., Welinder, P., Perona, P., Belongie, S.: The Caltech-UCSD Birds-200-2011 dataset. Technical report CNS-TR-2011-001, California Institute of Technology (2011)

32. Wang, Y., Zhang, J., Kan, M., Shan, S., Chen, X.: Self-supervised equivariant attention mechanism for weakly supervised semantic segmentation. In: Proceedings of the IEEE/CVF Conference on Computer Vision and Pattern Recognition, pp. 12275–12284 (2020)

33. Welling, M., Teh, Y.W.: Bayesian learning via stochastic gradient Langevin dynamics. In: Proceedings of the 28th International Conference on Machine Learning (ICML-11), pp. 681–688. Citeseer (2011)

34. Yang, Y., Bilen, H., Zou, Q., Cheung, W.Y., Ji, X.: Unsupervised foreground-background segmentation with equivariant layered GANs. arXiv preprint arXiv:2104.00483 (2021)

35. Zhang, Y., et al.: DatasetGAN: efficient labeled data factory with minimal human effort. In: Proceedings of the IEEE/CVF Conference on Computer Vision and Pattern Recognition, pp. 10145–10155 (2021)

36. Zhou, Y., Zhu, Y., Ye, Q., Qiu, Q., Jiao, J.: Weakly supervised instance segmentation using class peak response. In: Proceedings of the IEEE Conference on Computer Vision and Pattern Recognition, pp. 3791–3800 (2018)

37. Zhu, Y., Zhou, Y., Xu, H., Ye, Q., Doermann, D., Jiao, J.: Learning instance activation maps for weakly supervised instance segmentation. In: Proceedings of the IEEE/CVF Conference on Computer Vision and Pattern Recognition, pp. 3116–3125 (2019)

38. Zou, Y., Zhang, Z., Zhang, H., Li, C.L., Bian, X., Huang, J.B., Pfister, T.: PSEUDOSEG: designing pseudo labels for semantic segmentation. arXiv preprint arXiv:2010.09713 (2020)

What to Hide from Your Students: Attention-Guided Masked Image Modeling

Ioannis Kakogeorgiou[1(✉)], Spyros Gidaris[2], Bill Psomas[1], Yannis Avrithis[3,4], Andrei Bursuc[2], Konstantinos Karantzalos[1], and Nikos Komodakis[5,6]

[1] National Technical University of Athens, Athens, Greece
`gkakogeorgiou@central.ntua.gr`
[2] valeo.ai, Paris, France
[3] Institute of Advanced Research in Artificial Intelligence (IARAI), Vienna, Austria
[4] Athena RC, Athens, Greece
[5] University of Crete, Heraklion, Greece
[6] IACM-Forth, Heraklion, Greece

Abstract. Transformers and masked language modeling are quickly being adopted and explored in computer vision as *vision transformers* and *masked image modeling* (MIM). In this work, we argue that image token masking differs from token masking in text, due to the amount and correlation of tokens in an image. In particular, to generate a challenging pretext task for MIM, we advocate a shift from random masking to informed masking. We develop and exhibit this idea in the context of distillation-based MIM, where a teacher transformer encoder generates an attention map, which we use to guide masking for the student.

We thus introduce a novel masking strategy, called *attention-guided masking* (AttMask), and we demonstrate its effectiveness over random masking for dense distillation-based MIM as well as plain distillation-based self-supervised learning on classification tokens. We confirm that AttMask accelerates the learning process and improves the performance on a variety of downstream tasks. We provide the implementation code at https://github.com/gkakogeorgiou/attmask.

1 Introduction

Self-supervised learning (SSL) has attracted significant attention over the last years. Recently, several studies are shifting towards adapting SSL to transformer architectures. Originating in natural language processing, where self-supervised transformers [14,58] have revolutionized the field, these architectures were introduced to computer vision with the *vision transformer* (ViT) [16] as an alternative to convolutional neural networks [24,33,54]. ViT formulates an image as a sequence of tokens obtained directly from raw patches and then follows a pure

---

Supplementary Information The online version contains supplementary material available at https://doi.org/10.1007/978-3-031-20056-4_18.

transformer architecture. Despite the absence of image-specific inductive bias, ViT shows strong image representation learning capacity.

Considering that transformers are data-hungry, many studies advocate pre-training them on unsupervised pretext tasks, determined only by raw data. A prominent paradigm is to mask a portion of the input tokens—words in text or patches in images—and train the transformer to predict these missing tokens [2, 14,23,65,70]. This paradigm, called *masked language modeling* (MLM) in the language domain [14], is remarkably successful and extends to the vision domain as *masked image modeling* (MIM) [2,65,70].

MIM-based self-supervised methods have already shown impressive results on images. However, an important aspect that has not been well explored so far is how to choose which image tokens to mask. Typically, the selection is random, as has been the norm for text data. In this work, we argue that random token masking for image data is not as effective.

In text, random word masking is likely to hide high-level concepts that describe entire semantic entities such as objects (nouns) and actions (verbs). By contrast, an image has much more tokens than a sentence, which are highly redundant, and random masking is less likely to hide "interesting" parts; or when it does, the remaining parts still easily reveal the identity of the visual concepts. As shown in Fig. 1(b–d), unless masking is very aggressive, this is thus less likely to form challenging token reconstruction examples that would allow the transformer to develop strong comprehension skills.

The question we ask is this: *Can we develop a masking strategy that addresses this limitation and makes informed decisions on which tokens to mask?*

To this end, we propose to exploit the intrinsic properties of ViT and in particular its self-attention mechanism. Given an input sequence of image patches, we forward it through the transformer encoder, thereby obtaining an attention map in its output. We then mask the most attended tokens. As shown in Fig. 1(f–g), the motivation is that highly-attended tokens form more coherent image regions that correspond to more discriminative cues comparing with random tokens, thus leading to a more challenging MIM task.

This strategy, which we call *attention-guided masking* (AttMask), is an excellent fit to popular distillation-based self-supervised objectives, because it is the teacher encoder that sees the entire image and extracts the attention map, and the student encoder that sees the masked image and solves the reconstruction task. AttMask thus incurs zero additional cost.

We make the following contributions:

1. We introduce a novel masking strategy for self-supervised learning, called AttMask, that exploits the intrinsic properties of ViT by leveraging its self-attention maps to guide token masking (Subsect. 3.2).
2. We show how to efficiently incorporate this above masking strategy into teacher-student frameworks that use a MIM reconstruction objective and demonstrate significant performance improvements over random masking.
3. Through extensive experimental evaluation, we confirm that AttMask offers several benefits: it accelerates the learning process; it improves performance

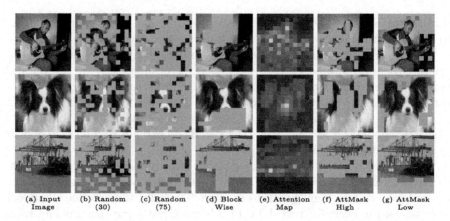

(a) Input Image (b) Random (30) (c) Random (75) (d) Block Wise (e) Attention Map (f) AttMask High (g) AttMask Low

Fig. 1. Different than random masking strategies (b–d), our *attention-guided masking* (AttMask) uses the attention map arising in the encoder (e) to mask the most highly attended by default (f), or the low-attended (g) patches. (b) is used by SimMIM [65], (c) by MAE [23], (d) by BEiT [2] and (g) by MST [36].

on a data-limited regime (Subsect. 4.2) and on a variety of downstream tasks (Subsect. 4.3); it increases the robustness against background changes, thus revealing that it reduces background dependency.

2 Related Work

Vision Transformers. Transformers are based on self-attention [58] and require pretraining on large unlabelled corpora [14]. Their adaptation to vision tasks is not straightforward. Representing pixels by tokens is impractical due to the quadratic complexity of self-attention, giving rise to approximations [10,25,46,60,62]. The idea of representing image patches by tokens is proposed in [12], where patches are of size 2×2, and is further studied in ViT [16], where patches are 16×16. Despite the absence of image-specific inductive bias, ViT is competitive to convolutional neural networks for ImageNet [13] and other smaller benchmark datasets [32,42]. Since it is pretrained on a large and private dataset [53], authors of DeiT [57] question its efficiency and propose an improved data-efficient version, which however is based on a strong teacher instead [49].

Self-supervised Learning. Early self-supervised learning methods follow the paradigm of training on an annotation-free *pretext task*, determined only by raw data [1,15,21,30,34,40,43,67]. This task can be *e.g.*the prediction of patch orderings [43] or rotation angles [21]. Starting from instance discrimination [63] and contrastive predictive coding [45], *contrastive learning* has become very popular [3,8,17,28,39,52,61]. These methods pull positives together and push negatives apart, where positives are typically determined by different views of the same example. Alternatively, contrastive learning often relies on clustering [4–6,19,35,66,71]. The requirement of negatives is eliminated in BYOL [22],

OBoW [20], SimSiam [9] and DINO [7], where the challenge is to avoid representation collapse, most notably by a form of *self-distillation* [55].

Using transformers, MIM as a pretext task is proposed in BEiT [2], which maps the images to discrete patch tokens and recovers tokens for masked patches, according to a block-wise random strategy. Other than that, MIM methods use continuous representations: SimMIM [65] randomly masks large patches and predicts the corresponding pixels by direct regression; MAE [23] randomly masks a large portion of patches and predicts the corresponding pixels using an autoencoder; MST [36] masks low-attended patches and reconstructs the entire input with a decoder; iBOT [70] extends the self-distillation loss of DINO to dense features corresponding to block-wise masked patches. Here, we advocate masking of *highly-attended* patches, in a sense the opposite of MST, and we exhibit this idea in the context of DINO and iBOT.

Regularization and Augmentation. As the complexity of a task increases, networks with more and more parameters are introduced. But with increased representational power comes increased need for more data or risk of overfitting. Several regularization and data augmentation methods have been proposed in this direction [13,27,50,51], combined with standard supervised tasks.

In this context, feature masking is introduced by Dropout [51], which randomly drops hidden neuron activations. To address the strong spatial correlation in convolutional feature maps, SpatialDropout [56] randomly drops entire channels. DropBlock [18] generalizes Dropout—or constrains SpatialDropout—by dropping features in a block, *i.e.*, a square region of a feature map. Attention Dropout [11] makes use of self-attention to mask the most discriminative part of an image. Feature-space masking, guided by attention from another network or branch, has been extensively studied as a mechanism to explore beyond the most discriminative object parts for weakly-supervised object detection [26,29,68]. Our work is a natural evolution of these ideas, where attention is an intrinsic mechanism of transformers; and the task becomes that of densely reconstructing the masked features. This is a pretext task, without need for supervision.

3   Method

A simplified overview of the method is shown in Fig. 2. We first discuss in Subsect. 3.1 preliminaries and background on vision transformers and self-supervision with distillation-based masked image modeling. In Subsect. 3.2, we then detail our attention-guided token masking strategy, called AttMask, and how we incorporate it into masked image modeling.

3.1   Preliminaries and Background

Vision Transformer [16]. We are given an input image $X \in \mathbb{R}^{h \times w \times c}$, where $h \times w$ is the spatial resolution and c is the number of channels. The first step is to tokenize it, *i.e.*, convert it to a sequence of token embeddings. The image is

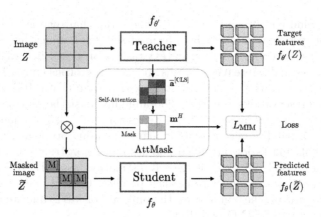

Fig. 2. Simplified overview of AttMask as incorporated in the masked image modelling (MIM) objective of iBOT [70]. A tokenized image Z (1) is given as input to a teacher encoder $f_{\theta'}$, generating target features $f_{\theta'}(Z)$ and an attention map $\overline{\mathbf{a}}^{[\text{CLS}]}$ (7). We then generate a mask $\mathbf{m}^H$ (9) on the most attended tokens and accordingly a masked version $\widetilde{Z}$ (10) of the image, which is given as input to a student encoder f_θ to generate the predicted features $f_\theta(\widetilde{Z})$. Using $\mathbf{m}^H$, loss L_{MIM} (3) is a dense distillation loss between predicted and target features of the masked tokens. Additionally, a global loss L_{G} (4) between [CLS] tokens is applied (not shown here).

divided into $n = hw/p^2$ non-overlapping patches $P_i \in \mathbb{R}^{p \times p \times c}$ for $i = 1, \ldots, n$, where $p \times p$ is the patch resolution. Each patch is flattened into a vector in $\mathbb{R}^{p^2 c}$ and projected to an embedding vector $\mathbf{z}_i \in \mathbb{R}^d$ using a linear layer, where d is the embedding dimension. A learnable embedding $\mathbf{z}^{[\text{CLS}]} \in \mathbb{R}^d$ of a "classification" token [CLS] is then prepended to form the *tokenized image*

$$Z = (\mathbf{z}^{[\text{CLS}]}; \mathbf{z}_1; \ldots; \mathbf{z}_n) \in \mathbb{R}^{(n+1) \times d}, \tag{1}$$

where ";" denotes row-wise stacking. The role of this special token is to represent the image at the output. A sequence of position embeddings is added to Z to retain positional information. The resulting sequence is the input to the *transformer encoder*. Each layer of the encoder consists of a *multi-head self-attention* (MSA) block followed by a *multi-layer perceptron* (MLP) block. Through all of its layers, the encoder uses a sequence of fixed length $n + 1$ of token embeddings of fixed dimension d, represented by a $(n + 1) \times d$ matrix. The embedding of the [CLS] token at the output layer serves as the image representation.

An MSA block consists of a number H of heads, each computing a *scaled dot-product self-attention* [58], *i.e.*, the relevance of each image patch to others, encoded as an $(n + 1) \times (n + 1)$ *attention matrix*. As discussed in Subsect. 3.2, we average attention matrices over all the heads of the last encoder layer and we use the row corresponding to the [CLS] token to generate token masks.

Distillation-Based Masked Image Modeling. *Self-distillation*, using a moving average of the student as teacher [55], is studied for self-supervision in

BYOL [22] and extended to vision transformers in DINO [7], which applies the distillation loss globally on the [CLS] token. iBOT [70] turns this task into *masked image modeling* (MIM) by applying the loss densely on masked tokens.

Given an input image X tokenized as $Z = (\mathbf{z}^{[\text{CLS}]}; \mathbf{z}_1; \ldots; \mathbf{z}_n)$, a *mask vector* $\mathbf{m} = (m_1, \ldots, m_n) \in \{0,1\}^n$ is generated, giving rise to a *masked tokenized image* $\widetilde{Z} = (\mathbf{z}^{[\text{CLS}]}; \tilde{\mathbf{z}}_1; \ldots; \tilde{\mathbf{z}}_n)$, with

$$\tilde{\mathbf{z}}_i = (1 - m_i) \cdot \mathbf{z}_i + m_i \cdot \mathbf{z}^{[\text{MASK}]} \tag{2}$$

for $i = 1, \ldots, n$, where $\mathbf{z}^{[\text{MASK}]} \in \mathbb{R}^d$ is a learnable embedding of a "mask" token [MASK]. Following the strategy of BEiT [2], the mask vector is generated with random *block-wise* token sampling, that is, defined in terms of random rectangles in the 2D layout of the n tokens as a $(h/p) \times (w/p)$ matrix.

Following DINO [7], the transformer encoder is followed by a head that includes an MLP and scaled softmax, such that output token embeddings can be interpreted as probabilities. We denote by f_θ the mapping that includes the addition of the position embeddings, the encoder and the head, while θ is the set of learnable parameters. Given a tokenized image Z, masked or not, we denote by $f_\theta(Z) \in \mathbb{R}^{(n+1) \times d}$ the output token sequence and by $f_\theta(Z)_i, f_\theta(Z)^{[\text{CLS}]} \in \mathbb{R}^d$ the embedding of the i-th and [CLS] token respectively. The teacher parameters θ' are obtained from the student parameters θ by *exponential moving average* (EMA) according to $\theta' \leftarrow \alpha\theta' + (1 - \alpha)\theta$.

For each input image, two standard resolution augmented *global views* are generated, with tokenized images Z^a, Z^b and mask vectors $\mathbf{m}^a, \mathbf{m}^b$. For each view v in $V = \{a, b\}$ and for each masked token, the MIM objective is to minimize the reconstruction loss between the student f_θ output for the masked input $\widetilde{Z}^v$ and the teacher $f_{\theta'}$ output for the non-masked input Z^v:

$$L_{\text{MIM}} = -\sum_{v \in V} \sum_{i=1}^{n} m_i^v f_{\theta'}(Z^v)_i \log(f_\theta(\widetilde{Z}^v)_i). \tag{3}$$

Following DINO [7], a similar loss is applied globally on the [CLS] tokens between the student output for one masked view $\widetilde{Z}^v$ and the teacher output for the other non-masked view Z^u:

$$L_{\text{G}} = -\sum_{(u,v) \in V^2} \mathbb{1}_{u \neq v} f_{\theta'}(Z^u)^{[\text{CLS}]} \log(f_\theta(\widetilde{Z}^v)^{[\text{CLS}]}). \tag{4}$$

Finally, as detailed in the supplementary, a *multi-crop* strategy applies, giving rise to a loss L_{LC} between local crops and global views. The overall loss of iBOT [70] is a weighted sum of L_{MIM} (3) and L_{G} (4) + L_{LC}. DINO itself uses the sum L_{G} (4) + L_{LC} without masking.

3.2 AttMask: Attention-Guided Token Masking

Prior MIM-based self-supervised methods use random or block-wise random token masking. In this section we describe our attention-guided token masking strategy, which hides tokens that correspond to the salient regions of an image and thus define a more challenging MIM objective.

Attention Map Generation. Given an input sequence $Y \in \mathbb{R}^{(n+1) \times d}$, a *multi-head self-attention* (MSA) layer uses three linear layers to map Y to the *query* Q_j, *key* K_j and *value* V_j sequences for $j = 1, \ldots, H$, where H is the number of heads, $Q_j, K_j, V_j \in \mathbb{R}^{(n+1) \times d'}$ and $d' = d/H$. Then, it forms the $(n+1) \times (n+1)$ *attention matrix*, where softmax is row-wise:

$$A_j = \mathrm{softmax}\left(Q_j K_j^\top / \sqrt{d'}\right). \tag{5}$$

To generate token masks from any layer of the transformer encoder, we average the attention matrices over all heads:

$$\overline{A} = \frac{1}{H} \sum_{j=1}^{H} A_j. \tag{6}$$

Now, each row of an attention matrix is a vector in $\mathbb{R}^{n+1}$, that corresponds to one token and, excluding the diagonal elements, determines an *attention vector* in $\mathbb{R}^n$ over all other tokens. We focus on the attention vector of the [CLS] token, which comprises all but the first elements of the first row of $\overline{A}$:

$$\overline{\mathbf{a}}^{[\mathrm{CLS}]} = \left(\overline{a}_{1,2}, \overline{a}_{1,3}, \ldots, \overline{a}_{1,n+1}\right), \tag{7}$$

where $\overline{a}_{i,j}$ is the element i, j of $\overline{A}$. This vector can be reshaped to $(h/p) \times (w/p)$ *attention map*, to be visualized as a 2D image, indicating the regions of the input image that the [CLS] token is attending.

Mask Generation: Highly-Attended Tokens. There is a permutation $\sigma_\downarrow : \{1, \ldots, n\} \to \{1, \ldots, n\}$ that brings the elements of $\overline{\mathbf{a}}^{[\mathrm{CLS}]}$ in descending order, such that $\overline{a}^{[\mathrm{CLS}]}_{\sigma_\downarrow(i)} \geq \overline{a}^{[\mathrm{CLS}]}_{\sigma_\downarrow(j)}$ for $i < j$, where $\overline{a}^{[\mathrm{CLS}]}_i$ is the i-th element of $\overline{\mathbf{a}}^{[\mathrm{CLS}]}$. Choosing a number $k = \lfloor rn \rfloor$ that is proportional to the total number n of tokens with *mask ratio* $r \in [0, 1]$, we define

$$M^H := \{\sigma_\downarrow(i), \ldots, \sigma_\downarrow(k)\} \tag{8}$$

as the set of indices of the top-k most attended tokens. We thus define the *high-attention mask vector* $\mathbf{m}^H$ with elements

$$m_i^H := \mathbb{1}_{M^H}(i) = \begin{cases} 1 & \text{if } i \in M^H \\ 0 & \text{otherwise} \end{cases} \tag{9}$$

for $i = 1, \ldots, n$. This masking strategy, which we call AttMask-High, essentially hides the patches that correspond to the most discriminative or salient regions of an image. By AttMask we shall refer to this strategy as default.

Low-Attended Tokens. We also examine the opposite approach of AttMask-High that masks the least attended tokens. In particular, we define the set of indices of the bottom-k least attended tokens $M^L = \{\sigma_\uparrow(i), \ldots, \sigma_\uparrow(k)\}$ and the *low-attention mask vector* $\mathbf{m}^L$ with $m_i^L := \mathbb{1}_{M^L}(i)$ based on the permutation $\sigma_\uparrow$

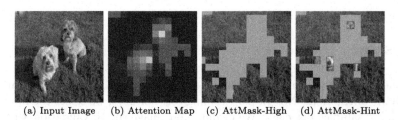

(a) Input Image   (b) Attention Map   (c) AttMask-High   (d) AttMask-Hint

Fig. 3. Given image (a), the mean attention map (b) is averaged over heads (6), (7). The AttMask-High strategy (c) masks the most attended patches, while AttMask-Hint (d) reveals few of them to leave hints about the identity of the masked object

that brings the elements of $\overline{\mathbf{a}}^{[\mathrm{CLS}]}$ in ascending order, that is, $\overline{a}^{[\mathrm{CLS}]}_{\sigma_\downarrow(i)} \leq \overline{a}^{[\mathrm{CLS}]}_{\sigma_\downarrow(j)}$ for $i < j$. This strategy, which we call AttMask-Low and is similar to the masking strategy of MST [36], hides patches of the image background. Our experiments show that AttMask-Low does not work well with the considered MIM-based loss.

Highly-Attended with Hints. Finally, because AttMask-High may be overly aggressive in hiding the foreground object of an image, especially when the mask ratio r is high, we also examine an alternative strategy that we call AttMask-Hint: While still masking highly attended tokens, we allow a small number of the most highly attended ones to be revealed, so as to leave hints about the identity of the masked object. In particular, we remove from the initial set M^H a small number $m = \lfloor sn \rfloor$ of tokens with *show ratio* $s < r$. These m tokens are randomly selected from the $\lfloor s_{\max} n \rfloor$ most attended tokens in M^H, where $s_{\max} > s$. An example comparing AttMask-Hint with AttMask-High is illustrated in Fig. 3.

Incorporating AttMask into Self-supervised Methods. Because the embedding of the [CLS] token at the output layer of the transformer encoder serves as the image representation, we generate token masks based on the attention vector precisely of the [CLS] token of the output layer. In particular, given a global view tokenized as $Z^v = (\mathbf{z}^{[\mathrm{CLS}]}; \mathbf{z}_1; \ldots; \mathbf{z}_n)$, we obtain the attention vector $\overline{\mathbf{a}}^{[\mathrm{CLS}]}$ (7) and the corresponding high-attention mask vector $\mathbf{m}^H$ (9) at the output layer of the teacher. Then, similarly to (2), we give as input to the student the masked version $\widetilde{Z}^v = (\mathbf{z}^{[\mathrm{CLS}]}; \tilde{\mathbf{z}}_1; \ldots; \tilde{\mathbf{z}}_n)$ with

$$\tilde{\mathbf{z}}_i = (1 - m_i^H) \cdot \mathbf{z}_i + m_i^H \cdot \mathbf{z}^{[\mathrm{MASK}]}. \tag{10}$$

We argue that masking highly attended regions using $\mathbf{m}^H$ helps in learning powerful representations. In Sect. 4, we also experiment with low-attended regions using $\mathbf{m}^L$, supporting further our argument.

AttMask can be incorporated into different methods to either replace the block-wise strategy of BEiT [2] or introduce masking. For iBOT [70], we use $\widetilde{Z}^v$ in L_{MIM} (3) and L_{G} (4). For DINO [7], we introduce masking by using $\widetilde{Z}^v$ for global views in L_{G} (4), but not for local crops in the L_{LC} loss (see supplementary).

4   Experiments

4.1   Setup

Datasets and Evaluation Protocol. We pretrain iBOT and DINO on 20% and 100% of the ImageNet-1k [13] training set. For 20%, we select the first 20% of training samples per class. We evaluate on ImageNet-1k validation set by k-NN or *linear probing*. For linear probing, we train a linear classifier on top of features using the same training protocol as in DINO [7]. With linear probing, we also validate robustness against background changes on ImageNet-9 (IN-9) [64]. For k-NN [63], we freeze the pretrained model and extract features of training images, then use a k-nearest neighbor classifier with $k = 20$. We also perform the same k-NN experiment, now extracting features only from $\nu \in \{1, 5, 10, 20\}$ examples per class. This task is more challenging and is similar to few-shot classification, only the test classes are the same as in representation learning.

We downstream to other tasks either with or without *finetuning*. We finetune on CIFAR10 [32], CIFAR100 [32] and Oxford Flowers [42] for *image classification* measuring accuracy; on COCO [37] for *object detection* and *instance segmentation* measuring mean average precision (mAP); and on ADE20K [69] for *semantic segmentation* measuring mean Intersection over Union (mIoU). Without finetuning, we extract features as with k-NN and we evaluate using dataset-specific evaluation protocol and metrics. We test on revisited $\mathcal{R}$Oxford and $\mathcal{R}$Paris [48] for *image retrieval* measuring mAP [48]; on Caltech-UCSD Birds (CUB200) [59], Stanford Cars (CARS196) [31], Stanford Online Products (SOP) [44] and In-Shop Clothing Retrieval (In-Shop) [38] for *fine-grained classification* measuring Recall@k [41]; and on DAVIS 2017 [47] for *video object segmentation* measuring mean region similarity $\mathcal{J}_m$ and contour-based accuracy $\mathcal{F}_m$ [47].

In supplementary, we provide more benchmarks, visualizations and ablations.

Implementation Details. As transformer encoder, we use ViT-S/16 [16]. The attention map (7) is generated from the last layer of the teacher encoder by default, *i.e.*, layer 12. We mask the input with probability $p = 0.5$, while the mask ratio r is sampled uniformly as $r \sim U(a, b)$ with $[a, b] = [0.1, 0.5]$ by default. For AttMask-Hint, we set $s_{\max} = 0.1$ and the show ratio s is sampled uniformly from $[s_{\max}a, s_{\max}b] = [0.01, 0.05]$. Following [7,70], we apply *multi-crop* [6] scheme. The overall loss of iBOT [70] is a weighted sum of L_{MIM} (3), with weight λ, and L_{G} (4) + L_{LC} (DINO [7]), with weight 1, where L_{LC} is the multi-crop loss. By default, $\lambda = 1$. Hyperparameters are ablated in Subsect. 4.4. Training details are given in the supplementary.

4.2   Experimental Analysis

We provide an analysis on 20% of ImageNet-1k training samples, incorporating AttMask into distillation-based MIM [70] or self-distillation only [7]. We also provide results on robustness against background changes.

Table 1. *Different masking strategies* for iBOT [70] pre-training on 20% of ImageNet. Top-1 accuracy for k-NN, linear probing on ImageNet validation set; fine-tuning on CIFAR10/100. †: default iBOT masking strategy from BEiT [2]. ‡: aggressive random masking strategy from MAE [23].

iBOT Masking	Ratio (%)	ImageNet-1k		CIFAR10	CIFAR100
		k-NN	Linear	Fine-tuning	
Random Block-Wise[†]	10–50	46.7	56.4	98.0	86.0
Random[‡]	75	47.3	55.5	97.7	85.5
Random	10–50	47.8	56.7	98.0	86.1
AttMask-Low (ours)	10–50	44.0	53.4	97.6	84.6
AttMask-Hint (ours)	10–50	49.5	57.5	98.1	**86.6**
AttMask-High (ours)	10–50	**49.7**	**57.9**	**98.2**	**86.6**

Table 2. Top-1 k-NN accuracy on ImageNet-1k validation for iBOT pre-training on different percentage (%) of ImageNet-1k. †: default iBOT masking strategy from BEiT [2].

% ImageNet-1k	5	10	20	100
Random Block-Wise[†]	15.7	31.9	46.7	71.5
AttMask-High (ours)	**17.5**	**33.8**	**49.7**	**72.5**

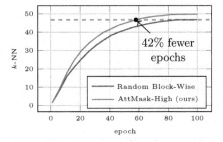

Fig. 4. Top-1 k-NN accuracy on ImageNet-1k validation for iBOT training *vs.* training epoch on 20% ImageNet training set. †: default iBOT masking strategy from BEiT [2].

Masking Strategies: Distillation-Based MIM. We explore a number of masking strategies using distillation-based MIM, by incorporating AttMask into iBOT [70]. We compare AttMask with random block-wise masking [2], which is the default in iBOT, random patch masking with the same ratio, as well as with a more aggressive ratio, following MAE [23]. AttMask masks the most attended tokens (AttMask-High) by default, but we also consider the least attended (AttMask-Low) and the most attended with hints (AttMask-Hint).

We evaluate performance using k-NN and linear probing evaluation protocol on the validation set, along with a fine-tuning evaluation on CIFAR10 and CIFAR100. As shown in Table 1, the AttMask-High outperforms all other masking strategies on all the evaluation metrics. In particular, AttMask-High achieves an improvement of +3.0% on k-NN and +1.5% on linear probing compared with the default iBOT strategy (random block-wise).

Interestingly, random patch masking outperforms the default iBOT strategy, while the more aggressive MAE-like strategy is inferior and AttMask-Low

Table 3. Top-1 k-NN accuracy on ImageNet-1k validation for DINO [7] pre-training on 20% of the ImageNet-1k training set using mask ratio of 10–50%. †: default DINO.

No Masking†	Random	AttMask-Low	AttMask-Hint	AttMask-High
43.0	43.4	42.7	**43.6**	43.5

Table 4. *Background robustness*: Linear probing of iBOT model on IN-9 [64] and its variations, when pre-trained on 20% ImageNet-1k under different masking strategies. †: default iBOT masking strategy from BEiT [2]. ‡: aggressive random masking.

iBOT Masking	Ratio (%)	OF	MS	MR	MN	NF	OBB	OBT	IN-9
Random Block-wise†	10-50	72.4	74.3	59.4	56.8	36.3	14.4	15.0	89.1
Random‡	75	73.1	73.8	58.8	55.9	35.6	13.7	14.5	87.9
Random	10-50	72.8	75.3	60.4	57.5	34.9	10.3	14.4	89.3
AttMask-Low (ours)	10-50	66.0	71.1	55.2	52.2	32.4	12.5	14.0	86.6
AttMask-Hint (ours)	10-50	74.4	75.9	61.7	58.3	39.6	**16.7**	**15.7**	89.6
AttMask-High (ours)	10-50	**75.2**	**76.2**	**62.3**	**59.4**	**40.6**	15.2	15.3	**89.8**

performs the lowest. Intuitively, this means that masking and reconstruction of non-salient regions does not provide a strong supervisory signal under a MIM objective. By contrast, our AttMask creates the more aggressive task of reconstructing the most salient regions and guides the model to explore the other regions. In this setup, AttMask-Hint is slightly lower than AttMask-High.

Data and Training Efficiency. Self-supervised methods on vision transformers typically require millions of images, which is very demanding in computational resources. We advocate that being effective on less data and fast training are good properties for a self-supervised method. In this direction, we assess efficiency on less data and training time, still with iBOT training. In Table 2 we observe that our AttMask-High consistently outperforms the default random block-wise masking strategy of iBOT at lower percentage of ImageNet-1k training set. In addition, in Fig. 4, AttMask-High achieves the same performance as random block-wise with 42% fewer training epochs.

Masking Strategies: Self-distillation Only. Here, we compare masking strategies using distillation only, without MIM reconstruction loss, by incorporating AttMask into DINO [7]. That is, we apply only the cross-view cross-entropy loss on the [CLS] token (4). In Table 3, AttMask-High improves k-NN by +0.5 compared with the default DINO (no masking), while AttMask-Low is inferior. This reveals that AttMask is effective even without a MIM loss. Moreover, AttMask-Hint is slightly better than AttMask-High in this setting.

Table 5. Top-1 accuracy on ImageNet validation set. (a) k-NN and linear probing using the full ImageNet training set; (b) k-NN using only $\nu \in \{1, 5, 10, 20\}$ examples per class. Pre-training on 100% ImageNet-1k for 100 epochs.

METHOD	(a) FULL		(b) FEW EXAMPLES			
	k-NN	LINEAR	$\nu = 1$	5	10	20
DINO [7]	70.9	74.6				
MST [36]	72.1	75.0				
iBOT [70]	71.5	74.4	32.9	47.6	52.5	56.4
iBOT+AttMask-High	72.5	75.7	37.1	51.3	55.7	59.1
iBOT+AttMask-Hint	**72.8**	**76.1**	**37.6**	**52.2**	**56.4**	**59.6**

Table 6. Fine-tuning for *image classification* on CIFAR10 [32], CIFAR100 [32] and Oxford Flowers [42]; *Object detection* (AP^b, %) and *instance segmentation* (AP^m, %) on COCO [37]; and *semantic segmentation* on ADE20K [69] (mIoU, %). Models pre-trained on 100% ImageNet-1k training set for 100 epochs.

METHOD	CIFAR10	CIFAR100	FLOWERS	COCO		ADE20K
		Accuracy		AP^b	AP^m	mIoU
iBOT	**98.8**	89.5	96.8	48.2	41.8	44.9
iBOT+AttMask	**98.8**	**90.1**	**97.7**	**48.8**	**42.0**	**45.3**

Robustness Against Background Changes. Deep learning models tend to depend on image background. However, to generalize well, they should be robust against background changes and rather focus on foreground. To analyze this property, we use ImageNet-9 (IN-9) dataset [64], which includes nine coarse-grained classes with seven background/foreground variations. In four datasets, the background is altered: Only-FG (OF), Mixed-Same (MS), Mixed-Rand (MR), and Mixed-Next (MN). In another three, the foreground is masked: No-FG (NF), Only-BG-B (OBB), and Only-BG-T (OBT).

In Table 4, we evaluate the impact of background changes on IN-9 and its variations, training iBOT under different masking strategies. We observe that, except for O.BB. and O.BT, AttMask-High is the most robust. On OBB and OBT where the foreground object is completely missing, AttMask-Hint exploits slightly better the background correlations with the missing object.

4.3   Benchmark

We pre-train iBOT with AttMask-High and AttMask-Hint on 100% of ImageNet-1k and compare it with baseline iBOT and other distillation-based methods.

ImageNet Classification. As shown in Table 5(a), AttMask-High brings an improvement of 1% k-NN and 1.3% linear probing over baseline iBOT [70]

Table 7. *Image retrieval* (mAP, %) on (a) $\mathcal{R}$Oxford and (b) $\mathcal{R}$Paris [48] and *video object segmentation* (mean region similarity $\mathcal{J}_m$ and contour-based accuracy $\mathcal{F}_m$, %) on (c) DAVIS 2017 [47], without fine-tuning. Models pre-trained on 100% ImageNet-1k training set for 100 epochs.

METHOD	(a) $\mathcal{R}$OXFORD		(b) $\mathcal{R}$PARIS		(c) DAVIS 2017		
	MEDIUM	HARD	MEDIUM	HARD	$(\mathcal{J}\&\mathcal{F})_m$	$\mathcal{J}_m$	$\mathcal{F}_m$
iBOT	31.0	11.7	56.2	28.9	60.5	59.5	61.4
iBOT+AttMask	**33.5**	**12.1**	**59.0**	**31.5**	**62.1**	**60.6**	**63.5**

Table 8. Fine-grained classification (R@k: Recall@k, %) [41] without fine-tuning. Models pre-trained on 100% ImageNet-1k training set for 100 epochs.

METHOD	CUB200			CARS196			SOP			IN-SHOP		
	R@1	2	4	R@1	2	4	R@1	10	100	R@1	10	20
iBOT	51.4	63.8	75.0	35.6	46.0	56.3	57.4	72.2	84.0	39.1	61.9	68.2
iBOT+AttMask	**57.2**	**69.4**	**80.3**	**39.8**	**50.4**	**61.4**	**59.0**	**73.9**	**85.4**	**40.7**	**63.7**	**70.3**

and is better than prior methods. AttMask-High is thus effective for larger datasets too. Table 5(b) shows results of the more challenging task where only $\nu \in \{1, 5, 10, 20\}$ training examples per class are used for the k-NN classifier. In this case, AttMask-High is very effective, improving the baseline iBOT masking strategy by 3–4%, demonstrating the quality of the learned representation. In this setup, AttMask-Hint offers a further small improvement over AttMask-High. For simplicity though, we use AttMask-High by default as AttMask.

Downstream Tasks with Fine-Tuning. We fine-tune the pre-trained models with iBOT and iBOT with AttMask for *image classification* on CIFAR10 [32], CIFAR100 [32] and Oxford Flowers [42], *object detection* and *instance segmentation* on COCO [37], and *semantic segmentation* on ADE20K [69]. In Table 6, we observe that AttMask brings small improvement on the baseline iBOT masking strategy on *image classification* fine-tuning in all cases. Furthermore, we observe that AttMask improves clearly the scores by 0.6% AP^b on object detection and 0.4% mIoU on semantic segmentation.

Downstream Tasks Without Fine-Tuning. Without finetuning, we use the pretrained models with iBOT and iBOT with AttMask to extract features as with k-NN and we evaluate using dataset-specific evaluation protocol and metrics. As shown in Table 7(a, b), AttMask is very effective on image retrieval, improving by 1–3% mAP the baseline iBOT masking strategy on $\mathcal{R}$Oxford and $\mathcal{R}$Paris [48], on both medium and hard protocols. More impressive the performance on fine-grained classification, improving by 2–6% R@1 on all datasets, as shown in Table 8. Finally, AttMask improves on video object segmentation on DAVIS 2017 [47] on all metrics, as shown in Table 7(c). These experiments are

Table 9. AttMask k-NN top-1 accuracy on ImageNet-1k validation for iBOT pretraining on 20% of ImageNet-1k *vs.*(a) layer from which the attention map (7) is generated; (b) masking probability p (using batch size 180); and (c) mask ratio r.

(a) LAYER				(b) MASKING PROB p					(c) MASK RATIO r (%)			
6	9	11	12	0	0.25	0.50	0.75	1	10–30	10–50	10–70	30
48.1	48.1	**49.8**	49.7	43.4	47.3	**49.4**	**49.4**	44.2	49.5	**49.7**	48.5	49.1

very important because they evaluate the quality of the pretrained features as they are, without fine-tuning and without even an additional layer, on datasets of different distribution than the pretraining set. AttMask improves performance by a larger margin in this type of tasks, compared with ImageNet.

4.4 Ablation Study

We provide an ablation for the main choices and hyperparameters of our masking strategy and loss function, incorporating AttMask into iBOT [70] and pretraining on 20% of ImageNet-1k training samples.

Layer for Attention Map Generation. The attention map (7) is generated from the last layer of the teacher encoder by default, that is, layer 12 of ViT-S. In Table 9(a), we aim to understand the impact of other layer choices on AttMask. We observe that the deeper layers achieve the highest k-NN performance. Although layer 11 works slightly better, we keep the choice of layer 12 for simplicity, since layer 12 embeddings are used anyway in the loss function.

Masking Probability and Mask Ratio. We mask the global views with probability $p = 0.5$ by default. Table 9(b) reports on other choices and confirms that this choice is indeed best. Therefore, it is useful that student network sees both masked and non-masked images.

The mask ratio r is sampled uniformly as $r \sim U(a, b)$ with $[a, b] = [0.1, 0.5]$ by default. Table 9(c) shows the sensitivity of AttMask with respect to the upper bound b, along with a fixed ratio $r = 0.3$. AttMask is relatively stable, with the default interval $[0.1, 0.5]$ working best and the more aggressive choice $[0.1, 0.7]$ worst. This is possibly due to the foreground objects being completely masked and confirms that masking the most attended patches is an effective strategy. The added variation around the fixed ratio $r = 0.3$ is beneficial.

5 Conclusion

By leveraging the self-attention maps of ViT for guiding token masking, our AttMask is able to hide from the student network discriminative image cues and thus lead to more challenging self-supervised objectives. We empirically demonstrate that AttMask offers several benefits over random masking when used in self-supervised pre-training with masked image modeling. Notably, it accelerates the learning process, achieves superior performance on a variety of downstream tasks, and it increases the robustness against background changes, thus revealing that it reduces background dependency. The improvement is most pronounced in more challenging downstream settings, like using the pretrained features without any additional learning or finetuning, or working with limited data. This reveals the superior quality of the learned representation.

Acknowledgments. We thank Shashanka Venkataramanan for his valuable contribution to certain experiments. This work was supported by computational time granted from GRNET in the Greek HPC facility ARIS under projects PR009017, PR011004 and PR012047 and by the HPC resources of GENCI-IDRIS in France under the 2021 grant AD011012884. NTUA thanks NVIDIA for the support with the donation of GPU hardware. This work has been supported by RAMONES and iToBos projects, funded by the EU Horizon 2020 research and innovation programme, under grants 101017808 and 965221, respectively.

References

1. Arandjelovic, R., Zisserman, A.: Look, listen and learn. In: Proceedings of the IEEE International Conference on Computer Vision, pp. 609–617 (2017)
2. Bao, H., Dong, L., Piao, S., Wei, F.: BEit: BERT pre-training of image transformers. In: International Conference on Learning Representations (2022)
3. Cai, T.T., Frankle, J., Schwab, D.J., Morcos, A.S.: Are all negatives created equal in contrastive instance discrimination? arXiv preprint arXiv:2010.06682 (2020)
4. Caron, M., Bojanowski, P., Joulin, A., Douze, M.: Deep clustering for unsupervised learning of visual features. In: Ferrari, V., Hebert, M., Sminchisescu, C., Weiss, Y. (eds.) Computer Vision – ECCV 2018. LNCS, vol. 11218, pp. 139–156. Springer, Cham (2018). https://doi.org/10.1007/978-3-030-01264-9_9
5. Caron, M., Bojanowski, P., Mairal, J., Joulin, A.: Unsupervised pre-training of image features on non-curated data. In: Proceedings of the IEEE/CVF International Conference on Computer Vision, pp. 2959–2968 (2019)
6. Caron, M., Misra, I., Mairal, J., Goyal, P., Bojanowski, P., Joulin, A.: Unsupervised learning of visual features by contrasting cluster assignments. In: Advances in Neural Information Processing Systems, vol. 33, pp. 9912–9924 (2020)
7. Caron, M., et al.: Emerging properties in self-supervised vision transformers. In: Proceedings of the IEEE/CVF International Conference on Computer Vision, pp. 9650–9660 (2021)
8. Chen, T., Kornblith, S., Norouzi, M., Hinton, G.: A simple framework for contrastive learning of visual representations. In: International Conference on Machine Learning, pp. 1597–1607. PMLR (2020)
9. Chen, X., He, K.: Exploring simple siamese representation learning. In: Proceedings of the IEEE/CVF Conference on Computer Vision and Pattern Recognition, pp. 15750–15758 (2021)
10. Child, R., Gray, S., Radford, A., Sutskever, I.: Generating long sequences with sparse transformers. arXiv preprint arXiv:1904.10509 (2019)
11. Choe, J., Shim, H.: Attention-based dropout layer for weakly supervised object localization. In: Proceedings of the IEEE/CVF Conference on Computer Vision and Pattern Recognition, pp. 2219–2228 (2019)

12. Cordonnier, J.B., Loukas, A., Jaggi, M.: On the relationship between self-attention and convolutional layers. In: International Conference on Learning Representations (2020)
13. Deng, J., Dong, W., Socher, R., Li, L.J., Li, K., Fei-Fei, L.: ImageNet: a large-scale hierarchical image database. In: IEEE Conference on Computer Vision and Pattern Recognition, pp. 248–255. IEEE (2009)
14. Devlin, J., Chang, M.W., Lee, K., Toutanova, K.: BERT: pre-training of deep bidirectional transformers for language understanding. In: Proceedings of the 2019 Conference of the North American Chapter of the Association for Computational Linguistics: Human Language Technologies, Volume 1 (Long and Short Papers), pp. 4171–4186 (2019)
15. Doersch, C., Gupta, A., Efros, A.A.: Unsupervised visual representation learning by context prediction. In: Proceedings of the IEEE International Conference on Computer Vision, pp. 1422–1430 (2015)
16. Dosovitskiy, A., et al.: An image is worth 16×16 words: transformers for image recognition at scale. In: International Conference on Learning Representations (2020)
17. Falcon, W., Cho, K.: A framework for contrastive self-supervised learning and designing a new approach. arXiv preprint arXiv:2009.00104 (2020)
18. Ghiasi, G., Lin, T.Y., Le, Q.V.: DropBlock: a regularization method for convolutional networks. In: Advances in Neural Information Processing Systems, vol. 31 (2018)
19. Gidaris, S., Bursuc, A., Komodakis, N., Pérez, P., Cord, M.: Learning representations by predicting bags of visual words. In: Proceedings of the IEEE Conference on Computer Vision and Pattern Recognition (2020)
20. Gidaris, S., Bursuc, A., Puy, G., Komodakis, N., Cord, M., Pérez, P.: OBoW: online bag-of-visual-words generation for self-supervised learning. In: Proceedings of the IEEE Conference on Computer Vision and Pattern Recognition (2021)
21. Gidaris, S., Singh, P., Komodakis, N.: Unsupervised representation learning by predicting image rotations. In: International Conference on Learning Representations (2018)
22. Grill, J.B., Strub, F., et al.: Bootstrap your own latent-a new approach to self-supervised learning. In: Advances in Neural Information Processing Systems, vol. 33, pp. 21271–21284 (2020)
23. He, K., Chen, X., Xie, S., Li, Y., Dollár, P., Girshick, R.: Masked autoencoders are scalable vision learners. In: Proceedings of the IEEE/CVF Conference on Computer Vision and Pattern Recognition (CVPR), pp. 16000–16009 (2022)
24. He, K., Zhang, X., Ren, S., Sun, J.: Deep residual learning for image recognition. In: Proceedings of the IEEE Conference on Computer Vision and Pattern Recognition, pp. 770–778 (2016)
25. Ho, J., Kalchbrenner, N., Weissenborn, D., Salimans, T.: Axial attention in multidimensional transformers. arXiv preprint arXiv:1912.12180 (2019)
26. Hou, Q., Jiang, P., Wei, Y., Cheng, M.M.: Self-erasing network for integral object attention. In: Advances in Neural Information Processing Systems (2018)
27. Ioffe, S., Szegedy, C.: Batch normalization: accelerating deep network training by reducing internal covariate shift. In: International Conference on Machine Learning, pp. 448–456. PMLR (2015)
28. Kalantidis, Y., Sariyildiz, M.B., Pion, N., Weinzaepfel, P., Larlus, D.: Hard negative mixing for contrastive learning. In: Advances in Neural Information Processing Systems, vol. 33, pp. 21798–21809 (2020)

29. Kim, D., Cho, D., Yoo, D., So Kweon, I.: Two-phase learning for weakly supervised object localization. In: Proceedings of the IEEE/CVF International Conference on Computer Vision (2017)
30. Kolesnikov, A., Zhai, X., Beyer, L.: Revisiting self-supervised visual representation learning. In: Proceedings of the IEEE/CVF Conference on Computer Vision and Pattern Recognition, pp. 1920–1929 (2019)
31. Krause, J., Stark, M., Deng, J., Li, F.F.: 3D object representations for fine-grained categorization. In: ICCVW (2013)
32. Krizhevsky, A., et al.: Learning multiple layers of features from tiny images (2009)
33. Krizhevsky, A., Sutskever, I., Hinton, G.E.: ImageNet classification with deep convolutional neural networks. In: Proceedings of the 25th International Conference on Neural Information Processing Systems, NIPS 2012, Red Hook, NY, USA, vol. 1, pp. 1097–1105. Curran Associates Inc. (2012)
34. Lee, H.Y., Huang, J.B., Singh, M., Yang, M.H.: Unsupervised representation learning by sorting sequences. In: Proceedings of the IEEE International Conference on Computer Vision, pp. 667–676 (2017)
35. Li, J., Zhou, P., Xiong, C., Hoi, S.: Prototypical contrastive learning of unsupervised representations. In: International Conference on Learning Representations (2021)
36. Li, Z., et al.: MST: masked self-supervised transformer for visual representation. In: Advances in Neural Information Processing Systems, vol. 34 (2021)
37. Lin, T.Y., et al.: Microsoft COCO: common objects in context. In: Fleet, D., Pajdla, T., Schiele, B., Tuytelaars, T. (eds.) ECCV 2014. LNCS, vol. 8693, pp. 740–755. Springer, Cham (2014). https://doi.org/10.1007/978-3-319-10602-1_48
38. Liu, Z., Luo, P., Qiu, S., Wang, X., Tang, X.: DeepFashion: powering robust clothes recognition and retrieval with rich annotations. In: Proceedings of the IEEE Conference on Computer Vision and Pattern Recognition (2016)
39. Misra, I., van der Maaten, L.: Self-supervised learning of pretext-invariant representations. In: Proceedings of the IEEE/CVF Conference on Computer Vision and Pattern Recognition, pp. 6707–6717 (2020)
40. Misra, I., Zitnick, C.L., Hebert, M.: Shuffle and learn: unsupervised learning using temporal order verification. In: Leibe, B., Matas, J., Sebe, N., Welling, M. (eds.) ECCV 2016. LNCS, vol. 9905, pp. 527–544. Springer, Cham (2016). https://doi.org/10.1007/978-3-319-46448-0_32
41. Musgrave, K., Belongie, S., Lim, S.-N.: A metric learning reality check. In: Vedaldi, A., Bischof, H., Brox, T., Frahm, J.-M. (eds.) ECCV 2020. LNCS, vol. 12370, pp. 681–699. Springer, Cham (2020). https://doi.org/10.1007/978-3-030-58595-2_41
42. Nilsback, M.E., Zisserman, A.: Automated flower classification over a large number of classes. In: Proceedings of the Indian Conference on Computer Vision, Graphics and Image Processing, December 2008
43. Noroozi, M., Favaro, P.: Unsupervised learning of visual representations by solving jigsaw puzzles. In: Leibe, B., Matas, J., Sebe, N., Welling, M. (eds.) ECCV 2016. LNCS, vol. 9910, pp. 69–84. Springer, Cham (2016). https://doi.org/10.1007/978-3-319-46466-4_5
44. Oh Song, H., Xiang, Y., Jegelka, S., Savarese, S.: Deep metric learning via lifted structured feature embedding. In: Proceedings of the IEEE Conference on Computer Vision and Pattern Recognition (2016)
45. van den Oord, A., Li, Y., Vinyals, O.: Representation learning with contrastive predictive coding. arXiv e-prints. arXiv-1807 (2018)
46. Parmar, N., et al.: Image transformer. In: International Conference on Machine Learning, pp. 4055–4064. PMLR (2018)

47. Perazzi, F., Pont-Tuset, J., McWilliams, B., Van Gool, L., Gross, M., Sorkine-Hornung, A.: A benchmark dataset and evaluation methodology for video object segmentation. In: Proceedings of the IEEE Conference on Computer Vision and Pattern Recognition (2016)
48. Radenović, F., Iscen, A., Tolias, G., Avrithis, Y., Chum, O.: Revisiting Oxford and Paris: large-scale image retrieval benchmarking. In: Proceedings of the IEEE Conference on Computer Vision and Pattern Recognition, pp. 5706–5715 (2018)
49. Radosavovic, I., Kosaraju, R.P., Girshick, R., He, K., Dollar, P.: Designing network design spaces. In: Proceedings of the IEEE/CVF Conference on Computer Vision and Pattern Recognition (2020)
50. Simonyan, K., Zisserman, A.: Very deep convolutional networks for large-scale image recognition. In: Bengio, Y., LeCun, Y. (eds.) International Conference on Learning Representations (2015)
51. Srivastava, N., Hinton, G., Krizhevsky, A., Sutskever, I., Salakhutdinov, R.: Dropout: a simple way to prevent neural networks from overfitting. J. Mach. Learn. Res. **15**(56), 1929–1958 (2014)
52. Stojnic, V., Risojevic, V.: Self-supervised learning of remote sensing scene representations using contrastive multiview coding. In: Proceedings of the IEEE/CVF Conference on Computer Vision and Pattern Recognition, pp. 1182–1191 (2021)
53. Sun, C., Shrivastava, A., Singh, S., Gupta, A.: Revisiting unreasonable effectiveness of data in deep learning era. In: Proceedings of the IEEE International Conference on Computer Vision, pp. 843–852 (2017)
54. Szegedy, C., et al.: Going deeper with convolutions. In: Proceedings of the IEEE Conference on Computer Vision and Pattern Recognition, pp. 1–9 (2015)
55. Tarvainen, A., Valpola, H.: Mean teachers are better role models: weight-averaged consistency targets improve semi-supervised deep learning results (2017)
56. Tompson, J., Goroshin, R., Jain, A., LeCun, Y., Bregler, C.: Efficient object localization using convolutional networks. In: Proceedings of the IEEE Conference on Computer Vision and Pattern Recognition, pp. 648–656 (2015)
57. Touvron, H., Cord, M., Douze, M., Massa, F., Sablayrolles, A., Jégou, H.: Training data-efficient image transformers & distillation through attention. In: International Conference on Machine Learning, pp. 10347–10357. PMLR (2021)
58. Vaswani, A., et al.: Attention is all you need. In: Advances in Neural Information Processing Systems, vol. 30 (2017)
59. Wah, C., Branson, S., Welinder, P., Perona, P., Belongie, S.: The Caltech-UCSD Birds-200-2011 dataset. Technical report, CNS-TR-2011-001, California Institute of Technology (2011)
60. Wang, H., Zhu, Y., Green, B., Adam, H., Yuille, A., Chen, L.-C.: Axial-DeepLab: stand-alone axial-attention for panoptic segmentation. In: Vedaldi, A., Bischof, H., Brox, T., Frahm, J.-M. (eds.) ECCV 2020. LNCS, vol. 12349, pp. 108–126. Springer, Cham (2020). https://doi.org/10.1007/978-3-030-58548-8_7
61. Wang, T., Isola, P.: Understanding contrastive representation learning through alignment and uniformity on the hypersphere. In: International Conference on Machine Learning, pp. 9929–9939. PMLR (2020)
62. Weissenborn, D., Täckström, O., Uszkoreit, J.: Scaling autoregressive video models. In: International Conference on Learning Representations (2020)
63. Wu, Z., Xiong, Y., Yu, S.X., Lin, D.: Unsupervised feature learning via non-parametric instance discrimination. In: Proceedings of the IEEE Conference on Computer Vision and Pattern Recognition, pp. 3733–3742 (2018)

64. Xiao, K., Engstrom, L., Ilyas, A., Madry, A.: Noise or signal: the role of image backgrounds in object recognition. In: International Conference on Learning Representations (2021)
65. Xie, Z., et al.: SimMIM: a simple framework for masked image modeling. In: Proceedings of the IEEE/CVF Conference on Computer Vision and Pattern Recognition (CVPR), pp. 9653–9663 (2022)
66. Asano, Y.M., Rupprecht, C., Vedaldi, A.: Self-labelling via simultaneous clustering and representation learning. In: International Conference on Learning Representations (2020)
67. Zhang, L., Qi, G.J., Wang, L., Luo, J.: AET vs. AED: unsupervised representation learning by auto-encoding transformations rather than data. In: Proceedings of the IEEE/CVF Conference on Computer Vision and Pattern Recognition, pp. 2547–2555 (2019)
68. Zhang, X., Wei, Y., Feng, J., Yang, Y., Huang, T.S.: Adversarial complementary learning for weakly supervised object localization. In: Proceedings of the IEEE Conference on Computer Vision and Pattern Recognition, June 2018
69. Zhou, B., Zhao, H., Puig, X., Fidler, S., Barriuso, A., Torralba, A.: Scene parsing through ADE20K dataset. In: Proceedings of the IEEE Conference on Computer Vision and Pattern Recognition, pp. 633–641 (2017)
70. Zhou, J., et al.: iBOT: image BERT pre-training with online tokenizer. In: International Conference on Learning Representations (2022)
71. Zhuang, C., Zhai, A.L., Yamins, D.: Local aggregation for unsupervised learning of visual embeddings. In: Proceedings of the IEEE/CVF International Conference on Computer Vision, pp. 6002–6012 (2019)

Pointly-Supervised Panoptic Segmentation

Junsong Fan[1,3], Zhaoxiang Zhang[1,2,3(✉)], and Tieniu Tan[1,2]

[1] Center for Research on Intelligent Perception and Computing,
Institute of Automation, Chinese Academy of Sciences, Beijing, China
{fanjunsong2016,zhaoxiang.zhang}@ia.ac.cn, tnt@nlpr.ia.ac.cn
[2] University of Chinese Academy of Sciences, Beijing, China
[3] Centre for Artificial Intelligence and Robotics, HKISI_CAS, HongKong, China

Abstract. In this paper, we propose a new approach to applying point-level annotations for weakly-supervised panoptic segmentation. Instead of the dense pixel-level labels used by fully supervised methods, point-level labels only provide a single point for each target as supervision, significantly reducing the annotation burden. We formulate the problem in an end-to-end framework by simultaneously generating panoptic pseudo-masks from point-level labels and learning from them. To tackle the core challenge, i.e., panoptic pseudo-mask generation, we propose a principled approach to parsing pixels by minimizing pixel-to-point traversing costs, which model semantic similarity, low-level texture cues, and high-level manifold knowledge to discriminate panoptic targets. We conduct experiments on the Pascal VOC and the MS COCO datasets to demonstrate the approach's effectiveness and show state-of-the-art performance in the weakly-supervised panoptic segmentation problem. Codes are available at https://github.com/BraveGroup/PSPS.git.

Keywords: Weakly-supervised learning · Panoptic segmentation

1 Introduction

Panoptic segmentation [23] aims at fully parsing all the pixels into nonoverlapping masks for both thing instances and stuff classes. It combines the semantic segmentation and the instance segmentation tasks simultaneously. Classical deep learning approaches require precise dense pixel-level labels to solve this problem. However, acquiring exact pixel- and instance-level annotations on large-scale datasets is very time-consuming, hindering the popularization and generalization of the approaches in new practical applications.

To alleviate the annotation burden for segmentation models, researchers recently proposed weakly-supervised learning (WSL) [4,51,52], which focuses on leveraging coarse labels to train dense pixel-level segmentation tasks. Typically, the weak supervision includes image-level [14–16], point-level [2,38], scribble-level [31,47], and bounding box-level labels [9], etc. These approaches tackle either semantic segmentation [36], instance segmentation [1,21], or panoptic

© The Author(s), under exclusive license to Springer Nature Switzerland AG 2022
S. Avidan et al. (Eds.): ECCV 2022, LNCS 13690, pp. 319–336, 2022.
https://doi.org/10.1007/978-3-031-20056-4_19

segmentation [27,41] tasks. Among them, the weakly-supervised panoptic segmentation (WSPS) problem is the most challenging since it requires both semantic and instance discrimination with only weak supervision. As a result, the WSPS got less attention in previous works, and its performance is far from satisfactory. The seminal work by Li et al. [27] manages to address the WSPS problem using bounding-box level labels. Later, JTSM [41] proposes to apply only image-level labels for the WSPS problem. Recently, PanopticFCN [29] tackles this problem by connecting multiple point labels into polygons. The performances of these approaches differ significantly with the different weak annotations.

In this paper, we propose a new WSPS paradigm to use only a single point for each target as the supervision, as illustrated in Fig. 1. Recall that the core of weakly-supervised segmentation is to release the annotation burden while still obtaining decent performance. In other words, balance the cost of annotation and the model performance. We are motivated to use the point-level labels because, on the one hand, the annotation time of point-level labels is only marginally above the image-level labels [2], saving much cost compared with the box-level or polygon labels. On the other hand, point labels can provide minimum spatial information to localize and discriminate different panoptic targets for the segmentation models.

A natural idea to estimate panoptic masks from point-level labels is to assign each pixel in the image to one of the points according to some principles. To this end, we propose tackling this problem by minimizing the pixel-to-point traversing cost, measured by the neighboring pixel affinities. There are two basic requirements to correctly assign pixels to point labels: semantic class matching and instance discrimination. The former ensures that the pixels are parsed with the correct class labels, and the latter is responsible for distinguishing different instances in the thing classes. Therefore, we consider three criteria to model the affinities: semantic similarity, low-level image cues, and high-level instance discrimination knowledge. Using these criteria, we model the pixel-to-point traversing costs and solve the assignment problem by finding the shortest path.

We base our approach on the transformer models [11,39,46], which have recently shown impressive results in computer vision tasks [3,8,30,44,56]. Specifically, our approach contains a group of semantic query tokens to parse semantic segmentation results and a group of panoptic query tokens responsible for the panoptic segmentation task [30]. In addition to the regular panoptic segmentation model, our approach contains a label generation model, which produces dense panoptic pseudo-masks depending on the point-level labels and the criteria above. The whole approach is end-to-end. After training, only the panoptic segmentation branch is kept for testing. Thus, it does not incur additional computation or memory overhead for usage. We conduct thorough experiments to analyze the proposed approach and the properties of the point-level labels. Meanwhile, we demonstrate new cutting-edge performance with the WSPS problem on the Pascal VOC [13] and the MS COCO [32] datasets.

In summary, the main contributions of this work are:

- We propose a new paradigm for the WSPS problem, which utilizes a single point for each target as supervision for training.

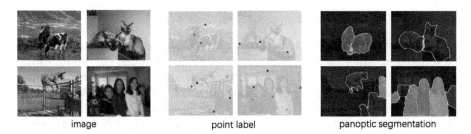

image   point label   panoptic segmentation

Fig. 1. Illustration of the proposed pointly-supervised panoptic segmentation. From left to right: input images, point labels as supervision, and panoptic segmentation predictions. The point labels provide a single point annotation for each target, including both thing instances and stuff classes, which are used at training time only. Please see Sect. 3 for details. Best viewed in color.

- A novel approach to estimating dense panoptic pseudo-masks by minimizing the pixel-to-point traversing distance is proposed.
- We implement the approach in an end-to-end framework with transformers, conduct analytical experiments to study the model and the point-level labels, and demonstrate state-of-the-art performance on the Pascal VOC and the MS COCO datasets.

2   Related Works

2.1   Panoptic Segmentation

The panoptic segmentation [23] task simultaneously incorporates semantic segmentation and instance segmentation, where each pixel is uniquely assigned to one of the stuff classes or one of the thing instances. This problem can be tackled by combining the semantic and instance segmentation results in a post-processing manner [23]. Later works such as JSIS [10] adopt a unified network combining a semantic segmentation branch and an instance segmentation branch. After that, many approaches have been proposed for improvement by using feature pyramids [22], automatic architecture searching [49], and unifying the pipeline [28], etc.

Recently, transformer-based approaches have shown impressive results across the NLP [11,39,46] and the CV [3,12,34,56] applications. The seminal work DETR [3] provides a clear and elegant solution for object detection and segmentation. The following work DeformableDETR [56] improves it by using the deformable transformers to reduce the computation burden and accelerate the convergence. K-Net [54] adopts an iterative refinement procedure to enhance the attention masks gradually. MaskFormer [8] proposes to separate the mask prediction and the classification process. Panoptic SegFormer [30] embraces a similar idea and adopts an auxiliary localization target to ease the model training. Our panoptic segmentation approach is based on these works, and we focus on alleviating the annotation burden by exploiting point-level annotations.

2.2   Weakly-Supervised Segmentation

Weakly supervised segmentation [4,52] aims to alleviate the annotation burden for segmentation tasks by using weak labels for training. According to the type of tasks, it concerns semantic segmentation [16,17,24,26,36,48], instance segmentation [1,45], and panoptic segmentation [27,41] problems. According to the kinds of supervision, these approaches use image-level [16,24,26,36,41,48], point-level [2,38], scribble-level [31,47], or box-level [9,43,45] labels for training. Among them, image-level label-based approaches are the most prevalent. These approaches generally rely on the CAM [40,55] to extract spatial information from classification models, which are trained by the image-level labels. Though great progress has been achieved by these approaches on the semantic segmentation task, it is generally hard to distinguish different instances of the same class with only image-level labels, especially on large-scale datasets with many overlapping instances. Li et al. [27] proposes to address this problem by additionally using bounding-box annotations, which however takes much more time to annotate. PanopticFCN [29] alternatively proposes to use coarse polygons to supervise the panoptic segmentation model, which are obtained by connecting multiple point annotations for each target. PSIS [7] proposes to address the instance segmentation problem by using sparsely sampled foreground and background points in each bounding box. Though these approaches achieve better results, their annotation burden is significantly heavier than image-level labels. In this paper, we try to use a new form of weak annotation for panoptic segmentation, i.e., a single point for each target. We demonstrate that this supervision can achieve competitive performance compared with previous approaches while significantly reducing the annotation burden.

2.3   Point-Level Labels in Visual Tasks

Recently point-level annotation has drawn interest in a broad range of computer vision tasks. Beside the works concerning the detection and segmentation tasks [2,7,29,38], some works adopt point-level labels to train crowd counting [33,50] models. SPTS [37] proposes to use points for the text spotting problem. Chen et al. [5] propose addressing weakly-supervised detection problems using point labels. Besides, point labels also play an essential role in interactive segmentation models, where users provide interactive hints through point-level clicks [35,42,53]. To the best of our knowledge, there are still no approaches to training panoptic segmentation models using only a single point per target.

3   Approach

In this section, we elaborate on the details of the proposed approach. Figure 2 illustrates the overall framework, which can be decomposed into two major components, a label generation model and a panoptic segmentation model. These two components share the same backbone and the transformer encoder [56]. The

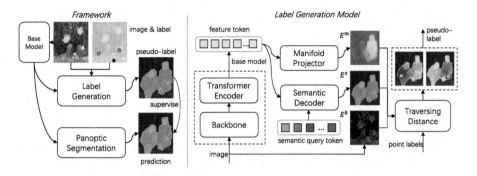

Fig. 2. Illustration of the proposed approach. Left: the overall framework, which contains a label generation model and a panoptic segmentation model. The former produces dense panoptic pseudo-labels from point-level labels, the latter is responsible for the final panoptic segmentation prediction. Right: the detailed pipeline of the label generation model. Please see Sect. 3 for more information. Best viewed in color.

label generation model is the core of the weakly-supervised learning, which is responsible for obtaining dense panoptic pseudo-masks from weak point-level labels. The panoptic segmentation model is the same as those fully-supervised ones and learns from the panoptic pseudo-masks. All these models are trained as a whole in an end-to-end manner. After the training stage, the label generation model can be removed, only leaving a standard panoptic segmentation model for usage. Hence, it does not bring any computation or memory overhead than other fully-supervised methods.

3.1   Dense Semantics from Point Supervision

Semantic parsing is the cornerstone of our approach to producing dense pixel-level pseudo-masks from sparse point-level labels. We decompose the panoptic pseudo-label generation problem into two steps: semantic parsing and instance discrimination. In the semantic parsing step, the semantic probabilities for all the pixels in the image are first obtained. By means of this, the latter problem could be reduced to partition pixels within each class into different instances, reducing the solution space and improving the estimation robustness.

To generate semantic segmentation results, we adopt a set of semantic query tokens, which has a one-to-one correspondence to the semantic classes, as shown in Fig. 2. The semantic decoder is made of transformer decoder layers following the Panoptic SegFormer [30]. It contains a mask branch to decode masks from tokens and a classification branch to decode the class probabilities. The semantic segmentation probabilities are then obtained by multiplying together the mask probabilities and the class probabilities.

Let $P \in \mathbb{R}^{HW \times C}$ denote the semantic segmentation probabilities of the C classes. Given a set of N point-level labels, it can be mapped to a set of N^s labeled semantic pixels, $Y = \{(x_i, c_i)\}_{i=1}^{N^s}$, where x_i and c_i are the coordinate and class index of the ith pixel, respectively. The mapping could be implemented by coloring the surrounding pixels of each point-level label and applying the same geometric augmentations as the input image. The partial cross-entropy loss for semantic segmentation is the average on labeled pixels:

$$\mathcal{L}_{sem} = -\frac{1}{N^s} \sum_{(x_i, c_i) \in Y} \log P_{x_i, c_i}, \tag{1}$$

To supplement the sparse partial cross-entropy loss, inspired by [45], we adopt the image texture-based constraints densely on all the pixels, a.k.a., color-prior loss. Let $P_i, P_j \in \mathbb{R}^C$ denote the class probabilities of the ith and jth pixels, respectively. The color prior loss is defined as:

$$\mathcal{L}_{col} = -\frac{1}{Z} \sum_{i=1}^{HW} \sum_{j \in \mathcal{N}(i)} A_{i,j} \log P_i^T P_j, \tag{2}$$

where $P_i^T P_j$ measures the predicted probability similarity of the pair, higher values indicate that the prediction of the pair tends to be the same class. $A_{i,j}$ is the color-prior affinity following [45], which is obtained by thresholding the pixel similarity computed in the LAB color space with threshold 0.3. $\mathcal{N}(i)$ is the set of neighbor pixel indices of i. $Z = \sum_{i=1}^{HW} \sum_{j \in \mathcal{N}(i)} A_{i,j}$ is the normalization factor. By optimizing Eq. 2, neighboring pixels owning similar colors are encouraged to derive the same semantic prediction. Experiments in Sect. 4.3 demonstrate this strategy can effectively improve the mask quality.

3.2 Traversing Distance and Mask Generation

After obtaining the semantic classes of each pixel, the challenge of generating panoptic masks is mainly reduced to discriminating different instances in the same class. We propose a principled approach to address this problem by assigning each pixel to the nearest point label, where the distance is defined by the proposed traversing distance, as illustrated in Fig. 3.

Denote the cost of traveling from pixel i to point label s by $\mathcal{D}_{i,s}$, the target is to find the nearest point label $\hat{s}$, and mark pixel i as the foreground of the corresponding segmentation target. Formally,

$$\mathcal{D}_{i,s} = \min_{\Gamma_{i,s}} \int E(x) \Gamma_{i,s}(x) dx, \tag{3}$$

where, $\Gamma_{i,s}$ is a path from pixel i to point label s. E describes the non-negative traversing cost along the path. In discrete digital images, the path is defined as a sequence of continual pixels under the 8-neighborhood connection.

In this framework, the question reduces to defining proper transferring cost E to help distinguish different instances. We consider three criteria to accomplish this task: semantic similarity, low-level boundary cues, and high-level instance-aware manifold knowledge. For clarity, we slightly abuse the notation to denote

Fig. 3. (a) Illustration of the traversing distance method. Each pixel finds the point label with the minimum traversing cost and is assigned to the corresponding target. (b) Example of a two-instance case, showing the traversing cost of each pixel to each point label. Highlighted regions have low costs. Please see Sect. 3.2 for details. Best viewed in color.

the cost between neighboring pixels i and j by $E_{i,j}$, which is composed of the three items:

$$E_{i,j} = E_{i,j}^s + \lambda_b E_{i,j}^b + \lambda_m E_{i,j}^m, \tag{4}$$

where, λ_b and λ_m are the weights controlling the relative importance.

$E_{i,j}^s$ reflects the semantic similarity, whose value is low if the neighboring pixels belong to the same class. It is defined by the aforementioned semantic probabilities:

$$E_{i,j}^s = \sum_{c=1}^{C} |P_{i,c} - P_{j,c}|, \tag{5}$$

where, $P_{i,c}$ is the probability of the ith pixel belonging to class c. By means of this, crossing pixels of different classes are costly. Thus, paths residing in the object interiors are encouraged. This strategy could help pixels be assigned to the point within a coherent class region rather than geometrically closer points but with different classes.

$E_{i,j}^b$ defines the boundary cost considering the low-level image textures. Given the boundary map $B \in \mathbb{R}^{HW}$ obtained by edge filters, $E_{i,j}^b$ is counted by the non-negative value at the target location. In this way, the paths are encouraged not to cross the boundaries:

$$E_{i,j}^b = |B_j|, \tag{6}$$

In this paper, we adopt the efficient Sobel filter to compute the boundary map. The boundary cost implicitly assumes that regions of coherent colors are more likely to belong to the same class and instance, which has been proved experimentally by previous works [24,25,45] in addressing the segmentation tasks.

$E_{i,j}^m$ provides high-level knowledge to distinguish instances, which is learned by the deep model online. We add a manifold projector to the transformer encoder to produce dense features to compute the instance similarity, as illustrated in Fig. 2. The manifold projector firstly reshapes the feature tokens back to 2D spatial features. Features from different pyramid levels are bilinearly sampled to the same size and summed together. Then, the projection is obtained by a 2-layer MLP model, implemented by two 1×1 convolution layers interleaved by a ReLU activation. Given the L2-normalized feature map $F \in \mathbb{R}^{HW \times D}$ produced by the manifold projector, the cost is defined by the non-negative cosine distance:

$$E_{i,j}^m = \max\{1 - F_i^T F_j, 0\}, \tag{7}$$

where, the projected features belonging to the same instance are similar and produce low costs. In this way, paths are encouraged not to cross different instances. To convey instance-aware knowledge, the manifold projection model should be trained by instance-aware constraints. For clarity, we postpone explaining the details in the Sect. 3.3.

After obtaining the criteria, the next step is finding the shortest path between each pair of pixels and point labels in the 8-neighborhood graph. Note that the graph is very sparse because each pixel only connects to its local neighbors. Let N denote the total number of point labels and M denote the number of pixels. Then, the minimum distance $\mathcal{D}_{i,s}$ in Eq. 3 can be efficiently solved by the shortest distance algorithm with time complexity $O(MN \log M)$.

It is noteworthy that the distance measurement in Eq. 3 can only produce connected components. As a result, if an instance is overlapped and separated into several parts by some region belonging to different classes, the farther parts would be assigned with the wrong class. To overcome this limitation, we use the class compatibility between the pixel and the point label to reweight the distance before assigning pixels to point labels.

$$\hat{s} = \operatorname{argmin}_s \left[\left(\hat{\mathcal{D}}_{i,s} - 1 \right) \cdot \left(P_i^T P_s \right) \right], \tag{8}$$

where, P_i is the probability of the ith pixel obtained by the semantic segmentation branch. P_s is the one-hot encoding of the point label's ground truth class. $\hat{\mathcal{D}}$ is the normalized version of $\mathcal{D}$ in range $[0, 1]$. Finally, we judge that pixel i is part of the instance holding point label $\hat{s}$ according to Eq. 8, and the whole image is parsed into non-overlapping regions, obtaining panoptic pseudo-masks.

3.3 Weakly-Supervised Training

In this section, we elaborate on training the whole model with the generated pseudo-masks. Firstly, the panoptic segmentation model, as illustrated in Fig. 2, is trained by the pseudo-masks. As aforementioned, we adopt the Panoptic Seg-Former architecture, which contains a localization decoder to help quickly converge to the target locations, a classification branch to predict class probabilities for each query token, and a mask decoder to decode masks. They are optimized by the localization loss, the focal loss, and the dice loss, respectively. For simplicity, here we denote all these losses to train the panoptic segmentation model as $\mathcal{L}_{pan}$. Please refer to the paper [30] for more details.

In addition to the panoptic segmentation model, the manifold projector used in Eq. 7 also needs to train to provide instance-aware representations. Here we utilize a contrastive learning strategy [6,19] to optimize the manifolds with the pseudo-masks. Let $\mathcal{M}_i \in \mathbb{R}^{HW}$ denote the pseudo-mask of target i that contains point label with coordinate x_i. The global representation of target i is the masked average of the projection $F \in \mathbb{R}^{HW \times D}$:

$$\bar{F}_i = \frac{1}{Z_i} \sum_{j=1}^{HW} \mathcal{M}_{i,j} F_j, \tag{9}$$

where, $Z_i = \sum_{j=1}^{HW} \mathcal{M}_{i,j}$ is for normalization, $F_j \in \mathbb{R}^D$ is the feature at pixel j.
The loss for the projector is the average of all point-to-target contrasts:

$$\mathcal{L}_{cl} = -\frac{1}{N} \sum_{i=1}^{N} \log \frac{\exp\left(F_{x_i}^T \bar{F}_i / \tau\right)}{\sum_{j=1}^{N} \exp\left(F_{x_i}^T \bar{F}_j / \tau\right)}, \tag{10}$$

where, N is the total number of point labels, τ is a scale factor and is set 0.07 following [19]. When the setting is extended to annotate each target with multiple points, the sum in the denominator of the contrasts should iterate over the number of targets. With this optimization target, the feature projections at the labeled points are encouraged to be coherent within the estimated instance region and distinctive from the others. The pseudo-mask estimation and the manifold projector mutually benefit each other and improve the model together.

Taking all the above components together, our final model is end-to-end:

$$\mathcal{L}_{all} = \mathcal{L}_{sem} + \mathcal{L}_{col} + \mathcal{L}_{pan} + \mathcal{L}_{cl}, \tag{11}$$

After training, only the panoptic segmentation model is kept for testing, thus not incurring any computation or memory overhead compared with previous fully-supervised panoptic segmentation models.

4 Experiments

In this section, we discuss the experiments. We first describe the experiment setting and implementation details and then elaborate on the analyses and comparison using the VOC and COCO datasets.

4.1 Datasets

Pascal VOC dataset [13,18] contains 10582 training images and 1449 validation images. It has 20 thing classes and one stuff class. By default, a single point label per target is sampled with the uniform distribution from the masks, which is fixed through all the experiments. To study the influence of point label distribution, we also adopt other sampling strategies in Sect. 4.3 for analyses. We analyze our approach with the panoptic quality (PQ), segmentation quality (SQ), recognition quality (RQ), and intersection over union (IoU) metrics.

MS COCO dataset [32] contains 118k images for training, 5k images for validation, and 20k images for testing. It contains 80 thing classes and 53 stuff classes. The same point sampling strategy and metrics are applied to the COCO.

4.2   Implementation Details

Architecture. We base our approach on the Panoptic SegFormer with a ResNet50 backbone [20]. As mentioned in Sect. 4.3, we adopt an extra group of semantic query tokens to produce the semantic segmentation results. Specifically, the C semantic tokens produce C masks and classification scores, which are multiplied together and projected by a linear layer followed by a Softmax function to produce semantic probabilities. The mask decoder contains 6 transformer decoder layers [30], which has the same architecture as the panoptic segmentation model. The color prior loss in Eq. 2 is constructed by sampling neighboring pixels with kernel size 5 and dilation rate 2, and the loss is amplified by factor 3. The image edge used in Eq. 6 is obtained by the Sobel filter in the LAB color space and its absolute values are normalized into the range $[0, 1]$. The panoptic segmentation model follows the same setting as [30], and the number of query tokens for panoptic segmentation is set to 300.

Optimization. We follow previous practice [30] for training, i.e., AdamW optimizer with learning rate 1.4×10^{-4}, weight decay 1.4×10^{-4}, and batch size 8. The learning rates for the backbone parameters are multiplied by the factor 0.1. To stabilize the training, we adopt a linear warm-up strategy for the losses $\mathcal{L}_{pan}$ and $\mathcal{L}_{cl}$ during the first training epoch, so that reliable pseudo-panoptic masks can be obtained, which depends on the well-learned semantic parsing results. The balancing weights λ_b and λ_m in Eq. 4 are all set 0.1 by default. In experiments, we extend each point label to a square region with a size of 17 pixels to facilitate the training of semantic segmentation, as explained in Eq. 1. The shorter sizes of input images are resized to 600 and 800 on the VOC and COCO, respectively. On the VOC, we train 20 epochs and decay the learning rate with a factor of 0.1 after epoch 15. On the COCO, we follow the $1\times$ schedule to train 12 epochs and decay the learning rate after epoch 8.

4.3   Ablation Studies

In this section, we conduct analytic experiments on the VOC dataset to reveal the properties of the proposed method with point-level supervision.

Instance Discrimination. We first conduct experiments to demonstrate the effectiveness of the proposed traversing distance-based instance discrimination approach. Table 1 shows the ablation results of the distance measurement criteria in Eq. 4. With only the semantic probabilities, the model achieves PQ 46.6% on the VOC val set. The boundary criterion and the manifold criterion improve the baseline result to 48.5% and 49.4%, respectively. We noticed that this improvement is mainly due to the PQth, which is improved from 44.5% to 46.5% and 47.4%, respectively. And the results of stuff classes are relatively similar, demonstrating that the low-level image cues and high-level instance-aware manifold can effectively help to identify different instances. Finally, with all the criteria, our approach achieves the final result of PQ 49.8% and PQth 47.8%.

Table 1. Ablation studies for the proposed traversing distance-based instance discrimination. Results are reported on the VOC val set. E^s, E^b, and E^m denote the criteria of semantic similarity, low-level boundary, and high-level manifold, respectively.

E^s	E^b	E^m	PQ	PQ^{th}	PQ^{st}
✓			46.6	44.5	89.1
✓	✓		48.5	46.5	89.3
✓		✓	49.4	47.4	89.2
✓	✓	✓	**49.8**	**47.8**	**89.5**

Table 2. Influence of the hyper-parameters in computing the traversing cost. Results are reported on the VOC val set. We conduct experiments by fixing one hyper-parameter and alter another.

λ_b	λ_m	PQ	PQ^{th}	PQ^{st}
0.0	0.1	49.4	47.4	89.2
0.1	0.1	**49.8**	**47.8**	**89.5**
0.5	0.1	48.3	46.3	89.1
1.0	0.1	48.4	46.3	89.4
0.1	0.0	48.5	46.5	89.3
0.1	0.1	**49.8**	**47.8**	**89.5**
0.1	0.5	49.3	47.3	89.2
0.1	1.0	48.9	47.0	89.1

Hyper-Parameter Sensitivity. We conduct experiments to study the sensitivity of the hyper-parameters used in Eq. 4. To save the search cost, we fix one parameter and adjust another. Results reported in Table 2 show that the scale of the additional criteria for the instance discrimination, i.e., the boundary and the feature manifold criteria, should be approximately one order of magnitude smaller than the semantic criterion. It is noteworthy that even larger values are not optimal, they still boost the baseline's performance from PQ 46.6% to 48.3% or higher, demonstrating the robustness of the proposed approach.

Point Sampling Strategies. We conduct experiments to study the influence of the position distribution bias of the point labels. In addition to the uniform sampling strategy, we also tried the center-biased and the border-biased sampling strategies. Specifically, we first compute the euclidean distance of each pixel to the centroid of the corresponding ground truth mask. Then, we build the probability density map according to the square of the euclidean distance. Finally, the points are sampled based on the normalized probability for each target to obtain border-biased labels. The center-biased labels are sampled in a similar way by reversing the probabilities. Results in Table 3 show that the center-biased labels achieve the best performance, and the border-biased labels perform worst.

Table 3. Influence of the point sampling strategy. Results are reported on the VOC val set. "Border" and "Center" refer to strategies that prefer target border regions and center regions, respectively.

Method	mIoU	PQ	SQ	RQ
Border	65.6	44.7	78.1	55.7
Uniform	67.5	49.8	78.4	62.0
Center	**67.7**	**50.9**	**79.1**	**62.8**

Table 4. Ablation study of the semantic segmentation submodule. Results are reported on the VOC val set.

Method	mIoU	PQ	SQ	RQ
w/o $\mathcal{L}_{col}$	62.2	41.3	74.3	54.0
w/ $\mathcal{L}_{col}$	67.5	49.8	78.4	62.0

While the SQ values of the three methods are relatively similar, the RQ of the border-biased strategy is much worse than the others, revealing that annotations near borders are harmful to discriminating different targets, while annotations at center regions provide more robust results. This phenomenon has positive meanings because center annotation accords with human intuition and is easier in practice.

Semantic Segmentation Module. In this section, we conduct ablation experiments to study the semantic segmentation submodule. Results in Table 4 demonstrate the low-level cues can effectively improve the segmentation performance from mIoU 62.2% to mIoU 67.5%. The improvement of the semantic segmentation quality not only improves the quality of the panoptic masks, i.e., SQ is improved from 74.3% to 78.4%, but also benefits the localization of the targets, i.e., a significant improvement of the RQ from 54.0% to 62.0%. We conjecture the reason is that more accurate semantic probabilities provide more reliable instance discrimination cues for Eq. 4 to distinguish different targets.

4.4 Comparison with Related Works

We compare our approach with the related works in Table 5. Compared to the JTSM [41] that uses image-level labels, our approach achieves significant improvement with the help of point-level labels, which improves the PQ with +10.8% on the VOC, and +24.0% on the COCO. It demonstrates that point-level labels are promising in addressing panoptic segmentation problems. As pointed out by Bearman et al. [2], the point-level labels only cost marginally above image-level labels. For example, on the VOC dataset, image labels cost on average 20.0 s/img, while point labels cost 22.1 s/img, where the difference

Table 5. Comparison with related works on the VOC and the COCO datasets. Results are reported on the COCO val set and the VOC val set. $\mathcal{M}$ mask annotation for fully-supervised learning, $\mathcal{B}$ bounding-box level supervision, $\mathcal{I}$ image-level supervision, $\mathcal{P}$ the proposed point-level supervision, $\mathcal{P}_{10}$ point-level supervision with 10 points per target.

Method	Backbone	Supervision	COCO			VOC		
			PQ	PQ^{th}	PQ^{st}	PQ	PQ^{th}	PQ^{st}
Panoptic FPN [22]	R50	$\mathcal{M}$	41.5	48.3	31.2	65.7	64.5	90.8
K-Net [54]	R50	$\mathcal{M}$	47.1	51.7	40.3	-	-	-
MaskFormer [8]	R50	$\mathcal{M}$	46.5	51.0	39.8	-	-	-
Panoptic SegFormer [30]	R50	$\mathcal{M}$	48.0	52.3	41.5	67.9	66.6	92.7
Li et.al. [27]	R101	$\mathcal{B}+\mathcal{I}$	-	-	-	59.0	-	-
JTSM [41]	R18-WS	$\mathcal{I}$	5.3	8.4	0.7	39.0	37.1	77.7
PanopticFCN [29]	R50	$\mathcal{P}_{10}$	31.2	35.7	24.3	48.0	46.2	85.2
Ours	R50	$\mathcal{P}$	29.3	29.3	29.4	49.8	47.8	89.5
Ours	R50	$\mathcal{P}_{10}$	33.1	33.6	32.2	56.6	54.8	91.4

is marginal compared with the full labels' 239.7 s/img. Compared to the PanopticFCN [29] using ten points to connect polygons for training, our approach achieves competitive performance when using only a single point as annotation, which is +1.8% on the VOC and −1.9% on the COCO in respect to the PQ. Note that these comparable results are achieved by using only 1/10 of the annotations of the PanopticFCN. When increasing the annotation to ten points per target, our approach achieves +8.6% and +1.9% improvements on the VOC and the COCO datasets compared with the PanopticFCN, demonstrating the scalability of our approach in utilizing more points per target.

To help qualitatively study the results, we visualize the predictions on the val set of VOC and COCO. Results in Fig. 4 show that our approach performs generally well in handling scenes with complex multiple instances and classes. We also show the results for hard examples, which contain extremely many instances with small scales. In these cases, some instances are missing in the prediction. Improving the performance with these small and thin objects when only accessing point-level labels may be a potential direction in future studies.

(a) Results on the VOC val set.

(b) Results on the COCO val set.

(c) Hard cases with multiple small and thin objects.

Fig. 4. Visualization of the panoptic segmentation results. The models are trained with a *single point* per target as annotation. Each group from left to right are the input, prediction, and ground truth, respectively. Best viewed in color.

5   Conclusions

In this paper, we propose a new paradigm for weakly-supervised panoptic segmentation using a single point label for each target. To tackle this problem, we propose a principled approach that generates panoptic pseudo-masks by solving the minimization problem of pixel-to-point traversing costs, which integrates semantic similarity, low-level texture cues, and high-level knowledge to distinguish different targets. We demonstrate its effectiveness and study the influence of point labels through analytical experiments. Besides, we achieve new state-of-the-art performance with point-level labels on the VOC and COCO datasets.

Acknowledgments. This work was supported in part by the Major Project for New Generation of AI (No. 2018AAA0100400), the National Natural Science Foundation of China (No. 61836014, No. U21B2042, No. 62072457, No. 62006231).

References

1. Ahn, J., Cho, S., Kwak, S.: Weakly supervised learning of instance segmentation with inter-pixel relations. In: Proceedings of the IEEE/CVF Conference on Computer Vision and Pattern Recognition, pp. 2209–2218 (2019)
2. Bearman, A., Russakovsky, O., Ferrari, V., Fei-Fei, L.: What's the point: semantic segmentation with point supervision. In: Leibe, B., Matas, J., Sebe, N., Welling, M. (eds.) ECCV 2016. LNCS, vol. 9911, pp. 549–565. Springer, Cham (2016). https://doi.org/10.1007/978-3-319-46478-7_34
3. Carion, N., Massa, F., Synnaeve, G., Usunier, N., Kirillov, A., Zagoruyko, S.: End-to-end object detection with transformers. In: Vedaldi, A., Bischof, H., Brox, T., Frahm, J.-M. (eds.) ECCV 2020. LNCS, vol. 12346, pp. 213–229. Springer, Cham (2020). https://doi.org/10.1007/978-3-030-58452-8_13
4. Chan, L., Hosseini, M.S., Plataniotis, K.N.: A comprehensive analysis of weakly-supervised semantic segmentation in different image domains. Int. J. Comput. Vis. **129**(2), 361–384 (2021). https://doi.org/10.1007/s11263-020-01373-4
5. Chen, L., Yang, T., Zhang, X., Zhang, W., Sun, J.: Points as queries: weakly semi-supervised object detection by points. In: Proceedings of the IEEE/CVF Conference on Computer Vision and Pattern Recognition, pp. 8823–8832 (2021)
6. Chen, T., Kornblith, S., Norouzi, M., Hinton, G.: A simple framework for contrastive learning of visual representations. In: International Conference on Machine Learning, pp. 1597–1607. PMLR (2020)
7. Cheng, B., Parkhi, O., Kirillov, A.: Pointly-supervised instance segmentation. In: Proceedings of the IEEE/CVF Conference on Computer Vision and Pattern Recognition, pp. 2617–2626 (2022)
8. Cheng, B., Schwing, A., Kirillov, A.: Per-pixel classification is not all you need for semantic segmentation. Adv. Neural. Inf. Process. Syst. **34**, 17864–17875 (2021)
9. Dai, J., He, K., Sun, J.: BoxSup: exploiting bounding boxes to supervise convolutional networks for semantic segmentation. In: Proceedings of the IEEE International Conference on Computer Vision, pp. 1635–1643 (2015)
10. De Geus, D., Meletis, P., Dubbelman, G.: Panoptic segmentation with a joint semantic and instance segmentation network. arXiv preprint arXiv:1809.02110 (2018)
11. Devlin, J., Chang, M.W., Lee, K., Toutanova, K.: Bert: pre-training of deep bidirectional transformers for language understanding. arXiv preprint arXiv:1810.04805 (2018)
12. Dosovitskiy, A., et al.: An image is worth 16 × 16 words: transformers for image recognition at scale. ICLR (2021)
13. Everingham, M., Van Gool, L., Williams, C.K., Winn, J., Zisserman, A.: The pascal visual object classes (VOC) challenge. Int. J. Comput. Vis. **88**(2), 303–338 (2010). https://doi.org/10.1007/s11263-009-0275-4
14. Fan, J., Zhang, Z., Song, C., Tan, T.: Learning integral objects with intra-class discriminator for weakly-supervised semantic segmentation. In: Proceedings of the IEEE/CVF Conference on Computer Vision and Pattern Recognition, pp. 4283–4292 (2020)

15. Fan, J., Zhang, Z., Tan, T.: Employing multi-estimations for weakly-supervised semantic segmentation. In: Vedaldi, A., Bischof, H., Brox, T., Frahm, J.-M. (eds.) ECCV 2020. LNCS, vol. 12362, pp. 332–348. Springer, Cham (2020). https://doi.org/10.1007/978-3-030-58520-4_20

16. Fan, J., Zhang, Z., Tan, T., Song, C., Xiao, J.: CIAN: cross-image affinity net for weakly supervised semantic segmentation. In: Proceedings of the AAAI Conference on Artificial Intelligence, vol. 34, pp. 10762–10769 (2020)

17. Fan, R., Hou, Q., Cheng, M.M., Yu, G., Martin, R.R., Hu, S.M.: Associating inter-image salient instances for weakly supervised semantic segmentation. In: Proceedings of the European Conference on Computer Vision, pp. 367–383 (2018)

18. Hariharan, B., Arbeláez, P., Bourdev, L., Maji, S., Malik, J.: Semantic contours from inverse detectors. In: Proceedings of the International Conference on Computer Vision, pp. 991–998. IEEE (2011)

19. He, K., Fan, H., Wu, Y., Xie, S., Girshick, R.: Momentum contrast for unsupervised visual representation learning. In: Proceedings of the IEEE/CVF Conference on Computer Vision and Pattern Recognition, pp. 9729–9738 (2020)

20. He, K., Zhang, X., Ren, S., Sun, J.: Deep residual learning for image recognition. In: Proceedings of the IEEE Conference on Computer Vision and Pattern Recognition, pp. 770–778 (2016)

21. Khoreva, A., Benenson, R., Hosang, J., Hein, M., Schiele, B.: Simple does it: weakly supervised instance and semantic segmentation. In: Proceedings of the IEEE Conference on Computer Vision and Pattern Recognition, pp. 876–885 (2017)

22. Kirillov, A., Girshick, R., He, K., Dollár, P.: Panoptic feature pyramid networks. In: Proceedings of the IEEE/CVF Conference on Computer Vision and Pattern Recognition, pp. 6399–6408 (2019)

23. Kirillov, A., He, K., Girshick, R., Rother, C., Dollár, P.: Panoptic segmentation. In: Proceedings of the IEEE/CVF Conference on Computer Vision and Pattern Recognition, pp. 9404–9413 (2019)

24. Kolesnikov, A., Lampert, C.H.: Seed, expand and constrain: three principles for weakly-supervised image segmentation. In: Leibe, B., Matas, J., Sebe, N., Welling, M. (eds.) ECCV 2016. LNCS, vol. 9908, pp. 695–711. Springer, Cham (2016). https://doi.org/10.1007/978-3-319-46493-0_42

25. Krähenbühl, P., Koltun, V.: Efficient inference in fully connected CRFs with gaussian edge potentials. In: Advances in Neural Information Processing Systems, pp. 109–117 (2011)

26. Lee, J., Kim, E., Lee, S., Lee, J., Yoon, S.: FickleNet: weakly and semi-supervised semantic image segmentation using stochastic inference. In: Proceedings of the IEEE Conference on Computer Vision and Pattern Recognition, pp. 5267–5276 (2019)

27. Li, Q., Arnab, A., Torr, P.H.: Weakly-and semi-supervised panoptic segmentation. In: Proceedings of the European Conference on Computer Vision, pp. 102–118 (2018)

28. Li, Q., Qi, X., Torr, P.H.: Unifying training and inference for panoptic segmentation. In: Proceedings of the IEEE/CVF Conference on Computer Vision and Pattern Recognition, pp. 13320–13328 (2020)

29. Li, Y., et al.: Fully convolutional networks for panoptic segmentation with point-based supervision. arXiv preprint arXiv:2108.07682 (2021)

30. Li, Z., et al.: Panoptic SegFormer: delving deeper into panoptic segmentation with transformers. In: Proceedings of the IEEE/CVF Conference on Computer Vision and Pattern Recognition, pp. 1280–1289 (2022)

31. Lin, D., Dai, J., Jia, J., He, K., Sun, J.: ScribbleSup: scribble-supervised convolutional networks for semantic segmentation. In: Proceedings of the IEEE Conference on Computer Vision and Pattern Recognition, pp. 3159–3167 (2016)

32. Lin, T.-Y., Maire, M., Belongie, S., Hays, J., Perona, P., Ramanan, D., Dollár, P., Zitnick, C.L.: Microsoft COCO: common objects in context. In: Fleet, D., Pajdla, T., Schiele, B., Tuytelaars, T. (eds.) ECCV 2014. LNCS, vol. 8693, pp. 740–755. Springer, Cham (2014). https://doi.org/10.1007/978-3-319-10602-1_48

33. Liu, Y., Xu, D., Ren, S., Wu, H., Cai, H., He, S.: Fine-grained domain adaptive crowd counting via point-derived segmentation. arXiv preprint arXiv:2108.02980 (2021)

34. Liu, Z., et al.: Swin transformer: hierarchical vision transformer using shifted windows. In: Proceedings of the IEEE/CVF International Conference on Computer Vision, pp. 10012–10022 (2021)

35. Maninis, K.K., Caelles, S., Pont-Tuset, J., Van Gool, L.: Deep extreme cut: from extreme points to object segmentation. In: Proceedings of the IEEE Conference on Computer Vision and Pattern Recognition, pp. 616–625 (2018)

36. Pathak, D., Krähenbühl, P., Darrell, T.: Constrained convolutional neural networks for weakly supervised segmentation. In: Proceedings of the IEEE International Conference on Computer Vision, pp. 1796–1804 (2015)

37. Peng, D., et al.: SPTS: single-point text spotting. arXiv preprint arXiv:2112.07917 (2021)

38. Qian, R., Wei, Y., Shi, H., Li, J., Liu, J., Huang, T.: Weakly supervised scene parsing with point-based distance metric learning. In: Proceedings of the AAAI Conference on Artificial Intelligence, vol. 33, pp. 8843–8850 (2019)

39. Radford, A., et al.: Language models are unsupervised multitask learners. OpenAI Blog **1**(8), 9 (2019)

40. Selvaraju, R.R., Cogswell, M., Das, A., Vedantam, R., Parikh, D., Batra, D.: Gradcam: visual explanations from deep networks via gradient-based localization. In: Proceedings of the IEEE International Conference on Computer Vision, pp. 618–626 (2017)

41. Shen, Y., et al.: Toward joint thing-and-stuff mining for weakly supervised panoptic segmentation. In: Proceedings of the IEEE/CVF Conference on Computer Vision and Pattern Recognition, pp. 16694–16705 (2021)

42. Sofiiuk, K., Petrov, I.A., Konushin, A.: Reviving iterative training with mask guidance for interactive segmentation. arXiv preprint arXiv:2102.06583 (2021)

43. Song, C., Huang, Y., Ouyang, W., Wang, L.: Box-driven class-wise region masking and filling rate guided loss for weakly supervised semantic segmentation. In: Proceedings of the IEEE Conference on Computer Vision and Pattern Recognition, pp. 3136–3145 (2019)

44. Strudel, R., Garcia, R., Laptev, I., Schmid, C.: Segmenter: transformer for semantic segmentation. In: Proceedings of the IEEE/CVF International Conference on Computer Vision, pp. 7262–7272 (2021)

45. Tian, Z., Shen, C., Wang, X., Chen, H.: BoxInst: high-performance instance segmentation with box annotations. In: Proceedings of the IEEE/CVF Conference on Computer Vision and Pattern Recognition, pp. 5443–5452 (2021)

46. Vaswani, A., et al.: Attention is all you need. Adv. Neural Inf. Proc. Syst. **30**, 1–11 (2017)

47. Vernaza, P., Chandraker, M.: Learning random-walk label propagation for weakly-supervised semantic segmentation. In: Proceedings of the IEEE Conference on Computer Vision and Pattern Recognition, vol. 3, p. 3 (2017)

48. Wei, Y., Xiao, H., Shi, H., Jie, Z., Feng, J., Huang, T.S.: Revisiting dilated convolution: a simple approach for weakly- and semi-supervised semantic segmentation. In: Proceedings of the IEEE Conference on Computer Vision and Pattern Recognition, pp. 7268–7277 (2018)
49. Wu, Y., Zhang, G., Xu, H., Liang, X., Lin, L.: Auto-panoptic: cooperative multi-component architecture search for panoptic segmentation. Adv. Neural. Inf. Process. Syst. **33**, 20508–20519 (2020)
50. Zand, M., Damirchi, H., Farley, A., Molahasani, M., Greenspan, M., Etemad, A.: Multiscale crowd counting and localization by multitask point supervision. In: ICASSP 2022–2022 IEEE International Conference on Acoustics, Speech and Signal Processing (ICASSP), pp. 1820–1824. IEEE (2022)
51. Zhang, D., Han, J., Cheng, G., Yang, M.H.: Weakly supervised object localization and detection: a survey. IEEE Trans. Pattern Anal. Mach. Intell. **44**, 5866–5885 (2021)
52. Zhang, M., Zhou, Y., Zhao, J., Man, Y., Liu, B., Yao, R.: A survey of semi-and weakly supervised semantic segmentation of images. Artif. Intell. Rev. **53**(6), 4259–4288 (2020)
53. Zhang, S., Liew, J.H., Wei, Y., Wei, S., Zhao, Y.: Interactive object segmentation with inside-outside guidance. In: Proceedings of the IEEE/CVF Conference on Computer Vision and Pattern Recognition, pp. 12234–12244 (2020)
54. Zhang, W., Pang, J., Chen, K., Loy, C.C.: K-net: towards unified image segmentation. Adv. Neural Inf. Proc. Syst. **34**, 10326–10338 (2021)
55. Zhou, B., Khosla, A., Lapedriza, A., Oliva, A., Torralba, A.: Learning deep features for discriminative localization. In: Proceedings of the IEEE Conference on Computer Vision and Pattern Recognition, pp. 2921–2929 (2016)
56. Zhu, X., Su, W., Lu, L., Li, B., Wang, X., Dai, J.: Deformable DETR: deformable transformers for end-to-end object detection. In: Proceedings of the International Conference on Learning Representations (2021)

MVP: Multimodality-Guided Visual Pre-training

Longhui Wei[1,2(✉)], Lingxi Xie[2], Wengang Zhou[1,3], Houqiang Li[1,3],
and Qi Tian[2]

[1] CAS Key Laboratory of Technology in GIPAS, EEIS Department,
University of Science and Technology of China, Hefei, China
`weilh2568@gmail.com`, {`zhwg,lihq`}`@ustc.edu.cn`
[2] Huawei Cloud, Shenzhen, China
`tian.qi1@huawei.com`
[3] Institute of Artificial Intelligence, Hefei Comprehensive National Science Center,
Hefei, China

Abstract. Recently, masked image modeling (MIM) has become a promising direction for visual pre-training. In the context of vision transformers, MIM learns effective visual representation by aligning the token-level features with a pre-defined space (*e.g.*, BEIT used a d-VAE trained on a large image corpus as the tokenizer). In this paper, we go one step further by introducing guidance from other modalities and validating that such additional knowledge leads to impressive gains for visual pre-training. The proposed approach is named Multimodality-guided Visual Pre-training (MVP), in which we replace the tokenizer with the vision branch of CLIP, a vision-language model pre-trained on 400 million image-text pairs. We demonstrate the effectiveness of MVP by performing standard experiments, *i.e.*, pre-training the ViT models on ImageNet and fine-tuning them on a series of downstream visual recognition tasks. In particular, pre-training ViT-Base/16 for 300 epochs, MVP reports a 52.4% mIoU on ADE20K, surpassing BEIT (the baseline and previous state-of-the-art) with an impressive margin of 6.8%.

Keywords: Visual pre-training · Masked image modeling · Multimodality

1 Introduction

Deep neural networks have been a fundamental tool for computer vision, yet they often require a large amount of labeled training data [9] and the model can sometimes bias towards the semantic labels. A promising direction to alleviate the issues is unsupervised visual pre-training, which has been attracting increasing attentions in both academia and industry. After the early efforts based on geometries [23,33] and image generation [24,31], the emerge of contrastive learning [4,6,16,27,28,34] has made a great progress in learning from large-scale

S. Avidan et al. (Eds.): ECCV 2022, LNCS 13690, pp. 337–353, 2022.
https://doi.org/10.1007/978-3-031-20056-4_20

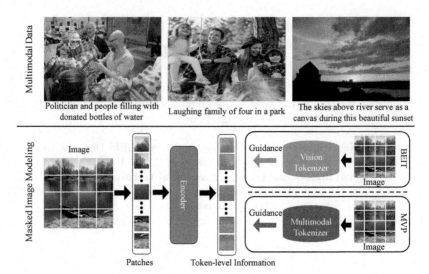

Fig. 1. The motivation of our MVP. The image-text pairs of CC3M [26] are shown at the top. For each case, the caption can depict some important semantic contents. The pipeline of masked image modeling is presented at the bottom, and our MVP simply replaces the vision tokenizer in BEIT with the multimodal tokenizer.

image data. Without semantic annotations, these approaches report competitive downstream transfer performance, sometimes even surpassing the supervised counterpart [17].

Recently, vision transformers [13,29] have been validated effective in a wide range of visual recognition tasks, but these models are also shown to heavily rely on large-scale training data. To alleviate the burden, researchers start investigating unsupervised pre-training. Besides applying contrastive learning [3,7], another interesting methodology is named masked image modeling (MIM)[1]. MIM [2,12,15,32,35,39] removes part of image patches from input and requires the target model to recover the missing contents. Currently, there are two main directions for MIM: one [2,12] is to predict the tokenized features (*e.g.*, by d-VAE [37] or VQ-VAE [30]), and the other [15,35] is to predict pixel-level information. MIM works particularly well for vision transformer models, *e.g.*, when the pre-trained backbone is allowed to be fine-tuned, state-of-the-art image classification accuracy is reported on ImageNet-1K [9]. But, we note that such models are weak when the backbone is frozen – for example, BEIT [2] reports a 37.6% accuracy in the linear probing test on ImageNet-1K; MAE [15] improves it to 67.8%, but it is still significantly lower than that reported by contrastive learning (*e.g.*, DINO reports 78.2%). This makes us conjecture that the pre-trained model learns relatively weak semantic features for visual representation.

The goal of this paper is to enhance the semantics for MIM. For this purpose, we present Multimodality-guided Visual Pre-training (MVP), a single yet

---

[1] It borrows the framework of masked language modeling (MLM) [11,19] from natural language processing.

effective framework that incorporates multimodal information into MIM, in particular, the BEIT framework [2]. As shown in Fig. 1, our motivation is simple that multimodal data can provide more semantic knowledge. Therefore, instead of using a tokenizer that was pre-trained with pure image data, we replace it with a tokenizer that is pre-trained with image-text pairs. We expect the latter to provide weak semantic guidance (since the tokenizer is required to align vision and language) and open-domain representation ability (the texts are not constrained by a set of pre-defined classes). To the best of our knowledge, this is the first work that investigates the use of multimodal pre-training on the MIM framework.

MVP is easily implemented upon BEIT, *i.e.*, directly changing the tokenizer. In particular, we refer to the pre-trained model of CLIP [25] that has seen 400 million image-text pairs, and directly take the vision branch as the tokenizer. It replaces the original tokenizer pre-trained by d-VAE [37]. Other parts of BEIT are nearly unchanged expect for the prediction pretext task. Interestingly, such a simple modification brings large benefits on a series of downstream tasks. MVP reports a 75.4% accuracy on ImageNet-1K linear probing, which significantly surpasses the numbers of BEIT (37.6%) and MAE (67.8%), demonstrating its strong ability of semantic learning. In the fine-tuning test, MVP reports 84.4% and 86.3% accuracy with ViT-Base/16 and ViT-Large/16 backbones, respectively, both of which surpass the BEIT baseline by more than 1%. Most notably, when the pre-trained backbone is transferred for semantic segmentation on ADE20K [38], MVP with a ViT-Base/16 backbone achieves a 52.4% mIOU, which outperforms all existing MIM-based methods by a remarkable margin of 3.6%.

The main contributions of this paper can be summarized as follows:

- We analyze the recent masked image modeling (MIM) based pre-training methods lack of semantics knowledge, and then firstly point out they can be enhanced with the guidance of other modalities.
- We design a simple yet effective algorithm to improve the transfer performance of MIM-based visual pre-training. By resorting to a tokenizer pre-trained with multimodal data (image-text pairs), MVP learns richer semantic knowledge for each image.
- We evaluate the effectiveness of MVP with extensive experiments, and the results clearly demonstrate the advantages of MVP over the recently proposed visual pre-training methods.

2   Related Work

In the deep learning era, a fundamental methodology for visual recognition is to train deep neural networks. In the scenarios with insufficient labeled training data, a popular pipeline is to pre-train the model with labeled/unlabeled data from other sources (*e.g.*, ImageNet [9]) and transfer the model to specific domains. This paper focuses on unsupervised (self-supervised) pre-training. In this section, we review two sub-topics in this field, namely, visual pre-training and multimodal pre-training.

2.1   Visual Pre-training

Currently, as self-supervised learning methods with contrastive loss [6,16,27,28] heavily boost the transfer performance of visual models, self-supervised learning has become the mainstream in the visual pre-training field. For example, He *et al.* [16] proposed a momentum contrast framework to reduce the limitation of requirement on batch size, and significantly pushed forward the transfer performance of pre-training models. Concurrently, SimCLR [4] has been proposed to verify the effect of different data augmentation strategies in contrastive learning based methods. Moreover, target to avoid the confusion of sampled negative noise, BYOL [14] was designed to achieve competitive results by simply pushing the positive pairs together. Recently, vision transformer based architectures [13,29] have been validated in a wide range of visual tasks compared with traditional convolutional networks. To improve the transfer performance of vision transformers, some self-supervised works [3,7] were further proposed for effectively pre-training the vision transformer backbones.

As masked language modeling (MLM) based methods [11,19] achieve great success in the natural language processing field, more and more researchers expect to design similar pretext tasks to enhance the visual pre-training models. Motivated by this, masked image modeling (MIM) based approaches have been designed recently and achieved competitive results. For example, by simply designing a pretext task with the visual token prediction of each masked image patch, BEIT [2] heavily enhanced the transfer performance of visual models. Moreover, with the pixel-level information reconstruction of each masked patch, MAE [15] further improved the final results. Concurrently, some similar MIM-based schemes [5,32,35] have been proposed and pushed forward the development of visual pre-training. In this work, we also utilize the MIM-based framework but design a special multimodality-driven pretext task to guide the visual models learning more multimodal semantic knowledge.

2.2   Multimodal Pre-training

Information is commonly reserved as different modalities in real scenarios. Because of its increasing importance, multimodal pre-training has been attracting more and more researchers [8,18,20,21,25]. The existing multimodal pre-training works can be mainly summarized with two mainstream directions according to the network architecture, *i.e.*, one-stream multimodal network architecture based methods and two-stream multimodal network architecture based methods. For most works with one-stream multimodal architecture [8,20,21], they usually encoded the language and image into discrete tokens, and then fused the information of these tokens in the early stage of network. Though these works can perform well on fusing different modalities, their inference efficiencies are relatively poor. To address this challenge, researchers tend to utilize two-stream network architecture [18,25] for processing the interaction of different modalities. For example, CLIP [25], a recent state-of-the-art multimodal pre-training approach, extracted each modality information with one alone branch, and then simply aligned the extracted feature from each branch into a common multimodal representation space. Benefiting from it pre-trained on 400 million image-text pairs, CLIP heavily pushed forward the transfer performance of multimodal models on a wide range of downstream tasks. In this work, we have no expects to design a new multimodal pre-training framework, but utilize a pre-trained multimodal model to guide the semantic knowledge learning of visual pre-training models.

3   Our Approach

3.1   Problem Setting

Given a large-scale image dataset $\mathcal{D} = \{\mathbf{I}_n\}_{n=1}^{N}$, the goal of visual pre-training is to guide a computational model to learn transferable knowledge on $\mathcal{D}$. After pre-training, the visual backbone with pre-trained parameters will be transferred into different visual downstream tasks for improving the corresponding performances. Currently, many self-supervised visual pre-training schemes are proposed to enhance the transfer performance of models by designing different pretext tasks. Given a pretext task as $\mathcal{L}(\cdot)$ and visual model as $f^{\text{vis}}(\mathbf{I}_n; \boldsymbol{\theta})$, the goal of self-supervised visual pre-training can be written as:

$$\min_{\boldsymbol{\theta}} \mathbb{E}_{\mathbf{I}_n \in \mathcal{D}}[\mathcal{L}(\mathbf{I}_n, f^{\text{vis}}(\cdot; \boldsymbol{\theta}))], \tag{1}$$

where $\mathbb{E}_{\mathbf{I}_n \in \mathcal{D}}[\cdot]$ denotes the expectation on the entire training dataset, $\mathcal{D}$.

3.2   Masked Image Modeling with Tokenizer

As presented in Eq. (1), the core of self-supervised visual pre-training is to design a proper pretext task. As vision transformers [3,13] achieve competitive results on visual recognition tasks, researchers [2,12] resort to BERT-style schemes in natural language processing and design masked image modeling (MIM) based pretext tasks to guide the visual pre-training. Given an image $\mathbf{I} \in \mathcal{R}^{H \times W \times 3}$, it can be divided into several image patches $\{\mathbf{p}_1, \mathbf{p}_2, \ldots, \mathbf{p}_M\}$, where M represents the number of patches, and these patches are further encoded as isolated tokens $\{\mathbf{t}_1, \mathbf{t}_2, \ldots, \mathbf{t}_M\}$ in the vision transformer backbone. MIM-based methods usually mask percentages of tokens as $\{\mathbf{t}_1, \ldots, \hat{\mathbf{t}}_m, \ldots, \mathbf{t}_M\}$, where $\hat{\mathbf{t}}_m$ represents that the m-th token is replaced by a MASK token. Then, MIM-based methods [2,12,32] utilize the pretext by predicting the information (provided by the Tokenizer) of these masked tokens for pre-training visual models.

Take BEIT (a current state-of-the-art MIM-based method) as an example, the optimization goal of MIM with Tokenizer can be formulated as:

$$\mathcal{L}_{\text{BEIT}} \doteq -\sum_{m \in \mathcal{M}} \log(\mathbf{z}_m^{\text{GT}} | \mathbf{z}_m^{\text{vis}}), \tag{2}$$

where the loss is computed between the extracted features,

$$\{\mathbf{z}_1^{\text{vis}}, \ldots, \mathbf{z}_m^{\text{vis}}, \ldots, \mathbf{z}_M^{\text{vis}}\} = f^{\text{head}}(f^{\text{vis}}(\{\mathbf{t}_{\text{CLS}}, \mathbf{t}_1, .., \hat{\mathbf{t}}_m .., \mathbf{t}_M\})), \tag{3}$$

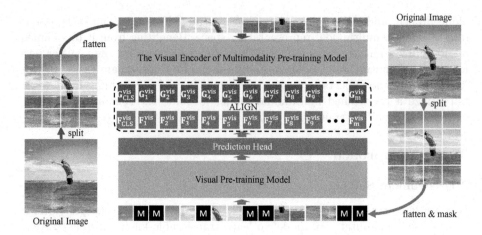

Fig. 2. Framework of the proposed MVP, where each M (MASK) denotes a masked token, and $\mathbf{F}_m^{vis}/\mathbf{G}_m^{vis}$ (or $\mathbf{F}_{CLS}^{vis}/\mathbf{G}_{CLS}^{vis}$) denotes the extracted features of each normal (or CLS) token. MVP is designed with the token-level multimodal information prediction pretext task to guide the pre-training of visual model.

and ground-truth guidance,

$$\{\mathbf{z}_1^{GT}, \ldots, \mathbf{z}_m^{GT}, \ldots, \mathbf{z}_M^{GT}\} = \text{Tokenizer}(\{\mathbf{p}_1, \ldots, \mathbf{p}_m, \ldots, \mathbf{p}_M\}). \qquad (4)$$

In the above equations, $\mathcal{M}$ denotes the set of masked tokens, Tokenizer($\cdot$) denotes the utilized vision tokenizer (*e.g.*, d-VAE in BEIT) to extract visual features from the given patches, $f^{head}(\cdot; \boldsymbol{\theta})$ represents the prediction head, and $\mathbf{t}_{CLS}$ denotes the CLS token in the vision transformer, respectively. In this work, we also utilize a similar framework with BEIT but modify the prediction target with the guidance of multimodal knowledge.

3.3   Multimodality-Guided Visual Pre-training

As described in Sect. 1, the semantic discrimination of representation learned by previous MIM-based methods is relatively weak, for that they lack explicit semantics learning guidance. Target to address this problem, we require the tokenizer in MIM-based methods [2,12] to be aware of semantic information. To leverage weak supervision but not bias towards a specific semantic space, we decide to use a tokenizer pre-trained by multimodal data. Specially, we resort to a pre-trained multimodal model to extract semantic knowledge of each token, and then pre-train visual models with a multimodal knowledge prediction task. The proposed scheme is named Multimodality-guided Visual Pre-training (MVP), and the overview of MVP is shown in Fig. 2. In the following, we will introduce the details of each module in MVP.

Multimodal Semantics Extraction. The goal of this module is to extract discriminative semantic knowledge but not bias towards a specific semantic space for the visual pre-training purpose. As shown in Fig. 1, the language can better describe the semantics inside each image compared with the single annotated label. Motivated by this, our MVP utilizes a recent state-of-the-art multimodal pre-training model (CLIP, which has been pre-trained on 400 million image-text pairs) to extract multimodal semantic knowledge. Given the large-scale image-text pairs as $\{(\mathbf{T}_n, \mathbf{J}_n)\}_{n=1}^{N'}$, where $\mathbf{T}_n$ describes the semantic content of each image $\mathbf{J}_n$ (to be distinguished from $\mathbf{I}_n$), the optimization goal of CLIP can be simply formulated as:

$$\text{Dist}(\mathbf{J}_n, \mathbf{T}_n) < \forall_{n' \neq n} \text{Dis}(\mathbf{J}_n, \mathbf{T}_{n'}), \tag{5}$$

in which

$$\text{Dis}(\mathbf{J}_n, \mathbf{T}_{n'}) = \langle g^{\text{vis}}(\mathbf{J}_n), g^{\text{lang}}(\mathbf{T}_{n'}) \rangle, \tag{6}$$

where $\langle \cdot, \cdot \rangle$ denotes the cosine distance measurement. $g^{\text{vis}}(\cdot)$ and $g^{\text{lang}}(\cdot)$ represent the vision and language branch of the multimodal model (i.e., CLIP), respectively. Benefiting from Eq. (5), whether the visual feature extracted by the vision branch or the text feature extracted by the language branch is finally projected into a common multimodal space, and the semantics of this space is discriminative undoubtedly for it pre-training on the huge image-text pairs.

To integrate with the MIM framework, our MVP chooses the transformer architecture as vision branch of CLIP to extract multimodal semantics. Thus, the corresponding extracted multimodal knowledge of each token can be represented as:

$$\{\mathbf{G}_{\text{CLS}}^{\text{vis}}, \mathbf{G}_1^{\text{vis}}, \ldots, \mathbf{G}_m^{\text{vis}}, \ldots, \mathbf{G}_M^{\text{vis}}\} = g^{\text{vis}}(\{\mathbf{t}_{\text{CLS}}, \mathbf{t}_1, \ldots, \mathbf{t}_m, \ldots, \mathbf{t}_M\}), \tag{7}$$

where $\mathbf{G}_m^{\text{vis}}$ denotes the feature of visual token $\mathbf{t}_m$, and $\mathbf{G}_{\text{CLS}}^{\text{vis}}$ represents the global feature extracted on the CLS token.

Multimodal Information Prediction. After obtaining the multimodal feature of each token, MVP further utilizes the designed multimodal information prediction pretext task to guide the pre-training of visual models. Same with BEIT, MVP firstly uses the Blockwise Masking scheme [2] to mask percentages of tokens, and then inputs these masked tokens and remained unmasked tokens into the visual model to extract visual features. Furthermore, one extra prediction head $P^{\text{head}}(\cdot)$ as BEIT is added to project these token-level visual features into the multimodal space. Therefore, the predicted multimodal information of each visual token can be formulated as:

$$\{\mathbf{F}_{\text{CLS}}^{\text{vis}}, \mathbf{F}_1^{\text{vis}}, \ldots, \mathbf{F}_m^{\text{vis}}, \ldots, \mathbf{F}_M^{\text{vis}}\} = f^{\text{head}}(f^{\text{vis}}(\{\mathbf{t}_{\text{CLS}}, \mathbf{t}_1 \ldots, \hat{\mathbf{t}}_m, \ldots, \mathbf{t}_M\})), \tag{8}$$

where $\mathbf{F}_m^{\text{vis}}$ denotes the predicted multimodal feature of visual token $\hat{\mathbf{t}}_m$ according to the visual models, and $\mathbf{F}_{\text{CLS}}^{\text{vis}}$ represents the predicted global multimodal feature of the CLS token.

After obtaining the predicted multimodal feature of each token according to Eq. (8) and the corresponding ground truth generated by Eq. (7), MVP can guide the pre-training of visual models by achieving the token-level alignment of these features:

$$\mathcal{L}_{\text{MVP}} \doteq -\frac{\langle \mathbf{F}_{\text{CLS}}^{\text{vis}}, \mathbf{G}_{\text{CLS}}^{\text{vis}} \rangle + \sum_{m=1}^{M} \langle \mathbf{F}_{m}^{\text{vis}}, \mathbf{G}_{m}^{\text{vis}} \rangle}{M+1}, \qquad (9)$$

Driven by the alignment of Eq. (9), MVP can guide the candidate visual model well to learn the common semantic knowledge of different modalities both in the global level (the alignment on the CLS token) and patch level (the alignment on each visual token). Thus, compared with recent self-supervised visual pre-training approaches, the pre-trained knowledge of visual models driven by MVP will contain more discriminative but relatively unbiased information. More evaluation and analysis of MVP are introduced in Sect. 4.

Implementation Details. Following most MIM-based approaches [2,12,15], we mainly utilize a series of ViT backbones [13] to evaluate the effectiveness of MVP. To achieve the token-level alignment as Eq. (9), we directly utilize the vision branch with ViT-Base/16 backbone of CLIP, to extract multimodal knowledge. Notably, whether pre-training the visual model with ViT-Base/16 or ViT-Large/16 backbone, the backbone of vision branch in CLIP is always selected with ViT-Base/16. During pre-training, the parameters of vision branch in CLIP are frozen, and only of the parameters in candidate pre-trained visual model are tuned. For all variants of ViT in this paper, the image resolution of the input is set as 224×224, and Blockwise Masking scheme is employed to mask 75 visual tokens as BEIT [2]. Additionally, AdamW optimizer and a cosine decay learning rate scheduler are utilized. The initial learning rate and weight decay are set as $1.5e-3$ and $5e-2$, respectively. Same with most previous works [3,32], MVP is pre-trained on ImageNet-1K lasting for 300 epochs. In the following of this paper, we denote ViT-Base/16 as ViT-B/16, and ViT-Large/16 as ViT-L/16 for short, respectively.

3.4   Relationship to Prior Work

Some concurrent works [10,36] seem similar to our MVP, which also utilize language to guide the pre-training of visual models. However, there are still differences in motivations and implementations with ours. Virtex [10] utilized a heavy-weight textual prediction head (vision transformer architecture) to process the visual feature extracted by the convolutional network, and then predict the corresponding caption of each image. Though Virtex has achieved competitive transfer performances on different visual downstream tasks, there still exists a problem that the pre-training capability of visual models heavily relies on the textual head. However, the image caption prediction task is very challenging for that each image can be described by different texts. Therefore, Virtex is hard to be pre-trained on super large-scale image-text datasets. Differently, our MVP simply designs the multimodal semantics prediction task on visual models with an additional light-weight prediction head (only one fully-connected layer), which guides the pre-training of visual models to learn the common semantic knowledge of different modalities (provided by CLIP).

Additionally, MaskFeat [32] is the most similar work with ours currently. It also designs a feature prediction task based on the masked image modeling framework. However, MaskFeat only utilizes the visual feature (*e.g.*, HOG feature) to supervise the pre-training of visual models, which is relatively weak from the view of semantics discrimination. Differently, the motivation of our MVP is resorting to the semantics guidance of different modalities. To achieve this, MVP utilizes a pre-trained multimodal model to replace the tokenizer in BEIT, and designs a corresponding feature prediction pretext task. Extensive experiments show our MVP enjoys lots of benefits on a wide range of downstream tasks compared with MaskFeat.

4   Experimental Results

4.1   Datasets and Downstream Evaluation Setup

Same with most previous works [2,12,15], MVP is mainly evaluated on image classification and semantic segmentation tasks. The details of our utilized datasets and experimental settings are introduced in the next.

Datasets. In this paper, MVP is mainly evaluated on the image classification task of ImageNet-1K, which contains about 130 million labeled images. Additionally, ADE20K [38] is a relatively challenging semantic segmentation dataset, and it contains 25K images of 150 categories. In this paper, we also conduct evaluations on the semantic segmentation task of ADE20K.

Image Classification Setup. While end-to-end fine-tuning the visual models pre-trained by MVP, we follow the most of hyper-parameter settings in the work [2]. AdamW optimizer is utilized, and the weight decay is set as $5e-2$. The initial learning rate is set with $4e-3$ for ViT-B/16, and $1e-3$ for ViT-L/16, respectively. Additionally, a cosine decay learning rate scheduler is applied. We fine-tune the ViT-B/16 last for 100 epochs with 20 warm-up epochs, and 50 epochs with 5 warm-up epochs for ViT-L/16.

Semantic Segmentation Setup. While fine-tuning the pre-trained visual models on semantic segmentation task of ADE20K, we also follow the most of hyper-parameter settings in BEIT [2], in which the resolution of input image is set as 512×512, AdamW optimizer is applied and the initial learning rate is set as $3e-4$ for ViT-B/16, and $2e-5$ for ViT-L/16, respectively. The batch size is set as 16, and the models are fine-tuned last for 160K steps.

4.2   Comparisons on Image Classification

In this section, we firstly conduct comparisons with recent state-of-the-art visual pre-training approaches on ImageNet-1K with end-to-end fine-tuning mode. As shown in Table 1, our MVP achieves consistently competitive results while

Table 1. Comparison to the state-of-the-arts on ImageNet-1K. All entries are firstly pre-trained on ImageNet-1K, and then further fine-tuned with end-to-end mode. The image resolution of the input for all entries is set as 224 × 224.

Method	Model	Pre-training epochs	Top-1 (%)
DINO [3]	ViT-B/16	300	82.8
BEIT [2]	ViT-B/16	800	83.2
MAE [15]	ViT-B/16	1600	83.6
MaskFeat [32]	ViT-B/16	1600	84.0
MVP (ours)	**ViT-B/16**	**300**	**84.4**
BEIT [2]	ViT-L/16	800	85.2
MAE [15]	ViT-L/16	1600	85.9
MVP (ours)	**ViT-L/16**	**300**	**86.3**

pre-training different visual models. For example, MVP achieves 84.4% Top-1 accuracy of ViT-B/16 on ImageNet-1K, which outperforms the baseline (BEIT) with 1.2%. As for the ViT/L-16 backbone, MVP also surpasses BEIT with 1.1% on Top-1 accuracy. Additionally, compared with MaskFeat, which also utilizes a feature prediction scheme similar to MVP, our work still shows better transfer performances while fine-tuning on ImageNet-1K, *e.g*, 0.4% improvement on ViT/B-16 and 0.6% improvement on ViT/L-16, respectively.

MVP is also evaluated on the linear probing test of ImageNet-1K, and it achieves 75.4% Top-1 accuracy, which significantly outperforms the current MIM-based methods (*e.g.*, BEIT reports a 37.6% accuracy and MAE achieves a 67.8% accuracy). The above consistent improvements clearly demonstrate the superiority of our multimodality-guided visual pre-training scheme. More evaluations and analysis can be seen in Sect. 4.4. We admit that there is still a weak performance gap in the linear probing task of MVP compared with previous self-supervised learning approaches (*e.g.*, DINO reports a 78.2% accuracy), which could own to the MIM framework and will be left for future study.

4.3   Comparisons on Semantic Segmentation

Different from the image classification where the single object is present in each image, semantic segmentation is a more challenging task and each image contains multiple instances. Given that the text can fully describe the presented instances and their relationships inside each image, our MVP driven by multimodal information should achieve much better transfer performance on semantic segmentation datasets.

To evaluate this, we conduct extensive comparisons with recent state-of-the-arts on ADE20K. As shown in Table 2, our MVP shows significant advantages on this task. For example, as for the recent MIM-based methods with different visual feature or pixel information reconstruction pretext tasks, they achieve the nearly same transfer performance, *e.g.*, 45.6% mIoU of BEIT and 48.1% mIoU

Table 2. Comparison to the state-of-the-arts on ADE20K. All models are pre-trained on ImageNet-1K and fine-tuned on ADE20K. The image resolution of the input for all entries is set as 512×512.

Method	Model	Pre-training epochs	mIoU (%)
BEIT [2]	ViT-B/16	800	45.6
MAE [15]	ViT-B/16	1600	48.1
MVP (ours)	**ViT-B/16**	**300**	**52.4**

Table 3. Comparisons of BEIT and our MVP pre-trained on different datasets. All evaluations are conducted on ADE20K, and the image resolution of the input for all models is set as 512×512. BEIT* represents that we reproduce its result on ADE20K with the officially released model.

Method	Model	Pre-training dataset	mIoU (%)
BEIT* [2]	ViT-B/16	ImageNet-21K	46.3
MVP (ours)	**ViT-B/16**	**ImageNet-1K**	**52.4**
BEIT* [2]	ViT-L/16	ImageNet-21K	51.8
MVP (ours)	**ViT-L/16**	**ImageNet-1K**	**54.3**

of MAE on ViT/B-16, respectively. Differently, with the guidance of multimodal semantic knowledge, our MVP heavily pushes forward the transfer results, *e.g.*, 3.6% improvement compared with the previous best reported performance of ViT-B/16.

It is admitted that the above significant improvements of our MVP could own to the super large-scale multimodal dataset while pre-training CLIP. To valid this, we also conduct comparisons with the BEIT model pre-trained on ImageNet-21K, which contains about 21K classes. As shown in Table 3, MVP still shows consistent advantages in transferring pre-trained knowledge. Notably, there are lots of coarse aligned image-text pairs on websites, and they are nearly free to be available. Therefore, the requirement of MVP with a pre-trained multimodal model is not a hard constrain for the visual pre-training community.

4.4 Ablation Study

The Effect of Different Pre-Training Epochs. In this section, we first verify the effect of different pre-training epochs on MVP. As shown in Table 4, with the pre-training epochs increasing, the transfer performance of MVP is gradually improved, *e.g.*, while enlarging the pre-training epochs from 100 to 300, there is a 0.5% improvement on Top-1 accuracy of ImageNet-1K and 0.4% improvement on mIoU metric of ADE20K, respectively.

The Effect of Guidance with Different Knowledge. There is another question is whether the improvement of MVP is taken by the designed feature prediction pretext task or the guidance of multimodal semantic knowledge. One

Table 4. The effect of different pre-training epochs on MVP.

Model	Epochs	ImageNet-1K (Top-1)	ADE20K (mIoU)
ViT-B/16	100	83.9	52.0
ViT-B/16	300	84.4	52.4

Table 5. The effect of utilizing different guidance on MVP.

Guidance	Model	Epochs	ImageNet-1K (Top-1)	ADE20K (mIoU)
DINO	ViT-B/16	300	83.6	47.0
CLIP	ViT-B/16	300	84.4	52.4

indirect evidence is that our MVP achieves much better transfer performances on downstream tasks compared with MaskFeat, a recent state-of-the-art with the pretext task of reconstructing the HOG feature. However, the discrimination of HOG feature is relatively weak. To better evaluate it, we resort to the guidance of a recent self-supervised visual pre-training method, DINO [3]. Similar to MVP, we firstly utilize the ViT-B/16 backbone pre-trained by DINO to extract its visual feature of each token, and then these features are regarded as the prediction target to guide the visual models pre-training. The comparisons are shown in Table 5. Generally, the model with guidance of a pre-trained multimodal model can achieve much better results compared with the model driven by visual pre-training model, especially evaluated on dense vision downstream task, *i.e.*, 5.4% improvement on ADE20K. The above significant improvement further evaluates the superiority of our multimodality-guided visual pre-training scheme.

Analysis of Representation Learning in MVP. Though MVP achieves excellent transfer performances on different downstream tasks, there remains a question of whether it learns dense visual features as the corresponding language describes. To evaluate this, we conduct visualization analysis on the representation of MVP. For that there is no explicit constrain on CLS token of BEIT to extract the global feature, we cannot conduct comparisons on the learned global representation of BEIT and our MVP. To analyze the character of representation in MVP, we utilize DINO, a recent state-of-the-art self-supervised learning method, to compare. For both MVP and DINO, we use CLS token as the query to look for the corresponding response map. We average their attention maps of all heads in ViT-B/16 backbone and then present the results in Fig. 3.

Generally, the previous self-supervised learning method (DINO) only focuses on the specified foreground (*e.g.*, the dog and the polar bear), but ignores other useful information. Differently, MVP can better describe the overall scene and instances inside each image, *e.g.*, "a man and his dog play together in the sofa", "the dog is seeing the sunset", and *etc.* Moreover, as for the complex images in ADE20K, *e.g*, "there are two chairs and one table in this room" and "peoples

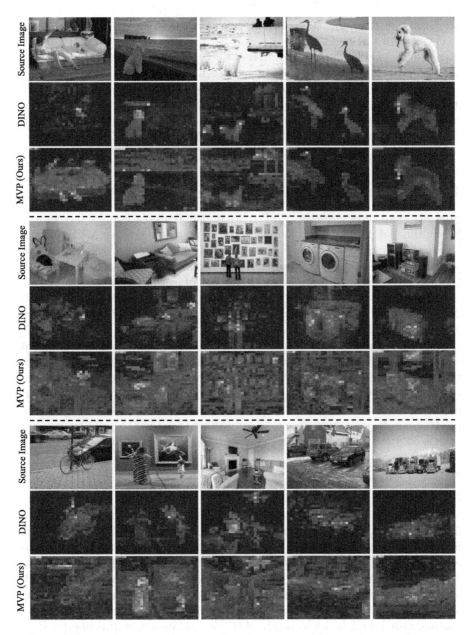

Fig. 3. Visualization of representation learned by different visual pre-training methods. The presented feature map is generated by averaging their attention maps of all heads in ViT-B/16 with CLS token as the query. Images in the first row are from ImageNet-1K, and images of the fourth and seventh row are from ADE20K. Generally, the previous self-supervised visual pre-training method (DINO) only attends on limited regions. Differently, with the guidance of multimodal semantics, MVP can handle the complex image and better describe the overall scene and instances inside each image.

are looking at the multiple murals on the wall", MVP seems to have the ability to extract the whole of its content inside each image from the view of attention map, which could be the reason of that MVP performs much better than previous visual pre-training works on the semantic segmentation task.

As discussed above, it is concluded that MVP can better learn the multi-grained dense semantic knowledge inside each image. This phenomenon further reflects the superiority of visual pre-training driven by multimodal semantic knowledge. In the future, we will evaluate our MVP on more dense vision downstream tasks.

4.5   Discussions and Future Perspectives

First, we shall recognize that MVP relies on the representation ability brought by multimodal pre-training. Therefore, the comparison between MVP and pure vision pre-training algorithms is not completely fair. However, this paper hopes to deliver the message that pure vision pre-training, especially the recent MIM-based approaches [2,15], suffers the limitations of learning semantic information – this seems not to be solved by simply using larger datasets (*e.g.*, ImageNet-21K, used by BEIT). We advocate for using of multimodal information towards a potential breakthrough.

Second, we notice that MVP, like BEIT, is built upon a pre-trained tokenizer and thus incurs extra training costs. On the other hand, provided a multimodal pre-trained model, MVP enjoys a higher training efficiency in the pure vision domain. Going further along this direction may enlighten the community to establish multimodal pre-training as an upstream task of single-modal pre-training. In the future, it will be interesting to extend the idea to more languages [22] and even more data modalities [1], observing their contribution to visual representation learning.

5   Conclusion

In this paper, we present Multimodality-guided Visual Pre-training (MVP), the first work to introduce guidance from other modalities on masked image modeling. By replacing the tokenizer with the vision branch of CLIP on BEIT and simply modifying the prediction task, MVP can better learn the multimodal semantic knowledge inside each image. Extensive experiments on a wide range of visual downstream tasks have clearly shown the effectiveness of MVP on pre-training visual models. Importantly, this work points a new direction for visual pre-training with other modalities. In the future, the effective visual pre-training schemes with more data modalities guidance will be designed.

Acknowledgments. This work was supported by the National Natural Science Foundation of China under Contract 61836011 and U20A20183. It was also supported by the GPU cluster built by MCC Lab of Information Science and Technology Institution, USTC.

References

1. Baevski, A., Hsu, W.N., Xu, Q., Babu, A., Gu, J., Auli, M.: Data2vec: a general framework for self-supervised learning in speech, vision and language. arXiv preprint arXiv:2202.03555 (2022)
2. Bao, H., Dong, L., Wei, F.: BEiT: BERT pre-training of image transformers. arXiv preprint arXiv:2106.08254 (2021)
3. Caron, M., et al.: Emerging properties in self-supervised vision transformers. In: Proceedings of the IEEE/CVF International Conference on Computer Vision, pp. 9650–9660 (2021)
4. Chen, T., Kornblith, S., Norouzi, M., Hinton, G.: A simple framework for contrastive learning of visual representations. arXiv preprint arXiv:2002.05709 (2020)
5. Chen, X., et al.: Context autoencoder for self-supervised representation learning. arXiv preprint arXiv:2202.03026 (2022)
6. Chen, X., Fan, H., Girshick, R., He, K.: Improved baselines with momentum contrastive learning. arXiv preprint arXiv:2003.04297 (2020)
7. Chen, X., Xie, S., He, K.: An empirical study of training self-supervised vision transformers. arXiv preprint arXiv:2104.02057 (2021)
8. Chen, Y.-C., et al.: UNITER: UNiversal Image-TExt Representation Learning. In: Vedaldi, A., Bischof, H., Brox, T., Frahm, J.-M. (eds.) ECCV 2020. LNCS, vol. 12375, pp. 104–120. Springer, Cham (2020). https://doi.org/10.1007/978-3-030-58577-8_7
9. Deng, J., Dong, W., Socher, R., Li, L.J., Li, K., Fei-Fei, L.: ImageNet: a large-scale hierarchical image database. In: 2009 IEEE Conference on Computer Vision and Pattern Recognition, pp. 248–255. IEEE (2009)
10. Desai, K., Johnson, J.: VirTex: learning visual representations from textual annotations. In: Proceedings of the IEEE/CVF Conference on Computer Vision and Pattern Recognition, pp. 11162–11173 (2021)
11. Devlin, J., Chang, M.W., Lee, K., Toutanova, K.: BERT: pre-training of deep bidirectional transformers for language understanding. arXiv preprint arXiv:1810.04805 (2018)
12. Dong, X., et al.: PeCo: perceptual codebook for BERT pre-training of vision transformers. arXiv preprint arXiv:2111.12710 (2021)
13. Dosovitskiy, A., et al.: An image is worth 16 × 16 words: transformers for image recognition at scale. arXiv preprint arXiv:2010.11929 (2020)
14. Grill, J.B., et al.: Bootstrap your own latent: a new approach to self-supervised learning. arXiv preprint arXiv:2006.07733 (2020)
15. He, K., Chen, X., Xie, S., Li, Y., Dollár, P., Girshick, R.: Masked autoencoders are scalable vision learners. arXiv preprint arXiv:2111.06377 (2021)
16. He, K., Fan, H., Wu, Y., Xie, S., Girshick, R.: Momentum contrast for unsupervised visual representation learning. In: Proceedings of the IEEE/CVF Conference on Computer Vision and Pattern Recognition, pp. 9729–9738 (2020)
17. He, K., Girshick, R., Dollár, P.: Rethinking ImageNet pre-training. In: Proceedings of the IEEE/CVF International Conference on Computer Vision, pp. 4918–4927 (2019)
18. Jia, C., et al.: Scaling up visual and vision-language representation learning with noisy text supervision. In: International Conference on Machine Learning, pp. 4904–4916. PMLR (2021)
19. Lan, Z., Chen, M., Goodman, S., Gimpel, K., Sharma, P., Soricut, R.: ALBERT: a lite BERT for self-supervised learning of language representations. arXiv preprint arXiv:1909.11942 (2019)

20. Li, L.H., Yatskar, M., Yin, D., Hsieh, C.J., Chang, K.W.: VisualBERT: a simple and performant baseline for vision and language. arXiv preprint arXiv:1908.03557 (2019)

21. Li, X., et al.: OSCAR: object-semantics aligned pre-training for vision-language tasks. In: Vedaldi, A., Bischof, H., Brox, T., Frahm, J.-M. (eds.) ECCV 2020. LNCS, vol. 12375, pp. 121–137. Springer, Cham (2020). https://doi.org/10.1007/978-3-030-58577-8_8

22. Ni, M., et al.: M3P: learning universal representations via multitask multilingual multimodal pre-training. In: Proceedings of the IEEE/CVF Conference on Computer Vision and Pattern Recognition, pp. 3977–3986 (2021)

23. Noroozi, M., Favaro, P.: Unsupervised Learning of visual representations by solving jigsaw puzzles. In: Leibe, B., Matas, J., Sebe, N., Welling, M. (eds.) ECCV 2016. LNCS, vol. 9910, pp. 69–84. Springer, Cham (2016). https://doi.org/10.1007/978-3-319-46466-4_5

24. Pathak, D., Krahenbuhl, P., Donahue, J., Darrell, T., Efros, A.A.: Context encoders: feature learning by inpainting. In: Proceedings of the IEEE Conference on Computer Vision and Pattern Recognition, pp. 2536–2544 (2016)

25. Radford, A., et al.: Learning transferable visual models from natural language supervision (2021)

26. Sharma, P., Ding, N., Goodman, S., Soricut, R.: Conceptual captions: a cleaned, hypernymed, image alt-text dataset for automatic image captioning. In: Proceedings of the 56th Annual Meeting of the Association for Computational Linguistics (Volume 1: Long Papers), pp. 2556–2565 (2018)

27. Tian, Y., Krishnan, D., Isola, P.: Contrastive multiview coding. arXiv preprint arXiv:1906.05849 (2019)

28. Tian, Y., Sun, C., Poole, B., Krishnan, D., Schmid, C., Isola, P.: What makes for good views for contrastive learning. arXiv preprint arXiv:2005.10243 (2020)

29. Touvron, H., Cord, M., Douze, M., Massa, F., Sablayrolles, A., Jégou, H.: Training data-efficient image transformers & distillation through attention. In: International Conference on Machine Learning, pp. 10347–10357. PMLR (2021)

30. Van Den Oord, A., et al.: Neural discrete representation learning. Adv. Neural Inf. Proc. Syst. **30**, 1–10 (2017)

31. Vincent, P., Larochelle, H., Bengio, Y., Manzagol, P.A.: Extracting and composing robust features with denoising autoencoders. In: Proceedings of the 25th International Conference on Machine Learning, pp. 1096–1103 (2008)

32. Wei, C., Fan, H., Xie, S., Wu, C.Y., Yuille, A., Feichtenhofer, C.: Masked feature prediction for self-supervised visual pre-training. arXiv preprint arXiv:2112.09133 (2021)

33. Wei, C., et al.: Iterative reorganization with weak spatial constraints: solving arbitrary jigsaw puzzles for unsupervised representation learning. In: Proceedings of the IEEE Conference on Computer Vision and Pattern Recognition, pp. 1910–1919 (2019)

34. Wei, L., Xie, L., Zhou, W., Li, H., Tian, Q.: Exploring the diversity and invariance in yourself for visual pre-training task. arXiv preprint arXiv:2106.00537 (2021)

35. Xie, Z., et al.: SimMIM: a simple framework for masked image modeling. arXiv preprint arXiv:2111.09886 (2021)

36. Yuan, X., et al.: Multimodal contrastive training for visual representation learning. In: Proceedings of the IEEE/CVF Conference on Computer Vision and Pattern Recognition, pp. 6995–7004 (2021)

37. Zhang, M., Jiang, S., Cui, Z., Garnett, R., Chen, Y.: D-VAE: a variational autoencoder for directed acyclic graphs. Adv. Neural Inf. Process. Syst. **32** (2019)
38. Zhou, B., et al.: Semantic understanding of scenes through the ade20k dataset. Int. J. Comput. Vis. **127**(3), 302–321 (2019)
39. Zhou, J., et al.: iBOT: image BERT pre-training with online tokenizer. arXiv preprint arXiv:2111.07832 (2021)

Locally Varying Distance Transform for Unsupervised Visual Anomaly Detection

Wen-Yan Lin[1]($\boxtimes$), Zhonghang Liu[1], and Siying Liu[2]

[1] Singapore Management University, Singapore, Singapore
daniellin@smu.edu.sg
[2] Institute for Infocomm Research, Singapore, Singapore

Abstract. Unsupervised anomaly detection on image data is notoriously unstable. We believe this is because many classical anomaly detectors implicitly assume data is low dimensional. However, image data is always high dimensional. Images can be projected to a low dimensional embedding but such projections rely on global transformations that truncate minor variations. As anomalies are rare, the final embedding often lacks the key variations needed to distinguish anomalies from normal instances. This paper proposes a new embedding using a set of locally varying data projections, with each projection responsible for persevering the variations that distinguish a local cluster of instances from all other instances. The locally varying embedding ensures the variations that distinguish anomalies are preserved, while simultaneously allowing the probability that an instance belongs to a cluster, to be statistically inferred from the one-dimensional, local projection associated with the cluster. Statistical agglomeration of an instance's cluster membership probabilities, creates a global measure of its affinity to the dataset and causes anomalies to emerge, as instances whose affinity scores are surprisingly low.

Keywords: Anomaly detection · Unsupervised · High dimensions · Bayesian

1 Introduction

As our attention is limited, we are often forced to trust data labels. What if the labels are wrong? The Internet's growth is driving an explosion of data and demands on our attention. This in turn creates a growing need for automated anomaly detectors to aid data curation. Unfortunately, visual (image based)

W.-Y. Lin and Z. Liu—Joint first author.

Supplementary Information The online version contains supplementary material available at https://doi.org/10.1007/978-3-031-20056-4_21.

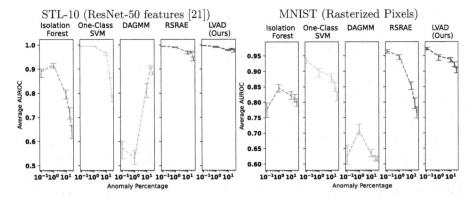

Fig. 1. Performance of anomaly detectors that are: distance based, Isolation Forest [34]; manifold based, OC-SVM [12]; and deep-learned, DAGMM [51], RSRAE [26]. Error bars represent performance fluctuations within the dataset. LVAD is notably robust to changes in feature, dataset and anomaly percentage.

anomaly detectors are notoriously unstable. This paper attempts to explain this instability and suggest a solution[1].

As anomalies are rare, most traditional anomaly detectors assume anomalous regions of a sample space are significantly less densely populated than normal regions, a cue which can be discovered through density (statistical) analysis. Unfortunately, the assumption is inappropriate for image data. Other things being equal, statistical sample spaces grow exponentially with the number of dimensions. As image data is high dimensional, image sample spaces tend to be so huge that all regions are sparsely populated, making traditional, density based anomaly detection ill-conditioned.

The conventional solution is to re-establish density by projecting image data to a low dimensional embedding. This can be achieved through global projections like representation learning [20,33,42] and dimensionality reduction [3,18,36]. This approach has proven to be effective on many vision problems but is inappropriate for anomaly detection. Anomalies are relatively rare. Thus, their associated variations make up a correspondingly minor fraction of the dataset's total variation. As dimensionality reduction algorithms can only preserve the major variations, the final embedding may well lack the minor variations that distinguish anomalies from normal instances.

This paper proposes an alternative approach to embedding. Let us assume local data clusters are outcomes of individual, high dimensional generative processes. Shell theory [30] suggests that instances of each generative process will be uniquely close to their mean. Thus, the likelihood an instance belongs to a specific cluster can be determined from its distance to the cluster mean. This leads to an embedding scheme in which data is embedded as a set of one-dimensional distance-from-mean projections, with each projection representing a space in

---

[1] Unless otherwise stated, the term anomaly detection is used to refer to unsupervised anomaly detection, where training data is unavailable [10].

which members of its associated cluster (generative process) are separable from all other instances.

Integrating shell theory [30] with Bayes Rule, we can infer the probability a given instance is a member of its associated cluster, from the sample density of its distance projection. Agglomerating the probabilities yields a statistical quantification of the affinity of each instance to the dataset. Instances with surprisingly low affinity scores are deemed anomalous. We term this Locally Varying Anomaly Detection or LVAD.

Unlike traditional anomaly detectors which infer class membership using all dimensions simultaneously, LVAD uses a bottom up inference scheme in which local cluster membership is inferred from individual, one dimensional projections. These inferences are then merged into an estimate of class membership. This effectively decouples inference stability from the number of projections, allowing LVAD to employ large numbers of local projections to model data variations as faithfully as possible. Experiments show LVAD is effective on a wide range of datasets, features and anomaly percentages.

1.1 Related Works

Conceptually, LVAD has many similarities with cluster based learning techniques [22,24,32,50]. These are widely employed in machine learning but are seldom used in anomaly detection. This may be because anomalous instances can potentially have low variance clusters which allow for self-validation. This would introduce instabilities that eliminate the gains made through clustering's ability to learn the normality structure. LVAD counteracts this trend through its statistical agglomeration process, creating an anomaly detector whose performance steadily improves with the number of clusters.

LVAD can be considered a classical anomaly detector. However, unlike most classical techniques, LVAD's distance based statistical formulation can accommodate high dimensions. This reduces the reliance on heuristic's like manifold fitting [12,31,40] or nearest neighbor assignment [5,34]; and avoids density based statistics [6,7,39] that are ill-conditioned in high dimensions. This statistically grounded approach may be contributing to LVAD's notably graceful degradation, with high accuracy on easy tasks, where anomaly percentages are low; and a slow drop in accuracy as anomaly percentages increase.

Beyond classical anomaly detectors, there is a range of deep anomaly detectors [8,9,15,26,28,37,43,49,51] which seek to simultaneously refine the image's feature representation and discover anomalies. This approach can lead to surprisingly high accuracy but can also cause unexpected failures, which arise because we lack a mathematical framework to analyze such detectors. LVAD is more conservative and assumes the image's feature representation is given. Nonetheless, LVAD's performance is respectable, with evaluations on a wide range of datasets and anomaly percentages, showing it to be consistently the best or close to the best algorithm.

While the focus is often of the anomaly detection algorithm, the impact of normalization pre-processing can be just as large. This has been noted in many

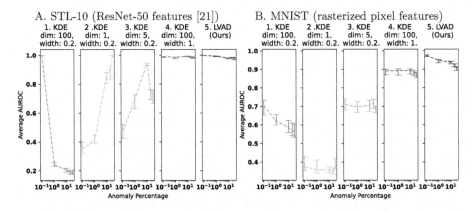

Fig. 2. Understanding anomaly detection with a naive algorithm. Kernel density estimation, KDE [39] is applied after normalizing the data (see Sect. 3.4) and projecting it onto Principal Components [18]. Density is used as the anomaly score. Number of dimensions and KDE bandwidth are given as dim and width respectively.

papers [16,30,46]; however, there is no consensus regarding which normalization scheme is most appropriate [25]. We contribute to this debate with a theoretical argument in favor of layer (instance) normalization [2], which significantly improves the performance of LVAD and many other traditional anomaly detectors.

Finally, LVAD draws inspiration from sources beyond the field of image anomaly detection. Most directly, we are influenced by adjacent fields of semi-supervised anomaly detection [4,23,41,44] and video anomaly detection [38,47]. From a theoretical perspective, our framework draws on works from high dimensional statistics [30,32,42] and dimensionality reduction [3,18,36]. We also take inspiration from many empirical studies, such as evaluation of data normalization [2,13,25,30], cluster based projections [1,11] and general discussions on open-set learning [45].

2 Understanding Anomaly Detection

We begin by studying a naive anomaly detector to better understand the problem of visual anomaly detection.

Let $\mathcal{S}$ be a set of images, a minority of which are anomalous. The ith image in $\mathcal{S}$ is denoted $\mathbf{x}_i \in \mathcal{S}$, with the binary random variable, Y, indicating if a given instance is anomalous:

$$Y = \begin{cases} 1, & \text{if instance is normal;} \\ 0, & \text{if instance is anomalous.} \end{cases} \tag{1}$$

Our goal is to develop an anomaly detection function, $a(\mathbf{x})$, that gives the likelihood an instance is normal. Ideally,

$$a(\mathbf{x}) = p\left(Y = 1 \mid \mathbf{x}\right), \tag{2}$$

where $p(Y = 1 \mid \mathbf{x})$ is the probability $\mathbf{x}$ is normal.

Assuming normal and anomalous instances are different and anomalies are in the minority, an estimated sample density can be a proxy for likelihood and thus anomaly probability; i.e.:

$$a(\mathbf{x}) = kde(\mathbf{x}), \tag{3}$$

where $kde(.)$ denotes the kernel density estimate, KDE [39].

As explained in the introduction, image data inhabits a huge, high dimensional sample space where data-points are sparsely scattered. Thus, we follow conventional wisdom, and re-establish density using PCA [18], to project data onto a low dimension embedding. The kernel density is estimated on the embedding. The performance of this naive anomaly detector is plotted in Fig. 2.

In Fig. 2A.1., density is estimated on the relatively high 100 dimensions. As predicted by conventional wisdom, the high dimensional density estimation is ill conditioned; and detector accuracy declines rapidly as anomaly percentages increase. Figure 2A.2. and Fig. 2A.3. are more interesting. In this case, a very low dimensional embedding is used. The resultant detector exhibits performance reversal, and is accurate on difficult cases, where anomaly percentages are high; but fails on simple cases, where anomaly percentages are low.

We suggest that performance reversal is caused by PCA's dimensionality reduction. Like many other dimensionality reduction algorithms, PCA achieves the low dimensional embedding by truncating away minor data variations. As anomalies form a small fraction of the dataset, the final embedding may no longer have the variations which distinguish anomalous instances, morphing an easy problem into a difficult one. When the anomaly percentage becomes large, dimensionality reduction is more stable and detection accuracy rises accordingly.

Figure 2A.4. and Fig. 2B.4. show another twist. If the number of dimensions is high but the density kernel is large enough to agglomerate almost all points, the naive anomaly detector is stable but somewhat inaccurate. The inaccuracies likely arise from an overly coarse agglomeration. Perhaps the key to anomaly detection lies in statically meaningful, fine-grained agglomeration.

3   Our Approach

Drawing a lesson from the previous section, we avoid explicit detection of anomalies, as this can be unstable when anomaly percentages are low. Rather, we seek to establish an affinity score between instances, with the goal of having anomalies emerge as instances whose affinity scores are surprisingly low.

3.1   The Anomaly Scoring Function

Let us assume each image instance, $\mathbf{x}_i \in \mathcal{S}$ is the outcome of one of m high dimensional generative processes:

$$\{a_j, \boldsymbol{\mu}_j \mid j \in \{1, 2, \ldots, m\}\}, \tag{4}$$

where a_j is the probability that the jth generative process is normal and μ_j is the generative process's mean. Y_j is used to indicate if a given instance is an outcome of the jth generator.

$$Y_j = \begin{cases} 1, & \text{if the instance derives from the } j\text{th generative process;} \\ 0, & \text{otherwise.} \end{cases} \tag{5}$$

Thus, the anomaly detection function of Eq. (2) becomes a sum of the probability of the given instance, $\mathbf{x}$, arising from each generative process, multiplied by the probability that the generative process is normal:

$$a(\mathbf{x}) = p\,(Y = 1\,|\,\mathbf{x}) = \sum_{j=1}^{m} a_j \times p\,(Y_j = 1\,|\,\mathbf{x}). \tag{6}$$

As explained in the introduction, the high dimensional nature of $\mathbf{x}$ means $p\,(Y_j = 1\,|\,\mathbf{x})$ is difficult to estimate directly. Thus, our first task is to find a low dimensional projection where the individual $p\,(Y_j = 1\,|\,\mathbf{x})$ terms can be estimated from data. These can then be agglomerated into an overall anomaly score.

Shell theory [30] argues that coincidental similarity between high dimensional instances is unlikely. Thus, each high dimensional generative process will have an associated distinctive-shell centered on it's mean. Instances of the generative process will almost surely lie on the distinctive-shell; and all other instances will almost surely fall outside the shell. i.e.

$$p\,(Y_j = 1\,|\,\mathbf{x}) = \begin{cases} 1, & \text{if } d_j(\mathbf{x}) = r_j; \\ 0, & \text{otherwise.} \end{cases} \qquad p\,(Y_j = 0\,|\,\mathbf{x}) = \begin{cases} 1, & \text{if } d_j(\mathbf{x}) > r_j; \\ 0, & \text{otherwise.} \end{cases} \tag{7}$$

where μ_j is the mean of the jth generator; r_j is the radius of its distinctive shell; and $d_j(\mathbf{x}) = \|\mu_j - \mathbf{x}\|$ is the distance of an instance $\mathbf{x}$ from μ_j.

Equation (7) suggests $p\,(Y_j = 1\,|\,d_j(\mathbf{x}))$, which we term the distance density functions, may be an excellent function for scoring membership in generator-j. This is because of two reasons. Firstly, the distance density functions is defined on one dimension and thus can potentially be estimated from data. Secondly, the distance density functions is highly sensitive to an instance's membership with generator-j:

$$\begin{aligned} p\,(Y_j = 1\,|\,\mathbf{x}) = p\,(Y_j = 1\,|\,d_j(\mathbf{x})) = 1, & \quad \text{if } \mathbf{x} \in \text{generator-}j; \\ p\,(Y_j = 1\,|\,\mathbf{x}) = p\,(Y_j = 0\,|\,d_j(\mathbf{x})) = 0, & \quad \text{if } \mathbf{x} \notin \text{generator-}j. \end{aligned} \tag{8}$$

Unfortunately, the distance density function is usually too sensitive to be practical, with minor errors in density estimation inducing large errors in the anomaly score. This motivates us to develop the bounded density function, which can identify generator membership but uses gentler penalty function.

Let τ_j denote some upper bound of an instance's distance to μ_j. An instance, $\mathbf{x}$, is considered to satisfy τ_j if:

$$d_j(\mathbf{x}) \leq \tau_j. \tag{9}$$

Given an instance satisfies τ_j, with some abuse of notation, the probability that it is also a member of generator-j, is written as:

$$p\left(Y_j = 1 \mid \tau_j\right) = \frac{\int_0^{\tau_j} p\left(Y_j = 1 \mid d_j(\mathbf{x}) = \theta_j\right) d\theta_j}{\int_0^{\tau_j} p\left(Y_j = 0 \mid d_j(\mathbf{x}) = \theta_j\right) d\theta_j + \int_0^{\tau_j} p\left(Y_j = 1 \mid d_j(\mathbf{x}) = \theta_j\right) d\theta_j}.$$

(10)

We term this the bounded probability density function.

From Eq. (7) and Eq. (10), we know the bounded probability density function is 1 when the bound is at the shell radius, $\tau_j = r_j$; and declines gradually as τ_j increases beyond r_j. Thus, if we set the bound to the actual distance of an instance $\mathbf{x}$ from μ_j, the density function can indicate if $\mathbf{x}$ is a member of generator-j:

$$\begin{aligned} p\left(Y_j = 1 \mid \tau_j = d_j(\mathbf{x})\right) = 1, \quad &\text{if } \mathbf{x} \in \text{generator-}j; \\ p\left(Y_j = 1 \mid \tau_j = d_j(\mathbf{x})\right) < 1, \quad &\text{if } \mathbf{x} \notin \text{generator-}j. \end{aligned}$$

(11)

Unlike the distance probability density of Eq. (8), the bounded probability density's non-member penalty is gentler, making it somewhat forgiving of errors in the estimated pdf.

Replacing the estimation of membership probability in Eq. (6) with the bounded probability density, we have the final anomaly score:

$$a_b(\mathbf{x}) = \sum_{j=1}^{m} a_j \times p\left(Y_j = 1 \mid \tau_j = d_j(\mathbf{x})\right).$$

(12)

Note that the anomaly score in Eq. (12) is slightly different but arguably more practical than the idealized score in Eq. (6).

3.2 Estimating the Bounded Probability Density Function

Bayes rule allows the bounded probability density to be decomposed into cumulative density functions which can be estimated from the data:

$$p\left(Y_j = 1 \mid \tau_j\right) = \frac{p\left(\tau_j \mid Y_j = 1\right) p\left(Y_j = 1\right)}{p\left(\tau_j\right)}.$$

(13)

where $p\left(\tau_j\right)$ is the probability that an instance is closer to mean μ_j than the bound τ_j; and $p\left(\tau_j \mid Y_j = 1\right)$ is the probability that an instance of generator-j is closer to μ_j than τ_j.

Unfortunately, when τ_j is less than r_j, Eq. (13) becomes numerically unstable. This is because, as shown in Eq. (7), distinctive-shells are hollow. Thus, if $\tau_o < r_j$,

$$p\left(\tau_j = \tau_o \mid Y_j = 1\right) \approx 0, \qquad p\left(\tau_j = \tau_o\right) \approx 0,$$

(14)

making both the numerator and denominator of Eq. (13) approximately zero. Such instability is not a problem in the ideal case, as the bound, τ_o will never be used for inference. However, in practice, instances are occasionally much closer to the shell mean, than the shell radius. If so, inference with Eq. (13) involves a numerically unstable division of two small numbers. To address this problem, we modify the bounded probability estimate to:

$$p\left(Y_j = 1 \mid \tau_j\right) = \frac{p\left(\tau_j \mid Y_j = 1\right) + \epsilon}{\left(p\left(\tau_j \mid Y_j = 1\right) + \epsilon\right) + p\left(\tau_j \mid Y_j = 0\right) \times \frac{p(Y_j=0)}{p(Y_j=1)}}. \tag{15}$$

where ϵ is a small constant. As $p\left(\tau_j = \tau_o \mid Y_j = 0\right) \ll p\left(\tau_j = \tau_o \mid Y_j = 1\right)$, Eq. (15) ensures $p\left(Y_j = 1 \mid \tau_j = \tau_o\right) \approx 1$, simultaneously providing numerical stability and intuitively validating instances that are usually close to μ_j, as members of generator-j.

3.3   Algorithmic Implementation

Pre-processing: By default, ResNet-50 features [21] are used as image representation; this is followed by instance (layer) normalization [2], detailed in Sect. 3.4.

Generator Parameters, a_j, μ_j: These generator parameters from Eq. (4) are obtained through K-Means clustering of the given features; where the default value for cluster number is 300. a_j is the fraction of features assigned to cluster-j; μ_j is the mean of cluster-j.

Bounded Density Function, $p\left(Y_j = 1 \mid \tau_j\right)$: This is estimated using Eq. (15). Computation of individual components is as follows:

1. $p\left(Y_j = 1\right)$: The probability an instance is created by the generator underlying cluster Y_j. As data is over-clustered, instances of a generator may be divided among multiple clusters. This can usually be ignored as subsequent agglomeration cancels out the effects of over-clustering. $p\left(Y_j = 1\right)$ is the exception and requires the actual fraction of instances deriving from the underlying generator.

Let n_j be the number of instances in cluster-j; r_j be the estimated shell radius of cluster-j; and s_j the standard deviation of cluster-j's points' distance to its mean μ_j from r_j,

$$r_j = \frac{1}{n_j} \sum_i \|\mathbf{x}_i - \mu_j\|, \; \forall \mathbf{x}_i \in cluster\text{-}j, \tag{16}$$

$$s_j = std\{\|d_j(\mathbf{x}_i) - r_j\| \mid \mathbf{x}_i \in cluster\text{-}j\}.$$

For all instances in the dataset, $\mathcal{S}$, we compute their distances from μ_j. If the distance falls within 3 times the standard deviation s_j, the instance is considered to belong to the generative process underlying Y_j. Thus, $p\left(Y_j = 1\right)$ is the percentage of instances in the dataset satisfying

$$\|d_j(\mathbf{x}) - r_j\| \leq 3s_j, \; \mathbf{x} \in \mathcal{S}. \tag{17}$$

2. $\frac{p(Y_j=0)}{p(Y_j=1)} = \frac{1 - p(Y_j=1)}{p(Y_j=1)}$. For stability, the fraction is capped at 100.

3. $p\left(\tau_j|Y_j=1\right)$ is the cumulative density function of within-cluster-j instance's distances to $\boldsymbol{\mu}_j$. $p\left(\tau_j|Y_j=0\right)$ is the cumulative density function of out-of-cluster-j instance's distances to $\boldsymbol{\mu}_j$.

Inference: The anomaly score of an instance $\mathbf{x}$ is inferred from Eq. (12) using the estimated bounded probability density functions, $p\left(Y_j=1\,|\,\tau_j\right)$, and the estimated fraction of instances in each cluster, a_j.[2]

3.4   Normalization

LVAD relies on shell theory [30], which assumes normalized data. Unfortunately, traditional normalization cannot be used in anomaly detection tasks. This leads us to suggest instance (layer) normalization [2] as an alternative.

Let $\mathbf{x}$ denote a normalized feature and $\widetilde{\mathbf{x}}$ its raw counterpart. $\mathbf{x}$ is related to $\widetilde{\mathbf{x}}$ via:

$$\mathbf{x} = n(\widetilde{\mathbf{x}}, \mathbf{v}) = \frac{\widetilde{\mathbf{x}} - \mathbf{v}}{\|\widetilde{\mathbf{x}} - \mathbf{v}\|}, \tag{18}$$

where $\mathbf{v}$ is the normalization vector, which in tradiotnal normalization, is set to the dataset mean. From the perspective of shell theory, generative processes arise form a natural hierarchy, rooted in a generator-of-everything. In this model, $\mathbf{v}$, should be the mean of a common ancestral generator of all normal and anomalous instances; and the worst possible choice of $\mathbf{v}$ is the mean of the normal generator. Unfortunately, as anomalies make up a small fraction of the dataset, in anomaly detection tasks, the dataset mean is likely the normal generator's mean. This makes traditional normalization terrible for anomaly detection tasks.

We suggest an alternative, inspired by the common signal processing assumption that generative processes are ergodic in their mean. If so, the mean of the hypothesized, distribution-of-everything can be estimated by averaging over all features and all instances. We term this ergodic-set normalization:

$$\mathbf{v}_{set} = \begin{bmatrix} m_e \ m_e \ \dots \ m_e \end{bmatrix}^T, \quad m_e = \frac{1}{n \times d} \sum_{i=1}^{n} \sum_{k=1}^{d} \widetilde{\mathbf{x}}_i[k]. \tag{19}$$

Ergodic-set normalization is similar to layer normalization [2] commonly employed in machine learning. In layer normalization, the averaging over the entire dataset is replaced with an average over the dimensions of each instance, giving each instance an individual normalization vector:

$$\mathbf{v}_i = \begin{bmatrix} m_i \ m_i \ \dots \ m_i \end{bmatrix}^T, \quad m_i = \frac{1}{d} \sum_{k=1}^{d} \widetilde{\mathbf{x}}_i[k]. \tag{20}$$

As LVAD has no layers, we term layer normalization as ergodic-instance normalization or instance normalization for short. As instance and ergodic-set normalization yield similar results, we use instance normalization to be our default, since readers will be more familiar with it. Its impact on anomaly detection tasks is illustrated in Fig. 3.

---

[2] Code is available at: https://www.kind-of-works.com/.

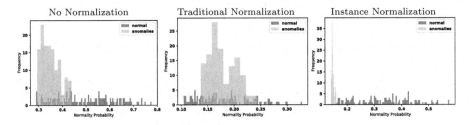

Fig. 3. Impact of normalization on LVAD, evaluated on STL-10 [14]. Our suggested instance normalization is notably effective.

4 Experiment

Experiments are divided into four sections: traditional anomaly detection, Sect. 4.1; an ablation study, Sect. 4.2; multi-normal anomaly detection, Sect. 4.3; and qualitative evaluation, Sect. 4.4.

4.1 Traditional Anomaly Detection Task

Unsupervised visual anomaly detectors are evaluated in Table 1. Both traditional and deep-learning anomaly detectors use ResNet-50 [21] as the image representation. Whenever possible, an instance (layer) normalization [2] is applied to the data. Although the deep-learning algorithms have the potential to discover the best representation from raw images, the performance is much worse on this setting; thus, it is not included in the evaluations.

For each dataset, one class at a time is chosen to provide normal instances; instances from the other classes are treated as anomalies. A test set is created by mixing anomalous and normal instances. The percentage of anomalies in the test set is varied from a low of 0.1% to a high of 30%. The anomaly detector is tasked with quantifying the normality of each instance. Algorithm performance is measured in terms of its Area Under Receiver Operating Characteristic curve (AUROC).

Deviation from Standard Protocol: Readers familiar with anomaly detection may find that some algorithms perform surprisingly well. This is partly because our focus is unsupervised anomaly detection, rather than the semi-supervised anomaly detection studied in most other papers. However, it may also stem from different experimental protocols. The changes we make in this paper are:

– Evaluations often do not normalize data [19,28,51], in part because the correct normalization for anomaly detection is unknown, as explained in Sect. 3.4. We alter the protocol by applying an instance (layer) normalization [2] whenever possible. This greatly improves the performance of some algorithms like OC-SVM [12] and RSRAE [26].

- Many papers designate only one class per dataset as normal [4,28,48]. This sometimes results in skipping of difficult cases, such as digit 5 of MNIST [27]. In our evaluation, the designation of normal is rotated through every class in the dataset.
- Evaluations are often performed at a single anomaly percentage [4,28,51] or across a narrow range of anomaly percentages [26]. As discussed in Sect. 2, many algorithms are sensitive to the percentage of anomalies. To capture this, we allow anomaly percentages to range from 0.1% to 30%.

Discussion: Interestingly, many algorithms in Table 1 exhibit the same performance reversal as the naive anomaly detector from Sect. 2. Thus, many of the best performing algorithms at high anomaly percentages, fail badly on low anomaly percentages. Notable examples are, Shell-Renormalization [30], DAGMM [51] and Deep-Unsup. [28]. While performance reversal is unfortunate, these results show that anomaly detection can be robust to high anomaly percentages.

The remaining anomaly detection algorithms appear to behave naturally, with performance declining as anomaly percentages increase. Notable examples being OC-SVM [12], LOF [5] and RSRAE [26]. Although increasing anomaly percentages is expected to induce performance degradation, the performance decline of many algorithms may be too sharp. After all, the previously discussed algorithms were clearly robust to high anomaly percentages.

LVAD seems to represents a good compromise between this two performance characteristics. While not always the best algorithm, LVAD is notably stable at low and high anomaly percentages, with performance that is usually quite close to the best. LVAD's performance on the MNIST dataset [27], where its AUROC on raw pixels, is easily comparable to deep learned solutions that learn an improved image representation.

4.2   Ablation Study

The experiments thus far have established LVAD as an effective anomaly detector. However, given the traditional brittleness of anomaly detection algorithms,

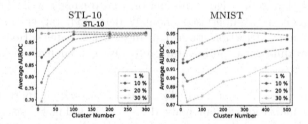

Fig. 4. Given sufficient data, LVAD's performance improves with the number of clusters used, as more clusters allow finer modeling of data variation.

Table 1. Average AUROC of unsupervised visual anomaly detectors. Ave. is the average score on a dataset; a high Ave. indicates accuracy. Diff. is the difference between the highest and lowest scores on a dataset; a small Diff. indicates stability. LVAD is consistently one of the best algorithms.

Dataset	Algorithm	Anomaly Percentage (%)					Ave.	Diff.
		0.1	1	10	20	30		
STL-10 (ResNet-50)	LVAD (Ours)	0.998	0.993	0.979	0.983	0.977	**0.986**	0.021
	Shell-Renorm. [30]	0.803	0.829	0.997	0.999	0.999	0.925	0.196
	OC-SVM [12]	0.996	0.995	0.967	0.877	0.777	0.922	0.219
	IF [34]	0.890	0.917	0.797	0.718	0.638	0.792	0.279
	KDE [39]	0.566	0.516	0.578	0.560	0.546	0.553	0.062
	LOF [5]	0.996	0.878	0.388	0.393	0.428	0.617	0.608
	ECOD [29]	0.965	0.964	0.937	0.894	0.846	0.921	0.119
	DAGMM [51]	0.574	0.477	0.826	0.911	0.883	0.734	0.434
	Deep-Unsup. [28]	0.384	0.956	0.906	0.869	0.866	0.796	0.572
	RSRAE [26]	0.995	0.992	0.972	0.971	0.944	0.975	0.051
Internet STL-10 (ResNet-50)	LVAD (Ours)	0.997	0.997	0.996	0.985	0.981	**0.991**	0.016
	Shell-Renorm. [30]	0.803	0.829	0.997	0.999	0.999	0.925	0.196
	OC-SVM [12]	0.999	0.997	0.985	0.908	0.817	0.941	0.182
	IF [34]	0.847	0.903	0.859	0.790	0.732	0.826	0.171
	KDE [39]	0.267	0.634	0.652	0.652	0.628	0.567	0.385
	LOF [5]	0.989	0.790	0.468	0.503	0.521	0.654	0.521
	ECOD [29]	0.926	0.949	0.913	0.868	0.804	0.892	0.145
	DAGMM [51]	0.543	0.512	0.791	0.836	0.921	0.721	0.409
	Deep-Unsup. [28]	0.429	0.960	0.867	0.855	0.849	0.792	0.531
	RSRAE [26]	0.998	0.997	0.979	0.993	0.973	0.988	0.025
MIT-Places-5 (RestNet-50)	LVAD (Ours)	0.955	0.941	0.922	0.891	0.867	**0.915**	0.088
	Shell-Renorm. [30]	0.676	0.794	0.996	0.995	0.978	0.888	0.302
	OC-SVM [12]	0.966	0.908	0.834	0.727	0.683	0.824	0.283
	IF [34]	0.779	0.659	0.600	0.545	0.522	0.621	0.257
	KDE [39]	0.614	0.457	0.330	0.336	0.355	0.418	0.284
	LOF [5]	0.926	0.640	0.368	0.414	0.420	0.554	0.558
	ECOD [29]	0.945	0.887	0.792	0.711	0.637	0.794	0.308
	DAGMM [51]	0.433	0.423	0.835	0.851	0.767	0.662	0.428
	Deep-Unsup. [28]	0.685	0.890	0.772	0.792	0.795	0.787	0.205
	RSRAE [26]	0.965	0.928	0.893	0.686	0.605	0.815	0.360
CIFAR-10 (ResNet-50)	LVAD (Ours)	0.930	0.940	0.903	0.854	0.816	**0.889**	0.124
	Shell-Renorm. [30]	0.740	0.756	0.895	0.896	0.894	0.836	0.156
	OC-SVM [12]	0.913	0.922	0.869	0.801	0.742	0.849	0.180
	IF [34]	0.894	0.876	0.786	0.721	0.661	0.788	0.233
	KDE [39]	0.649	0.590	0.575	0.561	0.552	0.585	**0.097**
	LOF [5]	0.907	0.613	0.477	0.485	0.497	0.596	0.430
	ECOD [29]	0.852	0.910	0.883	0.837	0.791	0.855	0.119
	DAGMM [51]	0.494	0.503	0.778	0.883	0.850	0.702	0.389
	Deep Unsup. [28]	0.841	0.847	0.732	0.702	0.689	0.762	0.158
	RSRAE [26]	0.901	0.911	0.800	0.814	0.739	0.833	0.172
CatVsDog (ResNet-50)	LVAD (Ours)	0.981	0.978	0.927	0.851	0.780	0.903	0.201
	Shell-Renorm. [30]	0.866	0.846	0.996	0.953	0.617	0.856	0.379
	OC-SVM [12]	0.989	0.982	0.892	0.799	0.737	0.880	0.252
	IF [34]	0.925	0.878	0.798	0.706	0.690	0.799	0.235
	KDE [39]	0.497	0.489	0.481	0.470	0.489	0.485	**0.027**
	LOF [5]	0.895	0.412	0.407	0.439	0.437	0.518	0.488
	ECOD [29]	0.936	0.905	0.852	0.793	0.738	0.845	0.198
	DAGMM [51]	0.784	0.710	0.960	0.914	0.846	0.843	0.250
	Deep-Unsup. [28]	0.545	0.862	0.801	0.773	0.740	0.744	0.317
	RSRAE [26]	0.982	0.981	0.961	0.917	0.835	**0.935**	0.147
MNIST (Rasterized Pixels)	LVAD (Ours)	0.974	0.948	0.938	0.923	0.904	**0.937**	0.070
	OC-SVM [12]	0.937	0.901	0.885	0.856	0.824	0.881	0.113
	IF [34]	0.777	0.846	0.821	0.812	0.797	0.811	**0.069**
	KDE [39]	0.636	0.488	0.489	0.487	0.489	0.518	0.149
	LOF [5]	0.982	0.932	0.540	0.507	0.505	0.693	0.477
	ECOD [29]	0.855	0.779	0.740	0.723	0.709	0.761	0.146
	DRAE [43]	0.739	0.794	0.669	0.672	0.657	0.706	0.137
	DAGMM [51]	0.624	0.708	0.629	0.616	0.613	0.638	0.095
	Deep-Unsup. [28]	0.525	0.891	0.847	0.779	0.835	0.775	0.366
	RSRAE [26]	0.966	0.948	0.851	0.794	0.763	0.864	0.203
	NCAE-UAD [46]	0.909	0.831	0.805	0.759	0.728	0.806	0.181
Fashion-MNIST (Rasterized Pixels)	LVAD (Ours)	0.896	0.909	0.899	0.884	0.868	0.891	0.041
	OC-SVM [12]	0.875	0.898	0.889	0.867	0.843	0.874	0.055
	IF [34]	0.908	0.917	0.915	0.902	0.889	**0.906**	0.028
	KDE [39]	0.437	0.511	0.507	0.511	0.515	0.496	0.078
	LOF [5]	0.756	0.522	0.433	0.429	0.441	0.516	0.327
	ECOD [29]	0.890	0.866	0.850	0.825	0.806	0.847	0.084
	DRAE [43]	0.870	0.815	0.671	0.657	0.680	0.739	0.231
	DAGMM [51]	0.784	0.793	0.788	0.780	0.769	0.783	**0.024**
	Deep-Unsup. [28]	0.765	0.868	0.878	0.884	0.856	0.850	0.119
	RSRAE [26]	0.900	0.854	0.748	0.711	0.689	0.780	0.211
	NCAE-UAD [46]	0.885	0.833	0.799	0.786	0.730	0.807	0.155

Table 2. LVAD works well with different feature representations. Evaluations are performed with 20% anomalies per test set.

Dataset	Feature representation	LVAD: Ave. AUROC
MIT-Places-Small	ResNet-50 [21]	0.891
	ViT [17]	0.870
	SWIN-B [35]	**0.899**
STL-10	ResNet-50 [21]	**0.983**
	ViT [17]	0.922
	SWIN-B [35]	0.963

there remains a concern regarding how sensitive the algorithm is to its two primary parameters: number of clusters and choice of features.

Number of Clusters: It was suggested in the introduction that LVAD decouples inference stability from the number of projections, allowing the use of huge number of projections to faithfully model data variations. If true, LVAD's performance should improve with the number of clusters (and hence projections). Figure 4 shows this to be the case. Thus, the number of clusters used in LVAD should be as large as practical; the primary limitations being quantity of available data and computational time. Our default number of clusters is 300.

Feature Representation: Table 2 illustrates LVAD's performance with different features. The performance varies little with feature choice. As such, we use the classic, ResNet-50 [21] feature, as the default image representation, since most researchers are familiar with its characteristics.

4.3   Quantifying Surprise: Multi-normal Anomaly Detection

Thus far the focus has been on traditional anomaly detection, where only one class is designated to be normal. This is reasonable in data curation; however, it does not correspond to a human's definition of an anomaly. We see many different classes in our daily lives; yet, we still have the capacity to be surprised. We hypothesize that the human definition of anomalies/surprise, corresponds to the very understudied field of multi-normal anomaly detection. If so, LVAD may be a good candidate for quantifying surprise, as its cluster based formulation is innately accommodative of multi-modal normality.

Table 3 provides preliminary results, which show all algorithms suffering a notable decline in performance. This may be inevitable, as multi-normality makes unsupervised anomaly detection less well conditioned. However, it can also be an indication of deeper flaws in current algorithms.

As expected, LVAD's multi-normal anomaly detection is relatively good; and it is noticeably more accurate than its close rival, OCSVM [12]. However, there is still considerable room for improvement.

Table 3. Multi-normal Anomaly Detection evaluated in terms of AUROC. For each dataset, a random set of classes are designated normal.

Dataset {normal class combination}	Algorithm	Anomaly Percentage (%)					Ave.	Diff.
		0.1	1	10	20	30		
STL-10	LVAD (Ours)	0.986	0.943	0.924	0.880	0.814	**0.909**	**0.172**
	IF [34]	0.834	0.730	0.649	0.554	0.489	0.651	0.345
{(0,1,2), (5,6,7), (1,4,8)}	Shell-Renorm. [30]	0.646	0.632	0.722	0.925	0.908	0.767	0.293
	OC-SVM [12]	0.956	0.915	0.797	0.652	0.568	0.778	0.388
	DAGMM [51]	0.469	0.567	0.671	0.452	0.464	0.525	0.219
	RSRAE [26]	0.897	0.879	0.779	0.684	0.647	0.777	0.250
Internet STL-10	LVAD (Ours)	0.987	0.992	0.960	0.938	0.927	**0.961**	**0.065**
	IF [34]	0.775	0.879	0.772	0.721	0.703	0.770	0.176
{(0,1,2), (5,6,7), (1,4,8)}	Shell-Renorm. [30]	0.697	0.726	0.992	0.979	0.948	0.868	0.295
	OC-SVM [12]	0.995	0.988	0.887	0.779	0.746	0.879	0.249
	DAGMM [51]	0.346	0.539	0.632	0.473	0.440	0.486	0.286
	RSRAE [26]	0.988	0.988	0.714	0.934	0.729	0.871	0.274
MIT-Places-5	LVAD (Ours)	0.910	0.888	0.808	0.726	0.687	0.804	0.223
	IF [34]	0.653	0.575	0.516	0.490	0.498	0.546	0.163
{(0, 2), (1,4), (3,4)}	Shell-Renorm. [30]	0.784	0.758	0.845	0.833	0.812	**0.806**	**0.087**
	OC-SVM [12]	0.888	0.895	0.709	0.640	0.616	0.750	0.279
	DAGMM [51]	0.363	0.476	0.589	0.582	0.627	0.527	0.264
	RSRAE [26]	0.871	0.900	0.671	0.641	0.585	0.734	0.315
CIFAR-10	LVAD (Ours)	0.850	0.833	0.770	0.702	0.648	**0.761**	0.202
	IF [34]	0.747	0.720	0.606	0.558	0.507	0.628	0.240
{(0,1,2), (5,6,7), (1,4,8)}	Shell-Renorm. [30]	0.554	0.533	0.463	0.461	0.433	0.489	0.121
	OC-SVM [12]	0.828	0.789	0.718	0.646	0.595	0.715	0.233
	DAGMM [51]	0.288	0.284	0.404	0.432	0.495	0.381	0.211
	RSRAE [26]	0.749	0.769	0.741	0.690	0.655	0.721	**0.114**
MNIST	LVAD (Ours)	0.849	0.804	0.765	0.735	0.710	**0.773**	0.139
	Isolation Forest [34]	0.665	0.640	0.613	0.596	0.585	0.620	0.080
{(0,5,7), (2,7,9), (0,7,8)}	Shell-Renorm. [30]	–	–	–	–	–	–	–
	OC-SVM [12]	0.676	0.701	0.687	0.657	0.633	0.671	0.068
	DAGMM [51]	0.426	0.425	0.445	0.441	0.437	0.435	**0.020**
	RSRAE [26]	0.897	0.809	0.773	0.720	0.657	0.771	0.240
Fashion-MNIST	LVAD (Ours)	0.842	0.831	0.796	0.783	0.757	0.802	0.085
	IF [34]	0.819	0.853	0.843	0.816	0.790	**0.824**	**0.063**
{(0,6,8), (0,7,9), (1,2,4)}	Shell-Renorm. [30]	–	–	–	–	–	–	–
	OC-SVM [12]	0.789	0.773	0.740	0.719	0.699	0.744	0.090
	DAGMM [51]	0.270	0.265	0.342	0.345	0.358	0.316	0.093
	RSRAE [26]	0.855	0.801	0.771	0.767	0.749	0.789	0.106

4.4 Qualitative Results

LVAD performs well on numerical evaluations; however, it is also important to assurance ourselves that the evaluation metrics correspond to human intuition. Figure 5 shows LVAD's ranking of internet crawled cars by their anomalousness. The result appears intuitive and suggest LVAD may be useful in data curation. It also provides a final sanity check of the earlier, numerical evaluations.

Fig. 5. Images crawled from the internet with search keyword "plane". Images are sorted by LVAD's normality score. Normality increases from left to right, top to bottom.

5   Conclusion

This paper proposes LVAD, a statistically grounded scheme for anomaly detection. Experiments show LVAD to be more stable and accurate than most prior techniques, with performance reaching levels where real world deployment may be a possibility. Some applications include, surveillance, self-driving cars and internet data curation.

References

1. Aytekin, C., Ni, X., Cricri, F., Aksu, E.: Clustering and unsupervised anomaly detection with l 2 normalized deep auto-encoder representations. In: 2018 International Joint Conference on Neural Networks (IJCNN), pp. 1–6. IEEE (2018)
2. Ba, J.L., Kiros, J.R., Hinton, G.E.: Layer normalization. arXiv preprint. arXiv:1607.06450 (2016)
3. Becht, E., et al.: Dimensionality reduction for visualizing single-cell data using UMAP. Nat. Biotechnol. **37**(1), 38–44 (2019)
4. Bergman, L., Hoshen, Y.: Classification-based anomaly detection for general data. arXiv preprint. arXiv:2005.02359 (2020)
5. Breunig, M.M., Kriegel, H.P., Ng, R.T., Sander, J.: Lof: identifying density-based local outliers. In: Proceedings of the 2000 ACM SIGMOD international Conference on Management of data, pp. 93–104 (2000)
6. Campello, R.J.G.B., Moulavi, D., Sander, J.: Density-based clustering based on hierarchical density estimates. In: Pei, J., Tseng, V.S., Cao, L., Motoda, H., Xu, G. (eds.) PAKDD 2013. LNCS (LNAI), vol. 7819, pp. 160–172. Springer, Heidelberg (2013). https://doi.org/10.1007/978-3-642-37456-2_14
7. Campello, R.J., Moulavi, D., Zimek, A., Sander, J.: Hierarchical density estimates for data clustering, visualization, and outlier detection. ACM Trans. Knowl. Discov. Data (TKDD) **10**(1), 1–51 (2015)
8. Chalapathy, R., Chawla, S.: Deep learning for anomaly detection: a survey. arXiv preprint. arXiv:1901.03407 (2019)
9. Chalapathy, R., Menon, A.K., Chawla, S.: Anomaly detection using one-class neural networks. arXiv preprint. arXiv:1802.06360 (2018)
10. Chandola, V., Banerjee, A., Kumar, V.: Anomaly detection: a survey. ACM comput. surv. (CSUR) **41**(3), 1–58 (2009)

11. Chang, Y., Tu, Z., Xie, W., Yuan, J.: Clustering driven deep autoencoder for video anomaly detection. In: Vedaldi, A., Bischof, H., Brox, T., Frahm, J.-M. (eds.) ECCV 2020. LNCS, vol. 12360, pp. 329–345. Springer, Cham (2020). https://doi.org/10.1007/978-3-030-58555-6_20

12. Chen, Y., Zhou, X.S., Huang, T.S.: One-class SVM for learning in image retrieval. In: ICIP, pp. 34–37. Citeseer (2001)

13. Cho, M., Kim, T., Kim, I.J., Lee, S.: Unsupervised video anomaly detection via normalizing flows with implicit latent features. arXiv preprint. arXiv:2010.07524 (2020)

14. Coates, A., Ng, A., Lee, H.: An analysis of single-layer networks in unsupervised feature learning. In: Proceedings of the 14th International Conference on Artificial Intelligence and Statistics, pp. 215–223. JMLR Workshop and Conference Proceedings (2011)

15. Di Mattia, F., Galeone, P., De Simoni, M., Ghelfi, E.: A survey on gans for anomaly detection. arXiv preprint. arXiv:1906.11632 (2019)

16. Dias, M.L., Mattos, C.L.C., da Silva, T.L., de Macedo, J.A.F., Silva, W.C.: Anomaly detection in trajectory data with normalizing flows. In: 2020 International Joint Conference on Neural Networks (IJCNN), pp. 1–8. IEEE (2020)

17. Dosovitskiy, A., et al.: An image is worth 16x16 words: transformers for image recognition at scale. arXiv preprint. arXiv:2010.11929 (2020)

18. F.R.S., K.P.: Liii. on lines and planes of closest fit to systems of points in space. Lond. Edinb. Dublin Philos. Mag. J. Sci. 2(11), 559–572 (1901). https://doi.org/10.1080/14786440109462720

19. Golan, I., El-Yaniv, R.: Deep anomaly detection using geometric transformations. arXiv preprint. arXiv:1805.10917 (2018)

20. Goodfellow, I., et al.: Generative adversarial nets. In: Advances in Neural Information Processing Systems, pp. 2672–2680 (2014)

21. He, K., Zhang, X., Ren, S., Sun, J.: Deep residual learning for image recognition. In: Proceedings of the IEEE Conference on Computer Vision and Pattern Recognition, pp. 770–778 (2016)

22. He, Z., Xu, X., Deng, S.: Discovering cluster-based local outliers. Pattern Recogn. Lett. **24**(9–10), 1641–1650 (2003)

23. Hendrycks, D., Mazeika, M., Kadavath, S., Song, D.: Using self-supervised learning can improve model robustness and uncertainty. In: Advances in Neural Information Processing Systems, vol. 32 (2019)

24. Herrera, J.L., Del-Blanco, C.R., Garcia, N.: Automatic depth extraction from 2d images using a cluster-based learning framework. IEEE Trans. Image Process. **27**(7), 3288–3299 (2018)

25. Kirichenko, P., Izmailov, P., Wilson, A.G.: Why normalizing flows fail to detect out-of-distribution data. In: Advances in Neural Information Processing Systems, vol. 33, pp. 20578–20589 (2020)

26. Lai, C.H., Zou, D., Lerman, G.: Robust subspace recovery layer for unsupervised anomaly detection. arXiv preprint. arXiv:1904.00152 (2019)

27. LeCun, Y., Cortes, C.: MNIST handwritten digit database (2010). http://yann.lecun.com/exdb/mnist/

28. Li, T., Wang, Z., Liu, S., Lin, W.Y.: Deep unsupervised anomaly detection. In: Proceedings of the IEEE/CVF Winter Conference on Applications of Computer Vision, pp. 3636–3645 (2021)

29. Li, Z., Zhao, Y., Hu, X., Botta, N., Ionescu, C., Chen, G.: Ecod: unsupervised outlier detection using empirical cumulative distribution functions. In: IEEE Transactions on Knowledge and Data Engineering (2022)

30. Lin, D., Liu, S., Li, H., Cheung, N.M., Ren, C., Matsushita, Y.: Shell theory: a statistical model of reality. In: IEEE Transactions on Pattern Analysis and Machine Intelligence (2021)
31. Lin, W.Y., Cheng, M.M., Zheng, S., Lu, J., Crook, N.: Robust non-parametric data fitting for correspondence modeling. In: Proceedings of the IEEE International Conference on Computer Vision, pp. 2376–2383 (2013)
32. Lin, W.Y., Liu, S., Lai, J.H., Matsushita, Y.: Dimensionality's blessing: Clustering images by underlying distribution. In: Proceedings of the IEEE conference on computer vision and pattern recognition. pp. 5784–5793 (2018)
33. Liou, C.Y., Cheng, W.C., Liou, J.W., Liou, D.R.: Autoencoder for words. Neurocomputing **139**, 84–96 (2014)
34. Liu, F.T., Ting, K.M., Zhou, Z.H.: Isolation forest. In: 2008 8th IEEE international Conference on Data Mining, pp. 413–422. IEEE (2008)
35. Liu, Z., et al.: Swin transformer: hierarchical vision transformer using shifted windows. In: ICCV, pp. 10012–10022 (2021)
36. Van der Maaten, L., Hinton, G.: Visualizing data using t-SNE. J. Mach. Learn. Res. **9**(11), 2579–2605 (2008)
37. Mishra, P., Verk, R., Fornasier, D., Piciarelli, C., Foresti, G.L.: Vt-adl: a vision transformer network for image anomaly detection and localization. In: 2021 IEEE 30th International Symposium on Industrial Electronics (ISIE), pp. 01–06. IEEE (2021)
38. Pang, G., Yan, C., Shen, C., Hengel, A.V.D., Bai, X.: Self-trained deep ordinal regression for end-to-end video anomaly detection. In: Proceedings of the IEEE/CVF Conference on Computer Vision and Pattern Recognition, pp. 12173–12182 (2020)
39. Parzen, E.: On estimation of a probability density function and mode. Ann. Math. Stat. **33**(3), 1065–1076 (1962)
40. Roweis, S.T., Saul, L.K.: Nonlinear dimensionality reduction by locally linear embedding. Science **290**(5500), 2323–2326 (2000)
41. Ruff, L., et al.: Deep one-class classification. In: International Conference on Machine Learning, pp. 4393–4402. PMLR (2018)
42. Wang, F., Liu, H.: Understanding the behaviour of contrastive loss. In: Proceedings of the IEEE/CVF Conference on Computer Vision and Pattern Recognition, pp. 2495–2504 (2021)
43. Xia, Y., Cao, X., Wen, F., Hua, G., Sun, J.: Learning discriminative reconstructions for unsupervised outlier removal. In: Proceedings of the IEEE International Conference on Computer Vision, pp. 1511–1519 (2015)
44. Yoon, S., Noh, Y.K., Park, F.: Autoencoding under normalization constraints. In: International Conference on Machine Learning, pp. 12087–12097. PMLR (2021)
45. Yoshihashi, R., Shao, W., Kawakami, R., You, S., Iida, M., Naemura, T.: Classification-reconstruction learning for open-set recognition. In: Proceedings of the IEEE/CVF Conference on Computer Vision and Pattern Recognition, pp. 4016–4025 (2019)
46. Yu, J., Oh, H., Kim, M., Kim, J.: Normality-calibrated autoencoder for unsupervised anomaly detection on data contamination. arXiv preprint. arXiv:2110.14825 (2021)
47. Zaheer, M.Z., Mahmood, A., Khan, M.H., Segu, M., Yu, F., Lee, S.I.: Generative cooperative learning for unsupervised video anomaly detection. In: Proceedings of the IEEE/CVF Conference on Computer Vision and Pattern Recognition, pp. 14744–14754 (2022)

48. Zenati, H., Foo, C.S., Lecouat, B., Manek, G., Chandrasekhar, V.R.: Efficient gan-based anomaly detection (2018)
49. Zhai, S., Cheng, Y., Lu, W., Zhang, Z.: Deep structured energy based models for anomaly detection. arXiv preprint. arXiv:1605.07717 (2016)
50. Zhang, Y., Liu, C., Zhou, Y., Wang, W., Wang, W., Ye, Q.: Progressive cluster purification for unsupervised feature learning. In: 2020 25th International Conference on Pattern Recognition (ICPR), pp. 8476–8483. IEEE (2021)
51. Zong, B., et al.: Deep autoencoding gaussian mixture model for unsupervised anomaly detection. In: International conference on learning representations (2018)

HRDA: Context-Aware High-Resolution Domain-Adaptive Semantic Segmentation

Lukas Hoyer[1]([✉])[ID], Dengxin Dai[2][ID], and Luc Van Gool[1,3][ID]

[1] ETH Zurich, Zürich, Switzerland
{lhoyer,vangool}@vision.ee.ethz.ch
[2] MPI for Informatics, Saarbrücken, Germany
ddai@mpi-inf.mpg.de
[3] KU Leuven, Leuven, Belgium

Abstract. Unsupervised domain adaptation (UDA) aims to adapt a model trained on the source domain (e.g. synthetic data) to the target domain (e.g. real-world data) without requiring further annotations on the target domain. This work focuses on UDA for semantic segmentation as real-world pixel-wise annotations are particularly expensive to acquire. As UDA methods for semantic segmentation are usually GPU memory intensive, most previous methods operate only on downscaled images. We question this design as low-resolution predictions often fail to preserve fine details. The alternative of training with random crops of high-resolution images alleviates this problem but falls short in capturing long-range, domain-robust context information. Therefore, we propose HRDA, a multi-resolution training approach for UDA, that combines the strengths of small high-resolution crops to preserve fine segmentation details and large low-resolution crops to capture long-range context dependencies with a learned scale attention, while maintaining a manageable GPU memory footprint. HRDA enables adapting small objects and preserving fine segmentation details. It significantly improves the state-of-the-art performance by 5.5 mIoU for GTA→Cityscapes and 4.9 mIoU for Synthia→Cityscapes, resulting in unprecedented 73.8 and 65.8 mIoU, respectively. The implementation is available at github.com/lhoyer/HRDA.

Keywords: Unsupervised domain adaptation · Semantic segmentation · Multi-resolution · High-resolution · Attention

1 Introduction

Even though neural networks currently are the unchallenged approach to solve many computer vision problems, their training often requires a large amount of annotated data. For certain tasks, such as semantic segmentation, providing the

Supplementary Information The online version contains supplementary material available at https://doi.org/10.1007/978-3-031-20056-4_22.

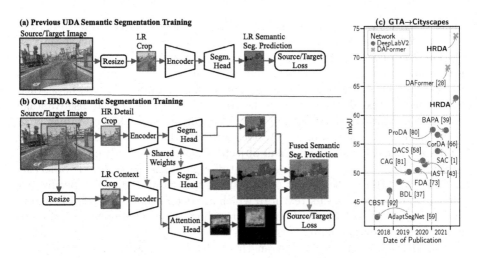

Fig. 1. (a) Most previous UDA methods were only trained with downscaled inputs to account for their high GPU memory footprint. (b) Our HRDA incorporates fine segmentation details from a random high-resolution (HR) detail crop and context information from a random low-resolution (LR) context crop. Their predictions are fused using a learned scale attention (best viewed zoomed-in). In that way, HRDA can utilize HR details and long-range context information while keeping a manageable memory footprint. (c) Compared to previous works, HRDA provides a major performance gain.

annotations is particularly labor-intensive as pixel-wise labels of the entire image are necessary, which can take more than one hour per image [11,51]. Therefore, several methods aim to reduce the annotation burden such as weakly-supervised learning [14,61,93], semi-supervised learning [17,27,35,53], and unsupervised domain adaption (UDA) [26,28,59,67,92]. In this work, we focus on UDA. To avoid the annotation effort for the target dataset, the network is trained on a source dataset with existing or cheaper annotations such as automatically labeled synthetic data [47,49]. However, neural networks are usually sensitive to domain shifts. This problem is approached in UDA by adapting the network, which is trained with source data, to unlabeled target images.

UDA methods are usually more GPU memory intensive than regular supervised learning as UDA training often requires images from multiple domains, additional networks (e.g. teacher model or domain discriminator), and additional losses, which consume significant additional GPU memory. Therefore, most UDA semantic segmentation methods so far (e.g. [1,28,39,58,59,66,73,90]) follow the convention of downscaling images due to GPU memory constraints (see Fig. 1 a). Taking Cityscapes as an example, current UDA methods use half the full resolution (i.e. 1024×512 pixels), while most supervised methods use the full resolution (i.e. 2048×1024 pixels). This is one of the key differences in the training setting of UDA and supervised semantic segmentation, possibly contributing to the gap between the state-of-the-art performance of UDA and supervised learning.

We question this design choice as predictions from low-resolution (LR) inputs often fail to recognize small objects such as distant traffic lights and to preserve fine segmentation details such as limbs of distant pedestrians. However, naively learning UDA with full high-resolution (HR) images is often difficult as the resolution quadratically affects the GPU memory consumption. A common remedy is training with random crops of the image. While training with HR crops allows to adapt small objects and preserve segmentation details, it limits the learned long-range context dependencies to the crop size. This is a crucial disadvantage for UDA as context information and scene layout are often domain-robust (e.g. rider on bicycle or sidewalk at the side of road) [31,71,89]. Further, while HR inputs are necessary to adapt small objects, they can be disadvantageous compared to LR inputs when adapting large stuff-regions such as close sidewalks (see Sect. 5.4). At HR, these regions often contain too detailed, domain-specific features (e.g. detailed sidewalk texture), which are detrimental to UDA. LR inputs 'hide away' these features, while still providing sufficient details to recognize large regions across domains.

To effectively combine the strength of these two approaches while maintaining a manageable GPU memory footprint, we propose *HRDA*, a novel multi-resolution framework for UDA semantic segmentation (see Fig. 1 b). First, HRDA uses a large LR *context crop* to adapt large objects without confusion from domain-specific HR textures and to learn long-range context dependencies as we assume that HR details are not crucial for long-range dependencies. Second, HRDA uses a small HR *detail crop* from the region within the context crop to adapt small objects and to preserve segmentation details as we assume that long-range context information play only a subordinate role in learning segmentation details. In that way, the GPU memory consumption is significantly reduced while still preserving the main advantages of a large crop size and a high resolution. Given that the importance of the LR context crop vs. the HR detail crop depends on the content of the image, HRDA fuses both using an input-dependent scale attention. During UDA, the attention learns to decide how trustworthy the LR and the HR predictions are in every image region. Previous multi-resolution frameworks for supervised learning [5,56,72] cannot naively be applied to state-of-the-art UDA due to GPU memory constraints as they operate on full LR and HR images. To adapt HRDA to the target domain, it can be trained with pseudo-labels fused from multiple resolutions. To further increase the robustness of the detail pseudo-labels with respect to different contexts, they are generated using an overlapping sliding window mechanism.

This work makes four contributions. To the best of our knowledge, it is the first work on UDA semantic segmentation (1) systematically studying the influence of resolution and crop size, (2) exploiting HR inputs for adapting small objects and fine segmentation details, (3) applying multi-resolution fusion with a learned scale attention for object-scale-dependent adaptation, and (4) fusing a nested large LR crop to capture long-range context and small HR crop to capture details for memory-efficient UDA training. HRDA provides significant performance gains when applied to various UDA strategies [28,58,59,62]. When used with the SOTA method DAFormer [28], HRDA gains +5.5 mIoU for GTA→Cityscapes and +4.9 mIoU for Synthia→Cityscapes, resulting in unprecedented 73.8 and 65.8 mIoU, respectively (see Fig. 1 c).

2   Related Work

Semantic Segmentation: Most semantic segmentation approaches are based on (convolutional) neural networks, which can be effectively trained in an end-to-end manner to perform pixel-wise classification as first shown by Long et al. [41]. This concept was further improved in different aspects including increasing the receptive field while preserving spatial details [2,3,6,48,65,74,83], integrating context information [30,75,76,78,91], attention mechanisms [18,32,69,84], refining boundaries [15,36,77], and Transformer-based architectures [40,54,68,70,85].

Several architectures [3,4,16,38,83] utilize intermediate features with different scales, which are generated from a single scale input, to aggregate context information. Furthermore, multi-scale input inference, where predictions from scaled versions of an image are combined via average or max pooling, is often used to obtain better results [4,6,9,75]. However, the naive pooling is independent of the image content, which can lead to suboptimal results. Therefore, Chen et al. [5] and Yang et al. [72] segment multi-scale inputs and learn an attention-weighted sum of the predictions. Tao et al. [56] further propose a hierarchical attention that is agnostic to the number of scales during inference.

Unsupervised Domain Adaptation (UDA): To adapt a semantic segmentation network to the target domain, several strategies have been proposed, while most can be grouped into adversarial training and self-training. In adversarial training [19,22], a domain discriminator is trained in order to provide supervision to align the domain distributions based on style-transferred inputs [21,25,37,45] or network features/outputs [26,59,60,62,64]. In self-training, the network is adapted to the target domain using high-confidence pseudo-labels. In order to regularize the training and to avoid pseudo-label drift, approaches such as confidence thresholding [43,92], pseudo-label prototypes [39,80,81], and consistency regularization [50,52,57] based on data augmentation [1,10,44,46], different context [35,89], domain-mixup [20,29,39,58,89], or multiple models [79,87,88] have been used. Several works also combine self-training and adversarial training [34,37,64,86], minimize the entropy [7,62,63], refine boundaries [39], use a curriculum [12,13,82], or learn auxiliary tasks [8,29,63,66]. The use of semantic segmentation networks with multi-scale *features* is quite common in UDA as many methods evaluate their approach with DeepLabV2 [3]. However, these features are generated from a single-scale input. While some works apply multi-scale average pooling for inference [1,64] or enforce scale consistency [23,33,55] of low-resolution inputs, they fall short in learning an input-adaptive multi-scale fusion. To the best of our knowledge, HRDA is the first work to learn a multi-resolution *input* fusion for UDA semantic segmentation. For that purpose, we newly extend scale attention [5,56] to UDA and reveal its significance for UDA by improving the adaptation process across different object scales. Further, we propose fusing nested crops with different scales and sizes, which successfully overcomes the pressing issue of limited GPU memory for multi-resolution UDA.

3 Preliminary

In UDA, a neural network f_θ is trained using source domain images $\mathcal{X}^S = \{x_{HR}^{S,m}\}_{m=1}^{N_S}$ with $x_{HR}^{S,m} \in \mathbb{R}^{H_S \times W_S \times 3}$ and target domain images $\mathcal{X}^T = \{x_{HR}^{T,m}\}_{m=1}^{N_T}$ with $x_{HR}^{T,m} \in \mathbb{R}^{H_T \times W_T \times 3}$ to achieve a good performance on the target domain. However, labels are only available for the source domain $\mathcal{Y}^S = \{y_{HR}^{S,m}\}_{m=1}^{N_S}$ with $y_{HR}^{S,m} \in \{0,1\}^{H_S \times W_S \times C}$. As the following definitions refer to the same source/target sample, we will drop index m to avoid convolution. Most previous UDA methods bilinearly downsample $\zeta(\cdot,\cdot)$ the images and labels x_{HR}^S, x_{HR}^T, and y_{HR}^S by a dataset-specific factor $s_S, s_T \geq 1$ to satisfy GPU memory constraints, e.g. $x_{LR}^T = \zeta(x_{HR}^T, 1/s_T) \in \mathbb{R}^{\frac{H_T}{s_T} \times \frac{W_T}{s_T} \times 3}$. Some methods such as [28,58,80] additionally crop the LR image but for simplicity, we consider full LR images in this section.

As only source labels are available, the supervised categorical cross-entropy loss can only be calculated for the source predictions $\hat{y}_{LR}^S = f_\theta(x_{LR}^S)$

$$\mathcal{L}^S = \mathcal{L}_{ce}(\hat{y}_{LR}^S, y_{LR}^S, 1)\,, \tag{1}$$

$$\mathcal{L}_{ce}(\hat{y}, y, q) = -\sum_{i=1}^{H(y)} \sum_{j=1}^{W(y)} \sum_{c=1}^{C} q_{ij} y_{ijc} \log \zeta(\hat{y}, \frac{H(y)}{H(\hat{y})})_{ijc}\,. \tag{2}$$

As the predictions are usually smaller than the input due to the output stride of the segmentation network, they are upsampled to the label size $H(y) \times W(y)$.

However, a model trained only with $\mathcal{L}^S$ usually does not generalize well to the target domain. In order to adapt the model to the target domain, UDA methods incorporate an additional loss for the target domain $\mathcal{L}^T$, which is added to the overall loss $\mathcal{L} = \mathcal{L}^S + \lambda \mathcal{L}^T$. The target loss can be defined according to the used training strategies such as adversarial training [59,60,64] or self-training [28, 43,58,80,81,92]. In this work, we mainly evaluate HRDA with the self-training method DAFormer [28], as it is the current state-of-the-art method for UDA semantic segmentation. In self-training, the model is iteratively adapted to the target domain by training it with pseudo-labels for target images, predicted by a teacher network g_ϕ:

$$p_{LR,ijc}^T = [c = \arg\max_{c'} g_\phi(x_{LR}^T)_{ijc'}]\,, \tag{3}$$

where $[\cdot]$ denotes the Iverson bracket. The pseudo-labels are used to additionally train the network f_θ on the target domain

$$\mathcal{L}^T = \mathcal{L}_{ce}(\hat{y}_{LR}^T, p_{LR}^T, q_{LR}^T)\,. \tag{4}$$

As the pseudo-labels are not necessarily correct, their quality is weighted by a confidence estimate q_{LR}^T [28,43,58,92]. After each training step t, the teacher model g_ϕ is updated with the exponentially moving average of the weights of f_θ, implementing a temporal ensemble to stabilize pseudo-labels, which is a common strategy in semi-supervised learning [17,52,57] and UDA [1,39,58]

$$\phi_{t+1} \leftarrow \alpha\phi_t + (1-\alpha)\theta_t\,. \tag{5}$$

Further, DAFormer [28] uses consistency training [50,52,57], i.e. the network f_θ is trained on augmented target data following DACS [58], while the teacher model g_ϕ generates the pseudo-labels using non-augmented target images. Besides self-training, DAFormer [28] uses a domain-robust Transformer network, rare class sampling, and feature regularization based on ImageNet features.

4   Methods

In this work, we propose a multi-resolution framework for UDA as small objects and segmentation details are easier to adapt with high-resolution (HR) inputs, while large stuff regions are easier to adapt with low-resolution (LR) inputs. As UDA methods require more GPU memory than regular supervised training, we design a training strategy based on a large LR context crop to learn long-range context dependencies and a small HR detail crop to preserve segmentation details while maintaining a manageable GPU memory footprint (Sect. 4.1). The strengths of both LR context and HR detail crop are combined by fusing their predictions with a learned scale attention (Sect. 4.2). For a robust pseudo-label generation, we further utilize overlapping slide inference to fuse predictions with different contexts (Sec. 4.3). The proposed method is designed to be applicable to common network architectures and can be combined with existing UDA methods.

4.1   Context and Detail Crop

Due to GPU memory constraints, it is not feasible to train state-of-the-art UDA methods with full-sized high-/multi-resolution inputs as images from multiple domains, additional networks, and additional losses are required for UDA training. Therefore, most previous works only use LR inputs. However, HR inputs are important to recognize small objects and produce fine segmentation borders. In order to still utilize HR inputs, random cropping is a possible solution. However, random cropping restricts learning context-aware semantic segmentation, especially for long-range dependencies and scene layout, which might be critical for UDA as context relations are often domain-invariant (e.g. car on road, rider on bicycle) [31,71,89]. In order to both train with long-range context as well as high resolution, we propose to combine different crop sizes for different resolutions, i.e. a large LR context crop and a small HR detail crop (see Fig. 2 a). The purpose of the context crop is to provide a large crop to learn long-range context relations. The purpose of detail crop is to focus on HR to recognize small objects and produce fine segmentation details, which does not necessarily require far-away context information. In order to segment the entire image during model validation, overlapping sliding window inference is used (see Sect. 4.3).

The context crop $x_c \in \mathbb{R}^{h_c \times w_c \times 3}$ is obtained by cropping from the original HR image $x_{HR} \in \mathbb{R}^{H \times W \times 3}$ and bilinear downsampling by the factor $s \geq 1$

$$x_{c,HR} = x_{HR}[b_{c,1} : b_{c,2}, b_{c,3} : b_{c,4}], \quad x_c = \zeta(x_{c,HR}, 1/s) \tag{6}$$

a) Multi-Resolution Training with Context and Detail Crop

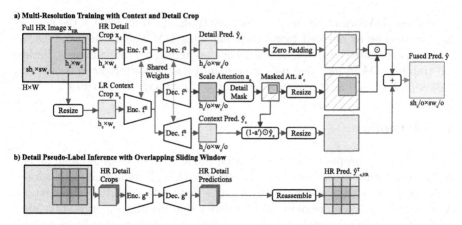

Fig. 2. (a) Multi-resolution training with low-resolution (LR) context and high-resolution (HR) detail crop. The prediction of the detail crop is fused into the context prediction within the region where it was cropped from by a learned scale attention. (b) For pseudo-label generation, multiple detail crops are generated using overlapping slide inference to cover the entire context crop. The pseudo-label is fused from HR pred. $\hat{y}_{c,HR}^T$ and LR pred. $\hat{y}_c^T$ with the full attention a_c^T similar to (a) (see Sect. 4.3).

The crop bounding box b_c is randomly sampled from a discrete uniform distribution within the image size while ensuring that the coordinates can be divided by $k = s \cdot o$ with $o \geq 1$ denoting the output stride of the segmentation network to ensure exact alignment in the later fusion process:

$$b_{c,1} \sim \mathcal{U}\{0, (H - sh_c)/k\} \cdot k, \qquad b_{c,2} = b_{c,1} + sh_c,$$
$$b_{c,3} \sim \mathcal{U}\{0, (W - sw_c)/k\} \cdot k, \qquad b_{c,4} = b_{c,3} + sw_c. \qquad (7)$$

The detail crop $x_d \in \mathbb{R}^{h_d \times w_d \times 3}$ is randomly cropped from within the context crop region, which is necessary to enable the fusion of context and detail predictions in the later process:

$$x_d = x_{c,HR}[b_{d,1} : b_{d,2}, b_{d,3} : b_{d,4}], \qquad (8)$$

$$b_{d,1} \sim \mathcal{U}\{0, (sh_c - h_d)/k\} \cdot k, \qquad b_{d,2} = b_{d,1} + h_d,$$
$$b_{d,3} \sim \mathcal{U}\{0, (sw_c - w_d)/k\} \cdot k, \qquad b_{d,4} = b_{d,3} + w_d. \qquad (9)$$

In this work, we use context and detail crops of the same dimension, i.e. $h_c = h_d$ and $w_c = w_d$, to balance the required resources for both crops and provide a good trade-off between context-aware and detailed predictions. The context downscale factor is $s = 2$ following the LR design of previous UDA methods [28,39,58], which means that the context crop covers 4 times more content at half the resolution compared to the detail crop.

Using a feature encoder f^E and a semantic decoder f^S, the context semantic segmentation $\hat{y}_c = f^S(f^E(x_c)) \in \mathbb{R}^{\frac{h_c}{o} \times \frac{w_c}{o} \times C}$ and the detail semantic segmentation $\hat{y}_d = f^S(f^E(x_d)) \in \mathbb{R}^{\frac{h_d}{o} \times \frac{w_d}{o} \times C}$ are predicted. The networks f^E and f^S

are shared for both HR and LR inputs. This not only saves memory usage but also increases the robustness of the network against different resolutions.

4.2   Multi-resolution Fusion

While the HR detail crop is well-suited to segment small objects such as poles or distant pedestrians, it lacks the ability to capture long-range dependencies, which is disadvantageous in segmenting large stuff regions such as large regions of sidewalk. The opposite is the case for the LR context crop. Therefore, we fuse the predictions from both crops using a learned scale attention [5] to predict in which image regions to trust predictions from context and detail crop. Additionally, the scale attention provides the advantage that it enables adapting objects at the better-suited scale. For example, small objects are easier to adapt at HR while large objects are easier to adapt at LR as the appearance of an object should have a resolution high enough to be discriminative but not too high to avoid that the network overfits to domain-specific detailed textures.

The scale attention decoder f^A learns to predict the scale attention $a_c = \sigma(f^A(f^E(x_c))) \in [0,1]^{\frac{h_c}{o} \times \frac{w_c}{o} \times C}$ to weigh the trustworthiness of LR context and HR detail predictions. The sigmoid function σ ensures a weight in $[0,1]$, where 1 means a focus on the HR detail crop. The attention is predicted from the context crop as it has a better grasp on the scene layout (larger context). As the predictions are smaller than the inputs due to the output stride o, the crop coordinates are scaled accordingly in the following steps. Outside of the detail crop c_d, the attention is set to 0 as there is no detail prediction available

$$a_c' \in \mathbb{R}^{\frac{h_c}{o} \times \frac{w_c}{o}}, \quad a_c'(i,j) = \begin{cases} a_c(i,j) & \text{if } \frac{b_{d,1}}{s \cdot o} \le i < \frac{b_{d,2}}{s \cdot o} \wedge \frac{b_{d,3}}{s \cdot o} \le j < \frac{b_{d,4}}{s \cdot o} \\ 0 & \text{otherwise} \end{cases}.$$

(10)

The detail crop is aligned with the (upsampled) context crop by padding it with zeros to a size of $\frac{sh_c}{o} \times \frac{sw_c}{o}$

$$\hat{y}_d'(i,j) = \begin{cases} \hat{y}_d(i - \frac{b_{d,1}}{o}, j - \frac{b_{d,3}}{o}) & \text{if } \frac{b_{d,1}}{o} \le i < \frac{b_{d,2}}{o} \wedge \frac{b_{d,3}}{o} \le j < \frac{b_{d,4}}{o} \\ 0 & \text{otherwise} \end{cases}.$$

(11)

The predictions from multiple scales are fused using the attention-weighted sum

$$\hat{y}_{c,F} = \zeta((1 - a_c') \odot \hat{y}_c, s) + \zeta(a_c', s) \odot \hat{y}_d'.$$

(12)

The encoder, segmentation head, and attention head are trained with the fused multi-scale prediction and the detail crop prediction

$$\mathcal{L}_{HRDA}^S = (1 - \lambda_d)\mathcal{L}_{ce}(\hat{y}_{c,F}^S, y_{c,HR}^S, 1) + \lambda_d \mathcal{L}_{ce}(\hat{y}_d^S, y_d^S, 1),$$

(13)

where the ground truth $y_{c,HR}^S/y_d^S$ is cropped according to Eq. 6/8. Additionally supervising the detail crop is helpful to learn more robust features for HR inputs even though the attention might favor the context crop in that region. An additional loss for $\hat{y}_c$ is not necessary as it is already directly supervised in regions without detail crop (see Eq. 10). The target loss $\mathcal{L}^T_{HRDA}$ is adapted accordingly

$$\mathcal{L}^T_{HRDA} = (1 - \lambda_d)\mathcal{L}_{ce}(\hat{y}^T_{c,F}, p^T_{c,F}, q^T_{c,F}) + \lambda_d\mathcal{L}_{ce}(\hat{y}^T_d, p^T_d, q^T_d). \quad (14)$$

For pseudo-label prediction, we also utilize multi-resolution fusion (see Sect. 4.3). Therefore, when predicting pseudo-labels the scale attention focuses on the better-suited resolution (e.g. HR for small objects). As the pseudo-labels are further used to train the model also with the worse-suited resolution (e.g. LR for small objects), it improves the robustness for both small and large objects.

4.3   Pseudo-Label Generation with Overlapping Sliding Window

For self-training with Eq. 14, it is necessary to generate a high-quality HRDA pseudo-label $p^T_{c,F}$ for the context crop $x^T_{c,HR}$. The underlying HRDA prediction $\hat{y}^T_{c,F}$ is fused from the LR prediction $\hat{y}^T_c$ and HR prediction $\hat{y}^T_{c,HR}$ using the full scale attention a^T_c similar to Eq. 12

$$\hat{y}^T_{c,F} = \zeta((1 - a^T_c) \odot \hat{y}^T_c, s) + \zeta(a^T_c, s) \odot \hat{y}^T_{c,HR}. \quad (15)$$

Therefore, the HR prediction $\hat{y}^T_{c,HR}$ is necessary for the entire context crop $x^T_{c,HR}$ instead of just the detail crop x_d. Note that for pseudo-label generation g_ϕ instead of f_θ is used for predictions. Even though large HR network inputs are problematic during training, they are not an issue during pseudo-label inference as no data for the backpropagation has to be stored. However, the used DAFormer [28], as well as other Vision Transformers [70,85], have a learned (implicit) positional embedding that works best if training and inference input size are the same. Therefore, we infer the HR prediction $\hat{y}^T_{c,HR}$ using a sliding window of size $h_d \times w_d$ over the HR context crop $x^T_{c,HR}$ (see Fig 2 b). The window is shifted with a stride of $h_d/2 \times w_d/2$ to generate overlapping predictions with different contexts, which are averaged to increase robustness. The crops of the sliding window can be processed in parallel as the images in a batch, which allows for efficient computation on the GPU.

For model validation or deployment, the full-scale HRDA semantic segmentation $\hat{y}_{F,HR}$ of the entire image x_{HR} is necessary. As the context crop is usually smaller than the entire image, $\hat{y}_{F,HR}$ is generated using an overlapping sliding window over the entire image x_{HR} with a size of $sh_c \times sw_c$ and a stride of $sh_c/2 \times sw_c/2$. Within the sliding window, the HRDA prediction is generated in the same way as $\hat{y}^T_{c,F}$ for the pseudo-label.

5   Experiments

5.1   Implementation Details

Datasets: As target data, the real-world Cityscapes dataset [11] of European street scenes with 2975 training and 500 validation images of 2048 × 1024 pixels

Table 1. Comparison with previous UDA methods. The results of HRDA are averaged over 3 random seeds. Further methods are shown in the supplement.

	Road	S.walk	Build	Wall	Fence	Pole	Tr.Light	Sign	Veget	Terrain	Sky	Person	Rider	Car	Truck	Bus	Train	M.bike	Bike	mIoU
GTA5 → Cityscapes																				
CBST [92]	91.8	53.5	80.5	32.7	21.0	34.0	28.9	20.4	83.9	34.2	80.9	53.1	24.0	82.7	30.3	35.9	16.0	25.9	42.8	45.9
DACS [58]	89.9	39.7	87.9	30.7	39.5	38.5	46.4	52.8	88.0	44.0	88.8	67.2	35.8	84.5	45.7	50.2	0.0	27.3	34.0	52.1
CorDA [66]	94.7	63.1	87.6	30.7	40.6	40.2	47.8	51.6	87.6	47.0	89.7	66.7	35.9	90.2	48.9	57.5	0.0	39.8	56.0	56.6
BAPA [39]	94.4	61.0	88.0	26.8	39.9	38.3	46.1	55.3	87.8	46.1	89.4	68.8	40.0	90.2	60.4	59.0	0.0	45.1	54.2	57.4
ProDA [80]	87.8	56.0	79.7	46.3	44.8	45.6	53.5	53.5	88.6	45.2	82.1	70.7	39.2	88.8	45.5	59.4	1.0	48.9	56.4	57.5
DAFormer [28]	95.7	70.2	89.4	53.5	48.1	49.6	55.8	59.4	89.9	47.9	92.5	72.2	44.7	92.3	74.5	78.2	65.1	55.9	61.8	68.3
HRDA (Ours)	96.4	74.4	91.0	61.6	51.5	57.1	63.9	69.3	91.3	48.4	94.2	79.0	52.9	93.9	84.1	85.7	75.9	63.9	67.5	73.8
Synthia → Cityscapes																				
CBST [92]	68.0	29.9	76.3	10.8	1.4	33.9	22.8	29.5	77.6	–	78.3	60.6	28.3	81.6	–	23.5	–	18.8	39.8	42.6
DACS [58]	80.6	25.1	81.9	21.5	2.9	37.2	22.7	24.0	83.7	–	90.8	67.6	38.3	82.9	–	38.9	–	28.5	47.6	48.3
BAPA [39]	91.7	53.8	83.9	22.4	0.8	34.9	30.5	42.8	86.6	–	88.2	66.0	34.1	86.6	–	51.3	–	29.4	50.5	53.3
CorDA [66]	93.3	61.6	85.3	19.6	5.1	37.8	36.6	42.8	84.9	–	90.4	69.7	41.8	85.6	–	38.4	–	32.6	53.9	55.0
ProDA [80]	87.8	45.7	84.6	37.1	0.6	44.0	54.6	37.0	88.1	–	84.4	74.2	24.3	88.2	–	51.1	–	40.5	45.6	55.5
DAFormer [28]	84.5	40.7	88.4	41.5	6.5	50.0	55.0	54.6	86.0	–	89.8	73.2	48.2	87.2	–	53.2	–	53.9	61.7	60.9
HRDA (Ours)	85.2	47.7	88.8	49.5	4.8	57.2	65.7	60.9	85.3	–	92.9	79.4	52.8	89.0	–	64.7	–	63.9	64.9	65.8

is used. As source data, the synthetic datasets GTA [47] with 24,966 images of 1914×1052 pixels and Synthia [49] with 9,400 images of 1280×760 pixels are used. Previous works [28,58,59,73] downsample Cityscapes to 1024×512 and GTA to 1280×720. Instead, we maintain the full resolution for Cityscapes. To train with the same scale ratio of source and target images as previous works, we resize GTA to 2560×1440 and Synthia to 2560×1520 pixels.

Network Architecture: Our default network is based on DAFormer [28]. It consists of an MiT-B5 encoder [70] and a context-aware feature fusion decoder [28]. For the scale attention decoder, we use the lightweight Seg-Former MLP decoder [70] with an embedding dimension of 256. When evaluating other UDA methods in Table 2, we use a ResNet101 [24] backbone with a DeepLabV2 [3] decoder both as segmentation and scale attention head.

Training: By default, we follow the DAFormer [28] self-training strategy (see Sect. 3) and training parameters, i.e. AdamW [42] with a learning rate of 6×10^{-5} for the encoder and 6×10^{-4} for the decoder, a batch size of 2, linear learning rate warmup, $\lambda_{st} = 1$, $\alpha = 0.999$, and DACS [58] data augmentation. For adversarial training and entropy minimization, we use SGD with a learning rate of 0.0025 and $\lambda_{adv} = \lambda_{ent} = 0.001$. The context and detail crop are generated using $h_c = w_c = h_d = w_d = 512$ with $s = 2$ to balance the required resources for both crops in the default case. The detail loss weight is chosen empirically $\lambda_d = 0.1$. The experiments are conducted on a Titan RTX GPU with 24 GB memory.

5.2   Comparison with State-of-the-Art UDA Methods

First, we compare the proposed HRDA with previous UDA methods in Table 1. It can be seen that HRDA outperforms the previously best state-of-the-art method by a significant margin of +5.5 mIoU on GTA→Cityscapes and +4.9 mIoU on Synthia→ Cityscapes. HRDA improves the IoU of almost all classes across both

Image   ProDA [80]   DAFormer [28]   HRDA (Ours)   Ground Truth

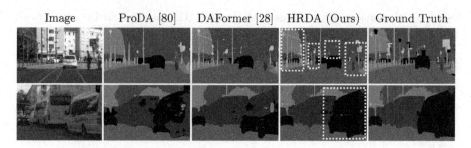

Fig. 3. Qualitative comparison of HRDA with previous methods on GTA→Cityscapes. HRDA improves the segmentation of small classes such as pole, traffic sign, traffic light, and rider as well as large and difficult classes such as bus.

Table 2. HRDA applied to different UDA methods on GTA→Cityscapes. Mean and standard deviation are provided over 3 random seeds.

	UDA Method	Network	w/o HRDA	w/ HRDA	Improvement
1	Entropy Min. [62]	DeepLabV2 [3]	$44.3_{\pm 0.4}$	$46.7_{\pm 1.2}$	+2.4
2	Adversarial [59]	DeepLabV2 [3]	$44.2_{\pm 0.1}$	$47.1_{\pm 1.0}$	+2.9
3	DACS [58]	DeepLabV2 [3]	$53.9_{\pm 0.6}$	$59.4_{\pm 1.2}$	+5.5
4	DAFormer [28]	DeepLabV2 [3]	$56.0_{\pm 0.5}$	$63.0_{\pm 0.4}$	+7.0
5	DAFormer [28]	DAFormer [28]	$68.3_{\pm 0.5}$	$73.8_{\pm 0.3}$	+5.5

datasets. The highest performance gains are achieved for classes with fine segmentation details such as pole, traffic light, traffic sign, person, rider, motorbike, and bike. But also large classes such as truck, bus, and train benefit from HRDA. This is also reflected in the visual examples in Fig. 3.

5.3   HRDA for Different UDA Methods

HRDA is designed to be applicable to most UDA methods. In Table 2, we compare the performance without and with HRDA of three further representative UDA methods. It can be seen that HRDA consistently improves the performance by at least +2.4 mIoU, demonstrating the importance of high- and multi-resolution inputs for UDA in general. Also, it shows that HRDA can be applied to different network architectures. The highest improvement is achieved for self-training methods (row 3–5) with +5.5 mIoU and more, which shows that the HRDA pseudo-labels positively reinforce the UDA process.

5.4   Influence of Resolution and Crop Size on UDA

In the following, we analyze the underlying principles of HRDA on GTA→ Cityscapes, starting with the influence of the resolution and crop size on UDA. For the comparison, we use the relative crop size $h/\frac{H_T}{s}$, which is normalized by

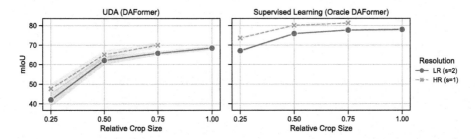

Fig. 4. Segmentation performance over the relative crop size $(h/\frac{H_T}{s})$ for different resolutions and for both the UDA method DAFormer [28] and the target-supervised oracle. There is no value for $HR_{1.0}$ due to GPU memory constraints. (Color figure online)

	Road	S.walk	Build.	Wall	Fence	Pole	T.Light	T.Sign	Veget.	Terrain	Sky	Person	Rider	Car	Truck	Bus	Train	M.bike	Bike	mIoU
$LR_{0.5}$	96	71	88	46	27	44	50	56	89	45	91	70	40	91	60	66	39	50	61	62
$HR_{0.5}$	93	63	89	47	27	52	56	62	90	40	91	76	41	92	61	66	67	56	67	65
$LR_{1.0}$	96	71	89	54	49	49	56	60	90	50	92	72	46	92	69	80	67	57	62	68
$LR_{1.0}+HR_{0.5}$	96	74	91	62	51	57	64	69	91	48	94	79	53	94	84	86	76	64	68	74

Fig. 5. Class-wise IoU for the UDA method DAFormer [28] for different crop resolutions XR ($s_{LR} = 2$, $s_{HR} = 1$) and relative crop sizes $a = h/\frac{H_T}{s_{XR}}$. Crops are denoted as XR_a. The colors indicate the difference to the first row. (Color figure online)

the image height at the corresponding resolution, to disentangle the crop size from the used image resolution. Figure 4 shows that both an increased resolution and crop size improve the performance for both UDA and supervised learning. A large crop size is even more important for UDA than for supervised learning, i.e. a 4 times smaller LR crop reduces the performance by 39% for UDA and by 14% for supervised training. The larger crop provides more context clues and improves the performance of all classes, especially the ones that are difficult to adapt such as wall, fence, truck, bus, and train (cf. row 1 and 3 in Fig. 5), probably, as the relevant context clues are more domain-invariant [31,71,89]. A higher input resolution improves the UDA performance by a similar amount as it improves supervised learning. The improvement originates from a higher IoU for small classes such as pole, traffic light, traffic sign, person, motorbike, and bicycle, while some large classes such as road, sidewalk, and terrain have a decreased performance (cf. row 1 and 2 in Fig. 5). This supports that large objects are easier to adapt at LR while small objects are easier to adapt at HR, which can be exploited by the multi-resolution fusion of HRDA.

5.5 Combining Crops from Multiple Resolutions with HRDA

Multi-resolution UDA: Next, we combine crops from LR and HR using the proposed multi-resolution training for UDA. Table 3 shows that training with multiple resolutions improves the performance over both LR-only and HR-

Table 3. HRDA context size. XR_a denotes crops with resolution XR ($s_{LR} = 2$, $s_{HR} = 1$) and relative crop size $a = h/\frac{H_T}{s_{XR}}$.

	Context Crop	Detail Crop	mIoU
1	$LR_{0.5}$	–	62.1 ± 2.1
2	–	$HR_{0.5}$	65.1 ± 1.9
3	$LR_{0.5}$	$HR_{0.5}$	68.5 ± 0.6
4	$LR_{0.75}$	$HR_{0.5}$	71.1 ± 1.7
5	$LR_{1.0}$	$HR_{0.5}$	73.8 ± 0.3

Table 4. HRDA detail size. XR_a denotes crops with resolution XR ($s_{LR} = 2$, $s_{HR} = 1$) and relative crop size $a = h/\frac{H_T}{s_{XR}}$.

	Context Crop	Detail Crop	mIoU
1	$LR_{1.0}$	–	68.5 ± 0.9
2	–	$HR_{0.25}$	47.7 ± 2.4
3	$LR_{1.0}$	$HR_{0.25}$	70.6 ± 0.7
4	$LR_{1.0}$	$HR_{0.375}$	71.7 ± 0.4
5	$LR_{1.0}$	$HR_{0.5}$	73.8 ± 0.3

Table 5. Comparison of HRDA with naive HR crops that have a comparable GPU memory footprint ($HR_{0.75}$).

	Context	Detail	Mem	mIoU
1	–	$HR_{0.75}$	22.0 GB	70.0 ± 1.2
2	$LR_{0.75}$	$HR_{0.375}$	13.5 GB	71.3 ± 0.3
3	$LR_{1.0}$	$HR_{0.5}$	22.5 GB	73.8 ± 0.3

Table 6. HRDA detail crop variants. Up-LR: LR crop upsampled to HR resolution.

	Context Crop	Detail Crop	mIoU
1	$LR_{1.0}$	–	68.5 ± 0.9
2	$LR_{1.0}$	$LR_{0.5}$	69.1 ± 0.4
3	$LR_{1.0}$	Up-$LR_{0.5}$	71.9 ± 1.5
4	$LR_{1.0}$	$HR_{0.5}$	73.8 ± 0.3

only training by +3.4 mIoU (cf. row 2 and 3), which demonstrates that multi-resolution fusion with scale attention results in better domain adaptation.

Context Crop Size: Based on the observation that large crops are important for UDA (Sect. 5.4), we increase the context crop size while keeping the detail crop size fixed, which further improves the performance by +5.3 mIoU (cf. row 3 and 5), demonstrating the effectiveness of the proposed small HR detail and large LR context crops. Figure 5 shows that the multi-resolution training combines the strength of the single-scale training with $HR_{0.5}$ and $LR_{1.0}$ as the multi-resolution IoU of each class is better than the best single-scale IoU (cf. row 2, 3, and 4).

Detail Crop Size: Already the combination of the context crop $LR_{1.0}$ with an even smaller detail crop $HR_{0.25}$ outperforms training with solely the context crop by +2.1 mIoU (cf. row 1 and 3 in Table 4), even though $HR_{0.25}$ alone performs -20.8 mIoU worse (cf. row 1 and 2). This shows that the multi-resolution fusion effectively exploits the strength of the small detail crop while compensating for its lacking long-range dependencies with the context crop. Further increasing the detail crop size, results in additional performance gains (cf. row 2 and 5). This shows that even though context information is not crucial for the detail crop, it is still helpful to some extent while being limited due to GPU memory constraints.

Detail Crop Variants: It is crucial for HRDA to use context/detail crops with different resolutions. Using LR instead of HR for the detail crop gives only a

Table 7. Component ablation of HRDA.

	Context	Detail	Scale attention	Overlapping detail	Detail loss	mIoU
1	–	✓	–	–	–	65.1 ±1.9
2	✓	–	–	–	–	68.5 ±0.9
3	✓	✓	Average	–	–	67.5 ±0.8
4	✓	✓	Learned	–	–	71.5 ±0.5
5	✓	✓	Learned	✓	–	72.4 ±0.1
6	✓	✓	Learned	✓	✓	73.8 ±0.3

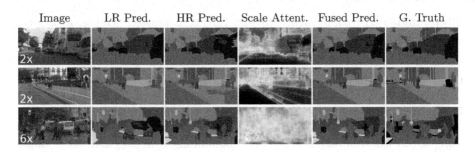

Image   LR Pred.   HR Pred.   Scale Attent.   Fused Pred.   G. Truth

Fig. 6. Visual examples of the different predictions and the scale attention of HRDA. Large objects are better segmented from LR while small objects are better segmented from HR. The scale attention learns to utilize this pattern for fusing LR and HR predictions. The examples are zoomed in (2x or 6x) for better visibility of the details.

marginal gain of +0.6 over the baseline (cf. row 1 and 2 in Table 6). However, using an LR crop that is bilinearly upsampled to HR as detail crop does improve the performance by +3.4 mIoU (cf. row 1 and 3 in Table 6) but is still -1.9 mIoU worse than using a real HR detail crop (cf. row 3 and 4 in Table 6). This shows that the improved performance of HRDA comes from both the additional zoomed-in context information as well as the additional details in the HR image.

Comparison with Naive HR: We compare HRDA with naive large HR crops ($HR_{0.75}$), which have a comparable GPU memory footprint as HRDA. This is a very strong baseline, which is already +1.7 mIoU better than DAFormer [28]. Table 5 shows that HRDA still outperforms $HR_{0.75}$ crops by +3.8 mIoU (cf. row 1 and 3). Even when reducing the crop size of HRDA to match the size of $HR_{0.75}$, HRDA is still +1.3 mIoU better while requiring 40% less GPU memory. This demonstrates that combining LR context crop and HR detail crop performs better than naively increasing the resolution, due to HRDA's capability of capturing large context information and multi-resolution fusion.

HRDA Component Ablations: The components of HRDA are ablated in Table 7. The most crucial component is the learned scale attention. While naively averaging the predictions from both scales gives no improvement over just using the context crop (cf. row 2 and 3), the learned scale attention improves the performance by +3.0 mIoU (cf. row 2 and 4). This shows that it is crucial to learn which scale is best-suited to adapt certain image regions. Generating pseudo-labels with different context views by overlapping slide detail crops results in a further gain of +0.9 mIoU (cf. row 4 and 5). Finally, additional supervision of the detail crop ($\lambda_d = 0.1$) further provides +1.4 mIoU (cf. row 5 and 6).

Qualitative Analysis: Figure 6 provides representative visual examples demonstrating that LR predictions work better for large objects such as a bus or sidewalk (row 1/2) while HR predictions work better for small objects and fine details (row 3). The scale attention focuses on LR for large objects and on HR for small objects and segmentation borders, combining the strength of both.

Supplement: The supplement provides further parameter studies, additional baseline comparisons, a runtime analysis, and an extended qualitative analysis.

6   Conclusions

In this work, we presented HRDA, a multi-resolution approach for UDA that combines the advantages of small HR detail crops and large LR context crops using a learned scale attention, while maintaining a manageable GPU memory footprint. It can be combined with various UDA methods and achieves a consistent, significant improvement. Overall, HRDA achieves an unprecedented performance of 73.8 mIoU on GTA→Cityscapes and 65.8 mIoU on Synthia→Cityscapes, which is a respective gain of +5.5 mIoU and +4.9 mIoU over the previous SOTA.

Acknowledgements. This work is supported by the European Lighthouse on Secure and Safe AI (ELSA) and a Facebook Academic Gift on Robust Perception (INFO224).

References

1. Araslanov, N., Roth, S.: Self-supervised augmentation consistency for adapting semantic segmentation. In: CVPR, pp. 15384–15394 (2021)
2. Chen, L.C., Papandreou, G., Kokkinos, I., Murphy, K., Yuille, A.L.: Semantic image segmentation with deep convolutional nets and fully connected crfs. In: ICLR, pp. 834–848 (2015)
3. Chen, L.C., Papandreou, G., Kokkinos, I., Murphy, K., Yuille, A.L.: Deeplab: semantic image segmentation with deep convolutional nets, atrous convolution, and fully connected crfs. PAMI **40**(4), 834–848 (2017)
4. Chen, L.C., Papandreou, G., Schroff, F., Adam, H.: Rethinking atrous convolution for semantic image segmentation. arXiv preprint. arXiv:1706.05587 (2017)
5. Chen, L.C., Yang, Y., Wang, J., Xu, W., Yuille, A.L.: Attention to scale: scale-aware semantic image segmentation. In: CVPR, pp. 3640–3649 (2016)
6. Chen, L.-C., Zhu, Y., Papandreou, G., Schroff, F., Adam, H.: Encoder-decoder with atrous separable convolution for semantic image segmentation. In: Ferrari, V., Hebert, M., Sminchisescu, C., Weiss, Y. (eds.) ECCV 2018. LNCS, vol. 11211, pp. 833–851. Springer, Cham (2018). https://doi.org/10.1007/978-3-030-01234-2_49

7. Chen, M., Xue, H., Cai, D.: Domain adaptation for semantic segmentation with maximum squares loss. In: ICCV, pp. 2090–2099 (2019)

8. Chen, Y., Li, W., Chen, X., Gool, L.V.: Learning semantic segmentation from synthetic data: a geometrically guided input-output adaptation approach. In: CVPR, pp. 1841–1850 (2019)

9. Cheng, B., et al.: Panoptic-deeplab: a simple, strong, and fast baseline for bottom-up panoptic segmentation. In: CVPR, pp. 12475–12485 (2020)

10. Choi, J., Kim, T., Kim, C.: Self-ensembling with gan-based data augmentation for domain adaptation in semantic segmentation. In: ICCV, pp. 6830–6840 (2019)

11. Cordts, M., et al.: The cityscapes dataset for semantic urban scene understanding. In: CVPR. pp. 3213–3223 (2016). https://www.cityscapes-dataset.com/license/

12. Dai, D., Sakaridis, C., Hecker, S., Van Gool, L.: Curriculum model adaptation with synthetic and real data for semantic foggy scene understanding. IJCV **128**(5), 1182–1204 (2020)

13. Dai, D., Van Gool, L.: Dark model adaptation: semantic image segmentation from daytime to nighttime. In: ITSC, pp. 3819–3824 (2018)

14. Dai, J., He, K., Sun, J.: Boxsup: exploiting bounding boxes to supervise convolutional networks for semantic segmentation. In: ICCV, pp. 1635–1643 (2015)

15. Ding, H., Jiang, X., Liu, A.Q., Thalmann, N.M., Wang, G.: Boundary-aware feature propagation for scene segmentation. In: ICCV, pp. 6819–6829 (2019)

16. Ding, X., Guo, Y., Ding, G., Han, J.: Acnet: strengthening the kernel skeletons for powerful cnn via asymmetric convolution blocks. In: ICCV, pp. 1911–1920 (2019)

17. French, G., Laine, S., Aila, T., Mackiewicz, M., Finlayson, G.: Semi-supervised semantic segmentation needs strong, varied perturbations. In: BMVC (2020)

18. Fu, J., Liu, J., Tian, H., Li, Y., Bao, Y., Fang, Z., Lu, H.: Dual attention network for scene segmentation. In: CVPR, pp. 3146–3154 (2019)

19. Ganin, Y., et al.: Domain-adversarial training of neural networks. JMLR **17**(1), 2030–2096 (2016)

20. Gao, L., Zhang, J., Zhang, L., Tao, D.: DSP: dual Soft-Paste for unsupervised domain adaptive semantic segmentation. In: ACMMM, pp. 2825–2833 (2021). arXiv:2107.09600

21. Gong, R., Li, W., Chen, Y., Dai, D., Van Gool, L.: Dlow: domain flow and applications. IJCV **129**(10), 2865–2888 (2021)

22. Goodfellow, I., et al.: Generative adversarial nets. In: NeurIPS, pp. 2672–2680 (2014)

23. Guan, D., Huang, J., Lu, S., Xiao, A.: Scale variance minimization for unsupervised domain adaptation in image segmentation. Pattern Recogn. **112**, 107764 (2021)

24. He, K., Zhang, X., Ren, S., Sun, J.: Deep residual learning for image recognition. In: CVPR, pp. 770–778 (2016)

25. Hoffman, J., et al.: Cycada: cycle-consistent adversarial domain adaptation. In: ICML, pp. 1989–1998 (2018)

26. Hoffman, J., Wang, D., Yu, F., Darrell, T.: Fcns in the wild: pixel-level adversarial and constraint-based adaptation. arXiv preprint. arXiv:1612.02649 (2016)

27. Hoyer, L., Dai, D., Chen, Y., Köring, A., Saha, S., Van Gool, L.: Three ways to improve semantic segmentation with self-supervised depth estimation. In: CVPR, pp. 11130–11140 (2021)

28. Hoyer, L., Dai, D., Van Gool, L.: DAFormer: improving network architectures and training strategies for domain-adaptive semantic segmentation. In: CVPR (2022)

29. Hoyer, L., Dai, D., Wang, Q., Chen, Y., Van Gool, L.: Improving semi-supervised and domain-adaptive semantic segmentation with self-supervised depth estimation. arXiv preprint. arXiv:2108.12545 (2021)

30. Hoyer, L., Munoz, M., Katiyar, P., Khoreva, A., Fischer, V.: Grid saliency for context explanations of semantic segmentation. In: NeurIPS, pp. 6462–6473 (2019)
31. Huang, J., Lu, S., Guan, D., Zhang, X.: Contextual-relation consistent domain adaptation for semantic segmentation. In: Vedaldi, A., Bischof, H., Brox, T., Frahm, J.-M. (eds.) ECCV 2020. LNCS, vol. 12360, pp. 705–722. Springer, Cham (2020). https://doi.org/10.1007/978-3-030-58555-6_42
32. Huang, Z., Wang, X., Huang, L., Huang, C., Wei, Y., Liu, W.: Ccnet: criss-cross attention for semantic segmentation. In: ICCV, pp. 603–612 (2019)
33. Iqbal, J., Ali, M.: Mlsl: multi-level self-supervised learning for domain adaptation with spatially independent and semantically consistent labeling. In: WACV, pp. 1864–1873 (2020)
34. Kim, M., Byun, H.: Learning texture invariant representation for domain adaptation of semantic segmentation. In: CVPR, pp. 12975–12984 (2020)
35. Lai, X., et al.: Semi-supervised semantic segmentation with directional context-aware consistency. In: CVPR, pp. 1205–1214 (2021)
36. Li, X., et al.: Improving semantic segmentation via decoupled body and edge supervision. In: Vedaldi, A., Bischof, H., Brox, T., Frahm, J.-M. (eds.) ECCV 2020. LNCS, vol. 12362, pp. 435–452. Springer, Cham (2020). https://doi.org/10.1007/978-3-030-58520-4_26
37. Li, Y., Yuan, L., Vasconcelos, N.: Bidirectional learning for domain adaptation of semantic segmentation. In: CVPR, pp. 6936–6945 (2019)
38. Lin, D., Shen, D., Shen, S., Ji, Y., Lischinski, D., Cohen-Or, D., Huang, H.: Zigzagnet: fusing top-down and bottom-up context for object segmentation. In: CVPR, pp. 7490–7499 (2019)
39. Liu, Y., Deng, J., Gao, X., Li, W., Duan, L.: Bapa-net: boundary adaptation and prototype alignment for cross-domain semantic segmentation. In: ICCV, pp. 8801–8811 (2021)
40. Liu, Z., et al.: Swin transformer: hierarchical vision transformer using shifted windows. In: ICCV, pp. 10012–1110022 (2021)
41. Long, J., Shelhamer, E., Darrell, T.: Fully convolutional networks for semantic segmentation. In: CVPR, pp. 3431–3440 (2015)
42. Loshchilov, I., Hutter, F.: Decoupled weight decay regularization. In: ICLR (2018)
43. Mei, K., Zhu, C., Zou, J., Zhang, S.: Instance adaptive self-training for unsupervised domain adaptation. In: Vedaldi, A., Bischof, H., Brox, T., Frahm, J.-M. (eds.) ECCV 2020. LNCS, vol. 12371, pp. 415–430. Springer, Cham (2020). https://doi.org/10.1007/978-3-030-58574-7_25
44. Melas-Kyriazi, L., Manrai, A.K.: Pixmatch: unsupervised domain adaptation via pixelwise consistency training. In: CVPR, pp. 12435–12445 (2021)
45. Pizzati, F., Charette, R.d., Zaccaria, M., Cerri, P.: Domain bridge for unpaired image-to-image translation and unsupervised domain adaptation. In: WACV, pp. 2990–2998 (2020)
46. Prabhu, V., Khare, S., Kartik, D., Hoffman, J.: Augco: augmentation consistency-guided self-training for source-free domain adaptive semantic segmentation. arXiv preprint. arXiv:2107.10140 (2021)
47. Richter, S.R., Vineet, V., Roth, S., Koltun, V.: Playing for data: ground truth from computer games. In: ECCV, pp. 102–118 (2016). https://download.visinf.tu-darmstadt.de/data/from_games/
48. Ronneberger, O., Fischer, P., Brox, T.: U-Net: convolutional networks for biomedical image segmentation. In: Navab, N., Hornegger, J., Wells, W.M., Frangi, A.F. (eds.) MICCAI 2015. LNCS, vol. 9351, pp. 234–241. Springer, Cham (2015). https://doi.org/10.1007/978-3-319-24574-4_28

49. Ros, G., Sellart, L., Materzynska, J., Vazquez, D., Lopez, A.M.: The synthia dataset: a large collection of synthetic images for semantic segmentation of urban scenes. In: CVPR, pp. 3234–3243 (2016). http://synthia-dataset.net/, dataset license: CC BY-NC-SA 3.0

50. Sajjadi, M., Javanmardi, M., Tasdizen, T.: Regularization with stochastic transformations and perturbations for deep semi-supervised learning. In: NeurIPS (2016)

51. Sakaridis, C., Dai, D., Van Gool, L.: ACDC:the adverse conditions dataset with correspondences for semantic driving scene understanding. In: ICCV, pp. 10765–10775 (2021)

52. Sohn, K., et al.: Fixmatch: simplifying semi-supervised learning with consistency and confidence. In: NeurIPS (2020)

53. Souly, N., Spampinato, C., Shah, M.: Semi supervised semantic segmentation using generative adversarial network. In: ICCV, pp. 5688–5696 (2017)

54. Strudel, R., Garcia, R., Laptev, I., Schmid, C.: Segmenter: transformer for semantic segmentation. In: ICCV, pp. 7262–7272 (2021)

55. Subhani, M.N., Ali, M.: Learning from scale-invariant examples for domain adaptation in semantic segmentation. In: Vedaldi, A., Bischof, H., Brox, T., Frahm, J.-M. (eds.) ECCV 2020. LNCS, vol. 12367, pp. 290–306. Springer, Cham (2020). https://doi.org/10.1007/978-3-030-58542-6_18

56. Tao, A., Sapra, K., Catanzaro, B.: Hierarchical multi-scale attention for semantic segmentation. arXiv preprint. arXiv:2005.10821 (2020)

57. Tarvainen, A., Valpola, H.: Mean teachers are better role models: weight-averaged consistency targets improve semi-supervised deep learning results. In: NeurIPS, pp. 1195–1204 (2017)

58. Tranheden, W., Olsson, V., Pinto, J., Svensson, L.: DACS: domain adaptation via cross-domain mixed sampling. In: WACV, pp. 1379–1389 (2021)

59. Tsai, Y.H., Hung, W.C., Schulter, S., Sohn, K., Yang, M.H., Chandraker, M.: Learning to adapt structured output space for semantic segmentation. In: CVPR, pp. 7472–7481 (2018)

60. Tsai, Y.H., Sohn, K., Schulter, S., Chandraker, M.: Domain adaptation for structured output via discriminative patch representations. In: ICCV, pp. 1456–1465 (2019)

61. Unal, O., Dai, D., Van Gool, L.: Scribble-supervised lidar semantic segmentation. In: CVPR, pp. 2697–2707 (2022)

62. Vu, T.H., Jain, H., Bucher, M., Cord, M., Pérez, P.: Advent: adversarial entropy minimization for domain adaptation in semantic segmentation. In: CVPR, pp. 2517–2526 (2019)

63. Vu, T.H., Jain, H., Bucher, M., Cord, M., Pérez, P.: Dada: depth-aware domain adaptation in semantic segmentation. In: ICCV, pp. 7364–7373 (2019)

64. Wang, H., Shen, T., Zhang, W., Duan, L.-Y., Mei, T.: Classes matter: a fine-grained adversarial approach to cross-domain semantic segmentation. In: Vedaldi, A., Bischof, H., Brox, T., Frahm, J.-M. (eds.) ECCV 2020. LNCS, vol. 12359, pp. 642–659. Springer, Cham (2020). https://doi.org/10.1007/978-3-030-58568-6_38

65. Wang, J., et al.: Deep high-resolution representation learning for visual recognition. PAMI **43**(10), 3349–3364 (2020)

66. Wang, Q., Dai, D., Hoyer, L., Fink, O., Van Gool, L.: Domain adaptive semantic segmentation with self-supervised depth estimation. In: ICCV, pp. 8515–8525 (2021)

67. Wang, Q., Fink, O., Van Gool, L., Dai, D.: Continual test-time domain adaptation. In: CVPR, pp. 7201–7211 (2022)

68. Wang, W., et al.: Pyramid vision transformer: a versatile backbone for dense prediction without convolutions. In: ICCV, pp. 568–578 (2021)
69. Wang, X., Girshick, R., Gupta, A., He, K.: Non-local neural networks. In: CVPR, pp. 7794–7803 (2018)
70. Xie, E., Wang, W., Yu, Z., Anandkumar, A., Alvarez, J.M., Luo, P.: SegFormer: simple and efficient design for semantic segmentation with transformers. In: NeurIPS (2021)
71. Yang, J., An, W., Yan, C., Zhao, P., Huang, J.: Context-aware domain adaptation in semantic segmentation. In: WACV, pp. 514–524 (2021)
72. Yang, S., Peng, G.: Attention to refine through multi scales for semantic segmentation. In: Hong, R., Cheng, W.-H., Yamasaki, T., Wang, M., Ngo, C.-W. (eds.) PCM 2018. LNCS, vol. 11165, pp. 232–241. Springer, Cham (2018). https://doi.org/10.1007/978-3-030-00767-6_22
73. Yang, Y., Soatto, S.: Fda: fourier domain adaptation for semantic segmentation. In: CVPR, pp. 4085–4095 (2020)
74. Yu, F., Koltun, V.: Multi-scale context aggregation by dilated convolutions. arXiv preprint. arXiv:1511.07122 (2015)
75. Yuan, Y., Chen, X., Wang, J.: Object-contextual representations for semantic segmentation. In: Vedaldi, A., Bischof, H., Brox, T., Frahm, J.-M. (eds.) ECCV 2020. LNCS, vol. 12351, pp. 173–190. Springer, Cham (2020). https://doi.org/10.1007/978-3-030-58539-6_11
76. Yuan, Y., Huang, L., Guo, J., Zhang, C., Chen, X., Wang, J.: OCNet: object context for semantic segmentation. Int. J. Comput. Vis. **129**(8), 2375–2398 (2021). https://doi.org/10.1007/s11263-021-01465-9
77. Yuan, Y., Xie, J., Chen, X., Wang, J.: SegFix: model-agnostic boundary refinement for segmentation. In: Vedaldi, A., Bischof, H., Brox, T., Frahm, J.-M. (eds.) ECCV 2020. LNCS, vol. 12357, pp. 489–506. Springer, Cham (2020). https://doi.org/10.1007/978-3-030-58610-2_29
78. Zhang, H., et al.: Context encoding for semantic segmentation. In: CVPR, pp. 7151–7160 (2018)
79. Zhang, K., Sun, Y., Wang, R., Li, H., Hu, X.: Multiple fusion adaptation: A strong framework for unsupervised semantic segmentation adaptation. In: BMVC (2021)
80. Zhang, P., Zhang, B., Zhang, T., Chen, D., Wang, Y., Wen, F.: Prototypical pseudo label denoising and target structure learning for domain adaptive semantic segmentation. In: CVPR, pp. 12414–12424 (2021)
81. Zhang, Q., Zhang, J., Liu, W., Tao, D.: Category anchor-guided unsupervised domain adaptation for semantic segmentation. In: NeurIPS, pp. 435–445 (2019)
82. Zhang, Y., David, P., Foroosh, H., Gong, B.: A curriculum domain adaptation approach to the semantic segmentation of urban scenes. PAMI **42**(8), 1823–1841 (2019)
83. Zhao, H., Shi, J., Qi, X., Wang, X., Jia, J.: Pyramid scene parsing network. In: CVPR, pp. 2881–2890 (2017)
84. Zhao, H., Zhang, Y., Liu, S., Shi, J., Loy, C.C., Lin, D., Jia, J.: PSANet: point-wise spatial attention network for scene parsing. In: Ferrari, V., Hebert, M., Sminchisescu, C., Weiss, Y. (eds.) ECCV 2018. LNCS, vol. 11213, pp. 270–286. Springer, Cham (2018). https://doi.org/10.1007/978-3-030-01240-3_17
85. Zheng, S., et al.: Rethinking semantic segmentation from a sequence-to-sequence perspective with transformers. In: CVPR, pp. 6881–6890 (2021)
86. Zheng, Z., Yang, Y.: Unsupervised scene adaptation with memory regularization in vivo. In: IJCAI, pp. 1076–1082 (2020)

87. Zheng, Z., Yang, Y.: Rectifying pseudo label learning via uncertainty estimation for domain adaptive semantic segmentation. Int. J. Comput. Vis. **129**(4), 1106–1120 (2021). https://doi.org/10.1007/s11263-020-01395-y

88. Zhou, Q., et al.: Uncertainty-aware consistency regularization for cross-domain semantic segmentation. arXiv preprint. arXiv:2004.08878 (2020)

89. Zhou, Q., et al.: Context-aware mixup for domain adaptive semantic segmentation. In: WACV, pp. 514–524 (2021)

90. Zhou, T., Brown, M., Snavely, N., Lowe, D.G.: Unsupervised learning of depth and ego-motion from video. In: CVPR, pp. 1851–1858 (2017)

91. Zhou, Y., Sun, X., Zha, Z.J., Zeng, W.: Context-reinforced semantic segmentation. In: CVPR, pp. 4046–4055 (2019)

92. Zou, Y., Yu, Z., Vijaya Kumar, B.V.K., Wang, J.: Unsupervised domain adaptation for semantic segmentation via class-balanced self-training. In: Ferrari, V., Hebert, M., Sminchisescu, C., Weiss, Y. (eds.) ECCV 2018. LNCS, vol. 11207, pp. 297–313. Springer, Cham (2018). https://doi.org/10.1007/978-3-030-01219-9_18

93. Zou, Y., Zhang, Z., Zhang, H., Li, C.L., Bian, X., Huang, J.B., Pfister, T.: Pseudoseg: Designing pseudo labels for semantic segmentation. In: ICLR (2021)

SPot-the-Difference Self-supervised Pre-training for Anomaly Detection and Segmentation

Yang Zou[1]([✉]), Jongheon Jeong[2], Latha Pemula[1], Dongqing Zhang[1], and Onkar Dabeer[1]

[1] AWS AI Labs, Seattle, USA
{yanzo,lppemula,zdongqin,onkardab}@amazon.com
[2] KAIST, Daejeon, South Korea
jongheonj@kaist.ac.kr

Abstract. Visual anomaly detection is commonly used in industrial quality inspection. In this paper, we present a new dataset as well as a new self-supervised learning method for ImageNet pre-training to improve anomaly detection and segmentation in 1-class and 2-class 5/10/high-shot training setups. We release the Visual Anomaly (VisA) Dataset consisting of 10,821 high-resolution color images (9,621 normal and 1,200 anomalous samples) covering 12 objects in 3 domains, making it the largest industrial anomaly detection dataset to date. Both image and pixel-level labels are provided. We also propose a new self-supervised framework - SPot-the-difference (SPD) - which can regularize contrastive self-supervised pre-training, such as SimSiam, MoCo and SimCLR, to be more suitable for anomaly detection tasks. Our experiments on VisA and MVTec-AD dataset show that SPD consistently improves these contrastive pre-training baselines and even the supervised pre-training. For example, SPD improves Area Under the Precision-Recall curve (AU-PR) for anomaly segmentation by 5.9% and 6.8% over SimSiam and supervised pre-training respectively in the 2-class high-shot regime. We open-source the project at http://github.com/amazon-research/spot-diff.

Keywords: Representation learning · Pre-training · Anomaly detection · Anomaly segmentation · Industrial anomaly dataset

1 Introduction

Visual surface anomaly detection and segmentation identify and localize defects in industrial manufacturing [3]. While anomaly detection and segmentation are

---

J. Jeong—Work done during an Amazon internship.

Supplementary Information The online version contains supplementary material available at https://doi.org/10.1007/978-3-031-20056-4_23.

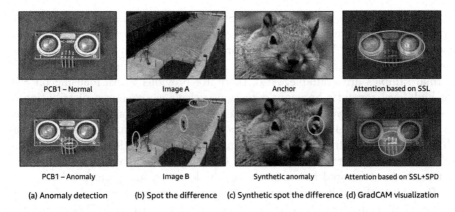

PCB1 – Normal   Image A   Anchor   Attention based on SSL

PCB1 – Anomaly   Image B   Synthetic anomaly   Attention based on SSL+SPD

(a) Anomaly detection   (b) Spot the difference   (c) Synthetic spot the difference   (d) GradCAM visualization

Fig. 1. (a) Normal and anomalous samples of VisA - PCB1 with real defect (molten metal), anomaly highlighted by red ellipse; (b) A pair of images for the spot-the-difference (SPD) puzzle [25]; (c) An anchor image and its variant augmented by SmoothBlend for synthetic spot-the-difference; (d) GradCAM attention visualization for PCB1 - Anomaly image based on self-supervised ImageNet pre-training w/wo proposed SPD. With SPD, attention is more focused on the local defects. (Color figure online)

instances of image classification and semantic segmentation problems, respectively, they have unique challenges. First, defects are rare, and it is hard to obtain a large number of anomalous images. Second, common types of anomalies, such as surface scratches and damages, are often small. Figure 1 (a) gives an example. Third, manufacturing is a performance sensitive domain and usually requires highly accurate models. Fourth, inspection in manufacturing spans a wide range of domains and tasks, from detecting leakages in capsules to finding damaged millimeter-sized components on a complex circuit board.

Upon the aforementioned challenges, previous surface anomaly detection models have been typically trained for a particular object and require re-training for different ones. For each object, there are only slight global differences in lighting and object pose/positions across images while the diversity in the defects on objects is large. Moreover, due to the rarity of anomalous data, there has been a predominant focus on 1-class anomaly detection, which only requires normal images for model training [6,10,14,26,33,44]. In mature manufacturing domains, anomalous samples are also available and sometimes sufficient. In such cases, one can improve over 1-class methods with a standard 2-class model [12,18,21,27] by incorporating the anomalous data in training, which is in fact a well-established practice in commercial visual inspection AI services [1,2]. For both setups, existing state-of-the-art methods for surface anomaly detection commonly leverage supervised representations pre-trained on ImageNet [16], either as feature extractors [14,33] or as initialization for fine-tuning on the target dataset [26,44].

Meanwhile, recent advances in self-supervised learning (SSL) have shown that pre-trained representations learned without categorical labels might be a better choice for transfer learning compared to those from supervised in object detection and segmentation [8,9,23]. However, their application to anomaly detection and segmentation is underdeveloped. SSL for surface anomaly detection was explored in CutPaste [26] to learn representation from downstream images for each specific object. However, such representations hardly generalize to different objects and can lead to overfitting in a practical setting where only 1–20 normal samples are available. Also, there are previous works focusing on SSL for high-level semantic anomaly detection such as cat among a distribution of dogs [11,13,37]. However, as [35] pointed out, surface anomaly detection aims to spot the low-level textual anomalies such as scratch and crack which has challenges different from semantic anomaly detection. Until now, the universal self-supervised pre-trained representation with good generalization ability have not yet been attempted for surface anomaly detection and segmentation.

Regarding the evaluation protocol, the community has been experiencing the lack of challenging benchmarks. The popular MVTec Anomaly Detection (AD) benchmark [3] is saturating with the Area Under the Receiver Operating Characteristic (AU-ROC) approaching $\sim$95% [14,26], and the benchmark is limited to the 1-class setup. But the anomaly detection problems in practice is still far from solved, demanding new datasets and metrics that better represent the real-world. In this paper, we introduce a new challenging Visual Anomaly (VisA) dataset. VisA is collected to present several new characteristics: objects with complex structures such as printed circuit board (PCB), multiple instances with different locations in a single view, 12 different objects spanning 3 domains, and multiple anomaly classes (up to 9) for each object. VisA contains 10,821 high-resolution color images - 9,621 normal and 1,200 anomalous - with both image and pixel-level labels. To our best knowledge, VisA is currently the largest and most challenging public dataset for anomaly classification and segmentation. Moreover, to cover different use cases in practice, we establish benchmarks not only in standard 1-class training setup but also 2-class training setups with 5/10/high-shot. For evaluation, we propose to use Area Under the Precision-Recall curve (AU-PR) in combination with standard AU-ROC. In the imbalanced defect dataset, AU-ROC might present inflated view of performances and AU-PR is more informative to measure anomaly detection performance [11,13,37].

In addition to an improved dataset, we also explore self-supervision to improve anomaly detection. As we argue below, our hypothesis is that previous contrastive SSL methods [8,9,23] are sub-optimal to transfer learning for anomaly detection. Specifically, SimCLR, MoCo and other methods regard globally augmented images of a given image as one class and other images in the same batch as negative classes. Transformations, such as cropping and color jittering, are applied globally to the anchor for positives generation. The InfoNCE or cosine similarity losses [8,9,23] encourage invariance to these global deformations, and capturing semantic information instead of local details [19]. However, anomaly detection relies on local textual details to spot defects. Thus the subtle and local intra-object (or intra-class) differences are important but not well modeled by previous methods. Figure 1 (d) illustrates the sub-optimality in one of the previous SSL methods using the GradCAM attention map [38]. As far as we know, improving representations by self-supervision for better downstream anomaly detection/segmentation has not been studied before and we explore this angle.

Inspired by the spot-the-difference puzzle shown in Fig. 1 (b), we propose a contrastive SPot-the-Difference (SPD) training to promote the local sensitivity of previous SSL methods. In the puzzle, players need to be sensitive to the subtle differences between the two globally alike images, which is similar to anomaly detection. In the contrastive SPD training, as shown in Fig. 1 (c), a novel augmentation called SmoothBlend is proposed to produce the local perturbations on SPD negatives for synthetic spot-the-difference. The (locally) augmented images are regarded as negatives, which is different from regarding (globally) augmented images as positives in SimCLR/MoCo. Moreover, weak global augmentations, such as weak cropping and color jittering, are also applied to the SPD negatives as anomaly detection should spot defects under slight global changes in lighting and object pose/position. Additionally, to prevent models from using the slight global changes as shortcuts to differentiate negatives, SPD positives are generated by applying weak global augmentations on the anchor. Lastly, SPD training minimizes the feature similarities between SPD negative pairs while maximizing the similarities between SPD positives, which encourages models to be locally sensitive to anomalous patterns and invariant to slight global variations.

Our main contributions are as follows:

1. We propose a new VisA dataset, $2\times$ larger than MVTec-AD, with both image and pixel-level annotations. It spans 12 objects across 3 domains, with challenging scenarios including complex structures in objects, multiple instances and object pose/location variations. Moreover, we establish both 1-class and 5/10/high-shot 2-class benchmarks to cover different use cases.
2. To promote the local sensitivity to anomalous patterns, a SPot-the-Difference (SPD) training is proposed to regularize self-supervised ImageNet pre-training, which benefits their transfer-learning ability for anomaly detection and localization. As far as we know, we are the first one to explore self-supervised pre-training on large-scale datasets for surface defect detection tasks.
3. Compared to strong self-supervised pre-training baselines such as SimSiam, MoCo and SimCLR, extensive experiments show our proposed SPD learning improves them for better anomaly detection and segmentation. We also show the SPD improves over supervised ImageNet pre-training for both tasks.

2   Related Works

Unsupervised Anomaly Detection and Segmentation use only normal samples to train models, which have drawn extensive attention. Many recent methods are proposed to detect low-level texture anomalies [35], such as scratches and cracks, which are common cases in industrial visual inspection [15,31,34,44]. SPADE [14] and PatchCore [33] extract features at patch level and use nearest neighbor methods to classify patches and images as anomalies. PaDiM [14] learns a parametric distribution over patches for anomaly detection. CutPaste [26] learns a representation based on images augmented by cut-and-pasted patches. The supervised ImageNet models are used in these methods either as feature extractors or initialization for fine-tuning. However, self-

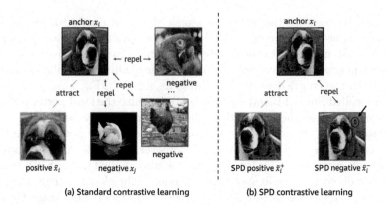

Fig. 2. (a) Contrastive learning in SimCLR, MoCo and SimSiam; (b) Contrastive learning in SPD training. Local deformation in SPD negative is highlighted by circle.

supervised pre-training on large-scale datasets is an unexplored area for quality inspection applications. In addition, several works [30,36,39,40] focus on high-level semantic anomaly detection. As mentioned in [35], semantic anomaly detection approaches can be less effective for texture anomaly detection as their challenges are different.

Self-supervised Learning (SSL) have gathered momentum in the last 5 years. Several surrogate tasks have been proposed for self-supervision, such as image colorization [46], rotation prediction [20], jigsaw puzzles [29]. Recently, multi-view based methods such as MoCo [23], SimCLR [8], SimSiam [9] and BYOL [22] present better or comparable performances than supervised pre-training in transfer learning tasks including image classification, object detection [43] and semantic segmentation [41]. Moreover, to promote spatial details of representations for localization tasks, several approaches proposed to encourage the invariance of patch features to global augmentations [7,28,41,42], although they may not lead to local sensitivity to tiny defects. As far as we know, none of these works explored their generalization ability to surface defect detection tasks.

3   SPot-the-Difference (SPD) Regularization

To promote local sensitivity of standard self-supervised contrastive learning, we propose a contrastive SPot-the-Difference (SPD) regularization. As mentioned earlier, SPD aims to increase model invariance to slight global changes by maximizing the feature similarity between an image and its weak global augmentation, while forcing dissimilarity for local perturbations, as shown in Fig. 2 (b). In the following, we first present background in contrastive learning, and then the augmentations used in SPD followed by the learning with SPD.

3.1   Background on Self-supervised Contrastive Learning

Many self-supervised learning methods, such as SimCLR [8] and MoCo [23], are based on contrastive learning. As shown in Fig. 2 (a), given an image, these

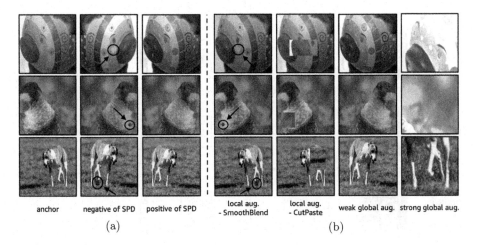

			local aug.	local aug.		
anchor	negative of SPD	positive of SPD	- SmoothBlend	- CutPaste	weak global aug.	strong global aug.
(a)			(b)			

Fig. 3. (a) Samples for synthetic spot-the-difference; (b) Augmentation comparison.

methods maximize the feature similarity between two strongly augmented samples x_i and $\hat{x}_i$ while minimizing the similarities between the anchor x_i and other images x_j's in the same batch of size N. Strong global augmentations, such as grayscaling, large cropping and strong color jittering, are used to get positives. Typically, an encoder extracts features $h_i, \hat{h}_i$ and h_j's which are inputs to a multilayer perceptron (MLP) head. The MLP head extracts the L2 normalized embeddings $z_i, \hat{z}_i$ and z_j's to compute the InfoNCE loss defined as follows.

$$\mathcal{L}_{\mathrm{NCE}}(x_i, \hat{x}_i) = -\log \frac{\exp(z_i \cdot \hat{z}_i / \tau)}{\exp(z_i \cdot \hat{z}_i / \tau) + \sum_{j=1}^{N} \mathbb{1}_{j \neq i} \exp(z_i, z_j / \tau)} \tag{1}$$

τ is a temperature scaling hyperparameter. In addition, SimSiam [9] shows that self-supervised models can be trained even without negatives where only similarity modeling is implemented for positives.

Remark: Images augmented by most strong global transformations in SSL, such as grayscaling and large cropping, share semantics with anchor but with different local details (a dog v.s. a dog head). Thus to maximize their similarity, the features are forced to be invariant about local details and capture the global semantics. This is even enforced by minimizing similarities between anchor and different images in a batch as they have different global structures [8,17]. This further motivates us to promote local sensitivity in SSL for anomaly detection.

3.2   Augmentations for SPD

Local Augmentation: In SPD, the locally deformed images, rather than other images of a batch in standard contrastive training, are used as negatives. Smooth-Blend is proposed to produce local deformations. The first column in Fig. 3 (b) presents the samples augmented by SmoothBlend. It is implemented by a smoothed alpha blending between an image and a small randomly cut patch of

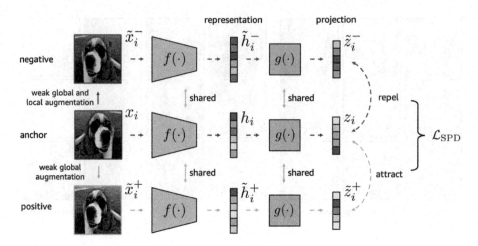

Fig. 4. The contrastive spot-the-difference learning.

the same image. Specifically, color jittering is applied to a cut patch. Then an all-zero foreground layer u is created with the patch pasted to a random location. An alpha mask α is created where the pixels corresponding to the pasted patch are set to 1 otherwise 0, followed by a Gaussian blur. Finally, the augmented sample is obtained by $\bar{x} = (1 - \alpha) \odot x + \alpha \odot u$. $\odot$ is the element-wise product.

Global Augmentation: To generate global variations for both SPD positives and negatives, we use weak global augmentation. Adding global variations to SPD is motivated by the potentially small global variations in realistic manufacturing environment, such as lighting, object positions, etc. To simulate such slight changes, we choose weak random cropping, Gaussian blurring, horizontal flipping and color jittering. Such weak global augmentations are different from strong transformations used in SimSiam, SimCLR and MoCo which is illustrated by last two columns in Fig. 3 (b). As we can see, there might be just 20% overlap between the anchor and strongly augmented positive. If the network is designed to maximize the distance between negatives with only subtle changes while minimizing the distance between positives with largely global transformations, it is a confusing task which might harm representation learning for anomaly detection.

Remark: SmoothBlend is a smoothed version of CutPaste augmentation proposed in [26]. Both of them can be used to generate structural local deformations, illustrated by the first two columns in Fig. 3 (b). Unlike the sharp edges of the CutPaste patches, the local and subtle perturbations with smooth edges from SmoothBlend provides a challenging puzzle for models.

3.3   Training with SPD

Based on the above augmentations, we propose the SPD learning illustrated by Fig. 4 with Fig. 3 (a) presents more SPD training samples. For an anchor image x_i, a negative $\tilde{x}_i^-$ is generated by applying weak global augmentations followed by SmoothBlend. The positive $\tilde{x}_i^+$ is produced by weak global transformations only.

Then a shared feature extractor $f(\cdot)$ extracts the representations $h_i, \tilde{h}_i^-, \tilde{h}_i^+$ (h_i's are used for downstream anomaly detection tasks). They are further inputted into a shared multilayer perceptron (MLP) $g(\cdot)$ to get the projections $z_i, \tilde{z}_i^-, \tilde{z}_i^+$. The cosine similarity between $z_i, \tilde{z}_i^-$ is minimized while similarity between $z_i, \tilde{z}_i^+$ is maximized. In summary, the SPD learning minimizes the following SPD loss.

$$\mathcal{L}_{\mathrm{SPD}}(x_i, \tilde{x}_i^-, \tilde{x}_i^+) = \cos(z_i, \tilde{z}_i^-) - \cos(z_i, \tilde{z}_i^+). \tag{2}$$

Standard Contrastive SSL with SPD: Regularizing SSL with SPD is simple. Taking SimCLR as an example baseline, for a given image, SimCLR generates the anchor x_i and positive $\hat{x}_i$ via strong global augmentations with other images x_j's in the same batch as negatives. Then SPD positives $\hat{x}_i^+$ and negatives $\hat{x}_i^-$ are generated by SmoothBlend and weak global augmentations. The shared encoder and MLP head in SimCLR are used to extract the image feature projections for loss computation. Finally the network is trained by the following combined loss.

$$\mathcal{L}(x_i, \hat{x}_i, \tilde{x}_i^-, \tilde{x}_i^+) = \mathcal{L}_{\mathrm{NCE}}(x_i, \hat{x}_i) + \eta \cdot \mathcal{L}_{\mathrm{SPD}}(x_i, \tilde{x}_i^-, \tilde{x}_i^+) \tag{3}$$

Similarly, we can apply SPD to MoCo. For SimSiam, $\mathcal{L}_{\mathrm{NCE}}(x_i, \hat{x}_i)$ loss is replaced by a cosine distance loss for positive pairs without considering negatives [9].

Standard Supervised Pre-training with SPD: With the class labels, standard supervised pre-trained features also capture global semantics to distinguish categories with less attention to local details, similar to SSL. Thus SPD could improve its local sensitivity. Specifically, on top of the last feature layer of the standard supervised model (ResNet-50 [24]), an auxiliary classifier is added to classify if an augmented SPD image has a local perturbation or not, which is trained by cross-entropy loss. The backbone is shared to extract features.

4   Visual Anomaly (VisA) Dataset

4.1   Dataset Description

The VisA dataset contains 12 subsets corresponding to 12 different objects. Figure 5 gives images in VisA. There are 10,821 images with 9,621 normal and 1,200 anomalous samples. Four subsets are different types of printed circuit boards (PCB) with relatively complex structures containing transistors, capacitors, chips, etc. For the case of multiple instances in a view, we collect four subsets: Capsules, Candles, Macaroni1 and Macaroni2.

Table 1. Overview of VisA dataset.

	Object	# Normal samples	# Anomaly samples	# Anomaly classes
Complex structure	PCB1	1,004	100	4
	PCB2	1,001	100	4
	PCB3	1,006	100	4
	PCB4	1,005	100	7
Multiple instances	Capsules	602	100	5
	Candle	1,000	100	8
	Macaroni1	1,000	100	7
	Macaroni2	1,000	100	7
Single instance	Cashew	500	100	9
	Chewing gum	503	100	6
	Fryum	500	100	8
	Pipe fryum	500	100	6

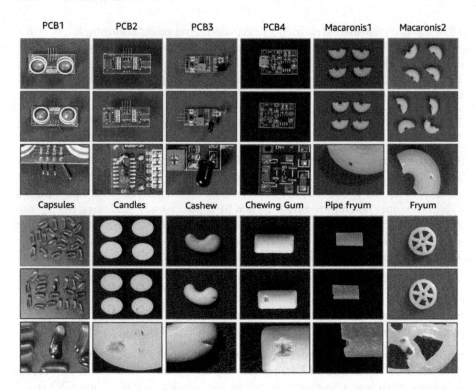

Fig. 5. Samples of VisA datasets. First row: normal images; Second row: anomalous images; Third row: anomalies viewed by zooming in.

Instances in Capsules and Macaroni2 largely differ in locations and poses. Moreover, we collect four subsets including Cashew, Chewing gum, Fryum and Pipe fryum, where objects are roughly aligned. The anomalous images contain various flaws, including surface defects such as scratches, dents, color spots or crack, and structural defects like misplacement or missing parts. There are 5–20 images per defect type and an image may contain multiple defects. The defects were manually generated to produce realistic anomalies. All images were acquired using a $4,000 \times 6,000$ high-resolution RGB sensor. Both image and pixel-level annotations are provided. Table 1 gives the statistics of VisA dataset.

Figure 6 illustrates the differences between VisA and MVTec-AD. First, VisA considers more complex structures, comparing the VisA - PCB3 with multiple electronic components to a single one of MVTec - transistor as an example. Second, multiple objects can appear in VisA (Capsules) as opposed to a single object in MVTec-AD. Third, large variation in object locations is covered by VisA (Capsules) while almost all objects in MVTec-AD are roughly aligned. Lastly, MVTec-AD has 5, 354 images and VisA is 2× larger with 10, 821 images.

4.2 Evaluation Protocol and Metrics

We establish three evaluation protocols for each of 12 objects in VisA dataset. First, following MVTec-AD 1-class protocol, we establish VisA 1-class protocol

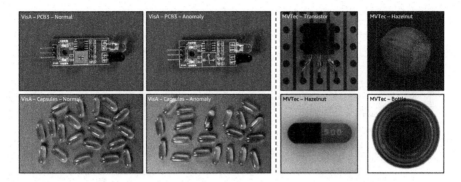

Fig. 6. Comparing VisA and MVTec-AD. VisA is more challenging due to the complex object structures, multiple instances, large variations of objects and scale.

by assigning 90% normal images to train set while 10% normal images and all anomalous samples are grouped as test set. Second, we establish 2-class high/low-shot evaluation protocols as proxies for realistic 2-class setups in commercial products [1,2]. In high-shot setup, for each object, 60%/40% normal and anomalous images are assigned to train/test set respectively. For low-shot benchmark, firstly, 20%/80% normal and anomalous images are grouped to train/test set respectively. Then the k-shot (k = 5,10) setup randomly samples k images from both classes in train set for training. The averaged performances over 5 random runs will be reported. Note that for both 1-class and 2-class training setups, test sets have samples from both classes. In addition, we report model performances averaged over all subsets of VisA and MVTec-AD in Sec. 5. The model performances for each subset are reported in Sec. D of supplementary.

For metrics, we report Area Under Precision-Recall curve (AU-PR) in combination with the Area Under Receiver Operator Characteristic curve (AU-ROC). AU-ROC is the most widely used metric for anomaly detection tasks [14,33,44]. But as pointed out in [11,13,37], in imbalanced dataset where performance of minor class is more important, AU-ROC might provide an inflated view of performance which may cause challenges in measuring models' true capabilities. This is true for anomaly detection where anomalies are often rare. In [3], the best method is Student-Teacher [5] with 92.2% AU-ROC which seems to be close to perfection. However, it only gets 59.9% AU-PR which is far-from satisfactory. The imbalance issue is more extreme in anomaly segmentation where normal pixels (negatives) can be tens/hundreds times more than anomalous pixels (positives). Even for a bad model, the false positive rate can be small due to numerous negatives, leading to a high AU-ROC. Thus we argue AU-PR is a better performance measurement. Our experiments also demonstrate this point.

5   Experiments

Datasets: For self-supervised as well as supervised pre-training, we use ImageNet 2012 classification dataset [16]. ImageNet consists 1,000 classes with 1.28

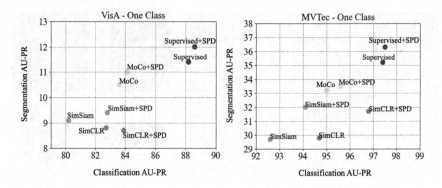

Fig. 7. Scatter plots for various ImageNet pre-training models in 1-class setup.

Table 2. 1-class performance evaluation of various ImageNet pre-training options on VisA and MVTec-AD with PaDiM. Bold numbers refers to the highest score. In the brackets are the gaps to the ImageNet supervised/self-supervised pre-training counterpart. In green are the gaps of at least $+0.5$ point.

	ImageNet labels	VisA (1-class)				MVTec-AD (1-class)			
		Classification		Segmentation		Classification		Segmentation	
		AU-PR	AU-ROC	AU-PR	AU-ROC	AU-PR	AU-ROC	AU-PR	AU-ROC
Sup. pre-train	✓	88.2	87.8	11.4	93.1	97.4	94.5	35.2	94.4
SimSiam	✗	80.2	78.1	9.1	93.1	92.6	83.9	29.7	92.1
+SPD	✗	82.8 (+2.6)	81.2 (+3.1)	9.4 (+0.3)	92.7 (-0.4)	94.1 (+1.5)	88.0 (+4.1)	32.0 (+2.3)	92.2 (+0.1)
MoCo	✗	83.6	83.4	10.5	93.4	95.0	90.4	33.2	93.4
+SPD	✗	84.1 (+0.5)	83.0 (-0.4)	11.0 (+0.5)	93.5 (+0.1)	95.6 (+0.6)	90.5 (+0.1)	33.5 (+0.3)	93.5 (+0.1)
SimCLR	✗	82.7	81.6	8.8	89.7	94.7	90.7	29.8	92.1
+SPD	✗	83.9 (+0.8)	82.6 (+1.0)	8.7 (-0.1)	89.9 (+0.2)	96.8 (+2.1)	93.8 (+3.1)	31.7 (+1.9)	92.9 (+0.8)
Sup. pre-train+SPD	✓	**88.6** (+0.4)	**87.8** (+0.0)	**12.0** (+0.6)	**93.8** (+0.7)	**97.5** (+0.1)	**94.6** (+0.1)	**36.3** (+1.1)	**94.6** (+0.2)

million training images. For downstream tasks, in addition to our VisA dataset, we use MVTec-AD dataset [4] as a 1-class training benchmark. MVTec-AD contains 15 sub-datasets with a total of $5,354$ images.

Anomaly Detection and Segmentation Algorithms: To evaluate the transfer learning performances of different pre-training, we adopt the following algorithms for anomaly detection and segmentation.

1-Class Anomaly Classification/Segmentation: We leverage PaDiM [14] which is one of the top performing 1-class anomaly detection/localization methods.

2-Class Anomaly Classification/Segmentation: We train a standard binary ResNet [24] as the supervised model for classification. A U-Net [32] is used as segmentation model. The focal loss [27] is used to overcome the data imbalance.

Implementation Details: Unless otherwise noted, we choose ResNet-50 as the major backbone. We adopt exactly the same hyperparameters in SimSiam, MoCo, SimCLR and supervised learning for pre-training. More implementation details are in the supplementary.

Table 3. 2-class fine-tuning with different pre-training on VisA high-shot setup.

	ImageNet labels	VisA (2-class, high-shot)			
		Classification		Segmentation	
		AU-PR	AU-ROC	AU-PR	AU-ROC
Sup. pre-train	✓	97.5	99.5	65.1	97.3
SimSiam	✗	88.7	97.9	53.8	97.3
+SPD	✗	93.2 (+4.5)	98.7 (+0.8)	59.7 (+5.9)	98.1 (+0.8)
MoCo	✗	93.9	98.8	62.4	98.0
+SPD	✗	94.2 (+0.3)	98.8 (+0.0)	64.4 (+2.0)	97.9 (-0.1)
SimCLR	✗	93.4	98.5	67.7	95.3
+SPD	✗	92.7 (-0.7)	98.6 (+0.1)	68.2 (+0.5)	95.7 (+0.4)
Sup. pre-train+SPD	✓	**98.3** (+0.8)	**99.7** (+0.2)	**71.9** (+6.8)	**98.5** (+1.2)

5.1   SPD in High-Shot 1-class/2-class Regimes

For the 1-class setting, the results of PaDiM with various pre-training options w/wo SPD are shown in Table 2. The results are also visualized as scatter plots in Fig. 7. We have several key observations. First, SPD improves performances of both anomaly detection and segmentation across almost all pre-training baselines on both VisA and MVTec-AD. While we report both AU-PR and AU-ROC, the former metric is more relevant to the application and we see that self-supervised methods are improved up to AU-PR of 2.6%. Note both metrics are averaged over the 12 objects in VisA. For different objects, the gains differ and are given in Sec. D of the supplementary. Second, the gap between self-supervised pre-training with SimSiam, SimCLR, MoCo, and supervised pre-training is large. SPD reduces this gap, but no combination of SSL and SPD beats supervised pre-training. This is in contrast to the low-shot regime in Sect. 5.2, where self-supervision has advantages in some cases. Third, PaDiM is one of the SOTA methods with >97% AU-ROC in MVTec. But it just achieves <90% AU-PR and AU-ROC in VisA - classification. For VisA ̄ - segmentation, PaDiM only achieves about 10% AU-PR. This shows the difficulty of the VisA 1-class benchmark. Moreover, the gap between low AU-PR and high AU-ROC for both VisA/MVTec segmentation justifies the inflated performance view of AU-ROC, in favor of AU-PR as a more suitable metric in imbalanced datasets. In addition, even in terms of AU-ROC, the SPD consistently improves almost all baselines.

In Table 3, we show the results for the 2-class high-shot regime on the VisA and observe similar trends as above. However, the AU-PR gains from SPD on top of SimSiam and supervised pre-training are higher at 5.9% and 6.8% respectively for segmentation. Another key point to note here is that the AU-ROC metrics are saturating even though AU-PR metrics show room for improvement, particularly for segmentation. This another data point for preferring AU-PR metric. Comparing Tables 2 and 3, there is a significant gap between 1-class and 2-class performance on VisA. As anomalies are harder to obtain compared to normal images, bridging the gap is an open challenge to the research community.

Table 4. Low-shot anomaly detection and segmentation on VisA.

	ImageNet labels	Classification (2-class, low-shot)				Segmentation (2-class, low-shot)			
		5-shot		10-shot		5-shot		10-shot	
		AU-PR	AU-ROC	AU-PR	AU-ROC	AU-PR	AU-ROC	AU-PR	AU-ROC
Sup. pre-train	✓	59.2	85.5	70.4	91.7	17.8	74.6	28.3	81.8
SimSiam	✗	51.9	82.3	65.0	89.4	17.3	75.2	28.5	81.6
+SPD	✗	56.1 (+4.2)	84.0 (+1.7)	67.6 (+2.6)	90.8 (+1.4)	18.2 (+0.9)	76.0 (+0.8)	29.7 (+1.2)	83.2 (+1.6)
MoCo	✗	56.1	83.8	68.7	90.6	21.5	80.5	32.3	**85.7**
+SPD	✗	56.4 (+0.3)	83.9 (+0.1)	68.0 (-0.7)	90.1 (-0.5)	**22.1** (+0.6)	78.5 (-2.0)	**32.8** (+0.5)	84.9 (-0.8)
SimCLR	✗	48.4	79.6	58.2	86.0	18.4	71.2	23.0	75.1
+SPD	✗	47.4 (-1.0)	79.9 (+0.3)	59.0 (+0.8)	86.1 (+0.1)	18.9 (+0.5)	74.5 (+3.3)	25.1 (+2.1)	78.2 (+3.1)
Sup. pre-train+SPD	✓	**59.8** (+0.6)	**85.9** (+0.4)	**71.2** (+0.8)	**92.1** (+0.4)	18.7 (+0.9)	75.9 (+1.3)	30.6 (+2.3)	81.8 (+0.0)

Table 5. Ablation study.

	VisA (1-class)				MVTec-AD (1-class)			
	Classification		Segmentation		Classification		Segmentation	
	AU-PR	AU-ROC	AU-PR	AU-ROC	AU-PR	AU-ROC	AU-PR	AU-ROC
SimSiam w/ Res50	80.2	78.1	9.1	93.1	92.6	83.9	29.7	92.1
+SPD ($\eta = 0.1$)	82.8	81.2	9.4	92.7	94.1	88.0	32.0	92.2
+SPD ($\eta = 0.5$)	80.5	79.3	8.7	93.0	93.3	84.9	30.1	91.9
+SPD ($\eta = 1.0$)	81.5	79.8	9.4	92.8	93.4	85.8	30.0	92.0
+SPD w/CutPaste	78.8	77.0	9.7	93.1	93.5	85.2	28.2	91.3
+SPD w/Xent	71.4	66.6	2.7	84.8	86.3	71.0	15.2	82.6
SimSiam w/WideRes50	80.3	77.7	9.9	93.6	93.0	84.7	31.3	92.2
+SPD	81.9	80.4	10.5	93.7	93.4	85.4	32.5	92.8

Table 6. 1-class performance evaluation on VisA and MVTec-AD with PatchCore.

Backbone: Wide ResNet50	VisA (1-class)				MVTec-AD (1-class)			
	Classification		Segmentation		Classification		Segmentation	
	AU-PR	AU-ROC	AU-PR	AU-ROC	AU-PR	AU-ROC	AU-PR	AU-ROC
Sup. pre-train	93.3	92.4	38.4	98.4	99.2	99.8	48.8	97.6
Sup. pre-train+SPD	93.8 (+0.5)	92.5 (+0.1)	39.3 (+0.9)	98.1 (-0.3)	99.0 (-0.2)	99.7 (-0.1)	49.3 (+0.5)	97.5 (-0.1)

5.2   SPD in Low-shot 2-Class Regime

Low-shot Anomaly Segmentation: With different ImageNet pre-training as initialization, a 2-class U-Net with ResNet-50 encoder is trained for each 5/10-shot segmentation setup. From Table 4, SPD again improves all baselines in both 5-shot and 10-shot evaluation, with AU-PR gain up to 2.3%. One departure from the high-shot regime is that for few-shot anomaly segmentation, MoCo+SPD is the best method, even outperforming supervised pre-training.

Low-shot Anomaly Detection: Initialized with different ImageNet pre-training, a 2-class ResNet-50 is trained in 5/10-shot setups for anomaly detection. From Table 4, overall the supervised pre-training with SPD outperforms both supervised pre-training only and other SSL's. Moreover, SPD significantly improves SimSiam with 4.2% AU-PR in 5-shot and 2.6% AU-PR in 10-shot, although it's still inferior to supervised pre-training.

5.3   Ablation Study

We conduct extensive ablation studies based on ImageNet SimSiam pre-training and PaDiM as the anomaly detection and segmentation algorithms trained in the 1-class setups of VisA and MVTec-AD. Results are shown in Table 5.

Sensitivity Analysis on SPD Loss Weight η: From Table 5, we see consistent improvement for $\eta = 0.1, 0.5, 1.0$ in at least one task for both datasets. SPD loss with $\eta = 0.1$ gives us the best performances in both datasets, which is chosen as the default SPD loss weight for all pre-training with SPD. So the SimSiam+SPD ($\eta = 0.1$) is regarded as SimSiam+SPD for better clarity.

Comparison Between SPD and CutPaste [26]: CutPaste and cross-entropy loss used in [26] for anomaly detection training can also be used in ImageNet pre-training. An ablation study is done to demonstrate the superiority of the proposed SmoothBlend and SPD loss. With $\mathcal{L}_{\mathrm{SPD}}$, SmoothBlend is arguably better than CutPaste by 4.0% and 3.8% AU-PR improvement in VisA - classification and MVTec - segmentation (+SPD v.s. +SPD w/ CutPaste). With the SmoothBlend, the SPD loss significantly outperforms cross-entropy loss (+SPD v.s. +SPD w/ Xent). Such results demonstrate the validity of proposed methods.

SPD with Different Backbones: ResNet-50 is adopted as the backbone for all major experiments in this paper. We demonstrate the SPD can generalize to different network architectures by experiments of SimSiam w/wo SPD on wide ResNet-50 [45]. As in Table 5, SPD still improves the baseline.

Results with PatchCore: In addition to PaDiM, we also evaluate supervised pre-trained models based on another state-of-the-art 1-class method Patch-Core [33]. Wide ResNet-50 is chosen as the backbone network. As in Table 6, on VisA, SPD improves supervised pre-trained model by 0.5% and 0.9% AU-PR for both classification and segmentation. On MVTec-AD, SPD improves by 0.5% AU-PR for segmentation with slightly performance decreased in classification.

Extending SPD to Other Tasks: Besides improvement on defect detection and segmentation, SPD also improves ImageNet supervised classification accuracy: 69.8% $\rightarrow$ 70.2% for ResNet-18 and 76.1% $\rightarrow$ 76.4% for ResNet-50. Pre-trained models with better ImageNet accuracy are expected to benefit downstream tasks more. Thus we speculate that SPD will work well for object recognition and detection, especially on fine-grained classification and small object detection as SPD promotes local sensitivity. In addition, we will leverage the proposed SPD training as a 1-class anomaly detection model to be trained by downstream data.

Qualitative Results: To qualitatively demonstrate the effectiveness of SPD regularization, we present attention maps of anomalous samples and anomaly segmentation results in Sec. E of the supplementary due to page limits.

6   Conclusions

In this work, we present a spot-the-difference (SPD) training to regularize pre-trained models' local sensitivity to anomalous patterns. We also present a novel

Visual Anomaly (VisA) dataset which is the largest industrial anomaly detection dataset. Extensive experiments demonstrate the benefits of SPD for various contrastive self-supervised and supervised pre-training for anomaly detection and segmentation. Compared to standard supervised pre-training, SimSiam with SPD obtains superior or competitive performances in low-shot regime while supervised learning with SPD presents better performances in various setups.

Acknowledgments. The authors would like to thank Fanyi Xiao, Erhan Bas, Aditya Deshpande and Joachim Stahl for idea brainstorming and providing insightful comments on the manuscript.

References

1. AWS Lookout for Vision. https://aws.amazon.com/lookout-for-vision/
2. Google Visual Inspection AI. https://cloud.google.com/solutions/visual-inspection-ai
3. Bergmann, P., Batzner, K., Fauser, M., Sattlegger, D., Steger, C.: The MVTec anomaly detection dataset: a comprehensive real-world dataset for unsupervised anomaly detection. Int. J. Comput. Vis. **129**(4), 1038–1059 (2021). https://doi.org/10.1007/s11263-020-01400-4
4. Bergmann, P., Fauser, M., Sattlegger, D., Steger, C.: MVTec AD-a comprehensive real-world dataset for unsupervised anomaly detection. In: Proceedings of the IEEE/CVF Conference on Computer Vision and Pattern Recognition, pp. 9592–9600 (2019)
5. Bergmann, P., Fauser, M., Sattlegger, D., Steger, C.: Uninformed students: student-teacher anomaly detection with discriminative latent embeddings. In: Proceedings of the IEEE/CVF Conference on Computer Vision and Pattern Recognition, pp. 4183–4192 (2020)
6. Caron, M., Misra, I., Mairal, J., Goyal, P., Bojanowski, P., Joulin, A.: Unsupervised learning of visual features by contrasting cluster assignments. In: Advances in Neural Information Processing Systems, vol. 33, pp. 9912–9924 (2020)
7. Chen, K., Hong, L., Xu, H., Li, Z., Yeung, D.Y.: MultiSiam: self-supervised multi-instance siamese representation learning for autonomous driving. In: Proceedings of the IEEE/CVF International Conference on Computer Vision, pp. 7546–7554 (2021)
8. Chen, T., Kornblith, S., Norouzi, M., Hinton, G.: A simple framework for contrastive learning of visual representations. In: International Conference on Machine Learning, pp. 1597–1607. PMLR (2020)
9. Chen, X., He, K.: Exploring simple siamese representation learning. In: Proceedings of the IEEE/CVF Conference on Computer Vision and Pattern Recognition, pp. 15750–15758 (2021)
10. Cohen, N., Hoshen, Y.: Sub-image anomaly detection with deep pyramid correspondences. arXiv preprint. arXiv:2005.02357 (2020)
11. Cook, J., Ramadas, V.: When to consult precision-recall curves. Stand. Genomic Sci. **20**(1), 131–148 (2020)
12. Cui, Y., Jia, M., Lin, T.Y., Song, Y., Belongie, S.: Class-balanced loss based on effective number of samples. In: Proceedings of the IEEE/CVF Conference on Computer Vision and Pattern Recognition, pp. 9268–9277 (2019)

13. Davis, J., Goadrich, M.: The relationship between precision-recall and ROC curves. In: Proceedings of the 23rd International Conference on Machine learning, pp. 233–240 (2006)
14. Defard, T., Setkov, A., Loesch, A., Audigier, R.: PaDiM: a patch distribution modeling framework for anomaly detection and localization. In: Del Bimbo, A., et al. (eds.) ICPR 2021. LNCS, vol. 12664, pp. 475–489. Springer, Cham (2021). https://doi.org/10.1007/978-3-030-68799-1_35
15. Deng, H., Li, X.: Anomaly detection via reverse distillation from one-class embedding. In: Proceedings of the IEEE/CVF Conference on Computer Vision and Pattern Recognition (CVPR), pp. 9737–9746 (2022)
16. Deng, J., Dong, W., Socher, R., Li, L.J., Li, K., Fei-Fei, L.: ImageNet: a large-scale hierarchical image database. In: 2009 IEEE Conference on Computer Vision and Pattern Recognition, pp. 248–255. IEEE (2009)
17. Ericsson, L., Gouk, H., Loy, C.C., Hospedales, T.M.: Self-supervised representation learning: Introduction, advances and challenges. arXiv preprint. arXiv:2110.09327 (2021)
18. Feng, T., Qi, Q., Wang, J., Liao, J.: Few-shot class-adaptive anomaly detection with model-agnostic meta-learning. In: 2021 IFIP Networking Conference (IFIP Networking), pp. 1–9. IEEE (2021)
19. Geirhos, R., Narayanappa, K., Mitzkus, B., Bethge, M., Wichmann, F.A., Brendel, W.: On the surprising similarities between supervised and self-supervised models. In: NeurIPS 2020 Workshop SVRHM (2020). https://openreview.net/forum?id=q2ml4CJMHAx
20. Gidaris, S., Singh, P., Komodakis, N.: Unsupervised representation learning by predicting image rotations. In: International Conference on Learning Representations (2018)
21. Görnitz, N., Kloft, M., Rieck, K., Brefeld, U.: Toward supervised anomaly detection. J. Artif. Intell. Res. **46**, 235–262 (2013)
22. Grill, J.B., et al.: Bootstrap your own latent-a new approach to self-supervised learning. In: Advances in Neural Information Processing Systems, vol. 33, pp. 21271–21284 (2020)
23. He, K., Fan, H., Wu, Y., Xie, S., Girshick, R.: Momentum contrast for unsupervised visual representation learning. In: Proceedings of the IEEE/CVF Conference on Computer Vision and Pattern Recognition, pp. 9729–9738 (2020)
24. He, K., Zhang, X., Ren, S., Sun, J.: Deep residual learning for image recognition. In: Proceedings of the IEEE Conference on Computer Vision and Pattern Recognition, pp. 770–778 (2016)
25. Jhamtani, H., Berg-Kirkpatrick, T.: Learning to describe differences between pairs of similar images. In: Proceedings of the 2018 Conference on Empirical Methods in Natural Language Processing (EMNLP) (2018)
26. Li, C.L., Sohn, K., Yoon, J., Pfister, T.: CutPaste: self-supervised learning for anomaly detection and localization. In: Proceedings of the IEEE/CVF Conference on Computer Vision and Pattern Recognition, pp. 9664–9674 (2021)
27. Lin, T.Y., Goyal, P., Girshick, R., He, K., Dollár, P.: Focal loss for dense object detection. In: Proceedings of the IEEE International Conference on Computer Vision, pp. 2980–2988 (2017)
28. Liu, S., Li, Z., Sun, J.: Self-EMD: self-supervised object detection without ImageNet. arXiv preprint. arXiv:2011.13677 (2020)
29. Noroozi, M., Favaro, P.: Unsupervised learning of visual representations by solving jigsaw puzzles. In: Leibe, B., Matas, J., Sebe, N., Welling, M. (eds.) ECCV 2016.

LNCS, vol. 9910, pp. 69–84. Springer, Cham (2016). https://doi.org/10.1007/978-3-319-46466-4_5

30. Reiss, T., Hoshen, Y.: Mean-shifted contrastive loss for anomaly detection. arXiv preprint. arXiv:2106.03844 (2021)
31. Ristea, N.C., et al.: Self-supervised predictive convolutional attentive block for anomaly detection. In: Proceedings of the IEEE/CVF Conference on Computer Vision and Pattern Recognition (2022)
32. Ronneberger, O., Fischer, P., Brox, T.: U-Net: convolutional networks for biomedical image segmentation. In: Navab, N., Hornegger, J., Wells, W.M., Frangi, A.F. (eds.) MICCAI 2015. LNCS, vol. 9351, pp. 234–241. Springer, Cham (2015). https://doi.org/10.1007/978-3-319-24574-4_28
33. Roth, K., Pemula, L., Zepeda, J., Schölkopf, B., Brox, T., Gehler, P.: Towards total recall in industrial anomaly detection. In: Proceedings of the IEEE/CVF Conference on Computer Vision and Pattern Recognition, pp. 14318–14328 (2022)
34. Rudolph, M., Wehrbein, T., Rosenhahn, B., Wandt, B.: Fully convolutional cross-scale-flows for image-based defect detection. In: Winter Conference on Applications of Computer Vision (WACV) (2022)
35. Ruff, L., et al.: A unifying review of deep and shallow anomaly detection. In: Proceedings of the IEEE, vol. 109, no. 5, pp. 756–795 (2021)
36. Ruff, L., et al.: Deep one-class classification. In: Proceedings of the 35th International Conference on Machine Learning, vol. 80, pp. 4393–4402 (2018)
37. Saito, T., Rehmsmeier, M.: The precision-recall plot is more informative than the roc plot when evaluating binary classifiers on imbalanced datasets. PLoS ONE 10(3), e0118432 (2015)
38. Selvaraju, R.R., Cogswell, M., Das, A., Vedantam, R., Parikh, D., Batra, D.: Grad-CAM: visual explanations from deep networks via gradient-based localization. In: Proceedings of the IEEE International Conference on Computer Vision, pp. 618–626 (2017)
39. Sohn, K., Li, C.L., Yoon, J., Jin, M., Pfister, T.: Learning and evaluating representations for deep one-class classification. In: International Conference on Learning Representations (2021). https://openreview.net/forum?id=HCSgyPUfeDj
40. Tack, J., Mo, S., Jeong, J., Shin, J.: CSI: novelty detection via contrastive learning on distributionally shifted instances. In: Advances in Neural Information Processing Systems, vol. 33, pp.11839–11852 (2020)
41. Wang, X., Zhang, R., Shen, C., Kong, T., Li, L.: Dense contrastive learning for self-supervised visual pre-training. In: Proceedings of the IEEE/CVF Conference on Computer Vision and Pattern Recognition (CVPR), pp. 3024–3033 (June 2021)
42. Xie, E., et al.: DetCo: unsupervised contrastive learning for object detection. In: Proceedings of the IEEE/CVF International Conference on Computer Vision, pp. 8392–8401 (2021)
43. Yang, C., Wu, Z., Zhou, B., Lin, S.: Instance localization for self-supervised detection pretraining. In: Proceedings of the IEEE/CVF Conference on Computer Vision and Pattern Recognition (CVPR), pp. 3987–3996 (2021)
44. Yi, J., Yoon, S.: Patch SVDD: patch-level svdd for anomaly detection and segmentation. In: Proceedings of the Asian Conference on Computer Vision (2020)
45. Zagoruyko, S., Komodakis, N.: Wide residual networks. In: British Machine Vision Conference 2016. British Machine Vision Association (2016)
46. Zhang, R., Isola, P., Efros, A.A.: Colorful image colorization. In: Leibe, B., Matas, J., Sebe, N., Welling, M. (eds.) ECCV 2016. LNCS, vol. 9907, pp. 649–666. Springer, Cham (2016). https://doi.org/10.1007/978-3-319-46487-9_40

Dual-Domain Self-supervised Learning and Model Adaption for Deep Compressive Imaging

Yuhui Quan[1,2], Xinran Qin[1(✉)], Tongyao Pang[2], and Hui Ji[2]

[1] School of Computer Science and Engineering, South China University of Technology, Guangzhou 510006, China
csyhquan@scut.edu.cn, csqinxinran@mail.scut.edu.cn
[2] Department of Mathematics, National University of Singapore, Singapore 119076, Singapore
{matpt,matjh}@nus.edu.sg

Abstract. Deep learning has been one promising tool for compressive imaging whose task is to reconstruct latent images from their compressive measurements. Aiming at addressing the limitations of supervised deep learning-based methods caused by their prerequisite on the ground truths of latent images, this paper proposes an unsupervised approach that trains a deep image reconstruction model using only a set of compressive measurements. The training is self-supervised in the domain of measurements and the domain of images, using a double-head noise-injected loss with a sign-flipping-based noise generator. In addition, the proposed scheme can also be used for efficiently adapting a trained model to a test sample for further improvement, with much less overhead than existing internal learning methods. Extensive experiments show that the proposed approach provides noticeable performance gain over existing unsupervised methods and competes well against the supervised ones.

Keywords: Self-supervised deep learning · Compressed sensing · Model adaption · Compressive imaging · Image reconstruction

1 Introduction

Compressed Sensing (CS) provides an acceleration technique for imaging, with a broad spectrum of applications in different domains, such as computed tomography (CT) and magnetic resonance imaging (MRI) in medicine, as well as

Yuhui Quan is also with Pazhou Lab, Guangzhou 510335, China. He would like to thank the support in part by National Natural Science Foundation of China under Grant 61872151 and in part by Natural Science Foundation of Guangdong Province under Grant 2022A1515011755.
Hui Ji would like to thank the support in part by Singapore MOE AcRF under Grant R-146-000-315-114.

Supplementary Information The online version contains supplementary material available at https://doi.org/10.1007/978-3-031-20056-4_24.

S. Avidan et al. (Eds.): ECCV 2022, LNCS 13690, pp. 409–426, 2022.
https://doi.org/10.1007/978-3-031-20056-4_24

energy-efficient cameras, holography and scanning microscopy in science. In general, CS captures a small number of linear measurements of an image and then reconstructs the image from these measurements. Let $x \in \mathbb{R}^N$ denote the image of interest, $y \in \mathbb{C}^M$ the measurements with $M \ll N$, and $\Phi \in \mathbb{C}^{M \times N}$ the sensing matrix. Then, compressive imaging (*i.e.* CS-based imaging) solves

$$y = \Phi x + \epsilon, \tag{1}$$

where $\epsilon \in \mathbb{C}^M$ denotes the measurement noise (*e.g.* Gaussian white noise). How to suppress the propagation of noise to the solution and how to resolve the solution ambiguity caused by the under-determinedness of Φ are two main concerns.

Deep learning has emerged as a promising tool for compressive imaging; see *e.g.*, [4,11,17,24,31,37,39,40,42–45]. These methods train a deep neural network (NN) in a supervised manner, *i.e.*, using an external dataset with many ground truth (GT) images and their measurements. The NN's performance depends on both the size of training data and the coherence between training and test data. Unfortunately, in many data-limited domains, *e.g.*, MRI and CT in medicine, it is often very difficult or costly to collect sufficient GT images. Then, the possible bias in a limited amount of training data can lead to poor generalization performance of a pre-trained model, *e.g.*, novel pathology not present in training data might disappear in the reconstructed images of test data.

Recently, there has been an increasing interest in developing deep learning methods for compressive imaging with relaxed requirements on training data. Nevertheless, existing works along this line have various issues in practice. The weakly-supervised learning method [14] takes unpaired images and measurements for training, which still requires the access to GT images. The unsupervised learning methods [2,3,21] avoid accessing GT images. However, their performance is not competitive with their supervised counterparts. The internal learning methods [25,28,41] learn an NN from the test sample itself by exploiting its internal statistics, whereas the millions of gradient updates on each test sample result in high computational cost, especially when processing many samples. There are also some unsupervised methods working on specific settings of sensing matrices, *e.g.*, paired ones [35] or varying ones [6,21]. The resulting specific sensing setups limit the wider adoption of these methods.

This paper is devoted to developing an self-supervised deep learning approach for compressive imaging, which enjoys competitive performance against existing supervised methods, while its training only requires measurements collected in a general sensing setup (*i.e.*, using a single fixed sensing matrix). Such an approach is applicable to data-limited environments and makes the sensing more flexible in practice than those using paired or varying sensing matrices.

Recall that the linear system in (1) is under-determined. It has a non-zero kernel (also called null space) defined by $\ker(\Phi) = \{x | \Phi x = 0\}$. Therefore, the measurement vector y only provides the noisy information of image x within $\operatorname{im}(\Phi^H) = \ker(\Phi)^{\perp}$ where $\operatorname{im}(\Phi^H)$ denotes the image (also called column space) of the adjoint operator of Φ, *i.e.*, its Hermitian transpose Φ^H. The remaining information of x in $\ker(\Phi)$, is not available in y. Then, two critical parts of an unsupervised approach are: *(a)* Training the NN to predict the image in $\text{im}(\mathbf{\Phi}^H)$ when only noisy measurements are available; and *(b)* Training the NN to predict the image in $\text{ker}(\mathbf{\Phi})$ when no information is available. Note that while the latter one can be partially addressed if the training dataset contains measurements from varied $\mathbf{\Phi}$, it is not assumed in our setup as mentioned before.

In this work, those two parts are implemented by a self-supervised training scheme. Regarding the first part, as the measurement vector $\boldsymbol{y}$ encodes the image $\boldsymbol{x}$ by $\mathbf{\Phi}\boldsymbol{x}$, we use $\boldsymbol{y}$ as the "labels" for self-supervision and train the NN to predict an image $\boldsymbol{x}'$ from $\boldsymbol{y}$ such that $\mathbf{\Phi}\boldsymbol{x}' \approx \boldsymbol{y}$ under some loss defined in the domain of measurements. Since $\boldsymbol{y}$ can be noisy, the key is then how to make the training robust to the measurement noise, which is treated by extending the self-supervised loss introduced in the self-supervised Gaussian denoiser [26] to the measurement domain. Built on a double-head symmetric noise injection, where the injected noise is drawn from the same distribution as measurement noise, the proposed loss is equivalent, in terms of expectation, to the loss with noise-free labels $\mathbf{\Phi}\boldsymbol{x}$ in the measurement domain. Such a loss enables us to train the NN to predict the GT in $\text{im}(\mathbf{\Phi}^H)$, in analogy with supervised learning. We also show that the loss has a close connection to Stein's unbiased risk estimator (SURE) [10,21] in the presence of Gaussian noise.

Regarding the second part, the training scheme above does not address the solution ambiguity caused by $\text{ker}(\mathbf{\Phi})$, as $\mathbf{\Phi}(\boldsymbol{x} + \boldsymbol{n}) = \mathbf{\Phi}(\boldsymbol{x}) \approx \boldsymbol{y}, \forall \boldsymbol{n} \in \text{ker}(\mathbf{\Phi})$. While no information of $\boldsymbol{x}$ in $\text{ker}(\mathbf{\Phi})$ exists in $\boldsymbol{y}$, the prediction from an NN with specific structures, *e.g.*, a convolutional NN (CNN) or an unfolding-based NN, is an estimate biased to smooth and regular structures; see *e.g.* [7,32]. Thus, one can utilize the intermediate prediction from an NN as another noisy observation of "labels" (GT images) for the self-supervision in $\text{ker}(\mathbf{\Phi})$. The training in $\text{ker}(\mathbf{\Phi})$ is implemented by defining a similar double-head symmetric noise-injected loss in image domain, which further refines the estimate from the NN regarding the information in both $\text{ker}(\mathbf{\Phi})$ and $\text{im}(\mathbf{\Phi})$. Note that the "noise" in this case refers to the residual of the intermediate GT estimate, whose statistical distribution is complex and unknown. We introduce random sign flipping to simulate the samples drawn from the distribution of the residuals.

The above ideas lead to a dual-domain loss for self-supervised learning of compressive imaging, which brings noticeable performance gain over existing unsupervised methods. Motivated by the benefits of internal learning, we also apply the proposed loss to adapting a trained model to each test sample, which alleviates possible bias of training data and possible inconsistency of sensing matrices between training and test data. Such a model adaption scheme brings further performance gain. See below for the summary of our main contributions.

- A dual-domain self-supervised loss is proposed for handling possible ambiguity and overfitting when only noisy measurements are available in training.
- A model adaption scheme is proposed to exploit specific internal characteristics of a test sample for performance improvement. It also provides much higher computational efficiency than existing internal learning methods.

– A self-supervised learning approach for compressive imaging is introduced with a relaxed requirement on training data. Its performance is noticeably better than existing unsupervised methods and is competitive against state-of-the-art supervised methods.

2 Related Work

Image priors play an important role in compressive imaging for regularizing the solution of (1). Traditional methods use handcrafted image priors, such as transform-induced sparsity [18], non-local low-rankness [9], and the denoising prior from some manually-designed denoiser [22]. These methods require solving an optimization problem with some time-consuming iterative scheme.

Deep learning-based methods encode image priors into a measurements-to-image reconstructive NN. For supervised learning, the effort is mainly on the design of NN architectures; see *e.g.* [1,8,29,30,38,45]. Among them, physics-aware NNs are the most prominent ones, which are often designed by an unfolding strategy that replaces the prior-related operations in a traditional iterative method by some NN blocks; see *e.g.* [19,24,39,40,42–44]. Dual-domain architectures are also superior in supervised methods; see *e.g.* [31,44,45]. In comparison to these works, the concept of dual domain used in the proposed approach is mainly for unsupervised training, rather than NN structures.

The prerequisite on many paired samples is one limitation of supervised methods. Plug-and-play methods (*e.g.* [12,15,34]) partially address this limitation by calling pre-trained models of denoising or generative NNs. These methods still require GT images in the target domain for model pre-training. When the target image is not in the domain of training data, the performance of these methods is likely to see a big drop. In the unpaired learning method [14], the prerequisite of GT images is still required.

To remove the prerequisite on GT images, there have been a few studies on unsupervised deep learning for compressive imaging. Xia *et al.* [35] used the measurement samples collected by two sensors. Cloe *et al.* [6] trained a generative adversarial NN using unpaired measurement samples collected by different sensing matrices. Both Metzler *et al.* [21] and Zhussip *et al.* [46] proposed to train a learned denoiser-approximate message passing NN with a SURE-based denoiser. The former addressed the ambiguity caused by the null space via using varied sensing matrices for collecting measurement data, while the latter mainly relies on the regularization provided by the SURE-based denoiser to resolve the ambiguity. Chen *et al.* [2,3] proposed to exploit the equivariance present in latent images so that the missing null-space information of one sample in can be supervised by the reconstructed range-space information of another sample. By assuming the equivariance, they showed that the unsupervised training with equivariant transforms is an unbiased estimator to the GT. In comparison, the proposed dual-domain training scheme uses the NN's prediction to refine the learning in both spaces and leads to further improvement.

Instead of leveraging a dataset, internal learning exploits the implicit image priors encoded by an untrained CNN which enables one to exploit sample-specific statistics for good performance. It is GT-free as it only takes test samples for learning. Inspired by the dropout-based unsupervised denoiser [27], Pang *et al.* [25] utilized the model uncertainty of a Bayesian CNN to refine the result of internal learning. For accelerated MRI, Zalbagi *et al.* [41] used an under-parameterized CNN with few and simplified convolutional layers for addressing the overfitting in internal learning. Wang *et al.* [33] proposed to run Monte Carlo sampling on the NN's weights to approximate the Bayesian estimator of latent images. These methods suffer from high computational costs due to sample-wise model learning. In comparison, the proposed model adaption scheme exploits internal statistics of test data with much higher computational efficiency.

3   Dual-Domain Self-supervised Training

Given a full row-rank matrix Φ, we have

$$\mathbb{C}^N = \mathrm{im}(\Phi^H) \oplus \mathrm{ker}(\Phi). \tag{2}$$

Recall that there are two issues to address in unsupervised training: measurement noise in $\mathrm{im}(\Phi^H)$ and solution ambiguity in $\mathrm{ker}(\Phi)$. Let $f_\Phi(\cdot;\omega) : \mathbb{C}^M \to \mathbb{R}^N$ denote a deep NN model parameterized by ω which predicts an image from input measurements with the sensing matrix Φ. We will omit the parameters ω or the subscript Φ if not causing notational confusion.

In supervised learning, by minimizing the error between the output $f(y)$ and GT x, one can train f to simultaneously minimize the prediction errors in both $\mathrm{im}(\Phi^H)$ and $\mathrm{ker}(\Phi)$. In unsupervised learning, as only y is available, we only have the noisy information of x in $\mathrm{im}(\Phi^H)$. Then, the key is how to train f for prediction with small prediction errors in both $\mathrm{im}(\Phi^H)$ and $\mathrm{ker}(\Phi)$. To address this, we propose a dual-domain self-supervised loss function $\mathcal{L}^{\mathrm{Dual}}$:

$$\mathcal{L}^{\mathrm{Dual}}(\omega) := \mathcal{L}^{\mathrm{Measure}}(\omega) + \lambda \mathcal{L}^{\mathrm{Image}}(\omega), \tag{3}$$

with a pre-defined hyper-parameter λ. The first part $\mathcal{L}^{\mathrm{Measure}}$ concerns the prediction error in $\mathrm{im}(\Phi^H)$. The second part $\mathcal{L}^{\mathrm{Image}}$ measures the prediction error in image domain $\mathbb{C}^N$ that covers the error in $\mathrm{ker}(\Phi)$.

3.1   Loss Function

For the prediction in $\mathrm{im}(\Phi^H)$, we use the noisy measurement y to train the NN. Motivated by [26], we run data augmentation on y to eliminate the noise effect. Let $y' = y + \gamma$ denote an augmented version of y with random noise γ. Consider

$$\Phi f_\Phi(y') \to y \approx \Phi x + \epsilon. \tag{4}$$

Once the measurement noise ϵ can be handled by $\mathcal{L}^{\mathrm{Measure}}$, f can learn accurate predictions in $\mathrm{im}(\Phi^H)$, as if using the noise-free measurements Φx.

Since y carries no information about x in $\mathrm{ker}(\Phi)$, we use the output of f, denoted by z, as a noisy version of the GT image for supervising the training. As the structure of a CNN itself imposes certain implicit prior on its prediction [7, 32], z can be viewed as a regularized solution that contains some information of x in $\ker(\boldsymbol{\Phi})$. Similarly, consider an augmented version of z: $z' = z + r$ with random noise r and the following scheme:

$$f_{\boldsymbol{\Phi}}(\boldsymbol{\Phi} z') \rightarrow z = x + e. \tag{5}$$

If the residual e can be effectively handled by the loss $\mathcal{L}^{\text{Image}}$, then the ambiguity in null-space prediction can be effectively alleviated during learning. Note that while f is expected to learn accurate prediction in $\text{im}(\boldsymbol{\Phi}^H)$ by the loss $\mathcal{L}^{\text{Measure}}$, the training with $\mathcal{L}^{\text{Image}}$ also provides certain refinement on its prediction in $\ker(\boldsymbol{\Phi})$ due to the implicit regularization of the NN structure.

To effectively handle the noise in y and the error in z, we define

$$\begin{aligned}
\mathcal{L}^{\text{Measure}}(\boldsymbol{\omega}) &:= \mathbb{E}_{y \sim \mathbb{Y}, \gamma} \| \boldsymbol{\Phi} f_{\boldsymbol{\Phi}}(y + \gamma; \boldsymbol{\omega}) - y + \gamma \|_2^2, \\
\mathcal{L}^{\text{Image}}(\boldsymbol{\omega}) &:= \mathbb{E}_{y \sim \mathbb{Y}, r} \| f_{\boldsymbol{\Phi}}(\boldsymbol{\Phi}(z + r); \boldsymbol{\omega}) - z + r \|_2^2,
\end{aligned} \tag{6}$$

where $z := f(y; \boldsymbol{\omega}_0)$ ($\boldsymbol{\omega}_0$ is the NN parameters obtained in the previous epoch), $\mathbb{Y}$ is the training dataset of measurement samples, and both γ and r are injected random noises drawn from some distributions. The resulting self-supervised loss $\mathcal{L}^{\text{Dual}}$ is connected to its supervised counterpart as shown in Proposition 1.

Proposition 1. *Consider $y = \boldsymbol{\Phi} x + \epsilon$. Let P_1 and P_2 denote the conditional distribution of ϵ and the residual $e := f_{\boldsymbol{\Phi}}(y; \boldsymbol{\omega}_0) - x$ on x respectively, where $\boldsymbol{\omega}_0$ denotes the NN parameters obtained in the previous step, i.e., $\epsilon | x \sim P_1$ and $e | x \sim P_2$. Assume the random noise γ (resp. r) is drawn from P_1 (resp. P_2) and independent from ϵ (resp. e) conditioned on x. Then, the loss function $\mathcal{L}^{\text{Dual}}$ defined by (3) and (6) satisfies*

$$\mathcal{L}^{\text{Dual}}(\boldsymbol{\omega}) = \mathbb{E}_{x,\epsilon,\gamma} \| \boldsymbol{\Phi} f_{\boldsymbol{\Phi}}(y + \gamma; \boldsymbol{\omega}) - \boldsymbol{\Phi} x \|_2^2 + \lambda \mathbb{E}_{x,\epsilon,r} \| f_{\boldsymbol{\Phi}}(\boldsymbol{\Phi}(z + r); \boldsymbol{\omega}) - x \|_2^2 + C,$$

where $z = f_{\boldsymbol{\Phi}}(y; \boldsymbol{\omega}_0)$ and C is a constant.

Proof. See supplementary materials for the proof.   □

Proposition 1 states both $\mathcal{L}^{\text{Measure}}$ and $\mathcal{L}^{\text{Image}}$ are the unbiased estimates of their supervised counterparts under certain conditions. Therefore, the proposed self-supervised loss enables us to train with only noisy measurements, provided that we can draw samples from P_1 and P_2. Sampling from P_1 is easy when the distribution of measurement noise is known, e.g., Gaussian white noise. Sampling from P_2 is hard as its distribution is in general complex and unknown.

Generation of Injected Noise r. To sample from P_2, one simple way is to approximate it using normal distribution $\mathcal{N}(0, \sigma_e^2 \mathbf{I})$. Such a treatment certainly is sub-optimal and how to set the noise level σ_e is non-trivial either. We develop a sign-flipping-based scheme to generate the samples which empirically approximate the samples from P_2 better.

Let $z' = f_{\boldsymbol{\Phi}}(\boldsymbol{\Phi} z + \gamma)$ denote an intermediate prediction during training which is detached from back prorogation. Suppose z' is a good estimate of x. Then the residual $e' = z - z'$ can be viewed as an approximation to the residual e. Using e' as the injected noise is sub-optimal, as it remains correlated to e. To reduce the correlation, we apply random sign-flipping to e' so as to generate new samples $\{r\}$, *i.e.*, r is generated by $r = e' \odot s$, where $\odot$ denotes element-wise product and $s(i)$ takes values from $\{1, -1\}$ with probability 0.5 for all i. It is easy to show that $\mathbb{E}(r^\top e) = 0$ (see supplementary materials). Although the zero covariance between r and e does not guarantee that they are independent, the correlation between them is likely to be reduced. Furthermore, if the distribution of e' is symmetric w.r.t. the origin (which is observed empirically; see Fig. 1), flipping sign does not destroy the statistics, *i.e.*, r follows the same distribution as e'. In summary, the noises generated by the random sign-flipping simulate the samples from P_2 better with weak correlation to z.

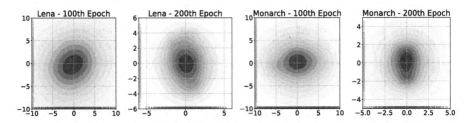

Fig. 1. Distribution of the residual $e = z - x$ at different epochs. The results are computed in the configuration of Gaussian sensing matrices with $\epsilon \sim \mathcal{N}(0, \frac{10}{255}\mathbf{I})$, using our NN trained with $\mathcal{L}^{\text{Measure}}$. Kernel density estimator is applied to the t-SNE projections of 1000 instances to show the distribution. It can be seen that e are roughly symmetrically distributed around the origin.

Relation to SURE. The proposed self-supervised loss is also closely related to the SURE-based loss. When applied to the measurements contaminated by Gaussian noise $\epsilon \sim \mathcal{N}(0, \sigma^2\mathbf{I})$, the SURE loss takes the form:

$$\mathcal{L}^{\text{SURE}}(\boldsymbol{\omega}) := \|\boldsymbol{\Phi} f_{\boldsymbol{\Phi}}(\boldsymbol{y}; \boldsymbol{\omega}) - \boldsymbol{y}\|_2^2 + 2\sigma^2 \text{tr}\left(\boldsymbol{\Phi}^{\text{H}} \frac{\partial f_{\boldsymbol{\Phi}}(\boldsymbol{y}; \boldsymbol{\omega})}{\partial \boldsymbol{y}}\right). \tag{7}$$

By injecting noise into the NN input, we modify the above SURE loss to be

$$\mathcal{L}^{\text{SURE+}}(\boldsymbol{\omega}) := \|\boldsymbol{\Phi} f_{\boldsymbol{\Phi}}(\boldsymbol{y} + \boldsymbol{\epsilon}'; \boldsymbol{\omega}) - \boldsymbol{y}\|_2^2 + 2\sigma^2 \text{tr}\left(\boldsymbol{\Phi}^{\text{H}} \frac{\partial f_{\boldsymbol{\Phi}}(\boldsymbol{y} + \boldsymbol{\epsilon}'; \boldsymbol{\omega})}{\partial \boldsymbol{y}}\right), \tag{8}$$

where $\boldsymbol{\epsilon}' \sim \mathcal{N}(0, \sigma^2\mathbf{I})$ is i.i.d. to $\boldsymbol{\epsilon}$. Then see below for the connection to SURE+.

Proposition 2. *Let $\boldsymbol{y} = \boldsymbol{\Phi}\boldsymbol{x} + \boldsymbol{\epsilon} \in \mathbb{R}^M$. Assume $\boldsymbol{\epsilon}, \boldsymbol{\epsilon}' \sim \mathcal{N}(0, \sigma^2\mathbf{I})$ are independent from each other and $\boldsymbol{x}$. Then,*

$$\mathbb{E}_{\boldsymbol{y}, \boldsymbol{\epsilon}'} \mathcal{L}^{\text{SURE+}} = \mathbb{E}_{\boldsymbol{y}, \boldsymbol{\epsilon}'} \mathcal{L}^{\text{Measure}} - M\sigma^2. \tag{9}$$

Proof. See supplementary materials for the proof.   □

Proposition 2 shows that, for Gaussian noise, training with the loss $\mathcal{L}^{\text{Measure}}$ can be roughly viewed as a data-augmented version of SURE applied to $\boldsymbol{y}$. Different from SURE, no regularization term on partial derivatives are introduced in $\mathcal{L}^{\text{Measure}}$, which results in more efficient computation. Together with $\mathcal{L}^{\text{Image}}$, the proposed loss $\mathcal{L}^{\text{Dual}}$ noticeably outperformed SURE-based methods.

3.2   NN Architecture

Motivated by the studies in [7] which show that the unfolding of the proximal gradient descent algorithm (PGDA) has a certain regularization effect on the NN's prediction during unsupervised learning, we adopt a similar NN that unfolds the PGDA for the problem: $\min_{\boldsymbol{x}} \|\boldsymbol{y} - \boldsymbol{\Phi x}\|_2^2 + \psi(\boldsymbol{x})$, with the regularization function $\psi : \mathbb{R}^N \rightarrow \mathbb{R}$. The iterative scheme of PGDA reads

$$\boldsymbol{x}^{(k)} = \text{prox}_{\psi}(\boldsymbol{x}^{(k-1)} - \rho\boldsymbol{\Phi}^{\text{H}}(\boldsymbol{\Phi x}^{(k-1)} - \boldsymbol{y})), \tag{10}$$

where prox_{ψ} is the proximal operator and ρ is a learnable step size. The NN is defined by replacing $\text{prox}_{\psi}^{\rho}$ with a convolutional block. It contains K phases, each of which mimics one iteration in (10). See Fig. 2 for the detailed structure.

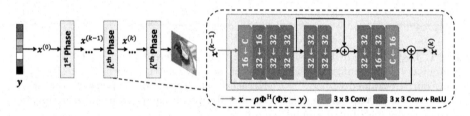

Fig. 2. NN architecture used in the proposed approach. The estimate $\boldsymbol{x}^{(0)}$ is initialized as the least-squares solution during training and initialized as the prediction from the pre-trained model during test-time adaption.

4   Inference with Test-Time Model Adaption

The proposed loss $\mathcal{L}^{\text{Dual}}$ not only can be used for unsupervised training, but also can be applied for adapting a deep model trained over an external dataset to unseen data. One such extension is adapting the model to a test sample under a specific sensing matrix (seen or unseen), so as to exploit sample-specific statistics for performance boost. Let $\widehat{\boldsymbol{\omega}}$ denote the NN parameters of a trained model. For a test sample $(\boldsymbol{y}^{\star}, \boldsymbol{\Phi}^{\star})$, we first initialize $\boldsymbol{\omega}^{\star} = \widehat{\boldsymbol{\omega}}$ and then update it by the gradient of (3) on $\boldsymbol{y}^{\star}$:

$$\boldsymbol{\omega}^{\star} := \boldsymbol{\omega}^{\star} - \tau\nabla_{\boldsymbol{\omega}^{\star}}\mathcal{L}_{\boldsymbol{y}^{\star}}^{\text{Dual}}(\boldsymbol{\omega}^{\star}), \tag{11}$$

with T steps. Once done, the final prediction is given by

$$\boldsymbol{x}^{\star} = f_{\boldsymbol{\Phi}^{\star}}(\boldsymbol{y}^{\star}; \boldsymbol{\omega}^{\star}), \tag{12}$$

with the adapted NN parameters $\boldsymbol{\omega}^{\star}$. See an algorithmic description of the whole adaption process in supplementary materials.

5   Experiments

The proposed approach is evaluated on three tasks compressive imaging in CT, MRI, and natural image reconstruction (NIR) respectively. The configuration is as follows: *(a)* NN: $K = 12$ for all tasks; *(b)* Initialization: Kaiming initialization is used for all learnable weights, except that the step size ρ and the bias terms are initialized by 0.5 and 0 respectively. *(c)* Training: We set $\lambda = 0.25$ in $\mathcal{L}^{\text{Dual}}$ and call the Adam optimizer with 500 epochs and with learning rate fixed at 10^{-4}; and *(d)* Adaption: The Adam optimizer is used with $T = 200$ epochs and with fixed learning rate 10^{-4}. The performance of the proposed approach is evaluated with and without using test-time adaption respectively, which are denoted by Ours-TA and Ours-NA correspondingly. For the comparison with existing methods, we quote their results directly from the literature whenever possible; or we use their reproducible codes with efforts on hyper-parameter tuning-up to obtain the results; otherwise we leave them blank in tables.

5.1   Sparse-View CT from Randon Measurements

Following [2], the CT measurements are taken by the discrete Radon transform based sensing matrix without noise. The 100 real in-vivo CT images of size 128×128 from the CT100 dataset [5], collected from the cancer imaging archive which consists of the middle slice of CT images taken from 69 patients, are used for the experiment: 90 for training and 10 for test. The methods for comparison include *(a)* two supervised methods: FBP [13] and FISTANet [36]; *(b)* an internal learning method: BCNN [25]; and *(c)* a very recent state-of-the-art unsupervised method: EI [2]. Since EI is an unsupervised method whose focus is on the training scheme design, for a fair comparison, we replace its NN with ours and retrain it with the same data as ours throughout the experiments, which brings performance improvement to the original EI.

The quantitative comparison is presented in Table 1. Ours-TA is the best performer among all methods including both the internal learning and unsupervised ones. Its performance is close to that of the supervised-trained FISTANet. Even without adaption, Ours-NA still performs noticeably better than other GT-free methods. Such results have indicated that the proposed approach is very effective for unsupervised compressive imaging. See also Fig. 3 for a demonstration.

Table 1. Mean PSNR (dB) and SSIM values in sparse-view CT reconstruction. The best results among GT-dependent methods, GT-free methods, and all methods are marked in green, marked in blue, and underlined respectively.

Metric	FBP	FISTANet	BCNN	EI	Ours-NA	Ours-TA
PSNR	30.24	41.85	39.82	40.48	41.35	41.99
SSIM	–	0.983	0.970	0.968	0.979	0.985

5.2   MRI Reconstruction from k-Space Measurements

Following [17,25], the k-space measurements in MRI are taken by $\boldsymbol{\Phi} : \boldsymbol{x} \rightarrow \boldsymbol{\beta} \odot (\mathbf{F}\boldsymbol{x})$, where $\boldsymbol{\beta}$ is a fixed binary mask for downsampling and $\mathbf{F}$ denotes the discrete Fourier transform. The measurement noise is generated by $\boldsymbol{\epsilon} = \boldsymbol{\Phi}(\epsilon_1 + i\epsilon_2)$, where $\epsilon_1, \epsilon_2 \sim \mathcal{N}(\mathbf{0}, \sigma^2 \mathbf{I})$. The 2D Gaussian masks and radial masks of different CS ratios are used for $\boldsymbol{\beta}$. The images from the Alzheimer's Disease Neuroimaging Initiative are used: 279 for training and 21 for test. Both the noiseless setting ($\sigma = 0$) and noisy setting ($\sigma = 0.1\max(\boldsymbol{x})$) are considered. We train an individual model for each sensing matrix and each noise setting. In each setting, each image is called only once for measurement generation. Then we have 279 measurement samples in total for training. In addition to the BCNN and EI, the methods for comparison include (a) a classic non-learning method: SparseMRI [18]; (b) five supervised methods: GAN [17], ADMMNet [39], DDN [1], CDDN [44] MACNet [11]; and (c) a very recent internal learning method: ConvDec [41].

Table 2. Mean values of PSNR(dB) (even rows) and SSIM (odd rows) in MRI reconstruction. The best results among GT-dependent methods, GT-free methods, and all methods are marked in green, marked in blue, and underlined respectively.

	Mask	Radial						2D Gaussian					
	Noise level	0			0.1*MaxValue			0			0.1*MaxValue		
	CS Ratio	1/3	1/4	1/5	1/3	1/4	1/5	1/3	1/4	1/5	1/3	1/4	1/5
GT-Dependent	GAN	34.49	32.29	30.10	26.72	25.55	25.02	35.12	32.96	31.79	26.49	26.31	25.79
		0.94	0.90	0.84	0.75	0.74	0.73	0.94	0.91	0.89	0.76	0.75	0.75
	ADMMNet	35.31	33.70	32.32	26.50	25.97	25.44	36.34	34.95	33.82	26.17	25.82	25.40
		0.94	0.93	0.92	0.60	0.61	0.59	0.95	0.94	0.93	0.56	0.60	0.61
	DDN	33.58	32.76	31.79	31.48	30.83	29.69	34.82	32.73	31.16	31.10	30.89	29.87
		0.92	0.88	0.89	0.85	0.85	0.82	0.91	0.89	0.87	0.85	0.84	0.84
	CDDN	36.58	34.70	33.46	30.71	30.79	30.28	37.93	36.01	34.76	30.90	30.93	30.74
		0.97	0.95	0.95	0.85	0.86	0.86	0.97	0.96	0.96	0.84	0.85	0.86
	MACNet	36.70	34.76	33.42	30.98	30.97	30.25	38.22	35.84	34.81	31.04	30.92	30.81
		0.98	0.97	0.95	0.87	0.87	0.86	0.98	0.96	0.96	0.86	0.86	0.86
GT-Free	SparseMRI	34.58	32.31	30.72	25.32	25.13	24.68	34.93	32.79	31.69	24.91	24.92	24.97
		0.94	0.90	0.86	0.49	0.49	0.49	0.93	0.90	0.89	0.47	0.49	0.51
	ConvDec	35.02	33.99	32.14	29.00	28.27	27.48	36.77	35.82	32.92	28.94	28.66	28.24
		0.94	0.94	0.91	0.85	0.83	0.71	0.94	0.96	0.91	0.85	0.84	0.84
	BCNN	35.58	34.08	32.28	29.58	29.47	28.38	37.60	36.10	33.81	29.46	29.20	29.17
		0.94	0.95	0.92	0.85	0.87	0.84	0.94	0.95	0.93	0.86	0.85	0.85
	EI	36.16	33.49	32.35	30.22	29.56	29.77	37.03	36.11	34.01	29.00	29.61	29.82
		0.94	0.92	0.90	0.81	0.75	0.76	0.93	0.95	0.92	0.72	0.72	0.73
	Ours-NA	36.25	34.32	33.47	30.66	30.62	30.16	37.42	36.20	34.80	30.87	30.65	30.29
		0.94	0.94	0.93	0.85	0.86	0.85	0.94	0.96	0.93	0.86	0.86	0.85
	Ours-TA	36.43	34.70	33.97	31.68	31.04	30.44	37.82	36.72	35.46	31.62	31.30	30.89
		0.95	0.95	0.95	0.86	0.88	0.87	0.95	0.96	0.95	0.87	0.86	0.86

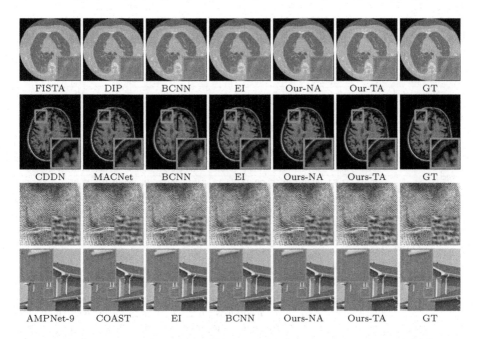

| FISTA | DIP | BCNN | EI | Our-NA | Our-TA | GT |

| CDDN | MACNet | BCNN | EI | Ours-NA | Ours-TA | GT |

| AMPNet-9 | COAST | EI | BCNN | Ours-NA | Ours-TA | GT |

Fig. 3. Visual results. The first row: CT reconstruction. The second row: MRI reconstruction from noisy measurements with radial mask of CS ratio 25% The last two rows: NIR from noiseless Gaussian measurements of CS ratio 40% and 25%.

See Table 2 for quantitative comparison. Ours-TA outperforms other GT-free methods in all settings. By exploiting both the external knowledge from training data and the internal statistics of a test sample, Ours-TA even outperforms the supervised methods in many settings. Without model adaption, Ours-NA still performs better than other GT-free methods overall, and competes with the supervised methods. See Fig. 3 for the visual comparison of some reconstruction results, where our result is closer to the GT in comparison with other GT-free methods. Both quantitative and qualitative results have clearly verified the effectiveness of the proposed approach.

5.3   NIR from Blockwise Gaussian Measurements

Following [16,42], the measurements are taken by a blockwise row-orthogonalized Gaussian matrix $\mathbf{\Phi} \in \mathbb{R}^{M \times N}$ with different CS ratios defined by M/N. Both the noiseless setting with $\epsilon = \mathbf{0}$ and the noisy setting with $\epsilon \sim \mathcal{N}(\mathbf{0}, \frac{10}{255}\mathbf{I})$ are considered. Same as the previous experiment, we train an individual model for each sensing matrix and each noise setting. The 88912 image blocks of size 33×33 (*i.e.* $N = 1089$) provided by [16] are used to generate 88912 measurement samples for the training. Two datasets including Set11 [42] and BSD68 [20] are used for test, each image of which is cropped into non-overlapping blocks of size 33×33 for measurement generation. In addition to DDN, BCNN, EI (its

Table 3. Mean values of PSNR(dB) (even rows) and SSIM (odd rows) in NIR. The best results among GT-dependent methods, GT-free methods, and all methods are marked in green, marked in blue, and underlined respectively.

Dataset		Set11						BSD68					
Noise level		0			10			0			10		
CS Ratio		0.40	0.25	0.10	0.40	0.25	0.10	0.40	0.25	0.10	0.40	0.25	0.10
GT-Dependent	ISTANet+	36.02	32.44	26.49	31.09	29.20	24.55	32.17	29.29	25.29	28.98	27.26	23.86
		0.96	0.92	0.80	0.89	0.86	0.70	0.92	0.85	0.70	0.83	0.77	0.60
	DDN	27.38	26.18	23.30	25.64	24.39	17.22	28.84	26.42	23.44	21.98	22.99	20.61
		0.80	0.78	0.70	0.73	0.69	0.35	0.85	0.78	0.64	0.49	0.52	0.46
	DPANet	35.04	31.74	26.99	30.17	29.31	25.13	31.43	29.21	25.88	28.95	27.25	24.39
		0.95	0.92	0.84	0.89	0.86	0.75	0.91	0.83	0.61	0.81	0.76	0.63
	AMPNet-9	35.75	32.08	25.95	29.00	28.06	24.53	32.41	29.38	25.33	27.50	26.64	24.03
		0.96	0.92	0.79	0.77	0.78	0.71	0.92	0.85	0.70	0.74	0.71	0.62
	COAST	36.94	33.85	28.34	31.16	29.37	25.71	33.02	30.07	26.25	29.15	27.43	24.02
		0.96	0.93	0.80	0.89	0.86	0.78	0.92	0.87	0.70	0.83	0.77	0.60
	SSLIP	33.73	30.42	25.02	30.58	28.71	24.48	30.72	28.26	24.72	28.47	26.91	24.25
		0.93	0.89	0.75	0.89	0.85	0.73	0.88	0.81	0.66	0.83	0.75	0.67
GT-Free	DAMP	33.51	28.31	21.18	29.19	26.34	20.79	28.06	25.54	21.93	26.54	24.83	21.72
		0.93	0.85	0.60	0.86	0.80	0.58	0.79	0.70	0.52	0.72	0.65	0.51
	LDAMP-SURE	33.36	31.37	25.12	28.79	28.16	23.39	31.83	28.77	23.17	27.82	26.81	23.65
		0.95	0.90	0.65	0.81	0.82	0.64	0.90	0.84	0.65	0.77	0.73	0.60
	BCNN	35.71	32.30	27.49	30.39	28.67	25.23	31.28	28.63	25.24	28.13	26.47	23.79
		0.95	0.92	0.83	0.88	0.84	0.76	0.90	0.84	0.71	0.81	0.75	0.64
	EI/REI	35.63	31.11	22.79	28.86	28.10	22.25	31.79	28.45	23.11	28.07	27.02	22.34
		0.95	0.90	0.64	0.76	0.76	0.33	0.90	0.82	0.63	0.68	0.72	0.44
	Ours-NA	36.37	32.70	26.89	31.42	29.17	25.41	32.17	28.97	25.61	28.24	27.23	24.10
		0.95	0.93	0.82	0.90	0.86	0.78	0.91	0.86	0.70	0.81	0.77	0.66
	Ours-TA	37.18	33.41	27.57	31.94	29.84	26.06	32.63	29.66	26.15	29.32	27.61	24.63
		0.96	0.94	0.84	0.91	0.87	0.79	0.92	0.87	0.72	0.84	0.78	0.68

robust version REI [3] is used for noisy cases), we also compare with *(a)* a non-learning method: DAMP [23]; *(b)* five supervised methods: ISTANet+ [42], DPANet [31], MACNet [4], AMPNet-9 [43], COAST [40]; *(c)* a plug-and-play method: SSLIP [15]; and *(d)* a recent unsupervised method: LDAMP-SURE [21].

The quantitative comparison is given in Table 3. Ours-TA is the best performer among the GT-free methods through all settings. Again, it is very competitive with the supervised methods and even outperformed them in nearly half settings. This is attributed to both the effectiveness of the unsupervised learning as well as the benefit from the model adaption. Without adaption, Ours-NA still performs competitively to supervised methods and is better than other GT-free methods. Particularly, with the dual-domain learning, it outperforms LDAMP-SURE significantly. We can observe a bigger improvement brought by model adaption in NIR than that in MRI. This is mainly because natural images exhibit larger variations between training and test samples, in comparison to the medical images in MRI. See also Fig. 3 for some visual comparison, where Ours-

TA produces more details than other GT-free methods. To conclude, the results have again demonstrated the effectiveness of the proposed approach.

5.4   Additional Analysis on Test-Time Model Adaption

The benefit of the proposed model adaption scheme has been demonstrated by the result comparison between Our-TA and Ours-NA in Table 1, 2 and 3. Those experiments use the same sensing matrix through training and test. We further examine the performance gain for the case when sensing matrices differ between training and test in MRI reconstruction. See Table 4 for the results. When dealing with Gaussian masks, the models trained on radial masks in Table 4 do not perform as well as the models trained on Gaussian masks in Table 2. However, their performance is noticeably improved after the model adaption.

Table 4. Mean PSNR(dB) values of MRI reconstructions in cross-mask adaption test.

Test / Train	Gaussian, Ratio = 20%		Gaussian, Ratio = 25%	
	w/o adaption	w/adaption	w/o adaption	w/adaption
Radial, Ratio = 25%	34.45/0.93	35.31/0.95	35.18/0.95	35.86/0.96
Gaussian, Ratio = 25%	34.80/0.94	35.46/0.95	36.39/0.96	36.72/0.96

Table 5. Running time (in seconds) of different methods for reconstructing all images in BSD68. All the tests are conducted on an RTX 3090Ti GPU.

CS Ratio	ISTANet+	DDNet	DPANet	COAST	LDAMP-SURE	BCNN	Ours-NA	Ours-TA
40%	2.56	0.06	2.94	3.28	310.21	90013	2.91	2178
25%	2.61	0.07	2.93	3.31	321.56	89652	2.86	2136
10%	2.29	0.05	2.80	3.30	320.43	91089	2.79	2134

While the model adaption brings notable performance gain by exploiting the internal statistics of a test sample, it also has a much less computational overhead than the internal learning methods. See Table 5 for the testing time of some selected methods on all images of BSD68, with the comparison to ours. The speed of Ours-NA is not bad among the compared methods. With an additional model adaptation process in the inference phase, Ours-TA is slower than Ours-NA but is significantly faster than BCNN. We also select the supervised methods including COAST and ISTANet+ for comparison.

5.5   Ablation Studies

See Table 6 for the ablation studies and results, whose details are as follows.

Without $\mathcal{L}^{Image}$. We retrain the NN by removing the loss $\mathcal{L}^{\text{Image}}$ in (3). Noticeable performance degradation is observed when compared to Our-NA. This has indicated the effectiveness of $\mathcal{L}^{\text{Image}}$ for handing the null-space ambiguity in unsupervised learning. It is interesting to see that using only the measurement-domain loss $\mathcal{L}^{\text{Measure}}$ may yield reasonable performance. This is probably because the measurement-domain training together with the unfolding-based architecture has certain implicit bias to smoothness on the NN's output, which resolves the null-space ambiguity to some degree.

Without $\mathcal{L}^{Measure}$. We remove the loss $\mathcal{L}^{\text{Measure}}$ in (3) and retrain the NN. It causes Ours-NA not to work. This is not surprising as the reconstruction from available measurements does play a critical role in the whole reconstruction and the effectiveness of the loss $\mathcal{L}^{\text{Image}}$ also relies on the success of the reconstruction in $\text{im}(\mathbf{\Phi}^{\text{H}})$ by sharing the NN weights during learning.

Without Outer Noise Injection. We only inject noise into the NN inputs y and z, and remove the outer noise injection in (3). A noticeable performance decrease is observed when compared to Ours-NA. The reason may be that the resulting loss function loses its connection to the supervised counterpart and leads to larger training error.

Using Gaussian Noise for Injected r. The sign-flipping-based generation scheme for injected noise is replaced by a simple scheme where $r \sim \mathcal{N}(0, \alpha\mathbf{I})$ with α estimated from e'. The PSNR results are fine but lower than that using the proposed generation scheme.

Supervised Training. We retrain our NN with a supervised ℓ_2 loss using the same paired data as those compared supervised methods. It leads to certain improvement over Ours-NA, but not significant. This demonstrates that the proposed dual-domain self-supervised loss is even as effective as the supervised loss, which coincides with Proposition 1.

Using Other NN Structures. We replace the NN structure with that of the ISTANet+, a representative NN in supervised compressive imaging. The resulting performance is very close to the original one. We also apply the test-time model adaption to the supervised ISTANet+. There is also a noticeable improvement over the original one in Table 3. All these results suggest the possible applicability of both our training and adaption schemes to other NNs.

Table 6. Results of ablation studies in terms of mean PSNR(dB) values on Set11.

Noise level		0			10		
CS Ratio		0.4	0.25	0.1	0.4	0.25	0.1
NA	w/o $\mathcal{L}^{\text{Image}}$	34.11	31.03	24.32	30.12	27.52	22.16
	w/o $\mathcal{L}^{\text{Measure}}$	16.67	15.09	11.25	15.21	14.16	10.32
	W/o Outer injection	28.20	20.83	15.66	27.33	18.37	13.24
	Gaussian injected r	35.67	31.65	26.18	31.39	29.31	24.81
	Supervised training	36.98	32.93	27.02	31.57	29.60	26.55
TA	Ours-NA	36.37	32.70	26.89	31.42	29.17	25.41
	Ours-TA (ISTANet+)	36.67	33.23	27.18	31.02	29.31	25.85
	Adaptive ISTA-Net+	36.70	<u>33.71</u>	27.34	31.48	29.63	<u>26.21</u>
	Ours-TA	<u>37.18</u>	33.41	<u>27.57</u>	<u>31.94</u>	<u>29.84</u>	26.06

6 Conclusion

We proposed an unsupervised deep learning approach for compressive imaging. It is based on a dual-domain self-supervised training scheme which not only allows effective learning in both measurement domain and image domain without any GT image, but also allows test-time model adaption for enjoying the advantages from both external and internal learning. The effectiveness of the proposed approach is grounded by mathematical analysis and has been demonstrated by extensive experiments on three imaging tasks. The developed techniques can be extended to solving other ill-posed problems, which is our future work.

References

1. Chen, D., Davies, M.E.: Deep decomposition learning for inverse imaging problems. In: Vedaldi, A., Bischof, H., Brox, T., Frahm, J.-M. (eds.) ECCV 2020. LNCS, vol. 12373, pp. 510–526. Springer, Cham (2020). https://doi.org/10.1007/978-3-030-58604-1_31
2. Chen, D., Tachella, J., Davies, M.E.: Equivariant imaging: learning beyond the range space. In: Proceedings of International Conference on Computer Vision (2021)
3. Chen, D., Tachella, J., Davies, M.E.: Robust equivariant imaging: a fully unsupervised framework for learning to image from noisy and partial measurements. In: Proceedings of IEEE Conference on Computer Vision and Pattern Recognition (2022)
4. Chen, J., Sun, Y., Liu, Q., Huang, R.: Learning memory augmented cascading network for compressed sensing of images. In: Vedaldi, A., Bischof, H., Brox, T., Frahm, J.-M. (eds.) ECCV 2020. LNCS, vol. 12367, pp. 513–529. Springer, Cham (2020). https://doi.org/10.1007/978-3-030-58542-6_31
5. Clark, K., et al.: The cancer imaging archive (TCIA): maintaining and operating a public information repository. J. Digit. Imaging **26**(6), 1045–1057 (2013)

6. Cole, E.K., Pauly, J.M., Vasanawala, S.S., Ong, F.: Unsupervised MRI reconstruction with generative adversarial networks. arXiv preprint arXiv:2008.13065 (2020)

7. Diamond, S., Sitzmann, V., Heide, F., Wetzstein, G.: Unrolled optimization with deep priors. arXiv preprint arXiv:1705.08041 (2017)

8. Ding, Q., Chen, G., Zhang, X., Huang, Q., Ji, H., Gao, H.: Low-dose CT with deep learning regularization via proximal forward-backward splitting. Phys. Med. Biol. **65**(12), 125009 (2020)

9. Dong, W., Shi, G., Li, X., Ma, Y., Huang, F.: Compressive sensing via nonlocal low-rank regularization. IEEE Trans. Image Process. **23**(8), 3618–3632 (2014)

10. Eldar, Y.C.: Generalized sure for exponential families: applications to regularization. IEEE Trans. Signal Process. **57**(2), 471–481 (2008)

11. Feng, C.M., Yang, Z., Chen, G., Xu, Y., Shao, L.: Dual-octave convolution for accelerated parallel MR image reconstruction. In: Proceedings of AAAI Conference on Artificial Intelligence (2021)

12. Jalal, A., Karmalkar, S., Dimakis, A.G., Price, E.: Instance-optimal compressed sensing via posterior sampling. In: Proceedings of International Conference on Machine Learning (2021)

13. Jin, K.H., McCann, M.T., Froustey, E., Unser, M.A.: Deep convolutional neural network for inverse problems in imaging. IEEE Trans. Image Process. **26**, 4509–4522 (2017)

14. Kabkab, M., Samangouei, P., Chellappa, R.: Task-aware compressed sensing with generative adversarial networks. In: Proceedings of AAAI Conference on Artificial Intelligence (2018)

15. Kadkhodaie, Z., Simoncelli, E.: Stochastic solutions for linear inverse problems using the prior implicit in a denoiser. In: Proceedings of Advances in Neural Information Processing Systems, vol. 34 (2021)

16. Kulkarni, K., Lohit, S., Turaga, P., Kerviche, R., Ashok, A.: ReconNet: noniterative reconstruction of images from compressively sensed measurements. In: Proceedings of IEEE Conference on Computer Vision and Pattern Recognition, pp. 449–458 (2016)

17. Liu, J., Kuang, T., Zhang, X.: Image reconstruction by splitting deep learning regularization from iterative inversion. In: Frangi, A.F., Schnabel, J.A., Davatzikos, C., Alberola-López, C., Fichtinger, G. (eds.) MICCAI 2018. LNCS, vol. 11070, pp. 224–231. Springer, Cham (2018). https://doi.org/10.1007/978-3-030-00928-1_26

18. Lustig, M., Donoho, D., Pauly, J.M.: Sparse MRI: the application of compressed sensing for rapid MR imaging. Magn. Reson. Med. **58**(6), 1182–1195 (2007)

19. Mardani, M., et al.: Neural proximal gradient descent for compressive imaging. In: Advances in Neural Information Processing Systems, vol. 31 (2018)

20. Martin, D., Fowlkes, C., Tal, D., Malik, J.: A database of human segmented natural images and its application to evaluating segmentation algorithms and measuring ecological statistics. In: Proceedings of International Conference on Computer Vision, IEEE, vol. 2, pp. 416–423. (2001)

21. Metzler, C., Mousavi, A., Heckel, R., Baraniuk, R.: Unsupervised learning with stein's unbiased risk estimator. arXiv preprint arXiv:1805.10531 (2018)

22. Metzler, C.A., Maleki, A., Baraniuk, R.: BM3D-AMP: a new image recovery algorithm based on BM3D denoising. In: Proceedings of International Conference on Image Processing, pp. 3116–3120. IEEE (2015)

23. Metzler, C.A., Maleki, A., Baraniuk, R.: From denoising to compressed sensing. IEEE Trans. Inf. Theory **62**(9), 5117–5144 (2016)

24. Metzler, C.A., Mousavi, A., Baraniuk, R.G.: Learned D-AMP: principled neural network based compressive image recovery. In: Proceedings of Conference on Neural Information Processing Systems (2017)
25. Pang, T., Quan, Y., Ji, H.: Self-supervised Bayesian deep learning for image recovery with applications to compressive sensing. In: Proceedings of European Conference on Computer Vision (2020)
26. Pang, T., Zheng, H., Quan, Y., Ji, H.: Recorrupted-to-recorrupted: unsupervised deep learning for image denoising. In: Proceedings of IEEE Conference on Computer Vision and Pattern Recognition (2021)
27. Quan, Y., Chen, M., Pang, T., Ji, H.: Self2self with dropout: learning self-supervised denoising from single image. In: Proceedings of IEEE Conference on Computer Vision and Pattern Recognition, pp. 1890–1898 (2020)
28. Quan, Y., Qin, X., Chen, M., Huang, Y.: High-quality self-supervised snapshot hyperspectral imaging. In: IEEE International Conference on Acoustics, Speech and Signal Processing. IEEE, pp. 1526–1530. (2022)
29. Shi, W., Jiang, F., Liu, S., Zhao, D.: Scalable convolutional neural network for image compressed sensing. In: Proceedings of IEEE Conference on Computer Vision and Pattern Recognition, pp. 12290–12299 (2019)
30. Shi, W., Jiang, F., Liu, S., Zhao, D.: Image compressed sensing using convolutional neural network. IEEE Trans. Image Process. **29**, 375–388 (2019)
31. Sun, Y., Chen, J., Liu, Q., Liu, B., Guo, G.: Dual-path attention network for compressed sensing image reconstruction. IEEE Trans. Image Process. **29**, 9482–9495 (2020)
32. Ulyanov, D., Vedaldi, A., Lempitsky, V.: Deep image prior. In: Proceedings of IEEE Conference on Computer Vision and Pattern Recognition, pp. 9446–9454 (2018)
33. Wang, W., Li, J., Ji, H.: Self-supervised deep image restoration via adaptive stochastic gradient langevin dynamics. In: Proceedings of the IEEE/CVF Conference on Computer Vision and Pattern Recognition, pp. 1989–1998 (2022)
34. Wei, K., Aviles-Rivero, A., Liang, J., Fu, Y., Schönlieb, C.B., Huang, H.: Tuning-free plug-and-play proximal algorithm for inverse imaging problems. In: Proceedings of International Conference on Machine Learning. PMLR, pp. 10158–10169 (2020)
35. Xia, Z., Chakrabarti, A.: Training image estimators without image ground-truth. In: Proceedings of Conference on Neural Information Processing Systems (2019)
36. Xiang, J., Dong, Y., Yang, Y.: FISTA-Net: learning a fast iterative shrinkage thresholding network for inverse problems in imaging. IEEE Trans. Med. Imaging **40**(5), 1329–1339 (2021)
37. Xin, B., Wang, Y., Gao, W., Wipf, D.: Maximal sparsity with deep networks? In: Proceedings of Conference on Neural Information Processing Systems (2016)
38. Xu, K., Zhang, Z., Ren, F.: LAPRAN: a scalable Laplacian pyramid reconstructive adversarial network for flexible compressive sensing reconstruction. In: Proceedings of European Conference on Computer Vision, pp. 485–500 (2018)
39. Yang, Y., Sun, J., Li, H., Xu, Z.: ADMM-CSNet: a deep learning approach for image compressive sensing. IEEE Trans. Pattern Anal. Mach. Intell. **42**(3), 521–538 (2019)
40. You, D., Zhang, J., Xie, J., Chen, B., Ma, S.: Coast: controllable arbitrary-sampling network for compressive sensing. IEEE Trans. Image Process. **30**, 6066–6080 (2021)
41. Zalbagi Darestani, M., Heckel, R.: Accelerated MRI with un-trained neural networks. In: IEEE Transactions on Computational Imaging. vol. 7, pp. 724–733 (2021)

42. Zhang, J., Ghanem, B.: ISTA-Net: interpretable optimization-inspired deep network for image compressive sensing. In: Proceedings of IEEE Conference on Computer Vision and Pattern Recognition, pp. 1828–1837 (2018)
43. Zhang, Z., Liu, Y., Liu, J., Wen, F., Zhu, C.: AMP-Net: denoising-based deep unfolding for compressive image sensing. IEEE Trans. Image Process. **30**, 1487–1500 (2021)
44. Zheng, H., Fang, F., Zhang, G.: Cascaded dilated dense network with two-step data consistency for MRI reconstruction. In: Proceedings of Conference on Neural Information Processing Systems (2019)
45. Zhou, B., Zhou, S.K.: DuDoRNet: learning a dual-domain recurrent network for fast MRI reconstruction with deep T1 prior. In: Proceedings of IEEE Conference on Computer Vision and Pattern Recognition, pp. 4273–4282 (2020)
46. Zhussip, M., Soltanayev, S., Chun, S.: Training deep learning based image denoisers from undersampled measurements without ground truth and without image prior. In: Proceedings of IEEE Conference on Computer Vision and Pattern Recognition, pp. 10255–10264 (2019)

Unsupervised Selective Labeling for More Effective Semi-supervised Learning

Xudong Wang, Long Lian, and Stella X. Yu

UC Berkeley/ICSI, Berkeley, USA
{xdwang,longlian,stellayu}@berkeley.edu

Abstract. Given an unlabeled dataset and an annotation budget, we study how to selectively label a fixed number of instances so that semi-supervised learning (SSL) on such a partially labeled dataset is most effective. We focus on *selecting* the right data to label, in addition to usual SSL's propagating labels from labeled data to the rest unlabeled data. This instance selection task is challenging, as without any labeled data we do not know what the objective of learning should be. Intuitively, no matter what the downstream task is, instances to be labeled must be *representative* and *diverse*: The former would facilitate label propagation to unlabeled data, whereas the latter would ensure coverage of the entire dataset. We capture this idea by selecting cluster prototypes, either in a pretrained feature space, or along with feature optimization, both without labels. Our unsupervised selective labeling consistently improves SSL methods over state-of-the-art active learning given labeled data, by 8–25× in label efficiency. For example, it boosts FixMatch by 10% (14%) in accuracy on CIFAR-10 (ImageNet-1K) with 0.08% (0.2%) labeled data, demonstrating that small computation spent on selecting what data to label brings significant gain especially under a low annotation budget. Our work sets a new standard for practical and efficient SSL.

Keywords: Semi-supervised learning · Unsupervised selective labeling

1 Introduction

Deep learning's success on natural language understanding [21], visual object recognition [41], and object detection [31] follow a straightforward recipe: better model architectures, more data, and scalable computation [32,36,42,73]. As training datasets get bigger, their full task annotation becomes infeasible [4,63].

Semi-supervised learning (SSL) deals with learning from both a small amount of labeled data *and* a large amount of unlabeled data: Labeled data directly supervise model learning, whereas unlabeled data help learn a desirable

---

X. Wang and L. Lian—Equal contribution.

Supplementary Information The online version contains supplementary material available at https://doi.org/10.1007/978-3-031-20056-4_25.

S. Avidan et al. (Eds.): ECCV 2022, LNCS 13690, pp. 427–445, 2022.
https://doi.org/10.1007/978-3-031-20056-4_25

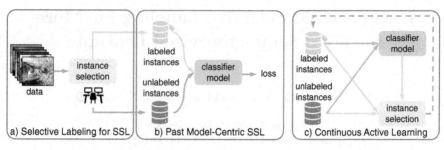

Fig. 1. Our unsupervised selective labeling is a novel aspect of semi-supervised learning (SSL) and different from active learning (AL). **a, b)** Existing SSL methods focus on optimizing the model *given* labeled and unlabeled data. Instead of such model-centric learning, we focus on optimizing the selection of training instances *prior to* their label acquisition. **c)** Existing AL methods alternate between classifier learning and instance selection, leveraging a classifier trained on initial labeled data and regularized on unlabeled data. In contrast, we select instances from unlabeled data without knowing the classification task.

model that makes consistent [4,5,43,58,63,65,69,72] and unambiguous [5,33,43] predictions.

Recent SSL methods approach fully supervised learning performance with a very small fraction of labeled data. For example, on ImageNet, SSL with 1% labeled data, i.e., only 13 instead of around 1300 labeled images per class, captures 95% (76.6% out of 80.5% in terms of top-1 accuracy) of supervised learning performance with 100% fully labeled data [15].

The lower the annotation level, the more important what the labeled instances are to SSL. While a typical image could represent many similar images, an odd-ball only represents itself, and labeled instances may even cover only part of the data variety, trapping a classifier in partial views with unstable learning and even model collapse.

A common assumption in SSL is that labeled instances are sampled randomly either over all the available data or over individual classes, the latter known as stratified sampling [4,5,63,69]. Each method has its own caveats: Random sampling can fail to cover all semantic classes and lead to poor performance and instability, whereas stratified sampling is utterly unrealistic: If we can sample data by category, we would already have the label of every instance!

Selecting the right data to label for the sake of model optimization is not new. In fact, it is the focus of active learning (AL): Given an initial set of labeled data, the goal is to select an additional subset of data to label (Fig. 1) so that a model trained over such partially labeled data approaches that over the fully labeled data [26,59,75]. Unlabeled data can also be exploited for model training by combining AL and SSL, resulting in a series of methods called semi-supervised active learning (SSAL).

However, existing AL/SSAL methods have several shortcomings.

1. They often require randomly sampled labeled data to begin with, which is sample-inefficient in low labeling settings that SSL methods excel at [13].

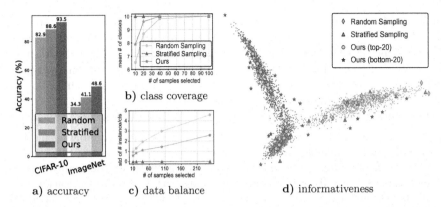

a) accuracy   c) data balance   d) informativeness

Fig. 2. Our instance selection outperforms random and stratified sampling by selecting a diverse set of representative instances. **a)** The classification accuracy using SSL method FixMatch increases with our selectively labeled instances. **b)** Our method covers all the semantic classes with only a few instances. **c)** Our selection is far more balanced than random sampling. **d)** On a toy dataset of 3 classes in ImageNet, our top-ranked instances cover informative samples across the entire space, whereas our bottom-ranked instances tend to be outliers.

2. AL/SSAL methods are designed with human annotators in a loop, working in multiple rounds of labeling and training. This could be cumbersome in low-shot scenario and leads to large labeling overhead.
3. AL's own training pipeline with a human-in-the-loop design makes its integration into existing SSL code implementation hard [64].
4. The requested labels are tightly coupled with the model being trained so that labels need to be collected anew every time a model is trained with AL/SSAL.

We address *unsupervised selective labeling* for SSL (Fig. 1), in stark contrast with supervised data selection for AL, which is conditioned on an initial labeled set and for the benefit of a certain task. Given only an annotation budget and an unlabeled dataset, among many possible ways to select a fixed number of instances for labeling, which way would lead to the best SSL model performance when it is trained on such partially labeled data?

Our instance selection task is challenging, as without any labeled data we do not know what the objective of learning should be. Intuitively, no matter what the downstream task is, instances to be labeled must be *representative* and *diverse*: The former would facilitate label propagation to unlabeled data, whereas the latter would ensure coverage of the entire dataset. We capture this idea by selecting cluster prototypes, either in a pretrained feature space, or along with feature optimization, both without labels.

Our pipeline has three steps: 1) Unsupervised feature learning that maps data into a discriminative feature space. 2) Select instances for labeling for maximum representativeness and diversity, without or with additional optimization. 3) Apply SSL (e.g., [15,63]) to the labeled data and the rest unlabeled data.

Figure 2 shows that our method has many benefits over random or stratified sampling for labeled data selection, in terms of accuracy, coverage, balance over classes, and representativeness. As it selects informative instances without initial labels, it can not only integrate readily into existing SSL methods, but also achieve higher label efficiency than SSAL methods. While most AL/SSAL methods only work on small-scale datasets such as CIFAR [40], our method scales up easily to large-scale datasets such as ImageNet [57], taking less than an hour for our data selection on a commodity GPU server.

Our work sets a new standard for practical SSL with these contributions.

1. We systematically analyze the impact of different selective labeling methods on SSL under low-label settings, a previously ignored aspect of SSL.
2. We propose two unsupervised selective labeling methods that capture representativeness and diversity without or along with feature optimization.
3. We benchmark extensively on our data selection with various SSL methods, delivering much higher sample efficiency over sampling in SSL or AL/SSAL.
4. We release our toolbox with AL/SSL implementations and a unified data loader, including benchmarks, selected instance indices, and pretrained models that combine selective labeling with various methods for fair comparisons.

2   Selective Labeling for Semi-supervised Learning

Suppose we are given an unlabeled dataset of n instances and an annotation budget of m. Our task is to select m $(m \ll n)$ instances for labeling, so that a SSL model trained on such a partially labeled dataset, with m instances labeled and $n - m$ unlabeled, produces the best classification performance.

Formally, let $\mathbb{D} = \{(x_i, y_i)\}_{i=1}^n$ denote n pairs of image x_i and its (*unknown*) class label y_i. Let $\mathbb{A}$ denote a size-m subset of $\mathbb{D}$ with *known* class labels. Our goal is to select $\mathbb{A} \subset \mathbb{D}$ for acquiring class labels, in order to maximize the performance of a given SSL model trained on labeled data $\mathbb{A}$ and unlabeled data $\mathbb{D} \backslash \mathbb{A}$.

Our unsupervised selective labeling is challenging, as we do not have any labels to begin with, i.e., we don't know what would make the SSL model perform the best. Our idea is to select m instances that are not only *representative* of most instances, but also *diverse* enough to broadly cover the entire dataset, so that we do not lose information prematurely before label acquisition.

Our SSL pipeline with selective labeling consists of three steps: **1)** unsupervised feature learning; **2)** unsupervised instance selection for annotation; **3)** SSL on selected labeled data $\mathbb{A}$ and remaining unlabeled data $\mathbb{D} \backslash \mathbb{A}$.

We propose two selective labeling methods in Step 2, training-free Unsupervised Selective Labeling (USL) and training-based Unsupervised Selective Labeling (USL-T), both aiming at selecting cluster prototypes in a discriminative feature space without label supervision.

2.1   Unsupervised Representation Learning

Our first step is to obtain lower-dimensional and semantically meaningful features with unsupervised contrastive learning [14,35,51,71], which maps x_i onto a d-dimensional hypersphere with L^2 normalization, denoted as $f(x_i)$. We use MoCov2 [17] (SimCLR [14] or CLD [68]) to learn representations on ImageNet (CIFAR [40]). See appendix for details.

2.2 Unsupervised Selective Labeling (USL)

We study the relationships between data instances using a weighted graph, where nodes $\{V_i\}$ denote data instances in the (normalized) feature space $\{f(x_i)\}$, and edges between nodes are attached with weights of pairwise feature similarity [7, 19,25,61], defined as $\frac{1}{D_{ij}}$, the inverse of feature distance D:

$$D_{ij} = \|f(x_i) - f(x_j)\|. \tag{1}$$

Intuitively, the smaller the feature distance, the better the class information can be transported from labeled nodes to unlabeled nodes. Given a labeling budget of m instances, we aim to select m instances that are not only similar to others, but also well dispersed to cover the entire dataset.

Representativeness: Select Density Peaks. A straightforward approach is to select well connected nodes to spread semantic information to nearby nodes. It corresponds to finding a density peak in the feature space. The K-nearest neighbor density (K-NN) estimation [28,52] is formulated as:

$$p_{\mathrm{KNN}}(V_i, k) = \frac{k}{n} \frac{1}{A_d \cdot D^d(V_i, V_{k(i)})} \tag{2}$$

where $A_d = \pi^{d/2}/\Gamma(\frac{d}{2} + 1)$ is the volume of a unit d-dimensional ball, d the feature dimension, $\Gamma(x)$ the Gamma function, $k(i)$ instance i's kth nearest neighbor. p_{KNN} is very sensitive to noise, as it only takes the kth nearest neighbor into account. For robustness, we replace the kth neighbor distance $D(V_i, V_{k(i)})$ with the average distance $\bar{D}(V_i, k)$ to all k nearest neighbors instead:

$$\hat{p}_{\mathrm{KNN}}(V_i, k) = \frac{k}{n} \frac{1}{A_d \cdot \bar{D}^d(V_i, k)}, \quad \text{where } \bar{D}(V_i, k) = \frac{1}{k} \sum_{j=1}^{k} D(V_i, V_{j(i)}). \tag{3}$$

We use $\hat{p}_{\mathrm{KNN}}(V_i, k)$ to measure the *representativeness* of node V_i. Since only the relative ordering matters in our selection process, the density peak corresponds to the sample with maximum $\hat{p}_{\mathrm{KNN}}(V_i, k)$ (i.e., maximum $1/\bar{D}(V_i, k)$).

Diversity: Pick One in Each Cluster. While instances of high feature density values are individually representative, a separate criterion is necessary to avoid repeatedly picking similar instances near the same density peaks (Fig. 3a). To select m diverse instances that cover the entire unlabeled dataset, we resort to K-Means clustering that partitions n instances into $m(\leq n)$ clusters, with each cluster represented by its centroid c [29,47] and every instance assigned to the cluster of the nearest centroid. Formally, we seek m-way node partitioning $\mathbb{S} = \{S_1, S_2, ..., S_m\}$ that minimizes the within-cluster sum of squares [39]:

$$\min_{\mathbb{S}} \sum_{i=1}^{m} \sum_{V \in S_i} \|V - c_i\|^2 = \min_{\mathbb{S}} \sum_{i=1}^{m} |S_i| \mathrm{Var}(S_i) \tag{4}$$

It is optimized iteratively with EM [48] from random initial centroids. We then pick the most representative instance of each cluster according to Eq. 3.

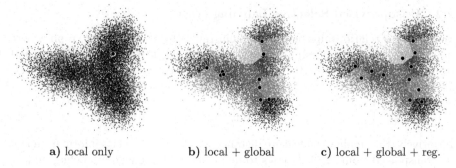

a) local only   b) local + global   c) local + global + reg.

Fig. 3. a) Points at density peaks are individually representative of their local neighborhoods, but lack broad coverage of the entire set. **b)** Hard constraint by K-Means greatly depends on clustering quality and only partially alleviates the problem. **c)** Soft regularization leads to more uniform and diversified queries.

Regularization: Inter-Cluster Information Exchange. So far we use K-Means clustering to find m hard clusters, and then choose the representative of each cluster *independently*. This last step is sub-optimal, as instances of high density values could be located along cluster boundaries and close to instances in adjacent regions (Fig. 3b). We thus apply a regularizer to inform each cluster of other clusters' choices and iteratively diversify selected instances (Fig. 3c).

Specifically, let $\hat{\mathbb{V}}^t = \{\hat{V}_1^t, ..., \hat{V}_m^t\}$ denote the set of m instances selected at iteration t, $\hat{V}_i^t$ for clusters S_i, where $i \in \{1, ..., m\}$. For each candidate V_i in cluster S_i, the farther it is away from those in other clusters in $\hat{\mathbb{V}}^{t-1}$, the more diversity it creates. We thus minimize the total inverse distance to others in a regularization loss $\mathrm{Reg}(V_i, t)$, with a sensitivity hyperparameter α:

$$\mathrm{Reg}(V_i, t) = \sum_{\hat{V}_j^{t-1} \notin S_i} \frac{1}{\|V_i - \hat{V}_j^{t-1}\|^\alpha}. \tag{5}$$

This regularizer is updated with an exponential moving average:

$$\overline{\mathrm{Reg}}(V_i, t) = m_{\mathrm{reg}} \cdot \overline{\mathrm{Reg}}(V_i, t-1) + (1 - m_{\mathrm{reg}}) \cdot \mathrm{Reg}(V_i, t) \tag{6}$$

where m_{reg} is the momentum. At iteration t, we select instance i of the maximum *regularized utility* $U'(V_i, t)$ within each cluster:

$$U'(V_i, t) = U(V_i) - \lambda \cdot \overline{\mathrm{Reg}}(V_i, t) \tag{7}$$

where λ is a hyperparameter that balances diversity and individual representativeness, utility $U(V_i) = 1/\bar{D}(V_i, k)$. In practice, calculating distances between every candidate and every selected instance in $\hat{\mathbb{V}}^{t-1}$ is no longer feasible for a large dataset, so we only consider h nearest neighbors in $\hat{\mathbb{V}}^{t-1}$. $\hat{\mathbb{V}}^t$ at the last iteration is our final selection for labeling.

2.3   Training-Based Unsupervised Selective Labeling (USL-T)

Our USL is a simple yet effective *training-free* approach to selective labeling. Next we introduce an end-to-end *training-based* Unsupervised Selective Labeling (USL-T), an alternative that integrates instance selection into representation learning and often leads to more balanced (Fig. 5) and more label-efficient (Table 2) instance selection. The optimized model implicitly captures semantics and provides a strong initialization for downstream tasks (Sec. 4.5).

Global Constraint via Learnable K-Means Clustering. Clustering in a given feature space is not trivial (Fig. 3c). We introduce a better alternative to K-Means clustering that jointly learns both the cluster assignment and the feature space for unsupervised instance selection.

Suppose that there are C centroids initialized randomly. For instance x with feature $f(x)$, we infer one-hot cluster assignment distribution $y(x)$ by finding the closest *learnable* centroid $c_i, i \in \{1, \ldots, C\}$ based on feature similarity s:

$$y_i(x) = \begin{cases} 1, & \text{if } i = \arg\min_{k \in \{1,\ldots,C\}} s(f(x), c_k) \\ 0, & \text{otherwise.} \end{cases} \tag{8}$$

We predict a soft cluster assignment $\hat{y}(x)$ by taking softmax over the similarity between instance x and each learnable centroid:

$$\hat{y}_i(x) = \frac{e^{s(f(x), c_i)}}{\sum_{j=1}^{C} e^{s(f(x), c_j)}}. \tag{9}$$

The hard assignment $y(x)$ can be regarded as pseudo-labels [43,63,67]. By minimizing $D_{\text{KL}}(y(x)\|\hat{y}(x))$, the KL divergence between soft and hard assignments, we encourage not only each instance to become more similar to its centroid, but also the learnable centroid to become a better representative of instances in the cluster. With soft predictions, each instance has an effect on all the centroids.

Hardening soft assignments has a downside: Initial mistakes are hard to correct with later training, degrading performance. Our solution is to ignore ambiguous instances with maximal softmax scores below threshold τ:

$$L_{\text{global}}(\{x_i\}_{i=1}^{n}) = \frac{1}{n} \sum_{\max(\hat{y}(x_i)) \geq \tau} D_{\text{KL}}(y(x_i)\|\hat{y}(x_i)) \tag{10}$$

where τ is the threshold hyper-parameter. This loss leads to curriculum learning: As instances are more confidently assigned to a cluster with more training, more instances get involved in shaping both feature $f(x)$ and clusters $\{c_i\}$.

Our global loss can be readily related to K-Means clustering.

Observation 1. *For $\tau = 0$ and fixed feature f, optimizing L_{global} is equivalent to optimizing K-Means clustering with a regularization term on inter-cluster distances that encourage additional diversity. See Appendix for derivations.*

Local Constraint with Neighbor Cluster Alignment. Our global constraint is the counterpart of K-Means clustering in USL. However, since soft assignments usually have low confidence scores for most instances at the beginning, convergence could be very slow and sometimes unattainable. We propose an additional local smoothness constraint by assigning an instance to the same cluster of its neighbors' in the unsupervisedly learned feature space to prepare confident predictions for the global constraint to take effect.

This simple idea as is could lead to two types of collapses: Predicting one big cluster for all the instances and predicting a soft assignment that is close to a uniform distribution for each instance. We tackle them separately.

1) For one-cluster collapse, we adopt a trick for long-tailed recognition [49] and adjust logits to prevent their values from concentrating on one cluster:

$$\hat{P}(z, \bar{z}) = z - \alpha \cdot \log \bar{z} \tag{11}$$

$$\bar{z} = \mu \cdot \sigma(z) + (1-\mu) \cdot \bar{z} \tag{12}$$

where α controls the intensity of adjustment, $\bar{z}$ is an exponential moving average of $\sigma(z)$, and $\sigma(\cdot)$ is the softmax function.

2) For even-distribution collapse, we use a sharpening function [2,4, 5] to encourage the cluster assignment to approach a one-hot probability distribution, where a temperature parameter t determines the spikiness.

Both anti-collapse measures can be concisely captured in a single function $P(\cdot)$ that modifies and turns logits z into a reference distribution:

$$[P(z, \bar{z}, t)]_i = \frac{\exp(\hat{P}(z_i, \bar{z}_i)/t)}{\sum_j \exp(\hat{P}(z_j, \bar{z}_j/t))} \tag{13}$$

We now impose our local labeling smoothness constraints with such modified soft assignments between x_i and its randomly selected neighbor x_i':

$$L_{\text{local}}(\{x_i\}_{i=1}^n) = \frac{1}{n} \sum_{i=1}^n D_{\text{KL}}(P(y(x_i'), \bar{y}(x_i'), t) || \hat{y}(x_i)). \tag{14}$$

We restrict x_i' to x's k nearest neighbors, selected according to the unsupervisedly learned feature prior to training and fixed for simplicity and efficiency. We show that our local constraint prevents both collapses.

Observation 2. *Neither one-cluster nor even-distribution collapse is optimal to our local constraint, i.e., $P(y(x'), \bar{y}(x'), t) \neq \hat{y}(x)$. See Appendix for more details.*

Our final loss adds up the global and local terms with loss weight λ:

$$L = L_{\text{global}} + \lambda L_{\text{local}} \tag{15}$$

Diverse and Representative Instance Selection in USL-T. Our USL-T is an end-to-end unsupervised feature learning method that directly outputs m

Table 1. Key properties of SSL, AL, SSAL, and our USL/USL-T pipelines. Among them, our approach is the only one that does not use any random labels.

Property	Semi-supervised learning	Active learning	Semi-supervised active learning	Ours
Uses no initial random labels	✗	✗	✗	✓
Actively queries for labels	✗	✓	✓	✓
Requires annotation only once	✓	✗	✗	✓
Leverages unlabeled data	✓	✗	✓	✓
Allows label reuse across runs	✓	✗	✗	✓

clusters for selecting m *diverse* instances. For each cluster, we then select the most *representative* instance, characterized by its highest confidence score, i.e. $\max \hat{y}(x)$. Just as USL, USL-T improves model learning efficiency by selecting diverse representative instances for labeling, without any label supervision.

2.4 Distinctions and Connections with SSL/AL/SSAL

Table 1 compares our USL with related SSL, AL, and SSAL settings.

1. Our USL has the advantage of AL/SSAL that seeks optimal instances to label, yet does not require inefficient initial random samples or multiple rounds of human interventions. USL has high label efficiency for selected instances in low label settings and does not need to trade off annotation budget allocation between initial random sampling and several interim annotation stages.
2. Compared to AL, our USL also leverages unlabeled data. Compared to SSAL, USL is much easier to implement because we keep existing SSL implementation intact, while SSAL requires a human-in-the-loop pipeline. Consequently, unlike AL/SSAL where instance selection is coupled with the model to be trained, our selection is *decoupled* from the downstream SSL model. The same selection from USL works well even across different downstream SSL methods, enabling label reuse across different SSL experiments.
3. Most notably, our work is the first *unsupervised* selective labeling method on large-scale recognition datasets that requests annotation only *once*.

3 Related Work

Semi-supervised Learning(SSL) integrates information from small-scale labeled data and large-scale unlabeled data. *Consistency-based regularization* [58,65,72] applies a consistency loss by imposing invariance on unlabeled data under augmentations. *Pseudo-labeling* [4,5,43,69] relies on the model's high confidence predictions to produce pseudo-labels of unlabeled data and trains them jointly with labeled data. FixMatch [63] integrates strong data augmentation [22] and pseudo-label filtering [46] and explores training on the most representative samples ranked by [10]. However, [10] is a supervised method that requires all labels. *Transfer learning* method SimCLRv2 [15] is a two-stage SSL method that applies contrastive learning followed by fine-tuning on labeled data. *Entropy-minimization* [5,33] assumes that classification boundaries do not pass through the high-density area of marginal distributions and enforces confident predictions on unlabeled data. Instead of competing with existing SSL methods, our USL enables more effective SSL by choosing the right instances to label *for* SSL, without any prior semantic supervision.

Active Learning (AL) aims to select a small subset of labeled data to achieve competitive performance over supervised learning on fully labeled data [6,20,56]. *Traditional AL* has three major types [55,60]: membership query synthesis [1], stream-based selective sampling [3,23], and pool-based active learning [37,50,66,70]. In *Deep AL*, Core-Set [59] approaches data selection as a set cover problem. [26] estimates distances from decision boundaries based on sensitivity to adversarial attacks. LLAL [75] predicts target loss of unlabeled data parametrically and queries instances with the largest loss for labels. *Semi-supervised Active Learning* (SSAL) combines AL with SSL. [64] merges uncertainty-based metrics with MixMatch [5]. [30] merges consistency-based metrics with consistency-based SSL. AL/SSAL often rely on initial labeled data to learn both the model and the instance sampler, requiring multiple (e.g. 10) rounds of sequential annotation and significant modifications of existing annotation pipelines. Recent *few-label transfer* [45] leverages features from a large source dataset to select instances in a smaller target dataset for annotation. It also requires a seed instance per class to be pre-labeled in the target dataset, whereas we do not need supervision anywhere for our instance selection.

Deep Clustering. DeepCluster [11] also jointly learns features and cluster assignments with k-Means clustering. However, USL-T, with end-to-end backprop to jointly optimize classifiers and cluster assignments, is much more *scalable* and *easy to implement*. UIC/DINO [12,16] incorporate neural networks with categorical outputs through softmax, but both methods focus on learning feature or attention maps for downstream applications instead of acquiring a set of instances that are representative and diverse. Recently, SCAN/NNM/RUC [24,53,67] produce image clusters to be evaluated against semantic classes via Hungarian matching. However, such methods are often compared *against* SSL methods [67], whereas our work is *for* SSL methods. See appendix for more discussions about **self-supervised learning** and **deep clustering** methods.

4   Experiments

We evaluate our USL and USL-T by integrating them into both pseudo-label based SSL methods (FixMatch [63], MixMatch [5], or CoMatch [44]) and transfer-based SSL methods (SimCLRv2 and SimCLRv2-CLD [15,68]). We also compare against various AL/SSAL methods. Lastly, we show several intriguing properties of USL/USL-T such as generalizability.

4.1 CIFAR-10

We compare against mainstream SSL methods such as FixMatch [63] and SimCLRv2-CLD [15,68] on extremely low-label settings to demonstrate our superior label efficiency. The labeling budget is 40 samples in total unless otherwise stated. Note that the self-supervised models used for instance selection are trained on CIFAR-10 from scratch entirely *without external data*. The SSL part, including backbone and hyperparameters, is untouched. See appendix for details.

Comparison with AL and SSAL. Table 2 compares ours against various recent AL/SSAL methods in terms of sample efficiency and accuracy. AL methods operate at a much larger labeling budget than ours (187× more), because they rely only on labeled samples to learn both features and classification. SSAL methods make use of unlabeled samples and have higher label efficiency. However, we achieve much higher accuracy with fewer labels requested.

To tease apart whether our performance gains come from SSL or selective labeling, we tune recent AL/SSAL methods with their public implementations and run experiments with the same total budget, i.e. 40 samples in a 20 random + 20 selected setting. We then apply AL/SSAL selections to the same SSL for a fair comparison (Table 3).

Table 2. USL and USL-T greatly outperform AL/SSAL methods in accuracy and label efficiency on CIFAR-10. †, ‡: results from [38] and [30], respectively.

CIFAR-10	Budget	Acc (%)
Active Learning (AL)		
CoreSet [59]†	7500	85.4
VAAL [62]†	7500	86.8
UncertainGCN [9]†	7500	86.8
CoreGCN [9]†	7500	86.5
MCDAL [18]	7500	87.2
Semi-supervised Active Learning (SSAL)		
TOD-Semi [38]	7500	87.8
CoreSetSSL [59]‡	250	88.8
CBSSAL [30]	150	87.6
MMA [64]	500	91.7
MMA+k-means [64]	500	91.5
REVIVAL [34]	150	88.0
Selective Labeling		
FixMatch + USL (Ours)	**40**	90.4
FixMatch + USL (Ours)	**100**	**93.2**
FixMatch + USL-T (Ours)	**40**	**93.5**

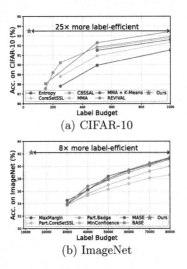

(a) CIFAR-10

(b) ImageNet

Fig. 4. Compared to SSAL, USL gets up to 25× higher label efficiency.

While AL performs better than random selection in SimCLRv2-CLD, its advantage saturates on FixMatch. Since AL relies on labeled samples to learn the right features, with 20 random samples, it is very difficult to learn meaningful features for selection. Instead, AL could only learn a very coarse selection criterion and hence limited gains.

SSAL methods have greater gains on SimCLRv2-CLD. However, since SSAL still depends on initial random selections which seldom cover all 10 classes, these methods do not have an accurate knowledge of the full dataset in the low-label setting, where many rounds of queries are infeasible. That is, there is a serious trade-off in the low-label regime: Allowing more samples (e.g., 30) in the initial random selection for better coverage means less annotation budget for AL/SSAL selection (e.g., 10). Such a dilemma manifests itself in the imbalanced selection in Fig. 5 and the poor performance on FixMatch.

USL/USL-T as a Universal Method. In addition to mainstream SSL, we also use SimCLRv2, MixMatch [5], and SOTA CoMatch [44] for a comprehensive evaluation in Table 4. We observe significant accuracy gains on all of them.

Table 3. The samples selected by USL and USL-T greatly outperform the ones from AL/SSAL on [15,63,68], with a budget of 40 labels on CIFAR-10. ‡: MMA⁺ is our improved MMA [64] based on Fix-Match. †: not a fair baseline.

CIFAR-10	S.v2-CLD	FixMatch
Random Selection	60.8	82.9
Stratified Selection†	66.5	88.6
UncertainGCN	63.0	77.3
CoreGCN	62.9	72.9
MMA⁺‡	60.2	71.3
TOD-Semi	65.1	83.3
USL (Ours)	**76.6 ↑11.5**	**90.4 ↑7.1**
USL-T (Ours)	**76.1 ↑11.0**	**93.5 ↑10.2**

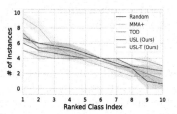

Fig. 5. Comparisons on the semantic class distributions of several methods over 3 runs. USL and USL-T get more balanced distribution.

Table 4. USL/USL-T is a universal method that brings significant accuracy gains to various SSL methods. Experiments are conducted on CIFAR-10 with 40 labels. †: practically infeasible, as it assumes perfectly balanced labeled instances.

CIFAR-10	MixMatch	SimCLRv2	SimCLRv2-CLD	FixMatch	CoMatch
Random	43.4	55.9	60.8	82.9	87.4
Stratified†	62.0	69.8	66.5	88.6	93.1
USL (Ours)	**61.6 ↑18.2**	**69.1 ↑13.2**	**76.6 ↑15.8**	**90.4 ↑7.5**	**93.4 ↑6.0**
USL-T (Ours)	**66.0 ↑22.6**	**71.5 ↑15.6**	**76.1 ↑15.3**	**93.5 ↑10.6**	**93.0 ↑5.6**

4.2   CIFAR-100

On CIFAR-100, we keep hyperparameters the same as the ones for CIFAR-10, except that we change the budget level to 400 to have 4 labels per class on average. Although we may benefit more from hyperparameter tuning, we already show *consistent gains* over other selection methods (Table 5).

4.3   ImageNet-100 and ImageNet-1k

To demonstrate our effectiveness on large-scale datasets, we benchmark on 100 random classes of ImageNet [67] and the full ImageNet [57].

ImageNet-100. On SimCLRv2 with a budget of 400 labels in total, we outperform baselines by 6.1% in this extremely low-label setting (Table 6).

ImageNet-1k: Setup. We experiment on SimCLRv2 and FixMatch with 1% (12, 820 labels) and 0.2% (2, 911 labels) labeled data. We also design a variant of our method that utilizes features provided by CLIP [54]. CLIP is trained on uncurated internet-crawled data in a wide range of domains. Following [8], we initialize FixMatch parameters with MoCov2. See appendix for more details.

Table 5. By selecting informative samples to label, USL and USL-T greatly improve performance of SSL methods on CIFAR-100 with 400 labels. †: practically infeasible, as it assumes perfectly balanced labeled instances.

CIFAR-100	S.v2-CLD Acc	FixMatch Acc
Random Selection	26.5	48.7
Stratified Selection†	30.6	51.2
USL (Ours)	**33.0** ↑**6.5**	**55.1** ↑**6.4**
USL-T (Ours)	**36.9** ↑**10.4**	**55.7** ↑**7.0**

Table 6. USL and USL-T scale well to high dimensional image inputs with many classes on ImageNet-100 [67]. †: practically infeasible.

ImageNet-100	SimCLRv2 Acc
Random	62.2
Stratified†	65.1
USL (Ours)	**67.5** ↑**5.3**
USL-T (Ours)	**68.3** ↑**6.1**

Table 7. Our proposed methods scale well on large-scale dataset ImageNet [57]. *: reported in [8]. USL-MoCo and USL-CLIP use MoCov2 features and CLIP features, respectively, to perform selective labeling. †: not a fair comparison.

	SimCLRv2		FixMatch	
ImageNet-1k	1%	0.20%	1%	0.20%
Random	49.7	33.2	58.8	34.3
Stratified†	52.0	36.4	60.9*	41.1
USL-MoCo (Ours)	51.5 ↑1.8	39.8 ↑6.6	61.6 ↑2.8	**48.6** ↑**14.3**
USL-CLIP (Ours)	**52.6** ↑**2.9**	**40.4** ↑**7.2**	**62.2** ↑**3.4**	47.5 ↑13.2

ImageNet-1k: Comparing With AL/SSAL Methods. As most AL/SSAL methods in Table 2 do not scale to ImageNet, we compare our USL with SSAL methods specifically designed for ImageNet-scale settings [27]. Figure 4b shows our 8× improvement in terms of label efficiency. Table 7 shows that our approach provides up to 14.3% (3.4%) gains in the 0.2% (1%) SSL setting.

ImageNet-1k: USL-CLIP. Table 7 shows samples selected according to both MoCov2 and CLIP features boost SSL performance. USL-MoCo performs 1.1% better than USL-CLIP in the FixMatch setting. We hypothesize that it is, in part, due to a mismatch between parameter initialization (MoCov2) and the feature space used for the sampling process (CLIP). However, for 1% case, USL-CLIP performs 0.6% better than USL-MoCo, showing a slight advantage of a model trained with sufficient general knowledge and explicit semantics.

4.4   Strong Generalizability

Cross-Dataset Generalizability with CLIP. Since CLIP does not use ImageNet samples in training and the downstream SSL task is not exposed to the CLIP model either, USL-CLIP's result shows strong cross-dataset generalizability in Table 7. It means that: **1)** When a new dataset is collected, we could use a general multi-modal model to skip self-supervised pretraining; **2)** Unlike AL where sample selection is strictly coupled with model training, our annotated instances work *universally* rather than with only the model used to select them.

Cross-Domain Generalizability. Such generalizability also holds *across domains*. We use a CLD model trained on CIFAR-10 to select 40 labeled instances in medical imaging dataset BloodMNIST [74]. Although our model has *not* been trained on any medical images, our model with FixMatch performs 10.9% (7.6%) better than random (stratified) sampling. See appendix for more details.

Table 8. The backbone weights learned as a by-product in USL-T capture more semantic information, thereby working as a good initialization.

Weights	Selection method	Accuracy
SimCLR[14]	Random	55.9
SimCLR[14]	USL-T (Ours)	71.5
CLD[68]	USL-T (Ours)	77.2
USL-T (Ours)	USL-T (Ours)	**85.4** ↑**8.2**

Table 9. Hyperparams for USL-T. Hyperparams for USL are in appendix.

Hyperparam	CIFAR-10/100	ImageNet-100/1k
Adjustment factor α	5	2.5
Temperature t	0.25	0.5
Loss term weight λ	5	0.5
Neighborhood size k	20	
Momentum μ	0.5	

4.5   USL-T for Representation Learning

Our USL-T updates feature backbone weights during selective labeling. The trained weights are not used as a model initializer in the downstream SSL experiments for fair comparisons. However, we discover surprising generalizability that greatly exceeds self-supervised learning models under the SimCLRv2 setting. Specifically, we compare the performance of classifiers that are initialized with various model weights and are optimized on samples selected by different methods. Table 8 shows that, even with these strong baselines, initializing the model with our USL-T weights surpasses baselines by 8.2%.

4.6   Hyperparameters and Run Time

Table 9 shows that our hyperparameters generalize within small-scale and large-scale datasets. Our computational overhead is negligible. On ImageNet, we only introduce about 1 GPU hour for selective labeling, as opposed to 2300 GPU hours for the subsequent FixMatch pipeline. See appendix for more analysis, including formulations and visualizations.

5   Summary

Unlike existing SSL methods that focus on algorithms that better integrate labeled and unlabeled data, our selective-labeling is the first to focus on unsupervised data selection for labeling and enable more effective subsequent SSL. By choosing a diverse representative set of instances for annotation, we show significant gains in annotation efficiency and downstream accuracy, with remarkable selection generalizability within and across domains.

Acknowledgements. The authors thank Alexei Efros and Trevor Darrell for helpful discussions and feedback on this work in their classes.

References

1. Angluin, D.: Queries and concept learning. Mach. Learn. **2**(4), 319–342 (1988)
2. Assran, M., et al.: Semi-supervised learning of visual features by non-parametrically predicting view assignments with support samples. In: Proceedings of the IEEE/CVF International Conference on Computer Vision, pp. 8443–8452 (2021)
3. Atlas, L.E., Cohn, D.A., Ladner, R.E.: Training connectionist networks with queries and selective sampling. In: Advances in Neural Information Processing Systems. Citeseer, pp. 566–573 (1990)
4. Berthelot, D., et al.: ReMixMatch: semi-supervised learning with distribution alignment and augmentation anchoring. arXiv preprint arXiv:1911.09785 (2019)
5. Berthelot, D., Carlini, N., Goodfellow, I., Papernot, N., Oliver, A., Raffel, C.: MixMatch: a holistic approach to semi-supervised learning. arXiv preprint arXiv:1905.02249 (2019)

6. Bilgic, M., Getoor, L.: Link-based active learning. In: NIPS Workshop on Analyzing Networks and Learning with Graphs, vol. 4 (2009)

7. Bondy, J.A., Murty, U.S.R., et al.: Graph Theory With Applications, vol. 290. Macmillan, London (1976)

8. Cai, Z., Ravichandran, A., Maji, S., Fowlkes, C., Tu, Z., Soatto, S.: Exponential moving average normalization for self-supervised and semi-supervised learning. In: Proceedings of the IEEE/CVF Conference on Computer Vision and Pattern Recognition, pp. 194–203 (2021)

9. Caramalau, R., Bhattarai, B., Kim, T.K.: Sequential graph convolutional network for active learning. In: Proceedings of the IEEE/CVF Conference on Computer Vision and Pattern Recognition, pp. 9583–9592 (2021)

10. Carlini, N., Erlingsson, U., Papernot, N.: Distribution density, tails, and outliers in machine learning: metrics and applications. arXiv preprint arXiv:1910.13427 (2019)

11. Caron, M., Bojanowski, P., Joulin, A., Douze, M.: Deep clustering for unsupervised learning of visual features. In: ECCV (2018)

12. Caron, M., et al.: Emerging properties in self-supervised vision transformers. In: Proceedings of the IEEE/CVF International Conference on Computer Vision, pp. 9650–9660 (2021)

13. Chan, Y.C., Li, M., Oymak, S.: On the marginal benefit of active learning: does self-supervision eat its cake? In: ICASSP 2021–2021 IEEE International Conference on Acoustics, Speech and Signal Processing (ICASSP). IEEE, pp. 3455–3459 (2021)

14. Chen, T., Kornblith, S., Norouzi, M., Hinton, G.: A simple framework for contrastive learning of visual representations. In: International Conference on Machine Learning. PMLR, pp. 1597–1607 (2020)

15. Chen, T., Kornblith, S., Swersky, K., Norouzi, M., Hinton, G.: Big self-supervised models are strong semi-supervised learners. arXiv preprint arXiv:2006.10029 (2020)

16. Chen, W., Pu, S., Xie, D., Yang, S., Guo, Y., Lin, L.: Unsupervised image classification for deep representation learning. In: Bartoli, A., Fusiello, A. (eds.) ECCV 2020. LNCS, vol. 12536, pp. 430–446. Springer, Cham (2020). https://doi.org/10.1007/978-3-030-66096-3_30

17. Chen, X., Fan, H., Girshick, R., He, K.: Improved baselines with momentum contrastive learning. arXiv preprint arXiv:2003.04297 (2020)

18. Cho, J.W., Kim, D.J., Jung, Y., Kweon, I.S.: MCDAL: maximum classifier discrepancy for active learning. arXiv preprint arXiv:2107.11049 (2021)

19. Chung, F.R., Graham, F.C.: Spectral Graph Theory. No. 92. American Mathematical Society (1997)

20. Cohn, D., Atlas, L., Ladner, R.: Improving generalization with active learning. Mach. Learn. **15**(2), 201–221 (1994)

21. Collobert, R., Weston, J., Bottou, L., Karlen, M., Kavukcuoglu, K., Kuksa, P.: Natural language processing (almost) from scratch. J. Mach. Learn. Res. **12**(ARTICLE), 2493–2537 (2011)

22. Cubuk, E.D., Zoph, B., Shlens, J., Le, Q.V.: RandAugment: practical automated data augmentation with a reduced search space. In: Proceedings of the IEEE/CVF Conference on Computer Vision and Pattern Recognition Workshops, pp. 702–703 (2020)

23. Dagan, I., Engelson, S.P.: Committee-based sampling for training probabilistic classifiers. In: Machine Learning Proceedings 1995. Elsevier, pp. 150–157 (1995)

24. Dang, Z., Deng, C., Yang, X., Wei, K., Huang, H.: Nearest neighbor matching for deep clustering. In: Proceedings of the IEEE/CVF Conference on Computer Vision and Pattern Recognition, pp. 13693–13702 (2021)

25. Deo, N.: Graph theory with applications to engineering and computer science. Networks **5**(3), 299–300 (1975)

26. Ducoffe, M., Precioso, F.: Adversarial active learning for deep networks: a margin based approach. arXiv preprint arXiv:1802.09841 (2018)

27. Emam, Z.A.S., et al.: Active learning at the ImageNet scale. arXiv preprint arXiv:2111.12880 (2021)

28. Fix, E., Hodges, J.L.: Discriminatory analysis. nonparametric discrimination: consistency properties. Int. Stat. Rev./ Rev. Int. Stat. **57**(3), 238–247 (1989)

29. Forgy, E.W.: Cluster analysis of multivariate data: efficiency versus interpretability of classifications. Biometrics **21**, 768–769 (1965)

30. Gao, M., Zhang, Z., Yu, G., Arık, S.Ö., Davis, L.S., Pfister, T.: Consistency-based semi-supervised active learning: towards minimizing labeling cost. In: Vedaldi, A., Bischof, H., Brox, T., Frahm, J.-M. (eds.) ECCV 2020. LNCS, vol. 12355, pp. 510–526. Springer, Cham (2020). https://doi.org/10.1007/978-3-030-58607-2_30

31. Girshick, R., Donahue, J., Darrell, T., Malik, J.: Rich feature hierarchies for accurate object detection and semantic segmentation. In: Proceedings of the IEEE Conference on Computer Vision and Pattern Recognition, pp. 580–587 (2014)

32. Goodfellow, I., Bengio, Y., Courville, A.: Deep Learning. MIT Press, Cambridge (2016)

33. Grandvalet, Y., Bengio, Y., et al.: Semi-supervised learning by entropy minimization. CAP **367**, 281–296 (2005)

34. Guo, J., et al.: Semi-supervised active learning for semi-supervised models: exploit adversarial examples with graph-based virtual labels. In: Proceedings of the IEEE/CVF International Conference on Computer Vision, pp. 2896–2905 (2021)

35. He, K., Fan, H., Wu, Y., Xie, S., Girshick, R.: Momentum contrast for unsupervised visual representation learning. In: Proceedings of the IEEE/CVF Conference on Computer Vision and Pattern Recognition, pp. 9729–9738 (2020)

36. Hestness, J.,et al.: Deep learning scaling is predictable, empirically. arXiv preprint arXiv:1712.00409 (2017)

37. Huang, S.J., Jin, R., Zhou, Z.H.: Active learning by querying informative and representative examples. In: Advances in Neural Information Processing Systems, vol. 23, pp. 892–900 (2010)

38. Huang, S., Wang, T., Xiong, H., Huan, J., Dou, D.: Semi-supervised active learning with temporal output discrepancy. In: Proceedings of the IEEE/CVF International Conference on Computer Vision, pp. 3447–3456 (2021)

39. Kriegel, H.P., Schubert, E., Zimek, A.: The (black) art of runtime evaluation: are we comparing algorithms or implementations? Know. Inf. Syst. **52**(2), 341–378 (2017)

40. Krizhevsky, A., Hinton, G., et al.: Learning multiple layers of features from tiny images (2009)

41. Krizhevsky, A., Sutskever, I., Hinton, G.E.: ImageNet classification with deep convolutional neural networks. In: Advances in Neural Information Processing Systems, vol. 25, pp 1097–1105 (2012)

42. LeCun, Y., Bengio, Y., Hinton, G.: Deep learning. Nature **521**(7553), 436–444 (2015)

43. Lee, D.H., et al.: Pseudo-label: the simple and efficient semi-supervised learning method for deep neural networks. In: Workshop on Challenges in Representation Learning. ICML, vol. 3 (2013)

44. Li, J., Xiong, C., Hoi, S.C.: CoMatch: semi-supervised learning with contrastive graph regularization. In: Proceedings of the IEEE/CVF International Conference on Computer Vision, pp. 9475–9484 (2021)

45. Li, S., et al.: Improve unsupervised pretraining for few-label transfer. In: Proceedings of the IEEE/CVF International Conference on Computer Vision, pp. 10201–10210 (2021)
46. Liu, B., Wu, Z., Hu, H., Lin, S.: Deep metric transfer for label propagation with limited annotated data. In: Proceedings of the IEEE/CVF International Conference on Computer Vision Workshops (2019)
47. Lloyd, S.: Least squares quantization in PCM. IEEE Trans. Inf. Theory **28**(2), 129–137 (1982)
48. McLachlan, G.J., Krishnan, T.: The EM Algorithm and Extensions, vol. 382. Wiley, Hoboken (2007)
49. Menon, A.K., Jayasumana, S., Rawat, A.S., Jain, H., Veit, A., Kumar, S.: Long-tail learning via logit adjustment. arXiv preprint arXiv:2007.07314 (2020)
50. Miao, Z., Liu, Z., Gaynor, K.M., Palmer, M.S., Yu, S.X., Getz, W.M.: Iterative human and automated identification of wildlife images. Nat. Mach. Intell. **3**(10), 885–895 (2021)
51. Oord, A.V.D., Li, Y., Vinyals, O.: Representation learning with contrastive predictive coding. arXiv preprint arXiv:1807.03748 (2018)
52. Orava, J.: K-Nearest Neighbour Kernel Density Estimation. The Choice of Optimal k. vol. 50. no. 1, pp. 39–50. Tatra Mountains Mathematical Publications, Poland, (2011)
53. Park, S., et al.: Improving unsupervised image clustering with robust learning. In: Proceedings of the IEEE/CVF Conference on Computer Vision and Pattern Recognition, pp. 12278–12287 (2021)
54. Radford, A., et al.: Learning transferable visual models from natural language supervision. arXiv preprint arXiv:2103.00020 (2021)
55. Ren, P., et al.: A survey of deep active learning. arXiv preprint arXiv:2009.00236 (2020)
56. Roy, N., Mccallum, A.: Toward optimal active learning through sampling estimation of error reduction. In: Proceedings of the 18th International Conference on Machine Learning (2001)
57. Russakovsky, O., et al.: ImageNet large scale visual recognition challenge. Int. J. Comput. Vis. (IJCV) **115**(3), 211–252 (2015). https://doi.org/10.1007/s11263-015-0816-y
58. Sajjadi, M., Javanmardi, M., Tasdizen, T.: Regularization with stochastic transformations and perturbations for deep semi-supervised learning. arXiv preprint arXiv:1606.04586 (2016)
59. Sener, O., Savarese, S.: Active learning for convolutional neural networks: a core-set approach. arXiv preprint arXiv:1708.00489 (2017)
60. Settles, B.: Active learning literature survey (2009)
61. Shi, J., Malik, J.: Normalized cuts and image segmentation. IEEE Trans. Pattern Anal. Mach. Intell. **22**(8), 888–905 (2000)
62. Sinha, S., Ebrahimi, S., Darrell, T.: Variational adversarial active learning. In: Proceedings of the IEEE/CVF International Conference on Computer Vision, pp. 5972–5981 (2019)
63. Sohn, K.,et al.: FixMatch: simplifying semi-supervised learning with consistency and confidence. In: Advances in Neural Information Processing Systems, vol. 33 (2020)
64. Song, S., Berthelot, D., Rostamizadeh, A.: Combining MixMatch and active learning for better accuracy with fewer labels. arXiv preprint arXiv:1912.00594 (2019)

65. Tarvainen, A., Valpola, H.: Mean teachers are better role models: weight-averaged consistency targets improve semi-supervised deep learning results. In: Proceedings of the 31st International Conference on Neural Information Processing Systems, pp. 1195–1204 (2017)
66. Tong, S., Koller, D.: Support vector machine active learning with applications to text classification. J. Mach. Learn. Res. 2(Nov), 45–66 (2001)
67. Van Gansbeke, W., Vandenhende, S., Georgoulis, S., Proesmans, M., Van Gool, L.: SCAN: learning to classify images without labels. In: Vedaldi, A., Bischof, H., Brox, T., Frahm, J.-M. (eds.) ECCV 2020. LNCS, vol. 12355, pp. 268–285. Springer, Cham (2020). https://doi.org/10.1007/978-3-030-58607-2_16
68. Wang, X., Liu, Z., Yu, S.X.: Unsupervised feature learning by cross-level instance-group discrimination. In: Proceedings of the IEEE/CVF Conference on Computer Vision and Pattern Recognition, pp. 12586–12595 (2021)
69. Wang, X., Wu, Z., Lian, L., Yu, S.X.: Debiased learning from naturally imbalanced pseudo-labels. In: Proceedings of the IEEE/CVF Conference on Computer Vision and Pattern Recognition, pp. 14647–14657 (2022)
70. Wei, K., Iyer, R., Bilmes, J.: Submodularity in data subset selection and active learning. In: International Conference on Machine Learning. PMLR, pp. 1954–1963 (2015)
71. Wu, Z., Xiong, Y., Yu, S.X., Lin, D.: Unsupervised feature learning via non-parametric instance discrimination. In: Proceedings of the IEEE Conference on Computer Vision and Pattern Recognition, pp. 3733–3742 (2018)
72. Xie, Q., Dai, Z., Hovy, E., Luong, T., Le, Q.: Unsupervised data augmentation for consistency training. In: Advances in Neural Information Processing Systems, vol. 33 (2020)
73. Xie, Q., Luong, M.T., Hovy, E., Le, Q.V.: Self-training with noisy student improves ImageNet classification. In: Proceedings of the IEEE/CVF Conference on Computer Vision and Pattern Recognition, pp. 10687–10698 (2020)
74. Yang, J., et al.: MedMNIST v2: a large-scale lightweight benchmark for 2D and 3D biomedical image classification. arXiv preprint arXiv:2110.14795 (2021)
75. Yoo, D., Kweon, I.S.: Learning loss for active learning. In: Proceedings of the IEEE/CVF Conference on Computer Vision and Pattern Recognition, pp. 93–102 (2019)

Max Pooling with Vision Transformers Reconciles Class and Shape in Weakly Supervised Semantic Segmentation

Simone Rossetti[1,2], Damiano Zappia[1], Marta Sanzari[2], Marco Schaerf[1,2], and Fiora Pirri[1,2(✉)]

[1] DeepPlants, Rome, Italy
{simone,damiano,fiora}@deepplants.com
[2] DIAG, Sapienza, Rome, Italy
{rossetti,sanzari,schaerf,pirri}@diag.uniroma1.it

Abstract. Weakly Supervised Semantic Segmentation (WSSS) research has explored many directions to improve the typical pipeline CNN plus class activation maps (CAM) plus refinements, given the image-class label as the only supervision. Though the gap with the fully supervised methods is reduced, further abating the spread seems unlikely within this framework. On the other hand, WSSS methods based on Vision Transformers (ViT) have not yet explored valid alternatives to CAM. ViT features have been shown to retain a scene layout, and object boundaries in self-supervised learning. To confirm these findings, we prove that the advantages of transformers in self-supervised methods are further strengthened by Global Max Pooling (GMP), which can leverage patch features to negotiate pixel-label probability with class probability. This work proposes a new WSSS method dubbed ViT-PCM (ViT Patch-Class Mapping), not based on CAM. The end-to-end presented network learns with a single optimization process, refined shape and proper localization for segmentation masks. Our model outperforms the state-of-the-art on baseline pseudo-masks (BPM), where we achieve 69.3% mIoU on PascalVOC 2012 *val* set. We show that our approach has the least set of parameters, though obtaining higher accuracy than all other approaches. In a sentence, quantitative and qualitative results of our method reveal that ViT-PCM is an excellent alternative to CNN-CAM based architectures.

Keywords: Weakly-supervised semantic segmentation · Vision transformers · Global max pooling · Image class-labels supervision

1 Introduction

Weakly supervised semantic segmentation (WSSS) is about segmenting object classes with no pixel-label supervision and using the less demanding supervision possible. The most economic supervision is via image-level class labels, out of

Supplementary Information The online version contains supplementary material available at https://doi.org/10.1007/978-3-031-20056-4_26.

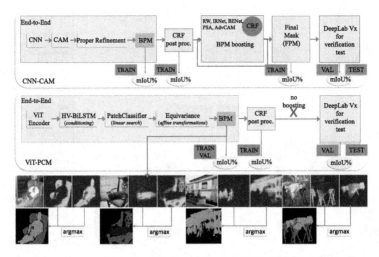

Fig. 1. The figure compares the basic structure of a CNN-CAM method, above in light blue, with our proposed ViT-PCM method, below in light green. ViT-PCM learns to estimate the BPM, shown in the last two strips, with a single optimization. Our BPM are then refined with a CRF (see Fig. 4) and, without further processing, are passed to the verification task (DeepLab). Differently from ViT-PCM, a CAM-based method demands a multi-stage optimization. All recent approaches require boosting the BPM, improved by the CRF, before passing them to the verification task. (Color figure online)

which a WSSS method computes pseudo-masks for each object class in an image. To test a WSSS method accuracy, a supervised segmentation network, such as DeepLab [7], is trained on the devised pseudo-masks, and the induced accuracy is compared with the fully supervised methods. The segmentation task, supervised by the pseudo-mask labels, is a *verification task* aiming at demonstrating the computed pseudo-mask quality. In principle, the verification task adds equal improvement to all methods (Fig. 1).

So far, methods based on image-level class labels generate pseudo-mask using class activation maps (CAM) [62]. CAM are obtained from a multi-label classification network, such as a CNN.

CAM limitations in estimating both shape and localization of the classes of interest [4,12,20,50] induce many researchers to resort to extra refinements between the baseline pseudo-masks (BPM), often called *seeds*, and the final pseudo-masks production for test verification. These refinements mostly often bring into play multi-stage architectures, as noted in PAMR [3]. Several authors resort to saliency maps as subsidiary supervision for good localization [32,47,52, 57,63]. Other authors adopt image operations such as region erasing [42,51], or region growing to expand the seed region during training [23,26], and multi-scale map fusion to improve background and foreground [53]. Jang *et Al.* [25] reviewed the feature layers selection for CAMs using attribute propagation methods [35]. Sun *et Al.* [45] estimate the similarity of the foreground features of the same

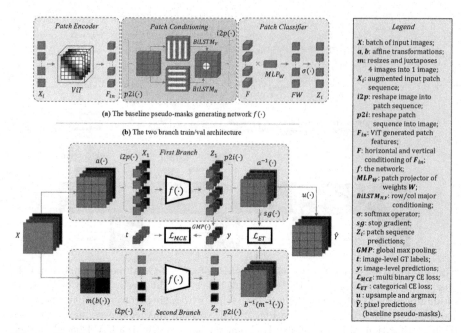

Fig. 2. The above schema shows the end-to-end ViT-PCM, a semantic segmentation method supervised by image-level class labels t. The plate in (a) shows the core network $f(\cdot)$ implementing the *linear search method*, which maps the image-level class labels to patch-labels. The plate (b) shows the two-branches architecture, including $f(\cdot)$ in both branches.

class with two co-attention networks to capture better the context and [19] look into relations across different images.

Yet, the greatest success in refinement strategies has been earned by IRNet [1], PSA [2], and AdvCAM [30]. Also, PAC [44] and BENet [9], have been recently used. For example, SEAM [50], Chang *et Al.* [6] and [41] use PSA; CONTA [14] and ReCAM [12] use IRNet while [30] using both. AFA [39] use PAC [44].

CRF [27] are trained on PascalVOC, fully supervised, and introduced in WSSS by [26]. CRF used as post-processing out of a training loop, improve the BPM, on average, 3–4% mIoU, on Pascal VOC 2012. On the other hand, multi-stage methods, refining BPM with IRNet [1], PSA [2], and AdvCAM [30] use dense CRF in the training loop, which gives a substantial boost in accuracy. Using dense CRF, optimized on PascalVOC, likewise using saliency (e.g. [22], which operates dense CRF too) in the refinement loop to obtain the final pseudo-mask, beside being resource intensive, fails to generalize a method beyond the PascalVOC dataset. This lack of generalization power is common to any WSSS approach using biased methods in a refinement training loop.

The challenge is to raise the bar of the baseline pseudo-mask accuracy so that the only supervision truly sticks to the image-level label. To this end, we introduce a new model for computing pseudo-masks, which bypasses the CAM bottleneck. The main contribution of the paper are the followings:

- We introduce a novel model for weakly supervised semantic segmentation (WSSS) based on ViT [15]. The model, dubbed ViT-PCM, is represented in Fig. 2.
- We propose a new pseudo-mask computation method *Explicit Search* without resorting to CAM. The method leverages the locality properties of ViT to come close to an effective mapping between multi-label classification and semantic segmentation. We use the Global Max Pooling (GMP) to fetch the relevance of each patch, given the patches' categorical distribution over the classes of interest. This way, we project the patch features to class predictions (PCM) using a multi-label BCE loss (MCE). We ensure equivariance to translation and scaling transformations defining two branches, see Fig. 2.
- The proposed pseudo-mask computation outperforms all state-of-the-art methods: we obtain BPM accuracy of 67.7 mIoU% on Pascal VOC 2012 *train* set which improves the current best BPM [39] of 3.91%. On average, we improve more than 5% mIoU than all the other competitors. On MS-COCO 2014 we obtain 45.03% mIoU on *val* set.
- For the verification task, using DeepLab as a segmentation method, we do not need to boost our BPM to obtain masks more suitable for DeepLab, yet we obtain comparable validation and test scores.
- We also prove the advantages of our method in terms of computational effort. In particular, we obtain the final segmentation with 89.4 M of parameter size, the minimal cost amid competitors.

Beyond the novelty of our contribution, which is the first proposal to compute pseudo-mask baselines bypassing CAM, we show that both quantitative and qualitative results prove that exploring new methods for baseline pseudo-masks can be rewarding. We establish a new state of art on baseline pseudo-mask computation, using image-level class labels without refinement.

2   Related Works

Current WSSS methods mostly operate with image-level class labels as the cheapest supervision. Approaches using image-level class labels are based so far on CAM [62] methods using a plain multi-label classification network. The class activation maps are obtained via the global average pooling (GAP) averaging the feature maps of the last layer, further concatenated into a weights vector. This last is connected with the class prediction, using a BCE prediction loss. More recently, Vision Transformers [15] are emerging as an alternative to generate CAM [39,58]. Our method is the first one using only ViT without CAM to generate baseline pseudo-masks.

CNN Plus CAM. These methods contribute to two complementary research directions: *Baseline Pseudo-Mask generation*, to control and expand the activation of CAM regions, and *Pseudo-Mask refinement* to obtain the full mask of objects.

Baseline Pseudo-Mask Generation. extends CAM by revising the loss, or by augmenting the dataset, or by perturbing CAM devised regions, or using pretrained saliency maps. In ReCAM [12] the authors propose softmax cross-entropy (SCE) as a valid solution for CAM, since it bypasses the non-exclusive class problem of BCE. In OoD [31] the authors propose an out of distribution dataset taken from OpenImages [28], to better capture background semantics. Other methods to expand CAM perturb the generated regions to capture new areas [29,30,43], by either erasing or masking. Since [52], pretrained methods for saliency detection and saliency maps have been adopted in [32,36,54,57,59,61], and in [24,25]. The latter propose an online attention accumulation (OAA) strategy based on attribute propagation methods. Pseudo-mask generation is contaminated by self-supervised learning in [50], via downstream tasks and transformations ensuring CAM features equivariance, or via contrastive representation learning, as in RCA [63], C2AM [56] and PPC [16].

Pseudo-Mask Refinement. In recent works, all CAM-based approaches explore refinement strategies, ensuring some control on pixel-level labelling. The most common strategies are PSA [2], AdvCAM [30] and IRNet [1]. PSA refines the baseline masks by propagating pixel semantic values to their neighbours, collecting confidence for the target classes. AdvCAM [30] uses iterative adversarial climbing performed on an image to iteratively involve its features in the classification to increase CAM confidence in activated regions. IRNet [1] explores class equivalence relations of pixels and refines pixel-labels by evaluating the displacement w.r.t. computed centroids. Recently BENet [9] has been used for pseudo-mask baseline refinement, too; it refines object boundaries, together with foreground and background. We observed in the introduction that all these strategies use in the training loop dense CRF of [27], which is trained on PascalVOC2012.

Transformers. ViT have so far gathered a significant success with self-supervised learning [15], as witnesses Dino [5], [11,33], and recently SDMP [37]. Dino [5] downstream task segments foreground from background for single class images, differing from WSSS. Only recently ViT contributed to WSSS with MCTformer [58] and AFA [39], though both resort to CAM. MCTformer exploits ViT attention mechanism to obtain localization maps. To generate pseudo-masks, they resort to PSA [2]. AFA uses ViT multi-head-self-attention (MSA) to capture global dependencies and develop an affinity-based attention module to propagate the initial pseudo-masks, namely the obtained CAM. Refinement of the initial pseudo-mask is attained by affinity propagation with RAWK [49], in turn, pretrained on a scribble dataset.

Differently from the above approaches, we use ViT as a backbone for building our explicit search method. Indeed, we devise an end-to-end internal refinement to obtain a baseline pseudo-mask (BMP) without resorting to external strategies.

3   Motivations of Using ViT and Bypass CAM

At the core of semantic segmentation, supervised by image-level labels, is the mapping between multilabel image classification and pixel-level classification. This mapping requires linking the abstract image feature space, encoding classes

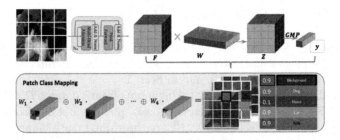

Fig. 3. PCM: Patch to class mapping.

into an index vector, to a completely different space in which features encode classes into a fine grid structure. How could this be possible? CNN have an inductive bias on the image features local structure because of convolution kernels, which CAM leverages. The inductive bias of CNN entitles CAM to indicate the pixels which mainly contribute to the specific class prediction. The produced map is appealing though misleading: it does not induce a mapping between image features and pixels (Fig. 3).

On the other hand, ViT [15] have much less bias because images are split into flattened patches and encoded. Thus, the spatial relations are learned from scratch using attention and position embedding. This learning from a *tabula rasa* generates a number of basis functions for each patch, specifying their internal structure. These basis functions account implicitly for the class a patch belongs to. On these grounds, the mapping problem amounts to unravelling the implicit class representation brought on by the patch principal components. Our proposed *explicit search method* models this mapping.

We describe here the intuition. Let us assume that patches are pixels, the classes (categories) are denoted by $\mathcal{C}$, having cardinality K and $X \in \mathbb{R}^{h \times w \times 3}$ is an image. Let also assume that the ViT inferring the image multiclass labels is the function $f(\cdot|\varphi)$ with parameters φ, mapping an image X to a vector of values in $(0,1)$ for each category in $\mathcal{C}$. On the other hand, let us represent the basis functions specifying the patches' internal structure, implicitly accounting for the patch classes, by a tensor Z. We shall see below how Z is computed. Z has height and width as the image X, and it also has a third axis for the categories $\mathcal{C}$. We make Z a stochastic tensor along the categories axis: summing up along that axis, we obtain a matrix of ones. Let $f(\cdot|\theta)$, with parameter θ, play the role of the segmentation model; namely, it evaluates the likelihood that a patch of the original image belongs to some precise class in $\mathcal{C}$.

We argue that Global Max Pooling (GMP) relates the two models $f(\cdot|\theta)$ and $f(\cdot|\varphi)$ as follows. Let Z^k be the slice of Z, along the categories axis, which should specify the patches internal structure for the category $k \in \mathcal{C}$. GMP selects the most relevant element of Z^k, namely the element with the highest confidence to belong to the category k, and returns a probability value y^k that it belongs to class $k \in \mathcal{C}$. The selected element Z_{ij}^k, at the same time, is the one in highest consideration to tell whether or not the category k appears in the image. In this way, GMP links image class prediction and patch class prediction.

4   The Explicit Search Method

This section considers the optimization method leading to estimating the map between image classes and patch classes. The end-to-end architecture enclosing the method is described in Fig. 2, and in Sect. 5.

Let us indicate by f the network taking inputs from a dataset $\mathcal{D} = \{\langle X_{in}, t \rangle\}$. Here $X_{in} \in \mathbb{R}^{h \times w \times 3}$ indicates an input images, possibly obtained from an augmented and transformed set, $t \in \{0, 1\}^K$ are the ground truth binary labels, and K is the number of classes defined by the category set $\mathcal{C} = \{0, 1, \ldots, K\}$. The output of f is a tensor $\hat{Y} \in \mathcal{C}^{h \times w}$ which is a *baseline pseudo-mask*.

ViT is part of f. We recall that ViT partitions the image X, resized image of the original X_{in}, into s patches of size $(d \times d \times 3)$. In particular, we are interested in the feature maps $F \in \mathbb{R}^{s \times e}$, with $s = (n/d)^2$, with $n = w = h$. The feature maps F are the encoded representations of the patches, obtained by ViT. F represent the basis functions specifying the patches internal structure.

Explicit Search by Global Max-Pooling. Given $F \in \mathbb{R}^{s \times e}$, we consider also a weight matrix $W \in \mathbb{R}^{e \times K}$ whose weights are taken into account in the optimization method described below. More precisely, we estimate the baseline pseudo-mask $\hat{Y}$, training the weights W with only image-level class labels as supervision, minimizing the multilabel classification error.

The first objective is to minimize the multilabel classification prediction error (MCE). Thus, given the ground truth binary labels t defined above, and recalling that K are the number of classes, we model the multi-label classification using K independent Bernoulli distributions and K binary cross-entropy losses (BCE):

$$\mathcal{L}_{MCE} = \frac{1}{K} \sum_{k \in \mathcal{C}} BCE(t_k, y_k) = -\frac{1}{K} \sum_{k \in \mathcal{C}} t_k \log(y_k) + (1 - t_k) \log(1 - y_k). \quad (1)$$

Let us consider first how $y \in \mathbb{R}^K$ is obtained. Let:

$$A = FW \quad \text{and} \quad Z = softmax(A), \text{ with } F \in \mathbb{R}^{s \times e}, W \in \mathbb{R}^{e \times K} \text{ hence } Z \in \mathbb{R}^{s \times K}. \quad (2)$$

Z represents the semantic segmentation predictions, needing to be projected into class predictions[1]. We do so using Global Max Pooling (GMP):

$$y_k = GMP(Z^k) = \max(Z^k) = Z_i^k, \text{ for some } i \in \{1, \ldots, s\}. \quad (3)$$

Here:

$$Z^k = softmax(A^k) \quad \text{and} \quad A_j^k = F_j W^k \quad (4)$$

The feature maps F are the encoded representation of patches U, and F_j is the feature map of patch U_j, while A_j^k is the logit of patch U_j, $j = 0, \ldots, s$ with respect to class $k \in \{0, 1, \ldots, K\}$.

---

[1] Note that we are representing here Z as a matrix, which is simply a reshaping of the tensor Z discussed in Sect. 3.

Given the vector y_k, we show how the optimization obtains the terms separating the feature space by the relative error backpropagation of $\mathcal{L}_{MCE}$, with respect to weights W. Computing the gradient of Eq. (1) w.r.t. the weight W, we obtain:

$$\frac{\partial \mathcal{L}_{MCE}}{\partial W} = \sum_{k \in \mathcal{C}} \frac{\partial BCE(t_k, y_k)}{\partial W} \tag{5}$$

Let us analyze the gradient of the weights W, with respect to each column h, of size e, with $h \in \{0, 1, \ldots K\}$. Applying the chain rule, w.r.t. the generic class k:

$$\frac{\partial BCE(t_k, y_k)}{\partial W^h} = \frac{\partial BCE(t_k, y_k)}{\partial y_k} \frac{\partial Z_i^k}{\partial A^h} \frac{\partial A^h}{\partial W^h} \tag{6}$$

Here we used the fact that $y_k = max(Z^k)$, and $max(Z^k) = Z_i^k$ from Eq. (3). Therefore, the gradient dimension is $\frac{\partial BCE(t_k, y_k)}{\partial W^h} \in \mathbb{R}^e$. The derivation of each term is provided in the supplementary.

Let us select, now, the column h of the weights W, this column will be updated by the quantity:

$$\frac{\partial \mathcal{L}_{MCE}}{\partial W^h} = \frac{\partial BCE(t_h, y_h)}{\partial W^h} + \sum_{k \in \mathcal{C}, k \neq h} \frac{\partial BCE(t_k, y_k)}{\partial W^h}$$

$$= -F_{i_h}(t_h - y_h) + \sum_{k \in \mathcal{C}, k \neq h} F_{i_k} Z_{i_k}^h \frac{t_k - y_k}{1 - y_k} \tag{7}$$

Note that here the subscripts i_h, i_k in F and Z^h indicate, respectively, the indexes at which Z_i have maximum value, w.r.t classes h and k, where F_i is obtained by the last two terms of Eq. 6, r.h.s. We are using these indexes only in the updating rule for the weights; we are not using them in the derivation.

Equation 7 specifies the linear-search mechanism of the proposed optimization, iteratively selecting the most representative features F_{i_h} of each category h. At each step, the optimization updates the full column rank matrix $W \in \mathbb{R}^{s \times e}$ and returns the minimum error norm solution, which separates the feature vector space $\mathbb{R}^e$ into K linear sub-spaces. Considering the optimization manifold, the vector W^h moves in the direction of the best representative feature vector F_{i_u}, with either u being of the same category of the chosen column h, or not. More precisely, at each iteration, W^h moves in the direction of F_{i_h} according to the error value $(t_h - y_h)$, and in the direction F_{i_k} according to the term $Z_{i_k}^h \frac{t_k - y_k}{1 - y_k}$, for any category k, with $k \neq h$.

More specifically, when the term $\frac{(t_k - y_k)}{1 - y_k} = 1$, and the category $k \neq h$ is considered, W^h moves in the direction opposite to the best representative feature vector F_{i_k}. On the other hand, when $t_k = 0$ the term considered is $-(Z_{i_k}^k \frac{y_k}{1 - y_k})$ which is added to W^h, for its updating. Note that, in this case, the update term is increasingly small, since $y_k \ll 1 - y_k$ as $y_k \to 0$. This optimization method, based on iterative learning and stochastic gradient descent, induces a separation in the space of patch features, according to the multilabel classification.

5   ViT-PCM Model Structure

The model architecture has two branches, as shown in Fig. 2. We describe its components in the following.

Augmentation. The batch of input images is augmented as usual in the first branch. In the second branch, images are translated, rotated and scaled. Furthermore, we merge four images from the batch into a single image after scaling them to have a different tiling of the images into patches.

ViT Patch Encoder. The Vision Transformer encoder takes as input the augmented batch of images and returns the features F_{in} and the n patches described in the *explicit search* method, Sect. 4.

HV-BiLSTM Patch Conditioning. Two bidirectional LSTM (BiLSTM) process row-wise and column-wise the features F_{in} transformed to a tensor grid. The two BiLSTM outputs are concatenated into a HV-BiLSTM (for Horizontal and Vertical), and their feature maps F are fed to the Patch Classifier. The HV-BiLSTM improves information amid neighbour patches by conditioning each patch on all other ones in horizontal (H) and vertical directions (V) [48].

Patch Classifier (PC). While ViT and the two BiLSTM encode class information into the patch features, the Patch Classifier implements the BPM generation, as described in the explicit search method, Sect. 4.

Two Branches for Equivariant Regularization. ViT are not equivariant to translations because of the absolute positional encoding used for self-attention. Romero *et Al.* [38] show that for self-attention to be equivariant to group transformations, they must act directly on positional encoding. In our ViT-based method, though GMP is independent of the positional encoding and is invariant to transformations, the BPM generation is not. To remedy we resort to typical self-supervised learning tasks, using two branches enabling the network to learn equivariance properties. Equivariance encourages the feature representation to change coherently to the transformation applied to the input [13]. As discussed above, we apply affine transformations to both the network branches in the preprocessing step. After the same processing steps of the main branch, the sibling one applies an inverse merging of the features and upscales them to obtain the n patches feature maps as in the main branch. Finally, inverse affine transformations are applied to both branches.

The outcome is that these transformations cope both with positional encoding and spatial transformations. The loss to be minimized is the cross entropy loss $\mathcal{L}_{ET}$, taking into account the transformations in the two branches:

$$
\mathcal{L}_{ET} = -\frac{1}{s} \sum_{i=0}^{s} \sum_{X \in \mathcal{X}} \nu_i(X) \log \mu_i(X)
$$
$$
\text{with } \mu_i(X) = a^{-1} f(a(X)) \text{ and } \nu_i(X) = c^{-1} f(c(X))
$$

(8)

Here, $\mathcal{X}$ is the images domain, $a(\cdot), b(\cdot)$ are affine transformations in the first and second branch, $m(\cdot)$ is the above defined merging operation, and $c = m(b(\cdot))$.

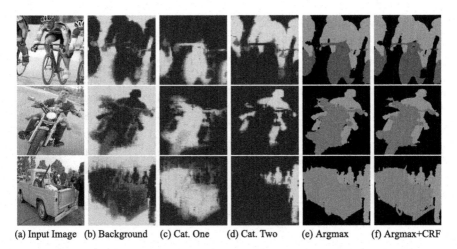

(a) Input Image   (b) Background   (c) Cat. One   (d) Cat. Two   (e) Argmax   (f) Argmax+CRF

Fig. 4. Columns (b)–(c)–(d) show the BPM inferred by our ViT-PCM, with probabilities highlighted by 60×60 heatmaps: values in yellow indicate the pixels' probability of belonging to the predicted class. Column (e) is the scaled BPM, obtained by selecting from the distribution of each patch the category indices with maximum probability (argmax). Column (f) displays the BPM argmax refined by CRF.

Final Loss. We have the $\mathcal{L}_{MCE}$ loss, conveying the mapping between image classification and patch classification, and $\mathcal{L}_{ET}$, which ensures equivariance and scales the images so that patches get pixel dimension. The final loss is then:

$$\mathcal{L} = \mathcal{L}_{MCE} + \mathcal{L}_{ET} \tag{9}$$

Training the end-to-end network by minimizing this final loss obtains the baseline pseudo-mask.

6   Experiments and Results

6.1   Set-Up

Datasets. We conducted our experiments on Pascal VOC 2012 [17] (20 categories) and on MS COCO 2014 [34] (80 categories), the additional background class is inferred. The Pascal VOC 2012 Dataset [17] is usually augmented with the SBD dataset [21]. The images in train sets of PASCAL VOC and MS COCO are annotated with image-level labels only. We report mean Intersection-Over-Union (mIoU) as the evaluation criteria.

Networks Configuration. For the ViT transformer backbones [15] we used ViT-S/16 and ViT-B/16 architectures, pre-trained on ImageNet22K and fine-tuned on ImageNet2012 [40]. We designed an MLP layer projecting the patch features into a categorical distribution on the K classes as a baseline model for ablation purposes. For the verification task, we used DeepLab V2 [8].

Table 1. Ablation on our ViT-PCM model for baseline pseudo-mask production, on PASCAL-VOC 2012 values in mIoU%.

Backbone	$\mathcal{L}_{MCE}$	$\mathcal{L}_{ET}$	HV-BiLSTM	CRF	Train	Val
ViT-S/16	✓				44.0	43.3
	✓	✓			59.2 +15.2	56.4 +13.1
	✓	✓	✓		63.6 +4.4	61.8+5.4
	✓	✓	✓	✓	67.1 +3.5	64.9+3.1
ViT-B/16	✓				45.6	44.1
	✓	✓			65.1 +19.5	62.4 +18.3
	✓	✓	✓		67.7 +2.6	66.0+3.6
	✓	✓	✓	✓	71.4 +3.7	69.3+3.3

Reproducibility. Images are resized to 384×384 for training and augmented by random colour jitter, random grayscale, $90°$ rotation, and vertical and horizontal flip. Initially, we freeze the backbone and ignore the output feature for the [cls] token. At the same time, we preserve the 24·24 encoded patch features as input to the BiLSTM conditioning, whose outcome features are passed to the Patch Classifier. We initialize the MLP layer with standard Gaussian distribution and use L2 regularization with coefficient $l_2 = 10^{-1}$. We ran our training sessions iterating over the entire dataset, each epoch measuring the mIoU (%) progresses on the PascalVOC 2012 and MS COCO2014 validation sets. We keep the input resolution to 384×384 to hasten the evaluation on a 4 NVIDIA Titan V GPUs with 12 GB RAM each, a deliberately limited resources setup. We use Adam optimization and schedule the learning rate as follows: 10^{-3} learning rate for the first two epochs with a frozen backbone; then, we unfreeze the last four backbone layers and keep training until convergence with 10^{-4} learning rate. At inference time, we scale the input image to 960×960 to get pseudo-label segmentation maps of shape 60×60. As expected, we noticed an increase in performance of about $2-3\%$ mIoU scores for validation in the training session, confirming that ViTs scales very well on larger input size.

6.2   Ablation Studies

In Table 1 we evaluate ViT-PCM computation both with backbone ViT-S/16 and ViT-B/16, considering each component of the end-to-end network. We adopted a patch size of 16 since the memory requirements grow quadratically with the number of patches. The low scores of the ($\mathcal{L}_{MCE}$) in Table 1 are due to the difficulty in encoding the background without equivariance. We observe that with the equivariance, $\mathcal{L}_{ET}$ there is an improvement of 15.2 mIoU% on the *train* set and 13.1 mIoU% on the *val* set for PascalVOC 2012. A further improvement of 4.4 on the *train* set and 5.4 mIoU% on the *val* set is obtained by conditioning the patches with HV-BiLSTM. Finally, we add the dCRF [27] as post-processing obtaining an improvement of 3.5 mIoU% on *train* set.

Table 2. mIoU(%) of BPM on PascalVOC 2012 *val* set. w/wo CRF

Method	bkg	plane	bike	bird	boat	btl	bus	car	cat	chair	cow	table	dog	horse	mbk	person	plant	sheep	sofa	train	tv	mIoU(%)
Pseudo-masks w/o CRF	87.2	66.4	36.9	61.0	61.1	63.0	86.8	76.0	76.9	41.1	80.7	39.0	82.3	77.4	75.7	55.9	50.6	85.0	50.9.6	78.9	54.7	66.0
Pseudo-masks w/ CRF	88.8	78.2	39.1	69.2	67.2	67.2	88.0	77.7	78.5	42.5	83.9	39.2	85.2	82.8	79.8	56.2	51.0	91.3	51.0	81.9	57.0	69.3

Figure 4 shows the BPM heat-maps for each class in the second, third and fourth columns, inferred by our end-to-end network, including the background. The BPM heat map highlights each pixel's likelihood of belonging to a specific category. Column (e) shows the pseudo-masks obtained by selecting the indices of the classes with maximum probability. Column (f) shows the pseudo-masks improved by CRF. We use these last masks for the verification task as input to DeepLab [7].

In Table 2 we report the BPM mIoU% on Pascal VOC val set for each category, w and w/o CRF.

6.3   Comparisons with State-of-the-Art

Comparison on Baseline Pseudo-Masks. We compare the mIoU (%) accuracy of our ViT-PCM method with other methods, which compute BPM and post-process them with CRF [27] similarly. Some methods such as CIAN [19] and EDAM [54] also incorporate saliency.

Results are reported in Table A. Here we can observe that CRF, used as BPM post-processing, improves the BPM, on average, by 3.97%, with a standard deviation of 1.87. The statistics show that CRF out of a training loop behaves similarly on all methods. Observe that we improved BPM state-of-the-art by 3.91 mIou% points and BPM+CRF by 5.4 mIoU%, both w.r.t. AFA [39], owning so far the best accuracy on both.

Table A: mIoU(%) on PascalVOC2012 train set.

Method	Backbone	BPM	BPM+CRF
ICD [18] CVPR'20	VGG16	57.00	62.20
SCE [6] CVPR'20	ResNet38	50.90	–
SEAM [50] CVPR'20	ResNet38	55.41	56.83
CIAN [19] AAAI'20	ResNet101	58.10	62.50
ECSNet [46] ICCV'20	ResNet38	56.60	58.60
PAMR [3] CVPR'20	ResNet38	59.7	62.7
AdvCAM [30] CVPR'21	ResNet50	55.60	62.10
CPN [60] ICCV'21	ResNet38	57.43	–
CSE [29] ICCV'21	ResNet38	56.0	62.8
EDAM [54] CVPR'21	ResNet101	52.83	58.18
MCTformer [58] CVPR'22	DeiT-S	61.70	–
PPC [16] CVPR'22	Resnet38	61.50	64.00
CLIMS [55] CVPR'22	Resnet50	56.60	–
SIPE [10] CVPR'22	Resnet50	58.60	64.70
AFA [39] CVPR'22	MiT-B1	63.80	66.00
IRN+W-OoD [31] CVPR'22	Resnet50	53.30	58.40
ViT-PCM Ours	ViT-B/16	**67.71**	**71.4**

Table C: mIoU(%) on MS-COCO 2014 val set.

Method	Backbone	Val
MCTformer [58] CVPR'22	Resnet38	42.0
SIPE [10] CVPR'22	Resnet38	43.6
ViT-PCM Ours	ViT-B/16	**45.0**

Table B: mIoU(%) on PascalVOC2012 val and test set.

Method	Backbone	Val	Test
IRNet [1] CVPR'19	ResNet50	63.5	64.8
SCE [6] CVPR'20	ReseNet101	66.1	65.9
SEAM [50] CVPR'20	ResNet38	64.5	65.7
CIAN [19] AAAI'20	ResNet101	64.3	65.3
ECSNet [46] ICCV'20	ResNet38	66.6	67.6
CONTA [14] NeurIPS'20	ResNet101	66.1	66.7
BES [9] ECCV'20	ResNet101	65.7	66.6
AdvCAM [30] CVPR'21	ResNet50	68.1	68.0
CPN [60] ICCV'21	ResNet38	67.8	68.5
EDAM [54] CVPR'21	ResNet101	52.83	58.18
CSE [29] ICCV'21	ResNet38	68.4	68.2
MCTformer [58] CVPR'22	Resnet38	71.9	71.6
CLIMS [55] CVPR'22	Resnet50	70.4	70.0
SIPE [10] CVPR'22	Resnet101	68.8	69.7
AdvCAM+W-OoD [31] CVPR'22	Resnet38	70.7	70.1
PAMR [3] CVPR'20	ResNet38	62.7	64.3
MCIS [45] ECCV'20	ResNet101	66.2	66.9
ICD [18] CVPR'20	Resnet101	64.1	64.3
AFA [39] CVPR'22	MiT-B1	66.0	66.3
MCTformer* [58] CVPR'22	Resnet38	68.2	68.4
ViT-PCM Ours	ResNet 101	**70.3**	**70.9**

Table D: mIoU(%) on PascalVOC2012 val set.

Method	ViT-S/8	ViT-S/16	ViT-B/16
DINO [5]	44.7	45.9	–
ViT-PCM Ours	–	**74.55**	**77.25**

Semantic Segmentation Verification Tasks. The verification task of the WSSS methods on PascalVOC 2012 tests the final pseudo-mask (FPM), and the results are reported in Table B. We divide the methods into two: those which are boosted (or, according to the definition in PAMR [3] are multi-stage) and those which are end-to-end, highlighted in grey. For the methods considered, the boosted ones improve the mIoU% w.r.t. the BPM on average of 9.8%, while the end-to-end methods improve on average 4.2%. Our ViT-PCM not being boosted improves by 2.39% on the val set and decreases on the test set. Our ViT-PCM has the best accuracy among the end-to-end methods, with 70.3% and 70.9% on *val* and *test* sets. Our method is second to MCT-Former [58] on the test set w.r.t. all methods (boosted and end-to-end). However, MCT-Former end-to-end version is second to ViT-PCM, on both the val and test sets.

In Table C we also evaluate our method on MS-COCO 2014 dataset [34]. Our ViT-PCM achieves 45.03 mIoU% on *val* set. We reported only the last methods (2022) with the highest performance. Table D compares our foreground maps with DINO [5] maps on the PascalVOC 2012 val set. Figure 5 shows the ratio between the parameters consumed to obtain the BPM and the final segmentation mask, against the mIoU% on the val set of PascalVOC2012. A ⋆ marker specifies the BPM, and a □ marker specifies the final segmentation mask, ours in red and the others in blue. Our ViT-PCM, with backbone ViT-S/16, is green-dashed, and ViT-B/16 is green-continuous. We can observe that most of the shown methods are multi-stage (see also [3,39]), and boosting the BPM asks for a significant increase of parameters. Table 3 shows the accuracy between CAM and PCM on different backbones and the amount of parameters required. We made this table to understand whether it would be profitable to use CAM with ViT. As shown in the table, we can see that the combination ViT and PCM is the best solution. Figure 6 compares our qualitative results on Pascal VOC 2012 val set with other approaches whose implementation we have used to generate the images; therefore, they might be biased.

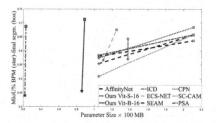

Fig. 5. Networks parameters consumed from the BPM to the final-segmentation in ours and other methods, against mIoU% on PascalVoc2012 val. set.

Table 3. Comparison between CAM [62] and PCM (our Patch Class Mapping) on PascalVOC2012 *val* set. The Table reports the best results obtained with Multi-Label BCE loss and L2 regularization loss in all experiments, for both CAM and PCM.

Backbone	Params (M)	Localization	mIoU (%)	pixAcc (%)
Resnet50v2	25	CAM	**27.8**	72.7
		PCM	25.2	**76.0**
Xception	23	CAM	**37.8**	76.5
		PCM	36.5	**79.5**
ViT-S/16	**22**	CAM	29.3	55.0
		PCM	**43.3**	**80.1**

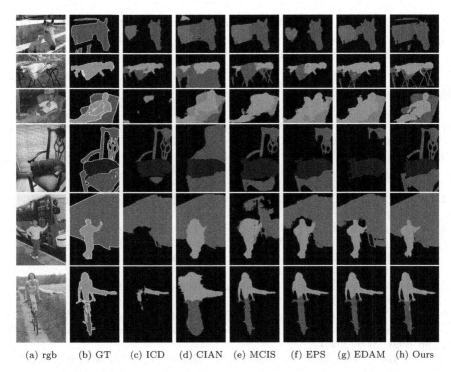

(a) rgb   (b) GT   (c) ICD   (d) CIAN   (e) MCIS   (f) EPS   (g) EDAM   (h) Ours

Fig. 6. Qualitative comparison on Pascal VOC 2012 validation set.

6.4 Limitations

We observed that ViT-PCM is biased on the most discriminative features. Many approaches to WSSS highlight the improvements due to processing pixel relations, boundaries, and neighbourhoods. We have used only the conditioning from HV-BiLSTM, which might not be the best solution. On the other hand, some recent approaches have explored contrastive loss for foreground-background learning with no image-level supervision. Since the background is our Achille's heel, we could have explored this idea. Another bottleneck of our approach is the final scaling to map patches to pixels, where we perform a rough scaling to keep the resources limited.

7   Conclusions

We presented an innovative, simple and end-to-end method, ViT-PCM, based on ViT for generating baseline pseudo-masks (BPM) with precise localization and higher quality than those obtained from the more involved CAM CNN-based architectures. We obtained new state-of-the-art in BPM generation with 67.7 % mIoU on PascalVOC 2012 *train set* and 71.4% mIoU using CRF only in post-processing. These results demonstrate this work's high contribution to the field of WSSS. Therefore, we hope that others will continue in this direction. In the supplementary files, we report more analysis and results. The code is available at https://github.com/deepplants/ViT-PCM.

References

1. Ahn, J., Cho, S., Kwak, S.: Weakly supervised learning of instance segmentation with inter-pixel relations. In: ICCV, pp. 2209–2218 (2019)
2. Ahn, J., Kwak, S.: Learning pixel-level semantic affinity with image-level supervision for weakly supervised semantic segmentation. In: CVPR, pp. 4981–4990 (2018)
3. Araslanov, N., Roth, S.: Single-stage semantic segmentation from image labels. In: CVPR, pp. 4253–4262 (2020)
4. Bae, W., Noh, J., Kim, G.: Rethinking class activation mapping for weakly supervised object localization. In: Vedaldi, A., Bischof, H., Brox, T., Frahm, J.-M. (eds.) ECCV 2020. LNCS, vol. 12360, pp. 618–634. Springer, Cham (2020). https://doi.org/10.1007/978-3-030-58555-6_37
5. Caron, M., et al.: Emerging properties in self-supervised vision transformers. In: ICCV, pp. 9650–9660 (2021)
6. Chang, Y.T., Wang, Q., Hung, W.C., Piramuthu, R., Tsai, Y.H., Yang, M.H.: Weakly-supervised semantic segmentation via sub-category exploration. In: CVPR, pp. 8991–9000 (2020)
7. Chen, L.C., Papandreou, G., Kokkinos, I., Murphy, K.P., Yuille, A.L.: DeepLab: semantic image segmentation with deep convolutional nets, atrous convolution, and fully connected CRFs. IEEE TPAMI **40**, 834–848 (2018)
8. Chen, L.-C., Zhu, Y., Papandreou, G., Schroff, F., Adam, H.: Encoder-decoder with atrous separable convolution for semantic image segmentation. In: Ferrari, V., Hebert, M., Sminchisescu, C., Weiss, Y. (eds.) ECCV 2018. LNCS, vol. 11211, pp. 833–851. Springer, Cham (2018). https://doi.org/10.1007/978-3-030-01234-2_49
9. Chen, L., Wu, W., Fu, C., Han, X., Zhang, Y.: Weakly supervised semantic segmentation with boundary exploration. In: Vedaldi, A., Bischof, H., Brox, T., Frahm, J.-M. (eds.) ECCV 2020. LNCS, vol. 12371, pp. 347–362. Springer, Cham (2020). https://doi.org/10.1007/978-3-030-58574-7_21
10. Chen, Q., Yang, L., Lai, J.H., Xie, X.: Self-supervised image-specific prototype exploration for weakly supervised semantic segmentation. In: Proceedings of the IEEE/CVF Conference on Computer Vision and Pattern Recognition, pp. 4288–4298 (2022)
11. Chen, X., Xie, S., He, K.: An empirical study of training self-supervised vision transformers. In: ICCV, pp. 9640–9649 (2021)
12. Chen, Z., Wang, T., Wu, X., Hua, X.S., Zhang, H., Sun, Q.: Class re-activation maps for weakly-supervised semantic segmentation. In: Proceedings of the IEEE/CVF Conference on Computer Vision and Pattern Recognition, pp. 969–978 (2022)
13. Dangovski, R., et al.: Equivariant self-supervised learning: encouraging equivariance in representations. In: ICLR (2021)
14. Dong, Z., Hanwang, Z., Jinhui, T., Xiansheng, H., Qianru, S.: Causal intervention for weakly supervised semantic segmentation. In: Neurips (2020)
15. Dosovitskiy, A., et al.: An image is worth $16 times 16$ words: transformers for image recognition at scale. arXiv preprint arXiv:2010.11929 (2021)

16. Du, Y., Fu, Z., Liu, Q., Wang, Y.: Weakly supervised semantic segmentation by pixel-to-prototype contrast. In: Proceedings of the IEEE/CVF Conference on Computer Vision and Pattern Recognition, pp. 4320–4329 (2022)

17. Everingham, M., Van Gool, L., Williams, C.K., Winn, J., Zisserman, A.: The pascal visual object classes (VOC) challenge. Int. J. of comput. vis. **88**(2), 303–338 (2010)

18. Fan, J., Zhang, Z., Song, C., Tan, T.: Learning integral objects with intra-class discriminator for weakly-supervised semantic segmentation. In: CVPR (2020)

19. Fan, J., Zhang, Z., Tan, T., Song, C., Xiao, J.: CIAN: cross-image affinity net for weakly supervised semantic segmentation. In: AAAI (2020)

20. Guo, H., Zheng, K., Fan, X., Yu, H., Wang, S.: Visual attention consistency under image transforms for multi-label image classification. In: ICCV, pp. 729–739 (2019)

21. Hariharan, B., Arbeláez, P., Bourdev, L., Maji, S., Malik, J.: Semantic contours from inverse detectors. In: 2011 International Conference on Computer Vision, pp. 991–998. IEEE (2011)

22. Hou, Q., Cheng, M.M., Hu, X., Borji, A., Tu, Z., Torr, P.H.: Deeply supervised salient object detection with short connections. In: Proceedings of the IEEE Conference on Computer Vision and Pattern Recognition, pp. 3203–3212 (2017)

23. Huang, Z., Wang, X., Wang, J., Liu, W., Wang, J.: Weakly-supervised semantic segmentation network with deep seeded region growing. In: CVPR, pp. 7014–7023 (2018)

24. Jiang, P.T., Han, L.H., Hou, Q., Cheng, M.M., Wei, Y.: Online attention accumulation for weakly supervised semantic segmentation. IEEE TPAMI (2021)

25. Jiang, P.T., Hou, Q., Cao, Y., Cheng, M.M., Wei, Y., Xiong, H.K.: Integral object mining via online attention accumulation. In: ICCV, pp. 2070–2079 (2019)

26. Kolesnikov, A., Lampert, C.H.: Seed, expand and constrain: three principles for weakly-supervised image segmentation. In: Leibe, B., Matas, J., Sebe, N., Welling, M. (eds.) ECCV 2016. LNCS, vol. 9908, pp. 695–711. Springer, Cham (2016). https://doi.org/10.1007/978-3-319-46493-0_42

27. Krähenbühl, P., Koltun, V.: Efficient inference in fully connected CRFs with gaussian edge potentials. In: Advances in neural information processing systems, vol. 24 (2011)

28. Kuznetsova, A., et al.: The open images dataset V4. Int. J. Comput. Vis. **128**(7), 1956–1981 (2020)

29. Kweon, H., Yoon, S.H., Kim, H., Park, D., Yoon, K.J.: Unlocking the potential of ordinary classifier: class-specific adversarial erasing framework for weakly supervised semantic segmentation. In: Proceedings of the IEEE/CVF International Conference on Computer Vision, pp. 6994–7003 (2021)

30. Lee, J., Kim, E., Yoon, S.: Anti-adversarially manipulated attributions for weakly and semi-supervised semantic segmentation. In: CVPR, pp. 4071–4080 (2021)

31. Lee, J., Oh, S.J., Yun, S., Choe, J., Kim, E., Yoon, S.: Weakly supervised semantic segmentation using out-of-distribution data. In: Proceedings of the IEEE/CVF Conference on Computer Vision and Pattern Recognition, pp. 16897–16906 (2022)

32. Lee, S., Lee, M., Lee, J., Shim, H.: Railroad is not a train: saliency as pseudo-pixel supervision for weakly supervised semantic segmentation. In: CVPR, pp. 5495–5505 (2021)

33. Li, C., et al.: Efficient self-supervised vision transformers for representation learning. arXiv preprint arXiv:2106.09785 (2021)

34. Lin, T.-Y., et al.: Microsoft COCO: common objects in context. In: Fleet, D., Pajdla, T., Schiele, B., Tuytelaars, T. (eds.) ECCV 2014. LNCS, vol. 8693, pp. 740–755. Springer, Cham (2014). https://doi.org/10.1007/978-3-319-10602-1_48

35. Montavon, G., Lapuschkin, S., Binder, A., Samek, W., Müller, K.R.: Explaining nonlinear classification decisions with deep Taylor decomposition. Pattern Recogn. **65**, 211–222 (2017)
36. Oh, S.J., Benenson, R., Khoreva, A., Akata, Z., Fritz, M., Schiele, B.: Exploiting saliency for object segmentation from image level labels. In: CVPR, pp. 5038–5047 (2017)
37. Ren, S., et al.: A simple data mixing prior for improving self-supervised learning. In: Proceedings of the IEEE/CVF Conference on Computer Vision and Pattern Recognition, pp. 14595–14604 (2022)
38. Romero, D.W., Cordonnier, J.B.: Group equivariant stand-alone self-attention for vision. arXiv preprint arXiv:2010.00977 (2020)
39. Ru, L., Zhan, Y., Yu, B., Du, B.: Learning affinity from attention: end-to-end weakly-supervised semantic segmentation with transformers. In: Proceedings of the IEEE/CVF Conference on Computer Vision and Pattern Recognition, pp. 16846–16855 (2022)
40. Russakovsky, O.: ImageNet large scale visual recognition challenge. Int. J. of comput. vis. **115**(3), 211–252 (2015)
41. Shimoda, W., Yanai, K.: Self-supervised difference detection for weakly-supervised semantic segmentation. In: ICCV, pp. 5208–5217 (2019)
42. Singh, K.K., Lee, Y.J.: Hide-and-seek: forcing a network to be meticulous for weakly-supervised object and action localization. In: ICCV, pp. 3544–3553 (2017)
43. Stammes, E., Runia, T.F., Hofmann, M., Ghafoorian, M.: Find it if you can: end-to-end adversarial erasing for weakly-supervised semantic segmentation. In: ICDIP, vol. 11878 (2021)
44. Su, H., Jampani, V., Sun, D., Gallo, O., Learned-Miller, E., Kautz, J.: Pixel-adaptive convolutional neural networks. In: Proceedings of the IEEE/CVF Conference on Computer Vision and Pattern Recognition, pp. 11166–11175 (2019)
45. Sun, G., Wang, W., Dai, J., Van Gool, L.: Mining cross-image semantics for weakly supervised semantic segmentation. In: Vedaldi, A., Bischof, H., Brox, T., Frahm, J.-M. (eds.) ECCV 2020. LNCS, vol. 12347, pp. 347–365. Springer, Cham (2020). https://doi.org/10.1007/978-3-030-58536-5_21
46. Sun, K., Shi, H., Zhang, Z., Huang, Y.: ECS-Net: improving weakly supervised semantic segmentation by using connections between class activation maps. In: ICCV, pp. 7283–7292 (2021)
47. Sun, W., Zhang, J., Barnes, N.: Inferring the class conditional response map for weakly supervised semantic segmentation. In: WACV, pp. 2878–2887 (2022)
48. Van Oord, A., Kalchbrenner, N., Kavukcuoglu, K.: Pixel recurrent neural networks. In: International conference on machine learning, pp. 1747–1756. PMLR (2016)
49. Vernaza, P., Chandraker, M.: Learning random-walk label propagation for weakly-supervised semantic segmentation. In: Proceedings of the IEEE Conference on Computer Vision and Pattern Recognition, pp. 7158–7166 (2017)
50. Wang, Y., Zhang, J., Kan, M., Shan, S., Chen, X.: Self-supervised equivariant attention mechanism for weakly supervised semantic segmentation. In: CVPR, pp. 12275–12284 (2020)
51. Wei, Y., Feng, J., Liang, X., Cheng, M.M., Zhao, Y., Yan, S.: Object region mining with adversarial erasing: a simple classification to semantic segmentation approach. In: CVPR, pp. 1568–1576 (2017)
52. Wei, Y., et al.: STC: a simple to complex framework for weakly-supervised semantic segmentation. IEEE TPAMI **39**(11), 2314–2320 (2016)

53. Wei, Y., Xiao, H., Shi, H., Jie, Z., Feng, J., Huang, T.S.: Revisiting dilated convolution: a simple approach for weakly-and semi-supervised semantic segmentation. In: CVPR, pp. 7268–7277 (2018)
54. Wu, T., et al.: Embedded discriminative attention mechanism for weakly supervised semantic segmentation. In: CVPR, pp. 16765–16774 (2021)
55. Xie, J., Hou, X., Ye, K., Shen, L.: CLIMS: cross language image matching for weakly supervised semantic segmentation. In: Proceedings of the IEEE/CVF Conference on Computer Vision and Pattern Recognition, pp. 4483–4492 (2022)
56. Xie, J., Xiang, J., Chen, J., Hou, X., Zhao, X., Shen, L.: C2AM: contrastive learning of class-agnostic activation map for weakly supervised object localization and semantic segmentation. In: Proceedings of the IEEE/CVF Conference on Computer Vision and Pattern Recognition, pp. 989–998 (2022)
57. Xu, L., Ouyang, W., Bennamoun, M., Boussaid, F., Sohel, F., Xu, D.: Leveraging auxiliary tasks with affinity learning for weakly supervised semantic segmentation. In: ICCV, pp. 6984–6993 (2021)
58. Xu, L., Ouyang, W., Bennamoun, M., Boussaid, F., Xu, D.: Multi-class token transformer for weakly supervised semantic segmentation. In: Proceedings of the IEEE/CVF Conference on Computer Vision and Pattern Recognition, pp. 4310–4319 (2022)
59. Yao, Y., et al.: Non-salient region object mining for weakly supervised semantic segmentation. In: CVPR, pp. 2623–2632 (2021)
60. Zhang, F., Gu, C., Zhang, C., Dai, Y.: Complementary patch for weakly supervised semantic segmentation. In: ICCV, pp. 7242–7251 (2021)
61. Zhang, T., Lin, G., Liu, W., Cai, J., Kot, A.: Splitting Vs. merging: mining object regions with discrepancy and intersection loss for weakly supervised semantic segmentation. In: Vedaldi, A., Bischof, H., Brox, T., Frahm, J.-M. (eds.) ECCV 2020. LNCS, vol. 12367, pp. 663–679. Springer, Cham (2020). https://doi.org/10.1007/978-3-030-58542-6_40
62. Zhou, B., Khosla, A., Lapedriza, A., Oliva, A., Torralba, A.: Learning deep features for discriminative localization. In: CVPR, pp. 2921–2929 (2016)
63. Zhou, T., Zhang, M., Zhao, F., Li, J.: Regional semantic contrast and aggregation for weakly supervised semantic segmentation. In: Proceedings of the IEEE/CVF Conference on Computer Vision and Pattern Recognition, pp. 4299–4309 (2022)

Dense Siamese Network for Dense Unsupervised Learning

Wenwei Zhang[1], Jiangmiao Pang[2], Kai Chen[2,3],
and Chen Change Loy[1(✉)]

[1] S-Lab, Nanyang Technological University, Singapore, Singapore
{wenwei001,ccloy}@ntu.edu.sg
[2] Shanghai AI Laboratory, Shanghai, China
[3] SenseTime Research, Shanghai, China
{pangjiangmiao,chenkai}@pjlab.org.cn

Abstract. This paper presents Dense Siamese Network (DenseSiam), a simple unsupervised learning framework for dense prediction tasks. It learns visual representations by maximizing the similarity between two views of one image with two types of consistency, *i.e.*, pixel consistency and region consistency. Concretely, DenseSiam first maximizes the pixel level spatial consistency according to the exact location correspondence in the overlapped area. It also extracts a batch of region embeddings that correspond to some sub-regions in the overlapped area to be contrasted for region consistency. In contrast to previous methods that require negative pixel pairs, momentum encoders or heuristic masks, DenseSiam benefits from the simple Siamese network and optimizes the consistency of different granularities. It also proves that the simple location correspondence and interacted region embeddings are effective enough to learn the similarity. We apply DenseSiam on ImageNet and obtain competitive improvements on various downstream tasks. We also show that only with some extra task-specific losses, the simple framework can directly conduct dense prediction tasks. On an existing unsupervised semantic segmentation benchmark, it surpasses state-of-the-art segmentation methods by 2.1 mIoU with 28% training costs. Code and models are released at https://github.com/ZwwWayne/DenseSiam.

1 Introduction

Dense prediction tasks, such as image segmentation and object detection, are fundamental computer vision tasks with many real-world applications. Beyond conventional supervised learning methods, recent research interests grow in unsupervised learning to train networks from large-scale unlabeled datasets. These methods either learn representations as pre-trained weights then fine-tune on downstream tasks [10,55] or directly learn for specific tasks [11].

Supplementary Information The online version contains supplementary material available at https://doi.org/10.1007/978-3-031-20056-4_27.

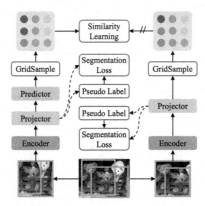

Fig. 1. Dense Siamese Network (DenseSiam) unanimously solves unsupervised pre-training and unsupervised semantic segmentation. The pair of images are first processed by the same encoder network and a convolutional projector. Then a predictor is applied on one side, and a stop-gradient operation on the other side. A grid sampling method is used to extract dense predictions in the overlapped area. DenseSiam can perform unsupervised semantic segmentation by simply adding a segmentation loss with pseudo labels produced by the projector.

In recent years, unsupervised pre-training has attracted a lot of attention. Much effort has been geared to learn global representation for image classification [6,8,10,20,21]. As the global averge pooling in these methods discards spatial information, it has been observed [6,8,20,55] that the learned representations are sub-optimal for dense uses. Naturally, some attempts conduct similarity learning at level [37,47,54] or region-level [25,39,51,52] and maintain the main structures in global ones to learn representations for dense prediction tasks.

Despite the remarkable progress in that field, the development in unsupervised learning for specific tasks is relatively slow-moving. For example, solutions in unsupervised semantic segmentation [11,28,36] rely more on clustering methods (such as k-means) that are also derived from unsupervised image classification [5,6,28]. When reflecting on these similar tasks from the perspective of unsupervised learning, we observe these tasks share the inherent goal of maximizing the similarity of dense predictions (either labels or embeddings) across images but differ in the task-specific training objectives.

In this paper, we propose *Dense Siamese Network* (DenseSiam) to unanimously solve these dense unsupervised learning tasks within a single framework (Fig. 1). It learns visual representations by maximizing two types of consistency, *i.e.*, pixel consistency and region consistency, with methods dubbed as *PixSim* and *RegionSim*, respectively. The encoder here can be directly fine-tuned for various downstream dense prediction tasks after unsupervised pre-training. By adding an extra segmentation loss to the projector and regarding the argmaxed prediction of projector as pseudo labels, the encoder and projector is capable of learning class-wise representations for unsupervised semantic segmentation.

Specifically, PixSim learns to maximize the pixel-level spatial consistency between the grid sampled predictions. Its training objective is constrained under

Table 1. Comparison of unsupervised dense representation learning methods.

Method	Base	Pixel	Region	Extra components	Correspondence
DenseCL [47]	MoCo v2 [9]	✓	✗	✗	Feature similarity
PixPro [54]	BYOL [20]	✓	✗	✗	Coordinate distance
VaDER [37]	MoCo v2	✓	✗	✗	Location
ReSim [51]	MoCo v2	✗	✓	✗	Dense region crops
SCRL [39]	BYOL [20]	✗	✓	✗	Sampled region crops
DetCo [52]	MoCo v2	✗	✓	✗	Image patches
SoCo [48]	BYOL	✗	✓	Selective search [44]	Sampled region crops
DetCon [25]	SimCLR [8]	✗	✓	FH masks [17]	Heuristic masks
CAST [42]	MoCo v2	✗	✓	DeepUSPS [34]	Saliency map
DenseSiam	SimSiam [10]	✓	✓	✗	Location + region embeddings

the exact location correspondence. In addition, the projected feature maps are multiplied with the features from encoder to generate a batch of region embeddings on each image, where each region embedding corresponds to a sub-region in the overlapped area. RegionSim then conducts contrastive learning between pairs of region embeddings and optimizes them to be consistent.

In contrast to previous unsupervised pre-training methods for dense prediction tasks, DenseSiam benefits from the simple Siamese network [10] that does not have negative pixel pairs [47,54] and momentum encoders [39,54]. Uniquely, DenseSiam optimizes the consistency of different granularities. The optimization for each granularity is simple as it neither requires heuristic masks [25] nor manual regions crops [39,51,52].

Extensive experiments show that DenseSiam is capable of learning strong representation for dense prediction tasks. DenseSiam obtains nontrivial 0.4 AP^{mask}, 0.7 mIoU, and 1.7 AP improvement in comparison with SimSiam when transferring its representation on COCO instance segmentation, Cityscapes semantic segmentation, and PASCAL VOC detection, respectively. For unsupervised semantic segmentation, DenseSiam makes the first attempt to discard clustering [11,28] while surpassing previous state-of-the-art method [11] by **2.1** mIoU with only ∼28% of the original training costs.

2 Related Work

Siamese Network. Siamese network [3] was proposed for comparing entities. They have many applications including object tracking [2], face verification [41,43], and one-shot recognition [29]. In conventional use cases, Siamese Network takes different images as input and outputs either a global embedding of each image for comparison [3,29,41,43] or outputs feature map of each image for cross-correlation [2]. DenseSiam uses the Siamese architecture to output pixel embeddings and maximizes similarity between embeddings of the same pixel from two views of an image to pre-train dense representations with strong transferability in dense prediction tasks.

Unsupervised Representation Learning. Representative unsupervised representation learning methods include contrastive learning [1,8,9,15,21,50] and clustering-based methods [5,6,45,56]. Notably, Siamese network has become a common structure in recent attempts [6,8,20], despite their different motivations and solutions to avoid the feature 'collapsing' problem. SimSiam [10] studies the minimum core architecture in these methods [6,8,20] and shows that a simple Siamese network with stopping gradient can avoid feature 'collapsing' and yield strong representations.

Given the different natures of image-level representation learning and dense prediction tasks, more recent attempts [14,25,37,39,42,47,48,51–55] pre-train dense representations specially designed for dense prediction tasks. Most of these methods conduct similarity learning with pixels [37,47,54], manually cropped patches of image or features [39,48,51–53], and regional features segmented by saliency map [42] or segmentation masks [25] obtained in unsupervised manners. These methods still need a momentum encoder [37,39,47,52,54] or negative pixel samples [37,47,54], although they [8,20] have been proven unnecessary [10] in image-level representation learning.

DenseSiam only needs a Siamese network with a stop gradient operation to obtain strong dense representations, without momentum encoder [37,39,47,52, 54] nor negative pixel pairs [37,47,54] (Table 1). It conducts contrastive learning among regional features inside an image emerged via pixel similarity learning. Thanks for the unique design, DenseSiam performs region-level similarity learning without saliency maps [42], region crops [39,51,52], nor heuristic masks [25].

Unsupervised Semantic Segmentation. Unsupervised semantic segmentation aims to predict labels for each pixel without annotations. There are a few attempts that introduce heuristic masks and conduct similarity learning between segments (regions) [26,46] with object-centric images. Most methods focus on natural scene images and exploit the assumption that semantic information should be invariant to photometric transformations and equivariant to geometric transformations no matter how the model predicts the labels, which is inherently consistent with the goal of unsupervised representation learning. However, these methods still rely on clustering [11,28,36] to predict the per-pixel labels and maximize the consistency of cluster assignments in different views of the image, which is cumbersome and difficult to be used for large-scale data.

DenseSiam conducts unsupervised semantic segmentation by adding a class-balanced cross entropy loss without clustering, significantly reduces the training costs and makes it scalable for large-scale data. RegionSim further boosts the segmentation accuracy by maximizing the consistency between regional features.

3 Dense Siamese Network

DenseSiam, as shown in Fig. 2, is a generic unsupervised learning framework for dense prediction tasks. The framework is inspired by SimSiam [10] but differs in its formulation tailored for learning dense representation (Sect. 3.1). In particular, it conducts dense similarity learning by PixSim (Sect. 3.2), which aims

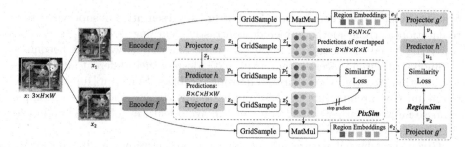

Fig. 2. Pipeline of DenseSiam. DenseSiam takes two randomly augmented views of an image x as inputs. The two views are processed by an encoder network f without global average pooling (GAP), followed by a projector network g. The predictor network h transforms the dense prediction of the projector of one view. Then GridSample module samples the same pixels inside the intersected regions of the two views and interpolates their feature grids. The similarity between feature grids from two views are maximized by PixSim. Then DenseSiam multiplies the features of encoder and the dense predictions by projector g in the overlapped area to obtain region embeddings of each image. These region embeddings are processed by a new projector g' and new predictor h' for region level similarity learning.

at maximizing pixel-level spatial consistency between grid sampled predictions. Based on the region embeddings derived from per-pixel predictions inferred in PixSim, DenseSiam further performs region-level contrastive learning through RegionSim (Sect. 3.3).

3.1 Siamese Dense Prediction

As shown in Fig. 2, DenseSiam takes two randomly augmented views x_1 and x_2 of an image x as inputs. The two views are processed by an encoder network f and a projector network g. The encoder network can either be a backbone network like ResNet-50 [24] or a combination of networks such as ResNet-50 with FPN [30]. As the encoder network f does not use global average pooling (GAP), the output of f is a *dense feature map* and is later processed by the projector g, which consists of three 1×1 convolutional layers followed by Batch Normalization (BN) and ReLU activation. Following the design in SimSiam [10], the last BN layer in g does not use learnable affine transformation [27]. The projector g projects the per-pixel embeddings to either a feature space for representation learning or to a labels space for segmentation. Given the dense prediction from g, noted as $z_1 \triangleq g(f(x_1))$, the predictor network h transforms the output of one view and matches it to another view [10]. Its output is denoted as $p_1 \triangleq h(g(f(x_1)))$.

The encoder and projector essentially form a Siamese architecture, which outputs two dense predictions (z_1 and z_2) for two views of an image, respectively. DenseSiam conducts similarity learning of different granularities using the Siamese dense predictions with the assistance of predictor [10,20]. After unsupervised pre-training, only the encoder network is fine-tuned for downstream dense

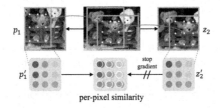

Fig. 3. Grid Sample module when grid size $K = 3$. Pixels at the same location in the original image should have similar predictions when they are transformed into two views. The Grid Sample module samples these pixels and interpolates their predictions in two views. The predictions of one view are learned to match those in another view.

prediction tasks, where the projector is only used during pre-training to improve the representation quality [8]. When directly learning the dense prediction tasks, the encoder and projector are combined to tackle the task.

3.2 PixSim

Dense Similarity Learning. We formulate the dense similarity learning to maximize the similarity of dense predictions inside the overlapping regions between p_1 and z_2. Specifically, given the relative coordinates of the intersected region in x_1 and x_2, we uniformly sample $K \times K$ point grids inside the intersected region from both views as shown in Fig. 3. These points in two views have exactly the same coordinates when they are mapped to the original image x; thus, their predictions should be consistent to those in another view. Assuming the sampled feature grids are $z_1' \triangleq \texttt{gridsample}(z_1)$ and $p_1' \triangleq \texttt{gridsample}(p_1)$, PixSim minimizes the distance of the feature grids by a symmetrical loss [10,20]:

$$\mathcal{L}_{dense} = \frac{1}{2}\mathcal{D}(p_1', \texttt{stopgrad}(z_2'))$$
$$+ \frac{1}{2}\mathcal{D}(p_2', \texttt{stopgrad}(z_1')), \tag{1}$$

where $\texttt{stopgrad}$ is the stop-gradient operation to prevent feature 'collapsing' [10] and $\mathcal{D}$ is a distance function that can have many forms [6,10]. Two representative distance functions are negative cosine similarity [10,20]

$$\mathcal{D}(p_1', z_2') = -\frac{p_1'}{\|p_1'\|_2} \cdot \frac{z_2'}{\|z_2'\|_2}, \tag{2}$$

and cross-entropy similarity

$$\mathcal{D}(p_1', z_2') = -\texttt{softmax}(p_1') \cdot \log \texttt{softmax}(z_2'). \tag{3}$$

Advantages to Image-Level Similarity Learning. Previous formulation of image-level representation learning faces two issues when transferring their representations for dense prediction tasks. First, it learns global embeddings for each image during similarity learning, where most of the spatial information is discarded during GAP. Hence, the spatial consistency is not guaranteed in its goal of representation learning, while dense prediction tasks like semantic segmentation and object detection rely on the spatial information of each pixel. Second, it is common that p_1 and z_2 contain different contents (see examples of x_1 and x_2 in Fig. 2) after heavy data augmentations like random cropping and resizing, but the global embeddings that encode these different contents are forced to be close to each other during training. This forcefully makes the embeddings of different pixel groups to be close to each other, breaking the regional consistency and is thus undesirable for dense prediction tasks.

PixSim resolves the above-mentioned issues by conducting pixel-wise similarity learning inside the intersected regions of two views, where the embeddings at identical locations of different views have different values due to augmentations [8] are forced to be similar to each other in training. Such a process learns dense representations that are invariant to data augmentations, which are more favorable dense representations for dense prediction tasks.

3.3   RegionSim

When using cross-entropy with softmax as the training objective, PixSim implicitly groups similar pixels together into the same regions/segments. The consistency of such regions can be further maximized by the proposed RegionSim to learn better dense representation. The connection between PixSim and Region-Sim is seamless - region-level similarity learning can be achieved without heuristic masks [25], saliency map [42], or manually cropping multiple regional features [39,51,52] as in previous studies.

Region Embedding Generation. As shown in Fig. 2, DenseSiam first obtains the feature grids of the intersected regions of each view by grid sampling from the features produced by the encoder f. This restricts RegionSim inside the intersected regions to ensure that the region embeddings to encode the similar contents. For simplicity, the region embeddings $e_1 \in \mathcal{R}^{N \times C}$ are obtained by the summation of multiplication between the masks and features as

$$e_1 = \sum_{i,j}^{K \times K} z_1'[i,j] \cdot \texttt{gridsample}(f(x_1))[i,j], \qquad (4)$$

where N and C represent the number of sub-regions and the number of feature channels, respectively. The process yields an embedding for each segment of each pseudo category, which will then be used for contrastive learning to increase the consistency between these region embeddings.

Region Similarity Learning. After obtaining the region embeddings, Region-Sim transforms them by a projector network g', which is a three-layer MLP head [8,10,20]. The output of g' is then transformed by h' for contrasting or matching with another view. RegionSim assumes each region embedding of a sub-region to be consistent with the embedding of the sub-region in another view. Therefore, Eq. 1 can be directly applied to these region embeddings to conduct region-level similarity learning. Meanwhile, we also enforce the region embedding to have low similarities with the embeddings of other region embeddings to make the feature space more compact. Consequently, by denoting the two outputs as $u_1 \triangleq h'(g'(e_1))$ and $v_2 \triangleq g'(e_2)$, RegionSim can also minimize the symmetrized loss function

$$\mathcal{L}_{region} = \frac{1}{2}\mathcal{L}_c(u_1, v_2) + \frac{1}{2}\mathcal{L}_c(u_2, v_1). \qquad (5)$$

The contrastive loss function [35] $\mathcal{L}_c$ can be written as

$$\mathcal{L}_c(u_1, v_2) = -\sum_s^N \log \frac{\exp(u_1^s \cdot v_2^s)}{\sum_{s'}^N \exp(u_1^s \cdot v_2^{s'})}. \qquad (6)$$

3.4   Learning Objective

When conducting unsupervised representation learning, DenseSiam also maintains a global branch to conduct image-level similarity learning to enhance the global consistency of representations, besides PixSim and RegionSim shown in Fig. 2. The architecture of the global branch remains the same as SimSiam [10]. The numbers of channels in the projectors and predictors of PixSim and RegionSim are set to 512 for efficiency. Denoting the loss of the global branch as $\mathcal{L}_{sim}$, DenseSiam optimizes the following loss

$$\mathcal{L} = \mathcal{L}_{sim} + \lambda_1 \mathcal{L}_{dense} + \lambda_2 \mathcal{L}_{region}, \qquad (7)$$

where λ_1 and λ_2 are loss weights of $\mathcal{L}_{dense}$ for PixSim and $\mathcal{L}_{region}$ for RegionSim, respectively. The encoder f is used for fine-tuning in downstream dense prediction tasks after pre-training.

4   Unsupervised Semantic Segmentation

The proposed framework is appealing in that it can be readily extended to address dense prediction tasks such as unsupervised semantic segmentation, by simply adding a task-specific losses and layers, without needing the offline and cumbersome clustering process [11,28,36].

Formally, when using cross-entropy similarity (Eq. 3) in PixSim, the softmax output $\texttt{softmax}(z)$ can be regarded as the probabilities of belonging to each of N pseudo-categories. In such a case, the projector g predicts a label for each pixel, which aligns with the formulation for unsupervised semantic segmentation.

DenseSiam uses ResNet with a simplified FPN [11,30] as the encoder g. The output channel N of PixSim is modified to match the number of classes in the dataset (e.g., 27 on COCO stuff-thing dataset [11,31]). Our experiment shows that a direct change in the number of output channels in PixSim without any further modification can already yield reasonable performance without feature 'collapsing'. Following previous method [11] that encourages the prediction scores to have a lower entropy (*i.e.*, more like one-hot scores), we add a cross entropy loss, denoted as $\mathcal{L}_{seg}$, when applying PixSim for unsupervised semantic segmentation with the pseudo labels obtained by `argmax`(z_1).

We also observe that the small number of categories undermines the training stability, which is also a common issue in clustering-based methods [11,28]. To solve this issue, DenseSiam introduces another set of projector and predictor in PixSim to keep a large number of pseudo categories following the over-clustering strategy [11,28]. This head only conducts similarity learning using Eq. 1, noted as $\mathcal{L}_{aux}$. Therefore, the overall loss of DenseSiam for unsupervised semantic segmentation is calculated as

$$\mathcal{L} = \lambda_1 \mathcal{L}_{dense} + \lambda_2 \mathcal{L}_{region} + \lambda_3 \mathcal{L}_{seg} + \lambda_4 \mathcal{L}_{aux}. \tag{8}$$

We use $\lambda_4 = \frac{\log N}{\log N + \log N_{aux}}$ and $\lambda_1 = \frac{\log N_{aux}}{\log N + \log N_{aux}}$ to prevent the auxiliary loss from overwhelming the gradients because it uses a larger number N_{aux} of pseudo categories [11]. Note that RegionSim is only used in training to enhance the region consistency of dense labels predicted by PixSim. Only the encoder f and projector g are combined to form a segmentation model at inference time.

5   Experiments

5.1   Experimental Settings

Datasets. For unsupervised pre-training, we compare with other methods on ImageNet-1k [40] (IN1k) dataset and conduct ablation studies on COCO [31] dataset as it is smaller. COCO and IN1k are two large-scale datasets that contain $\sim$118K and $\sim$1.28 million images, respectively. Though having more images, IN1k is highly curated and it mainly consists of object-centric images. Thus, the data is usually used for image classification. In contrast, COCO contains more diverse scenes in the real world and it has more objects ($\sim$7 objects *vs.* $\sim$1 in IN1k) in one image. Hence, it is mainly used for dense prediction tasks like object detection, semantic, instance, and panoptic segmentation.

For unsupervised semantic segmentation, the model is trained and evaluated on curated subsets [11,28] of COCO `train2017` split and `val2017` split, respectively. The training and validation set contain 49,629 images and 2,175 images, respectively. The semantic segmentation annotations include 80 thing categories and 91 stuff categories [4]. We follow previous methods [11,28] to merge these categories to form 27 (15 'stuff' and 12 'things') categories.

Training Setup. We closely follow the pre-training settings of SimSiam [10] when conducting unsupervised pre-training experiments of DenseSiam. Specifically, we use a learning rate of $lr \times$ BatchSize/256 following the linear scaling strategy [19], with a base $lr = 0.05$. The batch size is 512 by default. We use the cosine decay learning rate schedule [33] and SGD optimizer, where the weight decay is 0.0001 and the SGD momentum is 0.9. We pre-train DenseSiam for 800 epochs on COCO and for 200 epochs on IN1k. ResNet-50 [24] is used as default.

For unsupervised semantic segmentation, for a fair comparison, we follow PiCIE [11] to adopt the backbone pre-trained on IN1k in a supervised manner. The backbone is then fine-tuned with DenseSiam for unsupervised semantic segmentation using the same base learning rate, weight decay, and SGD momentum as those used in unsupervised representation learning. The batch size is 256 by default. We empirically find the constant learning schedule works better during training. The model is trained for 10 epochs. ResNet-18 [24] is used as default for a fair comparison with previous methods [11].

Evaluation Protocol of Transfer Learning. For unsupervised pre-training, we evaluate the transfer learning performance of the pre-trained representations following Wang *et al* [47]. We select different dense prediction tasks to comprehensively evaluate the transferability of the dense representation, including semantic segmentation, object detection, and instance segmentation. Challenging and popular dataset with representative algorithms in each task is selected.

When evaluating on semantic segmentation, we fine-tune a FCN [32] model and evaluate it with the Cityscapes dataset [13]. The model is trained on the `train_fine` set (2975 images) for 40k iterations and is tested on the `val` set. Strictly following the settings in MMSegmentation [12], we use FCN-D8 with a crop size of 769, a batch size of 16, and synchronized batch normalization. Results are averaged over five trials.

When evaluating on object detection, we fine-tune a Faster R-CNN [38] with C4-backbone by 24k iterations on VOC 2007 trainval + 2012 train set and is tested in VOC 2007 test set. Results are reported as an average over five trials.

We also evaluate the representation on object detection and instance segmentation on COCO dataset [31]. We fine-tune a Mask R-CNN with FPN [30] with standard multi-scale 1x schedule [7,49] on COCO `train2017` split and evaluate it on COCO `val2017` split. We apply synchronized batch normalization in backbone, neck, and RoI heads during training [22,47].

Evaluation of Unsupervised Semantic Segmentation. Since the model is trained without labels, a mapping between the model's label space and the ground truth categories needs be established. Therefore, we first let the model predicts on each image on the validation set, then we calculate the confusion matrix between the predicted labels and the ground truth classes. We use linear assignment to build a one-to-one mapping between the predicted labels and ground truth classes by taking the confusion matrix as the assignment cost. Then we calculate mean IoU over all classes based on the obtained mapping [11,28]. To more comprehensively understand the model's behavior, we also report mean IoU of stuff and things classes, noted as $mIoU^{St}$ and $mIoU^{Th}$, respectively.

5.2   Transfer Learning Results

The comparison on transfer learning in dense prediction tasks between DenseSiam and previous unsupervised representation learning methods [8,10,20,21,

Table 2. Transfer learning. All unsupervised methods are either based on 200-epoch pre-training in ImageNet ('IN1k'). *COCO instance segmentation* and *COCO detection*: Mask R-CNN [23] (1× schedule) fine-tuned in COCO `train2017`; *Cityscapes*: FCN fine-tuned on Cityscapes dataset [13]; *VOC 07+12 detection*: Faster R-CNN fine-tuned on VOC 2007 trainval + 2012 train, evaluated on VOC 2007 test; COCO `train2017`, evaluated on COCO `val2017`. All Mask R-CNN are with FPN [30]. All Faster R-CNN models are with the C4-backbone [18]. All VOC and Cityscapes results are averaged over 5 trials

Pre-train	COCO instance seg.			COCO detection			Cityscapes	VOC 07+12 detection		
	AP^{mask}	AP^{mask}_{50}	AP^{mask}_{75}	AP	AP_{50}	AP_{75}	mIoU	AP	AP_{50}	AP_{75}
scratch	29.9	47.9	32.0	32.8	50.9	35.3	63.5	32.8	59.0	31.6
supervised	35.9	56.6	38.6	39.7	59.5	43.3	73.7	54.2	81.6	59.8
BYOL [20]	34.9	55.3	37.5	38.4	57.9	41.9	71.6	51.9	81.0	56.5
SimCLR [8]	34.8	55.2	37.2	38.5	58.0	42.0	73.1	51.5	79.4	55.6
MoCo v2 [9]	36.1	56.9	38.7	39.8	59.8	43.6	74.5	57.0	82.4	63.6
SimSiam [10]	36.4	57.4	38.8	40.4	60.4	44.1	76.3	56.7	82.3	63.4
ReSim [51]	36.1	56.7	38.8	40.0	59.7	44.3	76.8	58.7	83.1	66.3
DetCo [52]	36.4	57.0	38.9	40.1	60.3	43.9	76.5	57.8	82.6	64.2
DenseCL [47]	36.4	57.0	39.2	40.3	59.9	44.3	75.7	58.7	82.8	65.2
PixPro [54]	36.6	57.3	39.1	40.5	60.1	44.3	76.3	**59.5**	**83.4**	**66.9**
DenseSiam	**36.8**	**57.6**	**39.8**	**40.8**	**60.7**	**44.6**	**77.0**	58.5	82.9	65.3

47,51] is shown in Table 2. The results of scratch, supervised, MoCo v2 [9], DenseCL [47], SimCLR [8], and BYOL [20] are reported from DenseCL [47]. For fair comparison, we fine-tune the model of ReSim-C4 [51] using the similar setting (Sect. 5.1). The model checkpoint is released by the paper authors[1]. We report the results of SimSiam [10], DetCo [52], and PixPro [54] based on our re-implementation.

COCO Instance Segmentation and Detection. As shown in the first two columns of Table 2, DenseSiam outperforms SimSiam by 0.4 AP^{mask} on COCO instance segmentation. The improvements over SimSiam is on-par with that of DenseCL and DetCo over MoCo v2 (0.4 *vs.* 0.3 AP^{mask}) and is better than ReSim (0.4 *vs.* 0 AP^{mask}). This further verifies the effectiveness of DenseSiam. Notably, DenseSiam outperforms ReSim, DetCo, DenseCL, and PixPro by 0.7, 0.4, 0.4, and 0.2 AP^{mask}, respectively. The results in COCO object detection is consistent with that in instance segmentation.

Cityscapes Semantic Segmentation. We compare DenseSiam with previous methods on semantic segmentation on Cityscapes dataset [13] and report the mean IoU (mIoU) of fine-tuned models. DenseSiam surpasses SimSiam by 0.7 mIoU and outperforms previous dense representation learning methods ReSim, DetCo, DenseCL, and PixPro by 0.2, 0.5, 1.3, and 0.7 mIoU, respectively. Notably, image-level unsupervised method such as SimCLR [8], BYOL [20] and SimSiam [10] show considerable performance gap against dense unsuper-

---

[1] https://github.com/Tete-Xiao/ReSim.

vised methods including DenseSiam, DenseCL, and ReSim, indicating that pre-training with image-level similarity learning is sub-optimal for dense prediction tasks.

PASCAL VOC Object Detection. We further compare DenseSiam with previous methods on PASCAL VOC [16] object detection. We report the original metric AP_{50} (AP calculated with IoU threshold 0.5) of VOC and further report COCO-style AP [49] and AP_{75}, which are stricter criteria in evaluating the detection performance. DenseSiam show a large improvement of 1.8 AP in comparison with SimSiam [10]. Notably, DenseSiam exhibits considerable improvements on AP_{75} than AP_{50}, suggesting the effectiveness of DenseSiam in learning accurate spatial information. Its improvement over SimSiam is more than that of DetCo [52] (0.8 AP) over MoCo v2, and is on-par with those of DenseCL [47] and ReSim [51] over MoCo v2 [9].

DenseCL, ReSim, and PixPro are 0.2, 0.2, and 1.0 AP better than DenseSiam, respectively. This phenomenon contradicts the results in the benchmarks of COCO dataset, although their improvements over their image-level counterparts are consistent across benchmarks. We hypothesize that the different backbones used in the two benchmarks leads to this phenomenon, where ResNet-50-C4 backbone [38] is used on PASCAL VOC but ResNet-50-FPN [30] is used on COCO. The hypothesis also explains the inferior performance of DetCo [52]: DetCo conducts contrastive learning on pyramid features but only one feature scale is used when fine-tuning Faster R-CNN on PASCAL VOC dataset.

Table 3. Unsupervised semantic segmentation. The model is trained and tested on the curated COCO dataset [11,28]. '+ aux.' denotes PiCIE or DenseSiam is trained with an auxiliary head

Method	mIoU	mIoUSt	mIoUTh	Time (h)
Modified Deep Clustering [5]	9.8	22.2	11.6	–
IIC [28]	6.7	12.0	13.6	–
PiCIE [11] + aux.	14.4	17.3	23.8	18
DenseSiam + aux.	**16.4**	**24.5**	**29.5**	5

5.3 Unsupervised Segmentation Results

In Table 3 we compare DenseSiam with previous state-of-the-art methods in unsupervised semantic segmentation. DenseSiam achieves new state-of-the-art performance of 16.4 mIoU, surpassing PiCIE by 2 mIoU over all classes. Imbalanced performance is observed in previous methods between thing and stuff classes, *e.g.*, PiCIE [11] and IIC [28] surpass Modified DeepClustering [5] on thing classes but fall behind on stuff classes. In contrast, DenseSiam consistently outperforms previous best results on both thing and stuff classes by more than 2 mIoU. The results reveal that clustering is unnecessary, whereas clustering is indispensable in previous unsupervised segmentation methods [11,28].

We also calculate the training costs of PiCIE and DenseSiam by measuring the GPU hours used to train the model with similar batch size and backbone. Because PiCIE needs clustering to obtain pseudo labels before each training epoch, its training time is comprised of the time of label clustering, data loading, and model's forward and backward passes. In contrast, DenseSiam does not rely on clustering. In the setting of single GPU training, DenseSiam saves ~72% training costs in comparison with PiCIE.

5.4   Ablation Study

Unsupervised Pre-training. We ablate the key components in DenseSiam as shown in Table 4. The baselines in Table 4a-e are SimSiam (53.5 AP).

i) Effective grid number K in PixSim: We study the effective number K used in grid sampling in PixSim in Table 4a. The greater the number, the more feature grids will be sampled from the intersected regions and will be used for similarity learning. With zero grid number DenseSiam degenerates to the SimSiam baseline where no pixel similarity learning is performed. The results in Table 4b shows that 7×7 feature grids is sufficient to improve the per-pixel consistency of dense representation. We also compare the training memory used in PixSim. The comparison shows that PixSim only brings 0.1%–0.3% extra memory cost in comparison with SimSiam.

ii) Loss weight of PixSim: We further study the loss weight λ_1 of $\mathcal{L}_{dense}$ used for per-pixel similarity learning. The comparative results in Table 4b show that with $\lambda_1 = 1$ we achieve the best performance, which is equal to the loss weight of the image-level similarity learning.

iii) Loss weight of RegionSim: We study the loss weight λ_2 of RegionSim as shown in Table 4c. We find that 0.1 works best and large value of λ_2 leads decreased performance.

iv) Orders of grid sample, projector, and predictor: As DenseSiam consists of encoder, projector, and predictor, we study the optimal position where the grid sampler should be introduced. The results in Table 4d show that it is necessary to put the grid sample module after the projector, but the predictor can perform equally well when it is before or behind the grid sample module.

v) Regions to focus in global branch: We also study the regions that should be focused in global branch in Table 4e, as an image-level similarity learning branch (SimSiam) is kept to facilitate training. The abbreviations 'global' and 'in.' indicate whether the similarity learning is conducted with the whole image or the intersected regions between two views. To maximize per-pixel consistency, PixSim is always conducted with the intersected regions. We find that the focusing on the whole image when conducting image-level similarity learning is always important in both SimSiam and DenseSiam. Only using the intersected regions will lead to feature 'collapsing' (second row with zero accuracy in downstream tasks) in SimSiam since it makes some learning shortcuts for the model (Table 4e).

Table 4. Ablation studies in unsupervised pre-trainings. All unsupervised representations are based on 800-epoch pre-training on COCO train2017. The representations are fine-tuned with Faster R-CNN [38] (C4-backbone) in VOC 2007 trainval + 2012 train and evaluated on VOC 2007 test. 'Mem.' indicates memory cost measured by Gigabyte (GB). The results of fine-tuning are averaged over 5 trials. Best settings are bolded and used as default settings

(a) The effective number K in PixSim

Gird Number	AP	AP$_{50}$	AP$_{75}$	Mem.
0	53.5	79.7	59.3	8.06
1	28.8	53.8	27.1	8.11
3	53.9	80.0	59.4	8.12
7	**54.9**	**80.8**	**60.9**	8.18
9	54.6	80.7	60.6	8.21
14	54.7	80.6	60.8	8.28

(b) The effective loss weight of PixSim

λ_1	AP	AP$_{50}$	AP$_{75}$
0	53.5	79.7	59.3
0.1	53.3	79.6	58.8
0.3	53.5	79.9	58.8
0.5	54.0	80.2	60.0
0.7	54.0	79.8	59.8
1.0	**54.9**	**80.8**	**60.9**

(c) The effective loss weight of RegionSim

λ_2	AP	AP$_{50}$	AP$_{75}$
0	53.5	79.7	59.3
0.01	55.3	81.0	61.3
0.05	55.0	80.9	60.6
0.1	**55.5**	**81.0**	**61.5**
0.2	55.3	81.0	61.0
0.5	55.3	80.9	61.1

(d) The effective order of grid sample, projector, and predictor in PixSim

Order	AP	AP$_{50}$	AP$_{75}$
-	53.5	79.7	59.3
grid. + proj. + pred.	53.4	79.6	59.0
proj. + grid. + pred.	54.7	80.6	60.4
proj. + pred. + grid.	**54.9**	**80.8**	**60.9**

(e) Regions to be focused in global branch. 'in.' indicates the intersected regions

Image-level	Pixel-level	AP	AP$_{50}$	AP$_{75}$
global	N/A	53.5	79.7	59.3
in.	N/A	0.0	0.0	0.0
global	in.	**54.9**	**80.8**	**60.9**
in.	in.	35.6	61.5	35.6

(f) Suitable start epoch of RegionSim epoch of RegionSim

Start epoch	AP	AP$_{50}$	AP$_{75}$
never	54.9	80.8	60.9
0.4	37.7	64.8	38.4
0.5	**55.3**	**81.1**	**61.5**
0.6	55.0	80.8	60.4
w/o PixSim	52.8	79.2	58.0

Table 5. Ablation study in unsupervised segmentation. 'Aux.' indicates auxiliary head

PixSim	Aux	CE	Region	mIoU	mIoUSt	mIoUTh
✓				10.1	19.0	17.7
✓	✓			11.1	20.4	22.3
✓	✓	✓		15.0	24.8	23.4
✓	✓	✓	✓	16.4	24.5	29.5

vi) Start point of RegionSim: The start point of RegionSim based on PixSim (54.9) matters as shown in Table 4f. The label prediction quality is not accurate and may lead to a wrong optimization direction if RegionSim is applied at a wrong time. Starting RegionSim at the middle point of training yields the best performance. We further try only using RegionSim without PixSim (last row in Table 4f). Only adding RegionSim degrades fine-tuning results on by 2.7 AP, this also implies that RegionSim needs PixSim to produce meaningful groups.

Unsupervised Semantic Segmentation. We also study the effectiveness of the components in DenseSiam for unsupervised semantic segmentation. Directly applying PixSim without any further modification yields 10.1 mIoU, which already surpasses many previous methods [5,28] (9.8 and 6.7 mIoU). Adding CE loss further improves the performance by making the feature space more compact and discriminative. After adding the auxiliary head, the model already surpasses the previous state-of-the-art method PiCIE. RegionSim further brings 1.4 mIoU of improvement.

6   Conclusion

Different dense prediction tasks essentially shares the similar goal of optimizing the spatial consistency between views of images. DenseSiam exploits such a property and unanimously solves unsupervised dense representation learning and unsupervised semantic segmentation within a Siamese architecture. DenseSiam optimizes similarity between dense predictions at pixel level by PixSim and at region level by RegionSim, with neither negative pixel pairs, momentum encoder, manual region crops, nor heuristic masks, which are *all unnecessary* as revealed by DenseSiam to obtain a strong dense representation for downstream tasks. Its unsupervised semantic segmentation performance also achieves the new state-of-the-art.

Acknowledgment. This study is supported under the RIE2020 Industry Alignment Fund Industry Collaboration Projects (IAF-ICP) Funding Initiative, as well as cash and in-kind contribution from the industry partner(s). The work is also suported by Singapore MOE AcRF Tier 2 (MOE-T2EP20120-0001) and NTU NAP Grant. Jiangmiao Pang and Kai Chen are partially supported by the Shanghai Committee of Science and Technology, China (Grant No. 20DZ1100800).

References

1. Bachman, P., Hjelm, R.D., Buchwalter, W.: Learning representations by maximizing mutual information across views. In: Wallach, H.M., Larochelle, H., Beygelzimer, A., d'Alché-Buc, F., Fox, E.B., Garnett, R. (eds.) NeurIPS (2019)
2. Bertinetto, L., Valmadre, J., Henriques, J.F., Vedaldi, A., Torr, P.H.S.: Fully-convolutional siamese networks for object tracking. In: Hua, G., Jégou, H. (eds.) ECCV 2016. LNCS, vol. 9914, pp. 850–865. Springer, Cham (2016). https://doi.org/10.1007/978-3-319-48881-3_56
3. Bromley, J., et al.: Signature verification using a "siamese" time delay neural network. In: NeurIPS (1993)
4. Caesar, H., Uijlings, J., Ferrari, V.: COCO-Stuff: thing and stuff classes in context. In: CVPR (2018)
5. Caron, M., Bojanowski, P., Joulin, A., Douze, M.: Deep clustering for unsupervised learning of visual features. In: Ferrari, V., Hebert, M., Sminchisescu, C., Weiss, Y. (eds.) Computer Vision – ECCV 2018. LNCS, vol. 11218, pp. 139–156. Springer, Cham (2018). https://doi.org/10.1007/978-3-030-01264-9_9
6. Caron, M., Misra, I., Mairal, J., Goyal, P., Bojanowski, P., Joulin, A.: Unsupervised learning of visual features by contrasting cluster assignments. In: NeurIPS (2020)
7. Chen, K., et al.: MMDetection: open MMlab detection toolbox and benchmark. arXiv preprint arXiv:1906.07155 (2019)
8. Chen, T., Kornblith, S., Norouzi, M., Hinton, G.E.: A simple framework for contrastive learning of visual representations. In: ICML (2020)
9. Chen, X., Fan, H., Girshick, R.B., He, K.: Improved baselines with momentum contrastive learning. CoRR abs/2003.04297 (2020)
10. Chen, X., He, K.: Exploring simple siamese representation learning. In: CVPR (2021)

11. Cho, J.H., Mall, U., Bala, K., Hariharan, B.: PiCIE: unsupervised semantic segmentation using invariance and equivariance in clustering. In: CVPR (2021)
12. Contributors, M.: MMSegmentation: openMMlab semantic segmentation toolbox and benchmark (2020). https://github.com/open-mmlab/mmsegmentation
13. Cordts, M., et al.: The cityscapes dataset for semantic urban scene understanding. In: CVPR (2016)
14. Dai, Z., Cai, B., Lin, Y., Chen, J.: UP-DETR: unsupervised pre-training for object detection with transformers. In: CVPR (2021)
15. Dosovitskiy, A., Fischer, P., Springenberg, J.T., Riedmiller, M.A., Brox, T.: Discriminative unsupervised feature learning with exemplar convolutional neural networks. TPAMI **8**(6), 1734–1747 (2016)
16. Everingham, M., Gool, L.V., Williams, C.K.I., Winn, J.M., Zisserman, A.: The pascal visual object classes (VOC) challenge. IJCV **88**(2), 303–338 (2010). https://doi.org/10.1007/s11263-009-0275-4
17. Felzenszwalb, P.F., Huttenlocher, D.P.: Efficient graph-based image segmentation. IJCV **59**, 167–181 (2004). https://doi.org/10.1023/B:VISI.0000022288.19776.77
18. Girshick, R., Radosavovic, I., Gkioxari, G., Dollár, P., He, K.: Detectron (2018). https://github.com/facebookresearch/detectron
19. Goyal, P., et al.: Accurate, large minibatch SGD: training imagenet in 1 hour. CoRR abs/1706.02677 (2017)
20. Grill, J., et al.: Bootstrap your own latent - a new approach to self-supervised learning. In: NeurIPS (2020)
21. He, K., Fan, H., Wu, Y., Xie, S., Girshick, R.B.: Momentum contrast for unsupervised visual representation learning. In: CVPR (2020)
22. He, K., Girshick, R., Dollar, P.: Rethinking ImageNet pre-training. In: ICCV (2019)
23. He, K., Gkioxari, G., Dollár, P., Girshick, R.B.: Mask R-CNN. In: ICCV (2017)
24. He, K., Zhang, X., Ren, S., Sun, J.: Deep residual learning for image recognition. In: CVPR (2016)
25. Hénaff, O.J., Koppula, S., Alayrac, J., van den Oord, A., Vinyals, O., Carreira, J.: Efficient visual pretraining with contrastive detection. In: ICCV (2021)
26. Hwang, J., et al.: SegSort: segmentation by discriminative sorting of segments. In: ICCV (2019)
27. Ioffe, S., Szegedy, C.: Batch normalization: accelerating deep network training by reducing internal covariate shift. In: ICML (2015)
28. Ji, X., Vedaldi, A., Henriques, J.F.: Invariant information clustering for unsupervised image classification and segmentation. In: ICCV (2019)
29. Koch, G., et al.: Siamese neural networks for one-shot image recognition. In: ICML deep learning workshop (2015)
30. Lin, T., Dollár, P., Girshick, R.B., He, K., Hariharan, B., Belongie, S.J.: Feature pyramid networks for object detection. In: CVPR (2017)
31. Lin, T.Y., et al.: Microsoft COCO: common objects in context. In: Fleet, D., Pajdla, T., Schiele, B., Tuytelaars, T. (eds.) ECCV 2014. LNCS, vol. 8693, pp. 740–755. Springer, Cham (2014). https://doi.org/10.1007/978-3-319-10602-1_48
32. Long, J., Shelhamer, E., Darrell, T.: Fully convolutional networks for semantic segmentation. In: CVPR (2015)
33. Loshchilov, I., Hutter, F.: SGDR: stochastic gradient descent with warm restarts. In: ICLR (2017)
34. Nguyen, D.T., et al.: DeepUSPS: deep robust unsupervised saliency prediction via self-supervision. In: NeurIPS (2019)
35. van den Oord, A., Li, Y., Vinyals, O.: Representation learning with contrastive predictive coding. CoRR abs/1807.03748 (2018)

36. Ouali, Y., Hudelot, C., Tami, M.: Autoregressive unsupervised image segmentation. In: Vedaldi, A., Bischof, H., Brox, T., Frahm, J.-M. (eds.) ECCV 2020. LNCS, vol. 12352, pp. 142–158. Springer, Cham (2020). https://doi.org/10.1007/978-3-030-58571-6_9

37. Pinheiro, P.O., Almahairi, A., Benmalek, R.Y., Golemo, F., Courville, A.C.: Unsupervised learning of dense visual representations. In: NeurIPS (2020)

38. Ren, S., He, K., Girshick, R., Sun, J.: Faster R-CNN: towards real-time object detection with region proposal networks. In: NeurIPS (2015)

39. Roh, B., Shin, W., Kim, I., Kim, S.: Spatially consistent representation learning. In: CVPR (2021)

40. Russakovsky, O., et al.: ImageNet large scale visual recognition challenge. IJCV 115, 211–252 (2015). https://doi.org/10.1007/s11263-015-0816-y

41. Schroff, F., Kalenichenko, D., Philbin, J.: FaceNet: a unified embedding for face recognition and clustering. In: CVPR (2015)

42. Selvaraju, R.R., Desai, K., Johnson, J., Naik, N.: CASTing your model: learning to localize improves self-supervised representations. In: CVPR (2021)

43. Taigman, Y., Yang, M., Ranzato, M., Wolf, L.: DeepFace: closing the gap to human-level performance in face verification. In: CVPR (2014)

44. Uijlings, J.R.R., van de Sande, K.E.A., Gevers, T., Smeulders, A.W.M.: Selective search for object recognition. IJCV 104, 154–171 (2013). https://doi.org/10.1007/s11263-013-0620-5

45. Van Gansbeke, W., Vandenhende, S., Georgoulis, S., Proesmans, M., Van Gool, L.: SCAN: learning to classify images without labels. In: Vedaldi, A., Bischof, H., Brox, T., Frahm, J.-M. (eds.) ECCV 2020. LNCS, vol. 12355, pp. 268–285. Springer, Cham (2020). https://doi.org/10.1007/978-3-030-58607-2_16

46. Van Gansbeke, W., Vandenhende, S., Georgoulis, S., Van Gool, L.: Unsupervised semantic segmentation by contrasting object mask proposals. In: ICCV (2021)

47. Wang, X., Zhang, R., Shen, C., Kong, T., Li, L.: Dense contrastive learning for self-supervised visual pre-training. In: CVPR (2021)

48. Wei, F., Gao, Y., Wu, Z., Hu, H., Lin, S.: Aligning pretraining for detection via object-level contrastive learning. In: NeurIPS (2021)

49. Wu, Y., Kirillov, A., Massa, F., Lo, W.Y., Girshick, R.: Detectron2 (2019). https://github.com/facebookresearch/detectron2

50. Wu, Z., Xiong, Y., Yu, S.X., Lin, D.: Unsupervised feature learning via non-parametric instance discrimination. In: CVPR (2018)

51. Xiao, T., Reed, C.J., Wang, X., Keutzer, K., Darrell, T.: Region similarity representation learning. In: ICCV (2021)

52. Xie, E., et al.: DetCo: unsupervised contrastive learning for object detection. In: ICCV (2021)

53. Xie, J., Zhan, X., Liu, Z., Ong, Y.S., Loy, C.C.: Unsupervised object-level representation learning from scene images. In: NeurIPS (2021)

54. Xie, Z., Lin, Y., Zhang, Z., Cao, Y., Lin, S., Hu, H.: Propagate yourself: exploring pixel-level consistency for unsupervised visual representation learning. In: CVPR (2021)

55. Yang, C., Wu, Z., Zhou, B., Lin, S.: Instance localization for self-supervised detection pretraining. In: CVPR (2021)

56. Zhan, X., Xie, J., Liu, Z., Ong, Y., Loy, C.C.: Online deep clustering for unsupervised representation learning. In: CVPR (2020)

Multi-granularity Distillation Scheme Towards Lightweight Semi-supervised Semantic Segmentation

Jie Qin[1,2,3], Jie Wu[2(✉)], Ming Li[2], Xuefeng Xiao[2], Min Zheng[2], and Xingang Wang[3(✉)]

[1] School of Artificial Intelligence, University of Chinese Academy of Sciences, Beijing, China
[2] ByteDance Inc., Beijing, China
wujie10558@gmail.com
[3] Institute of Automation, Chinese Academy of Sciences, Beijing, China
xingang.wang@ia.ac.cn

Abstract. Albeit with varying degrees of progress in the field of Semi-Supervised Semantic Segmentation, most of its recent successes are involved in unwieldy models and the lightweight solution is still not yet explored. We find that existing knowledge distillation techniques pay more attention to pixel-level concepts from labeled data, which fails to take more informative cues within unlabeled data into account. Consequently, we offer the first attempt to provide lightweight SSSS models via a novel multi-granularity distillation (MGD) scheme, where multi-granularity is captured from three aspects: i) complementary teacher structure; ii) labeled-unlabeled data cooperative distillation; iii) hierarchical and multi-levels loss setting. Specifically, MGD is formulated as a labeled-unlabeled data cooperative distillation scheme, which helps to take full advantage of diverse data characteristics that are essential in the semi-supervised setting. Image-level semantic-sensitive loss, region-level content-aware loss, and pixel-level consistency loss are set up to enrich hierarchical distillation abstraction via structurally complementary teachers. Experimental results on PASCAL VOC2012 and Cityscapes reveal that MGD can outperform the competitive approaches by a large margin under diverse partition protocols. For example, the performance of ResNet-18 and MobileNet-v2 backbone is boosted by **11.5%** and **4.6%** respectively under 1/16 partition protocol on Cityscapes. Although the FLOPs of the model backbone is compressed by **3.4–5.3×** (ResNet-18) and **38.7–59.6×** (MobileNetv2), the model manages to achieve satisfactory segmentation results.

Keywords: Semi-supervised semantic segmentation · Lightweight · Distillation · Multi-granularity

---

J. Qin and J. Wu—Equal contribution.
This work was done while Jie Qin interned at ByteDance.
Code is available at github.com/JayQine/MGD-SSSS.

© The Author(s), under exclusive license to Springer Nature Switzerland AG 2022
S. Avidan et al. (Eds.): ECCV 2022, LNCS 13690, pp. 481–498, 2022.
https://doi.org/10.1007/978-3-031-20056-4_28

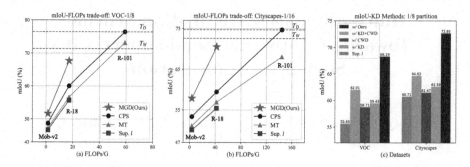

Fig. 1. (a)/(b) The mIoU-FLOPs trade-off between MGD and existing methods including Sup. l, MT [44] and CPS [7]. T_D and T_W denote two complementary teacher models. Sup. l denotes the model trained only with the labeled data under the corresponding partition. (c) The results of existing distillation methods (KD [46] and CWD [38]) for optimizing lightweight model of ResNet-18

1   Introduction

Semantic segmentation is a fundamental and crucial task due to extensive vision applications such as scene understanding and autonomous driving. However, this task is still extremely dependent on adequate granular pixel-level annotations [5,6,29,61], which requires a huge amount of manual effort. To alleviate such expensive and unwieldy annotations, some researchers attempt to address this task in the semi-supervised paradigm, where the model is merely accessible to a small amount of image-label pairs joint with abundant unlabeled images. This is an exceedingly favorable setting since such coarse unlabeled images are more readily available on the internet. The main challenge under this paradigm is how to take good advantage of unlabeled data to alleviate the drastic drop in performance when the labeled data is reduced. The recent state-of-the-art semi-supervised semantic segmentation approaches [7,18,33,65] mostly benefit from pseudo labeling and consistency regularization.

Despite semi-supervised semantic segmentation (SSSS) having witnessed prevailing success in a series of computer vision applications, most previous approaches [7,63,65] have resorted to unwieldy and cumbersome models. It is arduous to popularize these models that require tremendous computational costs, which becomes a critical bottleneck when such models are required to deploy on resource-constrained server platforms or even more lightweight mobile devices. As shown in Fig. 1, the performance of the existing competitive approaches suffers from drastic performance degradation when replacing the cumbersome backbone with a lightweight one such as ResNet-18 [15] or MobileNet-v2 [37]. We also leverage the existing distillation methods [38,46,50] to optimize lightweight models but also get unimpressive results. It may due to the fact that existing distillation methods mainly transfer pixel-level knowledge, which lacks diverse and hierarchical distillation signals. Furthermore, these approaches are designed for labeled data and fail to take the data characteristic of unlabeled data into account, hence they are not well adapted to the SSSS task.

These observations motivate us to raise a question: *how to obtain a lightweight SSSS model with a lighter computation cost joint with high performance?* Compared with traditional semi-supervised semantic segmentation, lightweight solution confronts three additional challenges: (i) How to design teacher models to efficiently assist in boosting the capacity of the lightweight model? (ii) How to fully leverage both limited labeled and sufficient unlabeled data in the semi-supervised distillation setting? (iii) Are there more granularity concepts that can be resorted to refine the lightweight model for this fine-grained task?

To answer these questions, we propose a novel ***Multi-Granularity Distillation (MGD)*** scheme to obtain a lightweight SSSS model with impressive performance and lite computational costs. This scheme elaborately designs triplet-branches to leverage complementary teacher models and hierarchical auxiliary supervision to distill the lightweight model. Specifically, we capture multi-level concepts to formulate the hierarchical optimization objectives, which can be regarded as diverse granularity supervision signals and play a key role to break through the bottleneck of the capacity of the lightweight student model. The contributions of this work are summarized into four folds:

- To the best of our knowledge, we offer the first attempt to obtain the lightweight model for semi-supervised semantic segmentation. We provide efficient solutions for the challenges of this newly-raised task and alleviate the issue of performance degradation during model compression. We believe our work provides the foundation and direction for lightweight research in the field of semi-supervised semantic segmentation.
- We propose a novel multi-granularity distillation (MGD) scheme that employs triplet-branches to distill task-specific concepts from two complementary teacher models into a student one. The deep-and-thin and shallow-and-wide teachers help to provide comprehensive and diverse abstractions to boost the lightweight model.
- The labeled-unlabeled data cooperative distillation is designed to make full use of the characteristics of extensive unlabeled data in the semi-supervised setting. Then we design a hierarchical loss paradigm to provide multi-level (image-level/region-level/pixel-level) auxiliary supervision for unlabeled data, which supervises the lightweight model to grasp the high-level categorical abstraction and low-level contextual information.
- Extensive experiments on PASCAL VOC2012 and Cityscape demonstrate that MGD can outperform the competitive approaches by a large margin under diverse partition protocols. Although the FLOPs of the model backbone is compressed by **3.4–5.3×** (ResNet-18) and **38.7–59.6×** (MobileNetv2), the model still can achieve satisfactory performance.

2   Related Work

2.1   Semantic Segmentation

Semantic segmentation is a fundamental and crucial task in the field of computer vision [5, 6, 34, 61]. It aims to perform a pixel-level prediction to cluster parts of an image together that belong to the same object class. Many approaches [2,32,36] employ the encoder-decoder structure to resume the resolution of features step by step and accomplish pixel-level classification simultaneously. In order to capture the long-range relationships, DeepLab v3+ [5] make use of dilated convolution [55] to increase the receptive field of networks. [53,60,61] use the pyramid pooling to capture multi-scale features and integrate pyramid features to obtain global context information. [12,17,45,62,64] use the attention mechanism to aggregate the global contexts that benefit dense prediction. HRNet [42] maintains the context of images by holding the resolution of features.

2.2   Semi-supervised Learning

Semi-supervised learning aims to utilize limit labeled data and a large amount of unlabeled data to improve the model capacity [14,20,24,26]. The consistency regularization technique applies different perturbations or augmentations and encourages the model to produce invariant outputs [31,44,51]. For example, VAT [31] applies adversarial perturbations to the output and Temporal Model [23] incorporates the outputs over epochs and makes them consistent. Data augmentations or mixing are performed to generate the different perturbed data to train networks [3,4]. FixMatch [39] takes advantage of the weak augmentation to generate the pseudo labels and supervise the images with strong augmentation. MT [44] generates the predictions by exponential moving average (EMA). Self-supervised learning [58], GAN-based methods [9,25,41] and self-training [10,52] are also exploited to assist semi-supervised learning.

2.3   Semi-supervised Semantic Segmentation

Semi-supervised semantic segmentation is proposed to accomplish the segmentation task with limited image-label pairs and ample unlabeled images. GAN-based methods [18,30,40] are proposed to synthesize additional training data or generate the pseudo labels by using adversarial loss on predictions. From the perspective of consistency regularization, data augmentations [56,59], feature space pertubations [33] and network initialization [7,19] are applied to generate the different types of predictions and compute consistency losses. CCT [33] exploits the consistent supervision on the outputs of the main decoder and several auxiliary decoders with different perturbations. GCT [19] employs two segmentation networks with the same structure but different initialization and enforces the consistency between the predictions. PC^{2}Seg [63] and [1,22] take advantage of the contrastive learning to improve the representation ability on the unlabeled data. PseudoSeg [65] uses the weak augmented images to generate the pseudo labels, which are used to supervise the strong augmented images.

2.4   Knowledge Distillation

Knowledge Distillation [13,16] is a knowledge transfer technique that optimizes a lightweight student model with effective information transfer and supervision of a larger teacher model or ensembles. Besides the knowledge transfer in the outputs, the feature maps [28, 35] in the intermediate layers of networks are used to improve the performance of the student networks. Moreover, some methods attempt to transfer the attention concepts [47–49] of feature maps from each channel in intermediate layers. Some approaches try to exploit the knowledge distillation on the dense prediction tasks [27, 38, 46, 50]. In addition, [54] indicates that multiple teacher networks can provide more effective information for training a lightweight and ascendant student network. In this paper, we design a deeper and a wider model to play as the complementary teachers and provide multi-granularity auxiliary supervision.

3   Methodology

In this section, we first illustrate the overview of the proposed multi-granularity distillation (MGD) framework. Then the complementary teacher distillation and the novel labeled-unlabeled data cooperative distillation are presented in Sect. 3.2 and Sect. 3.3, respectively. The hierarchical and multi-level distillation for unlabeled data is introduced Sect. 3.4.

3.1   Multi-granularity Distillation Scheme

Due to limited labeled data and restricted learning capacity of lightweight models, conventional consistency regularization approaches [7, 33, 65] suffer from a drastic degradation in performance when they are directly applied on the lightweight models (refer to Fig. 1). Furthermore, we also tried a series of existing distillation methods to relieve significant performance degradation but found that they are not so effective under the setting of semi-supervised segmentation. Therefore, we propose a multi-granularity distillation scheme to leverage task-oriented knowledge distillation techniques to guide the learning procedure of the lightweight model, as shown in Fig. 2. Specifically, multi granularity denotes that the distillation process is carried out synergistically from diverse aspects. Firstly, we design dual teachers to provide complementary distillation abstractions. Secondly, we formulate a labeled-unlabeled data cooperative distillation to optimize the network via the data characteristics of semi-supervision. Thirdly, we employ image-level, region-level and pixel-level visual cues from complementary teacher models to formulate a hierarchical and multi-level optimization objective.

3.2   Complementary Teacher Distillation

Solution for "How to design teacher models to efficiently assist in boosting the capacity of the lightweight model?"

Although [54] has proved that multiple teacher models can provide more effective information for students, the research on diverse teacher structures is still insufficient. For the fine-grained task of semantic segmentation, complementary teacher networks can bring two advantages: i) help to capture more

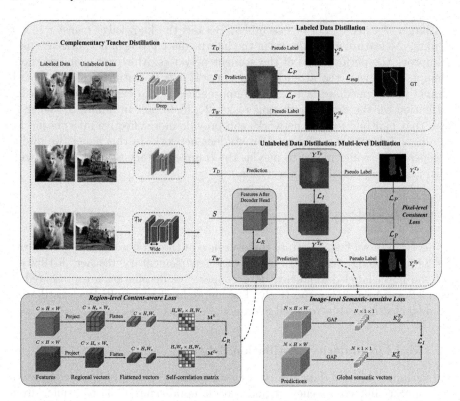

Fig. 2. The pipeline of Multi-Granularity Distillation (MGD) Scheme. MGD is formulated as triplet-branches, where there are two structurally-complementary teacher models (*i.e.*, T_D and T_W) and a target student model S. T_D indicates the deep-and-thin teacher model, T_W denotes the shallow-and-wide teacher model, and the student network S is a shallow and thin model. Image-level semantic-sensitive loss, region-level content-aware loss, and pixel-level consistency loss are designed to form the hierarchical and multi-level loss setting

comprehensive visual cues and boost the performance of the student model from different aspects; ii) suppress over-fitting issue that is common in the distillation. Hence in this paper, the teacher model is expanded from two complementary dimensions compared to the student model, *i.e.*, depth and width. Specifically, the complementary teachers contain a deep-and-thin teacher model T_D (such as ResNet-101 [15]) and a wide-and-shallow teacher model T_W (such as Wide ResNet-34 [57]). These two complementary teacher models can achieve comparable performance while tending to contain diverse potential characteristics.

T_D has proven its ability in extracting high-level semantic and global categorical abstractions [43], which helps to achieve promising results in the classification-oriented task. Hence, we attempt to extract the global semantic knowledge $K_G^{T_D}$ from T_D to enhance the global perception ability of the student model. Furthermore, T_W is conducive to capturing the diverse content-aware information due to the sufficient channels, which is beneficial for modeling the contextual relationship between regions. In this paper, we first follow CPS [7] to pre-train two teacher models and freeze their parameters to conduct an offline distillation procedure for refining the student model.

3.3   Labeled-Unlabeled Data Cooperative Distillation

Solution for "How to fully leverage both limited labeled and sufficient unlabeled data in the semi-supervised distillation setting?"

The existing distillation techniques are mainly carried out under the full supervision setting and lack of distillation practice for unlabeled data. So we involve a novel labeled-unlabeled data cooperative distillation scheme in MGD. As for labeled data (X_l) distillation, the student model is optimized by ground truth labels $\hat{Y}$ with the supervision loss $\mathcal{L}^l_{Sup}$:

$$\mathcal{L}^l_{Sup}(Y, \hat{Y}) = -\frac{1}{H \times W} \sum_{i=1}^{H \times W} (\hat{y}_i log(y_i)), \tag{1}$$

where y_i represents the prediction of the student model and the $\hat{y}_i$ illustrates the ground truth label. Superscript l represents labeled data.

Furthermore, we design the pixel-level consistency loss to maintain that the multiple predictions of the same input are consistent. Specifically, both output of the teacher model T_D and T_W can be regarded as pseudo label Y_p for the student model S. Pixel-level consistency loss is set as:

$$\begin{aligned} \mathcal{L}^l_P(Y, Y_p) &= \mathcal{L}_{ce}(Y, Y_p^{T_D}) + \mathcal{L}_{ce}(Y, Y_p^{T_W}) \\ &= -\frac{1}{H \times W} \sum_{i=1}^{H \times W} [y_{pi}^{T_D} log(y_i) + y_{pi}^{T_W} log(y_i)], \end{aligned} \tag{2}$$

where $y_{pi}^{T_D}$ and $y_{pi}^{T_W}$ are the pseudo labels generated by T_D and T_W respectively. $H \times W$ denotes the number pixels of prediction masks. The $\mathcal{L}^l_{Sup}$ and $\mathcal{L}^l_P$ are combined to form the labeled distillation loss $\mathcal{L}_{label}$. Besides labeled data distillation, we further design a hierarchical and multi-level loss setting for unlabeled data distillation $\mathcal{L}_{unlabel}$ in Sect. 3.4.

3.4   Hierarchical and Multi-level Distillation

Solution for "Are there more granularity concepts that can be resorted to refine the lightweight model for this fine-grained task?"

To capture the multi-granularity features oriented for segmentation task, we design a hierarchical and multi-level distillation scheme for unlabeled data, which helps to provide students with holistic and local concepts in various aspects. Because there is no ground-truth supervision for unlabeled data, we introduce image-level semantic-sensitive loss, region-level content-aware loss, and pixel-level consistency loss to achieve a more comprehensive distillation procedure on unlabeled data.

Image-Level Semantic-sensitive Loss. Image-level semantic-sensitive loss is introduced to distill the high-dimensional semantic abstraction from the deeper teacher model T_D into the lightweight one. After obtaining the predictions $Y \in \mathcal{R}^{N \times H \times W}$ from T_D, we employ global average pooling (GAP) operation to calculate the global semantic vector of each category, which is illustrated as:

$$K_G^{T_D} = G(Y^{N \times H \times W}), \tag{3}$$

where $K_G^{T_D} \in \mathcal{R}^{N \times 1 \times 1}$ summarizes the global semantic knowledge of Nth categories. G denotes the global average pooling operation in each channel. We further calculate the global semantic representation K_G^S of student model and employ image-level semantic-sensitive loss $\mathcal{L}_I^u$ to supervise it:

$$\mathcal{L}_I^u \left(K_G^S, K_G^{T_D} \right) = \frac{1}{N} \sum_{i=1}^{N} \| k_{Gi}^S - k_{Gi}^{T_D} \|_1, \tag{4}$$

where k_{Gi}^S and $k_{Gi}^{T_D}$ denote the semantic category of the student S and the teacher T_D respectively. N represents the number of categories and u represents unlabeled data. In this way, the student model attempts to learn higher-dimensional semantic representations, which helps to provide global guidance on distinguishing task-specific categories with respect to the semantic segmentation task.

Region-Level Content-Aware Loss. Region-level content-aware loss aims to take advantage of channels advantage of wider teacher model T_W to provide plentiful regional context information. It leverages correlation between image patches from T_W to guide the student S to model contextual relationships between regions, which is effective to better understand image regional details and relationships. The decoders output features (F^{T_W} and F^S) from T_W and S are extracted to calculate the content-aware loss. Firstly, $F \in \mathcal{R}^{C \times H \times W}$ are projected into the regional content vectors $V \in \mathcal{R}^{C \times H_v \times W_v}$ via projection heads. Each vector $v \in \mathcal{R}^{C \times 1 \times 1}$ in V represents the regional content of the patch features with size $C \times H/H_v \times W/W_v$. The projection heads are employed with the adaptive average pooling. Then, the regional content vectors V are used to calculate the self-correlation matrix $M \in \mathcal{R}^{H_v W_v \times H_v W_v}$:

$$M = sim(V^T V), \text{ with } m_{ij} = \frac{v_i^T v_j}{\|v_i\| \|v_j\|}, \tag{5}$$

where m_{ij} denotes the value of self-correlation matrix at the coordinate of row i and column j produced with the cosine similarity $sim()$. The v_i and v_j are the ith and j^{th} vectors of flattened $V \in \mathcal{R}^{C \times H_v W_v}$. The self-correlation matrix represents the regional relationship among features F, which can reflect the correlation between image regions. The region-level content-aware loss is set up to minimize the difference between M^{T_W} and M^S:

$$\mathcal{L}_R^u\left(\mathbf{M}^S, \mathbf{M}^{Tw}\right) = \frac{1}{H_v W_v \times H_v W_v} \sum_{i=1}^{H_v W_v} \sum_{j=1}^{H_v W_v} (m_{ij}^S - m_{ij}^{Tw})^2, \tag{6}$$

where m_{ij}^S and m_{ij}^{Tw} denote the self-correlation values of student model and teacher model. $H_v W_v \times H_v W_v$ is the size of self-correlation matrices.

Pixel-Level Consistency Loss. The pixel-level consistency loss is also employed on the unlabeled data X_u, which is the same as Eq. (2) and denoted as $\mathcal{L}_P^u$. To sum up, the total loss function in our multi-granularity distillation scheme is summarized as:

$$\mathcal{L} = \underbrace{\mathcal{L}_{Sup}^l + \mathcal{L}_P^l}_{\mathcal{L}_{label}} + \underbrace{\mathcal{L}_P^u + \lambda_1 \mathcal{L}_I^u + \lambda_2 \mathcal{L}_R^u}_{\mathcal{L}_{unlabel}}, \tag{7}$$

where the λ_1 and λ_2 are the trade-off parameters for the loss functions.

4 Experiment

4.1 Datasets and Evaluation Metrics

Datasets. PASCAL VOC2012 [11] is a widely used benchmark for semantic segmentation, which consists of 20 foreground objects classes and one background class. Following [7,19], we adopt 10,582 augmented images as the full training set and 1,449 images for validation. Cityscapes [8] is a real urban scene dataset that consists of 2,974 images for training, 500 images for validation, and 1,525 for testing with 19 semantic classes. We follow [7,19] to use the public 1/16, 1/8, 1/4, and 1/2 subsets of the training set as the labeled data and the remaining images in the training set as the unlabeled data.

Evaluation Metrics. To verify the performance of the segmentation model, we calculate the mean Intersection-over-Union (mIoU) of all classes. We also compare the parameters and FLOPs of the model backbone for fair evaluation.

4.2 Implementation Details

We initialize the weights of the lightweight backbones (ResNet-18 [15] and MobileNetv2 [37]) with pre-trained weights on ImageNet [21]. We employ DeepLabv3+ [6] segmentation architecture in our framework, which consists of a visual backbone and an ASPP based segmentation heads. The deep-and-thin teacher model ResNet-101 and the wide-and-shallow teacher model Wide ResNet-34 [57] are pre-trained via CPS [7] and do not update their parameters in the procedure of optimizing student models. We leverage SGD algorithm for network optimization with a 0.0005 weight decay and a 0.9 momentum. We set the hyper-parameters of the coefficients of the loss functions as $\lambda_1 = 0.002$ and $\lambda_2 = 100$. There is currently no researches on lightweight semi-supervised semantic segmentation. We replace the backbone of competitive methods *i.e.*,

Table 1. Comparison with SOTAs on the VOC2012 Val set with 512×512 input size under different partition protocols. The first split reports the results of the complementary teacher models. The second and third splits denote the results of employing ResNet-18 and MobileNetv2 as the lightweight backbone, respectively. Sup. l denotes training with only labeled data under the corresponding partition.

Method	Backbone	Params	FLOPs	1/16 (662)	1/8 (1323)	1/4 (2646)	1/2 (5291)
CPS [7]	ResNet-101 (T_D)	42.63M	59.13G	73.98	76.43	77.61	78.64
CPS [7]	Wide ResNet-34 (T_W)	66.83M	91.12G	68.17	71.38	74.78	75.85
Sup. l	ResNet-18	11.19M	17.20G	42.17	55.65	62.52	65.39
MT [44]	ResNet-18	(3.81× w.r.t. T_D)	(3.44× w.r.t. T_D)	44.61	56.62	61.79	66.48
CPS [7]	ResNet-18	(5.97× w.r.t. T_W)	(5.30× w.r.t. T_W)	47.13	60.05	65.89	68.69
KD [46]	ResNet-18			56.37	62.01	66.23	68.55
CWD [38]	ResNet-18			50.45	58.71	63.96	65.82
Ours (MGD)	ResNet-18			**66.86**	**68.29**	**69.71**	**71.59**
Sup. l	MobileNetv2	1.81M	1.52G	46.02	46.66	48.19	49.61
MT [44]	MobileNetv2	(23.55× w.r.t. T_D)	(38.90× w.r.t. T_D)	45.11	47.20	49.15	49.63
CPS [7]	MobileNetv2	(36.92× w.r.t. T_W)	(59.95× w.r.t. T_W)	46.57	48.75	49.94	50.52
KD [46]	MobileNetv2			47.99	49.30	50.07	50.68
CWD [38]	MobileNetv2			46.13	47.45	48.89	49.70
Ours (MGD)	MobileNetv2			**50.95**	**52.27**	**53.92**	**55.88**

CPS [7] and MT [44] with ResNet-18 and MobileNetv2 to make a comparison with our approach. The classical distillation methods KD [46] (KL Divergence) and CWD [38] are employed on our complementary teacher models to distill the lightweight models.

4.3   Comparison with State-of-the-Art Methods

In this section, we compare MGD with several state-of-the-art methods in terms of computation cost and accuracy under all partition protocols. We employ ResNet-18 and MobileNetv2 as the lightweight backbones and report the results on PASCAL VOC2012 and Cityscapes in Table 1, 2, 3 and Fig. 3. We summarize the FLOPs and parameters of the model backbone, and the corresponding segmentation heads in these models are compressed proportionately.

PASCAL VOC2012. The experimental results on PASCAL VOC2012 are shown in Table 1, which can be summarized as the following observations: 1) Replacing the large model with a small model directly will result in obvious performance degradation. For example, it decreased from 73.97% (ResNet-101) to 47.13% (ResNet-18) under 1/16 partition protocols, with a serious decline of 26.8%. 2) Employing the existing distillation method obtain minor improvement, while our approach contributes to alleviating the performance drop effectively. As shown in Fig. 3, MGD shows significant performance improvement under diverse partition protocols, and the growth trend is more obvious when the amount of labeled data is less. Compared with CPS, MGD helps to boost the performance from 47.13 to 66.86 in the 1/16 partition setting. In more detail, the improvement is 19.73%, 8.24%, 3.82%, and 2.90% under 1/16, 1/8, 1/4, and 1/2 partition protocols, respectively. 3) Furthermore, although the model with ResNet-18 backbone is compressed by **3.44×** (**5.30×**) FLOPs and **3.81×** (**5.97×**) parameters,

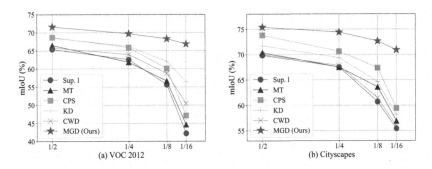

Fig. 3. Performance of different methods under different partition protocols with ResNet-18 backbone

Table 2. Comparison for few-supervision on PASCAL VOC2012. We follow the same partition protocols as PseudoSeg [65].

Method	Backbone	1/16 (92)	1/8 (183)	1/4 (366)	1/2 (732)
CPS [7]	ResNet-101	64.07	67.42	71.71	75.88
CPS [7]	Wide ResNet-34	60.01	63.32	67.84	72.03
Sup. l	ResNet-18	15.54	22.43	35.78	51.47
MT [44]	ResNet-18	12.58	18.15	33.71	50.02
CPS [7]	ResNet-18	24.53	36.19	47.61	56.85
Ours	ResNet-18	**58.03**	**61.94**	**64.97**	**67.40**

it only exists a small gap from the result of T_W. It fully demonstrates the effectiveness of our method. 4) Although the lightweight model with MobileNetv2 compresses more calculational costs (**38.90×** (**59.95×**) FLOPs and **23.55×** (**36.92×**) parameters), MGD manages to achieve an impressive performance. For example, MGD with MobileNetv2 (50.95) even surpasses the CPS method with ResNet-18 backbone (47.13) under 1/16 partition protocol.

Few Supervision on PASCAL VOC2012. To evaluate the robustness of our method on the few labeled case, we conduct the experiments on PASCAL VOC 2012 with few supervision by following the same partition protocols adopted in PseudoSeg [65]. As shown in Table 2, it can observe that our method still can achieve impressive results with fewer labeled samples, which far exceed MT [44] and CPS [7]. Surprisingly, the performance of MGD (58.03) trained with only 1/16 partition data can surpass CPS (56.85) under 1/2 partition protocols. The few supervision experiments further reveal that MGD is suitable for lightweight model optimization with few or even very few samples.

Cityscapes. We conduct the experiments under different partition protocols on Cityscapes and summarize the result in Table 3. From the Table 3 and Fig. 3, we observe a similar performance gain and trend under different partition protocols as PASCAL VOC2012. Our method can establish state-of-the-art results among all partition protocols with both ResNet-18 and MobileNetv2 backbones.

Table 3. Comparison with state-of-the-arts on the Cityscapes val set with the input size of 800×800 under different partition protocols.

Method	Backbone	Params	FLOPs	1/16 (662)	1/8 (1323)	1/4 (2646)	1/2 (5291)
CPS [7]	ResNet-101(T_D)	42.63M	144.32G	74.72	77.62	78.85	79.58
CPS [7]	Wide ResNet-34(T_W)	66.83M	222.45G	72.56	75.41	77.68	78.37
Sup. l	ResNet-18	11.19M	42.01G	55.39	60.71	67.51	69.83
MT [44]	ResNet-18	(3.81× w.r.t. T_D)	(3.43× w.r.t. T_D)	56.92	63.61	67.46	70.38
CPS [7]	ResNet-18	(5.97× w.r.t. T_W)	(5.30× w.r.t. T_W)	59.43	67.35	70.64	73.81
KD [46]	ResNet-18			58.10	64.62	69.35	71.76
CWD [38]	ResNet-18			55.88	61.47	67.80	70.02
Ours (MGD)	ResNet-18			**70.91**	**72.65**	**74.42**	**75.40**
Sup. l	MobileNetv2	1.81M	3.73G	50.06	51.97	54.03	56.86
MT [44]	MobileNetv2	(23.55× w.r.t. T_D)	(38.69× w.r.t. T_D)	51.10	53.85	56.21	57.25
CPS [7]	MobileNetv2	(36.92× w.r.t. T_W)	(59.64× w.r.t. T_W)	53.34	55.61	57.98	59.20
KD [46]	ResNet-18			53.45	54.89	55.28	57.90
CWD [38]	ResNet-18			51.52	52.64	54.37	57.01
Ours (MGD)	MobileNetv2			**58.00**	**59.27**	**61.36**	**62.55**

Table 4. Analysis of different teacher setting on VOC2012 and Cityscapes under 1/8 partition with student ResNet-18. T_D: ResNet-101, T_W: Wide ResNet-34.

First teacher		Second teacher		VOC	Cityscapes
T_D	T_W	T_D	T_W		
√				64.85	69.63
	√			64.36	68.98
√		√		66.14	71.19
	√		√	65.78	70.92
√			√	**68.29**	**72.65**

For example, MGD obtains 70.91/58.00 under the 1/16 partition protocol with ResNet-18/MobileNetv2 backbone, which outperforms CPS by 11.48%/4.66%.

Qualitative Results. As illustrated in Fig. 4, we compare our method with the competitive approach CPS [7] and Sup. l in terms of segmentation results on PASCAL VOC2012 Val [11]. From the figure, we find that Sup. l and CPS fail to capture the internal pixels of the target or mistake the object categories. On the contrary, our approach manages to obtain the integral masks closer to the ground truth labels, which further proves the superiority of the MGD scheme and its multi-level setting.

4.4   Ablation Study

Analysis of Teacher Setting. To evaluate the significance of the complementary teacher scheme, we employ different teacher model combinations to optimize the lightweight model. As shown in Table 4, employing two teacher models in the distillation procedure is better than a single model. Furthermore, adopting different structural-based teachers can achieve more impressive performance

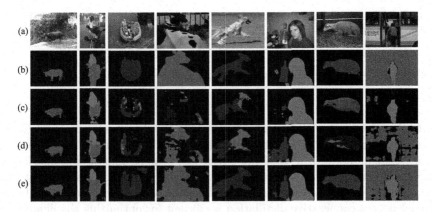

Fig. 4. Qualitative results on the PASCAL VOC2012 Val. (a) Input images. (b) Ground truth labels. (c) The segmentation results from Sup. l. (d) The segmentation results from CPS [7]. (e) The segmentation results from MGD

Table 5. The performance with different loss setting on the VOC2012 and Cityscapes under 1/8 partition protocol with student ResNet-18.

(a) Results of different levels distillation.

Pixel-level		Image-level		Region-level		VOC	City
$\mathcal{L}_{Sup}$	$\mathcal{L}_P$	$\mathcal{L}_I^{T_D}$	$\mathcal{L}_I^{T_W}$	$\mathcal{L}_R^{T_D}$	$\mathcal{L}_R^{T_W}$		
✓						55.65	60.71
✓	✓					63.61	69.05
✓	✓	✓				66.01	71.03
✓	✓				✓	66.02	71.15
✓	✓	✓			✓	**68.29**	**72.65**
✓	✓	✓	✓	✓	✓	67.51	71.96

(b) Performance of labeled and unlabeled data distillation losses.

$\mathcal{L}_{label}$		$\mathcal{L}_{unlabel}$			VOC	City
$\mathcal{L}_{Sup}$	$\mathcal{L}_P^l$	$\mathcal{L}_P^u$	$\mathcal{L}_I^{T_D}$	$\mathcal{L}_R^{T_W}$		
✓	✓				58.24	63.98
✓	✓	✓	✓	✓	**68.29**	**72.65**

than leveraging the same combination, which indicates that teacher models with different architectures help to provide complementary concepts and success in optimizing lightweight models from different dimensions.

Analysis of Loss Setting. To investigate the distillation loss setting, we conduct extensive experiments and analyze the components in the multi-level distillation loss and the cooperative distillation loss in Table 5. As shown in Table 5a, the variant with the $\mathcal{L}_P^{u,l}$ can obtain a notable improvement than the supervised baseline. $\mathcal{L}_I^u$ and $\mathcal{L}_R^u$ further boost the performance of the lightweight model to 66.01/71.03% and 66.02/71.15%, which proves the effectiveness of region-level content-aware loss and image-level semantic-sensitive loss. We employ $\mathcal{L}_I^u$ and $\mathcal{L}_R^u$ on different branches to further explore the optimal configuration for these two losses. The experimental results show that when applying $\mathcal{L}_I^u$ to the deeper teacher model and $\mathcal{L}_R^u$ to a wider model can achieve the best results, *i.e.*, 68.29%/72.65%. It may be because the deeper teacher is beneficial to provide the corresponding global semantic characteristics while the wider model has the advantage in capturing local context information. The results in Table 5a also

Table 6. Different size of H_v and W_v on VOC2012 under 1/8 partition protocol with student ResNet-18.

$H_v \times W_v$	3×3	5×5	7×7	9×9	11×11
mIoU	66.83	67.01	**68.29**	67.75	67.38

reveal that the distillation losses from image-level, region-level and pixel-level are all essential for breaking through the bottleneck of the capacity of the lightweight model. As summarized in Table 5b, MGD can achieve 10.05% and 8.67% performance improvement via unlabeled data distillation, which demonstrates the effectiveness of the unlabeled distillation loss. And it further reveals the labeled-unlabeled data cooperative distillation is efficient for optimizing the lightweight SSSS model.

Analysis of Size of Regional Content Vectors. The regional content vectors $\mathbf{V} \in \mathcal{R}^{C \times H_v \times W_v}$ are generated by the adaptive average pooling operation. To determine the optimal size of $H_v \times W_v$, we follow the dataset characteristic to set $H_v = W_v$ and conduct the experiments on PASCAL VOC2012. As shown in Table 6, the MGD can achieve the best result when $H_v \times W_v = 7 \times 7$.

5   Discussion

In this paper, we provide an effective solution on how to obtain a lightweight segmentation model in a semi-supervised setting. Furthermore, there are still many aspects worthy of further study: i) How to formulate the whole optimization process into a one-stage procedure? ii) How to further narrow the performance gap between the lightweight model and the large model? iii) Is there any data selection strategy such as the active learning algorithm that can improve the performance? We hope that our work can provide inspired insight and encourage more researchers to involve in the field of lightweight semi-supervised models.

6   Conclusion

In this paper, we offer the first attempt to obtain lightweight SSSS models via a novel multi-granularity distillation (MGD) scheme. MGD employs triplet-branches to distill diverse granularity concepts from two complementary teacher models into a student one. Within MGD, the labeled-unlabeled data cooperative distillation scheme is set up to take full advantage of semi-supervised data characteristics. Furthermore, MGD designs a hierarchical and multi-level loss setting for unlabeled data, which consists of an image-level semantic-sensitive loss, a region-level content-aware loss, and a pixel-level consistency loss. This novel hierarchical loss setting plays a key role to break through the bottleneck of the capacity of the lightweight model. We conduct extensive experiments on two benchmarks to demonstrate the effectiveness of the proposed approach and analyze the key factors that contribute more to addressing this task.

References

1. Alonso, I., Sabater, A., Ferstl, D., Montesano, L., Murillo, A.C.: Semi-supervised semantic segmentation with pixel-level contrastive learning from a class-wise memory bank. arXiv preprint arXiv:2104.13415 (2021)
2. Badrinarayanan, V., Kendall, A., Cipolla, R.: SegNet: a deep convolutional encoder-decoder architecture for image segmentation. TPAMI **39**, 2481–2495 (2017)
3. Berthelot, D., et al.: ReMixMatch: semi-supervised learning with distribution alignment and augmentation anchoring. arXiv preprint arXiv:1911.09785 (2019)
4. Berthelot, D., Carlini, N., Goodfellow, I., Papernot, N., Oliver, A., Raffel, C.: MixMatch: a holistic approach to semi-supervised learning. arXiv preprint arXiv:1905.02249 (2019)
5. Chen, L.C., Papandreou, G., Kokkinos, I., Murphy, K., Yuille, A.L.: DeepLab: Semantic image segmentation with deep convolutional nets, atrous convolution, and fully connected CRFs. TPAMI **40**, 834–848 (2017)
6. Chen, L.-C., Zhu, Y., Papandreou, G., Schroff, F., Adam, H.: Encoder-decoder with atrous separable convolution for semantic image segmentation. In: Ferrari, V., Hebert, M., Sminchisescu, C., Weiss, Y. (eds.) ECCV 2018. LNCS, vol. 11211, pp. 833–851. Springer, Cham (2018). https://doi.org/10.1007/978-3-030-01234-2_49
7. Chen, X., Yuan, Y., Zeng, G., Wang, J.: Semi-supervised semantic segmentation with cross pseudo supervision. In: CVPR (2021)
8. Cordts, M., et al.: The cityscapes dataset for semantic urban scene understanding. In: CVPR (2016)
9. Dai, Z., Yang, Z., Yang, F., Cohen, W.W., Salakhutdinov, R.: Good semi-supervised learning that requires a bad GAN. arXiv preprint arXiv:1705.09783 (2017)
10. Dong-DongChen, W., WeiGao, Z.H.: Tri-net for semi-supervised deep learning. In: IJCAI (2018)
11. Everingham, M., Van Gool, L., Williams, C.K., Winn, J., Zisserman, A.: The pascal visual object classes (VOC) challenge. IJCV **88**, 303–338 (2010)
12. Fu, J., et al.: Dual attention network for scene segmentation. In: CVPR (2019)
13. Gou, J., Yu, B., Maybank, S.J., Tao, D.: Knowledge distillation: a survey. Int. J. Comput. Vision **129**(6), 1789–1819 (2021)
14. Grandvalet, Y., Bengio, Y., et al.: Semi-supervised learning by entropy minimization. CAP (2005)
15. He, K., Zhang, X., Ren, S., Sun, J.: Deep residual learning for image recognition. In: CVPR (2016)
16. Hinton, G., Vinyals, O., Dean, J.: Distilling the knowledge in a neural network. arXiv preprint arXiv:1503.02531 (2015)
17. Huang, Z., Wang, X., Huang, L., Huang, C., Wei, Y., Liu, W.: CCNet: criss-cross attention for semantic segmentation. In: ICCV (2019)
18. Hung, W.C., Tsai, Y.H., Liou, Y.T., Lin, Y.Y., Yang, M.H.: Adversarial learning for semi-supervised semantic segmentation. arXiv preprint arXiv:1802.07934 (2018)
19. Ke, Z., Qiu, D., Li, K., Yan, Q., Lau, R.W.H.: Guided collaborative training for pixel-wise semi-supervised learning. In: Vedaldi, A., Bischof, H., Brox, T., Frahm, J.-M. (eds.) ECCV 2020. LNCS, vol. 12358, pp. 429–445. Springer, Cham (2020). https://doi.org/10.1007/978-3-030-58601-0_26
20. Kipf, T.N., Welling, M.: Semi-supervised classification with graph convolutional networks. arXiv preprint arXiv:1609.02907 (2016)

21. Krizhevsky, A., Sutskever, I., Hinton, G.E.: ImageNet classification with deep convolutional neural networks. In: NeurIPS (2012)
22. Lai, X., et al.: Semi-supervised semantic segmentation with directional context-aware consistency. In: CVPR (2021)
23. Laine, S., Aila, T.: Temporal ensembling for semi-supervised learning. arXiv preprint arXiv:1610.02242 (2016)
24. Lee, D.H., et al.: Pseudo-label: the simple and efficient semi-supervised learning method for deep neural networks. In: ICMLW (2013)
25. Li, C., Xu, K., Zhu, J., Zhang, B.: Triple generative adversarial nets. arXiv preprint arXiv:1703.02291 (2017)
26. Liu, B., Wu, Z., Hu, H., Lin, S.: Deep metric transfer for label propagation with limited annotated data. In: ICCVW (2019)
27. Liu, Y., Chen, K., Liu, C., Qin, Z., Luo, Z., Wang, J.: Structured knowledge distillation for semantic segmentation. In: Proceedings of the IEEE/CVF Conference on Computer Vision and Pattern Recognition, pp. 2604–2613 (2019)
28. Liu, Y., Shu, C., Wang, J., Shen, C.: Structured knowledge distillation for dense prediction. TPAMI (2020)
29. Long, J., Shelhamer, E., Darrell, T.: Fully convolutional networks for semantic segmentation. In: CVPR (2015)
30. Mittal, S., Tatarchenko, M., Brox, T.: Semi-supervised semantic segmentation with high-and low-level consistency. TPAMI **43**, 1369–1379 (2019)
31. Miyato, T., Maeda, S.I., Koyama, M., Ishii, S.: Virtual adversarial training: a regularization method for supervised and semi-supervised learning. TPAMI **41**, 1979–1993 (2018)
32. Noh, H., Hong, S., Han, B.: Learning deconvolution network for semantic segmentation. In: ICCV (2015)
33. Ouali, Y., Hudelot, C., Tami, M.: Semi-supervised semantic segmentation with cross-consistency training. In: CVPR (2020)
34. Qin, J., Wu, J., Xiao, X., Li, L., Wang, X.: Activation modulation and recalibration scheme for weakly supervised semantic segmentation. In: Proceedings of the AAAI Conference on Artificial Intelligence, vol. 36, no. 2, pp. 2117–2125 (2022)
35. Romero, A., Ballas, N., Kahou, S.E., Chassang, A., Gatta, C., Bengio, Y.: FitNets: hints for thin deep nets. arXiv preprint arXiv:1412.6550 (2014)
36. Ronneberger, O., Fischer, P., Brox, T.: U-net: convolutional networks for biomedical image segmentation. In: Navab, N., Hornegger, J., Wells, W.M., Frangi, A.F. (eds.) MICCAI 2015. LNCS, vol. 9351, pp. 234–241. Springer, Cham (2015). https://doi.org/10.1007/978-3-319-24574-4_28
37. Sandler, M., Howard, A., Zhu, M., Zhmoginov, A., Chen, L.C.: MobileNetV 2: inverted residuals and linear bottlenecks. In: CVPR (2018)
38. Shu, C., Liu, Y., Gao, J., Yan, Z., Shen, C.: Channel-wise knowledge distillation for dense prediction. In: Proceedings of the IEEE/CVF International Conference on Computer Vision, pp. 5311–5320 (2021)
39. Sohn, K., et al.: FixMatch: simplifying semi-supervised learning with consistency and confidence. arXiv preprint arXiv:2001.07685 (2020)
40. Souly, N., Spampinato, C., Shah, M.: Semi supervised semantic segmentation using generative adversarial network. In: ICCV (2017)
41. Springenberg, J.T.: Unsupervised and semi-supervised learning with categorical generative adversarial networks. arXiv preprint arXiv:1511.06390 (2015)
42. Sun, K., Xiao, B., Liu, D., Wang, J.: Deep high-resolution representation learning for human pose estimation. In: CVPR (2019)

43. Szegedy, C., et al.: Going deeper with convolutions. In: Proceedings of the IEEE Conference on Computer Vision and Pattern Recognition, pp. 1–9 (2015)
44. Tarvainen, A., Valpola, H.: Mean teachers are better role models: weight-averaged consistency targets improve semi-supervised deep learning results. arXiv preprint arXiv:1703.01780 (2017)
45. Wang, X., et al.: MVSTER: epipolar transformer for efficient multi-view stereo. arXiv preprint arXiv:2204.07346 (2022)
46. Wang, Y., Zhou, W., Jiang, T., Bai, X., Xu, Y.: Intra-class feature variation distillation for semantic segmentation. In: Vedaldi, A., Bischof, H., Brox, T., Frahm, J.-M. (eds.) ECCV 2020. LNCS, vol. 12352, pp. 346–362. Springer, Cham (2020). https://doi.org/10.1007/978-3-030-58571-6_21
47. Wu, J., Hu, H., Wu, Y.: Image captioning via semantic guidance attention and consensus selection strategy. TOMM **14**, 1–19 (2018)
48. Wu, J., Hu, H., Yang, L.: Pseudo-3D attention transfer network with content-aware strategy for image captioning. TOMM **15**, 1–19 (2019)
49. Wu, J., Xie, S., Shi, X., Chen, Y.: Global-local feature attention network with reranking strategy for image caption generation. In: Yang, J., et al. (eds.) CCCV 2017. CCIS, vol. 771, pp. 157–167. Springer, Singapore (2017). https://doi.org/10.1007/978-981-10-7299-4_13
50. Xie, J., Shuai, B., Hu, J.F., Lin, J., Zheng, W.S.: Improving fast segmentation with teacher-student learning. arXiv preprint arXiv:1810.08476 (2018)
51. Xie, Q., Dai, Z., Hovy, E., Luong, M.T., Le, Q.V.: Unsupervised data augmentation for consistency training. arXiv preprint arXiv:1904.12848 (2019)
52. Xie, Q., Luong, M.T., Hovy, E., Le, Q.V.: Self-training with noisy student improves ImageNet classification. In: CVPR (2020)
53. Yang, M., Yu, K., Zhang, C., Li, Z., Yang, K.: DenseASPP for semantic segmentation in street scenes. In: CVPR (2018)
54. You, S., Xu, C., Xu, C., Tao, D.: Learning from multiple teacher networks. In: SIGKDD (2017)
55. Yu, F., Koltun, V.: Multi-scale context aggregation by dilated convolutions. arXiv preprint arXiv:1511.07122 (2015)
56. Yun, S., Han, D., Oh, S.J., Chun, S., Choe, J., Yoo, Y.: CutMix: regularization strategy to train strong classifiers with localizable features. In: ICCV (2019)
57. Zagoruyko, S., Komodakis, N.: Wide residual networks. arXiv preprint arXiv:1605.07146 (2016)
58. Zhai, X., Oliver, A., Kolesnikov, A., Beyer, L.: S4l: self-supervised semi-supervised learning. In: ICCV (2019)
59. Zhang, H., Cisse, M., Dauphin, Y.N., Lopez-Paz, D.: Mixup: beyond empirical risk minimization. arXiv preprint arXiv:1710.09412 (2017)
60. Zhao, H., Qi, X., Shen, X., Shi, J., Jia, J.: ICNet for real-time semantic segmentation on high-resolution images. In: Ferrari, V., Hebert, M., Sminchisescu, C., Weiss, Y. (eds.) ECCV 2018. LNCS, vol. 11207, pp. 418–434. Springer, Cham (2018). https://doi.org/10.1007/978-3-030-01219-9_25
61. Zhao, H., Shi, J., Qi, X., Wang, X., Jia, J.: Pyramid scene parsing network. In: CVPR (2017)
62. Zhao, H., et al.: PSANet: point-wise spatial attention network for scene parsing. In: Ferrari, V., Hebert, M., Sminchisescu, C., Weiss, Y. (eds.) ECCV 2018. LNCS, vol. 11213, pp. 270–286. Springer, Cham (2018). https://doi.org/10.1007/978-3-030-01240-3_17
63. Zhong, Y., Yuan, B., Wu, H., Yuan, Z., Peng, J., Wang, Y.X.: Pixel contrastive-consistent semi-supervised semantic segmentation. In: ICCV (2021)

64. Zhu, Z., Xu, M., Bai, S., Huang, T., Bai, X.: Asymmetric non-local neural networks for semantic segmentation. In: ICCV (2019)
65. Zou, Y., Zhang, Z., Zhang, H., Li, C.L., Bian, X., Huang, J.B., Pfister, T.: PSEUDOSEG: designing pseudo labels for semantic segmentation. arXiv preprint arXiv:2010.09713 (2020)

CP²: Copy-Paste Contrastive Pretraining for Semantic Segmentation

Feng Wang[1], Huiyu Wang[2], Chen Wei[2], Alan Yuille[2], and Wei Shen[3(✉)]

[1] Department of Automation, Tsinghua University, Beijing, China
[2] Department of Computer Science, Johns Hopkins University, Baltimore, USA
[3] MoE Key Lab of Artificial Intelligence, AI Institute, Shanghai Jiao Tong University, Shanghai, China
shenwei1231@gmail.com

Abstract. Recent advances in self-supervised contrastive learning yield good image-level representation, which favors classification tasks but usually neglects pixel-level detailed information, leading to unsatisfactory transfer performance to dense prediction tasks such as semantic segmentation. In this work, we propose a pixel-wise contrastive learning method called CP² (**C**opy-**P**aste **C**ontrastive **P**retraining), which facilitates both image- and pixel-level representation learning and therefore is more suitable for downstream dense prediction tasks. In detail, we copy-paste a random crop from an image (the foreground) onto different background images and pretrain a semantic segmentation model with the objective of 1) distinguishing the foreground pixels from the background pixels, and 2) identifying the composed images that share the same foreground. Experiments show the strong performance of CP² in downstream semantic segmentation: By finetuning CP² pretrained models on PASCAL VOC 2012, we obtain 78.6% mIoU with a ResNet-50 and 79.5% with a ViT-S. Code and models are available at https://github.com/wangf3014/CP2.

Keywords: Dense contrastive learning · Semantic segmentation

1 Introduction

Learning invariant *image-level* representation and transferring to downstream tasks has became a common paradigm in self-supervised contrastive learning. Specifically, the objective of these methods is either to minimize the Euclidean (ℓ_2) distance [13,26] or cross entropy [5,6] between the *image-level* features of augmented views of the same image, or to distinguish the positive image feature from a set of negative image features by optimizing an InfoNCE [38] loss [10–12,14,28,41].

Supplementary Information The online version contains supplementary material available at https://doi.org/10.1007/978-3-031-20056-4_29.

In spite of the success in downstream classification tasks, these contrastive objectives build on the assumption that every pixel in an image belongs to a single label and lack the perception of spatially varying image content. We argue that these *classification-oriented* objectives are not ideal for downstream dense prediction tasks such as semantic segmentation where the model should distinguish different semantic labels in an image. For the task of semantic segmentation, current contrastive learning models may easily over-fit to learning the *image-level* representation and neglect pixel-level variances.

Moreover, there is an architectural misalignment in the current pretraining finetuning paradigm for downstream semantic segmentation tasks: 1) The semantic segmentation model usually requires a large atrous rate and a small output stride than those in the classification-oriented pretrained backbones [8,34]; 2) The finetuning of the well pretrained backbone and the randomly initialized segmentation head can be out of sync, *e.g.* the random head may generate random gradients that poison the pretrained backbone, negatively affecting the performance. These two issues prevent the classification-oriented pretrained backbone from facilitating dense prediction tasks such as semantic segmentation.

In this paper, we propose a novel self-supervised pretraining method designed for downstream semantic segmentation, named **C**opy-**P**aste **C**ontrastive **P**retraining (CP²). Specifically, we pretrain a semantic segmentation model with Copy-Pasted input images which are composed by cropping random crops from a foreground image and pasting them onto different background images. Examples of the composed images are shown in Fig. 2. Aside from the image-wise contrastive loss for learning instance discrimination [2,28,44, 47], we introduce a pixel-wise con-

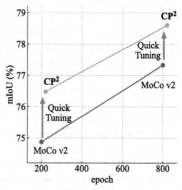

Fig. 1. Quick Tuning MoCo v2 with CP², evaluated by semantic segmentation on PASCAL VOC. A 20-epoch Quick Tuning with CP² yields large mIoU improvements.

trastive loss to enhance dense prediction. The segmentation model is trained by maximizing cosine similarity between the foreground pixels while minimizing cosine similarity between the foreground and background pixels. Overall, CP² yields pixel specific dense representation and has two key advantages for downstream segmentation: 1) CP² pretrains both backbone and segmentation head, addressing the issue of architectural misalignment; 2) CP² pretrains the model with a dense prediction objective, building up the model's perception of spatially varying information in an image.

Furthermore, we find that a considerably short period of CP² training is able to adapt pretrained classification-oriented models quickly to the semantic segmentation task and therefore yields better downstream performance. In particular, we first initialize the backbone with the weights of a pretrained classification-oriented model (*e.g.* a ResNet-50 [29] pretrained by MoCo v2 [12]), attach a randomly initialized segmentation head, and then tune the entire segmentation model by CP^2 for additional 20 epochs. As a result, the performance of the entire segmentation model on downstream semantic segmentation is significantly improved, *e.g.* **+1.6%** mIoU on PASCAL VOC 2012 [23] dataset. We denote this training protocol as **Quick Tuning**, as it is efficient and practical for transfer learning from image-level instance discrimination to pixel-level dense prediction.

For technical details, we mostly follow MoCo v2 [12], including its architecture, data augmentation, and the instance contrastive loss, in order to fully isolate the effectiveness of our newly introduced copy-paste mechanism and dense contrastive loss, and therefore MoCo v2 [12] serves as a direct baseline to CP^2. In the empirical evaluations of semantic segmentation, the CP^2 200-epoch model achieves 77.6% mIoU on PASCAL VOC 2012 [23], outperforming the MoCo v2 [12] 200-epoch model by **+2.7%** mIoU. Also, as illustrated in Fig. 1, the Quick Tuning protocol for CP^2 yields **+1.5%** and **+1.4%** mIoU improvements over the MoCo v2 200-epoch and 800-epoch model respectively. The improvement also generalizes to other segmentation datasets and vision transformers.

2   Related Work

Self-supervised Learning and Pretext Tasks. Self-supervised learning for visual understanding leverages the intrinsic properties of images as the supervisory information for training, for which the capability of visual representation heavily depends on the formulation of pretext tasks. Prior to the recent popularity of instance discrimination [2,28,44,47], people have explored numerous pretext tasks, including image denoising and reconstruction [3,39,51], adversarial learning [19,20,22], and heuristic tasks such as image colorization [50], jigsaw puzzle [36,43], context and rotation prediction [18,33], and deep clustering [4].

The emergence of contrastive learning, or more specifically, the scheme of instance discrimination [2,28,44,47] has made a break-through in unsupervised learning, as MoCo [28] achieves superior transfer performance than supervised training in a wide range of downstream tasks. Inspired by this success, many follow-up works conduct deeper explorations in self-supervised contrastive learning and put forward different optimization objectives [5,6,26,41,42,54], model architectures [13], and training strategies [10,12,14].

Dense Contrastive Learning. To obtain better adaptation in dense prediction tasks, a recent work [37] extends the image-level contrastive loss into a pixel-level. Despite the extension of contrastive loss helps the model learn finer grained features, it is not able to establish the model's perception of spatially varying information, and therefore the model has to be re-purposed in downstream finetuning. More recent works try to enhance the model's understanding

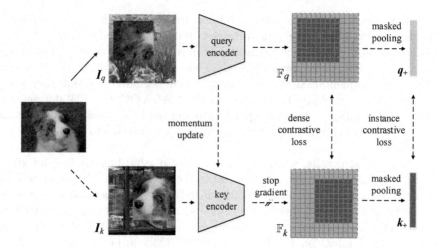

Fig. 2. Pipeline. We enrich the spatial information of unannotated images by randomly pasting two crops of foreground images onto different backgrounds. A dense contrastive loss is applied to their encoded feature maps and an instance contrastive loss is applied to the average of the foreground feature vectors (masked pooling). We follow the training architecture of momentum update in MoCo and BYOL.

of positional information in images by encouraging the consistency of pixel-level representations [45], or by employing heuristic masks [1,24] and applying a patch-wise contrastive loss [30].

Copy-Paste for Contrastive Learning. Copy-paste, *i.e.*, copying crops of one image and pasting them onto another image, once serves as a data augmentation method in *supervised* instance segmentation and semantic segmentation [25] for its simplicity and significant effect in enriching images' positional and semantic information. Similarly, by mixing images [31,49] or image crops [48] as data augmentation, the *supervised* models also attain considerable performance improvements in various tasks. The use of copy-paste is also reported in recent works of self-supervised object detection [30,46]. Inspired by the success of copy-paste, we utilize this approach in our dense contrastive learning method as the self-supervisory information.

3 Method

In this section, we present our CP^2 objective and loss function for learning a pixel-wise dense representation. We also discuss our model architecture and propose a Quick Tuning protocol for efficient training of CP^2.

3.1 Copy-Paste Contrastive Pretraining

We propose a novel pretraining method called CP^2, through which we desire the pretrained model to learn both instance discrimination and dense prediction. To this end, we manually synthesize image compositions by pasting foreground crops onto backgrounds. Specifically, as illustrated in Fig. 2, we generate two random crops from the foreground image and then overlay them onto two different background images. The objective of CP^2 is to 1) discriminate the foreground from background within each composed image and 2) identify the composed images with the same foreground from negative samples.

Copy-Paste. Given an original foreground image I^{fore}, we first generate two different views of it I_q^{fore}, $I_k^{fore} \in \mathbb{R}^{224 \times 224 \times 3}$ by data augmentation, one being query and the other being the positive key. The augmentation strategy follows SimCLR [10] and MoCo v2 [12], *i.e.*, the image is first randomly resized and cropped to 224×224 resolutions followed by color jittering, gray scale, Gaussian blurring and horizontal flipping. Next, we generate one view for each of two random background images using the same augmentation, denoted as I_q^{back}, $I_k^{back} \in \mathbb{R}^{224 \times 224 \times 3}$. We compose the image pairs by binary foreground-background masks $M_q, M_k \in \{0, 1\}^{224 \times 224}$, in which each element $m = 1$ denotes a foreground pixel and $m = 0$ denotes a background pixel. Formally, the composed images are generated by

$$
\begin{aligned}
I_q &= I_q^{fore} \odot M_q + I_q^{back} \odot (1 - M_q), \\
I_k &= I_k^{fore} \odot M_k + I_k^{back} \odot (1 - M_k),
\end{aligned}
\tag{1}
$$

where $\odot$ denotes element-wise product. Now we get two composed images I_q and I_k who share the foreground source image but have different backgrounds.

Contrastive Objectives. The composed images are then processed by a semantic segmentation model which we detail in Sect. 3.2. Given the input I_q, the output of the segmentation model is a set of $r \times r$ features $\mathbb{F}_q = \{f_q^i \in \mathbb{R}^C | i = 1, 2, \ldots, r^2\}$, where C is the number of output channels and r is the feature map resolution. For a 224×224 input image, $r = 14$ when the output stride $s = 16$. Among all the output features $f_q \in \mathbb{F}_q$, we denote the foreground features, *i.e.*, the features that correspond to foreground pixels as $f_q^+ \in \mathbb{F}_q^+ \subset \mathbb{F}_q$, where $\mathbb{F}_q^+$ is the foreground feature subset. Similarly, we have all the features $f_k \in \mathbb{F}_k$ for the input image I_k, among which foreground features are denoted as $f_k^+ \in \mathbb{F}_k^+ \subset \mathbb{F}_k$.

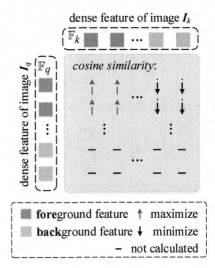

Fig. 3. Dense contrastive loss that maximizes the similarity of each foreground pair while minimizes that of each foreground-background pair.

We use two loss terms, one *dense* contrastive loss and one *instance* contrastive loss. The contrastive loss $\mathcal{L}_{dense}$ learns local and fine-grained features by distinguishing between foreground and background features, helping with downstream semantic segmentation tasks, while the instance contrastive loss aims to keep the global, instance-level representation.

In dense contrastive loss, we desire all the foreground features $\forall \boldsymbol{f}_q^+ \in \mathbb{F}_q^+$ of image $\boldsymbol{I}_q$ to be similar to all the foreground features $\forall \boldsymbol{f}_k^+ \in \mathbb{F}_k^+$ of image $\boldsymbol{I}_k$, and be dissimilar to the background features $\mathbb{F}_k^- = \mathbb{F}_k \backslash \mathbb{F}_k^+$ of image $\boldsymbol{I}_k$. Formally, for each foreground feature $\forall \boldsymbol{f}_q^+ \in \mathbb{F}_q^+$ and $\forall \boldsymbol{f}_k^+ \in \mathbb{F}_k^+$, the dense contrastive loss is obtained by

$$\mathcal{L}_{dense} = -\frac{1}{|\mathbb{F}_q^+||\mathbb{F}_k^+|} \sum_{\forall \boldsymbol{f}_q^+ \in \mathbb{F}_q^+, \forall \boldsymbol{f}_k^+ \in \mathbb{F}_k^+} \log \frac{\exp\left(\boldsymbol{f}_q^+ \cdot \boldsymbol{f}_k^+ / \tau_{dense}\right)}{\sum_{\forall \boldsymbol{f}_k \in \mathbb{F}_k} \exp\left(\boldsymbol{f}_q^+ \cdot \boldsymbol{f}_k / \tau_{dense}\right)}, \quad (2)$$

where τ_{dense} is a temperature coefficient. This dense contrastive loss is also illustrated in Fig. 3. Following supervised contrastive learning methods [32,52], we put the summation outside the log.

Besides the dense contrastive loss, we keep the instance contrastive loss that aims to learn the global, instance-level representation. We mostly follow the practice of MoCo [12,28], where given the query image, the model is required to distinguish the positive key from a memory bank of negative keys. But in our case, we use the composed image $\boldsymbol{I}_q$ as the query image, and the composed image $\boldsymbol{I}_k$ as the positive key image that shares the foreground with image $\boldsymbol{I}_q$. In addition, instead of using the global average pooling feature as the representation in MoCo, we use the normalized masked averaging of only the foreground features as illustrated in Fig. 2. Formally, the instance contrastive loss is computed as

$$\mathcal{L}_{ins} = -\log \frac{\exp(\boldsymbol{q}_+ \cdot \boldsymbol{k}_+ / \tau_{ins})}{\exp(\boldsymbol{q}_+ \cdot \boldsymbol{k}_+ / \tau_{ins}) + \sum_{n=1}^N \exp(\boldsymbol{q}_+ \cdot \boldsymbol{k}_n / \tau_{ins})}, \quad (3)$$

where $\boldsymbol{q}_+$, $\boldsymbol{k}_+$ are normalized masked averaging of $\mathbb{F}_q^+$ and $\mathbb{F}_k^+$:

$$\boldsymbol{q}_+ = \frac{\sum_{\forall \boldsymbol{f}_q^+ \in \mathbb{F}_q^+} \boldsymbol{f}_q^+}{\|\sum_{\forall \boldsymbol{f}_q^+ \in \mathbb{F}_q^+} \boldsymbol{f}_q^+\|_2}, \quad \boldsymbol{k}_+ = \frac{\sum_{\forall \boldsymbol{f}_k^+ \in \mathbb{F}_k^+} \boldsymbol{f}_k^+}{\|\sum_{\forall \boldsymbol{f}_k^+ \in \mathbb{F}_k^+} \boldsymbol{f}_k^+\|_2}. \quad (4)$$

$\boldsymbol{k}_n$ denotes the representations of negative samples from a memory bank [28,44] of N vectors, and τ_{ins} is a temperature coefficient.

The total loss $\mathcal{L}$ is simply a linear combination of the dense and the instance contrastive loss

$$\mathcal{L} = \mathcal{L}_{ins} + \alpha \mathcal{L}_{dense}, \quad (5)$$

where α is a trade-off coefficient for the two losses.

3.2   Model Architecture

Next, we discuss in detail our CP^2 model architecture that consists of a backbone and a segmentation head for both pretraining and finetuning. Different from existing contrastive learning frameworks [12, 28] that pretrain only the backbone, CP^2 enables the pretraining of both the backbone and the segmentation head, almost the same architecture as the one used for downstream segmentation tasks. In this way, CP^2 prevents the finetuning misalignment issue (Sect. 1), *i.e.*, finetuning the downstream models with a well-pretrained backbone and a randomly initialized head. This misalignment can require careful hyper-parameter tuning (*e.g.*, a larger learning rate on the head) and result in degradation of the transferring performance, especially when a heavy randomly initialized head is used. Therefore, CP^2 is able to achieve better performance for segmentation and also enables the usage of stronger segmentation heads.

In particular, we study two families of backbones, CNNs [29] and vision transformers [21]. For CNN backbones, we use the original ResNet-50 [29] with a 7 × 7 convolution as the first layer, instead of an inception stem [40] commonly used in segmentation tasks [7–9]. This setting ensures fair comparisons with previous self-supervised learning methods. In order to adapt the ResNet backbone to segmentation, we follow common segmentation settings [7, 8, 28] and use atrous rate 2 and stride 1 for the 3 × 3 convolutions in the last stage. For vision transformer backbones, we choose ViT-S [21] with 16 × 16 patch size, which has a similar number of parameters as ResNet-50. Note that both of our ResNet-50 and ViT-S have an output stride $s = 16$ which makes our backbones compatible with most existing segmentation heads.

Given the backbone output features with an output stride $s = 16$, we study two types of segmentation heads. By default, we employ the common DeepLab v3 [8] segmentation head (*i.e.* ASPP head with image pooling), as it is able to extract multi-scale spatial features and yield very competitive results. In addition to the DeepLab v3 ASPP head, we also study the lightweight FCN head [34] usually adopted for evaluation of self-supervised learning methods.

On top of the backbone and segmentation head that are trained for both pretraining and finetuning, we make as little change as possible. Specifically, for CP^2 pretraining, we add two 1 × 1 convolution layers to the segmentation head output, projecting the pixel-wise dense features to a 128-dimensional latent space (*i.e.*, $C = 128$). The latent features at each pixel are then ℓ_2 normalized individually. Our dense projection design is analogous to the 2-layer MLP design in common contrastive learning frameworks [12] followed by an ℓ_2 normalization. After the CP^2 training converges, we simply replace the 2-layer convolution projection by a segmentation output convolution that projects the segmentation head feature to the number of output classes, similar to the typical design in image-wise contrastive frameworks [10, 28]. Following MoCo [28], we momentum update the key encoder consisting of both the backbone and the segmentation head by the weights in the query encoder.

3.3   Quick Tuning

In order to train our CP^2 models quickly within a manageable computational budget, we propose a new training protocol called Quick Tuning that initializes our backbone with existing backbone checkpoints available online. These backbones typically have been trained by image-wise contrastive loss with extremely long schedules (*e.g.* 800 epochs [12] or 1000 epochs [10]). On top of these existing checkpoints that encode good image-level semantic representations, we apply our CP^2 training for just a few epochs (*e.g.*, 20 epochs) in order to finetune the representation still on ImageNet without human labels but for semantic segmentation. Specifically, we attach a randomly initialized segmentation head on top of the pretrained backbone with proper atrous rates and train this entire segmentation model with our CP^2 loss function. Finally, the learned segmentation model on ImageNet without using any label is further finetuned on various downstream segmentation datasets for evaluation of the learned representations.

Quick Tuning enables efficient and practical training for self-supervised contrastive learning, as it exploits the heavily-pretrained self-supervised backbones and let them quickly adapt to the desired objective or downstream tasks. According to our empirical evaluations, 20 epochs of Quick Tuning is sufficient to yield significant improvements on various datasets (for example, the finetuning mIoU on PASCAL VOC 2012 is improved by 1.6% after a 20-epoch Quick Tuning). This is particularly helpful for pretraining segmentation models efficiently, because segmentation models are usually much heavier than the backbone in terms of computational cost due to the atrous convolutions in the backbone and the ASPP module. In this case, Quick Tuning saves a large amount of computational resources by demonstrating significant improvements with a short period of segmentation model self-supervised pretraining.

4 Experiments

4.1 Experimental Setup

Our MoCo v2 implementation follows the official open source code [12], and our semantic segmentation implementation uses the MMSegmentation [15] library.

Datasets. We pretrain CP^2 and the baselines on ImageNet [17] (~1.28 million training images) and finetune on semantic segmentation tasks of PASCAL VOC [23], Cityscapes [16], and ADE20k [53]. For PASCAL VOC, we train on the augmented training set [27] with 10582 images and evaluate on VOC2012 validation set. For Cityscapes, we train on the "train-fine" set with 2975 images and evaluate on its validation set. For ADE20k, we train on the training set with 20210 images and evaluate on the validation set.

Segmentation and Projection Heads. Our DeepLab v3 ASPP head follows the default setting in MMSegmentation which uses 512 output channels for both the atrous convolutions and the output projection. Our CP^2 projection head consists of two layers of 512-channel 1×1 convolutions, ReLU, and a $C = 128$ channel 1×1 convolution. For the FCN head, we follow the settings in prior works [28,30] for fair comparison, *i.e.*, two layers of 256-channel 3×3 convolutions with atrous rate=6 followed by BN and ReLU. The CP^2 projection for the FCN-based model consists of two layers of 256-channel 1×1 convolutions, ReLU, and a $C = 128$ channel 1×1 convolution.

Baselines. We compare CP^2 with the self-supervised contrastive learning methods with classification-oriented [10,12,26,28,41], detection-oriented [30,46], and dense prediction [45] objectives. All the pretrained ResNet-50 models of are downloaded from their official implementations. For InsLoc [46], we use the backbone of its ResNet50-FPN model which has been pretrained for 400 epochs. For DetCon [30], we use the model pretrained 1000 epochs with DetCon-B manner for the most competitive baseline. The pretrained ViT-S model of MoCo v2 is borrowed from DINO [6]. Moreover, to compare with supervised methods, we load a pretrained ResNet-50 model in torchvision official model zoo, which has a top-1 accuracy of 76.13% on ImageNet validation set [17].

Hyper-parameters. For ResNet-backed models, we pretrain by SGD optimizer with 0.03 learning rate, 0.9 momentum, 0.0001 weight decay, and a mini-batch size of 256 on ImageNet. We finetune them by SGD with 0.9 momuntum, 0.0005 weight decay, and 0.003, 0.01, 0.01 learning rate for PASCAL, Cityscapes, and ADE20k, respectively. For ViT-backed models, we also pretrain with a mini-batch size of 256 on ImageNet but apply an AdamW [35] optimizer with $\beta_1 = 0.9$, $\beta_2 = 0.999$, 0.00005 learning rate, 0.01 weight decay for both pretraining and finetuning. We pretrain and finetune with 4 GPUs. We find that for CP^2 pretrained models, the use of weight decay in finetuning stage usually leads to $\sim$0.2% mIoU decrease. This is possibly because for the baseline methods, the segmentation head is randomly initialized in finetuning and relies on weight decay for better generalization. However, as CP^2 pretrains both the backbone and segmentation head with a proper weight decay, the ewights of segmentation head have been decayed into a lower scale and do not require further decaying during finetuning. Thus, in the finetuning stage, we use weight decay for those baseline models with random segmentation head and turn off weight decay for CP^2 models. We adopt a memory bank of $N = 65536$, $C = 128$ dimensional vectors, with k_+, the normalized masked average representation of image I_k in the current mini-batch enqueued and the oldest vectors dequeued. For instance contrastive loss $\mathcal{L}_{ins}$, we set the temperature $\tau_{ins} = 0.2$ in accordance with MoCo v2 [12]. We assign a weight of $\alpha = 0.2$ and set the temperature $\tau_{dense} = 1$ for $\mathcal{L}_{dense}$, according to grid search. For PASCAL VOC, we use crop size 512×512 and train with batch size 16 for 40k iterations. For Cityscapes, we use crop size 512×1024 and train with batch size 8 for 60k iterations. For ADE20k, we use crop size 512×512 and train with batch size 16 for 80k iterations.

4.2   Main Results

MoCo v2 [12] is a direct baseline to our method as we follow its model architecture, contrastive formulation, and the technical setups. For ease of reference, we use the following abbreviations to denote MoCo v2 pretrained models:

– **r.200, r.800:** ResNet-50 pretrained by MoCo v2 for 200, 800 epochs.

Table 1. Evaluation results (mIoU) with DeepLab v3 segmentation head. QT denotes Quick Tuning with CP^2 initialized by a MoCo v2 pre-trained backbone. Our results are marked in gray . The best results are **bolded**. Epochs that are consumed by the initialization model are de-emphasized.

Method	Backbone	Epoch	PASCAL	Cityscapes	ADE20k
supervised	ResNet-50	–	76.0	76.3	39.5
MoCo [28]	ResNet-50	200	73.2	75.8	38.6
SimCLR [10]	ResNet-50	1000	77.3	76.5	40.1
BYOL [26]	ResNet-50	300	77.4	76.5	40.2
InfoMin [41]	ResNet-50	800	77.2	76.5	39.6
InsLoc [46]	ResNet-50	400	75.6	76.3	40.3
DetCon [30]	ResNet-50	1000	78.1	77.1	40.6
PixPro [45]	ResNet-50	400	77.5	76.6	40.3
MoCo v2 [12]	ResNet-50	200	74.9	76.2	39.2
CP^2	ResNet-50	200	77.6	77.3	40.5
CP^2 QT r.200	ResNet-50	200+20	76.5	77.2	40.7
MoCo v2 [12]	ResNet-50	800	77.2	76.4	39.7
CP^2 QT r.800	ResNet-50	800+20	**78.6**	**77.4**	**41.3**
MoCo v2 [12]	ViT-S/16	300	78.8	77.2	41.3
CP^2 QT v.300	ViT-S/16	300+20	**79.5**	**77.6**	**42.2**

– **v.300:** ViT-S/16 pretrained by MoCo v2 for 300 epochs.

Results with DeepLab v3 Segmentation Head. We first present the evaluation results of DeepLab v3 semantic segmentation models (a backbone attached by an ASPP head with image pooling) [8]. As summarized in Table 1, CP^2 achieves 77.6% mIoU on PASCAL VOC with 200 epochs pretraining from scratch using a ResNet-50 backbone, which outperforms MoCo v2 by **+2.7%**. Also, the Quick Tuning protocol is demonstrated to be effective as it yields **+1.6%** mIoU on PASCAL VOC when tuning a 200-epoch MoCo v2 checkpoint for only another 20 epochs with CP^2, and **+1.4%** mIoU when tuning an 800-epoch MoCo v2 checkpoint. Moreover, by Quick Tuning the 800-epoch MoCo v2 model, CP^2 achieves the best performance among all ResNet-50 based methods on three evaluated datasets. Notably, it yields **+0.5%** mIoU on PASCAL VOC and **+0.7%** mIoU on ADE20k compared with the most competitive DetCon [30], in spite of DetCon's heavier computational cost and longer training schedule. For ViT based models, CP^2 also outperforms its MoCo v2 baseline by **+0.7%** mIoU on PASCAL, **+0.4%** mIoU on Cityscapes, and **+0.9%** mIoU on ADE20k when Quick Tuning for another 20 epochs.

Results with FCN Segmentation Head. Table 2 summarizes the evaluation results with the light-weight FCN [34] head (two hidden layers of atrous convolutions and a classification layer). Similarly, CP^2 achieves the highest mIoU on

Table 2. Evaluation results (mIoU) with FCN head. QT denotes Quick Tuning with CP^2 initialized by a MoCo v2 pre-trained backbone. Our results are marked in gray . The best results are **bolded**. Epochs that are consumed by the initialization model are de-emphasized.

Method	Backbone	Epoch	PASCAL	Cityscapes	ADE20k
supervised	ResNet-50	–	73.7	75.8	37.4
MoCo v2 [12]	ResNet-50	200	74.4	75.8	37.4
CP^2	ResNet-50	200	75.4	76.4	38.4
CP^2 QT r.200	ResNet-50	200+20	75.2	76.4	38.0
MoCo v2 [12]	ResNet-50	800	74.8	75.9	37.9
CP^2 QT r.800	ResNet-50	800+20	**75.7**	**76.5**	**39.2**
MoCo v2 [12]	ViT-S/16	300	77.7	76.6	40.4
CP^2 QT v.300	ViT-S/16	300+20	**78.6**	**77.0**	**41.2**

the three datasets with both ResNet-backed and ViT-backed architectures. In particular, compared to the baseline MoCo v2, CP^2 obtains up to +1.0% mIoU on PASCAL using ResNet-50 and +0.9% mIoU using ViT-S.

Overall, CP^2 yields significant performance improvements in the downstream task of semantic segmentation with both strong (ASPP) and light-weight (FCN) segmentation heads. Aside from demonstrating the effectiveness and robustness of CP^2 in terms of different segmentation heads, we further dissect the performance improvements from various factors and components in our ablation study. The more in-depth discussion and results in the ablation study show that our improvements on downstream segmentation tasks do not merely come from pretraining the segmentation head.

4.3 Ablation Study

In this section, we first question if CP^2 benefits downstream semantic segmentation tasks only because it offers a pretrained segmentation head, or the proposed dense contrastive loss ($\mathcal{L}_{dense}$) also helps? Second, we explore the effect of various types of copy-paste masks, ranging from a simple rectangle mask to masking random patches. Third, we study the effect of the training schedule in Quick Tuning. Fourth, we study the effect of two key hyper-parameters, the loss coefficient (α) and temperature (τ_{dense}) of the dense contrastive loss.

Segmentation Head Initialization. Intuitively, CP^2 can benefit the downstream segmentation tasks in two aspects. First, CP^2 provides the downstream semantic segmentation with a well-pretrained decoder head. Second, CP^2 pretrains the model with a segmentation-oriented objective (the dense contrastive loss), which is expected to enable the backbone to extract pixel-level features. To ablate the benefit of each component, we dissect the CP^2 trained model and examine the benefits of its backbone and segmentation head respectively.

Table 3 summarizes the results. By pretraining the ResNet-50 based model for 200 epochs from scratch and finetuning on PASCAL, CP^2 achieves 77.6%

Table 3. Ablation study of segmentation head pretraining on PASCAL VOC. The results are based on ASPP segmentation head. We use Quick Tuning for CP^2 in the settings of (ResNet-50, 800 epochs) and (ViT-S/16, 300 epochs).

Mode	Backbone	Head	mIoU
ResNet-50, 200 epochs	MoCo v2	Random	74.9
	CP^2	Random	76.3 (+1.4)
	CP^2	CP^2	**77.6 (+2.7)**
ResNet-50, 800 epochs	MoCo v2	Random	77.2
	CP^2 QT	Random	78.2 (+1.0)
	CP^2 QT	CP^2 QT	**78.6 (+1.4)**
ViT-S/16, 300 epochs	MoCo v2	Random	78.8
	CP^2 QT	Random	79.3 (+0.5)
	CP^2 QT	CP^2 QT	**79.5 (+0.7)**

mIoU, which is 2.7% higher than that of its MoCo v2 baseline. If we use the CP^2 pretrained backbone but still randomly initialize the segmentation head in the finetuning stage, it also attains 1.4% points higher mIoU than MoCo v2, demonstrating that the backbone representation is also improved for downstream segmentation thanks to our segmentation-oriented objective.

Similarly, the same phenomenon is observed for CP^2 Quick Tuning protocol as well. For example, by Quick Tuning the MoCo v2 800-epoch ResNet-50 and finetuning on PASCAL, we obtain +1.4% mIoU over MoCo v2. While finetuning the CP^2 pretrained backbone with a randomly initialized segmentation head also yields +1.0% mIoU over its baseline.

According to the observation above, CP^2 yields both a better backbone and a pretrained segmentation head for downstream semantic segmentation, thanks to our design of CP^2 that enables segmentation head pretraining and employs the segmentation-oriented contrastive objective.

Foreground-Background Mask. We further explore the effect of various types of copy-paste masking for CP^2. The experiments are conducted using our Quick Transfer protocol, initialized by the 800-epoch MoCo v2 checkpoint when using a ResNet-50 backbone and the 300-epoch MoCo v2 checkpoint when using a ViT-S backbone, on PASCAL VOC dataset.

First, we consider a baseline when copy-paste masking is not applied. Specifically, the augmented views of the foreground image will *not* be composed with random backgrounds but serve as the model inputs directly. And the model will be trained with only the image-wise contrastive loss ($\mathcal{L}_{ins}$) since there is no background to construct the dense contrastive loss. In other words, the segmentation model (a backbone followed by segmentation head) is simply trained with a MoCo loss that operates on average pooled features over the whole image. We denote this setup as *no copy-paste*. As shown in Table 4, *no copy-paste* yields relatively poor performance. Compared to the baseline performance of 77.2% mIoU

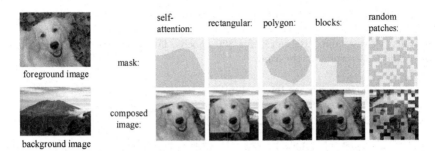

Fig. 4. Examples of masking strategies and composed images. The self-attention mask (DINO mask) is smoothed by Gaussian blur.

Table 4. Evaluation results of foreground-background masks on PASCAL VOC. Note that for the full mask, the models are trained without dense contrastive loss. Our default setting is marked in gray .

Mode	Random	mIoU	
		ResNet-50	ViT-S/16
Baseline MoCo v2	–	77.2	78.8
No copy-paste	–	77.6	78.9
DINO self-attention mask [6]	✗	77.9	79.3
Rectangular mask	✓	**78.6**	**79.5**
Polygon mask	✓	78.1	79.0
Random blocks	✓	77.3	78.7
Random patches	✓	75.3	78.9

with ResNet-50 and 78.8% mIoU with ViT-S (Table 1), *no copy-paste* training attains only marginal improvements of 0.4% and 0.1% mIoU respectively. This result indicates that pretraining the segmentation head with classification-oriented objectives cannot yield significant improvements on the downstream performance for semantic segmentation. This suggests that the improvement of CP^2 mainly comes from the copy-paste training and the dense contrastive loss.

We also explore various types of image masking, including the self-attention masks generated by DINO [6] and different shapes of random masking. The random masks include rectangular masks, polygon masks, random blocks, and random patches, for which we provide examples in Fig. 4. In order to ablate the influence of mask area, we limit the foreground ratio of each random mask to 0.5–0.8, which we find usually yields better empirical results. The self-attention masks are generated by the DINO [6] pretrained ViT-B/16 model. Specifically, for each image, we average their 12 heads of last layer self-attentions and then up-sample the averaged attention map to the original shape of the image. For denoising purpose, we also apply Gaussian blur to the self-attention DINO masks.

Table 5. Evaluation results of hyper-parameter search on PASCAL VOC. The results are based on ResNet50-ASPP models, where the base backbone is loaded from the MoCo v2 pretrained ResNet50 for 800 epochs. Our default setting is marked in gray . The best results are **bolded**.

(a) loss weight and temperature

Weight	Temperature(τ_{dense})			
	2	1	0.5	0.2
10	77.4	77.0	76.9	77.2
1	77.3	77.9	77.3	77.4
0.5	77.2	78.0	77.3	77.1
0.2	76.9	**78.6**	77.3	76.7
0.1	76.0	77.7	77.5	75.8

(b) Quick Tuning epochs

Epoch	mIoU
0	77.2
10	77.7 (+0.5)
20	**78.6 (+1.4)**
40	78.7 (+1.5)

Empirically, the random rectangular mask achieves the highest performance with both ResNet-50 and ViT-S/16 models in Table 4. This is possibly because the rectangular masks contain mostly the real continuous foreground of an image (compared with random patch masks) and also introduce randomness in the masks (compared with DINO masks). This result indicates that simple foreground-background information is sufficient for the models to learn semantic features, and applying the random rectangular masks yields consistent performance gain with both of the backbone architectures. Therefore, we use this simple and easy-to-implement masking strategy in CP^2 for the best performance.

Moreover, the ViT-backed model performs more robustly to various shapes of the mask than the ResNet-backed model. It is worth-noting that the **random patches** mask appears to mislead the ResNet-backed model as it yields 75.3% mIoU, which is 3.3% lower than the result of rectangular mask and even 1.9% lower than the MoCo v2 baseline before Quick Tuning. But the ViT model is robust to this random patch masking although no improvement is observed.

Hyper-parameter Search. It is important to consider the trade-off between the image-wise and pixel-wise objective. Two hyper-parameters, the weight and temperature (τ_{dense}) of pixel-wise contrastive loss (setting the weight of image-wise loss to 1), play decisive roles influencing this trade-off. We conduct grid search of these two parameters and summarize the results in Table 5a. As reported, the parameter pair we use in the main experiments, (weight=0.2, τ_{dense} = 1), achieves the peak performance. For better efficiency, we recommend a training time of 20 epochs on ImageNet when using Quick Tuning. As listed in Table 5b, 20 epochs of Quick Tuning yields 78.6% mIoU (1.4% higher than MoCo v2) while the 40-epoch Quick Tuning brings only 0.1% extra improvement.

5   Conclusion

In this work, we propose a segmentation-oriented contrastive learning method CP^2, in which we encourage the model to learn both image-level and pixel-level representation by pretraining it with both instance and dense contrastive losses.

We point out two key merits of CP^2: First, CP^2 trains the entire semantic segmentation model, pretraining both the backbone and decoder head, which directly addresses the issue of architectural misalignment when finetuning in downstream semantic segmentation. Second, CP^2 is trained on copy-pasted images (images with foreground and background) with a pixel-level dense objective, which helps the model learn localized or spatially varying features that benefit the downstream segmentation task. Our results demonstrate a significant margin over existing methods on semantic segmentation.

Acknowledgment. This work was supported by ONR N00014-21-1-2812, NSFC 62176159, Natural Science Foundation of Shanghai 21ZR1432200 and Shanghai Municipal Science and Technology Major Project 2021SHZDZX0102.

References

1. Arbeláez, P., Pont-Tuset, J., Barron, J.T., Marques, F., Malik, J.: Multiscale combinatorial grouping. In: CVPR (2014)
2. Bachman, P., Hjelm, R.D., Buchwalter, W.: Learning representations by maximizing mutual information across views. In: NeurIPS (2019)
3. Belghazi, M., Oquab, M., Lopez-Paz, D.: Learning about an exponential amount of conditional distributions. In: NeurIPS (2019)
4. Caron, M., Bojanowski, P., Joulin, A., Douze, M.: Deep clustering for unsupervised learning of visual features. In: Ferrari, V., Hebert, M., Sminchisescu, C., Weiss, Y. (eds.) Computer Vision – ECCV 2018. LNCS, vol. 11218, pp. 139–156. Springer, Cham (2018). https://doi.org/10.1007/978-3-030-01264-9_9
5. Caron, M., Misra, I., Mairal, J., Goyal, P., Bojanowski, P., Joulin, A.: Unsupervised learning of visual features by contrasting cluster assignments. In: NeurIPS (2020)
6. Caron, M., et al.: Emerging properties in self-supervised vision transformers. In: ICCV (2021)
7. Chen, L.C., Papandreou, G., Kokkinos, I., Murphy, K., Yuille, A.L.: DeepLab: semantic image segmentation with deep convolutional nets, atrous convolution, and fully connected CRFs. IEEE TPAMI **40**, 834–848 (2017)
8. Chen, L.C., Papandreou, G., Schroff, F., Adam, H.: Rethinking atrous convolution for semantic image segmentation. In: CVPR (2017)
9. Chen, L.-C., Zhu, Y., Papandreou, G., Schroff, F., Adam, H.: Encoder-decoder with atrous separable convolution for semantic image segmentation. In: Ferrari, V., Hebert, M., Sminchisescu, C., Weiss, Y. (eds.) ECCV 2018. LNCS, vol. 11211, pp. 833–851. Springer, Cham (2018). https://doi.org/10.1007/978-3-030-01234-2_49
10. Chen, T., Kornblith, S., Norouzi, M., Hinton, G.: A simple framework for contrastive learning of visual representations. In: ICML (2020)
11. Chen, T., Kornblith, S., Swersky, K., Norouzi, M., Hinton, G.: Big self-supervised models are strong semi-supervised learners. In: NeurIPS (2020)
12. Chen, X., Fan, H., Girshick, R., He, K.: Improved baselines with momentum contrastive learning. arXiv preprint arXiv:2003.04297 (2020)
13. Chen, X., He, K.: Exploring simple siamese representation learning. In: CVPR (2021)
14. Chen, X., Xie, S., He, K.: An empirical study of training self-supervised vision transformers. In: ICCV (2021)

15. Contributors, M.: MMSegmentation: OpenMMLab semantic segmentation toolbox and benchmark (2020). https://github.com/open-mmlab/mmsegmentation
16. Cordts, M., et al.: The cityscapes dataset for semantic urban scene understanding. In: CVPR (2016)
17. Deng, J., Dong, W., Socher, R., Li, L.J., Li, K., Fei-Fei, L.: ImageNet: a large-scale hierarchical image database. In: CVPR (2009)
18. Doersch, C., Gupta, A., Efros, A.A.: Unsupervised visual representation learning by context prediction. In: ICCV (2015)
19. Donahue, J., Krähenbühl, P., Darrell, T.: Adversarial feature learning. In: ICLR (2016)
20. Donahue, J., Simonyan, K.: Large scale adversarial representation learning. In: NeurIPS (2019)
21. Dosovitskiy, A., et al.: An image is worth 16×16 words: transformers for image recognition at scale. In: ICLR (2021)
22. Dumoulin, V., et al.: Adversarially learned inference. In: ICLR (2016)
23. Everingham, M., Eslami, S.A., Van Gool, L., Williams, C.K., Winn, J., Zisserman, A.: The pascal visual object classes challenge: a retrospective. IJCV **111**, 98–136 (2015)
24. Felzenszwalb, P.F., Huttenlocher, D.P.: Efficient graph-based image segmentation. IJCV **59**, 167–181 (2004)
25. Ghiasi, G., et al.: Simple copy-paste is a strong data augmentation method for instance segmentation. In: CVPR (2021)
26. Grill, J.B., et al.: Bootstrap your own latent a new approach to self-supervised learning. In: NeurIPS (2020)
27. Hariharan, B., Arbeláez, P., Bourdev, L., Maji, S., Malik, J.: Semantic contours from inverse detectors. In: ICCV (2011)
28. He, K., Fan, H., Wu, Y., Xie, S., Girshick, R.: Momentum contrast for unsupervised visual representation learning. In: CVPR (2020)
29. He, K., Zhang, X., Ren, S., Sun, J.: Deep residual learning for image recognition. In: CVPR (2016)
30. Hénaff, O.J., Koppula, S., Alayrac, J.B., Oord, A.V.D., Vinyals, O., Carreira, J.: Efficient visual pretraining with contrastive detection. In: ICCV (2021)
31. Hendrycks, D., Mu, N., Cubuk, E.D., Zoph, B., Gilmer, J., Lakshminarayanan, B.: AugMix: a simple data processing method to improve robustness and uncertainty. In: ICLR (2019)
32. Khosla, P., et al.: Supervised contrastive learning. In: NeurIPS (2020)
33. Komodakis, N., Gidaris, S.: Unsupervised representation learning by predicting image rotations. In: ICLR (2018)
34. Long, J., Shelhamer, E., Darrell, T.: Fully convolutional networks for semantic segmentation. In: CVPR (2015)
35. Loshchilov, I., Hutter, F.: Decoupled weight decay regularization. In: ICLR (2019)
36. Noroozi, M., Favaro, P.: Unsupervised learning of visual representations by solving jigsaw puzzles. In: Leibe, B., Matas, J., Sebe, N., Welling, M. (eds.) ECCV 2016. LNCS, vol. 9910, pp. 69–84. Springer, Cham (2016). https://doi.org/10.1007/978-3-319-46466-4_5
37. O Pinheiro, P.O., Almahairi, A., Benmalek, R., Golemo, F., Courville, A.C.: Unsupervised learning of dense visual representations. In: NIPS (2020)
38. Oord, A.V.D., Li, Y., Vinyals, O.: Representation learning with contrastive predictive coding. arXiv preprint arXiv:1807.03748 (2018)
39. Pathak, D., Krahenbuhl, P., Donahue, J., Darrell, T., Efros, A.A.: Context encoders: feature learning by inpainting. In: CVPR (2016)

40. Szegedy, C., Ioffe, S., Vanhoucke, V., Alemi, A.A.: Inception-V4, inception-ResNet and the impact of residual connections on learning. In: AAAI (2017)
41. Tian, Y., Sun, C., Poole, B., Krishnan, D., Schmid, C., Isola, P.: What makes for good views for contrastive learning? In: NeurIPS (2020)
42. Wei, C., Wang, H., Shen, W., Yuille, A.: CO2: consistent contrast for unsupervised visual representation learning. In: ICLR (2021)
43. Wei, C., et al.: Iterative reorganization with weak spatial constraints: solving arbitrary jigsaw puzzles for unsupervised representation learning. In: CVPR (2019)
44. Wu, Z., Xiong, Y., Yu, S.X., Lin, D.: Unsupervised feature learning via nonparametric instance discrimination. In: CVPR (2018)
45. Xie, Z., Lin, Y., Zhang, Z., Cao, Y., Lin, S., Hu, H.: Propagate yourself: exploring pixel-level consistency for unsupervised visual representation learning. In: CVPR (2021)
46. Yang, C., Wu, Z., Zhou, B., Lin, S.: Instance localization for self-supervised detection pretraining. In: CVPR (2021)
47. Ye, M., Zhang, X., Yuen, P.C., Chang, S.F.: Unsupervised embedding learning via invariant and spreading instance feature. In: CVPR (2019)
48. Yun, S., Han, D., Oh, S.J., Chun, S., Choe, J., Yoo, Y.: CutMix: regularization strategy to train strong classifiers with localizable features. In: ICCV (2019)
49. Zhang, H., Cisse, M., Dauphin, Y.N., Lopez-Paz, D.: Mixup: beyond empirical risk minimization. In: ICLR (2017)
50. Zhang, R., Isola, P., Efros, A.A.: Colorful image colorization. In: Leibe, B., Matas, J., Sebe, N., Welling, M. (eds.) ECCV 2016. LNCS, vol. 9907, pp. 649–666. Springer, Cham (2016). https://doi.org/10.1007/978-3-319-46487-9_40
51. Zhang, R., Isola, P., Efros, A.A.: Split-brain autoencoders: unsupervised learning by cross-channel prediction. In: CVPR (2017)
52. Zhao, X., et al.: Contrastive learning for label efficient semantic segmentation. In: ICCV (2021)
53. Zhou, B., et al.: Semantic understanding of scenes through the ADE20K dataset. IJCV **127**, 302–321 (2019)
54. Zhou, J., et al.: iBOT: image BERT pre-training with online tokenizer. In: ICLR (2022)

Self-Filtering: A Noise-Aware Sample Selection for Label Noise with Confidence Penalization

Qi Wei⬤, Haoliang Sun$^{(\boxtimes)}$⬤, Xiankai Lu⬤, and Yilong Yin$^{(\boxtimes)}$⬤

School of Software, Shandong University, Jinan, China
haolsun.cn@gmail.com , ylyin@sdu.edu.cn

Abstract. Sample selection is an effective strategy to mitigate the effect of label noise in robust learning. Typical strategies commonly apply the small-loss criterion to identify clean samples. However, those samples lying around the decision boundary with large losses usually entangle with noisy examples, which would be discarded with this criterion, leading to the heavy degeneration of the generalization performance. In this paper, we propose a novel selection strategy, **S**elf-**F**iltering (SFT), that utilizes the fluctuation of noisy examples in historical predictions to filter them, which can avoid the selection bias of the small-loss criterion for the boundary examples. Specifically, we introduce a memory bank module that stores the historical predictions of each example and dynamically updates to support the selection for the subsequent learning iteration. Besides, to reduce the accumulated error of the sample selection bias of SFT, we devise a regularization term to penalize the confident output distribution. By increasing the weight of the misclassified categories with this term, the loss function is robust to label noise in mild conditions. We conduct extensive experiments on three benchmarks with variant noise types and achieve the new state-of-the-art. Ablation studies and further analysis verify the virtue of SFT for sample selection in robust learning.

Keywords: Label noise · Sample selection · Confidence penalization

1 Introduction

Neural networks exhibit notorious vulnerability to low-quality annotation. Especially, the generalization performance would heavily degrade when label noise arises. However, most existing datasets [18,19] are commonly collected by Web crawlers, which inevitably contains label noise. Therefore, learning with noisy labels (LNL) poses great challenges for modern deep models [28].

Sample selection [3,14,23,32,44] is an effective strategy to mitigate the effect of label noise in LNL. The main idea is to select the clean instances from the

Supplementary Information The online version contains supplementary material available at https://doi.org/10.1007/978-3-031-20056-4_30.

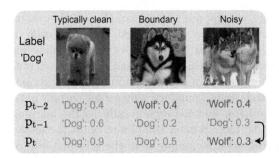

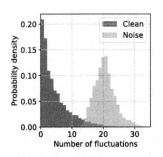

Fig. 1. Illustration of *fluctuation* during model learning. Given a sample (x, y), the fluctuation event is **correlated with predicted results and can be defined as the prediction** $p_{t-1} = y$ **at** $t - 1$ **moment while** $p_{t^*} \neq y$ $(t^* > t - 1)$ **at subsequent moments.** The line with the arrow indicates the *fluctuation* arises.

Fig. 2. Distributions of fluctuations number across synthetic CIFAR-10 with 40% symmetric label noise after 100 epochs.

corrupted dataset by using a certain criterion and reduce the bias of the training set. Inspired by the *memorization effect* that DNNs learn simple patterns shared by majority examples before fitting the noise [9], existing works [3, 9, 12, 14, 23, 32, 41, 44] commonly apply the small-loss criterion that selects samples with loss value lower than a pre-defined threshold and treats them as clean instances. Although these methods exhibit favorable properties for LNL, selecting samples with small losses would discard those boundary examples, since they are with large losses and usually entangled with noisy instances. However, those boundary examples are essential for learning a good decision boundary. Moreover, the selection bias would be accumulated and further degenerate the generalization performance as the learning proceeds [9, 32]. Besides, the loss threshold in this strategy is a crucial hyper-parameter that is usually carefully tuned by cross-validation, suffering from the issue of scalability and sensitivity.

In this paper, we have an interesting observation of the *fluctuation* in LNL, which has the potential for identifying noisy samples and retaining boundary samples. As shown in Fig. 1, a fluctuation event occurs when *a sample classified correctly at the current moment is misclassified in the following learning step*. Intuitively, as the learning proceeds, the discriminability of the classifier will be enhanced gradually, leading to a more accurate prediction for boundary examples rather than the noisy ones. Thus, the fluctuation would frequently occur for noisy samples but gradually disappear for boundary examples. On the other hand, more and more boundary samples are added to the training set via the fluctuation criterion, which can subsequently promote the learning of the classifier. To show the disparity between clean examples and noisy examples, we plot the distribution of the number of the fluctuation event in Fig. 2. The clean and noisy sample can be essentially separated by the proposed fluctuation criterion.

Based on the above observation, we propose a novel sample selection strategy, Self-Filtering (SFT), that filters out noisy samples with the fluctuation in historical predictions. We store the historical predictions of each example for different training iterations in an external memory bank and detect the fluctuation event for each sample in the current moment. By applying this criterion, SFT can filter out noisy samples and retain boundary samples for current optimization. Meanwhile, the memory bank updates dynamically as the learning proceeds, which can support selecting more reliable samples to boost the model learning. To reduce the accumulated error stemming from the selection bias of SFT, we design a regularization term to penalize the confident output distribution. By assigning the weight of the misclassified categories for the loss function, the model can avoid overconfidence of the correct prediction and further improve the robustness of our framework for severe label noise. We also integrate a semi-supervised method, FixMatch [26], into our framework to explore the useful information in the abandoned noisy samples, which has significantly advanced the model performance for noise-robust learning.

The contribution can be summarized in four aspects.

- We rethink the sample selection in LNL and propose a new strategy to select clean samples by using the fluctuation of historical predictions.
- We design a regularization term to penalise the confident output of the network, which can faithfully mitigate the sample selection bias.
- We build a novel learning framework, Self-Filtering (SFT), and achieve the new state-of-the-art on three benchmarks with variant noise types.
- We apply the proposed strategy to the prevailing learning framework and achieve a significant performance promotion, demonstrating its considerable versatility in LNL.

2   Related Work

Sample Selection. The majority of previous works exploit the memorization of DNNs and utilize the small-loss criterion to select clean samples [9,12,32,41]. One representative work is MentorNet [12] that proposes a teacher network to select clean samples for a student network with the small-loss trick. Similarly, Co-teaching [9,32,41] constructs a double branches network to select clean samples for each branch. A surrogate loss function [22] is introduced to identify clean samples and theoretically guaranteed in [6]. To avoid tuning the threshold in the small-loss trick, Beta Mixture Model [2] or Gaussian Mixture Model [14] is introduced to separate clean and noisy examples among the training loss automatically. Zhang et al. [43] designs a meta-network trained with extra clean meta-data to identify noisy samples. Recently, to achieve the stable prediction for sample selection, Model Ensemble (or Mean Teacher) [23] is introduced to compute the exponential moving-average predictions over past iterations and replace current predictions, which performs well to confront the more complex noise type (*e.g.* instance-dependent label noise). As a homologous approach that also aims to select the boundary samples, Me-Momentum [3] modifies the training strategy and introduces two-loop training in curriculum learning.

Robust Loss Function. A majority of robust loss functions have been theoretically analysed. Compared with the categorical cross-entropy (CCE) loss, mean absolute error (MAE) has been theoretically guaranteed to be robust to label noise [7]. Based on this analysis, a novel generalized cross-entropy loss that combined CCE and MAE has been proposed in [42] where its convergence and robustness are also analysed. Inspired by the symmetric Kullback-Leibler Divergence, a symmetric cross entropy (SCE) [31] has been designed to mitigate the effect of noisy labels. To exploit the virtue of variant noise-robust losses, a meta-learning method is designed to learn to combine the four loss functions [1,7,8,31] adaptively. Recently, a new family of loss functions, the peer loss [17] are proposed to punish the agreement between outputs of the network and noisy labels by adding a regularization term to cross-entropy. It has also been proved that minimizing those robust loss functions with corrupted labels is equivalent to minimise the cross entropy loss on the clean set under mild noise ratios.

Label Correction. The pioneering methods correct the noisy labels by an additional inference phase (*e.g.* knowledge graphs [15] or graphical models [37]). Recently, two types of correction functions are proposed to correction. Firstly, transition matrix approaches [11,36,40] aim to construct a matrix that stores the flipping probability between the true label and the noisy one and is estimated with a set of clean data. Secondly, another family of methods utilize the output of the network to rectify labels. For example, Song et al. [27] proposes to select the clean samples by co-teaching framework [9] and progressively refurbish noisy samples with the prediction confidence. To achieve learning the correction function in a data-driven way, Wu et al. [33] builds a meta-correcter to generate labels with the input of the true label and previous predictions of meta-net.

Compared with Me-Momentum [3] that selects samples in current epoch, we construct the memory bank and propose a novel criterion based on fluctuation by leveraging the historical predictions. Also, compared with existing works that select clean samples based on historical predictions (SELFIE [27] computes the entropy value from predictions histories and RoCL [44] utilizes the variance of the training loss), our framework exhibits two advantages: (i) Less hyper-parameter. Our criterion contains only one hyper-parameter, namely, the size of historical predictions. However, the selection criteria in these works both contain another statistic threshold except the history size (*e.g.*, an entropy threshold in [27] and a loss variance threshold in [44]). (ii) Less sensitive. The setting of these thresholds is related to noise ratios, requiring more cross-validation processes. Those merits facilitate the application of our criterion to more general scenarios.

3   Methods

3.1   Problem Definition and Overall

Supposing that we have the training set $\mathcal{D} = \{(\mathbf{x}^i, y^i)\}_{i=1}^n \in (\mathcal{X}, \mathcal{Y})$ with corrupted labels and $y^i \in [\mathrm{K}] = \{1, 2, ..., k\}$, the output distribution of a classifier f_θ

after t training epochs can be written as $\mathbf{p}^{(t)} = f(\mathbf{x}; \theta)$. Here, θ is the learnable parameters. Learning with label noise (LNL) aims to find the optimal parameter θ^* which can achieve admirable generalization performance on the clean testing set.

For a majority of sample selection methods [3,9,14,23,32,41,44], the robust training process for classifier f can be summarized as the following phases.

- Phase 1: select the reliable set $\tilde{\mathcal{D}}$ from the polluted dataset $\mathcal{D}$ via a certain selection strategy. (e.g. small-loss criterion is designed to select the top $\tau\%$ of samples with the smaller loss values in the current mini-batch as the clean samples, where $\tau\%$ is the noise ratio estimated by cross-validation).
- Phase 2: train the classifier f on the selected set $\tilde{\mathcal{D}}$, and update the parameter as $\theta^{(t+1)} = \theta^t - \eta\nabla(\frac{1}{|\tilde{\mathcal{D}}|}\sum_{(\mathbf{x},y)\in\tilde{\mathcal{D}}}\mathcal{L}(\mathbf{x}, y; \theta^t))$, where η and $\mathcal{L}$ are the given learning rate and loss function, respectively.
- Phase 3: repeat the above phases until finding the optimal parameter θ^*, then return the classifier f.

Our approach modifies the aforementioned two phases to render the network more robust on noisy labels. First, a novel criterion is proposed to select more boundary examples, which provides more decision information in the subset set $\tilde{\mathcal{D}}$. Second, we introduce a confidence regularization term to enable the loss function $\mathcal{L}$ more robust while tackling noisy labels. Eventually, we present the learning framework, Self-Filtering (SFT), for LNL that contains two stages of warming-up and main learning. To further exploit the useful knowledge in the discarded examples, we adopt the idea of semi-supervised learning and incorporate FixMatch into our SFT.

3.2   Selecting with the Fluctuation

The key step in our selection strategy is to go through the historical prediction stored in the dynamically updated memory bank module. As shown in Fig. 3(b), we collect all predictions of the training set $\mathcal{D}$ for the epoch t and store them in the memory bank $\mathcal{M}$. Specifically, this module contains those predictions of T epochs in the memory bank, where the size of $\mathcal{M}$ is $n \times T$. $\mathcal{M}$ maintains a queen data structure with the principle of first-in-first-out (FIFO). Therefore, for epoch t, $\mathcal{M}$ stores predictions of the last T epochs. Finally, for the example $(\mathbf{x}, y)$ in the current epoch t, the criterion for identifying it as the fluctuated sample can be formulated as

$$\beta = (\arg\max(\mathbf{p}^{t_1}) = y) \wedge (\arg\max(\mathbf{p}^{t_2}) \neq y), \qquad (1)$$

when $t_1, t_2 \in \{t-T, ..., t\}, T \geq 2$ and $t_1 < t_2$. A fluctuation event occurs when the sample classified correctly at the epoch t_1 is misclassified in the epoch t_2. By computing β for each sample with $\mathcal{M}$, we discard these examples where $\beta = 1$. Therefore, the clean samples selected by fluctuation criterion can be represented as:

$$\tilde{\mathcal{D}} = \{(\mathbf{x}^i, y^i) \in \mathcal{D} | \beta^i \neq 1\}_{i=1}^n. \qquad (2)$$

The selected clean samples will be utilized in the following learning stage.

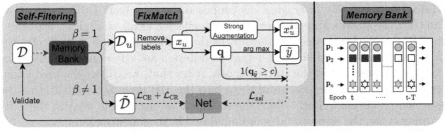

(a) Flowchart of Self-Filtering+   (b) Illustration of memory bank

Fig. 3. (a) The blue and red dashed line denote the update of memory bank and model parameter, respectively. For selected set $\tilde{\mathcal{D}}$, the objective function is $\mathcal{L}_{CE} + \mathcal{L}_{CR}$. For the set $\mathcal{D}_u$, we remove their labels and input them to *FixMatch* framework. (b) MB stores the past T epoch prediction of each sample, and select the samples without fluctuation event to train the model. The updated classifier produces the prediction of the whole dataset to update MB. (Color figure online)

3.3 Learning with Selected Examples

SFT contains two stages: warming-up and main learning. We firstly conduct a warming-up of a few epochs to gain the basic discriminability for the network and achieve initialization for the memory bank module. Then, the main learning proceeds with clean samples selected via the fluctuation criterion. Also, the external memory bank module is dynamically updated for each epoch.

Warming Up. It is necessary to warm up with the whole training set for the network before the main learning stage. However, it is usually vulnerable for pair noise that has a certain pattern for noise transition, especially under the extreme ratio (*e.g.* 40%). Therefore, we penalize the confidence for the output of the network to avoid radically moving forward in warm-up stage. Let $\mathbf{p}_y$ denotes the element in $\mathbf{p}$ for the label y, we formulate the confident-penalization regularization term as

$$\mathcal{R} = -\alpha(\mathbf{p}_j) \cdot \log \mathbf{p}_j \tag{3}$$

where $\mathbf{p}_j$ is the element with the second largest confidence of prediction $\mathbf{p}$. Under the condition of the pair noise, we consider that the class j could be the correct category for the noisy instance. $\alpha(\mathbf{p}_j)$ is an adaptive weight that can be computed by

$$\alpha(\mathbf{p}_j) = \max(0, \Gamma - \frac{\mathbf{p}_j}{\mathbf{p}_y}). \tag{4}$$

Here, Γ is a hyper-parameter of the confidence threshold. If the network is over-confident in class y, it would be penalized with a larger $\alpha(\mathbf{p}_j)$. Finally, we can write our objective function of cross-entropy loss with the regularizer in the warming-up stage as

$$\mathcal{L} = \mathbb{E}_{(\mathbf{x},y) \in \mathcal{D}}[\mathcal{L}_{CE}(f(\mathbf{x},\theta),y) + \mathcal{R}(f(\mathbf{x},\theta),y)], \tag{5}$$

Main Learning. By leveraging the proposed memory bank (MB) module, we can train the classification network with the selected clean examples. Meanwhile, the MB module is updated dynamically as the learning proceeds. Specifically, the clean sample is selected via the fluctuation criterion and subsequently utilized for training the network in the current epoch. After that, we collect the predictions for the whole examples and store them into the MB module for facilitating the selection in the next epoch. Since the classification network is weak in the early learning stage, the error would be accumulated in the following iteration step [9], leading to the selection bias. To tackle this problem, we propose a regularization term $\mathcal{L}_{\text{CR}}$ to penalize the confident output distribution for an example $(\mathbf{x}, y)$ as following

$$\mathcal{L}_{\text{CR}} = -\frac{1}{K} \sum_{k \in [K]} \alpha(\mathbf{p}_k) \cdot \log \mathbf{p}_k, \tag{6}$$

where the coefficient $\alpha(\mathbf{p}_k)$ can be computed by Eq. (4). The regularizer penalizes the confident output of the model by minimizing the expectation of the loss for each class. This is similar with the label smoothing (LS) [20] term. Recall LS of

$$\mathcal{L}_{\text{LS}} = -\log \mathbf{p}_y - \sum_{k \in [K]} \varepsilon \log \mathbf{p}_k, \tag{7}$$

where ε is a fixed smoothing coefficient and the later term can be regarded as a confidence regularization term. Compared with LS, our coefficient $\alpha(\mathbf{p}_k)$ is adaptively computed by using the predictive value for each class, which can avoid tuning the hyper-parameter and can be more robust to the variant noise ratios.

Let $\tilde{\mathcal{D}}$ denotes the selected samples, the loss function for the main learning stage can be formulated as

$$\mathcal{L} = \mathbb{E}_{(\mathbf{x}, y) \in \tilde{\mathcal{D}}}[\mathcal{L}_{\text{CE}}(f(\mathbf{x}, \theta), y) + \lambda \mathcal{L}_{\text{CR}}(f(\mathbf{x}, \theta), y)], \tag{8}$$

where λ is a hyper-parameter set by cross-validation.

3.4   Improving with FixMatch

Our framework for sample selection is flexible, which can be combined with the state-of-the-art semi-supervised method. Hence, to further explore the knowledge in the discarded noise set, we introduce FixMatch [26] to the main learning stage. Since FixMatch is play-and-plug for SFT, we denote Self-Filtering with FixMatch as SFT+ in the following section. The SFT framework is flexible, which can be implemented by commonly-used differentiation tools. The whole learning framework is summarised in Fig. 3(a). More details can be found in the supplemental material.

4   Experiments

To evaluate the performance of our proposed method, we implement experiments in several dimensions: (1) **Task variety:** we select three visual tasks with various dataset including CIFAR-10 [13], CIFAR-100 [13] and a real-world task Clothing1M [37]. (2) **Noise condition:** we manually corrupt the partial labels with three noise types (*e.g.* symmetric, pair and instance dependent noise) on CIFAR-10&100 and various noise ratios ranging from 20% to 80%. The code is available at https://github.com/1998v7/Self-Filtering.

4.1   Noise Types

To simulate the actual noise condition in real-world, we refer to [3] manually construct three noise types: symmetric, pair and instance-dependent label noise. Specially, we introduce a transition matrix T to corrupt the clean label y into a wrong label $\hat{y}$. Given a noise ratio τ, for each sample $(\mathbf{x}, y)$, the T is defined as $T_{ij}(\mathbf{x}) = P(\hat{y} = j | y = i)$, where T_{ij} denotes that the true label transits from clean label i to noisy label j.

(1) For **symmetric** label noise, the diagonal entries of the symmetric transition matrix are $1 - \tau$ and the off-diagonal entries are $\tau/(k-1)$, where k denotes the number of categories.

(2) For **pair-flipped** label noise, the diagonal entries of the symmetric transition matrix are $1 - \tau$ and there exists other value τ in each row.

(3) For **instance-dependent** label noise, we stay the same construct algorithm with [3,34]. The actual flip rate relies on the pre-setting noise ratio τ and the representation of images. The detail algorithm is provided in Appendix 1.

(4) For **open-set** label noise, it's reported as the combination of aforementioned type noise. We select a real-world datasets to verify the effectiveness of our framework. Clothing1M [37] contains one million images of 14 categories and its noise ratio is around 39.46%.

4.2   Network Structure and Experimental Setup

We adopt ResNet-18 [10] and ResNet-34 [10] to implement SFT on CIFAR-10 and CIFAR-100, respectively. The setting for the optimizer is listed as follows that SGD is with the momentum 0.9, the weight decay is 5e-4, the batch size is 32, and the initial learning rate is 0.02, and decayed with the factor 10 at 60 epoch. The number of epoch is set to be 75 for CIFAR-10 and 100 for CIFAR-100. For the warming-up stage, we train the network for 10 epochs and 30 epochs for CIFAR-10 and CIFAR-100, respectively, which is similar to Me-Momentum [3]. Typical data augmentations including randomly cropping and horizontally flipping are applied in our experiments.

For Clothing1M, we utilize the same architecture of ResNet-50 pre-trained on ImageNet. For image preprocessing and data augmentations, we resize the image to 256 × 256 and crop them into 224 × 224. The horizontally flipping is adopted. We train the classifier network for 15 epochs using SGD with 0.9 momentum, weight decay of 0.0005, and the batch size of 32. The warming-up stage is one epoch. The learning rate is set as 0.02 and decayed with the factor of 10 after 10

Table 1. Test accuracy (%) on CIFAR-10 (the *top*) and CIFAR-100 (the *bottom*). The mean accuracy (±std) over 5 repetitions are reported.

Method	Symm.		Pair.		Inst.	
	20%	40%	20%	40%	20%	40%
DMI [39]	88.18 ± 0.36	83.98 ± 0.48	89.44 ± 0.41	84.37 ± 0.78	89.14 ± 0.36	84.78 ± 1.97
Peer Loss [17]	88.97 ± 0.47	84.29 ± 0.52	89.61 ± 0.66	85.18 ± 0.87	89.94 ± 0.51	85.77 ± 1.19
Co-teaching [9]	87.16 ± 0.11	83.59 ± 0.28	86.91 ± 0.37	82.77 ± 0.57	86.54 ± 0.11	80.98 ± 0.39
JoCoR [32]	88.69 ± 0.19	85.44 ± 0.29	87.75 ± 0.46	83.91 ± 0.49	87.31 ± 0.27	82.49 ± 0.57
SELFIE [27]	90.18 ± 0.25	86.27 ± 0.31	89.29 ± 0.19	85.71 ± 0.30	89.24 ± 0.27	84.16 ± 0.44
CDR [35]	89.68 ± 0.38	86.13 ± 0.44	89.19 ± 0.29	85.79 ± 0.41	90.24 ± 0.39	83.07 ± 1.33
Me-Momentum [3]	91.44 ± 0.33	88.39 ± 0.34	90.91 ± 0.45	87.49 ± 0.56	90.86 ± 0.21	86.66 ± 0.91
PES [4]	92.38 ± 0.41	87.45 ± 0.34	91.22 ± 0.42	89.52 ± 0.91	**92.69 ± 0.42**	89.73 ± 0.51
SFT (ours)	**92.57 ± 0.32**	**89.54 ± 0.27**	**91.53 ± 0.26**	**89.93 ± 0.47**	91.41 ± 0.32	**89.97 ± 0.49**
DMI [39]	58.73 ± 0.70	49.81 ± 1.22	59.41 ± 0.69	48.13 ± 0.52	58.05 ± 0.20	47.36 ± 0.68
Peer Loss [17]	58.41 ± 0.55	50.53 ± 1.31	58.73 ± 0.51	50.17 ± 0.42	58.91 ± 0.41	48.61 ± 0.78
Co-teaching [9]	59.28 ± 0.47	51.60 ± 0.49	58.07 ± 0.61	49.79 ± 0.69	57.24 ± 0.69	49.39 ± 0.99
JoCoR [32]	64.17 ± 0.19	55.97 ± 0.46	60.42 ± 0.35	50.97 ± 0.58	61.98 ± 0.39	50.59 ± 0.71
SELFIE [27]	67.19 ± 0.30	61.29 ± 0.39	65.18 ± 0.23	58.67 ± 0.51	65.44 ± 0.43	53.91 ± 0.66
CDR [35]	66.52 ± 0.24	60.18 ± 0.22	66.12 ± 0.31	59.49 ± 0.47	67.06 ± 0.50	56.86 ± 0.62
Me-Momentum [3]	68.03 ± 0.53	63.48 ± 0.72	68.42 ± 0.19	59.73 ± 0.47	68.11 ± 0.57	58.38 ± 1.28
PES [4]	68.89 ± 0.41	64.90 ± 0.57	69.31 ± 0.25	59.08 ± 0.81	70.49 ± 0.72	65.68 ± 0.44
SFT (ours)	**71.98 ± 0.26**	**69.72 ± 0.31**	**71.23 ± 0.29**	**69.29 ± 0.42**	**71.83 ± 0.42**	**69.91 ± 0.54**

Table 2. Comparison results with SSL with symmetric (**S**), pair (**P**) and instance (**I**) label noise.

Methods	SSL	CIFAR-10			CIFAR-100		
		S 50%	**P** 40%	**I** 40%	**S** 50%	**P** 40%	**I** 40%
SELF [23]	Mean teacher	91.4	90.9	90.4	71.8	70.7	69.1
CORES^{2*} [5]	UDA	93.1	92.4	92.2	73.1	72.0	71.9
DivideMix [14]	MixMatch	94.6	<u>93.4</u>	93.0	74.6	72.1	71.7
ELR+ [16]	MixMatch	93.8	92.7	92.2	72.4	<u>74.4</u>	72.6
SFT+	FixMatch	<u>94.8</u>	92.9	**94.4**	**75.4**	74.2	<u>74.1</u>
SFT+*	MixMatch	**94.9**	**93.7**	<u>94.1</u>	<u>75.2</u>	**74.9**	**74.6**

epochs. Following the convention from [14], we sample 1000 mini-batches from the training data while ensuring the labels (noisy) are balanced.

Hyper-parameter Setup. We set memory bank size $T = 3$ and confidence threshold $\Gamma = 0.2$ for all experiments. We set the trade-off coefficient λ in loss function as 1 and the threshold c in FixMatch as 0.95 following [26].

4.3   Comparison with State-of-the-Arts

Baseline. We evaluate our method against the following state-of-the-art methods. (1) Robust loss function: DMI [39], Peer loss [17]. (2) Sample selection

Table 3. Test accuracy (%) on
the Clothing1M.

Method		Acc.
No SSL	Cross entropy	64.54
	MentorNet [12]	67.14
	Co-teaching [9]	68.51
	JoCoR [32]	70.30
	Forward [24]	69.84
	Joint Optim [29]	72.23
	Me-Momentum [3]	73.13
	SFT	**74.16**
SSL	DivideMix [14]	74.76
	ELR+ [16]	74.81
	SFT+*	**75.08**

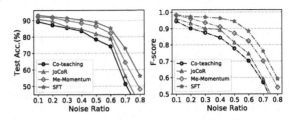

Fig. 4. Illustration of the performance of variant methods as the noise ratio changes. Notably, SFT can produce considerable performance under extreme noise ratios.

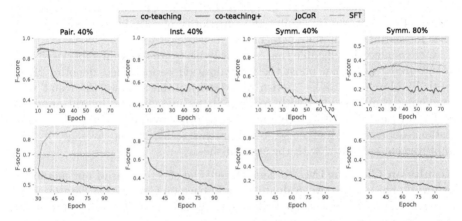

Fig. 5. SFT achieves the highest F-score for sample selection results on CIFAR-10 (the *top*) and CIFAR-100 (the *bottom*).

methods: Co-teaching [9], JoCoR [32], SELFIE [27], Me-Momentum [3]. Note that both of them explore the memorization effect and utilize the small-loss criterion to select clean examples. (3) Sample selection methods with SSL: SELF [23], CORES^{2}* [5], DivideMix [14] and ELR+ [16]. Specially, SELF and CORES^{2}* use the SSL methods of Mean Teacher [30] and UDA [38], respectively. DivideMix and ELR+ both utilize MixMatch. (4) Others: CDR [35], PES [4].

Results on CIFAR-10 & 100. To evaluate the performance of SFT, we conduct experiments on CIFAR-10 and CIFAR-100 under three noise types with variant noise ratios $\tau \in \{0.2, 0.4\}$. Since SSL can dramatically improve the performance, we split the table of each benchmark into two parts for a fair comparison. The bottom part includes methods using SSL, while the top part does not. As shown in Table 1, our SFT outperforms the almost state-of-the-art on two datasets with three noise types. Compared with the homologous approach Me-Momentum, SFT achieves the higher accuracy of 89.97% and gains the sig-

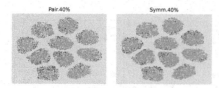
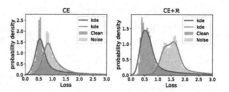

Fig. 6. Most boundary examples can be selected by SFT. The clusters with green dots are samples in the same categories. The red dots are the selected clean samples in the last ten epochs. (Color figure online)

Fig. 7. The losses distribution of noisy CIFAR-10 with Pair.40% after warming-up. There exists an obvious disparity between clean and noisy samples by using the reguliazer $\mathcal{R}$ during warming-up.

nificant improvement of **6.24%** in *Symm.*-40%, **9.56%** in *Pair.*-40% and **11.53%** in *Inst.*-40%. The results exhibit the superiority of SFT in handling the noise issue for learning with more categories.

Our framework is flexible that can easily integrate the semi-supervised technology (SSL) to further boost the generalization performance, denoting SFT+ (with FixMatch) or SFT+* (with MixMatch). Table 2 shows the result when combining vanilla models with recent SSL techniques. The hybrid approach, SFT+ (or SFT+*) consistently outperforms other methods. Especially, for the instance-dependent label noise, our approach achieves the average of **1.7%** improvement compared with the state-of-the-art.

Results on Clothing1M. To demonstrate the effectiveness of our method on real-world noisy labels, we evaluate our approach on Clothing1M dataset, which is a real-world benchmark in LNL tasks. As shown in Table 3, our proposal obtains the state-of-the-art performance. For a fair comparison, we divide the table into two parts according to using the semi-supervised technique or not. Our SFT+* (with MixMatch) outperforms other methods and achieves the improvement of **0.27%** over ELR+, demonstrating its effectiveness for the real-world application.

4.4 Further Analysis

Robustness. To validate the robustness of SFT in a more challenging noisy environment, we compare it with three robust methods [3,9,32] under a more noise ratio setting $\tau \in \{0.1, ..., 0.8\}$. We plot the test accuracy and F-score as the *Symm.* noise ratio increases. As shown in Fig. 4, SFT produces a good performance, even on the challenging condition with a far higher noise ratio. Compared with the homologous approach Me-Momentum, SFT exhibits the favorable property of selecting the clean samples and consistently outperforms Me-Momentum on variant noise ratios. SFT also exhibits considerable robustness under extreme noise conditions as shown in Fig. 4.

Effectiveness. We evaluate the effectiveness of SFT from these three aspects.

Table 4. The significant gain with our selection criterion for other methods.

Method		CIFAR-10				CIFAR-100			
		P 40%	I 40%	S 40%	S 80%	P 40%	I 40%	S 40%	S 80%
Co-teaching	Base	82.7	80.8	83.5	34.6	49.8	49.3	51.6	19.2
	After	84.9 (2.2)	83.9 (3.1)	85.2 (1.7)	39.7 (5.1)	52.1 (2.3)	51.9 (2.6)	54.1 (2.5)	23.6 (4.4)
JoCoR	Base	83.9	82.4	85.4	38.0	51.0	50.6	56.0	22.7
	After	86.8 (2.9)	85.6 (3.2)	87.1 (1.7)	41.6 (3.6)	53.6 (2.6)	53.6 (3.0)	58.4 (2.4)	26.8 (4.1)
DivideMix	Base	93.4	94.5	94.7	93.0	71.0	70.9	72.9	57.9
	After	94.1 (0.7)	94.7 (0.2)	94.6 (0.1)	92.8 (0.2)	72.4 (1.4)	72.0 (1.1)	73.3 (0.4)	59.1 (1.2)

Table 5. Comparison of the total training time (hours) on CIFAR-10.

Co-teaching [9]	MW-Net [25]	MSLC [33]	CORES^2 [5]	DivideMix [14]	Me-Momentum [3]	SFT	SFT+
2.9 h	4.7 h	4.1 h	2.6 h	4.4 h	4.8 h	**2.4 h**	4.1 h

(1) *How accurate is the sample selection strategy?* We conduct the comparison experiments on CIFAR-10 & 100 and plot the curves of F-score for the selection result. As shown in Fig. 5, SFT achieves the highest F-score on all noise types as the training proceeds. Under 40% noise ratios, SFT attains average 0.97 F1-score, indicating it obtains high selection accuracy and recall scores.

(2) *Are the boundary examples selected?* We conduct the experiment with *Inst. & Pair*-40% and record the selected set in different epoch to illustrate the dynamic selecting process by t-SNE [21]. As illustrated in Fig. 6, most of selected samples (red) lie around the decision boundary, demonstrating the effectiveness of the fluctuation criterion for selecting boundary examples.

(3) *How effective is the framework in the warming-up stage?* We plot the distribution of training losses for all instances after warming-up in Fig. 7. The blue and red parts represent the losses of clean and noise labels, respectively. By introducing the regularizer during the warming-up stage, there exists an obvious disparity between clean and noisy samples, verifying the effect of $\mathcal{R}$ in mitigating the overconfidence during warming-up.

Versatility. Our fluctuation criterion is flexible and play-and-plug that can be applied on other modern methods [9,14,32]. We replace the sample selection phase with our selection module and conduct experiments on CIFAR-10 & 100 under four settings of noise. As shown in Table 4, by introducing the fluctuation criterion, these three methods almost outperform the basic version that uses the small-loss criterion. Even in the current SOTA work DivideMix, the improvement of performance on CIFAR-100 is remarkable. The fluctuation criterion gains a significant average improvement of almost **2.0%** under all settings. These results demonstrate the great flexibility of our proposed selection strategy.

Efficiency. We compare the training time with typical methods to show its efficiency. We evaluate them on CIFAR-10 and obtain the mean value of train-

Table 6. The hyper-parameter selection of Γ. Test acc. is reported.

CIFAR-10	0.2	0.4	0.6	0.8
Symm. 40%	**89.67**	89.51	89.27	89.29
Pair. 40%	89.74	**90.11**	89.51	89.43
Inst. 40%	**89.93**	89.61	89.37	89.29
CIFAR-100	0.2	0.4	0.6	0.8
Symm. 40%	**69.88**	69.61	69.17	69.34
Pair. 40%	**69.23**	69.07	68.71	68.66
Inst. 40%	69.84	**69.91**	69.52	69.37

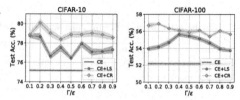

Fig. 8. Comparison confidence regularization (CR) with label smooth (LS). Γ, ε denote the confidence threshold and smooth coefficient respectively.

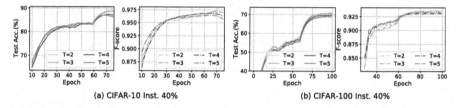

(a) CIFAR-10 Inst. 40%   (b) CIFAR-100 Inst. 40%

Fig. 9. The hyper-parameter selection of memory bank size T. Test accuracy (%) and F-score are reported.

ing time with the 40% rate of three noise types. All models are trained on a single Geforce-3090. As shown in Table 5, SFT is consistently faster than other methods since it can directly back-propagate with selected and does not rely on sophisticated learning strategies, *e.g.*, two-loop training in Me-Momentum [3].

4.5   Hyper-parameter Selection

The confidence threshold Γ and the size T of the memory bank are two hyper-parameters that need tuning with cross-validation. To study the impact of T and Γ, we conduct ablation studies and compared the confidence regularization (CR) with label smoothing (LS) as shown in Table 6, Fig. 8 and Fig. 9.

Confidence threshold Γ. We conduct the experiments from two aspects. First, in Table 6, we compare different setting of Γ on our framework and the value of Γ belongs to $\{0.2, 0.4, 0.6, 0.8\}$. As shown, the different values of Γ slightly affect the generalization performance of the model and a relatively small Γ is more preferred in our learning framework.

Further, to verify that this confidence regularization can be regarded as a robust loss function in a mild noisy condition, we compare CR with LS on two benchmarks with 40% symm. label noise. As shown in Fig. 8, our model achieves the best performance when $\Gamma = 0.2$ for all benchmarks. For the smooth coefficient ε, the setting is variant for different benchmarks (*e.g.* 0.1 for CIFAR-10, 0.4 for CIFAR-100). Therefore, we recommend $\Gamma = 0.2$ for most cases.

Memory Bank Size T. We conduct experiments with variant settings and plot the testing accuracy and F-score for sample selection in Fig. 9. Intuitively,

Table 7. Ablation study of each components. The results of *test accuracy* and *F-score* on variant noise labels are reported.

CIFAR-10	Pair. 40%		Inst. 40%	
	Acc.	F-score	Acc.	F-score
SFT	**89.74**	**0.963**	**90.06**	**0.969**
w. Voting	85.11	0.862	83.92	0.846
w/o. $\mathcal{R}$	88.79	0.952	88.83	0.961
w/o. $\mathcal{L}_{CR}$	87.14	0.944	87.36	0.948
w/o. $\mathcal{R}$ & $\mathcal{L}_{CR}$	86.05	0.940	86.31	0.946

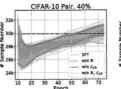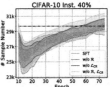

Fig. 10. Ablation study of selected samples number. The solid lines and dashed lines denote the number of selected set $\tilde{\mathcal{D}}$ and the clean labels in $\tilde{\mathcal{D}}$, respectively. The horizontal dashed line denotes the actual clean samples number.

the larger size T tends to detect more fluctuation events in the memory bank and further mitigate the selection of boundary examples. As we expected, the classification results and selection accuracy illustrate that our model attains the best performance with a smaller T. Therefore, we set $T = 3$ for all experiments.

4.6 Ablation Study

Selection Criterion. The majority voting strategy can select samples with high probability of consistent prediction results (right or wrong) in memory bank. Thus, we conduct an ablation study that replaces our criterion with the voting strategy. In Table 7, the significant improvement of test accuracy and F-score compared with voting strategy verifies the superiority of the fluctuation criterion.

Regularization Terms. To directly validate the effectiveness of regularization terms for warming-up and main learning, we remove them in different stages and retrain the model. We evaluate them with the classification accuracy and F-score for the selected results. As shown in Table 7, by removing each component, the performance of the model is degraded. Specifically, test accuracy and F-score averagely decrease **3.72%** and **0.023** on 40% noise ratio without $\mathcal{R}$ and $\mathcal{L}_{CR}$. We also plot the selection curve in Fig. 10. With the support of the two terms, the selected subset contains less noisy labels. Meanwhile, red dashed lines in two figures are close to the horizontal dashed line, indicating the boundary samples are almost selected by our framework.

5 Conclusion

In this paper, we propose a simple but effective framework, Self-Filtering, to select clean samples from the noisy training set. We build a memory bank module to store the historical predictions and design the fluctuation criterion for selection. Compared with the small-loss criterion, the fluctuation strategy takes the boundary sample into account and improves the generalization performance for learning with noisy labels. To reduce the accumulated error of the sample selection bias, we propose a confidence-penalization term. By increasing the weight of the misclassified categories with this term, we mitigate the noise effect in learning proceeding and thus the algorithm is robust to label noise. Extensive experiments and studies exhibit the great properties of the proposed framework.

Acknowledgment. This work was supported in part by National Natural Science Foundation of China (No. 62106129, 62106128, 62176139), Natural Science Foundation of Shandong Province (No. ZR2021ZD15, ZR2021QF053, ZR2021QF001), Young Elite Scientists Sponsorship Program by CAST (No. 2021QNRC001), and China Postdoctoral Science Foundation (No. 2021TQ0195, 2021M701984).

References

1. Amid, E., Warmuth, M.K., Anil, R., Koren, T.: Robust bi-tempered logistic loss based on Bregman divergences. In: NeurIPS (2019)
2. Arazo, E., Ortego, D., Albert, P., O'Connor, N., McGuinness, K.: Unsupervised label noise modeling and loss correction. In: ICML (2019)
3. Bai, Y., Liu, T.: ME-MOMENTUM: extracting hard confident examples from noisily labeled data. In: ICCV (2021)
4. Bai, Y., et al.: Understanding and improving early stopping for learning with noisy labels. In: NeurIPS (2021)
5. Cheng, H., Zhu, Z., Li, X., Gong, Y., Sun, X., Liu, Y.: Learning with instance-dependent label noise: a sample sieve approach. In: ICLR (2021)
6. Cheng, J., Liu, T., Ramamohanarao, K., Tao, D.: Learning with bounded instance and label-dependent label noise. In: ICML (2020)
7. Ghosh, A., Kumar, H., Sastry, P.: Robust loss functions under label noise for deep neural networks. In: AAAI (2017)
8. Gong, M., Li, H., Meng, D., Miao, Q., Liu, J.: Decomposition-based evolutionary multiobjective optimization to self-paced learning. IEEE Trans. Evol. Comput. **23**, 288–302 (2018)
9. Han, B., et al.: Co-teaching: robust training of deep neural networks with extremely noisy labels. In: NeurIPS (2018)
10. He, K., Zhang, X., Ren, S., Sun, J.: Deep residual learning for image recognition. In: CVPR (2016)
11. Hendrycks, D., Mazeika, M., Wilson, D., Gimpel, K.: Using trusted data to train deep networks on labels corrupted by severe noise. In: NeurIPS (2018)
12. Jiang, L., Zhou, Z., Leung, T., Li, L.J., Fei-Fei, L.: MentorNet: learning data-driven curriculum for very deep neural networks on corrupted labels. In: ICML (2018)
13. Krizhevsky, A., Hinton, G., et al.: Learning multiple layers of features from tiny images (2009)
14. Li, J., Socher, R., Hoi, S.C.: DivideMix: learning with noisy labels as semi-supervised learning. In: ICLR (2020)
15. Li, Y., Yang, J., Song, Y., Cao, L., Luo, J., Li, L.J.: Learning from noisy labels with distillation. In: ICCV (2017)
16. Liu, S., Niles-Weed, J., Razavian, N., Fernandez-Granda, C.: Early-learning regularization prevents memorization of noisy labels. In: NeurIPS (2020)

17. Liu, Y., Guo, H.: Peer loss functions: learning from noisy labels without knowing noise rates. In: ICML (2020)
18. Lu, X., Ma, C., Shen, J., Yang, X., Reid, I., Yang, M.H.: Deep object tracking with shrinkage loss. IEEE Trans. Pattern Anal. Mach. Intell. (2020)
19. Lu, X., Wang, W., Shen, J., Crandall, D., Van Gool, L.: Segmenting objects from relational visual data. IEEE Trans. Pattern Anal. Mach. Intell. **44**, 7885–7897 (2021)
20. Lukasik, M., Bhojanapalli, S., Menon, A., Kumar, S.: Does label smoothing mitigate label noise? In: ICML (2020)
21. Van der Maaten, L., Hinton, G.: Visualizing data using t-SNE. J. Mach. Learn. Res. **9**(11) (2008)
22. Natarajan, N., Dhillon, I.S., Ravikumar, P.K., Tewari, A.: Learning with noisy labels. In: NeurIPS (2013)
23. Nguyen, D.T., Mummadi, C.K., Ngo, T.P.N., Nguyen, T.H.P., Beggel, L., Brox, T.: SELF: learning to filter noisy labels with self-ensembling. In: ICLR (2020)
24. Patrini, G., Rozza, A., Krishna Menon, A., Nock, R., Qu, L.: Making deep neural networks robust to label noise: a loss correction approach. In: CVPR (2017)
25. Shu, J., et al.: Meta-weight-net: learning an explicit mapping for sample weighting. In: NeurIPS (2019)
26. Sohn, K., et al.: FixMatch: Simplifying semi-supervised learning with consistency and confidence. In: NeurIPS (2020)
27. Song, H., Kim, M., Lee, J.G.: SELFIE: refurbishing unclean samples for robust deep learning. In: ICML (2019)
28. Sun, H., Guo, C., Wei, Q., Han, Z., Yin, Y.: Learning to rectify for robust learning with noisy labels. Pattern Recogn. **124**, 108467 (2022)
29. Tanaka, D., Ikami, D., Yamasaki, T., Aizawa, K.: Joint optimization framework for learning with noisy labels. In: CVPR (2018)
30. Tarvainen, A., Valpola, H.: Mean teachers are better role models: weight-averaged consistency targets improve semi-supervised deep learning results. In: NeurIPS (2017)
31. Wang, Y., Ma, X., Chen, Z., Luo, Y., Yi, J., Bailey, J.: Symmetric cross entropy for robust learning with noisy labels. In: ICCV (2019)
32. Wei, H., Feng, L., Chen, X., An, B.: Combating noisy labels by agreement: a joint training method with co-regularization. In: CVPR (2020)
33. Wu, Y., Shu, J., Xie, Q., Zhao, Q., Meng, D.: Learning to purify noisy labels via meta soft label corrector. In: AAAI (2021)
34. Xia, X., et al.: Robust early-learning: hindering the memorization of noisy labels. In: ICLR (2020)
35. Xia, X., Liu, T., Han, B., Gong, C., Wang, N., Ge, Z., Chang, Y.: Robust early-learning: hindering the memorization of noisy labels. In: ICLR (2021)
36. Xia, X., Liu, T., Wang, N., Han, B., Gong, C., Niu, G., Sugiyama, M.: Are anchor points really indispensable in label-noise learning? In: NeurIPS (2019)
37. Xiao, T., Xia, T., Yang, Y., Huang, C., Wang, X.: Learning from massive noisy labeled data for image classification. In: CVPR (2015)
38. Xie, Q., Dai, Z., Hovy, E.H., Luong, T., Le, Q.: Unsupervised data augmentation for consistency training. In: NeurIPS (2020)
39. Xu, Y., Cao, P., Kong, Y., Wang, Y.: L_DMI: an information-theoretic noise-robust loss function. In: NeurIPS (2019)
40. Yao, Y., et al.: Dual T: reducing estimation error for transition matrix in label-noise learning. In: NeurIPS (2020)

41. Yu, X., Han, B., Yao, J., Niu, G., Tsang, I., Sugiyama, M.: How does disagreement help generalization against label corruption? In: ICML (2019)
42. Zhang, Z., Sabuncu, M.R.: Generalized cross entropy loss for training deep neural networks with noisy labels. In: NeurIPS (2018)
43. Zhang, Z., Zhang, H., Arik, S.O., Lee, H., Pfister, T.: Distilling effective supervision from severe label noise. In: CVPR (2020)
44. Zhou, T., Wang, S., Bilmes, J.: Robust curriculum learning: from clean label detection to noisy label self-correction. In: ICLR (2020)

RDA: Reciprocal Distribution Alignment for Robust Semi-supervised Learning

Yue Duan[1], Lei Qi[2], Lei Wang[3], Luping Zhou[4], and Yinghuan Shi[1(✉)]

[1] Nanjing University, Nanjing, China
syh@nju.edu.cn
[2] Southeast University, Nanjing, China
[3] University of Wollongong, Wollongong, Australia
[4] University of Sydney, Sydney, Australia

Abstract. In this work, we propose Reciprocal Distribution Alignment (RDA) to address semi-supervised learning (SSL), which is a hyperparameter-free framework that is independent of confidence threshold and works with both the matched (conventionally) and the mismatched class distributions. Distribution mismatch is an often overlooked but more general SSL scenario where the labeled and the unlabeled data do not fall into the identical class distribution. This may lead to the model not exploiting the labeled data reliably and drastically degrade the performance of SSL methods, which could not be rescued by the traditional distribution alignment. In RDA, we enforce a reciprocal alignment on the distributions of the predictions from two classifiers predicting pseudo-labels and complementary labels on the unlabeled data. These two distributions, carrying complementary information, could be utilized to regularize each other without any prior of class distribution. Moreover, we theoretically show that RDA maximizes the input-output mutual information. Our approach achieves promising performance in SSL under a variety of scenarios of mismatched distributions, as well as the conventional matched SSL setting. Our code is available at: https://github.com/NJUyued/RDA4RobustSSL.

Keywords: Distribution alignment · Mismatched distributions

1 Introduction

Semi-supervised learning (SSL) leverages the abundant unlabeled data to alleviate the lack of labeled data for machine learning [5,24,32]. Lately, *confidence-based pseudo-labeling* [21,23] and *distribution alignment* [2,4,10,21] have been introduced to SSL, boosting the performance to a new height. These techniques

---

Y. Duan, Y. Shi are with the National Key Laboratory for Novel Software Technology and the National Institute of Healthcare Data Science, Nanjing University.

Supplementary Information The online version contains supplementary material available at https://doi.org/10.1007/978-3-031-20056-4_31.

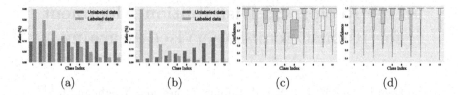

(a)   (b)   (c)   (d)

Fig. 1. Some examples of mismatched distributions in SSL. The x-axis represents the index of classes in CIFAR-10. In (a) and (b), the figures show the distributions of the labeled and unlabeled data. In (c) and (d), the figures show the confidences of FixMatch's predictions on the unlabeled data. Letter-value plots [14] are displayed for multi-level quantile information. In (a) and (c), we show imbalanced labeled data and balanced unlabeled data with 40 labels $N_0 = 10$. In (b) and (d), the labeled and unlabeled data are mismatched and imbalanced with 100 labels, $N_0 = 40$ and $\gamma = 10$. More details about imbalance ratio N_0 and γ can be found in Sect. 4.2. In (c) and (d), we can see that the confidences of FixMatch's predictions on the unlabeled data of different classes are totally irregular, which means it is difficult for us to adjust the confidence threshold to judge whether the prediction is correct. *i.e.*, confidence-based pseudo-labeling is also not suitable for the mismatched distributions.

improve the label imputation for unlabeled data, which alleviates the confirmation bias [1]. In brief, pseudo-labeling aims to achieve entropy minimization [11] by producing hard labels. Recently, FixMatch [23] utilizes the confidence-based threshold to select more accurate pseudo-labels and proves the superiority of this technique. Despite this threshold preventing the model from risk of noisy pseudo-labels, since the learning difficulties of different classes are different, a fixed threshold is not a "silver bullet" for all scenarios of SSL. Although [27,30] demonstrate the potential to dynamically adjust the threshold, the adjustment is complicated and the waste of unlabeled data with low confidence will become a latent limitation [9]. We try to ask—*is the confidence-based threshold really necessary for pseudo-labeling?*

Motivated by this, we rethink pseudo-labeling in a hyperparameter-free way while noticing that distribution alignment (DA) has been introduced to SSL [2,10,21]. DA scales the predictions on unlabeled data by prior information about labeled data distribution for strong regularization on the pseudo-labels, which can mitigate the confirmation bias. Inspired by this, we consider only using DA to improve the pseudo-labels without additional hyperparameters, *i.e.*, DA is enough for pseudo-labeling. Meanwhile, DA shows great potential in addressing the SSL under long-tailed distribution [26]. We expect that this technique can play a positive role in SSL in a more general scope. However, even though DA could help us improve pseudo-labeling by protecting SSL from noise, it is based on a strong assumption: *"labeled data and unlabeled data share the same distribution,"* *e.g.*, they are all balanced in CIFAR-10. The scenarios of *mismatched distributions* have not been widely discussed, *i.e.*, the distribution of labeled data doesn't match that of unlabeled data, which is illustrated in Fig. 1. Some typical scenarios lead to mismatched distributions, such as biased sampling, label missing not at random [13] and so on. Mismatched distributions might cause biased pseudo-labels, significantly degrading the SSL model performance

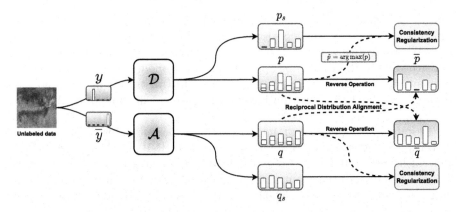

Fig. 2. Diagram of proposed Reciprocal Distribution Alignment (RDA). We use ground-truth label y and complementary label $\bar{y}$ (dash line means $\bar{y}$ is selected randomly from classes excluding ground-truth label) of labeled data to train Default Classifier $\mathcal{D}$ and Auxiliary Classifier $\mathcal{A}$, respectively. Given an unlabeled sample u, $\mathcal{D}$ predicts pseudo-label p and $\mathcal{A}$ predicts complementary label q for its weakly-augmented version. RDA is applied on p and q by reciprocally scaling each other to the distributions of their reversed versions obtained by *Reverse Operation* (Proposition 1). We then enforce consistency regularization on the aligned pseudo-label and complementary label against corresponding predictions for strongly-augmented u, *i.e.*, p_s (from $\mathcal{D}$) and q_s (from $\mathcal{A}$).

which is demonstrated by experimental results in Sect. 5.2. Under mismatched distributions, we cannot simply use the distribution of the labeled data to align predictions on unlabeled data with a very different distribution. This drives us to explore a more general distribution alignment to meet the above challenge of mismatched distributions.

Given motivations mentioned above, we propose Reciprocal Distribution Alignment (**RDA**) to establish a promising semi-supervised learning paradigm, which provides an integrated scheme to handle both the matched and mismatched scenarios in SSL. To relax the assumption about the class distribution of unlabeled data, we consider starting from the model itself to tap the potential guidance of distribution by regularizing the predictions from complementary perspectives. Inspired by [16, 18, 22], we consider simultaneously predict the class labels and their complementary labels (*i.e.*, indicating what class a sample is not), and utilize their distributions to regularize each other. Thus, we introduce two classifiers to RDA, one is Default Classifier (**DC**) and the other is Auxiliary Classifier (**AC**). Specifically, DC and AC are used to predict pseudo-labels and complementary labels for unlabeled data, respectively. The pseudo-labels and the complementary labels could be transformed into each other through their reversed version using the *Reverse Operation* defined in Proposition 1 in Sect. 3.3. Then a reciprocal alignment is employed to adjust the distributions of DC's predictions and AC's predictions by scaling them according to their corresponding reversed versions. We prove that RDA produces a "high-entropy" form of prediction distribution, which lead to maximizing the objective of input-output mutual information [2,4]. With the aligned pseudo-labels and complementary labels, the commonly used consistency regularization is further applied on DC and AC, respectively, which helps the model remain unchanged prediction on perturbed data. RDA could be applied to help the model improve pseudo-labels without suffering from the threat of mismatched distributions since no prior information about class distribution of data is used. A diagram of RDA is shown in Fig. 2.

Despite its simplicity, our method shows superior performance in various settings, *e.g.*, on widely-used SSL benchmark CIFAR-10, RDA achieves an accuracy of $92.03 \pm 2.01\%$ with only 20 labels in the conventional setting, and in mismatched distributions, outperforms CoMatch [21], a recently-proposed algorithm for SSL, by up to a 52.09% gain on accuracy. Besides the significant performance improvement, our contributions can be presented as follows:

- We propose Reciprocal Distribution Alignment (RDA), a novel SSL algorithm, which can improve pseudo-labels in a hyperparameter-free way.
- RDA can be safely applied to SSL in both the conventional setting and the scenarios of mismatched distributions.
- We theoretical show that RDA could optimize the objective of mutual information between input data and predictions [2,4] under the premise of rational use of class distribution guidance information.

2   Related Work

Pseudo-labeling Based Entropy Minimization. Entropy minimization is a significant idea in recent SSL methods, which is closely related to pseudo-labeling (*i.e.*, convert model's predictions to hard labels to reduce entropy) [20,21,23,28]. In another word, pseudo-labeling results in a form of entropy minimization [11]. This idea argues that model should ensure classes are well-separated while utilizing unlabeled data, which can be achieved by encouraging the model output prediction with low entropy [11]. Recent SSL algorithms like [21,23,27,31] set a confidence-based threshold to refine the pseudo-labels and obtain outstanding performance. However, the existence of confidence threshold leads to a waste of unlabeled samples with low confidence because they were filtered out. Moreover, it will lead to a significant increase in the cost of dynamic adjustment on confidence threshold like [27,30]. Meanwhile, under mismatched distributions, it is not reasonable to use a fixed threshold for all classes to filter pseudo-labels, because the model will also be affected by the unlabeled data with a potential risk of unknown distribution. In this work, we use distribution alignment to improve pseudo-labeling in a hyperparameter-free way which can achieve a better performance than algorithms introducing confidence threshold.

Distribution Alignment in SSL. Distribution alignment is proposed in [4] and originally applied to SSL in [2]. Briefly, [2] integrates it into pseudo-label inference step without additional loss terms or hyper-parameters. The main idea is the marginal distribution of predictions on unlabeled data and the marginal distribution of ground-truth labels should be consistent. This alleviates the confirmation bias [1] by improving pseudo-labels with the help of distributional guidance information. For class-imbalanced semi-supervised learning, [26] improves this technique by replacing the distribution of ground-truth labels with a smoothed form, resulting in superior performance in this setting. This improved distribution alignment in [26] helps the model benefit from rebalancing distribution.

In short, the objective of distribution alignment is to maximize the mutual information between the predictions and input data, *i.e.*, input-output mutual information [2,4]. Denoting the input data as x, the class prediction for x as y, and the predicted class distribution as $P(y|x)$, we can formalize this objective as:

$$\mathcal{I}(y; x) = \mathcal{H}(\mathbb{E}_x[P(y|x)]) - \mathbb{E}_x[\mathcal{H}(P(y|x))], \tag{1}$$

where $\mathcal{H}(\cdot)$ refers to entropy. For specific, distribution alignment aims to maximize the term $\mathcal{H}(\mathbb{E}_x[P(y|x)])$. However, the implementation of this technique in both [2] and [26] is based on an idealized assumption: *"labeled and unlabeled data fall in the same distribution."* More realistically, we cannot guarantee that the distribution of labeled data matches that of unlabeled data. Such mismatched distributions can cause the distribution alignment in [2,26] to fail and is even detrimental to the model's predictions on unlabeled data. In this work, we propose Reciprocal Distribution Alignment without the assumption of matched distributions and any prior information about the labeled data distribution.

3   Method

In this section, we discuss the setting of mismatched distributions in SSL and propose a novel SSL algorithm called Reciprocal Distribution Alignment (**RDA**) without additional hyper-parameters to improve pseudo-labeling in various scenarios of SSL. Moreover, we theoretically analyze the effectiveness of our method.

3.1   Matched and Mismatched Distributions in SSL

In semi-supervised learning, we have a training set divided into labeled portion $\mathcal{X}$ and unlabeled portion $\mathcal{U}$. We denote class distribution of $\mathcal{X}$ as $\mathcal{C}_x$ and class distribution of $\mathcal{U}$ as $\mathcal{C}_u$. Note that $\mathcal{C}_u$ is inaccessible in training. Given $x \in \mathcal{X}$ with corresponding label y and unlabeled data $u \in \mathcal{U}$, we can review the SSL algorithms as the following optimization task:

$$\min \mathcal{L} = \mathcal{L}_{sup}(x, y; \theta) + \mathcal{L}_{unsup}(u; \theta), \tag{2}$$

where θ is the parameters of the model, $\mathcal{L}_{sup}$ is supervised loss for the labeled data and $\mathcal{L}_{unsup}$ is unsupervised loss for the unlabeled data. Recent pseudo-labeling based SSL methods try to impute the unknown label of u for $\mathcal{L}_{unsup}$. Therefore, the accuracy of pseudo-labels has become the top priority. In the traditional SSL setting, we assume $\mathcal{C}_x \approx \mathcal{C}_u$. Under this assumption, we can use $\mathcal{C}_x$ to guide the prediction for u by distribution alignment [2,21], which can improve the performance of consistentency-based or pseudo-labeling based methods [2,10,21,23]. Unfortunately, this assumption is too impractical and idealistic. More in line with the actual situation is $C_x \not\approx C_u$, which is called *mismatched distributions* in SSL. Unlike the conventional SSL, in mismatched distributions, the model learns a distribution from C_x that differs from C_u, so it cannot correctly predict the pseudo-labels. In other words, the distribution gap caused by mismatch leads to strong confirmation bias [1], which could affect the performance of the model. It is worth noting that the distribution alignment used in [26] to solve the SSL under long-tail distribution also cannot be applied to the mismatched scenarios because [26] still depends on the assumption of matched distributions. To design a method that can tackle mismatched scenarios in SSL, we must face to $C_x \not\approx C_u$, and abandon prior of C_x used in previous method [2,26].

3.2   Overview

We introduce two classifiers for our method. One is called Default Classifier (DC) $\mathcal{D}$ and the other is called Auxiliary Classifier (AC) $\mathcal{A}$. In a nut shell, for an unlabeled image, $\mathcal{D}$ is used to predict pseudo-label and $\mathcal{A}$ is used to predict complementary label. We obtain labeled data $\mathcal{X} = \{(x_b, y_b)\}_{b=1}^{B}$ consisting of B images and unlabeled data $\mathcal{U} = \{(u_b)\}_{b=1}^{\mu B}$ consisting of μB images in a batch of data. At first, we construct complementary label $\overline{y}$ for every labeled data by their ground-truth. Complementary label [15,16] represents which class the sample does not belong to. Denoting $y \in \mathcal{Y} = \{1, \ldots, n\}$ as the ground-truth label of x where n is the number of classes, following [18], the complementary label of x is randomly selected from $\mathcal{Y} \setminus \{y\}$, which is denoted as $\overline{y}$.

Following [23], we integrate *consistency regularization* into RDA. Weak and strong augmentations are performed on images then we enforce consistency regularization on $\mathcal{D}$ and $\mathcal{A}$. Denoting u_w as the weakly-augmented image and u_s as the strongly-augmented image for the same unlabeled data u, let y_c be the class prediction for input image. $P_G(y_c|\cdot)$ refers to the predicted class distribution outputted by classifier G for input. We can obtain pseud-labels $p = P_{\mathcal{D}}(y_c|u_w)$, $p_s = P_{\mathcal{D}}(y_c|u_s)$, and complementary labels $q = P_{\mathcal{A}}(y_c|u_w)$, $q_s = P_{\mathcal{A}}(y_c|u_s)$ respectively. Note that p, q are n-dimensional vectors of class probability where n is the number of classes. p_i, q_i represent the probability of belonging to the i-th class in the predictions. Then, dual consistency regularization can be achieved by minimizing the default consistency loss $\mathcal{L}_{cd}$ and auxiliary consistency loss $\mathcal{L}_{ca}$:

$$\mathcal{L}_{cd} = \frac{1}{\mu B} \sum_{n=1}^{\mu B} H(\hat{p}_n, p_{s,n}), \tag{3}$$

$$\mathcal{L}_{ca} = \frac{1}{\mu B} \sum_{n=1}^{\mu B} H(q_n, q_{s,n}), \tag{4}$$

where $H(\cdot, \cdot)$ refers to the cross-entropy loss and $\hat{p} = \arg\max(p)$, which means we use hard labels for consistency regularization on $\mathcal{D}$. Differently, soft labels are used for $\mathcal{A}$ instead. RDA exploits all unlabeled data for training, whereas previous consistency-based methods waste low-confidence data [21,23,27].

In addition, we enforce cross-entropy loss on $\mathcal{D}$ between weakly-augmented version of x (denoted as x_w) and y, and on $\mathcal{A}$ between x_w and $\overline{y}$ respectively:

$$\mathcal{L}_{sd} = \frac{1}{B} \sum_{n=1}^{B} H(y_n, P_{\mathcal{D}}(y_c|x_{w,n})),$$ (5)

$$\mathcal{L}_{sa} = \frac{1}{B} \sum_{n=1}^{B} H(\overline{y}_n, P_{\mathcal{A}}(y_c|x_{w,n})),$$ (6)

where $\mathcal{L}_{sd}$ is default supervised loss for $\mathcal{D}$ and $\mathcal{L}_{sa}$ is auxiliary supervised loss for $\mathcal{A}$. To sum up, RDA jointly optimizes four losses mentioned above:

$$\mathcal{L} = \mathcal{L}_{sd} + \lambda_a \mathcal{L}_{sa} + \lambda_{cd} \mathcal{L}_{cd} + \lambda_{ca} \mathcal{L}_{ca},$$ (7)

where λ_a, λ_{cd} and λ_{ca} are trade-off coefficients and are all set to 1 for simplicity.

Previous entropy minimization based methods like [21,23,27] achieve superior performance in SSL by pseudo-labeling. Their key to success is the confidence threshold set to control the selection of pseudo-labels. To eliminate this hyperparameter that becomes cumbersome in mismatched distributions, we consider a way to improve pseudo-labels using only distribution alignment. According to Eq. (1), we can formalize the objective of distribution alignment for $\mathcal{D}$ as:

$$\max_{\mathcal{D}} \mathcal{H}[\mathbb{E}_u(P_{\mathcal{D}}(y_c|u_w))],$$ (8)

where $\mathcal{H}(\cdot)$ refers to the entropy. Likewise, we formalize the objective of distribution alignment for $\mathcal{A}$ as:

$$\max_{\mathcal{A}} \mathcal{H}[\mathbb{E}_u(P_{\mathcal{A}}(y_c|u_w))].$$ (9)

This two objectives encourage model to make predictions with equal frequency but these are not necessarily useful when dataset's class distribution of ground-truth is not uniform. We use Reciprocal Distribution Alignment descried in next paragraph to incorporate these two objectives.

3.3   Reciprocal Distribution Alignment

Following [2], we notice that making one distribution approach to another (distribution of labeled data is used in [2]) can achieve the purpose of maximizing Eq. (1). In this way, a form of "high entropy" could be achieved for the objective described by Eqs. (8) and (9). In brief, we define the objective over $\mathcal{D}$ and $\mathcal{A}$ as:

$$\max_{\mathcal{D},\mathcal{A}} h(\mathcal{D}, \mathcal{A}) = \mathcal{H}[\mathbb{E}_u(p)] + \mathcal{H}[\mathbb{E}_u(q)].$$ (10)

However, due to the existence of mismatched scenarios, the class distribution of labeled data cannot be directly used for alignment like [2]. So, next we will use the distribution of class predictions (*i.e.*, $\mathbb{E}_u(p)$) and the distribution of complementary class predictions (*i.e.*, $\mathbb{E}_u(q)$) to build a reciprocal alignment. Considering there is no strong correlation between the distribution of class predictions and that of complementary class predictions, we assume that $\mathcal{A}$ is used to predict pseudo-label $\bar{q}$ (a "reversed" version of q), so that the "reversed" version of $\mathbb{E}_u(q)$ (*i.e.*, $\mathbb{E}_u(\bar{q})$) can be used to align $\mathbb{E}_u(p)$.

Proposition 1 (Reverse Operation). *In the case of using $\mathcal{A}$ to predict pseudo-labels, we have $\bar{q} = Norm(\mathbb{1} - q)$, where $\mathbb{1}$ is all-one vector and $Norm(x)$ is the normalized operation defined as $x_i' = x_i / \sum_{j=1}^n x_j$, $i \in (1, \dots, n)$.*

Proof. Assuming we use $\mathcal{A}$ to predict pseudo-label $\bar{q}$, ideally, the probability of one class (*i.e.*, q_i) should randomly fall on a class which is different from the class predicted currently (*i.e.*, $\bar{q}_j$ where $j \neq i$). Thus, for any $\bar{q}_j \in \bar{q}$, its value is the sum of the values randomly assigned to it by all q_i:

$$\bar{q}_j = \sum_{i=1, i\neq j}^n \frac{q_i}{n-1} = \frac{1-q_j}{n-1}. \tag{11}$$

Rewriting it we obtain:

$$\bar{q}_j = \frac{1-q_j}{n - \sum_{k=1}^n q_k} = \frac{1-q_j}{(1-q_1) + \cdots + (1-q_n)}$$
$$= \frac{1-q_j}{\sum_{k=1}^n (1-q_k)} = Norm(1-q_j). \tag{12}$$

Now, $\bar{q} = Norm(1-q)$ follows by combining the similar proof for any $q_i \in q$. $\square$

Likewise, if we use $\mathcal{D}$ to predict complementary label $\bar{p}$, it can be calculated as $\bar{p} = Norm(\mathbb{1} - p)$. By Eq. (11), we notice that Reverse Operation does not change the relative relationship between classes in the class distribution, but just reverses the order, which allows us to still obtain helpful guidance information from the pseud-label and complementary label perspectives.

Then, distribution alignment is conducted on $\mathbb{E}_u(p)$ by scaling it to $\mathbb{E}_u(\bar{q})$. Reciprocally, we align $\mathbb{E}_u(q)$ by scaling it to $\mathbb{E}_u(\bar{p})$. Following [2], we also integrate distribution alignment into RDA without hyper-parameters. We compute the moving average $\Psi(\cdot)$ of p, q, and their reversed version $\bar{p}$, $\bar{q}$ over last 128 batches, which can respectively serve as the estimation of $\mathbb{E}_u(p)$, $\mathbb{E}_u(q)$, $\mathbb{E}_u(\bar{p})$ and $\mathbb{E}_u(\bar{q})$. Given an unlabeled image u, we scale the prediction of $\mathcal{D}$, *i.e.*, pseudo-label p by:

$$\tilde{p} = Norm(p \times \frac{\Psi(\bar{q})}{\Psi(p)}), \tag{13}$$

where $\tilde{p}$ is an aligned probability distribution. Then, $\hat{p} = \arg\max \tilde{p}$ is used as hard pseudo-label for default consistency loss $\mathcal{L}_{cd}$. Meanwhile, we scale the prediction of $\mathcal{A}$, *i.e.*, complementary label q by:

$$\tilde{q} = Norm(q \times \frac{\Psi(\bar{p})}{\Psi(q)}), \tag{14}$$

where $\tilde{q}$ is an aligned probability distribution. Then $\tilde{q}$ is used as soft complementary label for auxiliary consistency loss $\mathcal{L}_{ca}$. The following theorem shows why RDA results in maximizing the objective Eq. (10). In this way, the input-output mutual information could be maximized, boosting the model's performance [2,4].

Theorem 1. *For pseudo-label p and the reversed pseudo-label $\bar{p}$ obtained by **Reverse Operation**, we show that the entropy of $\bar{p}$ is larger than that of p:*

$$\mathcal{H}(\bar{p}) \geq \mathcal{H}(p). \tag{15}$$

Proof. We sort the sequence $p_1, \ldots, p_n$ in descending order and denote the sorted sequence as $p_1 \geq \cdots \geq p_n$ for simplicity. Considering the case where $p_1 < \frac{1}{2}$ firstly, we prove a equivalent form of Theorem 1:

$$\sum_{i=1}^{n} [p_i \log p_i - \frac{(1-p_i)}{n-1} \log \frac{(1-p_i)}{n-1}] \geq 0. \tag{16}$$

We define the function as

$$f(x) = x \log x - \frac{1-x}{n-1} \log \frac{1-x}{n-1}, \tag{17}$$

where $x \in [0, \frac{1}{2})$ by $\frac{1}{2} \geq p_1 \geq \cdots \geq p_n$. The second derivative of this function is

$$f''(x) = \frac{1}{x} - \frac{1}{(n-1)(1-x)} = \frac{(n-1) - nx}{x(n-1)(1-x)} \tag{18}$$

Let $f''(x) \geq 0$, we obtain $x \leq \frac{n-1}{n}$. Considering $n \geq 2$, the minimum of the term $\frac{n-1}{n}$ is $\frac{1}{2}$. By $x \leq \frac{1}{2}$, $f''(x) \geq 0$ holds, which means the $f(x)$ is a convex function. Thus, by Jensen's Inequality, we have

$$\frac{1}{n} \sum_{i=1}^{n} f(x_i) \geq f(\frac{1}{n} \sum_{i=1}^{n} x_i) \tag{19}$$

Substituting in $x_i = p_i$, by Eq. (19), we obtain

$$\frac{1}{n} \sum_{i=1}^{n} (p_i \log p_i - \frac{1-p_i}{n-1} \log \frac{1-p_i}{n-1}) \geq \frac{1}{n} \log \frac{1}{n} - \frac{1-\frac{1}{n}}{n-1} \log \frac{1-\frac{1}{n}}{n-1} = 0 \tag{20}$$

$\square$

The proofs of this theorem when $p_1 \geq \frac{1}{2}$ and the version of complementary label q are provided in Sec. A of Supplementary Material. Given the above proof, $\mathcal{D}$ and $\mathcal{A}$ are optimized to output predictions $\bar{p}$ and $\bar{q}$ with larger entropy, *i.e.*,

$$\mathcal{H}[\mathbb{E}_u(p)] + \mathcal{H}[\mathbb{E}_u(q)] \leq \mathcal{H}[\mathbb{E}_u(\bar{p})] + \mathcal{H}[\mathbb{E}_u(\bar{q})]. \tag{21}$$

RDA maximizes the objective Eq. (10) by aligning $\mathbb{E}_u(p)$ to $\mathbb{E}_u(\overline{q})$ and aligning $\mathbb{E}_u(q)$ to $\mathbb{E}_u(\overline{p})$ reciprocally, so as the input-output mutual information objective Eq. (1) could be maximized.

With *Reverse Operation*, we can apply distribution alignment while ensuring that the relative relationship between classes in the class distribution can be utilized, so as RDA could achieve a more reasonable form of "high entropy" for the objective of distribution alignment without using prior about C_x. So far, we construct hyperparameter-free Reciprocal Distribution Alignment (**RDA**), which is robust to SSL under both mismatched distributions and the conventional setting. The whole algorithm is presented in Sec. B of Supplementary Material.

4   Experimental Setup

We evaluate RDA on various standard benchmarks of SSL image classification task under diverse settings, including mismatched distributions (*i.e.*, $C_x \not\approx C_u$) and the conventional SSL setting (*i.e.*, $C_x \approx C_u$ and they are all balanced). Experiments show that RDA outperforms significantly over current state-of-the-art (SOTA) SSL methods under most settings. We also conduct further ablation studies on the effectiveness of each components in our method.

4.1   Datasets

RDA is evaluated on four datasets used in SSL widely: CIFAR-10/100 [19], STL-10 [6] and mini-ImageNet [25]. CIFAR-10/100, are composed of 60,000 images from 10/100 classes. Both of them are divided into training set with 50,000 images and test set with 10,000 images. STL-10 is composed of 5,000 labeled images and 100,000 unlabeled images which extracted from a broader distribution. mini-ImageNet is a subset of ImageNet [8] consisting of 100 classes, and each class has 600 images.

4.2   Settings of C_x and C_u

In addition to the conventional matched setting (*i.e.*, both C_x and C_u are balanced), we verify the efficacy of our method in more realistic mismatched scenarios, as discussed in Sect. 3.1. In view of the complexity of this problem, we mainly use the following three scenarios to summary our experimental protocol:

- Training with imbalanced C_x and balanced C_u. We are interested in the impact of mismatched distributions resulting from this simple setting. A graphical explanation of this setting is shown in Fig. 1(a).
- Training with mismatched and imbalanced C_x, C_u, which is shown in Fig. 1(b). This challenging setting can fully test the robustness of RDA.
- Training with balanced C_x and imbalanced C_u.

For experiments in above scenarios, we randomly select samples from dataset to construct imbalanced C_x and C_u. For C_x, the number of labeled data N_i in each class is fixed by N_0. N_i is calculated as $N_i = N_0 \times \gamma_x^{-\frac{i-1}{n-1}}$, where n is the number of classes and $i \in (1, \ldots, n)$. For fairness, we hold N_0 and search a proper γ_x for each N_i to keep the total number of labeled data consistent with we set. Details on searching for γ_x are shown in Sec. C.2 of Supplementary Material.

Specially, C_u is constructed in a form similar to reversely ordered C_x for more challenging setting. After a random selection of unlabeled data from dataset, the remaining data is seen as unlabeled data. The number of unlabeled data M_i of each class is fixed by: $M_i = M_0 \times \gamma^{-\frac{n-i}{n-1}}$, where $M_0 = 5000$ in CIFAR-10, $M_0 = 500$ in mini-ImageNet. In this way, we construct C_u as a *"reversed"* version of C_x as shown in Fig. 1(b). Likewise, DARP's protocol [17] also produces datasets with mismatched distributions from CIFAR-10 and STL-10. So we also make a fair comparison with DARP under this protocol. More details about DARP's protocol can be found in Sec. C.1 of Supplementary Material.

4.3   Baselines

We compare RDA mainly with three recent state-of-the-art SSL methods: (1) FixMatch [23], combining consistency regularization and entropy minimization; (2) FixMatch with distribution alignment [2]; (3) CoMatch [21], combining graph-based contrastive learning and consistency regularization. Moreover, we provide more comparisons with MixMatch [3], AlphaMatch [10], and DARP [17].

4.4   Implementation Details

Unless noted otherwise, we adopt Wide ResNet [29] and Resnet-18 [12] as the backbone for experiments. For specific, WRN-28-2 is used for CIFAR-10, WRN-28-8 is used for CIFAR-100 and Resnet-18 is used for STL-10/mini-ImageNet. Following [23], RandAugment [7] is used for strong augmentation. For simplicity, we train models using SGD with a momentum of 0.9 and a weight decay of 0.0005 in all experiments. In addition, we use a learning rate of 0.03 with cosine decay schedule to train the models for 1024 epochs. For hyper-parameters, we set $\mu = 7, B = 64, \lambda_a = \lambda_{cd} = \lambda_{ca} = 1$ for all experiments. Particularly, we report the results averaged on five folds and the standard deviation is calculated.

5   Results and Analysis

5.1   Conventional Setting (Matched Distributions)

For a fair comparison with baseline SSL methods, we conduct experiments in the conventional setting, *i.e.*, both C_x and C_w are balanced. We test the accuracy of RDA on CIFAR-10, mini-ImageNet, and STL-10 by varying the number of labeled data. Table 1 shows that the performance of RDA is compatible to (if not

Table 1. Results of accuracy (%) in the conventional matched SSL setting. Results with * are copied from CoMatch [21] and with † are copied from AlphaMatch [10]. Results of other baselines are based on our reimplementation.

Method	CIFAR-10				mini-ImageNet	STL-10
	20 labels	40 labels	80 labels	100 labels	1000 labels	1000 labels
MixMatch*	27.84±10.63	51.90±11.76	80.79±1.28	-	-	38.02±8.29
AlphaMatch†	-	91.35±3.38	-	-	-	-
FixMatch	84.97±10.37	89.18±1.54	91.99±0.71	93.14±0.76	39.03±0.66	65.38±0.42*
CoMatch	88.43±7.22	93.21±1.55	94.08±0.31	**94.55±0.27**	43.72±0.58	79.80±0.38*
RDA	**92.03±2.01**	**94.13±1.22**	**94.24±0.42**	94.35±0.25	**46.91±1.16**	**82.63±0.54**

Table 2. Results of accuracy (%) in the mismatched scenario with imbalanced C_x (*i.e.*, alter N_0) and balanced C_u. Experiments are conducted on CIFAR-10, CIFAR-100 and mini-ImageNet varying the number of labels and N_0. Baseline methods are using our reimplementation. Results with **DA** are achieved by combining the original *distribution alignment* in [2]. **Note that CoMatch [21] also integrates DA technique.**

Method	CIFAR-10				CIFAR-100		mini-ImageNet	
	40 labels		100 labels		400 labels	1000 labels	1000 labels	
	$N_0 = 10$	20	40	80	40	80	40	80
FixMatch	85.72±0.93	76.53±3.03	93.01±0.72	71.57±1.88	25.66±0.46	40.22±1.00	36.20±0.36	28.33±0.41
FixMatch w. DA	71.23±1.25	47.85±1.99	56.78±1.28	34.18±0.86	22.66±1.53	31.06±0.51	33.87±0.40	23.53±0.72
CoMatch	60.27±3.22	39.48±2.20	52.82±2.03	26.91±0.75	23.97±0.62	28.35±1.20	30.24±1.37	21.47±0.86
RDA	**92.57±0.53**	**81.78±6.44**	**94.23±0.36**	**79.00±2.67**	**30.86±0.78**	**41.29±0.43**	**42.73±0.84**	**36.73±1.01**

better than) that of the conventional SSL methods under matched class distributions. This results also confirm our view that with our design, the distribution alignment alone is enough for pseudo-labeling. RDA outperforms CoMatch by 3.60% when labels are scarce (with 20 labels). Moreover, on datasets with more classes, our method consistently achieves improvement on accuracy than the best baseline, *e.g.*, 46.91% (ours) vs 43.72% (CoMatch) on mini-ImageNet with 1000 labels. RDA's superior performance benefits from improving the pseudo-labels with the co-regularization of complementary class distribution and utilizing the entire unlabeled data, whereas low-confidence samples are discarded in [21,23].

5.2   Mismatched Distributions

Imbalanced C_x and Balanced C_u. We keep balanced distribution in the unlabeled data and vary N_0 to change the imbalance degree of C_x while the total number of labeled data remains unchanged in the way described in Sect. 4.2. Table 2 shows the results on CIFAR-10, CIFAR-100, and mini-ImageNet. RDA outperforms all baseline methods by a large margin. *e.g.*, on CIFAR-10, with 100 labels and $N_0 = 80$, RDA outperforms FixMatch by 7.43% and CoMatch by

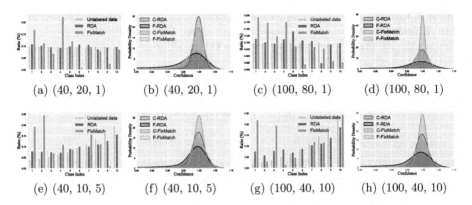

(a) $(40, 20, 1)$ (b) $(40, 20, 1)$ (c) $(100, 80, 1)$ (d) $(100, 80, 1)$

(e) $(40, 10, 5)$ (f) $(40, 10, 5)$ (g) $(100, 40, 10)$ (h) $(100, 40, 10)$

Fig. 3. In the caption, (x,y,z) denotes (labels, N_0, γ). In (a), (b), (c) and (d), C_x is imbalanced and C_u is balanced. In (e), (f), (g) and (h), C_x and C_u are imbalanced and they mismatch. In (a), (c), (e) and (g), the x-axis represents the index of classes in CIFAR-10 and the y-axis represents the ratio of label to the total. $RDA/FixMatch$ in figures indicates the class predictions from RDA/FixMatch and *Unlabeled data* indicates the ground-truth label of unlabeled samples. In (b), (d), (f) and (h), the x-axis represents the confidence of prediction from RDA/FixMatch and the y-axis represents the probability density of confidence estimated by kernel density estimation (KDE). *C-X* and *F-X* indicate the correct and false class predictions of *X*, respectively.

52.09%. We witness that mismatched C_x and C_u significantly decrease the models' performance. Notably, the traditional distribution alignment, assuming the labeled and unlabeled data share the same distribution, significantly degrades the performance of model when the distributions mismatch, whereas our method improves this situation by utilizing guidance of distribution information without any prior. As shown in Figs. 3(a) and 3(c), RDA resists the impact of imbalanced C_x and computes a more balanced pseudo-label distribution than FixMatch, demonstrating the effectiveness of RDA in this mismatched distributions scenario. Additionally, Figs. 3(b) and 3(d) show that the predictions of RDA are not necessarily more confident than that of FixMatch, but RDA reduces the overfitting on false pseudo-labels, *i.e.*, RDA is not as overconfident as FixMatch on the pseudo-labels that may be wrong. Since there is no prior requirement for the distribution of labeled data, RDA can be safely applied to this mismatched scenario without being overwhelmingly affected by the distribution gap, thus exhibiting robust performance improvement.

Mismatched and Imbalanced C_x, C_u. Results of the more challenging setting are summarized in Table 3. While FixMatch and CoMatch fail to correct the severely biased prediction on unlabeled data caused by reversely ordered labeled data, RDA shows its superior performance in this setting and outperforms baseline methods significantly once again. As shown in Figs. 3(e) and 3(g), while imbalanced and mismatched C_x, C_u lead to strong bias on FixMatch's predictions, RDA shows extraordinary robustness to this scenario. Additionally, in

Table 3. Results of accuracy (%) with mismatched and imbalanced C_x, C_u (*i.e.*, alter both N_0 and γ at the same time). Baseline methods are based on our reimplementation. We omit the results of baselines that combine DA considering their poor performance.

Method	CIFAR-10				mini-ImageNet
	40 labels, $N_0 =10$		100 labels, $N_0 =40$		1000 labels, $N_0 =40$
	$\gamma = 2$	5	5	10	10
FixMatch	74.97±5.80	64.62±6.13	58.72±3.61	57.49±4.56	21.40±0.53
RDA	**88.58±4.05**	**79.90±2.80**	**79.33±1.37**	**70.93±2.91**	**25.99±0.19**

contrast to FixMatch, RDA effectively prevents the model from overfitting to the false pseudo-labels, as shown in Figs. 3(f) and 3(h).

Balanced C_x and Imbalanced C_u. As shown in Table 4, RDA shows the compatibility to this scenario and also outperforms baselines combining distribution alignment. Mismatched distributions caused by balanced C_x and imbalanced C_u also lead to poor performance of methods with original distribution alignment.

Table 4. Accuracy (%) on CIFAR-10 with balanced C_x and imbalanced C_u (*i.e.*, alter γ).

Method	40 labels, $\gamma = 200$
FixMatch w. DA	41.37±1.22
CoMatch	38.85±2.19
RDA	**46.50±1.07**

Other Mismatched Settings. We also show results of RDA within the DARP's protocol averaged on all five runs. As shown in Table 5, RDA consistently outperforms current class-imbalanced SSL method DARP [17] and shows the largest gains in all settings with mismatched C_x and C_u. More discussions on generalized settings of mismatched distributions can be found in Sec. D of Supplementary Material.

Table 5. Accuracy (%) under DARP's protocol (see Sec. C.1 of Supplementary Material for more details). WRN-28-2 is adopted as the backbone for all datasets.

Method	CIFAR-10 ($\gamma_l =100$)				STL-10 ($\gamma_l \neq \gamma_u$)	
	$\gamma_u = 1$	50	150	100 (reversed)	$\gamma_l = 10$	20
FixMatch	68.90±1.95	73.90±0.25	69.60±0.60	65.50±0.05	72.90±0.09	63.40±0.21
DARP	85.40±0.55	77.30±0.17	72.90±0.24	74.90±0.51	77.80±0.33	69.90±0.40
RDA	**93.35±0.24**	**79.77±0.06**	**74.48±0.24**	**79.25±0.52**	**87.21±0.44**	**83.21±0.52**

Table 6. Accuracy (%) of ablation studies on CIFAR-10 with two alternative alignment strategies. "/" represents the conventional setting and $\gamma = 1$ represents balanced C_u.

Method	40 labels			100 labels		
	$N_0, \gamma = /$	20,1	10, 5	/	80,1	40, 10
$\mathbb{E}_u(p) \Rightarrow \mathbb{E}_u(\overline{q})$	91.88±1.46	73.54±3.44	74.83±2.99	94.14±0.52	54.88±11.79	62.96±3.43
$\mathbb{E}_u(q) \Rightarrow \mathbb{E}_u(\overline{p})$	93.35±0.12	58.90±3.50	57.38±3.63	**94.60±0.08**	54.26±4.34	55.39±14.14
RDA	**94.13±1.22**	**81.78±6.44**	**79.90±2.88**	94.35±0.25	**79.00±2.67**	**70.93±2.91**

5.3 Ablation Study

To prove the effectiveness of each component in RDA, we conduct ablation studies on CIFAR-10 using consistent experimental setup with Sect. 4.4. We mainly conduct experiments in three settings described in Sect. 4.2 and change the strategy performing distribution alignment from each direction as follows:

$\mathbb{E}_u(p) \Rightarrow \mathbb{E}_u(\overline{q})$. We keep Eq. (13) and discard Eq. (14). *i.e.*, we align distribution of class predictions to "reversed" distribution of complementary predictions.

$\mathbb{E}_u(q) \Rightarrow \mathbb{E}_u(\overline{p})$. We keep Eq. (14) and discard Eq. (13). *i.e.*, we align distribution of complementary predictions to "reversed" distribution of class predictions.

As shown in Table 6, the performance of default RDA in mismatched distributions is dominant. RDA helps the model better maximize the objective Eq. (10) while obtaining helpful guidance information of class distribution without prior.

6 Conclusion

In this work, we propose a semi-supervised learning approach which is robust to both the conventional SSL and SSL in mismatched distributions. First, we describe a scenario that has not been discussed extensively by recently-proposed SSL work: mismatched distributions. Second, we improve distribution alignment by proposed RDA so that this technique could be applied into mismatched scenario safely. Then we show RDA results in a form of maximizing the input-out mutual information without any prior information. Finally, we demonstrate that our method outperforms existing baselines significantly under various scenarios.

Acknowledgements. This work is supported by projects from NSFC Major Program (62192783), CAAI-Huawei MindSpore (CAAIXSJLJJ-2021-042A), China Postdoctoral Science Foundation (2021M690609), Jiangsu NSF (BK20210224), and CCF-Lenovo Bule Ocean. Thanks to Prof. Penghui Yao's helpful discussions.

References

1. Arazo, E., Ortego, D., Albert, P., O'Connor, N.E., McGuinness, K.: Pseudo-labeling and confirmation bias in deep semi-supervised learning. In: International Joint Conference on Neural Networks (2020)

2. Berthelot, D., et al.: ReMixMatch: semi-supervised learning with distribution matching and augmentation anchoring. In: International Conference on Learning Representations (2020)
3. Berthelot, D., Carlini, N., Goodfellow, I., Papernot, N., Oliver, A., Raffel, C.A.: MixMatch: a holistic approach to semi-supervised learning. In: Advances in Neural Information Processing Systems (2019)
4. Bridle, J.S., Heading, A.J., MacKay, D.J.: Unsupervised classifiers, mutual information and 'phantom targets'. In: Advances in Neural Information Processing Systems (1992)
5. Chapelle, O., Scholkopf, B., Zien, A.: Semi-supervised learning. IEEE Trans. Neural Netw. **20**(3), 542–542 (2009)
6. Coates, A., Ng, A.Y., Lee, H.: An analysis of single-layer networks in unsupervised feature learning. In: International Conference on Artificial Intelligence and Statistics (2011)
7. Cubuk, E.D., Zoph, B., Shlens, J., Le, Q.: RandAugment: practical automated data augmentation with a reduced search space. In: Advances in Neural Information Processing Systems (2020)
8. Deng, J., Dong, W., Socher, R., Li, L.J., Li, K., Fei-Fei, L.: ImageNet: a large-scale hierarchical image database. In: IEEE/CVF Conference on Computer Vision and Pattern Recognition (2009)
9. Duan, Y., et al.: MutexMatch: semi-supervised learning with mutex-based consistency regularization. arXiv preprint arXiv:2203.14316 (2022)
10. Gong, C., Wang, D., Liu, Q.: AlphaMatch: improving consistency for semi-supervised learning with alpha-divergence. In: IEEE/CVF Conference on Computer Vision and Pattern Recognition (2021)
11. Grandvalet, Y., Bengio, Y.: Semi-supervised learning by entropy minimization. In: Advances in Neural Information Processing Systems (2005)
12. He, K., Zhang, X., Ren, S., Sun, J.: Deep residual learning for image recognition. In: IEEE/CVF Conference on Computer Vision and Pattern Recognition (2016)
13. Hernán, M.A., Robins, J.M.: Causal Inference: What If. Chapman & Hall/CRC, Boca Raton (2020)
14. Hofmann, H., Kafadar, K., Wickham, H.: Letter-value plots: boxplots for large data. Technical report (2011)
15. Ishida, T., Niu, G., Hu, W., Sugiyama, M.: Learning from complementary labels. In: Advances in Neural Information Processing Systems (2017)
16. Ishida, T., Niu, G., Menon, A.K., Sugiyama, M.: Complementary-label learning for arbitrary losses and models. In: International Conference on Machine Learning (2018)
17. Kim, J., Hur, Y., Park, S., Yang, E., Hwang, S.J., Shin, J.: Distribution aligning refinery of pseudo-label for imbalanced semi-supervised learning. In: Advances in Neural Information Processing Systems (2020)
18. Kim, Y., Yim, J., Yun, J., Kim, J.: NLNL: negative learning for noisy labels. In: IEEE/CVF International Conference on Computer Vision (2019)
19. Krizhevsky, A., Hinton, G., et al.: Learning multiple layers of features from tiny images. Technical report, University of Toronto (2009)
20. Lee, D.H., et al.: Pseudo-label: the simple and efficient semi-supervised learning method for deep neural networks. In: Workshop on Challenges in Representation Learning, International Conference on Machine Learning (2013)
21. Li, J., Xiong, C., Hoi, S.C.: CoMatch: semi-supervised learning with contrastive graph regularization. In: IEEE/CVF International Conference on Computer Vision (2021)

22. Rizve, M.N., Duarte, K., Rawat, Y.S., Shah, M.: In defense of pseudo-labeling: an uncertainty-aware pseudo-label selection framework for semi-supervised learning. In: International Conference on Learning Representations (2021)
23. Sohn, K., et al.: FixMatch: simplifying semi-supervised learning with consistency and confidence. In: Advances in Neural Information Processing Systems (2020)
24. Van Engelen, J.E., Hoos, H.H.: A survey on semi-supervised learning. Mach. Learn. **109**(2), 373–440 (2020)
25. Vinyals, O., Blundell, C., Lillicrap, T., Wierstra, D., et al.: Matching networks for one shot learning. In: Advances in Neural Information Processing Systems (2016)
26. Wei, C., Sohn, K., Mellina, C., Yuille, A., Yang, F.: CReST: a class-rebalancing self-training framework for imbalanced semi-supervised learning. In: IEEE/CVF Conference on Computer Vision and Pattern Recognition (2021)
27. Xu, Y., et al.: Dash: semi-supervised learning with dynamic thresholding. In: International Conference on Machine Learning (2021)
28. Yang, L., Zhuo, W., Qi, L., Shi, Y., Gao, Y.: Mining latent classes for few-shot segmentation. In: IEEE/CVF International Conference on Computer Vision, pp. 8721–8730 (2021)
29. Zagoruyko, S., Komodakis, N.: Wide residual networks. In: British Machine Vision Conference (2016)
30. Zhang, B., et al.: FlexMatch: boosting semi-supervised learning with curriculum pseudo labeling. In: Advances in Neural Information Processing Systems (2021)
31. Zhao, Z., Zhou, L., Wang, L., Shi, Y., Gao, Y.: LaSSL: label-guided self-training for semi-supervised learning. In: AAAI Conference on Artificial Intelligence (2022)
32. Zhu, X.: Semi-supervised learning. In: Encyclopedia of Machine Learning and Data Mining, pp. 1142–1147 (2017)

MemSAC: Memory Augmented Sample Consistency for Large Scale Domain Adaptation

Tarun Kalluri$^{(\boxtimes)}$, Astuti Sharma, and Manmohan Chandraker

University of California San Diego, La Jolla, CA 92093, USA
{sskallur,asharma,mkchandraker}@eng.ucsd.edu

Abstract. Practical real world datasets with plentiful categories introduce new challenges for unsupervised domain adaptation like small inter-
class discriminability, that existing approaches relying on domain invariance alone cannot handle sufficiently well. In this work we propose
MemSAC, which exploits sample level similarity across source and target domains to achieve discriminative transfer, along with architectures
that scale to a large number of categories. For this purpose, we first
introduce a memory augmented approach to efficiently extract pairwise
similarity relations between labeled source and unlabeled target domain
instances, suited to handle an arbitrary number of classes. Next, we
propose and theoretically justify a novel variant of the contrastive loss
to promote local consistency among within-class cross domain samples
while enforcing separation between classes, thus preserving discriminative transfer from source to target. We validate the advantages of Mem-
SAC with significant improvements over previous state-of-the-art on multiple challenging transfer tasks designed for large-scale adaptation, such
as DomainNet with 345 classes and fine-grained adaptation on Caltech-
UCSD birds dataset with 200 classes. We also provide in-depth analysis
and insights into the effectiveness of MemSAC. Code is available on the
project webpage https://tarun005.github.io/MemSAC.

1 Introduction

It is well known that deep neural networks often do not generalize well when
the distribution of test samples differ significantly from those in training.
Unsupervised domain adaptation seeks to improve transferability in the presence of such domain shift, for which a variety of approaches have been proposed [3–6,13,18,20,24,38–41,43,54,60–62,72]. Despite impressive gains, most
approaches have been largely demonstrated on datasets with a limited number
of categories [48,50].

We first ask the question of whether existing domain adaptation methods
scale to a large number of categories. Surprisingly, the answer is usually no.

Supplementary Information The online version contains supplementary material
available at https://doi.org/10.1007/978-3-031-20056-4_32.

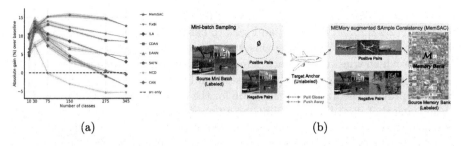

(a)   (b)

Fig. 1. (a) Accuracy(%) of various methods proposed for unsupervised domain adaptation with respect to the number of training classes from DomainNet [47] ($\mathbf{R}{\rightarrow}\mathbf{C}$). While most methods perform equally well for smaller number of categories (10–30), the benefits diminish with increasing number of classes in the dataset, to the extent that the performance drops *even below the source-only baseline* for few methods. In contrast, proposed MemSAC obtains significant gains ($\sim$15%) even on large scale datasets with many classes [47]. (b) **MEMory augmented SAmple Consistency (MemSAC)** The proposed method uses a memory bank and a sample consistency loss to identify source samples across a large number of categories that likely belong to the same class as an unlabeled target example, then pulls them together in feature space while pushing away samples from all other classes. Notice that without the proposed feature aggregation, a target anchor sample might not find any positive pairs ($\emptyset$) leading to noisy consistency estimates.

To illustrate this, consider Fig. 1a, which plots the absolute gain over a source-only model obtained by well-known adaptation methods (including DANN [20], MCD [55], SAFN [72], CAN [32], FixBi [43]) with respect to number of classes sampled from the DomainNet dataset [47]. While all methods provide similar benefits over a source-only model in smaller-scale settings with 10–30 classes, the gains reduce significantly when faced with a few hundred classes, where accuracies may even become *worse than a source-only model.*

We postulate that the above limitations with a larger number of categories arise due to lower inter-class separation and a greater possibility of negative transfer. Our key design choices stem from simple yet effective mechanisms developed in other areas such as self-supervised learning that can significantly benefit many-class domain adaptation. The resulting method, MemSAC (MEMory augmented SAmple Consistency), achieves impressive performance gains to establish new state-of-the-art on datasets such as DomainNet (345 classes) and CUB (200 classes). In the same illustration above, MemSAC obtains large improvements of 14.6% over a source-only baseline for 275 classes and 12.7% for 345 classes.

Our first insight for many-class domain adaptation pertains to class confusion, where several classes possibly look similar to each other. Classical adversarial approaches [20,32,55,71,72] which rely on domain alignment alone do not acknowledge this, giving rise to negative transfer as two seemingly close classes might align with each other. This problem is exacerbated in the extreme case of fine-grained datasets, where all the classes look similar to each other. On the other hand, class specific alignment strategies [18,32,43,46,54] suffer from noisy psuedo-labels leading to poor transfer. We observe that the contrastive loss is shown to be highly successful in learning better transferable features [11,12,22,23,27,29,42,70] and seek to extend those benefits to many-class domain adaptation. We achieve this with a novel *cross-domain sample consistency* loss which tries to align each sample in source domain with related samples in target domain, achieving tighter clusters and improved adaptation in the process. We provide theoretical justification for the effectiveness of our proposed loss by showing that it is akin to minimizing an upper bound to the input-consistency regularization recently proposed in [68], thereby ensuring that locally consistent prediction provides accuracy guarantees on unlabeled target data for unsupervised domain adaptation.

Our second insight pertains to architectural choices for training with a large number of categories. While having access to plentiful positive and negative pairwise relations per training iteration is desirable to infer local structure, the number of possible pairs are inherently restricted by the batch-size which is in turn limited by the GPU memory. We efficiently tackle this challenge in MemSAC by augmenting the adaptation framework with a lightweight, non-parametric memory module. Distinct from prior works [27,67], the memory module in our setting aggregates the *labeled* source domain features from multiple recent mini-batches, thus providing *unlabeled* target domain anchors meaningful interactions from sizeable positive and negative pairs even with reasonably small batch sizes that do not incur explosive growth in memory (Fig. 1b). Our architecture scales remarkably well with the number of categories, including the case of fine-grained adaptation [66] where all classes belong to a single subordinate category [7,77]. Moreover, MemSAC incurs negligible overhead in terms of speed and GPU memory during training and testing, making it an attractive choice for real-world usage of large-scale adaptation.

To summarize, in contrast to prior works, MemSAC achieves scalability in domain adaptation with a large number of classes. Our main contributions are:

1. A novel cross-domain sample consistency loss to enforce closer clustering of same category samples across source and target domains by exploiting pairwise relationships, thus achieving improved domain transfer even with many categories (Sect. 3.1).
2. A memory-based mechanism to handle limited batch-sizes by storing past features and effectively extracting similarity relations over a larger context for large scale datasets (Sect. 3.2).
3. Theoretical justification of the proposed losses in terms of the input-consistency regularization proposed in [68] for domain adaptation (Sect. 3.3).
4. A new state-of-the-art that outperforms all prior approaches by a significant margin on datasets with a large number of categories, such as 4.02% and 4.65% improvements in accuracy over the baseline which does not use our loss on the challenging DomainNet dataset with 345 categories and CUB-Drawings with 200 categories, respectively (Sect. 4).

2   Related Work

Unsupervised Domain Adaptation. A suite of tools have been proposed recently under the umbrella of unsupervised domain adaptation (UDA) that enable training on a labeled source domain and deploy models on a different target domain with few or no labels. A large body of these works aim to minimize some notion of divergence [3,4,50] between the source and target using an adversarial objective, resulting in domain invariant features [10,20,31,39,55,60–62,71]. Since domain invariance alone does not guarantee discriminative features in target [35], recent approaches propose class aware adaptation to align class conditional distributions across source and target [16,18,32,43,46,53,57,69,71]. ATT [53] assigns pseudo-labels based on predictions from classifiers, MADA [46] uses separate adversarial networks for each class, ILA [57] computes pairwise similarity between samples within a mini-batch for instance aware adaptation while SAFN [72] proposes re-normalizing features to achieve transferability. However, none of these works explicitly address the issue of scalability to adaptation with a large number of categories. Moreover, many clustering based methods [32,45] and instance based methods [57,65] proposed for UDA are not readily scalable to large datasets.

While partial adaptation [8,9,76], open set adaptation [44,56] and universal adaptation [52] allow training on real world source datasets with many categories, they are only focused on adaptation across those categories that are shared between source and target which are generally few in number, and do not address the problem of discriminative transfer across *all* the categories which is a different practical problem, and focus of this work.

Fine Grained Domain Adaptation. Fine grained visual categorization deals with classifying images that belong to a single subordinate category, such as birds, trees or animal species [63,64]. While fine grained classification on within domain samples has received much attention [7,37,58,77–80], the problem of unsupervised domain adaptation across fine-grained categories is relatively less studied [17,21,66,73]. All prior works often demand additional annotations in the form of attributes [21], weak supervision [17], part annotations [73] or hierarchical relationships [66] in one of the domains which might not be universally available. In contrast, we propose a method that performs fine-grained adaptation requiring no such additional knowledge.

Contrastive Learning. The success of contrastive learning [1,25,26,68] in extracting visual representations from data has attracted wide interest in self-supervised [11,12,15,22,23,27,29,42,70], semi-supervised [2] and supervised learning [34]. A unifying idea in those works is to encourage positive pairs, which are often augmented versions of the same image, to have similar representations in the feature space while pushing negative pairs far away. However, all those prior works assume that all positive and negative pairs in the contrastive loss come from the same domain. In contrast, we propose a variant of contrastive loss to handle multi-class discriminative transfer by enforcing sample consistency across similar samples extracted from different domains.

3   Unsupervised Adaptation Using MemSAC

Problem Description. In unsupervised domain adaptation, we have labeled samples $\mathcal{X}^s$ from a source domain with a corresponding source probability

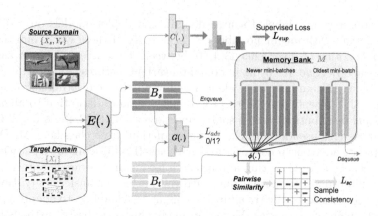

Fig. 2. An overview of MemSAC for domain adaptation During each iteration, the 256-dim source feature embeddings computed using $\mathcal{E}$, along with their labels, are added to a memory bank $\mathcal{M}$ and the oldest set of features are removed. Pairwise similarities between each target feature in mini-batch and all source features in memory bank are used to extract possible within-class and other-class source samples from the memory bank. Using the proposed consistency loss ($\mathcal{L}_{sc}$) on these similar and dissimilar pairs, along with adversarial loss ($\mathcal{L}_{adv}$), we achieve both local alignment and global adaptation.

distribution P_s, labeled according to a true labeling function f^*, and $\mathcal{Y}^s = f^*(\mathcal{X}^s)$. We are also given unlabeled data points $\mathcal{X}^t$ sampled according to the target distribution P_t. We follow a *covariate shift assumption* [3], where we assume that the marginal source and target distributions P_s and P_t are different, while the true labeling function f^* is same across the domains. The labels belong to a fixed category set $\mathcal{Y} = \{1, 2, \ldots, C\}$ with C different categories. Provided with this information, the goal of any learner is to output a predictor that achieves good accuracy on the target data $\mathcal{X}_t$. A key novelty in our instantiation of this framework lies in proposing an adaptation approach that works well even with a large number of classes C, by efficiently handling class confusion and discriminative transfer. The overview of the proposed architecture is shown in Fig. 2. $\mathcal{E}$ and $\mathcal{C}$ are the feature extractor and the classifier respectively. The objective function for MemSAC is given by

$$\min_{\theta} \mathcal{L}_{sup}(\mathcal{X}^s, \mathcal{Y}^s; \theta) + \lambda_{adv}\mathcal{L}_{adv}(\mathcal{X}^s, \mathcal{X}^t; \theta) + \lambda_{sc}\mathcal{L}_{sc}(\mathcal{X}^s, \mathcal{Y}^s, \mathcal{X}^t; \theta), \quad (1)$$

where $\mathcal{L}_{sup}$ is the supervised loss on source data, or the cross-entropy loss between the predicted class probability distributions and ground truths computed on source data. $\mathcal{L}_{adv}$ is the domain adversarial loss which we implement using a class conditional discriminator (Eq. 2) and $\mathcal{L}_{sc}$ is our novel cross-domain sample-consistency loss which is used to enforce the local similarity (or dissimilarity) between samples from source and target domains (Eq. 4). λ_{adv} and λ_{sc} are the corresponding loss coefficients. We use $\mathcal{B}_s(\in \mathcal{X}^s)$ and $\mathcal{B}_t(\in \mathcal{X}^t)$ to denote labeled source and unlabeled target mini-batches respectively, which are chosen randomly at each iteration from the dataset.

Class Conditional Adversarial Loss. We adopt the widely used adversarial strategy to learn domain-invariant feature representations using a domain discriminator $\mathcal{G}(.,\omega)$ parametrized by ω. To address the novel challenges presented by the current setting with large number of classes, we adopt the multilinear conditioning proposed in CDAN [39] to fuse information from the deep features as well as the classifier predictions. Denoting $f = \mathcal{E}(x)$ and $g = \mathcal{C}(\mathcal{E}(x))$, the input $h(x)$ to the discriminator $\mathcal{G}$ is given by $h(x) = T_\otimes(g, f)(x) = f(x) \otimes g(x)$, where $\otimes$ refers to the multilinear product (or flattened outer product) between the feature embedding and the softmax output of the classifier. The discriminator and adversarial losses are then computed as

$$\mathcal{L}_d = \frac{1}{|\mathcal{B}_s|} \sum_{i \in \mathcal{B}_s} -\log(\mathcal{G}(h_i;\omega)) + \frac{1}{|\mathcal{B}_t|} \sum_{i \in \mathcal{B}_t} -\log(1 - \mathcal{G}(h_i;\omega)) \qquad \mathcal{L}_{adv} = -\mathcal{L}_d. \quad (2)$$

We note that our contributions are complementary to the type of alignment objective used. In Table 3, we show significant gains starting from another adversarial objective (DANN [20]) and MMD objectives (CAN [33]) as well.

3.1 Cross Domain Sample Consistency

To achieve category specific transfer from source to target, we propose using much finer sample-level information to enforce consistency between similar samples, while also separating dissimilar samples across domains. Since our final goal is to transfer the class discriminative capability from source to target, we define the notions of similarity and dissimilarity as follows. For each target sample x_t from a target mini-batch $\mathcal{B}_t$ as the anchor, we construct a *similar set* $\mathcal{B}_{s+}^{x_t} = \{x \in \mathcal{B}_s | f^*(x) = f^*(x_t)\}$ and dissimilar set $\mathcal{B}_{s-}^{x_t} = \mathcal{B}_s \setminus \mathcal{B}_{s+}^{x_t}$ consisting of source samples and use this knowledge of sample-level similarity in the following *sample consistency loss*

$$\mathcal{L}_{sc,\mathcal{B}} = \frac{1}{|\mathcal{B}_t|} \sum_{j \in \mathcal{B}_t} -\log \left\{ \sum_{i \in \mathcal{B}_{s+}^j} \frac{\exp(\phi_{ij}/\tau)}{\sum_{i \in \mathcal{B}_s} \exp(\phi_{ij}/\tau)} \right\} \quad (3)$$

where ϕ_{ij} measures the cosine similarity metric between two feature vectors i and j, $(\phi_{ij} = \phi(f_i, f_j) = \frac{f_i \cdot f_j}{||f_i|| ||f_j||})$ and τ is the temperature parameter used to scale the contributions of positive and negative pairs [11,30]. $\mathcal{L}_{sc,\mathcal{B}}$ denotes the sample consistency loss computed using the mini-batch. Distinct from standard constrative loss [11,42] that typically derives positive pairs from augmented versions of the same image, our loss in Eq. (3) is well-suited to handle multiple positive and negative pairs for each anchor, similar to SupCon loss [34]. However, in contrast to SupCon, our modified consistency loss allows us to scale domain adaptation to many-class settings.

kNN-Based Pseudo-labeling. There are two challenges in directly using the sample consistency loss in (3). Firstly, unlike prior approaches [11,29,42] that use random transformations of same image to construct positives and negatives, the target data in unsupervised domain adaptation is completely unlabeled, so we do not have the similarity information readily ($f^*(x_t)$ is unknown). To address this issue, we use a k-NN based psuedo-labeling trick for all the target samples in a mini-batch. In every iteration of the training, for each target sample x_t from the target training mini-batch $\mathcal{B}_t$, we find k nearest neighbors from the source training mini-batch $\mathcal{B}_s$, which are computed using the feature similarity scores ϕ_{i,x_t}. x_t is then assigned the label corresponding to the majority class occurring among its neighbors. We use a value of $k=5$. Such an approach for psuedo-labeling is independent of, thus less sensitive to, noisy classifier boundaries helping us extract reliable target psuedo-labels during training. Once $\mathcal{B}_t$ is psuedo-labeled, it is straightforward to compute $\mathcal{B}_{s+}^{x_t}$ in (3). The second challenge is lack of representation for all classes in a mini-batch, which we address next.

3.2   Memory Augmented Similarity Extraction

From Eq. (3), we can observe that if the source and target mini-batches $\mathcal{B}_s$ and $\mathcal{B}_t$ contain completely non-intersecting classes, then the pseudo labeling of targets and the subsequent sample consistency loss would be noisy and lead to negative impact. This problem is exacerbated in our setting with a large number of classes, as randomly sampled $\mathcal{B}_s$ and $\mathcal{B}_t$ usually contain images with mutually non-intersecting categories. While one solution is to increase the size of mini-batch, it comes with significant growth in memory which is not scalable.

Therefore, we propose using a non-parametric memory bank $\mathcal{M}$ that aggregates the computation-free features, along with the corresponding labels, across multiple past mini-batches from the source dataset. We note that if the size of the memory bank $|\mathcal{M}|$ is sufficiently large, then source samples from all the classes would be adequately present in $\mathcal{M}$, providing us with authentic positive and negative samples for use in the sample consistency loss. Furthermore, since the memory overhead of storing the features in the memory bank itself is negligible (we only store the computation-free features), proposed adaptation approach can be scaled to handle arbitrarily large number of classes, as datasets with larger classes only requires us to correspondingly increase the size of $\mathcal{M}$, thus decoupling the similarity computation with mini-batch size or dataset size. Different from prior approaches that augment training with memory module [27,67,70], our approach aggregates features from multiple source batches, thus helping target samples to extract meaningful pairwise relationships from different classes.

Initializing and Updating Memory Bank. To initialize the memory bank, we first bootstrap the feature extractor for few hundred iterations by training only using $\mathcal{L}_{sup}$ and $\mathcal{L}_{adv}$ losses, and then introduce our consistency loss $\mathcal{L}_{sc}$ and start populating $\mathcal{M}$. After this, we follow a queue based approach for updating the memory bank similar to XBM [67]. In each iteration, We remove (*dequeue*) the oldest batch of features from the queue and insert (*enqueue*) the fresh mini-batch of source features (computed as $\{\mathcal{E}(x)|x \in \mathcal{B}_s\}$) along with the corresponding source labels. Alternative strategies for updating $\mathcal{M}$, such as a momentum encoder [27], yield similar results (details in the supplementary).

Sample Consistency Using Memory Bank. We can now use $\mathcal{M}$ as a proxy for $\mathcal{B}_s$ (and similar set $\mathcal{M}_+^{x_t}$ as a proxy for $\mathcal{B}_{s+}^{x_t}$) in assigning the target psuedo labels and in the sample consistency loss in (3). $|\mathcal{M}|$ is often much higher than $|\mathcal{B}_s|$, so access to larger number of source samples from $\mathcal{M}$ provides k-NN pseudo labels that are more reliable, with richer variety of positive and negative pairwise relations (more details in the supplementary). The final sample consistency loss used in MemSAC is

$$\mathcal{L}_{sc} = \frac{1}{|\mathcal{B}_t|} \sum_{j \in \mathcal{B}_t} - \log \left\{ \sum_{i \in \mathcal{M}_+^j} \frac{\exp(\phi_{ij}/\tau)}{\sum_{i \in \mathcal{M}} \exp(\phi_{ij}/\tau)} \right\}. \tag{4}$$

3.3 Theoretical Insight

Recently, Wei et al. [68] provide theoretical validation for contrastive learning. Specifically, under an *expansion* assumption which states that class conditional distribution of data is locally continuous, they bound the target error of a classifier C parametrized by θ by encouraging consistent predictions on neighboring examples. The regularization objective $R(\theta)$ is given by $R(\theta) \equiv \min_\theta \mathbb{E}_x[\max_{x' \in \mathcal{N}(x)} \mathbf{1}(C(x;\theta) \neq C(x';\theta))]$, where $\mathcal{N}(x)$ is the neighborhood of a sample x (Eq 1.2 in [68]). We now show the connections that can be drawn between our loss and the theory proposed in [68]. For this purpose, we work with the following approximations. Firstly, we approximate the neighborhood $\mathcal{N}(x)$ of a sample x with the *similar set* defined in Sect. 3.1, that is $\mathcal{N}(x) = \mathcal{B}_+^x$. Next, we approximate the hard condition that the classifier outputs of two images be equal $\mathbf{1}(C(x;\theta) \neq C(x';\theta))$, with the soft probability $\mathbf{Pr}(C(x;\theta) \neq C(x';\theta))$. Starting with the above objective, we have

$$\max_{x' \in \mathcal{N}(x)} \mathbf{1}(C(x;\theta) \neq C(x';\theta))$$

$$\leq \sum_{x' \in \mathcal{N}(x)} \mathbf{Pr}(C(x;\theta) \neq C(x';\theta))$$

$$\approx |\mathcal{B}_+^x| - \sum_{x' \in \mathcal{B}_+^x} \mathbf{Pr}(C(x;\theta) = C(x';\theta))$$

$$\leq |\mathcal{B}_+^x| - \sum_{x' \in \mathcal{B}_+^x} \frac{\exp(\phi_{x,x'})}{\sum_{x' \in \mathcal{B}} \exp(\phi(x,x'))}$$

$$\implies R(\theta) \equiv \max_\theta \mathbb{E}_x \left[\sum_{x' \in \mathcal{B}_+^x} \frac{\exp(\phi_{x,x'})}{\sum_{x' \in \mathcal{B}} \exp(\phi(x,x'))} \right]$$

where we used the softmax similarity between samples x, x' in the feature space as a proxy for the equality of their classifier outputs and changed max to sum with the bound. Under these specific assumptions, we can now see that the input-regularization objective $R(\theta)$ is strongly reminiscent of our sample consistency loss. Using Eq. (4), we minimize the negative log-likelihood of the similarity probability, which is equivalent to maximizing the similarity probability of like samples. Therefore, our sample consistency objective is akin to minimizing an upper bound on the input consistency regularization proposed in [68]. Furthermore, optimizing such an objective is shown to achieve bounded target error for unsupervised domain adaptation. Specifically, under the assumption that the psuedo label accuracy on target data is above a certain threshold, [68] showed that bounded error on target data is achievable using the consistency regularization (Theorem 4.3). In MemSAC, we realize this assumption by first training the feature extractor only using supervised ($\mathcal{L}_{sup}$) and adversarial ($\mathcal{L}_{adv}$) losses as explained in Sect. 3.2 before introducing our proposed sample consistency loss. To the best of our knowledge, we are the first to instantiate the regularization proposed in [68] for large scale domain adaptation, and showcase its effectiveness in achieving significant empirical gains.

4   Experiments and Analysis

Datasets. Consistent with the key motivations that distinguish MemSAC from prior literature in domain adaptation, we focus on large-scale datasets with many categories to underline its benefits.

DomainNet [47] is a large-scale dataset for UDA covering 6 domains and a total of 500k images from 345 different categories. It is an order of magnitude larger compared to prior benchmarks and serves as a useful testbed for evaluating many-class adaptation models. We follow the protocol established in prior works [49,51,59] to use data from 4 domains, namely real (**R**), clipart (**C**), sketch (**S**) and painting (**P**), showing results on all 12 transfer tasks across these 4 domains. In the supplementary material, we also provide results using a 126-class subset of DomainNet which contains much lesser label noise [36,51,75]. Nevertheless, our benefits persist on both these splits.

CUB (Caltech-UCSD birds) [64] is a challenging dataset originally proposed for fine-grained classification of 200 categories of birds, while *CUB-Drawings* [66] consists of paintings corresponding to the 200 categories of birds in CUB. We use this dataset pair, consisting of 14k images in total, for evaluation of adaptation on images with fine-grained categories. This setting can be challenging as appearance variations across species can be subtle, while pose variations within a class can be high. Thus, discriminative transfer requires precisely mapping category-specific information from source to target to avoid negative transfer. Results on other fine-grained datasets like Birds-123 and CompCars [74] are present in the supplementary material.

Training Details. We use a Resnet-50 [28] backbone pretrained on Imagenet, followed by a projection layer as the encoder $\mathcal{E}$ to obtain 256 dimensional feature embeddings. The discriminator $\mathcal{G}$ is implemented using an MLP with two hidden layers of 1024 dimensions. We use a standard batch size of 32 for both source

Table 1. Accuracy scores on DomainNet-345 using Resnet-50 backbone. Best values are in **bold** and the next best are underlined. MemSAC performs better than all other methods on most of the tasks. [†]Uses hierarchical label annotation. [‡]prediction uses ensemble classifiers. [§]Uses class-balanced sampling.

Source target	Real→			Clipart→			Painting→			Sketches→			Avg.
	C	P	S	R	P	S	R	C	S	R	C	P	
ResNet-50	41.61	42.79	29.66	42.41	27.24	32.15	49.52	32.55	26.73	38.75	40.89	27.5	35.98
MSTN [71]	27.25	32.98	24.35	28.17	21.14	24.15	30.74	19.85	22.5	24.31	26.22	23.56	25.44
RSDA [24]	27.28	35.83	24.35	36.98	24.94	31.12	41.32	26.1	24.71	29.46	26.22	27.79	29.68
BSP [13]	34.51	39.14	27.57	40.56	26.71	30.72	40.83	24.56	25.7	36.54	32.37	28.08	32.37
MCD [55][‡]	36.34	36.58	24.95	40.32	25.83	32.12	43.65	29.66	25.7	34.16	39.11	26.89	32.94[‡]
ILADA [57][§]	46.45	39.01	35.4	47.94	26.68	36.33	43.00	26.62	27.3	48.85	47.68	32.23	38.12[§]
SAFN [72]	38.11	45.96	29.20	45.96	30.00	34.65	54.44	34.74	30.64	45.29	47.43	38.01	39.54
DANN [20]	45.93	44.51	35.47	46.85	30.52	36.77	48.02	34.76	32.15	47.1	46.45	38.47	40.58
CAN [32][§]	40.71	37.77	33.7	**54.93**	31.41	37.37	51.05	33.64	30.95	52.13	42.19	32.04	39.82[§]
PAN [66][†]	49.25	48.18	36.46	49.66	33.27	38.78	51.89	36.01	32.94	49.12	50.94	39.89	43.03 [†]
CDAN [39]	50.15	48.35	39.01	50.02	33.39	39.3	52.21	36.44	33.68	48.46	49.27	38.65	43.24
HDAN [16]	46.30	47.52	34.39	49.91	33.98	37.98	55.26	40.82	32.77	49.04	49.77	40.04	43.15
FixBi [43][‡]	51.18	49.19	39.65	50.02	34.59	41.17	52.21	36.44	33.68	50.84	53.51	41.67	44.51[‡]
ToAlign [69]	50.82	50.72	35.17	49.52	33.88	41.41	57.92	43.51	36.29	47.96	**55.46**	41.61	45.45
MemSAC [Ours]	**54.34**$^{\pm.5}$	**52.27**$^{\pm.3}$	**41.74**$^{\pm.3}$	54.4$^{\pm.3}$	**36.87**$^{\pm.4}$	**42.45**$^{\pm.0}$	53.24$^{\pm.2}$	41.39$^{\pm.4}$	**37.22**$^{\pm.2}$	**53.33**$^{\pm.3}$	55.31$^{\pm.2}$	**44.56**$^{\pm.3}$	**47.26**
Tgt. Supervised	72.50	62.66	65.12	80.92	62.66	65.12	80.92	72.50	65.12	80.92	72.50	62.66	70.32

and target in all experiments and for all methods. The reported accuracies are computed on the complete unlabeled target data for CUB-200 dataset following established protocol for UDA [39,55,66,72], and the provided testset for Domain-Net. The crucial hyper-parameters in our method are λ_{sc}, temperature τ and memory bank size $|\mathcal{M}|$. For all datasets, we choose $\lambda_{sc} = 0.1$ and $\tau = 0.07$ based on the adaptation performance on the $C \rightarrow D$ setting on the CUB-200 dataset. We use a memory bank size of 48k on DomainNet dataset, but 24k on CUB-200 dataset owing to its smaller size. For experiments on MemSAC, we report mean and standard deviation over 3 random seeds. We compare MemSAC against traditional adversarial approaches (DANN [20], CDAN [39], MCD [55]) as well as the current state-of-the art (SAFN [72], BSP [13], RSDA [24], CAN [32], ILADA [57], FixBi [43], HDAN [16] and ToAlign [69]).

MemSAC Significantly Outperforms Others on Many-Class Adaptation. The results for the 12 transfer tasks on DomainNet are provided in Table 1. Firstly, methods such as RSDA (29.68%) and SAFN (39.54%) that achieve best performance on smaller scale datasets (like Office-31 [50] and visDA-2017 [48]) provide only marginal or no benefits over the more traditional adversarial approaches such as DANN (40.58%) and CDAN (43.24%) on DomainNet with 345 classes, indicating that large-scale datasets need different techniques for adaptation. Next, we compare against PAN [66], which requires a label hierarchy as additional information for training. For this supervision, we use the one level of hierarchy proposed in DomainNet [47]. Even when provided with access to hierarchical grouping labels in source, PAN (43.03%) achieves no improvement over CDAN (43.24%). In contrast, our method MemSAC that combines global adaptation using a conditional adversarial approach and local alignment using sample consistency to alleviate negative achieves an average accuracy of 47.26%, with a significantly better performance than all the prior approaches across most

Table 2. Results on fine-grained adaptation on 200 categories from CUB-Drawings dataset. Bold and underline indicate the best and second best methods respectively. †Uses hierarchical label annotation. §Uses class-balanced sampling.

	Resnet-50	MCD [55]	SAFN [72]	CAN§ [32]	RSDA [24]	DANN [20]	HDAN [16]	FixBi [43]	CDAN [39]	ToAlign [69]	PAN† [66]	MemSAC
C → D	60.88	50.18	60.29	52.18	61.04	62.09	60.25	68.20	68.12	64.43	70.53	**73.97**
D → C	42.07	38.56	41.34	50.05	44.20	47.73	52.40	49.47	53.83	50.54	55.38	**61.94**
Avg.	51.47	44.37	50.82	51.11	52.62	54.91	56.33	58.84	60.98	57.48	62.96	**67.95**

of the tasks. These trends and benefits also hold for the 126-class version of the DomainNet dataset, and results are presented in the supplementary material.

MemSAC Achieves New State-of-the-Art in Fine-Grained Adaptation. We also illustrate the benefit of using MemSAC for adaptation on fine-grained categories in Table 2 on the CUB-Drawings dataset. Although fine-grained visual recognition is a well-studied area [7,14,19,77,78], domain adaptation for fine grained categories is a relevant but less-addressed problem. Notably, methods like MCD, SAFN and RSDA perform worse or only marginally better than a source only baseline. PAN [66] uses supervised hierarchical label relations in source across 3 levels and obtains an average accuracy of 62.96%, while MemSAC obtains a state-of-the art accuracy of 67.95% using only single level source labels, thus outperforming all prior approaches on this challenging setting with minimal assumptions. This underlines the benefit of enforcing sample consistency using MemSAC for adaptation even in the presence of fine-grained categories in order to effectively counter negative alignment issues.

MemSAC Complements Multiple Adaptation Methods. The proposed memory-augmented consistency loss is generic enough to improve many adaptation backbones. As shown in Table 3 for the case of R→C and C→R transfer tasks from DomainNet, MemSAC can be used with most adversarial as well as MMD based approaches. MemSAC improves adversarial approaches DANN and CDAN by 3.35% and 4.29% respectively, and MMD-based approach CAN by 1.75% indicating that our proposed framework is competitive yet complementary to many existing adaptation approaches. Complete table for all the 12 transfer tasks is provided in supplementary material.

MemSAC Improves Adaptation Even with Larger Backbones. We employ Resnet-101 as a backbone in Table 3 and compare against other adaptation approaches with the same backbone. We note that the benefits obtained by MemSAC over prior adaptation approaches also hold for larger backbones, as shown for R→C and C→R of DomainNet dataset, and complete table containing results on all transfer tasks is presented in the supplementary material.

4.1   Analysis and Discussion

Ablation Studies. We show the influence of various design choices of our method in Table 4 on the CUB-200 dataset. First, we show in Table 4a that both the global domain adversarial method, which we implement using CDAN,

Table 3. MemSAC is also complementary to most adversarial and adaptation methods, as shown in (a). We show the results using a larger backbone (Resnet-101) for training in (b). MemSAC adds negligible memory and time overhead to the training even with large queues, and zero overhead during inference, as shown in (c)

(a) MemSAC complements existing UDA methods.

	R→C	C→R	Avg.
DANN [20]	45.93	46.85	46.39
DANN+MemSAC	49.67	49.81	**49.74**(+3.35%)
CAN [32]	40.71	54.93	47.82
CAN+MemSAC	43.79	55.36	**49.57**(+1.75%)
CDAN [39]	50.15	50.02	50.08
CDAN+MemSAC	54.34	54.40	**54.37**(+4.29%)

(b) Results using Resnet-101 backbone

	R→C	C→R	Avg.
Resnet-101	45.62	41.96	43.79
DANN [20]	47.71	48.33	48.02
MCD [55]	41.11	40.77	40.94
CDAN [39]	52.47	46.63	49.55
SAFN [72]	44.93	37.20	41.06
ToAlign [69]	50.09	50.23	50.16
MemSAC	**56.25**	**53.52**	**54.88**

(c) Training times of various methods.

Method	Peak GPU Mem.	Training Time	Avg. Acc
DANN	7.9GB	11.7 Hrs	40.58%
CDAN	8.2GB	12 Hrs	43.24%
PAN	8.9GB	16.2 Hrs	43.03%
ToAlign	9.22GB	24.21 Hrs	45.45%
MemSAC	8.5GB	12.63 Hrs	47.26%

as well as local sample level consistency loss are important to achieve best accuracy, as evident from the drop in accuracy without either of those components. Next, we investigate the effect of the temperature parameter τ in Table 4b which we use to suitably scale the contributions of positive and negative pairs in $\mathcal{L}_{sc}$ loss function (Eq. (4)). We find that $\tau = 0.07$ gives the best performance on the cosine similarity metric. Finally, in Table 4c, we note that the performance using other choices of the similarity function $\phi(.)$, namely *Euclidean* similarity and *Gaussian* similarity is inferior to using *Cosine* similarity. We also observed that *cosine* similarity is more stable to train under severe domain shifts.

Why Does MemSAC Help with Large Number of Classes? We propose our sample consistency loss in (4) to encourage tighter clustering of samples within each class, which is important in many-class datasets where class confusion is a significant problem. The main motivation of the proposed sample consistency loss is to bring within-class samples (that is, samples from the same class across source and target domains) closer to each other, so that a source classifier can be transferred to the target. To understand this further, in Fig. 3, we plot the *mean similarity score* during the training process. We define the *mean similarity score* as $\sum_{i \in \mathcal{M}_+^j} \phi_{ij}$, averaged over all the target samples $j \in \mathcal{B}_t$ in a mini-batch, which indicates the affinity score between same-class samples across domains. We observe that using the proposed loss, the similarity score is much higher and improves with training compared to the baseline without the consistency loss, which reflects in the overall accuracy (Table 1, Table 2).

MemSAC Achieves Larger Gains with Finer-Grained Classes. We show the appreciating benefits provided by MemSAC as the fine-grainedness of the dataset becomes more pronounced. For this purpose, we chose the 4 levels of label hierarchy provided by PAN [66] on the CUB-Drawings dataset. The levels L3, L2, L1 and L0 contain different granularity of bird species, grouped into 14, 38, 122 and 200 classes, respectively. The L0 level contains the finest separation of classes, while the level L3 with 14 classes contains the coarsest separation. We observe from Fig. 4 that with coarser granularity, MemSAC performs as good as the baseline method CDAN, whereas with finer separation of the categories

Table 4. Ablation results. Effect of (a) Loss coefficients, (b) temperature scaling, and (c) choice of similarity functions on accuracy of MemSAC on the CUB-Drawing adaptation.

(a) Effect of various compo-(b) Effect of the temper-(c) Accuracy using various nents of loss function in (1). ature τ in (4). choices for ϕ_{ij}.

Method	$\mathcal{L}_{adv}$	$\mathcal{L}_{sc}$	C→D	D→C	Avg. Acc
Source	✗	✗	60.88	42.07	51.47
CDAN	✓	✗	68.12	53.83	60.98
$\mathcal{L}_{sc}$ Only	✗	✓	64.45	41.13	52.79
MemSAC	✓	✓	**73.97**	**61.94**	**67.95**

τ	C→D	D→C	Avg. Acc
1.0	68.36	53.46	60.91
0.07	**73.97**	**61.94**	**67.95**
0.007	71.25	57.21	64.23

Similarity	ϕ_{ij}	C→D	D→C	Avg. Acc
Inv. Euc.	$(1+\|f_i - f_j\|^2)^{-1}$	71.00	57.21	64.23
Gaussian	$exp(-\|f_i - f_j\|^2)$	70.10	50.84	60.47
Cosine	$f_i \cdot f_j$	**73.97**	**61.94**	**67.95**

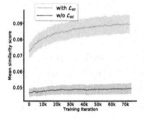 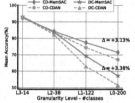 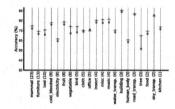

Fig. 3. Mean similarity score for *within-class* samples vs. training iteration shown for **D→C** on CUB-Drawings.

Fig. 4. Comparison of accuracy vs. granularity of labels on CUB-Drawings dataset for 4 levels of label hierarchy.

Fig. 5. Category wise gain/ drop in accuracy on **R→C** on DomainNet, compared to CDAN [39].

(L3 → L0), use of sample consistency loss provides much higher benefit (>3% improvement on both tasks). This confirms our intuition that sample level consistency benefits accuracies in fine-grained domain adaptation.

MemSAC Alleviates Class Confusion for Similar Classes. In Fig. 5 we use the DomainNet dataset to show the accuracies on every *coarse* category, along with the number of finer classes in each coarse category. We find that MemSAC provides consistent improvement over CDAN (marked by ↑) on most categories and any drops in accuracy (marked by ↓) are negligible. Our improvements are especially greater on categories with fine-grained classes like *trees (+13.3%)*, *vegetables (+6.7%)* and *birds (+5.6%)*, underlining the advantage of MemSAC to overcome class confusion within dense categories. Similar plots for other tasks in DomainNet are provided with the supplementary material.

Larger Memory Banks Improve Accuracy. A key design choice that we need to make in MemSAC is the size of the memory bank $\mathcal{M}$. Intuitively, small memory banks would not provide sufficient negative pairs in the sample consistency loss and lead to noisy gradients. We show in Fig. 6 for the two tasks in CUB-Drawings that accuracy indeed increases with larger sizes of memory banks (a memory size of 32, which is same as batch-size, indicates no memory at all and performs worse). We also find that the optimum capacity of the mem-

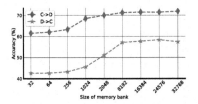

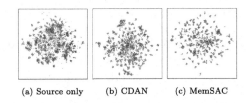

(a) Source only   (b) CDAN   (c) MemSAC

Fig. 6. Effect of memory bank size on CUB-Drawings dataset.

Fig. 7. tSNE for **R→C** on DomainNet. The two colors are source and target features. Notice improved alignment and feature separation with MemSAC.

ory bank may even be much higher than the size of the dataset. For example, the "drawing" domain has around 4k examples, but from Fig. 6, **D→C** achieves best accuracy at memory size of 25k. Since the feature encoder is simultaneously trained while updating memory bank, two copies of the same instance need not necessarily be exact duplicates of each other, but instead provide complementary "views" of the same sample. Thus, large queues help in enriching the positive and negative sample set, improving the accuracy (Fig. 7).

Computational Cost and Resources. We show the training time and GPU memory consumed for MemSAC compared to other baseline approaches in Table 3c. In summary, MemSAC incurs negligible overhead in memory during training and no overhead during inference even for large queues.

Limitations, Future Work and Impact. Although we report outstanding performance using MemSAC, we assume that the list of categories present in the data is known beforehand. Therefore, an avenue of future work is to relax this assumptions and extend MemSAC to open world adaptation approaches. While domain adaptation may have the positive impact of equitable performance of machine learning across geographic or social factors, MemSAC shares with other deep domain adaptation approaches the limitation of lack of explainability, which may have a negative impact on applications where decisions based on domain adaptation have a bearing on safety. We further note that significant room for improvement remains in achieving unsupervised domain adaptation that approach fully supervised performances.

5 Conclusion

We proposed MemSAC, a simple and effective approach for unsupervised domain adaptation designed to handle a large number of categories. We propose a sample consistency loss that pulls samples from similar classes across domains closer together, while pushing dissimilar samples further apart. Since minibatch sizes are limited, we devise a novel memory-based mechanism to effectively extract similarity relations for a large number of categories. We provide both theoretical intuition and empirical insights into the effectiveness of MemSAC for large-scale domain alignment and discriminative transfer. In extensive experiments and analysis across the main paper and supplementary, we showcase the strong improvements achieved by MemSAC over prior works, setting new state-of-the-arts across challenging many-class adaptation on DomainNet (126 and 345 classes) and fine-grained adaptation on CUB-Drawings (200 classes).

Acknowledgements. We thank NSF CAREER 1751365, NSF Chase-CI 1730158, Google Award for Inclusion Research and IPE PhD Fellowship.

References

1. Arora, S., Khandeparkar, H., Khodak, M., Plevrakis, O., Saunshi, N.: A theoretical analysis of contrastive unsupervised representation learning. arXiv preprint arXiv:1902.09229 (2019)
2. Assran, M., et al.: Semi-supervised learning of visual features by non-parametrically predicting view assignments with support samples. In: Proceedings of the IEEE/CVF International Conference on Computer Vision, pp. 8443–8452 (2021)
3. Ben-David, S., Blitzer, J., Crammer, K., Kulesza, A., Pereira, F., Vaughan, J.W.: A theory of learning from different domains. Mach. Learn. **79**(1–2), 151–175 (2010)
4. Ben-David, S., Blitzer, J., Crammer, K., Pereira, F.: Analysis of representations for domain adaptation. In: Advances in Neural Information Processing Systems, vol. 19, pp. 137–144 (2006)
5. Bousmalis, K., Silberman, N., Dohan, D., Erhan, D., Krishnan, D.: Unsupervised pixel-level domain adaptation with generative adversarial networks. In: Proceedings of the IEEE Conference on Computer Vision and Pattern Recognition, pp. 3722–3731 (2017)
6. Bousmalis, K., Trigeorgis, G., Silberman, N., Krishnan, D., Erhan, D.: Domain separation networks. In: Advances in Neural Information Processing Systems, pp. 343–351 (2016)
7. Branson, S., Van Horn, G., Belongie, S., Perona, P.: Bird species categorization using pose normalized deep convolutional nets. arXiv preprint arXiv:1406.2952 (2014)
8. Cao, Z., Long, M., Wang, J., Jordan, M.I.: Partial transfer learning with selective adversarial networks. In: Proceedings of the IEEE Conference on Computer Vision and Pattern Recognition, pp. 2724–2732 (2018)
9. Cao, Z., Ma, L., Long, M., Wang, J.: Partial adversarial domain adaptation. In: Proceedings of the European Conference on Computer Vision (ECCV), pp. 135–150 (2018)
10. Chen, C., et al.: Progressive feature alignment for unsupervised domain adaptation. In: Proceedings of the IEEE Conference on Computer Vision and Pattern Recognition, pp. 627–636 (2019)
11. Chen, T., Kornblith, S., Norouzi, M., Hinton, G.: A simple framework for contrastive learning of visual representations. arXiv preprint arXiv:2002.05709 (2020)
12. Chen, X., Fan, H., Girshick, R., He, K.: Improved baselines with momentum contrastive learning. arXiv preprint arXiv:2003.04297 (2020)
13. Chen, X., Wang, S., Long, M., Wang, J.: Transferability vs. discriminability: batch spectral penalization for adversarial domain adaptation. In: International Conference on Machine Learning, pp. 1081–1090. PMLR (2019)

14. Chen, Y., Bai, Y., Zhang, W., Mei, T.: Destruction and construction learning for fine-grained image recognition. In: Proceedings of the IEEE/CVF Conference on Computer Vision and Pattern Recognition, pp. 5157–5166 (2019)
15. Cole, E., Yang, X., Wilber, K., Mac Aodha, O., Belongie, S.: When does contrastive visual representation learning work? arXiv preprint arXiv:2105.05837 (2021)
16. Cui, S., Jin, X., Wang, S., He, Y., Huang, Q.: Heuristic domain adaptation. In: Advances in Neural Information Processing Systems, vol. 33, pp. 7571–7583. Curran Associates, Inc. (2020)
17. Cui, Y., Song, Y., Sun, C., Howard, A., Belongie, S.: Large scale fine-grained categorization and domain-specific transfer learning. In: Proceedings of the IEEE Conference on Computer Vision and Pattern Recognition, pp. 4109–4118 (2018)
18. Du, Z., Li, J., Su, H., Zhu, L., Lu, K.: Cross-domain gradient discrepancy minimization for unsupervised domain adaptation. In: The IEEE Conference on Computer Vision and Pattern Recognition (CVPR) (2021)
19. Dubey, A., Gupta, O., Raskar, R., Naik, N.: Maximum-entropy fine-grained classification. arXiv preprint arXiv:1809.05934 (2018)
20. Ganin, Y., Lempitsky, V.: Unsupervised domain adaptation by backpropagation. In: International Conference on Machine Learning, pp. 1180–1189. PMLR (2015)
21. Gebru, T., Hoffman, J., Fei-Fei, L.: Fine-grained recognition in the wild: a multi-task domain adaptation approach. In: Proceedings of the IEEE International Conference on Computer Vision, pp. 1349–1358 (2017)
22. Gordon, D., Ehsani, K., Fox, D., Farhadi, A.: Watching the world go by: representation learning from unlabeled videos. arXiv preprint arXiv:2003.07990 (2020)
23. Grill, J.B., et al.: Bootstrap your own latent: a new approach to self-supervised learning. arXiv preprint arXiv:2006.07733 (2020)
24. Gu, X., Sun, J., Xu, Z.: Spherical space domain adaptation with robust pseudo-label loss. In: Proceedings of the IEEE/CVF Conference on Computer Vision and Pattern Recognition, pp. 9101–9110 (2020)
25. Gutmann, M., Hyvärinen, A.: Noise-contrastive estimation: a new estimation principle for unnormalized statistical models. In: Proceedings of the Thirteenth International Conference on Artificial Intelligence and Statistics, pp. 297–304 (2010)
26. Hadsell, R., Chopra, S., LeCun, Y.: Dimensionality reduction by learning an invariant mapping. In: 2006 IEEE Computer Society Conference on Computer Vision and Pattern Recognition (CVPR 2006), vol. 2, pp. 1735–1742. IEEE (2006)
27. He, K., Fan, H., Wu, Y., Xie, S., Girshick, R.: Momentum contrast for unsupervised visual representation learning. In: Proceedings of the IEEE/CVF Conference on Computer Vision and Pattern Recognition, pp. 9729–9738 (2020)
28. He, K., Zhang, X., Ren, S., Sun, J.: Deep residual learning for image recognition. In: Proceedings of the IEEE Conference on Computer Vision and Pattern Recognition, pp. 770–778 (2016)
29. Hénaff, O.J., et al.: Data-efficient image recognition with contrastive predictive coding. arXiv preprint arXiv:1905.09272 (2019)
30. Hinton, G., Vinyals, O., Dean, J.: Distilling the knowledge in a neural network. arXiv preprint arXiv:1503.02531 (2015)
31. Kalluri, T., Varma, G., Chandraker, M., Jawahar, C.: Universal semi-supervised semantic segmentation. In: Proceedings of the IEEE International Conference on Computer Vision, pp. 5259–5270 (2019)
32. Kang, G., Jiang, L., Yang, Y., Hauptmann, A.G.: Contrastive adaptation network for unsupervised domain adaptation. In: Proceedings of the IEEE Conference on Computer Vision and Pattern Recognition, pp. 4893–4902 (2019)

33. Kang, G., Zheng, L., Yan, Y., Yang, Y.: Deep adversarial attention alignment for unsupervised domain adaptation: the benefit of target expectation maximization. In: Proceedings of the European Conference on Computer Vision (ECCV), pp. 401–416 (2018)
34. Khosla, P., et al.: Supervised contrastive learning. arXiv preprint arXiv:2004.11362 (2020)
35. Kumar, A., et al.: Co-regularized alignment for unsupervised domain adaptation. In: Advances in Neural Information Processing Systems, pp. 9345–9356 (2018)
36. Liang, J., Hu, D., Feng, J.: Combating domain shift with self-taught labeling. arXiv preprint arXiv:2007.04171 (2020)
37. Lin, T.Y., RoyChowdhury, A., Maji, S.: Bilinear CNN models for fine-grained visual recognition. In: Proceedings of the IEEE International Conference on Computer Vision, pp. 1449–1457 (2015)
38. Long, M., Cao, Y., Wang, J., Jordan, M.: Learning transferable features with deep adaptation networks. In: International Conference on Machine Learning, pp. 97–105. PMLR (2015)
39. Long, M., Cao, Z., Wang, J., Jordan, M.I.: Conditional adversarial domain adaptation. In: Advances in Neural Information Processing Systems, pp. 1640–1650 (2018)
40. Long, M., Wang, J., Ding, G., Sun, J., Yu, P.S.: Transfer feature learning with joint distribution adaptation. In: Proceedings of the IEEE International Conference on Computer Vision, pp. 2200–2207 (2013)
41. Long, M., Zhu, H., Wang, J., Jordan, M.I.: Unsupervised domain adaptation with residual transfer networks. In: Advances in Neural Information Processing Systems, pp. 136–144 (2016)
42. Misra, I., van der Maaten, L.: Self-supervised learning of pretext-invariant representations. In: Proceedings of the IEEE/CVF Conference on Computer Vision and Pattern Recognition, pp. 6707–6717 (2020)
43. Na, J., Jung, H., Chang, H.J., Hwang, W.: FixBi: bridging domain spaces for unsupervised domain adaptation. In: Proceedings of the IEEE/CVF Conference on Computer Vision and Pattern Recognition, pp. 1094–1103 (2021)
44. Panareda Busto, P., Gall, J.: Open set domain adaptation. In: Proceedings of the IEEE International Conference on Computer Vision, pp. 754–763 (2017)
45. Park, C., Lee, J., Yoo, J., Hur, M., Yoon, S.: Joint contrastive learning for unsupervised domain adaptation. arXiv preprint arXiv:2006.10297 (2020)
46. Pei, Z., Cao, Z., Long, M., Wang, J.: Multi-adversarial domain adaptation. arXiv preprint arXiv:1809.02176 (2018)
47. Peng, X., Bai, Q., Xia, X., Huang, Z., Saenko, K., Wang, B.: Moment matching for multi-source domain adaptation. In: Proceedings of the IEEE/CVF International Conference on Computer Vision, pp. 1406–1415 (2019)
48. Peng, X., Usman, B., Kaushik, N., Hoffman, J., Wang, D., Saenko, K.: VisDA: the visual domain adaptation challenge. arXiv preprint arXiv:1710.06924 (2017)
49. Prabhu, V., Khare, S., Kartik, D., Hoffman, J.: SENTRY: selective entropy optimization via committee consistency for unsupervised domain adaptation. In: Proceedings of the IEEE/CVF International Conference on Computer Vision, pp. 8558–8567 (2021)
50. Saenko, K., Kulis, B., Fritz, M., Darrell, T.: Adapting visual category models to new domains. In: Daniilidis, K., Maragos, P., Paragios, N. (eds.) ECCV 2010. LNCS, vol. 6314, pp. 213–226. Springer, Heidelberg (2010). https://doi.org/10.1007/978-3-642-15561-1_16

51. Saito, K., Kim, D., Sclaroff, S., Darrell, T., Saenko, K.: Semi-supervised domain adaptation via minimax entropy. In: Proceedings of the IEEE/CVF International Conference on Computer Vision, pp. 8050–8058 (2019)
52. Saito, K., Kim, D., Sclaroff, S., Saenko, K.: Universal domain adaptation through self supervision. arXiv preprint arXiv:2002.07953 (2020)
53. Saito, K., Ushiku, Y., Harada, T.: Asymmetric tri-training for unsupervised domain adaptation. arXiv preprint arXiv:1702.08400 (2017)
54. Saito, K., Ushiku, Y., Harada, T., Saenko, K.: Adversarial dropout regularization. arXiv preprint arXiv:1711.01575 (2017)
55. Saito, K., Watanabe, K., Ushiku, Y., Harada, T.: Maximum classifier discrepancy for unsupervised domain adaptation. In: Proceedings of the IEEE Conference on Computer Vision and Pattern Recognition, pp. 3723–3732 (2018)
56. Saito, K., Yamamoto, S., Ushiku, Y., Harada, T.: Open set domain adaptation by backpropagation. In: Proceedings of the European Conference on Computer Vision (ECCV), pp. 153–168 (2018)
57. Sharma, A., Kalluri, T., Chandraker, M.: Instance level affinity-based transfer for unsupervised domain adaptation. In: Proceedings of the IEEE/CVF Conference on Computer Vision and Pattern Recognition, pp. 5361–5371 (2021)
58. Sun, M., Yuan, Y., Zhou, F., Ding, E.: Multi-attention multi-class constraint for fine-grained image recognition. In: Proceedings of the European Conference on Computer Vision (ECCV), pp. 805–821 (2018)
59. Tan, S., Peng, X., Saenko, K.: Class-imbalanced domain adaptation: an empirical odyssey. In: Bartoli, A., Fusiello, A. (eds.) ECCV 2020. LNCS, vol. 12535, pp. 585–602. Springer, Cham (2020). https://doi.org/10.1007/978-3-030-66415-2_38
60. Tzeng, E., Hoffman, J., Darrell, T., Saenko, K.: Simultaneous deep transfer across domains and tasks. In: Proceedings of the IEEE International Conference on Computer Vision, pp. 4068–4076 (2015)
61. Tzeng, E., Hoffman, J., Saenko, K., Darrell, T.: Adversarial discriminative domain adaptation. In: Proceedings of the IEEE Conference on Computer Vision and Pattern Recognition, pp. 7167–7176 (2017)
62. Tzeng, E., Hoffman, J., Zhang, N., Saenko, K., Darrell, T.: Deep domain confusion: maximizing for domain invariance. arXiv preprint arXiv:1412.3474 (2014)
63. Van Horn, G., et al.: The iNaturalist species classification and detection dataset. In: Proceedings of the IEEE Conference on Computer Vision and Pattern Recognition, pp. 8769–8778 (2018)
64. Wah, C., Branson, S., Welinder, P., Perona, P., Belongie, S.: The Caltech-UCSD Birds-200-2011 Dataset. Technical report. CNS-TR-2011-001, California Institute of Technology (2011)
65. Wang, R., Wu, Z., Weng, Z., Chen, J., Qi, G.J., Jiang, Y.G.: Cross-domain contrastive learning for unsupervised domain adaptation. arXiv preprint arXiv:2106.05528 (2021)
66. Wang, S., Chen, X., Wang, Y., Long, M., Wang, J.: Progressive adversarial networks for fine-grained domain adaptation. In: Proceedings of the IEEE/CVF Conference on Computer Vision and Pattern Recognition, pp. 9213–9222 (2020)
67. Wang, X., Zhang, H., Huang, W., Scott, M.R.: Cross-batch memory for embedding learning. In: Proceedings of the IEEE/CVF Conference on Computer Vision and Pattern Recognition, pp. 6388–6397 (2020)
68. Wei, C., Shen, K., Chen, Y., Ma, T.: Theoretical analysis of self-training with deep networks on unlabeled data. In: 9th International Conference on Learning Representations, ICLR 2021, Virtual Event, Austria, 3–7 May 2021. OpenReview.net (2021). https://openreview.net/forum?id=rC8sJ4i6kaH

69. Wei, G., Lan, C., Zeng, W., Zhang, Z., Chen, Z.: ToAlign: task-oriented alignment for unsupervised domain adaptation. In: NeurIPS (2021)

70. Wu, Z., Xiong, Y., Yu, S.X., Lin, D.: Unsupervised feature learning via non-parametric instance discrimination. In: Proceedings of the IEEE Conference on Computer Vision and Pattern Recognition, pp. 3733–3742 (2018)

71. Xie, S., Zheng, Z., Chen, L., Chen, C.: Learning semantic representations for unsupervised domain adaptation. In: International Conference on Machine Learning, pp. 5423–5432 (2018)

72. Xu, R., Li, G., Yang, J., Lin, L.: Larger norm more transferable: an adaptive feature norm approach for unsupervised domain adaptation. In: Proceedings of the IEEE International Conference on Computer Vision, pp. 1426–1435 (2019)

73. Xu, Z., Huang, S., Zhang, Y., Tao, D.: Webly-supervised fine-grained visual categorization via deep domain adaptation. IEEE Trans. Pattern Anal. Mach. Intell. **40**(5), 1100–1113 (2016)

74. Yang, L., Luo, P., Change Loy, C., Tang, X.: A large-scale car dataset for fine-grained categorization and verification. In: Proceedings of the IEEE Conference on Computer Vision and Pattern Recognition, pp. 3973–3981 (2015)

75. Yang, L., et al.: MiCo: mixup co-training for semi-supervised domain adaptation. arXiv preprint arXiv:2007.12684 (2020)

76. Zhang, J., Ding, Z., Li, W., Ogunbona, P.: Importance weighted adversarial nets for partial domain adaptation. In: Proceedings of the IEEE Conference on Computer Vision and Pattern Recognition, pp. 8156–8164 (2018)

77. Zhang, N., Donahue, J., Girshick, R., Darrell, T.: Part-based R-CNNs for fine-grained category detection. In: Fleet, D., Pajdla, T., Schiele, B., Tuytelaars, T. (eds.) ECCV 2014. LNCS, vol. 8689, pp. 834–849. Springer, Cham (2014). https://doi.org/10.1007/978-3-319-10590-1_54

78. Zhang, N., Farrell, R., Darrell, T.: Pose pooling kernels for sub-category recognition. In: 2012 IEEE Conference on Computer Vision and Pattern Recognition, pp. 3665–3672. IEEE (2012)

79. Zheng, H., Fu, J., Mei, T., Luo, J.: Learning multi-attention convolutional neural network for fine-grained image recognition. In: Proceedings of the IEEE International Conference on Computer Vision, pp. 5209–5217 (2017)

80. Zheng, H., Fu, J., Zha, Z.J., Luo, J.: Looking for the devil in the details: learning trilinear attention sampling network for fine-grained image recognition. In: Proceedings of the IEEE/CVF Conference on Computer Vision and Pattern Recognition, pp. 5012–5021 (2019)

United Defocus Blur Detection and Deblurring via Adversarial Promoting Learning

Wenda Zhao[1]([✉]), Fei Wei[1], You He[2], and Huchuan Lu[1]

[1] Dalian University of Technology, Dalian, China
{zhaowenda,lhchuan}@dlut.edu.cn, fwei@mail.dlut.edu.cn
[2] Naval Aviation University, Yantai, China

Abstract. Understanding blur from a single defocused image contains two tasks of defocus detection and deblurring. This paper makes the earliest effort to jointly learn both defocus detection and deblurring without using pixel-level defocus detection annotation and paired defocus deblurring ground truth. We build on the observation that these two tasks are supplementary to each other: Defocus detection can segment the focused area from the defocused image to guide the defocus deblurring; Conversely, to achieve better defocus deblurring, an accurate defocus detection as the guide is essential. Therefore, we implement an adversarial promoting learning framework to jointly handle defocus detection and defocus deblurring. Specifically, a defocus detection generator G_{ws} is implemented to represent the defocused image as a layered composition of two elements: defocused image I_{df} and a focused image I_f. Then, I_{df} and I_f are fed into a self-referenced defocus deblurring generator G_{sr} to generate a deblurred image. Two generators of G_{ws} and G_{sr} are optimized alternately in an adversarial manner against a discriminator D with unpaired realistic fully-clear images. Thus, G_{sr} will produce a deblurred image to fool D, and G_{ws} is forced to generate an accurate defocus detection map to effectively guide G_{sr}. Comprehensive experiments on two defocus detection datasets and one defocus deblurring dataset demonstrate the effectiveness of our framework. Code and model are available at: https://github.com/wdzhao123/APL.

Keywords: Defocus blur detection · Defocus deblurring · Adversarial promoting learning

1 Introduction

Defocus blur is common in an image that is captured under optical imaging systems. Detecting defocus blur can provide important clues for various scene understanding, such as salient region detection [9] and depth estimation [8,21]. Sequentially, defocus deblurring is of great interest for the downstream computer vision tasks, such as object segmentation [16,17] and tracking [6,7], *etc.* Thus,

S. Avidan et al. (Eds.): ECCV 2022, LNCS 13690, pp. 569–586, 2022.
https://doi.org/10.1007/978-3-031-20056-4_33

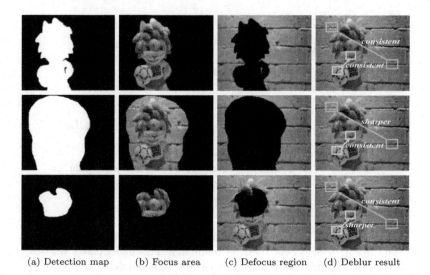

(a) Detection map   (b) Focus area   (c) Defocus region   (d) Deblur result

Fig. 1. Correlation illustration of defocus detection and deblurring. First row: An accurate focus detection can effectively segment the focus area and defocus region, thereby generating a natural deblurred image with consistent clarity. Second row: Excessive focus detection makes deblurred image still contain blurred area. Third row: Deficient focus detection makes deblurred image be not consistent in clarity, *e.g.*, over-sharpened focus area.

developing an efficient method for simultaneous defocus detection and deblurring is desirable. However, existing researches handle these two tasks separately.

Previous defocus detection methods can be mainly divided into two categories. One is prior knowledge-based methods [18,22,26,31,37], *e.g.*, gradient [2,10,31] and contrast [18,26,27]. Since the priors may dissatisfy some complicated scenes, the performance of defocus detection cannot be guaranteed. The other one is deep learning-based methods [11,30,32,43,44,47,49]. Their effectiveness usually relies on fully-supervised training with pixel-level annotation whose acquisition is time-consuming and expensive.

Existing defocus deblurring researches commonly compute a defocus map to guide the deblurring [23,41], where the defocus map is estimated through synthetic defocus image [13] or utilizing some prior knowledge, *e.g.*, edge [10, 19]. However, synthetic data results in a domain gap and prior knowledge has the scene dependency, which will hinder the performance of defocus deblurring. Recently, methods [1,14,25] propose end-to-end deep learning frameworks for defocus deblurring. Unfortunately, they are limited by the requirement of paired pixel-level ground truth.

Essentially, defocus detection and deblurring are supplementary to each other, as shown in Fig. 1. Blur detection can guide deblur generator to achieve defocusing. Sequentially, deblur generator can build the bridge between blur detection generator and discriminator to finetune defocus detection in an adversarial manner. Therefore, we explore the joint learning of defocus detection

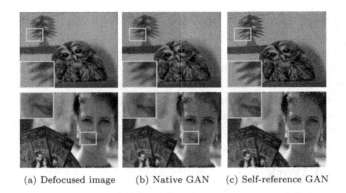

(a) Defocused image   (b) Native GAN   (c) Self-reference GAN

Fig. 2. Qualitative comparison of different defocus deblurring solutions. Native GAN produces hallucination (*e.g.*, blur and color distortion). We address this through using focused area to provide a clarity reference that guides the defocused area to deblur from the defocused image itself.

and defocus deblurring, and propose an adversarial promoting learning framework (MPLF) to tackle the problems of training defocus detection model with pixel-level annotation and learning defocus deblurring with paired ground truth. Specifically, MPLF includes three models: a defocus detection generator G_{ws}, a self-referenced defocus deblurring generator G_{sr} and a discriminator D. G_{ws} is implemented to generate a defocus detection map, and then the focused area and unfocused region are segmented from the defocused image to feed into G_{sr}. Two generators of G_{ws} and G_{sr} are optimized alternately in an adversarial manner against a discriminator D with unpaired realistic fully-clear images. Through this adversarial process, G_{sr} will produce a deblurred image to fool D to believe that the deblurred image is a natural fully-clear image, and G_{ws} is forced to produce an accurate defocus detection map without pixel-level supervision.

In particular, a potential solution is to implement generative adversarial networks (GAN) [3,12] to overcome the dependency on paired data in defocus deblurring. However, purely feeding an unpaired full-focused image to the discriminator often cannot optimize the generator well in the adversarial process, which easily degrades the deblurring image, *e.g.*, blur and color distortion (see Fig. 2(b)). Therefore, we design a self-referenced GAN that utilizes the focused area in the defocused image to guide the defocus region to deblur. Specifically, the defocused image is firstly represented as a layered composition of two elements: a defocused image I_{df} and a focused image I_f. Then, we build the self-referenced generator G_{sr} to deblur I_{df} with the reference of I_f. However, directly combining the defocused region with focused area as inputs, or concatenating focused area features with intermediate deep features can hardly make an efficient utilization of the focused area information. To address this problem, we propose an unpaired feature affine transformation model (UFAT) to recursively insert into G_{sr}. In UFAT, the focused area contents are referenced by influencing the feature affine transformation of the defocused region in the process of deblurring, thereby achieving better deblurring performance (see Fig. 2(c)).

In short, our contributions are as follows. 1) We make the earliest effort to explore the joint learning of defocus detection and defocus deblurring, fully utilizing their mutual promotion to obtain superior performances on these two tasks. 2) We propose an adversarial promoting learning framework to produce defocus detection in a weakly-supervised fashion, while generating a defocus deblurred image without using paired ground truth. 3) We validate the effectiveness of the proposed method on two defocus detection datasets and one defocus deblurring dataset.

2   Related Work

Fully-Supervised Defocus Detection. Benefitting from defocus detection datasets [22,47,48] with pixel-level annotation, deep convolutional neural networks-based methods [11,15,28–30,32,40] have been proposed to boost the performance of defocus detection. Among these methods, a main research route is multi-level feature integration. For example, Kim *et al.* [11] adopt long skip connections between encoder features and decoder features to combine multi-level contextual features. Tang *et al.* [32] implement a cross-layer feature fusion strategy to improve performance. Zhao *et al.* [43] design an image-scale-symmetric cooperative network to fuse multi-scale and multi-level features. In addition, some other mechanisms are effectively applied to defocus detection, such as ensemble network [44,49], cut-and-paste strategy [39] and depth distillation [5]. However, these methods are trained with abundant pixel-level ground truth whose acquisition is expensive and time-consuming. Thus, Zhao *et al.* [45] propose a weakly-supervised recurrent constraint network for focus region detection, where bounding box annotations are used.

Unsupervised Defocus Detection. Unsupervised defocus detection methods are usually concentrated on designing hand-crafted features [18,31,42]. For instance, Shi *et al.* [22] study a few blur feature representations, such as gradient, Fourier domain, and data-driven local filters. Golestaneh *et al.* [2] explore sorted transform coefficients of gradient magnitudes and multiscale fusion strategy. Yi *et al.* [37] adopt local binary patterns (LBP) to measure defocus blur. Hand-crafted features-based methods provide some efficient priors of understanding defocus blur, which may help us further design unsupervised or weakly-supervised deep defocus detection models.

Defocus Deblurring. On one hand, defocus deblurring methods [10,41] are concerned on estimating a defocus detection map, and then utilize a non-blind deconvolution technology to achieve deblurring. Shi *et al.* [23] establish the correspondence between sparse edge representation and blur strength to obtain defocus detection map. Park *et al.* [19] combine multi-scale deep and hand-crafted features for defocus estimation. Lee *et al.* [13] build synthetically blurred images with paired ground truth and implement domain adaptation to generate defocus blur maps of real defocused images. On the other hand, works [1,14,25] propose end-to-end defocus deblurring network which are trained with paired pixel-level ground truth.

In contrast, we focus on designing a weakly-supervised defocus deblurring framework without using paired pixel-level ground truth. Particularly, we adopt the focused area directly segmented from the defocused image itself as a reference to guide the defocus to deblur.

GAN-Based Deblurring. GAN has achieved impressive results in various vision tasks, such as image inpainting [36], shadow removal [34], image denoising [4] and image super-resolution [3]. The main idea is using an adversarial loss with a targeted image that forces the generated image to be high-quality. This provides a potential solution that implements GAN to overcome the dependency on paired data in defocus deblurring. However, purely adopting an unpaired full-focused image as the target in the adversarial process will produce hallucination (see Fig. 2(b)).

Different from existing GAN-based low-level image processing methods, we design a self-referenced GAN that utilizes the focused area segmented by defocus detection as a guide to optimize the defocus deblurring generator better, as shown in Fig. 2(c). Interestingly, this builds a bridge between defocus detection and defocus deblurring, allowing us to alternately optimize them in an adversarial manner, thereby producing an accurate defocus detection map without using pixel-level annotation.

3   Adversarial Promoting Learning

3.1   Motivation and Framework

Existing defocus detection and deblurring methods [33,48] usually train deep networks by recursive strategy in a fully-supervised manner. Let's denote the space of defocused images by $\mathcal{X}$, the space of defocus detection by $\mathcal{Y}$, and the space of deblurring images by $\mathcal{Z}$. Given an input defocused image $x \in \mathcal{X}$, defocus detection or deblurring aims to generate its corresponding detection map $y \in \mathcal{Y}$ or deblurring image $z \in \mathcal{Z}$. Most of the recursive strategy based methods iteratively optimize defocus detection mapping function Φ or deblurring mapping function Ψ, $i.e.$,

$$\Phi(x, y; \phi_1) \rightarrow \Phi(x, y_1, y; \phi_2) \rightarrow \Phi(x, y_2, y; \phi_3) \cdots, \tag{1}$$

$$\Psi(x, z; \psi_1) \rightarrow \Psi(x, z_1, z; \psi_2) \rightarrow \Psi(x, z_2, z; \psi_3) \cdots, \tag{2}$$

where $\{y_1, y_2, \cdots\}$ and $\{z_1, z_2, \cdots\}$ are the subspaces of detection maps and deblurring images, and $\{\phi_1, \phi_2, \cdots\}$ and $\{\psi_1, \psi_2, \cdots\}$ are the parameters of different optimization times of Φ and Ψ, respectively. As illustrated in Fig. 3(a)–(b), defocus detection and deblurring optimize their mapping functions in their own space, lacking communication with each other. Moreover, they train deep networks in a fully-supervised manner with pixel-level detection annotation or paired deblurring ground truth. The GAN methods [3,12,46] can partially dilute this issue through adversarial training with unpaired data. However, when the scene is complex, GAN methods can hardly produce clear deblurring images with realistic details (Fig. 2(b)). Therefore, [46] adds an adversarial discriminator and

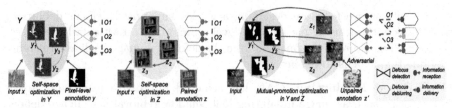

(a) Recursive detection (b) Recursive deblurring   (c) Adversarial promoting framework

Fig. 3. Illustrations of our motivation and framework. Existing defocus detection and deblurring methods [33,48] recursively optimize results (e.g., O1, O2 and O3) in their own space via a fully-supervised fashion (see (a) and (b)). In contrast, we utilize their mutual benefits to propose an adversarial promoting learning framework in a weakly-supervised manner without using pixel-level detection annotation and paired deblurring label (see (c)).

a classifier to assist in network optimization. But the parameter search space becomes large and the training is difficult to converge.

Different from previous methods [1,14,25,33,46,48], we design an adversarial promoting learning framework to handle defocus detection and deblurring tasks jointly. As is presented in Fig. 3(c), a defocus detection generator G_{ws} is implemented to generate defocus detection maps and a self-referenced deblurring generator G_{sr} is built to produce deblurring images. G_{ws} and G_{sr} are optimized alternately in an adversarial manner against a discriminator D with unpaired realistic fully-clear images, i.e.,

$$G_{ws}(x, z_1, z'; g_{ws}^1) \rightarrow G_{sr}(x, y_1, z'; g_{sr}^2) \rightarrow$$
$$G_{ws}(x, z_2, z'; g_{ws}^2) \rightarrow G_{sr}(x, y_2, z'; g_{sr}^3) \rightarrow \qquad (3)$$
$$G_{ws}(x, z_3, z'; g_{ws}^3) \cdots,$$

where $\{g_{ws}^1, g_{ws}^2, g_{ws}^3, \cdots\}$ and $\{g_{sr}^1, g_{sr}^2, g_{sr}^3, \cdots\}$ are the parameters of different optimization times of G_{ws} and G_{sr}, respectively. z' is the unpaired realistic fully-clear image. Therefore, G_{sr} gradually produces a deblurred image with the guidance of defocus detection map of G_{ws} in the adversarial process with unpaired fully-clear image, and G_{ws} is forced to find the accurate defocus detection map to effectively guide G_{sr}, where pixel-level detection annotation is not used. The network architecture of our model is shown in Fig. 4, which will be explained in detail as follows.

3.2 Architecture

Our MPLF is built on the successful applications of GAN, which contains three network models: a defocus detection generator G_{ws}, a self-referenced defocus deblurring generator G_{sr} and a discriminator D.

Self-referenced Deblurring Generator G_{sr}. Unpaired GANs are easy to produce hallucination (see Fig. 2(b)). One underlying reason is that the generator is under-constrained. In practice, we observe that the focused area in a

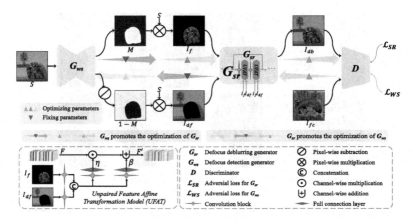

Fig. 4. Architecture of the proposed adversarial promoting learning. Defocus detection generator G_{ws} is encouraged to produce an accurate defocus detection map M that guides G_{sr} to generate better defocus deblurred image. Sequentially, self-referenced generative model G_{sr} is built to utilize the focused area segmented by M from the input image itself for defocus deblurring. Generators G_{ws} and G_{sr} are alternately optimized in an adversarial manner against the discriminator D, where only unpaired realistic fully-clear images are used. Especially, unpaired feature affine transformation model (UFAT) is recursively inserted to G_{sr}, addressing the issue that unpaired GANs produce hallucination.

defocused image contains important information (*e.g.*, clarity degree), which can be adopted to assist defocus deblurring. Therefore, we design a self-referenced generative model G_{sr} to dilute this issue. Consider a defocused image I with size $h \times w \times c$, where h and w are the height and width, and c denotes the number of channels. We define the representation of I as a layered composition of two elements: a defocused image I_{df} and a focused image I_f. I_{df} and I_f are defined through a defocus detection map M with each element belonging to $[0,1]$ as follows

$$I_{df} = (1 - M) \otimes I, I_f = M \otimes I, \tag{4}$$

where $\otimes$ expresses a pixel-wise multiplication operation.

Here, we focus on exploiting I_f to guide the defocus deblurring of I_{df}. However, directly combining I_f and I_{df}, or concatenating intermediate deep features of I_f and I_{df} can hardly obtain good performance (objective analysis is provided in Sect. 4.2). The potential cause is that their spatial contents are not aligned. Inspired by spatial feature transform [35], we introduce an unpaired feature affine transformation model (UFAT), where we extract feature affine transformation vectors η and β by consulting I_f to influence feature reconstruction of I_{df} in the defocus deblurring process.

$$UFAT(F, I_f, I_{df}) = \eta \odot F \uplus \beta, \tag{5}$$

where F represents a deep feature, $\odot$ and $\uplus$ stand for the channel-wise multiplication and addition operation, respectively.

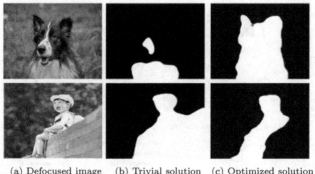

(a) Defocused image   (b) Trivial solution   (c) Optimized solution

Fig. 5. Qualitative comparison of different optimization solutions for defocus detection.

Figure 4 illustrates the network architecture of UFAT. In particular, UFAT firstly obtains the concatenated features of I_f and I_{df}, and then generates feature affine transformation vectors η and β. Sequentially, η and β are used to help F restructure the feature F'. Further, we utilize UFAT to build our self-referenced generative model G_{sr}. Specifically, G_{sr} is structured with two residual convolution blocks, and UFAT is recursively inserted to help feature reconstruction of I_{df} in the defocus deblurring process. In addition, a global skip connection is implemented to ease the training of the deep network. Notice that the spatial contents of I_f and I_{df} are unaligned, thus UFAT does not generate spatial feature transform. This is different from [35] where spatial-wise transformation is implemented. Our self-referenced generative model achieves better deblurring performance compared with native GAN-based method (see Fig. 2(c)). Objective analysis is provided in Sect. 4.2.

Defocus Detection Generator G_{ws} and Discriminator D. G_{ws} is built to produce a defocus detection map M, which is used to calculate I_f and I_{df} to feed into G_{sr}. Inspired by the U-Net architecture [20], G_{ws} is designed by an encoder-decoder framework with skip connections. The encoder is built with the first four convolution blocks of VGG16 [24] to extract multi-level features. Then, a decoder including four corresponding deconvolution blocks to produce a defocus detection map.

Discriminator D is implemented to distinguish whether the defocus deblurring image is fully-clear, where the first three convolution blocks of VGG16 are used to extract high-level features. Then, three full connection layers are added to output a one-element vector.

3.3   Optimization

Generators G_{ws} and G_{sr} are optimized alternately in an adversarial manner against the discriminator D with unpaired realistic fully-clear images. The optimization loss of G_{sr} can be expressed as

$$\mathcal{L}_{SR} = \min_{g_{ws},g_{sr}} \max_{d} \mathbb{E}_{I_{fc} \sim P_{fc}} log D(I_{fc}; d) +$$
$$\mathbb{E}_{I \sim P_{df}} log(1 - D(G_{sr}(G_{ws}(I) \otimes I, \qquad (6)$$
$$(1 - G_{ws}(I)) \otimes I); g_{ws}, g_{sr}))),$$

where d is weight parameter of D. P_{fc} and P_{df} illustrate empirical distributions of fully-clear images and defocused images, respectively. I_{fc} stands for a fully-clear image.

Optimization starts with G_{sr} which is pretrained using a set of simulated defocus pairs (synthesis strategy is given in Sect. 4.1). Then, G_{ws} is optimized to produce an accurate defocus detection map to help G_{sr} achieve better defocus deblurring performance. However, only using adversarial supervision to train G_{ws} is extremely under-constrained, and G_{ws} easily produces a trivial solution (see Fig. 5(b)). Thus, we utilize blur priors to provide an auxiliary supervision for training G_{ws} as

$$\mathcal{L}_{WS} = \mathcal{L}_{SR} + ||G_{ws}(I) - B(I)||_1, \qquad (7)$$

where $B(I)$ is a blur prior model for the input image I. Here, we adopt local contrast knowledge (refer to [37] for details). Using this loss, G_{ws} can generate more accurate defocus detection maps, as shown in Fig. 5(c).

3.4   Training Details

Our framework is implemented using Pytorch library on a NVIDIA RTX 2080Ti GPU. Adam with momentum 0.9 is adopted as the optimizer. The mini-batch size is taken to 1, and the learning rate is set to 0.0002. G_{sr}, D_1 and D are initialized with random values. We firstly optimize G_{sr} with simulated defocus pairs for 100 epochs. Then, we alternately optimize G_{ws} and G_{sr}, and each alternation is trained in an adversarial manner with D for 100 epochs. Considering memory capacity, we resize the image to 160×160 to verify the effectiveness of the proposed method.

4   Experiments

4.1   Configuration

Datasets. Two widely-used defocus detection datasets of CUHK [22] and DUT [48] are adopted to train and test our framework. The same strategy with [48] is implemented that training images and testing images are divided into 604 and 100 in CUHK, and 600 and 500 in DUT, respectively. It is worth noting that we train our framework without pixel-level defocus detection annotation. Besides, we utilize DP dataset [1] including 76 testing defocus images to evaluate the performance of defocus deblurring.

In addition, to initialize the self-referenced generative defocus deblurring model, we construct a simulated defocus dataset. Specifically, we firstly collect

Table 1. Effect study of defocus detection in the mutual promotion process using F_{max} and MAE scores on both CUHK and DUT datasets. G_{ws}_On stands for the nth optimization of G_{ws}.

Setting	CUHK		DUT	
	F_{max}	MAE	F_{max}	MAE
Single G_{ws}	0.785	0.173	0.679	0.232
G_{ws}_O1	0.790	0.155	0.696	0.213
G_{ws}_O2	0.801	0.133	0.682	0.212
G_{ws}_O3	**0.831**	**0.125**	**0.722**	**0.196**

Table 2. Effect study of defocus deblurring in the mutual promotion process using $PSNR$, $SSIM$ and MAE scores on DP dataset. G_{sr}_On stands for the nth optimization of G_{sr}.

Setting	$PSNR$	$SSIM$	MAE
Single G_{sr}	22.02	0.782	0.063
G_{sr}_O1	24.05	0.785	0.050
G_{sr}_O2	24.99	0.821	0.044
G_{sr}_O3	**25.71**	**0.842**	**0.041**

500 full-focused images with manifold scenes. Then, inspired by [38], we adopt a Gaussian filter with a standard deviation randomly sampled from 0.1 to 10 and window size 15×15 to blur a part (60%–70%) of each full-focused image. This process is repeated five times to produce 2500 defocused images.

Evaluations. We utilize two metrics of mean absolute error (MAE) and F-measure score (F_{max}) [32,48,49], to evaluate the performance of defocus detection. A smaller MAE demonstrates a more accurate result. A larger F_{max} indicates a better performance. Besides, peak signal to noise ratio ($PSNR$), structural similarity ($SSIM$) and MAE are adopted to measure defocus deblurring's performance [1]. A larger $PSNR$ or $SSIM$ stands for a better defocus deblurring.

4.2   Ablation Study

Adversarial Promotion Between Defocus Detection and Deblurring. Our adversarial promoting learning handles defocus detection G_{ws} and deblurring G_{sr} jointly. Defocus detection and deblurring are optimized alternately. Specifically, defocus detection maps of G_{ws} guide G_{sr} to generate deblurred images. Conversely, to effectively guide G_{sr}, G_{ws} is forced to produce accurate defocus detection maps. We implement the following settings to demonstrate the validity of the mutual promotion learning.

Firstly, we study the effects of single detection and single deblurring, *i.e.*, the one task's performance if the other task fails. Single G_{ws}: Training G_{ws} with the

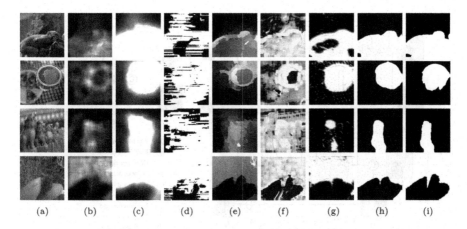

(a)   (b)   (c)   (d)   (e)   (f)   (g)   (h)   (i)

Fig. 6. Visual results of defocus detection produced by different methods. (a)–(i) are source, SVD [26], HiFST [2], KSFV [18], SS [31], DBDF [22], SGNet [46], Ours, and ground truth, respectively.

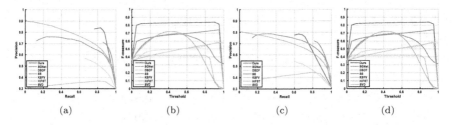

(a)   (b)   (c)   (d)

Fig. 7. Comparison of PR curves and F-measure curves of different methods on both CUHK and DUT datasets. (a)–(d) are PR curve on CUHK, F-measure curve on CUHK, PR curve on DUT and F-measure curve on DUT.

supervision of the local contrast prior model [37]. Single G_{sr}: Training G_{sr} in a adversarial manner with D using unpaired full-focused images. Secondly, we implement their adversarial promoting optimization, denoted as G_{ws}_On and G_{sr}_On ($n = 1, 2, 3$).

Table 1 and Table 2 present objective results. Compared with single detection and single deblurring, our mutual promotion learning improves their performances on all measure scores. With the optimization number increases, the performances of G_{sr} and G_{ws} are promoted. Especially, G_{ws}_O3 and G_{sr}_O3 obtain the best measure scores respectively, improving F_{max}/MAE by 5.9%/27.7% and 6.3%/15.5% than single detection on CUHK and DUT datasets, and raising $PSNR/SSIM/MAE$ by 16.8%/7.7%/34.9% than single deblurring on DP dataset.

Self-referenced Deblurring Generator. In Sect. 3.2, we propose a self-referenced deblurring generator to relieve the problem that unpaired GANs are easy to produce hallucination. The core idea is to utilize the focused area I_f in the

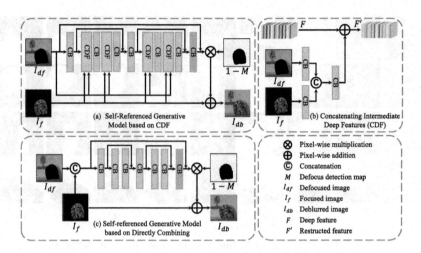

Fig. 8. Illustrations of DC-based and CDF-based self-referenced generative defocus deblurring models. CB stands for a convolution block with three convolution layers.

Table 3. Importance study of self-referenced deblurring generator using $PSNR$, $SSIM$ and MAE scores on DP dataset.

Metric	U-GAN	DC-GAN	CDF-GAN	UFAT-GAN
$PSNR$	22.02	24.16	24.80	**25.71**
$SSIM$	0.782	0.808	0.838	**0.842**
MAE	0.063	0.045	0.043	**0.041**

defocused image itself to guide the defocused region I_{df} to deblur. Structurally, we design UFATs to recursively insert into G_{sr}, making an efficient information utilization of the focused area, named as UFAT-GAN. Here, two aspects are studied to illustrate the effectiveness of the self-referenced deblurring generator.

On one hand, unpaired GAN is implemented for comparing where deblurring generator does not contain UFAT, denoted as U-GAN. On the other hand, UFAT's two variants are compared: directly making a combination of I_f and I_{df}, and concatenating intermediate deep features of I_f and I_{df}, named as DC-GAN and CDF-GAN. Detailed network structures of DC-GAN and CDF-GAN are shown in Fig. 8.

As can be seen in Table 3, implementing our self-referenced mechanism can improve performance, and DC-GAN outperforms U-GAN by 9.7%, 3.3% and 28.6% on $PSNR$, $SSIM$ and MAE, respectively. UFAT-GAN achieves the best performance, especially outperforming DC-GAN and CDF-GAN by 6.4% and 3.7% on $PSNR$. The underlying reason is that UFAT relieves the problem of unpaired spatial contents between I_f and I_{df} through two channel-wise attention vectors η and β.

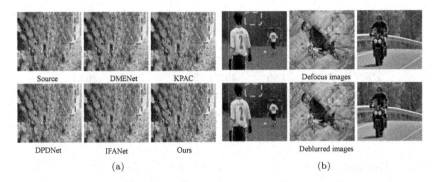

Fig. 9. Qualitative defocus deblurring results. (a) and (b) are visual comparison of different methods on DP and visual results of our method on CUHK and DUT. Our method achieves a uniform clarity in deblurred images.

Table 4. Defocus detection comparison with the state-of-the-art approaches using F_{max} and MAE scores on CUHK and DUT datasets. Average time is calculated on a workstation with a RTX 2080Ti GPU.

	Metric	SVD [26]	HiFST [2]	KSFV [18]	SS [31]	DBDF [22]	SGNet [46]	Ours
CUHK	F_{max}	0.764	0.583	0.420	0.759	0.626	0.732	**0.831**
	MAE	0.267	0.429	0.492	0.316	0.422	0.199	**0.125**
DUT	F_{max}	0.712	0.617	0.489	0.733	0.592	**0.731**	0.722
	MAE	0.288	0.399	0.404	0.320	0.454	0.204	**0.196**
Time	Second	2.153	17.93	4.937	0.336	31.55	0.007	**0.003**

4.3 Comparison with State-of-the-Art Methods

Defocus Detection. Our weakly-supervised defocus detection (Ours) is compared with the following five unsupervised state-of-the-art methods: singular value decomposition (SVD) [26], high-frequency multi-scale fusion and sort transform of gradient magnitudes (HiFST) [2], classifying discriminative features (KSFV) [18], spectral and spatial approach (SS) [31] and discriminative blur detection features (DBDF) [22]. Moreover, one weakly-supervised deep learning method of SGNet [46] is compared. To compare fairly, we utilize the available codes and recommended parameter settings released by authors.

Table 4 shows the quantitative defocus detection results. Ours outperforms the previous state-of-the-art results in general. Especially, ours achieves better performance of MAE by 37.2% and 3.9% than the second-best SGNet on CUHK and DUT, respectively. Besides, ours is highly efficient, which achieves the average testing time of 0.003 s. Figure 7 shows their PR curves and F-measure curves, comprehensively verifying the better performance of our method. Qualitative comparison is shown in Fig. 6, including of various scenes, such as complex background, unfocused foreground. Our method consistently generates defocus detection results closest to the ground truth.

Table 5. Quantitative comparison of different defocus deblurring methods using *PSNR*, *SSIM* and *MAE* scores on DP dataset.

Metric	EBDB	DMENet	Ours	DPDNet	IFANet	KPAC
PSNR	23.89	24.99	**25.71**	24.01	24.20	26.51
SSIM	0.813	0.767	**0.842**	0.734	0.797	0.861
MAE	0.050	0.044	**0.041**	0.047	0.045	0.038

Defocus Deblurring. Our weakly-supervised self-referenced defocus deblurring model is compared with five state-of-the-art methods, including two defocus maps based methods of EBDB [10] and DMENet [13], and three fully-supervised methods DPDNet [1], IFANet [14] and KPAC [25]. For a fair comparison, we implement the networks with their released codes to produce results. Notably, DPDNet is implemented with center view images since its corresponding parameters are not released. The images with resolution of 160×160 are used based on the memory capacity.

As shown in Table 5, our model achieves the best performance compared with weakly-supervised EBDB and DMENet. Moreover, our method obtains competitive performance compared with the fully-supervised methods, achieving the gaps of 0.8, 0.019 and 0.003 than the best *PSNR*, *SSIM* and *MAE*, respectively. Figure 9 presents qualitative results of different defocus deblurring methods. Our method shows a more uniform clarity in any areas of a deblurred image.

4.4   Limitation

Our framework is implemented in weakly-supervised manner, and can achieve better performances on both defocus detection and deblurring of various defocus blurs. However, it may have limitations in addressing ambiguous boundaries (see the second row in Fig. 6) and large blurs (see yellow dashed boxes in Fig. 9). Maybe physics-based blur prior can relieve this issue, and we will study it.

5   Conclusion

We present an efficient joint learning framework for defocus detection and deblurring without using pixel-level defocus detection annotation and paired defocus deblurring ground truth. The core idea is utilizing their correlations to build an adversarial promoting learning framework in an adversarial manner. A self-referenced defocus deblurring generator G_{sr} is firstly proposed to obtain the ability of defocus deblurring. In particular, UFAT is designed to recursively insert into G_{sr}, relieving the unpaired spatial contents between the focused area and defocused region through influencing the feature affine transformation of the defocused region. Then, a defocus detection generator G_{ws} is introduced and combines with G_{sr} to jointly learn in an adversarial manner against a discriminator. Thus, G_{ws} is encouraged to produce an accurate defocus detection without pixel-level annotation. Extensive qualitative and quantitative experiment results on three datasets verify the effectiveness of our method.

Acknowledgements. This work is supported by National Natural Science Foundation of China under Grant Nos. 62176038 and U1903215, and Science and Technology Star of Dalian under Grant No. 2021RQ054.

References

1. Abuolaim, A., Brown, M.S.: Defocus deblurring using dual-pixel data. In: Vedaldi, A., Bischof, H., Brox, T., Frahm, J.-M. (eds.) ECCV 2020. LNCS, vol. 12355, pp. 111–126. Springer, Cham (2020). https://doi.org/10.1007/978-3-030-58607-2_7
2. Alireza Golestaneh, S., Karam, L.J.: Spatially-varying blur detection based on multiscale fused and sorted transform coefficients of gradient magnitudes. In: Proceedings of the IEEE Conference on Computer Vision and Pattern Recognition, pp. 5800–5809 (2017)
3. Bulat, A., Yang, J., Tzimiropoulos, G.: To learn image super-resolution, use a GAN to learn how to do image degradation first. In: Proceedings of the European Conference on Computer Vision (ECCV), pp. 185–200 (2018)
4. Chen, J., Chen, J., Chao, H., Yang, M.: Image blind denoising with generative adversarial network based noise modeling. In: Proceedings of the IEEE Conference on Computer Vision and Pattern Recognition, pp. 3155–3164 (2018)
5. Cun, X., Pun, C.-M.: Defocus blur detection via depth distillation. In: Vedaldi, A., Bischof, H., Brox, T., Frahm, J.-M. (eds.) ECCV 2020. LNCS, vol. 12358, pp. 747–763. Springer, Cham (2020). https://doi.org/10.1007/978-3-030-58601-0_44
6. Ding, J., Huang, Y., Liu, W., Huang, K.: Severely blurred object tracking by learning deep image representations. IEEE Trans. Circuits Syst. Video Technol. **26**(2), 319–331 (2015)
7. Guo, Q., Feng, W., Gao, R., Liu, Y., Wang, S.: Exploring the effects of blur and deblurring to visual object tracking. IEEE Trans. Image Process. **30**, 1812–1824 (2021)
8. Gur, S., Wolf, L.: Single image depth estimation trained via depth from defocus cues. In: IEEE Conference on Computer Vision and Pattern Recognition, pp. 7683–7692 (2019)
9. Jiang, P., Ling, H., Yu, J., Peng, J.: Salient region detection by UFO: uniqueness, focusness and objectness. In: IEEE International Conference on Computer Vision, pp. 1976–1983 (2013)
10. Karaali, A., Jung, C.R.: Edge-based defocus blur estimation with adaptive scale selection. IEEE Trans. Image Process. **27**(3), 1126–1137 (2017)
11. Kim, B., Son, H., Park, S.J., Cho, S., Lee, S.: Defocus and motion blur detection with deep contextual features. In: Computer Graphics Forum, vol. 37, pp. 277–288 (2018)
12. Kupyn, O., Martyniuk, T., Wu, J., Wang, Z.: DeblurGAN-v2: deblurring (orders-of-magnitude) faster and better. In: Proceedings of the IEEE/CVF International Conference on Computer Vision, pp. 8878–8887 (2019)
13. Lee, J., Lee, S., Cho, S., Lee, S.: Deep defocus map estimation using domain adaptation. In: Proceedings of the IEEE Conference on Computer Vision and Pattern Recognition, pp. 12222–12230 (2019)

14. Lee, J., Son, H., Rim, J., Cho, S., Lee, S.: Iterative filter adaptive network for single image defocus deblurring. In: Proceedings of the IEEE/CVF Conference on Computer Vision and Pattern Recognition, pp. 2034–2042 (2021)
15. Li, J., et al.: Layer-output guided complementary attention learning for image defocus blur detection. IEEE Trans. Image Process. **30**, 3748–3763 (2021)
16. Luo, B., Cheng, Z., Xu, L., Zhang, G., Li, H.: Blind image deblurring via super-pixel segmentation prior. IEEE Trans. Circuits Syst. Video Technol. **32**, 1467–1482 (2021)
17. Pan, L., Dai, Y., Liu, M., Porikli, F., Pan, Q.: Joint stereo video deblurring, scene flow estimation and moving object segmentation. IEEE Trans. Image Process. **29**, 1748–1761 (2019)
18. Pang, Y., Zhu, H., Li, X., Li, X.: Classifying discriminative features for blur detection. IEEE Trans. Cybern. **46**(10), 2220–2227 (2015)
19. Park, J., Tai, Y.W., Cho, D., So Kweon, I.: A unified approach of multi-scale deep and hand-crafted features for defocus estimation. In: Proceedings of the IEEE Conference on Computer Vision and Pattern Recognition, pp. 1736–1745 (2017)
20. Ronneberger, O., Fischer, P., Brox, T.: U-Net: convolutional networks for biomedical image segmentation. In: Navab, N., Hornegger, J., Wells, W.M., Frangi, A.F. (eds.) MICCAI 2015. LNCS, vol. 9351, pp. 234–241. Springer, Cham (2015). https://doi.org/10.1007/978-3-319-24574-4_28
21. Sakurikar, P., Narayanan, P.: Composite focus measure for high quality depth maps. In: Proceedings of the IEEE International Conference on Computer Vision, pp. 1614–1622 (2017)
22. Shi, J., Xu, L., Jia, J.: Discriminative blur detection features. In: Proceedings of the IEEE Conference on Computer Vision and Pattern Recognition, pp. 2965–2972 (2014)
23. Shi, J., Xu, L., Jia, J.: Just noticeable defocus blur detection and estimation. In: Proceedings of the IEEE Conference on Computer Vision and Pattern Recognition, pp. 657–665 (2015)
24. Simonyan, K., Zisserman, A.: Very deep convolutional networks for large-scale image recognition. arXiv:1409.1556, pp. 1–14 (2014)
25. Son, H., Lee, J., Cho, S., Lee, S.: Single image defocus deblurring using kernel-sharing parallel atrous convolutions. In: Proceedings of the IEEE International Conference on Computer Vision (2021)
26. Su, B., Lu, S., Tan, C.L.: Blurred image region detection and classification. In: Proceedings of the 19th ACM International Conference on Multimedia, pp. 1397–1400 (2011)
27. Tai, Y.W., Brown, M.S.: Single image defocus map estimation using local contrast prior. In: 2009 16th IEEE International Conference on Image Processing (ICIP), pp. 1797–1800. IEEE (2009)
28. Tang, C., Liu, X., An, S., Wang, P.: BR^{2}Net: defocus blur detection via bidirectional channel attention residual refining network. IEEE Trans. Multimed. **23**, 624–635 (2020)
29. Tang, C., et al.: DeFusionNET: defocus blur detection via recurrently fusing and refining discriminative multi-scale deep features. IEEE Trans. Pattern Anal. Mach. Intell. **PP**(99), 1 (2020)
30. Tang, C., et al.: R^{2}MRF: defocus blur detection via recurrently refining multi-scale residual features. In: Proceedings of the AAAI Conference on Artificial Intelligence, vol. 34, pp. 12063–12070 (2020)

31. Tang, C., Wu, J., Hou, Y., Wang, P., Li, W.: A spectral and spatial approach of coarse-to-fine blurred image region detection. IEEE Signal Process. Lett. **23**(11), 1652–1656 (2016)
32. Tang, C., Zhu, X., Liu, X., Wang, L., Zomaya, A.: DeFusionNet: defocus blur detection via recurrently fusing and refining multi-scale deep features. In: IEEE Conference on Computer Vision and Pattern Recognition, pp. 2700–2709 (2019)
33. Tao, X., Gao, H., Shen, X., Wang, J., Jia, J.: Scale-recurrent network for deep image deblurring. In: Proceedings of the IEEE Conference on Computer Vision and Pattern Recognition, pp. 8174–8182 (2018)
34. Wang, J., Li, X., Yang, J.: Stacked conditional generative adversarial networks for jointly learning shadow detection and shadow removal. In: Proceedings of the IEEE Conference on Computer Vision and Pattern Recognition, pp. 1788–1797 (2018)
35. Wang, X., Yu, K., Dong, C., Loy, C.C.: Recovering realistic texture in image super-resolution by deep spatial feature transform. In: Proceedings of the IEEE Conference on Computer Vision and Pattern Recognition, pp. 606–615 (2018)
36. Xiong, W., et al.: Foreground-aware image inpainting. In: Proceedings of the IEEE/CVF Conference on Computer Vision and Pattern Recognition, pp. 5840–5848 (2019)
37. Yi, X., Eramian, M.: LBP-based segmentation of defocus blur. IEEE Trans. Image Process. **25**(4), 1626–1638 (2016)
38. Zhang, K., Zuo, W., Zhang, L.: Learning a single convolutional super-resolution network for multiple degradations. In: Proceedings of the IEEE Conference on Computer Vision and Pattern Recognition, pp. 3262–3271 (2018)
39. Zhang, N., Yan, J.: Rethinking the defocus blur detection problem and a real-time deep DBD model. In: Vedaldi, A., Bischof, H., Brox, T., Frahm, J.-M. (eds.) ECCV 2020. LNCS, vol. 12355, pp. 617–632. Springer, Cham (2020). https://doi.org/10.1007/978-3-030-58607-2_36
40. Zhang, S., Shen, X., Lin, Z., Mech, R., Costeira, J.P., Moura, J.M.F.: Learning to understand image blur. In: IEEE Conference on Computer Vision and Pattern Recognition, pp. 6586–6595 (2018)
41. Zhang, X., Wang, R., Jiang, X., Wang, W., Gao, W.: Spatially variant defocus blur map estimation and deblurring from a single image. J. Vis. Commun. Image Represent. **35**, 257–264 (2016)
42. Zhang, Z., Liu, Y., Xiong, Z., Li, J., Zhang, M.: Focus and blurriness measure using reorganized DCT coefficients for an autofocus application. IEEE Trans. Circuits Syst. Video Technol. **28**(1), 15–30 (2016)
43. Zhao, F., Lu, H., Zhao, W., Yao, L.: Image-scale-symmetric cooperative network for defocus blur detection. IEEE Trans. Circuits Syst. Video Technol. **32**(5), 2719–2731 (2021)
44. Zhao, W., Hou, X., He, Y., Lu, H.: Defocus blur detection via boosting diversity of deep ensemble networks. IEEE Trans. Image Process. **30**, 5426–5438 (2021)
45. Zhao, W., Hou, X., Yu, X., He, Y., Lu, H.: Towards weakly-supervised focus region detection via recurrent constraint network. IEEE Trans. Image Process. **29**, 1356–1367 (2019)
46. Zhao, W., Shang, C., Lu, H.: Self-generated defocus blur detection via dual adversarial discriminators. In: Proceedings of the IEEE/CVF Conference on Computer Vision and Pattern Recognition, pp. 6933–6942 (2021)
47. Zhao, W., Zhao, F., Wang, D., Lu, H.: Defocus blur detection via multi-stream bottom-top-bottom fully convolutional network. In: IEEE Conference on Computer Vision and Pattern Recognition, pp. 3080–3088 (2018)

48. Zhao, W., Zhao, F., Wang, D., Lu, H.: Defocus blur detection via multi-stream bottom-top-bottom network. IEEE Trans. Pattern Anal. Mach. Intell. **42**(8), 1884–1897 (2020)
49. Zhao, W., Zheng, B., Lin, Q., Lu, H.: Enhancing diversity of defocus blur detectors via cross-ensemble network. In: IEEE Conference on Computer Vision and Pattern Recognition, pp. 8905–8913 (2019)

Synergistic Self-supervised and Quantization Learning

Yun-Hao Cao[1] , Peiqin Sun[2]([⊠]) , Yechang Huang[2] , Jianxin Wu[1] ,
and Shuchang Zhou[2]

[1] State Key Laboratory for Novel Software Technology,
Nanjing University, Nanjing, China
`caoyunhao1997@gmail.com`, `wujx2001@gmail.com`
[2] MEGVII Technology, Beijing, China
{`sunpeiqin,huangyechang,zsc`}`@megvii.com`

Abstract. With the success of self-supervised learning (SSL), it has become a mainstream paradigm to fine-tune from self-supervised pre-trained models to boost the performance on downstream tasks. However, we find that current SSL models suffer severe accuracy drops when performing low-bit quantization, prohibiting their deployment in resource-constrained applications. In this paper, we propose a method called synergistic self-supervised and quantization learning (SSQL) to pretrain quantization-friendly self-supervised models facilitating downstream deployment. SSQL contrasts the features of the quantized and full precision models in a self-supervised fashion, where the bit-width for the quantized model is randomly selected in each step. SSQL not only significantly improves the accuracy when quantized to lower bit-widths, but also boosts the accuracy of full precision models in most cases. By only training once, SSQL can then benefit various downstream tasks at different bit-widths simultaneously. Moreover, the bit-width flexibility is achieved without additional storage overhead, requiring only one copy of weights during training and inference. We theoretically analyze the optimization process of SSQL, and conduct exhaustive experiments on various benchmarks to further demonstrate the effectiveness of our method.

Keywords: Quantization · Self-supervised learning · Transfer learning

1 Introduction

Deep supervised learning has achieved great success in the last decade. However, traditional supervised learning approaches rely heavily on a large set of annotated training data. Self-supervised learning (SSL) has gained popularity because of its ability to avoid the cost of annotating large-scale datasets as well as the ability to obtain task-agnostic representations [26]. After the emergence of the

Supplementary Information The online version contains supplementary material available at https://doi.org/10.1007/978-3-031-20056-4_34.

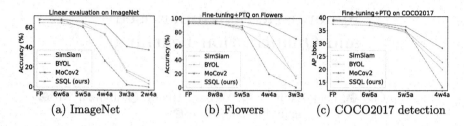

(a) ImageNet   (b) Flowers   (c) COCO2017 detection

Fig. 1. ImageNet linear evaluation and transfer results using ImageNet pretrained models. Directly applying current self-supervised contrastive methods does not work well for low-bit quantization when transferring, while our method (SSQL) leads to a dramatic performance boost. See Sect. 4.3 for details. '2w4a' means the weights are quantized to 2 bits and activations to 4 bits, etc.

contrastive learning (CL) paradigm [4,16], SSL has clearly gained momentum and several recent works [5,6,13] have achieved comparable or even better accuracy than the supervised pretraining when transferring to downstream tasks. A standard pipeline for SSL is to learn representations (i.e., pretrained backbone networks) on unlabeled datasets and then transfer to various downstream tasks (e.g., image classification [18] and object detection [17]) by fine-tuning.

With the fast development of self-supervised learning, an increasing proportion of the models that need to be deployed in downstream tasks are fine-tuned from SSL pretrained models. When we want to deploy them on some resource-constrained devices, it is essential to reduce the memory consumption and latency of the neural network. To facilitate deployment, several model compression techniques have been proposed, including lightweight architecture design [35,42], knowledge distillation [19], network pruning [14,27], and quantization [9,43]. Among them, quantization is one of the most effective methods and is directly supported by most current hardware. But severe accuracy degradation is often encountered during quantization, especially in the case of low bit-widths. As shown in Fig. 1, although current state-of-the-art self-supervised learning methods achieve impressive performance with full precision (FP) models, they all incur severe drop in accuracy when bit-width goes below 5. Inspired by SSL that can learn a good representation shared by various downstream tasks, we are thus motivated to ask a question: "Can we learn a quantization-friendly representation such that the pretrained model can be quantized more easily to facilitate deployment when transferring to different downstream tasks?".

We propose Synergistic Self-supervised and Quantization Learning (SSQL) by contrasting features of the quantized and full precision models as our solution: *SSL and quantization become synergistic—they help each other*. On one hand, the contrastive loss encourages similarity of the quantized and FP models. On the other hand, quantization improves SSL by encouraging feature consistency under differently augmented weights/activations. Our contributions are:

- To the best of our knowledge, we are the first to propose quantization-friendly training for SSL. We design an effective method called SSQL, which not only greatly improves the performance when quantized to low bit-widths, but also boosts the performance of full precision models in most cases.

- With SSQL, models only need to be trained *once* and can then be customized for a variety of downstream tasks at different bit-widths, allowing flexible speed-accuracy trade-off for real-world deployment. The bit-width flexibility is achieved without additional storage overhead, as only *one copy of weights* needs to be kept, both in the training and inference stage.
- SSQL is versatile. First, it can be combined with existing negative-based/free CL methods. Second, the pretrained models of SSQL are compatible with existing quantization methods to further boost the performance when quantizing.
- We provide theoretical analysis about the synergy between SSL and quantization in SSQL. Exhaustive experimental results further show that our SSQL achieves better performance on various benchmarks at all bit-widths.

2   Related Works

Network Quantization. Quantization is a method that converts the weights and activations in networks from full precision (i.e., 32-bit floating-point) to fixed-point integers. According to whether or not quantization is introduced into the training process, network quantization can be divided into two categories: Quantization-Aware Training (QAT) and Post-Training Quantization (PTQ). QAT methods [7,9,43] introduce a simulated quantization operation in the training stage. While it generally closes the gap to full precision accuracy compared to PTQ for low-bit quantization, it requires more effort in training and potentially hyperparameter tuning. In contrast, PTQ methods [20,23,29] take a trained full precision network and quantize it with little or no data [30], which requires minimal hyperparameter tuning and no end-to-end training. In this work, we introduce quantization into self-supervised learning to get a quantization-friendly pretrained model. Our pretrained model is compatible with existing QAT and PTQ methods when transferred to downstream tasks and hence can be combined to further improve performance.

AdaBits [21] enables adaptive bit-widths of weights and activations, but is a supervised learning method. Our pretrained model can adapt to different bit-widths, thus our work is also a method that only trains once for all bits, but in an unsupervised manner. More importantly, AdaBits focuses on the current task while we investigate the transfer ability of our models and also evaluate the quantization property on downstream tasks. OQAT [36] explores extremely low-bit architecture search by combining network architecture search methods with quantization. There are also works that study quantization-friendly properties. GDRQ [40] reshapes weights or activations into a uniform-like distribution dynamically. [15] proposes a bin regularization algorithm to improve low-bit network quantization. [38] proposes a quantization-friendly separable convolution for MobileNets. In contrast, we consider quantization-friendly properties from the perspective of pretraining under the self-supervised paradigm.

Self-supervised Learning. To avoid time-consuming and expensive data annotations and to explore better representations, many self-supervised methods were

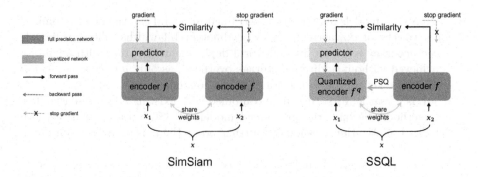

Fig. 2. Illustration of our method. Left: SimSiam [6]. Right: The proposed method SSQL. 'PSQ' denotes post step quantization, see Sect. 3.2 for details.

proposed to learn visual representations from large-scale unlabeled images or videos [2,8,12,31,41]. As the driving force of state-of-the-art SSL methods, contrastive learning methods greatly improve the performance of representation learning in recent years [3,4,6,13,16,32]. Contrastive learning is a discriminative approach that aims at pulling similar samples closer and pushing diverse samples far from each other. SimCLR [4] and MoCo [16] both employ a contrastive loss function InfoNCE [32], which requires negative samples. A more radical step is made by BYOL [13], which discards negative sampling in contrastive learning but achieves even better results in case a momentum encoder is used. [6] proposes a follow-up work SimSiam and demonstrates that simple siamese networks can learn meaningful representations even without the momentum encoder. However, previous works did not consider whether the pretrained model is quantization-friendly when transferring to downstream tasks.

SEED [11] uses self-supervised knowledge distillation for SSL with small models. S^2-BNN [37] investigates training self-supervised binary neural networks (BNN) by distilling knowledge from real networks. However, they all require a pretrained model as the teacher for distillation while ours does not. Moreover, [37] is tailored for BNN while our method is adaptive to different bit-widths. More importantly, our method can improve the performance of the full precision (FP) model over the baseline counterpart by encouraging feature consistency under differently augmented weights/activations via quantization.

3 Method

In this section, we introduce our approach, which we called synergistic self-supervised quantization learning (SSQL). We begin with the basic notation and a brief review of previous works, followed by our algorithm and analysis.

3.1 Background and Notation

Let x_1 and x_2 denote two randomly augmented views from an input image x. Let f denote an encoder network consisting of a backbone (e.g., ResNet [18]) and a projection MLP head [4]. By default we use SimSiam [6] as the baseline counterpart to develop our algorithm, as shown in Fig. 2.

SimSiam maximizes the similarity between two augmentations of one image. A prediction MLP head [13], denoted as h, transforms the output of one view and matches it to the other view. The output vectors for $\boldsymbol{x}_1$ is denoted as $\boldsymbol{z}_1 \triangleq f(\boldsymbol{x}_1)$ and $\boldsymbol{p}_1 \triangleq h(f(\boldsymbol{x}_1))$, and $\boldsymbol{z}_2$ and $\boldsymbol{p}_2$ are defined similarly.

The negative cosine similarity is defined as $D(\boldsymbol{p}, \boldsymbol{z}) \triangleq -\frac{\boldsymbol{p}}{\|\boldsymbol{p}\|_2} \cdot \frac{\boldsymbol{z}}{\|\boldsymbol{z}\|_2}$ and we assume both $\boldsymbol{z}$ and $\boldsymbol{p}$ have been l_2-normalized for simplicity in the following. Let $SG(\cdot)$ denote the stop-gradient operation. Then, the objective to be minimized in SimSiam is then:

$$L_{\text{SimSiam}} = D(\boldsymbol{p}_1, SG(\boldsymbol{z}_2)) + D(\boldsymbol{p}_2, SG(\boldsymbol{z}_1)). \tag{1}$$

3.2   Our Method

Our motivation is to train a quantization-friendly pretrained model, hence we proposed to introduce quantization into contrastive learning. We denote f^q as the quantized version of f, where q is the assigned quantization bit-width. Correspondingly, the resulting outputs become $\boldsymbol{z}^q$ and $\boldsymbol{p}^q$. We simply adopt the commonly used uniform quantizer for both weights and activations:

$$X_{int} = clip\left(\lfloor \frac{X}{S} + Z \rceil, 0, 2^q - 1\right), \tag{2}$$

$$X_q = (X_{int} - Z)S, \tag{3}$$

where S (scale) and Z (zero-point) are quantization parameters determined by the lower bound l and the upper bound u of X, while X can be either the model weights or activations. We use minimum and maximum values for l and u:

$$l = \min(X), u = \max(X), \tag{4}$$

$$S = \frac{u - l}{2^q - 1}. \tag{5}$$

Our solution SSQL is to let the quantized encoder f^q predict the output of the full precision (FP) encoder f (i.e., use FP outputs as the target):

$$L_{SSQL} = D(\boldsymbol{p}_1^q, SG(\boldsymbol{z}_2)) + D(\boldsymbol{p}_2^q, SG(\boldsymbol{z}_1)). \tag{6}$$

It is worth noting that we need only one copy of the model weights, which is f. f^q can be obtained directly from f using (2) and (3). Further, we can add the auxiliary SimSiam loss to improve performance by combining (1) and (6):

$$L_{SSQL\text{-}aux} = L_{SimSiam} + L_{SSQL}. \tag{7}$$

In order to make the model quantization-friendly to different bit-widths, we *randomly select* values from a set of candidate bit-widths *in each step* for the assignment of q. In addition, we also find that this random selection operation, as a kind of augmentation, brings a performance boost. We use 2∼8 and 4∼8 bits for weight and activation, respectively, in all our experiments. Also, we quantize f to get f^q after each step to ensure consistency, which we name as *post step quantization* (PSQ). Notice that we calculate S and Z during the forward pass of f and hence PSQ brings negligible overhead. During the backward pass, we adopt the straight-through estimator (STE) [1] for the quantization step. Notice that the quantized network and the full precision network *share weights*, hence when we backprop on the quantized network f_q using STE, the gradients will directly operate on the full precision network f. We will discuss the impact of the choice of loss functions and the candidate bit-widths set in Sect. 4.4.

3.3   The Synergy Between SSL and Quantization

Following the notations and analyses in [6], the optimization process can be viewed as an implementation of an Expectation-Maximization (EM) like algorithm. The loss function of SSQL can be organized in the following form:

$$\mathcal{L}(\theta, \eta) = \mathbb{E}_{x, \mathcal{T}, q}[\|\mathcal{F}_\theta^q(\mathcal{T}(x)) - \eta_x\|_2^2], \tag{8}$$

where $\mathcal{F}_\theta$ is a network parameterized by θ, $\mathcal{F}_\theta^q$ is obtained by quantizing $\mathcal{F}_\theta$, $\mathcal{T}$ is the augmentation and x is an image. The expectation $\mathbb{E}[\cdot]$ is over the distribution of images, augmentations and bit-widths. η_x is the representation of image x.

With the formulation of Eq. (8), we consider solving

$$\min_{\theta, \eta} \mathcal{L}(\theta, \eta). \tag{9}$$

The problem in (9) can be solved by alternating between two subproblems:

$$\theta^t \leftarrow \arg\min_\theta \mathcal{L}(\theta, \eta^{t-1}); \quad \eta^t \leftarrow \arg\min_\eta \mathcal{L}(\theta^t, \eta). \tag{10}$$

Here t is the index of alternation and "←" means assigning. The optimization step for η^t is the same as [6] and we analyze the optimization step for θ^t:

$$\theta^{t+1} \leftarrow \arg\min_\theta \mathbb{E}_{x, \mathcal{T}, q}\Big[\|\mathcal{F}_\theta^q(\mathcal{T}(x)) - \mathcal{F}_{\theta^t}(\mathcal{T}'(x))\|_2^2\Big]. \tag{11}$$

Here $\mathcal{T}'$ implies another view and detailed derivation of (11) is included in the appendix. Moreover, we have

$$\mathbb{E}_{x, \mathcal{T}, q}\Big[\|\mathcal{F}_\theta^q(\mathcal{T}(x)) - \mathcal{F}_{\theta^t}(\mathcal{T}'(x))\|_2^2\Big] \tag{12}$$

$$= \mathbb{E}_{x, \mathcal{T}, q}\Big[\|\mathcal{F}_\theta^q(\mathcal{T}(x)) - \mathcal{F}_\theta(\mathcal{T}(x)) + \mathcal{F}_\theta(\mathcal{T}(x)) - \mathcal{F}_{\theta^t}(\mathcal{T}'(x))\|_2^2\Big] \tag{13}$$

$$= \underbrace{\mathbb{E}_{x, \mathcal{T}, q}\Big[\|\mathcal{F}_\theta^q(\mathcal{T}(x)) - \mathcal{F}_\theta(\mathcal{T}(x))\|_2^2\Big]}_{\text{Q term (quantization term)}} + \underbrace{\mathbb{E}_{x, \mathcal{T}, q}\Big[\|\mathcal{F}_\theta(\mathcal{T}(x)) - \mathcal{F}_{\theta^t}(\mathcal{T}'(x))\|_2^2\Big]}_{\text{CL term (contrastive learning term)}} \tag{14}$$

$$+ \underbrace{2\mathbb{E}_{x, \mathcal{T}, q}\Big[\big(\mathcal{F}_\theta^q(\mathcal{T}(x)) - \mathcal{F}_\theta(\mathcal{T}(x))\big)^T \big(\mathcal{F}_\theta(\mathcal{T}(x)) - \mathcal{F}_{\theta^t}(\mathcal{T}'(x))\big)\Big]}_{\text{cross term}}. \tag{15}$$

It is reasonable to assume that the quantization error and the contrastive learning error are at most weakly correlated (see appendix for empirical verification), hence we can remove the cross term and are left with two objectives in the optimization step for θ. The Q term minimizes the distance between the quantized network $\mathcal{F}_\theta^q$ and the FP network $\mathcal{F}_\theta$, which naturally leads to the desired quantization-friendly property. The CL term is the original optimization term in SimSiam to learn image representations. Also notice that we take expectations over 3 terms, where the extra q term can be seen as one kind of augmentation on weights/activations. It is well-known that strong image augmentations are essential in SSL [4]. Hence, the quantization can potentially assist the learning of SSL, by encouraging feature consistency under differently augmented weights/activations via quantization. In conclusion, the design of our loss function makes quantization and SSL work in a synergistic fashion.

4 Experiments

We introduce the implementation details in Sect. 4.1. We experiment on CIFAR-10 and CIFAR-100 [22] in Sect. 4.2 and ImageNet [34] (IN) in Sect. 4.3. Then, we evaluate the transfer performance of ImageNet pretrained models on downstream classification and object detection benchmarks in Sect. 4.3. Finally, we study the effects of different components and hyper-parameters in our algorithm in Sect. 4.4.

4.1 Implementation Details

Datasets. The main experiments are conducted on three benchmark datasets, i.e., CIFAR-10, CIFAR-100 [22] and ImageNet [34]. We also conduct transfer experiments on 7 recognition benchmarks (see appendix for details) as well as 2 detection benchmarks Pascal VOC 07&12 [10] and COCO2017 [25].

Backbones. Apart from the commonly used ResNet-50 [18] in recent SSL papers, we also adopt 2 smaller networks, i.e., ResNet-18 [18] and ResNet-34 [18] for our experiments. We use the same settings as [6] for prediction and projection MLP. Sometimes we abbreviate ResNet-18/50 to R-18/50.

Training Details. We follow the training setup in SimSiam [6] for our method. More specifically, we use SGD for pretraining, with batch size of 256 and a base lr=0.05. The learning rate has a cosine decay schedule. The weight decay is 0.0001 and the SGD momentum is 0.9. We pretrain for 400 epochs on CIFAR-10 and CIFAR-100 and 100 epochs on ImageNet unless otherwise specified. Please see appendix for more training details for linear evaluation and fine-tuning.

Evaluation Protocols. Following previous works [16], we adopt linear evaluation and fine-tuning to evaluate the pretrained representations. Moreover, we want to evaluate the performance of the representations after quantization. Hence, we make corresponding adjustments and propose a new evaluation protocol when combining quantization and SSL, as shown in Fig. 3. More specifically,

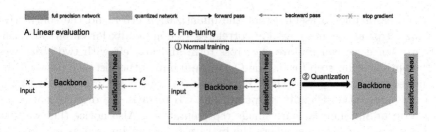

Fig. 3. Illustration of the evaluation protocols adopted in our paper.

Table 1. Linear evaluation results on CIFAR-10. All pretrained for 400 epochs. SimSiam-PACT trains 7 models separately and we color it grey.

Backbone	Method	Linear evaluation accuracy (%)							
		FP	8w8a	6w6a	5w5a	4w4a	3w3a	2w8a	2w4a
ResNet-18	SimSiam [6]	**90.7**	90.7	**90.6**	90.3	88.9	66.0	70.1	63.8
	BYOL [13]	89.3	89.3	89.4	89.3	88.0	75.1	71.9	63.3
	SimSiam-PACT [7]	-	89.2	89.2	89.3	89.2	88.2	89.3	88.3
	SSQL (ours)	**90.7**	90.8	**90.6**	90.6	90.1	85.6	88.0	86.5
	SimCLR [4]	**89.4**	89.3	89.2	88.8	87.1	73.9	65.6	55.6
	MoCov2 [5]	88.9	88.8	88.4	88.2	86.8	72.2	66.4	50.7
	SSQL-NCE (ours)	89.0	89.0	89.0	**88.8**	87.9	82.9	87.1	84.9
ResNet-50	SimSiam [6]	90.9	90.9	91.0	90.6	89.5	74.1	55.1	57.1
	BYOL [13]	90.3	90.3	90.0	89.7	87.5	58.5	82.4	67.8
	SSQL (ours)	**91.1**	**91.1**	**91.1**	**91.1**	**90.0**	77.4	89.5	87.2
	SimCLR [4]	91.5	91.4	91.3	90.5	88.1	59.6	63.5	42.4
	MoCov2 [5]	90.2	90.2	90.2	89.4	87.9	72.1	68.8	49.5
	SSQL-NCE (ours)	**92.1**	**92.1**	**92.0**	**91.9**	**89.8**	74.0	**88.6**	84.9

we freeze and quantize the backbone and only update the classification head for linear evaluation (i.e., backbone weights frozen). For fine-tuning, we first train the backbone as well as the classification head as normal (i.e., backbone weights updated). Then, based on the fine-tuned FP model, we conduct either PTQ or QAT to evaluate the performance after quantization. We adopt PTQ after fine-tuning in our experiments by default. We use '$nwma$' to denote that we quantize weight to n-bit and quantize activation to m-bit in this paper (e.g., 4w4a).

4.2 CIFAR Results

We compare our method with popular SSL methods BYOL [13], SimSiam [6], SimCLR [4] and MoCov2 [5]. We evaluate the linear evaluation accuracy under different bit-widths after quantization, as mentioned in Sect. 4.1. Notice that we only pretrain one full precision (FP) model and then use it for evaluation on different bit-widths. To better illustrate the effectiveness of our method, we also

Table 2. Linear evaluation results on CIFAR-100. All pretrained for 400 epochs.

Backbone	Method	Linear evaluation accuracy (%)							
		FP	8w8a	6w6a	5w5a	4w4a	3w3a	2w8a	2w4a
ResNet-18	SimSiam [6]	65.5	65.5	65.4	64.6	62.6	41.6	40.1	36.9
	BYOL [13]	62.6	62.6	62.5	62.0	60.6	47.9	44.1	38.8
	SimCLR [4]	59.2	59.2	59.0	57.9	54.4	34.1	38.4	28.8
	MoCov2 [5]	62.5	62.5	62.1	61.5	59.5	43.5	40.1	30.8
	SSQL (ours)	**66.9**	**66.8**	**66.9**	**65.8**	**65.0**	**57.4**	**53.9**	**50.6**
ResNet-50	SimSiam [6]	64.3	64.2	64.1	62.9	61.3	44.9	32.9	32.6
	BYOL [13]	66.7	66.5	65.0	59.6	47.2	14.5	55.3	27.2
	SimCLR [4]	66.2	66.1	65.9	64.8	60.1	40.2	43.8	24.7
	MoCov2 [5]	66.5	66.5	66.3	65.4	61.9	44.2	41.1	28.5
	SSQL (ours)	**68.0**	**67.9**	**67.8**	**67.8**	**67.8**	**59.9**	**62.9**	**61.5**

create one strong baseline SimSiam-PACT, by combining PACT [7] and SimSiam during pretraining. Notice that it is not a fair comparison with other methods because it needs to pretrain different models for different bit-widths (i.e., need 7 pretrained models for 7 bit-widths). In other words, it is not flexible and the training overhead is unbearable for large data volumes. Experimental results on CIFAR-10 and CIFAR-100 are shown in Table 1 and Table 2, respectively.

As shown in Table 1, take ResNet-18 as an example, our SSQL achieves comparable performance with the baseline counterpart SimSiam under linear evaluation in full precision on CIFAR-10. However, when we lower the bit-width (from 8w8a to 2w4a), our advantages over the baseline SimSiam will become more and more obvious. For instance, our SSQL achieves **19.6%** and **22.7%** higher accuracy than SimSiam at 3w3a and 2w4a, respectively. When comparing with SimSima-PACT, we can find that our SSQL achieves higher accuracy at 4w4a and above. However, SimSiam-PACT achieves slightly higher accuracy than our method at 3w3a and below but the gap is within 3%. Moreover, we achieve higher accuracy than SimSiam under ResNet-50 at FP, and the advantages when reducing bit-widths are consistent. Finally, our SSQL can also be combined with InfoNCE [32] based methods, e.g., SimCLR and we name it SSQL-NCE. We can observe similar trends as above and it demonstrates that our SSQL is compatible with both negative-based and negative-free CL methods.

As shown in Table 2, our SSQL achieves the highest accuracy on CIFAR-100 in all cases. For instance, when comparing the first column (FP), our SSQL is significantly better than baseline counterpart SimSiam: up to **+1.4%** and **+3.7%** accuracy for ResNet-18 and ResNet-50, respectively. Our advantages become bigger when we further lower the bit-widths: up to **+6.5%**, **+15%** and **+28.9%** accuracy at 4w4a, 3w3a and 2w4a, respectively, for ResNet-50.

To demonstrate the effectiveness of the proposed method in a more intuitive way, we visualize the feature spaces learned by different methods in Fig. 4. First,

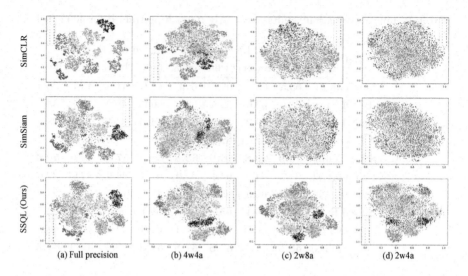

Fig. 4. t-SNE [28] visualization of CIFAR-10 using ResNet-18. The column (a) shows the results using FP backbone. The column (b), (c) and (d) shows the results at 4w4a, 2w8a and 2w4a, respectively. This figure is best viewed in color.

Table 3. Linear evaluation results on ImageNet. All pretrained for 100 epochs, except for MoCov2. [†] denotes that we use the official MoCov2 200ep checkpoint. SimSiam-PACT trains 5 models separately and we color it grey.

Backbone	Method	Linear evaluation accuracy (%)					
		FP	8w8a	5w5a	4w4a	3w3a	2w4a
ResNet-18	SimSiam [6]	55.0	54.7	53.9	36.7	6.3	1.5
	BYOL [13]	54.1	54.0	51.9	42.4	13.6	3.6
	SimSiam-PACT [7]	-	52.8	52.8	52.3	51.0	51.6
	SSQL (ours)	**57.6**	**57.6**	**56.7**	**52.8**	**41.0**	**43.1**
ResNet-50	SimSiam [6]	**68.1**	**67.9**	65.0	52.4	15.0	3.1
	BYOL [13]	64.6	64.4	61.7	53.6	16.8	6.4
	MoCov2[†] [5]	67.7	67.0	60.3	26.3	2.3	0.1
	SSQL (ours)	67.9	**67.9**	**66.1**	**63.0**	**40.8**	**37.4**

three models are trained on the CIFAR-10 dataset by using SimCLR, SimSiam and SSQL, respectively. After that, 5,000 samples in CIFAR-10 are represented accordingly and then are reduced to a two-dimensional space by t-SNE [28]. As seen, the samples are more separable in the feature space learned by SSQL than both SimCLR and SimSiam (especially at 2w8a and 2w4a), showing that SSQL can learn better feature representations after quantization.

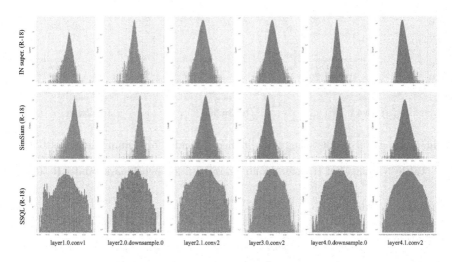

Fig. 5. Visualization of weight distribution for ResNet-18. The first, second and third row are the results of ImageNet supervised, SimSiam and ours, respectively.

Table 4. Fine-tuning+PTQ results on ImageNet subsets. Here we adopt the fine-tuning settings on 1%/10% labeled data and report Top-5 accuracy (%).

Backbone	Method	1% labels				10% labels			
		FP	6w6a	5w5a	4w4a	FP	6w6a	5w5a	4w4a
ResNet-18	SimSiam [6]	43.7	43.4	42.4	37.5	**76.1**	75.8	74.3	64.5
	BYOL [13]	36.7	36.5	35.5	31.2	75.5	75.1	73.9	65.2
	SSQL (ours)	**47.7**	**47.6**	**47.1**	**45.0**	76.1	**75.9**	**75.0**	**70.7**
ResNet-50	SimSiam [6]	53.2	52.8	51.5	36.4	82.5	81.7	79.0	67.9
	BYOL [13]	47.3	47.2	46.4	40.4	81.1	80.7	79.6	69.9
	SSQL (ours)	**55.2**	**55.0**	**54.4**	**51.8**	**83.0**	**82.7**	**81.0**	**76.7**

4.3 ImageNet and Transfer Learning Results

In this section, we do unsupervised pretraining on the large-scale ImageNet training set [34] without using labels. The linear evaluation results on ImageNet are shown in Table 3. Also, we evaluate the transfer ability of the learned representations on ImageNet later. We train SSQL, SimSiam and BYOL for 100 epochs on ImageNet and directly use the official checkpoint for MoCov2.

As shown in Table 3, when comparing the first column (FP), our SSQL achieves higher accuracy than the baseline counterpart SimSiam (57.6 v.s. 55.0) under ResNet-18. When comparing the fourth column (4w4a), our SSQL achieves 16.1% and 10.6% gains for ResNet-18 and ResNet-50, respectively. In short, our SSQL achieves comparable or better accuracy at full precision and is more quantization-friendly at lower bit-widths. When compared with SimSiam-PACT, our SSQL achieves better results at 4 bits or higher, *with only one copy of weights*.

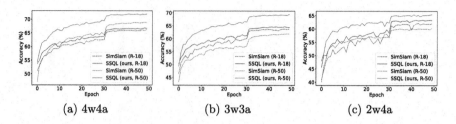

(a) 4w4a   (b) 3w3a   (c) 2w4a

Fig. 6. ImageNet results using LSQ [9]. See appendix for training details of LSQ.

Table 5. ImageNet transfer results on recognition benchmarks under R-50.

Datasets	Method	Linear evaluation					Fine-tuning				
		FP	8w8a	5w5a	4w4a	3w3a	FP	8w8a	5w5a	4w4a	3w3a
CIFAR-10	SimSiam	86.3	86.2	84.4	70.7	48.0	95.9	95.9	92.0	51.7	14.6
	SSQL (ours)	89.3	89.2	89.1	87.1	71.9	96.3	96.3	95.1	89.2	69.3
CIFAR-100	SimSiam	58.9	58.7	52.5	39.0	20.2	82.9	82.5	76.7	66.0	5.3
	SSQL (ours)	68.7	68.6	68.8	66.4	49.7	83.3	83.3	82.0	74.7	39.3
Flowers	SimSiam	78.7	82.5	81.9	66.6	49.3	94.0	93.8	83.8	57.8	16.2
	SSQL (ours)	90.7	90.7	91.3	90.9	84.0	95.3	95.3	94.6	90.3	70.6
Food-101	SimSiam	67.1	67.1	64.7	56.0	27.7	86.2	86.2	80.4	54.4	2.2
	SSQL (ours)	72.6	72.5	71.5	68.4	51.6	85.5	85.5	84.5	70.4	11.2
Pets	SimSiam	79.7	79.6	74.3	70.9	32.2	87.5	87.4	81.3	59.3	10.9
	SSQL (ours)	83.6	83.9	83.3	82.3	73.8	86.9	86.8	85.9	84.6	73.6
Dtd	SimSiam	69.9	69.7	69.1	63.4	46.6	73.4	73.6	70.5	60.4	8.8
	SSQL (ours)	74.4	74.3	74.3	73.4	64.4	73.7	73.7	71.9	70.1	56.6
Caltech-101	SimSiam	80.2	80.4	78.6	66.7	31.4	86.9	86.6	85.0	76.8	7.9
	SSQL (ours)	86.9	87.2	85.2	83.8	65.9	86.4	86.3	85.5	82.9	59.7

As shown in Fig. 1, the ImageNet linear evaluation performance can somehow indicate the performance at downstream tasks at different bit-widths (i.e., the trend is consistent). We plot the weight distribution of different pretrained models in Fig. 5. As seen, the weights of our model (third row) are more quantization-friendly when compared with the two baseline counterparts in terms of 3 aspects: more uniform distribution, smaller ranges, and much fewer outliers. (There is a similar phenomenon after fine-tuning on downstream tasks, too, see appendix).

Fine-Tuning with Partial Labels. Following common practices, we also fine-tune the pretrained models on ImageNet with 1% and 10% labeled data in Table 4. As seen, SSQL achieves the best performance in all cases. We also report the PTQ performance and our advantages become greater as the bit-width decreases. For instance, when fine-tuned using 10% labels under R-50, SSQL achieves 0.5% and 8.8% higher accuracy than SimSiam at FP and 4w4a, respectively.

Combining with QAT Method. To further illustrate the effectiveness of SSQL, we combine different pretrained models with the state-of-the-art QAT

Table 6. Object detection results on VOC2007 under R18-C4. The best results are in **boldface** and the second best results are <u>underlined</u>.

Method	FP			8w8a			6w6a			5w5a			4w4a		
	AP_{50}	AP	AP_{75}	AP_{50}	AP	AP_{75}	AP_{50}	AP	AP_{75}	AP_{50}	AP	AP_{75}	AP_{50}	AP	AP_{75}
random init	58.9	32.1	30.5	58.7	31.9	30.2	58.4	31.6	30.2	57.0	30.4	28.9	42.4	20.8	17.0
IN supervised	**73.9**	44.6	46.5	**74.1**	44.2	46.2	73.0	43.4	44.5	68.9	39.4	39.3	33.1	16.7	14.0
BYOL	72.8	44.7	46.3	72.4	44.4	46.0	72.2	44.2	45.6	62.7	38.0	39.4	52.7	28.9	27.8
SimSiam	72.8	44.4	46.6	72.9	44.4	46.3	72.4	44.0	46.0	69.7	42.0	43.1	50.4	26.4	23.8
SimSiam-200ep	72.5	44.3	46.5	72.5	44.3	46.5	72.0	43.9	46.3	69.2	41.4	42.7	53.7	29.8	29.0
SSQL (ours)	<u>73.4</u>	<u>44.7</u>	<u>46.8</u>	<u>73.5</u>	**45.0**	<u>46.8</u>	73.1	<u>44.5</u>	<u>46.4</u>	**71.6**	<u>42.8</u>	<u>44.4</u>	**61.2**	<u>34.1</u>	<u>33.4</u>
SSQL-200ep (ours)	73.2	**45.0**	**47.3**	73.2	**45.0**	**47.0**	<u>72.9</u>	**44.8**	**46.8**	<u>71.3</u>	**43.3**	**45.0**	**61.2**	**35.1**	**35.0**

Table 7. Object detection/segmentation results on COCO2017 under R50-FPN.

Method	FP						6w6a					
	AP^{bb}	AP^{bb}_{50}	AP^{bb}_{75}	AP^{mk}	AP^{mk}_{50}	AP^{mk}_{75}	AP^{bb}	AP^{bb}_{50}	AP^{bb}_{75}	AP^{mk}	AP^{mk}_{50}	AP^{mk}_{75}
IN supervised	38.2	56.0	42.0	34.8	56.0	37.2	37.6	58.3	41.4	34.3	55.2	36.8
SimSiam	**38.9**	**59.8**	**42.3**	**35.2**	**56.7**	**37.7**	38.1	58.7	41.5	34.5	55.7	36.8
BYOL	37.4	57.9	40.6	34.1	54.9	36.4	37.0	57.4	40.2	33.7	54.3	36.0
SSQL (ours)	38.7	59.2	**42.3**	**35.2**	56.2	**37.7**	**38.3**	**58.8**	**41.7**	**34.8**	**55.8**	**37.3**
	5w5a						4w4a					
IN supervised	35.2	55.5	38.4	31.9	52.3	34.0	23.4	38.6	24.6	21.4	36.3	22.1
SimSiam	34.3	54.0	36.7	30.9	50.6	32.6	19.9	33.6	20.6	18.1	31.3	18.3
BYOL	34.9	54.4	37.7	31.8	51.4	33.8	22.7	37.4	24.0	20.9	35.2	21.7
SSQL (ours)	**36.5**	**56.9**	**39.4**	**33.3**	**53.6**	**35.5**	**28.2**	**43.1**	**27.5**	**26.0**	**43.1**	**27.5**

method LSQ [9]. We initialize LSQ with ImageNet linear evaluated FP models (i.e., FP column in Table 3). As seen from the learning curves in Fig. 6, our SSQL provides a better starting point. Take R-50 4w4a as an example, SSQL achieves 7% higher accuracy than SimSiam after the first epoch, while the initial accuracy of the FP model is about the same. Consequently, our SSQL achieves higher final accuracy and it shows that our pretrained model can serve as a better initialization when combined with QAT methods to boost performance.

Transferring to Recognition Benchmarks. We transfer the ImageNet learned representations of R-50 to downstream recognition tasks in Table 5. The results of R-18 and more training details are included in the appendix. As shown in Table 5, our method improves a lot on all recognition benchmarks, especially under linear evaluation. When comparing the fine-tuning results at FP, we can see that our SSQL achieves comparable results with SimSiam. When we further conduct PTQ, we can observe larger improvements as the bit-width decreases, which is consistent with the properties observed in upstream pretraining. Take R-50 on CIFAR-10 as an example, SSQL is slightly better than SimSiam at FP but the improvement expands to 37.5% at 4w4a and 54.7% at 3w3a. In conclusion, the quantization-friendly properties are also well-preserved by SSQL when we fine-tune the weights during transferring. This again confirms our motivation that quantization-friendly pretraining is both important and feasible.

Table 8. Ablation studies on CIFAR-10 using ResNet-34.

ID	Q Pred	Q Target	Aux	W Bit	A Bit	Linear evaluation accuracy (%)					
						FP	6w6a	4w4a	3w3a	2w4a	Avg
(a)	✗	✗	✗	-	-	89.0	89.0	87.2	75.6	55.3	79.2
(b)	✗	✓	✗	4~16	4~16	87.6	87.5	85.8	70.4	58.5	78.0
(c)	✓	✓	✗	4~16	4~16	90.5	90.4	88.9	79.2	73.7	84.5
(d)	✓	✗	✗	4~16	4~16	**91.0**	**91.0**	89.5	83.0	65.2	83.9
(e)	✓	✗	✗	6	6	90.0	89.9	87.9	69.1	62.1	79.8
(f)	✓	✗	✗	4	4	36.0	35.9	36.4	29.2	29.7	33.4
(g)	✓	✓	✗	2~8	4~8	88.3	88.2	86.9	80.3	85.4	85.8
(h)	✓	✗	✗	2~8	4~8	89.6	89.5	88.2	82.9	81.5	86.3
(i)	✓	✗	✓	2~8	4~8	90.9	90.8	**89.6**	**83.2**	**86.8**	**88.3**

Transferring to Object Detection. We investigate the downstream object detection performance on Pascal VOC07&12 [10] in Table 6 and COCO2017 [25] in Table 7. The detector is Faster R-CNN [33] with a backbone of R18-C4 [17] for VOC and Mask R-CNN [17] with R50-FPN [24] backbone for COCO, implemented in [39]. We follow the same settings in [5] and we evaluate the performance of post-training quantization models (i.e., the fine-tuning+PTQ pipeline).

As shown in Table 6, our SSQL performs better than SimSiam and BYOL on Pascal VOC at FP. Also, as we lower the bit-width, our SSQL is more significantly better than baseline counterparts: up to **+1.9** and **+7.5** AP_{50} over *the best results among other methods* at 5w5a and 4w4a, respectively. We can reach similar conclusions on COCO2017 from Table 7. Although our SSQL achieves slightly lower accuracy than SimSiam at FP on COCO, we achieve **+2.2** and **+8.3** AP^{bb} points higher at 5w5a and 4w4a, respectively. In conclusion, the results show that the quantization-friendly property of our pretrained model can be well-preserved even after fine-tuning on downstream detection tasks.

4.4 Ablation Studies

We conduct ablation studies on CIFAR-10 in Table 8 and we keep the training settings the same as in Sect. 4.2. 'Q Pred' denotes whether to quantize the prediction branch and the same for 'Q Target'. 'Aux' denotes whether to add the auxiliary SimSiam loss. 'W/A Bit' represents the candidate bit-widths set for weight/activation. We can have the following conclusions from Table 8:

- Quantizing the target branch only degenerates the performance. The row (b) is the worst among the first four rows, which indicates that only using the quantized output as the target makes training more difficult (learning noisy targets). In other words, it is essential to update the quantized branch with the gradients (both row (c) and (d) perform better than the baseline row (a)).

- Random selection of bit-widths for training is better than training with a single bit-width. We can observe that the row (d) surpasses the row (e) and (f) at all bit-widths, where the latter two are trained using a single bit-width. It shows that the random selection operation in our method is beneficial to improve performance, by providing stronger randomness and augmentations.
- Using a reasonable bit perturbation range further improves the performance at lower bit-widths. When comparing the row (d) and (h), we can observe a big boost at 2w4a (81.5 v.s. 65.2) at the expense of FP accuracy. When comparing the row (c) and (g), we can find that quantizing both branches at the same time results in a larger drop in FP accuracy.
- The row (i) achieves the best trade-off among all settings, which is also the default setting for all our experiments. When comparing the row (i) and (h), we can see that the addition of the auxiliary loss makes the full precision model produce better targets, thus improving the accuracies at all bit-widths.

5 Conclusion

In this paper, we proposed a method called SSQL for pretraining quantization-friendly models to facility flexible deployment in resource constrained applications. We provide theoretical analysis for the proposed approach, and experimental results on various benchmarks show that our method not only greatly improves the performance when quantized to lower bits, but also boosts the performance of full precision models. It has also been verified that our method is compatible with PTQ or QAT methods, and the quantization-friendly property can be well-preserved when transferring to downstream tasks. In the future, we will explore applications of SSQL to other architectures, notably Transformers. Also, we will explore fine-tuning methods that can better preserve the quantization-friendly property of our models.

References

1. Bengio, Y., Léonard, N., Courville, A.: Estimating or propagating gradients through stochastic neurons for conditional computation. arXiv preprint arXiv:1308.3432 (2013)
2. Caron, M., Bojanowski, P., Joulin, A., Douze, M.: Deep clustering for unsupervised learning of visual features. In: The European Conference on Computer Vision. LNCS, vol. 11218, pp. 132–149. Springer, Cham (2018)
3. Caron, M., Misra, I., Mairal, J., Goyal, P., Bojanowski, P., Joulin, A.: Unsupervised learning of visual features by contrasting cluster assignments. In: Advances in Neural Information Processing Systems, pp. 9912–9924 (2020)
4. Chen, T., Kornblith, S., Norouzi, M., Hinton, G.: A simple framework for contrastive learning of visual representations. In: The International Conference on Machine Learning, pp. 1597–1607 (2020)
5. Chen, X., Fan, H., Girshick, R., He, K.: Improved baselines with momentum contrastive learning. arXiv preprint arXiv:2003.04297 (2020)

6. Chen, X., He, K.: Exploring simple Siamese representation learning. In: The IEEE Conference on Computer Vision and Pattern Recognition, pp. 15750–15758 (2021)

7. Choi, J., Wang, Z., Venkataramani, S., Chuang, P.I.J., Srinivasan, V., Gopalakrishnan, K.: PACT: parameterized clipping activation for quantized neural networks. In: The International Conference on Learning Representations, pp. 1–12 (2018)

8. Doersch, C., Gupta, A., Efros, A.A.: Unsupervised visual representations learning by context prediction. In: The IEEE International Conference on Computer Vision, pp. 1422–1430 (2015)

9. Esser, S.K., McKinstry, J.L., Bablani, D., Appuswamy, R., Modha, D.S.: Learned step size quantization. In: The International Conference on Learning Representations, pp. 1–12 (2020)

10. Everingham, M., Gool, L.V., Williams, C.K., Winn, J., Zisserman, A.: The pascal visual object classes (VOC) challenge. Int. J. Comput. Vis. **88**(2), 303–338 (2010)

11. Fang, Z., Wang, J., Wang, L., Zhang, L., Yang, Y., Liu, Z.: SEED: self-supervised distillation for visual representation. In: The International Conference on Learning Representations, pp. 1–12 (2021)

12. Gidaris, S., Singh, P., Komodakis, N.: Unsupervised representation learning by predicting image rotations. In: The International Conference on Learning Representations, pp. 1–14 (2015)

13. Grill, J.B., et al.: Boostrap your own latent: a new approach to self-supervised learning. In: Advances in Neural Information Processing Systems, pp. 21271–21284 (2020)

14. Han, S., Mao, H., Dally, W.J.: Deep compression: compressing deep neural networks with pruning, trained quantization and Huffman coding. In: The International Conference on Learning Representations, pp. 1–14 (2016)

15. Han, T., Li, D., Liu, J., Tian, L., Shan, Y.: Improving low-precision network quantization via bin regularization. In: The IEEE International Conference on Computer Vision, pp. 5261–5270 (2021)

16. He, K., Fan, H., Wu, Y., Xie, S., Girshick, R.: Momentum contrast for unsupervised visual representation learning. In: The IEEE Conference on Computer Vision and Pattern Recognition, pp. 9729–9738 (2020)

17. He, K., Gkioxari, G., Dollár, P., Girshick, R.: Mask R-CNN. In: The IEEE International Conference on Computer Vision, pp. 2961–2969 (2017)

18. He, K., Zhang, X., Ren, S., Sun, J.: Deep residual learning for image recognition. In: The IEEE Conference on Computer Vision and Pattern Recognition, pp. 770–778 (2016)

19. Hinton, G., Vinyals, O., Dean, J.: Distilling the knowledge in a neural network. arXiv preprint arXiv:1503.02531 (2015)

20. Hubara, I., Nahshan, Y., Hanani, Y., Banner, R., Soudry, D.: Accurate post training quantization with small calibration sets. In: The International Conference on Machine Learning, pp. 4466–4475 (2021)

21. Jin, Q., Yang, L., Liao, Z.: AdaBits: neural network quantization with adaptive bitwidths. In: The IEEE Conference on Computer Vision and Pattern Recognition, pp. 2146–2156 (2020)

22. Krizhevsky, A., Hinton, G.E.: Learning multiple layers of features from tiny images. Technical report, University of Toronto (2009)

23. Li, Y., et al.: BRECQ: pushing the limit of post-training quantization by block reconstruction. In: The International Conference on Learning Representations, pp. 1–16 (2021)

24. Lin, T.Y., Dollár, P., Girshick, R., He, K., Hariharan, B., Belongie, S.: Feature pyramid networks for object detection. In: The IEEE Conference on Computer Vision and Pattern Recognition, pp. 2177–2125 (2017)
25. Lin, T.-Y., et al.: Microsoft COCO: common objects in context. In: Fleet, D., Pajdla, T., Schiele, B., Tuytelaars, T. (eds.) ECCV 2014. LNCS, vol. 8693, pp. 740–755. Springer, Cham (2014). https://doi.org/10.1007/978-3-319-10602-1_48
26. Liu, X., et al.: Self-supervised learning: generative or contrastive. arXiv preprint arXiv:2006.08218 (2020)
27. Luo, J.H., Wu, J., Lin, W.: ThiNet: a filter level pruning method for deep neural network compression. In: The IEEE International Conference on Computer Vision, pp. 5058–5066 (2017)
28. van der Maaten, L., Hinton, G.: Visualizing data using t-SNE. J. Mach. Learn. Res. **9**(86), 2579–2605 (2008)
29. Nagel, M., Amjad, R.A., van Baalen, M., Louizos, C., Blankevoort, T.: Up or down? Adaptive rounding for post-training quantization. In: The International Conference on Machine Learning, pp. 7197–7206 (2020)
30. Nagel, M., van Baalen, M., Blankevoort, T., Welling, M.: Data-free quantization through weight equalization and bias correction. In: The IEEE International Conference on Computer Vision, pp. 1325–1334 (2019)
31. Noroozi, M., Favaro, P.: Unsupervised learning of visual representations by solving jigsaw puzzles. In: Leibe, B., Matas, J., Sebe, N., Welling, M. (eds.) ECCV 2016. LNCS, vol. 9910, pp. 69–84. Springer, Cham (2016). https://doi.org/10.1007/978-3-319-46466-4_5
32. van den Oord, A., Li, Y., Vinyals, O.: Representation learning with contrastive predictive coding. arXiv preprint arXiv:1807.03748 (2018)
33. Ren, S., He, K., Girshick, R., Sun, J.: Faster R-CNN: towards real-time object detection with region proposal networks. In: Advances in Neural Information Processing Systems, pp. 91–99 (2015)
34. Russakovsky, O., et al.: ImageNet large scale visual recognition challenge. Int. J. Comput. Vis. **115**(3), 211–252 (2015)
35. Sandler, M., Howard, A., Zhu, M., Zhmoginov, A., Chen, L.C.: MobileNetV2: inverted residuals and linear bottlenecks. In: The IEEE Conference on Computer Vision and Pattern Recognition, pp. 4510–4520 (2018)
36. Shen, M., et al.: Once quantization-aware training: high performance extremely low-bit architecture search. In: The IEEE International Conference on Computer Vision, pp. 5340–5349 (2021)
37. Shen, Z., Liu, Z., Qin, J., Huang, L., Cheng, K.T., Savvides, M.: S2-BNN: bridging the gap between self-supervised real and 1-bit neural networks via guided distribution calibration. In: The IEEE Conference on Computer Vision and Pattern Recognition, pp. 2165–2173 (2021)
38. Sheng, T., Feng, C., Zhuo, S., Zhang, X., Shen, L., Aleksic, M.: A quantization-friendly separable convolution for mobilenets. arXiv preprint arXiv:1803.08607 (2018)
39. Wu, Y., Kirillov, A., Massa, F., Lo, W.Y., Girshick, R.: Detectron2 (2019). www.github.com/facebookresearch/detectron2
40. Yu, H., Wen, T., Cheng, G., Sun, J., Han, Q., Shi, J.: Low-bit quantization needs good distribution. In: The IEEE Conference on Computer Vision and Pattern Recognition Workshops (2020)
41. Zhang, R., Isola, P., Efros, A.A.: Colorful image colorization. In: Leibe, B., Matas, J., Sebe, N., Welling, M. (eds.) ECCV 2016. LNCS, vol. 9907, pp. 649–666. Springer, Cham (2016). https://doi.org/10.1007/978-3-319-46487-9_40

42. Zhang, X., Zhou, X., Lin, M., Sun, J.: ShuffleNet: an extremely efficient convolutional neural network for mobile. In: The IEEE Conference on Computer Vision and Pattern Recognition, pp. 6848–6856 (2018)
43. Zhou, S., Wu, Y., Ni, Z., Zhou, X., Wen, H., Zou, Y.: DoReFa-Net: training low bitwidth convolutional neural networks with low bitwidth gradients. arXiv preprint arXiv:1606.06160 (2016)

Semi-supervised Vision Transformers

Zejia Weng[1,2], Xitong Yang[3], Ang Li[4], Zuxuan Wu[1,2(✉)],
and Yu-Gang Jiang[1,2(✉)]

[1] Shanghai Key Laboratory of Intelligent Information Processing, School of CS,
Fudan University, Shanghai, China
zxwu@fudan.edu.cn
[2] Shanghai Collaborative Innovation Center on Intelligent Visual Computing,
Shanghai, China
[3] Meta AI, Menlo Park, USA
[4] Baidu Apollo, Beijing, China

Abstract. We study the training of Vision Transformers for semi-supervised image classification. Transformers have recently demonstrated impressive performance on a multitude of supervised learning tasks. Surprisingly, we show Vision Transformers perform significantly worse than Convolutional Neural Networks when only a small set of labeled data is available. Inspired by this observation, we introduce a joint semi-supervised learning framework, Semiformer, which contains a transformer stream, a convolutional stream and a carefully designed fusion module for knowledge sharing between these streams. The convolutional stream is trained on limited labeled data and further used to generate pseudo labels to supervise the training of the transformer stream on unlabeled data. Extensive experiments on ImageNet demonstrate that Semiformer achieves 75.5% top-1 accuracy, outperforming the state-of-the-art by a clear margin. In addition, we show, among other things, Semiformer is a general framework that is compatible with most modern transformer and convolutional neural architectures. Code is available at https://github.com/wengzejia1/Semiformer.

Keywords: Vision transformers · CNNs · Semi-supervised learning

1 Introduction

Vision transformers (ViT) have achieved remarkable performance recently on a variety of supervised computer vision tasks [8,15,18]. Their success is largely fueled by high capacity models with self-attention layers trained on massive data. However, it is not always feasible to collect sufficient annotated data in many real world applications. When only a small number of labeled samples are provided,

Z. Weng and X. Yang—Equal contributions.

Supplementary Information The online version contains supplementary material available at https://doi.org/10.1007/978-3-031-20056-4_35.

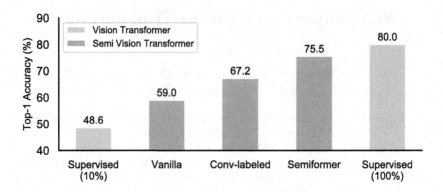

Fig. 1. Three semi-supervised vision transformers using 10% labeled and 90% unlabeled data (colored in green) vs. fully supervised vision transformers (colored in blue) using 10% and 100% labeled data. Our approach `Semiformer` achieves competitive performance, 75.5% top-1 accuracy. (Color figure online)

semi-supervised learning (SSL) [4,41] is a powerful paradigm to achieve better performance by leveraging a huge amount of unlabeled data. Despite the success of Vision Transformers in fully supervised scenarios, the understanding of its effectiveness in SSL is still an empty space.

We perform a series of studies with Vision Transformers (ViT) [8] in the semi-supervised learning (SSL) setting on ImageNet. Surprisingly, the results show that simply training a ViT using a popular SSL approach, FixMatch [23], still leads to much worse performance than a CNN trained even without FixMatch. We believe this results from the fact that pseudo labels from CNNs are more accurate, possibly due to their encoded inductive bias.

To validate our hypothesis, we use CNNs to produce pseudo labels for the joint semi-supervised training of CNNs and transformers. By doing so, we are able to significantly improve the top-1 accuracy of the ViT by 8+% (c.f. `Conv-labeled` and `Vanilla` in Fig. 1). This highlights that labels derived from CNNs are also helpful for training transformers under the SSL setting. While pseudo labels from CNNs are effective, the final ViT is still slightly weaker than the "teacher" CNN. We posit that simply performing pseudo labeling (PL) with CNNs to derive supervisory signals for transformers is not sufficient. Instead, we hypothesize that a joint knowledge sharing mechanism at the architecture level is required to fully explore knowledge in CNNs.

In light of these, we introduce a novel semi-supervised learning framework for Vision Transformers, which we term as `Semiformer`. In particular, `Semiformer` composes of a convolutional stream and a transformer stream. It leverages labels produced by CNNs as supervisory signals to train the CNN and the transformers jointly using a popular SSL strategy. The two streams are further connected with a cross-stream feature interaction module, enabling streams to complement each other. Benefited from more accurate labels and the interaction design, `Semiformer` can be readily used for SSL.

We conduct extensive experiments to evaluate `Semiformer`. In particular, `Semiformer` achieves 75.5% top-1 accuracy on ImageNet and outperforms the state-of-the-art using 10% of labeled samples. We also show `Semiformer` out-performs alternative methods by clear margins under different labeling ratios. In addition, we empirically demonstrate `Semiformer` is a generic framework compatible with modern CNN and transformer architectures. We also provide qualitative evidence that `Semiformer` is better than ViTs in the SSL setting.

Contributions. Our contributions are three-folded:

1. We are the first to investigate the application of Vision Transformers for semi-supervised learning. We reveal that Vision Transformers perform poorly when labeled samples are limited, yet they can be improved by utilizing unlabeled data together with the help from Convolutional neural networks.
2. We propose a generic framework `Semiformer` for the semi-supervised learning of Vision Transformers, which not only explores predictions as supervisory signals but also feature-level clues from CNNs to improve the ViTs in the low-data learning regime.
3. We perform extensive experiments and studies to evaluate `Semiformer`. `Semiformer` achieves 75.5% top-1 accuracy on ImageNet and outperforms state-of-the-art methods in semi-supervised learning. Additional ablation studies are further conducted to understand its effectiveness.

2   Related Work

Vision Transformers. A variety of Vision Transformers [8,15,17,25,28–30,37] have refreshed the state-of-the-art performance on ImageNet, demonstrating their powerful representation capability in solving vision tasks. Among them, the Vision Transformer (ViT) [8] is the first to prove that purely using the transformer structure can perform well on image classification tasks. It divides each image into a sequence of patches and then applies multiple transformer layers [27] to model their global relations. T2T-ViT [37] recursively aggregates neighboring tokens into one token for better modeling of local structures such as edges and lines among neighboring pixels, which outperforms ResNets [13] and also achieves comparable performance to light CNNs by directly training on ImageNet. Swin Transformer [18] creates a shifted windowing scheme cooperated with stacked local transformers for better information interaction among patches. With the continuous improvements of Vision Transformers, transformer based networks have achieved higher accuracy on medium-scale and large-scale datasets. Although transformers have been proven effective at solving visual tasks, it is known inferior to some CNNs when training from scratch on small-sized datasets mainly because ViTs lack image-specific inductive bias [8].

Touvron *et al.* [25] distill the knowledge of CNNs to ViTs, easing the training process of transformers to be more data efficient. The hard distillation idea is similar to the pseudo label approach in SSL. However, it differs from our work in that the teacher model in distillation is pre-trained in a fully supervised setting and frozen while we also use the pseudo labels to continuously updating the convolutional stream in our framework.

Semi-supervised Learning. Effective supervised learning using deep neural networks usually requires annotating a large amount of data. However, creating such large datasets is costly and labor-intensive. A promising solution is SSL, which leverages unlabeled data to improve model performance. Existing SSL methods are designed from the aspects of pseudo labeling where model predictions are converted to hard labels (*e.g.*, [16,22,36]), and consistency regularization where the model is constrained to have consistent outputs under different perturbations [1,2,21,24,34]. FixMatch [23] combines these two classic semi-supervised learning strategies. It predicts hard pseudo labels under weak perturbations and guides the model to learn on unlabeled data with strong perturbations. Our work is built upon FixMatch to explore the potential of semi-supervised Vision Transformers. The noisy student [35] extends the idea of self-training and distillation with larger student models and add noise to the student. [39] applies transformers to automated speech recognition using semi-supervised learning. Their superior performance is obtained by large scale pre-training and iterative self-training using the noisy student training approach.

As the advances of self-supervised learning approaches [3,5], a new trend for semi-supervised learning becomes first utilizing the large scale unlabeled data for self-supervised pre-training and then use the labeled data for fine-tuning. Chen *et al.* [6] show that a big ResNet pre-trained using SimCLRv2 can achieve competitive semi-supervised performance after fine-tuning.

Joint Modeling of CNNs and Transformers. CNNs and Transformers use two different ways to enforce geometric structure priors. A convolution operator is applied on patches of an image, which naturally results in a local geometric inductive bias. However, a Vision Transformer model utilizes the global self-attention to learn the relationships between global image elements [8]. From a complementary point of view, combining the advantages of CNNs in processing local visual structures and the advantages of transformer in processing global relationships is potentially a better approach for image modeling.

One research direction is to imitate the CNN operations into a Vision Transformer or vice versa [15,30,33,37]. For example, Pooling-based Vision Transformer (PiT) [15] applies pooling operations to shrink the feature maps and gradually increases the channel dimension at the same time, similar to the practice of CNN. PyramidViT [30] and CvT [32] also adopt a similar hierarchical design. T2T-ViT [37] designs a progressive tokenization module to aggregate neighboring tokens. [33] replaces the ViT stem by a small number of stacked convolutions and observes it improves the stability of model training. They also keep the network deep and narrow, inspired by CNNs.

Probably the most relevant approaches are [9,12,19,31] that aim to find ways to combine convolution and transformer into a single model. For example, the non-local network [31] adds self-attention layers to CNN backbones. SpeechConformer [12] attempts to use convolution to enhance the capabilities of the transformer, while ConVit [9] introduces gated positional self-attention (GPSA) module which becomes equipped with a "soft" convolutional inductive bias. VisualConformer [19] decouples CNN and Vision Transformer streams and design a module for feature communication across streams. However, these studies are all

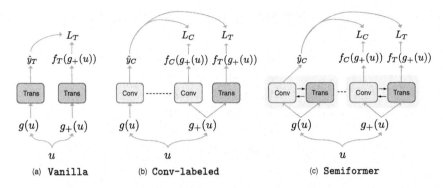

Fig. 2. We explore a variety of ways to apply vision transformer into semi-supervised learning task. Dotted line refers to weights sharing. u refers to the input image, g and g_+ refer to weak and strong data augmentation. $\hat{y}_T$ and $\hat{y}_C$ refer to pseudo labels produced by transformer and convolutional streams. $f_T(\cdot)$ and $f_C(\cdot)$ represent model predictions of transformer and convolutional streams respectively.

focused on supervised learning while we propose a generic framework for training semi-supervised vision transformers. Another major difference lies in that, even though we follow the same direction of fusing convolutions and transformers, our approach does not treat the combined architecture as an entirety, *e.g.*, the pseudo labels have to be generated by the convolutional stream only.

3   A Study with Vision Transformers for SSL

We start by presenting two frameworks that use pseudo labels for SSL. Although the two attempts are surprisingly unsatisfactory, their results reveal two important lessons which eventually inspire us to develop our framework. Below we provide the details of the two studies and our learned lessons.

Unlabeled Data Improves Vision Transformers. A natural approach to leverage unlabeled data is to do pseudo labeling through Vision Transformers. Our first hypothesis is that *a Vision Transformer can be improved when the total number of input-output training pairs increases (though many of them are pseudo labels)*. We verify this with a `Vanilla` framework, which uses the same architecture (*e.g.*, CNN or Transformer) and builds upon FixMatch [23] for SSL. In particular, FixMatch uses two types of augmentations, a strong one and a weak one. The pseudo label of the unlabeled data is obtained by applying the model on weakly augmented images. And the model is trained using the strongly augmented inputs with the pseudo labels.

Results in Table 1 show that after adding the other 90% images from the ImageNet as unlabeled training data, the transformer-based model can have an accuracy improvement by 10.4%, which is greater than the accuracy improvement of CNN's 8.3%. This validates our hypothesis, *i.e.*, large-scale data helps the Vision Transformer to learn better even when many of them are pseudo

Table 1. Results and comparisons with two different SSL frameworks, and comparisons with the supervised baselines.

Architecture	Method	Top-1 Acc (%)
CNN	`Sup. only (10%)`	60.2
	`Vanilla`	**68.5**
Transformer	`Sup. only (10%)`	48.6
	`Vanilla`	59.0
	`Conv-labeled`	67.2

labeled. However, despite the score increases, the performance of Vision Transformers in semi-supervised learning is still unsatisfactory, even inferior to the accuracy of fully supervised CNN training on only 10% of the labeled data.

Pseudo Labels from CNNs are More Accurate. We suspect that *the weak performance of* `Vanilla` *is due to the inaccurate pseudo labels generated by the transformer.* Vision Transformer contains less image-specific inductive bias, leading to poor performance on small-scale data and thus requires more data for representation learning. In contrast, CNNs are shown to possess strong image-specific inductive bias due to its convolution and pooling design. A natural question is: *what if we use a CNN to generate pseudo labels for Vision Transformer?*

We introduce a new SSL framework, `Conv-labeled`, which uses labels from CNNs for the SSL of CNN and transformers jointly, as illustrated in Fig. 2(b). As is seen in Table 1, the `Conv-labeled` approach results in 67.2% top-1 accuracy using the predictions from the ViT on ImageNet, improving the `Vanilla` approach by 8.2%, which suggests that CNNs provide better pseudo labels.

Conv-Based Pseudo Labeling is Not Enough. Although the ViT's performance is boosted by a CNN pseudo-label generator, the final performance of the ViT (67.2%) is still worse than the CNN (68.5%), observed from Table 1. This suggests that the knowledge from the CNN is not yet fully utilized through the simple pseudo labeling approach. One major problem here is that the two models are mostly decoupled except for the unilateral supervision given by the CNN. On the one hand, knowledge from the CNN is not directly injected into the transformer model. On the other hand, the CNN does not gain any information from the ViT. This motivates us to consider jointly modeling both a convolution network and a transformer, which becomes the proposed `Semiformer` framework.

4   Our Approach: `Semiformer`

We introduce `Semiformer` (illustrated in Fig. 2(c) and Fig. 3), which jointly fuses a CNN architecture and a Transformer for semi-supervised learning.

Notation. We use $f(x; \theta)$ to represent the mapping function of our `Semiformer`, given the input x and the model parameter θ. $f_T(x)$ and $f_C(x)$ are the vectorized

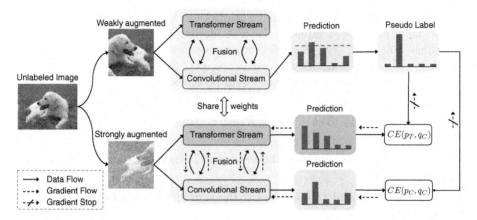

Fig. 3. Diagram of the `Semiformer` framework. For an unlabeled image, its weakly-augmented version (top) is fed into the model. The prediction of CNN is used for generating pseudo labels with a confidence threshold (dotted line). Then we compute the model's prediction for the strong augmented version of the same image (bottom). We expect both transformer and convolutional streams to match the pseudo label via cross-entropy losses. Streams complement each other with the feature-level modules.

output probability for each label from the transformer stream and the convolutional stream, respectively, and θ is omitted for simplicity. Additionally, a weak data augmentation function $g(\cdot)$ and a strong data augmentation function $g_+(\cdot)$ are used in our approach. We assume the semi-supervised dataset contains N_l labeled examples and N_u unlabeled examples. We use index i for labeled data, index j for unlabeled and index k for the label space.

Loss for Labeled Data. Formally, the total loss for labeled data is

$$\mathcal{L}_l = \sum_{i=1}^{N_l} \mathcal{L}_{xent}(y_i, f_T(g_+(x_i))) + \mathcal{L}_{xent}(y_i, f_C(g_+(x_i))) \tag{1}$$

where x_i is the i-th labeled example and y_i is its corresponding one-hot label vector. $\mathcal{L}_{xent}$ is the cross-entropy loss function, *i.e.*, $\mathcal{L}_{xent}(p, q) = \sum_k p_k \log q_k$.

Loss for Unlabeled Ddddata. Given an unlabeled image u_j, we first perform strong data augmentation $g_+(\cdot)$ and weak data augmentation $g(\cdot)$, according to FixMatch [23], to obtain the two views of the same input image. However, only the prediction output of the convolutional stream $f_C(g(u_j))$ is used to generate the pseudo label. The probability p_j of an unlabeled input u_j becomes

$$p_j = f_C(g(u_j)). \tag{2}$$

We define the pseudo labels as the class with maximum probability, *i.e.*, $\hat{p}_j = \arg\max_k p_{jk}$. We use $\hat{y}_j$ to represent the one-hot vector corresponding to pseudo label $\hat{p}_j$. These pseudo labels will in turn be used to calculate the cross entropy loss to back-propagate both the convolutional and the transformer streams with the strongly augmented inputs $g_+(u_j)$. A filtering by threshold $\max_k p_{jk} \geq \tau$, equivalent to $\langle \hat{y}_j, p_j \rangle \geq \tau$, is applied to remove pseudo labels without sufficient certainty. The remaining pseudo labels are used to guide the semi-supervised learning. The total loss for unlabeled data becomes

$$\mathcal{L}_u = \sum_{j=1}^{N_u} \left(\mathcal{L}_{xent}(\hat{y}_j, f_T(g_+(u_j))) + \mathcal{L}_{xent}(\hat{y}_j, f_C(g_+(u_j))) \right) \delta[\langle \hat{y}_j, p_j \rangle \geq \tau], \quad (3)$$

where $\delta[\cdot]$ is the delta function whose value is 1 when the condition is met and 0 otherwise.

Total Loss. The total training loss is the sum of both labeled and unlabeled losses such that

$$\mathcal{L} = \mathcal{L}_l + \lambda \mathcal{L}_u, \quad (4)$$

where λ is a trade-off. A more detailed study of λ can be found in Sect. 5.4.

Stream Fusion. Let M_T be the Vision Transformer feature map in a certain layer with the shape (d_T, h_T, w_T) representing depth, height and width, respectively. Let $M_{T,i}$ be the i-th patch feature according to M_T with the shape $(d_T, 1, 1)$. So, $M_{T,i}$ corresponds to a specific area of the original image and we denote the CNN sub-feature map who also corresponds to the same area as $M_{C,i}$ with the shape (d_C, h_C, w_C). Motivated by [19], we exchange information between patch features and its related CNN sub-feature map, described as Eq. (5) and Eq. (6):

$$M_{T,i} \mathrel{+}= \mathtt{layernorm}(\mathtt{pooling}(\mathtt{align}(M_{C,i}))), \quad (5)$$

$$M_{C,i} \mathrel{+}= \mathtt{batchnorm}(\mathtt{upsample}(\mathtt{align}(M_{T,i}))), \quad (6)$$

where the `align` operator refers to mapping features to the same dimensional space, `pooling` refers to downsampling, `upsample` refers to upsampling, `layernorm` refers to layer normalization and BN refers to batch normalization. Specifically, a `Conv1x1` layer is used for embedding dimension alignment (the `align` operator). The average pooling and spatial interpolation methods are used for spatial dimension alignment, *i.e.*, the `pooling` operator and the `upsample` operator, respectively.

To summarize, our framework consists of two parts, including carrying out a hard-way distillation manner by a convolutional stream to guide the transformer's learning from unlabeled data, and carrying out feature-level information interaction between the two streams so that the CNN's knowledge can be injected into the transformer and the convolutional stream can also be enhanced with a better global spatial information organization capability.

Inference. During training, we use the pseudo labels derived by the convolutional stream to train both the CNN and the Vision Transformer in a semi-supervised setting. For inference, we simply average combine predictions from the both streams as final scores, which is slightly better than using the transformer stream alone, as will be shown empirically.

5   Experiments

5.1   Experimental Setup

Datasets and Evaluation Metrics. To evaluate the effectiveness of Semiformer, we mainly conduct experiments on IMAGENET [7], which contains 1,000 classes and 1.3M images. In addition, we provide experimental results on PLACES205 [40]. Unlike IMAGENET that contains generic categories, PLACES205 is a place-focused dataset, which contains 2.5M images annotated into 205 classes. We use top-1 accuracy as our evaluation metric. Through all experiments, following [23], we mainly select 10% labeled samples and leave the other 90% samples as unlabeled data, unless specified otherwise.

Models. The Semiformer framework emphasizes how to complement the characteristics of the CNN and the ViT to achieve improved results. For the convolutional stream, we use a ResNet-like model and a personalized ConvMixer [26], while within transformer stream, we experiment with both a slightly modified ViT-S [25] and the PiT-S [15] as backbone networks.

Implementation Details. The initial learning rate is set to 10^{-3} and is decayed towards 10^{-5} following the cosine decay scheduler. We use 5 epochs to warm-up our models and another 25 epochs to train models on the labeled data before starting the semi-supervised learning process. In the training of ViT-ConvMixer model, the batch size of each GPU is 84, while in the training of ViT-Conv and PiT-Conv model, the batch size is 108 per GPU. We train models with 600 epochs using 32 NVIDIA V100 GPUs to produce our best top-1 accuracy by setting the number ratio of labeled and unlabeled images in each batch as 1:7. In order to avoid gains brought by data augmentation, we do not apply mixup, cutmix and repeat augmentation in our SSL process. We choose random augmentation, random erasing and color jitter as the strong data augmentation, and use random flipping and random cropping as the weak data augmentation. The value of λ which is the balance factor between loss terms is set as 4.0. In the semi-supervised learning with 5% IMAGENET labeled samples, we reduce the number ratio of labeled and unlabeled images per batch to 1:9. All the experiments share the same G.T. data split.

For ablation studies and discussion, we train 300 epochs to speed up the experiments and we set the number ratio of labeled and unlabeled images in each batch as 1:5 and use the label smoothing trick on ground-truth labels.

5.2   Main Results

Comparisons with State-of-the-Art. We first compare with state-of-the-art semi-supervised methods, such as UDA [34], FixMatch [23], S4L [38], MPL [20] and CowMix [10], as well as recent self-supervised methods. Experimental results in Table 2 show that our approach achieves better results by clear margins compared with alternative methods. For example, Semiformer is better than S4L [38] and CowMix [10] by 2.3% and 1.6% with only 11% and 67% of parameters of their models, respectively. In addition, while we follow the design the

Table 2. The results of `Semiformer` and comparisons with state-of-the-art methods. `Semiformer` achieves 75.5% top-1 accuracy and outperforms all Convolutional neural network based methods, while still keeping a reasonable parameter size. Here, the params does not include the final classifier.

Method	Architecture	Params	Top-1 Acc(%)
Sup. (10%)	ViT-S	23M	48.6
	Conv	13M	60.2
Self-supervised pretraining			
CPC [14]	ResNet-161	305M	71.5
SimCLR [5,6]	ResNet-50	24M	65.6
SimCLR [5,6]	ResNet-50 (2×)	94M	71.7
BYOL [11]	ResNet-50	24M	68.8
BYOL [11]	ResNet-50 (2×)	94M	73.5
DINO [3]	ViT-S	21M	72.2
Semi-supervised methods			
UDA [34]	ResNet-50	24M	68.8
FixMatch [23]	ResNet-50	24M	71.5
S4L [38]	ResNet-50 (4×)	375M	73.2
MPL [20]	ResNet-50	24M	73.9
CowMix [10]	ResNet-152	60M	73.9
Semiformer	ViT-S + Conv	40M	**75.5**

principle of FixMatch to generate pseudo labels, the knowledge sharing mechanism in `Semiformer` brings about 4% performance gain compared to FixMatch. Although MPL has a smaller model size, training MPL is computationally expensive as it requires meta updates. In addition, MPL uses complicated data augmentations, *i.e.*, AutoAugment, while we only use basic augmentations. Similarly, CowMix [10] introduces a new data augmentation strategy for SSL. We would like to point that `Semiformer` is a generic SSL framework that explores pseudo labels and knowledge in CNNs to promote the results of transformers. We believe it is in tandem with more advanced pseudo label generation strategies like MPL [20] and more complex augmentation methods [10]. In addition to SSL methods, we also compare with self-supervised learning results such as [6,11,14], which firstly learn representations with self-supervised methods and then perform finetuning on limited data. We see that `Semiformer` also performs favorably compared to this line of methods.

Effectiveness of `Semiformer` with Different Backbones. We evaluate the performance of `Semiformer` instantiated with different CNN and transformer backbones using 10% of labeled samples. We compare with the supervised training baseline (`Sup.`), the `Vanilla` method where the pseudo label generator share the same backbone used for SSL, and `Conv-labeled` that trains transformers with labels produced by CNNs. The results are summarized in Table 3. As the `Vanilla` results shown in the second block of Table 3, CNNs obviously achieve higher image classification accuracy than Vision Transformers under the SSL

Table 3. Ablation Study: The effectiveness of `Semiformer` with various backbones and comparisons with alternative methods (*i.e.*, vanilla and conv-labeled). All models are trained with 300 epochs and without pseudo label smoothing. For `Conv-labeled` and `Semiformer`, A/B in the last column: A indicates scores from the transformer stream only and B indicates averaged predictions from CNNs and transformers.

Method	Backbone	Pseudo labels	Top-1 Acc(%)
Sup. (10%)	ViT-S	-	48.6
	PiT-S	-	50.0
Vanilla	Conv	Conv	68.5
	ConvMixer	ConvMixer	69.3
	ViT-S	ViT-S	59.0
	PiT-S	PiT-S	63.0
Conv-labeled	ViT-S + Conv	Conv	67.2/70.2
	PiT-S + Conv	Conv	67.8/70.5
	ViT-S + ConvMixer	ConvMixer	66.7/70.2
Semiformer	ViT-S + Conv	Conv	72.4/73.5
	PiT-S + Conv	Conv	70.8/71.6
	ViT-S + ConvMixer	ConvMixer	72.9/**73.8**

setting, verifying that labels from CNNs are more accurate. ConvMixer [26] achieves the best results among all `Vanilla` models, offering a top-1 accuracy of 69.3%. This possibly results from the fact ConvMixer integrates the architectural advantages of both transformers and CNNs. Results in the third block of Table 3 show that using CNNs instead of Vision Transformers to generate pseudo labels significantly improves the performance of the Vision Transformer, allowing PiT-S and ViT-S to reach an accuracy of 67.2% and 67.8% respectively, with the same CNN architecture. The improved accuracy is close to that of the `Vanilla` semi-supervised CNN, suggesting the quality of the pseudo labels makes a difference to the semi-supervised learning process of Vision Transformers.

Results in the last block of Table 3 show that `Semiformer` significantly improves the performance of Vision Transformers. This highlights the effectiveness of `Semiformer` in exploring the interactions of CNNs and transformers. Taking the combination of ViT-S and Conv as an example, after applying the feature-level interaction to accomplish the dual information exchange, the accuracy of ViT-S is improved by 5.2% from 67.2% to 72.4%, revealing the efficacy of our `Semiformer` framework. We also observe that `Semiformer` is a versatile framework compatible with modern CNN and transformer architectures. In addition, by further combining the predictions from both the convolutional and transformer streams, we observe consistent performance gains under all settings for `Conv-labeled` and `Semiformer`.

The Ratio of Labeled Samples. we further experiment with 5% and 20% of labeled samples for SSL and compare with alternative methods. Except that

Table 4. SSL with different ratios of labeled samples on IMAGENET.

Dataset	Ratio	ViT-S		Conv		ViT-S + Conv	
		Sup.	Vanilla	Sup.	Vanilla	Conv-labeled	Semiformer
IMAGENET	5 %	28.6	45.7 ($\uparrow$17.1)	44.2	61.3 ($\uparrow$17.1)	62.0	66.3 ($\uparrow$4.3)
	10 %	48.6	59.0 ($\uparrow$10.4)	60.2	68.5 ($\uparrow$8.3)	70.2	73.5 ($\uparrow$3.3)
	20 %	52.9	69.8 ($\uparrow$16.9)	63.5	73.6 ($\uparrow$10.1)	74.8	78.1 ($\uparrow$3.3)

Table 5. Top-1 Accuracy of `Semiformer` on 5% labeled subset of Places205.

Dataset	Ratio	ViT-S		Conv		ViT-S + Conv	
		Sup.	Vanilla	Sup.	Vanilla	Conv-labeled	Semiformer
PLACES205	5 %	36.0	46.9 ($\uparrow$3.9)	44.3	51.6 ($\uparrow$7.3)	52.5	53.8 ($\uparrow$1.3)

we decrease the number of labeled and unlabeled images in each batch from 1:5 to 1:9 for 5% labeled samples, all the experimental settings are kept the same as those of using 10% labeled samples. Table 4 presents the results. Vision transformer performs poorly when only 5% labels are available, with an accuracy of only 28.6%, which is 15.6% lower than the Conv accuracy of 44.2%. With the increase of the number of labeled samples, the performance gain of ViTs is more significant than that of CNNs. For example, with ViTs, the accuracy increases by 20% and 14.3% respectively, when the number labeled samples grows from 5% to 10% and from 10% to 20%, respectively, suggesting that the training of Vision Transformers is more sensitive to the number of labels. In addition, we see that pseudo labels from CNNs are more accurate and help ViT learn better.

Extension to Places205. We also conduct experiments on PLACES205 to further evaluate the effectiveness of `Semiformer`. As PLACES205 is roughly 2 times larger than IMAGENET, we use 5% of labeled samples to assure the semi-supervised experiments on 5% PLACES205 and 10% IMAGENET have approximately the same number of labeled samples. We see from Table 5 that `Semiformer` consistently produces the best results. For example, `Semiformer` is 1.3% and 6.9% better than `Conv-labeled` and `Vanilla-ViT-S`, respectively. Similar trends can be observed by comparing across Table 4 and Table 5, which further confirms the efficacy of `Semiformer`.

5.3   Qualitative Results

We visualize in Fig. 4 the attention maps of ViT and `Semiformer`. Thanks to the guidance of pseudo label generator CNN and its supplementary help of injecting the local information extraction ability, `Semiformer` can retain more local information of images and can correctly focus on the key local positions of the images. For example, when analyzing the Fig. 4(a) which corresponds to the class of *bow*, `Semiformer` is particularly more focused on the man's hand holding the bow, the man's head and the quiver carried by the person, and those attended areas are

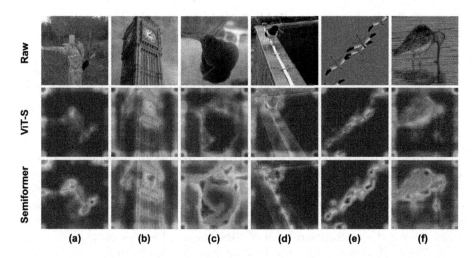

Raw

ViT-S

Semiformer

(a)   (b)   (c)   (d)   (e)   (f)

Fig. 4. Attention map of ViTs and Semiformer using samples from ImageNet. Compared to ViTs where the attention scores are scattered, Semiformer focuses more on critical objects.

critical for identifying the bow category. In addition, Semiformer covers essential objects precisely. In Fig. 4(f), we can see the attention map of Semiformer not only covers the animal completely, but also covers the contours more tightly. And for images with many small objects, for instance, Fig. 4(e), Semiformer shows stronger ability to concentrate on key local areas and coverage the essential areas.

5.4   Discussion

What Model Should Be Used to Produce Pseudo Labels? Although models in our Semiformer framework interact with each other, the CNN model still outperforms the vision transformer especially in the early training stage, making it important to retain the CNN hard-way distillation mode. To verify this, we replace the teacher stream which is responsible for generating pseudo labels. We use the following three strategies to produce pseudo labels: CNNs only, transformers only, and averaged predictions from CNNs and transformers. As shown in Table 6, using the CNNs as the teacher network brings the highest accuracy, *i.e.* 73.5%, while using the transformer stream to generate pseudo labels performs worst (*i.e.*, 67.4%). As the quality of pseudo labels generated by vision transformers are limited, we do not get better results by simply averaging CNN and Vision Transformer outputs as pseudo labels under the same setting. This further confirms the effectiveness of our pseudo labeling strategy.

Does Semiformer Performs Well Because of Larger Models? To clear up the confusion on the relationship between the number of parameters and accuracy, we ablate on the model architecture of Semiformer using different backbones. We experiment with different versions of ResNet [13] including ResNet-50

Table 6. Results by different pseudo labels.

PL Type	Acc@1(%)
CNN	**73.5**
Trans	67.4
Fusion	71.1

Table 7. Model size analysis. V and C refer to ViT-S and CNN, respectively. R represents ResNet.

Architecture	R50	R101	R152	C	V	C+C	V+V	V+C
Params	24M	43M	58M	13M	23M	35M	47M	40M
Top-1 Acc(%)	68.3	70.8	71.8	68.5	59.0	66.9	59.6	**73.5**

(R50), ResNet-101 (R101), ResNet-152 (R152). Results are presented in Table 7. We observe that by adding more layers to ResNet, the top-1 accuracy of semi-supervised learning does gradually increase. However, it is still lower than that of `Semiformer`. Even though the ResNet152 model contains 18M more parameters than `Semiformer`, its accuracy is still 1.7% worse than that of `Semiformer`, which proves the performance gain of `Semiformer` does not come from model sizes. We further instantiate the two streams of `Semiformer` with the same backbone, *i.e.* C+C and V+V respectively, and modify the stream connection correspondingly. Note that this is different from `Vanilla` as the two streams exchange information. Table 7 reveals that these combinations are significantly worse than `Semiformer`. For example, `Semiformer` outperforms V+V by 13.9% with 7M fewer parameters, which again shows the effectiveness of `Semiformer` is not due to extra parameters.

The Impact of Hyper-parameters. The default set of hyperparameters are: label and unlabeled data ratio is 1:5, confidence threshold is 0.7 and λ is set as 4. Based on the default setting, we control other variables unchanged and observe how the accuracy rate changes after independently changing the following three factors: different confidence threshold (0.65, 0.7, 0.75, 0.8); different λ value (1, 2, 3, 4); different proportion of the number of labeled and unlabeled data (1:3, 1:5, 1:7). `Semiformer` offers the best results with 0.7 confidence threshold, 1:7 labeled-unlabeled ratio, and $\lambda = 4$.

6   Conclusion

We presented `Semiformer`, the first framework to train Vision Transformers for semi-supervised learning. We found directly training a `Vanilla` transformer on semi-supervised data is ineffective. The proposed framework combines a CNN and a Vision Transformer using a cross fusion approach. The optimal semi-supervised learning performance is achieved by using only the convolutional stream to generate the pseudo labels. The final fused framework achieves 75.5% top-1 accuracy on ImageNet and outperforms the state-of-the-art in semi-supervised image classification.

Acknowledgement. Y.-G. Jiang was sponsored in part by "Shuguang Program" supported by Shanghai Education Development Foundation and Shanghai Municipal Education Commission (No. 20SG01). Z. Wu was supported by NSFC under Grant No. 62102092.

References

1. Bachman, P., Alsharif, O., Precup, D.: Learning with pseudo-ensembles. In: NeurIPS (2014)
2. Berthelot, D., et al.: ReMixMatch: semi-supervised learning with distribution alignment and augmentation anchoring. arXiv preprint arXiv:1911.09785 (2019)
3. Caron, M., et al.: Emerging properties in self-supervised vision transformers. In: ICCV (2021)
4. Chapelle, O., Scholkopf, B., Zien, A.: Semi-supervised Learning (Chapelle, O., et al. (eds.) 2006) [Book Reviews]. TNN (2009)
5. Chen, T., Kornblith, S., Norouzi, M., Hinton, G.: A simple framework for contrastive learning of visual representations. In: ICML (2020)
6. Chen, T., Kornblith, S., Swersky, K., Norouzi, M., Hinton, G.E.: Big self-supervised models are strong semi-supervised learners. In: NeurIPS (2020)
7. Deng, J., Dong, W., Socher, R., Li, L.J., Li, K., Fei-Fei, L.: ImageNet: a large-scale hierarchical image database. In: CVPR (2009)
8. Dosovitskiy, A., et al.: An image is worth 16 × 16 words: transformers for image recognition at scale. arXiv preprint arXiv:2010.11929 (2020)
9. d'Ascoli, S., Touvron, H., Leavitt, M.L., Morcos, A.S., Biroli, G., Sagun, L.: ConViT: improving vision transformers with soft convolutional inductive biases. In: ICML (2021)
10. French, G., Oliver, A., Salimans, T.: Milking cowmask for semi-supervised image classification. arXiv preprint arXiv:2003.12022 (2020)
11. Grill, J.B., et al.: Bootstrap your own latent-a new approach to self-supervised learning. In: NeurIPS (2020)
12. Gulati, A., et al.: Conformer: convolution-augmented transformer for speech recognition. arXiv preprint arXiv:2005.08100 (2020)
13. He, K., Zhang, X., Ren, S., Sun, J.: Deep residual learning for image recognition. In: CVPR (2016)
14. Henaff, O.: Data-efficient image recognition with contrastive predictive coding. In: ICML (2020)
15. Heo, B., Yun, S., Han, D., Chun, S., Choe, J., Oh, S.J.: Rethinking spatial dimensions of vision transformers. In: ICCV (2021)
16. Lee, D.H., et al.: Pseudo-label: the simple and efficient semi-supervised learning method for deep neural networks. In: ICMLW (2013)
17. Li, Y., Yao, T., Pan, Y., Mei, T.: Contextual transformer networks for visual recognition. IEEE TPAMI (2022)
18. Liu, Z., et al.: Swin transformer: hierarchical vision transformer using shifted windows. In: ICCV (2021)
19. Peng, Z., et al.: Conformer: local features coupling global representations for visual recognition. In: ICCV (2021)
20. Pham, H., Dai, Z., Xie, Q., Le, Q.V.: Meta pseudo labels. In: CVPR (2021)
21. Rasmus, A., Berglund, M., Honkala, M., Valpola, H., Raiko, T.: Semi-supervised learning with ladder networks. In: NeurIPS (2015)
22. Rosenberg, C., Hebert, M., Schneiderman, H.: Semi-supervised self-training of object detection models (2005)
23. Sohn, K., et al.: FixMatch: simplifying semi-supervised learning with consistency and confidence. In: NeurIPS (2020)
24. Tarvainen, A., Valpola, H.: Mean teachers are better role models: weight-averaged consistency targets improve semi-supervised deep learning results. In: NeurIPS (2017)

25. Touvron, H., Cord, M., Douze, M., Massa, F., Sablayrolles, A., Jégou, H.: Training data-efficient image transformers & distillation through attention. In: ICML (2021)
26. Trockman, A., Kolter, J.Z.: Patches are all you need? arXiv preprint arXiv:2201.09792 (2022)
27. Vaswani, A., et al.: Attention is all you need. In: NeurIPS (2017)
28. Wang, J., Yang, X., Li, H., Wu, Z., Jiang, Y.G.: Efficient video transformers with spatial-temporal token selection. In: ECCV (2022)
29. Wang, R., et al.: BEVT: BERT pretraining of video transformers. In: CVPR (2022)
30. Wang, W., et al.: Pyramid vision transformer: a versatile backbone for dense prediction without convolutions. In: ICCV (2021)
31. Wang, X., Girshick, R., Gupta, A., He, K.: Non-local neural networks. In: CVPR (2018)
32. Wu, H., et al.: CVT: introducing convolutions to vision transformers. In: ICCV (2021)
33. Xiao, T., Dollar, P., Singh, M., Mintun, E., Darrell, T., Girshick, R.: Early convolutions help transformers see better. In: Advances in Neural Information Processing Systems (2021)
34. Xie, Q., Dai, Z., Hovy, E., Luong, T., Le, Q.: Unsupervised data augmentation for consistency training. In: NeurIPS (2020)
35. Xie, Q., Luong, M.T., Hovy, E., Le, Q.V.: Self-training with noisy student improves imagenet classification. In: CVPR (2020)
36. Yang, L., et al.: Deep co-training with task decomposition for semi-supervised domain adaptation. In: ICCV (2021)
37. Yuan, L., et al.: Tokens-to-token ViT: training vision transformers from scratch on imagenet. In: ICCV (2021)
38. Zhai, X., Oliver, A., Kolesnikov, A., Beyer, L.: S4L: self-supervised semi-supervised learning. In: ICCV (2019)
39. Zhang, Y., et al.: Pushing the limits of semi-supervised learning for automatic speech recognition. arXiv preprint arXiv:2010.10504 (2020)
40. Zhou, B., Lapedriza, A., Xiao, J., Torralba, A., Oliva, A.: Learning deep features for scene recognition using places database. In: Advances in Neural Information Processing Systems, vol. 27 (2014)
41. Zhu, X.J.: Semi-supervised learning literature survey. Technical report, University of Wisconsin-Madison Department of Computer Sciences (2005)

Domain Adaptive Video Segmentation via Temporal Pseudo Supervision

Yun Xing[1], Dayan Guan[2], Jiaxing Huang[1], and Shijian Lu[1(✉)]

[1] Nanyang Technological University, Singapore, Singapore
shijian.lu@ntu.edu.sg
[2] Mohamed bin Zayed University of Artificial Intelligence, Abu Dhabi, UAE

Abstract. Video semantic segmentation has achieved great progress under the supervision of large amounts of labelled training data. However, domain adaptive video segmentation, which can mitigate data labelling constraints by adapting from a labelled source domain toward an unlabelled target domain, is largely neglected. We design temporal pseudo supervision (TPS), a simple and effective method that explores the idea of consistency training for learning effective representations from unlabelled target videos. Unlike traditional consistency training that builds consistency in spatial space, we explore consistency training in spatiotemporal space by enforcing model consistency across augmented video frames which helps learn from more diverse target data. Specifically, we design cross-frame pseudo labelling to provide pseudo supervision from previous video frames while learning from the augmented current video frames. The cross-frame pseudo labelling encourages the network to produce high-certainty predictions, which facilitates consistency training with cross-frame augmentation effectively. Extensive experiments over multiple public datasets show that TPS is simpler to implement, much more stable to train, and achieves superior video segmentation accuracy as compared with the state-of-the-art. Code is available at https://github.com/xing0047/TPS.

Keywords: Video semantic segmentation · Unsupervised domain adaptation · Consistency training · Pseudo labeling

1 Introduction

Video semantic segmentation [12,15,43,49,55], which aims to predict a semantic label for each pixel in consecutive video frames, is a challenging task in computer vision research. With the advance of deep neural networks in recent years, video

---

Y. Zing and D. Guan—Equal Contribution.

Supplementary Information The online version contains supplementary material available at https://doi.org/10.1007/978-3-031-20056-4_36.

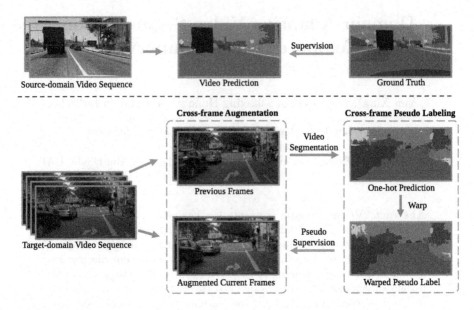

Fig. 1. The proposed temporal pseudo supervision (TPS) handles domain adaptive video segmentation by introducing *Cross-frame Augmentation* and *Cross-frame Pseudo Labelling* for consistency training in target domain. Specifically, the *Cross-frame Pseudo Labelling* obtains one-hot predictions (taken as pseudo labels) for *Previous Frames* and warps the predicted pseudo labels to the current video frames to supervise the learning from the *Augmented Current Frames* that are generated by the *Cross-frame Augmentation*.

semantic segmentation has achieved great progress [17,24,31,34,35,38,44,59] by learning from large-scale and annotated video data [4,11]. However, the annotation in video semantic segmentation involves pixel-level dense labelling which is prohibitively time-consuming and laborious to collect and has become one major constraint in supervised video segmentation. An alternative approach is to resort to synthetic data such as those rendered by game engines where pixel-level annotations are self-generated [22,56]. On the other hand, video segmentation models trained with such synthetic data often experience clear performance drops [19] while applied to real videos that usually have different distributions as compared with synthetic data.

Domain adaptive video segmentation aims for bridging distribution shifts across different video domains. Though domain adaptive image segmentation has been studied extensively, domain adaptive video segmentation is largely neglected despite its great values in various practical tasks. To the best of our knowledge, DA-VSN [19] is the only work that explores adversarial learning and temporal consistency regularization to minimize the inter-domain temporal discrepancy and inter-frame discrepancy in target domain. However, DA-VSN relies heavily on adversarial learning which cannot guarantee a low empirical error on unlabelled target data [6,37,70], leading to negative effects on temporal consistency regularization in target domain. Consistency training is a prevalent semi-supervised learning technique that can guarantee a low empirical error on unlabelled data by enforcing model outputs to be invariant to data augmentation [53,60,68]. It has recently been explored in domain adaptation tasks for guaranteeing a low empirical error on unlabelled target data [1,48,62].

Motivated by consistency training in semi-supervised learning, we design a method named temporal pseudo supervision (TPS) that explores consistency training in spatiotemporal space for effective domain adaptive video segmentation. TPS works by enforcing model predictions to be invariant under the presence of cross-frame augmentation that is applied to the unlabelled target-domain video frames as illustrated in Fig. 1. Specifically, TPS introduces cross-frame pseudo labelling that predicts pseudo labels for previous video frames. The predicted pseudo labels are then warped to the current video frames to enforce consistency with the prediction of the augmented current frames. Meanwhile, they also provide pseudo supervision for the domain adaptation model for learning from the augmented current frames. Compared with DA-VSN involving unstable adversarial learning, TPS is simpler to implement, more stable to train and achieve superior video segmentation performance consistently across multiple public datasets.

The major contributions of this work can be summarized in three aspects. First, we introduce a domain adaptive video segmentation framework that addresses the challenge of absent target annotations from a perspective of consistency training. Second, we design an innovative consistency training method that constructs consistency in spatiotemporal space between the prediction of the augmented current video frames and the warped prediction of previous video frames. Third, we demonstrate that the proposed method achieves superior video segmentation performance consistently across multiple public datasets.

2 Related Works

2.1 Video Semantic Segmentation

Video Semantic Segmentation is the challenging task of assigning a human-defined category to each pixel in each frame of a given video sequence. To tackle this challenge, the most natural and straightforward solution is to directly apply image segmentation approaches to each frame individually, in which way the model tends to ignore the temporal continuity in the video while training. A great many works explore on leveraging temporal consistency across frames by optical-flow guided feature fusion [17,34,44,72], sequential network based representation aggregation [52] or joint learning of segmentation as well as optical flow estimation [13,32].

Although video semantic segmentation has achieved great success under a supervised learning paradigm given a large amount of annotated data, pixel-wise video annotations are laborious and usually deficient to train a well-behaved network. Semi-supervised video segmentation aims at exploiting sparsely annotated video frames for segmenting unannotated frames of the same video. To make better use of unannotated data, a stream of work investigates on learning video segmentation network under annotation efficient settings by exploiting optical flow [13,51,52,72], patch matching [2,5], motion cues [61,73], pseudo-labeling [7], or self-supervised learning [33,39,66].

To further ease the burden of annotating, a popular line of study explores training segmentation network for real scene with synthetic data that can be automatically annotated, by either adversarial learning [19,27,28,30,54,63,65] or self-training [9,25,26,29,36,41,42,47,48,69,71,74], which is known as domain adaptation. For domain adaptive video segmentation, DA-VSN [19] is the only work that addresses the problem by incorporating adversarial learning to bridge the domain gap in temporal consistency. However, DA-VSN is largely constrained by adversarial learning that is unstable during training with high empirical risk. Different from adversarial learning [18,21,23,45,64,67], consistency training [1,48,60,68] is widely explored in semi-supervised learning and domain adaptation recently with the benefits of its higher training stability and lower empirical risk. In this work, we propose to address the domain adaptive video segmentation by introducing consistency training across frames.

2.2 Consistency Training

Consistency training is a prevalent semi-supervised learning scheme that regularizes network predictions to be invariant to input perturbations [10,20,53,60,68]. It intuitively makes sense as the model is supposed to be robust to small changes on inputs. Recent studies that focus on consistency training differ in how and where to set up perturbation. A great many works introduce random perturbation by Gaussian noise [16], stochastic regularization [40,58] or adversarial noise [50] at input level to enhance consistency training by enlarging sample space. More recently, it has been shown that stronger image augmentation [3,60,68] can better improve the consistency training. Conceptually, the strong augmentation on images enriches the sample space of data, which can benefit the semi-supervised learning significantly.

Aside from the effectiveness of consistency training in semi-supervised learning, a line of recent studies explore adapting the strategy in domain adaptation tasks [1,48,62]. SAC [1] tackles domain adaptive segmentation by ensuring consistency between predictions from different augmented views. DACS [62] performs augmentation by mixing image patches from the two domains with swapping labels and pseudo labels accordingly. Derived from FixMatch [60] which performs consistency training under the scenario of image classification, PixMatch [48] explores on various image augmentation strategies for domain adaptive image segmentation task. Unlike the aforementioned works involving consistency training in spatial space, we adopt consistency training in spatiotemporal space by enforcing model outputs invariant to cross-frame augmentation at the input level, which is devised to enrich the augmentation set and thus benefit the consistency training on unlabeled target videos.

3   Method

3.1   Background

Consistency training is a prevalent semi-supervised learning technique that enforces consistency between predictions on unlabeled images and the corresponding perturbed ones. Motivated by consistency training in semi-supervised learning, PixMatch [48] presents strong performance on domain adaptive segmentation by exploiting effective data augmentation on unlabeled target images. The idea is based on the assumption that a well-performed model should predict similarly when fed with strongly distorted inputs for unlabeled target data. Specifically, PixMatch performs pseudo labeling to provide pseudo supervision from original images for model training fed with augmented counterparts. As in FixMatch [60], the use of a hard label for consistency training in PixMatch encourage the model to obtain predictions with not only augmentation robustness but also high certainty on unlabeled data. Given a source-domain image $x^{\mathbb{S}}$ and its corresponding ground truth $y^{\mathbb{S}}$, together with an unannotated image $x^{\mathbb{T}}$ from the target domain, the training objective of PixMatch can be formulated as follows:

$$\mathcal{L}_{\text{PixMatch}} = \mathcal{L}_{ce}(\mathcal{F}(x^{\mathbb{S}}), y^{\mathbb{S}}) + \lambda_T \mathcal{L}_{ce}(\mathcal{F}(\mathcal{A}(x^{\mathbb{T}})), \mathcal{P}(\mathcal{F}(x^{\mathbb{T}}), \tau)). \tag{1}$$

where $\mathcal{L}_{ce}$ is the cross-entropy loss, $\mathcal{F}$ and $\mathcal{A}$ denote the segmentation network and the transformation function for image augmentation, respectively. $\mathcal{P}$ represents the operation that selects pseudo labels given a confidence threshold of τ. λ_T is a hyperparameter that controls the trade-off between source and target losses while training.

3.2   Temporal Pseudo Supervision

This work focus on the task of domain adaptive video segmentation. Different from PixMatch [48] that explored consistency training in spatial space for image-level domain adaptation, we propose a Temporal Pseudo Supervision (TPS) method to tackle the video-level domain adaptation by exploring spatio-temporal consistency training. Specifically, TPS introduces cross-frame augmentation for spatio-temporal consistency training to expand the diversity of image augmentation designed for spatial consistency training [48]. For the video-specific domain adaptation problem, we take adjacent frames as a whole in the form of $X_k = \mathcal{S}(x_{k-1}, x_k)$, where $\mathcal{S}$ is a notation for stack operation.

As for cross-frame augmentation in TPS, we apply image augmentation $\mathcal{A}$ defined in Eq. 1 on the current frames $X_k^{\mathbb{T}}$ and such process is treated as performing cross-frame augmentation $\mathcal{A}^{cf}$ on previous frames $X_{k-\eta}^{\mathbb{T}}$, where η is referred to as propagation interval which measures the temporal distance between the previous frames and the current frames. In this way, TPS can construct consistency training in spatiotemporal space by enforcing consistency between predictions on $\mathcal{A}^{cf}(X_{k-\eta}^{\mathbb{T}})$ and $X_{k-\eta}^{\mathbb{T}}$, which is different from PixMatch [48] that enforces spatial consistency between predictions on $\mathcal{A}(x^{\mathrm{T}})$ and x^{T} (as in Eq. 1). Formally, the cross-frame augmentation $\mathcal{A}^{cf}$ is defined as:

$$\mathcal{A}^{cf}(X^{\mathrm{T}}_{k-\eta}) = \mathcal{S}(\mathcal{A}(x^{\mathrm{T}}_{k-1}), \mathcal{A}(x^{\mathrm{T}}_{k})). \tag{2}$$

Remark 1. *It is worth highlighting that the image augmentation $\mathcal{A}$ plays a crucial role in consistency training by strongly perturbing inputs to construct unseen views. As for the augmentation set $\mathcal{A}$, there have been studies [3,60,68] presenting that stronger augmentation can benefit the consistency training more. To expand the diversity in image augmentation for the video task, we take the temporal deviation in video as a new kind of data augmentation for the video task and combine it with $\mathcal{A}$, noted as $\mathcal{A}^{cf}$. To validate the effectiveness of cross-frame augmentation, we empirically compare TPS (using $\mathcal{A}^{cf}$) with PixMatch [48] (using $\mathcal{A}$) in Table 1 and 2.*

With the constructed spatio-temporal space from cross-frame augmentation, TPS performs cross-frame pseudo labelling to provide pseudo supervision from previous video frames for network training fed with augmented current video frames. The cross-frame pseudo labelling has two roles: 1) facilitate the cross-frame consistency training that applies data augmentations across frames; 2) encourage the network to output video predictions with high certainty on unlabeled frames.

Given a video sequence in target domain, we first forward previous video frames $X^{\mathrm{T}}_{k-\eta}$ through a video segmentation network $\mathcal{F}$ to obtain the previous frame prediction, and use FlowNet [14] to produce the optical flow $o_{k-\eta \to k}$ estimated from the previous frame $x^{\mathrm{T}}_{k-\eta}$ and the current frame x^{T}_{k}. Subsequently, the obtained previous frame prediction is warped using the estimated optical flow $o_{k-\eta \to k}$ to ensure the warped prediction is in line with the current frame temporally. We then perform pseudo labeling by utilizing a confidence threshold τ to filter out warped predictions with low confidence. In a nutshell, the process of cross-frame pseudo labelling can be formulated as:

$$\mathcal{P}^{cf}(\mathcal{F}(X^{\mathrm{T}}_{k-\eta}), o_{k-\eta \to k}, \tau) = \mathcal{P}(\mathcal{W}(\mathcal{F}(X^{\mathrm{T}}_{k-\eta}), o_{k-\eta \to k}), \tau). \tag{3}$$

Remark 2. *we would like to note that the confidence threshold τ is set to pick out high-confident predictions as pseudo labels for consistency training. There exist hard-to-transfer classes in the domain adaptive segmentation task (e.g. light, sign and rider in SYNTHIA-Seq $\to$ Cityscapes-Seq) that tend to produce low confidence scores as compared to dominant classes, thus more possibly being ignored in pseudo labelling. To retain the pseudo label of hard-to-transfer classes as much as possible, we take 0 as the threshold τ for our experiments and further discussion about the effect of τ in Table 3.*

The training objective of TPS resembles Eq. 1 in both source and target domain except that: 1) instead of feeding single images to the model, TPS takes adjacent video frames as inputs for video segmentation; 2) TPS replaces $\mathcal{A}$ in Eq. 1 with a more diverse version $\mathcal{A}^{cf}$ to enrich the augmentation set by incorporating cross-frame augmentation; 3) in lieu of the straightforward pseudo labeling in Eq. 1, TPS resorts to cross-frame pseudo labeling that propagates video prediction from previous frames across optical flow $o_{k-\eta \to k}$ before further step. In a nutshell, given source-domain video frames $X^{\mathbb{S}}$ along with the target-domain video sequence, we formulate our TPS as:

$$\mathcal{L}_{\mathrm{TPS}} = \mathcal{L}_{ce}(\mathcal{F}(X^{\mathbb{S}}), y^{\mathbb{S}}) + \lambda_T \mathcal{L}_{ce}(\mathcal{F}(\mathcal{A}^{cf}(X_{k-\eta}^{\mathbb{T}})), \mathcal{P}^{cf}(\mathcal{F}(X_{k-\eta}^{\mathbb{T}}), o_{k-\eta \to k}, \tau)). \tag{4}$$

Remark 3. *We should point out that λ_T is set to balance the training between source and target domain as in DA-VSN. In spite of the effectiveness of DA-VSN on domain adaptive video segmentation task, the training process of adversarial learning is inherently unstable with feeding complex or irrelevant cues to the discriminator while training [45]. To alleviate the effect, DA-VSN set λ_T to 0.001 to stabilize the training process whereas compromise the domain adaptation performance. Different from the previous work, we leverage the inherent stability of consistency training and naturally set λ_T to 1.0 for our TPS to treat learning of source and target equally. We further make comparison on the stability of training process between DA-VSN and TPS by visualization in Fig. 3 and explore on the effect of λ_T on the performance in Table 5.*

4   Experiments

4.1   Experimental Setting

Datasets. To validate our method, we conduct comprehensive experiments under two challenging synthetic-to-real benchmarks for domain adaptive video segmentation: SYNTHIA-Seq [57] → Cityscapes-Seq [11] and VIPER [56] → Cityscapes-Seq. As in [19], we treat either SYNTHIA-Seq or VIPER as source-domain data and take Cityscapes-Seq as the target-domain data.

Implementation Details. As in [19], we take ACCEL [34] as the video segmentation framework, which is composed of double segmentation branches and an optical flow estimation branch, together with a fusion layer at the output level. Specifically, both branches for segmentation forward a single video frame through Deeplab [8]. Meanwhile, the branch of optical flow estimation [14] produces the corresponding optical flow of the adjacent video frames, which can be further used in a score fusion layer to integrate frame prediction from different views. As regard to the training process, we use SGD as the optimizer with momentum and weight decay set to 0.9 and 5×10^{-4} respectively. The model is trained with a learning rate of 2.5×10^{-4} for 40k iterations. As in [48,60], we incorporate multiple augmentations in our experiments, including gaussian blur, color jitter and random scaling. The mean intersection-over-union (mIoU) is used to evaluate all methods. For the efficiency of training and inference, we apply bicubic interpolation to resize every video frame in Cityscapes-Seq and VIPER to 512×1024, 720×1280, respectively. All the experiments are implemented on a single GPU with 11 GB memory.

Table 1. Quantitative comparisons over the benchmark of SYNTHIA-Seq → Cityscapes-Seq: TPS outperforms multiple domain adaptation methods by large margins. These methods include the only domain adaptive video segmentation method [19], the most related domain adaptive segmentation method [48] and other domain adaptive segmentation approaches [27,30,54,65,69,74,75] which serve as baselines. Note that "Source only" denotes the network trained with source-domain data solely

SYNTHIA-Seq → Cityscapes-Seq

Methods	road	side.	buil.	pole	light	sign	vege.	sky	pers.	rider	car	mIoU
Source only	56.3	26.6	75.6	25.5	5.7	15.6	71.0	58.5	41.7	17.1	27.9	38.3
AdvEnt [65]	85.7	21.3	70.9	21.8	4.8	15.3	59.5	62.4	46.8	16.3	64.6	42.7
CBST [75]	64.1	30.5	78.2	**28.9**	14.3	21.3	75.8	62.6	46.9	20.2	33.9	43.3
IDA [54]	87.0	23.2	71.3	22.1	4.1	14.9	58.8	67.5	45.2	17.0	73.4	44.0
CRST [74]	70.4	31.4	**79.1**	27.6	11.5	20.7	**78.0**	67.2	49.5	17.1	39.6	44.7
CrCDA [30]	86.5	26.3	74.8	24.5	5.0	15.5	63.5	64.4	46.0	15.8	72.8	45.0
RDA [27]	84.7	26.4	73.9	23.8	7.1	18.6	66.7	68.0	48.6	9.3	68.8	45.1
FDA [69]	84.1	32.8	67.6	28.1	5.5	20.3	61.1	64.8	43.1	19.0	70.6	45.2
DA-VSN [19]	89.4	31.0	77.4	26.1	9.1	20.4	75.4	**74.6**	42.9	16.1	82.4	49.5
PixMatch [48]	90.2	49.9	75.1	23.1	17.4	34.2	67.1	49.9	55.8	14.0	84.3	51.0
TPS (Ours)	**91.2**	**53.7**	74.9	24.6	**17.9**	**39.3**	68.1	59.7	**57.2**	**20.3**	**84.5**	**53.8**

4.2   Comparison with State-of-the-art

We compare the proposed TPS mainly with the most related methods DA-VSN [19] and PixMatch [48], considering the fact that DA-VSN is current state-of-the-art method on domain adaptive video segmentation (the same task as in this work) and PixMatch is the state-of-the-art method on domain adaptive image segmentation using consistency training (the same learning scheme as in this work). Quantitative comparisons are shown in Table 1 and 2. We note that TPS surpasses DA-VSN by a large margin on the benchmark of both SYNTHIA-Seq→Cityscapes-Seq (4.3% in mIoU) and VIPER→Cityscapes-Seq (1.1% in mIoU), which presents the superiority of consistency training over adversarial learning for domain adaptive video segmentation. Additionally, we highlight that our method TPS outperforms PixMatch on both benchmarks (a mIoU of 2.8% and 2.2%, respectively) which corroborates the effectiveness of the cross-frame augmentation for consistency training on video-specific task. In addition, we also compare our method with multiple baselines [27,30,54,65,69,74,75] which were originally devised for domain adaptive image segmentation. These baselines are based on adversarial learning [30,54,65] and self-training [27,69,74,75]. As in [19], We apply these approaches by simply replacing the image segmentation model with our video segmentation backbone and implement domain adaptation similarly. As presented in Table 4.1 and 4.2, TPS surpasses all baselines by large margins, demonstrating the advantage of our video-specific approach as compared to image-specific ones.

Table 2. Quantitative comparisons over the benchmark of VIPER → Cityscapes-Seq: TPS outperforms multiple domain adaptation methods by large margins

VIPER → Cityscapes-Seq																
Methods	road	side.	buil.	fence	light	sign	vege.	terr.	sky	pers.	car	truck	bus	mot.	bike	mIoU
Source only	56.7	18.7	78.7	6.0	22.0	15.6	81.6	18.3	80.4	59.9	66.3	4.5	16.8	20.4	10.3	37.1
AdvEnt [65]	78.5	31.0	81.5	22.1	29.2	26.6	81.8	13.7	80.5	58.3	64.0	6.9	38.4	4.6	1.3	41.2
CBST [75]	48.1	20.2	**84.8**	12.0	20.6	19.2	83.8	18.4	**84.9**	59.2	71.5	3.2	38.0	23.8	**37.7**	41.7
IDA [54]	78.7	33.9	82.3	22.7	28.5	26.7	82.5	15.6	79.7	58.1	64.2	6.4	41.2	6.2	3.1	42.0
CRST [74]	56.0	23.1	82.1	11.6	18.7	17.2	**85.5**	17.5	82.3	60.8	73.6	3.6	38.9	**30.5**	35.0	42.4
CrCDA [30]	78.1	33.3	82.2	21.3	29.1	26.8	82.9	28.5	80.7	59.0	73.8	16.5	41.4	7.8	2.5	44.3
RDA [27]	72.0	25.9	80.8	15.1	27.2	20.3	82.6	**31.4**	82.2	56.3	75.5	22.8	48.3	19.1	6.7	44.4
FDA [69]	70.3	27.7	81.3	17.6	25.8	20.0	83.7	31.3	82.9	57.1	72.2	22.4	**49.0**	17.2	7.5	44.4
PixMatch [48]	79.4	26.1	84.6	16.6	28.7	23.0	85.0	30.1	83.7	58.6	75.8	34.2	45.7	16.6	12.4	46.7
DA-VSN [19]	**86.8**	36.7	83.5	**22.9**	**30.2**	27.7	83.6	26.7	80.3	60.0	79.1	20.3	47.2	21.2	11.4	47.8
TPS (Ours)	82.4	**36.9**	79.5	9.0	26.3	**29.4**	78.5	28.2	81.8	**61.2**	**80.2**	**39.8**	40.3	28.5	31.7	**48.9**

Furthermore, we present the qualitative result in Fig. 2 to demonstrate the superiority of our method. We point out that despite the impressive adaptation performance of DA-VSN and PixMatch, both approaches are inferior in video segmentation as compared to TPS. As regard to DA-VSN, in spite of its excellence in retaining temporal consistency, the learnt network using DA-VSN produces less accurate segmentation (e.g. sidewalk in Fig. 2). Such outcome demonstrates the superiority of consistency training over adversarial learning in minimizing empirical error. As for PixMatch, we notice that the performance of learnt network with PixMatch is unsatisfying on retaining temporal consistency, which corroborates the necessity of introducing cross-frame augmentation in consistency training. Based on the observation of qualitative results, we conclude that TPS performs better in either keeping temporal consistency or producing accurate segmentation, which is in accordance with the quantitative result in Table 1.

4.3 Ablation Studies

We perform extensive ablation studies to better understand why TPS can achieve superior performance on video adaptive semantic segmentation. All the ablation studies are performed on the benchmark of SynthiaSeq→Cityscapes, where TPS achieves a mIoU of 53.8% under the default setting. We present complete ablation results and concrete analysis, including the propagation interval η in Eq. 2 the confidence threshold τ in Eq. 3, and the balancing parameter λ_T in Eq. 4.

Propagation Interval. The propagation interval η in Eq. 2 represents temporal variance between previous and current frames in cross-frame augmentation. We note that increasing propagation interval η will expand temporal variance and thus enrich cross-frame augmentation. We present our result of the ablation study on propagation interval in Table 3. Despite all results surpassing current methods in Table 1, we note that the network suffers from a performance drop while increasing propagation interval, especially on the segmentation of small

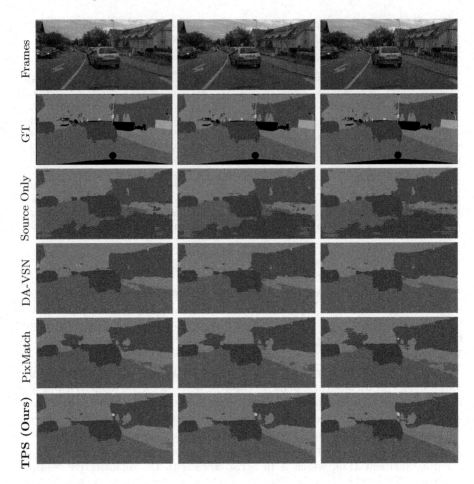

Fig. 2. Qualitative comparison of TPS with the state-of-the-art over domain adaptive video segmentation benchmark "SYNTHIA-Seq → Cityscapes-Seq": TPS produces much more accurate segmentation as compared to "source only", indicating the effectiveness of our approach on addressing domain adaptation issue. Moreover, TPS generates better segmentation than PixMatch and DA-VSN as shown in rows 4–5, which is consistent with our quantitative result. Best viewed in color.

objects, which can be ascribed to the increased warping error caused by propagating video prediction with optical flow.

Confidence Threshold. The confidence threshold τ in Eq. 3 is closely related to the quality of the produced pseudo labels. A common solution is to set a confidence threshold $\tau \in (0, 1)$ to filter out the low-confident predictions while pseudo labelling whereas retains high-confident ones. Despite its potential effectiveness in retaining the quality of pseudo labels, the consistency training in TPS tends to suffer from the inherent class-imbalance distribution in a real-world dataset

Table 3. Results of TPS with different propagation interval η: TPS achieves the best performance when $\eta = 1$. For the classes of small objects (*e.g.*, pole, light, sign, person and rider), the performance may suffer from warping error while increasing η

SYNTHIA-Seq $\rightarrow$ Cityscapes-Seq											
η	road	side.	buil.	pole	light	sign	vege.	sky	pers.	rider	car	mIoU
3	88.9	49.5	75.4	23.4	14.1	31.6	73.5	61.0	54.3	15.2	82.2	51.7
2	91.2	52.1	74.9	19.2	14.2	31.7	71.1	61.6	55.9	19.0	84.5	52.3
1	91.2	53.7	74.9	**24.6**	**17.9**	**39.3**	68.1	59.7	**57.2**	**20.3**	84.5	**53.8**

(target domain), which prevents the network to produce high confidence scores for some hard-to-transfer classes. To explore the effect of the threshold τ on the performance of TPS, we perform relevant experiments and present our results in Table 4. We note that the best result is obtained when τ is set to 0. We highlight that the segmentation on hard-to-transfer classes in our task (e.g. pole, light, sign and rider) suffers from performance drops as expected while confidence threshold τ is adopted when pseudo labeling.

Table 4. Results of TPS with different confidence threshold τ: The best result is obtained when $\tau = 0$. It can be noticed that the hard-to-transfer classes (*e.g.*, pole, light, sign, rider) experience performance drop while setting $\tau > 0$ to filter out low-confident predictions when pseudo labeling

SYNTHIA-Seq $\rightarrow$ Cityscapes-Seq											
τ	road	side.	buil.	pole	light	sign	vege.	sky	pers.	rider	car	mIoU
0.50	91.1	54.0	76.5	23.7	14.1	34.5	71.7	59.7	56.4	18.5	84.3	53.1
0.25	88.1	48.1	77.2	21.2	16.2	38.5	74.1	64.1	57.6	17.4	86.0	53.5
0.00	91.2	53.7	74.9	**24.6**	**17.9**	**39.3**	68.1	59.7	57.2	**20.3**	84.5	**53.8**

Table 5. Parameter analysis on the balancing weight λ_T. We observe that either prioritizing training process on source or target domain degrades the segmentation performance

SYNTHIA-Seq $\rightarrow$ Cityscapes-Seq						
λ_T	0.1	0.2	0.5	1.0	1.5	2.0
TPS (Ours)	50.0	51.2	52.6	**53.8**	53.4	53.3

Balancing Weight. The balancing weight λ_T in Eq. 4 contributes to our solution by balancing training process between source and target domain nicely. Both supervised learning in source domain with dense annotations and consistency training in target domain should be taken good care of. We present our result of ablation study on λ_T in Table 5. As presented in Table 5, the best result is retrieved while λ_T is set to 1.0. We can observe that all results of various λ_T surpass the result of previous work DA-VSN (achieved a mIoU of 49.5 in Table 1) on the benchmark of SYNTHIA-Seq→Cityscapes-Seq, which demonstrates the superiority of consistency training in TPS.

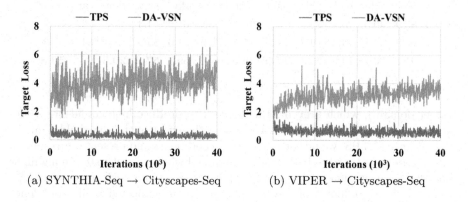

(a) SYNTHIA-Seq → Cityscapes-Seq   (b) VIPER → Cityscapes-Seq

Fig. 3. Target losses from TPS and DA-VSN for two domain adaptation benchmarks: (a) SYNTHIA-Seq → Cityscapes-Seq and (b) VIPER → Cityscapes-Seq. We point out that the degradation of target loss in TPS is more stable than that in DA-VSN for both two benchmarks. Best viewed in color.

4.4   Discussion

Training Stability. To compare the training stability of DA-VSN with TPS on two benchmarks, we visualize the target-domain training processes of both DA-VSN and TPS by calculating the target losses for every 20 iterations. As illustrated in Fig. 3, the decay of target loss with TPS is much less noisy than in DA-VSN, along with lower empirical error on average in target domain on both benchmarks, indicating the effectiveness of consistency training on the domain adaptive video segmentation task. In contrast, the target loss in DA-VSN degrades more unsteadily and harder to converge due to the adversarial learning module in DA-VSN, and such negative effect is stronger under the scenario of SYNTHIA-Seq→Cityscapes-Seq. The performance differences between benchmarks can be explained by the fact that SYNTHIA-Seq has larger domain gap with Cityscapes-Seq than VIPER, and we also point out that the notable advance on the benchmark of SYNTHIA-Seq→Cityscapes-Seq brought by TPS further demonstrates the superiority of consistency training over adversarial learning approach on bridging larger domain gap between different video distribution. This merit is important for real-world applications, since real scenarios could be very different from pre-built synthetic environment.

Feature Visualization. To delve deeper and investigate on the effectiveness of TPS, we visualize the target-domain video representation with t-SNE [46]

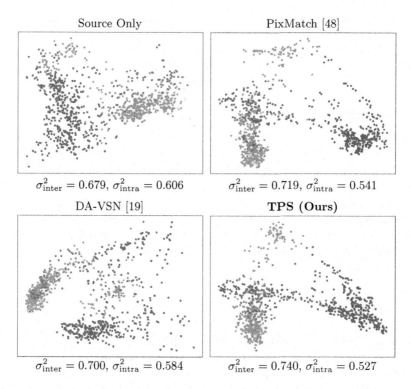

Source Only   PixMatch [48]

$\sigma^2_{\text{inter}} = 0.679,\ \sigma^2_{\text{intra}} = 0.606$ $\sigma^2_{\text{inter}} = 0.719,\ \sigma^2_{\text{intra}} = 0.541$

DA-VSN [19]   **TPS (Ours)**

$\sigma^2_{\text{inter}} = 0.700,\ \sigma^2_{\text{intra}} = 0.584$ $\sigma^2_{\text{inter}} = 0.740,\ \sigma^2_{\text{intra}} = 0.527$

Fig. 4. Visualization of temporal feature representations in the target domain via t-SNE [46] (different colors represent different categories): the proposed TPS surpasses Source Only, PixMatch [48] and DA-VSN [19] clearly with higher inter-class variance and lower intra-class variance. Note that we obtain the temporal features by stacking features extracted from two consecutive frames as in [19], and perform PCA with whitening on the obtained temporal features to retrieve principal components with unit component-wise variances. The visualization is based on the domain adaptive video segmentation benchmark SYNTHIA-Seq → Cityscapes-Seq. Best viewed in color.

presented in Fig. 4, together with visualization for source only, PixMatch and DA-VSN for comparison. We observe that TPS outperforms source-only training by a large margin, which reveals the outstanding adaptation performance of our consistency-training-based approach. Furthermore, we also spot that TPS surpasses the previous works on domain adaptive video segmentation task by achieving largest inter-class variance while keeping smallest intra-class variance, which is a proper indicator that the upstream class-wise representation from TPS are more distinguishable.

Complementary Study. We further conduct experiments to explore if TPS complements the domain adaptive video segmentation network DA-VSN [19] by performing additional cross-frame consistency training on target-domain data. The results of our complementary study are summarized in Table 6. It can be

Table 6. Complementary Study on TPS: the proposed TPS can be easily integrated with the state-of-the-art work DA-VSN [19] with a clear performance gain over two challenging domain adaptation benchmarks for video segmentation

	SYNTHIA-Seq $\to$ Cityscapes-Seq			VIPER $\to$ Citycapes-Seq		
Method	Base	+TPS	Gain	Base	+TPS	Gain
DA-VSN	49.5	55.1	+5.6	47.8	50.2	+2.4

observed that the integration of TPS improves the performance of DA-VSN by a large margin over two benchmarks, indicating that consistency training in TPS complements the adversarial learning in DA-VSN productively. Moreover, TPS complements with DA-VSN [19] by surpassing "TPS only" (achieved a mIoU of 53.8 and 48.9 in Table 1 and 2 respectively), which proves that the effects of adversarial learning and consistency training on the domain adaptive video segmentation task are orthogonal.

5   Conclusion

This paper proposes a temporal pseudo supervision method that introduces cross-frame augmentation and cross-frame pseudo labeling to address domain adaptive video segmentation from the perspective of consistency training. Specifically, cross-frame augmentation is designed to expand the diversity of image augmentation in traditional consistency training and thus effectively exploit unlabeled target videos. To facilitate consistency training with cross-frame augmentation, cross-frame pseudo labelling provides pseudo supervision from previous video frames for network training fed with augmented current video frames, where the introduction of pseudo labeling encourages the network to output video predictions with high certainty. Comprehensive experiments demonstrate the effectiveness of our method in domain adaption for video segmentation. In the future, we will investigate how the idea of temporal pseudo supervision perform in other video-specific tasks with unlabeled data, such as semi-supervised video segmentation and domain adaptive action recognition.

Acknowledgement. This study is supported under the RIE2020 Industry Alignment Fund - Industry Collaboration Projects (IAF-ICP) Funding Initiative, as well as cash and in-kind contribution from Singapore Telecommunications Limited (Singtel), through Singtel Cognitive and Artificial Intelligence Lab for Enterprises.

References

1. Araslanov, N., Roth, S.: Self-supervised augmentation consistency for adapting semantic segmentation. In: Proceedings of the IEEE/CVF Conference on Computer Vision and Pattern Recognition, pp. 15384–15394 (2021)

2. Badrinarayanan, V., Galasso, F., Cipolla, R.: Label propagation in video sequences. In: Proceedings of IEEE Computer Society Conference on Computer Vision and Pattern Recognition, pp. 3265–3272. IEEE (2010)
3. Berthelot, D., et al.: Remixmatch: semi-supervised learning with distribution alignment and augmentation anchoring. arXiv preprint arXiv:1911.09785 (2019)
4. Brostow, G.J., Shotton, J., Fauqueur, J., Cipolla, R.: Segmentation and recognition using structure from motion point clouds. In: Forsyth, D., Torr, P., Zisserman, A. (eds.) ECCV 2008. LNCS, vol. 5302, pp. 44–57. Springer, Heidelberg (2008). https://doi.org/10.1007/978-3-540-88682-2_5
5. Budvytis, I., Sauer, P., Roddick, T., Breen, K., Cipolla, R.: Large scale labelled video data augmentation for semantic segmentation in driving scenarios. In: Proceedings of the IEEE International Conference on Computer Vision Workshops, pp. 230–237 (2017)
6. Chen, C., et al.: Progressive feature alignment for unsupervised domain adaptation. In: Proceedings of the IEEE/CVF Conference on Computer Vision and Pattern Recognition, pp. 627–636 (2019)
7. Chen, L.C., et al.: Naive-student: leveraging semi-supervised learning in video sequences for urban scene segmentation. In: Vedaldi, A., Bischof, H., Brox, T., Frahm, J.-M. (eds.) ECCV 2020. LNCS, vol. 12354, pp. 695–714. Springer, Cham (2020). https://doi.org/10.1007/978-3-030-58545-7_40
8. Chen, L.C., Papandreou, G., Kokkinos, I., Murphy, K., Yuille, A.L.: DeepLab: semantic image segmentation with deep convolutional nets, atrous convolution, and fully connected CRFs. IEEE Trans. Pattern Anal. Mach. Intell. **40**(4), 834–848 (2017)
9. Chen, M., Xue, H., Cai, D.: Domain adaptation for semantic segmentation with maximum squares loss. In: Proceedings of the IEEE/CVF International Conference on Computer Vision, pp. 2090–2099 (2019)
10. Chen, X., Yuan, Y., Zeng, G., Wang, J.: Semi-supervised semantic segmentation with cross pseudo supervision. In: Proceedings of the IEEE/CVF Conference on Computer Vision and Pattern Recognition, pp. 2613–2622 (2021)
11. Cordts, M., et al.: The cityscapes dataset for semantic urban scene understanding. In: Proceedings of the IEEE Conference on Computer Vision and Pattern Recognition, pp. 3213–3223 (2016)
12. Couprie, C., Farabet, C., LeCun, Y., Najman, L.: Causal graph-based video segmentation. In: 2013 IEEE International Conference on Image Processing. IEEE, pp. 4249–4253 (2013)
13. Ding, M., Wang, Z., Zhou, B., Shi, J., Lu, Z., Luo, P.: Every frame counts: joint learning of video segmentation and optical flow. In: Proceedings of the AAAI Conference on Artificial Intelligence. vol. 34, pp. 10713–10720 (2020)
14. Dosovitskiy, A., et al.: Flownet: learning optical flow with convolutional networks. In: Proceedings of the IEEE international Conference on Computer Vision, pp. 2758–2766 (2015)
15. Floros, G., Leibe, B.: Joint 2D–3D temporally consistent semantic segmentation of street scenes. In: 2012 IEEE Conference on Computer Vision and Pattern Recognition. IEEE, pp. 2823–2830. (2012)
16. French, G., Mackiewicz, M., Fisher, M.: Self-ensembling for visual domain adaptation. arXiv preprint arXiv:1706.05208 (2017)
17. Gadde, R., Jampani, V., Gehler, P.V.: Semantic video CNNs through representation warping. In: Proceedings of the IEEE International Conference on Computer Vision (ICCV) (2017)

18. Guan, D., Huang, J., Lu, S., Xiao, A.: Scale variance minimization for unsupervised domain adaptation in image segmentation. Pattern Recogn. **112**, 107764 (2021)

19. Guan, D., Huang, J., Xiao, A., Lu, S.: Domain adaptive video segmentation via temporal consistency regularization. In: Proceedings of the IEEE/CVF International Conference on Computer Vision, pp. 8053–8064 (2021)

20. Guan, D., Huang, J., Xiao, A., Lu, S.: Unbiased subclass regularization for semi-supervised semantic segmentation. In: Proceedings of the IEEE/CVF Conference on Computer Vision and Pattern Recognition, pp. 9968–9978 (2022)

21. Guan, D., Huang, J., Xiao, A., Lu, S., Cao, Y.: Uncertainty-aware unsupervised domain adaptation in object detection. IEEE Trans. Multimedia **24**, 2502–2514 (2021)

22. Hernandez-Juarez, D., et al.: Slanted Stixels: representing San Francisco's steepest streets. arXiv preprint arXiv:1707.05397 (2017)

23. Hoffman, J., et al.: CyCADA: cycle-consistent adversarial domain adaptation. arXiv preprint arXiv:1711.03213 (2017)

24. Hu, P., Caba, F., Wang, O., Lin, Z., Sclaroff, S., Perazzi, F.: Temporally distributed networks for fast video semantic segmentation. In: Proceedings of the IEEE/CVF Conference on Computer Vision and Pattern Recognition, pp. 8818–8827 (2020)

25. Huang, J., Guan, D., Xiao, A., Lu, S.: Cross-view regularization for domain adaptive panoptic segmentation. In: Proceedings of the IEEE/CVF Conference on Computer Vision and Pattern Recognition, pp. 10133–10144 (2021)

26. Huang, J., Guan, D., Xiao, A., Lu, S.: Model adaptation: historical contrastive learning for unsupervised domain adaptation without source data. In: Advances in Neural Information Processing Systems, vol. 34, pp. 3635–3649 (2021)

27. Huang, J., Guan, D., Xiao, A., Lu, S.: RDA: robust domain adaptation via Fourier adversarial attacking. arXiv preprint arXiv:2106.02874 (2021)

28. Huang, J., Guan, D., Xiao, A., Lu, S.: Multi-level adversarial network for domain adaptive semantic segmentation. Pattern Recogn. **123**, 108384 (2022)

29. Huang, J., Guan, D., Xiao, A., Lu, S., Shao, L.: Category contrast for unsupervised domain adaptation in visual tasks. In: Proceedings of the IEEE/CVF Conference on Computer Vision and Pattern Recognition, pp. 1203–1214 (2022)

30. Huang, J., Lu, S., Guan, D., Zhang, X.: Contextual-relation consistent domain adaptation for semantic segmentation. In: Vedaldi, A., Bischof, H., Brox, T., Frahm, J.-M. (eds.) ECCV 2020. LNCS, vol. 12360, pp. 705–722. Springer, Cham (2020). https://doi.org/10.1007/978-3-030-58555-6_42

31. Huang, P.Y., Hsu, W.T., Chiu, C.Y., Wu, T.F., Sun, M.: Efficient uncertainty estimation for semantic segmentation in videos. In: Proceedings of the European Conference on Computer Vision (ECCV), pp. 520–535 (2018)

32. Hur, J., Roth, S.: Joint optical flow and temporally consistent semantic segmentation. In: Hua, G., Jégou, H. (eds.) ECCV 2016. LNCS, vol. 9913, pp. 163–177. Springer, Cham (2016). https://doi.org/10.1007/978-3-319-46604-0_12

33. Jabri, A., Owens, A., Efros, A.A.: Space-time correspondence as a contrastive random walk. In: Advances in Neural Information Processing Systems (2020)

34. Jain, S., Wang, X., Gonzalez, J.E.: Accel: a corrective fusion network for efficient semantic segmentation on video. In: Proceedings of the IEEE/CVF Conference on Computer Vision and Pattern Recognition, pp. 8866–8875 (2019)

35. Kim, D., Woo, S., Lee, J.Y., Kweon, I.S.: Video panoptic segmentation. In: Proceedings of the IEEE/CVF Conference on Computer Vision and Pattern Recognition, pp. 9859–9868 (2020)

36. Kim, M., Byun, H.: Learning texture invariant representation for domain adaptation of semantic segmentation. arXiv preprint arXiv:2003.00867 (2020)

37. Kumar, A., et al.: Co-regularized alignment for unsupervised domain adaptation. In: Advances in Neural Information Processing Systems, vol. 31 (2018)
38. Kundu, A., Vineet, V., Koltun, V.: Feature space optimization for semantic video segmentation. In: Proceedings of the IEEE Conference on Computer Vision and Pattern Recognition, pp. 3168–3175 (2016)
39. Lai, Z., Lu, E., Xie, W.: MAST: a memory-augmented self-supervised tracker. In: Proceedings of the IEEE/CVF Conference on Computer Vision and Pattern Recognition, pp. 6479–6488 (2020)
40. Laine, S., Aila, T.: Temporal ensembling for semi-supervised learning. arXiv preprint arXiv:1610.02242 (2016)
41. Li, Y., Yuan, L., Vasconcelos, N.: Bidirectional learning for domain adaptation of semantic segmentation. In: Proceedings of the IEEE Conference on Computer Vision and Pattern Recognition, pp. 6936–6945 (2019)
42. Lian, Q., Lv, F., Duan, L., Gong, B.: Constructing self-motivated pyramid curriculums for cross-domain semantic segmentation: a non-adversarial approach. In: The IEEE International Conference on Computer Vision (ICCV) (2019)
43. Liu, B., He, X.: Multiclass semantic video segmentation with object-level active inference. In: Proceedings of the IEEE Conference on Computer Vision and Pattern Recognition, pp. 4286–4294 (2015)
44. Liu, Y., Shen, C., Yu, C., Wang, J.: Efficient semantic video segmentation with per-frame inference. In: Vedaldi, A., Bischof, H., Brox, T., Frahm, J.-M. (eds.) ECCV 2020. LNCS, vol. 12355, pp. 352–368. Springer, Cham (2020). https://doi.org/10.1007/978-3-030-58607-2_21
45. Luo, Y., Liu, P., Guan, T., Yu, J., Yang, Y.: Significance-aware information bottleneck for domain adaptive semantic segmentation. In: Proceedings of the IEEE/CVF International Conference on Computer Vision, pp. 6778–6787 (2019)
46. Maaten, L.v.d., Hinton, G.: Visualizing data using t-SNE. J. Mach. Learn. Res. 9, 2579–2605 (2008)
47. Mei, K., Zhu, C., Zou, J., Zhang, S.: Instance adaptive self-training for unsupervised domain adaptation. In: Vedaldi, A., Bischof, H., Brox, T., Frahm, J.-M. (eds.) ECCV 2020. LNCS, vol. 12371, pp. 415–430. Springer, Cham (2020). https://doi.org/10.1007/978-3-030-58574-7_25
48. Melas-Kyriazi, L., Manrai, A.K.: PixMatch: unsupervised domain adaptation via pixelwise consistency training. In: Proceedings of the IEEE/CVF Conference on Computer Vision and Pattern Recognition, pp. 12435–12445 (2021)
49. Miksik, O., Munoz, D., Bagnell, J.A., Hebert, M.: Efficient temporal consistency for streaming video scene analysis. In: ICRA. IEEE, pp. 133–139. (2013)
50. Miyato, T., Maeda, S.i., Koyama, M., Ishii, S.: Virtual adversarial training: a regularization method for supervised and semi-supervised learning. IEEE Trans. Pattern Anal. Mach. Intell. 41(8), 1979–1993 (2018)
51. Mustikovela, S.K., Yang, M.Y., Rother, C.: Can ground truth label propagation from video help semantic segmentation? In: Hua, G., Jégou, H. (eds.) ECCV 2016. LNCS, vol. 9915, pp. 804–820. Springer, Cham (2016). https://doi.org/10.1007/978-3-319-49409-8_66
52. Nilsson, D., Sminchisescu, C.: Semantic video segmentation by gated recurrent flow propagation. In: Proceedings of the IEEE Conference on Computer Vision and Pattern Recognition, pp. 6819–6828 (2018)
53. Ouali, Y., Hudelot, C., Tami, M.: Semi-supervised semantic segmentation with cross-consistency training. In: Proceedings of the IEEE/CVF Conference on Computer Vision and Pattern Recognition, pp. 12674–12684 (2020)

54. Pan, F., Shin, I., Rameau, F., Lee, S., Kweon, I.S.: Unsupervised intra-domain adaptation for semantic segmentation through self-supervision. arXiv preprint arXiv:2004.07703 (2020)
55. Patraucean, V., Handa, A., Cipolla, R.: Spatio-temporal video autoencoder with differentiable memory. arXiv preprint arXiv:1511.06309 (2015)
56. Richter, S.R., Hayder, Z., Koltun, V.: Playing for benchmarks. In: Proceedings of the IEEE International Conference on Computer Vision, pp. 2213–2222 (2017)
57. Ros, G., Sellart, L., Materzynska, J., Vazquez, D., Lopez, A.M.: The synthia dataset: a large collection of synthetic images for semantic segmentation of urban scenes. In: Proceedings of the IEEE Conference on Computer Vision and Pattern Recognition, pp. 3234–3243 (2016)
58. Sajjadi, M., Javanmardi, M., Tasdizen, T.: Regularization with stochastic trans-formations and perturbations for deep semi-supervised learning. In: Advances in Neural Information Processing Systems, vol. 29, pp. 1163–1171 (2016)
59. Shelhamer, E., Rakelly, K., Hoffman, J., Darrell, T.: Clockwork convnets for video semantic segmentation. In: Hua, G., Jégou, H. (eds.) ECCV 2016. LNCS, vol. 9915, pp. 852–868. Springer, Cham (2016). https://doi.org/10.1007/978-3-319-49409-8_69
60. Sohn, K.,et al.: FixMatch: simplifying semi-supervised learning with consistency and confidence. arXiv preprint arXiv:2001.07685 (2020)
61. Tokmakov, P., Alahari, K., Schmid, C.: Weakly-supervised semantic segmentation using motion cues. In: Leibe, B., Matas, J., Sebe, N., Welling, M. (eds.) ECCV 2016. LNCS, vol. 9908, pp. 388–404. Springer, Cham (2016). https://doi.org/10.1007/978-3-319-46493-0_24
62. Tranheden, W., Olsson, V., Pinto, J., Svensson, L.: DACS: domain adaptation via cross-domain mixed sampling. In: Proceedings of the IEEE/CVF Winter Confer-ence on Applications of Computer Vision, pp. 1379–1389 (2021)
63. Tsai, Y.H., Hung, W.C., Schulter, S., Sohn, K., Yang, M.H., Chandraker, M.: Learning to adapt structured output space for semantic segmentation. In: Pro-ceedings of the IEEE Conference on Computer Vision and Pattern Recognition, pp. 7472–7481 (2018)
64. Tsai, Y.H., Sohn, K., Schulter, S., Chandraker, M.: Domain adaptation for struc-tured output via discriminative patch representations. In: Proceedings of the IEEE International Conference on Computer Vision, pp. 1456–1465 (2019)
65. Vu, T.H., Jain, H., Bucher, M., Cord, M., Pérez, P.: Advent: adversarial entropy minimization for domain adaptation in semantic segmentation. In: Proceedings of the IEEE Conference on Computer Vision and Pattern Recognition, pp. 2517–2526 (2019)
66. Wang, X., Jabri, A., Efros, A.A.: Learning correspondence from the cycle-consistency of time. In: Proceedings of the IEEE/CVF Conference on Computer Vision and Pattern Recognition, pp. 2566–2576 (2019)
67. Xiao, A., Huang, J., Guan, D., Zhan, F., Lu, S.: Transfer learning from synthetic to real lidar point cloud for semantic segmentation. In: Proceedings of the AAAI Conference on Artificial Intelligence, vol. 36, pp. 2795–2803 (2022)
68. Xie, Q., Dai, Z., Hovy, E., Luong, T., Le, Q.: Unsupervised data augmentation for consistency training. In: Advances in Neural Information Processing Systems, vol. 33, pp. 6256–6268 (2020)
69. Yang, Y., Soatto, S.: FDA: Fourier domain adaptation for semantic segmentation. In: Proceedings of the IEEE/CVF Conference on Computer Vision and Pattern Recognition, pp. 4085–4095 (2020)

70. Zhang, P., Zhang, B., Zhang, T., Chen, D., Wang, Y., Wen, F.: Prototypical pseudo label denoising and target structure learning for domain adaptive semantic segmentation. In: Proceedings of the IEEE/CVF Conference on Computer Vision and Pattern Recognition, pp. 12414–12424 (2021)
71. Zheng, Z., Yang, Y.: Rectifying pseudo label learning via uncertainty estimation for domain adaptive semantic segmentation. Int. J. Comput. Vis. **129**, 1–15 (2021). https://doi.org/10.1007/s11263-020-01395-y
72. Zhu, X., Xiong, Y., Dai, J., Yuan, L., Wei, Y.: Deep feature flow for video recognition. In: Proceedings of the IEEE Conference on Computer Vision and Pattern Recognition, pp. 2349–2358 (2017)
73. Zhu, Y., et al.: Improving semantic segmentation via video propagation and label relaxation. In: Proceedings of the IEEE/CVF Conference on Computer Vision and Pattern Recognition, pp. 8856–8865 (2019)
74. Zou, Y., Yu, Z., Liu, X., Kumar, B., Wang, J.: Confidence regularized self-training. In: Proceedings of the IEEE/CVF International Conference on Computer Vision, pp. 5982–5991 (2019)
75. Zou, Y., Yu, Z., Vijaya Kumar, B., Wang, J.: Unsupervised domain adaptation for semantic segmentation via class-balanced self-training. In: Proceedings of the European Conference on Computer Vision (ECCV), pp. 289–305 (2018)

Diverse Learner: Exploring Diverse Supervision for Semi-supervised Object Detection

Linfeng Li[1,2], Minyue Jiang[1], Yue Yu[1], Wei Zhang[1], Xiangru Lin[1], Yingying Li[1], Xiao Tan[1(✉)], Jingdong Wang[1], and Errui Ding[1]

[1] Baidu Inc., Beijing, China
e0724289@u.nus.edu,
{jiangminyue,yuyue15,zhangwei99,liyingying05,dingerrui}@baidu.com
[2] National University of Singapore, Singapore, Singapore

Abstract. Current state-of-the-art semi-supervised object detection methods (SSOD) typically adopt the teacher-student framework featured with pseudo labeling and Exponential Moving Average (EMA). Although the performance is desirable, many remaining issues still need to be resolved, for example: (1) the teacher updated by the student using EMA tends to lose its distinctiveness and hence generates similar predictions comparing with student and causes potential noise accumulation as the training proceeds; (2) the exploitation of pseudo labels still has much room for improvement. We present a diverse learner semi-supervised object detection framework to tackle these issues. Concretely, to maintain distinctiveness between teachers and students, our framework consists of two paired teacher-student models with diverse supervision strategy. In addition, we argue that the pseudo labels which are typically regarded as unreliable and obsoleted by many existing methods are of great value. A particular training strategy consisting of Multi-threshold Classification Loss (MTC) and Pseudo Label-Aware Erasing (PLAE) is hence designed to well explore the full set of all pseudo labels. Extensive experimental results show that our diverse learner framework outperforms the previous state-of-the-art method on the MS-COCO dataset by 2.10%, 1.50% and 0.83% when training with only 1%, 5% and 10% labeled data, demonstrating the effectiveness of our proposed framework. Moreover, our approach also performs well with larger amount of data, e.g. using full COCO training set and 123K unlabeled images from COCO, reaching a new state-of-the-art performance of 44.86% mAP.

Keywords: Semi-supervised object detection · Diverse learner · Multi-threshold loss · Pseudo label-aware erasing

L. Li, M. Jiang and Y. Yu—These authors contributed equally to this work.
This work was done when Linfeng Li was an intern at Baidu Inc.

Supplementary Information The online version contains supplementary material available at https://doi.org/10.1007/978-3-031-20056-4_37.

S. Avidan et al. (Eds.): ECCV 2022, LNCS 13690, pp. 640–655, 2022.
https://doi.org/10.1007/978-3-031-20056-4_37

1   Introduction

Machine vision systems have witnessed a remarkable progress over the last decades in the wave of deep neural networks, including image classification [5,6], object detection [16,17], and image segmentation [3,18], etc. Recent years, object detection task is dominated by the deep neural network based approaches [11,14,30] which require a large amount of labeled training data. However, obtaining large-scale labeled object detection data is laborious and time-consuming. To mitigate this issue, semi-supervised object detection (SSOD) is proposed [7,20], where it exploits theoretically unlimited and cost-free unlabeled data to boost the performance of the fully-supervised object detector. Current state-of-the-art SSOD methods typically follow the teacher-student framework featured with pseudo labeling [15,31] and exponential moving average [22]. In most existing teacher-student framework, reliable pseudo labels of the unlabeled data are selected, e.g. by thresholding the outputs of the teacher, and then they are used to train the student model. Afterwards, an EMA form strategy is employed to update the teacher model for temporally ensembling the student models in different time steps, which alleviates the detrimental effect caused by the imbalanced and noisy pseudo labels. Although the performance of this popular framework is competitive, according to our observation, there are two unresolved problems: (1) existing teacher-student frameworks suffer from erroneous pseudo labels especially in the late of training stage when the teacher and the student models become nearly identical and lose their distinctiveness. (2) the exploitation of pseudo labels is naive and more sophisticated methods are preferable. For example, STAC [20] and Unbiased Teacher [13] only exploit a single-thresholding method to pick some reliable pseudo labels and disregard all the rest.

To illustrate the first problem, we delve into the EMA updating equation, which is defined as follows,

$$\theta_{tea} = \alpha\theta_{tea} + (1 - \alpha)\theta_{stu}, \tag{1}$$

where θ_{tea} and θ_{stu} are the parameters of the teacher and the student respectively. α is the blending hyper-parameter balancing the historical teacher's parameters and current student's parameters. Normally, α is set to 0.999, accumulating more historical information for model stability concerns. However, given traditional one pair of teacher-student model, since EMA updates the teacher model in each training iteration, the model weights of the teacher becomes extremely similar to those of the student especially when the learning rate is small at the last phase of the training process. This will lead to the fact that the prediction of the teacher model and the student model become nearly identical, which hinders the teacher model from digging information from the unlabeled data to supervise the student. To address this problem, we propose a diverse learner framework consisting of two-paired teacher-student models to maintain the distinctiveness of the teacher against the student. DL introduces diverse supervision for each learner from the counterpart which is important to alleviate the less informative teacher problem during the later training process.

On the other hand, the exploitation of pseudo labeling in existing teacher-student framework is severely underexplored. Previous works [13,20] typically use a single high value threshold to generate high confident pseudo labels and the performance depends heavily on the choice of the threshold. Even worse, the quality of the pseudo labels produced by the teacher is misaligned with the image-level erasing operator [28], a typical operation of strong augmentation used in existing weak-strong augmentation module [24,29] of SSOD methods. Specifically, the operator may erase the entire foreground object due to the lack of ground-truth foreground information on the unlabeled images.

To make full use of pseudo labels, we divide the pseudo labels into certain and uncertain categories and propose a multi-threshold classification loss, which uses hard labels for certain pseudo labels and soft labels for uncertain pseudo labels. This ensures the high quality of pseudo labels, meanwhile, increases the number of available foreground pseudo labels. Therefore, the recall of foreground objects is enhanced without sacrificing precision. Additionally, to take full advantage of the high-quality certain foreground pseudo labels, we devise a pseudo label-aware erasing module by masking the contents of certain foreground objects in the unlabeled images according to the bounding box coordinates of the high-quality certain pseudo labels, guiding the erasing operator to become more focused on the foreground objects, which leads to a more generalized model and shows superior performance according to our experiments.

To conclude, this paper has the following contributions:

- We investigate the defects of existing EMA mechanism in SSOD and propose a diverse learner framework with diverse supervision that maintains the distinctiveness of the teacher against the student as the training proceeds.
- We introduce a more favorable pseudo labeling strategy. Specifically, we divide the pseudo labels into two different categories and propose a multi-threshold classification loss to smoothly combine high quality pseudo labels with potential foreground pseudo labels. Thanks to this strategy, our approach is capable to achieve a much higher recall rate of foreground objects at the same precision against existing SOTA methods.
- We extend the exploitation of pseudo labeling. Concretely, we introduce a simple yet efficient pseudo label-aware erasing module that guides the image-level erasing operator to become more focused on the foreground objects.
- Extensive experiments show that our method outperforms all previous state-of-the-art methods by clear margins under various SSOD settings on the MS COCO benchmark dataset.

2   Related Works

2.1   Semi-supervised Image Classification

Recent semi-supervised image classification methods can be roughly divided into two categories: consistency based methods [9,22,23] and pseudo labeling based methods [1,2,19]. The consistency based methods are predicated on the assumption that modest data disturbances should not change the predictions of images. There are several ways to implement perturbations. UDA [23] proposes image augmentations on unlabeled images to boost the performance of model. Temporal Ensembling [9] introduces an exponential moving average of label predictions on each training example. Mean Teacher [22] develops Temporal Ensembling [9] by averaging student model's parameters instead of predictions to obtain superior teacher models. The pseudo labeling based approaches annotate unlabeled data by generating pseudo labels with a strict threshold. Mixmatch and Remixmatch [1,2] apply stochastic data augmentation to unlabeled images and obtain pseudo labels by averaging the corresponding predictions. Fixmatch [19] generates pseudo labels on weakly-augmented unlabeled images and then trained to predict the pseudo-label when fed a strongly-augmented version of the same image. Flexmatch [26] sets a flexible thresholds for different classes at each time step to let pass informative unlabeled data and their pseudo labels. However, due to the complexity of object detection task, these image classification methods can not be directly applied to semi-supervised target detection field.

2.2 Semi-supervised Object Detection

Similar to semi-supervised image classification task, consistency based and pseudo labeling based methods are widely utilized in semi-supervised object detection methods [7,8,13,20,21,24,25,29]. Consistency based methods enforce models to generate consistent predictions on augmented images. CSD [7] is typical of consistency based methods, which constrains the consistency of features between original images and horizontal flip images. ISD [8] further proposes a mixup data augmentation method specially designed for semi-supervised object detection to create data perturbations.

For its excellent performance, the mainstream method in semi-supervised object detection is pseudo labeling based method and our method also belongs to this category. STAC [20] firstly proposes a teacher-student framework in semi-supervised object detection task which uses weak augmented images for teacher model to generate pseudo labels and trains student model to match the respective pseudo labels. Many other works [13,21,24,25] further improve the performance based on STAC [20]. In Unbiased Teacher [13], focal loss is introduced to solve the class imbalance issue. Soft Teacher [24] assesses the uncertainty of bounding boxes by box jittering and selects certain bounding boxes for regression. However, all these pseudo labeling based methods inevitably suffer from minor updates in the late training process since the teacher model is deeply related to the student model due to EMA mechanism. In contrast, we design a diverse learner framework with a diverse supervision strategy to keep discrepancy between teacher and student model which is beneficial for training process. Recently, data augmentations have proven to be an effective strategy for boosting model performance in semi-supervised object detection [4,28]. Some works [13,20,21,24] apply random erasing in strong augmentation, Instant Teaching [29] further combines Mixup and Mosaic augmentations to increase data perturbations. However, these augmentations operate on image level and neglect the information of pseudo labels. By introducing pseudo box location information, we propose a pseudo label-aware erasing module that encourages the random erasing operator to concentrate on the foreground objects.

3   Methodology

Preliminary. We follow the conventional setting of the semi-supervised object detection task, where the training set consists of two types of images: labeled images $D_s = \{s_i, y_i\}_{i=1}^{N_s}$ and unlabeled images $D_u = \{u_i\}_{i=1}^{N_u}$, where N_s and N_u are the number of labeled images s and unlabeled images u respectively. y represents the annotations for s.

Previous semi-supervised object detection works [13,24] mostly use Faster RCNN [17] and apply the pseudo labeling method in their framework, we also follow this setting. We denote the pseudo label of the j-th bounding box in image i as p_i^j. Specifically, p_i^j consists of bounding box locations $b_i^j \in \mathbb{R}^4$ and confidence $c_i^j \in \mathbb{R}$ which is the highest classification score in all categories. There are two types of training loss: unsupervised loss L_u and supervised loss L_s. Both L_s and L_u consist of the classification loss L_{cls} and regression loss L_{reg}. For more details, please refer to Faster RCNN [17]. The overall loss for semi-supervised object detection is defined as:

$$L = L_s + \lambda L_u, \tag{2}$$

$$L_s = \frac{1}{N_s}(\sum_{i=1}^{N_s}(L_{cls}(s_i, y_i) + (L_{reg}(s_i, y_i)))), \tag{3}$$

$$L_u = \frac{1}{N_u}(\sum_{i=1}^{N_u}(L_{cls}(u_i, p_i) + (L_{reg}(u_i, p_i)))), \tag{4}$$

where λ indicates unsupervised loss weight.

3.1   Diverse Learner

Existing most semi-supervised object detection methods adopt teacher-student framework. However, in the traditional framework teacher and student models tend to lose their distinctiveness in the late of training stage and this will cause a less informative teacher problem. We further illustrate this phenomenon in Fig. 1 where the similarity metric is calculated by

$$Similarity = \frac{1}{N_c} \sum_{i=1}^{N_c} \frac{M_{tea}^c \bigcap M_{stu}^c}{M_{tea}^c \bigcup M_{stu}^c}, \tag{5}$$

where N_c is the number of classes. M_{tea}^c is obtained by aggregating all detection results of class c produced by the teacher. The aggregation process is performed

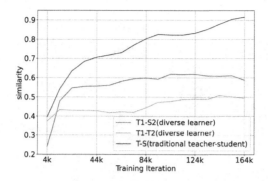

Fig. 1. Evaluation of models trained with 1% labeled images on *COCO-val* dataset. Similarity between predictions of two models. T1, T2, S2 denote teacher1, teacher2, student2 models respectively in our diverse learner framework. T and S represent teacher and student models in a traditional one paired teacher-student model correspondingly. (Color figure online)

by setting the foreground area to 1 and background area to 0, thus generating a binary mask for each class. M_{stu}^{c} is generated by similar process. This similarity metric measures the prediction consistency between the teacher and the student. Obviously, as the training iteration increases, the predictions of the teacher and the student tend to be more similar, which manifests that the teacher becomes less informative and thus limits further performance improvement (the blue line in Fig. 1).

We observe in Fig. 1 that for two pairs of randomly initialized teacher-student models, the teachers exhibit a small similarity score at the beginning of the training (the orange line in Fig. 1). This leads us to ponder: *can this discrepancy be maintained in the two paired teacher-student models where the teacher in one pair supervises the student in the other pair?* In this paper, we argue that the diverse supervision strategy does create distinctive teachers as the training proceeds (see the red and orange lines in Fig. 1). The underlying working principle is three-fold: (1) our diverse learner framework creates two different learners of the same unlabeled input image through differently initialized teachers; (2) the evolution of one pair of teacher-student models receive diverse supervisory signal (pseudo labels) from the other pair, which alleviates the less informative teacher problem mentioned above; (3) the teacher in one pair is regularized by its corresponding student to maintain its distinctiveness, which prevents itself from overfitting to the supervision signal from the other pair.

Our proposed diverse learner adopts diverse supervision strategy, as shown in Fig. 2(a), students are supervised by the counterpart teacher instead of the paired teacher. Specifically, we apply two randomly chosen weak augmentations W_1, W_2 to the unlabeled input images U and feed them to each teacher to obtain pseudo labels P_{tea1}, P_{tea2} correspondingly. P_{tea1}, P_{tea2} act as diverse supervising

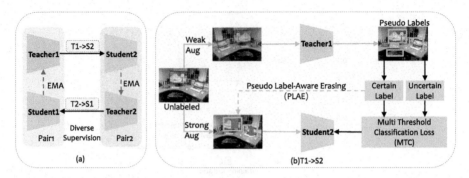

Fig. 2. Overview of our proposed **Diverse Learner** (DL) framework. (a) **Framework Abstraction**. It contains two learners, each consists of a pair of teacher-student models, where the teacher is updated by the student using EMA. In order to maintain the distinctiveness of the teacher against the student in each learner, each student receives diverse supervision from the teacher of the counterpart learner in each training iteration. All these models are randomly initialized. (b) **Detailed Framework and Training Procedure**. For simplicity, here we only illustrate supervision process of teacher1 and student2 on the unlabeled data in each training iteration, and the process of teacher2 and student1 is similar. Specifically, weak-augmented unlabeled images are fed to teacher1 to generate pseudo labels. Then we divide pseudo labels into certain labels and uncertain labels. On one hand, we devise a Pseudo Label-Aware Erasing (PLAE) module to enhance the strong augmentation for the training samples of the student2 model. On the other hand, we propose to calculate a Multi-Threshold Classification Loss (MTC) which treats certain labels and uncertain labels differently for supervising student2.

signal for the counterpart student student2, student1. Formally:

$$P_{tea1} = f_t\left(W_1(U), \theta_{tea1}\right), \tag{6}$$

$$P_{tea2} = f_t\left(W_2(U), \theta_{tea2}\right), \tag{7}$$

where $f_t(*)$ represents the inference process of teacher, θ_{tea1}, θ_{tea2} are the network parameters of teacher1 and teacher2, respectively. In order to further introduce diversity between two learners, both θ_{tea1} and θ_{tea2} are randomly initialized.

Similarly, students' inputs are generated by two randomly chosen strong augmentation operations S_1, S_2. We define the unsupervised loss as:

$$L_u = L_u^{stu1} + L_u^{stu2}, \tag{8}$$

$$L_u^{stu1} = L_u(f_s(S_1(U), \theta_{stu1}), P_{tea2}), \tag{9}$$

$$L_u^{stu2} = L_u(f_s(S_2(U), \theta_{stu2}), P_{tea1}), \tag{10}$$

where $f_s(*)$ represents the prediction process of student, θ_{stu1}, θ_{stu2} are the network parameters of the two students. In each training iteration, the teacher is updated by the student in the same pair learner via EMA,

$$\theta_{tea1} \leftarrow \alpha\theta_{tea1} + (1 - \alpha)\theta_{stu1}, \tag{11}$$

Fig. 3. Examples of the pseudo labels generated by diverse learner. Red boxes denote false predictions while green boxes stand for correct predictions. (a) Predictions of teacher1; (b) Predictions of teacher2. (Color figure online)

$$\theta_{tea2} \leftarrow \alpha\theta_{tea2} + (1 - \alpha)\theta_{stu2}, \tag{12}$$

Besides, when only one single pair of teacher-student is applied, once the teacher produces a wrong pseudo label for the unlabeled data, there is little chance that the noise can eliminated in the subsequent training process. However, our proposed diverse learner framework makes this rectification possible. As shown in Fig. 3, although some wrong pseudo labels such as the red boxes exist in one teacher model, another teacher still keeps the opportunity for generating correct labels.

3.2   Multi-threshold Classification Loss

A common way [13,20,24] to ensure the precision of pseudo labels is setting a high threshold to filter unreliable labels, while this strategy brings another problem that only few pseudo labels can remain after the filtering so that many correct labels are treated as background by mistake. Figure 4 shows that in standard teacher-student framework, high precision of pseudo labels comes with the cost of low recall. On the contrary, when confidence threshold decreases, although recall of pseudo labels increases, precision declines significantly. Thus, it is not feasible to simply set a threshold to determine whether the pseudo label is foreground or background.

Based on such observation, we propose a Multi-Threshold Classification Loss, which deals with the pseudo labels differently according to the classification score. Specifically, we denote a lower bound threshold as δ_l and an upper bound threshold as δ_u. Then, we divide the pseudo labels p^j into two categories: uncertain pseudo labels $p^j_{uncertain}$ and certain pseudo labels $p^j_{certain}$:

$$p^j = \begin{cases} p^j_{uncertain} & \delta_l \leq c^j \leq \delta_u \\ p^j_{certain} & otherwise \end{cases} \tag{13}$$

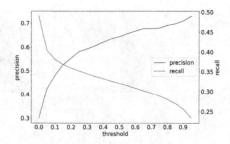

Fig. 4. Precision and recall under different threshold in traditional teacher-student framework

For the pseudo labels whose c^j are higher than δ_u or lower than δ_l, we believe that these $p^j_{certain}$ are reliable thus we follow the standard object detection task's setting, which adopts one-hot label y^j_{hard} and cross entropy loss.

For those $p^j_{uncertain}$ whose c^j are in the uncertain interval $[\delta_l, \delta_u]$, we use the classification score of $p^j_{uncertain}$ as soft label y^j_{soft} instead of one hot label y^j_{hard} since soft labels retain the estimations over all categories thus tolerate noisy predictions well in the uncertain interval. Next, to deal with these uncertain pseudo labels, we mainly propose following three methods:

1. **Neglect loss**: neglect all $P_{uncertain}$, i.e. loss function is not calculated.
2. **Binary cross entropy loss**: neglect the specific class of $P_{uncertain}$, only compute the binary cross entropy loss of foreground/background.
3. **KL divergence loss**: compute the KL divergence loss of $P_{uncertain}$.

We find that the KL divergence loss achieves the best performance (see Table 5), thus the final Multi-Threshold Classification Loss for unlabeled data is defined as follows:

$$L^j_{MTC} = \begin{cases} KL(y^j_{soft}||p^j_{uncertain}), & \delta_l \leq c^j \leq \delta_u \\ CE(y^j_{hard}, p^j_{certain}), & otherwise \end{cases} \tag{14}$$

where KL and CE stand for KL divergence loss and cross entropy loss, respectively. By replacing L_{cls} with L_{MTC}, the final unsupervised loss L_U is:

$$L_u = \frac{1}{N_u}(\sum_{i=1}^{N_u}(L_{MTC}(u_i, p_i) + (L_{reg}(u_i, p_i)))) \tag{15}$$

3.3 Pseudo Label-Aware Erasing

In addition to employing Multi-Threshold Classification loss in classification branch, in order to further make full utilization of certain foreground pseudo labels, we introduce pseudo label-aware erasing which randomly erases some content inside these high confidence pseudo boxes.

(a)   (b)   (c)   (d)

Fig. 5. (a) the original images; (b) green boxes mean pseudo labels; (c) the effect of random erasing; (d) the effect of our pseudo label-aware erasing. Red boxes indicate erasing regions. (Color figure online)

In previous works [20,21,24], random erasing [28] on the whole image are widely utilized as a way of strong augmentation. We observe two major drawbacks when the random erasing is performed on the whole image. Firstly, the erased areas are likely to locate in the background, as shown in the first row of Fig. 5(c). This is ineffective for training object detection models since the appearance of foreground objects are unchanged. Secondly, for object detection task, image level random erasing is possible to obscure objects completely, as shown in the second row in Fig. 5(c). This will definitely mislead students and harms the whole training process.

Figure 5(d) shows our proposed pseudo label-aware erasing strategy on the unlabeled data. We take the pseudo label's location information into account and only random erase the objects inside the pseudo bounding box according to a certain proportion. Comparing with image level random erasing method, this erasing strategy pays more attention to foreground area and does not have the risk of dispelling the objects completely.

4 Experiments

4.1 Experiments Setting

Datasets. We validate the efficacy of our method on the MS-COCO dataset [12]. The original *COCO-standard* set contains 118K labeled images, *COCO-additional* set contains 123K unlabeled images and *COCO-val* set contains 5K images. Following the previous works [13,24], two experimental settings are used: (1) Partially labeled data: we randomly sample 1%, 5% and 10% of the labeled training data from *COCO-standard* as a labeled training set and form the rest data into the unlabeled training data. (2) Fully Labeled data: we utilize the full labeled data in *COCO-standard* as training data set and *COCO-additional* as the unlabeled data set. We analyze the above settings on *COCO-val* set using mean average precision (mAP) as the evaluation metrics.

Implementation Detail. For fair comparison, we follow the previous works [13, 20,24], using Faster-RCNN [17] with FPN [10] as our detection framework. We initialize the parameters of backbones in four models with the Resnet-50 [5] pre-trained on ImageNet and the parameters of detection heads randomly. In regression branch, we use box-jittering strategy mentioned in Soft Teacher [24].

For partially labeled data, we train models for 180k iterations, and set unsupervised loss weight λ to 4.0, batch size to 40, unlabeled data sampling ratio to 0.2. For fully labeled data, we train models for 720k iterations, and set unsupervised loss weight λ to 2.0, batch size to 64, unlabeled data sampling ratio to 0.5. And we set EMA update parameter α to 0.999 in both partially labeled data and fully labeled data setting.

For the multi-threshold classification loss, we set lower bound confidence threshold $\delta_l = 0.8$ and upper bound confidence threshold $\delta_u = 0.9$. We apply pseudo label-aware erasing strategy to bounding boxes with confidence score higher than 0.9 since 80000 iteration to meet the demand of accurate bounding box locations. Besides, we utilize random resize and horizontal flip as weak augmentation and strong augmentation contains random erasing, rotation, color jittering, etc.

In inference, since two teacher models both achieve high performance, we report the performance of the better teacher model.

4.2   Results

Partially Labeled Data. We first compare our method with previous state-of-the-art methods with 1%, 5% and 10% labeled data from MS-COCO. As shown in Table 1, our method achieves the SOTA performance under all three settings. Diverse learner outperforms the latest best method Soft Teacher [24] by 2.10%, 1.50% and 0.83% under 1%, 5% and 10% setting respectively. It is worth mentioning that diverse learner outperforms other methods especially when labeled data is extremely rare.

Fully Labeled Data. Aside from the excellent performance on the partially labeled dataset, we also show that our method can surpass other methods trained on fully labeled dataset. As shown in Table 2, our method exceeds Soft Teacher [24] by 0.81% and reaches 44.86%, demonstrating the effectiveness of diverse learner in case of large amount of labeled data and unlabeled data.

4.3   Ablation Study

In this section, in order to validate our key designs, we conduct extensive ablation experiments using 1% labeled MS-COCO dataset. We choose the popular STAC [20] framework as our baseline method which contains one pair of teacher-student models with EMA strategy. Additionally, we apply the box jittering techniques [24] to enhance the performance of the regression branch. Based on

Table 1. Comparison with CSD [7], STAC [20], Unbiased Teacher [13], Humble Teacher [21], Instant Teaching [29] and Soft Teacher [24] on MS-COCO dataset with partially labeled data setting.

Method	1%COCO	5%COCO	10%COCO
Supervised	10.0	20.92	26.94
CSD [7]	10.51	18.63	22.46
STAC [20]	13.97	21.18	26.18
Humble Teacher [21]	16.98	27.70	31.61
Instant Teaching [29]	18.05	26.75	30.40
Unbiased Teacher [13]	20.75	28.27	31.50
Soft Teacher [24]*	21.62	30.42	33.78
Ours	**23.72**	**31.92**	**34.61**

*Metrics reported on Soft Teacher's official Github repo.

Table 2. Results on fully labeled data comparison with CSD [7], STAC [20], Unbiased Teacher [13], Humble Teacher [21], Instant Teaching [29] and Soft Teacher [24]

Method	mAP
Supervised	40.89
CSD [7]	38.82
STAC [20]	39.21
Humble Teacher [21]	42.37
Instant Teaching [29]	40.20
Unbiased Teacher [13]	41.30
Soft Teacher [24]*	44.05
Ours	**44.86**

*Metrics reported on Soft Teacher's official Github repo.

the baseline method, we gradually integrate our proposed key designs and ablate the effectiveness.

Effectiveness of MTC. Result No. 1 and No. 2 in Table 3 illustrate that training with MTC surpasses the baseline method over 1.5 points. For a better understanding of the effectiveness of MTC, we analyze the precision and recall values during the training progress. As shown in Fig. 6, when MTC is applied, the recall increases significantly while the precision is maintained comparing with the baseline.

Effectiveness of PLAE. As demonstrated by the result No. 2 and No. 3 in Table 3, a further improvement of 0.6% mAP is achieved when PLAE strategy is applied.

Table 3. Effect of all the key designs, we denote multi-threshold classification loss as MTC, pseudo-label aware erasing as PLAE, diverse learner as DL and mutual learning as ML.

No	MTC	PLAE	DL	ML	mAP
1					20.6
2	$\checkmark$				22.1(+1.5)
3	$\checkmark$	$\checkmark$			22.7(+2.1)
4	$\checkmark$	$\checkmark$		$\checkmark$	19.0(−1.6)
5	$\checkmark$	$\checkmark$	$\checkmark$		**23.7**(+3.1)

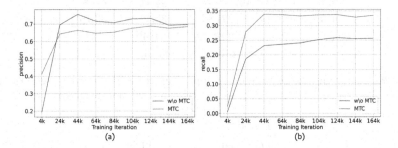

Fig. 6. Evaluation on *COCO-val* dataset under iou threshold = 0.5. (a) Diverse learner with multi-threshold classification loss (MTC) achieves almost the same precision as diverse learner without MTC. (b) Diverse learner with MTC achieves much higher recall than diverse learner without MTC.

Effectiveness of Diverse Learner. Here we first ablate the effect of incorporating our proposed DL framework. As shown in result No. 5 in Table 3, DL achieves another 1% improvement in mAP, reaching 23.7% mAP, which is 3.1% better than our baseline. Secondly, in order to further ablate the effects of using a teacher-student pair instead of one single model in each learner, we conduct experiment of integrating the conventional mutual learning method [27]. As shown in Fig. 7, directly integrating mutual learning strategy (green line) leads to an unstable training process thus harms the performance. We observe a severe drop (1.6%) in mAP, as shown in the result No. 4 in Table 3. On the contrary, our proposed DL framework enjoys merits from the mutual learning strategy while successfully stabilizes the training using the teacher-student pair with the EMA updating mechanism in each learner.

We calculate the average layer-wise cosine similarity of random-initialized layers' parameters between the teacher and student to measure the similarity of the teacher student pair. Results show that our proposed DL successfully reduces the similarity of the teacher and student from 0.9987 (traditional one paired teacher student) to 0.1498 (teacher1 and student2 in diverse learner).

Table 4. The comparison of choosing different lower threshold in MTC. The upper threshold is fixed to 0.9.

	mAP@$\delta_l = 0.6$	mAP@$\delta_l = 0.7$	mAP@$\delta_l = 0.8$
Ours (w\o DL)	22.6	23.1	22.7
Ours	23.2	23.4	**23.7**

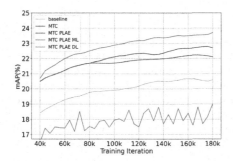

Fig. 7. The curves of mAP values corresponding to each setting in Table 3 during the training stage. (Color figure online)

Threshold Choice in MTC. We simply set upper threshold δ_u to 0.9 in our experiment and explore the choice of lower threshold δ_l from 0.6 to 0.8 (shown in Table 4) and 0.8 is the most suitable value for diverse learner.

Loss Type for Uncertain Pseudo Labels. As mentioned in Sect. 3.2, we experiment three types of loss functions to deal with the uncertain pseudo labels: neglect loss, binary cross entropy loss and KL divergence loss. The results of applying different loss functions on the baseline with PLAE module are shown in Table 5, KL divergence loss obtains the best performance.

Table 5. Effect of different types of loss functions for the uncertain pseudo labels.

Loss type	mAP
Neglect	21.2
Binary cross entropy loss	22.2
KL divergence loss	**22.7**

5   Conclusions

We present a diverse learner framework with diverse supervision that could maintain the distinctiveness of the teacher against the student. We also introduce a multi-threshold classification loss for a better utilization of both high-quality pseudo labels and potential uncertain pseudo labels and devise a simple yet efficient pseudo label-aware erasing strategy. Extensive experiments demonstrate the superiority of our method on the MS-COCO benchmark dataset. We will extend diverse learner to more learners in the future work, and study more elaborate supervision signals between multiple learners.

References

1. Berthelot, D., et al.: Remixmatch: semi-supervised learning with distribution alignment and augmentation anchoring. arXiv preprint arXiv:1911.09785 (2019)
2. Berthelot, D., Carlini, N., Goodfellow, I., Papernot, N., Oliver, A., Raffel, C.: Mixmatch: a holistic approach to semi-supervised learning. arXiv preprint arXiv:1905.02249 (2019)
3. Chen, L.C., Papandreou, G., Schroff, F., Adam, H.: Rethinking atrous convolution for semantic image segmentation. arXiv preprint arXiv:1706.05587 (2017)
4. DeVries, T., Taylor, G.W.: Improved regularization of convolutional neural networks with cutout. arXiv preprint arXiv:1708.04552 (2017)
5. He, K., Zhang, X., Ren, S., Sun, J.: Deep residual learning for image recognition. In: Proceedings of the IEEE Conference on Computer Vision and Pattern Recognition, pp. 770–778 (2016)
6. Iandola, F., Moskewicz, M., Karayev, S., Girshick, R., Darrell, T., Keutzer, K.: Densenet: implementing efficient convnet descriptor pyramids. arXiv preprint arXiv:1404.1869 (2014)
7. Jeong, J., Lee, S., Kim, J., Kwak, N.: Consistency-based semi-supervised learning for object detection. Adv. Neural. Inf. Process. Syst. **32**, 10759–10768 (2019)
8. Jeong, J., Verma, V., Hyun, M., Kannala, J., Kwak, N.: Interpolation-based semi-supervised learning for object detection. In: Proceedings of the IEEE/CVF Conference on Computer Vision and Pattern Recognition, pp. 11602–11611 (2021)
9. Laine, S., Aila, T.: Temporal ensembling for semi-supervised learning. arXiv preprint arXiv:1610.02242 (2016)
10. Lin, T.Y., Dollár, P., Girshick, R., He, K., Hariharan, B., Belongie, S.: Feature pyramid networks for object detection. In: Proceedings of the IEEE Conference on Computer Vision and Pattern Recognition, pp. 2117–2125 (2017)
11. Lin, T.Y., Goyal, P., Girshick, R., He, K., Dollár, P.: Focal loss for dense object detection. In: Proceedings of the IEEE International Conference on Computer Vision, pp. 2980–2988 (2017)
12. Lin, T.-Y., et al.: Microsoft COCO: common objects in context. In: Fleet, D., Pajdla, T., Schiele, B., Tuytelaars, T. (eds.) ECCV 2014. LNCS, vol. 8693, pp. 740–755. Springer, Cham (2014). https://doi.org/10.1007/978-3-319-10602-1_48
13. Liu, Y.C., et al.: Unbiased teacher for semi-supervised object detection. arXiv preprint arXiv:2102.09480 (2021)
14. Liu, Z., et al.: Swin transformer: hierarchical vision transformer using shifted windows. In: Proceedings of the IEEE/CVF International Conference on Computer Vision, pp. 10012–10022 (2021)
15. Radosavovic, I., Dollár, P., Girshick, R., Gkioxari, G., He, K.: Data distillation: towards omni-supervised learning. In: Proceedings of the IEEE Conference on Computer Vision and Pattern Recognition, pp. 4119–4128 (2018)

16. Redmon, J., Farhadi, A.: Yolov3: an incremental improvement. arXiv preprint arXiv:1804.02767 (2018)
17. Ren, S., He, K., Girshick, R., Sun, J.: Faster R-CNN: towards real-time object detection with region proposal networks. Adv. Neural. Inf. Process. Syst. **28**, 91–99 (2015)
18. Ronneberger, O., Fischer, P., Brox, T.: U-Net: convolutional networks for biomedical image segmentation. In: Navab, N., Hornegger, J., Wells, W.M., Frangi, A.F. (eds.) MICCAI 2015. LNCS, vol. 9351, pp. 234–241. Springer, Cham (2015). https://doi.org/10.1007/978-3-319-24574-4_28
19. Sohn, K., et al.: Fixmatch: simplifying semi-supervised learning with consistency and confidence. arXiv preprint arXiv:2001.07685 (2020)
20. Sohn, K., Zhang, Z., Li, C.L., Zhang, H., Lee, C.Y., Pfister, T.: A simple semi-supervised learning framework for object detection. arXiv preprint arXiv:2005.04757 (2020)
21. Tang, Y., Chen, W., Luo, Y., Zhang, Y.: Humble teachers teach better students for semi-supervised object detection. In: Proceedings of the IEEE/CVF Conference on Computer Vision and Pattern Recognition, pp. 3132–3141 (2021)
22. Tarvainen, A., Valpola, H.: Mean teachers are better role models: weight-averaged consistency targets improve semi-supervised deep learning results. arXiv preprint arXiv:1703.01780 (2017)
23. Xie, Q., Dai, Z., Hovy, E., Luong, M.T., Le, Q.V.: Unsupervised data augmentation for consistency training. arXiv preprint arXiv:1904.12848 (2019)
24. Xu, M., et al.: End-to-end semi-supervised object detection with soft teacher. In: Proceedings of the IEEE/CVF International Conference on Computer Vision (ICCV) (2021)
25. Yang, Q., Wei, X., Wang, B., Hua, X.S., Zhang, L.: Interactive self-training with mean teachers for semi-supervised object detection. In: Proceedings of the IEEE/CVF Conference on Computer Vision and Pattern Recognition, pp. 5941–5950 (2021)
26. Zhang, B., et al.: Flexmatch: boosting semi-supervised learning with curriculum pseudo labeling. In: Advances in Neural Information Processing Systems, vol. 34 (2021)
27. Zhang, Y., Xiang, T., Hospedales, T.M., Lu, H.: Deep mutual learning. In: Proceedings of the IEEE Conference on Computer Vision and Pattern Recognition, pp. 4320–4328 (2018)
28. Zhong, Z., Zheng, L., Kang, G., Li, S., Yang, Y.: Random erasing data augmentation. In: Proceedings of the AAAI Conference on Artificial Intelligence, vol. 34, pp. 13001–13008 (2020)
29. Zhou, Q., Yu, C., Wang, Z., Qian, Q., Li, H.: Instant-teaching: an end-to-end semi-supervised object detection framework. In: Proceedings of the IEEE/CVF Conference on Computer Vision and Pattern Recognition, pp. 4081–4090 (2021)
30. Zhu, X., Su, W., Lu, L., Li, B., Wang, X., Dai, J.: Deformable detr: deformable transformers for end-to-end object detection. arXiv preprint arXiv:2010.04159 (2020)
31. Zoph, B., et al.: Rethinking pre-training and self-training. Adv. Neural. Inf. Process. Syst. **33**, 3833–3845 (2020)

A Closer Look at Invariances
in Self-supervised Pre-training
for 3D Vision

Lanxiao Li$^{(\boxtimes)}$ ⓘ and Michael Heizmann ⓘ

Institute of Industrial Information Technology, Karlsruhe Institute of Technology,
Karlsruhe, Germany
{lanxiao.li,michael.heizmann}@kit.edu

Abstract. Self-supervised pre-training for 3D vision has drawn increasing research interest in recent years. In order to learn informative representations, a lot of previous works exploit invariances of 3D features, *e.g.*, perspective-invariance between views of the same scene, modality-invariance between depth and RGB images, format-invariance between point clouds and voxels. Although they have achieved promising results, previous researches lack a systematic and fair comparison of these invariances. To address this issue, our work, for the first time, introduces a unified framework, under which various pre-training methods can be investigated. We conduct extensive experiments and provide a closer look at the contributions of different invariances in 3D pre-training. Also, we propose a simple but effective method that jointly pre-trains a 3D encoder and a depth map encoder using contrastive learning. Models pre-trained with our method gain significant performance boost in downstream tasks. For instance, a pre-trained VoteNet outperforms previous methods on SUN RGB-D and ScanNet object detection benchmarks with a clear margin.

Keywords: 3D Vision · Self-supervised learning · Contrastive learning · Invariances · Point clouds · Depth maps

1 Introduction

In order to cope with challenging tasks *e.g.*, object detection, scene understanding, and large-scale semantic segmentation, neural networks for 3D vision are continuously becoming deeper, more complicated, and thus, more data-hungry. In recent years, self-supervised pre-training has shown promising progress in natural language processing and computer vision. By learning powerful representations on non-annotated data, the models gain better performance and convergence in downstream tasks. Self-supervised pre-training is especially appealing in 3D vision because 3D annotation is more costly than the 2D counterpart.

Supplementary Information The online version contains supplementary material available at https://doi.org/10.1007/978-3-031-20056-4_38.

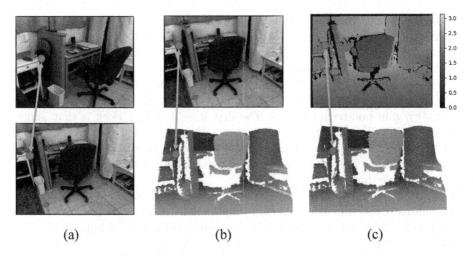

(a)   (b)   (c)

Fig. 1. Invariances in contrastive learning for 3D vision. Without loss of generality, we only consider the local correspondence here. Each column includes two views of the same scene. The exemplary correspondences across two views are illustrated with arrows, which means the two points/pixels have the same coordinate in the 3D space. In self-supervised pre-training, the similarity between corresponding local features is maximized, which forces networks to learn invariance between views. **(a) Perspective-invariance** in two views of the same scene from different view angles. We visualize RGD images instead of point clouds for better clarity. **(b) Modality-invariance** in an aligned image-point cloud pair. The data formats are also different in this case. But we still refer to it as modality-invariance to distinguish it from the format-invariance within a single modality. **(c) Format-invariance** between a depth map and a point cloud converted from it.

Self-supervised pre-training for 3D vision has already gained some research interests. A lot of previous works use contrastive learning as a pretext task to pre-train models, as it has shown superior performance in other domains [22,29, 56,62]. One classic hypothesis in contrastive learning is that a powerful representation should model view-invariant factors. A common approach to creating different views is data augmentation. Moreover, a 3D scene can be captured from various view angles, with different sensors (*e.g.*, RGB and depth cameras) and represented with different formats (*e.g.*, voxels, point clouds, and depth maps)[1], whereas the major semantic information in the scene is not changed by these factors. Thus, previous works exploit the perspective- [22,56], modality- [29] and format-invariance [62] of 3D features in self-supervised learning, as shown in Fig. 1. Although these works have shown impressive results, the contribution of the invariances is still under-explored, and a fair and systematic comparison of them hasn't been performed yet.

---

[1] To avoid ambiguity, we use the term *data format* instead of *data representation* in this work.

In this work, we first establish a unified framework for 3D self-supervised learning. Our framework takes into account the local point/pixel-level correspondence as well as the global instance-level correspondence. Also, our framework unifies contrastive learning with different input data formats and network structures, including Depth-Depth, Point-Point, Depth-Point, Image-Point, and Point-Voxel. By comparing various training strategies exploiting different invariances, we gain non-trivial results. The first insight of this work is that jointly pre-training a 3D encoder and a 2D encoder (Image-Point, Depth-Point) brings better performance than pre-training them separately or jointly pre-training two encoders with the same dimension (*e.g.*, a voxel and a point cloud encoder, which are both three dimensional).

Also, we propose the simple but effective idea to exploit the format-invariances between depth maps and point clouds/voxels. Our intuition is that depth maps are complementary to point clouds and voxels, although they contain almost the same information. The depth map format has the advantage that it's the natural view of the scene and clearly shows the perspective relationship between objects. Also, real-world depth maps usually contain bad pixels, which means the depth values are unmeasurable. In depth maps, the outlines of unmeasurable regions are sharp and clear, *e.g.*, the chair leg in Fig. 1(c). On the contrary, this information is lost if depth maps are lifted into 3D space. Moreover, thanks to its efficiency, the 2D encoder allows high-resolution depth maps as input, which preserves more fine-grained details in data. However, point or voxel-based networks usually take down-sampled or quantized input to avoid the excessive computational cost and memory usage, which results in inevitable information loss. On the other hand, point clouds and voxels are 3D formats and the corresponding networks can directly capture accurate 3D geometry, whereas depth map-based networks learn spatial relationships indirectly. Also, depth maps alone don't contain the information of camera calibrations. By contrasting the features extracted from two complementary data formats, the two networks learn appreciated properties from each other. This simple idea has less requirements on pre-training data and outperforms previous methods in our experiments.

The contribution of this work is many-fold:

1. We introduce a unified self-supervised pre-training framework for *all* major network types and data formats in 3D vision.
2. We provide a closer look at invariances in 3D pre-training, *e.g.*, format-, perspective- and modality-invariance.
3. We propose a novel approach for 3D self-supervised pre-training, which is based on the format-invariance between depth maps and points/voxels.
4. Our method reaches new SOTA results in multiple downstream tasks *e.g.*, object detection on SUN RGB-D dataset [48] and ScanNet [11] dataset.
5. The proposed method is also the first self-supervised pre-training approach for depth map-based networks.

2 Related Works

Feature Learning with 3D Data. PointNet [43] is the pioneer in deep learning methods for point clouds. To aggregate local information, PointNet++ [44] down-samples and groups point clouds hierarchically. Recent works [27,51,54] define point convolution on point clouds. Voxel-based methods convert irregular point clouds to regular 3D grids and apply 3D convolution [34,64] or deep sliding windows [49]. Also, some works [10,16] introduce sparse CNNs to reduce the computational cost and memory footprint. Some other works use 2D CNNs to extract features from depth maps [26,57,58], LiDAR range images [4,24,28] or pseudo images [23]. Also, a lot of works use more than one format of 3D data [12,23,28,33,47]. They and our work share the same motivation to combine the advantages of different data formats. However, our method learns the appreciated property via contrastive learning in the pretext task. In fine-tuning for downstream tasks, only one format is used.

Self-supervised Pre-training in Computer Vision. A lot of pretext tasks for self-supervised learning has been proposed. Some generative approaches recover images under some corruption, *e.g.*, auto-encoders for colorization [60,61] and denoising [50]. Some discriminative approaches generate pseudo-labels for *e.g.*, rotation prediction [15], Jigsaw puzzle solving [36] and objects tracking [52]. Recently, contrastive learning achieved impressive performance in self-supervised learning [3,7,8,19,35,37]. Besides the instance-level discrimination, some works also exploit the local correspondence for better transfer in tasks which need dense features, *e.g.*, object detection and semantic segmentation [5,39,53].

Self-supervised Pre-training for 3D Data. Some works [1,18,45,46] perform self-supervised learning on synthetic data *e.g.*, ShapeNet [55]. However, these approaches don't transfer well to real-world data [56]. PointContrast [56] first uses real-world point cloud data for self-supervised training. It learns perspective-invariance by predicting point-wise correspondence between two partially overlapping point clouds. Liu *et al.* [29] pre-train a 3D encoder by using a pre-trained 2D encoder as teacher. On the other hand, Liu *et al.* [32] propose a distillation pipeline to improve 2D encoders by using geometry guidance from 3D encoders. DepthContrast [62] extends the successful MoCo [8,19] pipeline to 3D domain and exploits the cross-format contrast between point clouds and voxels. Hou *et al.* [22] propose spatial partition to improve the contrastive learning and investigate the data-efficiency and label-efficiency of pre-trained models.

Multi-modal Feature Fusion. The idea of learning from two complementary sources is similar to data fusion. In 3D computer vision, a common practice is to fuse the color and geometry information. A lot of fusing approaches have been proposed, *e.g.*, for object detection [21,40,42,59] and salient object detection [14,25,57,63]. Some other works use self-supervised pre-training to improve the feature fusion [30,31]. The difference between fusing and contrasting multi-modal features is that fusion enriches features by combining complementary information from different modalities, while contrastive learning maximizes the shared information between modalities.

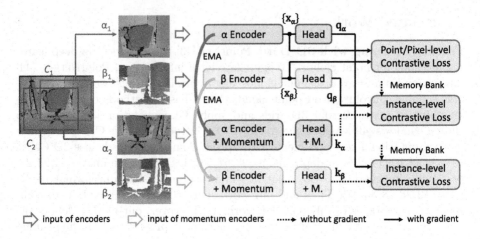

Fig. 2. A unified framework for 3D contrastive learning. Here, α and β refer to data types, *e.g.*, point clouds, images, and depth maps.

3 Method

In this work, we intend to research the invariances in 3D self-supervised learning, including perspective-, modality- and format-invariance. For a fair comparison, it's meaningful to investigate them under a unified framework. In this section, we first briefly revisit some representative works. Then, we introduce a unified framework to which all previous methods fit. Moreover, we introduce several contrastive learning methods under the unified framework. At last, we provide technical details of the framework.

3.1 Unified Framework for 3D Constrastive Learning

In this work, we pay attention to three previous works. (1) PointContrast [56]: it generates two views of the same scene from different perspectives and learns the local correspondence between 3D points using a contrastive loss. (2) DepthContrast [62]: following the successful MoCo pipeline [8,19], it augments two views of the same point cloud to build positive pairs and learn global correspondences by distinguishing the positive samples from a large number of negative samples. Also, it proposes to exploit cross-format contrast between point clouds and voxels. (3) Pixel-to-point [29]: its overall pipeline is similar to PointContrast. However, it learns local correspondences between point clouds and RGB images, in order to benefit from strong pre-trained RGB encoders.

Therefore, a unified framework must support both the local and global correspondence of 3D data and at least two different input types, either from different modalities (*e.g.*, RGB images and point clouds) or with different data formats (*e.g.*, depth maps and point clouds).

We show our framework in Fig. 2, which uses a single-view depth map or RGB-D image for simplicity. However, experiments show that the pre-trained weights generalize well on reconstructed multi-view 3D scans. Without loss of generality, we assume the input of the framework is a depth map in this section. We randomly crop the input to get crop C_1, which is further randomly augmented and converted into views α_1 and β_1. Here α and β refer to data formats (e.g., depth maps and point clouds, as visualized in Fig. 2). Then, α_1 and β_1 go through respective encoders and are encoded into pixelwise or pointwise features $\{\mathbf{x}_\alpha\}$ and $\{\mathbf{x}_\beta\}$. Note that the α and β encoders are usually different networks matching the input formats. But in the case of $\alpha = \beta$, they share the weights, following [56]. As α_1 and β_1 are generated from the same crop C_1, the dense correspondence between $\{\mathbf{x}_\alpha\}$ and $\{\mathbf{x}_\beta\}$ can be easily calculated without camera extrinsic. In this work, we follow [56] and use InfoNCE loss to train dense local correspondence, which is further explained in Sect. 3.3.

In order to learn informative representations, our framework also considers the global correspondence between views. Following [62], we perform instance discrimination based on global features $\mathbf{q}_\alpha$ and $\mathbf{q}_\beta$, which are globally pooled and projected from $\{\mathbf{x}_\alpha\}$ and $\{\mathbf{x}_\beta\}$. To preserve a large number of negative samples for effective contrastive learning, we use memory banks and momentum encoders, following the successful MoCo pipeline [8,19]. However, in supplementary material, we further show that our methods can be generalized to other pipelines, e.g., BYOL [17] and SimSiam [9].

Analog to crop C_1, we randomly crop C_2 from the same depth map, generate α_2 and β_2 and feed them to the momentum encoders. We refer to the globally pooled and projected features from momentum encoders as $\mathbf{k}_\alpha$ and $\mathbf{k}_\beta$, respectively. They are dynamically saved and updated in memory banks during training. Note that unlike [62] our work only contrasts features from different input formats, as we empirically found the gains from additional contrast within the formats are marginal.

3.2 Variants of Strategies

As the overall framework is shown, we now introduce various contrastive learning strategies under this framework. As shown in Fig. 3, we investigate the following variants in this work:

1. DPCo (Depth-Point Contrast), our proposed method, which learns *format-invariance* between depth maps and point clouds.
2. DVCo (Depth-Voxel Contrast), our proposed method, which learns *format-invariance* between depth maps and voxels.
3. PVCo (Point-Voxel Contrast), which learns *format-invariance* between point clouds and voxels. It's extended from PointContrast [62].
4. PPCo (Point-Point Contrast), which only uses point clouds as input. It serves as a baseline method as it only learns invariance against data augmentation.
5. IPCo (Image-Point Contrast), which learns *modality-invarince* between RGB images and point clouds. It's inspired by Pixel-to-point [29].
6. PointContrast [56], which learns *perspective-invariance* between view angles. It can be interpreted as a special case of our unified framework, since it

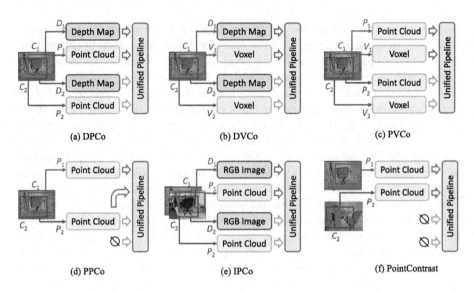

Fig. 3. Contrastive learning strategies under a unified framework.

generates the crops C_1 and C_2 from two overlapping depth maps from different view angles and only considers the local correspondence.

In this work, we propose to contrast a 3D format and a 2D format of the same geometric data (*i.e.*, DPCo and DVCo). Although they represent the same 3D scene, the two formats are complementary to some extent. As discussed in Sect. 1, point clouds and voxels directly represent 3D geometry while having inevitable information loss due to sampling and bad pixels. On the contrary, depth maps reserve more information but only represent the 3D scene indirectly. Experiment results show that our methods bring significantly better performance than PPCo and PVCo, which contrast only 3D formats.

3.3   Details

Point Cloud Encoder. We use a U-shaped PointNet++ [44] and follow the network configuration in [41], which consists of 4 down-sampling and 2 up-sampling modules. We use 20K points as input in the pre-training. The number of output points is fixed to 1024.

Voxel Encoder. We use a sparse residual U-Net [10] with 34 convolution layers to encode voxel inputs, following previous works [22,56]. We use the implementation of sparse convolution in [10]. For geometry-only input, we set all input features to 1. For input with colors, we use normalized RGB values as input features. In pre-training, we quantize inputs with the voxel size of 2.5 cm. The output of the voxel encoder has the same resolution as the input.

Depth Map Encoder. We use the U-shaped 2D CNN in [26] as depth map encoder. The network is a modified ResNet-34 [20] with relative depth convolution [26] and extra up-sampling layers. The input is resized and zero-padded to 352×352. The output is a feature map down-sampled with factor 8.

Color Image Encoder. Analog to the depth map encoder, we use a ResNet-34 with extra up-sampling layers to encoder the RGB images. We initialize this encoder with the pre-trained weights on ImageNet [13], following the setup in [29].

Momentum Encoders and Projection Heads. The momentum encoders have the same structure as the encoders. Their weights are updated via exponential moving average (EMA) from the corresponding encoders instead of back-propagation. We use global max pooling to aggregate the global features. The pooling layer is followed by an MLP consisting of 3 fully connected layers. The intermediate and the output layer have 512 and 128 channels, respectively. The projection heads of momentum encoders are updated via EMA as well.

Loss Functions. Our loss function consists of a local sub-loss L_l and a global sub-loss L_g. The local sub-loss is an InfoNCE loss which optimizes the local dense correspondence:

$$L_{l,\,\alpha\beta} = -\sum_i \log \frac{\exp(\mathbf{x}_{\alpha,\,i} \cdot \mathbf{x}_{\beta,\,i}/\tau)}{\exp(\mathbf{x}_{\alpha,\,i} \cdot \mathbf{x}_{\beta,\,i}/\tau) + \sum_{j \neq i} \exp(\mathbf{x}_{\alpha,\,i} \cdot \mathbf{x}_{\beta,\,j}/\tau)} \tag{1}$$

with $\mathbf{x}_{\alpha,\,i} \in \{\mathbf{x}_\alpha\}$ and $\mathbf{x}_{\beta,\,j} \in \{\mathbf{x}_\beta\}$. If the corresponding 3D coordinates of feature vector $\mathbf{x}_{\alpha,\,i}$ and $\mathbf{x}_{\beta,\,j}$ are close, they're considered as a positive pair and have $i = j$. The temperature τ is a hyperparameter and is set to 0.07 in this work. All features are L2-normalized before being fed into the loss function.

The global sub-loss is applied to optimize an instance discrimination task:

$$L_{g,\,\alpha\beta} = -\log \frac{\exp(\mathbf{q}_\alpha \cdot \mathbf{k}_\beta/\tau)}{\exp(\mathbf{q}_\alpha \cdot \mathbf{k}_\beta/\tau) + \sum_{n=1}^{N-1} \exp(\mathbf{q}_\alpha \cdot \mathbf{k}_{\beta,\,n}/\tau)} \tag{2}$$

The vector $\mathbf{q}_\alpha$ refers to the global feature from the α encoder and $\mathbf{k}_\beta$ the global feature from the β momentum encoder. Since $\mathbf{q}_\alpha$ and $\mathbf{k}_\beta$ are generated from the same data sample, they make a positive pair. Features $\mathbf{k}_{\beta,\,n}$ correspond to other samples and are read from a memory bank with the size N. We use $N = 2^{15}$ in this work. Following previous works, we make our loss symmetric to α and β. The total loss can be formulated as

$$L = L_l + L_g = 0.25 \cdot (L_{l,\,\alpha\beta} + L_{l,\,\beta\alpha} + L_{g,\,\alpha\beta} + L_{g,\,\beta\alpha}). \tag{3}$$

Principally, L can be a weighted sum of L_l and L_g and the weighting factors can be tuned. But we empirically found that the simple arithmetic average already generates good results.

Data Augmentation. We randomly crop C_1 and C_2. Also, we randomly drop a square area in each crop. We apply random rotation, scaling, and flipping to the point clouds and voxels. We randomly rotate depth maps around principal points and set 20% pixels on the depth map to zero. For RGB images, we apply random color jitter, grayscale, and Gaussian blur.

Dataset. We use ScanNet [11] for the pre-training, following previous works [22, 31, 56, 62]. ScanNet is a large-scale indoor dataset, which contains about 1500 scans reconstructed from 2.5M RGB-D frames. We follow the official train/val split and sample 78K frames (one in every 25 frames) from the train set.

Training. We pre-train the encoders for 120 epochs. We use SGD optimizer with momentum of 0.9 and an initial learning rate of 0.03. We train models on two NVIDIA Tesla V100 GPUs with a total of 64 GB memory and use as large batch size as it fits. The batch size of different strategies varies from 32 to 64. The learning rate is decayed with a cosine schedule. The pre-training takes from two to four days using PyTorch with Distributed Data Parallel.

More technical details can be found in the supplementary material.

4 Experiments and Results

In this section, we first briefly introduce the experimental setups. Then, we compare and analyze different contrastive learning strategies in detail under our unified framework, to clarify the contribution of the invariances. Then, we compare our method (DPCo) with state-of-the-art methods in the point cloud object detection task. At last, we show transfer learning results of our methods on voxels and depth maps. More experimental results can be found in the supplementary material.

4.1 Invariances in 3D Self-supervised Pre-training

In this subsection, we focus on the performance of transfer learning on point cloud-based 3D detection task, since we believe the 3D detection reflects the encoder's capability of capturing both semantic (*i.e.*, objects classification) and geometric (*i.e.*, bounding box regression) information and is thus representative. Also, 3D detection using raw points is well studied in previous works [6, 40–42]. In this work, we fine-tune a VoteNet [41] with a PointNet++ backbone on SUN RGB-D [48] and ScanNet [11] object detection benchmark. The evaluation metrics are the mean Average Precision over the representative classes with the threshold of 25% and 50% 3D-IoU (*i.e.*, AP25 and AP50).

Comparison Under the Unified Framework. In this experiment, we compare various contrastive learning strategies under our unified framework. As shown in Table 1, all pre-training methods deliver better results than training from scratch in both 3D detection benchmarks. Note that ScanNet benchmark uses point clouds reconstructed from multiple views. Our unified framework, which assumes that the pre-training data are independent single depth maps or RGB-D images, still significantly improves the detection results on this dataset. It implies that the weights pre-trained on single-view data generalize well on multi-view data.

Table 1. VoteNet fine-tuning performance of self-supervised pre-training strategies with different invariances. We reproduce the results without pre-training using the open-source code of [41], which are slightly better than the original publication.

Method	Invariance	Correspond	SUN RGB-D		ScanNet	
			AP25	AP50	AP25	AP50
From scratch	-	-	58.4	33.3	60.0	37.6
PPCo	Augmentation	Local+Global	58.6	34.9	62.6	39.5
PointContrast	Perspective	Local	59.6	34.1	62.8	38.1
PVCo	Format (3D-3D)	Local+Global	59.3	34.9	62.8	39.5
IPCo	Modality	Local+Global	**60.2**	35.5	63.9	40.9
DPCo (Ours)	Format (2D-3D)	Local+Global	59.8	**35.6**	**64.2**	**41.5**

The baseline strategy PPCo utilizes solely the invariance against data augmentation. However, it surpasses PointContrast, which relies on extrinsic parameters, in two out of four metrics. It implies that with a proper design (in our case, the local dense contrast and the MoCo-style instance discrimination), the perspective-invariance is unnecessary in pre-training. A similar observation is also reported in [62]. We hypothesize that in the instance discrimination subproblem, the network has to distinguish inputs from very similar view angles, as we extract training data from continuous RGB-D videos. This can be interpreted as hard example mining, which forces the network to focus on perspective-relevant details. Thus, with the help of global correspondence in pre-training, the encoders implicitly learn perspective-relevant information, but not necessarily the invariance in this case.

Moreover, PVCo, which contrasts features from point clouds and voxels, brings slightly better though very similar results as PPCo. It's probably due to the nature of point clouds and voxels as they both represent 3D coordinates directly. Also, PointNet++ is similar to 3D ConvNets, as it conducts convolution-like local aggregation, uses shared weights in a sliding window manner, and has a hierarchical topology with sub- and up-sampling. Thus, jointly pre-training voxel and point cloud encoders bring limited benefits to the point cloud encoder, compared to pre-training it alone. In this case, incorporating voxel features can be interpreted as a strong data augmentation to point clouds.

However, IPCo and DPCo, which contrast a 2D data format (*e.g.*, color images or depth maps) and a 3D format (*e.g.*, point clouds) achieve significantly better results than PPCo and PVCo, which utilize only 3D formats. It confirms our intuition that the 2D data format is complementary to the 3D format and the correspondence between them can provide strong contrast in self-supervised pre-training. More interestingly, our proposed method DPCo, which uses solely the geometrical information, reaches on-par or better performance as the one using both geometrical and color inputs (IPCo). This is an important advantage in practice, as our method is applicable even if the RGB images are not available or hard to align with depth maps. It also implies that the performance gains of

IPCo come probably not from the color information, but from other factors *e.g.*, different resolutions and perspective fields of 2D and 3D networks. Another advantage of DPCo is that it trains faster than PPCo and PVCo, thanks to the efficiency of 2D CNN.

Local and Global Correspondence. Our unified framework supports both the local and global correspondence of 3D data in the pre-training. In the following experiments, we investigate the contribution of each type of correspondence separately. As shown in Table 2 and Table 3, using local and global correspondence alone in the pre-training improves the performance of encoders. Also, comparing with Table 1, it's clear that combining them can bring further improvement, which is also observed in 2D pre-training, as discussed in [53]. Moreover, Table 2 and Table 3 show similar trends as Table 1, where IPCo and DPCo show superior performance over others. Interestingly, in Table 2 IPCo and DPCo achieve better results than PointContrast even without the global correspondence.

Table 2. Different choices of local correspondence in pre-training.

Contrast	SUN RGB-D		ScanNet	
	AP25	AP50	AP25	AP50
w/o	58.4	33.3	60.0	37.6
PPCo	58.7	34.8	62.2	38.8
PVCo	59.1	34.6	62.2	39.0
PointCo	59.6	34.1	62.8	38.1
IPCo	**60.1**	**35.6**	62.5	39.4
DPCo	59.6	35.1	**64.2**	**40.5**

Table 3. Different choices of global correspondence in pre-training.

Contrast	SUN RGB-D		ScanNet	
	AP25	AP50	AP25	AP50
w/o	58.4	33.3	60.0	37.6
PPCo	59.3	35.1	62.7	39.3
PVCo	59.0	**35.3**	62.5	39.6
IPCo	**59.4**	34.5	63.3	40.2
DPCo	**59.4**	34.9	**63.8**	**41.0**

Summary. Our observations concerning the invariances can be summarized as follows:

1. Explicit perspective-invariance in 3D self-supervised learning is unnecessary.
2. Format-invariance between 3D formats (*e.g.*, point clouds and voxels) improves the performance but the gains are marginal.
3. Format-invariance between depth map and a 3D formats (*e.g.*, depth maps and point clouds) significantly improves the performance, which is slightly better than modality-invariance between point clouds and RGB-images but has fewer requirements on the training data.

4.2   Comparison with SOTA Methods

In the previous subsection, our proposed method DPCo shows the best performance among all variants. In this subsection, we compare it with other SOTA self-supervised pre-training methods. Still, we use the fine-tuning performance

Table 4. Fine-tuning results of VoteNet on SUN RGB-D and ScanNet (scan-level) object detection benchmark with different pre-training methods. The absent values are not reported in original publications. We report the results of PointContrast and pixel-to-point with our own implementations, as the original papers use a voxel-based backbone instead of a PointNet++. Grayed methods refer to results with extra data or annotations. Specifically, DepthContrast† [62] uses a scaled PointNet++ backbone with 3× more parameters and is pre-trained on both ScanNet and Redwood indoor RGB-D scan dataset [38].

Pre-training	SUN RGB-D		ScanNet	
	AP25	AP50	AP25	AP50
From scatch	58.4	33.3	60.0	37.6
PointContrast [56]	-	34.8	-	38.0
PointContrast (Ours)	59.5	34.0	61.6	38.2
Hou *et al.* [22]	-	-	-	39.2
Pixel-to-point [29]	57.2	33.9	59.7	38.9
Pixel-to-point (Ours)	60.1	**35.6**	62.5	39.4
DepthContrast [62]	**60.4**	-	61.3	-
DPCo (Ours)	59.8	**35.6**	**64.2**	**41.5**
DepthContrast† [62]	61.6	35.5	64.0	42.9
Supervised	62.0	36.3	61.9	38.6

in point cloud object detection task as the metric. To obtain a strong supervised baseline, we follow the setup in [26] and generate bounding box annotations for single frames in ScanNet. Then, we pre-train a VoteNet with full supervision. For a fair comparison, the supervised baseline and other self-supervised methods use exactly the same number of frames for pre-training.

In Table 4, we compare our methods with PointContrast [56], DepthContrast [62], pixel-to-point [29] and the method of Hou *et al.* [22], which are already discussed in Sect. 2 and Sect. 3.1. As Table 4 shows, our method outperforms other self-supervised pipelines in three metrics out of four. It even outperforms the fully supervised baseline on ScanNet AP25 and AP50. Also, our method has on-par performance on SUN RGB-D AP50 und ScanNet AP25 with the up-scaled version of DepthContrast [62], which uses a 3-times larger network and is pre-trained with 5-times more data. This result implies that the contribution of format-invariance between point clouds and depth maps is comparable with scaling up the model capacity and the data amount. Also note that besides depth maps (or the equivalence *e.g.*, range images) and camera intrinsic, which are available in almost all 3D datasets, our method doesn't require any extra data, *e.g.*, color images and camera extrinsic, while a lot of SOTA methods do [22,29,56].

4.3   Data Efficiency

One important goal of pre-training is to transfer the features to very small datasets. To simulate this scenario, we randomly sample a small partition from the downstream datasets (*e.g.*, 5%, 10%) and fine-tune a VoteNet with the backbone pre-trained by DPCo. Experiments with the same percentage share the same data samples. The validation set is not sampled. As shown in Fig. 4 and Fig. 5, the pre-training brings more improvement, when less fine-tuning data are available. The trend is more obvious on ScanNet, as it contains fewer training samples than SUN RGB-D (1.2K *vs.* 5K in total). Especially, the DPCo pre-training boosts the AP25 on ScanNet from 13.3% to 36.5% and the AP50 from 2.4% to 14.4%, when only 5% of training data are used.

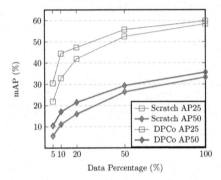

Fig. 4. Detection results on SUN RGB-D with reduced amount of data.

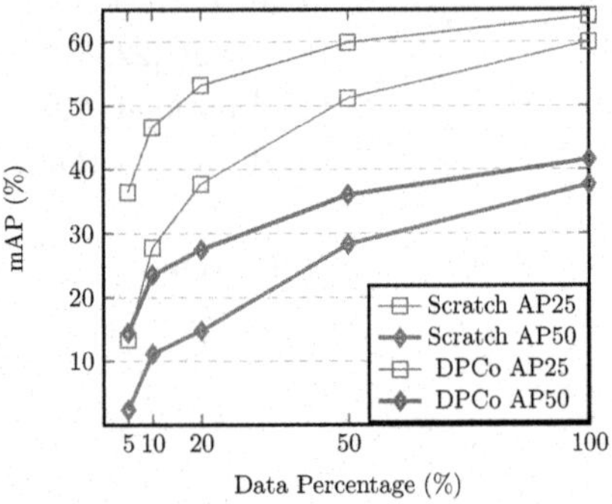

Fig. 5. Detection results on ScanNet with reduced amount of data.

4.4   Transfer on Depth Map and Voxel Encoders

Till now, we only showed the transfer learning results of point cloud encoders (PointNet++). In this subsection, we investigate the generalization of our methods (DPCo and DVCo) on the depth map and voxel encoders.

Depth Map Encoders. We fine-tune a 2.5D-VoteNet [26], which is a variant of VoteNet with a depth map-based backbone, by initializing its backbone with the pre-trained weights. In order to clarify the contribution of format-invariance, we also pre-train the depth map encoder with solely depth map input. This strategy is similar to PPCo in Fig. 3 and we name it DDCo (Depth-Depth Contrast). Since 2.5D-VoteNet doesn't support multi-view input, we only fine-tune it on SUN RGB-D dataset. One surprising result in Table 5 is that the pre-training using DDCo degrades the performance. As a depth map is an indirect representation of 3D coordinates, we hypothesize that DDCo makes the depth map encoder focus on the 2D textures instead of the true 3D geometry, which can be interpreted as cheating in the pre-training. It also implies that the pre-training of depth map encoders is non-trivial and requires a careful design. However, our proposed methods DPCo and DVCo consistently improve the detection results. Since the point cloud and voxel encoders are able to capture 3D geometrical information by their nature, they can provide guidance to the depth map encoder and prevent the depth map encoder from paying too much attention to 2D patterns. Also, combined with the results in Table 4, it's worth noticing that DPCo improves the 3D and 2D encoders at the same time. It proves that the principle of our methods is different from knowledge distillation (KD), which uses a stronger model as a teacher to improve a weaker student model.

Table 5. Fine-tuning results of 2.5D-VoteNet on SUN RGB-D dataset with different contrasting strategies.

Pre-training	AP25	AP50
From scratch	60.8	36.9
DDCo	56.0	31.2
DVCo	61.0	**39.3**
DPCo	**61.4**	38.8

Table 6. Fine-tuning results of Sparse 3D ResNet in semantic segmentation tasks. The evaluation metric is mean IoU over classes (mIoU).

Pre-training	S3DIS	ScanNet
From scratch	66.1	69.6
PVCo	66.6	70.3
DVCo	**67.2**	**70.5**

Voxel Transfer. To evaluate our methods on voxel-based networks, we use DVCo to pre-train a voxel encoder and fine-tune it for semantic segmentation on ScanNet [11] and S3DIS [2] dataset. We compare the performance with the not pre-trained baseline and PVCo. As shown in Table 6, DVCo brings significant improvement to the baseline on both segmentation tasks. The performance is also higher than PVCo, which is consistent with the transfer learning results of point cloud encoders.

5 Conclusion and Future Works

In this work, we establish a unified framework to fairly compare the contribution of perspective-, format- and modality-invariance in 3D self-supervised learning. With the help of our framework, we find out that contrasting a 3D data format (*e.g.* point clouds and voxels) with a 2D data format (*e.g.* images and depth maps) is especially beneficial. Moreover, we propose to contrast point clouds or voxels with depth maps instead of RGB images, which brings better performance and has fewer requirements on the training data than previous methods. Experimental results show that our methods improve all types of encoders in 3D vision, including point cloud, voxel, and depth map encoders.

Furthermore, some concerns deserve more research effort. For instance, in our framework, we jointly pre-train two different encoders. Although they both gain performance boost in downstream tasks, it's still unclear, whether each encoder has reached the optimum in the pre-training. In future work, we intend to investigate the optimization and convergence of the joint pre-training.

Acknowledgement. Parts of this work were financed by Baden-Württemberg Stiftung gGmbH within the project KOMO3D.

References

1. Achlioptas, P., Diamanti, O., Mitliagkas, I., Guibas, L.: Learning representations and generative models for 3D point clouds. In: International Conference on Machine Learning (ICML) (2018)
2. Armeni, I., Sax, S., Zamir, A.R., Savarese, S.: Joint 2D–3D-semantic data for indoor scene understanding. CoRR arXiv:1702.01105 (2017)
3. Bachman, P., Hjelm, R.D., Buchwalter, W.: Learning representations by maximizing mutual information across views. In: Neural Information Processing Systems (2019)
4. Bewley, A., Sun, P., Mensink, T., Anguelov, D., Sminchisescu, C.: Range conditioned dilated convolutions for scale invariant 3D object detection. CoRR arXiv:2005.09927 (2020)
5. Chaitanya, K., Erdil, E., Karani, N., Konukoglu, E.: Contrastive learning of global and local features for medical image segmentation with limited annotations. In: Neural Information Processing Systems (2020)
6. Chen, J., Lei, B., Song, Q., Ying, H., Chen, D.Z., Wu, J.: A hierarchical graph network for 3D object detection on point clouds. In: Proceedings of the IEEE/CVF Conference on Computer Vision and Pattern Recognition (CVPR), June 2020
7. Chen, T., Kornblith, S., Swersky, K., Norouzi, M., Hinton, G.E.: Big self-supervised models are strong semi-supervised learners. CoRR arXiv:2006.10029 (2020)
8. Chen, X., Fan, H., Girshick, R.B., He, K.: Improved baselines with momentum contrastive learning. CoRR arXiv:2003.04297 (2020)
9. Chen, X., He, K.: Exploring simple siamese representation learning. In: Proceedings of the IEEE/CVF Conference on Computer Vision and Pattern Recognition (CVPR), pp. 15750–15758, June 2021
10. Choy, C., Gwak, J., Savarese, S.: 4D spatio-temporal convnets: minkowski convolutional neural networks. In: The IEEE Conference on Computer Vision and Pattern Recognition (CVPR), pp. 3075–3084, June 2019
11. Dai, A., Chang, A.X., Savva, M., Halber, M., Funkhouser, T., Nießner, M.: ScanNet: richly-annotated 3D reconstructions of indoor scenes. In: Proceedings of Computer Vision and Pattern Recognition (CVPR). IEEE (2017)
12. Dai, A., Nießner, M.: 3DMV: joint 3D-multi-view prediction for 3D semantic scene segmentation. In: Ferrari, V., Hebert, M., Sminchisescu, C., Weiss, Y. (eds.) ECCV 2018. LNCS, vol. 11214, pp. 458–474. Springer, Cham (2018). https://doi.org/10.1007/978-3-030-01249-6_28
13. Deng, J., Dong, W., Socher, R., Li, L., Li, K., Fei-Fei, L.: ImageNet: a large-scale hierarchical image database. In: 2009 IEEE Conference on Computer Vision and Pattern Recognition, pp. 248–255 (2009)
14. Fan, D.-P., Zhai, Y., Borji, A., Yang, J., Shao, L.: BBS-Net: RGB-D salient object detection with a bifurcated backbone strategy network. In: Vedaldi, A., Bischof, H., Brox, T., Frahm, J.-M. (eds.) ECCV 2020. LNCS, vol. 12357, pp. 275–292. Springer, Cham (2020). https://doi.org/10.1007/978-3-030-58610-2_17
15. Gidaris, S., Singh, P., Komodakis, N.: Unsupervised representation learning by predicting image rotations. CoRR (2018). arXiv:1803.07728

16. Graham, B., Engelcke, M., van der Maaten, L.: 3D semantic segmentation with submanifold sparse convolutional networks. In: Proceedings of the IEEE Conference on Computer Vision and Pattern Recognition (CVPR), June 2018
17. Grill, J.B., et al.: Bootstrap your own latent - a new approach to self-supervised learning. In: Advances in Neural Information Processing Systems, vol. 33, pp. 21271–21284 (2020)
18. Hassani, K., Haley, M.: Unsupervised multi-task feature learning on point clouds. In: ICCV (2019)
19. He, K., Fan, H., Wu, Y., Xie, S., Girshick, R.: Momentum contrast for unsupervised visual representation learning. In: Proceedings of the IEEE/CVF Conference on Computer Vision and Pattern Recognition (CVPR), June 2020
20. He, K., Zhang, X., Ren, S., Sun, J.: Deep residual learning for image recognition. In: The IEEE Conference on Computer Vision and Pattern Recognition (CVPR), pp. 770–778, June 2016
21. Hou, J., Dai, A., Niessner, M.: 3D-SIS: 3D semantic instance segmentation of RGB-D scans. In: The IEEE Conference on Computer Vision and Pattern Recognition (CVPR), pp. 4421–4430, June 2019
22. Hou, J., Graham, B., Nießner, M., Xie, S.: Exploring data-efficient 3D scene understanding with contrastive scene contexts. In: Proceedings of the IEEE/CVF Conference on Computer Vision and Pattern Recognition, pp. 15587–15597 (2021)
23. Lang, A.H., Vora, S., Caesar, H., Zhou, L., Yang, J., Beijbom, O.: PointPillars: fast encoders for object detection from point clouds. In: Proceedings of the IEEE/CVF Conference on Computer Vision and Pattern Recognition (CVPR), June 2019
24. Li, B., Zhang, T., Xia, T.: Vehicle detection from 3D lidar using fully convolutional network. CoRR (2016). arXiv:1608.07916
25. Li, G., Liu, Z., Ye, L., Wang, Y., Ling, H.: Cross-modal weighting network for RGB-D salient object detection. In: Vedaldi, A., Bischof, H., Brox, T., Frahm, J.-M. (eds.) ECCV 2020. LNCS, vol. 12362, pp. 665–681. Springer, Cham (2020). https://doi.org/10.1007/978-3-030-58520-4_39
26. Li, L., Heizmann, M.: 2.5D-VoteNet: depth map based 3D object detection for real-time applications. In: British Machine Vision Conference (BMVC) (2021)
27. Li, Y., Bu, R., Sun, M., Wu, W., Di, X., Chen, B.: PointCNN: convolution on X-transformed points. In: Bengio, S., Wallach, H., Larochelle, H., Grauman, K., Cesa-Bianchi, N., Garnett, R. (eds.) Advances in Neural Information Processing Systems, vol. 31, pp. 820–830. Curran Associates, Inc. (2018)
28. Liang, Z., Zhang, M., Zhang, Z., Zhao, X., Pu, S.: RangeRCNN: towards fast and accurate 3D object detection with range image representation. CoRR (2020). arXiv:2009.00206
29. Liu, Y., et al.: Learning from 2D: pixel-to-point knowledge transfer for 3D pre-training. CoRR arXiv:2104.04687 (2021)
30. Liu, Y., Fan, Q., Zhang, S., Dong, H., Funkhouser, T.A., Yi, L.: Contrastive multimodal fusion with tupleinfonce. CoRR arXiv:2107.02575 (2021)
31. Liu, Y., Yi, L., Zhang, S., Fan, Q., Funkhouser, T.A., Dong, H.: P4contrast: contrastive learning with pairs of point-pixel pairs for RGB-D scene understanding. CoRR arXiv:2012.13089 (2020)
32. Liu, Z., Qi, X., Fu, C.W.: 3D-to-2D distillation for indoor scene parsing. In: Proceedings of the IEEE/CVF Conference on Computer Vision and Pattern Recognition (CVPR), pp. 4464–4474, June 2021
33. Liu, Z., Tang, H., Lin, Y., Han, S.: Point-voxel CNN for efficient 3D deep learning. In: Wallach, H., Larochelle, H., Beygelzimer, A., d'Alché-Buc, F., Fox, E., Garnett,

R. (eds.) Advances in Neural Information Processing Systems, vol. 32, pp. 965–975. Curran Associates, Inc. (2019)

34. Maturana, D., Scherer, S.: VoxNet: a 3D convolutional neural network for real-time object recognition. In: 2015 IEEE/RSJ International Conference on Intelligent Robots and Systems (IROS), pp. 922–928 (2015)

35. Misra, I., Maaten, L.V.D.: Self-supervised learning of pretext-invariant representations. In: Proceedings of the IEEE/CVF Conference on Computer Vision and Pattern Recognition (CVPR), June 2020

36. Noroozi, M., Favaro, P.: Unsupervised learning of visual representations by solving jigsaw puzzles. In: Leibe, B., Matas, J., Sebe, N., Welling, M. (eds.) ECCV 2016. LNCS, vol. 9910, pp. 69–84. Springer, Cham (2016). https://doi.org/10.1007/978-3-319-46466-4_5

37. van den Oord, A., Li, Y., Vinyals, O.: Representation learning with contrastive predictive coding. CoRR arXiv:1807.03748 (2018)

38. Park, J., Zhou, Q.Y., Koltun, V.: Colored point cloud registration revisited. In: ICCV (2017)

39. Pinheiro, P.O., Almahairi, A., Benmalek, R.Y., Golemo, F., Courville, A.C.: Unsupervised learning of dense visual representations. In: Neural Information Processing Systems (2020)

40. Qi, C.R., Chen, X., Litany, O., Guibas, L.J.: ImVoteNet: boosting 3D object detection in point clouds with image votes. In: The IEEE/CVF Conference on Computer Vision and Pattern Recognition (CVPR), pp. 4404–4413, June 2020

41. Qi, C.R., Litany, O., He, K., Guibas, L.J.: Deep Hough voting for 3D object detection in point clouds. In: The IEEE International Conference on Computer Vision (ICCV), pp. 9277–9286, October 2019

42. Qi, C.R., Liu, W., Wu, C., Su, H., Guibas, L.J.: Frustum PointNets for 3D object detection from RGB-D data. In: The IEEE Conference on Computer Vision and Pattern Recognition (CVPR), pp. 918–927, June 2018

43. Qi, C.R., Su, H., Mo, K., Guibas, L.J.: PointNet: deep learning on point sets for 3D classification and segmentation. In: The IEEE Conference on Computer Vision and Pattern Recognition (CVPR), pp. 652–660, July 2017

44. Qi, C.R., Yi, L., Su, H., Guibas, L.J.: PointNet++: deep hierarchical feature learning on point sets in a metric space. In: Guyon, I., et al. (eds.) Advances in Neural Information Processing Systems, vol. 30, pp. 5099–5108. Curran Associates, Inc. (2017)

45. Sanghi, A.: Info3D: representation learning on 3D objects using mutual information maximization and contrastive learning. In: Vedaldi, A., Bischof, H., Brox, T., Frahm, J.-M. (eds.) ECCV 2020. LNCS, vol. 12374, pp. 626–642. Springer, Cham (2020). https://doi.org/10.1007/978-3-030-58526-6_37

46. Sauder, J., Sievers, B.: Self-supervised deep learning on point clouds by reconstructing space. In: NeurIPS (2019)

47. Shi, S., et al.: PV-RCNN: point-voxel feature set abstraction for 3D object detection. In: Proceedings of the IEEE/CVF Conference on Computer Vision and Pattern Recognition (CVPR), June 2020

48. Song, S., Lichtenberg, S.P., Xiao, J.: SUN RGB-D: a RGB-D scene understanding benchmark suite. In: The IEEE Conference on Computer Vision and Pattern Recognition (CVPR), pp. 567–576, June 2015

49. Song, S., Xiao, J.: Deep sliding shapes for amodal 3D object detection in RGB-D images. In: The IEEE Conference on Computer Vision and Pattern Recognition (CVPR), pp. 808–816, June 2016

50. Vincent, P., Larochelle, H., Bengio, Y., Manzagol, P.A.: Extracting and composing robust features with denoising autoencoders. In: Proceedings of the 25th International Conference on Machine Learning, ICML 2008, pp. 1096–1103. Association for Computing Machinery, New York, July 2008. https://doi.org/10.1145/1390156.1390294

51. Wang, S., Suo, S., Ma, W.C., Pokrovsky, A., Urtasun, R.: Deep parametric continuous convolutional neural networks. In: Proceedings of the IEEE Conference on Computer Vision and Pattern Recognition (CVPR), June 2018

52. Wang, X., Gupta, A.: Unsupervised learning of visual representations using videos. In: Proceedings of the IEEE International Conference on Computer Vision (ICCV), December 2015

53. Wang, X., Zhang, R., Shen, C., Kong, T., Li, L.: Dense contrastive learning for self-supervised visual pre-training. In: Proceedings of the IEEE/CVF Conference on Computer Vision and Pattern Recognition (CVPR), pp. 3024–3033, June 2021

54. Wu, W., Qi, Z., Fuxin, L.: PointConv: deep convolutional networks on 3D point clouds. In: Proceedings of the IEEE/CVF Conference on Computer Vision and Pattern Recognition (CVPR), June 2019

55. Wu, Z., et al.: 3D shapenets: a deep representation for volumetric shapes. In: Proceedings of the IEEE Conference on Computer Vision and Pattern Recognition (CVPR), June 2015

56. Xie, S., Gu, J., Guo, D., Qi, C.R., Guibas, L., Litany, O.: PointContrast: unsupervised pre-training for 3D point cloud understanding. In: Vedaldi, A., Bischof, H., Brox, T., Frahm, J.-M. (eds.) ECCV 2020. LNCS, vol. 12348, pp. 574–591. Springer, Cham (2020). https://doi.org/10.1007/978-3-030-58580-8_34

57. Xing, Y., Wang, J., Chen, X., Zeng, G.: 2.5D convolution for RGB-D semantic segmentation. In: 2019 IEEE International Conference on Image Processing (ICIP), pp. 1410–1414 (2019). https://doi.org/10.1109/ICIP.2019.8803757

58. Xing, Y., Wang, J., Zeng, G.: Malleable 2.5D convolution: learning receptive fields along the depth-axis for RGB-D scene parsing. In: Vedaldi, A., Bischof, H., Brox, T., Frahm, J.-M. (eds.) ECCV 2020. LNCS, vol. 12364, pp. 555–571. Springer, Cham (2020). https://doi.org/10.1007/978-3-030-58529-7_33

59. Xu, D., Anguelov, D., Jain, A.: PointFusion: deep sensor fusion for 3D bounding box estimation. In: The IEEE Conference on Computer Vision and Pattern Recognition (CVPR), pp. 244–253, June 2018

60. Zhang, R., Isola, P., Efros, A.A.: Colorful image colorization. In: Leibe, B., Matas, J., Sebe, N., Welling, M. (eds.) ECCV 2016. LNCS, vol. 9907, pp. 649–666. Springer, Cham (2016). https://doi.org/10.1007/978-3-319-46487-9_40

61. Zhang, R., Isola, P., Efros, A.A.: Split-brain autoencoders: unsupervised learning by cross-channel prediction. In: Proceedings of the IEEE Conference on Computer Vision and Pattern Recognition (CVPR), July 2017

62. Zhang, Z., Girdhar, R., Joulin, A., Misra, I.: Self-supervised pretraining of 3D features on any point-cloud. CoRR arXiv:2101.02691 (2021)

63. Zhao, J.X., Cao, Y., Fan, D.P., Cheng, M.M., Li, X.Y., Zhang, L.: Contrast prior and fluid pyramid integration for RGBD salient object detection. In: Proceedings of the IEEE/CVF Conference on Computer Vision and Pattern Recognition (CVPR), June 2019

64. Zhou, Y., Tuzel, O.: VoxelNet: end-to-end learning for point cloud based 3D object detection. In: The IEEE Conference on Computer Vision and Pattern Recognition (CVPR), pp. 4490–4499, June 2018

ConMatch: Semi-supervised Learning with Confidence-Guided Consistency Regularization

Jiwon Kim[1,2(✉)], Youngjo Min[1], Daehwan Kim[3], Gyuseong Lee[1],
Junyoung Seo[1], Kwangrok Ryoo[1], and Seungryong Kim[1]

[1] Korea University, Seoul, Korea
{naancoco,1320harry,jpl358,se780,kwangrok21,seungryong_kim}@korea.ac.kr
[2] NAVER AI Lab, Seongam, Korea
[3] Samsung Electro-Mechanics, Suwon, Korea
daehwan85.kim@samsung.com

Abstract. We present a novel semi-supervised learning framework that intelligently leverages the consistency regularization between the model's predictions from two strongly-augmented views of an image, weighted by a confidence of pseudo-label, dubbed ConMatch. While the latest semi-supervised learning methods use weakly- and strongly-augmented views of an image to define a directional consistency loss, how to define such direction for the consistency regularization between two strongly-augmented views remains unexplored. To account for this, we present novel confidence measures for pseudo-labels from strongly-augmented views by means of weakly-augmented view as an anchor in non-parametric and parametric approaches. Especially, in parametric approach, we present, for the first time, to learn the confidence of pseudo-label within the networks, which is learned with backbone model in an end-to-end manner. In addition, we also present a stage-wise training to boost the convergence of training. When incorporated in existing semi-supervised learners, ConMatch consistently boosts the performance. We conduct experiments to demonstrate the effectiveness of our ConMatch over the latest methods and provide extensive ablation studies. Code has been made publicly available at https://github.com/JiwonCocoder/ConMatch.

1 Introduction

Semi-supervised learning has emerged as an attractive solution to mitigate the reliance on large labeled data, which is often laborious to obtain, and intelligently

---

J. Kim—Work done in Korea University.
J. Kim, Y. Min and D. Kim—Equal contribution.

Supplementary Information The online version contains supplementary material available at https://doi.org/10.1007/978-3-031-20056-4_39.

leverage a large amount of unlabeled data, to the point of being deployed in many computer vision applications, especially image classification [38,50,52]. Generally, this task have adopted pseudo-labeling [1,19,29,38,44,49,58] or consistency regularization [17,23,28,34,46,50]. Some methods [4,5,40,45,49,51,55] proposed to integrate both approaches in a unified framework, which is often called holistic approach. As one of pioneering works, FixMatch [45] first generates a pseudo-label from the model's prediction on the weakly-augmented instance and then encourages the prediction from the strongly-augmented instance to follow the pseudo-label. Their success inspired many variants that use, e.g., curriculum learning [51,55].

On the other hand, concurrent to the race for better semi-supervised learning methods [45,51,55], substantial progress has been made in self-supervised representation learning, especially with contrastive learning [3,6,8,10,20,22], aiming at learning a task-agnostic feature representation without any supervision, which can be well transferred to the downstream tasks. Formally, they encourage the features extracted from two differently-augmented images to be pulled against each other, which injects some invariance or robustness into the models. Not surprisingly, semi-supervised learning frameworks can definitely benefit from self-supervised representation learning [24,32,33] in that good representation from the feature encoder yields better performance with semi-supervised learning, and thus, some methods [24,32] attempt to combine the aforementioned two paradigms to boost the performance by achieving the better feature encoder.

Extending techniques presented in existing self-supervised representation learning [3,6,8,10,20,22], which only focus on learning feature encoder, to further consider the model's prediction itself would be an appealing solution to effectively combine the two paradigms, which allows for boosting not only feature encoder but also classifier. However, compared to feature representation learning [3,6,8,10,20,22], the consistency between the model's predictions from two different augmentations should be defined by considering which direction is better to achieve not only invariance but also high accuracy in image classification. Without this, simply pulling the model's predictions as done in [3,6,8,10,20,22] may hinder the classifier output, thereby decreasing the accuracy.

In this paper, we present a novel framework for semi-supervised learning, dubbed ConMatch, that intelligently leverages the confidence-guided consistency regularization between the model's predictions from two strongly-augmented images. Built upon conventional frameworks [45,55], we consider two strongly-augmented images and one weakly-augmented image, and define the consistency between the model's predictions from two strongly-augmented images, while still using an unsupervised loss between the model's predictions from one of the strongly-augmented images and the weakly-augmented image, as done in [45,55]. Since defining the direction of consistency regularization between two strongly-augmented images is of prime importance, rather than selecting in a deterministic manner, we present a probabilistic technique by measuring the confidence of pseudo-labels from each strongly-augmented image, and weighting the consis-

Table 1. Comparison of our ConMatch to other relevant works which have a form of consistency regularization combining pseudo-labeling [5,24,32,33,45,51,55].

	MixMatch [5]	FixMatch [45]	FlexMatch [55]	Dash [51]	SelfMatch [24]	CoMatch [33]	LESS [32]	ConMatch (Ours)
Using pseudo-labeling	✗	✓	✓	✓	✓	✓	✓	✓
Using two strong branches	✗	✗	✗	✗	✓	✓	✗	✓
Learning confidence measure	✗	✗	✗	✗	✗	✗	✗	✓
Using stage-wise training	✗	✗	✗	✗	✓	✗	✗	✓

tency loss with this confidence. To measure the confidence of pseudo-labels, we present two techniques, including non-parametric and parametric approaches. With this confidence-guided consistency regularization, our framework dramatically boosts the performance of existing semi-supervised learners [45,55]. In addition, we also present a stage-wise training scheme to boost the convergence of training. Our framework is a plug-and-play module, and thus various semi-supervised learners [4,24,32,33,45,49,51,55] can benefit from our framework. We briefly summarize our method with other highly relevant works in semi-supervised learning in Table 1. Experimental results and ablation studies show that the proposed framework not only boosts the convergence but also achieves the state-of-the-art performance on most standard benchmarks [12,27,35].

2   Related Works

Semi-supervised Learning. Semi-supervised learning has been an effective paradigm for leveraging an abundance of unlabeled data along with limited labeled data. For this task, various methods such as pseudo-labeling [19,29] and consistency regularization [28,42,46] have been proposed. In pseudo-labeling [29], a model uses unlabeled samples with high confidence as training targets, which reduces the density of data points at the decision boundary [19,41]. Consistency regularization has been first introduced by π-model [42], which is further improved by numerous following works [17,23,28,34,46,50]. In the consistency regularization, the model should minimize the distance between the model's predictions when fed perturbed versions of the input [23,28,34, 37,46,49,50] or the model [23,28,37,46,50,56]. Very recently, advanced consistency regularization methods [4,45,49] have been introduced by combining with pseudo-labeling. These methods show high accuracy, comparable to supervised learning in a fully-labeled setting, e.g., ICT [48], MixMatch [5], UDA [49], ReMixMatch [4], and FixMatch [45]. The aforementioned methods can be highly boosted by simultaneously considering the techniques proposed in recent self-supervised representation learning methods [3,6,8,20,22].

Self-supervised Representation Learning. Self-supervised representation learning has recently attracted much attention [3,6,8,16,18,20,22,36,57] due to its competitive performance. Specifically, contrastive learning [3,6,8,20,22] becomes a dominant framework. It formally maximizes the agreement between

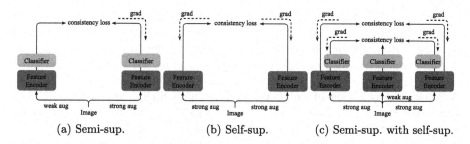

(a) Semi-sup.   (b) Self-sup.   (c) Semi-sup. with self-sup.

Fig. 1. Conceptual illustration of existing methods that leverage unlabeled data: (a) semi-supervised learning- the model uses the model's prediction itself to produce a pseudo-label for unlabeled data [4,5,17,28,29,34,42,45,46,48,49], (b) self-supervised representation learning- the model is learned to generate the same feature embedding for two augmented views from unlabeled data [3,6,8,10,20,20,22], and (c) semi-supervised learning with self-supervision representation learning- the model simultaneously learns a feature representation with self-supervised representation loss, while learning all the networks with semi-supervised learning [24,32,33].

different augmented views of the same image [16,18,36,57]. Most previous methods benefit from a large amount of negative pairs to preclude constant outputs and avoid a collapse problem [8]. An alternative to approximate the loss is to use cluster-based approach by discriminating between groups of images with similar features [6]. Some methods [10,20] mitigated to use negative samples by using a momentum encoder [20] and a stop-gradient technique [10]. The aforementioned methods applied the consistency loss at the feature-level, unlike recent semi-supervised learning methods [45,55] that consider the consistency loss in the logit-level, which may not be optimal to be incorporated with semi-supervised learners. Formulating the consistency loss in the logit-level as self-supervision is challenging because a direction between two augmented views should be determined. Without this, simply pulling the model's predictions as done in [3,6,8,10,20,22] may hinder the classifier output, thereby decreasing the accuracy (Fig. 1).

Self-supervision in Semi-supervised Learning. Many recent state-of-the-art semi-supervised learning methods adopt the self-supervised representation learning methods [9,54] to jointly learn good feature representation. Self-supervised pre-training, followed by supervised fine-tuning, has shown strong performance on semi-supervised learning settings. Specifically, SelfMatch [24] adopted SimCLR [8] for self-supervised pre-training and FixMatch [45] for semi-supervised fine-tuning. However, it may learn sub-optimal representation for the image classification task due to the task-agnostic learning. On the other hand, some methods [30,32] unify pseudo-labeling and self-supervised learning. [31] alternates between self- and semi-supervised learning. There lacks a study to effectively use self-supervision, rather than simply adopting this.

Confidence Estimation in Semi-supervised Learning. In semi-supervised learning, a confidence-based strategy has been widely used along with pseudo labeling so that the unlabeled data are used only when the predictions are sufficiently confident. Such confidence in pseudo-labeling has been often measured by the peak values of the predicted probability distribution [40,45,49,51,55]. Although the selection of unlabeled samples with high confidence predictions moves decision boundaries to low density regions [7], many of these selected predictions are incorrect due to the poor calibration of neural networks [21], which has the discrepancy between the confidence level of a network's individual predictions and its overall accuracy and leads to noisy training and poor generalization [14,15]. However, there was no study how to learn the confidence of pseudo-labels, which is the topic of this paper.

3   Methodology

3.1   Preliminaries

Let us define a batch of *labeled* instances as $\mathcal{X} = \{(x_b, y_b)\}_{b=1}^{B}$, where x_b is an instance and y_b is a label representing one of Y labels. In addition, let us define a batch of *unlabeled* instances as $\mathcal{U} = \{u_b\}_{b=1}^{\mu B}$, where μ is a hyper-parameter that determines the size of $\mathcal{U}$ relative to $\mathcal{X}$. The objective of semi-supervised learning is to use both $\mathcal{X}$ and $\mathcal{U}$ to train a model with parameters θ taking an instance $r \in \mathcal{X} \cup \mathcal{U}$ as input and outputting a distribution over class labels y such that $p_{\text{model}}(y|r; \theta)$. The model generally consists of an feature encoder $f(\cdot)$ and a classifier $g(\cdot)$, and thus, $p_{\text{model}}(y|r; \theta) = g(f(r))$.

For semi-supervised learning, most state-of-the-art methods are based on consistency regularization approaches [2,28,42] that rely on the assumption that the model should generate similar predictions when perturbed versions of the same instance are fed, e.g., using data augmentation [34], or model perturbation [28,46]. These methods formally extract a pseudo-label from one branch, filtered by confidence, and use this as a target for another branch. For instance, FixMatch [45] utilizes two types of augmentations such as *weak* and *strong*, denoted by $\alpha(\cdot)$ and $\mathcal{A}(\cdot)$, and a pseudo-label from weakly-augmented version of an image is used as a target for strongly-augmented version of the same image. This loss function is formally defined such that

$$\mathcal{L}_{\text{un}} = c(r)\mathcal{H}\left(q(r), p_{\text{model}}\left(y|\mathcal{A}(r); \theta\right)\right), \tag{1}$$

where $c(r)$ denotes a confidence of $q(r)$, and $q(r)$ denotes a pseudo-label generated from $p_{\text{model}}(y|\alpha(r); \theta)$, which can be either an one-hot label [40,45,51,55] or a sharpened one [4,5,49], and $\mathcal{H}(\cdot, \cdot)$ is often defined as a cross-entropy loss. In this framework, measuring confidence $c(r)$ is of prime importance, but conventional methods simply measure this, e.g., by the peak value of the softmax predictions [40,45,49,51,55].

On the other hands, semi-supervised learning framework can definitely benefit from existing self-supervised representation learning [24,32,33] in that good

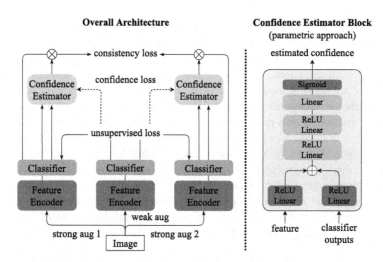

Fig. 2. Network configuration of ConMatch. A semi-supervised learning framework built upon consistency loss with an additional strong branch to leverage confidence loss between two strong branches. In the parametric approach, the confidence estimator block takes a concatenated heterogeneous feature as an input and produces the estimated confidence of pseudo label.

representation from the feature encoder $f(\cdot)$ yields better performance with semi-supervised learner. In this light, some methods attempted to combine semi-supervised learning and self-supervised representation learning to achieve the better feature encoder [24,32]. Concurrent to the race for better semi-supervised learning methods, substantial progress has been made in self-supervised representation learning, especially with contrastive learning [3,6,8,10,20,22]. The loss function for this task can also be defined as a consistency regularization loss, similar to [40,45,49,51,55] but in the feature-level, such that

$$\mathcal{L}_{\text{self}} = \mathcal{D}(F_i(r), F_j(r)), \qquad (2)$$

where $F_i(r) = f(\mathcal{A}_i(r))$ and $F_j(r) = f(\mathcal{A}_j(r))$ extracted from images with two different strongly-augmented images $\mathcal{A}_i(\cdot)$ and $\mathcal{A}_j(\cdot)$, respectively. $\mathcal{D}(\cdot, \cdot)$ can be defined as contrastive loss [22] or negative cosine similarity [10]. Even though this loss helps to boost learning the feature encoder $f(\cdot)$, the mechanism that simply pulls the features $F_i(r)$ and $F_j(r)$ may not be optimal to boost a semi-supervised learner and break the latent feature space, without considering a direction representing which branch is better.

3.2 Formulation

To combine the semi- and self-supervised learning paradigm in a boosting fashion, unlike [24,32,33], we present to effectively exploit a self-supervision between two *strong* branches tailored for boosting semi-supervised learning, called ConMatch. Unlike existing self-supervised representation learning methods, e.g.,

SimSiam [10], we formulate the consistency regularization loss at class logit-level[1], as done in semi-supervised learning methods [45,55], and estimate the confidences of each pseudo-label from two *strongly*-augmented images, $\mathcal{A}_i(r)$ and $\mathcal{A}_j(r)$ for r, and use them to consider the probability of each direction between them. Since measuring such confidences is notoriously challenging, we present novel confidence estimators by using the output from *weak*-augmented image $\alpha(r)$ as an anchor in non-parametric and parametric approaches.

An overview of our ConMatch is illustrated in Fig. 2. Specifically, there exist two branches for *strongly*-augmented images (called strong branches) and one branch for *weakly*-augmented image (called weak branch). Similar to existing semi-supervised representation learning methods [45,51,55], we attempt to apply the consistency loss between a pair of each strong branch and weak branch. But, tailored to semi-supervised learning, we present a confidence-guided consistency regularization loss $\mathcal{L}_{\mathrm{ccr}}$ between two strong branches such that

$$\mathcal{L}_{\mathrm{ccr}} = c_i(r)\mathcal{H}(q_i(r), p_{\mathrm{model}}(y|\mathcal{A}_j(r); \theta)) + c_j(r)\mathcal{H}(q_j(r), p_{\mathrm{model}}(y|\mathcal{A}_i(r); \theta)), \quad (3)$$

where $q_i(r)$ and $q_j(r)$ denote the pseudo-labels generated from $p_{\mathrm{model}}(y|\mathcal{A}_i(r); \theta)$ and $p_{\mathrm{model}}(y|\mathcal{A}_j(r); \theta)$, respectively. $c_i(r)$ and $c_j(r)$ denote estimated confidences of $q_i(r)$ and $q_j(r)$. Our proposed loss function is different from conventional self-supervised representation learning loss $\mathcal{L}_{\mathrm{self}}$ in that the consistency is applied in the logit-level (not feature-level) similar to [45,55], and adjusted by the estimated confidence. However, unlike [40,45,49,51,55], we can learn the better feature representation by considering two strongly-augmented views, while improving semi-supervised learning performance at the same time. It should be noted that this simple loss function can be incorporated with any semi-supervised learners, e.g., FixMatch [45] or FlexMatch [55].

To measure the confidences $c_i(r)$ and $c_j(r)$, we present two kinds of confidence estimators, based on non-parametric and parametric approaches. In the following, we explain how to measure these confidences in detail.

3.3 Measuring Confidence: Non-parametric Approach

Existing semi-supervised learning methods [29,42,45] have selected unlabeled samples with high confidence as training targets (i.e., pseudo-labels) in a straightforward way; which can be viewed as a form of entropy minimization [19]. It has been well known that it is non-trivial to set an appropriate threshold for such handcrafted confidence estimation, and thus, confidence-based strategies commonly suffer from a dilemma between pseudo-label exploration and accuracy depending on the threshold [1,33].

In our framework, estimating the confidence of pseudo-labels from strong branches may suffer from similar limitations if the conventional handcrafted methods [29,42,45] are simply used. To overcome this, we present a novel way to measure the confidences, $c_i(r)$ and $c_j(r)$, based on the similarity between outputs of *strongly*-augmented images and *weakly*-augmented images. Based on the

---

[1] In the paper, class logit means the output of the network, i.e., $p_{\mathrm{model}}(y|r; \theta)$ for r.

Algorithm 1: ConMatch-P (Parametric Approach)

1: **Notation:** strong augmentation $\mathcal{A}$, weak augmentation α, model $p_{\mathrm{model}}(\cdot; \theta)$ consisting of feature encoder f and classifier g, confidence estimator $h(\cdot; \theta_{\mathrm{conf}})$, pseudo label q, leranable confidence c

2: **Input:** $\mathcal{X} = \{(x_b, y_b) : b \in (1, \ldots, B)\}$, $\mathcal{U} = \{u_b : b \in (1, \ldots, \mu B)\}$

3: **for** $b = 1$ to B **do**

4:     $F(\alpha(x_b)), L(\alpha(x_b)) = f(\alpha(x_b)), g(f(\alpha(x_b)))$

5:     $c(\alpha(x_b)) = h(F(\alpha(x_b)), L(\alpha(x_b)); \theta_{\mathrm{conf}})$

6:     **if** $y_b == \mathrm{argmax}_y p_{\mathrm{model}}(y|\alpha(x_b); \theta))$ **then**

7:         $c_{\mathrm{GT}}(\alpha(x_b)) = 1$

8:     **else**

9:         $c_{\mathrm{GT}}(\alpha(x_b)) = 0$

10:     **end if**

11: **end for**

12: $\mathcal{L}_{\mathrm{sup}} = \sum_{b=1}^{B} \mathcal{H}(y_b, p_{\mathrm{model}}(y|\alpha(x_b); \theta))$

13: $\mathcal{L}_{\mathrm{conf-sup}} = \mathcal{H}(c_{\mathrm{GT}}(\alpha(x_b)), h(F(\alpha(x_b)), L(\alpha(x_b)); \theta_{\mathrm{conf}}))$

14: **for** $b = 1$ to μB **do**

15:     $(F_i, F_j), (L_i, L_j) = f(\mathcal{A}_i(u_b), \mathcal{A}_j(u_b)), g(f(\mathcal{A}_i(u_b), \mathcal{A}_j(u_b)))$

16:     $c_i, c_j = h(F_i, L_i; \theta_{\mathrm{conf}}), h(F_j, L_j; \theta_{\mathrm{conf}})$

17:     Generate pseudo labels for differently augmented versions $\alpha, \mathcal{A}_i, \mathcal{A}_j$

18: **end for**

19: Calculate $\mathcal{L}_{\mathrm{un}}$ using c, q from $\alpha(u_b)$, and $p_{\mathrm{model}}(y|\mathcal{A}(u_b); \theta)$ via Eq. 2

20: Calculate $\mathcal{L}_{\mathrm{ccr}}$ using c, q from $\mathcal{A}(u_b)$ and $p_{\mathrm{model}}(y|\mathcal{A}(u_b); \theta)$ via Eq. 3

21: Calculate $\mathcal{L}_{\mathrm{conf}}$ using c from $\mathcal{A}(u_b)$ and $p_{\mathrm{model}}(y|\alpha(u_b); \theta)$ via Eq. 6

22: Update θ by minimizing $\mathcal{L}_{\mathrm{sup}}, \mathcal{L}_{\mathrm{un}}$ and $\mathcal{L}_{\mathrm{ccr}}$

23: Update θ_{conf} by minimizing $\mathcal{L}_{\mathrm{conf-sup}}$ and $\mathcal{L}_{\mathrm{conf}}$

24: **Return:** Model parameters $\{\theta, \theta_{\mathrm{conf}}\}$

---

hypothesis that the similarity between the logits or probabilities from strongly-augmented images and weakly-augmented images can be directly used as a confidence estimator, we present to measure confidence of each strong branch loss by the cross-entropy loss value itself between strongly-augmented and weakly-augmented images. Specifically, we measure such a confidence with the following:

$$s_i(r) = \frac{1}{\mathcal{H}(p_{\mathrm{model}}(y|\alpha(r); \theta), p_{\mathrm{model}}(y|\mathcal{A}_i(r); \theta))}, \qquad (4)$$

where the smaller $\mathcal{H}(p_{\mathrm{model}}(y|\alpha(r); \theta), p_{\mathrm{model}}(y|\mathcal{A}_i(r); \theta))$, the higher $s_i(r)$ is. $s_j(r)$ can be similarly defined with $\alpha(r)$ and $\mathcal{A}_j(r)$. Finally, $c_i(r)$ is computed such that $c_i(r) = s_i(r)/(s_i(r) + s_j(r))$, and $c_j(r)$ is similarly computed.

In this case, the total loss for the non-parametric approach is as follows:

$$\mathcal{L}_{\mathrm{total}}^{\mathrm{np}} = \lambda_{\mathrm{sup}} \mathcal{L}_{\mathrm{sup}} + \lambda_{\mathrm{un}} \mathcal{L}_{\mathrm{un}} + \lambda_{\mathrm{ccr}} \mathcal{L}_{\mathrm{ccr}}, \qquad (5)$$

where λ_{sup}, λ_{un}, and λ_{ccr} are weights for $\mathcal{L}_{\mathrm{sup}}$, $\mathcal{L}_{\mathrm{un}}$, and $\mathcal{L}_{\mathrm{ccr}}$, respectively. Note that for weakly-augmented labeled images $\alpha(x_b)$ with labels y_b, a simple classification loss $\mathcal{L}_{\mathrm{sup}}$ is applied as $\mathcal{H}(y_b, p_{\mathrm{model}}(y|\alpha(x_b); \theta))$, as done in [45].

3.4   Measuring Confidence: Parametric Approach

Even though the above confidence estimator with non-parametric approach yields comparable performance to some extent (which will be discussed in experiments), it solely depends on each image, and thus it may be sensitive to outliers or errors without any modules to learn a prior from the dataset. To overcome this, we present an additional parametric approach for confidence estimation. Motivated by stereo confidence estimation [11,39,43,47], obtaining a confidence measure from the networks by extracting the confidence features from input and predicting the confidence with a classifier, we also introduce a learnable confidence measure for pseudo-labels. Unlike existing methods that simply use the model output as confidence [40,45,49,51,55], such learned confidence can intelligently select a subset of pseudo-labels that are less noisy, which helps the network to converge significantly faster and achieve improved performance by utilizing the false negative samples excluded from training by high threshold at early training iterations.

Specifically, we define an additional network for learnable confidence estimation such that $c(r) = h(F(r), L(r); \theta_{\mathrm{conf}})$, where $h(\cdot)$ is a confidence estimator with model parameters θ_{conf}, $F(r)$ is a feature, and $L(r)$ is a logit from an instance r, as shown in Fig. 2. For the network architecture, the concatenation of feature $F(r)$ and logit $L(r)$ transformed by individual non-linear projection heads is used, based on the intuition that a direct concatenation of two their heterogeneous confidence features does not provide an optimal performance [25], followed by the final classifier for confidence estimation. The detailed network architecture is described in the supplementary material.

The confidence estimator is learned with the following loss function:

$$\mathcal{L}_{\mathrm{conf}} = c_i(r)\mathcal{H}(p_{\mathrm{model}}(y|\alpha(r); \theta_{\mathrm{freeze}}), p_{\mathrm{model}}(y|\mathcal{A}_i(r); \theta_{\mathrm{freeze}})) + \log(1/c_i(r)), \tag{6}$$

where θ_{freeze} is a freezed network parameter with a stop gradient. The intuition behind is that during the confidence network training, we just want to make the network learn the confidence itself, rather than collapsing to trivial solution to learn the feature encoder simultaneously. In addition, we also use the supervised loss for confidence estimator $\mathcal{L}_{\mathrm{conf-sup}} = \mathcal{H}(c_{\mathrm{GT}}, h(F(\alpha(x_b)), L(\alpha(x_b)); \theta_{\mathrm{conf}}))$; $c_{\mathrm{GT}} = 1$ if y_b is equal to $\mathrm{argmax}_y\, p_{\mathrm{model}}(y|\alpha(x_b); \theta)$, and $c_{\mathrm{GT}} = 0$ otherwise.

The total loss for the parametric case can be written as

$$\mathcal{L}_{\mathrm{total}}^{\mathrm{param}} = \lambda_{\mathrm{sup}}\mathcal{L}_{\mathrm{sup}} + \lambda_{\mathrm{un}}\mathcal{L}_{\mathrm{un}} + \lambda_{\mathrm{conf}}\mathcal{L}_{\mathrm{conf}} + \lambda_{\mathrm{conf-sup}}\mathcal{L}_{\mathrm{conf-sup}} + \lambda_{\mathrm{ccr}}\mathcal{L}_{\mathrm{ccr}} \tag{7}$$

where λ_{conf} and $\lambda_{\mathrm{conf-sup}}$ are the weights for $\mathcal{L}_{\mathrm{conf}}$ and $\mathcal{L}_{\mathrm{conf-sup}}$, respectively. We explain an algorithm for ConMatch of parametric approach in Algorithm 1.

3.5   Stage-Wise Training

Even though our framework can be trained in an end-to-end manner, we further propose a stage-wise training strategy to boost the convergence of training. This stage-wise training consists of three stages, 1) pre-training for the feature encoder, 2) pre-training for the confidence estimator (for parametric approach only), and 3) fine-tuning for both feature encoder and confidence estimator (for parametric approach only). Specifically, we first warm up the feature encoder by solely using the standard semi-supervised loss functions with $\mathcal{L}_{sup}$ and $\mathcal{L}_{un}$. We then train the confidence estimator based on the outputs of the pre-trained feature encoder in the parametric approach. As mentioned in [26], this kind of simple technique highly boosts the convergence to discriminate between confident and unconfident outputs from the networks. Finally, we fine-tune all the networks with the proposed confidence-guided self-supervised loss $\mathcal{L}_{ccr}$. We empirically demonstrate the effectiveness of the stage-wise training by achieving state-of-the-art results on standard benchmark datasets [12,27,35].

4 Experiments

4.1 Experimental Settings

In experiments, we extensively evaluate the performance of our ConMatch on various standard datasets [12,27,35] with various label fraction settings in comparison to state-of-the-art algorithms, such as UDA [49], FixMatch [45], Flex-Match [55], SelfMatch [24], LESS [33] and Dash [51]. Our proposed methods have two variants; ConMatch-NP (non-parametric approach), and ConMatch-P (parametric approach) integrated to FlexMatch [55], which is the state-of-the-art semi-supervised learner, even though it can be easily integrated to others [32,45,49].

Datasets.   We consider four standard benchmarks, including CIFAR-10/100 [27], SVHN [35], and STL-10 [12]. CIFAR-10 [27] contains 50,000 training images and 10,000 test images, which have resolution 32×32 with ten classes. Similar to CIFAR-10, CIFAR-100 [27] has the same number of training/test images and image size, but it differently classifies as 100 fine-grained classes. SVHN [35] consists of 73,257 training images with 26,032 test images, having also 32×32 resolution images, belonging to ten different classes of numeric digits. STL-10 [12] contains 5,000 labeled images with size of 96×96 from 10 classes and 100,000 unlabeled images with size of 96×96.

Evaluation Metrics.   For quantitative evaluation, we compute the mean and standard deviation of error rates, when trained on 3 different folds for labeled data, based on the standard evaluation protocol of selecting a subset of the training data while keeping the remainder unlabeled. In addition, as in [32,55], we evaluate the quality of pseudo labels by training curves of precision, recall, and F1 values.

4.2 Implementation Details

For a fair comparison, we generally follow the same hyperparameters with Fix-Match [45]. Specifically, we use Wide ResNet (WRN) [53] as a feature encoder

Table 2. Comparison on error rates on CIFAR-10 [27] and CIFAR-100 [27] benchmarks on 3 different folds.

Methods	CIFAR-10			CIFAR-100	
	40	250	4,000	400	2,500
UDA [49]	29.05 ± 5.93	8.82 ± 1.08	4.88 ± 0.18	59.28 ± 0.88	33.13 ± 0.22
FixMatch (RA) [45]	13.81 ± 3.37	5.07 ± 0.65	4.26 ± 0.06	48.85 ± 1.75	28.29 ± 0.11
FlexMatch [55]	4.97 ± 0.06	4.98 ± 0.09	4.19 ± 0.01	$\underline{39.94 \pm 1.62}$	$\underline{26.49 \pm 0.20}$
SelfMatch [24]	6.81 ± 1.08	4.87 ± 0.26	$\underline{4.06 \pm 0.08}$	-	-
CoMatch [32]	6.91 ± 8.47	4.91 ± 0.33	-	-	-
LESS [33]	6.80 ± 1.10	4.90 ± 0.80	-	48.70 ± 12.40	-
Dash (RA) [51]	13.22 ± 3.75	$\mathbf{4.56 \pm 0.13}$	4.08 ± 0.06	44.76 ± 0.96	27.18 ± 0.21
ConMatch-NP	$\underline{4.89 \pm 0.07}$	5.00 ± 0.37	4.36 ± 0.42	44.90 ± 1.34	26.91 ± 1.35
ConMatch-P	$\mathbf{4.43 \pm 0.13}$	$\underline{4.70 \pm 0.25}$	$\mathbf{3.92 \pm 0.08}$	$\mathbf{38.89 \pm 2.18}$	$\mathbf{25.39 \pm 0.20}$

for the experiments, especially WRN-28-2 for CIFAR-10 [27] and SVHN [35], WRN-28-8 for CIFAR-100 [27], and WRN-37-2 for STL-10 [12]. We use a batch size of labeled data $B = 64$, the ratio of unlabeled data $\mu = 7$, and SGD optimizer with a learning rate starting from 0.03, The detailed hyperparameter settings are described in the supplementary material. For a weakly-augmented sample, we use a crop-and-flip, and for a strongly-augmented sample, we use RandAugmnet [13].

4.3   Comparison to State-of-the-Art Methods

On standard semi-supervised learning benchmarks, we evaluate the performance of our frameworks, ConMatch-P and ConMatch-NP, compared to various state-of-the-art methods, as shown in Table 2 and Table 3. We observe that the performance difference between ConMatch-NP and ConMatch-P is not large, except in the label-scare setting. This may be explained by the fact that non-parametric method highly depends on baseline performance since it does not consider other samples which can be modeled as a prior. We show our superiority on most benchmarks with extensive label setting, but we mainly focus the label-scare setting, since it corresponds to the central goal of semi-supervised learning, reducing the need for labeled data. We achieves 4.43% and 38.89% error rate for CIFAR-10 and CIFAR-100 settings [27] with only 4 labels per class respectively. Compared to the results of SelfMatch [24] and CoMatch [32], closely related to ours, adopting self-supervised methods, we can prove the competitiveness of our method by achieving 2.38% and 2.48% improvements at CIFAR-10 with 40 labels. On the other datasets, CIFAR-100 [35] and STL-10 [12], we record the lowest error rate of 38.89% and 25.39% with 400 and 2500 labels setting, and also slightly better than baseline [55] by recording 5.26% in STL-10 dataset.

Table 3. Comparison on error rates on SVHN [35] and STL-10 [12] benchamarks on 3 different folds.

Method	SVHN		STL-10
	40	250	1,000
UDA [49]	52.63 ± 20.51	5.69 ± 2.76	7.66 ± 0.56
FixMatch (RA) [45]	$\mathbf{3.96 \pm 2.17}$	$\underline{2.48 \pm 0.38}$	7.98 ± 1.50
FlexMatch [55]	4.97 ± 0.06	4.98 ± 0.09	$\underline{5.77 \pm 0.18}$
SelfMatch [24]	3.42 ± 1.02	2.63 ± 0.43	-
CoMatch [32]	6.91 ± 8.47	4.91 ± 0.33	20.20 ± 0.38
Dash (RA) [51]	$\mathbf{3.03 \pm 1.59}$	2.17 ± 0.10	7.26 ± 0.40
ConMatch-NP	6.20 ± 3.44	5.80 ± 0.74	6.02 ± 0.08
ConMatch-P	$\underline{3.14 \pm 0.57}$	3.13 ± 0.72	$\mathbf{5.26 \pm 0.04}$

Table 4. Ablation study of different semi-supervised baselines. We evaluate non-parametric (ConMatch-NP) and parametric (ConMatch-P) approaches with different baselines, Fixmatch [45] and FlexMatch [55].

Methods	CIFAR-10		CIFAR-100
	40	250	400
FixMatch [45]	13.81	5.07	48.85
ConMatch-NP w/[45]	$\underline{6.83}$	4.73	$\underline{48.73}$
ConMatch-P w/[45]	$\mathbf{5.13}$	4.64	$\mathbf{48.00}$
FlexMatch [55]	4.97	4.98	$\underline{39.94}$
ConMatch-NP w/[55]	$\underline{4.84}$	$\underline{4.74}$	44.90
ConMatch-P w/[55]	$\mathbf{4.68}$	$\mathbf{4.70}$	$\mathbf{38.89}$

Table 5. Ablation study of training schemes. E means end-to-end training and S means stage-wise training.

Methods	Status	CIFAR-10		CIFAR-100
		40	250	400
ConMatch w/FixMatch [45]	E	4.85	4.77	47.81
	S	5.13	4.60	48.00
ConMatch w/FlexMatch [55]	E	4.68	4.70	57.16
	S	4.43	4.70	38.89

4.4 Ablation Study

Effects of Different Baseline. We first evaluate our ConMatch with two baselines, FixMatch [45] and FlexMatch [55], in both parametric (ConMatch-P) and non-parametric (ConMatch-NP) approaches as shown in Table 4. ConMatch-P w/[45] boosts the performance significantly on CIFAR-10 with 40 labels from

Table 6. Ablation study of our component on CIFAR-10 [27] with 40 labels.

	Three branches	Logit-level self-sup.	Confidence net. input		Error rate
			Logits	Features	
(I)	✓	✗	✗	✗	18.11
(II)	✓	✓	✗	✗	77.50
(III)	✓	✓	✓	✗	7.05
(IV)	✓	✓	✓	✓	5.13

13.81% to 5.13%, achieving the state-of-the-art result. The performance gains of ConMatch-P w/[45] is relatively higher than one w/[55] on most setting since [45] does not adaptively adjust the threshold depending on the difficulty level of samples. Note that the thresholds of FixMatch [45] and FlexMatch [55] are used only for $\mathcal{L}_{un}$.

Effectiveness of Confidence Measure. In Table 4, we evaluate two confidence measures in non-parametric and parametric approach. In extremely label-scare setting, such as CIFAR-10 with 4 labels per class, the non-parametric approach achieves relatively lower performance, 1.70% and 0.16%, in both Fix-Match and FlexMatch baseline, while the parametric approach (ConMatch-P w/[55]) reaches the state-of-the-art performance. But, as the number of labels increases, the gap between non-parametric and parametric approach decreases, indicating that a certain number of labeled samples are required to measure the confidence without the confidence estimator.

Effectiveness of Stage-Wise Training. In Table 5, we report the performance difference between end-to-end training and stage-wise training. We can observe that ConMatch-P has obtained meaningful enhancements in both training schemes, but stage-wise training shows more larger gap between baseline.

Architecture. Here we analyze the key components of ConMatch, the confidence estimator and guided consistency regularization as shown in Table 6. For the fair comparison, we construct three branches on FixMatch [45] as baseline **(I)**, one branch for a weakly-augmented sample and two branches for strongly-augmented samples. **(II)** uses logit-level self-supervised loss, but not weighted by confidence, i.e., $\mathcal{L}_{ccr}$ with $c_i(r), c_j(r) = 1/2$. **(III)** and **(IV)** weight confidences of strongly-augmented instances to logit-level self-supervised loss. **(III)** only takes logits as an input of confidence estimator while both logits and features are fed into **(IV)**. The result of this ablation study shows that logit-level self-supervised loss without confidence guidance causes network collapse. The collapse occurred in **(II)** is one of the reasons why other semi-supervised methods [32] could not use self-supervision at logit-level and should use negative pairs.

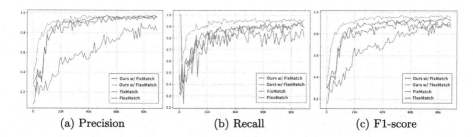

| (a) Precision | (b) Recall | (c) F1-score |

Fig. 3. Plots of evolution of pseudo-labeling between ours and baselines [45, 55] **as training progresses on CIFAR-10** [27] **with 40 labels:** in terms of (a) Precision, (b) Recall, and (c) F1-Score.

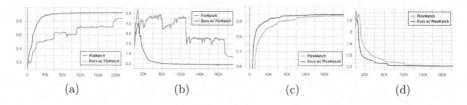

| (a) | (b) | (c) | (d) |

Fig. 4. Convergence analysis of baselines [45,55] **and ConMatch:** A comparison of top-1-accuracy and loss between FixMatch [45] and ConMatch w/[45] are shown at (a) and (b). A comparison between FlexMatch [55] and ConMatch w/[55] is shown at (c) and (d). Evaluations are done every 200K iterations on CIFAR-10 with 40 labels.

(III) and **(IV)** show a significant performance improvement compared to **(I)** without such collapse.

Evaluating Confidence Estimation. To evaluate the effectiveness of our confidence estimator, we measure precision, recall, and F1-score of ConMatch and FixMatch [45] as evolving the training iterations on CIFAR-10 [27] with 40 labels as shown in Fig. 3. The confident sample is defined as an unlabeled sample having max probability over than threshold in the baseline and confidence measures over than 0.5 in ConMatch. The quality of the confident sample is important to determine precisely to prevent the confirmation bias problem, significantly degrading the performances. The three classification metric, precision, recall and F1-score, are effective to evaluate the quality of the confidence. By Fig. 3, we can observe that ConMatch, starting from the scratch for the fair comparison, shows higher values in all metric compared to the baseline.

4.5   Analysis

Convergence Speed. One of the advantages of our ConMatch is its superior convergence speed. Based on the results as shown in Fig. 4(b) and (d), the loss of ConMatch decreases much faster and smoother than corresponding baseline [45], demonstrating our superior convergence speed. Furthermore, the result of the accuracy in Fig. 4(a) also proves that the global optimum is quickly reached. We also prove our effectiveness of our method by comparing the another baseline, FlexMatch [55]. The convergence speed gap is relatively smaller than FixMatch since it dynamically adjust class-wise thresholds at each time step, leading to the stable training, but ConMatch achieves fast convergence at all time step from the early phase where the predictions of the model are still unstable. It is manifest that the introduction of ConMatch successfully encourages the model to proactively improve the overall learning effect.

5   Conclusion

In this paper, we have proposed a novel semi-supervised learning framework built upon conventional consistency regularization frameworks with an additional strong branch to define the proposed confidence-guided consistency loss between two strong branches. To account for the direction of such consistency loss, we present confidence measures in non-parametric and parametric approaches. Also, we also presented a stage-wise training to boost the convergence of training. Our experiments have shown that our framework boosts the performance of base semi-supervised learners, and is clearly state-of-the-art on several benchmarks.

Acknowledgements. This research was supported by the MSIT, Korea (IITP-2022-2020-0-01819, ICT Creative Consilience program), and National Research Foundation of Korea (NRF-2021R1C1C1006897).

References

1. Arazo, E., Ortego, D., Albert, P., O'Connor, N.E., McGuinness, K.: Pseudo-labeling and confirmation bias in deep semi-supervised learning. In: IJCNN (2020)
2. Bachman, P., Alsharif, O., Precup, D.: Learning with pseudo-ensembles. In: NeurIPS (2014)
3. Bachman, P., Hjelm, R.D., Buchwalter, W.: Learning representations by maximizing mutual information across views. In: NeurIPS (2019)
4. Berthelot, D., et al.: Remixmatch: semi-supervised learning with distribution alignment and augmentation anchoring. arXiv:1911.09785 (2019)
5. Berthelot, D., Carlini, N., Goodfellow, I., Papernot, N., Oliver, A., Raffel, C.A.: Mixmatch: a holistic approach to semi-supervised learning. In: NeurIPS (2019)
6. Caron, M., Misra, I., Mairal, J., Goyal, P., Bojanowski, P., Joulin, A.: Unsupervised learning of visual features by contrasting cluster assignments. In: NeurIPS (2020)
7. Chapelle, O., Zien, A.: Semi-supervised classification by low density separation. In: AISTATS Workshops (2005)
8. Chen, T., Kornblith, S., Norouzi, M., Hinton, G.: A simple framework for contrastive learning of visual representations. In: ICML (2020)
9. Chen, T., Kornblith, S., Swersky, K., Norouzi, M., Hinton, G.E.: Big self-supervised models are strong semi-supervised learners. In: NeurIPS (2020)
10. Chen, X., He, K.: Exploring simple siamese representation learning. In: CVPR (2021)

11. Choi, H., et al.: Adaptive confidence thresholding for monocular depth estimation. In: ICCV (2021)
12. Coates, A., Ng, A., Lee, H.: An analysis of single-layer networks in unsupervised feature learning. In: AISTATS (2011)
13. Cubuk, E.D., Zoph, B., Shlens, J., Le, Q.V.: Randaugment: practical automated data augmentation with a reduced search space. In: CVPR Workshops (2020)
14. Dawid, A.P.: The well-calibrated Bayesian. JASA **77**(379), 605–610 (1982)
15. DeGroot, M.H., Fienberg, S.E.: The comparison and evaluation of forecasters. J. Roy. Stat. Soc. Ser. D (Stat.) **32**(1–2), 12-22 (1983)
16. Donahue, J., et al.: Decaf: a deep convolutional activation feature for generic visual recognition. In: ICML (2014)
17. French, G., Mackiewicz, M., Fisher, M.: Self-ensembling for visual domain adaptation. arXiv:1706.05208 (2017)
18. Gidaris, S., Singh, P., Komodakis, N.: Unsupervised representation learning by predicting image rotations. arXiv:1803.07728 (2018)
19. Grandvalet, Y., Bengio, Y.: Semi-supervised learning by entropy minimization. In: NeurIPS (2004)
20. Grill, J.B., et al.: Bootstrap your own latent-a new approach to self-supervised learning. In: NeurIPS (2020)
21. Guo, C., Pleiss, G., Sun, Y., Weinberger, K.Q.: On calibration of modern neural networks. In: ICML (2017)
22. He, K., Fan, H., Wu, Y., Xie, S., Girshick, R.: Momentum contrast for unsupervised visual representation learning. In: CVPR (2020)
23. Ke, Z., Wang, D., Yan, Q., Ren, J., Lau, R.W.: Dual student: breaking the limits of the teacher in semi-supervised learning. In: ICCV (2019)
24. Kim, B., Choo, J., Kwon, Y.D., Joe, S., Min, S., Gwon, Y.: Selfmatch: combining contrastive self-supervision and consistency for semi-supervised learning. arXiv:2101.06480 (2021)
25. Kim, S., Min, D., Kim, S., Sohn, K.: Unified confidence estimation networks for robust stereo matching. TIP **28**(3), 1299–1313 (2018)
26. Kim, S., Min, D., Kim, S., Sohn, K.: Adversarial confidence estimation networks for robust stereo matching. T-ITS **22**(11), 6875–6889 (2020)
27. Krizhevsky, A., Hinton, G., et al.: Learning multiple layers of features from tiny images (2009)
28. Laine, S., Aila, T.: Temporal ensembling for semi-supervised learning. arXiv:1610.02242 (2016)
29. Lee, D.H., et al.: Pseudo-label: the simple and efficient semi-supervised learning method for deep neural networks. In: ICML Workshops (2013)
30. Lee, D., Kim, S., Kim, I., Cheon, Y., Cho, M., Han, W.S.: Contrastive regularization for semi-supervised learning. arXiv:2201.06247 (2022)
31. Lerner, B., Shiran, G., Weinshall, D.: Boosting the performance of semi-supervised learning with unsupervised clustering. arXiv:2012.00504 (2020)
32. Li, J., Xiong, C., Hoi, S.C.: Comatch: semi-supervised learning with contrastive graph regularization. In: ICCV (2021)
33. Lucas, T., Weinzaepfel, P., Rogez, G.: Barely-supervised learning: Semi-supervised learning with very few labeled images. arXiv:2112.12004 (2021)
34. Miyato, T., Maeda, S.I., Koyama, M., Ishii, S.: Virtual adversarial training: a regularization method for supervised and semi-supervised learning. TPAMI **41**(8), 1979–1993 (2018)
35. Netzer, Y., Wang, T., Coates, A., Bissacco, A., Wu, B., Ng, A.Y.: Reading digits in natural images with unsupervised feature learning (2011)

36. Noroozi, M., Favaro, P.: Unsupervised learning of visual representations by solving jigsaw puzzles. In: Leibe, B., Matas, J., Sebe, N., Welling, M. (eds.) ECCV 2016. LNCS, vol. 9910, pp. 69–84. Springer, Cham (2016). https://doi.org/10.1007/978-3-319-46466-4_5

37. Park, S., Park, J., Shin, S.J., Moon, I.C.: Adversarial dropout for supervised and semi-supervised learning. In: AAAI (2018)

38. Pham, H., Dai, Z., Xie, Q., Le, Q.V.: Meta pseudo labels. In: CVPR (2021)

39. Poggi, M., Mattoccia, S.: Learning from scratch a confidence measure. In: BMVC (2016)

40. Rizve, M.N., Duarte, K., Rawat, Y.S., Shah, M.: In defense of pseudo-labeling: an uncertainty-aware pseudo-label selection framework for semi-supervised learning. arXiv:2101.06329 (2021)

41. Sajjadi, M., Javanmardi, M., Tasdizen, T.: Mutual exclusivity loss for semi-supervised deep learning. In: ICIP (2016)

42. Sajjadi, M., Javanmardi, M., Tasdizen, T.: Regularization with stochastic transformations and perturbations for deep semi-supervised learning. In: NeurIPS (2016)

43. Seki, A., Pollefeys, M.: Patch based confidence prediction for dense disparity map. In: BMVC (2016)

44. Shi, W., Gong, Y., Ding, C., Tao, Z.M., Zheng, N.: Transductive semi-supervised deep learning using min-max features. In: ECCV (2018)

45. Sohn, K., et al.: Fixmatch: simplifying semi-supervised learning with consistency and confidence. In: NeurIPS (2020)

46. Tarvainen, A., Valpola, H.: Mean teachers are better role models: weight-averaged consistency targets improve semi-supervised deep learning results. In: NeurIPS (2017)

47. Tosi, F., Poggi, M., Benincasa, A., Mattoccia, S.: Beyond local reasoning for stereo confidence estimation with deep learning. In: ECCV (2018)

48. Verma, V., Kawaguchi, K., Lamb, A., Kannala, J., Bengio, Y., Lopez-Paz, D.: Interpolation consistency training for semi-supervised learning. arXiv:1903.03825 (2019)

49. Xie, Q., Dai, Z., Hovy, E., Luong, T., Le, Q.: Unsupervised data augmentation for consistency training. In: NeurIPS (2020)

50. Xie, Q., Luong, M.T., Hovy, E., Le, Q.V.: Self-training with noisy student improves imagenet classification. In: CVPR (2020)

51. Xu, Y., et al.: Dash: semi-supervised learning with dynamic thresholding. In: ICML (2021)

52. Yalniz, I.Z., Jégou, H., Chen, K., Paluri, M., Mahajan, D.: Billion-scale semi-supervised learning for image classification. arXiv:1905.00546 (2019)

53. Zagoruyko, S., Komodakis, N.: Wide residual networks. arXiv:1605.07146 (2016)

54. Zhai, X., Oliver, A., Kolesnikov, A., Beyer, L.: S4L: self-supervised semi-supervised learning. In: ICCV (2019)

55. Zhang, B., et al.: Flexmatch: boosting semi-supervised learning with curriculum pseudo labeling. In: NeurIPS (2021)

56. Zhang, L., Qi, G.J.: WCP: worst-case perturbations for semi-supervised deep learning. In: CVPR (2020)

57. Zhang, R., Isola, P., Efros, A.A.: Colorful image colorization. In: Leibe, B., Matas, J., Sebe, N., Welling, M. (eds.) ECCV 2016. LNCS, vol. 9907, pp. 649–666. Springer, Cham (2016). https://doi.org/10.1007/978-3-319-46487-9_40

58. Zoph, B., et al.: Rethinking pre-training and self-training. In: NeurIPS (2020)

FedX: Unsupervised Federated Learning with Cross Knowledge Distillation

Sungwon Han[1,2](✉)📧, Sungwon Park[1,2]📧, Fangzhao Wu[3]📧, Sundong Kim[2]📧, Chuhan Wu[4]📧, Xing Xie[3]📧, and Meeyoung Cha[1,2]📧

[1] School of Computing, KAIST, Daejeon, South Korea
{lion4151,psw0416}@kaist.ac.kr
[2] Data Science Group, Institute for Basic Science, Daejeon, South Korea
{sundong,mcha}@ibs.re.kr
[3] Microsoft Research Asia, Beijing, China
xingx@microsoft.com
[4] Tsinghua University, Beijing, China

Abstract. This paper presents FedX, an unsupervised federated learning framework. Our model learns unbiased representation from decentralized and heterogeneous local data. It employs a two-sided knowledge distillation with contrastive learning as a core component, allowing the federated system to function without requiring clients to share any data features. Furthermore, its adaptable architecture can be used as an add-on module for existing unsupervised algorithms in federated settings. Experiments show that our model improves performance significantly (1.58–5.52pp) on five unsupervised algorithms.

Keywords: Unsupervised representation learning · Self-supervised learning · Federated learning · Knowledge distillation · Data privacy

1 Introduction

Most deep learning techniques assume unlimited access to data during training. However, this assumption does not hold in modern distributed systems, where data is stored at client nodes for privacy reasons [28,34]. For example, personal data stored on mobile devices cannot be shared with central servers, nor can patient records in hospital networks. *Federated learning* is a new branch of collaborative technique to build a shared data model while securing data privacy; it is a method to run machine learning by involving multiple decentralized edge devices without exchanging locally bounded data [2,36].

In federated systems, supervised methods have been used for a variety of downstream tasks such as object detection [22], image segmentation [31], and

---

S. Han and S. Park—Equal contribution to this work.

Supplementary Information The online version contains supplementary material available at https://doi.org/10.1007/978-3-031-20056-4_40.

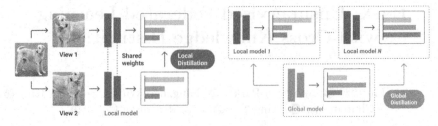

(a) Local knowledge distillation   (b) Global knowledge distillation

Fig. 1. Illustration of two knowledge flows in FedX: (a) local knowledge distillation progressively learns augmentation-invariant features, and (b) global knowledge distillation regularizes local models from bias.

person re-identification [45]. The main challenge here is the data's decentralized and heterogeneous nature (i.e., non-IID setting), which obscures the global data distribution. To address this issue, several methods have been proposed, including knowledge distillation [45], control variates [13], and contrastive learning [19]. These methods necessitate that local clients have high-quality data labels.

Nowadays, the need for *unsupervised* federated learning is increasing to handle practical scenarios that lack data labels. This is the new frontier in federated learning. There have been a few new ideas; for instance, Zhang *et al.* proposed FedCA, a model that uses local data features and external datasets to alleviate inconsistency in the representation space [42]. Wu *et al.* proposed FCL, which exchanges encrypted local data features for privacy and introduces a neighborhood matching approach to cluster the decentralized data across clients [38]. However, these approaches allow data sharing among local clients and raise privacy concerns.

We present FedX, a new advancement in unsupervised learning on federated systems that learns semantic representation from local data and refines the central server's knowledge via *knowledge distillation*. Unlike previous approaches, this model is privacy-preserving and does not rely on external datasets. The model introduces two novel considerations to the standard FedAvg [23] framework: *local knowledge distillation* to train the network progressively based on local data and *global knowledge distillation* to regularize data bias due to the non-IID setting. This two-sided knowledge flow distinguishes our model.

Local knowledge distillation (Fig. 1a) maximizes the embedding similarity between two different views of the same data instance while minimizing that of other instances—this process is defined by the *contrastive loss*. We designed an additional loss that relaxes the contrastive loss via soft labeling. Soft labels are computed as similarities between an anchor and randomly selected instances, called *relationship vectors*. We minimize the distance between relationship vectors of two different views in order to transfer structural knowledge and achieve fast training speed—this process is modulated by the *relational loss*.

Global knowledge distillation (Fig. 1b) treats the sample representation passed by the global model as an alternative view that should be placed near the embedding of the local model. This process is also modulated by contrastive loss and relational loss. Concurrent optimization allows the model to learn semantic information while eliminating data bias through regularization. These objectives do not require additional communication rounds or costly computation. Moreover, they do not share sensitive local data or use external datasets.

1. We propose an unsupervised federated learning algorithm, FedX, that learns data representations via a unique two-sided knowledge distillation at local and global levels.
2. Two-sided knowledge distillation helps discover meaningful representation from local data while eliminating bias by using global knowledge.
3. FedX can be applied to extant algorithms to enhance performance by 1.58–5.52pp in top-1 accuracy and further enhance training speed.
4. Unlike other unsupervised federated learning approaches, FedX preserves privacy between clients and does not share data directly. It is also lightweight and does not require complex communication for sending data features.
5. FedX is open-sourced at https://github.com/Sungwon-Han/FEDX.

2   Related Work

2.1   Unsupervised Representation Learning

There are two common approaches to unsupervised representation learning. One approach is to use generative models like autoencoder [33] and adversarial learning [30] that learn the latent representation by mimicking the actual data distribution. Another method is to use discriminative models with contrastive learning [5, 27, 40]. Contrastive learning approaches teach a model to pull the representations of the anchor and its positive samples (i.e., different views of the image) in embedding space, while pushing the anchor apart from negative samples (i.e., views from different images) [7, 18].

In contrastive learning, SimCLR [3] employs data augmentation to generate positive samples. MoCo [8] introduces a momentum encoder and dynamic queue to handle negative samples efficiently. BYOL [6] reduces memory costs caused by a large number of negative samples. ProtoCL [18] uses prototypes to group semantically similar instances into local clusters via an expectation-maximization framework. However, under distributed and non-IID data settings, as in federated systems, these methods show a decrease in accuracy [42].

2.2   Federated Learning

Federated Averaging (FedAvg) by McMahan *et al.* is a standard framework for supervised federated learning [23]. Several subsequent studies improved the local update or global aggregation processes of FedAvg. For instance, external dataset [43], knowledge distillation [45], control variates [13, 20], and contrastive learning [19] can be applied for better local update process. Similarly, global aggregation process can be improved via Bayesian non-parametric approaches [35], momentum updates [11], or normalization methods [37].

Unsupervised federated learning is more difficult to implement because no labels are provided and clients must rely on locally-defined pretext tasks that may be biased. This is a less explored field, with only a few methods proposed. FedCA [42] shares local data features and uses an external dataset to reduce the mismatch in representation space among clients. FCL [38] encrypts the local data features before exchanging them. Because of the explicit data sharing, these methods raise new privacy concerns. We, on the other hand, consider a completely isolated condition that does not permit any local data sharing. FedU [44] is another approach in the field that improves on the global aggregation method. It decides how to update predictors selectively based on the divergence of local and global models. Our model is orthogonal to FedU, and both concepts can be used in tandem.

2.3   Knowledge Distillation

Knowledge distillation aims to effectively train a network (i.e., student) by distilling the knowledge of a pretrained network (i.e., teacher). Knowledge can be defined over the features at the intermediate hidden layers [15,16], logits at the final layer [10], or structural relations among training samples [24,29,32]. Self-knowledge distillation uses the student network itself as a teacher network and progressively uses its knowledge to train the model [12,14]. We leverage this concept to efficiently train the local model while preserving the knowledge of the global model. FedX is the first-of-a-kind approach that uses the knowledge distillation concept for unsupervised federated learning.

3   Model

3.1   Overview

Problem Statement. Consider a federated system in which data can only be viewed locally at each client and cannot be shared outside. Our goal is to train a single unsupervised embedding model F_ϕ that maps data points from each client to the embedding space. Let us denote local data and model from client m as $\mathcal{D}^m$ and f_θ^m respectively (i.e., $m \in \{1, ..., M\}$). The main objective for the global model F_ϕ is as follows:

$$\arg \min_\phi \mathcal{L}(\phi) = \sum_{m=1}^{M} \frac{|\mathcal{D}^m|}{|\mathcal{D}|} \mathcal{L}_m(\phi),$$

$$\text{where } \mathcal{L}_m(\phi) = \mathbb{E}_{\mathbf{x} \in \mathcal{D}^m}[l_m(\mathbf{x}; \phi)]. \tag{1}$$

$\mathcal{L}_m$ represents the local objective in client m and l_m is the empirical loss objective of $\mathcal{L}_m$ over $\mathcal{D}^m$. For simplicity, we hereafter denote the local model f_θ^m at client m and global model F_ϕ as f^m and F.

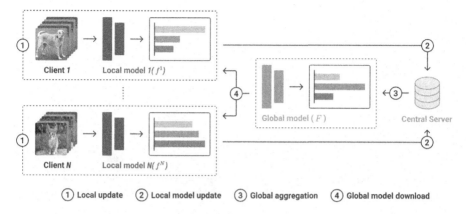

Fig. 2. Illustration of the FedAvg framework [23], which is used as the base structure of many federated systems. FedX modifies the local update process ①.

We use FedAvg [23] as the underlying structure, and the data flow is depicted in Fig. 2. Four processes run in each communication round: Process ① on local update is when each local client trains a model f^m with its data $\mathcal{D}^m$ for E local epochs; Process ② on local model upload occurs when clients share the trained model weights with the server; Process ③ on global aggregation occurs when the central server averages the received model weights and generates a shared global model F; Process ④ on global model download is when clients replace their local models with the downloaded global model (i.e., averaged weights). These processes run for R communication rounds.

FedX modifies the Process ① by redesigning loss objectives in order to distill knowledge at both the local and global scales. The following sections introduce the design components of our unsupervised federated learning model (Fig. 3).

3.2 Local Knowledge Distillation

The first significant change takes place with local clients, whose goal is to learn meaningful representations from local data. Let us define a data pair; $\mathbf{x}_i$ and $\tilde{\mathbf{x}}_i$ be two augmented views of the same data instance. The *local contrastive loss* L_c^{local} learns semantic representation by maximizing the agreement between $\mathbf{x}_i$ and $\tilde{\mathbf{x}}_i$ while minimizing the agreement of views from different instances (i.e., negative samples). We showcase the proposed contrastive loss from two of the unsupervised representation learning methods as vanilla baselines.

* SimCLR [3] utilizes a contrastive objective based on the InfoNCE loss [26]. Given a batch $\mathcal{B}$ with size n and its augmented version $\tilde{\mathcal{B}}$, each anchor has a single positive sample and considers all other $(2n - 2)$ data points to be negative samples. The following is the definition of this $(2n - 1)$-way instance

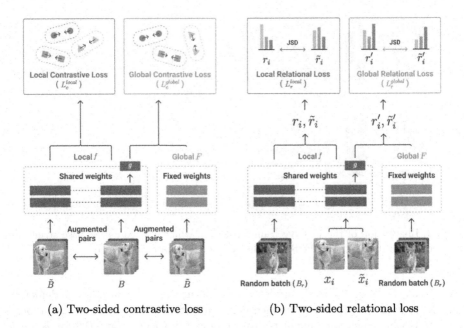

(a) Two-sided contrastive loss   (b) Two-sided relational loss

Fig. 3. The overall architecture of FedX, with the local model f^m, the projection head h^m, and the global model F at local client m. Two-sided (a) contrastive loss and (b) relational loss enable the model to learn semantic information from local data while regularizing the bias by distilling knowledge from the global model. FedX modifies the process ① on local update in Fig. 2.

discrimination loss, where τ is the temperature used to control the entropy value and $\text{sim}(\cdot)$ is the cosine similarity function between two embeddings:

$$L_c^{\text{local}} = -\log \frac{\exp(\text{sim}(\mathbf{z}_i, \tilde{\mathbf{z}}_i)/\tau)}{\sum_{k \in (\mathcal{B} \cup \tilde{\mathcal{B}} - \{i\})} \exp(\text{sim}(\mathbf{z}_i, \mathbf{z}_k)/\tau)}, \tag{2}$$

$$\text{where } \mathbf{z}_i = f^m(\mathbf{x}_i), \ \tilde{\mathbf{z}}_i = f^m(\tilde{\mathbf{x}}_i). \tag{3}$$

∗ BYOL [6] does not train on negative samples. Instead, an asymmetric architecture is used to prevent the model from learning trivial solutions. The model f^m with a prediction layer g^m is trained to predict a view from the exponential moving average model f^m_{ema}. The loss is defined as follows:

$$L_c^{\text{local}} = \left\| \mathbf{z}_i/\|\mathbf{z}_i\| - \mathbf{z}^{\tilde{\text{ema}}}_i/\|\mathbf{z}^{\tilde{\text{ema}}}_i\| \right\|^2, \tag{4}$$

$$\text{where } \mathbf{z}_i = g^m \circ f^m(\mathbf{x}_i), \ \mathbf{z}^{\tilde{\text{ema}}}_i = f^m_{\text{ema}}(\tilde{\mathbf{x}}_i). \tag{5}$$

We consider another design aspect to help the model learn structural knowledge more effectively. Motivated by the concept of relational knowledge distillation [1,41], structural knowledge represented as relations among samples is extracted from the local model and progressively transferred back to itself. This entails selecting a set of instances at random $\mathcal{B}_r$ and computing the cosine similarity between the embeddings of two different views $\mathbf{x}_i$, $\tilde{\mathbf{x}}_i$ and random instances $\mathcal{B}_r$. We then apply the softmax function to the similarity vector to compute relationship probability distributions $\mathbf{r}_i$ and $\tilde{\mathbf{r}}_i$ (Eq. 6). In vector notation, the superscript j represents the j-th component value of a given vector.

$$\mathbf{r}_i^j = \frac{\exp(\mathrm{sim}(\mathbf{z}_i, \mathbf{z}_j)/\tau)}{\sum_{k \in \mathcal{B}_r} \exp(\mathrm{sim}(\mathbf{z}_i, \mathbf{z}_k)/\tau)}, \quad \tilde{\mathbf{r}}_i^j = \frac{\exp(\mathrm{sim}(\tilde{\mathbf{z}}_i, \mathbf{z}_j)/\tau)}{\sum_{k \in \mathcal{B}_r} \exp(\mathrm{sim}(\tilde{\mathbf{z}}_i, \mathbf{z}_k)/\tau)} \quad (6)$$

The above concept, *local relational loss*, is defined as the Jensen-Shannon divergence (JSD) between two relationship probability distributions $\mathbf{r}_i$ and $\tilde{\mathbf{r}}_i$ (Eq. 7). Minimizing the discrepancy between two distributions make the model to learn structural knowledge invariant to data augmentation. In contrastive learning with soft targets, this divergence loss can also be interpreted as relaxing the InfoNCE objective.

$$L_r^{\mathrm{local}} = \frac{1}{2}\mathrm{KL}(\mathbf{r}_i \| \mathbf{r}_i^{\mathrm{target}}) + \frac{1}{2}\mathrm{KL}(\tilde{\mathbf{r}}_i \| \mathbf{r}_i^{\mathrm{target}}), \text{ where } \mathbf{r}_i^{\mathrm{target}} = \frac{1}{2}(\mathbf{r}_i + \tilde{\mathbf{r}}_i) \quad (7)$$

The total loss term for local knowledge distillation is given in Eq. 8:

$$L_{\mathrm{local\text{-}KD}} = L_c^{\mathrm{local}} + L_r^{\mathrm{local}}. \quad (8)$$

3.3   Global Knowledge Distillation

The second major change is to regularize the bias contributed by the inconsistency between local and overall data distribution. The inconsistency addresses the issue of decentralized non-IID settings, where local clients are unaware of global data distribution. Training the local model f^m will be suboptimal in this case because the local update process becomes biased towards local minimizers [42]. Such data inconsistency among local clients can be resolved by distilling knowledge on a global scale.

We consider two kinds of losses: *global contrastive loss* and *global relational loss*. Because the global model simply aggregates model weights at the local clients in FedAvg, we can think of the sample's embedding from the global model as an alternate view of the same data instance. The global contrastive loss maximizes the agreement between the views of the local and global models from the same instance while minimizing that of all other views from different instances.

Each communication round assumes that the central server sends a fixed set of averaged model weights (i.e., global model F) to the client. The batch $\mathcal{B}$ and its augmented version $\tilde{\mathcal{B}}$ are then used to train the local model f^m as in Eq. 9 with the InfoNCE loss. To match the embedding space between the local and global models, we consider an additional prediction layer h^m on top of local models. Similar method has been used in [4,6].

$$L_c^{\mathrm{global}} = -\log \frac{\exp(\mathrm{sim}(\mathbf{z}_i^l, \tilde{\mathbf{z}}_i^g)/\tau)}{\sum\limits_{k \in (\mathcal{B}-\{i\})} \exp(\mathrm{sim}(\mathbf{z}_i^l, \mathbf{z}_k^l)/\tau) + \sum\limits_{k \in (\tilde{\mathcal{B}}-\{i\})} \exp(\mathrm{sim}(\mathbf{z}_i^l, \mathbf{z}_k^g)/\tau)},$$

where $\mathbf{z}_i^l = h^m \circ f^m(\mathbf{x}_i)$, $\tilde{\mathbf{z}}_i^l = h^m \circ f^m(\tilde{\mathbf{x}}_i)$, $\mathbf{z}_i^g = F(\mathbf{x}_i)$, $\tilde{\mathbf{z}}_i^g = F(\tilde{\mathbf{x}}_i)$. $\quad (9)$

We introduce the *global relational loss* on top of the global contrastive loss. This loss is defined in the same way as the local relational loss (Eq. 7), but it includes global model embeddings. It regularizes the model by penalizing any mismatch between two augmented views over the global embedding space after the prediction layer h^m. As a result, the model maintains its local knowledge based on local data while learning augmentation-invariant knowledge using the global contrastive loss.

Given two different views $\mathbf{x}_i$, $\tilde{\mathbf{x}}_i$ and random instances $\mathcal{B}_r$, the relationship probability distributions for global relational loss, $\mathbf{r}_i'$ and $\tilde{\mathbf{r}}_i'$, are defined (Eq. 10). We again adopt the JS divergence between two relationship probability vectors $\mathbf{r}_i'$ and $\tilde{\mathbf{r}}_i'$ as the global relational loss (Eq. 11).

$$\mathbf{r}_i'^j = \frac{\exp(\text{sim}(\mathbf{z}_i^l, \mathbf{z}_j^g)/\tau)}{\sum_{k \in \mathcal{B}_r} \exp(\text{sim}(\mathbf{z}_i^l, \mathbf{z}_k^g)/\tau)}, \quad \tilde{\mathbf{r}}_i'^j = \frac{\exp(\text{sim}(\tilde{\mathbf{z}}_i^l, \mathbf{z}_j^g)/\tau)}{\sum_{k \in \mathcal{B}_r} \exp(\text{sim}(\tilde{\mathbf{z}}_i^l, \mathbf{z}_k^g)/\tau)} \quad (10)$$

$$L_r^{\text{global}} = \frac{1}{2}\text{KL}(\mathbf{r}_i' \| \mathbf{r}_i'^{\text{target}}) + \frac{1}{2}\text{KL}(\tilde{\mathbf{r}}_i' \| \mathbf{r}_i'^{\text{target}}), \text{ where } \mathbf{r}_i'^{\text{target}} = \frac{1}{2}(\mathbf{r}_i' + \tilde{\mathbf{r}}_i') \quad (11)$$

The total loss for global knowledge distillation is given in Eq. 12. The overall model then combines losses from knowledge distillation at the local and global levels, as shown in Eq. 13. The detailed algorithm is described in the appendix.

$$L_{\text{global-KD}} = L_c^{\text{global}} + L_r^{\text{global}} \quad (12)$$

$$L_{\text{total-KD}} = L_{\text{local-KD}} + L_{\text{global-KD}} \quad (13)$$

4   Experiment

Using multiple datasets, we compared the performance of our model to other baselines and investigated the role of model components and hyperparameters. We also used embedding analysis to examine how the proposed model achieves the performance gain. Finally, we applied the model in a semi-supervised setting.

4.1   Performance Evaluation

Data Settings. Three benchmark datasets are used. CIFAR-10 [17] contains 60,000 images of 32×32 pixels from ten classes that include airplanes, cats, and dogs. SVHN [25] contains 73,257 training images and 26,032 test images with small cropped digits of of 32×32 pixels. F-MNIST [39] contains 70,000 images of 28×28 pixels from ten classes, including dresses, shirts, and sneakers.

We used the Dirichlet distribution to enforce the non-IID property of local clients. Let $Dir_N(\beta)$ denote the Dirichlet distribution with N clients and β as the concentration parameter. We take a sample $p_{k,j}$ from $Dir_N(\beta)$ and assign class k to client j based on the sampled proportion $p_{k,j}$. With this data allocation strategy, each client will be assigned a few data samples for each class (or even none) to ensure bias. By default, N and β are to 10 and 0.5, respectively, similar to other research [19].

Table 1. Performance improvement with FedX on classification accuracy over three datasets. Both the final round accuracy and the best accuracy show that our model brings substantial improvement for all baseline algorithms.

Method	CIFAR-10		SVHN		F-MNIST	
	Last	Best	Last	Best	Last	Best
FedSimCLR	51.31	52.88	75.19	76.50	77.66	79.44
+ FedX	**56.88**	**57.95**	**77.19**	**77.70**	**81.98**	**82.47**
FedMoCo	56.74	57.82	70.69	70.99	82.31	83.58
+ FedX	**58.23**	**59.43**	**73.57**	**73.92**	**83.62**	**84.65**
FedBYOL	52.24	53.14	65.95	67.32	81.45	82.37
+ FedX	**56.49**	**57.79**	**68.94**	**69.05**	**83.18**	**84.30**
FedProtoCL	51.33	52.12	49.85	50.19	81.76	**83.57**
+ FedX	**55.36**	**56.76**	**69.31**	**69.75**	**82.74**	83.34
FedU	50.79	50.79	66.02	66.22	80.59	82.03
+ FedX	**56.15**	**57.26**	**68.13**	**68.39**	**83.73**	**84.12**

Implementation Details. The model was trained for 100 communication rounds, with 10 local epochs in each round. The ResNet18 backbone [9] and the SGD optimizer with a learning rate of 0.01 were used. SGD weight decay was set to 1e–5, SGD momentum was set to 0.9, and batch size was set to 128. For all objectives, the temperature τ was set as 0.1. Augmentations included random crop, random horizontal flip, and color jitter. We used four A100 GPUs.

Baselines. We implemented five baselines: (1) FedSimCLR based on Sim-CLR [3], (2) FedMoCo based on MoCo [8], (3) FedBYOL based on BYOL [6], and (4) FedProtoCL based on ProtoCL [18]. These are unsupervised models that are built on top of FedAvg [23]. The final baseline (5) FedU [44] is built over Fed-BYOL and downloads a global model by divergence-aware module (see process ④ in Fig. 2). For a fair comparison, we applied the same experimental settings on these baselines, including the backbone network, optimizer, augmentation strategy, number of local epochs, and communication rounds. We used the original implementations and hyper-parameter settings for FedU. Unless otherwise specified, we refer to FedSimCLR as the representative baseline in the remainder of this section.

Evaluation. All models were compared using the linear evaluation protocol, which is a method for training a linear classifier on top of representations [42, 44]. We freeze the backbone network of each trained model after training. Then, for the next 100 epochs, a new classifier is appended and trained with ground-truth labels. The top-1 classification accuracy over the test set is reported as an evaluation metric.

Results. Table 1 summarizes the performance comparison, where FedX brings meaningful performance improvements over the baseline algorithms. On average,

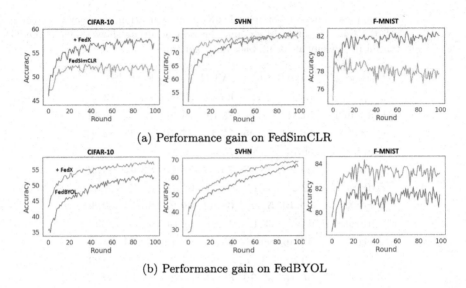

(a) Performance gain on FedSimCLR

(b) Performance gain on FedBYOL

Fig. 4. Performance comparison between two vanilla baselines (i.e., FedSimCLR and FedBYOL) and FedX-enhanced versions over communication rounds. FedX helps models outperform in all three benchmark datasets and continues to bring advantage with increasing communication rounds.

our model improves CIFAR-10 by 4.29% points (pp), SVHN by 5.52pp, and F-MNIST by 1.58pp across all baselines. One exception is F-MNIST, where FedProtoCL by itself has a slightly higher best accuracy. However, adding FedX still contributes to improved final round accuracy, implying that the model has good training stability.

We then examine how quickly the model improves baselines across the various communication rounds. Figure 4 shows the trajectory for two example baselines on FedSimCLR and FedBYOL.[1] These plots confirm that model-enhanced models outperform vanilla baselines; most plots show this benefit early in the communication rounds. We see that local bias can degrade the performance of a baseline model during the early training phase in some cases (see the F-MNIST case in Fig. 4a). This is most likely due to the biased contrastive objective caused by locally sampled negatives. In contrast, adding FedX prevents such deterioration and even continues to improve accuracy as communication rounds increase.

4.2 Component Analyses

Ablation Study. FedX used learning objectives at the local and global levels separately, with two types of losses: contrastive loss and relational loss. In this section, we look at ablations by removing each learning objective or loss component and testing the added value of each design choice to overall performance.

---

[1] Results for other baselines are presented in the Appendix.

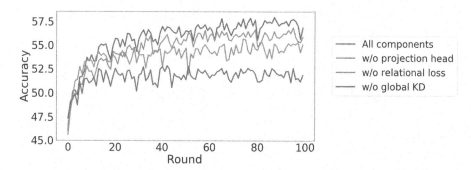

Fig. 5. Performance comparison of ablations over communication rounds for CIFAR-10. Removing any module leads to performance degradation. Ablation on contrastive loss L_c showed the best accuracy of 35.13% and hence excluded.

Table 2. Ablation results with different global-scale regularization methods. The proposed global knowledge distillation performs the best among them.

Method	CIFAR-10		SVHN		F-MNIST	
	Last	Best	Last	Best	Last	Best
$L_{\text{local-KD}}$ only	51.89	52.85	76.64	77.20	79.79	80.42
$L_{\text{local-KD}}$ + SCAFFOLD	52.73	53.20	75.18	75.52	79.45	80.36
$L_{\text{local-KD}}$ + FedProx	52.48	53.34	**77.43**	**77.79**	79.83	80.24
$L_{\text{local-KD}}$ + $L_{\text{global-KD}}$	**56.88**	**57.95**	77.19	77.70	**81.98**	**82.47**

Figure 5 plots the performance comparison of different ablations across the communication round. The complete model has the highest accuracy, implying that removing any component reduces performance. It also confirms the importance of a global knowledge distillation objective.

FedX used global knowledge distillation to convey global model knowledge and regularize the local bias caused by the inconsistency between local and overall data distribution. Several studies in supervised settings have addressed a similar challenge using extra regularization or gradient update processes. We replaced the global knowledge distillation loss ($L_{\text{global-KD}}$ – Eq. 12) with extant strategies, such as FedProx [21] or SCAFFOLD [13] and verified its efficacy. The performance comparison of different ablations across three benchmark datasets is summarized in Table 2. The findings imply that our global knowledge distillation technique is more effective than alternative designs.

Robustness Test. The model's robustness is then tested by varying key hyperparameters in different simulation settings. This allows us to test the system in difficult scenarios, such as (a) when each client is only allowed to hold a small amount of data (i.e., data size $|\mathcal{D}|$), (b) when more clients participate in the federated system (i.e., client count N), and (c) when communication with the central server becomes limited and costly (i.e., the number of communication

Table 3. Analysis of accuracy on CIFAR-10 over varying hyper-parameters indicates FedX consistently enhances the baseline performance.

(a) Effect of the data size $|\mathcal{D}|$

Data size	Baseline		Baseline+FedX	
	Last	Best	Last	Best
10%	46.80	47.37	51.03	53.96
25%	48.42	49.79	52.84	54.45
50%	51.17	52.04	54.62	55.85
100%	51.31	52.88	56.88	57.95

(b) Effect of the client count N

Clients #	Baseline		Baseline+FedX	
	Last	Best	Last	Best
5	52.87	53.87	58.55	58.55
10	51.31	52.88	56.88	57.95
15	52.31	53.06	55.12	56.82
20	50.70	52.89	56.56	56.56

(c) Effect of the communication round count R

Communication round	Baseline		Baseline+FedX	
	Last	Best	Last	Best
20	52.01	52.80	56.97	56.97
50	51.95	53.53	57.29	57.29
100	51.31	52.88	56.88	57.95
200	52.79	53.23	57.35	57.58

rounds R) [36]. We test how our model performs under these scenarios in Table 3. We note that when varying the communication rounds R, we also changed the number of local epochs E accordingly such that $R \times E = 1000$.

The table summarizes the effect of each hyperparameter for the baseline model (FedSimCLR) and the FedX-enhanced model. We make several observations. First, reducing the data size $|\mathcal{D}|$ degrades performance. The drop, however, is not severe and remains nearly 5pp drop even when clients only hold 10% of the data. Second, increasing the number of clients N will add complexity and degrade performance. However, when N increases from 10 to 20, the drop is only marginal near 1pp. Third, while increasing communication rounds generally provides additional benefits, the gain appears to be marginal after some rounds, as shown in the example. Regardless of these changes, FedX consistently leads to nontrivial improvements over baseline.

4.3   Analysis of the Embedding Space

We next quantitatively examine the embedding space characteristics to see how well FedX distills global knowledge into the local model and encodes data semantic structure. We calculated the angle difference between the normalized embeddings passed by local model f and global model F as a quality metric:

$$\text{Angle}(\mathbf{x}) = \arccos\left(\text{sim}(f(\mathbf{x}), F(\mathbf{x}))\right), \tag{14}$$

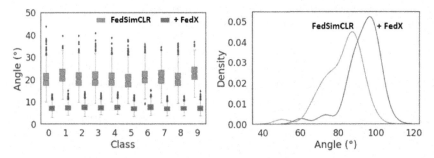

(a) Box plot on local vs. global models   (b) Histogram on inter-class difference

Fig. 6. Embedding analysis of baseline and FedX-enhanced models on CIFAR-10 comparing the angle difference of the embedded features.

where $\mathbf{x}$ is an instance from the test data $\mathcal{D}_{test}$ and sim($\cdot$) is the cosine similarity function. It should be noted that a larger angle represents more significant deviance in the embedding distributions of the two models.

Figure 6a visualizes, for each of the ten classes in CIFAR-10, the angle difference between the embedding of each item between the local model and the global model computed by Eq. 14. Compared to the baseline (FedSimCLR), FedX-enhanced model reports a remarkably lower angle difference between the local and global models. This indicates that the local model can learn the refined knowledge of the global model through knowledge distillation.

When it comes to the embedding space of different class items, it is best to have a large gap. Given $\mathcal{D}_{test}^c$ as a set of instances from class c, we can compute a representative class prototype by averaging embeddings from $\mathcal{D}_{test}^c$ (Eq. 15). Then, the inter-class angle difference can be defined between any pair of class prototypes (Eq. 16). Figure 6b plots the histogram of the inter-class angle difference of every class pair, showing that FedX-enhanced models have larger angles of 93.15° on average than the baseline model of 82.36°. This demonstrates that our model can better discriminate between different class items.

$$\mathbf{z}_c = \frac{1}{|\mathcal{D}_{test}^c|} \sum_{\mathbf{x} \in \mathcal{D}_{test}^c} f(\mathbf{x}) \tag{15}$$

$$\text{Angle}(c_i, c_j) = \arccos(\text{sim}(\mathbf{z}_{c_i}, \mathbf{z}_{c_j})) \tag{16}$$

4.4   Extension to Semi-supervised Settings

Finally, as a practical extension, consider a scenario in which each client has a small set of partially labeled data. This may be a more natural setting in many real-world federated systems [44]. To convert our model to a semi-supervised setting, we first trained it without supervision and then fine-tuned it with an additional classifier on labeled data for an additional 100 epochs. For fine-tuning, an SGD optimizer with a learning rate of 1e–3 was used.

Table 4. Classification accuracy in a semi-supervised setting on CIFAR-10. FedX enhances the baseline performance even with a small set of labels.

Label ratio	FedSimCLR		FedMoCo		FedBYOL		FedProtoCL		FedU	
	Vanilla	FedX	Vanilla	FedX	Vanilla	FedX	Vanilla	FedX	Vanilla	FedX
1%	21.37	**23.33**	23.02	**25.18**	18.10	**21.86**	18.44	18.17	**21.41**	21.23
5%	30.68	**35.86**	34.24	**37.63**	29.77	**34.48**	19.64	**26.66**	32.19	**35.41**
10%	31.14	**39.40**	38.15	**39.32**	32.23	**37.89**	22.90	**27.54**	34.51	**37.51**

Table 4 shows the performance results on CIFAR-10 in the semi-supervised setting with varying label ratios of 1%, 5%, and 10%. As expected, increasing the labeling ratio from 1% to 5% brings an immediate performance gain. FedX-enhanced models outperform most cases in the semi-supervised setting for multiple baselines. Only minor exceptions can be seen with a 1% labeling rate, where our model performs similarly to the baseline. Our model, on the other hand, benefits more quickly from increasing the label ratio and can learn the data representation from distributed local clients.

5   Conclusion

This work presented the first-of-its-kind unsupervised federated learning approach called FedX. We elaborate the local update process of the common federated learning framework and the model does not share any data directly across local clients. Its unique two-sided knowledge distillation can efficiently handle data bias in a non-IID setting while maintaining privacy. It is straightforward and does not require any complex communication strategy.

The substantial performance gain of FedX shows great potential for many future applications. For example, distributed systems with strict data privacy and security requirements, such as learning patterns of new diseases across hospital data or learning tending content in a distributed IoT network, can benefit from our model. Unsupervised learning is facilitated even when local clients lack data labels and contain heterogeneous data. This versatile and robust trait makes unsupervised learning the new frontier in federated systems. We hope that our technique and implementation details will be useful in tackling difficult problems with decentralized data.

Acknowledgements. We thank Seungeon Lee and Xiting Wang for their insights and discussions on our work. This research was supported by the Institute for Basic Science (IBS-R029-C2, IBS-R029-Y4), Microsoft Research Asia, and Potential Individuals Global Training Program (2021-0-01696) by the Ministry of Science and ICT in Korea.

References

1. Bhat, P., Arani, E., Zonooz, B.: Distill on the go: online knowledge distillation in self-supervised learning. In: Proceedings of the IEEE/CVF Conference on Computer Vision and Pattern Recognition, pp. 2678–2687 (2021)
2. Bonawitz, K., et al.: Towards federated learning at scale: system design. Proc. Mach. Learn. Syst. **1**, 374–388 (2019)
3. Chen, T., Kornblith, S., Norouzi, M., Hinton, G.: A simple framework for contrastive learning of visual representations. In: Proceedings of the International Conference on Machine Learning, pp. 1597–1607. PMLR (2020)
4. Chen, X., He, K.: Exploring simple siamese representation learning. In: Proceedings of the IEEE/CVF Conference on Computer Vision and Pattern Recognition, pp. 15750–15758 (2021)
5. Gidaris, S., Singh, P., Komodakis, N.: Unsupervised representation learning by predicting image rotations. In: International Conference on Learning Representations (2018)
6. Grill, J.B., et al.: Bootstrap your own latent-a new approach to self-supervised learning. Adv. Neural. Inf. Process. Syst. **33**, 21271–21284 (2020)
7. Han, S., Park, S., Park, S., Kim, S., Cha, M.: Mitigating embedding and class assignment mismatch in unsupervised image classification. In: Vedaldi, A., Bischof, H., Brox, T., Frahm, J.-M. (eds.) ECCV 2020. LNCS, vol. 12369, pp. 768–784. Springer, Cham (2020). https://doi.org/10.1007/978-3-030-58586-0_45
8. He, K., Fan, H., Wu, Y., Xie, S., Girshick, R.: Momentum contrast for unsupervised visual representation learning. In: Proceedings of the IEEE/CVF Conference on Computer Vision and Pattern Recognition, pp. 9729–9738 (2020)
9. He, K., Zhang, X., Ren, S., Sun, J.: Deep residual learning for image recognition. In: Proceedings of the IEEE/CVF Conference on Computer Vision and Pattern Recognition, pp. 770–778 (2016)
10. Hinton, G., Vinyals, O., Dean, J., et al.: Distilling the knowledge in a neural network. arXiv preprint arXiv:1503.02531 (2015)
11. Hsu, T.M.H., Qi, H., Brown, M.: Measuring the effects of non-identical data distribution for federated visual classification. arXiv preprint arXiv:1909.06335 (2019)
12. Ji, M., Shin, S., Hwang, S., Park, G., Moon, I.C.: Refine myself by teaching myself: feature refinement via self-knowledge distillation. In: Proceedings of the IEEE/CVF Conference on Computer Vision and Pattern Recognition, pp. 10664–10673 (2021)
13. Karimireddy, S.P., Kale, S., Mohri, M., Reddi, S., Stich, S., Suresh, A.T.: Scaffold: stochastic controlled averaging for federated learning. In: Proceedings of the International Conference on Machine Learning, pp. 5132–5143. PMLR (2020)
14. Kim, K., Ji, B., Yoon, D., Hwang, S.: Self-knowledge distillation with progressive refinement of targets. In: Proceedings of the IEEE/CVF International Conference on Computer Vision, pp. 6567–6576 (2021)
15. Komodakis, N., Zagoruyko, S.: Paying more attention to attention: improving the performance of convolutional neural networks via attention transfer. In: Proceedings of the International Conference on Learning Representations (2017)
16. Koratana, A., Kang, D., Bailis, P., Zaharia, M.: Lit: learned intermediate representation training for model compression. In: Proceedings of the International Conference on Machine Learning, pp. 3509–3518. PMLR (2019)
17. Krizhevsky, A.: Learning multiple layers of features from tiny images. Technical report, Citeseer (2009)

18. Li, J., Zhou, P., Xiong, C., Hoi, S.: Prototypical contrastive learning of unsupervised representations. In: Proceedings of the International Conference on Learning Representations (2020)
19. Li, Q., He, B., Song, D.: Model-contrastive federated learning. In: Proceedings of the IEEE/CVF Conference on Computer Vision and Pattern Recognition, pp. 10713–10722 (2021)
20. Li, T., Sahu, A.K., Talwalkar, A., Smith, V.: Federated learning: challenges, methods, and future directions. IEEE Signal Process. Mag. **37**(3), 50–60 (2020)
21. Li, T., Sahu, A.K., Zaheer, M., Sanjabi, M., Talwalkar, A., Smith, V.: Federated optimization in heterogeneous networks. Proc. Mach. Learn. Syst. **2**, 429–450 (2020)
22. Liu, Y., et al.: Fedvision: an online visual object detection platform powered by federated learning. In: Proceedings of the Association for the Advancement of Artificial Intelligence, vol. 34, pp. 13172–13179 (2020)
23. McMahan, B., Moore, E., Ramage, D., Hampson, S., Arcas, B.A.: Communication-efficient learning of deep networks from decentralized data. In: Proceedings of the Artificial Intelligence and Statistics, pp. 1273–1282. PMLR (2017)
24. Mitrovic, J., McWilliams, B., Walker, J.C., Buesing, L.H., Blundell, C.: Representation learning via invariant causal mechanisms. In: International Conference on Learning Representations (2020)
25. Netzer, Y., Wang, T., Coates, A., Bissacco, A., Wu, B., Ng, A.Y.: Reading digits in natural images with unsupervised feature learning (2011)
26. Oord, A.V.D., Li, Y., Vinyals, O.: Representation learning with contrastive predictive coding. arXiv preprint arXiv:1807.03748 (2018)
27. Park, S., et al.: Improving unsupervised image clustering with robust learning. In: Proceedings of the IEEE/CVF Conference on Computer Vision and Pattern Recognition, pp. 12278–12287 (2021)
28. Park, S., Kim, S., Cha, M.: Knowledge sharing via domain adaptation in customs fraud detection. arXiv preprint arXiv:2201.06759 (2022)
29. Park, W., Kim, D., Lu, Y., Cho, M.: Relational knowledge distillation. In: Proceedings of the IEEE/CVF Conference on Computer Vision and Pattern Recognition, pp. 3967–3976 (2019)
30. Radford, A., Metz, L., Chintala, S.: Unsupervised representation learning with deep convolutional generative adversarial networks. In: Proceedings of the International Conference on Learning Representations (2016)
31. Sheller, M.J., Reina, G.A., Edwards, B., Martin, J., Bakas, S.: Multi-institutional deep learning modeling without sharing patient data: a feasibility study on brain tumor segmentation. In: Crimi, A., Bakas, S., Kuijf, H., Keyvan, F., Reyes, M., van Walsum, T. (eds.) BrainLes 2018. LNCS, vol. 11383, pp. 92–104. Springer, Cham (2019). https://doi.org/10.1007/978-3-030-11723-8_9
32. Tejankar, A., Koohpayegani, S.A., Pillai, V., Favaro, P., Pirsiavash, H.: ISD: self-supervised learning by iterative similarity distillation. In: Proceedings of the IEEE/CVF International Conference on Computer Vision, pp. 9609–9618 (2021)
33. Vincent, P., Larochelle, H., Bengio, Y., Manzagol, P.A.: Extracting and composing robust features with denoising autoencoders. In: Proceedings of the 25th International Conference on Machine Learning, pp. 1096–1103 (2008)
34. Voigt, P., von dem Bussche, A.: The EU General Data Protection Regulation (GDPR): A Practical Guide. Springer, Cham (2017). https://doi.org/10.1007/978-3-319-57959-7

35. Wang, H., Yurochkin, M., Sun, Y., Papailiopoulos, D., Khazaeni, Y.: Federated learning with matched averaging. In: Proceedings of the International Conference on Learning Representations (2020)
36. Wang, J., et al.: A field guide to federated optimization. arXiv preprint arXiv:2107.06917 (2021)
37. Wang, J., Liu, Q., Liang, H., Joshi, G., Poor, H.V.: Tackling the objective inconsistency problem in heterogeneous federated optimization. Adv. Neural. Inf. Process. Syst. **33**, 7611–7623 (2020)
38. Wu, Y., Wang, Z., Zeng, D., Li, M., Shi, Y., Hu, J.: Federated contrastive representation learning with feature fusion and neighborhood matching (2021). https:// openreview.net/forum?id=6LNPEcJAGWe
39. Xiao, H., Rasul, K., Vollgraf, R.: Fashion-MNIST: a novel image dataset for benchmarking machine learning algorithms. arXiv preprint arXiv:1708.07747 (2017)
40. Xu, Y.Z., Han, S., Park, S., Cha, M., Li, C.T.: A comprehensive and adversarial approach to self-supervised representation learning. In: 2020 IEEE International Conference on Big Data (Big Data), pp. 709–717. IEEE (2020)
41. Yang, C., An, Z., Cai, L., Xu, Y.: Mutual contrastive learning for visual representation learning. In: Proceedings of the AAAI Conference on Artificial Intelligence, vol. 36, pp. 3045–3053 (2022)
42. Zhang, F., et al.: Federated unsupervised representation learning. arXiv preprint arXiv:2010.08982 (2020)
43. Zhao, Y., Li, M., Lai, L., Suda, N., Civin, D., Chandra, V.: Federated learning with non-IID data. arXiv preprint arXiv:1806.00582 (2018)
44. Zhuang, W., Gan, X., Wen, Y., Zhang, S., Yi, S.: Collaborative unsupervised visual representation learning from decentralized data. In: Proceedings of the IEEE/CVF International Conference on Computer Vision, pp. 4912–4921 (2021)
45. Zhuang, W., et al.: Performance optimization of federated person re-identification via benchmark analysis. In: Proceedings of the 28th ACM International Conference on Multimedia, pp. 955–963 (2020)

W2N: Switching from Weak Supervision to Noisy Supervision for Object Detection

Zitong Huang[1], Yiping Bao[2], Bowen Dong[1], Erjin Zhou[2],
and Wangmeng Zuo[1,3(✉)]

[1] Harbin Institute of Technology, Harbin, China
wmzuo@hit.edu.cn
[2] MEGVII Technology, Beijing, China
[3] Peng Cheng Laboratory, Shenzhen, China

Abstract. Weakly-supervised object detection (WSOD) aims to train an object detector only requiring the image-level annotations. Recently, some works have managed to select the accurate boxes generated from a well-trained WSOD network to supervise a semi-supervised detection framework for better performance. However, these approaches simply divide the training set into labeled and unlabeled sets according to the image-level criteria, such that sufficient mislabeled or wrongly localized box predictions are chosen as pseudo ground-truths, resulting in a sub-optimal solution of detection performance. To overcome this issue, we propose a novel WSOD framework with a new paradigm that switches from weak supervision to noisy supervision (W2N). Generally, with given pseudo ground-truths generated from the well-trained WSOD network, we propose a two-module iterative training algorithm to refine pseudo labels and supervise better object detector progressively. In the localization adaptation module, we propose a regularization loss to reduce the proportion of discriminative parts in original pseudo ground-truths, obtaining better pseudo ground-truths for further training. In the semi-supervised module, we propose a two tasks instance-level split method to select high-quality labels for training a semi-supervised detector. Experimental results on different benchmarks verify the effectiveness of W2N, and our W2N outperforms all existing pure WSOD methods and transfer learning methods. Our code is publicly available at https://github.com/1170300714/w2n_wsod.

Keywords: Weakly supervised learning · Object detection

1 Introduction

Different from fully supervised object detection (FSOD) [10,24] which heavily relys on instance-level bounding box annotations, weakly supervised object detection (WSOD) aims to use only image-level labels as supervision to train an

---

Supplementary Information The online version contains supplementary material available at https://doi.org/10.1007/978-3-031-20056-4_41.

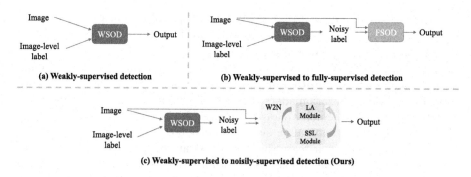

Fig. 1. Training paradigms with three different weakly supervised object detection frameworks: (a) Basic weakly-supervised detection. (b) Weakly-supervised to fully-supervised detection framework. (c) Our W2N framework.

object detector. Compared to the time-consuming instance-level ground-truth annotating process, image-level category labels are easy to obtain relatively, which is more time-saving and economy. Therefore, WSOD has become a hot and meaningful research topic. Existing WSOD methods [2,5,25,30,31] usually follow the multiple instance learning (MIL) framework, which is based on precomputed region proposals [33] and is formulated as a proposals classification task, as shown in Fig. 2(a). However, without accurate bounding box ground-truths, the localization ability of model is severely limited by inaccurate region proposals. Specifically, the WSOD network tends to focus on the discriminative part instead of the whole object for some typical categories (person, cat, dog, etc.). As shown in Fig. 2(b), some works [15,30,31,35,38,41] proposed pseudo ground-truth (PGT) excavation algorithm to generate pseudo ground-truths from prediction by a MIL-based weakly-supervised object detector and use it to deploy a supervised detector, trying to apply the FSOD training paradigm to WSOD task. However, the improvement of detection precision is still limited because some low-quality boxes in the pseudo ground-truths make the WSOD network converge to the sub-optimal solution.

To reduce the negative effect from low-quality pseudo ground-truths, some semi-supervised learning [22,28] approaches have been proposed and applied into weakly supervised object detection tasks. *e.g.*, the recently proposed SoS [29] combines a novel labeled-unlabeled dataset split method as well as the state-of-the-art semi-supervised detection method [22] into the WSOD training to improve the detection performance. The main idea of this method is paying more attention to relatively high-quality pseudo labels and carry out a dynamic label updating for noisy labels to improve the performance of detector progressively.

Inspired by this semi-supervised learning formula, we argue that the pseudo ground-truths can been seen as an inaccurate instance-level bounding box annotation, so it's significant to formulate the multi-phase WSOD problem as a noisy-label object detection task. To this end, we propose our novel weakly supervised object detection framework namely Weakly-supervision to Noisy-supervision (W2N). The noisy labels of the training image set are generated by any well-trained WSOD and then fed into W2N framework for further training procedure. An overview of the contrast between the existing WSOD framework and our framework is presented in Fig. 2(c).

We formulate W2N framework to an iterative refinement process including several **localization adaptation modules** and **semi-supervised learning modules**. In the localization adaptation module, we initialize a fully supervised detector training on the noisy dataset generated by WSOD. During the training phase, we generate a proposal outside each noisy box annotation and then store the decoded boxes of their regression results. Meanwhile, the decoded boxes are used to calculate a regularization loss to optimize the detector. After training, we use this detector to generate pseudo ground-truth again to reduce the proportion of bounding box located at discriminative part and then step into the semi-supervised learning module. And in the semi-supervised learning module, we first split the dataset with pseudo ground-truths into labeled set and a unlabeled set by the hybrid-level dataset split method. And then a semi-supervised object detection framework is performed to train a detector on these two sets. Finally, we execute these two modules iteratively and construct an iterative training framework for better detection performance with only image-level annotations.

Extensive experiments and ablation studies have been conducted to evaluate the effectiveness our proposed method. The experimental results demonstrate that our W2N framework brings huge improvement for all baselines on different benchmark datasets. In conclusion, the contributions of this paper are summarized as follows:

1) We propose a new multi-phase WSOD paradigm, which formulates the multi-phase weakly supervised object detection problem as a noisy-label object detection problem to reduce the negative effect from low-quality pseudo ground-truths.
2) To tackle the noisy-label training problem, we proposed an iterative learning framework including localization adaptation module and semi-supervised learning module, which improves the quality of pseudo ground-truths and the performance of detector.
3) Experimental results on different benchmark datasets show that our proposed method bring a huge improvement for all WSOD baseline and achieve state-of-the-art performance on WSOD tasks.

2   Related Work

2.1   Weakly Supervised Object Detection

Existing WSOD methods [2,27,30,31] are usually based on multiple instance learning (MIL) [7], which formulate this task as a proposal classification problem. Nevertheless, most of the WSOD algorithms tend to recognize the discriminative parts of some objects and optimizing into local-minima, which promote the proposals of several approaches [4,11,25]. Recently, some works [3,8,42] have leveraged transfer learning paradigm with an external fully-annotated source

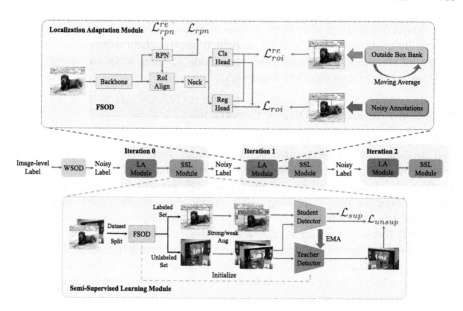

Fig. 2. The illustration of our Weak-to-Noisy (W2N) method, which executes localization adaptation modules (LA module) and semi-supervised learning modules (SSL module) iteratively to generate more accurate pseudo labels and supervise a better object detector. Specifically, the localization adaptation module focus on handling bounding boxes of discriminative parts in $\mathbb{X}_p$ to enlarge the corresponding bounding box and cover more parts of the object, and the semi-supervised learning module leverages the pseudo ground-truth of $\mathbb{X}_p$ with higher detection precision to enhance the final detection performance.

dataset to further improve the detection performance of WSOD. In addition, some work managed to convert weak supervision into other paradigms. For example, W2F [41] combined the weakly-supervised detector and the fully-supervised detector by our pseudo ground-truth mining algorithm. SoS [29] harness all potential supervisory signals in WSOD and split the dataset into labeled and unlabeled images to execute a SSOD framework. To the best of our knowledge, we are the first to formulate the weakly supervised object detection problem as a noisy-label object detection problem. In addition, we explore the noise characteristic of every instance-level annotation and design two learning modules to enhance their accuracy, which is not explored in previous works.

2.2 Learning with Noisy Labels

Some work are engaged in exploring how to train an image classifier with noisy labels. To address this problem, DivideMix [16] used two networks to perform sample selection via a two-component mixture model. Pleiss *et al.* [23] introduced the *Area Under the Margin* statistic which measures the average difference between the logit of a sample's assigned class and its highest non-assigned to separate correctly-labeled data from mislabeled data. Liu *et al.* [20] found that model learns to predict the true labels during the early learning stage but eventually memorizes the wrong labels, which inspires them to leverage the early output of the model. We absorb the inspiration of these work and adapt them to noisy label object detection framework.

2.3 Semi Supervised Object Detection

Semi-supervised learning aims to training networks with both a few of labeled and amount of unlabeled data. In this setting, Jeong *et al.* [12] proposed a consistency-based method, which enforces the predictions of an input image and its flipped version to be consistent. STAC [28] proposes to use a weak data augmentation for model training and a strong data augmentation is used for performing pseudo-label. Liu *et al.* [22] proposed a simple yet effective method, Unbiased Teacher, to address the pseudolabeling bias issue caused by class-imbalance existing in ground-truth labels and the overfitting issue caused by the scarcity of labeled data. Xu.*et al.* [36] proposed a soft teacher mechanism as well as a box jittering approach to improve the overall detection performance with semi-supervised manner.

3 Proposed Method

Definition. Let $\mathbb{X} = \{(\mathbf{I}, \mathbb{P}, \mathbf{y})\}$ denotes the weakly annotated dataset including C individual object categories, where $\mathbf{I}$ means the input image, $\mathbb{P}$ means the set of proposals w.r.t. $\mathbf{I}$, and $\mathbf{y} = [y_1, y_2, \ldots, y_C]^T$ is the image classification label. WSOD targets at learning an object detector g with only image-level supervision.

3.1 Overview

With given dataset $\mathbb{X}$, we first train a weakly supervised object detector g following previous state-of-the-art methods [8,11,25,31] and then adopt the multi-phase training strategy [41] to generate pseudo ground-truth (PGT) on the training images. Now we obtain a new dataset with supervised signal: $\mathbb{X}_p = \{(\mathbf{I}, \{\mathbf{S}\})\}$, $\mathbf{S} = (\mathbf{b}, c)$, where $\mathbf{b} = [x, y, w, h]$ denotes the instance-level bounding box by its center coordinate (x, y), width w, height h, and c denotes the category of this box. We propose $\mathbb{X}_p$ can be regarded as a noisy annotation due to the low accuracy in terms of classification or localization, and the WSOD task can be converted to an object detection task with noisy annotations. To train an object detector on such noisy dataset, we propose a novel training framework namely Weakly-to-Noisy (W2N), which executes localization adaptation modules and semi-supervised learning modules iteratively to generate more accurate pseudo labels and supervise a better object detector. The overall pipeline of W2N is shown as Fig. 2. Specifically, the localization adaptation module focus on handling discriminative parts bounding box in $\mathbb{X}_p$ to enlarge the corresponding bounding box and cover more parts of the object, and the semi-supervised learning module leverages the high-quality part of the pseudo ground-truths in $\mathbb{X}_p$ to enhance the final detection performance of object detector.

| 200 iters | 400 iters | 600 iters | 3000 iters | 5000 iters |

Training process

Fig. 3. An example of regression results of a proposals outside the discriminative part pseudo ground-truth during training. Blue box indicates the real ground-truth, red box indicates the discriminative part pseudo ground-truth and the yellow box indicates the outer box of the red one. Yellow box is regressed to the blue box at early stage of training process, but finally overfits to the red box. (Color figure online)

3.2   Noisy Label Generation

Due to the lack of instance-level supervision during the training procedure of WSOD, the prediction results from the pretrained WSOD network g is not accurate enough [2,31,41], *e.g.*, the wrong prediction in Fig. 4, mislabel or low location accuracy. Following [29,41], we treat the pretrained object detector g as a generator of noisy labels to generate the pseudo ground-truths. We select three WSOD baseline methods to play the role of generators: *OICR+REG* [31], *CASD* [11], and *LBBA* [8]. After training on $\mathbb{X}$, the weakly-supervised detector g inference on training Image **I** and we filter the original predictions, convert it to pseudo ground-truth and obtain $\mathbb{X}_p$ according to the Pseudo Ground-Truth Excavation method proposed by W2F [41].

3.3   Learning Detector with Noisy Annotations

After generating the noisy labels, we feed the labels into the W2N training framework to supervise better object detector progressively. Following [16,20], we propose an training framework W2N, which iterates between localization adaptation module and semi-supervised learning module for several steps. The following subsections will illustrate these two modules in details.

Localization Adaptation Module. In semi-supervised learning module which will be mentioned below, the quality of labeled set will effect the performance of the detector [29]. The more accurate label in labeled set, the higher performance the model achieve. However, we argue that the dataset split can not recognize and filter the discriminative-part noisy labels among several categories (e.g., like the "person" prediction box Fig. 4. The main reason is that too many discriminative-part noisy labels appear in the $\mathbb{X}_p$ such that network tends to overfit them easily during training and then obtain low detection precision.

Fig. 4. An example of noisy label. Notice that the orange box has precise bounding box but mislabeled to bicycle (the ground-truth is motorbike), while the category of red box is correct but its bounding box is incorrect. (Color figure online)

To deal with this problem, we revisit the characteristic of discriminative-part noisy labels and dig out such regular pattern, which is shown in Fig. 3. First, the discriminative-part noisy labels are usually inside the corresponding real ground-truths. Second, if we use the $\mathbb{X}_p$ to train a supervised object detector f, the outer proposals of the discriminative part noisy labels will regress toward the real ground-truth during the early stage during of training phase. But as training continues, it tends to overfit toward the discriminative part noisy labels again. Based on this observation, we refer to the method of using early output in noisy-label image classification task and design a regularization loss to handle the "discriminative part problem".

As mentioned above, with regard to a discriminative part noisy labels, their corresponding outer proposals will regress toward a more accurate location at early stage learning phase. Therefore we store these proposals as the extra supervision to optimize the fully supervised detector f. Specifically, given a pseudo ground-truth box $\mathbf{b} = [x, y, w, h]$ at iteration t during training phase, we randomly generate a outer box extending from $\mathbf{b}$ it by random sampling the transformation δ^t:

$$
\begin{aligned}
\delta_x^t, \delta_y^t &\sim \mathcal{U}(-\alpha, \alpha) \\
\delta_w^t, \delta_h^t &\sim \mathcal{U}(\sqrt{3}, 2)
\end{aligned}
\tag{1}
$$

$\mathcal{U}(-\alpha, \alpha)$ denotes an uniform distribution in the range $[-\alpha, \alpha]$. Then a random outer box $\tilde{\mathbf{b}}^\mathbf{t} = [\tilde{x}^t, \tilde{y}^t, \tilde{w}^t, \tilde{h}^t]$ is obtained by:

$$
[\tilde{x}^t, \tilde{y}^t, \tilde{w}^t, \tilde{h}^t] = [x + \delta_x^t \cdot w, y + \delta_y^t \cdot h, w \cdot \delta_w^t, h \cdot \delta_h^t].
\tag{2}
$$

The outer boxes $\tilde{\mathbf{b}}^\mathbf{t}$ are fed into the object detector and then obtain the decode boxes $\hat{\mathbf{b}}^\mathbf{t}$. To measure the quality of $\hat{\mathbf{b}}^\mathbf{t}$, we only select the boxes whose prediction scores are higher than a threshold τ_{score} while the IoU with corresponding $\mathbf{b}$ are lower than the label assigning threshold τ_{assign} (e.g., 0.5). Finally, to obtain more precision outer boxes, we adopt the moving average strategy to synthesize all $\hat{\mathbf{b}}$ before iteration t and obtain the extra supervision for regularization, shown as Eq. (3):

$$
\hat{\mathbf{b}}_{re}^t = \beta \hat{\mathbf{b}}_{re}^{t-1} + (1 - \beta) \hat{\mathbf{b}}^\mathbf{t},
\tag{3}
$$

where β is the moving average value of bounding box. Then we use $\{(\mathbf{b}, c)\}$ and $\{(\hat{\mathbf{b}}_{re}^{t}, c)\}$ as the supervision signal to optimize detector f, and calculate loss function $\mathcal{L}_{rpn}$, $\mathcal{L}_{roi}$, $\mathcal{L}_{rpn}^{re}$ and $\mathcal{L}_{roi}^{re}$, where $\mathcal{L}_{rpn}$ and $\mathcal{L}_{roi}$ indicate the loss supervised with noisy labels $\{(\mathbf{b}, c)\}$ of RPN and RoI head while $\mathcal{L}_{rpn}^{re}$ and $\mathcal{L}_{roi}^{re}$ is calculated with extra supervision $\{(\hat{\mathbf{b}}_{re}^{t}, c)\}$ as regularization terms. Each of them is the combination of Smooth L1 Loss (regression loss) and Cross-Entropy Loss (classification loss), which are the same formulation as [24]. The whole loss function $\mathcal{L}_{fsod}$ for optimization f is shown as Eq. (4):

$$\mathcal{L}_{fsod} = \mathcal{L}_{rpn} + \mathcal{L}_{roi} + \lambda_{re}(\mathcal{L}_{rpn}^{re} + \mathcal{L}_{roi}^{re}) \tag{4}$$

where λ_{re} indicates the regularization weight.

After the process above, we use the well-trained detector f to re-generate the pseudo ground-truths on the training set, which can reduce the proportion of low-quality pseudo ground-truths and improve the performance of the next semi-supervised learning module.

Semi-supervised Learning Module. In this module, we design a hybrid-level dataset split algorithm as well as a pseudo-label based semi-supervised training algorithm.

Dataset split method is crucial for turning noisy-label learning into semi-supervised approach. A basic solution is that splitting the whole dataset according to the training loss of each image. The training data with small loss is regarded as the sample from labeled set, vise versa. SoS [29] proposed the "image-level split method", which accumulated the losses from the RPN module and that from the detection head and then obtained the image-level split loss function. Given image $\mathbf{I}$, the image-level split loss $\mathcal{L}_{split}(\mathbf{I})$ is defined as Eq. (5):

$$\mathcal{L}_{split}(\mathbf{I}) = \underset{i}{\text{avg}}(\mathcal{L}_{split}^{rpn}(R_i, t_i)) + \underset{j}{\text{avg}}(\mathcal{L}_{split}^{roi}(R_j, t_j)). \tag{5}$$

And the $\mathcal{L}_{split}^{rpn}$ and $\mathcal{L}_{split}^{roi}$ are shown as Eq. (6) and (7):

$$\mathcal{L}_{split}^{rpn}(R_i, t_i) = \mathcal{L}_{rpn}^{cls}(R_i, t_i) + \mathcal{L}_{rpn}^{reg}(R_i, t_i), \tag{6}$$

$$\mathcal{L}_{split}^{roi}(R_j, t_j) = \mathcal{L}_{roi}^{cls}(R_j, t_j) + \mathcal{L}_{roi}^{reg}(R_j, t_j), \tag{7}$$

where R_i is the i-th foreground RoI, t_i indicates the assigned target label of R_i, $\mathcal{L}_{rpn}$ and $\mathcal{L}_{roi}$ are RPN and RoI head losses, and cls and reg stand for classification task and box regression task, respectively. $\mathcal{L}_*^{cls}$ is Cross-Entropy Loss and $\mathcal{L}_*^{reg}$ is Smooth L1 Loss. And the $\text{avg}(\cdot)$ means the mean average operation. Then, we rank all instances with their $\mathcal{L}_{split}(\mathbf{I})$ by the ascending order, keeping the number of p percent of image annotations with small loss value to be the labeled set. However, we find that a training image may contain multiple instance labels, and the accurate labels and noisy labels often appear at the same time. Therefore, we proposed the second split method namely "instance-level split method", in which every instance is be seen to the smallest split unit. And the aggregated loss in Eq. (5) will be modified to Eq. (8):

$$\mathcal{L}_{split}(\mathbf{S}) = \underset{i}{\mathrm{avg}}(\mathcal{L}_{split}^{rpn}(R_i, t_i)) + \underset{j}{\mathrm{avg}}(\mathcal{L}_{split}^{roi}(R_j, t_j)), \tag{8}$$

where $\mathbf{S}$ indicates to one instance label and $\mathrm{avg}(\cdot)$ means the mean average operation. Then we rank all instances according to the $\mathcal{L}_{split}(\mathbf{S})$ by the ascending order, and then keep the top p percent of the instance labels with small loss value to be the labeled set $\mathbb{X}_l = \{(\mathbf{I}_l, \{\mathbf{S}_l\})\}$, and the other instances are keeping unlabeled.

In SoS [29], the labeled set are used for supervising the training for classification and regression sub-tasks. However, we can not make sure that each pseudo label is correct in terms of both classification and localization. As shown in Fig. 4, a box with high location information may be mislabeled of category while a box with correct category may cover part of an object. From this perspective, we introduce two tags $\lambda_{cls}, \lambda_{reg}$ for one instance label indicating their confidence for two sub-task respectively. The final formulation of labeled set is modified to $\mathbb{X}_l = \{(\mathbf{I}_l, \{(\mathbf{S}_l, \lambda_{cls}, \lambda_{reg})\})\}$, where $\lambda_{cls}, \lambda_{reg} \in \{0, 1\}, \lambda_{cls} + \lambda_{reg} \neq 0$. $\lambda_{cls} = 1$ means the category label of this instance is correct, while $\lambda_{cls} = 0$ means not, similar meaning for λ_{reg}. To decide the value of $\lambda_{cls}, \lambda_{reg}$, we propose "two tasks instance-level split" method, which is shown as Eq. (9):

$$\begin{aligned}
\mathcal{L}_{split}^{cls}(\mathbf{S}) &= \underset{i}{\mathrm{avg}}(\mathcal{L}_{rpn}^{cls}(R_i, t_i)) + \underset{j}{\mathrm{avg}}(\mathcal{L}_{roi}^{cls}(R_j, t_j)), \\
\mathcal{L}_{split}^{reg}(\mathbf{S}) &= \underset{i}{\mathrm{avg}}(\mathcal{L}_{rpn}^{reg}(R_i, t_i)) + \underset{j}{\mathrm{avg}}(\mathcal{L}_{roi}^{reg}(R_j, t_j)),
\end{aligned} \tag{9}$$

where $\mathcal{L}_{split}^{cls}(\mathbf{S})$ only accumulates the classification loss for each foreground proposal while $\mathcal{L}_{split}^{reg}(\mathbf{S})$ only accumulates the regressions loss for each foreground proposal. Then, we rank the instance according to $\mathcal{L}_{split}^{cls}(\mathbf{S})$ and $\mathcal{L}_{split}^{reg}(\mathbf{S})$ by the ascending order, respectively. Finally, we set $\lambda_{cls} = 1$ for the top p percent of the instances in terms of $\mathcal{L}_{split}^{cls}(\mathbf{S})$ and set $\lambda_{reg} = 1$ for the top p percent of the instances in terms of $\mathcal{L}_{split}^{reg}(\mathbf{S})$. In Sect. 4, we will discuss the effect of three data split proposed above.

After splitting the noisy dataset, we introduce a novel semi-supervised object detection method for weakly-to-noisy label training. The difference between [22] and our semi-supervised detection method is two-fold. First, we use labeled set $\mathbb{X}_l$ as labeled set to optimize model with the supervised loss $\mathcal{L}_{sup}$. Combining with our *two tasks instance-level split* method, we modify the origin supervised loss function with adding the value of $(\lambda_{cls}, \lambda_{reg})$. Specifically, $\mathcal{L}_{sup}$ is shown as Eq. (10):

$$\begin{aligned}
\mathcal{L}_{sup}(\mathbf{I}) = &\underset{i}{\mathrm{avg}}(\lambda_{cls}^{t_i}\mathcal{L}_{rpn}^{cls}(R_i, t_i) + \lambda_{reg}^{t_i}\mathcal{L}_{rpn}^{reg}(R_i, t_i)) \\
&+ \underset{j}{\mathrm{avg}}(\lambda_{cls}^{t_j}\mathcal{L}_{roi}^{cls}(R_j, t_j) + \lambda_{reg}^{t_j}\mathcal{L}_{roi}^{reg}(R_j, t_j)) \\
&+ \underset{k}{\mathrm{avg}}(\mathcal{L}_{bg}(R_k)),
\end{aligned} \tag{10}$$

where $\mathcal{L}_{bg}(R_i)$ indicates the background loss of corresponding proposals. Particularly, only the target label of which $\lambda_{cls}^{t_i} = 1$ ($\lambda_{reg}^{t_i} = 1$) can contribute to $\mathcal{L}_{sup}$ in classification (regression) task. The loss function used on the labeled set is shown as Eq. (11):

$$\mathcal{L}_{sup} = \frac{1}{N_l} \sum_i \mathcal{L}_{sup}(\mathbf{I}_i), \tag{11}$$

where N_l is the number of image in $\mathbb{X}_l$. Second, the regression loss of the unlabeled data are not adopted in the whole training process of [22]. In our method we adopt the box jittering strategy proposed by [36] and add the regression loss of the unlabeled data in origin $\mathcal{L}_{unsup}$ [22]. Finally, the whole loss function of SSOD module is shown as Eq. (12):

$$\mathcal{L}_{ssod} = \mathcal{L}_{sup} + \lambda_u \mathcal{L}_{unsup}, \tag{12}$$

where λ_u is the weight of $\mathcal{L}_{unsup}$.

Iterative Training Framework. Finally, we propose the two-phase iterative training framework based on these two modules. The whole training process of our framework is given in Algorithm 1, which is summarized as follows. Specifically, the first phase is the conventional weakly-supervised object detection pre-training module, we train a WSOD network g and then generated the pseudo ground-truths for each training image in the training dataset $\mathbb{X}_p^0$. The second phase is our proposed weakly-to-noisy training framework. Given the pseudo ground-truths, we first execute the localization adaptation module to initialize a fully-supervised detector f_t and then refine $\mathbb{X}_p^t$ to reduce the proportion of the discriminative part. Then we excute the two tasks instance-level split method and split the whole training set $\mathbb{X}_p^t$ into labeled set and unlabeled set. With the splitted training sets, we execute the semi-supervised object detection module to supervise a better object detector f_t'. Generally, we use f_t' to update the $\mathbb{X}_p^t$ to $\mathbb{X}_p^{t+1}$ and then perform these two modules iteratively for T times. And finally, the last object detector f_T' with corresponding parameters θ_f^T is saved for usage.

4   Experiments

4.1   Experiment Settings

Datasets. Following [25,32,42], we evaluate our method on four benchmarks: PASCAL VOC 2007, PASCAL VOC 2012 [9], MS-COCO [19], and ILSVRC 2013 [6] detection dataset. **Evaluation Metrics.** We use mean average precision (mAP) to evaluate the detection performance over categories, and CorLoc to measure the localization accuracy.

Algorithm 1. Weak Supervision to Noisy Supervision for Object Detection

---

Input: Iteration number T, weakly annotated dataset $\mathbb{X}$;
Output: An updated detector $f_T^{'}$;
1: Train the weakly supervised detector g on $\mathbb{X}$;
2: Obtain the noisy annotations dataset $\mathbb{X}_p^0$ by pretrained weakly supervised detector g;
3: **for** $t = 0...T - 1$ **do**
4:     **Localization Adaptation module:**
5:         Initialize an object detector f_t on $\mathbb{X}_p^t$;
6:         Refine $\mathbb{X}_p^t$ by f_t;
7:     **Semi-Supervised Learning module:**
8:         Split $\mathbb{X}_p^t$ into labeled set and unlabeled set by f_t;
9:         Execute the semi-supervised object detection approach to optimize f_t to $f_t^{'}$;
10:        Update the $\mathbb{X}_p^t$ to $\mathbb{X}_p^{t+1}$ by $f_t^{'}$;

4.2   Comparison with State-of-the-Arts

We *state the implementation details in the suppl.* And here we compare our method with several state-of-the-art WSOD approaches in terms of mAP and CorLoc on PASCAL VOC 2007 [9] reported by Table 1 and Table 2. Our all results are obtained with single-scale testing approach. Based on these results, we obtain the following observations: First, our W2N framework outperforms all WSOD baselines in terms of both mAP and CorLoc. Specifically, on PASCAL VOC 2007 dataset, it outperforms OICR+REG by 8.7% mAP and 3.8% CorLoc, outperforms CASD by 11.4% mAP and 12.6% CorLoc, and outperforms LBBA by 9.5% mAP and 10.8% CorLoc. Performance on PASCAL VOC 2012 also demonstrates favorable performance improvement.

Second, our W2N outperforms all of the state-of-the-art WSOD methods as well as transfer learning based methods. Specifically, CASD+W2N achieves 65.4% mAP on PASCAL VOC 2007 test set, which outperforms CASD by 8.6% mAP and outperforms CaT5 by 1.9% mAP. Moreover, LBBA+W2N obtains 68.6% mAP and 83.4% CorLoc, which achieves a new state-of-the-arts for WSOD problem and bridges the performance gap with fully supervised methods (Faster R-CNN) [24]. In the supplementary we will show more results on other datasets and give analyze for comparison between [29] and ours.

4.3   Ablation Study

In this section, we discuss the effect of key components of W2N on PASCAL VOC 2007 dataset [9].

Effect of Two Modules. Table 3 shows the ablation study of each module on LBBA baseline. Simply re-training Faster R-CNN(FRCNN*) with pseudo GT only brings 0.3% mAP gain. By introducing localization adaption and semi-supervised learning separately, these improvements respectively outperform the baseline by 1.2% and 7.0% in terms of mAP. Specifically, as illustrated in Fig. 5,

Table 1. Comparison of our method on PASCAL VOC 2007 test set to state-of-the-art WSOD methods in terms of mAP (%), where [+] means the results with multi-scale testing.

Methods	Aero	Bike	Bird	Boat	Bottle	Bus	Car	Cat	Chair	Cow	Table	Dog	Horse	Motor	Person	Plant	Sheep	Sofa	Train	TV	AP
Pure WSOD:																					
WSDDN [2]	39.4	50.1	31.5	16.3	12.6	64.5	42.8	42.6	10.1	35.7	24.9	38.2	34.4	55.6	9.4	14.7	30.2	40.7	54.7	46.9	34.8
OICR[+] [31]	58.0	62.4	31.1	19.4	13.0	65.1	62.2	28.4	24.8	44.7	30.6	25.3	37.8	65.5	15.7	24.1	41.7	46.9	64.3	62.6	41.2
PCL[+] [30]	54.4	69.0	39.3	19.2	15.7	62.9	64.4	30.0	25.1	52.5	44.4	19.6	39.3	67.7	17.8	22.9	46.6	57.5	58.6	63.0	43.5
Yang et al.[+] [38]	57.6	70.8	50.7	28.3	27.2	72.5	69.1	65.0	26.9	64.5	47.4	47.7	53.5	66.9	13.7	29.3	56.0	54.9	63.4	65.2	51.5
C-MIDN[+] [37]	53.3	71.5	49.8	26.1	20.3	70.3	69.9	68.3	28.7	65.3	45.1	62.3	58.0	71.2	20.0	27.5	54.9	54.9	69.4	63.5	52.6
Arun et al. [1]	66.7	69.5	52.8	31.4	24.7	74.5	74.1	67.3	14.6	53.0	46.1	52.9	69.9	70.8	18.5	28.4	54.6	60.7	67.1	60.4	52.9
WSOD2[+] [40]	65.1	64.8	57.2	39.2	24.3	69.8	66.2	61.0	29.8	64.6	42.5	60.1	71.2	70.7	21.9	28.1	58.6	59.7	52.2	64.8	53.6
GradingNet-C-MIL [13]	-	-	-	-	-	-	-	-	-	-	-	-	-	-	-	-	-	-	-	-	54.3
MIST-Full [25]	68.8	77.7	57.0	27.7	28.9	69.1	74.5	67.0	32.1	73.2	48.1	45.2	54.4	73.7	35.0	29.3	64.1	53.8	65.3	65.2	54.9
IM-CFB[+] [39]	63.3	77.5	48.3	36.0	32.6	70.8	71.9	73.1	29.1	68.7	47.1	69.4	56.6	70.9	22.8	24.8	56.0	59.8	73.2	64.6	55.8
CASD [11]	-	-	-	-	-	-	-	-	-	-	-	-	-	-	-	-	-	-	-	-	56.8
SoS [29]	72.9	79.4	59.6	20.4	49.8	81.2	82.9	84.0	31.5	76.6	57.4	60.7	74.7	75.1	33.0	34.3	66.3	61.1	80.6	71.8	62.7
SoS[+] [29]	77.9	81.2	58.9	26.7	54.3	82.5	84.0	83.5	36.3	76.5	57.5	58.4	78.5	78.6	33.8	37.4	64.0	63.4	81.5	74.0	64.4
OICR+REG (reproduce)	54.0	61.9	43.9	22.6	31.7	73.8	65.1	60.6	14.4	68.0	17.0	48.8	58.3	69.9	12.8	22.0	53.9	53.6	69.7	60.4	48.3
CASD (reproduce)	68.8	67.2	53.9	38.2	21.5	70.4	69.7	68.9	23.6	66.3	48.8	62.3	56.4	70.6	17.3	24.9	55.9	58.9	66.0	69.1	54.0
OICR+REG+W2N (Ours)	71.0	74.2	60.8	28.8	44.6	78.0	72.6	80.3	16.7	74.3	24.3	58.2	64.6	75.1	13.3	29.9	60.3	65.3	80.1	67.6	**57.0(+8.7)**
CASD+W2N (Ours)	74.0	81.7	71.2	48.9	51.0	78.6	82.3	83.5	29.1	76.9	51.5	82.1	76.9	79.1	28.5	34.3	65.0	64.2	75.2	74.8	**65.4(+11.4)**
WSOD with transfer learning:																					
MSD-Ens[+] [18]	70.5	69.2	53.3	43.7	25.4	68.9	68.7	56.9	18.4	64.2	15.3	72.0	74.4	65.2	15.4	25.1	53.6	54.4	45.6	61.4	51.1
OICR+UBBR [14]	59.7	44.8	54.0	36.1	29.3	72.1	67.4	70.7	23.5	63.8	31.5	61.5	63.7	61.9	37.9	15.4	55.1	57.4	69.9	63.6	52.0
LBBA[+] [8]	70.3	72.3	48.7	38.7	30.4	74.3	76.6	69.1	33.4	68.2	50.5	67.0	49.0	73.6	24.5	27.4	63.1	58.9	66.0	69.2	56.6
Zhong et al. (R50-C4)[+] [42]	64.8	50.7	65.5	45.3	46.4	75.7	74.0	80.1	31.3	77.0	26.2	79.3	74.8	66.5	57.9	11.5	68.2	59.0	74.7	65.5	59.7
TraMaS[+] [21]	68.6	61.1	69.6	48.1	49.9	76.3	77.8	80.9	34.9	77.0	31.1	80.9	78.5	66.3	64.0	19.1	69.1	62.3	74.4	69.1	62.9
CaTs [3]	74.0	70.7	60.0	31.1	50.0	75.9	82.0	70.7	32.8	74.3	69.5	70.2	69.5	77.0	37.5	45.8	67.0	61.1	72.4	68.0	63.0
LBBA (reproduce)	70.2	75.5	49.2	41.9	30.5	80.5	78.2	72.8	36.4	73.8	52.3	67.0	46.4	76.2	34.6	29.4	67.9	66.6	68.3	74.1	59.1
LBBA+W2N (Ours)	71.8	83.0	69.9	50.3	54.5	79.0	83.9	83.9	39.4	79.2	52.9	82.2	83.6	79.2	62.6	32.7	68.5	66.1	75.8	74.5	**68.6(+9.5)**
Upper bounds:																					
Faster R-CNN (Res50+FPN) [24]	82.8	84.2	75.2	62.4	67.0	81.4	87.1	82.6	57.3	82.5	64.9	83.0	84.0	82.7	83.7	54.0	76.1	73.4	81.8	76.1	**76.1**

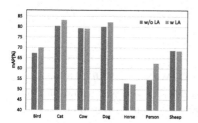

Fig. 5. Effect of location adaption module on animal categories and person category with LBBA+W2N.

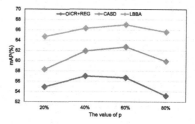

Fig. 6. Effect of different size of the labeled set on VOC 2007 for different WSOD+W2Ns.

W2N+LBBA with location adaption module improves the detection performance of categories which suffer from the discriminative part problem, especially for person category. Furthermore, our full method combining these two modules can further improve the detection performance to 67.0% mAP. More ablation study about effect of two modules can be found in the suppl.

Effect of Iterative Training. Generally, more training iterations means better predictions. Thus we analyze the effect of training iteration T. Table 4 shows the performance of W2N with different iteration numbers T using three different methods, respectively. Generally, as the T increases, the performance first increase and then begin to oscillate near the highest point. And the highest performance for all baseline are outperforming beyond 1.5% mAP than the settings

Table 2. Comparison of our method on PASCAL VOC 2007 trainval set to state-of-the-art WSOD methods in terms of CorLoc (%), where $^+$ means the results with multi-scale testing.

Methods	Aero	Bike	Bird	Boat	Bottle	Bus	Car	Cat	Chair	Cow	Table	Dog	Horse	Motor	Person	Plant	Sheep	Sofa	Train	TV	CorLoc
Pure WSOD:																					
WSDDN [2]	65.1	58.8	58.5	33.1	39.8	68.3	60.2	59.6	34.8	64.5	30.5	43.0	56.8	82.4	25.5	41.6	61.5	55.9	65.9	63.7	53.5
OICR+ [31]	81.7	80.4	48.7	49.5	32.8	81.7	85.4	40.1	40.6	79.5	35.7	33.7	60.5	88.8	21.8	57.9	76.3	59.9	75.3	81.4	60.6
PCL+ [30]	79.6	85.5	62.2	47.9	37.0	83.8	83.4	43.0	38.3	80.1	50.6	30.9	57.8	90.8	27.0	58.2	75.3	68.5	75.7	78.9	62.7
Li+ [17]	85.0	83.9	58.9	59.6	43.1	79.7	85.2	77.9	31.3	78.1	50.6	75.6	76.2	88.4	49.7	56.4	73.2	62.6	77.2	79.9	68.6
C-MIL+ [34]	-	-	-	-	-	-	-	-	-	-	-	-	-	-	-	-	-	-	-	-	65.0
Yang et al.+ [38]	80.0	83.9	74.2	53.2	48.5	82.7	86.2	69.5	39.3	82.9	53.6	61.4	72.4	91.2	22.4	57.5	83.5	64.8	75.7	77.1	68.0
MIST (Full)+ [25]	87.5	82.4	76.0	58.0	44.7	82.2	87.5	71.2	49.1	81.5	51.7	53.3	71.4	92.8	38.2	52.8	79.4	61.0	78.3	76.0	68.8
WSOD2+ [40]	87.1	80.0	74.8	60.1	36.6	79.2	83.8	70.6	43.5	88.4	46.0	74.7	87.4	90.8	44.2	52.4	81.4	61.8	67.7	79.9	69.5
Arun et al. [1]	88.6	86.3	71.8	53.4	51.2	87.6	89.0	65.3	33.2	86.6	58.8	65.9	87.7	93.3	30.9	58.9	83.4	67.8	78.7	80.2	70.9
GradingNet-C-MIL [13]	-	-	-	-	-	-	-	-	-	-	-	-	-	-	-	-	-	-	-	-	72.1
IM-CFB+ [39]	-	-	-	-	-	-	-	-	-	-	-	-	-	-	-	-	-	-	-	-	72.2
OICR+REG (reproduce)	91.6	78.3	62.6	46.0	44.8	86.4	87.7	80.3	34.4	87.1	30.1	69.4	81.1	90.8	31.3	44.8	76.0	76.1	83.1	60.5	67.4
CASD (reproduce)	68.8	67.2	53.9	38.2	21.5	70.4	69.7	68.9	23.6	66.3	48.8	62.3	56.4	70.6	17.3	24.9	55.9	58.9	66.0	69.1	68.5
OICR+REG+W2N (Ours)	87.4	86.0	69.7	50.8	59.8	80.8	88.4	86.9	37.5	86.5	26.0	69.8	84.0	95.1	31.6	57.6	78.12	75.6	85.8	77.3	**71.2(+3.8)**
CASD+W2N (Ours)	92.0	90.5	82.4	71.3	73.0	85.5	94.7	89.0	46.3	89.4	63.5	87.9	92.7	96.7	47.1	70.2	84.4	75.1	82.4	87.5	**80.1(+12.6)**
WSOD with transfer learning:																					
OICR+UBBR [14]	47.9	18.9	63.1	39.7	10.2	62.3	69.3	61.0	27.0	79.0	24.5	67.9	79.1	49.7	28.6	12.8	79.4	40.6	61.6	28.4	47.6
WSLAT-Ens [26]	78.6	63.4	66.4	56.4	19.7	82.3	74.8	69.1	22.5	72.3	31.0	63.0	74.9	78.4	48.6	29.4	64.6	36.2	75.9	69.5	58.8
MSD-Ens+ [18]	89.2	75.7	75.1	66.5	58.8	78.2	88.9	66.9	28.2	86.3	29.7	83.5	83.3	92.8	23.7	40.3	85.6	48.9	70.3	68.1	66.8
Zhong et al.(R50-C4)+ [42]	87.5	64.7	87.4	69.7	67.9	86.3	88.8	88.1	44.4	93.8	31.9	89.1	92.9	86.3	71.5	22.7	94.8	56.5	88.2	76.3	74.4
LBBA+ [8]	93.3	90.6	71.8	69.2	59.5	90.9	94.4	78.5	55.4	96.6	51.0	82.3	72.5	93.2	48.5	52.8	100.0	66.7	78.3	87.5	76.7
TraMaS+ [21]	90.6	67.4	89.7	70.5	72.8	86.6	91.7	89.8	51.0	96.1	34.0	93.7	94.8	90.3	73.0	26.5	95.2	68.2	89.8	83.1	77.7
CaTs [3]	-	-	-	-	-	-	-	-	-	-	-	-	-	-	-	-	-	-	-	-	80.3
LBBA (reproduce)	86.9	84.5	74.6	65.6	55.1	85.4	86.8	84.4	42.5	88.0	45.0	83.3	82.3	88.6	47.6	49.1	88.3	50.8	81.1	84.3	72.7
LBBA+W2N (Ours)	89.5	93.4	83.9	70.2	73.4	87.1	94.5	92.0	58.9	95.7	64.0	91.0	94.8	93.5	80.7	64.1	91.7	78.2	84.3	89.1	**83.5(+10.8)**
Upper bounds:																					
Faster R-CNN (Res50+FPN) [24]	91.7	93.7	92.6	75.0	84.0	95.4	95.3	93.2	76.5	94.5	86.9	92.3	96.0	93.2	93.0	76.8	94.9	89.2	85.7	90.4	**89.5**

Table 3. Effect of two modules on VOC 2007.

WSOD	FRCNN*	LA	SSL	ITER	mAP
LBBA					59.1
	✓				59.4
		✓			60.3
			✓		66.1
		✓	✓		67.0
		✓	✓	✓	**68.6**

Table 4. The mAP results of our W2N with different iteration times T on Pascal VOC 2007 dataset.

Methods	0	1	2	3	4
OICR+REG+W2N	56.8	**57.0**	56.8	56.8	56.9
CASD+W2N	62.7	64.5	**65.4**	65.4	65.2
LBBA+W2N	67	67.9	**68.6**	68.4	68.4

of $T = 0$, which proves that the iterative training strategy is effective for further improving detection performance. In addition, for LBBA and CASD, it reaches the highest performance when $T = 2$; while for OICR+REG, $T = 1$ is the best optimal solution. This result indicates that the iterative training process will converge quickly on relative small T, which reveals the high efficiency of W2N.

Effect of Hybrid-Level Dataset Split. We combined three different WSOD methods with three different split methods and then obtained nine different experiment settings. We conducted experiments on all of the settings at iteration 0 and demonstrate the results in Table 5. Experimental results prove that the two tasks instance-level split method achieves the best performance among them, higher than the instance-level split method. In addition, both two tasks instance-level split method and instance-level split method outperform the image-level

Table 5. Comparisons of different dataset split methods on VOC 2007.

Methods	Image-level	Instance-level	Two tasks instance-level	mAP
OICR+REG+W2N	✓			55.4
OICR+REG+W2N		✓		56.8
OICR+REG+W2N			✓	**56.8**
CASD+W2N	✓			61.9
CASD+W2N		✓		62.6
CASD+W2N			✓	**62.7**
LBBA+W2N	✓			65.4
LBBA+W2N		✓		66.8
LBBA+W2N			✓	**67.0**

split method more than about 1.5% mAP, which proves that it is more effective and reasonable to treat the instance-level as the smallest division unit.

Proportion of Clean Split p. The proportion of clean split p determines the quality of pseudo labels, therefore here we explore the effect of different p. We deploy varying p to decide the size of labeled set for three different WSOD methods at iteration 0. Figure 6 shows that for LBBA and CASD, $p = 60\%$ is the best choice, while for OICR+REG, $p = 40\%$ is better. Generally, when p is small, as p increases, the performance of W2Ns improves, while p further increases, the performance of W2Ns begin to drop significantly. This is reasonable that too small leads to a small size of high quality pseudo label in labeled set, which is not conducive to model learning. While too large clean size will involve more noisy labels. Therefore, we propose that a moderate size is beneficial for training.

5   Conclusion

In this paper, we propose a weakly supervised object detection method namely Weakly-supervision to Noisy-supervision (W2N). We treat the pseudo labels generated by the pretrained weakly detector as noisy labels and propose an iterative training procedure, which includes the localization adaptation module and the semi-supervised learning module. The localization adaptation module refines the original pseudo ground-truths to reduce the proportion of low-quality bounding boxes. The semi-supervised learning module split the dataset with pseudo ground-truths into a high-quality labeled set as well as an unlabeled set and supervises the object detector with a well-designed semi-supervised object detection manner with these two datasets. Extensive experiments on different datasets show that our proposed method performs favorably against other state-of-the-art WSOD methods.

Acknowledgement. This work was supported in part by the National Key R&D Program of China under Grant No. 2021ZD0112100, and the Major Key Project of

PCL under Grant No. PCL2021A12. This work was done when Zitong was an intern at MEGVII Tech.

References

1. Arun, A., Jawahar, C., Kumar, M.P.: Dissimilarity coefficient based weakly supervised object detection. In: 2019 IEEE/CVF Conference on Computer Vision and Pattern Recognition (CVPR), June 2019. https://doi.org/10.1109/cvpr.2019.00966
2. Bilen, H., Vedaldi, A.: Weakly supervised deep detection networks. In: Proceedings of the IEEE Conference on Computer Vision and Pattern Recognition, pp. 2846–2854 (2016)
3. Cao, T., Du, L., Zhang, X., Chen, S., Zhang, Y., Wang, Y.F.: Cat: weakly supervised object detection with category transfer. In: Proceedings of the IEEE/CVF International Conference on Computer Vision (ICCV), pp. 3070–3079, October 2021
4. Chen, Z., Fu, Z., Jiang, R., Chen, Y., Hua, X.: SLV: spatial likelihood voting for weakly supervised object detection. In: 2020 IEEE/CVF Conference on Computer Vision and Pattern Recognition (CVPR), pp. 12992–13001 (2020)
5. Cinbis, R.G., Verbeek, J., Schmid, C.: Weakly supervised object localization with multi-fold multiple instance learning. IEEE Trans. Pattern Anal. Mach. Intell. **39**(1), 189–203 (2016)
6. Deng, J., Dong, W., Socher, R., Li, L.J., Li, K., Fei-Fei, L.: Imagenet: a large-scale hierarchical image database. In: 2009 IEEE Conference on Computer Vision and Pattern Recognition, pp. 248–255. IEEE (2009)
7. Dietterich, T.G., Lathrop, R.H., Lozano-Pérez, T.: Solving the multiple instance problem with axis-parallel rectangles. Artif. Intell. **89**, 31–71 (1997)
8. Dong, B., Huang, Z., Guo, Y., Wang, Q., Niu, Z., Zuo, W.: Boosting weakly supervised object detection via learning bounding box adjusters. In: Proceedings of the IEEE/CVF International Conference on Computer Vision, pp. 2876–2885 (2021)
9. Everingham, M., Van Gool, L., Williams, C.K., Winn, J., Zisserman, A.: The pascal visual object classes (VOC) challenge. Int. J. Comput. Vision **88**(2), 303–338 (2010)
10. Girshick, R.: Fast R-CNN. In: International Conference on Computer Vision (ICCV) (2015)
11. Huang, Z., Zou, Y., Bhagavatula, V., Huang, D.: Comprehensive attention self-distillation for weakly-supervised object detection. In: NeurIPS (2020)
12. Jeong, J., Lee, S., Kim, J., Kwak, N.: Consistency-based semi-supervised learning for object detection. Adv. Neural. Inf. Process. Syst. **32**, 10759–10768 (2019)
13. Jia, Q., Wei, S., Ruan, T., Zhao, Y., Zhao, Y.: Gradingnet: towards providing reliable supervisions for weakly supervised object detection by grading the box candidates. In: Proceedings of the AAAI Conference on Artificial Intelligence, vol. 35, no. 2, pp. 1682–1690, May 2021. https://ojs.aaai.org/index.php/AAAI/article/view/16261
14. Lee, S., Kwak, S., Cho, M.: Universal bounding box regression and its applications. In: Jawahar, C.V., Li, H., Mori, G., Schindler, K. (eds.) ACCV 2018. LNCS, vol. 11366, pp. 373–387. Springer, Cham (2019). https://doi.org/10.1007/978-3-030-20876-9_24
15. Li, D., Huang, J.B., Li, Y., Wang, S., Yang, M.H.: Weakly supervised object localization with progressive domain adaptation. In: Proceedings of the IEEE Conference on Computer Vision and Pattern Recognition, pp. 3512–3520 (2016)

16. Li, J., Socher, R., Hoi, S.C.: Dividemix: learning with noisy labels as semi-supervised learning. In: International Conference on Learning Representations (2019)
17. Li, X., Kan, M., Shan, S., Chen, X.: Weakly supervised object detection with segmentation collaboration. In: Proceedings of the IEEE/CVF International Conference on Computer Vision (ICCV), October 2019
18. Li, Y., Zhang, J., Zhang, J., Huang, K.: Mixed supervised object detection with robust objectness transfer. IEEE Trans. Pattern Anal. Mach. Intell. **41**(3), 639–653 (2018). https://doi.org/10.1109/TPAMI.2018.2810288
19. Lin, T.-Y., et al.: Microsoft COCO: common objects in context. In: Fleet, D., Pajdla, T., Schiele, B., Tuytelaars, T. (eds.) ECCV 2014. LNCS, vol. 8693, pp. 740–755. Springer, Cham (2014). https://doi.org/10.1007/978-3-319-10602-1_48
20. Liu, S., Niles-Weed, J., Razavian, N., Fernandez-Granda, C.: Early-learning regularization prevents memorization of noisy labels. In: Advances in Neural Information Processing Systems, vol. 33 (2020)
21. Liu, Y., Zhang, Z., Niu, L., Chen, J., Zhang, L.: Mixed Supervised Object Detection by Transferring Mask Prior and Semantic Similarity. arXiv e-prints arXiv:2110.14191 (2021)
22. Liu, Y.C., et al.: Unbiased teacher for semi-supervised object detection. In: International Conference on Learning Representations (2020)
23. Pleiss, G., Zhang, T., Elenberg, E., Weinberger, K.Q.: Identifying mislabeled data using the area under the margin ranking. In: Larochelle, H., Ranzato, M., Hadsell, R., Balcan, M.F., Lin, H. (eds.) Advances in Neural Information Processing Systems, vol. 33, pp. 17044–17056. Curran Associates, Inc. (2020). https://proceedings.neurips.cc/paper/2020/file/c6102b3727b2a7d8b1bb6981147081ef-Paper.pdf
24. Ren, S., He, K., Girshick, R., Sun, J.: Faster R-CNN: towards real-time object detection with region proposal networks. In: Advances in Neural Information Processing Systems (NIPS) (2015)
25. Ren, Z., et al.: Instance-aware, context-focused, and memory-efficient weakly supervised object detection. In: IEEE/CVF Conference on Computer Vision and Pattern Recognition (CVPR) (2020)
26. Rochan, M., Wang, Y.: Weakly supervised localization of novel objects using appearance transfer. In: 2015 IEEE Conference on Computer Vision and Pattern Recognition (CVPR), pp. 4315–4324 (2015). https://doi.org/10.1109/CVPR.2015.7299060
27. Shen, Y., Ji, R., Wang, Y., Wu, Y., Cao, L.: Cyclic guidance for weakly supervised joint detection and segmentation. In: The IEEE Conference on Computer Vision and Pattern Recognition (CVPR), June 2019
28. Sohn, K., Zhang, Z., Li, C.L., Zhang, H., Lee, C.Y., Pfister, T.: A simple semi-supervised learning framework for object detection. arXiv preprint arXiv:2005.04757 (2020)
29. Sui, L., Zhang, C.L., Wu, J.: Salvage of supervision in weakly supervised detection (2021)
30. Tang, P., et al.: PCL: proposal cluster learning for weakly supervised object detection. IEEE Trans. Pattern Anal. Mach. Intell. **42**(1), 176–191 (2018)
31. Tang, P., Wang, X., Bai, X., Liu, W.: Multiple instance detection network with online instance classifier refinement. In: CVPR (2017)
32. Uijlings, J., Popov, S., Ferrari, V.: Revisiting knowledge transfer for training object class detectors. In: Proceedings of the IEEE Conference on Computer Vision and Pattern Recognition, pp. 1101–1110 (2018)

33. Uijlings, J.R., Van De Sande, K.E., Gevers, T., Smeulders, A.W.: Selective search for object recognition. Int. J. Comput. Vision **104**(2), 154–171 (2013)
34. Wan, F., Liu, C., Ke, W., Ji, X., Jiao, J., Ye, Q.: C-mil: continuation multiple instance learning for weakly supervised object detection. 2019 IEEE/CVF Conference on Computer Vision and Pattern Recognition (CVPR), June 2019
35. Wan, F., Wei, P., Jiao, J., Han, Z., Ye, Q.: Min-entropy latent model for weakly supervised object detection. In: 2018 IEEE/CVF Conference on Computer Vision and Pattern Recognition, June 2018. https://doi.org/10.1109/cvpr.2018.00141
36. Xu, M., et al.: End-to-end semi-supervised object detection with soft teacher. arXiv preprint arXiv:2106.09018 (2021)
37. Yan, G., et al.: C-MIDN: coupled multiple instance detection network with segmentation guidance for weakly supervised object detection. In: 2019 IEEE/CVF International Conference on Computer Vision (ICCV), pp. 9833–9842 (2019). https://doi.org/10.1109/ICCV.2019.00993
38. Yang, K., Li, D., Dou, Y.: Towards precise end-to-end weakly supervised object detection network. In: Proceedings of the IEEE International Conference on Computer Vision, pp. 8372–8381 (2019)
39. Yin, Y., Deng, J., Zhou, W., Li, H.: Instance mining with class feature banks for weakly supervised object detection. In: Proceedings of the AAAI Conference on Artificial Intelligence, vol. 35, no. 4, pp. 3190–3198, May 2021. https://ojs.aaai.org/index.php/AAAI/article/view/16429
40. Zeng, Z., Liu, B., Fu, J., Chao, H., Zhang, L.: WSOD2: learning bottom-up and top-down objectness distillation for weakly-supervised object detection. In: Proceedings of the IEEE/CVF International Conference on Computer Vision (ICCV), October 2019
41. Zhang, Y., Bai, Y., Ding, M., Li, Y., Ghanem, B.: W2F: a weakly-supervised to fully-supervised framework for object detection. In: Proceedings of the IEEE Conference on Computer Vision and Pattern Recognition, pp. 928–936 (2018)
42. Zhong, Y., Wang, J., Peng, J., Zhang, L.: Boosting weakly supervised object detection with progressive knowledge transfer. In: Vedaldi, A., Bischof, H., Brox, T., Frahm, J.-M. (eds.) ECCV 2020. LNCS, vol. 12371, pp. 615–631. Springer, Cham (2020). https://doi.org/10.1007/978-3-030-58574-7_37

Decoupled Adversarial Contrastive Learning for Self-supervised Adversarial Robustness

Chaoning Zhang[1]([⊠]), Kang Zhang[1], Chenshuang Zhang[1], Axi Niu[2], Jiu Feng[3], Chang D. Yoo[1], and In So Kweon[1]

[1] Korea Advanced Institute of Science and Technology (KAIST), Daejeon, Korea
chaoningzhang1990@gmail.com, zhangkang@kaist.ac.kr
[2] Northwestern Polytechnical University, Xi'an, China
[3] Sichuan University, Chengdu, China

Abstract. *Adversarial training* (AT) for robust representation learning and *self-supervised learning* (SSL) for unsupervised representation learning are two active research fields. Integrating AT into SSL, multiple prior works have accomplished a highly significant yet challenging task: learning robust representation without labels. A widely used framework is adversarial contrastive learning which couples AT and SSL, and thus constitutes a very complex optimization problem. Inspired by the divide-and-conquer philosophy, we conjecture that it might be simplified as well as improved by solving two sub-problems: non-robust SSL and pseudo-supervised AT. This motivation shifts the focus of the task from seeking an optimal integrating strategy for a coupled problem to finding sub-solutions for sub-problems. With this said, this work discards prior practices of directly introducing AT to SSL frameworks and proposed a two-stage framework termed <u>De</u>coupled <u>A</u>dversarial <u>C</u>ontrastive <u>L</u>earning (DeACL). Extensive experimental results demonstrate that our DeACL achieves SOTA self-supervised adversarial robustness while significantly reducing the training time, which validates its effectiveness and efficiency. Moreover, our DeACL constitutes a more explainable solution, and its success also bridges the gap with semi-supervised AT for exploiting unlabeled samples for robust representation learning. The code is publicly accessible at https://github.com/pantheon5100/DeACL.

Keywords: Adversarial contrastive learning · Adversarial training · Self-supervised learning · Adversarial robustness

1 Introduction

Despite the phenomenal success in a wide range of applications [27,30,60,63], deep neural networks (DNNs) are widely recognized to be vulnerable to adversar-

C. Zhang and K. Zhang—Equal Contribution.

Supplementary Information The online version contains supplementary material available at https://doi.org/10.1007/978-3-031-20056-4_42.

ial examples [21,48]. Adversarial training (AT) and its variants have become the de facto standard approach for learning an adversarially robust model [36,66]. AT targets robust generalization [46] which requires more data than standard training. In practice, however, samples with ground-truth (GT) labels are much more difficult to obtain than their unlabeled counterparts. To partly or fully remove the dependence on human annotation, unlabeled samples can be exploited for learning robust representation.

Multiple works [7,38,50,59] have independently shown that unlabeled samples improve adversarial robustness in the semi-supervised setting. The performance of such semi-supervised AT, however, is often reported to be poor when only a small amount of labelled samples are available. Therefore, an interesting question is whether reasonable robustness can be achieved with *only* unlabeled samples. The past few years have witnessed substantial progress in the field of self-supervised learning (SSL) [10,12,25] for representation learning without GT labels. Inspired by such progress, multiple works [19,31,32,56] have shown the success of adversarial contrastive learning (CL) for achieving robustness without labels, which constitutes a positive answer to the above question.

Nonetheless, robust SSL has been often recognized as a challenging problem due to its two mixed challenging goals: (a) *unsupervised* representation learning; (b) *robust* representation learning. The first goal can be readily realized by SOTA SSL frameworks, such as contrastive learning (CL)-based SimCLR [10], MoCo [26], while AT constitutes a go-to solution for the second goal. Thus, a line of works [19,31,32,56] choose a natural strategy by introducing AT into SimCLR or MoCo to perform adversarial CL. Despite having such off-the-shelf solutions for both SSL and AT, how to effectively integrate the two techniques as an optimal solution remains not fully clear. Searching for such an optimal combining strategy is non-trivial because the two goals are entangled in the optimization. Moreover, SSL and AT often require different configuration choices for their respective goals, and combining them inevitably involves a trade-off between them. Inspired by the design philosophy of the divide-and-conquer algorithm, we conjecture that the task might be simplified by solving two sub-problems in a decoupled manner. This frustratingly simple motivation brings a fundamental shift for the focus of robust SSL: from *seeking an optimal combining strategy for a coupled problem* to *finding sub-solutions for sub-problems*.

To this end, this work discards the prior practice [19,31,32,56] of introducing AT to SSL frameworks and proposes a new two-stage framework termed <u>De</u>coupled <u>A</u>dversarial <u>C</u>ontrastive <u>L</u>earning (DeACL). At stage 1, we perform standard (*i.e.* non-robust) SSL to learn instance-wise representation as a target vector. At stage 2, the obtained target vectors can be used for facilitating AT in a **pseudo-supervised** manner for learn-

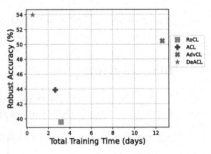

Fig. 1. Comparison of different methods on robust accuracy and total training time.

ing robust representation. We find that DeACL significantly benefits from the configuration for second-stage AT being set differently from that of first-stage SSL.

Except for enabling flexible yet simple configuration choices, another important side benefit of our DeACL is to require much fewer computation resources. At first sight, it might be counter-intuitive that two-stage approaches can be much faster than single-stage counterparts. Ignoring specific implementation details, the basic rationale is as follows. SSL typically requires M times more iterations than their supervised counterpart, and AT is often N times slower than standard training. Compared with supervised standard training, combining them into a single-stage makes it $M \times N$ times slower, while our DeACL makes it only $M + N$ times slower due to the disentangling effect. As shown in Fig. 1, with SimCLR as the baseline SSL, our DeACL achieves state-of-the-art robustness while significantly reducing the required training time. The superior performance of our approach is also confirmed under adversarial full fine-tuning.

Overall, this work studies self-supervised robust representation learning. We summarize the contributions as follows:

- In contrast to existing works seeking an optimal strategy for combing SSL and AT to achieve robust SSL, our work investigates a different approach by solving two sub-problems in a divide-and-conquer manner, which yields a novel two-stage DeACL framework for robust SSL.
- The proposed DeACL has two advantages: (a) enabling flexible configuration for the two sub-problems; (b) requiring much fewer computation resources. Extensive experiments demonstrate that DeACL achieves SOTA robustness while significantly reducing the training time.
- Our DeACL also constitutes a more explainable solution for robust SSL and its success also bridges the gap with semi-supervised AT for exploiting unlabeled samples for robust representation learning.

2   Related Works

The task of robust SSL lies in the intersection between SSL and AT to learn robust feature representation without GT labels. SSL and AT are two active research fields, for which we summarize their recent progress.

Development in SSL. The success of SSL has been demonstrated in a wide range of applications, ranging from natural language processing [16,33,39,43,47] to more recent vision tasks [13,17,34]. Without the need for GT labels annotated by the human, early SSL approaches leverage handcrafted "pretext" tasks, like solving Jigsaw puzzle [20] or predicting image rotation [40], while recent methods seek to learn augmentation-invariant representation [2,8,10,24,26]. To make the encoder augmentation-invariant, a commonly adopted practice is to minimize the distance between a positive pair, *i.e.* two views augmented from the same image based on a Siamese network architecture. A widely known issue in SSL is that the network might output an undesired constant, for which contrastive learning (CL) provides a satisfactory solution by maximizing the distance between negative samples, *i.e.* views of different images. CL has been widely investigated in [2, 10,26,28,29,41,49,51–53,57,68], contributing to the progress of SSL. Recently, multiple works [3,12,18,24,58] have also explored non-contrastive SSL. A unified perspective on contrasitve and non-contrastive SSL is provided in [64,65].

Development in AT. To improve adversarial robustness, early works have attempted with various image processing or detection techniques, most of which, however, are found to give a false sense of robustness [1,6,15]. Currently, AT and its variants are widely recognized as powerful solutions to improve model robustness, among which Mardy-AT [36] and Trades-AT [66] are two widely used baselines. From the perspective of model architecture, AT often requires a larger model capacity [50,55]. Moreover, [42,54] have found that a smooth activation function, like parametric softplus, is often but not always [23] helpful for AT. From the perspective of tricks, [42] has performed a comprehensive evaluation for bags of tricks in AT and found that most of them provide no or trivial performance boost over Mardy-AT and Trades-AT if basic hyperparameters, such as weight decay, are set to proper values. From the perspective of data, [7,50,67] have shown that unlabeled data can be helpful for robustness improvement over a basic supervised baseline. However, those approaches still depend on a large amount of labeled samples. For example, [7,50,59] have shown that robust accuracy drops significantly when only 10% of the CIFAR10 labels are available. Universal AT [5] has also been investigated for defending against universal adversarial perturbations [4,37,61,62].

Self-supervised Adversarial Robustness. Clearly, self-supervised AT, *i.e.* achieving robustness with only unlabeled samples, can be even more challenging than the semi-supervised AT setting. Nonetheless, multiple recent works [9,19,22,31,32] have demonstrated encouraging success in this challenging yet highly significant direction. Prior attempts mainly focused on finding effective techniques to combine SSL and AT. What differentiates our approach from prior attempts [19,22,31,32,56] lies in disentangling robust SSL into two decoupled sub-problems (SSL and AT) which can be solved in two stages. In the following section, we will detail existing single-stage frameworks as well as the motivation behind our two-stage framework.

3   Proposed Method

To avoid ambiguity, we start by presenting the problem of our interest, *i.e.* robust SSL, and common fine-tuning methods for evaluating the learned robust representation. Then, we briefly summarize how prior attempts [9,19,22,31,32] solve this problem in a single-stage framework. Compared with standard supervised training, either SSL or AT makes the optimization more complex, while simultaneously realizing SSL and AT clearly makes the problem complexity to an even higher level thus is difficult to solve. Inspired by the philosophy of the divide-and-conquer algorithm, we divide the complex robust SSL problem into two sub-problems: non-robust SSL and pseudo-supervised AT, and sequentially conquer them. We identify multiple important details that need to be configured differently for AT at stage 2 from standard SSL at stage 1.

3.1 Problem Statement

Robust SSL. The goal of robust SSL is to learn robust feature representation with only unlabeled samples so that the model can be trained by a self-supervision loss, such as InfoNCE in CL-based SSL frameworks [10,26]. Note that this is different from a semi-supervised setting, where labeled samples are used together with unlabeled dataset. By contrast, robust SSL *exclusively only* utilizes unlabeled dataset.

Standard Linear Finetuning. For quantitatively evaluating the learned representation, a common practice is to train a linear classifier (denoted as ϕ_{θ_c}) on top of the pretrained encoder (denoted as f_{θ_e}) as:

$$\text{SLF: } \min_{\theta_c} \mathbb{E}_{(x,y) \in \mathcal{D}} \ell_{CE}(\phi_{\theta_c} \circ f_{\theta_e}(x), y), \tag{1}$$

where ℓ_{CE} represents the supervised CE loss with GT-labels y over a certain dataset $\mathcal{D}$. This is often termed *standard linear finetuning* (SLF) [19,31] since only a linear classifier is updated on Clean Examples (CEs). Training such a linear classifier allows access to the ground-truth labels; otherwise, the learned representation in the encoder cannot be evaluated. To not break the rule of the SSL task, the backward gradient can only be propagated to the linear classifier so that the pretrained encoder is fixed during the evaluation. The quality of learned robust representation is finally evaluated on the full model $\phi_{\theta_c} \circ f_{\theta_e}$ by measuring its robust accuracy under PGD attack [36] or autoattack [15]. **Adversarial full finetuning.** Except for the above linear finetuning as the primary evaluation metric, one can also make the constraint less strict in the finetuning stage to perform adversarial full finetuning [32] (AFF). AFF allows the encoder to be updated during the finetuning as:

$$\text{AFF: } \min_{\theta_c, \theta_e} \mathbb{E}_{(x,y) \in \mathcal{D}} \ell_{CE}(\phi_{\theta_c} \circ f_{\theta_e}(x + \delta), y), \tag{2}$$

where σ is adversarial perturbation. It is worth highlighting that the weight initialization from robust SSL significantly improves the convergence speed of supervised AT together with a non-trivial performance boost. Note that we do not consider standard full finetuning because it cannot generate a robust model.

Basic Setup. Following [19,31,32], we adopt ResNet18 as the encoder architecture and investigate robustness on CIFAR10. Under the l_∞ constraint, we set the maximum allowable perturbation budget ϵ to $8/255$ during both training and evaluation. Following AdvCL [19], we evaluate the learned robust representation on three metrics: Standard Accuracy (SA), Robust Accuracy (RA) and Autoattack Accuracy (AA). SA is the classification evaluated on clean examples, while RA is evaluated on adversarial examples generated by 20-step PGD attacks. AA evaluates the model accuracy under Autoattack [15] for mitigating the concerns for the phenomenon of obfuscated gradient. We follow [19] for the settings of SLF and AFF (see the supplementary for a detailed setup).

3.2   Existing Single-Stage Framework for Robust SSL

Since contrastive learning (CL) is a widely proven effective technique in SSL for representation learning without labels, for which SimCLR [10] is a popular representative. Therefore, multiple works [19,31,32] have adopted SimCLR as the baseline SSL method and improved its robustness by combining it with AT. Let us briefly recap how SimCLR framework works. The optimization goal of CL is to make the anchor sample be attracted close to its positive sample, *i.e.* a different view augmented from the same image while being pushed away from its negative samples. The pipeline takes a batch of image samples as the input and processes it with a backbone encoder followed by a projector which is an MLP [10]. The output is a latent vector denoted as z. With $\cdot$ indicating the cosine similarity between vectors and N indicating the number of negative samples, the contrastive InfoNCE is shown as:

$$\mathcal{L}_{CL} = -\log \frac{\exp(z_a \cdot z_b / \tau)}{\exp(z_a \cdot z_b / \tau) + \sum_{i=1}^{N} \exp(z_a \cdot z_i / \tau)}, \tag{3}$$

where z_a and z_b are a positive pair. τ denotes the temperature hyperparameter. The negative samples are included to prevent a collapse mode where the model outputs a constant regardless of the inputs. Note that the above loss can be simplified to a cosine similarity loss by excluding negative samples.

RoCL. Introducing AT to the above CL, [32] is one of the pioneering works to propose a robust contrastive learning (RoCL) framework. Following the procedure in vanilla AT [36], RoCL first generates adversarial examples (z_a^{adv}) by maximizing its cosine distance from z_b with multi-step PGD attacks and then updates the network by minimizing the cosine distance between all positive samples. In contrast to standard SSL, RoCL has three positive samples, z_a, z_b and z_a^{adv}, which forms three contrastive losses for training the network.

ACL. Concurrent to RoCL [32], another work [31] proposes a similar SimCLR-based approach coined as adversarial contrastive learning (ACL). [31] has explored to improve the robustness of SimCLR with various attempts, among which a dual stream consisting of a standard2standard (S2S) and adversarial2adversarial (A2A) performs the best. S2S is a normal CL as introduced in Eq. 3, while A2A replaces z_a and z_b with adversarial examples z_a^{adv} and z_b^{adv} which are generated by maximizing their cosine distance to each other.

AdvCL. Very recently, another SimCLR-based adversarial contrastive learning framework, which is coined as AdvCL in [19] to differentiate from ACL, has been proposed. In essence, without dual-stream design, AdvCL is more similar to RoCL than ACL. What differentiates AdvCL from them is its two distinctive components: (a) introducing another positive view which is augmented by keeping only high-frequency content; (b) adopting another supervision loss by utilizing an additional encoder pretrained on a much larger dataset (ImageNet). Empirically, these two designs improve its performance over RoCL and ACL by a large margin. As reported in [19], this performance boost is at the cost of being three times slower than RoCL and AdvCL. If the pretraining time on ImageNet is considered, the required computation resources can be more intimidating.

3.3 Decomposed Adversarial Contrastive Learning

Motivation. Divide-and-conquer is a widely used algorithm paradigm in ML to break down a complex problem into two (or more) sub-problems which can be easier to solve. Inspired by such design philosophy, we propose to divide the complex robust SSL into two sub-problems, *i.e.* (a) (non-robust) SSL and (b) (pseudo-)supervised AT. Such a decoupled optimization procedure simplifies the robust SSL by shifting the task focus from seeking an optimal strategy to combine SSL and AT to finding sub-solutions to sub-problems. Overall, with the motivation to decompose robust SSL, we propose a new two-stage framework, termed DeACL. For differentiation, we denote the encoder at stage 1 as $f_{\theta 1}$ and that at stage 2 $f_{\theta 2}$.

Stage 1: non-robust SSL for optimizing $f_{\theta 1}$. Following [19,31,32], this work mainly adopts SimCLR as the SSL method. Following [14], we train the model for 1000 epochs. A detailed setup is listed in the supplementary. The purpose of non-robust SSL is to obtain label-alike pseudo-targets for guiding the following pseudo-supervised AT.

Stage 2: pseudo-supervised AT for optimizing $f_{\theta 2}$. In vanilla supervised AT, the model training is guided by GT labels. Conceptually, the term "label" is often associated with human predefined classes, cat or dog for instance, which do not exist in the SSL. Thus, the representation vectors obtained from SSL are termed *targets* to differentiate from *labels*. Moreover, since the targets are generated by a SSL pretrained model instead of human annotation, we term them *pseudo-targets*. Specifically, the pseudo-targets refer to the instance-wise representation vectors by feeding the samples to a pretrained backbone encoder. They serve a similar role as GT labels to guide the supervised AT.

Loss Design. We use the default SSL loss (Eq. 3 for instance) to optimize $f_{\theta 1}$ at stage 1 of our DeACL. At stage 2, we optimize the encoder $f_{\theta 2}$ with the loss as:

$$L_{stage2} = CosSim(f_{\theta 2}(x), z_1) + \lambda CosSim(f_{\theta 2}(x^{\mathrm{adv}}), f_{\theta 2}(x)), \qquad (4)$$

where $CosSim$ indicates cosine similarity loss and z_1 indicates target vector generated from the pretrained $f_{\theta 1}$. The adversarial example x^{adv} is generated by maximizing $CosSim(f_{\theta 2}(x^{\mathrm{adv}}), z_1)$. Following AdvC [19], 5-step PGD (with the step size $\alpha = 2/255$) is adopted to generate x^{adv}. Eq. 4 consists of two terms where the first one increases accuracy and the second one acts as a regularization loss to increase robustness. λ is a hyper-parameter for achieving a trade-off between accuracy and robustness. In this work, we set λ to 2 (see supplementary

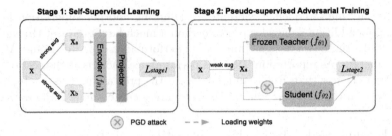

Fig. 2. Overall framework of DeACL. It consists of two stages. At stage 1, DeACL performs a standard SSL to obtain a non-robust encoder. At stage 2, the pretrained encoder act as a teacher model to generate pseudo-targets for guiding a supervised AT on a student model. After two stages of training, the student model is the model of our interest.

for the ablation study). This design is inspired by a SOTA loss in (supervised) Trades-AT [66]. A major difference from [66] is that we use *CosSim* instead of KL divergence to measure the distance. We empirically find that *CosSim* outperforms KL by a large margin. An alternative loss could be designed to directly minimize $CosSim(f_{\theta 2}(x^{\mathrm{adv}}), z_1)$. Its performance is worse than Eq. 4 (see the supplementary for ablation study), which aligns with the finding in prior works [42,66].

Overall Framework. The overall framework of our DeACL is shown in Fig. 2, where the pretrained encoder in stage 1 is loaded and then frozen in stage 2 as a teacher model for generating pseudo-targets.

At stage 2, we can initialize $f_{\theta 2}$ with random weights or pretrained weights by loading $f_{\theta 1}$ to the student model. Empirically, we find that this only yields a small performance variation as shown in Table 1. In the beginning, loading pretrained (non-robust) weights boosts the convergence speed (see

Table 1. Influence of weight initialization for the student model.

	AA	RA	SA
DeACL	45.31	53.95	80.17
Student scratch	44.63	54.06	79.47

the supplementary), which is well expected. Since this convergence and performance boost is free, our DCL by default adopts this practice.

4   Advantages of Our DeACL

4.1   Flexible Configuration for SSL and at

It has been shown in [42] that training configurations (*e.g.*, weight decay) can have a significant influence on robustness in supervised AT. However, it is not clear how to choose the optimal configurations in robust SSL, especially considering the differences of main configurations in SSL and supervised AT, as shown in Table 2. Since recent works [19,31,32] all train the model in a single stage, it is not clear whether configurations of SSL or supervised AT should be applied.

RoCL and ACL both follow the configuration as standard SSL, such as small weight decay, strong augmentation, adopting a projector head, and preventing collapse with InfoNCE loss. For the weight decay, AdvCL adopts a value that lies between those for SSL and AT. For augmentation, AdvCL adopts strong augmentation on CEs and weak augmentation on AEs. [19] shows that their AdvCL performance drops by a large margin if strong augmentation is applied on AEs. A major drawback for existing single-stage frameworks lies in seeking an optimal configuration that simultaneously fits both SSL and AT.

Table 2. Summarization of four configuration details in various settings.

Configuration	SSL	AT	Single-stage frameworks			Two-stage DeACL	
			RoCL	ACL	AdvCL	SSL	AT
Weight decay	1e-5	5e-4	1e-6	1e-6	1e-4	1e-5	5e-4
Data augmentation	Strong	Weak	Strong	Strong	Strong/weak	Strong	Weak
Projector head	Yes	No	Yes	Yes	Yes	Yes	No
Collapse prevention	Yes	No	Yes	Yes	Yes	Yes	No

By contrast, our DeACL enables stage-specific configuration. In other words, we can freely choose the optimal experimental configurations during each stage. For the first stage which aims to train a standard model, we follow the open source SSL library [14] for optimal configuration. In the following, we detail why and how each configuration is set at stage 2 of our DeACL.

Weight Decay. SSL typically has a strong regularization effect due to strong augmentation and the weight decay is often set to a relatively small value, 1e-5 for instance [14]. Supervised AT, however, often suffers from robust overfitting [44] and requires a large weight decay [42]. [42] has performed an extensive study on a bag of tricks on supervised AT, and has found that weight decay is the most significant factor, which has a much higher influence than tricks reported in most works.

Table 3. Influence of weight decay at stage 2 with the SSL results on CIFAR10.

Weight decay	SLF		
	AA	RA	SA
1e-6	34.77	40.45	81.88
1e-5	36.33	44.21	80.29
1e-4	43.26	52.39	80.21
5e-4	45.31	53.95	80.17
1e-3	43.07	53.32	78.24
5e-3	24.80	33.45	55.76

With the weight decay set to 5e-4, [42] has shown that most tricks bring no or marginal performance boost over the widely used Madry-AT [36] and Trades-AT [66]. Table 3 shows that a relatively large weight, *i.e.* 5e-4, is required for achieving high robustness and accuracy. Note that [42] also shows that 5e-4 is the optimal weight decay for vanilla supervised AT on the same dataset CIFAR10.

Data Augmentation. SSL is widely known to require strong augmentation to learn augmentation-invariant representation, while supervised training (either standard or adversarial one) typically often adopts weak augmentation. On the CIFAR10 dataset, the strong augmentation consists of random resized crop, color jittering, color change, Gaussian blur, solarization

Table 4. Influence of data augmentation at stage 2 with the SSL results on CIFAR10.

Augmentation		SLF		
AE	CE	AA	RA	SA
Weak	Weak	45.31	53.95	80.17
Strong	Strong	6.93	17.43	48.12
Weak	Strong	34.47	45.45	74.85
Strong	Weak	7.62	18.36	79.93

and horizontal crop, while the weak augmentation only consists of random crop (after padding) and horizontal flip. The results in Table 4 show that applying strong augmentation on either clean examples (CEs) or adversarial examples (AEs) in Eq. 4 yields significantly inferior performance.

Projector Head. Projector head has become a de facto standard component in SSL to be added after the backbone during training for performance boost [10,11,45]. After the training is done, only the backbone is kept for the downstream task. In the case of supervised AT [36], no projector is used during training. The results in Table 5

Table 5. Influence of projector head at stage 2 with the SSL results on CIFAR10.

	AA	RA	SA
w/o projector	45.31	53.95	80.17
w/projector	42.48	50.60	78.80

show that adding the projector at stage 2 of our DeACL is harmful to both robustness and accuracy.

Collapse Prevention. A widely known phenomenon in SSL is that the model output a constant output, *i.e.* collapse, if the loss only maximizes the cosine similarity between a pair of positive samples. A widely used approach to mitigate this phenomenon is to introduce a contrastive component, *i.e.* simultaneously

Table 6. Influence of collapse prevention at stage 2 with the SSL results on CIFAR10.

	AA	RA	SA
w/o collapse prevention	45.31	53.95	80.17
w/collapse prevention	34.18	39.32	72.19

minimizing the cosine similarity between negative samples (See Eq. 3). The results in Table 6 show that adding a contrastive component decreases the performance by a large margin. At stage 2 of our DeACL, there is low or no risk of collapse because it is supervised by distinctive pseudo-targets.

Takeaway on the Configuration. Overall, our above investigation shows that our DeACL significantly benefits from the fact that the configurations for AT in our DeACL can be set differently from those in SSL. The best configurations at stage 2 of our DeACL are the same as those in supervised AT, which is reasonable considering the second stage our DeACL conducts a *i.e.* pseudo-supervised AT. As shown in Table 7, thanks to the flexible configuration, our DeACL achieves superior performance over existing single-stage frameworks. Notably, our proposed DeACL achieves the highest robustness for both AA and RA on both CIFAR10 and CIFAR100. For SA, our DeACL outperforms all existing methods except for AdvCL on CIFAR10. On CIFAR100, our DeACL outperforms all existing methods by a large margin.

Table 7. SLF results on CIFAR10 and CIFAR100. All the methods are evaluated with ResNet18 under the same condition following [19]. We report three metrics (Auto Attack (AA), Robust Accuracy (RA), Standard Accuracy (SA)) as well as the pre-training time (in days). For all metrics, the best performance is highlighted in **bold**.

Method	CIFAR10			CIFAR100			Computation resource		
	AA (%)	RA (%)	SA (%)	AA (%)	RA (%)	SA (%)	Time	GPU	Total
AP-DPE	16.07	18.22	78.30	4.17	6.23	47.91	10.11	1	10.11
RoCL	23.38	39.54	79.90	8.66	18.79	49.53	1.59	2	3.18
ACL	39.13	42.87	77.88	16.33	20.97	47.51	2.65	1	2.65
AdvCL	42.57	50.45	**80.85**	19.78	27.67	48.34	3.15	4	12.60
DeACL	**45.31**	**53.95**	80.17	**20.34**	**30.74**	**52.79**	0.45	1	**0.45**

Performing a similar investigation on existing single-stage frameworks might also bring a performance boost. However, it is not guaranteed considering the configuration trade-off between SSL and AT. Moreover, such a search for optimal configuration in single-stage frameworks can be intimidating if taking computation resources into account. In the following, we discuss another advantage of our DeACL for significantly reducing the training time.

4.2   Two-Stage DeACL is Faster Than Single-Stage Frameworks

As shown in Table 7, among the three single-stage frameworks (RoCL, ACL, AdvCL), the very recent AdvCL achieves the best robustness but at the cost of significantly more training time. As noted in [19], their superior performance is partly attributed to introducing additional views as well as additional pseudo supervision regularization from encoder pretrained on ImageNet. These two design choices are also the reason that makes their AdvCL significantly slower. Compared with them, our DeACL requires the least training time, which is mainly attributed to the effect of disentangling SSL and AT. It is worth highlighting that our DeACL achieves a significant performance boost over RoCL and ACL, without relying on additional high-frequency views or additional supervision from ImageNet pretrained models. These two techniques might further improve the performance of our DeACL, and we leave such investigation for future work. We do not include them in this work to make our DeACL simple and fast.

Rationale for why DeACL is Fast. Given that RoCL and ACL do not use the two design choices as AdvCL, why are they still significantly slower than our DeACL? At first sight, it seems counterintuitive that the two-stage DeACL can be faster. The rationale is briefly discussed as follows. SSL and AT are both widely known to require much longer training time than their standard supervised counterpart. Specifically, SSL often requires M (10 for instance) times more training iterations (epochs) due to the lack of GT labels. AT makes the iteration-wise training time N (7 for instance) times longer because generating adversarial examples with the commonly used multi-step PGD attack is very slow. Directly solving a robust SSL requires $M \times N$ times more training time, while disentangling them into two stages is expected to only require $M + N$ times more training time. In practice, training time can be more than complex than the above reasoning rationale, depending on the implementation details.

Table 8. AFF results on CIFAR10 and CIFAR100. All the methods are evaluated with ResNet18 under the same condition following [19]. For all metrics (AA, RA, SA), our DeACL achieves the best performance which is highlighted in **bold**.

SSL-AT	CIFAR10			CIFAR100		
	AA(%)	RA(%)	SA(%)	AA(%)	RA(%)	SA(%)
Supervised	46.19	49.89	79.86	21.61	25.86	52.22
AP-DPE	48.13	51.52	81.19	22.53	26.89	55.27
RoCL	47.88	51.35	81.01	22.28	27.49	55.10
ACL	49.27	52.82	82.19	23.63	29.38	56.61
AdvCL	49.77	52.77	83.62	24.72	28.73	56.77
DeACL	**50.39**	**54.18**	**83.95**	**25.48**	**29.65**	**59.86**

5   Additional Experimental Results

The results in the above section demonstrate that our DeACL outperforms existing single-stage frameworks by a large margin while requiring significantly less training time. Here, we further conduct extra experiments to verify the effectiveness of our approach from different angles.

AFF Results. Table 8 reports the AFF results on both CIFAR10 and CIFAR100. Compared to the results in Table 7, for all methods, AFF brings a consistent performance boost over SLF, which is expected since AFF also allows the encoder to be updated. Similar to the trend with SLF, we observe that our DeACL achieves SOTA performance for all the three considered metrics on both CIFAR10 and CIFAR100.

Influence of Attack Steps and Perturbation Magnitude. For the RA, by default we use 20-step PGD, *i.e.* PGD-20, with ϵ set to l_∞ 8/255. Here, we evaluate with various steps and ϵ values. The results in Fig. 3 show that our DeACL consistently outperforms existing methods by a non-trivial margin.

Qualitative Results. With t-SNE [35], the visualization of learned representation on CIFAR10 is shown in Fig. 4, where each point is colored by its GT label.

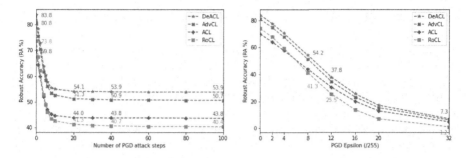

Fig. 3. RA on CIAR10 with various PGD steps and ϵ. Our DeACL consistently achieves the best performance.

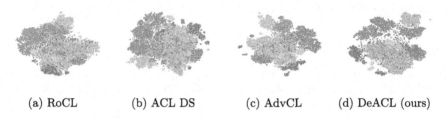

(a) RoCL   (b) ACL DS   (c) AdvCL   (d) DeACL (ours)

Fig. 4. Visualization of robust representation learned with different methods. Our method gives a more clear classification boundary than existing methods.

The class boundary of our DeACL is clearer than that of existing methods, which suggests that DeACL might be more robust to adversarial perturbation.

6   Implications of Our Findings

6.1   Towards a More Explainable Solution

It is desirable to have a more explainable solution for a given task. For the task of robust SSL, the success of existing solutions based on a single-stage framework is much more difficult to explain because it couples two sub-problems. Our DeACL decouples the task, which makes the solution significantly more explainable. For example, an interesting question

Table 9. Results on Cifar10 with various SSL frameworks at stage 1 of our DeACL.

SSL frameworks	SLF		
	AA	RA	SA
SimCLR [10]	45.31	53.95	80.17
MoCo v2 [11]	46.29	53.97	80.56
BYOL [24]	44.14	52.42	80.89
BarlowTwins [58]	41.31	50.47	80.88
VICReg [3]	43.65	50.56	82.10

to ask in robust SSL is how much the SSL framework choice influences the performance. With the existing single-stage framework, such influence is much more difficult to analyze due to its interaction with AT. Note that SSL framework often has its optimal configuration setting. As we can see from Sect. 4.1, such configuration detail can have a significant influence when considering AT.

With our DeACL, we can adopt a unified configuration in the second-stage AT to exclude such influence of configuration on AT. With this said, Table 9 reports the influence of SSL frameworks. We observe an interesting phenomenon that CL-based frameworks tend to outperform non-CL-based frameworks for achieving higher robustness but possibly at the cost of slightly lower accuracy. [56] claims that adversarial momentum contrastive learning (AMOC) outperforms adversarial contrastive learning by showing a non-trivial performance gain of their AMOC over ACL. Since many configurations in MoCov2 and SimCLR are different and many other details like how to generate adversarial examples are also very different, their conclusion might be not fully convincing. Our results in Table 9 show that MoCov2 and SimCLR achieve comparable RA and SA, suggesting their non-trivial performance boost is likely to be caused by the influence of different configurations on AT.

6.2   Towards a Unified Perspective on Semi/self-Supervised at

It is worth noting that a similar two-stage approach is also used in semi-supervised AT for exploiting unlabeled dataset. The success of such a two-stage approach in both semi-supervised and self-supervised settings suggests a new unified perspective on how to effectively exploit unlabelled dataset for learning robust representation. Intuitively, in the semi-supervised settings, the unlabeled dataset can also be used to improve the robustness in a single-stage manner through a regularization loss for instance. However, [50] has found that such a single-stage approach achieves inferior performance than the two-stage approach. Given that our two-stage DeACL also outperforms existing single-stage SOTA baselines in self-supervised setting, it suggests a unified understanding on semi-supervised and self-supervised AT: pseudo-targets (either pseudo-labels or pseudo-vectors) are all you need for exploiting unlabeled dataset to learn robust representation.

Despite such a unified perspective, it is also important to note distinctions between them. Their core distinction lies in their different motivations. A semi-supervised setting allows access to labeled datasets and the motivation of using unlabelled images is to use more samples. Note that more samples are used for training a robust model at stage 2 of semi-supervised AT than those used at stage 1 for training a non-robust model. By contrast, our DeACL in the self-supervised setting is *not* motivated to increase the sample size and the second stage uses the same number of samples as those at stage 1. Instead, the motivation of the two-stage procedure in our DeACL lies in decomposing the robust SSL. Moreover, what connects the two stages is the supervision targets which are pseudo-labels and pseudo-vectors in semi-supervised and self-supervised settings, respectively. Due to this difference, at stage 2, our DeACL needs to adopt the cosine similarity loss instead of the commonly adopted CE loss.

7 Conclusion

This work revisits the task of robust SSL for learning robust representation without labels. Discard the practice of seeking an optimal strategy to combine SSL and AT, we propose a novel two-stage framework termed DeACL. Our DeACL enables independent configuration for SSL and AT for achieving SOTA robustness by using significantly smaller training resources. Extensive results confirm the effectiveness and efficiency of our DeACL over existing single-stage frameworks by a significant margin. Our findings also have non-trivial implications for pushing (a) towards a more explainable solution for robust SSL and (b) towards a unified perspective of understanding on semi/self-supervised AT regarding how to effectively exploit unlabeled samples for robust representation learning.

Acknowledgments. This work was partly supported by the National Research Foundation of Korea (NRF) grant funded by the Korea government (MSIT) (No. 2022R1A2C201270611), and Institute of Information & communications Technology Planning & Evaluation (IITP) grant funded by the Korea government (MSIT) (No. 2022-0-00951, Development of Uncertainty-Aware Agents Learning by Asking Questions).

References

1. Athalye, A., Carlini, N., Wagner, D.: Obfuscated gradients give a false sense of security: circumventing defenses to adversarial examples. In: ICML (2018)
2. Bachman, P., Hjelm, R.D., Buchwalter, W.: Learning representations by maximizing mutual information across views. In: NeurIPS (2019)
3. Bardes, A., Ponce, J., LeCun, Y.: Vicreg: variance-invariance-covariance regularization for self-supervised learning. arXiv preprint arXiv:2105.04906 (2021)
4. Benz, P., Zhang, C., Imtiaz, T., Kweon, I.S.: Double targeted universal adversarial perturbations. In: ACCV (2020)
5. Benz, P., Zhang, C., Karjauv, A., Kweon, I.S.: Universal adversarial training with class-wise perturbations. In: ICME (2021)
6. Carlini, N., Wagner, D.: Adversarial examples are not easily detected. In: ACM Workshop on Artificial Intelligence and Security (2017)
7. Carmon, Y., Raghunathan, A., Schmidt, L., Liang, P., Duchi, J.C.: Unlabeled data improves adversarial robustness. In: NeurIPS (2019)
8. Caron, M., Misra, I., Mairal, J., Goyal, P., Bojanowski, P., Joulin, A.: Unsupervised learning of visual features by contrasting cluster assignments. arXiv preprint arXiv:2006.09882 (2020)
9. Chen, T., Liu, S., Chang, S., Cheng, Y., Amini, L., Wang, Z.: Adversarial robustness: from self-supervised pre-training to fine-tuning. In: CVPR (2020)
10. Chen, T., Kornblith, S., Norouzi, M., Hinton, G.: A simple framework for contrastive learning of visual representations. In: ICML (2020)
11. Chen, X., Fan, H., Girshick, R., He, K.: Improved baselines with momentum contrastive learning. arXiv preprint arXiv:2003.04297 (2020)
12. Chen, X., He, K.: Exploring simple siamese representation learning. In: CVPR (2021)

13. Chen, X., Xie, S., He, K.: An empirical study of training self-supervised vision transformers. In: ICCV (2021)
14. da Costa, V.G.T., Fini, E., Nabi, M., Sebe, N., Ricci, E.: Solo-learn: a library of self-supervised methods for visual representation learning. JMLR (2022)
15. Croce, F., Hein, M.: Reliable evaluation of adversarial robustness with an ensemble of diverse parameter-free attacks. In: ICML (2020)
16. Devlin, J., Chang, M.W., Lee, K., Toutanova, K.: BERT: pre-training of deep bidirectional transformers for language understanding. In: Proceedings of the 2019 Conference of the North American Chapter of the Association for Computational Linguistics: Human Language Technologies, Volume 1 (Long and Short Papers) (2019)
17. El-Nouby, A., et al.: XCiT: cross-covariance image transformers. arXiv preprint arXiv:2106.09681 (2021)
18. Ermolov, A., Siarohin, A., Sangineto, E., Sebe, N.: Whitening for self-supervised representation learning. In: ICML. PMLR (2021)
19. Fan, L., Liu, S., Chen, P.Y., Zhang, G., Gan, C.: When does contrastive learning preserve adversarial robustness from pretraining to finetuning? In: NeurIPS (2021)
20. Gidaris, S., Singh, P., Komodakis, N.: Unsupervised representation learning by predicting image rotations. In: ICLR (2018)
21. Goodfellow, I.J., Shlens, J., Szegedy, C.: Explaining and harnessing adversarial examples. In: ICLR (2015)
22. Gowal, S., Huang, P.S., van den Oord, A., Mann, T., Kohli, P.: Self-supervised adversarial robustness for the low-label, high-data regime. In: ICLR (2021)
23. Gowal, S., Qin, C., Uesato, J., Mann, T., Kohli, P.: Uncovering the limits of adversarial training against norm-bounded adversarial examples. arXiv preprint arXiv:2010.03593 (2020)
24. Grill, J.B., et al.: Bootstrap your own latent-a new approach to self-supervised learning. In: Advances in Neural Information Processing Systems (2020)
25. He, K., Fan, H., Wu, Y., Xie, S., Girshick, R.: Momentum contrast for unsupervised visual representation learning. arXiv preprint arXiv:1911.05722 (2019)
26. He, K., Fan, H., Wu, Y., Xie, S., Girshick, R.: Momentum contrast for unsupervised visual representation learning. In: CVPR (2020)
27. He, K., Zhang, X., Ren, S., Sun, J.: Deep residual learning for image recognition. In: CVPR (2016)
28. Henaff, O.: Data-efficient image recognition with contrastive predictive coding. In: ICML (2020)
29. Hjelm, R.D., et al.: Learning deep representations by mutual information estimation and maximization. arXiv preprint arXiv:1808.06670 (2018)
30. Huang, G., Liu, Z., Van Der Maaten, L., Weinberger, K.Q.: Densely connected convolutional networks. In: CVPR (2017)
31. Jiang, Z., Chen, T., Chen, T., Wang, Z.: Robust pre-training by adversarial contrastive learning. In: NeurIPS (2020)
32. Kim, M., Tack, J., Hwang, S.J.: Adversarial self-supervised contrastive learning. arXiv preprint arXiv:2006.07589 (2020)
33. Lan, Z., Chen, M., Goodman, S., Gimpel, K., Sharma, P., Soricut, R.: Albert: a lite bert for self-supervised learning of language representations. In: ICLR (2020)
34. Li, C., et al.: Efficient self-supervised vision transformers for representation learning. arXiv preprint arXiv:2106.09785 (2021)
35. Van der Maaten, L., Hinton, G.: Visualizing data using t-SNE. J. Mach. Learn. Res. (2008)

36. Madry, A., Makelov, A., Schmidt, L., Tsipras, D., Vladu, A.: Towards deep learning models resistant to adversarial attacks. In: ICLR (2018)
37. Moosavi-Dezfooli, S.M., Fawzi, A., Fawzi, O., Frossard, P.: Universal adversarial perturbations. In: CVPR (2017)
38. Najafi, A., Maeda, S.i., Koyama, M., Miyato, T.: Robustness to adversarial perturbations in learning from incomplete data. In: NeurIPS (2019)
39. Nie, P., Zhang, Y., Geng, X., Ramamurthy, A., Song, L., Jiang, D.: DC-BERT: decoupling question and document for efficient contextual encoding. In: Proceedings of the 43rd International ACM SIGIR Conference on Research and Development in Information Retrieval (2020)
40. Noroozi, M., Favaro, P.: Unsupervised learning of visual representations by solving jigsaw puzzles. In: Leibe, B., Matas, J., Sebe, N., Welling, M. (eds.) ECCV 2016. LNCS, vol. 9910, pp. 69–84. Springer, Cham (2016). https://doi.org/10.1007/978-3-319-46466-4_5
41. Oord, A.V.D., Li, Y., Vinyals, O.: Representation learning with contrastive predictive coding. arXiv preprint arXiv:1807.03748 (2018)
42. Pang, T., Yang, X., Dong, Y., Su, H., Zhu, J.: Bag of tricks for adversarial training. arXiv preprint arXiv:2010.00467 (2020)
43. Radford, A., Wu, J., Child, R., Luan, D., Amodei, D., Sutskever, I., et al.: Language models are unsupervised multitask learners. OpenAI Blog (2019)
44. Rice, L., Wong, E., Kolter, Z.: Overfitting in adversarially robust deep learning. In: ICML (2020)
45. Richemond, P.H., et al.: Byol works even without batch statistics. arXiv preprint arXiv:2010.10241 (2020)
46. Schmidt, L., Santurkar, S., Tsipras, D., Talwar, K., Madry, A.: Adversarially robust generalization requires more data. In: NeurIPS (2018)
47. Su, W., Zhu, X., Cao, Y., Li, B., Lu, L., Wei, F., Dai, J.: VL-bert: pre-training of generic visual-linguistic representations. In: ICLR (2020)
48. Szegedy, C., et al.: Intriguing properties of neural networks. arXiv preprint arXiv:1312.6199 (2013)
49. Tian, Y., Krishnan, D., Isola, P.: Contrastive multiview coding. In: Vedaldi, A., Bischof, H., Brox, T., Frahm, J.-M. (eds.) ECCV 2020. LNCS, vol. 12356, pp. 776–794. Springer, Cham (2020). https://doi.org/10.1007/978-3-030-58621-8_45
50. Uesato, J., Alayrac, J.B., Huang, P.S., Stanforth, R., Fawzi, A., Kohli, P.: Are labels required for improving adversarial robustness? In: NeurIPS (2019)
51. Wang, T., Isola, P.: Understanding contrastive representation learning through alignment and uniformity on the hypersphere. In: ICML (2020)
52. Wang, X., Zhang, R., Shen, C., Kong, T., Li, L.: Dense contrastive learning for self-supervised visual pre-training. In: Proceedings of IEEE Conference on Computer Vision and Pattern Recognition (CVPR) (2021)
53. Wu, Z., Xiong, Y., Yu, S.X., Lin, D.: Unsupervised feature learning via non-parametric instance discrimination. In: CVPR (2018)
54. Xie, C., Tan, M., Gong, B., Yuille, A., Le, Q.V.: Smooth adversarial training. arXiv preprint arXiv:2006.14536 (2020)
55. Xie, C., Yuille, A.: Intriguing properties of adversarial training at scale. In: ICLR (2020)
56. Xu, C., Yang, M.: Adversarial momentum-contrastive pre-training. arXiv preprint arXiv:2012.13154 (2020)
57. Yeh, C.H., Hong, C.Y., Hsu, Y.C., Liu, T.L., Chen, Y., LeCun, Y.: Decoupled contrastive learning. arXiv preprint arXiv:2110.06848 (2021)

58. Zbontar, J., Jing, L., Misra, I., LeCun, Y., Deny, S.: Barlow twins: self-supervised learning via redundancy reduction. In: ICML (2021)
59. Zhai, R., et al.: Adversarially robust generalization just requires more unlabeled data. arXiv preprint arXiv:1906.00555 (2019)
60. Zhang, C., et al.: Resnet or densenet? Introducing dense shortcuts to resnet. In: WACV (2021)
61. Zhang, C., Benz, P., Imtiaz, T., Kweon, I.S.: Understanding adversarial examples from the mutual influence of images and perturbations. In: CVPR (2020)
62. Zhang, C., Benz, P., Karjauv, A., Kweon, I.S.: Universal adversarial perturbations through the lens of deep steganography: towards a fourier perspective. In: AAAI (2021)
63. Zhang, C., et al.: Revisiting residual networks with nonlinear shortcuts. In: BMVC (2019)
64. Zhang, C., Zhang, K., Pham, T.X., Yoo, C., Kweon, I.S.: Dual temperature helps contrastive learning without many negative samples: towards understanding and simplifying MoCo. In: CVPR (2022)
65. Zhang, C., Zhang, K., Zhang, C., Pham, T.X., Yoo, C.D., Kweon, I.S.: How does simsiam avoid collapse without negative samples? A unified understanding with self-supervised contrastive learning. In: ICLR (2022)
66. Zhang, H., Yu, Y., Jiao, J., Xing, E.P., Ghaoui, L.E., Jordan, M.I.: Theoretically principled trade-off between robustness and accuracy. In: ICML (2019)
67. Zhang, J., Han, B., Niu, G., Liu, T., Sugiyama, M.: Where is the bottleneck of adversarial learning with unlabeled data? arXiv preprint arXiv:1911.08696 (2019)
68. Zhuang, C., Zhai, A.L., Yamins, D.: Local aggregation for unsupervised learning of visual embeddings. In: ICCV (2019)

Author Index

Printed in the United States
by Baker & Taylor Publisher Services